PHILIP'S

STREET ATLAS

Gloucestershire

First published in 2001 by

Philip's, a division of
Octopus Publishing Group Ltd
2–4 Heron Quays, London E14 4JP

First edition 2001
Second impression with revisions 2003

ISBN 0-540-08099-3 (spiral)

Printed and bound in Spain
by Cayfosa-Quebecor

Contents

III **Key to map symbols**

IV **Key to map pages**

VI **Route planning**

VIII **Administrative and Postcode boundaries**

1 **Street maps** at 3½ inches to 1 mile

140 **Street maps** at 1¾ inches to 1 mile

190 **Street maps** at 3½ inches to 1 mile

193 **Street maps of centres of Cheltenham, Bristol and Gloucester** at 7 inches to 1 mile

197 **Town maps** of Chipping Norton, Evesham, Faringdon and Ross-on-Wye

199 **Index** of towns and villages

201 **Index** of streets, hospitals, industrial estates, railway stations, schools, shopping centres, universities and places of interest

Digital Data

The exceptionally high-quality mapping found in this atlas is available as digital data in TIFF format, which is easily convertible to other bitmapped (raster) image formats.

The index is also available in digital form as a standard database table. It contains all the details found in the printed index together with the National Grid reference for the map square in which each entry is named.

For further information and to discuss your requirements, please contact Philip's on 020 7531 8438 or james.mann@philips-maps.co.uk

Key to map symbols

22a	**Motorway** with junction number
	Primary route – dual/single carriageway
	A road – dual/single carriageway
	B road – dual/single carriageway
	Minor road – dual/single carriageway
	Other minor road – dual/single carriageway
	Road under construction
	Pedestrianised area
DY7	**Postcode boundaries**
	County and unitary authority boundaries
	Railway
	Railway under construction
	Tramway, miniature railway
	Rural track, private road or narrow road in urban area
	Gate or obstruction to traffic (restrictions may not apply at all times or to all vehicles)
	Path, bridleway, byway open to all traffic, road used as a public path
	The representation in this atlas of a road, track or path is no evidence of the existence of a of a right of way
185 / 106	**Adjoining page indicators** (The colour of the arrow indicates the scale of the adjoining page - see scales below)
196 / 192	**The map areas within the pink and blue bands are shown at a larger scale on the page, indicated by the red and blue blocks and arrows**

Walsall	**Railway station**
	Private railway station
	Bus, coach station
	Ambulance station
	Coastguard station
	Fire station
	Police station
	Accident and Emergency entrance to hospital
H	**Hospital**
	Place of worship
i	**Information Centre** (open all year)
P	**Parking**
P&R	**Park and Ride**
PO	**Post Office**
	Camping site
	Caravan site
	Golf course
	Picnic site
Prim Sch	**Important buildings, schools, colleges, universities and hospitals**
River Medway	**Water name**
	River, stream
	Lock, weir
	Water
	Tidal water
	Woods
	Houses
Church	**Non-Roman antiquity**
ROMAN FORT	**Roman antiquity**

Acad	**Academy**	Mkt	**Market**
Allot Gdns	**Allotments**	Meml	**Memorial**
Cemy	**Cemetery**	Mon	**Monument**
C Ctr	**Civic Centre**	Mus	**Museum**
CH	**Club House**	Obsy	**Observatory**
Coll	**College**	Pal	**Royal Palace**
Crem	**Crematorium**	PH	**Public House**
Ent	**Enterprise**	Recn Gd	**Recreation Ground**
Ex H	**Exhibition Hall**	Resr	**Reservoir**
Ind Est	**Industrial Estate**	Ret Pk	**Retail Park**
IRB Sta	**Inshore Rescue Boat Station**	Sch	**School**
Inst	**Institute**	Sh Ctr	**Shopping Centre**
Ct	**Law Court**	TH	**Town Hall/House**
L Ctr	**Leisure Centre**	Trad Est	**Trading Estate**
LC	**Level Crossing**	Univ	**University**
Liby	**Library**	Wks	**Works**
		YH	**Youth Hostel**

■ The small numbers around the edges of the maps identify the 1 kilometre National Grid lines ■ The dark grey border on the inside edge of some pages indicates that the mapping does not continue onto the adjacent page

The scale of the maps on the pages numbered in blue is 5.52 cm to 1 km • 3½ inches to 1 mile • 1: 18103

0 ¼ ½ ¾ 1 mile
0 250 m 500 m 750 m 1 kilometre

The scale of the maps on pages numbered in green is 2.76 cm to 1 km • 1¾ inches to 1 mile • 1: 36206

0 ¼ ½ ¾ 1 mile
0 250m 500m 750m 1kilometre

The scale of the maps on pages numbered in red is 11.04 cm to 1 km • 7 inches to 1 mile • 1: 9051.4

0 220 yards 440 yards 660 yards ½ mile
0 125 m 250 m 375 m ½ kilometre

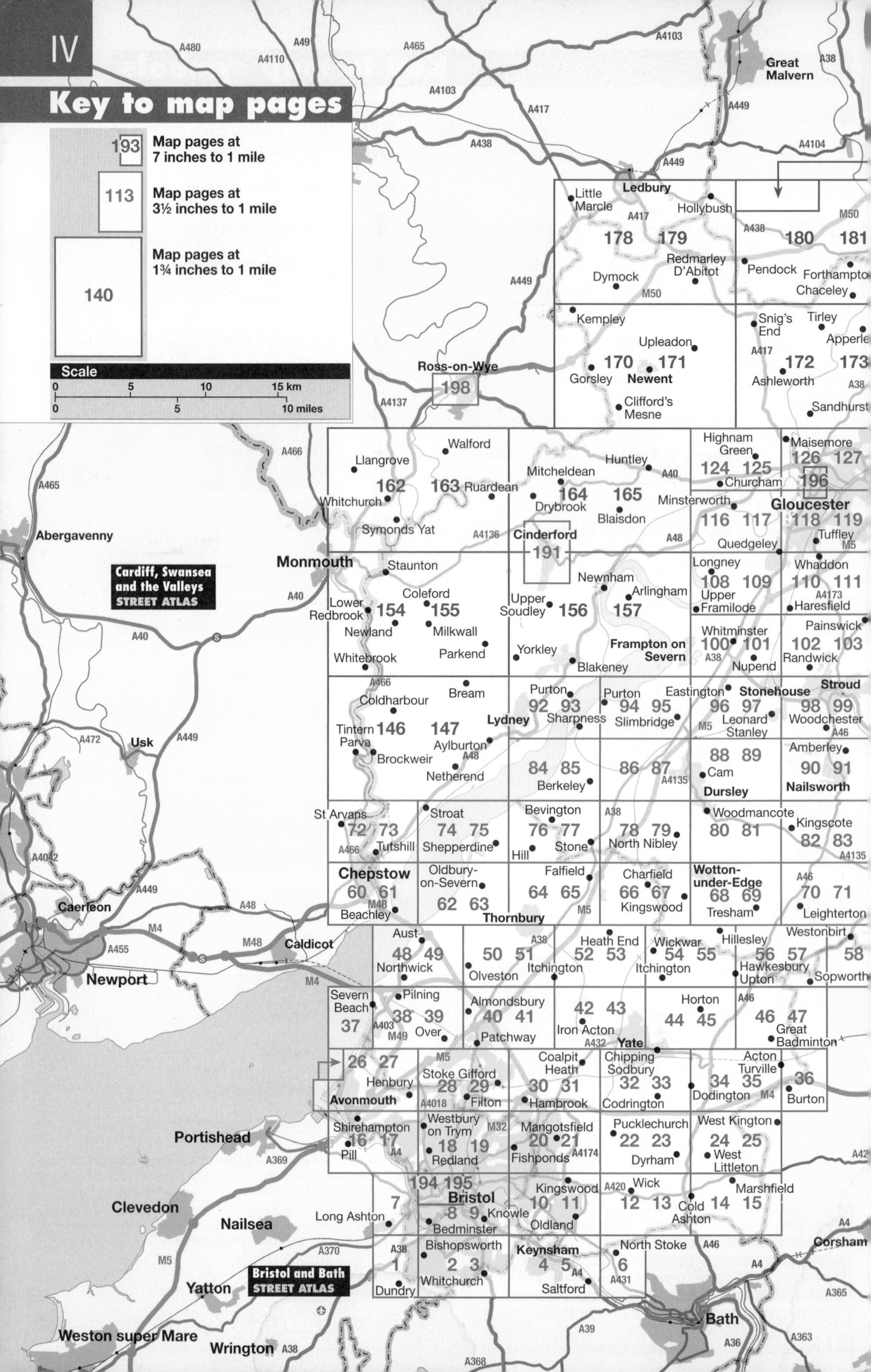
IV
Key to map pages
193 Map pages at 7 inches to 1 mile
113 Map pages at 3½ inches to 1 mile
140 Map pages at 1¾ inches to 1 mile
Scale
0 5 10 15 km
0 5 10 miles
Great Malvern
Ledbury
Little Marcle
Hollybush
178 179 180 181
Redmarley D'Abitot
Dymock
Pendock
Forthampton
Chaceley
Kempley
Snig's End
Tirley
Apperley
Upleadon
170 171 172 173
Gorsley
Newent
Ashleworth
Clifford's Mesne
Sandhurst
Ross-on-Wye
198
Walford
Llangrove
Highnam Green
Maisemore
Huntley
Mitcheldean
124 125 126 127
162 163 Ruardean 164 165
Churcham
196
Whitchurch
Drybrook
Blaisdon
Minsterworth
Gloucester
116 117 118 119
Symonds Yat
Cinderford
Quedgeley
Tuffley
191
Abergavenny
Monmouth
Staunton
Longney
Whaddon
Cardiff, Swansea and the Valleys STREET ATLAS
Newnham
Arlingham
108 109 110 111
Coleford
Upper Soudley
Upper Framilode
Haresfield
Lower Redbrook 154 155 156 157
Newland
Milkwall
Painswick
Whitminster
Frampton on Severn
100 101 102 103
Parkend
Yorkley
Whitebrook
Nupend
Randwick
Blakeney
Bream
Purton
Purton
Eastington
Stonehouse
Stroud
Coldharbour
92 93 94 95 96 97 98 99
Lydney
Sharpness
Slimbridge
Leonard Stanley
Woodchester
Tintern Parva 146 147
Usk
Aylburton
Amberley
Brockweir
88 89
Netherend
84 85 86 87
90 91
Cam
Berkeley
Dursley
Nailsworth
St Arvans
Stroat
Bevington
Woodmancote
72 73 74 75 76 77 78 79 80 81
Kingscote
82 83
Tutshill
Shepperdine
Hill
Stone
North Nibley
Chepstow
Oldbury-on-Severn
Falfield
Charfield
Wotton-under-Edge
60 61 62 63 64 65 66 67 68 69 70 71
Caerleon
Beachley
Thornbury
Kingswood
Tresham
Leighterton
Aust
Heath End
Wickwar
Hillesley
Westonbirt
48 49 50 51 52 53 54 55 56 57 58
Caldicot
Northwick
Olveston
Itchington
Itchington
Hawkesbury Upton
Sopworth
Newport
Severn Beach
Pilning
Almondsbury
Horton
37 38 39 40 41 42 43 44 45 46 47
Over
Patchway
Iron Acton
Yate
Great Badminton
26 27
Coalpit Heath
Chipping Sodbury
Acton Turville
Henbury
Stoke Gifford
28 29 30 31 32 33 34 35 36
Avonmouth
Filton
Hambrook
Codrington
Dodington
Burton
Shirehampton
Westbury on Trym
Mangotsfield
Pucklechurch
West Kington
Portishead
16 17 18 19 20 21 22 23 24 25
Pill
Redland
Fishponds
Dyrham
West Littleton
194 195
Bristol
Kingswood
Wick
Marshfield
Clevedon
7 8 9 10 11 12 13 14 15
Nailsea
Long Ashton
Knowle
Oldland
Cold Ashton
Bedminster
Corsham
Bishopsworth
Keynsham
North Stoke
1 2 3 4 5 6
Yatton
Bristol and Bath STREET ATLAS
Dundry
Whitchurch
Saltford
Bath
Weston super Mare
Wrington

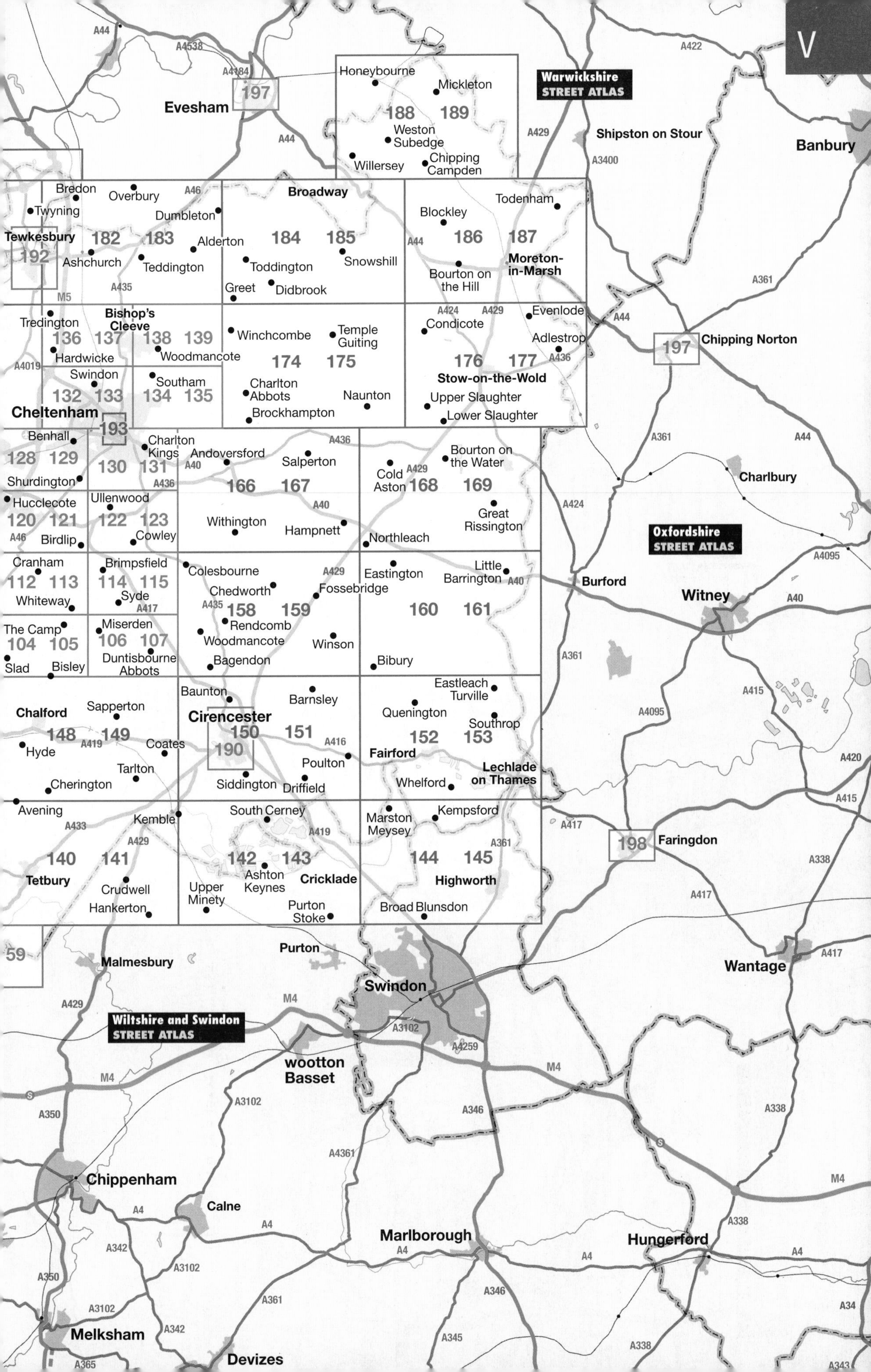

V
Warwickshire STREET ATLAS
Oxfordshire STREET ATLAS
Wiltshire and Swindon STREET ATLAS
Evesham
197
Honeybourne
Mickleton
188 189
Weston Subedge
Willersey
Chipping Campden
Shipston on Stour
Banbury
Bredon
Overbury
Twyning
Dumbleton
Tewkesbury
192
182 183
Ashchurch
Alderton
Teddington
Broadway
184 185
Toddington
Snowshill
Greet
Didbrook
Blockley
Todenham
186 187
Bourton on the Hill
Moreton-in-Marsh
Tredington
Bishop's Cleeve
136 137 138 139
Hardwicke
Woodmancote
Winchcombe
Temple Guiting
174 175
Charlton Abbots
Brockhampton
Naunton
Evenlode
Condicote
Adlestrop
176 177
Stow-on-the-Wold
Upper Slaughter
Lower Slaughter
Chipping Norton
197
Swindon
Southam
132 133 134 135
Cheltenham
193
Benhall
128 129
Charlton Kings
130 131
Shurdington
Andoversford
Salperton
166 167
Cold Aston
168 169
Bourton on the Water
Charlbury
Hucclecote
Ullenwood
120 121 122 123
Birdlip
Cowley
Withington
Hampnett
Northleach
Great Rissington
Cranham
Brimpsfield
112 113 114 115
Whiteway
Syde
Colesbourne
Chedworth
Fossebridge
158 159
Eastington
Little Barrington
160 161
Burford
Witney
The Camp
Miserden
104 105 106 107
Rendcomb
Woodmancote
Winson
Slad
Bisley
Duntisbourne Abbots
Bagendon
Bibury
Baunton
Cirencester
Barnsley
Eastleach Turville
Quenington
Southrop
Chalford
Sapperton
148 149
150 151
190
152 153
Hyde
Coates
Poulton
Fairford
Lechlade on Thames
Tarlton
Cherington
Siddington
Driffield
Whelford
Avening
Kemble
South Cerney
Marston Meysey
Kempsford
140 141 142 143 144 145
Tetbury
Crudwell
Hankerton
Ashton Keynes
Cricklade
Upper Minety
Purton Stoke
Highworth
Broad Blunsdon
Faringdon
198
Wantage
59
Malmesbury
Purton
Swindon
wootton Basset
Chippenham
Calne
Marlborough
Hungerford
Melksham
Devizes
A44 A4538 A4184 A429 A3400 A422 A46 A435 M5 A4019 A424 A436 A40 A417 A433 A419 A416 A361 A4095 A415 A420 A338 A417 M4 A3102 A4259 A346 A350 A4361 A4 A342 A3102 A345 A34 A365 A343

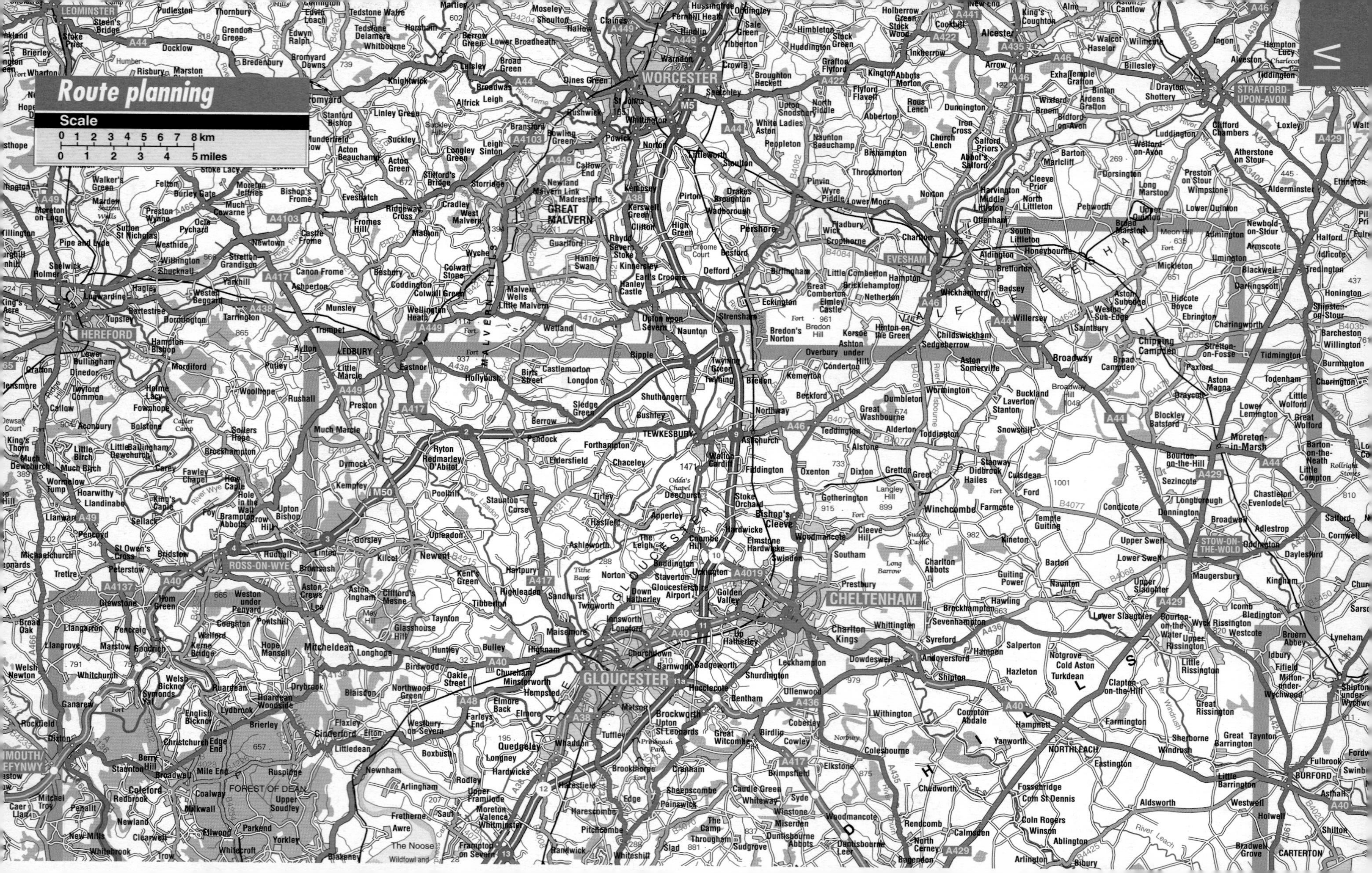

VI
Route planning
Scale
0 1 2 3 4 5 6 7 8 km
0 1 2 3 4 5 miles
WORCESTER
STRATFORD-UPON-AVON
LEOMINSTER
HEREFORD
GREAT MALVERN
LEDBURY
EVESHAM
TEWKESBURY
CHELTENHAM
GLOUCESTER
ROSS-ON-WYE
STOW-ON-THE-WOLD
BURFORD
NORTHLEACH
CARTERTON
FOREST OF DEAN
VALE OF EVESHAM
MALVERN HILLS
VALE OF GLOUCESTER
COTSWOLD HILLS

VII
STROUD
CIRENCESTER
SWINDON
MARLBOROUGH
CHIPPENHAM
MALMESBURY
TETBURY
CALNE
DEVIZES
MELKSHAM
TROWBRIDGE
BRADFORD-ON-AVON
BATH
BRISTOL
KEYNSHAM
KINGSWOOD
CHEPSTOW
THORNBURY
CHIPPING SODBURY
YATE
NAILSWORTH
CRICKLADE
HIGHWORTH
LECHLADE ON THAMES
FAIRFORD
WOOTTON BASSETT
MIDSOMER NORTON
RADSTOCK
Avonmouth
VALE OF BERKELEY
COTSWOLDS
VALE OF PEWSEY
Marlborough Downs
Savernake Forest

Major administrative and Postcode boundaries

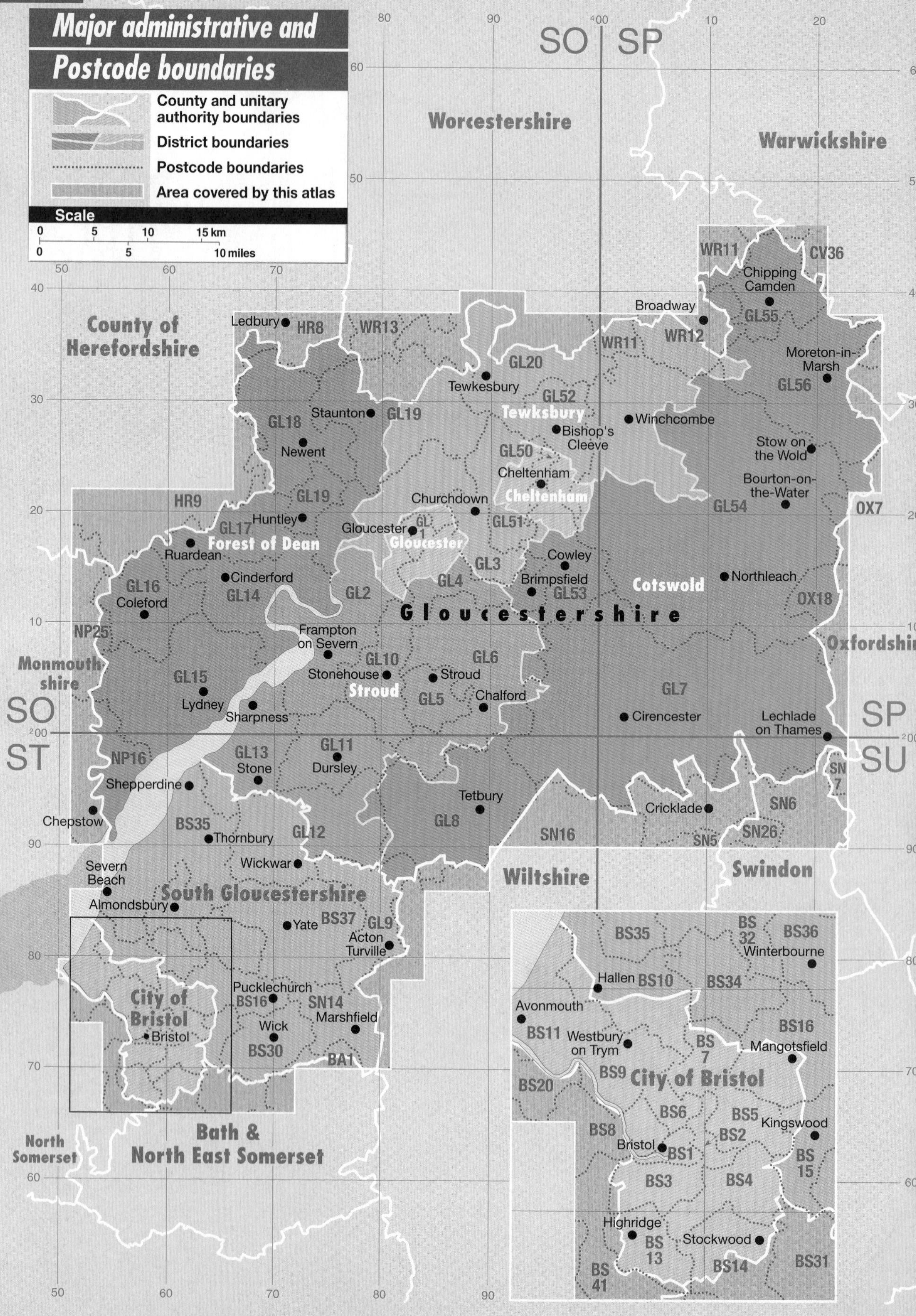

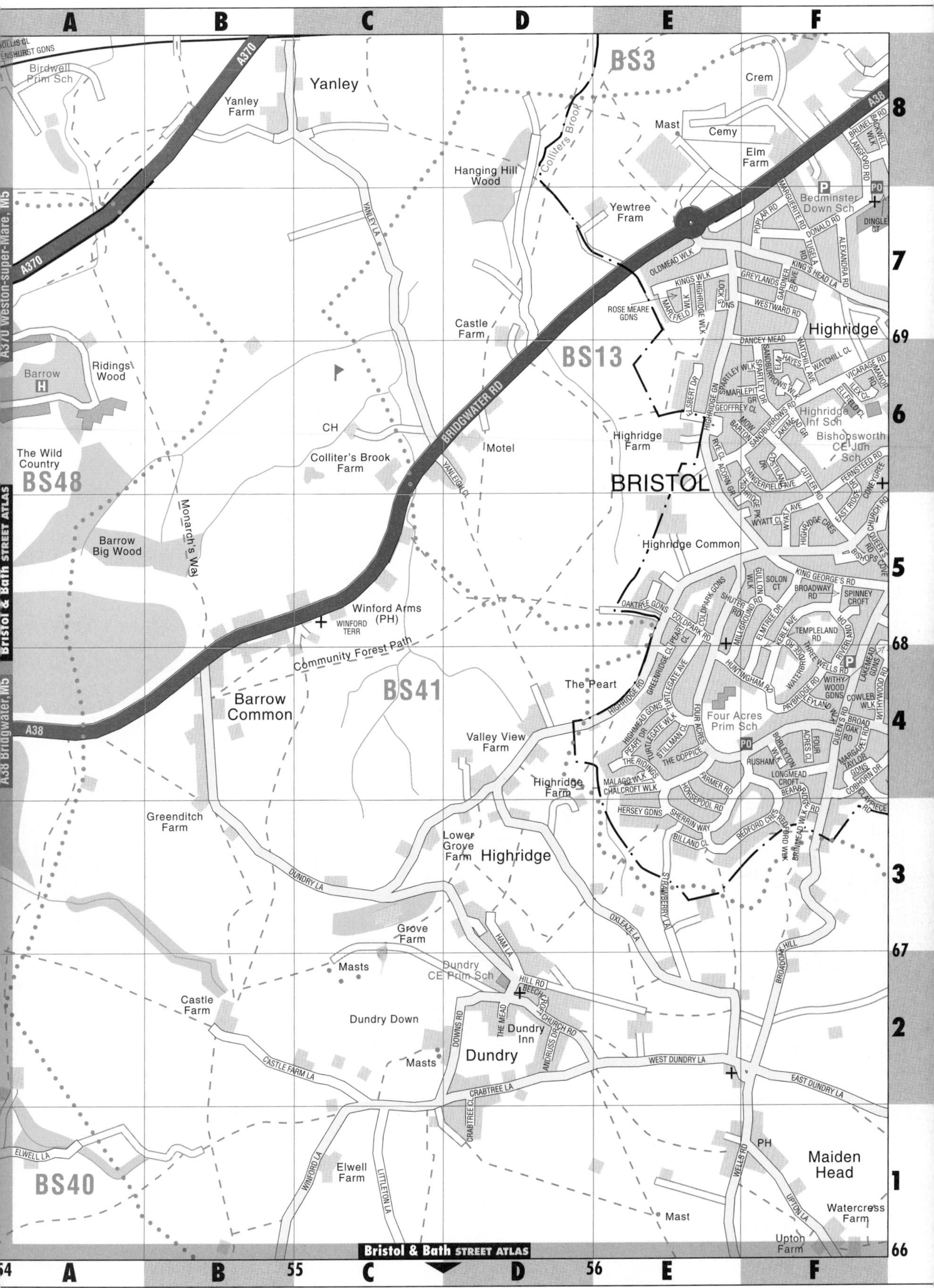
A B C D E F
8 7 69 6 5 68 4 3 67 2 1 66
54 55 56
Yanley
Yanley Farm
Birdwell Prim Sch
A370
BS3
Crem
Mast
Cemy
Elm Farm
Hanging Hill Wood
Colliters Brook
Yewtree Fram
Bedminster Down Sch
A38
A370 Weston-super-Mare, M5
Yanley La
Castle Farm
BS13
Highridge
Barrow
Ridings Wood
Highridge Inf Sch
Bishopsworth CE Jun Sch
CH
Colliter's Brook Farm
Motel
Highridge Farm
The Wild Country
BS48
BRISTOL
Bridgwater Rd
Barrow Big Wood
Monarch's Way
Highridge Common
Winford Arms (PH)
Winford Terr
Community Forest Path
BS41
Barrow Common
The Peart
Four Acres Prim Sch
A38 Bridgwater, M5
Valley View Farm
Highridge Farm
Greenditch Farm
Lower Grove Farm
Highridge
Dundry La
Grove Farm
Masts
Dundry CE Prim Sch
Castle Farm
Dundry Down
Dundry Inn
Dundry
Masts
Castle Farm La
West Dundry La
East Dundry La
Crabtree La
Elwell La
BS40
Elwell Farm
Winford Rd
Littleton La
PH
Maiden Head
Wells Rd
Upton La
Watercress Farm
Mast
Upton Farm
Oxleaze La
Strawberry La
Broadoak Hill
Bristol & Bath STREET ATLAS

1
8

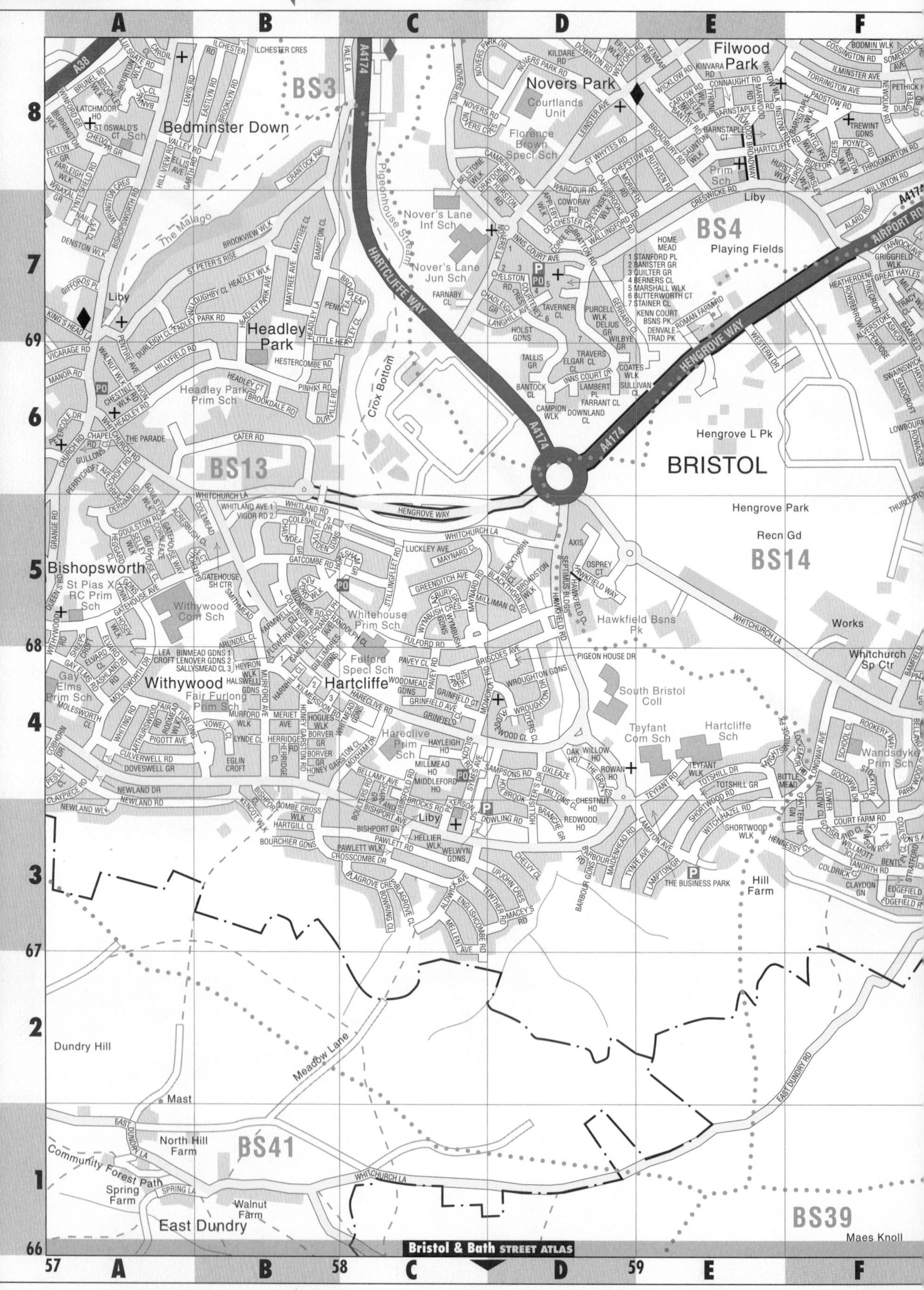
Bedminster Down
Novers Park
Filwood Park
Headley Park
BS3
BS4
BS13
BS14
BS41
BS39
BRISTOL
Bishopsworth
Withywood
Hartcliffe
Hengrove Park
Hengrove L Pk
Playing Fields
Recn Gd
Works
Whitchurch Sp Ctr
South Bristol Coll
Teyfant Com Sch
Hartcliffe Sch
Hawkfield Bsns Pk
Dundry Hill
Mast
North Hill Farm
Spring Farm
Walnut Farm
East Dundry
Community Forest Path
Meadow Lane
Maes Knoll
Hill Farm
HARTCLIFFE WAY
HENGROVE WAY
AIRPORT RD
A4174
A38
Crox Bottom
Pigeonhouse Stream
The Malago
Nover's Lane Inf Sch
Nover's Lane Jun Sch
Florence Brown Specl Sch
Courtlands Unit
Headley Park Prim Sch
Withywood Com Sch
Whitehouse Prim Sch
Fulford Specl Sch
Hareclive Prim Sch
Fair Furlong Prim Sch
Gay Elms Prim Sch
St Pias X RC Prim Sch
Wansdyke Prim Sch
THE BUSINESS PARK
EAST DUNDRY RD
WHITCHURCH LA
A B C D E F
57 58 59
66 67 68 69
1 2 3 4 5 6 7 8

1

9
4

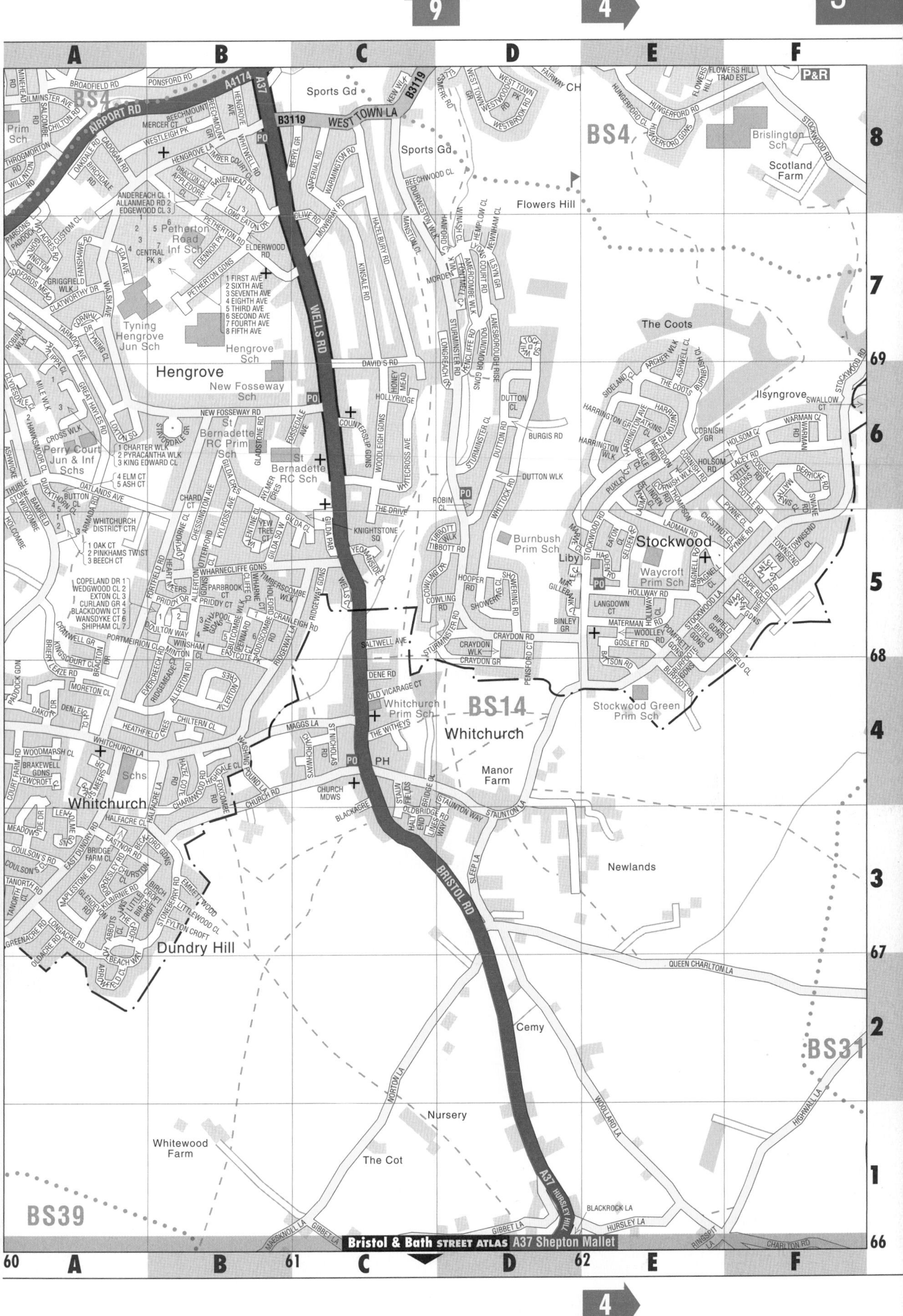
A
B
C
D
E
F
8
7
69
6
5
68
4
3
67
2
1
66
60
61
62
BS4
BS14
BS31
BS39
A4174
A37
B3119
AIRPORT RD
WEST TOWN LA
WELLS RD
BRISTOL RD
Sports Gd
Flowers Hill
Brislington Sch
Scotland Farm
P&R
Petherton Road Inf Sch
Tyning Hengrove Jun Sch
Hengrove Sch
Hengrove
New Fosseway Sch
NEW FOSSEWAY RD
St Bernadette RC Prim Sch
St Bernadette RC Sch
Perry Court Jun & Inf Schs
The Coots
Ilsyngrove
Stockwood
Burnbush Prim Sch
Waycroft Prim Sch
Liby
Stockwood Green Prim Sch
Whitchurch Prim Sch
Whitchurch
Manor Farm
Schs
Newlands
Dundry Hill
QUEEN CHARLTON LA
Cemy
Nursery
Whitewood Farm
The Cot
BLACKROCK LA
HURSLEY LA
HURSLEY HILL
GIBBET LA
MAESKNOLL LA
CHARLTON RD
Bristol & Bath STREET ATLAS A37 Shepton Mallet

4

3
10

A
B
C
D
E
F
8
7
69
6
5
68
4
3
67
2
1
66
63
64
65
BS4
BS15
BS30
BS14
BS31
Hicks Gate
A4
BATH RD
IRONMOULD LA
A4174
A4175
DURLEY HILL
Avon Walkway
River Avon
Keysham Hams
Factory
Scotland Bottom
Somerdale
STOCKWOOD RD
Oaklease Farm
Durleypark
DURLEY LA
Cemy
KEYNSHAM BY-PASS
Recn Gd
CROSS ST
HAMS RD
SOMERDALE RD
Community Forest Path
DRYLEAZE
CHANDOS RD
SUMMER LEAZE
SOMERDALE RD
THE AVENUE
STOCKWOOD HILL
Stockwood Vale
CH
Wood Covert
BRISTOL RD
OLD VICARAGE GN
STATION RD
KEYNSHAM RD
Keynsham
ABBEY PK
ABBEY CL
THE PARK
Broadlands Sch
BROADLANDS AVE
MILWARD RD
ST JOHNS CT
ST MARKS CL
CULVERS RD
B3116 HIGH ST
ST FRANCIS RD
ST LADOC RD
CRANMORE AVE
ST MARGARET'S CL
ST ANNE'S AVE
ST ANNE'S CT
AVON MILL LA
AVON CL
VANDYCK AVE
TENNYSON CL
CONSTABLE CL
Charlton Bottom
Broadlands House
ORCHARD CL
WINSCOMBE CL
ST GEORGE'S RD
WESTBOURNE AVE
WEST VIEW RD
ASHTON WAY
BACK LA
REGENTS
Temple Jun Sch
DRAGONS HILL CL
GASTON AVE
WHEATHILL CL
LOCKINGWELL RD
MENDIP CL
SELWORTHY CL
HOLCOMBE GR
ASHCROFT AVE
PARK CL
ST KEYNA RD
MAYE
KELDS
B3116
THE CENTRE
Liby
BATH HILL
AVON RD
DRAGONS HILL
ST PATRICKS CT
ROCK RD
TEMPLE CT
THE LABBOTT
RIVER TERR
L Ctr
Ct
HEATHFIELD CL
DOWNFIELD
CLEEVE GR
STAPLE GR
HANDEL RD
HAWTHORNS LA
CARPENTERS LA
TEMPLE ST
ST KENYA CT
FOX AND HOUNDS LA
BATH RD B3116
WESTFIELD CL
Keynsham Prim Sch
CHARLTON PK
St John's Prim Sch
SHERWOOD CL
TAMSIN CT
ST CADOC HO
HOMEAVON HO
Temple Hill Inf Sch
MONMOUTH CL
CHEPSTOW WLK
COURTLANDS
SHERWOOD RD
DAPPS HILL
LUDLOW CL
KELSTON RD
ALBERT RD
LAYS DR
ARUNDEL WLK
BARNARD WLK
DONNINGTON WLK
TINTAGEL CL
PRINCESS CL
CAMERONS CL
PARK RD
STIRLING WAY
JOFFE CRES
FAIRFAX CRES
ST CLEMENTS RD
CHEW COTTS
STEEL MILLS
SEVERN WAY
GLEBE WLK
RAGLAN WLK
DARTMOUTH WLK
QUEENS RD
WINDSOR AVE
BALMORAL RD
EDINBURGH RD
VICTORIA HO
EDWARD CT
CAROLINE CL
LINCOLN CL
CAERNARVON RD
WORTH CL
DURHAM GR
TENBY RD
BERKELEY GDNS
Lays Bsns Ctr
NORFOLK GR
KENT WAY
WARWICK RD
RICHMOND CL
LULWORTH RD
DUDLEY CL
COMPTON GN
ROCKHILL EST
Lays Farm
PINE CT
ELM CT
FIRS CT
ROWAN WLK
WALTON WLK
FARLEIGH RD
AMBERLEY CL
CORONATION AVE
ORWELL DR
BOX WLK
LONGMEADOW RD
MAPLE WLK
TAMWORTH RD
CHELMER GR
WALNUT WLK
LIME CT
BIRCH CT
ACACIA CT
CHERRY TREE CL
WILLOW WLK
Castle Prim Sch
DUNSTER RD
CHANDAG RD
CLYDE AVE
HOLMOAK RD
CEDAR DR
NEWLANDS RD
HURN LA
LILAC CL
SALLUT CL
OAK TREE WLK
HOLLY WLK
THE BRAMBLES
CHARLTON RD
HORNBEAM WLK
LABURNUM WLK
MAY TREE WLK
ST CLEMENTS CT
River Chew
WELLSWAY
MANOR RD
KEYNSHAM
Parkhouse Lane
LYNDHURST RD
SUNNYMEAD
Queen Charlton
Parkhouse Farm
OAKFIELD RD
HIGHFIELD RD
Manor Farm
QUEEN CHARLTON LA
PARKHOUSE LA
Chewton Place
CHEWTON RD
HIGHWALL LA
Wellfield House
Manor Farm
COURTENAY RD
THE HOMESTEAD
REDLYNCH LA
Chew Keynsham
Poplars Cottage
DARWELL LA
Warners Farm
Harvey's Ditch
Charlton Field

3

11
6

Londonderry Farm
Community Forest Path
KEYNSHAM RD
A4175
Nursery
Field Grove Farm
Monarch's Way
The Meadows Prim Sch
A431
BATH RD
CLAY LA
CROFT CL
KINGS SQ
HAYMAN RIDGE
Works
Mill
MILL LA
PO
GOLDEN VALLEY LA
Bitton
Nursery
Barrow Hill
PH
HARRINGTON CL
EDWIN SHORT CL
HIGH ST
AUBREY MEADS
BREWERY HILL
CHURCH LA
CHURCH RD
CHURCH FARM PADDOCK
BS30
River Boyd
Nursery
BATH RD
A431
Broad Mead
Works
Mickle Mead
River Avon
Holm Mead
Avon Walkway
Sewage Works
WANSDYKE WORKSHOPS
BROADMEAD LA
Mill
Avon Valley Country Park
Avon Farm
Bristol & Bath Rly Path
CONSTABLE CL
UNITY RD
UNITY CT
Superstore
Ashmead Road Ind Est
KEYNSHAM BY-PASS
GASTON AVE
LYTTON GR
TA Ctr
ASHMEAD RD
Ellsbridge Ho
Norton Radstock Coll
Pixash Bsns Ctr
PIXASH LA
BATH RD
B3116
Wellsway Sec Sch
1 NASH CL
2 RUBENS CL
3 CHELSEA CL
4 HILLS CL
5 REYNOLDS CL
6 TURNER CL
ELLSBRIDGE CL
HARDING PL
WORLD'S END LA
AVON LA
DERWENT GR
SEVERN WAY
Chandag Jun & Inf Sch
CHANDAG RD
TAMAR DR
TRENT GR
ORWELL DR
LAMBOURN RD
CHERWELL RD
WINDRUSH GN
TEVIOT RD
WINDRUSH RD
WANSBECK RD
CALDER CL
WALDEN RD
CHELMER GR
TORRIDGE RD
DEVERON GR
MARDEN RD
MINSMERE RD
COLNE GN
Nurseries
Glenavon Farm
COPSE RD
MEAD LA
WEDMORE RD
CHELWOOD RD
KELSTON CL
BROADWAY
STRATTON RD
CAMERTON CL
SALTFORD CT
QUEEN SQ
PH
HIGH ST
THE BATCH
MEDWAY CL
HURN LA
CONWAY GN
EVENLODE WAY
WITHAM RD
MEDWAY DR
WAVENEY RD
BS31
BATH RD
WICK HOUSE CL
BROCKLEY RD
NORMAN RD
JENA CT
IFORD CL
HINTON CL
HOMEFIELD CL
HOMEFIELD RD
ROUNDMOOR CL
BEECH RD
CHESTNUT WLK
P
River Avon
THE SHALLOWS
Playing Field
WAYFORD CL
MARLOCK RD
GRANGE RD
HOWARD CL
BOYD RD
VICTORIA RD
CLAVERTON RD
LANSDOWN RD
FENTON CL
VERNON CL
WITNEY CL
JUSTICE AVE
Liby
PO
YATES CL
CARY RD
RHODE CL
MANSEL CL
KINGSTON AVE
HERMES CL
CAVENDISH CL
KEPPEL CL
TRENCHARD RD
NUNNEY CL
HUTTON CL
LAWSON CL
CABOT CL
ANSON CL
CLAVERTON RD
OAKFIELD RD
TILLEY CL
GAINWELL CL
Keynsham Manor
Eastover Farm
MORGAN CL
DRAKE CL
MELLS CL
MANOR RD
RALEIGH CL
MONTAGUE RD
PEPYS CL
Saltford CE Prim Sch
COLLINGWOOD CL
TYNING RD
COURTENAY RD
CADBURY RD
CHATFIELD CL
HARDINGTON DR
RODNEY RD
UPLANDS DR
MAESBURY RD
SILBURY RISE
Saltford
HASELBURY GR
GOLF CLUB LA
HARCOURT CL
SOMERVILLE CL
FAIRWAYS
BERESFORD CL
UPLANDS RD
THE FOLLY
CH
THE GLEN
A4
WELLSWAY
Uplands
Burnett Bsns Pk
B3116
BA2
Folly Wood
A B C D E F
8 7 69 6 5 68 4 3 67 2 1 66
66 67 68

6

5
12

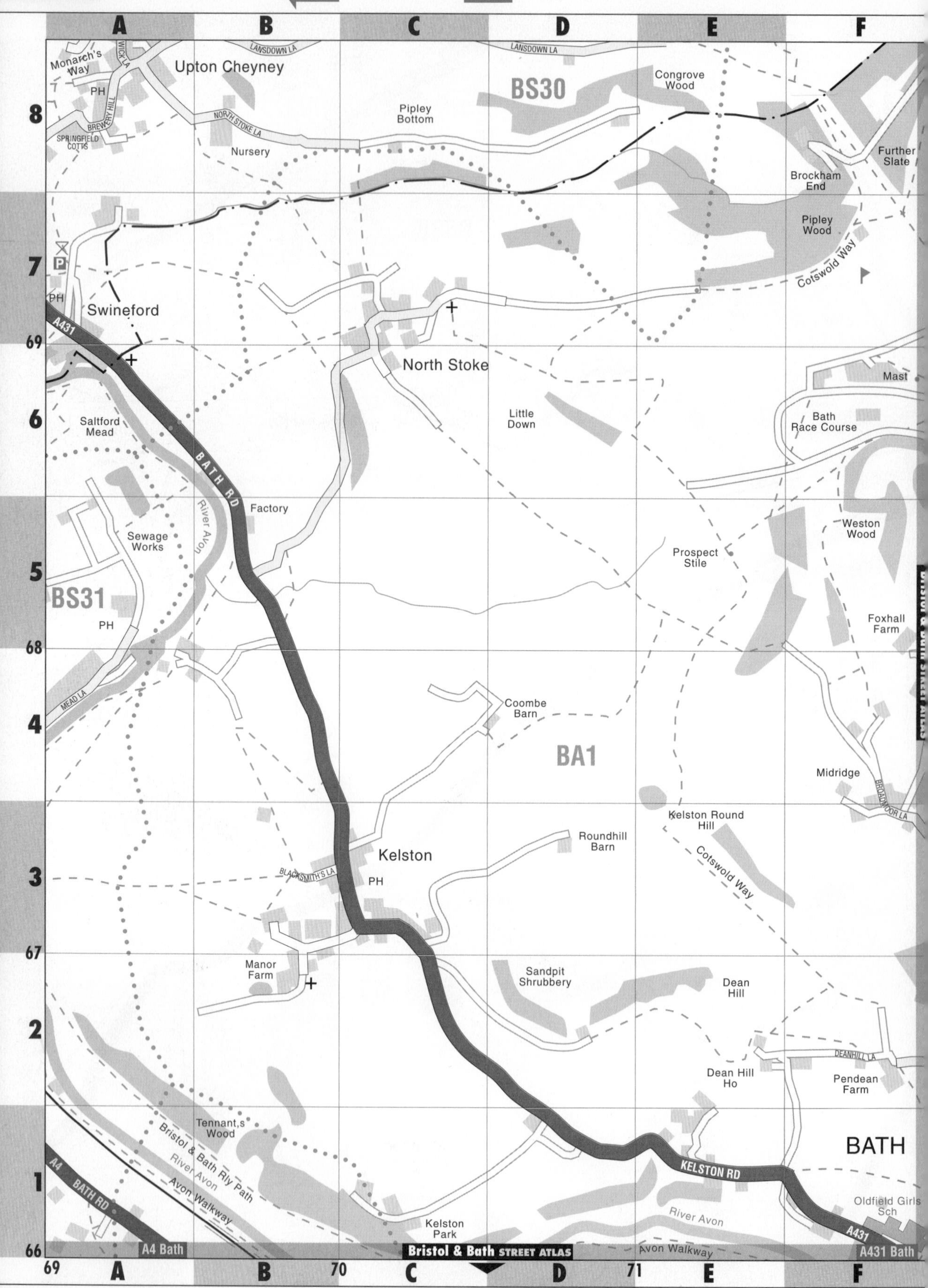
A
B
C
D
E
F
8
7
69
6
5
68
4
3
67
2
1
66
69
70
71
LANSDOWN LA
Monarch's Way
WICK LA
Upton Cheyney
PH
BREWERY HILL
SPRINGFIELD COTTS
NORTH STOKE LA
Nursery
Pipley Bottom
BS30
Congrove Wood
Further Slate
Brockham End
Pipley Wood
Cotswold Way
PH
Swineford
A431
North Stoke
Mast
Little Down
Bath Race Course
Saltford Mead
BATH RD
River Avon
Factory
Sewage Works
Weston Wood
Prospect Stile
BS31
PH
Foxhall Farm
MEAD LA
Coombe Barn
BA1
Midridge
BROADMOOR LA
Kelston Round Hill
Roundhill Barn
Kelston
BLACKSMITH'S LA
PH
Cotswold Way
Manor Farm
Sandpit Shrubbery
Dean Hill
DEANHILL LA
Dean Hill Ho
Pendean Farm
Tennant,s Wood
Bristol & Bath Rly Path
River Avon
Avon Walkway
BATH
KELSTON RD
A4
BATH RD
River Avon
Oldfield Girls Sch
Kelston Park
A431
A4 Bath
Bristol & Bath STREET ATLAS
Avon Walkway
A431 Bath

5

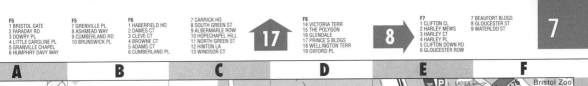

F5
1 BRISTOL GATE
2 FARADAY RD
3 DOWRY PL
4 LITTLE CAROLINE PL
5 GRANVILLE CHAPEL
6 HUMPHRY DAVY WAY

F5
7 GRENVILLE PL
8 ASHMEAD WAY
9 CUMBERLAND RD
10 BRUNSWICK PL

F6
1 HABERFIELD HO
2 DAWES CT
3 CLEVE CT
4 BROWNE CT
5 ADAMS CT
6 CUMBERLAND PL
7 CARRICK HO
8 SOUTH GREEN ST
9 ALBERMARLE ROW
10 HOPECHAPEL HILL
11 NORTH GREEN ST
12 HINTON LA
13 WINDSOR CT

17

F6
14 VICTORIA TERR
15 THE POLYGON
16 GLENDALE
17 PRINCE'S BLDGS
18 WELLINGTON TERR
19 OXFORD PL

8

F7
1 CLIFTON CL
2 HARLEY MEWS
3 HARLEY CT
4 HARLEY PL
5 CLIFTON DOWN RD
6 GLOUCESTER ROW
7 BEAUFORT BLDGS
8 GLOUCESTER ST
9 WATERLOO ST

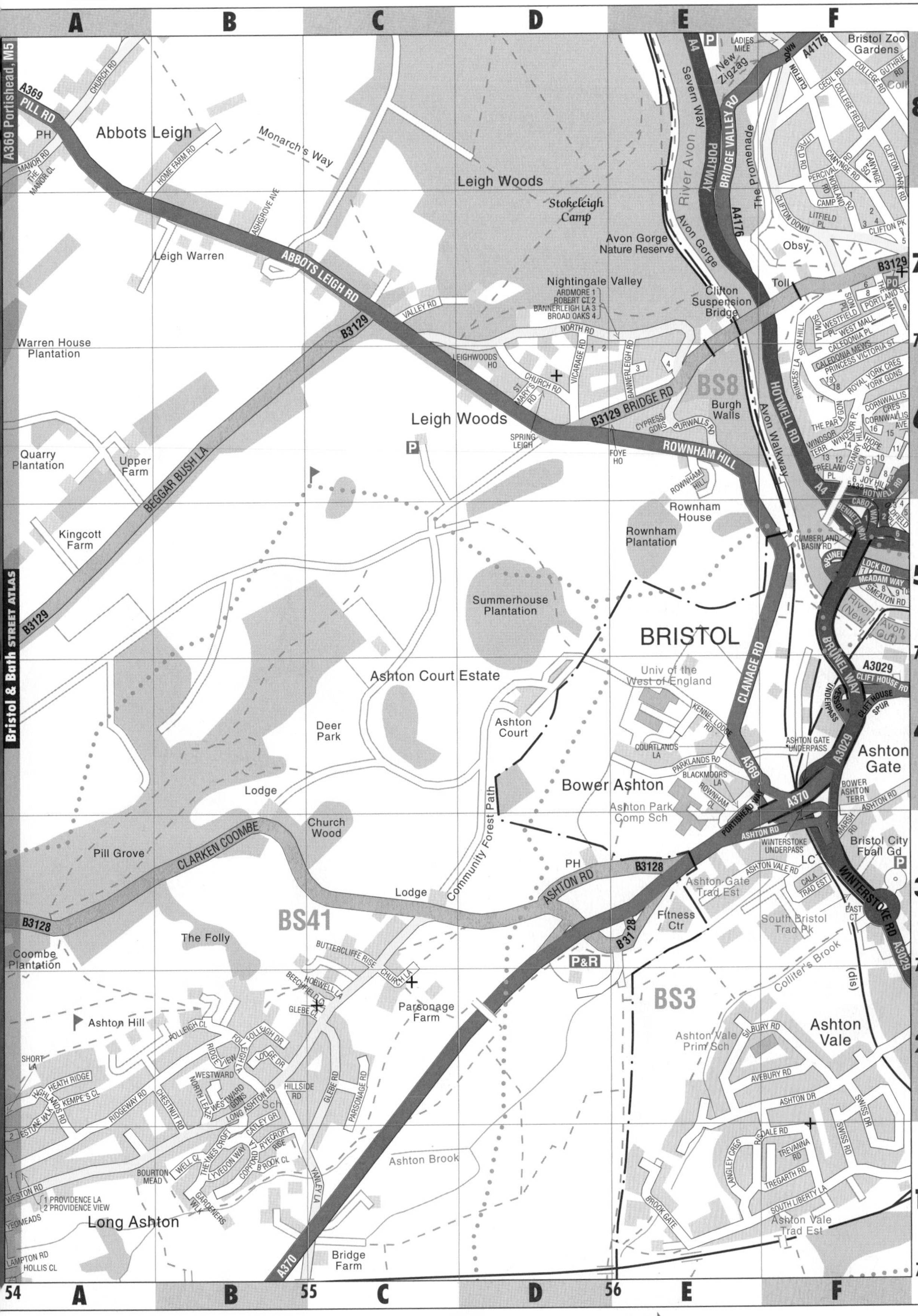

1
8

8
D4
1 DEAN CRES
2 ST PAUL'S RD
3 HOLLIDGE GDNS
4 BERCHEL HO
5 BERRY CROFT
6 LEICESTER ST
7
D4
7 ST CATHERINES PL
8 PERCY ST
9 DOVETON ST
10 BEDMINSTER PL
11 NELSON PAR
18
F4
1 CLIFTON VIEW
2 RICHMOND CT
3 DUNMORE ST
4 HIGHAM ST
5 VERNON ST
6 BELLEVUE RD
7 BELLE CT
8 CHEAPSIDE ST
9 WYCLIFFE ROW
10 BUSH CT
11 BARRINGTON CT
For full street detail of the highlighted area see pages 194 and 195.
A
B
C
D
E
F
8
7
73
6
5
72
4
3
71
2
1
70
57
58
59
194
195
Kingsdown
St Pauls
Clifton
Clifton Coll
Tyndall's Park
Victoria Park
Univ of Bristol
BRISTOL
Clifton Wood
Brandon Hill
Cabot Twr
SS Gt Britain
Canon's Marsh
Hotwells
Floating Harbour
Bristol Harbour Rly
Avon Walkway
River Avon (New Cut)
CORONATION RD
HOTWELL RD
ANCHOR RD
PARK ROW
PARK ST
WHITELADIES RD
QUEEN'S RD
JACOB'S WELLS RD
VICTORIA ST
TEMPLE WAY
TEMPLE WAY UNDERPASS
BALDWIN ST
REDCLIFFE WAY
The Exploratory (Science Ctr)
Temple Meads
Southville
Bedminster
Windmill Hill
Victoria Park
Malago Vale
City of Bristol Coll
Lower Knowle
Knowle
Bedminster Down
Barnack Trad Est
Bristol Vale Ctr For Ind
Novers Hill Trad Est
Nover's Common
Merrywood Sch
Liberty Ind Pk
Duckmoor Road Ind Est
Superstore
Works
Fball Gd
Mast
BS3
BS4
BS13
NORTH ST
WEST ST
WINTERSTOKE RD
BEDMINSTER DOWN RD
BEDMINSTER RD
PARSON ST
HARTCLIFFE WAY
ST JOHN'S LA
REDCATCH RD
WEDMORE VALE
YORK RD
BATH RD
A
B
C
D
E
F
A3
1 WINTERSTOKE HO
2 SOUTHBOW HO
3 WHITEMEAD HO
A4
1 CHALCROFT HO
2 VAUXHALL TERR
3 ASHTON GATE TERR
4 TOLL HOUSE CT
5 ST FRANCIS RD
6 NORTH RD
B2
1 WINTERSTOKE CTR
2 SOUTH LIBERTY LA
3 TRAFALGAR TERR
4 AVONLEIGH CT
5 WINTERSTOKE CL
6 CHESSEL CT
7 CHAPEL BARTON
8 CHURCHLANDS RD
9 BRIGHTON TERR
7
B2
10 OSBORNE TERR
2
B3
1 THISTLE ST
2 MARTIN ST
3 LINDREA ST
4 CROWTHER ST
5 PARKER ST
6 DORSET ST
7 GAYWOOD HO
8 ASHFIELD TERR
9 AUBREY HO
C3
1 ALBERT PL
2 CLYDE CT
3 CLYDE TERR
4 GRAHAM RD
5 STANLEY ST
6 PALMERSTON ST
7 PROSPECT PL
8 WESTBOURNE GR
9 HEBRON RD
10 SION RD
11 SOUTH RD
12 STANLEY ST N
13 SHEENE CT
14 EATON ST
15 NEW JOHN ST
C4
1 KINGSLEY PL
2 FRY CT
3 SMYTH TERR
4 SUMMER ST
5 MERRYWOOD CL
6 ARGYLE ST
7 ACRAMAN'S RD
8 DEAN CRES
9 MURRY ST
10 NORTHFIELD HO
11 MAWDELEY HO

A6
1 KINGSLAND CL
2 UNION RD
3 KINGSLAND ROAD BRIDGE
4 DINGS WLK
5 BIRKIN ST
6 BARTON VALE

A8
1 HARLESTON ST
2 WINSFORD ST
3 PENNYWELL CT
4 BEAUFORT ST
5 ASHMAN CL
6 BEAUMONT TERR
7 RAWNSLEY HO

B7
1 THE ARCHES
2 BAYNTON HO
3 KINGSMARSH HO
4 HEMMINGS PAR
5 BRENTRY AVE
6 CATTYBROOK ST
7 THOMAS ST
8 CASHMORE HO
9 ROWAN CT
10 STRAWBRIDGE RD
11 BEAUFORT HO
12 ST LUKE ST

19

B7
13 HARWOOD HO
14 ERNEST BARKER CL
15 ROBERT ST
16 CHARLTON ST
17 ATCHLEY ST
18 WILLIAM MASON CL

10

F6
1 BARTON CL
2 RIVERSIDE CT
3 BUTLERS WLK
4 QUAYSIDE LA
5 PORT SIDE CL
6 RIVERSIDE WLK
7 ST ANNES CL
8 PARFITT'S HILL
9 CORKER'S HILL
10 ST GEORGES AVE
11 DE LA WARRE CT
12 ELIZABETHS MEWS

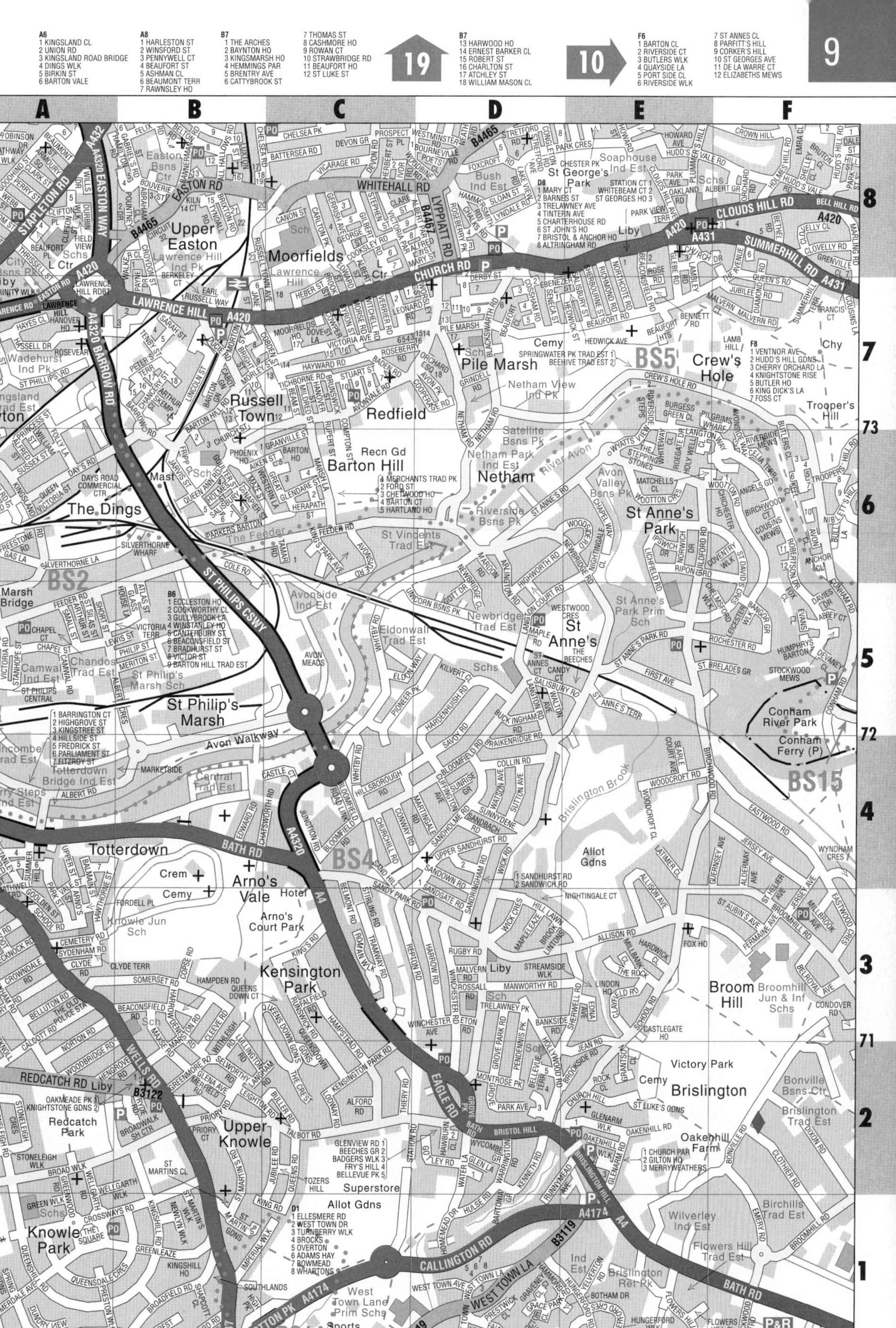

B8
1 CROYDON HO
2 LANSDOWNE CT
3 SHAW CL
4 VINING WLK
5 HILTON CT
6 LANSDOWN RD
7 THOMSON RD
8 WESTBOURNE RD
9 EASTBOURNE RD
10 ELMGROVE AVE
11 ALL HALLOWS CT
12 ADELAIDE PL
13 COMBFACTORY LA
14 LAWNWOOD IND UNITS
15 LAWNWOOD RD
16 BRIGHTON PK
17 KILBURN CT
18 OWEN ST
19 KILBURN ST
20 WINDSOR GR
21 CLAYTON ST
22 BRIXTON ROAD MEWS
23 CATTYBROOK ST

C7
1 MILTON PK
2 WEIGHT RD
3 DRAPER CT
4 CHESTER CT
5 BARKER CT
6 ADRYEN CT
7 OXFORD ST
8 CAMBRIDGE ST
9 YORK ST
10 LANCASTER ST
11 CORBETT HO
12 ASHMEAD HO
13 LONGLANDS HO
14 GARVEY HO
15 OSPREY RD
16 HOWETT RD
17 MATTHEW'S RD
18 RUSSELL TOWN IND PK

3

C8
1 JOHNSONS RD
2 IDA RD
3 SAMUEL ST
4 WHITEHALL TRAD EST
5 LILLIAN ST
6 ALBION ST
7 ARTHUR ST
8 WILLIAM ST
9 LYNTON PL

10

D7
1 SENECA PL
2 HANDEL AVE
3 PARKFIELD AVE
4 WESTON AVE
5 SPEEDWELL AVE
6 BLACKSWARTH HO
7 PADMORE CT
8 SHAFTESBURY TERR
9 LEWIN ST
10 CLAREMONT TERR
11 GEORGE & DRAGON LA
12 GLADSTONE ST
13 TERRELL GDNS
14 GIBBS CT
15 FRAMPTON CT
16 EDWARDS CT
17 DILLON CT
18 ORCHARD CT

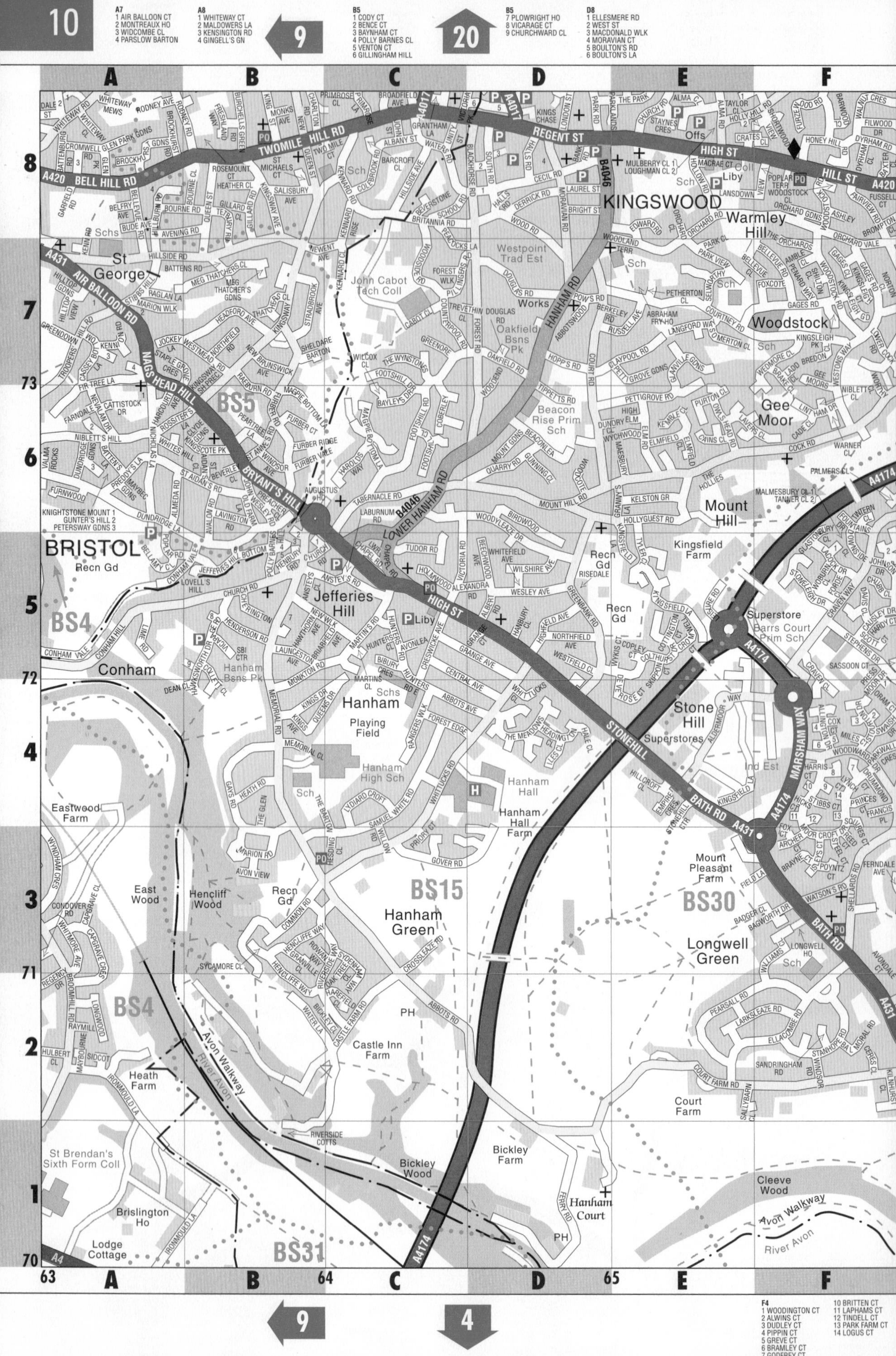

10
A7
1 AIR BALLOON CT
2 MONTREAUX HO
3 WIDCOMBE CL
4 PARSLOW BARTON
A8
1 WHITEWAY CT
2 MALDOWERS LA
3 KENSINGTON RD
4 GINGELL'S GN
9
B5
1 CODY CT
2 BENCE CT
3 BAYNHAM CT
4 POLLY BARNES CL
5 VENTON CT
6 GILLINGHAM HILL
20
B5
7 PLOWRIGHT HO
8 VICARAGE CT
9 CHURCHWARD CL
D8
1 ELLESMERE RD
2 WEST ST
3 MACDONALD WLK
4 MORAVIAN CT
5 BOULTON'S RD
6 BOULTON'S LA
A
B
C
D
E
F
8
7
73
6
5
72
4
3
71
2
1
70
63
64
65
A420
BELL HILL RD
TWOMILE HILL RD
REGENT ST
HIGH ST
HILL ST
A4017
B4046
KINGSWOOD
Warmley Hill
St George
A431
AIR BALLOON RD
NAGS HEAD HILL
BRYANT'S HILL
BS5
John Cabot Tech Coll
Westpoint Trad Est
Works
Oakfield Bsns Pk
HANHAM RD
Woodstock
Gee Moor
Beacon Rise Prim Sch
LOWER HANHAM RD
Mount Hill
A4174
BRISTOL
Recn Gd
KNIGHTSTONE MOUNT 1
GUNTER'S HILL 2
PETERSWAY GDNS 3
Kingsfield Farm
Jefferies Hill
HIGH ST
BS4
Conham
Hanham Bsns Pk
Superstore
Barrs Court Prim Sch
Hanham
Playing Field
Stone Hill
Superstores
MARSHAM WAY
STONEHILL
Ind Est
Hanham High Sch
Hanham Hall
Hanham Hall Farm
BATH RD
Eastwood Farm
East Wood
Hencliff Wood
BS15
Hanham Green
Mount Pleasant Farm
BS30
Longwell Green
BS4
Avon Walkway
River Avon
Castle Inn Farm
PH
Heath Farm
Court Farm
St Brendan's Sixth Form Coll
Bickley Farm
Bickley Wood
Cleeve Wood
Brislington Ho
Hanham Court
Lodge Cottage
BS31
A4
9
4
F4
1 WOODINGTON CT
2 ALWINS CT
3 DUDLEY CT
4 PIPPIN CT
5 GREVE CT
6 BRAMLEY CT
7 GODFREY CT
8 FRAMPTON CT
9 TURNERS CT
10 BRITTEN CT
11 LAPHAMS CT
12 TINDELL CT
13 PARK FARM CT
14 LOGUS CT

A5
1 HENRY WILLIAMSON CT
2 BETJEMAN CT
3 LAURIE LEE CT
4 DYLAN THOMAS CT

A8
1 FILWOOD DR
2 DYRHAM RD
3 LYNTON
4 CHARFIELD

C6
1 ASHCOMBE CL
2 ASHBOURNE CL
3 CHARGROVE
4 HIGHCROFT

21
12

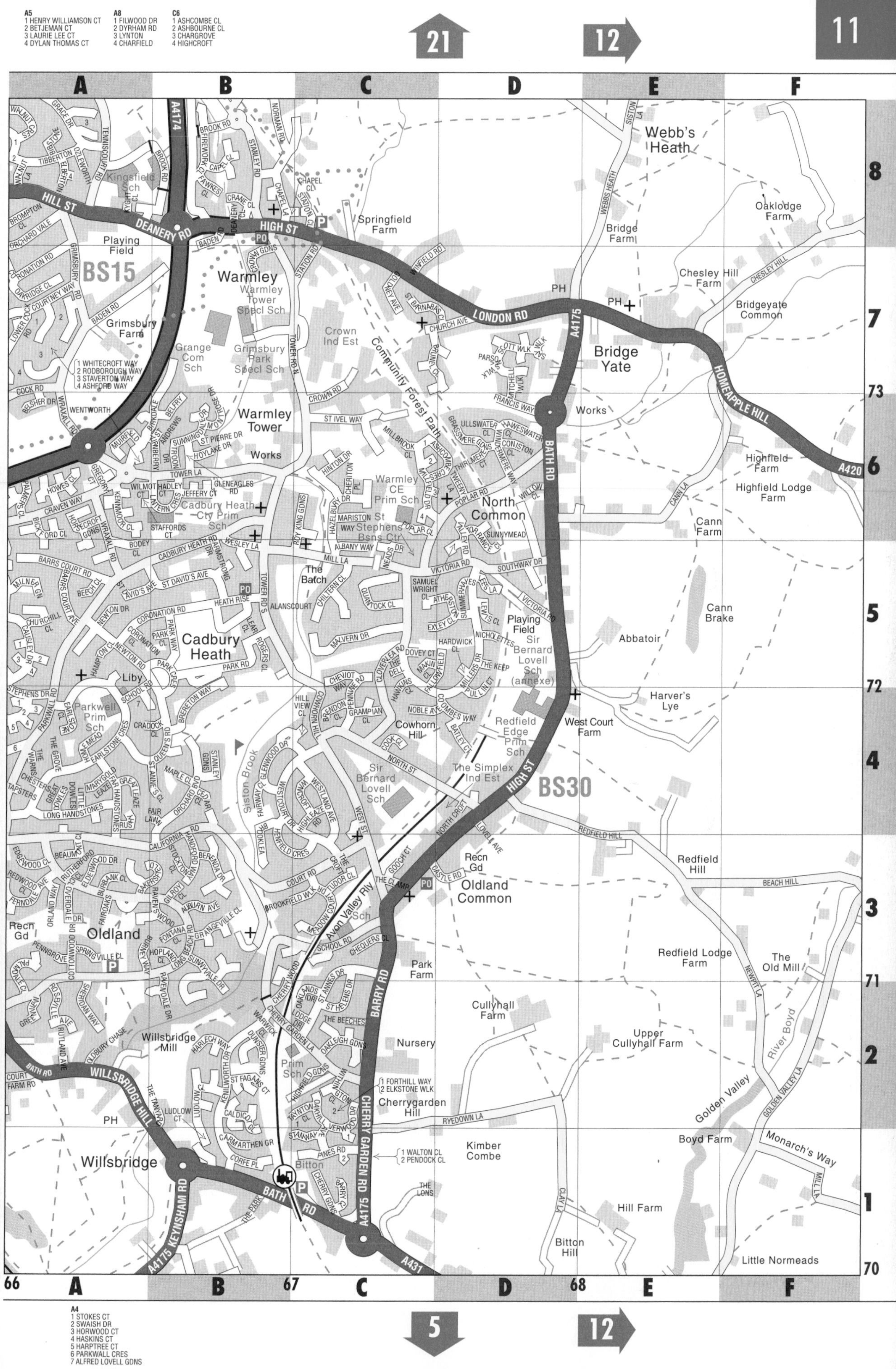

A4
1 STOKES CT
2 SWAISH DR
3 HORWOOD CT
4 HASKINS CT
5 HARPTREE CT
6 PARKWALL CRES
7 ALFRED LOVELL GDNS

5
12

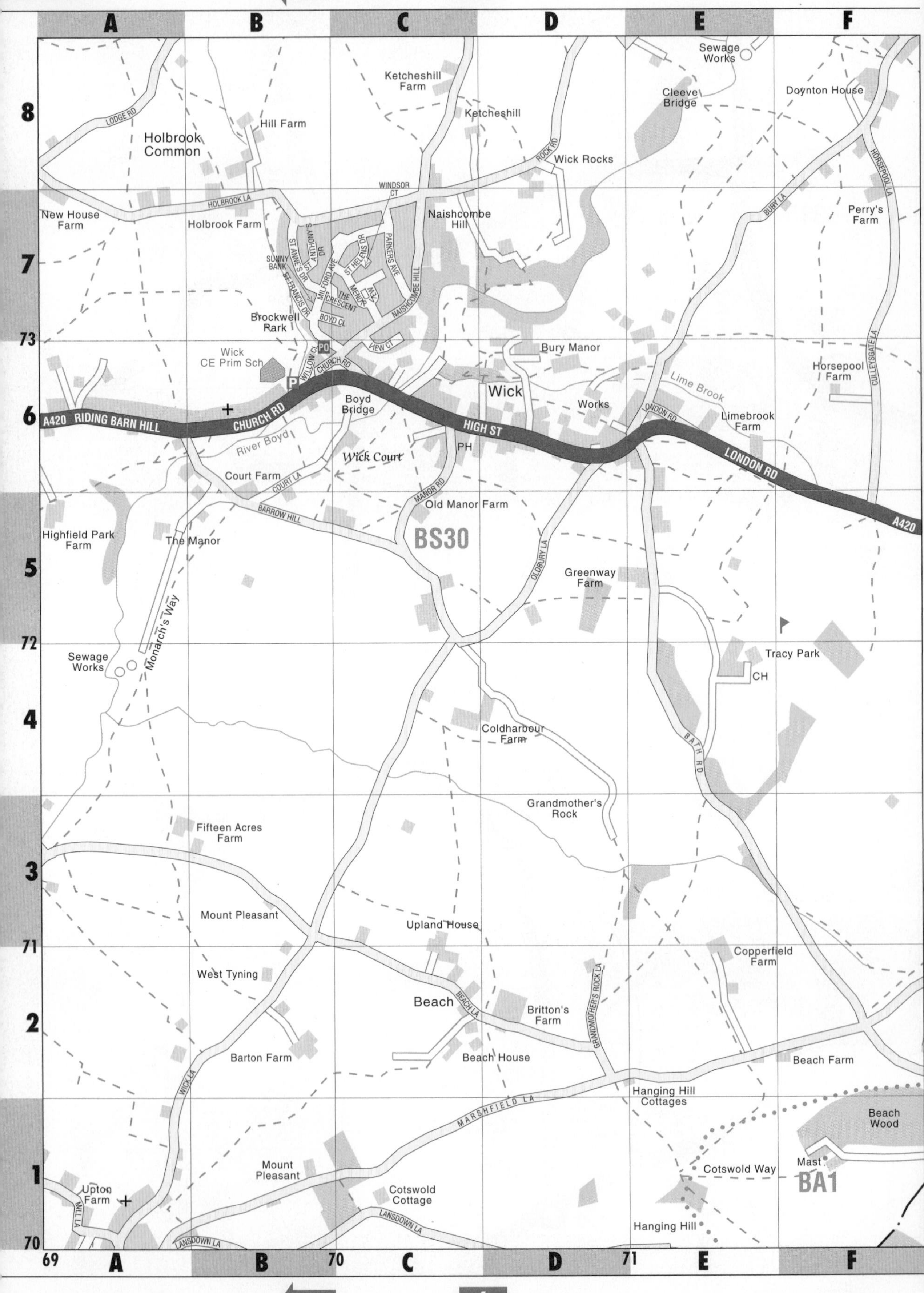
11
22
A
B
C
D
E
F
Sewage Works
Ketcheshill Farm
Cleeve Bridge
Doynton House
Ketcheshill
Hill Farm
Holbrook Common
LODGE RD
ROCK RD
Wick Rocks
HORSEPOOL LA
WINDSOR CT
HOLBROOK LA
New House Farm
Holbrook Farm
Naishcombe Hill
BURY LA
Perry's Farm
ST ANTHONYS DR
ST ANNE'S DR
SUNNY BANK
ST HELENS DR
PARKERS AVE
MILFORD AVE
ST FRANCIS DR
THE CRESCENT
THE MENOR
NAISHCOMBE HILL
Brockwell Park
BOYD CL
PO
NEW CT
Bury Manor
Wick CE Prim Sch
WILLOW CL
CHURCH RD
P
Lime Brook
Horsepool Farm
CULLEYSGATE LA
Wick
Boyd Bridge
Works
LONDON RD
Limebrook Farm
A420
RIDING BARN HILL
CHURCH RD
HIGH ST
River Boyd
PH
Wick Court
LONDON RD
Court Farm
COURT LA
MANOR RD
Old Manor Farm
BARROW HILL
A420
Highfield Park Farm
The Manor
BS30
OLDBURY LA
Greenway Farm
Monarch's Way
Sewage Works
Tracy Park
CH
Coldharbour Farm
BATH RD
Grandmother's Rock
Fifteen Acres Farm
Mount Pleasant
Upland House
Copperfield Farm
West Tyning
GRANDMOTHER'S ROCK LA
Beach
BEACH LA
Britton's Farm
Barton Farm
Beach House
Beach Farm
WICK LA
Hanging Hill Cottages
MARSHFIELD LA
Beach Wood
Mount Pleasant
Mast
Cotswold Way
BA1
Upton Farm
WILL LA
Cotswold Cottage
LANSDOWN LA
Hanging Hill
LANSDOWN LA
8
7
73
6
5
72
4
3
71
2
1
70
69
70
71
11
6

23
14

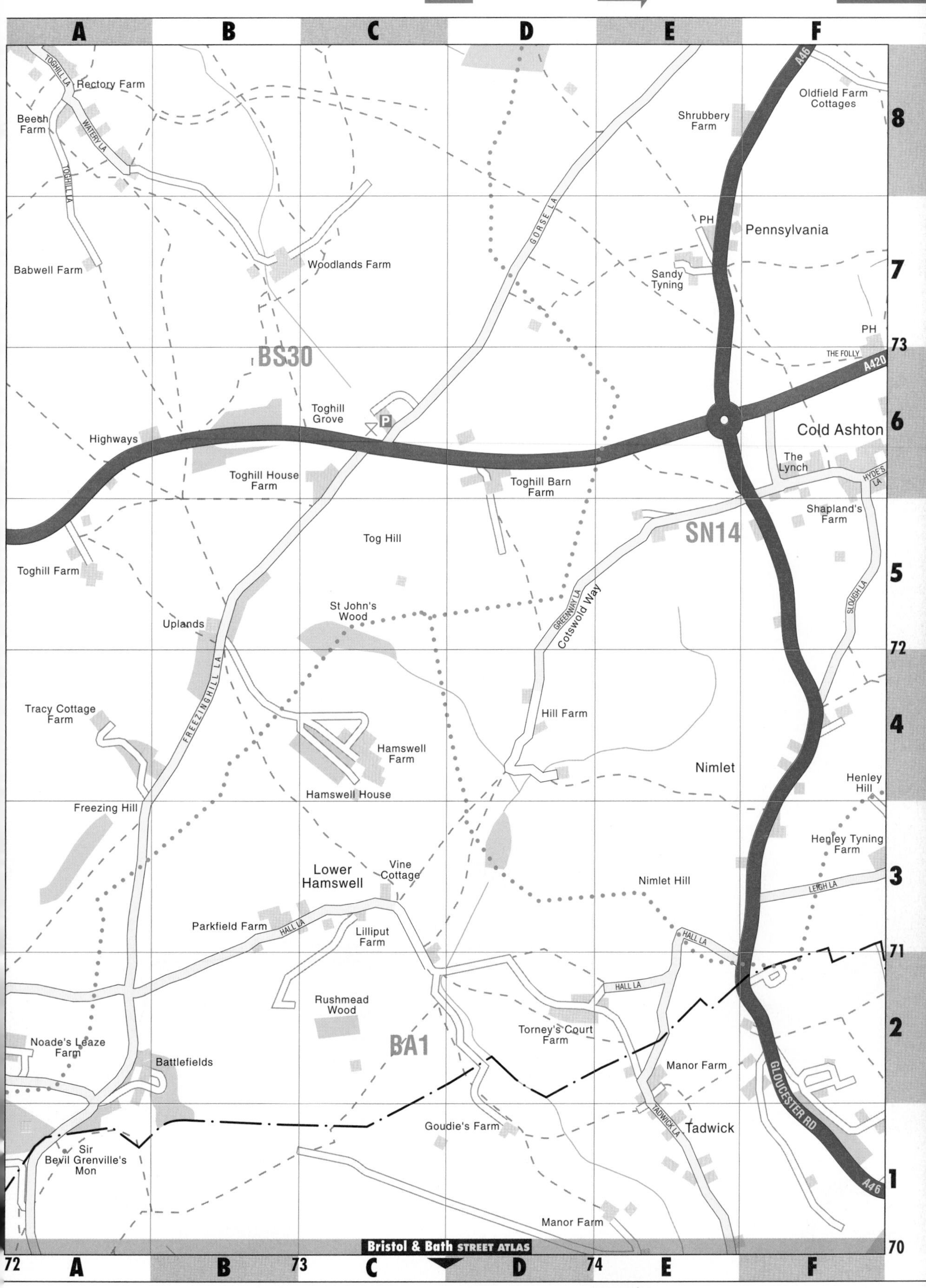
A
B
C
D
E
F
Rectory Farm
Beech Farm
TOGHILL LA
WATERY LA
Oldfield Farm Cottages
Shrubbery Farm
A46
8
Babwell Farm
Woodlands Farm
GORSE LA
PH
Pennsylvania
Sandy Tyning
7
BS30
PH
THE FOLLY
A420
73
Toghill Grove
Highways
Cold Ashton
6
Toghill House Farm
Toghill Barn Farm
The Lynch
HYDE'S LA
Shapland's Farm
SN14
Tog Hill
Toghill Farm
5
St John's Wood
GREENWAY LA
Cotswold Way
SLOUGH LA
Uplands
72
FREEZINGHILL LA
Tracy Cottage Farm
Hill Farm
4
Hamswell Farm
Nimlet
Hamswell House
Henley Hill
Freezing Hill
Henley Tyning Farm
Lower Hamswell
Vine Cottage
Nimlet Hill
3
LEIGH LA
Parkfield Farm
HALL LA
Lilliput Farm
HALL LA
71
HALL LA
Rushmead Wood
2
Torney's Court Farm
Noade's Leaze Farm
BA1
Battlefields
Manor Farm
GLOUCESTER RD
Goudie's Farm
TADWICK LA
Tadwick
Sir Bevil Grenville's Mon
A46
1
Manor Farm
70
72
73
74

14

13
24
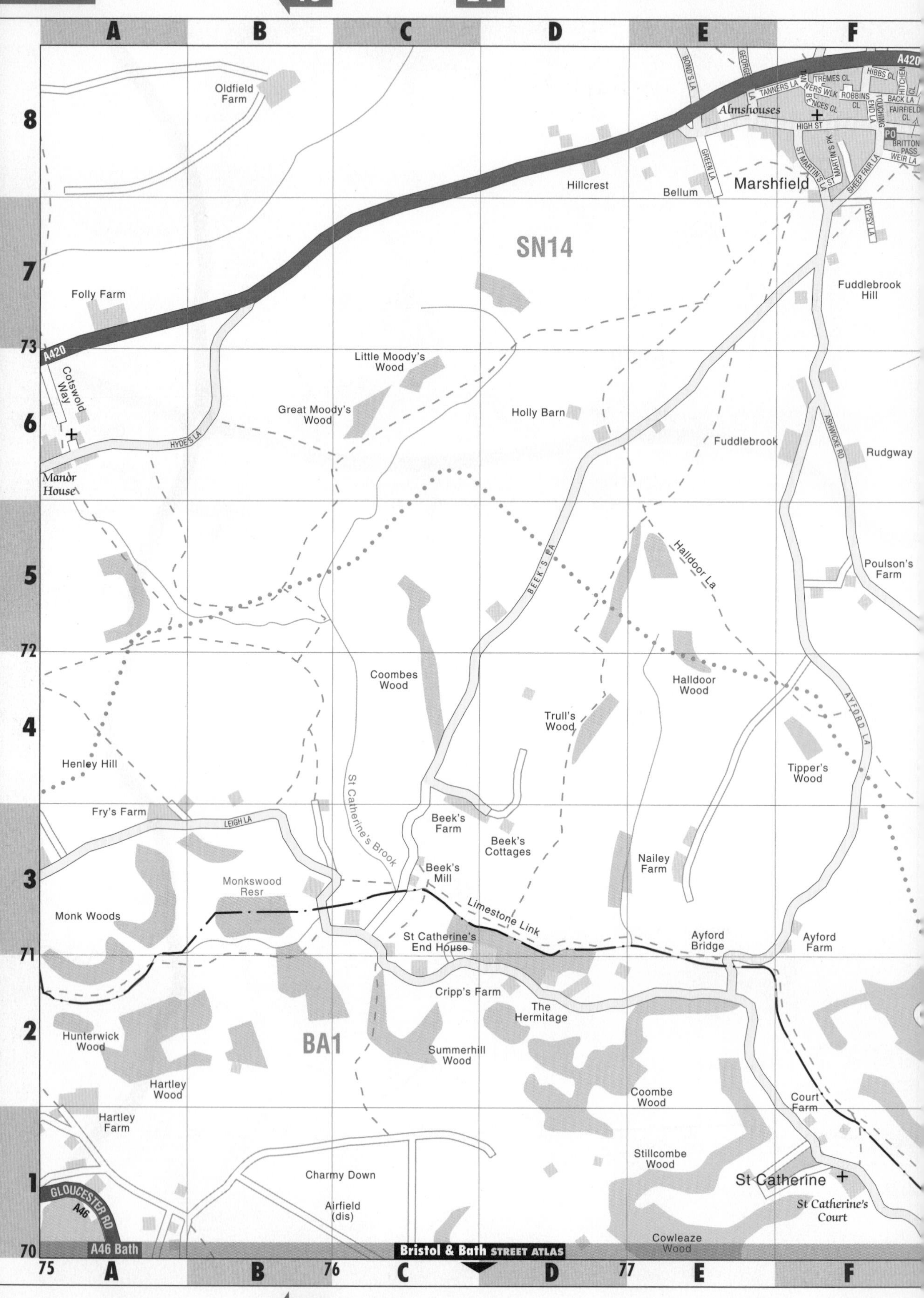
A
B
C
D
E
F
8
7
73
6
5
72
4
3
71
2
1
70
75
76
77
A420
Oldfield Farm
Almshouses
Marshfield
Hillcrest
Bellum
SN14
Folly Farm
Fuddlebrook Hill
Cotswold Way
Little Moody's Wood
Great Moody's Wood
Holly Barn
Fuddlebrook
Rudgway
HYDE'S LA
Manor House
BEEK'S LA
Halldoor La
Poulson's Farm
ASHWICKE RD
Coombes Wood
Halldoor Wood
Trull's Wood
AYFORD LA
Tipper's Wood
Henley Hill
St Catherine's Brook
Fry's Farm
LEIGH LA
Beek's Farm
Beek's Cottages
Beek's Mill
Nailey Farm
Monkswood Resr
Monk Woods
Limestone Link
St Catherine's End House
Ayford Bridge
Ayford Farm
Cripp's Farm
The Hermitage
Hunterwick Wood
BA1
Summerhill Wood
Hartley Wood
Coombe Wood
Court Farm
Hartley Farm
Stillcombe Wood
Charmy Down
Airfield (dis)
St Catherine
St Catherine's Court
GLOUCESTER RD
A46
A46 Bath
Cowleaze Wood
BOND'S LA
GEORGE LA
TANNERS LA
TANNERS WLK
TREMES CL
ROBBINS CL
BENCES CL
HIGH ST
HIBBS CL
KITCHEN CL
BACK LA
FAIRFIELD CL
TOUCHING END LA
PO
BRITTON PASS
WEIR LA
GREEN LA
ST MARTIN'S LA
ST MARTIN'S PK
SHEEP FAIR LA
GYPSY LA

13

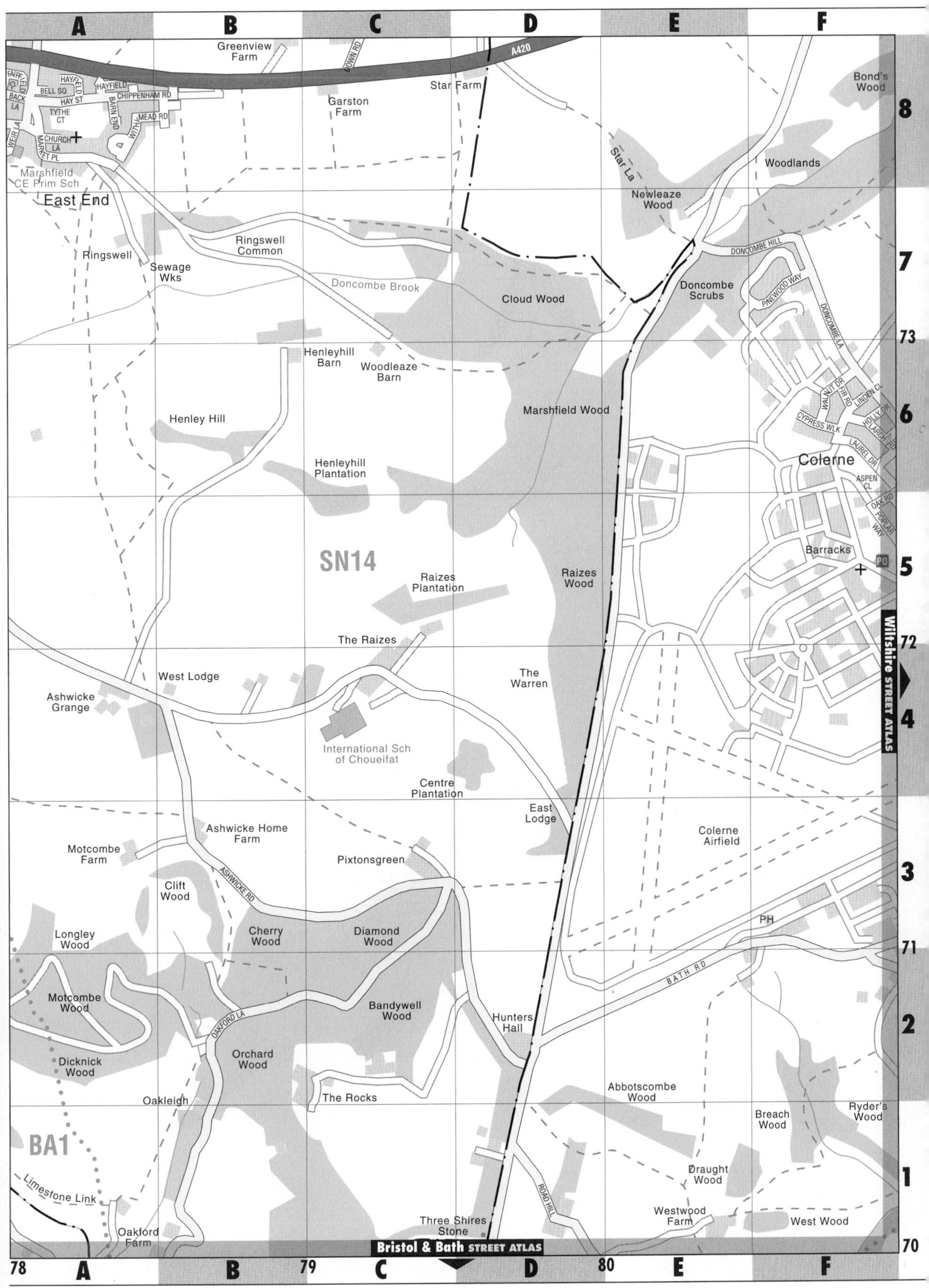

Wiltshire STREET ATLAS

Bristol & Bath STREET ATLAS

26

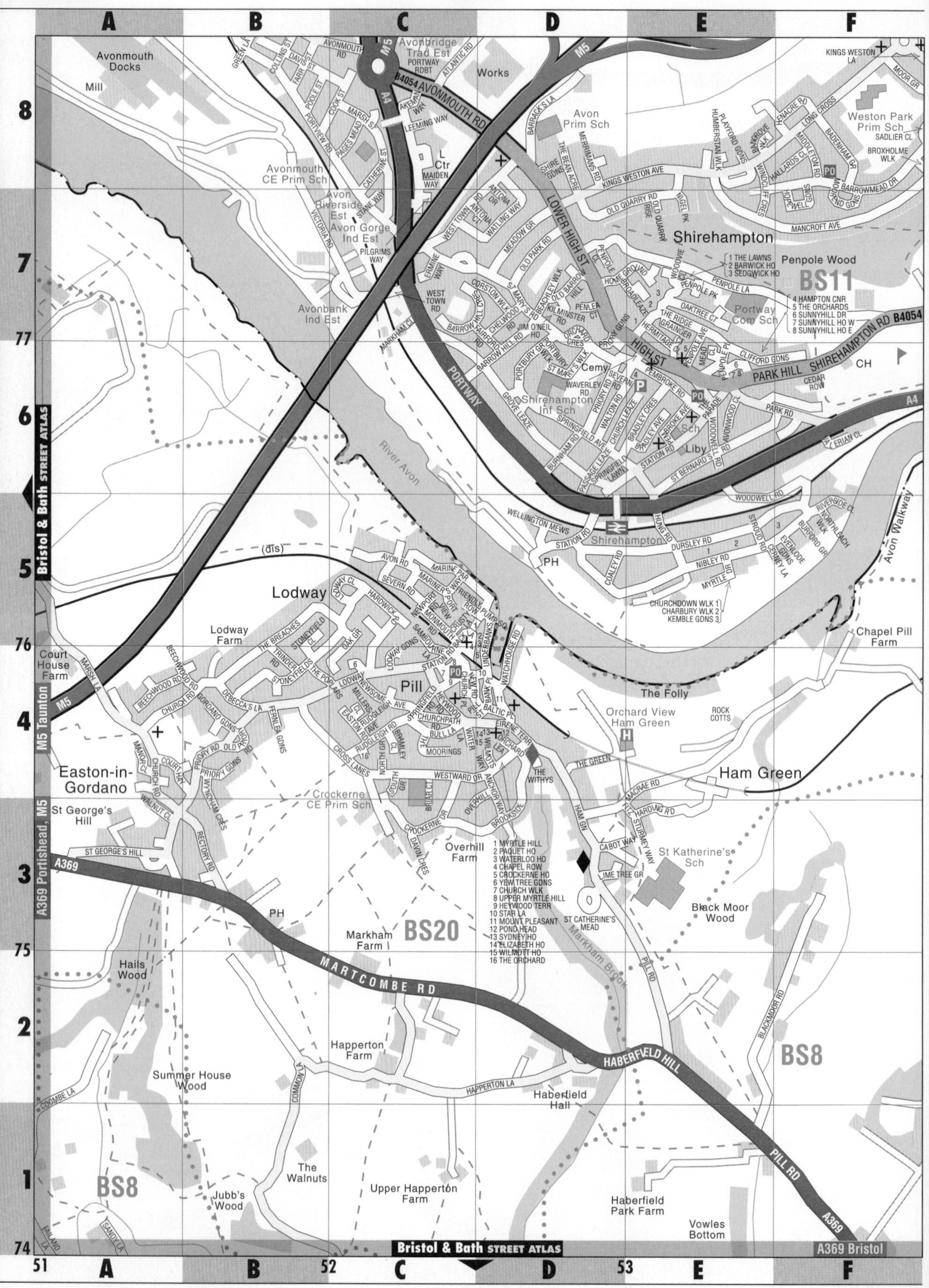
A
B
C
D
E
F
Avonmouth Docks
Mill
Avonbridge Trad Est
PORTWAY RDBT
Works
B4054 AVONMOUTH RD
M5
A4
Avon Prim Sch
KINGS WESTON LA
Weston Park Prim Sch
SADLIER CL
BROXHOLME WLK
Avonmouth CE Prim Sch
Avon Riverside Est
Avon Gorge Ind Est
PILGRIMS WAY
L Ctr
MAIDEN WAY
LEEMING WAY
KINGS WESTON AVE
OLD QUARRY RD
LOWER HIGH ST
Shirehampton
MANCROFT AVE
Penpole Wood
BS11
1 THE LAWNS
2 BARWICK HO
3 SEDGWICK HO
4 HAMPTON CNR
5 THE ORCHARDS
6 SUNNYHILL DR
7 SUNNYHILL HO W
8 SUNNYHILL HO E
Portway Com Sch
B4054
SHIREHAMPTON RD
PARK HILL
CH
CEDAR ROW
HIGH ST
Cemy
Shirehampton Inf Sch
Liby
Sch
PORTWAY
PARK RD
Avonbank Ind Est
WEST TOWN RD
River Avon
WELLINGTON MEWS
STATION RD
Shirehampton
DURSLEY RD
NIBLEY RD
MYRTLE DR
CHURCHDOWN WLK 1
CHARBURY WLK 2
KEMBLE GDNS 3
WOODWELL RD
Avon Walkway
Chapel Pill Farm
PH
(dis)
Lodway
Lodway Farm
Court House Farm
MARSH LA
Pill
The Folly
Orchard View Ham Green
ROCK COTTS
Ham Green
Easton-in-Gordano
St George's Hill
ST GEORGE'S HILL
Crockerne CE Prim Sch
THE WITHYS
Overhill Farm
St Katherine's Sch
Black Moor Wood
1 MYRTLE HILL
2 PAQUET HO
3 WATERLOO HO
4 CHAPEL ROW
5 CROCKERNE HO
6 YEW TREE GDNS
7 CHURCH WLK
8 UPPER MYRTLE HILL
9 HEYWOOD TERR
10 STAR LA
11 MOUNT PLEASANT
12 POND HEAD
13 SYDNEY HO
14 ELIZABETH HO
15 WILMOTT HO
16 THE ORCHARD
ST CATHERINE'S MEAD
Markham Brook
A369
PH
Markham Farm
BS20
MARTCOMBE RD
Hails Wood
Happerton Farm
HAPPERTON LA
HABERFIELD HILL
Haberfield Hall
BS8
Summer House Wood
COOMBE LA
COMMON LA
The Walnuts
Upper Happerton Farm
Jubb's Wood
BS8
Haberfield Park Farm
Vowles Bottom
PILL RD
BLACKMOOR RD
M5 Taunton
A369 Portishead, M5
Bristol & Bath STREET ATLAS
A369 Bristol
8
7
77
6
5
76
4
3
75
2
1
74
51
52
53

27
18

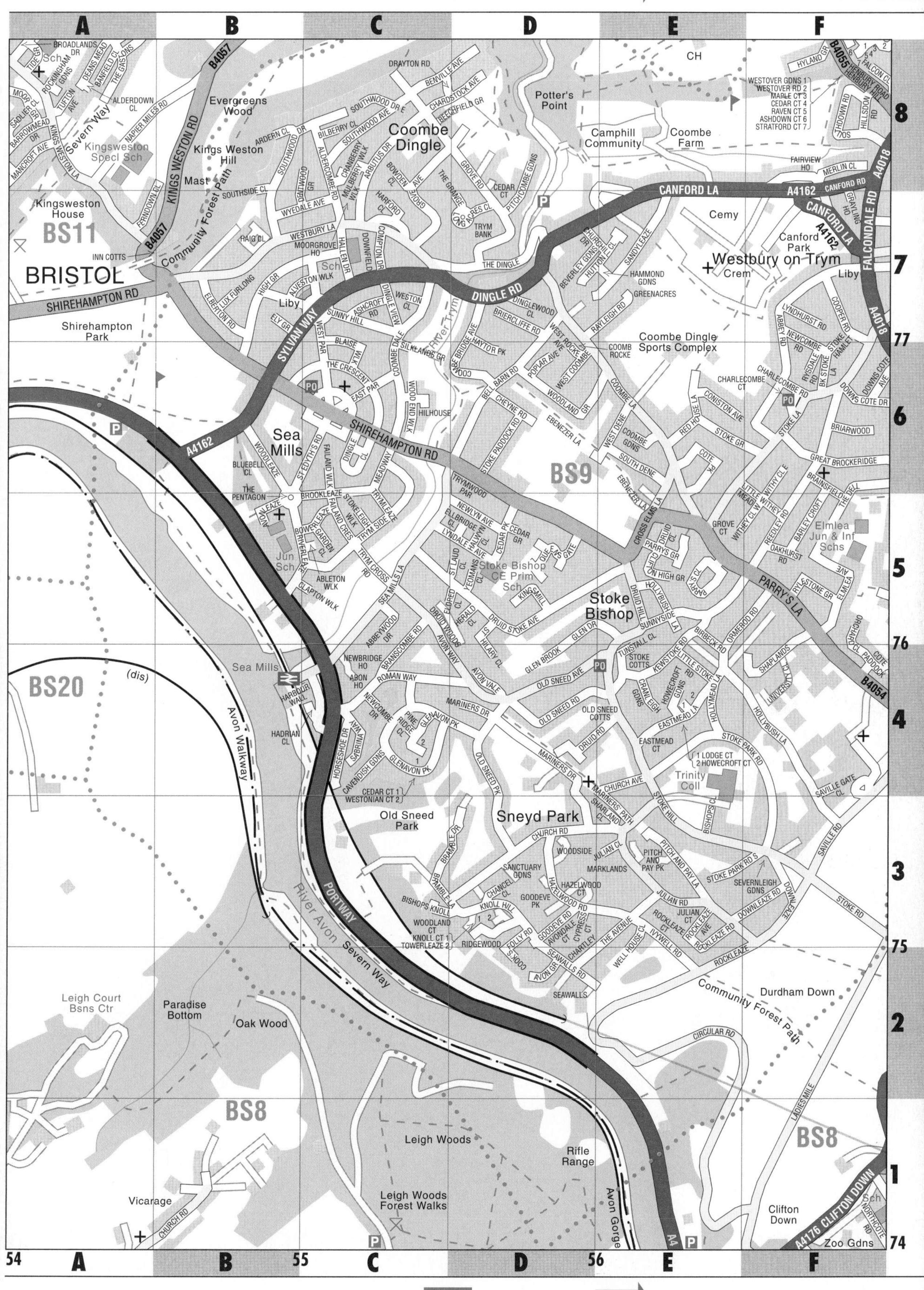
BRISTOL
BS11
BS9
BS20
BS8
Coombe Dingle
Sea Mills
Stoke Bishop
Sneyd Park
Westbury on Trym
Shirehampton Park
Kingsweston House
Evergreens Wood
Kings Weston Hill
Potter's Point
Camphill Community
Coombe Farm
Coombe Dingle Sports Complex
Old Sneed Park
Leigh Woods
Leigh Woods Forest Walks
Durdham Down
Clifton Down
Paradise Bottom
Oak Wood
Rifle Range
Avon Gorge
River Avon
Severn Way
Avon Walkway
Community Forest Path
PORTWAY
SHIREHAMPTON RD
DINGLE RD
SYLVAN WAY
CANFORD LA
PARRY'S LA
FALCONDALE RD
KINGS WESTON RD
A4162
A4018
B4057
B4054
B4055
A4
A4176 CLIFTON DOWN
Zoo Gdns
Trinity Coll
Cemy
Crem
Leigh Court Bsns Ctr
Vicarage

7
18

A7
1 WESTMINSTER CL
2 CARLTON HO
3 CARLTON CT

B6
1 CRANFORD CT
2 BLANDFORD CL
3 ST PETER'S WLK

F1
1 BUDD HO
2 CARY CT

17

F1
3 CARR HO
4 WINKWORTH PL
5 BEVIN CT
6 COREY CL
7 LANGSDOWN HO
8 DAVEY TERR
9 NEWFOUNDLAND RD

28

F1
10 FRANKLYN LA
11 DERMOT ST
12 CAIRNS' CRES
13 LOWER ASHLEY RD
14 GORDON RD
15 MARY CARPENTER PL

F2
1 SOMMERVILLE RD S
2 ASHLEY COURT RD
3 BALMORAL MANS
4 FALKLAND RD
5 CUMBERLAND GR
6 ASHLEY TRAD EST
7 ASHLEY GROVE RD
8 MINTO ROAD IND CTR
9 MINTO RD
10 PARKWAY TRAD EST
11 LYNMOUTH RD

A B C D E F

Westbury-on-Trym, Eastfield, Henleaze, Golden Hill, Horfield, Westbury Park, Bishopston, Ashley Down, Redland, Montpelier, Woolcott Park, Cotham, Durdham Down

57 A B 58 C D 59 E F

A2
1 ST VINCENT'S HILL
2 YORK ST
3 HIGHLAND CRES
4 HIGHLAND SQ
5 BELGRAVE HILL
6 RICHMOND DALE
7 RICHMOND CT
8 QUARRY STEPS
9 SUTHERLAND PL
10 WORRALL MEWS
11 WORRALL PL
12 HAYDON CT
13 HIGHLAND PL
14 MORNINGTON RD
15 ANGLESEA PL
16 NORMANTON RD

B1
1 KING'S PARADE AVE
2 GROSVENOR CT
3 COMPTON LODGE
4 COLLINGWOOD RD
5 PLIMSOLL HO
6 OAKLAND RD
7 TYNDALE CT
8 IMPERIAL RD
9 WHATLEY CT
10 CLIFTON METRO
11 CLIFTON DOWN SH CTR
12 GEORGE CT

17

13 HOPKINS CT
14 BHIRRAFF CT
15 COTHAM GDNS
16 PITVILLE PL
17 HAMPTON LA

B2
1 FERNLEIGH CT
2 LOWER REDLAND MEWS
3 EAST SHRUBBERY
4 SHRUBBERY COTTS

8

5 WEST SHRUBBERY
6 SOUTH TERR
7 FITZROY TERR
8 REDLAND TERR
9 BURLINGTON CT
10 GREENWAY HO

C2
1 ERMLEET RD
2 FERNBANK CT
3 CLYDE MEWS

D1
1 ELMGROVE PK
2 CHELTENHAM CRES
3 LLANARTH VILLAS
4 ARLEY COTTS
5 HILLSIDE HO
6 VICTORIA CT
7 VICTORIA GDNS
8 FREMANTLE LA
9 THORPE LODGE

D1
10 ST MATTHEW'S AVE
11 PRIOR'S HILL
12 THOMAS ST N

D2
1 PROSPECT PL
2 BROOKFIELD LA
3 BROOKFIELD RD

E1
1 MILLBROOK CT

E1
2 ARMIDALE AVE
3 ARMIDALE COTTS
4 WOODMANCOTE RD
5 NORRISVILLE RD
6 NINE TREE HILL
7 DOVE ST
8 ARMADA HO
9 ARMADA PL
10 HEPBURN RD

E1
11 DALRYMPLE RD
12 BARNABAS ST
13 BRIGHTON ST

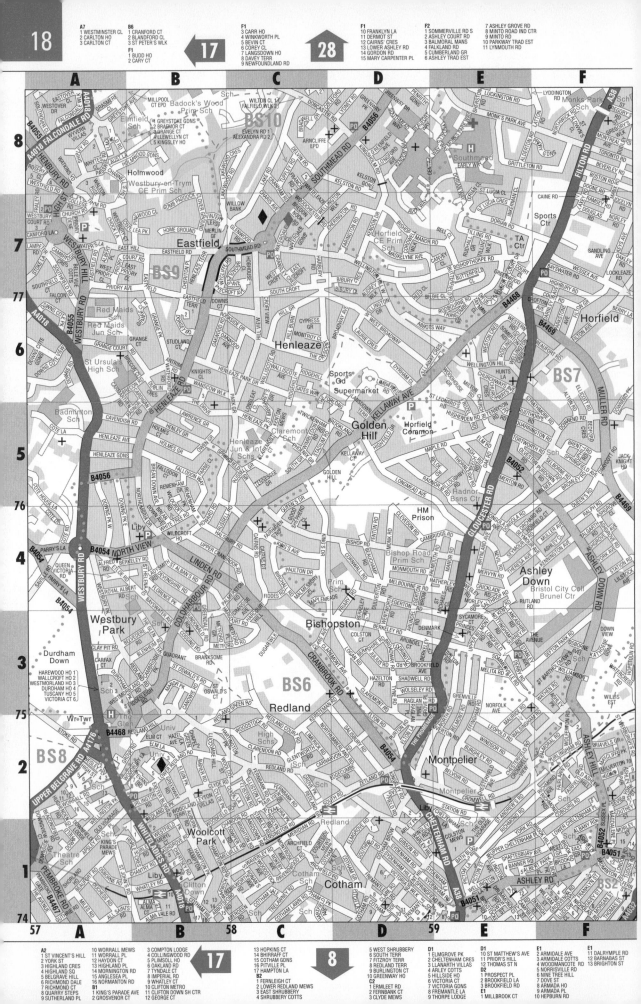

A1
1 ASHLEY GROVE RD
2 CONDUIT PL
3 SUMMERS TERR
4 SUMMERS RD
5 BYRON ST
6 NEWFOUNDLAND RD
7 GABLE RD
8 WAVERLEY ST
9 MILLPOND ST
10 MILL HO
11 BEAN ST
12 KENSINGTON PK
13 RAWNSLEY HO

A2
1 RYLAND PL
2 BOUCHER PL
3 LYNMOUTH RD
4 SEDDON RD
5 TREEFIELD PL
6 WEEDON CL
7 TRENTHAM CL
8 MINTO ROAD IND CTR
9 DORSET GR
10 DURHAM RD
11 TEWKESBURY RD
12 MERSTHAM RD

29

B1
1 ST MARK'S AVE
2 CHAPEL RD
3 CHURCH AVE
4 ST MARKS CHURCH HO
5 HENRIETTA ST
6 MANOR HO
7 WARWICK AVE

20

B1
8 ST MARK'S GR
9 MANOR CT
10 ST NICHOLAS PK
11 ST MARK'S TERR
12 RENE RD
13 ST MARKS HO
14 OXFORD PL
15 ROSHNI GAR W
16 ROSHNI GAR E
17 MOORHILL ST
18 NORTHCOTE ST
19 BELTON RD
20 NORMANBY RD
21 GRAHAM RD

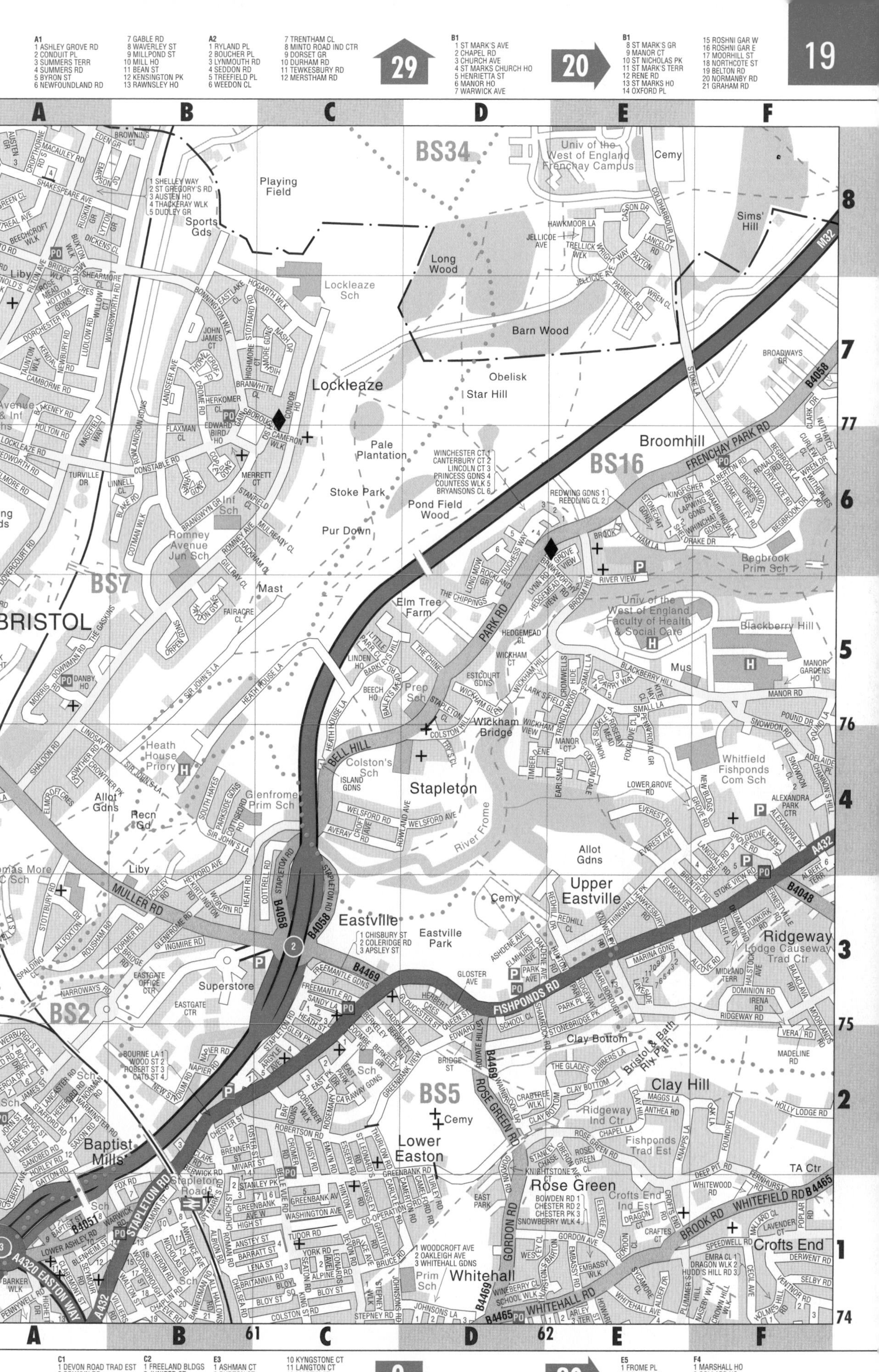

C1
1 DEVON ROAD TRAD EST
2 COLWYN RD
3 LENA AVE
4 LITTLETON ST
5 GREENHAVEN
6 CARTLEDGE RD
7 PRUDHAM ST

C2
1 FREELAND BLDGS
2 JUNIPER CT
3 FOUNTAINE CT
4 BOSWELL ST
5 ARGYLE ST

E3
1 ASHMAN CT
2 BURTON CT
3 COLSTONE CT
4 DAINES CT
5 ELLYOTT CT
6 FRANKLYN CT
7 GOLDNEY CT
8 HAYTHORNE CT
9 JEFFREYS CT
10 KYNGSTONE CT
11 LANGTON CT
12 MARTIN CT
13 MARLBOROUGH AVE

9

20

E5
1 FROME PL
2 SCHOOL LA
3 GLENSIDE PK
4 SPIRES VIEW
5 BLACKBERRY AVE

F4
1 MARSHALL HO
2 COLLARD HO
3 GROVE AVE
4 FEATHERSTONE RD
5 STOKE VIEW PK
6 WHARF RD

19
30

D5
1 BRITANNIA CT
2 OVERNHURST CT
3 GARTON HO
4 PLEASANT HO
5 PENDENNIS HO
6 SHRUBBERY CT
7 BERKELEY HO
8 NELSON HO

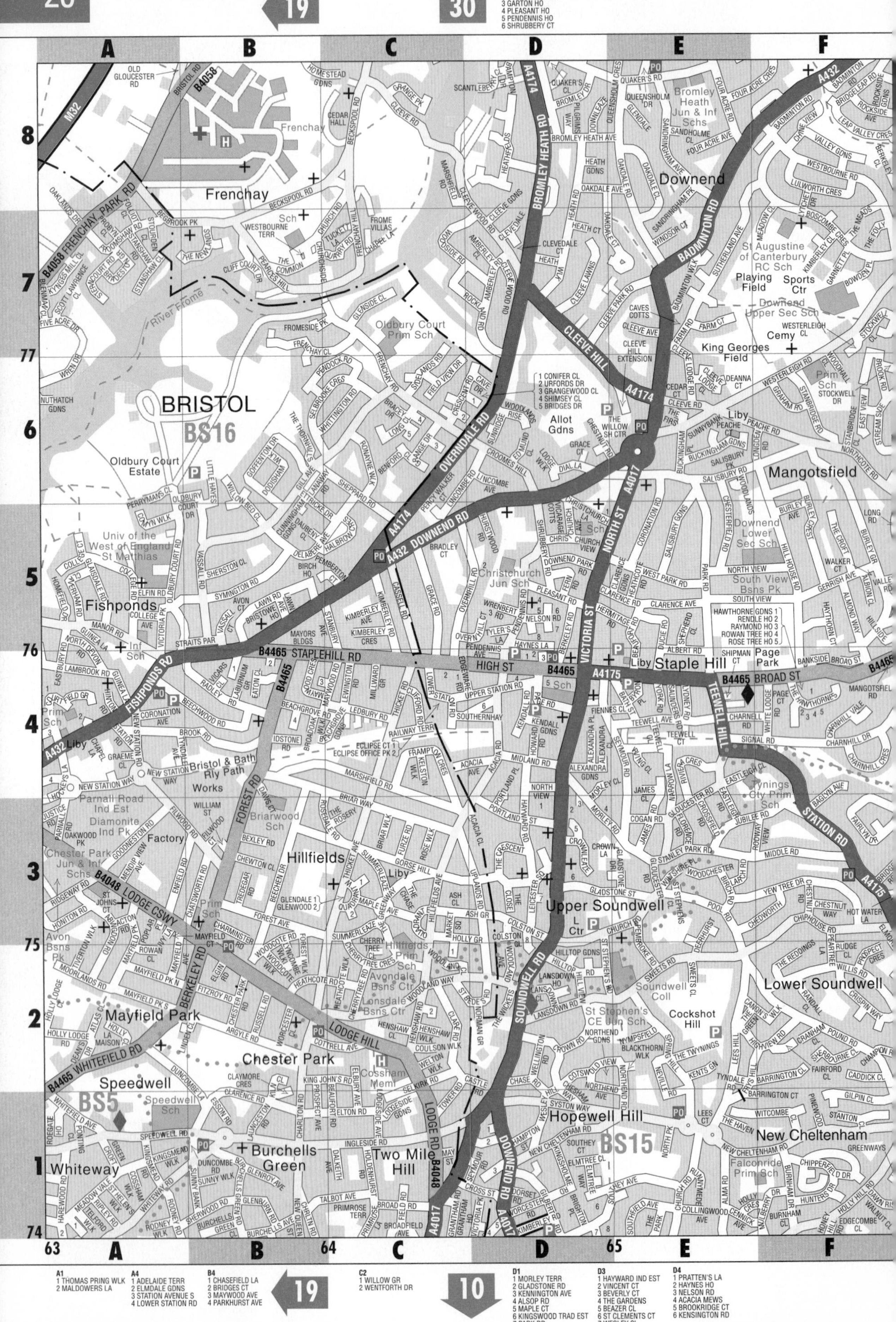

A1
1 THOMAS PRING WLK
2 MALDOWERS LA

A4
1 ADELAIDE TERR
2 ELMDALE GDNS
3 STATION AVENUE S
4 LOWER STATION RD

B4
1 CHASEFIELD LA
2 BRIDGES CT
3 MAYWOOD AVE
4 PARKHURST AVE

19

C2
1 WILLOW GR
2 WENTFORTH DR

10

D1
1 MORLEY TERR
2 GLADSTONE RD
3 KENNINGTON AVE
4 ALSOP RD
5 MAPLE CT
6 KINGSWOOD TRAD EST
7 PARK RD
8 HICKLING CT

D3
1 HAYWARD IND EST
2 VINCENT CT
3 BEVERLY CT
4 THE GARDENS
5 BEAZER CL
6 ST CLEMENTS CT
7 WESLEY CL
8 WHITFIELD CL

D4
1 PRATTEN'S LA
2 HAYNES HO
3 NELSON RD
4 ACACIA MEWS
5 BROOKRIDGE CT
6 KENSINGTON RD

A7
1 WAKEFORD RD
2 WESTBOURNE CL

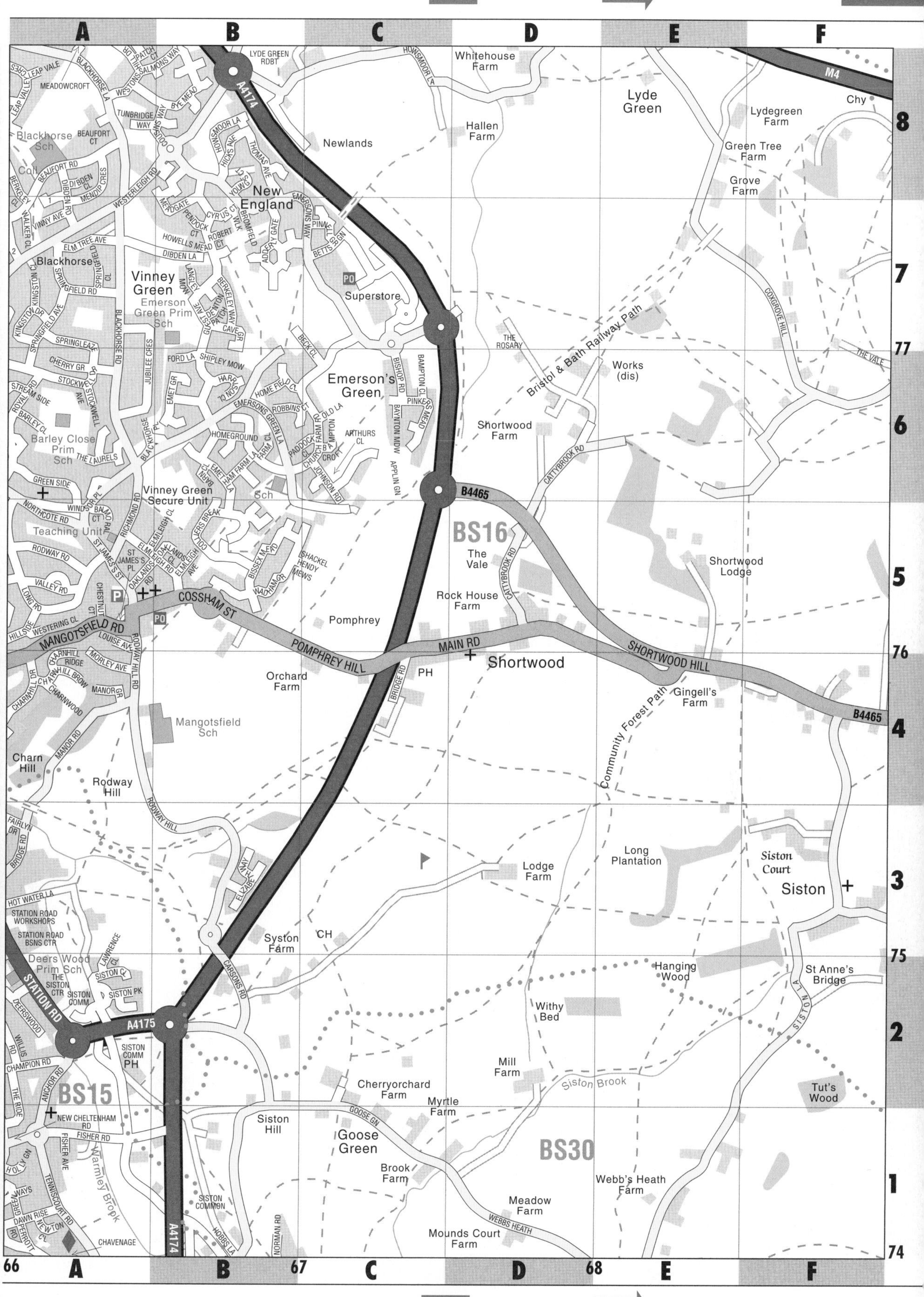

21
32
BS37
BS37
M4
M4
B4465
BATCHFIELD LA
Park Farm
Ivy Cottage
Monarch's Way
St Aldam's Ash Farm
Parkfield
WESTERLEIGH RD
Barleyclose Farm
PARKFIELD RD
PH
Lower Fields Farm
Bridehill Farm
Pucklechurch CE Prim Sch
Cranford Farm
King's La
EDMUND CT
Feltham Farm
Feltham Brook
SN14
LANSDOWN RD
CASTLE RD
PH
FELTHAM RD
BS16
HILL VIEW RD
Pucklechurch
QUEEN'S RD
PO
HOMEFIELD RD
Marsh Farm
Home Farm
ORCHARD RD
MAPLE WLK
POPLAR DR
CHERRYTREE CT
Churchmead Farm
BIRCH DR
CEDAR WAY
HOLLY CL
DENNISWORTH
Dennisworth Farm
BECKET CT
ST ALDAMS DR
HAWTHORNE CL
HAWTHORNE RIDGE DR
HODDON LA
KESTREL DR
EAGLE CRES
GOLDFINCH WAY
Pucklechurch Trad Est
OAK TREE AVE
MERLIN RIDGE
WOODPECKER CRES
PARTRIDGE RD
SHORTWOOD RD
BECKET CT
COSSHAM RD
HM Remand Centre
B4465
SHORTWOOD RD
Back La
BACK LA
REDFORD LA
Redford La
Sewage Works
ABSON RD
ROOKERY LA
Trunk House
Primrose Wood
Northmead Farm
Rookery Farm
Overscourt Farm
Collin's Farm
Church Farm
Abson
Woodlands Farm
Wilton Farm
Bottoms Farm
BS30
Abson Edith Farm
LODGE RD
Doynton Mill
Feltham Brook
Wilkes' Farm
MILL LA
Boyd Bridge
River Boyd
Clovermead Farm
CLEEVE LA
Gatherham Farm
HAM LA
Monarch's Way
HIGH ST
Blue Lodge
PH
A
B
C
D
E
F
8
7
77
6
5
76
4
3
75
2
1
74
69
70
71

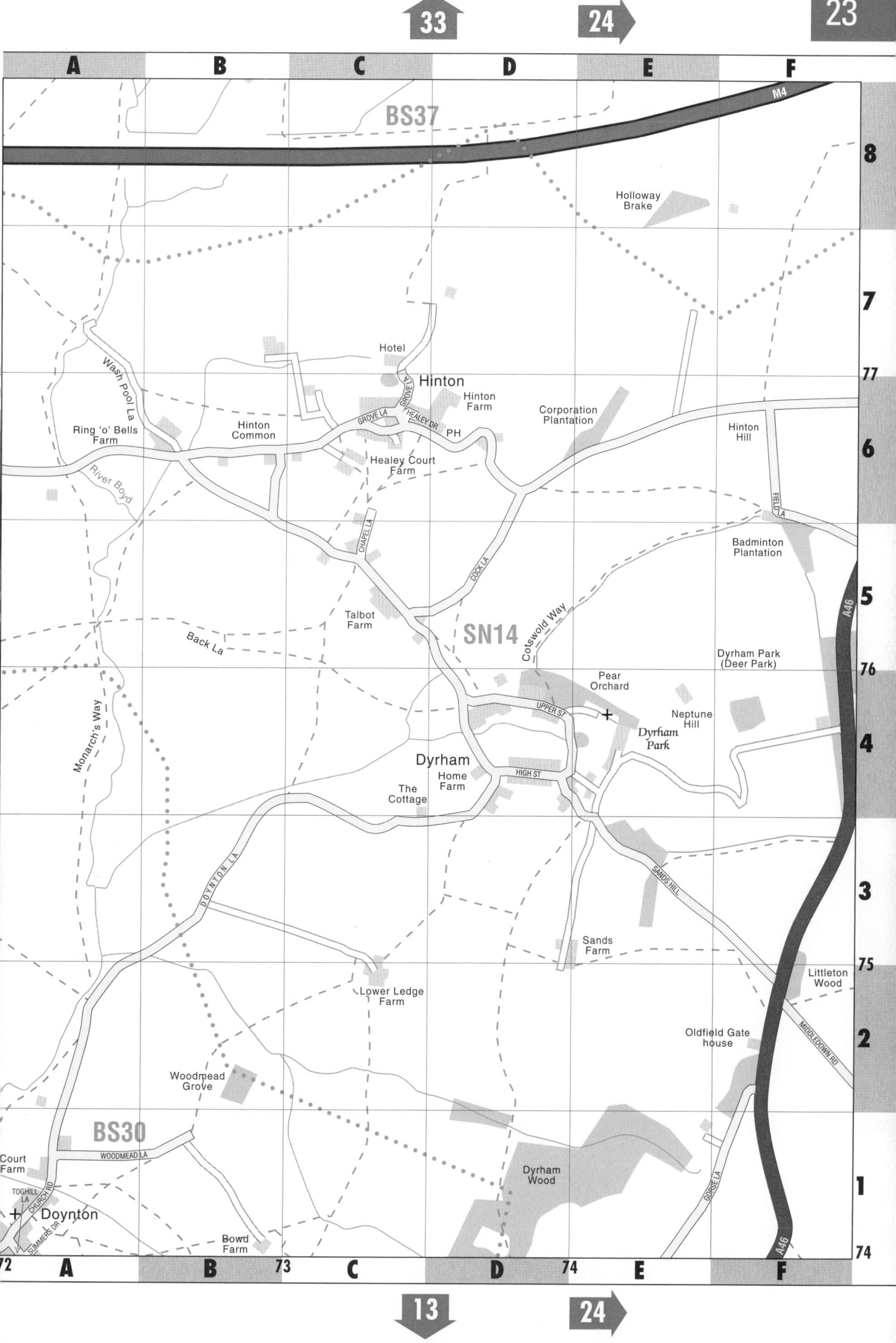
33
24
A
B
C
D
E
F
BS37
M4
8
Holloway Brake
7
Hotel
Hinton
77
Hinton Farm
Corporation Plantation
Wash Pool La
GROVE LA
HEALEY DR
Ring 'o' Bells Farm
Hinton Common
PH
Hinton Hill
6
Healey Court Farm
River Boyd
FIELD LA
CHAPEL LA
Badminton Plantation
COCK LA
5
A46
Cotswold Way
Talbot Farm
SN14
Back La
Dyrham Park (Deer Park)
76
Pear Orchard
UPPER ST
Neptune Hill
Monarch's Way
Dyrham Park
4
Dyrham
Home Farm
HIGH ST
The Cottage
SANDS HILL
DOYNTON LA
3
Sands Farm
75
Littleton Wood
Lower Ledge Farm
2
Oldfield Gate house
MIDDLEDOWN RD
Woodmead Grove
BS30
WOODMEAD LA
Court Farm
Dyrham Wood
1
TOGHILL LA
CHURCH RD
GORSE LA
Doynton
SUMMERS DR
Bowd Farm
A46
74
72
73
74
13
24

23
34

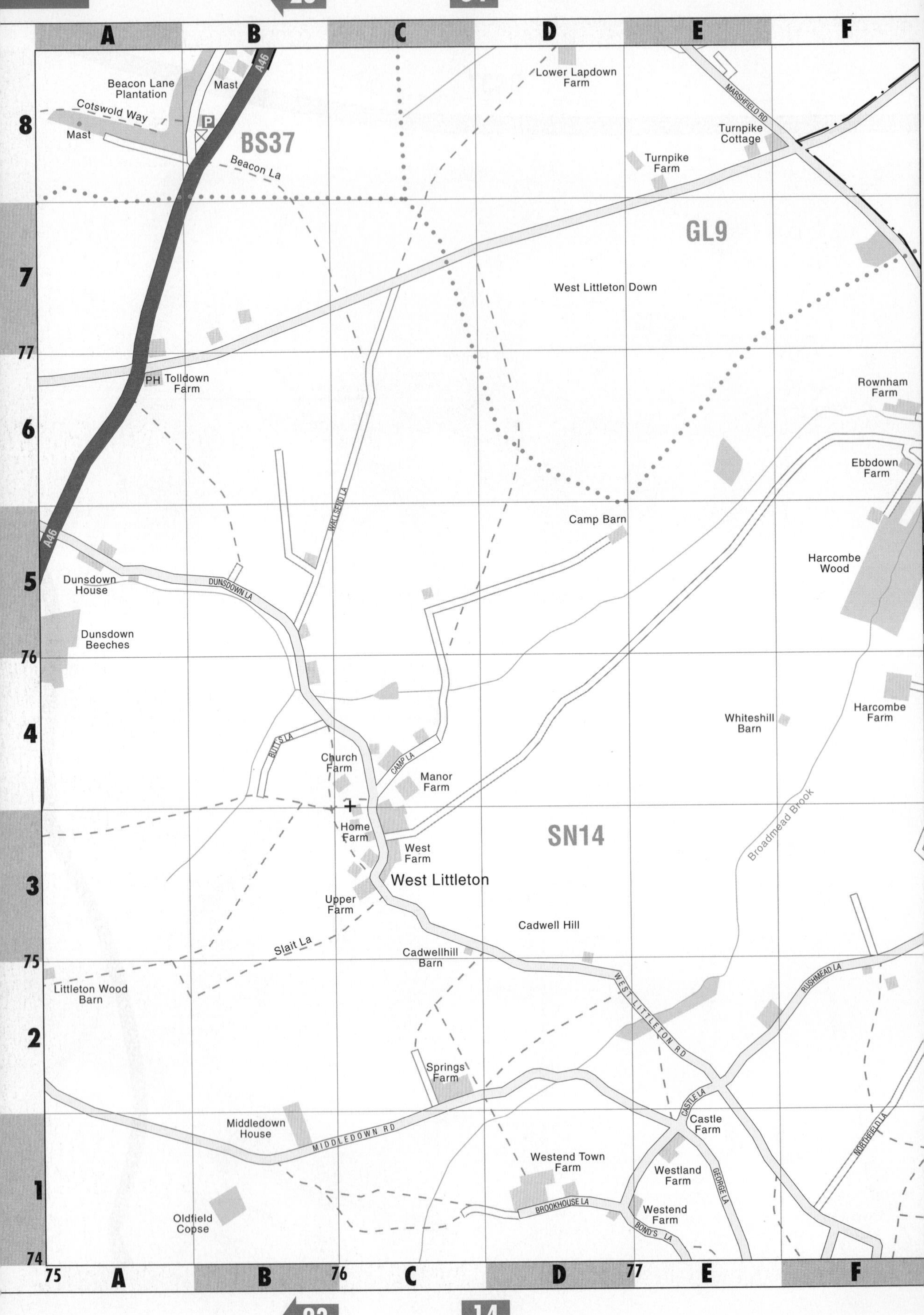
A
B
C
D
E
F
8
7
77
6
5
76
4
3
75
2
1
74
75
76
77
Beacon Lane
Plantation
Mast
Cotswold Way
Mast
A46
BS37
Beacon La
Lower Lapdown
Farm
MARSHFIELD RD
Turnpike
Cottage
Turnpike
Farm
GL9
West Littleton Down
PH
Tolldown
Farm
Rownham
Farm
Ebbdown
Farm
Camp Barn
WALLSEND LA
Harcombe
Wood
Dunsdown
House
DUNSDOWN LA
Dunsdown
Beeches
Whiteshill
Barn
Harcombe
Farm
BUTTS LA
Church
Farm
CAMP LA
Manor
Farm
Home
Farm
SN14
Broadmead Brook
West
Farm
West Littleton
Upper
Farm
Cadwell Hill
Slait La
Cadwellhill
Barn
WEST LITTLETON RD
RUSHMEAD LA
Littleton Wood
Barn
Springs
Farm
CASTLE LA
Castle
Farm
Middledown
House
MIDDLEDOWN RD
NORTHFIELD LA
Westend Town
Farm
Westland
Farm
GEORGE LA
BROOKHOUSE LA
Westend
Farm
Oldfield
Copse
BOND'S LA

23
14

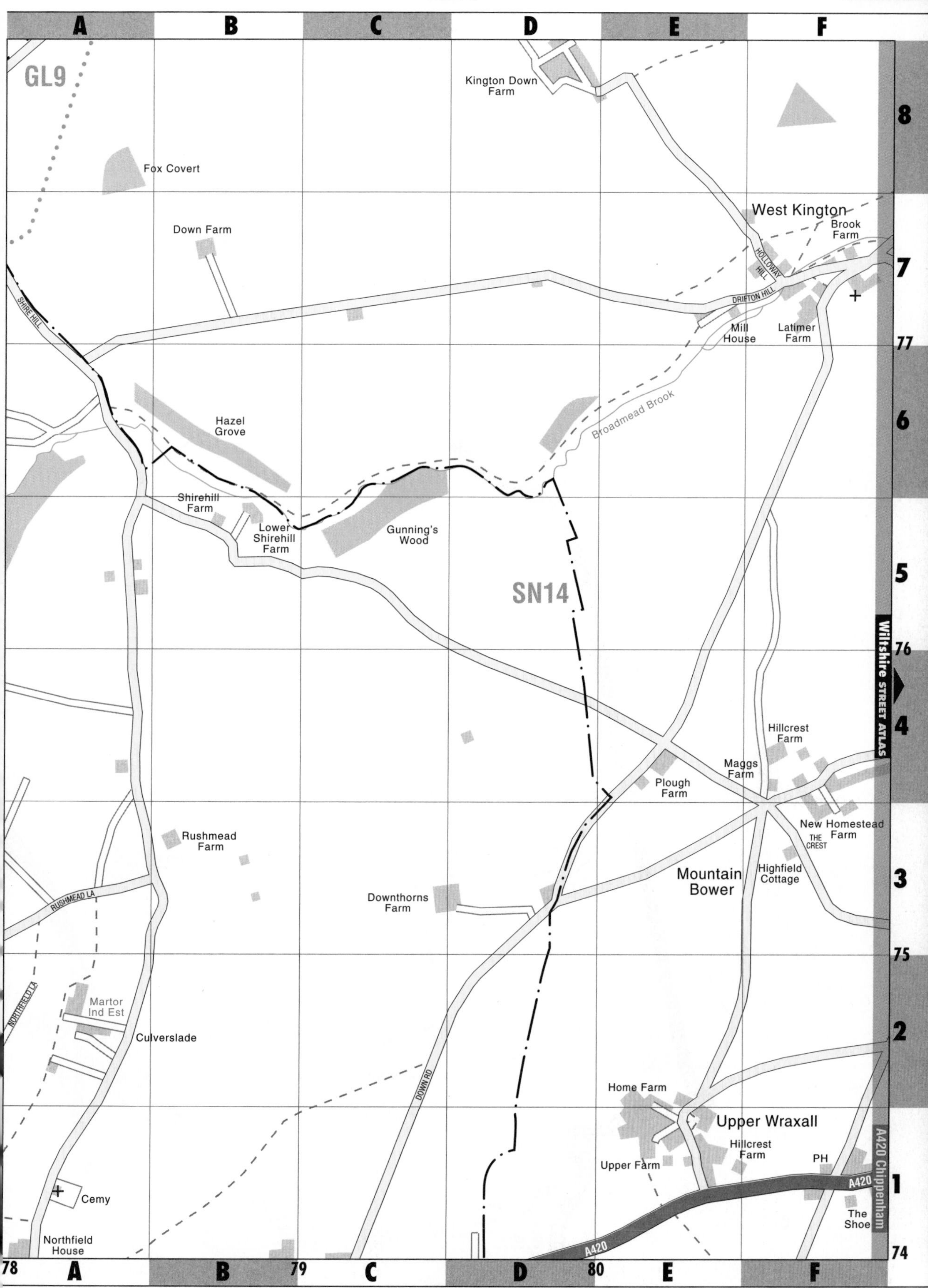
A
B
C
D
E
F
GL9
Kington Down Farm
Fox Covert
Down Farm
West Kington
Brook Farm
HOLLOWAY HILL
DRIFTON HILL
Mill House
Latimer Farm
SHIRE HILL
Hazel Grove
Broadmead Brook
Shirehill Farm
Lower Shirehill Farm
Gunning's Wood
SN14
Hillcrest Farm
Maggs Farm
Plough Farm
New Homestead Farm
THE CREST
Rushmead Farm
Mountain Bower
Highfield Cottage
Downthorns Farm
RUSHMEAD LA
NORTHFIELD LA
Martor Ind Est
Culverslade
DOWN RD
Home Farm
Upper Wraxall
Hillcrest Farm
Upper Farm
PH
A420
A420 Chippenham
Cemy
The Shoe
Northfield House
Wiltshire STREET ATLAS
8
7
77
6
5
76
4
3
75
2
1
74
78
79
80

37

Jetty (dis)
Piers
Docks
BS11
River Avon
Swash Channel
BS20
River Rd
505
79
81
Holes Mouth
River Severn
Fuel Storage Depot
Hallen Marsh Junction
Smoke La
A403
Severn Rd
Chittening Rd
Docks Ind Est
Bank Rd
Worthy Rd
Greensplott Rd
LC's
Works
Severn Rd
Washingpool La
West House Farm
BS10
Severn Way
Works
LC
Dean Rd
Ironchurch Rd
Burcott Rd
Humber Way
Lawrence Weston Rd
Moorend Farm Ave
Cabot Pk
Moorhouse La
Severnside Trad Est
Fuel Storage Depot
BS11
LC
Stores Rd
Cadmium Rd
Severn Rd
Workshop Rd
Spar Rd
Acid Rd
Zinc Rd
Retort Rd
I.S.F. Rd
Boundary Rd
Works
LC's
St Andrews Road
St Andrew's Rd
Katherine Farm
Poplar Farm
Sewage Works
Mere Bank Rhine
Kings Weston La
M49
M5
St Georges Ind Est
Royal Edward Dock
Royal Edward Dock
Avonmouth Docks
International Trad Est
Jubilee Way
St Andrews Trad Est
Haslemere Ind Est
Third Way
Ballast La
18a
St Andrews Gate Rdbt
Fire Station La
Avonmouth
King Road Ave
A4 Crowley Way
Avonmouth Way W
Motorway Distribution Ctr
St Brendans Rdbt
Nova Way
First Way
Willment Way
Fifth Way
Avonmouth Way
The Polygon
Fourth Way
Second Way
Lescren Way
Bristol Broadway
Neale Way
Jutland Rd
Lennox Ho
Richmond Terr
King St
East
Napier Sq
Queen St
Clayton St
Meadow
Gloucester Rd
Portview Rd
Avonmouth Rd
St Andrew's Rd
Liby
St Brendan's Way
Smyths Cl
Collins St
Napier Rd
Green La
PO
Avonmouth
A4
Avonbridge Trad Est
Atlantic Rd
M5
18
1 Campbell Farm
2 Campbell Ct
Campbell Farm Dr
Ableton La
Bristol & Bath Street Atlas
8
7
6
5
80
4
3
79
2
1
78
51
52
53
A B C D E F

16

38
28

A
B
C
D
E
F
8
7
81
6
5
80
4
3
79
2
1
78
55
56
M49
M5
Minor's Farm
MINOR'S LA
Works
Red Rhine
Elmington Manor Farm
BERWICK CL
Spaniorum Farm
Compton Greenfield
Bishop's Farm
BERWICK LA
BOWSTREET LA 1
HOLLYWOOD LA 2
BS35
Manor Farm
Spaniorum Hill
Hallen Ind Est
Sampson House Bsns Pk
Community Forest Path
Hakes Hill Wood
SEVERN RD
BERWICK LA
Sampson Farm
Berwick Lodge
Camp (dis)
Stowick Farm
BS10
Berwick Farm
Berwick
Berwick Wood
Berwick Lodge Farm
Hallen Marsh
Hallen Farm
BERWICK CT
Hallen
King William the IVth (PH)
Norton Farm
A4018
CRIBBS CSWY
THE CLOSE
Sports Gd
B4055
Haw Wood
MOORHOUSE LA
Moor House
Wellinghouse Farm
OAKHILL LA
Mount Skitham
WINDSOR CR
NETTLESTONE CL
MEADOWLAND RD
GREENLANDS WAY
STATION RD
GIFFORD RD
TORMARTON CRES
CRANDELL CL
LOVERINGE CL
MOUNT PLEASANT
STONE'S COTTS
HALLEN RD
ISON HILL RD
SEVERN GRANGE
TREVERDOWE WLK
MARISSAL RD
COTRITH GR
BIRDALE CL
PO
DOWDESWELL CL
LANGFIELD CL
MODECOMBE GR
TRATMAN WLK
BICKERTON CL
FITCHETT WLK
PASSAGE RD
PEVERELL CL
PEVERELL DR
CHAMPNEYS AVE
Severn House
GREENSIDE CL 1
COUSINS CL 2
HILL END DR
COOMBE CL
WINDMILL LA
GLENEAGLES
SPRINGWOOD
Henbury Sch
MARISSAL CL
DOLMAN CL
MARMION CRES
LOWLIS CL
VAUGHAN CL
VIMPANY CL
HARMER CL
THE CHALET
TREVELYAN WLK
STANDFAST RD
MACHIN CL
MACHIN RD
BARLANDS HO
BROOKRIDGE HO
P
CONVENT CL
ROYAL CL
GREEN DELL CL
WOODSIDE GR
HALLEN CL
B4057
AVONMOUTH WAY
HENBURY CT
Henbury Court Prim Sch
Common Gout
LAWRENCE WESTON RD
BATTERSBY WAY
SCANDRETT CL
Henbury Manor Sch
CROW LA
ELLSWORTH RD
Severn Way
Moorgrove Wood
BLAISE HAMLET
HALLEN RD
Bank Leaze Prim Sch
ATWOOD DR
AYLMINTON WLK
CORBETT CL
HOLLY HO
MUSGROVE CL
WOODGROVE RD
CHURCH CL
HENBURY RD
Blaise Prim Sch
RICHESON CL
RICHESON WLK
St Bede's RC Sch
WESCOTT GR
Miniature Rly
Mus
Hazel Brook
TRYMWOOD CL
THE ELMS
LORAIN WLK
SATCHFIELD CL
CHALLENDER AVE
BS11
LONG CROSS
GORHAM CL
VINCENT CL
DE CLIFFORD RD
ROMAN FARM CT
Cemy
KINGS WESTON RD
P
BRISTOL
Henbury
HENBURY GDNS
SATCHFIELD CRES
ARNALL DR
BLETHWIN CL
STANDISH CL
BLAISDON CL
Lawrence Weston
Lawrence Weston Sch
Liby
SALTMARSH DR
STILE ACRES
UPPER TERR
DEERING CL
QUARRY LA
THE QUARRY
Blaise Castle
Community Forest Path
COMMONFIELD RD
AWDELETT CL
LITTLE MEAD
FERNHILL LA
ROCKWELL AVE
BELLHOUSE WLK
Greenhill Plantation
Kingsweston Down Nature Res
Limekiln Wood
CHESTERFIELD HO
FRANCES GREEVES CT
Wesley Theological Coll
COLLEGE PARK DR
DIDSBURY CL
BURYCOURT CL
SHORTLANDS RD
RIDINGLEAZE
OTTERY CL
BROADLANDS DR
CAPEL RD
OAKHANGER DR
PO
KIRKBY RD
ASTRY CL
BROOKTHORPE AVE
THE GASTONS
MEERE BANK
FERNHILL CT
GOLDSBURY WLK
GOODRING HILL
B4057
BS9
Blaise Castle Estate
BS9
Coombe Hill
CH
COOMBE WAY
WESTOVER RD
SOMERFORD CT
HENBURY HILL
B4055
NORTHOVER RD
WESTOVER CL
A
B
55
C
D
56
E
F

17
28

27 39

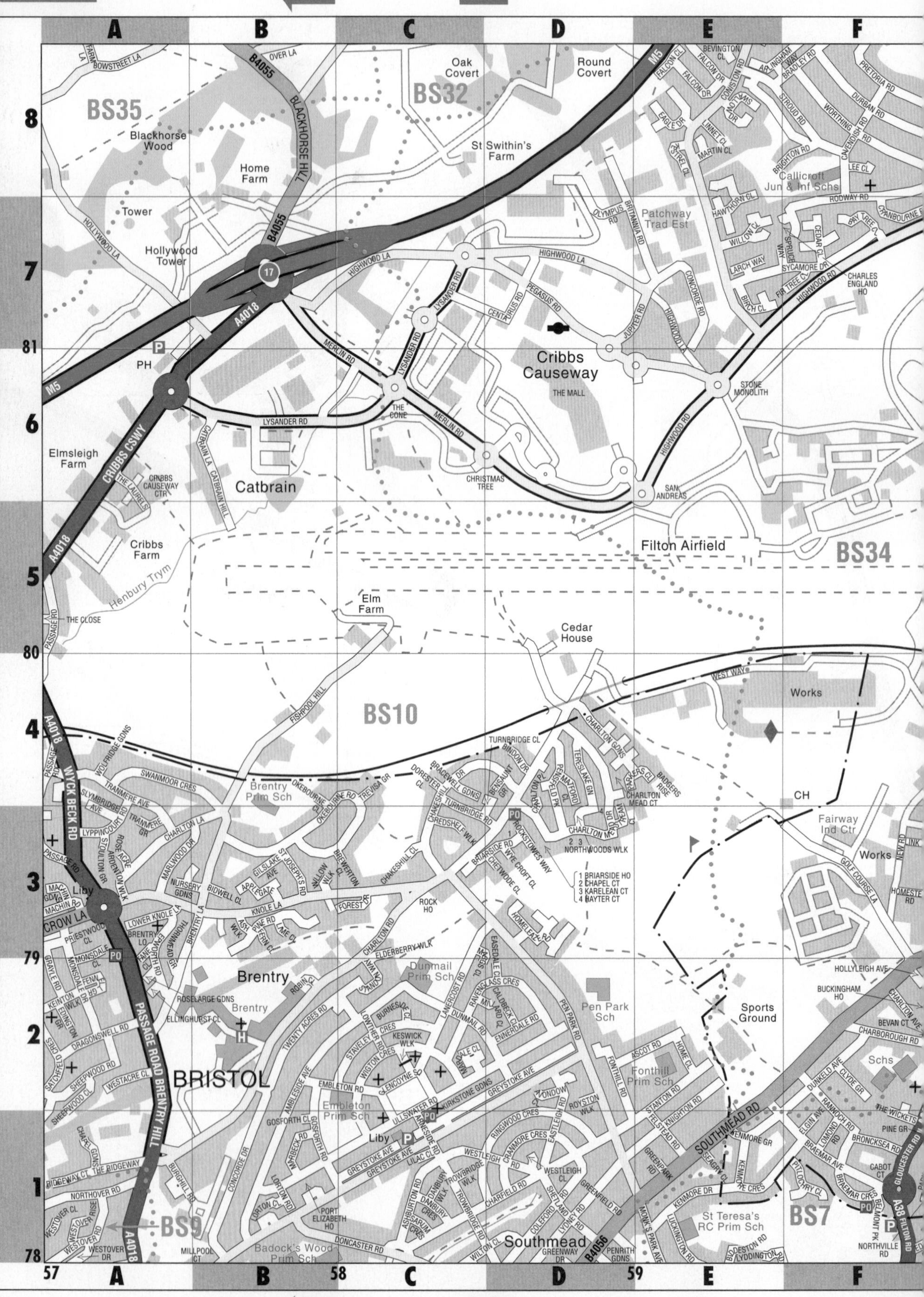
A B C D E F
8 7 81 6 5 80 4 3 79 2 1 78
57 58 59
BS35
BS32
BS34
BS10
BS9
BS7
Blackhorse Wood
Home Farm
Oak Covert
Round Covert
St Swithin's Farm
Tower
Hollywood Tower
Hollywood La
Bowstreet La
Over La
B4055
Blackhorse Hill
M5
A4018
17
PH
Highwood La
Lysander Rd
Merlin Rd
Centaurus Rd
Pegasus Rd
Jupiter Rd
Concorde Rd
Olympus Rd
Britannia Rd
Patchway Trad Est
Cribbs Causeway
The Mall
The Cone
Christmas Tree
San Andreas
Stone Monolith
Highwood Rd
Callicroft Jun & Inf Schs
Charles England Ho
Rodway Rd
Cranbourne Rd
Falcon Cl
Falcon Dr
Eagle Dr
Kestrel Cl
Linnet Cl
Martin Cl
Bevington Cl
Coniston Rd
Aplingham Way
Bradley Rd
Stroud Rd
Pretoria Rd
Durban Rd
Worthing Rd
Cavendish Rd
Brighton Rd
Lee Cl
Hawthorn Cl
Willow Cl
Larch Way
Birch Cl
Spruce Way
Cedar Cl
Sycamore Dr
Fir Tree Cl
Bay Tree Cl
Elmsleigh Farm
Cribbs Cswy
Cribbs Causeway Ctr
The Laurels
Catbrain La
Catbrain Hill
Catbrain
Cribbs Farm
Filton Airfield
Henbury Trym
The Close
Passage Rd
Elm Farm
Cedar House
Fishpool Hill
West Way
Works
CH
Fairway Ind Ctr
Golf Course La
Wolfridge Gdns
Swanmoor Cres
Tranmere Ave
Tranmere Gr
Slymbridge Ave
Lyppincourt Rd
Stoulton Gr
Rose Acre
Arden Ton Wlk
Charlton La
Marlwood Dr
Nursery Gdns
Bidwell Cl
Gilslake Ave
Applegate
St Joseph's Rd
Willow Cl
Brewerton Cl
Chakeshill Cl
Forest Dr
Rock Ho
Knole La
Lower Knole La
Brentry Prim Sch
Okebourne Rd
Trevisa Gr
Dorester Cl
Bracewell Gdns
Turnbridge Rd
Turnbridge Cl
Bindon Dr
Bensaunt Gr
Gredshelf Wlk
Carlton Pl
Pensfield Pk
Tereslake Gn
Charlton Gdns
Badgers Rise
Charlton Mead Ct
Charlton Mead Dr
Northwoods Wlk
Rockstowes Way
Briarside Rd
Wye Croft Cl
Chetwode Cl
1 Briarside Ho
2 Chapel Ct
3 Karelean Ct
4 Hayter Ct
Homeleaze Rd
Crow La
Liby
Priestwood Cl
Monsdale Cl
Brentry Lo
Brentry La
Elderberry Wlk
Charlton Rd
Dunmail Prim Sch
Brentry
Roselarge Gdns
Ellinghurst Cl
Twenty Acres Rd
Burneside Cl
Lanercost Rd
Ravenglass Cres
Caldbeck Cl
Easedale Cl
Dunmail Rd
Ennerdale Rd
Pen Park Rd
Pen Park Sch
Keswick Wlk
Staveley Cres
Wigton Cres
Glencoyne Sq
Embleton Rd
Embleton Prim Sch
Ambleside Ave
Gosforth Cl
Gosforth Rd
Kirkstone Gdns
Greystoke Ave
Ullswater Rd
Armside Rd
Lilac Cl
Ringwood Cres
Cranmore Cres
Westleigh Cl
Royston Wlk
Eastleigh Rd
Fonthill Rd
Fonthill Prim Sch
Ascot Rd
Home Cl
Stanton Rd
Knighton Rd
Sports Ground
Southmead Rd
Kenmore Gr
Kenmore Cres
Kenmore Dr
Seagry Cl
Greenpark Rd
St Teresa's RC Prim Sch
Hollyleigh Ave
Buckingham Ho
Charborough Rd
Bevan Ct
Dunkeld Ave
Clyde Gr
Elgin Ave
Lomond Rd
Rannoch Rd
Braemar Ave
Braemar Cres
Pitlochry Cl
Bronckesea Rd
Pine Gr
Cabot Ct
The Wickets
Schs
Homeste Rd
Gloucester Rd
Filton Rd
A38
Belmont Pk
Northville Rd
Keinton Wlk
Grayle Rd
Dragonswell Rd
Sheepwood Rd
Westacre Cl
Sheepwood Cl
Satchfield Cres
BRISTOL
Passage Road Brentry Hill
Concorde Dr
Burghill Rd
Mayrbeck Rd
Lorton Rd
Port Elizabeth Ho
Doncaster Rd
Ashburton Rd
Danbury Wlk
Danbury Cres
Trowbridge Wlk
Trowbridge Rd
Westleigh Rd
Charfield Rd
Shetland Rd
Lydney Rd
Greenfield Rd
Coleford Rd
Wilton Cl
Southmead
Greenway Dr
Penrith Gdns
B4056
Monk's Park Ave
Luckington Rd
Bideston Rd
Lyddington Rd
Chapel Gdns
The Ridgeway
Ridgeway Ct
Northover Rd
Westover Cl
Westover Rise
Westover Dr
Millpool Ct
Badock's Wood Prim Sch
Wyck Beck Rd

27 18

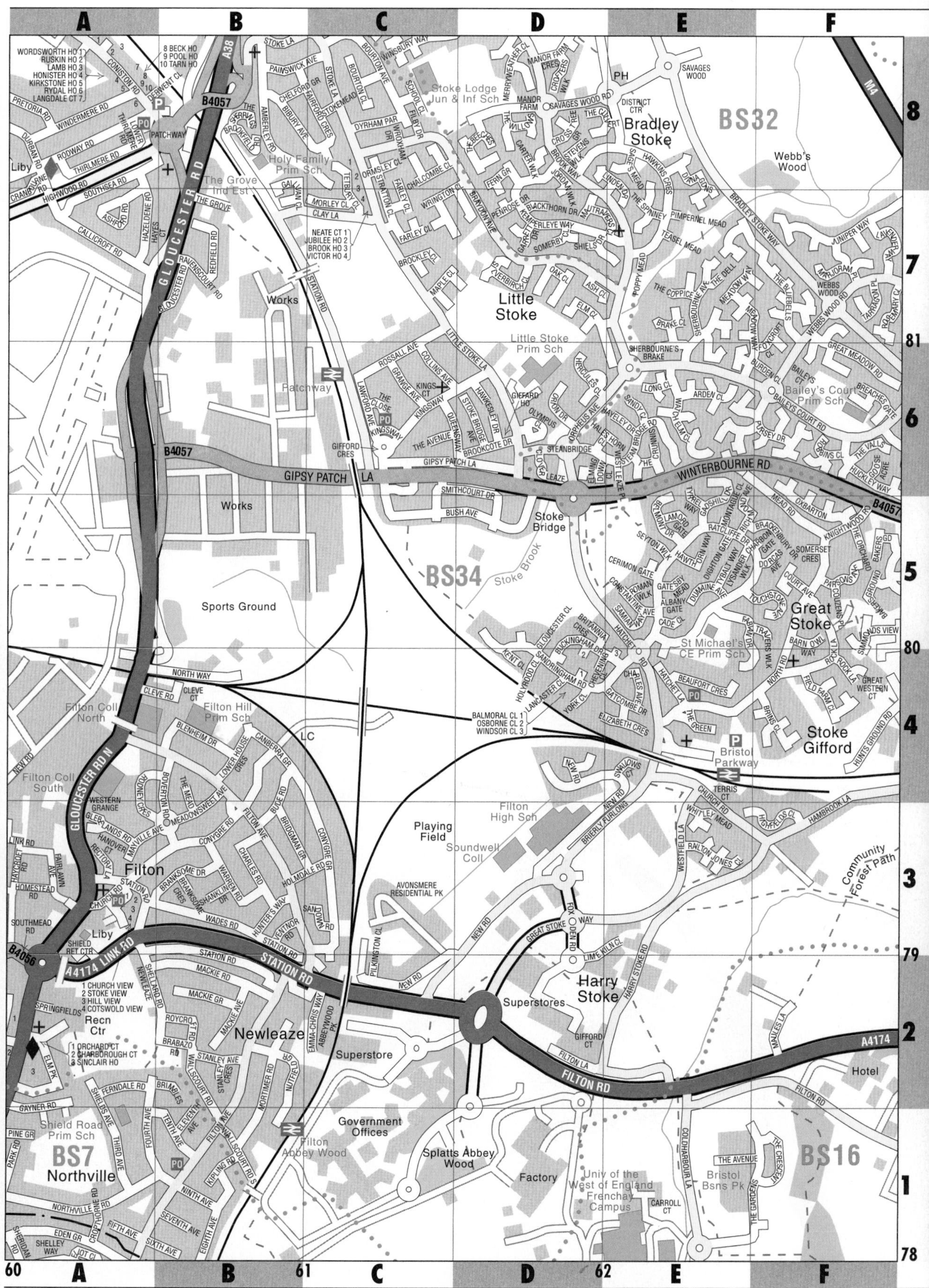
40
30
A
B
C
D
E
F
BS32
Bradley Stoke
Little Stoke
Webb's Wood
Stoke Lodge Jun & Inf Sch
Holy Family Prim Sch
The Grove Ind Est
Works
Patchway
Little Stoke Prim Sch
Bailey's Court Prim Sch
GLOUCESTER RD
GIPSY PATCH LA
WINTERBOURNE RD
Stoke Bridge
BS34
Stoke Brook
Sports Ground
Great Stoke
St Michael's CE Prim Sch
Filton Coll North
Filton Hill Prim Sch
Filton Coll South
Stoke Gifford
Bristol Parkway
Playing Field
Filton High Sch
Soundwell Coll
Filton
Community Forest Path
AVONSMERE RESIDENTIAL PK
Liby
Harry Stoke
Superstores
Recn Ctr
Newleaze
Superstore
STATION RD
A4174 LINK RD
FILTON RD
Hotel
Government Offices
Splatts Abbey Wood
Factory
Univ of the West of England Frenchay Campus
Bristol Bsns Pk
BS16
Shield Road Prim Sch
BS7
Northville
Filton Abbey Wood
M4
B4057
B4056
A4174
A38
60
61
62
78
79
80
81
8
7
6
5
4
3
2
1
19
30

29
41

A
B
C
D
E
F
8
7
81
6
5
80
4
3
79
2
1
78
63
64
65
BS32
BS36
BS16
M4
M32
B4427
B4057
B4058
A4174
A432
Oakdale
Firlea
Northwood Farm
Matford Bridge
Langley
High La
Swan La
Bristol Rd
Playing Field
Henroost Farm
Ferndale Farm
Old Gloucester Rd
St Marys RC Prim Sch
Silverhill Sch (Jun)
PH
Watley's End
Chequers Ct
Green Acres Farm
Court Farm
Church La
Green La
High St
Elm Park Prim Sch
Bradley Brook
The Ridings High Sch
St Michaels CE Prim Sch
Winterbourne
Beacon La
Winterbourne Rd
Great Stoke
Winterbourne Hill
Flaxpits
Liby
Hicks Common
Bristol Parkway N
Parkway N
Parkway
Mulgrove Farm
Huckford
Hunts Ground Rd
Hillside Farm
Winterbourne Down
Sturden Court
Pye Corner
Brook Farm
Damsons Bridge
Hoodland
Hambrook La
Community Forest Path
Frome Valley Walkway
River Frome
Hambrook Prim Sch
Bury Hill
Saw Mill
Whiteshill
Moorend
Hambrook Hotel
Mast
Faber Farm
Buryhill Farm
The Stream
The Meads
Common Mead La
Baugh Farm
Bromley Heath
Filton Rd
Fernbrook Cl
Penn Dr
Park Cres
Elliott Ave
Riverwood Rd
Bellfields La
Queensholm Cres
Greenleaze Ave
Queensholm Cl
Four Acre Rd
1 TANNERS CT
2 THE HORNBEAMS
3 THE ROWANS
4 BERKELEY GN
5 THE ALDERS
6 THE LIMES
7 THE BEECHES
8 WELLINGTON PL
9 THE WILLOWS
10 THE ELMS
11 BEAUFORT
12 ASHTON
13 BADMINTON
14 DYRHAM
15 BOWOOD
16 LANSDOWNE
DOWN FARM HO 1
WHITEGATES 2
BAMPTON DR 1
QUAKER'S RD 2
KEMPTON CL 1
BADMINTON RD 2
BLACKHORSE LA 3

29
20

42
32
Frampton Cotterell
Frampton End
Frampton End Farm
Church Bridge
Frampton Cotterell CE Sch
Frampton Court
Parsonage Bridge
Nightingale's Bridge
Frome Valley Walkway
Mayshill Farm
Ox Bridge
Oxbridge Farm
Says Court Farm
Mast
Depot
PH
Highcroft Jun Sch
Brockeridge Inf Sch
Coalpit Heath
The Manor Prim Sch
Froglane Farm
New Plantation
Burn Wood
Cloisters
River Frome
BS36
Blackberry Brake
Woodlands Farm
Ram Hill Bsns Pk
The Dramway Footpath
GREENACRES PARK HOMES (Caravan Site)
Ram Hill
Ramhill Wood
Ivoryhill Farm
Ivory Hill
Hotwater Brake
Box Hedge Farm
Kendleshire Farm
Kendleshire
Serridge House
Martin Croft Brake
Bitterwell Lake
Henfield
BS37
Branch Pool Wood
Kendalshire Farm
Cloverlea Bsns Ctr
Rogers Farm
Henfield Farm
Parkgate Farm
Coalsack Farm
Windmill Farm
Community Forest Path
Folly Brook
Lydegreen Bridge
Folly Bridge
Weston Farm
BS16
Mast
BADMINTON RD
A432
A4174
M4
WESTERLEIGH RD
67
68
81
80
79
78
21
32

31
43

A
B
C
D
E
F
8
7
81
6
5
80
4
3
79
2
1
78
69
70
71
Westerleigh Common
YATE
Says Court Farm
BS36
Beech Hill
Say's Wood
Elm Farm
Rodford
BS37
Pool Farm
Wapley Bushes
Cliff Farm
Wapley Common
Dodmoor Farm
Grove Farm
(dis)
Jorrocks Ind Est
Wychwell Farm
Church Farm
Brook Farm
Westerleigh
PH
Wapley
Beanwood Farm
Bean Wood
Brice's Farm
Mill House Farm
Bush's Farm
B4465
WESTERLEIGH RD
KIDNEY HILL
SUNNYBANK
Westerleigh Hill Farm
Mast
Westerleigh Hill
Abattoir
Dewshill Wood
Cliff Farm
Burbarrow La
Crem
Gorse Covert
LEIGH LA
Leigh Farm
BATCHFIELD LA
BS16
Rodford Prim Sch
Culverhill Sch
Abbotswood Jun & Inf Schs
Wellesley Prim Sch
Chescombe Farm
St Paul's RC Prim Sch
Kings Court Prim Sch
Kingsgate Park
Raysfield Inf & Jun Schs
SHIRE WAY
BESOM LA
SHORTHILL RD
WAPLEY HILL
WAYLEAZE
BROAD LA
MILL CRES
NEWMAN CL
IVY TERR
OLD MILL CL
THE QUADRANGLE
WESTERLEIGH RD
WOODWARD AVE
CHEDWORTH
RODBOROUGH
PITCHCOMBE
WITCOMBE
BROCKWORTH
EDGEWORTH
BADGEWORTH
KINGSCOTE
CHERINGTON
MAISEMORE
WOODCHESTER
LITTLEDEAN
BLAISDON
BREDON
KELSTON CL
RODFORD WAY
GLENFALL
CHARGROVE
HARDWICKE
BISLEY
DEERHURST
BARNWOOD RD
PRESTBURY
LONGFORD
QUEDGELEY
ELMORE
PRESCOTT
BROOKTHORPE
ST BRIAVELS DR
WOODMANCOTE
NORTHFIELD
LANSDOWN
HATHERLEY
CHATCOMBE
SUNDRIDGE PK
STANSHAWES COURT DR
KINGSGATE PARK
AVONLEA
OAK LODGE
STANSHAWES DR
LYDBROOK CL
TODDINGTON CL
BIRKDALE
SUNNINGDALE
DOVECOTE
HARESCOMBE
SLIMBRIDGE CL
GOLDCREST RD
HERON WAY
SCOTT WAY
KENILWORTH
SHACKLETON AVE
HUDSON CL
MERLIN WAY
KESTREL CL
ROBIN WAY
TURNBERRY
PARK VIEW
FINCH RD
COLESBORNE CL
APPERLEY CL
CHALFORD CL
HIGHWORTH CRES

44
34

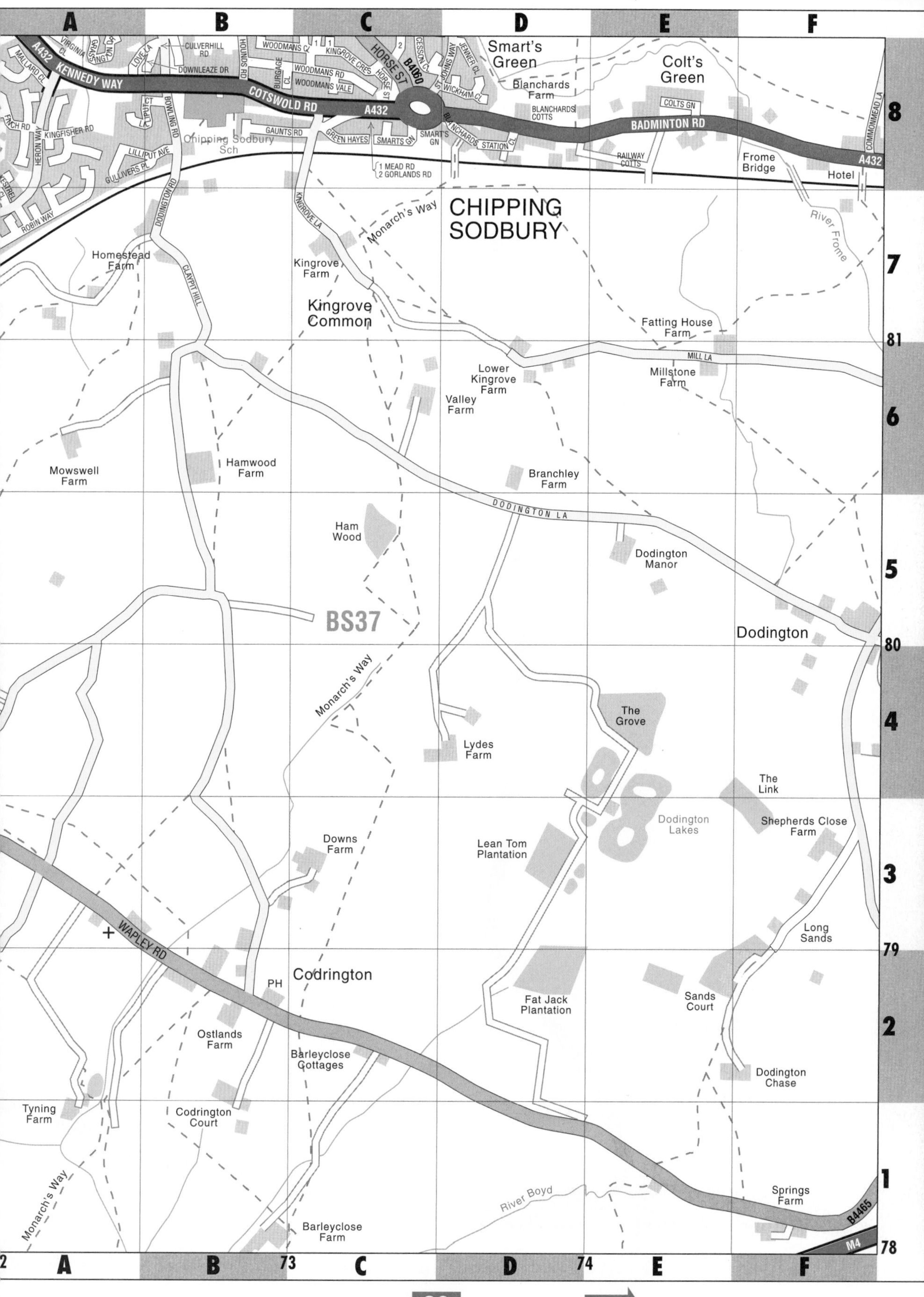
A
B
C
D
E
F
CHIPPING SODBURY
Smart's Green
Colt's Green
Blanchards Farm
KENNEDY WAY
A432
COTSWOLD RD
BADMINTON RD
HORSE ST
B4060
Chipping Sodbury Sch
Kingrove Farm
Kingrove Common
Homestead Farm
Monarch's Way
Frome Bridge
Hotel
River Frome
Fatting House Farm
MILL LA
Millstone Farm
Lower Kingrove Farm
Valley Farm
Mowswell Farm
Hamwood Farm
Branchley Farm
DODINGTON LA
Ham Wood
Dodington Manor
BS37
Dodington
The Grove
Lydes Farm
The Link
Dodington Lakes
Shepherds Close Farm
Downs Farm
Lean Tom Plantation
Long Sands
WAPLEY RD
Codrington
PH
Fat Jack Plantation
Sands Court
Ostlands Farm
Barleyclose Cottages
Dodington Chase
Tyning Farm
Codrington Court
River Boyd
Springs Farm
B4465
Barleyclose Farm
M4
8
7
81
6
5
80
4
3
79
2
1
78
72
73
74

23
34

33
45

A
B
C
D
E
F
8
7
81
6
5
80
4
3
79
2
1
78
75
76
77
COMMONMEAD LA
Haye's Farm
Old Sodbury CE Prim Sch
Lyegrove Wood
Lyegrove House
Lyegrove Farm
A46
A432
PO
COTSWOLD LA
CHURCH LA
Old Sodbury
Tyning La
PH
Overndale Sch
Plough Farm
Sodbury Tunnel
BADMINTON RD
HILL LA
Hotel
WESTMORLAND TERR
B4040
B404
CHAPEL LA
MILL LA
Windylands
CATCHPOT LA
Coomb's End
Hammerdown Clump
Bennett's Gorse
BS37
Frenchpiece Wood
The Clovers
Dodington House
Dodington
Dodington Park
BATH RD
Sheepcot Barn
Cotswold Way
Long Plantation
Vineyard Clump
Bailey Clump
River Frome
Black Brake
Dodington Wood
Old Farm
PH
Old Hundred
PH
GL9
Southfield Clump
Dodington Ash
Tormarton
Watt's Barn
B4465
LAPDOWN LA
MARSHFIELD RD
Hawkes Tyning Clump
TORMARTON INTERCHANGE
18
M4

33
24

46
36
A
B
C
D
E
F
Lyegrove Wood
Egg Clump
LIME AVE
OLD DOWN RD
Withy Moor
STATION RD
Sodbury Tunnel
Limes Farm
Newhouse Farm
Acton Turville
B4040
B4039
BURTON RD
B4039
PH
GL9
TORMARTON RD
OAKES LA
Vicarage Cottage
Warren Barn
Fagot Pile
M4
Pike Cottage
Old Warren
Wall Leaze Wood
Parks Farm
Brotton Hill Wood
Warren Gorse
Westfield Farm
Phyldornick
Little Westfield
SN14
Fox Covert
8
7
81
6
5
80
4
3
79
2
1
78
78
79
80
25
36

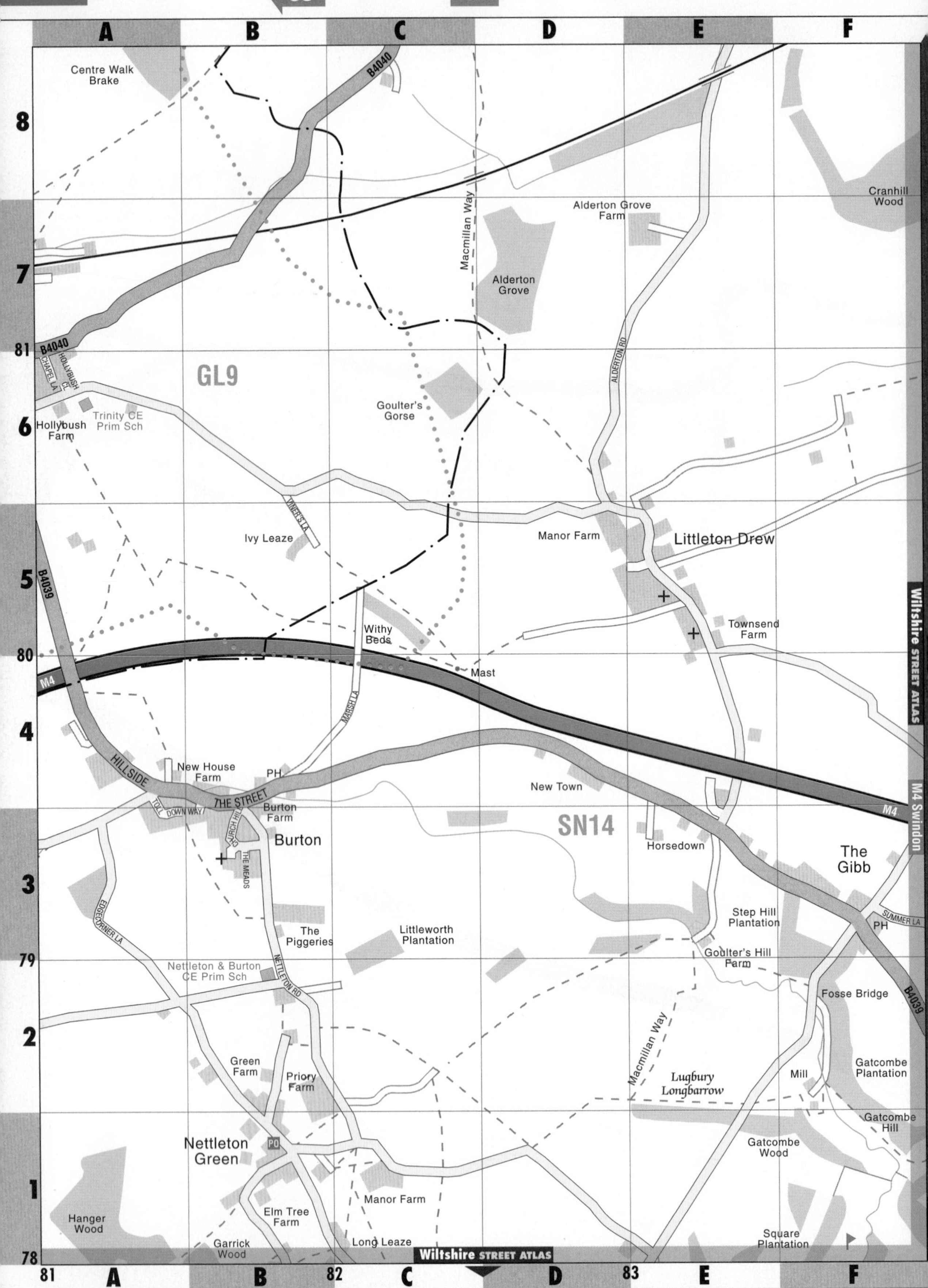
A
B
C
D
E
F
8
7
81
6
5
80
4
3
79
2
1
78
Centre Walk Brake
B4040
Macmillan Way
Alderton Grove Farm
Cranhill Wood
Alderton Grove
GL9
CHAPEL LA
HOLLYBUSH CL
Trinity CE Prim Sch
Hollybush Farm
Goulter's Gorse
ALDERTON RD
Ivy Leaze
Manor Farm
Littleton Drew
B4039
Withy Beds
Townsend Farm
M4
Mast
MARSH LA
HILLSIDE
New House Farm
PH
THE STREET
New Town
TOLL DOWN WAY
Burton Farm
CHURCH HILL
SN14
Burton
THE MEADS
Horsedown
The Gibb
EDGECORNER LA
The Piggeries
Littleworth Plantation
Step Hill Plantation
SUMMER LA
PH
Goulter's Hill Farm
Nettleton & Burton CE Prim Sch
NETTLETON RD
Fosse Bridge
Green Farm
Priory Farm
Lugbury Longbarrow
Mill
Gatcombe Plantation
Gatcombe Hill
Nettleton Green
PO
Gatcombe Wood
Manor Farm
Hanger Wood
Elm Tree Farm
Garrick Wood
Long Leaze
Square Plantation
Wiltshire STREET ATLAS
M4 Swindon
81
82
83

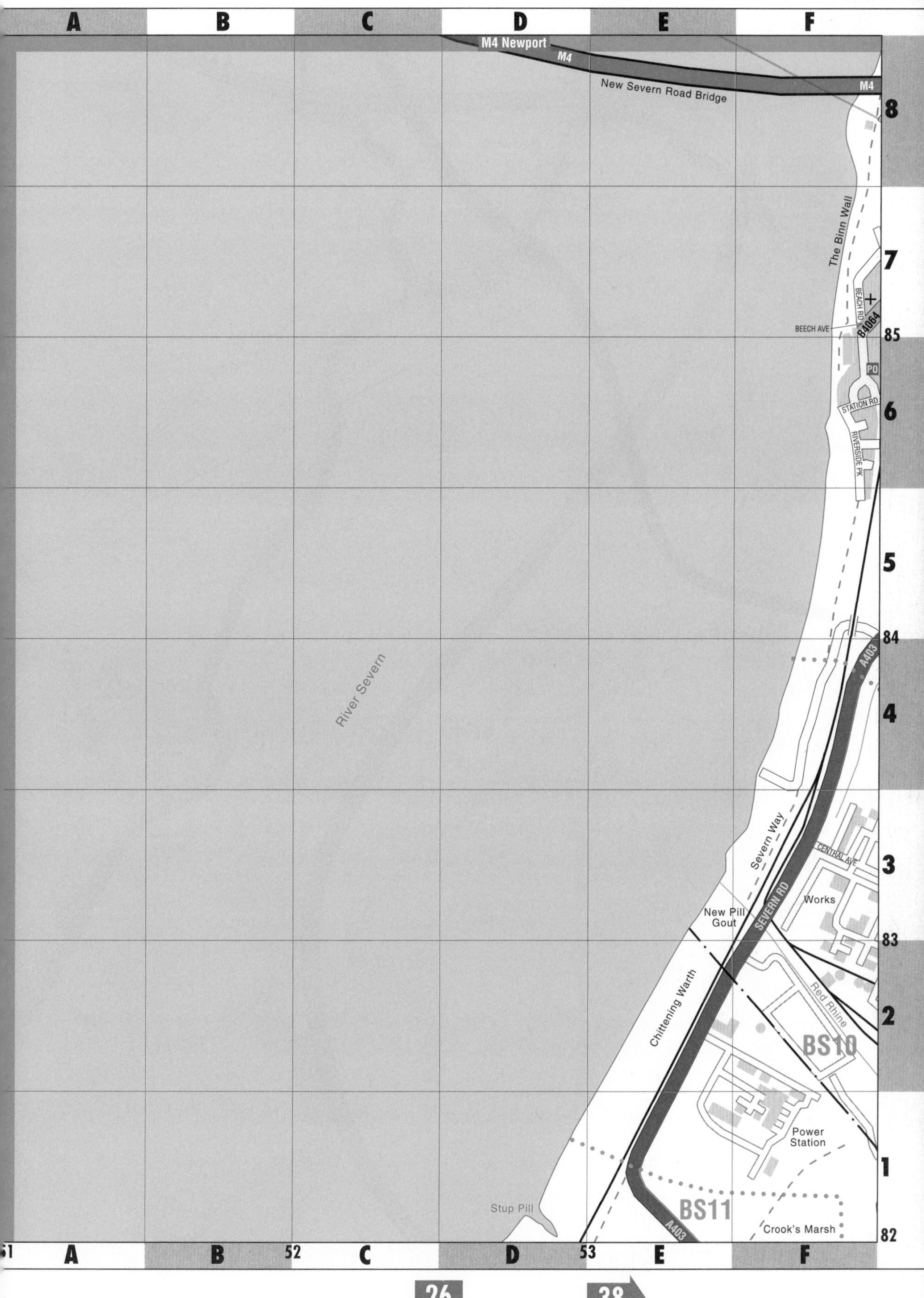
A
B
C
D
E
F
M4 Newport
M4
New Severn Road Bridge
M4
8
The Binn Wall
7
BEACH RD
B4064
BEECH AVE
85
PO
STATION RD
6
RIVERSIDE PK
5
84
A403
River Severn
4
Severn Way
CENTRAL AVE
3
SEVERN RD
Works
New Pill Gout
83
Chittening Warth
Red Rhine
2
BS10
Power Station
1
Stup Pill
BS11
A403
Crook's Marsh
82
51
52
53

37
48

A
B
C
D
E
F
8
7
85
6
5
84
4
3
83
2
1
82
54
55
56
M4
22
M49
B4064
A403
B4055
Nursery
Southworthy Farm
PH
REDWICK RD
Redwick
NORTHWICK RD
Laurel Farm
REDHAM LA
Works
SHAFT RD
GREEN LA
Salthouse Farm
Kings Arms Inn
The Pill
WICK RD
CHESSELL AVE
VICARAGE RD
KEENS GR
Pilning
BEACH RD
OSBORNE RD
BEACH AVE
LITTLE GREEN LA
WHITEHOUSE RD
THE GLEBE
REDWICK GDNS
PO
St Peter's Farm
East Redham Farm
GORSE COVER RD
WAINBRIDGE CRES
CROSS HANDS RD
JACKSON CL
CHURCH RD
CRANMOOR GN
NORTHOVER CT
BANK RD
Gumhurn Farm
Torrs Farm
PH
CHURCH RD
STATION RD
Severn Beach
SEVERN RD
Redwick Common Rhine
Severn Beach Prim Sch
Severn Beach
Whitehouse Farm
MARSH COMM
PILNING ST
ALBERT RD
VICTORIA CRES
SCHOOL WAY
DENNY ISLE DR
PROSPECT RD
ABLETON LA
Ellinghurst Rhine
The Plough (PH)
Depot
Pilning
ABBOTT RD
SEVERNWOOD GDNS
Ellinghurst Farm
Grove Farm
WESTERN APPROACH DISTRIBUTION PK
SHAYMOOR LA
STATION RD
Gilslake
BS35
GOVIER WAY
HOLLOWAY RD
Marsh Common
Dyer's Common
COLLINS DR
PALMER AVE
Noor Rhine
Swanmoor Bridge
Swanmoor Rhine
Middle Compton Rhine
ROAD TWO
CENTRAL AVE
Avlon Works
Mast
Severnside Works
Upper Compton Rhine
SPANIORUM VIEW
THE LANE
FARM LA
LC
GREEN LA
Lyde Brook
ABLETON LA
BS10
Brook Farm
How Street Rhine
VIMPENNYS LA
Crook's Marsh
BERWICK LA

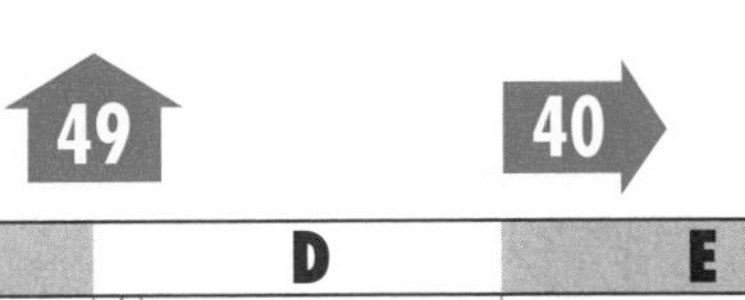
49
40

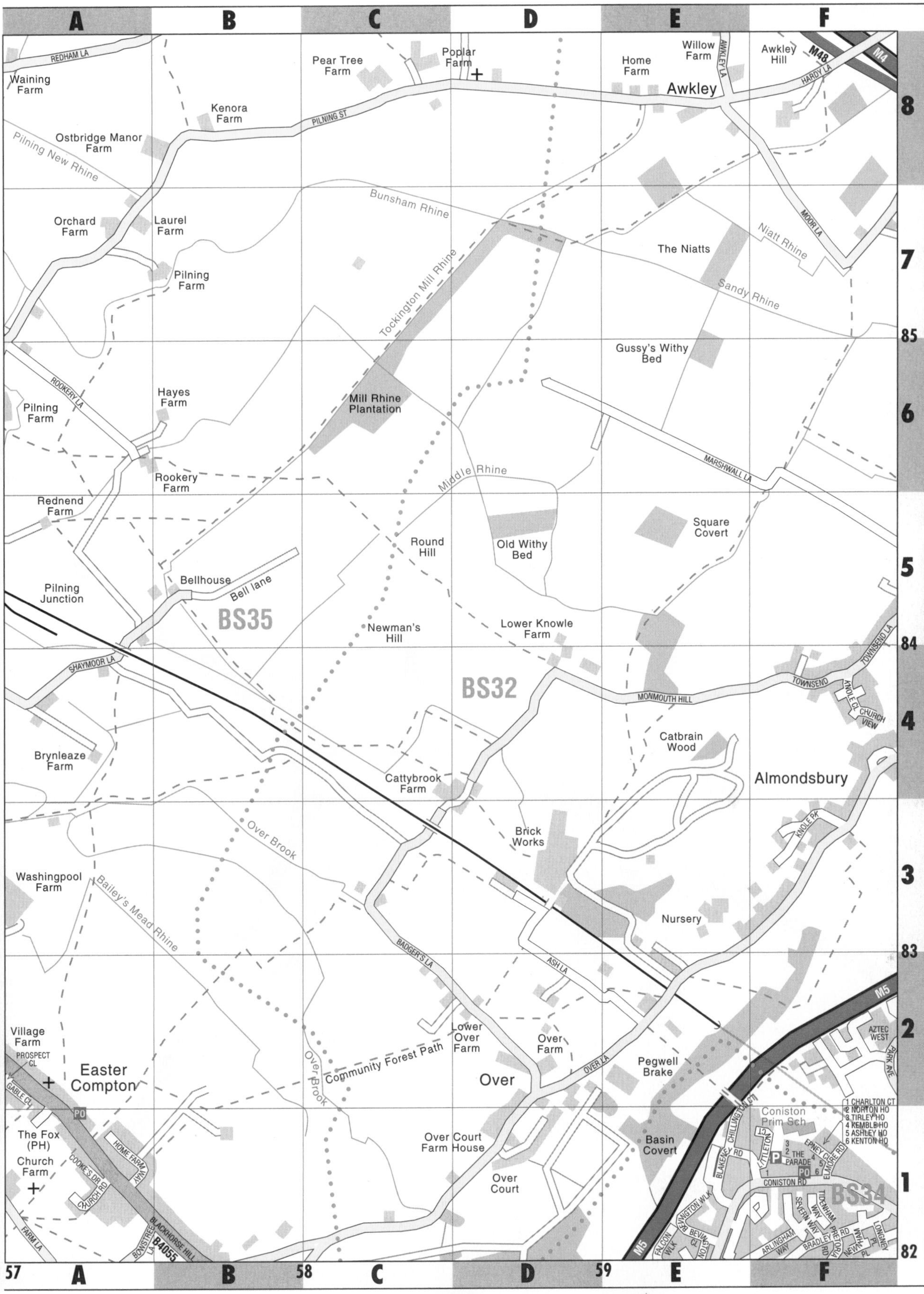

A B C D E F
Waining Farm
Redham La
Pear Tree Farm
Poplar Farm
Home Farm
Willow Farm
Awkley La
Awkley Hill
M48
M4
Awkley
Hardy La
Kenora Farm
Pilning St
Ostbridge Manor Farm
Pilning New Rhine
Orchard Farm
Laurel Farm
Bunsham Rhine
The Niatts
Niatt Rhine
Moor La
Pilning Farm
Tockington Mill Rhine
Sandy Rhine
Gussy's Withy Bed
Hayes Farm
Pilning Farm
Rookery La
Mill Rhine Plantation
Marshwall La
Rookery Farm
Middle Rhine
Rednend Farm
Round Hill
Old Withy Bed
Square Covert
Bellhouse
Bell lane
Pilning Junction
BS35
Newman's Hill
Lower Knowle Farm
Shaymoor La
BS32
Monmouth Hill
Townsend
Townsend La
Knole Cl
Church View
Catbrain Wood
Brynleaze Farm
Cattybrook Farm
Almondsbury
Brick Works
Over Brook
Knole Pk
Washingpool Farm
Bailey's Mead Rhine
Nursery
Badger's La
Ash La
M5
Aztec West
Park Ave
Village Farm
Lower Over Farm
Over Farm
Pegwell Brake
Prospect Cl
Easter Compton
Community Forest Path
Over Brook
Over
Over La
Gable Cl
PO
Chillington Ct
Coniston Prim Sch
1 Charlton Ct
2 Norton Ho
3 Tirley Ho
4 Kemble Ho
5 Ashley Ho
6 Kenton Ho
The Fox (PH)
Home Farm Way
Over Court Farm House
Basin Covert
Lytleton
The Parade
Epney Cl
Elmore Rd
Blakeney Rd
Church Farm
Cooke's Dr
Church Rd
Over Court
Coniston Rd
Bevington Wlk
BS34
Tidenham Way
Severn Way
Farm La
Blackhorse Hill
B4055
Bowstreet La
Falcon Wlk
Bevington Cl
Arlingham Way
Bradley Rd
Pretoria Rd
Newent Pl
Longney Pl
8 7 6 5 4 3 2 1
85 84 83 82
57 58 59
28
40

39
50

A
B
C
D
E
F
8
7
85
6
5
84
4
3
83
2
1
82
60
61
62
Sewage Works
MOOR LA
M4
M48
LOWER TOCKINGTON RD
The Roundabout
Lower Woodhouse Farm
Harts
A38
BS35
Gatten's Brake
TOCKINGTON PARK LA
Tockington Park Farm
Woodcock Hill
Woodhouse
FERNHILL
Woodhouse Down
Fernhill Farm
FERNDALE CL
WOODHOUSE AVE
Tockington Park wood
TOCKINGTON LA
FERNHILL CT
WOODHOUSE CL
SOUTH RD
Sewage Works
Meerbrook Farm
Hortham Wood
Cemy
BISHOP'S WOOD
OLD AUST RD
GLOUCESTER RD
THE QUARRIES
Lower Almondsbury
Hortham Farm
Lower Court Farm
Almondsbury
HORTHAM LA
CHESTERMASTER CL
COURT VIEW CL
FOREST HILLS
FLORENCE PK
COPE PK
M5
LOWER COURT RD
MARSHWALL LA
WALNUT TREE CL
THE SCOP
PO
Colony Farm
WOODLANDS LA
TOWNSEND LA
THE POUND
CHURCH RD
PH
GLEBE FIELD
Woodlands Wood
CAVENDISH DR
Almondsbury CE Prim Sch
HOLLOW RD
THE HILL
SUNDAYS HILL
RED HOUSE LA
PH
20
OVER LA
BS32
Hortham Brook
15
OAKLANDS DR
Almondsbury Hill
ALMONDSBURY INTERCHANGE
Mast
RAC Twr
BROTHERSWOOD CT
Sports Gd
WEST POINT ROW
ST JAMES CT
Almondsbury Bsns Ctr
APEX CT
Mast
ALMONDSBURY RDBT
INTERPLEX 16
EQUINOX
Mast
WOODLANDS
NORTH CT
SOUTH CT
BUCKINGHAM CT
BLENHEIM CT
HAWKLEY DR
16
ORPEN PK
Eagles Wood Bsns Pk
FOUNTAIN CT
NEW LEAZE
GREAT PARK RD
WOODLANDS PK
ASH RIDGE RD
QUADRANT
WOODLANDS LA
CROWS GR
LIME KILN GDNS
Mast
OTTRELLS MEAD
THE QUADRANT
COOKS CL
BADGERS CL
FOXFIELD AVE
WARREN CL
PYE CROFT
OXEN LEAZE
WOODLANDS CT
THE PARK
Holy Trinity Prim Sch
WESTFIELD WAY
PADDOCK CL
CH
PO
GRANGE CL
APSELEYS MEAD
PEAR TREE RD
CHESSEL CL
TEAL CL
RUSH CL
FOXBOROUGH GDNS
BULLENS CL
PERRYS LEA
HONEYSUCKLE CL
TRENCH LA
West Country Water Park
PARK AVE
BRADLEY PAVS
BROAD CROFT
KITES CL
MALLARD CL
LAPWING CL
BOWSLAND WAY
PRIMROSE CL
TRESHAM CL
STANLEY MEAD
THE AZTEC CTR
AZTEC WEST
OAKTREE CRES
STANSHAWS CL
PATCHWAY BROOK
CAMPION DR
BOWSLAND
Patchway
Sch
KINGSWEAR CL
ELLICKS CL
ORMONDS CL
BS36
PARK AVE
HEMPTON LA
MANOR RD
THE AVENUE
THE CLOSE
FERNDENE
BRACKENDENE
BRADLEY STOKE WAY
Patchway Brook
WATERSIDE DR
ATWELL DR
ALBION TERR
THE COMMON
THE COMMON (EAST)
Wheatfield Prim Sch
Community Forest Path
WHEATFIELD DR
CRANHAM DR
CORNFIELD CL
HARVEST CL
Playing Field
Patcham High Sch
STAVERTON CL
SHELLMOR AVE
STANDISH AVE
Patchway CE Prim Sch
SAXON WAY
BROOK WAY
DEWFALLS DR
Savage's Wood
HIGHNAM CL
SANDHURST CL
COURTLANDS
WINSBURY WAY
STOKE MDWS
SHELLMOR CL
MANOR FARM CRES
Superstore
L Ctr & Liby
LONGNEY PL
COLERIDGE HO
CONISTON RD
SHELLEY HO
BS34
MAISEMORE AVE
SHELLMOR CL
RUDFORD CL
ELMS GR
A38
M4
M5

39
29

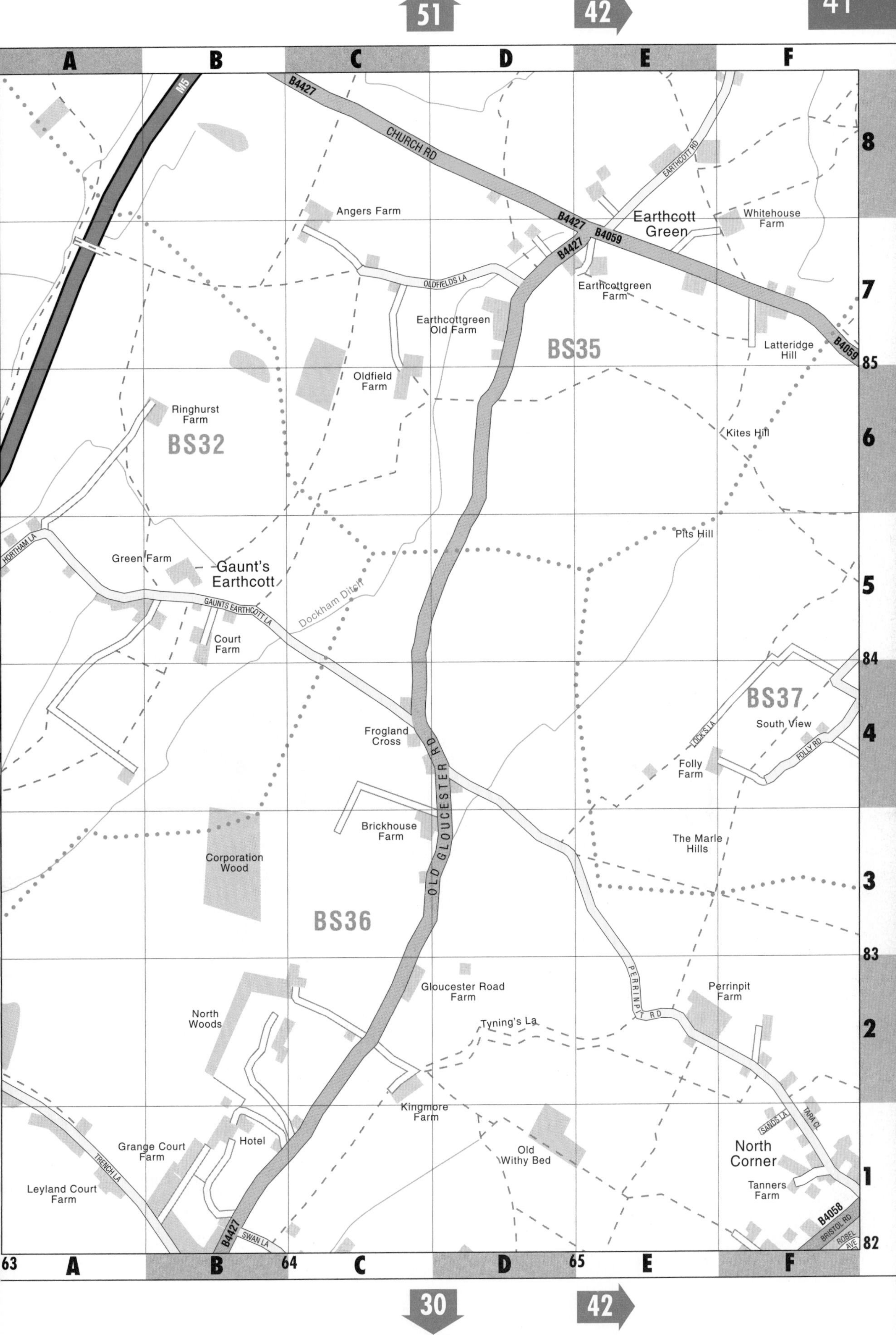
51
42
A
B
C
D
E
F
M5
B4427
CHURCH RD
EARTHCOTT RD
Angers Farm
Earthcott Green
Whitehouse Farm
B4427
B4059
OLDFIELDS LA
Earthcottgreen Farm
Earthcottgreen Old Farm
BS35
Latteridge Hill
B4059
Oldfield Farm
Ringhurst Farm
BS32
Kites Hill
Pits Hill
HORTHAM LA
Green Farm
Gaunt's Earthcott
GAUNTS EARTHCOTT LA
Dockham Ditch
Court Farm
BS37
South View
LOCK'S LA
FOLLY RD
Frogland Cross
OLD GLOUCESTER RD
Folly Farm
Brickhouse Farm
The Marle Hills
Corporation Wood
BS36
Gloucester Road Farm
Perrinpit Farm
PERRINPIT RD
North Woods
Tyning's La
Kingmore Farm
SANDS LA
TARA CL
North Corner
Grange Court Farm
Hotel
Old Withy Bed
TRENCH LA
Leyland Court Farm
Tanners Farm
B4058
BRISTOL RD
ROBEL AVE
B4427
SWAN LA
8
7
85
6
5
84
4
3
83
2
1
82
63
64
65
30
42

41
52

A B C D E F

8
7
85
6
5
84
4
3
83
2
1
82

Lower Lark's Farm
BS35
LATTERIDGE LA
LARK'S LA
Dowell's Farm
Patch Elm Farm
PATCH ELM LA
Mudgedown Farm
B4059
NORTHMEAD LA
Northend Farm
CHAINGATE LA
Chaingate House
Ladden Bows Bridge
Latteridge
WOTTON RD
BECKFIELD FARM
Two Pools Farm
LC
Acton Court
FOLLY RD
Sheephouse Farm
Ladden Brook
BS37
Acton Lodge
Hill House
LATTERIDGE RD
PARK ST
B4058
PH
HIGH ST
Laddenside Farm
Iron Acton
Isle of Rhee
Elm Farm
STATION RD
HOLLY HILL
Iron Acton CE Prim Sch
YATE RD
Cogmill La
CHILLWOOD CL
ALGARS DR
BRISTOL RD
River Frome
Brake Farm
Algars Manor
Robins Wood
NIBLEY LA
Lavenham Farm
Frome Valley Walkway
Cog Mill Farm
FRAMPTON END RD
Hover's La
BS36
Tubb's Bottom
Chestnut Farm
A432
BADMINTON RD
CONIFER CL
CHURCH RD
WESTERN AVE
SCHOOL RD
MILL LA
Cemy
Mayshill

66 A B 67 C D 68 E F

41
31

A B C D E F

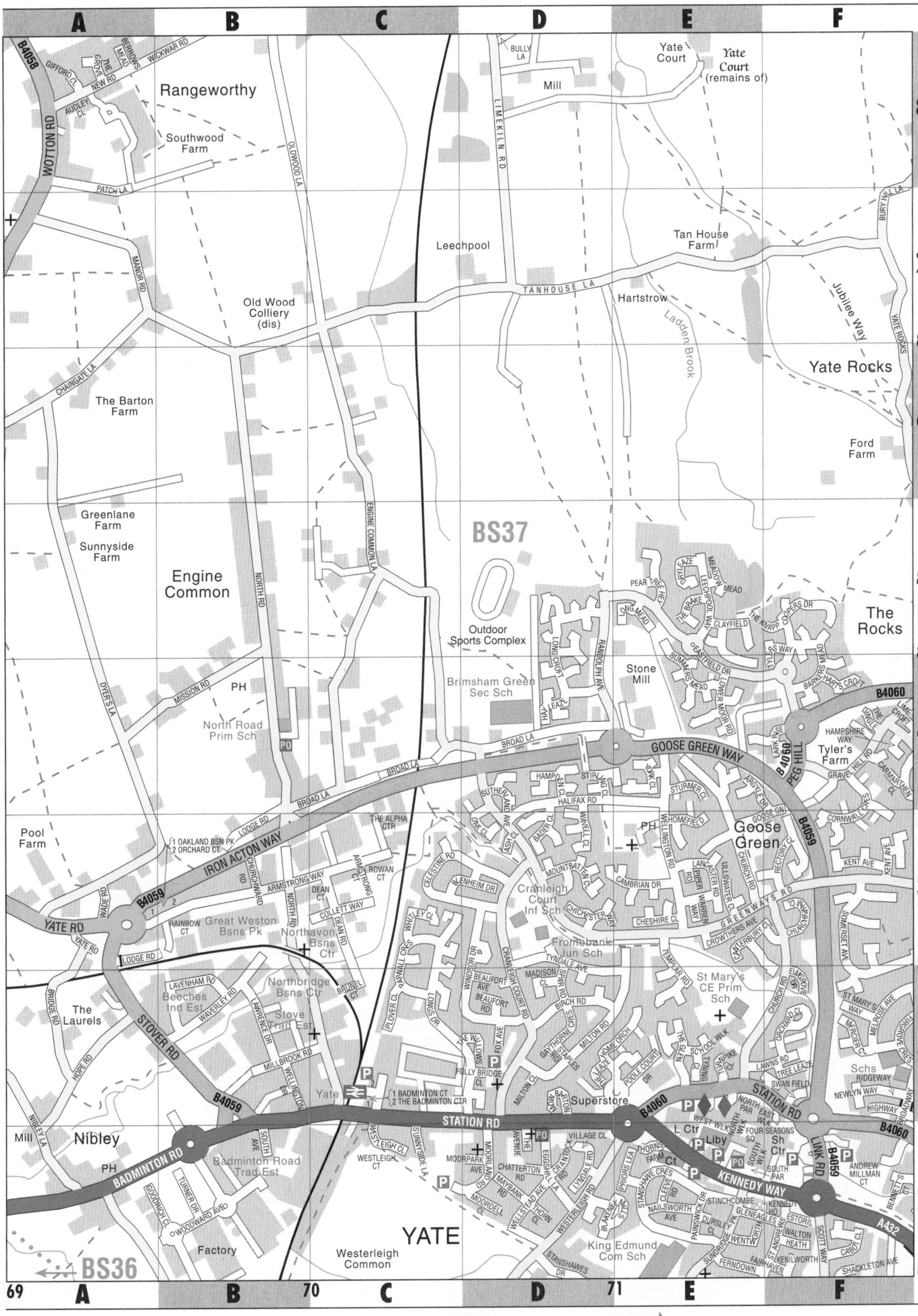

8
B4058
WOTTON RD
GIFFORD CL
THE GROVE
BERROWS MEAD
WICKWAR RD
NEW RD
AUDLEY CL
Rangeworthy
Southwood Farm
PATCH LA
OLDWOOD LA
LIMEKILN RD
BULLY LA
Mill
Yate Court
Yate Court (remains of)

7
MANOR RD
Old Wood Colliery (dis)
Leechpool
TANHOUSE LA
Tan House Farm
Hartstrow
Ladden Brook
Jubilee Way
BURY HILL LA
YATE ROCKS
85
Yate Rocks

6
CHAINGATE LA
The Barton Farm
Ford Farm
Greenlane Farm
Sunnyside Farm
ENGINE COMMON LA
BS37

5
Engine Common
NORTH RD
Outdoor Sports Complex
PEAR TREE HEY
DRYLEAZE
MEADOW MEAD
LECHPOOL WAY
THE BRAKE
LONG MEAD
CLAYFIELD
THE KNAPP
COOPERS DR
The Rocks
84
LONG CROFT
RANDOLPH AVE
Stone Mill
EASTFIELD DR
SUMMERS MEAD
LOWER MOOR RD
TYLERS WAY
BARKERS MEAD
HARTS CROFT
DYER'S LA
MISSION RD
PH
Brimsham Green Sec Sch
THE LEAZE

4
North Road Prim Sch
PO
BROAD LA
GOOSE GREEN WAY
B4060
LARK RISE
PEG HILL
THE DINGLE
LIME CROFT
HAMPSHIRE WAY
Tyler's Farm
GRAVEL HILL RD
CARMARTHEN CL
HAMPDEN CL
STIRLING CL
YORK CL
SUTHERLAND AVE
HALIFAX RD
STURMER CL
ARGYLE DR
LODGE RD
IRON ACTON WAY
THE ALPHA CTR
OAK CL
ASH CL
BADER CL
WAVELL CL
HOMEFIELD
GOOSE GN
Goose Green
B4059
CORNWALL CRES
Pool Farm
1 OAKLAND BSN PK
2 ORCHARD CT
PH
WELLINGTON RD
KENT AVE

3
CHURCHWARD RD
ARMSTRONG WAY
ARMSTRONG CT
ROWAN CT
CELESTINE RD
BLENHEIM DR
MOUNTBATTEN CL
LANCASTER RD
ULLSWATER CL
CHURCH RD
RECTORY CL
GREENWAYS RD
WADE RD
DEAN CT
COLLETT WAY
Cranleigh Court Inf Sch
CAMBRIAN DR
PIPER RD
WARREN WAY
CHESHIRE CL
CHICHESTER WAY
GREENWAYS AVE
CROWTHERS AVE
CANTERBURY CL
CHURCH CL
SOMERSET AVE
YATE RD
RAINBOW CT
Great Western Bsns Pk
Northavon Bsns Ctr
NORTH RD
DEAN RD
WHITLEY CL
Frome bank Jun Sch
TYNDALE AVE
LODGE RD
83
LAVENHAM RD
Northbridge Bsns Ctr
BRUNEL CT
RAYMILL CRES
WINDSOR DR
CRANLEIGH COURT RD
MADISON CL
BEAUFORT AVE
BEAUFORT RD
SPAR RD
BIRCH RD
TEMPLAR RD
St Mary's CE Prim Sch
ELMGROVE DR
ST MARY'S WAY
MELROSE AVE
THIRLMERE CRES
MERCIER CL

2
Beeches Ind Est
WAVERLEY RD
LAWRENCE DR
BRIDGE RD
The Laurels
STOVER RD
Stove Trad Est
PLOVER CL
LONGS DR
THE WILLOWS
FOX AVE
GAYTHORNE CRES
MILTON RD
HOME ORCH
THE GLEN
SCHOOL WALK
TYNING CL
TURNPIKE CL
ORCHARD CL
LAWNS RD
TREE LEAZE
SWAN FIELD
HOPE RD
MILLBROOK RD
WELLINGTON DR
STAPLES RD
THE LEAZE
POOLE COURT DR
Schs
RIDGEWAY
NEWLYN WAY
HIGHWAY
FOLLY BRIDGE CL
Yate
1 BADMINTON CT
2 THE BADMINTON CTR
MILTON CL
BARTON CT
Superstore
STATION RD
B4060
NORTH PAR
EAST WALK
WEST WALK
NORTH WALK
BROADWAY
B4059
Mill
NIBLEY LA
Nibley
SOUTH AVE
L Ctr
Liby
FOUR SEASONS SQ
SOUTH WALK
Sh Ctr
LINK RD
B4060

1
PH
BADMINTON RD
Badminton Road Trad Est
WESTLEIGH CL
SUNNYSIDE LA
MOORPARK AVE
MOORLAND RD
THE AVENUE
PO
VILLAGE CL
THORNS FARM
Ct
ANDREW MILLMAN CT
BENNETT'S CT
WESTLEIGH CT
CHATTERTON RD
EGGSHILL LA
CRANTOCK RD
LYNDALE RD
PRIORS LEA
STANSHAWE CRES
CLEEVE RD
KENNEDY WAY
SOUTH PAR
GOODRICH CL
TURNER DR
WOODWARD AVE
MAYBANK RD
WELLSTEAD AVE
THORN CL
WESTERLEIGH RD
BLAKENEY RD
STALL ST
NAILSWORTH AVE
STINCHCOMBE
PAINSWICK DR
KENNEDY HO
GLENEAGLES
ESTORIL
WALTON
HEATH
A432
MOORDELL CL
DURSLEY CL
BOWLERS PK
WENTWORTH
ST ANDREWS
SCOTT WAY
CABOT CL
Factory
YATE
Westerleigh Common
King Edmund Com Sch
SUNDRIDGE PK
FERNDOWN
FAIRHAVEN
KENILWORTH
SHACKLETON AVE
82
BS36
STANSHAWES DR

69 A B 70 C D 71 E F

43
54

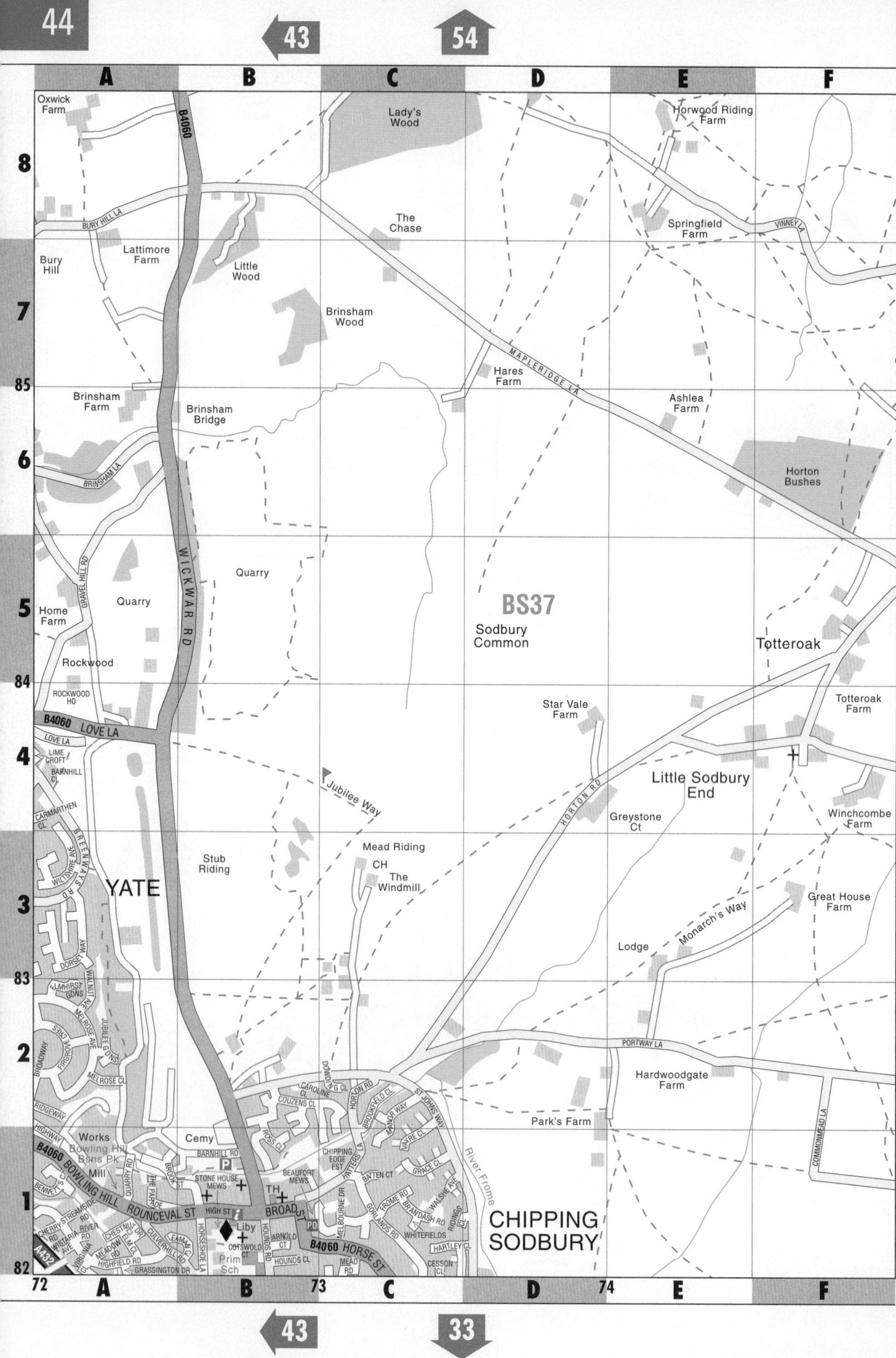
A
B
C
D
E
F
8
7
85
6
5
84
4
3
83
2
1
82
72
73
74
Oxwick Farm
B4060
Lady's Wood
Horwood Riding Farm
BURY HILL LA
The Chase
Springfield Farm
VINNEY LA
Bury Hill
Lattimore Farm
Little Wood
Brinsham Wood
MAPLERIDGE LA
Hares Farm
Ashlea Farm
Brinsham Farm
Brinsham Bridge
BRINSHAM LA
Horton Bushes
WICKWAR RD
Quarry
GRAVEL HILL RD
BS37
Home Farm
Sodbury Common
Totteroak
Rockwood
ROCKWOOD HO
Star Vale Farm
Totteroak Farm
B4060 LOVE LA
LOVE LA
LIME CROFT
BARNHILL CL
Jubilee Way
Little Sodbury End
HORTON RD
CARMARTHEN CL
GREENWAYS RD
Greystone Ct
Winchcombe Farm
Mead Riding
CH
The Windmill
WILTSHIRE AVE
Stub Riding
YATE
Great House Farm
Monarch's Way
DORSET WAY
WALNUT AVE
Lodge
ELMHIRST GDNS
MELROSE AVE
JUBILEE GDNS
FIRGROVE CRES
BROADWAY
PORTWAY LA
Hardwoodgate Farm
MELROSE CL
CAROLINE CL
DOWDING CL
HORTON RD
COUZENS CL
BROOKFIELD CL
ST JOHNS WAY
MANOR WAY
RIDGEWAY
HIGHWAY
Works
Bowling Hill Bsns Pk
Cemy
ROSS CL
Park's Farm
VAYRE CL
BARNHILL RD
CHIPPING EDGE EST
HATTERS LA
GRACE CL
COMMONMEAD LA
River Frome
Mill
QUARRY RD
BROOK ST
STONE HOUSE MEWS
TH
BEAUFORT MEWS
BATTEN CT
B4060 BOWLING HILL
ROUNCEVAL ST
BENNETTS CT
FROME RD
WALSHE AVE
HIGH ST
BROAD ST
PO
MELBOURNE DR
GORLANDS RD
BRANDASH RD
CHIPPING SODBURY
STREAMSIDE
CHERRY RD
WISTARIA AVE
RIVER RD
CHESTNUT DR
ELM CL
MEADOW RD
LEAMAN CL
CULVERHILL RD
HORSESHOE LA
Liby
COTSWOLD CT
HOUNDS RD
ARNOLD CT
WHITEFIELDS
RIDINGS CL
VIRGINIA CL
HIGHFIELD RD
GRASSINGTON DR
Prim Sch
HOUNDS CL
B4060 HORSE ST
MEAD RD
HARTLEY CL
CESSON CL
A432

43
33

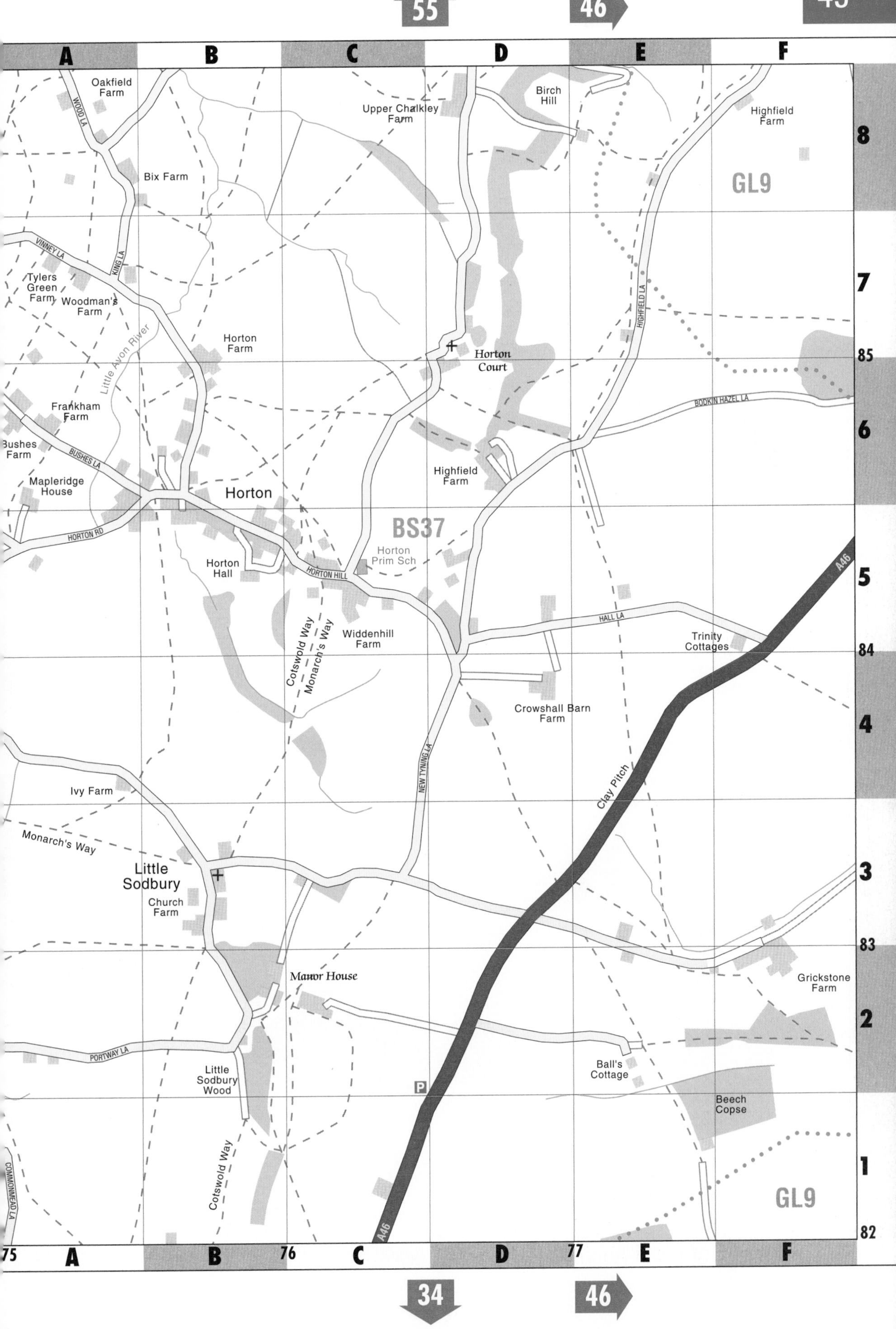
55
46
34
46
A
B
C
D
E
F
8
7
85
6
5
84
4
3
83
2
1
82
75
76
77
Oakfield Farm
WOOD LA
Upper Chalkley Farm
Birch Hill
Highfield Farm
GL9
Bix Farm
VINNEY LA
KING LA
Tylers Green Farm
Woodman's Farm
Horton Farm
Little Avon River
HIGHFIELD LA
Horton Court
BODKIN HAZEL LA
Frankham Farm
Bushes Farm
BUSHES LA
Highfield Farm
Mapleridge House
Horton
HORTON RD
BS37
Horton Hall
Horton Prim Sch
HORTON HILL
A46
HALL LA
Cotswold Way
Monarch's Way
Widdenhill Farm
Trinity Cottages
Crowshall Barn Farm
NEW TYNING LA
Clay Pitch
Ivy Farm
Monarch's Way
Little Sodbury
Church Farm
Manor House
Grickstone Farm
PORTWAY LA
Little Sodbury Wood
Ball's Cottage
P
Beech Copse
COMMONMEAD LA
Cotswold Way
GL9
A46

45
56

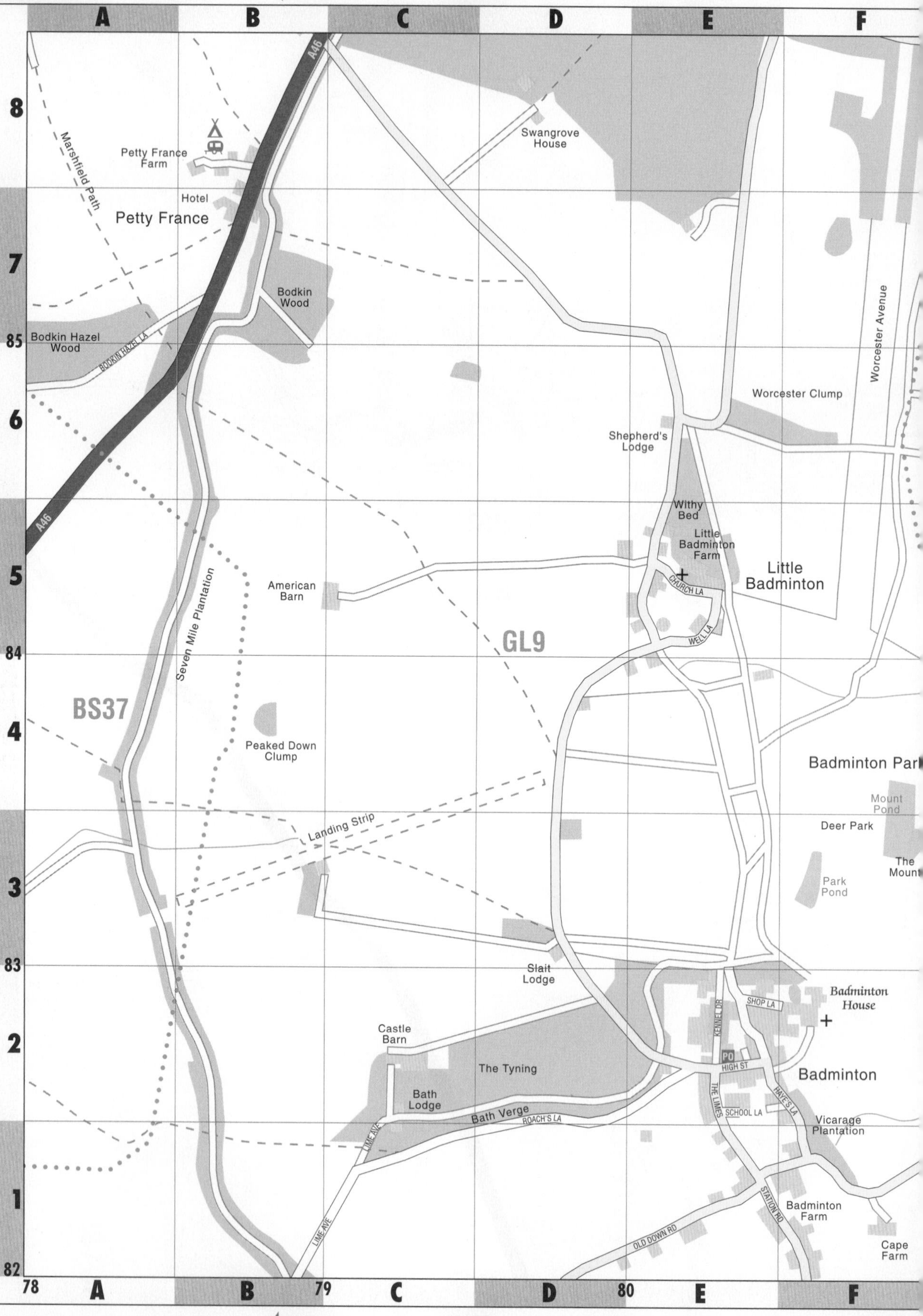

A B C D E F

8
Marshfield Path
Petty France Farm
Swangrove House
Hotel
Petty France
A46
7
Bodkin Wood
85
Bodkin Hazel Wood
BODKIN HAZEL LA
Worcester Avenue
Worcester Clump
6
Shepherd's Lodge
Withy Bed
Little Badminton Farm
Little Badminton
5
American Barn
CHURCH LA
WELL LA
Seven Mile Plantation
GL9
84
BS37
4
Peaked Down Clump
Badminton Park
Mount Pond
Deer Park
Landing Strip
3
The Mount
Park Pond
83
Slait Lodge
Badminton House
SHOP LA
KENNEL DR
2
Castle Barn
The Tyning
PO
HIGH ST
Badminton
Bath Lodge
Bath Verge
ROACH'S LA
THE LIMES
SCHOOL LA
HAYE'S LA
Vicarage Plantation
LIME AVE
1
STATION RD
Badminton Farm
OLD DOWN RD
Cape Farm
82

78 A B 79 C D 80 E F

45
35

57
A
B
C
D
E
F
Duchess's Clump
GL9
Badminton Down
Luckley Brake
Hundred Acres Farm
Sandy Farm
SHALLOWBROOKS LA
Ivy Leaze Cottage
Luckley Farm
Wick Farm
Lord's Copse
SN14
Cherry Orchard
CHERRY ORCHARD LA
North End Farm
North End House
Brook End
SHERSTON RD
B4040
Luckington Court
Luckington Cty Prim Sch
SOPWORTH RD
PH
Lyppiatt Barn
The Farm
Luckington Court Gardens
THE MERCHANTS
PO
CHURCH RD
CHAPEL ROW
HOLLIS GDNS
AVON RISE
THE STREET
POLAR GDNS
Luckington
Hermit's Cell
Allengrove Farm
ALLENGROVE LA
Allen Grove
Oak Plantation
Hebden Leaze Farm
BRISTOL RD
Macmillan Way
GL9
Giant's Cave
Alderton
Townfield Farm
Splash Pond
Fatting Barn
Hebden Leaze
Hebden Farm
B4040
Wiltshire STREET ATLAS
8
7
85
6
5
84
4
3
83
2
1
82
81
82
83
36

61

A B C D E F

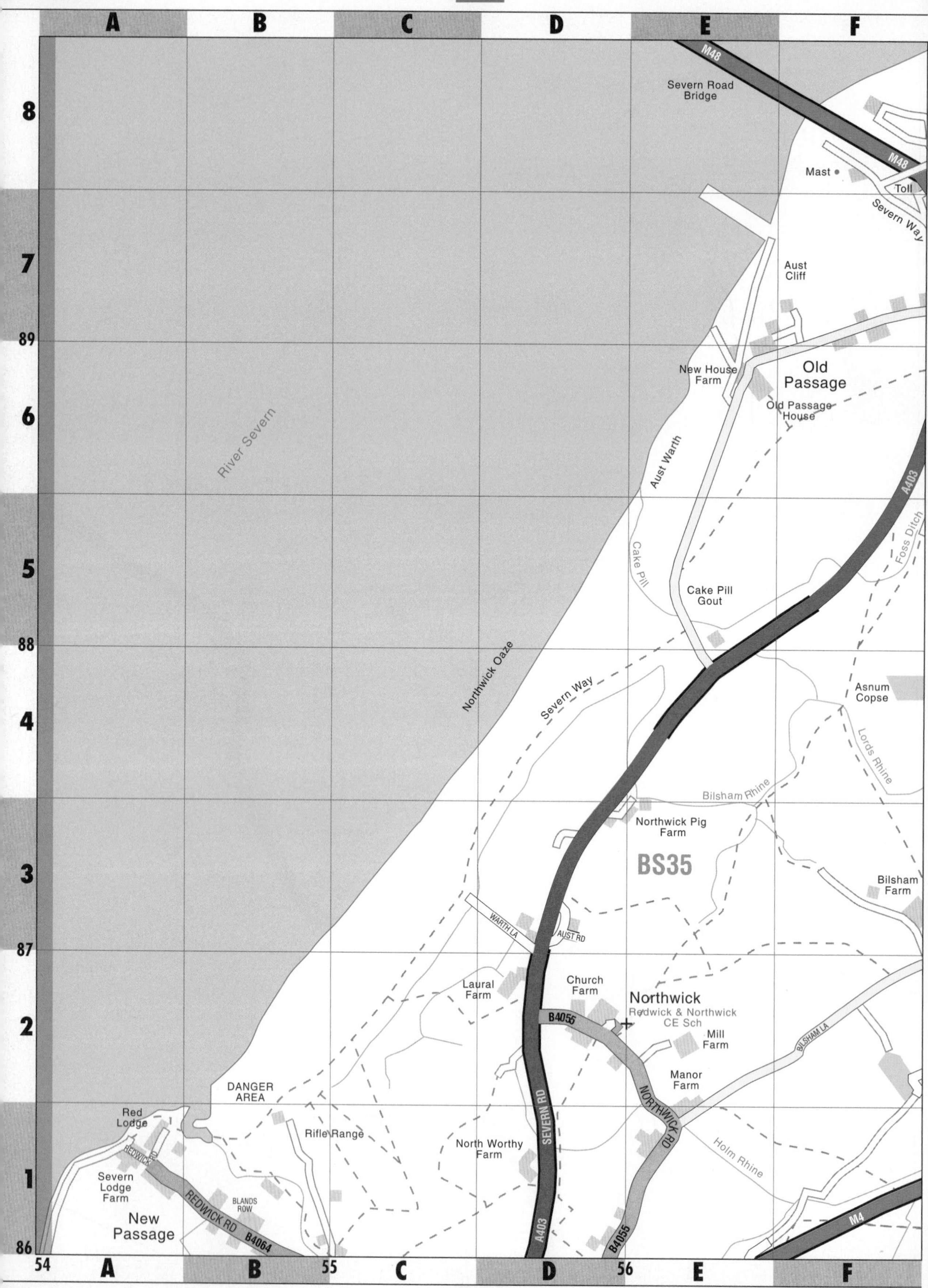

A B C D E F

38

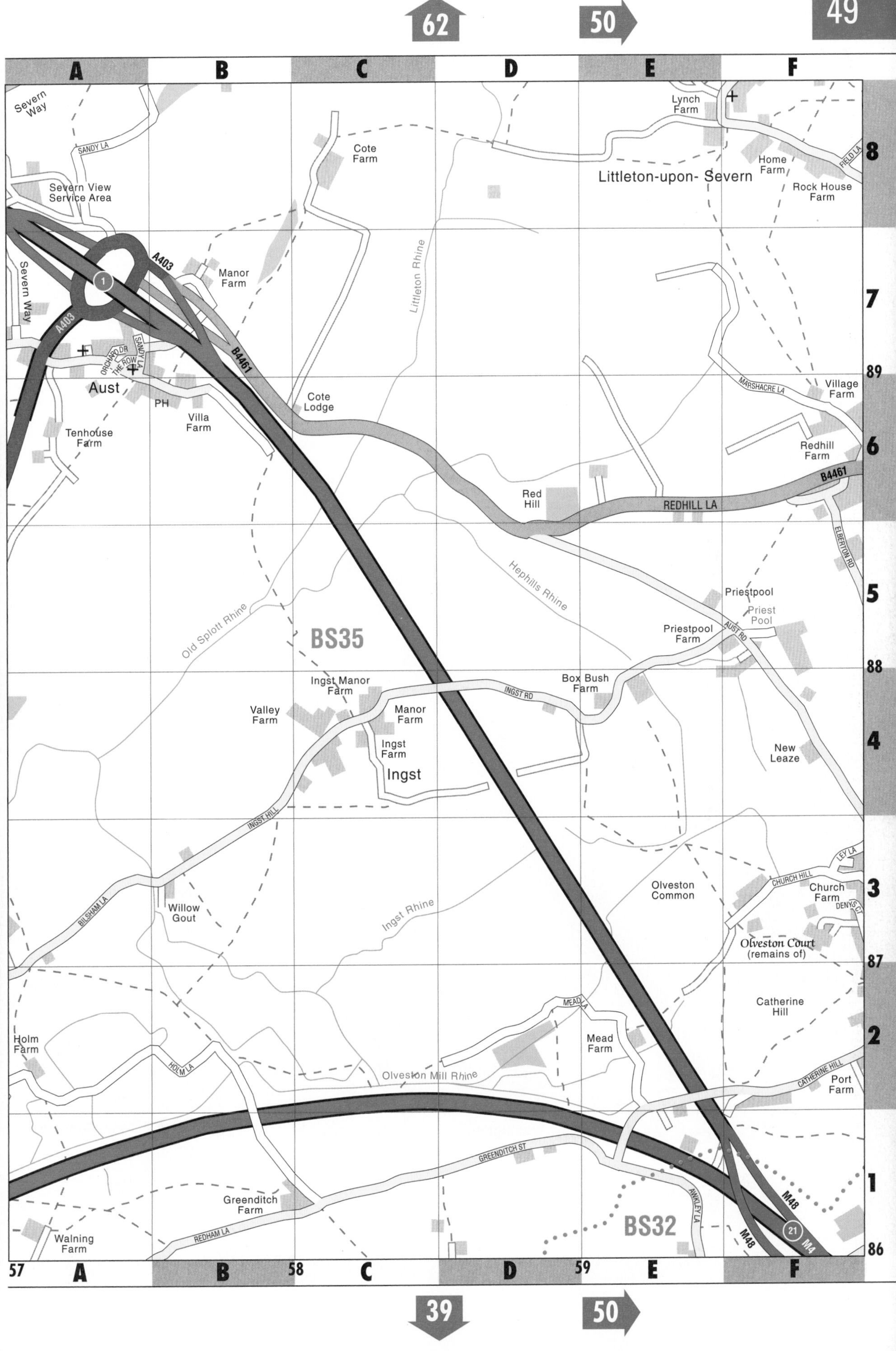
62
50
A
B
C
D
E
F
Severn Way
Sandy La
Severn View Service Area
Cote Farm
Lynch Farm
Littleton-upon- Severn
Home Farm
Field La
Rock House Farm
8
A403
Manor Farm
Littleton Rhine
7
Orchard Dr
The Row
Sandy La
B4461
Aust
PH
Villa Farm
Tenhouse Farm
Cote Lodge
Marshacre La
Village Farm
89
Redhill Farm
6
Red Hill
Redhill La
B4461
Elberton Rd
Hephills Rhine
Priestpool
Priest Pool
5
Old Splott Rhine
BS35
Priestpool Farm
Aust Rd
88
Ingst Manor Farm
Box Bush Farm
Ingst Rd
Valley Farm
Manor Farm
Ingst Farm
Ingst
New Leaze
4
Ingst Hill
Ley La
Church Hill
Olveston Common
Church Farm
3
Denys Ct
Bilsham La
Willow Gout
Ingst Rhine
Olveston Court (remains of)
87
Mead La
Catherine Hill
Holm Farm
Mead Farm
2
Holm La
Olveston Mill Rhine
Catherine Hill
Port Farm
Greenditch St
1
M48
Greenditch Farm
Awkley La
BS32
M48
M4
21
Walning Farm
Redham La
86
57
58
59
39
50

49
63

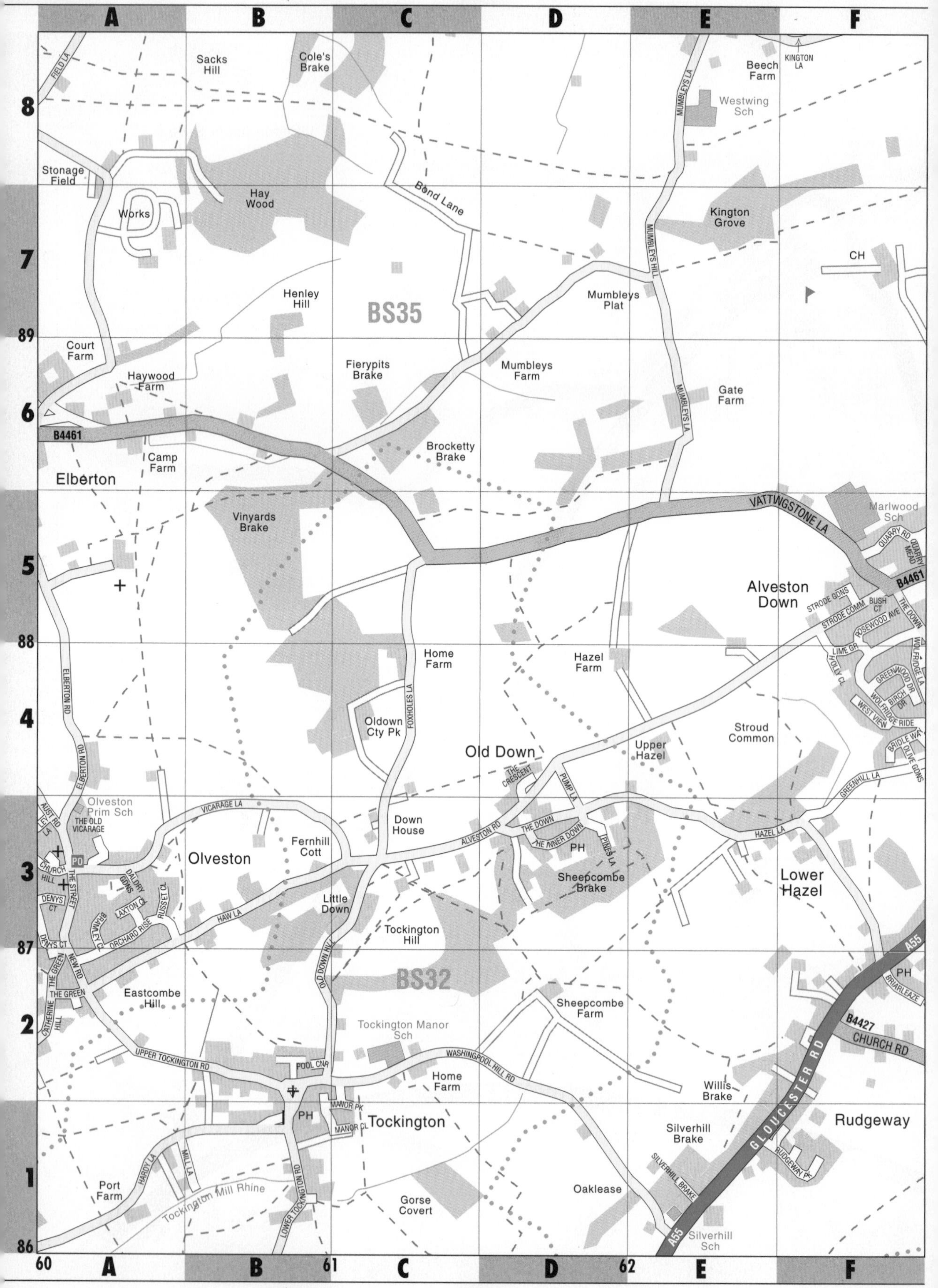

A B C D E F
8 7 89 6 5 88 4 3 87 2 1 86
60 61 62
Sacks Hill
Cole's Brake
Field La
Beech Farm
Kington La
Westwing Sch
Mumbleys La
Stonage Field
Hay Wood
Works
Bond Lane
Kington Grove
Mumbleys Hill
CH
Henley Hill
BS35
Mumbleys Plat
Court Farm
Fierypits Brake
Mumbleys Farm
Haywood Farm
Gate Farm
B4461
Camp Farm
Brocketty Brake
Elberton
Vinyards Brake
Vattingstone La
Marlwood Sch
Quarry Rd
Quarry Mead
B4461
Alveston Down
Strode Gdns
Strode Comm.
Bush Ct
Rosewood Ave
The Down
Lime Gr
Wolfridge La
Holly Cl
Greenwood Dr
Birch Dr
Home Farm
Hazel Farm
Elberton Rd
Oldown Cty Pk
Foxholes La
West View
Wolfridge Ride
Stroud Common
Bridle Way
Olive Gdns
Old Down
Upper Hazel
The Crescent
Pump La
Greenhill La
Olveston Prim Sch
Aust Rd
Ley La
The Old Vicarage
Vicarage La
Down House
Alveston Rd
The Down
The Inner Down
Hazel La
PO
Fernhill Cott
PH
Pines La
Olveston
Church Hill
The Street
Daldry Gdns
Russet Cl
Sheepcombe Brake
Lower Hazel
Denys Ct
Bramley Cl
Laxton Cl
Little Down
Orchard Rise
Haw La
Tockington Hill
Denys Ct
The Green
New Rd
Old Down Hill
BS32
A55
PH
The Green
Eastcombe Hill
Sheepcombe Farm
Briarleaze
Catherine Hill
Tockington Manor Sch
B4427
Church Rd
Upper Tockington Rd
Pool Cnr
Washingpool Hill Rd
Home Farm
Willis Brake
Gloucester Rd
PH
Manor Pk
Tockington
Manor Cl
Silverhill Brake
Rudgeway
Hardy La
Mill La
Rudgeway Pk
Port Farm
Tockington Mill Rhine
Lower Tockington Rd
Gorse Covert
Oaklease
Silverhill Brake
A55
Silverhill Sch

49
40

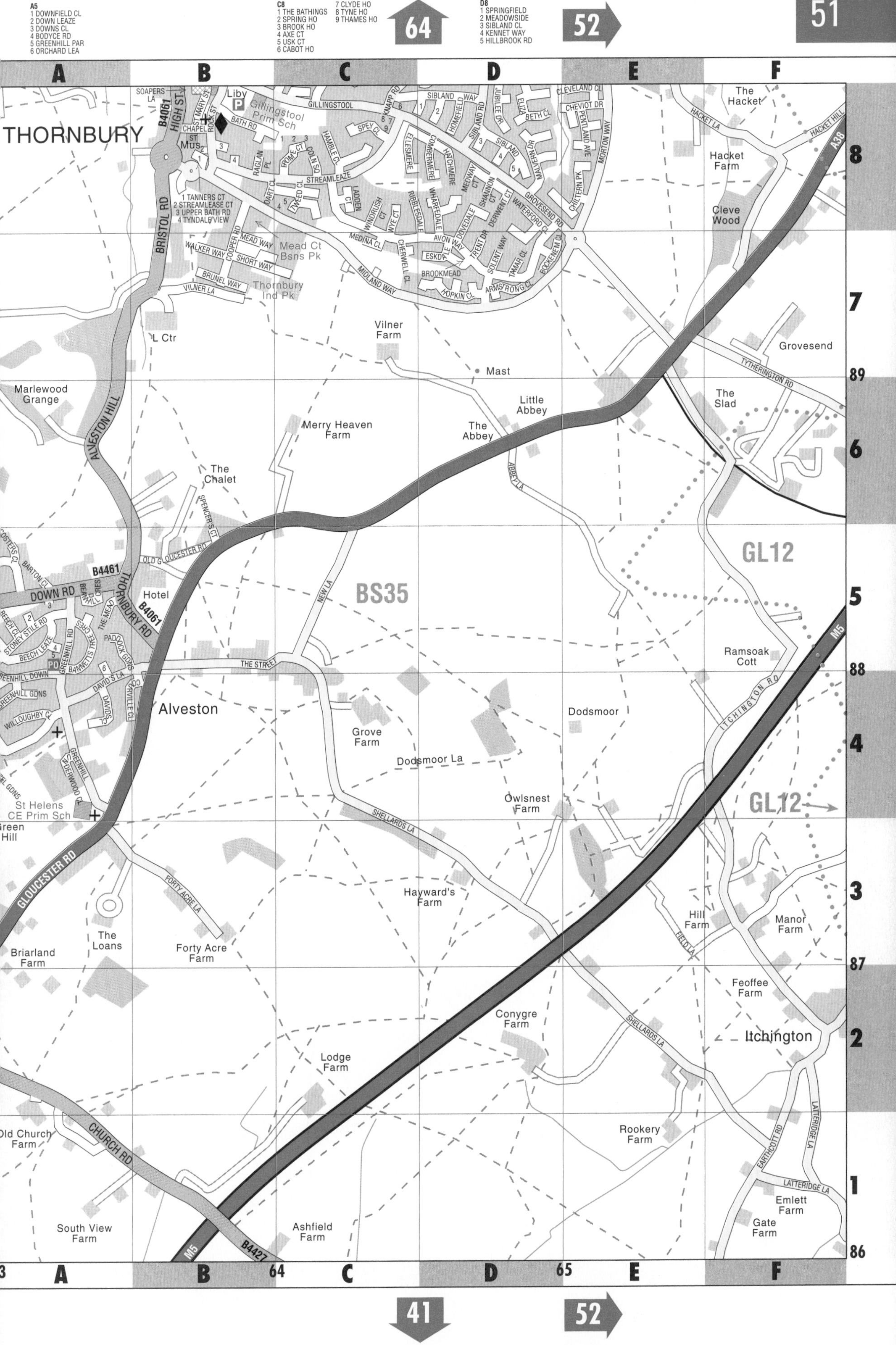

A5
1 DOWNFIELD CL
2 DOWN LEAZE
3 DOWNS CL
4 BODYCE RD
5 GREENHILL PAR
6 ORCHARD LEA
C8
1 THE BATHINGS
2 SPRING HO
3 BROOK HO
4 AXE CT
5 USK CT
6 CABOT HO
7 CLYDE HO
8 TYNE HO
9 THAMES HO
64
D8
1 SPRINGFIELD
2 MEADOWSIDE
3 SIBLAND CL
4 KENNET WAY
5 HILLBROOK RD
52
51
THORNBURY
1 TANNERS CT
2 STREAMLEAZE CT
3 UPPER BATH RD
4 TYNDALE VIEW
Gillingstool Prim Sch
Mead Ct Bsns Pk
Thornbury Ind Pk
L Ctr
Vilner Farm
Mast
Grovesend
The Hacket
Hacket Farm
Cleve Wood
The Slad
Little Abbey
The Abbey
Merry Heaven Farm
Marlewood Grange
The Chalet
Hotel
Alveston
BS35
GL12
Ramsoak Cott
Dodsmoor
Grove Farm
Dodsmoor La
Owlsnest Farm
St Helens CE Prim Sch
Green Hill
Hayward's Farm
Hill Farm
Manor Farm
The Loans
Briarland Farm
Forty Acre Farm
Feoffee Farm
Conygre Farm
Itchington
Lodge Farm
Rookery Farm
Old Church Farm
Emlett Farm
Gate Farm
South View Farm
Ashfield Farm
BRISTOL RD
ALVESTON HILL
GLOUCESTER RD
THORNBURY RD
DOWN RD
THE STREET
NEW LA
SHELLARDS LA
FORTY ACRE LA
CHURCH RD
ABBEY LA
TYTHERINGTON RD
ITCHINGTON RD
EARTHCOTT RD
LATTERIDGE LA
HACKET LA
HACKET HILL
MIDLAND WAY
GILLINGSTOOL
GROVESEND RD
A38
M5
B4061
B4461
B4427
89
88
87
86
64
65
8
7
6
5
4
3
2
1
A
B
C
D
E
F
41
52

51
65

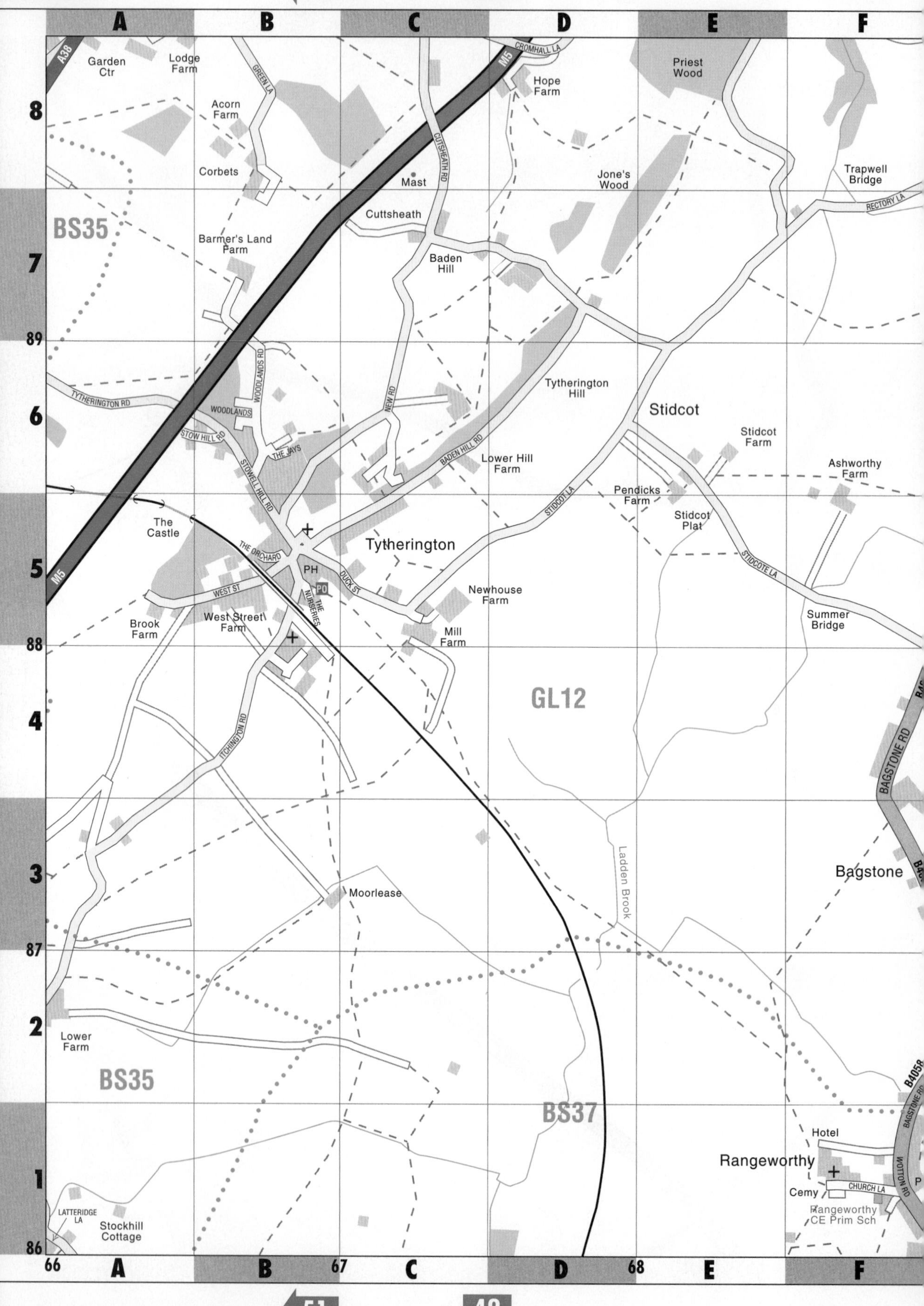
A
B
C
D
E
F
8
7
89
6
5
88
4
3
87
2
1
86
66
67
68
Garden Ctr
Lodge Farm
Acorn Farm
Corbets
Mast
Cuttsheath
Hope Farm
Priest Wood
Jone's Wood
Trapwell Bridge
RECTORY LA
BS35
Barmer's Land Farm
Baden Hill
Tytherington Hill
Stidcot
Stidcot Farm
Ashworthy Farm
Lower Hill Farm
Pendicks Farm
Stidcot Plat
The Castle
Tytherington
PH
PO
Newhouse Farm
Summer Bridge
Brook Farm
West Street Farm
Mill Farm
GL12
Moorlease
Ladden Brook
Bagstone
Lower Farm
BS35
BS37
Hotel
Rangeworthy
Cemy
Rangeworthy CE Prim Sch
Stockhill Cottage
A38
M5
GREEN LA
CROMHALL LA
CUTTSHEATH RD
NEW RD
WOODLANDS RD
WOODLANDS
TYTHERINGTON RD
STOW HILL RD
THE JAYS
STOWELL HILL RD
BADEN HILL RD
STIDCOT LA
STIDCOTE LA
THE ORCHARD
WEST ST
THE NURSERIES
DUCK ST
ITCHINGTON RD
BAGSTONE RD
B4058
CHURCH LA
WOTTON RD
LATTERIDGE LA

51
42

66
54
A
B
C
D
E
F
8
7
89
6
5
88
4
3
87
2
1
86
69
70
71
43
54
Heathend House Farm
THE GREEN
B4058
Heath End
Cole's Bridge
RECTORY LA
JUBILEE LA
Cromhall Common
BRISTOL RD
Lake Copse
B4509
THE DOWNS
The Cliffs
Cowship Farm
COWSHIP LA
The Meads Farm
West End
GL12
BAGSTONE RD
Newlands Farm
RAG LA
WESTEND RD
Barber's Court Farm
Westend Farm
England's Farm
Whitehouse Farm
Oldclose Farm
Ladden Brook
Wixoldbury Farm
Frith Farm
FRITH LA
Little Bagstone Court Farm
Firingsclose Farm
Hall End Farm
Hillhouse Cottage
Bagstone
Shepherds Close
Hall End
HALL END LA
Greenview Farm
GREEN LA
Jubilee Way
Yate Lower Common
LIMEKILN RD
LC
Hall End Farm
Hillhouse Farm
Oat Field Farm
Yate Lower Common
BS37
NEW RD
Newhouse Farm
WICKWAR RD
BULLY LA
WOTTON RD

53
67

A
B
C
D
E
F
8
7
89
6
5
88
4
3
87
2
1
86
72
73
74
Bunsall Bridge
B4060
Southwood Farm
Archfield Nursery
Cherryrock Farm
Haroldsfield Farm
Cherryrock Brake
Mounteney's Farm
Station House
STATION RD
Trad Est
Kites Farm
Chasehouse Farm
MOUNTENEY'S LA
CHASE LA
Chaselane Farm
B4509
CHURCH LA
THE DOWNS
WESTEND RD
Chase Hill
Saltmoors Ditch
Inglestone Farm
PH
AVON CRES
AVON CRES
COTSWOLD VIEW
NORTH ST
HONEYBORNE WAY
ARKELLS CT
HIGH ST
GL12
South Moon Ridings
Arnolds Field Trad Est
TH
BACK LA
INGLESTONE RD
The Alexander Hosea Prim Sch
Sturt Farm
The Walk
PO
Sturt Bridge
SOUTHEND HO
BURLEIGH WAY
Little Stanley Wood
Lower Woods Lodge
Wickwar
AMBERLEY WAY
CANTERS LEAZE
Little Avon River
GL9
South Farm
POPLAR LA
Horwood Farm
Wetmoor Nature Reserve
Poplar Farm
HORWOOD LA
SODBURY RD
Bishop's Hill Wood
Upper Wetmoor
Lower Wetmoor Wood
Littley Wood
FRITH LA
Hill View Farm
PINCOTS LA
Pincots Farm
Bishop's Hill Brook
Sturgeon Wood
Burnt Wood
Bedford's Wood
Bays Wood
BS37
Shortwood Farm
Stonybridge Wood
Little Shortwood Farm
Haskin's Farm
WOOD LA
Birdsbush Farm
B4060

53
44

68
56

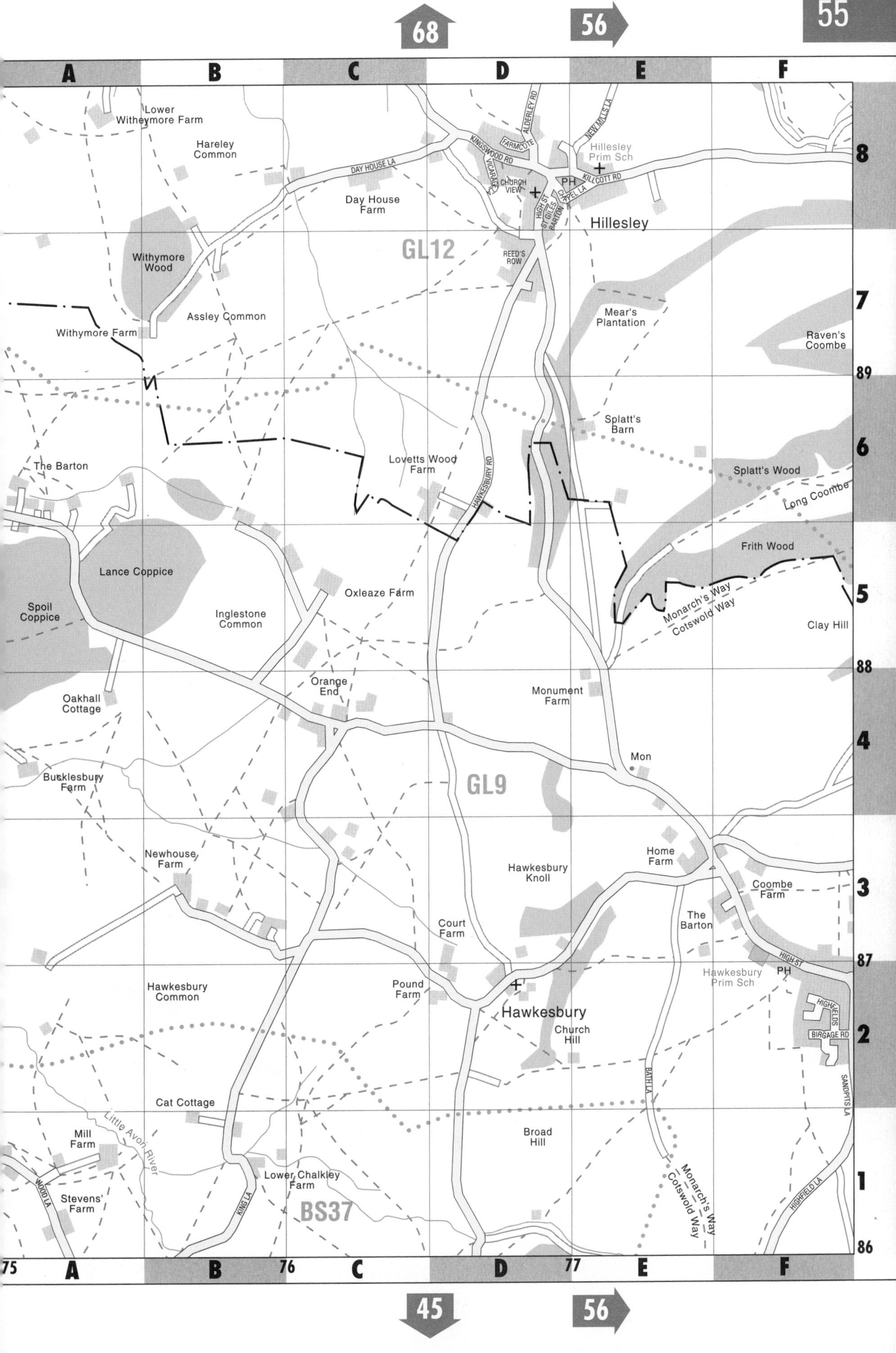
A
B
C
D
E
F
Lower Witheymore Farm
Hareley Common
DAY HOUSE LA
Day House Farm
KINGSWOOD RD
FARMCOTE
ALDERLEY RD
NEW MILLS LA
Hillesley Prim Sch
PH
KILLCOTT RD
CHAPEL LA
VICARAGE
CHURCH VIEW
HIGH ST
ST GILES BARTON
Hillesley
GL12
REED'S ROW
Withymore Wood
Assley Common
Withymore Farm
Mear's Plantation
Raven's Coombe
Splatt's Barn
Lovetts Wood Farm
HAWKESBURY RD
Splatt's Wood
Long Coombe
The Barton
Frith Wood
Lance Coppice
Oxleaze Farm
Monarch's Way
Cotswold Way
Spoil Coppice
Inglestone Common
Clay Hill
Orange End
Monument Farm
Oakhall Cottage
Mon
Bucklesbury Farm
GL9
Newhouse Farm
Hawkesbury Knoll
Home Farm
Coombe Farm
The Barton
Court Farm
HIGH ST
Hawkesbury Prim Sch
PH
Pound Farm
Hawkesbury Common
Hawkesbury
HIGHFIELDS
BIRGAGE RD
Church Hill
BATH LA
SANDPITS LA
Cat Cottage
Little Avon River
Broad Hill
Mill Farm
Lower Chalkley Farm
WOOD LA
Stevens' Farm
KING LA
BS37
Monarch's Way
Cotswold Way
HIGHFIELD LA
8
7
89
6
5
88
4
3
87
2
1
86
75
76
77

45
56

55
69

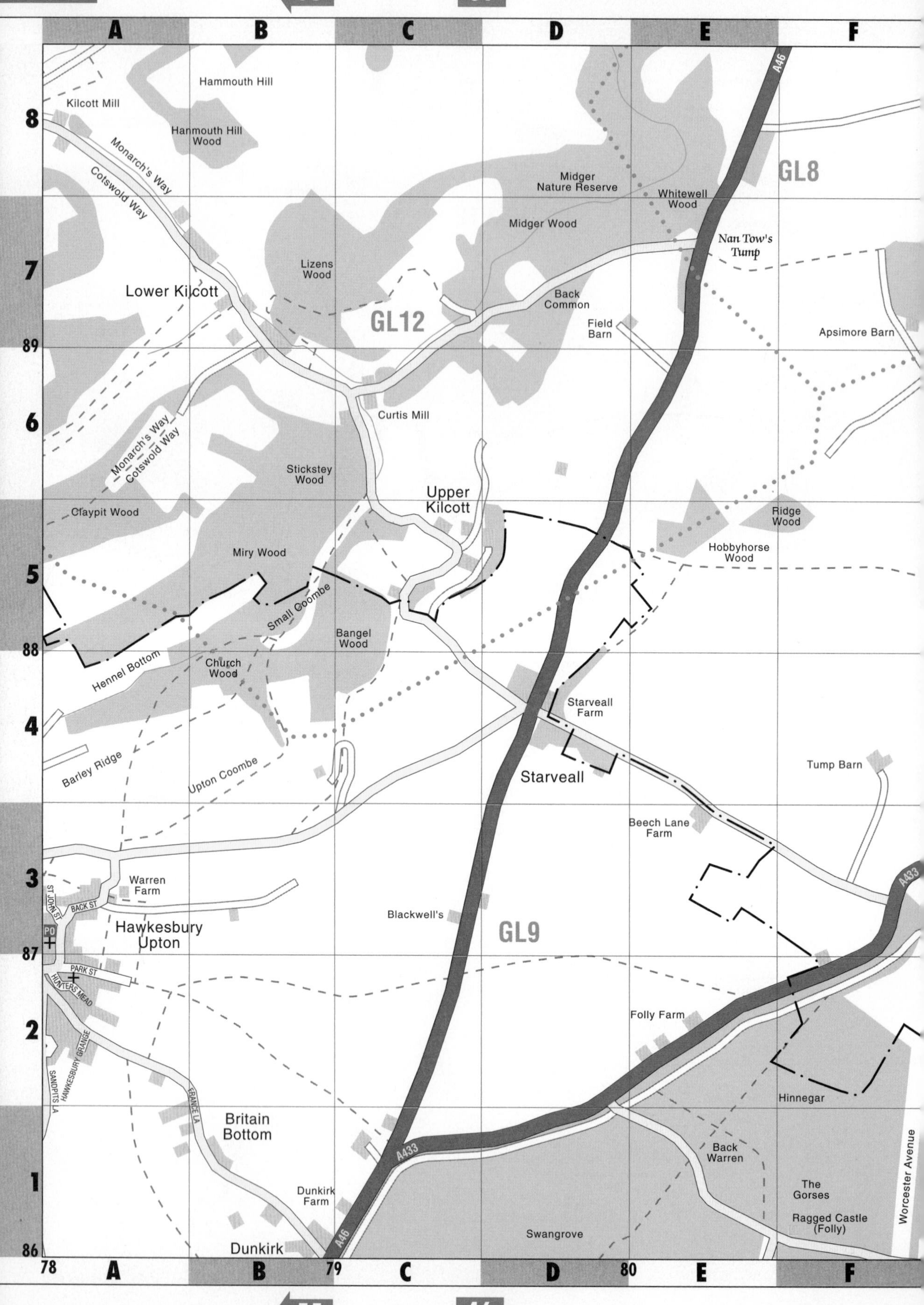
A
B
C
D
E
F
Hammouth Hill
Kilcott Mill
8
Hanmouth Hill Wood
Monarch's Way
Cotswold Way
Midger Nature Reserve
Whitewell Wood
GL8
A46
Midger Wood
Nan Tow's Tump
Lizens Wood
7
Lower Kilcott
GL12
Back Common
Field Barn
Apsimore Barn
89
Curtis Mill
6
Monarch's Way
Cotswold Way
Stickstey Wood
Upper Kilcott
Claypit Wood
Ridge Wood
Miry Wood
Hobbyhorse Wood
5
Small Coombe
Bangel Wood
88
Hennel Bottom
Church Wood
Starveall Farm
4
Barley Ridge
Upton Coombe
Starveall
Tump Barn
Beech Lane Farm
3
Warren Farm
ST JOHN ST
BACK ST
A433
Blackwell's
Hawkesbury Upton
GL9
PO
87
PARK ST
HUNTERS MEAD
Folly Farm
2
HAWKESBURY GRANGE
SANDPITS LA
FRANCE LA
Hinnegar
Britain Bottom
A433
Back Warren
Worcester Avenue
1
Dunkirk Farm
The Gorses
Ragged Castle (Folly)
Swangrove
86
Dunkirk
A46
78
79
80

55
46

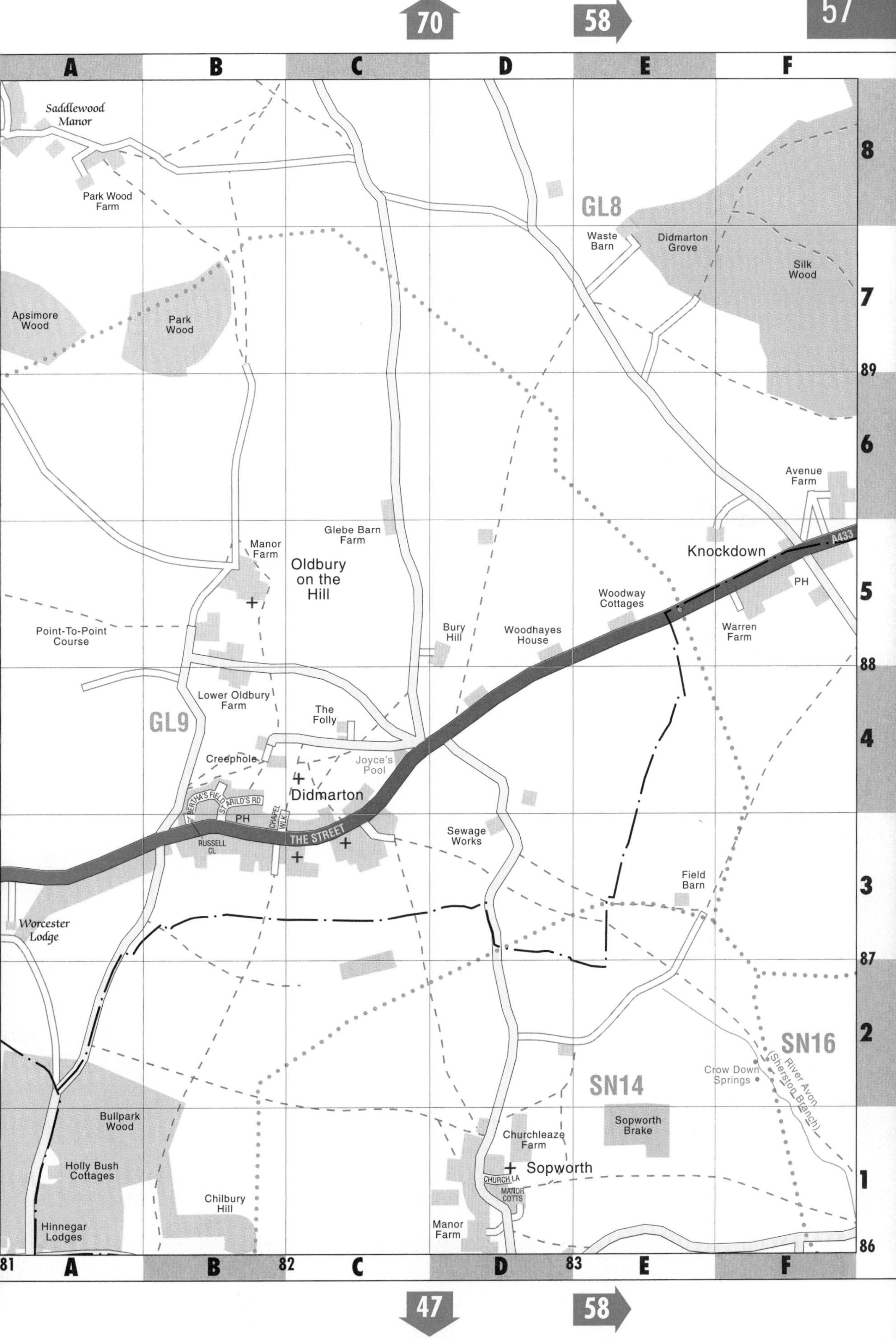
A
B
C
D
E
F
Saddlewood Manor
Park Wood Farm
GL8
Waste Barn
Didmarton Grove
Silk Wood
Apsimore Wood
Park Wood
Avenue Farm
Glebe Barn Farm
Manor Farm
Oldbury on the Hill
Knockdown
A433
PH
Woodway Cottages
Point-To-Point Course
Bury Hill
Woodhayes House
Warren Farm
Lower Oldbury Farm
GL9
The Folly
Creephole
Joyce's Pool
Didmarton
BERTHA'S FIELD
ST ARILD'S RD
CHAPEL WLK
PH
THE STREET
RUSSELL CL
Sewage Works
Field Barn
Worcester Lodge
SN16
Crow Down Springs
River Avon (Sherston Branch)
SN14
Bullpark Wood
Sopworth Brake
Churchleaze Farm
Holly Bush Cottages
Sopworth
CHURCH LA
MANOR COTTS
Chilbury Hill
Hinnegar Lodges
Manor Farm
8
7
89
6
5
88
4
3
87
2
1
86
81
82
83

57
71

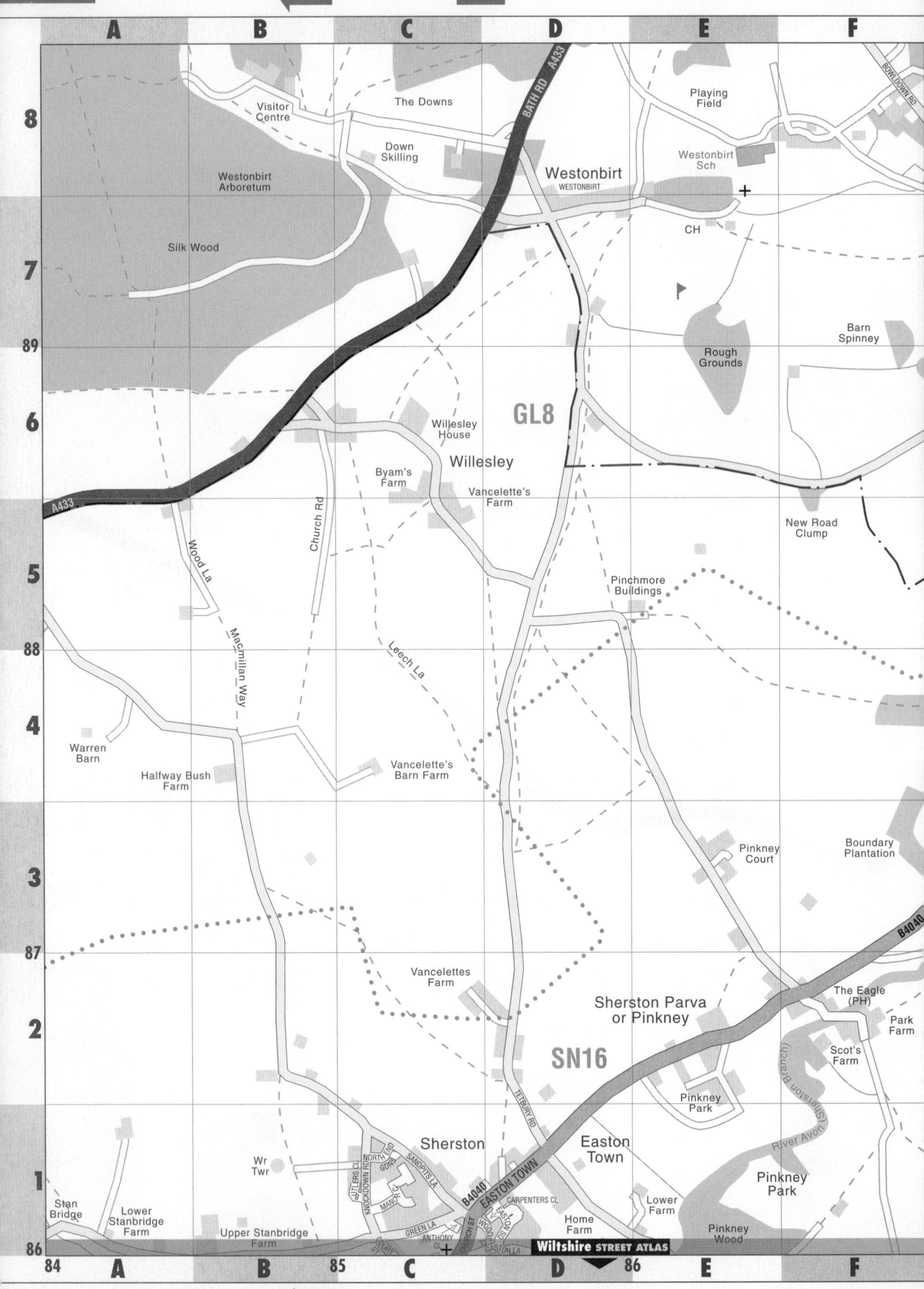
A
B
C
D
E
F
8
7
89
6
5
88
4
3
87
2
1
86
84
85
86
The Downs
Visitor Centre
Down Skilling
Westonbirt Arboretum
Silk Wood
BATH RD A433
Westonbirt
WESTONBIRT
Playing Field
Westonbirt Sch
CH
BOWLDOWN RD
Barn Spinney
Rough Grounds
GL8
Willesley House
Willesley
Byam's Farm
Vancelette's Farm
A433
Church Rd
Wood La
New Road Clump
Pinchmore Buildings
Macmillan Way
Leech La
Warren Barn
Halfway Bush Farm
Vancelette's Barn Farm
Pinkney Court
Boundary Plantation
B4040
Vancelettes Farm
Sherston Parva or Pinkney
The Eagle (PH)
Park Farm
SN16
Scot's Farm
Pinkney Park
River Avon (Sherston Branch)
TETBURY RD
Sherston
Easton Town
Wr Twr
NORTH END GDNS
SANDPITS LA
BUTLERS CL
KNOCKDOWN RD
MANOR CL
B4040
EASTON TOWN
CARPENTERS CL
Pinkney Park
Stan Bridge
Lower Stanbridge Farm
Upper Stanbridge Farm
GREEN LA
ANTHONY CL
CHURCH ST
COURT ST
GASTON LA
Home Farm
Lower Farm
Pinkney Wood

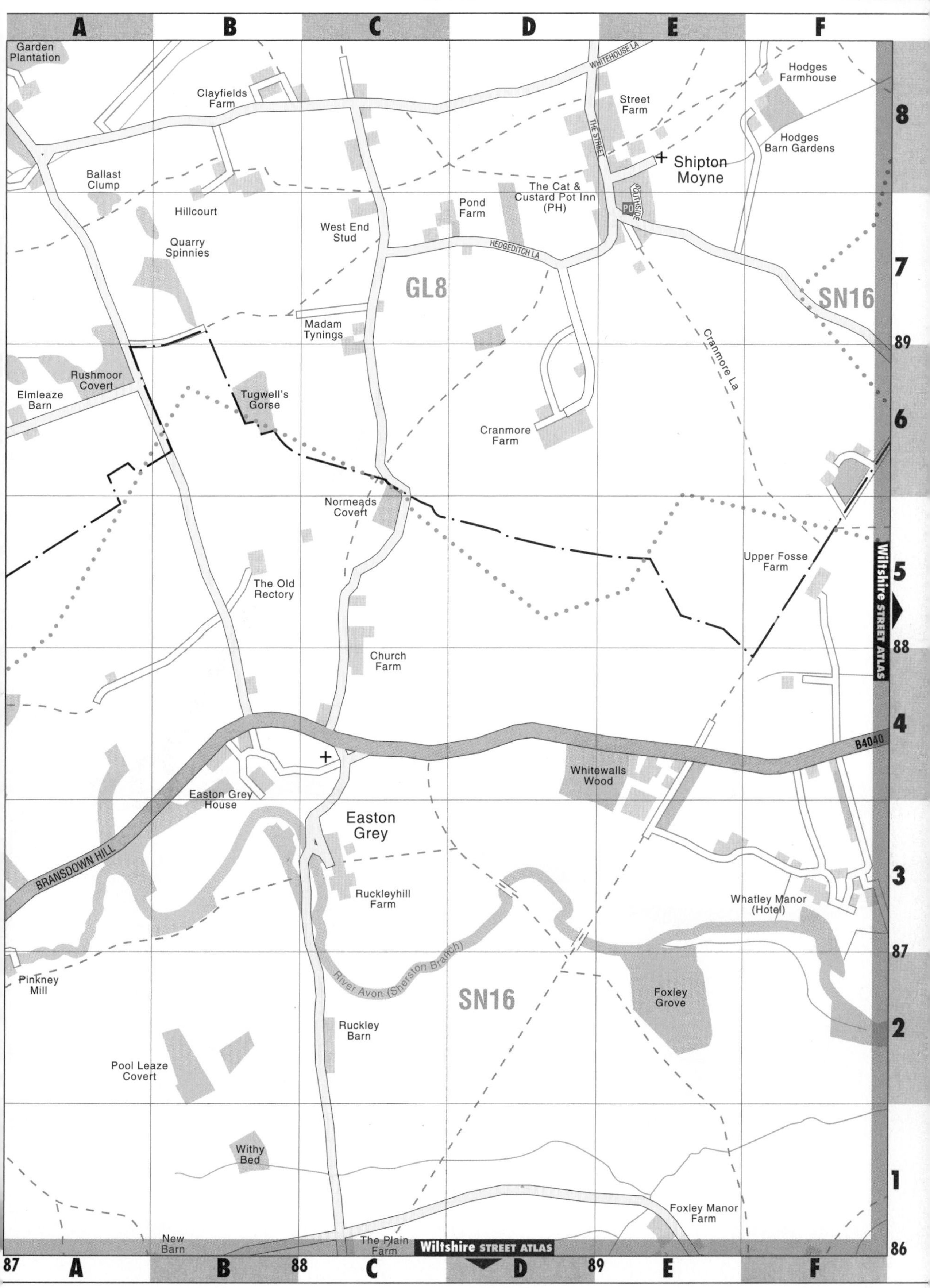

Wiltshire STREET ATLAS
Wiltshire STREET ATLAS

72

A
B
C
D
E
F
8
7
93
6
5
92
4
3
91
2
1
90
51
52
53
Great Barnets Woods
Bayfield Cottage
Bayfield
Traphill Wood
Barnetts Farm
Trap Hill
Mounton
Mounton House Sch
Bigs Wood
Brynderwin
Woodlands Grove
Chepstow Com
St Lawrence House
MOUNTON RD
ST LAWRENCE LA
SMOOTH STONES
ST LAWRENCE RD
WYE VALLEY LINK RD
A466
A48
NEWPORT RD
HARDWICK HILL
MOUNT PLEASANT
WELSH ST
B4293
Liby
LANCASTER WAY
HUNTFIELD RD
MEADOW WLK
PENTERRY PK
TEMPEST DR
MOUNTON HTS
MOUNTON RD
BADGERS DENE
VAUXHALL RD
PORTWALL RD
VINE COTTS
GREEN ST
Port Wall
1 OLD BELL CHAMBERS
2 HOCKER HILL ST
3 BEAUFORT SQ
4 BANK SQ
5 MIDDLE ST
6 ST MARY ST
7 ST MARY STREET ARC
8 OXFORD ST
9 SCHOOL HILL IND EST
10 RESTWAY WALL
11 GARDEN CITY WAY
Chepstow
Station Yard Ind Est
Hardwick
River Wye
(Afon Gwy)
LARKFIELD HO
Sch
High Beech
HIGH BEECH LA
Cemy
Pembroke Jun & Inf Sch
Bulwark
Chepstow Bulwark
CHEPSTOW
(CAS-GWENT)
WILLOW CL
Trelenny
Pwllmeric
(Pwllmeurig)
New Inn (PH)
New Hall
ORCHARD AVE
St Tewdric
Home Farm
MATHERN RD
NP16
The Bungalow
Newton Green
Wylands
East Wood
Mathern Mill (dis)
BAILEY'S HAY
LADY MARGARET CT 1
CIDERMILL CL 2
WELL CL 3
THORN TREE DR 4
FOUNTAIN WAY
The Buftons
A48 Newport
PH
Mathern
STEPASIDE
M48
M48 Newport (M4)
Sewage Works
Newhouse Farm Ind Est
St Tewdric's Well
Mathern House
Innage
Moynes Court
Moynes Court
LC
Mathern Palace
St Pierre
St Pierre Golf & Country Club
Boat House
The Cottage
Caldicot Level
NP26
Palace Farm
St Pierre Farm

73
62

A
B
C
D
E
F
Mast
Sch
Sedbury Bsns Pk
Badams Court
Baker's Wood
Hitchen's Grove
Offa's Dyke Path
PH
Sedbury
Sewage Works
THE BELFREY
Sedbury Park
Sedbury Cliffs
Pennsylvania Farm
Buttington Trump
Offa's Dyke Path
The Combe
Buttington Farm
NP16
INNER LOOP RD
LOOP RD
Slimeroad Sand
Warren Slade
Works
River Severn
Slime Road
Park Redding
River Wye (Afon Gwy)
ST GEORGES WAY
APPRENTICE CL
BEACHLEY RD
POTTERS CROFT
1 PHOENIX DR
2 CLARENDON CL
3 ALMA DR
4 BRITON CL
Whirls End
Beachley
Beachley Barracks
LC
Hunger Pill
Hen And Chickens
The Old Ferry Hotel
IRB Sta
Sports Gd
Leary Rock
Severn Road Bridge
Upper Bench
Beachley Point
M48
Aust Rock
8
7
93
6
5
92
4
3
91
2
1
90
54
55
56

48
62

61
74

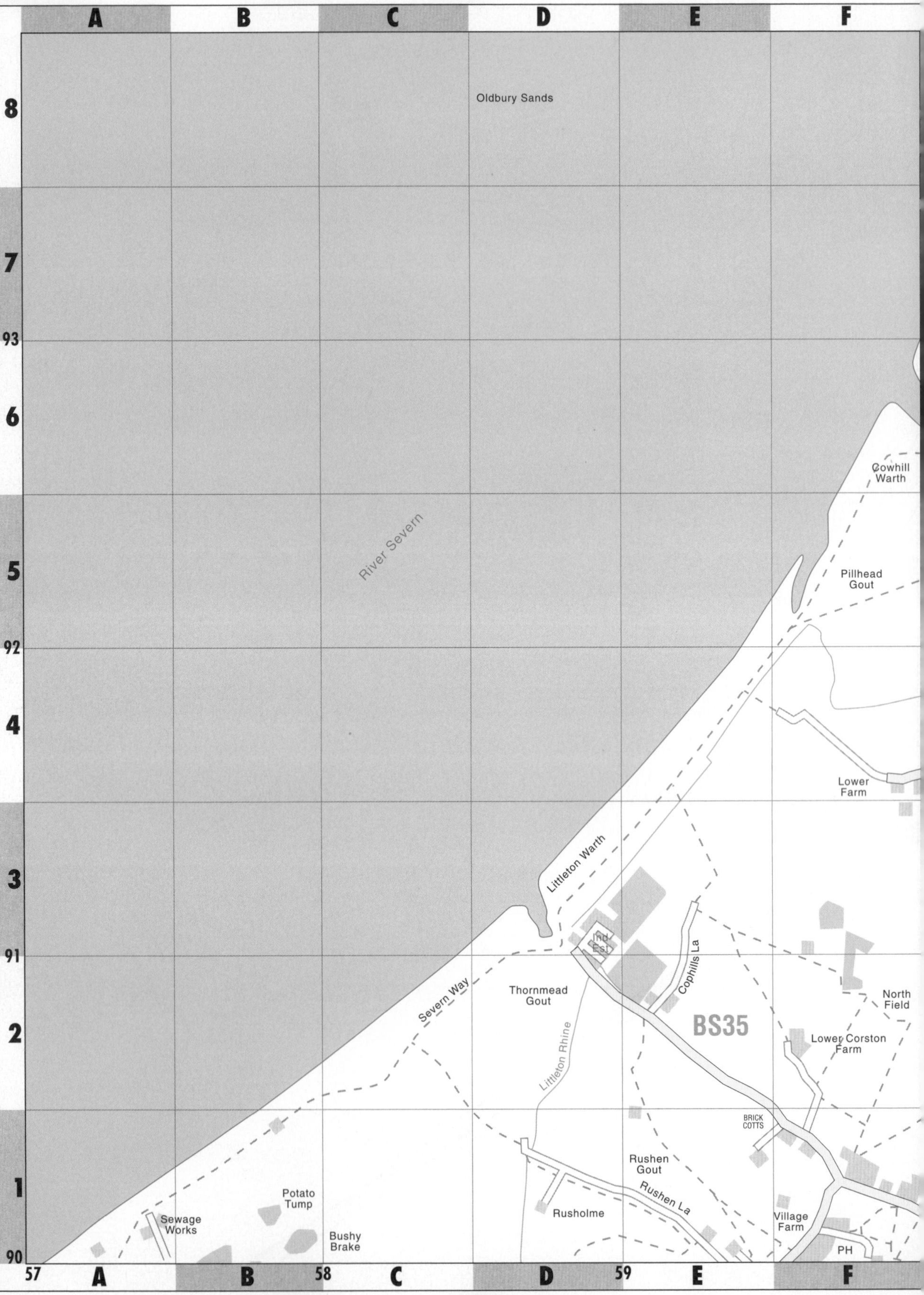

Oldbury Sands
River Severn
Cowhill Warth
Pillhead Gout
Lower Farm
Littleton Warth
Ind Est
Cophills La
Severn Way
Thornmead Gout
North Field
BS35
Littleton Rhine
Lower Corston Farm
BRICK COTTS
Rushen Gout
Rushen La
Potato Tump
Rusholme
Village Farm
Sewage Works
Bushy Brake
PH

A B C D E F
8 7 93 6 5 92 4 3 91 2 1 90
57 58 59

61
49

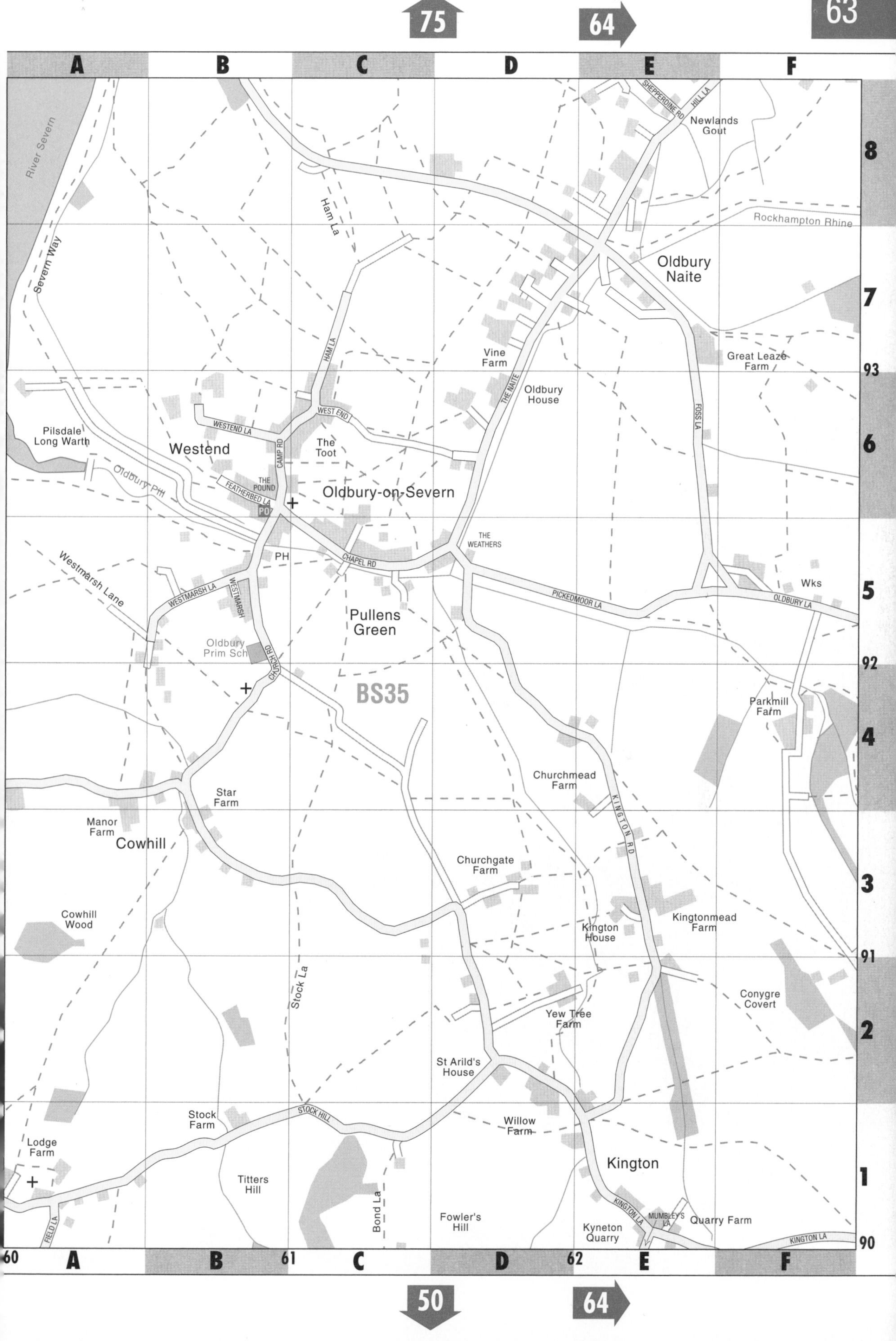
75
64
A
B
C
D
E
F
8
7
93
6
5
92
4
3
91
2
1
90
60
61
62
River Severn
Severn Way
Ham La
SHEPPERDINE RD
HILL LA
Newlands
Gout
Rockhampton Rhine
Oldbury
Naite
Vine
Farm
HAM LA
THE NAITE
Great Leaze
Farm
Oldbury
House
FOSS LA
Pilsdale
Long Warth
WESTEND LA
WEST END
The
Toot
Westend
CAMP RD
Oldbury Pill
THE
POUND
FEATHERBED LA
PO
Oldbury-on-Severn
THE
WEATHERS
Westmarsh Lane
PH
CHAPEL RD
WESTMARSH LA
WESTMARSH
PICKEDMOOR LA
Wks
OLDBURY LA
Pullens
Green
Oldbury
Prim Sch
CHURCH RD
BS35
Parkmill
Farm
Star
Farm
Churchmead
Farm
Manor
Farm
Cowhill
KINGTON RD
Churchgate
Farm
Cowhill
Wood
Kington
House
Kingtonmead
Farm
Stock La
Conygre
Covert
Yew Tree
Farm
St Arild's
House
Stock
Farm
STOCK HILL
Willow
Farm
Lodge
Farm
Kington
Titters
Hill
Bond La
Fowler's
Hill
KINGTON LA
MUMBLEY'S LA
Quarry Farm
Kyneton
Quarry
FIELD LA
KINGTON LA
50
64

63
76

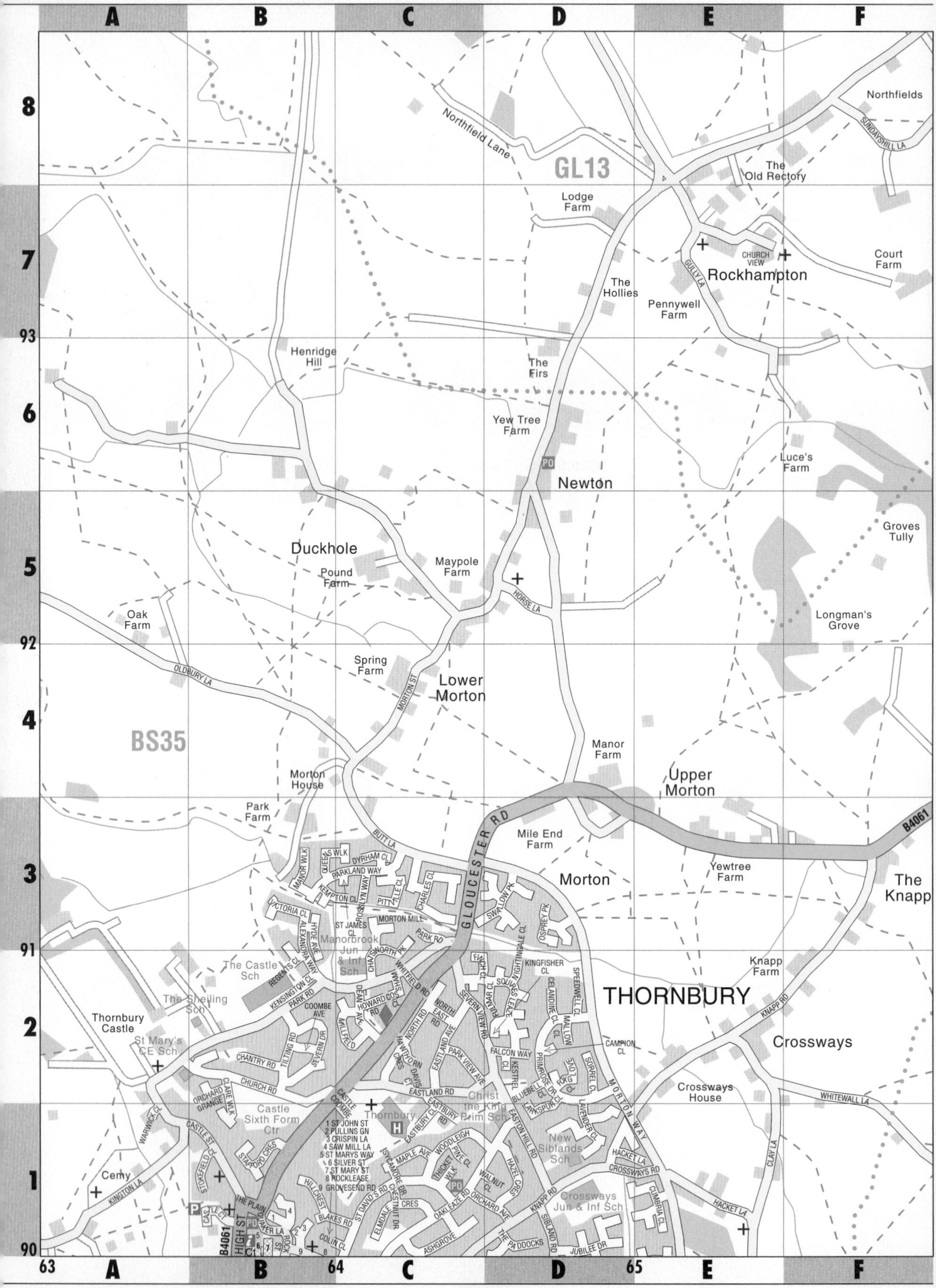

A B C D E F

8
7
93
6
5
92
4
3
91
2
1
90

Northfield Lane
GL13
Northfields
SUNDAYSHILL LA
The Old Rectory
Lodge Farm
CHURCH VIEW
GULLY LA
Rockhampton
Court Farm
The Hollies
Pennywell Farm
Henridge Hill
The Firs
Yew Tree Farm
PO
Newton
Luce's Farm
Duckhole
Pound Farm
Maypole Farm
HORSE LA
Groves Tully
Longman's Grove
Oak Farm
OLDBURY LA
Spring Farm
MORTON ST
Lower Morton
BS35
Manor Farm
Upper Morton
Morton House
Park Farm
Mile End Farm
B4061
GLOUCESTER RD
BUTT LA
Morton
Yewtree Farm
The Knapp
MANOR WLK
QUEENS WLK
DYRHAM CL
PARKLAND WAY
KEMPTON CL
ROSSLYN WAY
PITTVILLE CL
CHARLES CL
SWALLOW PK
OSPREY PK
VICTORIA CL
HYDE AVE
ALEXANDRA WAY
ST JAMES CL
MORTON MILL
PARK RD
NIGHTINGALE CL
Manorbrook Jun & Inf Sch
CHATSWORTH PK
WHITFIELD RD
FINCH CL
KINGFISHER CL
SPEEDWELL CL
The Castle Sch
REGENTS CL
KENSINGTON CL
SQUIRES LEAZE
FULMAR CL
CELANDINE CL
MALLOW CL
THORNBURY
Knapp Farm
The Sheiling Sch
PARK RD
COOMBE AVE
DEAN AVE
HOWARD RD
COSSHAM CL
NORTH EAST RD
SEVERN VIEW RD
KNAPP RD
Thornbury Castle
MILLFIELD
NORTH RD
HAWTHORN CRES
DAVIS CT
EASTLAND AVE
PARK VIEW AVE
FALCON WAY
CAMPION CL
Crossways
St Mary's CE Sch
CHANTRY RD
TILTING RD
SEVERN DR
KESTREL CL
PRIMROSE DR
FOXGLOVE CL
SORREL CL
CHURCH RD
CASTLE COOMBE
EASTLAND RD
BLUEBELL CL
LARKSPUR CL
MORTON WAY
Crossways House
WHITEWALL LA
ORCHARD GRANGE
CLARE WLK
Castle Sixth Form Ctr
Thornbury
H
EASTBURY CL
EASTBURY RD
Christ the King Prim Sch
EASTON HILL RD
LAVENDER CL
WARWICK CL
CASTLE ST
1 ST JOHN ST
2 PULLINS GN
3 CRISPIN LA
4 SAW MILL LA
5 ST MARYS WAY
6 SILVER ST
7 ST MARY ST
8 ROCKLEASE
9 GROVESEND RD
STAFFORD CRES
SYCAMORE DR
MAPLE AVE
WOODLEIGH
PINE CL
THICKET WLK
WALNUT CL
HAZEL CRES
New Siblands Sch
HACKET LA
CROSSWAYS RD
CLAY LA
Cemy
KINGTON LA
STOKEFIELD CL
HILLCREST
PO
ST DAVID'S RD
CHESTNUT DR
ORCHARD AVE
KNAPP RD
Crossways Jun & Inf Sch
CUMBRIA CL
HACKET LA
P
THE PLAIN
CASTLE CT
B4061
HIGH ST
PO
QUAKER LA
ROCK ST
BLAKES RD
COLIN CL
ELMDALE
CRES
OAKLEAZE RD
ASHGROVE
THE PADDOCKS
SIBLAND RD
JUBILEE DR
Ct

63 A B 64 C D 65 E F

63
51

77
66
A
B
C
D
E
F
The Elms
Oakhall Farm
Sundayshill Farm
Sundayshill
Gables Hotel
MOORSLADE LA
Heneage Farm
Heneage Court
HENEAGE LA
Falfield
SUNDAYSHILL LA
B4509
ERMILL CL
MILL LA
M5
GL13
The Copse
EASTLEY CL
CHURCH AVE
14
B4509
HM Young Offender Institution
PH
PO
Sewage Works
Eastwood Park
Mount Pleasant
Pound House Farm
Larch Covert
Home Farm House
GAMBRIL LA
Stump's Wood
BS35
GL12
Hotel
Morton Farm
Pool Farm
Whitfield Farm
GLOUCESTER RD
B4061
B4061
IRON HOGG LA
Whitfield
OLD GLOUCESTER RD
Brinkmarsh Farm
Buckover Farms
Brinkmarsh Lane Farm
Abbotside Farm
BRINKMARSH LA
Abbotside
Stanley Wood
Abbots-side Hill
B4061
PH
Rudge Wood
Horseshoe Farm
Milbury Heath
WHITEWALL LA
CHAPEL LA
Buckover
Mast
GREEN LA
CUTSHEATH RD
CROMHALL LA
Priest Wood
A38
M5
A38
8
7
93
6
5
92
4
3
91
2
1
90
66
67
68
52
66

65
78

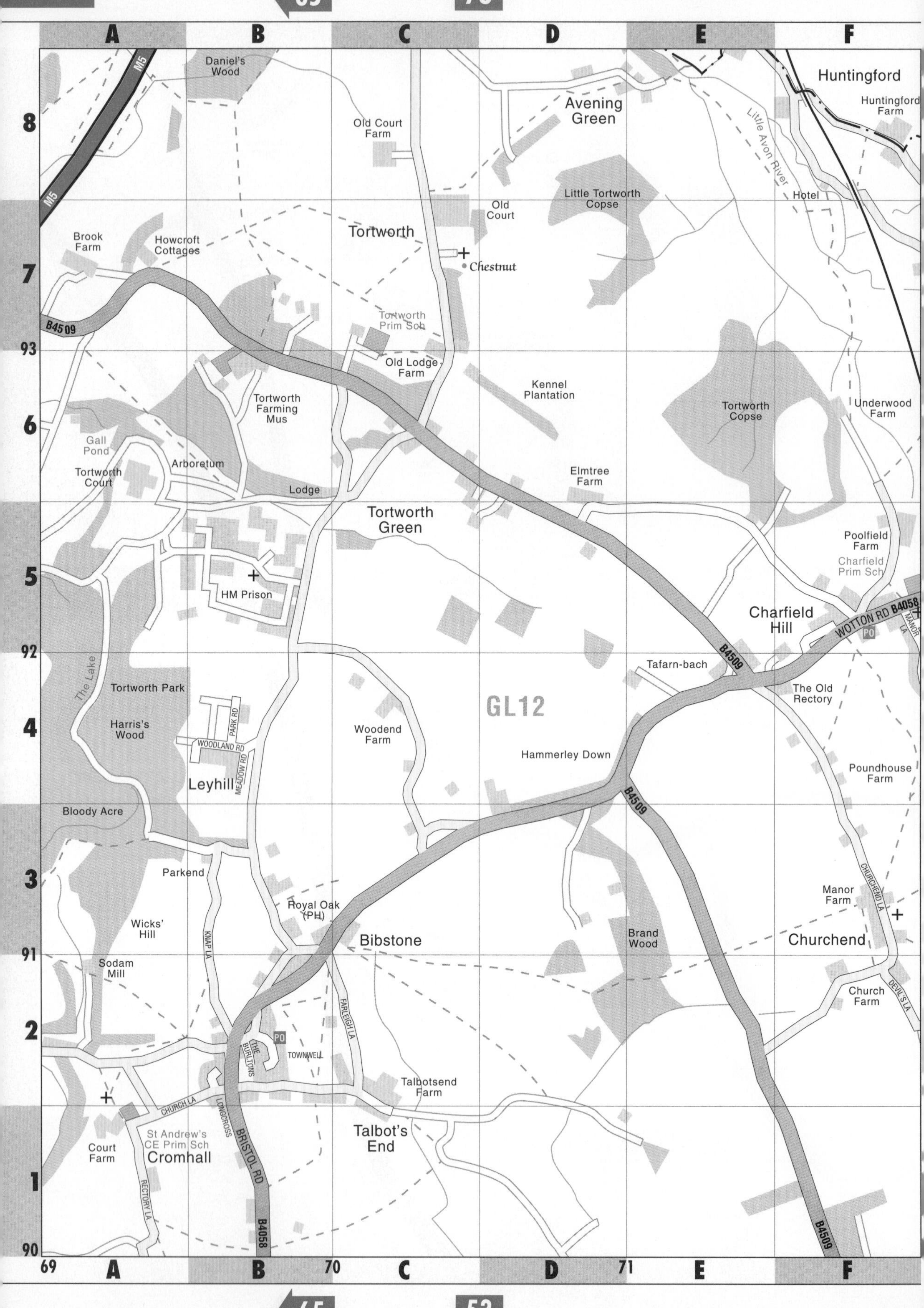
A
B
C
D
E
F
8
7
93
6
5
92
4
3
91
2
1
90
69
70
71
M5
Daniel's Wood
Old Court Farm
Avening Green
Huntingford
Huntingford Farm
Little Avon River
Hotel
Old Court
Little Tortworth Copse
Brook Farm
Howcroft Cottages
Tortworth
Chestnut
B4509
Tortworth Prim Sch
Old Lodge Farm
Kennel Plantation
Tortworth Farming Mus
Tortworth Copse
Underwood Farm
Gall Pond
Tortworth Court
Arboretum
Lodge
Elmtree Farm
Tortworth Green
Poolfield Farm
Charfield Prim Sch
HM Prison
Charfield Hill
WOTTON RD
B4058
MANOR LA
PO
The Lake
Tafarn-bach
The Old Rectory
Tortworth Park
GL12
Harris's Wood
PARK RD
WOODLAND RD
Woodend Farm
Hammerley Down
Poundhouse Farm
Leyhill
MEADOW RD
Bloody Acre
Parkend
CHURCHEND LA
Manor Farm
Royal Oak (PH)
Wicks' Hill
KNAP LA
Bibstone
Brand Wood
Churchend
Sodam Mill
FARLEIGH LA
Church Farm
DEVIL'S LA
THE BURLTONS
TOWNWELL
Talbotsend Farm
CHURCH LA
LONGCROSS
St Andrew's CE Prim Sch
Court Farm
Cromhall
BRISTOL RD
Talbot's End
B4058

65
53

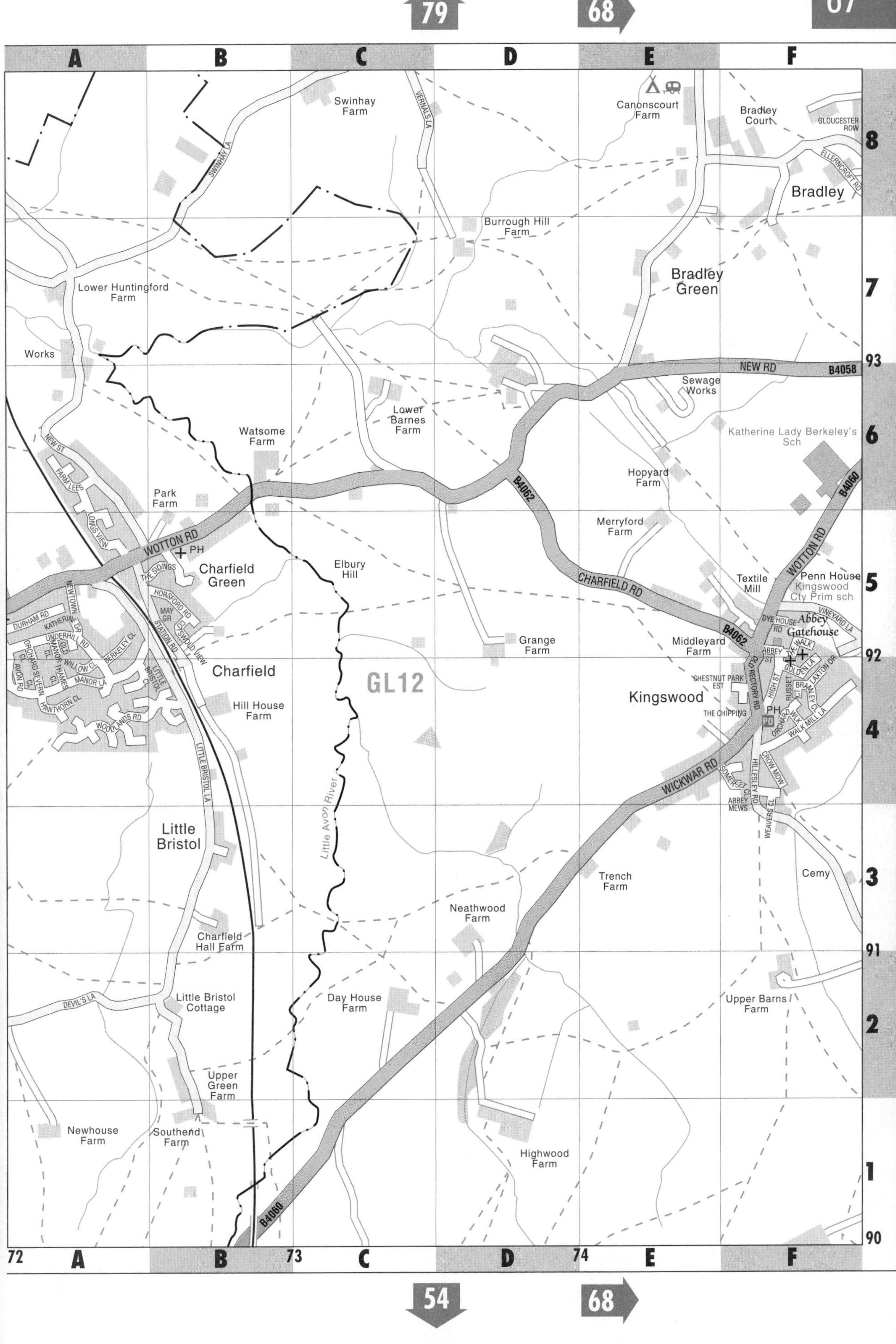
79
68
A
B
C
D
E
F
Swinhay Farm
VERNALS LA
SWINHAY LA
Canonscourt Farm
Bradley Court
GLOUCESTER ROW
ELLERNCROFT RD
Bradley
8
Burrough Hill Farm
Lower Huntingford Farm
Bradley Green
7
Works
NEW RD
B4058
93
Sewage Works
Lower Barnes Farm
Watsome Farm
Katherine Lady Berkeley's Sch
6
NEW ST
FARM LEES
Hopyard Farm
B4062
B4060
Park Farm
LONGS VIEW
Merryford Farm
WOTTON RD
PH
Charfield Green
THE SIDINGS
Elbury Hill
WOTTON RD
Textile Mill
Penn House
Kingswood Cty Prim sch
5
HORSFORD RD
MAY GR
COTSWOLD VIEW
STATION RD
CHARFIELD RD
VINEYARD LA
DYE HOUSE RD
Abbey Gatehouse
DURHAM RD
KATHERINE DR
NEWTOWN
UNDERHILL RD
OLD MANOR CL
BERKELEY CL
WILLOW CL
Grange Farm
Middleyard Farm
B4062
ABBEY ST
THE WALK
GOLDEN LA
LAXTON DR
92
ORCHARD CL
AVON RD
SEVERN CL
THAMES CL
MANOR LA
LITTLE BRISTOL CL
Charfield
GL12
CHESTNUT PARK EST
OLD RECTORY RD
HIGH ST
RUSSET CT
BRAMLEY CL
HAWTHORN CL
Hill House Farm
Kingswood
THE CHIPPING
PH
PO
ORCHARD WLK
WALK MILL LA
WOODLANDS RD
4
LITTLE BRISTOL LA
WICKWAR RD
SOMERSET CL
HILLESLEY RD
CROW MDW
ABBEY MEWS
WEAVERS CL
Little Bristol
Little Avon River
Trench Farm
Cemy
3
Neathwood Farm
Charfield Hall Farm
91
DEVIL'S LA
Little Bristol Cottage
Day House Farm
Upper Barns Farm
2
Upper Green Farm
Newhouse Farm
Southend Farm
Highwood Farm
1
B4060
90
72
73
74
54
68

67
80

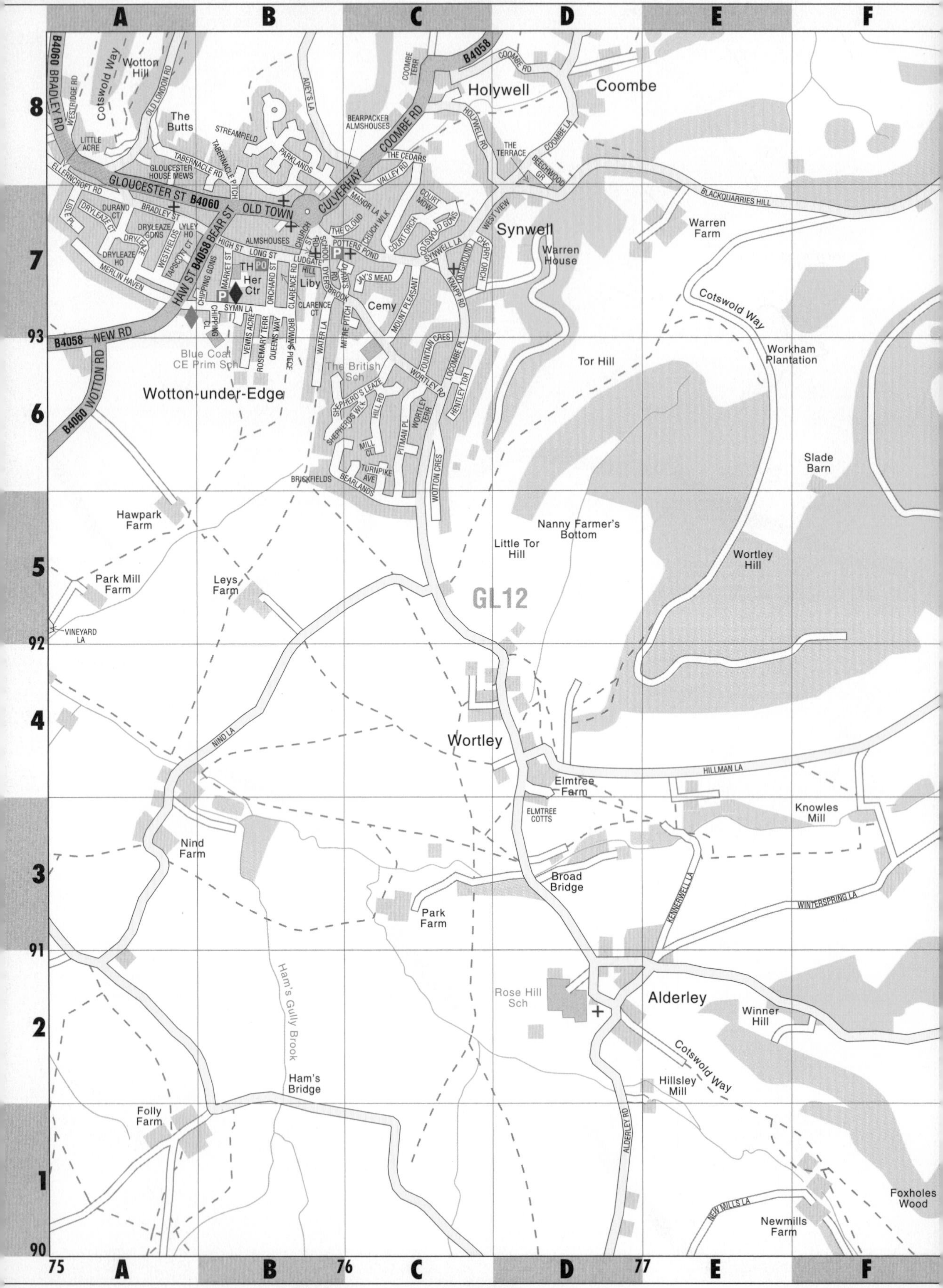

A B C D E F

8
7
93
6
5
92
4
3
91
2
1
90

B4060 BRADLEY RD
Cotswold Way
Wotton Hill
WESTRIDGE RD
OLD LONDON RD
The Butts
LITTLE ACRE
STREAMFIELD
TABERNACLE RD
TABERNACLE PITCH
GLOUCESTER HOUSE MEWS
ELLERNCROFT RD
GLOUCESTER ST B4060
OLD TOWN
PARKLANDS
ADEY'S LA
COOMBE TERR
BEARPACKER ALMSHOUSES
COOMBE RD
B4058
COOMBE RD
Holywell
Coombe
HOLYWELL RD
THE TERRACE
COOMBE LA
BEECHWOOD GR
THE CEDARS
VALLEY RD
CULVERHAY
MANOR LA
BLACKQUARRIES HILL
LISLE PL
DRYLEAZE CT
DURAND CT
BRADLEY ST
DRYLEAZE GDNS
DRYLEAZE
WESTFIELDS
LYLEY HO
TAPSCOTT CT
BEAR ST
B4058
HIGH ST
ALMSHOUSES
LONG ST
CHURCH ST
THE CLOUD
SCHOOL RD
CHURCH WLK
COURT MDW
COURT ORCH
COTSWOLD GDNS
POTTERS POND
SYNWELL LA
WEST VIEW
CHERRY ORCH
Synwell
Warren House
Warren Farm
DRYLEAZE HO
MERLIN HAVEN
HAW ST
CHIPPING GDNS
MARKET ST
TH PO
Her Ctr
ORCHARD ST
LUDGATE HILL
CLARENCE RD
Liby
DYERS BROOK
JAY'S MEAD
KNAPP RD
OATGROUND
SYMN LA
CHIPPING CL
CLARENCE CT
Cemy
MOUNT PLEASANT
Cotswold Way
B4058 NEW RD
VENNS ACRE
ROSEMARY TERR
QUEENS WAY
BROWNS PIECE
WATER LA
MITRE PITCH
FOUNTAIN CRES
LOCOMBE PL
Blue Coat CE Prim Sch
The British Sch
Tor Hill
Workham Plantation
B4060 WOTTON RD
Wotton-under-Edge
SHEPHERD'S LEAZE
SHEPHERDS WLK
HILL RD
WORTLEY RD
WORTLEY TERR
HENTLEY TOR
MILL CL
PITMAN PL
TURNPIKE AVE
WOTTON CRES
BRICKFIELDS
BEARLANDS
Slade Barn
Hawpark Farm
Nanny Farmer's Bottom
Little Tor Hill
Wortley Hill
Park Mill Farm
Leys Farm
GL12
VINEYARD LA
NIND LA
Wortley
HILLMAN LA
Elmtree Farm
ELMTREE COTTS
Knowles Mill
Nind Farm
Broad Bridge
KENNERWELL LA
WINTERSPRING LA
Park Farm
Ham's Gully Brook
Rose Hill Sch
Alderley
Winner Hill
Cotswold Way
Ham's Bridge
Hillsley Mill
Folly Farm
ALDERLEY RD
Foxholes Wood
NEW MILLS LA
Newmills Farm

75 A B 76 C D 77 E F

67
55

81 70

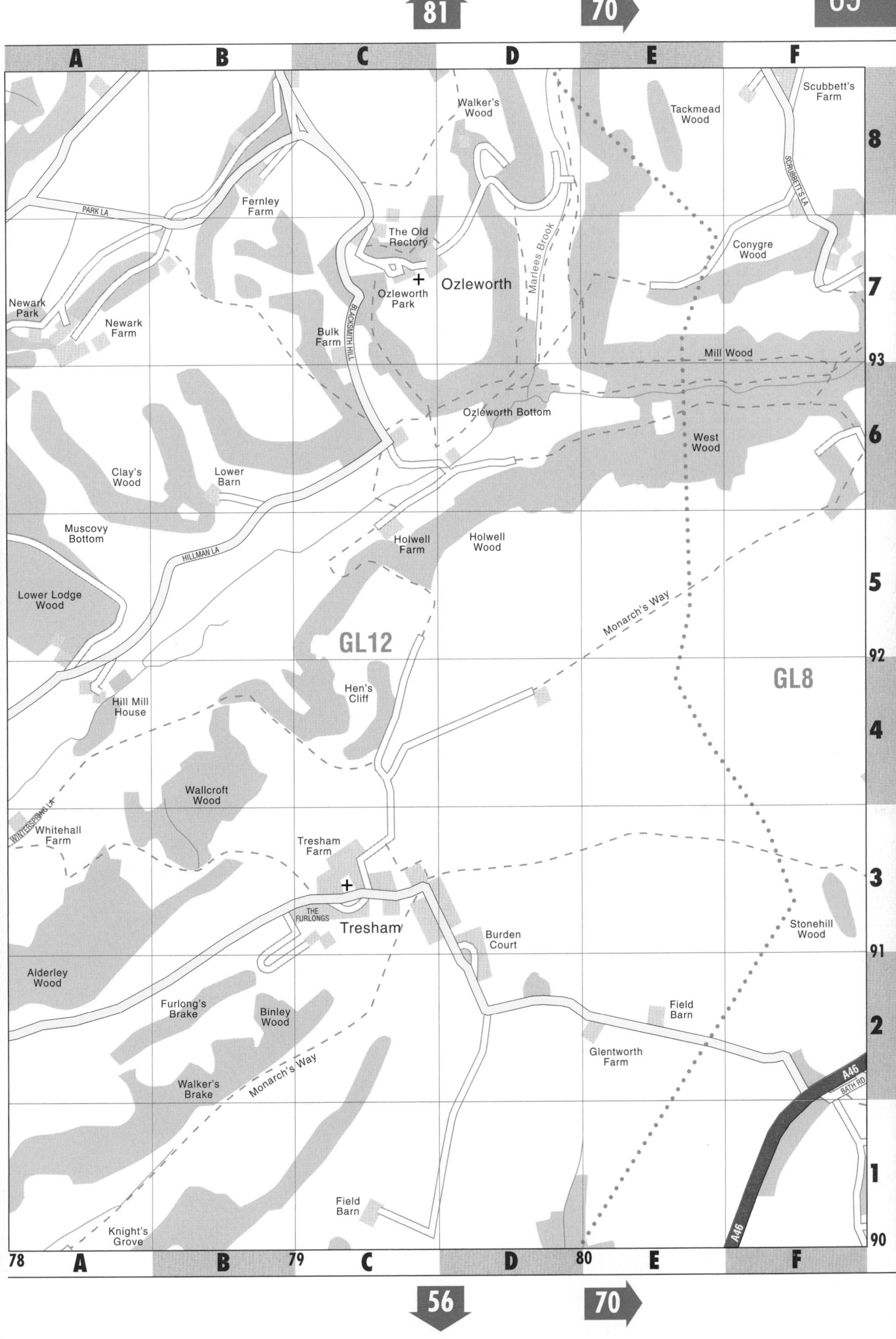
A
B
C
D
E
F
Scubbett's Farm
Walker's Wood
Tackmead Wood
8
SCRUBBETT'S LA
PARK LA
Fernley Farm
The Old Rectory
Conygre Wood
Ozleworth
Ozleworth Park
Marlees Brook
7
Newark Park
Newark Farm
Bulk Farm
BLACKSMITH HILL
Mill Wood
93
Ozleworth Bottom
West Wood
6
Clay's Wood
Lower Barn
Muscovy Bottom
Holwell Farm
Holwell Wood
HILLMAN LA
5
Lower Lodge Wood
Monarch's Way
GL12
92
GL8
Hill Mill House
Hen's Cliff
4
Wallcroft Wood
WINTERSPRING LA
Whitehall Farm
Tresham Farm
3
THE FURLONGS
Tresham
Burden Court
Stonehill Wood
91
Alderley Wood
Furlong's Brake
Binley Wood
Field Barn
2
Glentworth Farm
Monarch's Way
Walker's Brake
A46
BATH RD
1
Field Barn
Knight's Grove
A46
90
78
79
80

56 70

69
82

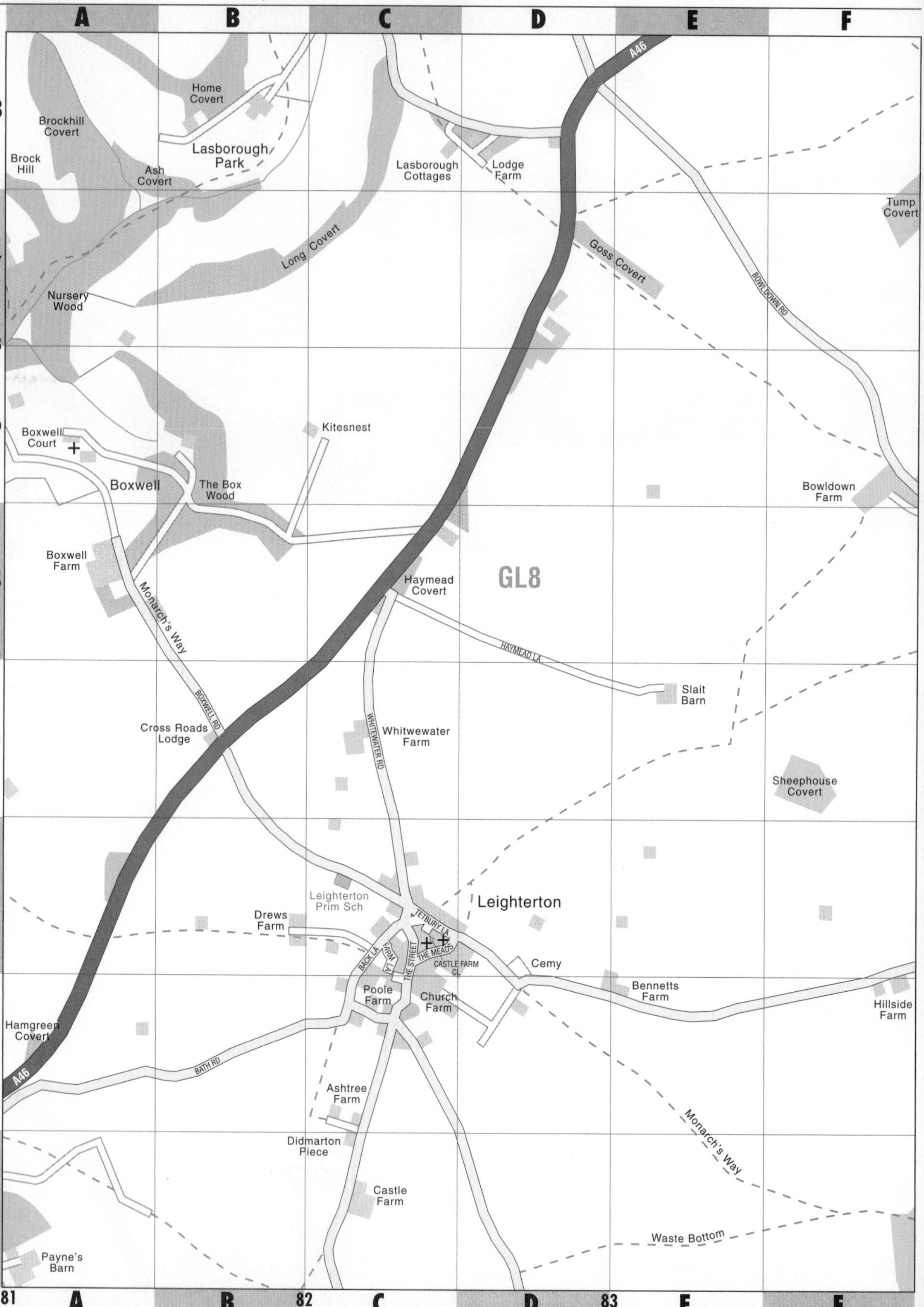

A B C D E F
8
7
93
6
5
92
4
3
91
2
1
90
Home Covert
Brockhill Covert
Lasborough Park
Brock Hill
Ash Covert
Lasborough Cottages
Lodge Farm
A46
Tump Covert
Long Covert
Goss Covert
Nursery Wood
BOWLDOWN RD
Kitesnest
Boxwell Court
Boxwell
The Box Wood
Bowldown Farm
Boxwell Farm
Haymead Covert
GL8
Monarch's Way
HAYMEAD LA
Slait Barn
BOXWELL RD
WHITEWATER RD
Cross Roads Lodge
Whitwewater Farm
Sheephouse Covert
Leighterton Prim Sch
Leighterton
Drews Farm
TETBURY LA
BACK LA
FARM LA
THE STREET
THE MEADS
CASTLE FARM CL
Cemy
Bennetts Farm
Poole Farm
Church Farm
Hillside Farm
Hamgreen Covert
BATH RD
Ashtree Farm
Didmarton Piece
Monarch's Way
Castle Farm
Waste Bottom
Payne's Barn
81 A B 82 C D 83 E F

69
57

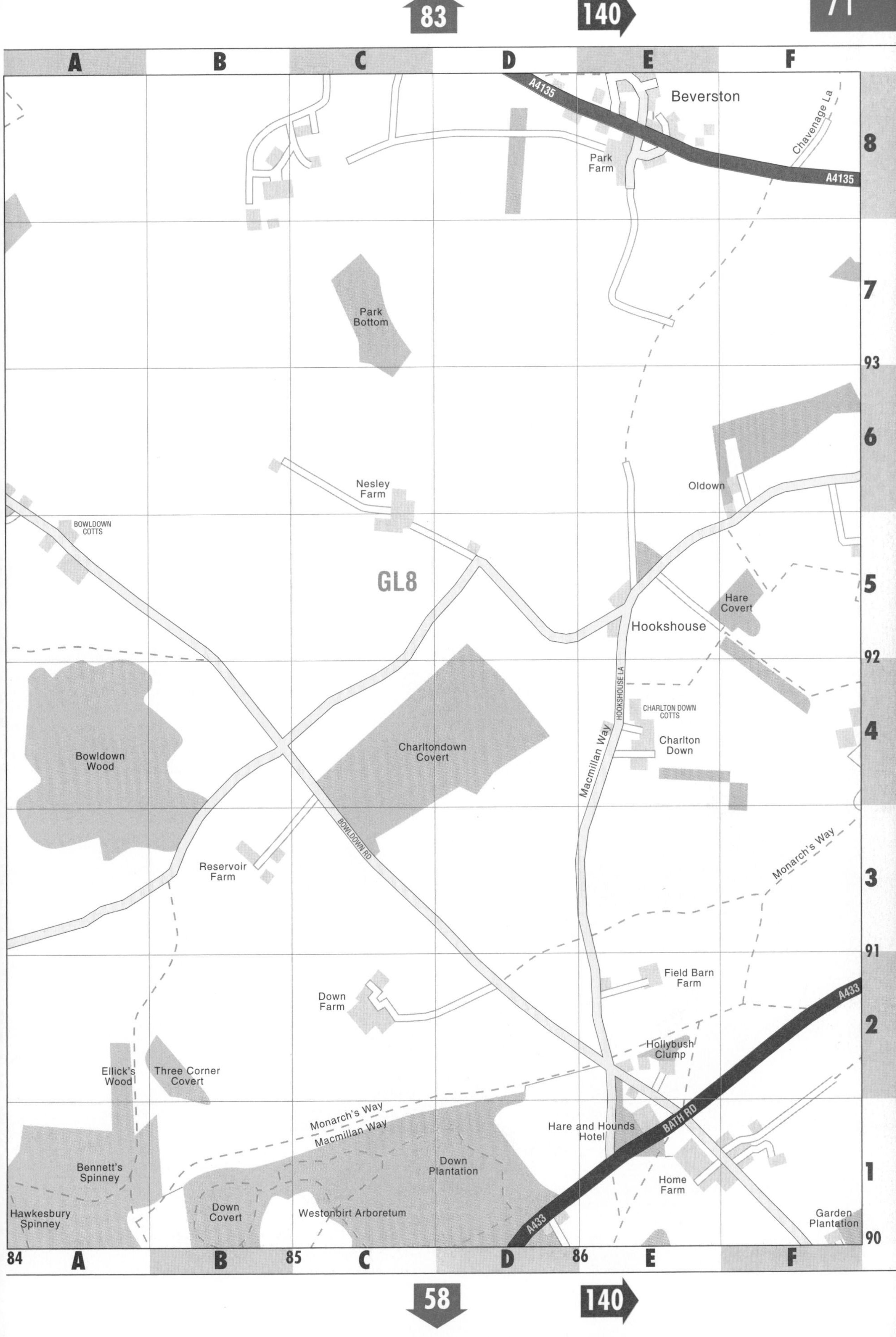
83
140
A
B
C
D
E
F
A4135
Beverston
Chavenage La
Park
Farm
A4135
8
Park
Bottom
7
93
6
Nesley
Farm
Oldown
BOWLDOWN
COTTS
GL8
5
Hare
Covert
Hookshouse
92
HOOKSHOUSE LA
CHARLTON DOWN
COTTS
Macmillan Way
Charltondown
Covert
Charlton
Down
4
Bowldown
Wood
BOWLDOWN RD
Reservoir
Farm
Monarch's Way
3
91
Field Barn
Farm
Down
Farm
A433
2
Hollybush
Clump
Ellick's
Wood
Three Corner
Covert
Monarch's Way
Macmillan Way
Hare and Hounds
Hotel
BATH RD
Down
Plantation
Bennett's
Spinney
Home
Farm
1
Down
Covert
Hawkesbury
Spinney
Westonbirt Arboretum
A433
Garden
Plantation
90
84
A
B
85
C
D
86
E
F
58
140

146

A
B
C
D
E
F
8
7
97
6
5
96
4
3
95
2
1
94
51
52
53
Wet Wood
Gaer Hill
Gaer Hill Farm
Minepit Wood
Liveoaks Grove
A466
Livox Cottages
Wynd Cliff
Livox Farm
Wet Wood
Wyndcliffe Court
PENTERRY LA
Moss Cottage
Liveoaks Brake
Mill Farm
DEVAUDEN RD
Nature Trail
Lower Wyndcliff Wood
Lower Martridge Wood
WOODLANDS CL
St Arvans
Lover's Leap
Ban-y-gor Wood
GRANGE PK
GRANGE RD
LAIRD PK
The New Temple
Barn
FORGE GDNS
COURT GDNS
Lancaut
LANCAUT LA
CHURCH LA
THE ROW
SYCAMORE CT
WYNDCLIFFE VIEW
MANOR VIEW
FOROWICH CL
PH
PIERCEFIELD TERR
Sewage Works
Cave Wood
Giant's Cave
River Wye (Afon Gwy)
Wye Valley Walk
Piercefield Cliffs
NP16
Oakgrove
Stables
Stables
Piercefield
Pierce Wood
Piercefield Park
Chepstow Race Course
Longhope Reach
Offa's Dyke Path
Fryth Wood
Rossfield
B4228
GOWER COTTS
COLEFORD RD
Chapelhouse Wood
MOPLA RD
B4293
ITTON RD
Goldenhill Farm
Sandy Way
CASTLEFORD HILL
CASTLEFORD GDNS
PO
St John's-on-the-hill Sch
Cockshoot Wood
Crossway Green
Chepstow Comp Sch
River Wye (Afon Gwy)
B4293
B4235
B4235
ST LAWRENCE RD
PIERCEFIELD AVE
PARK VIEW
WINTOUR CL
L Ctr
ST MAUR GDNS
ELMDALE
ROCK VILLA LA
1 SOMERSET COTTS
2 RIVERSIDE MILL
3 ORCHARD GDNS
4 KENDALL SQ
5 CHURCH ROW
WELSH ST
KINGSMARK LA
NORMANDY WAY
Great Barnets Woods
Bishop's Barnets Wood
TURNPIKE CL
A466
HUNTFIELD RD
DEANS GDNS
STUART CL
CASTLE GDNS
MOUNT WAY
OAKFIELD AVE
The Dell Prim Sch
Chepstow Castle
Mus
BRIDGE ST
ST ANN ST
THE BACK
HOLLINGS CL
LOWER CHURCH ST
DAVIS CT
CHURCH RD
MYRTLE PL
A48
TUDOR DR
B4293

60

146
74

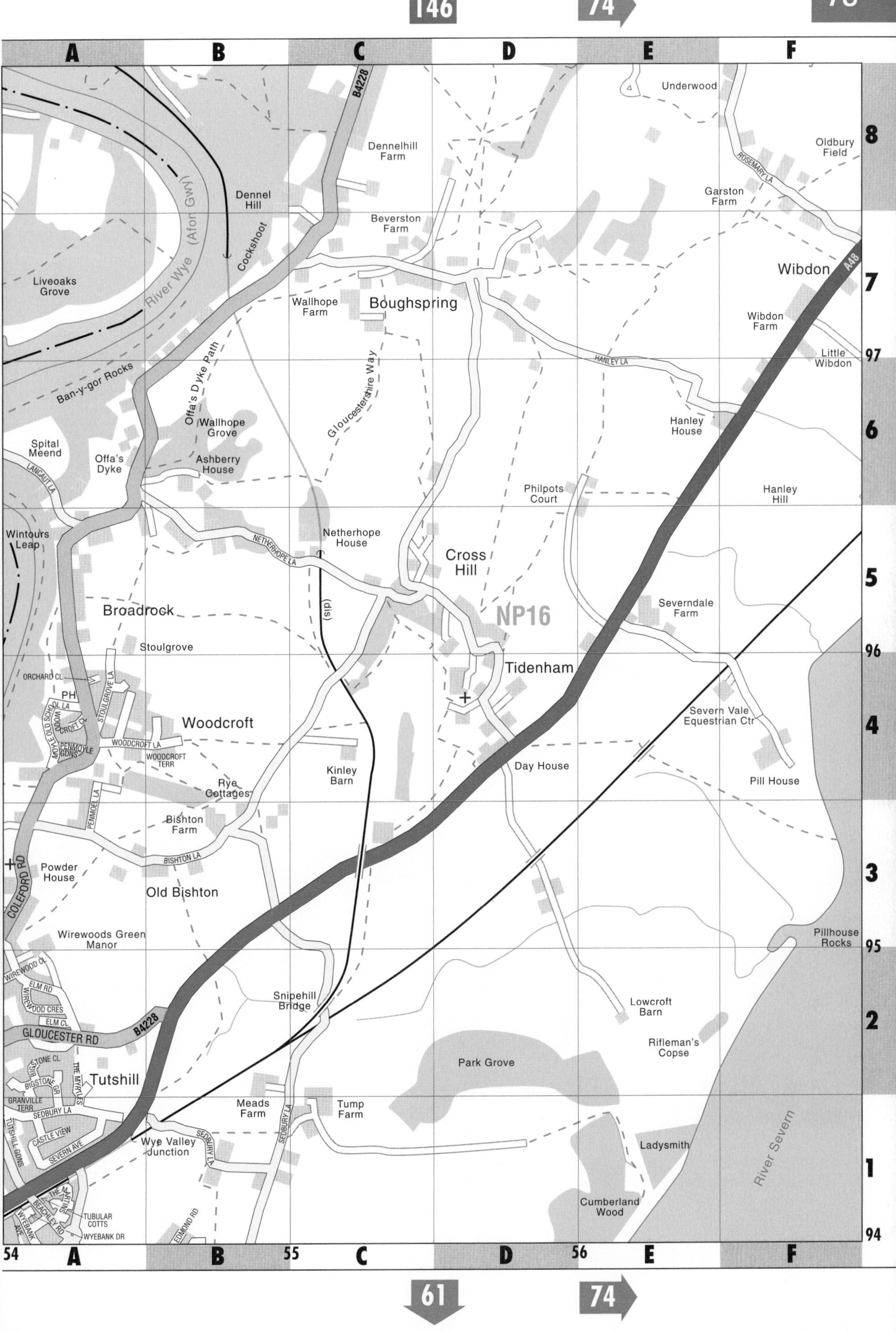
A
B
C
D
E
F
B4228
Underwood
Dennelhill
Farm
Oldbury
Field
8
ROSEMARY LA
Dennel
Hill
River Wye (Afon Gwy)
Cockshoot
Beverston
Farm
Garston
Farm
Liveoaks
Grove
Wibdon
A48
7
Wallhope
Farm
Boughspring
Wibdon
Farm
Offa's Dyke Path
Ban-y-gor Rocks
Gloucestershire Way
HANLEY LA
Little
Wibdon
97
Wallhope
Grove
Hanley
House
Spital
Meend
Offa's
Dyke
Ashberry
House
6
LANGAUT LA
Philpots
Court
Hanley
Hill
Wintours
Leap
Netherhope
House
NETHERHOPE LA
Cross
Hill
5
(dis)
Broadrock
NP16
Severndale
Farm
Stoulgrove
96
ORCHARD CL
Tidenham
PH
STOULGROVE LA
OLD SCHOOL LA
CROFT CL
Woodcroft
Severn Vale
Equestrian Ctr
4
PENMOYLE GDNS
WOODCROFT LA
WOODCROFT TERR
Day House
Kinley
Barn
Rye
Cottages
Pill House
PENMOEL LA
Bishton
Farm
BISHTON LA
Powder
House
3
COLEFORD RD
Old Bishton
Wirewoods Green
Manor
Pillhouse
Rocks
95
WIREWOOD CL
ELM RD
WIREWOOD CRES
ELM CL
Snipehill
Bridge
Lowcroft
Barn
2
GLOUCESTER RD
B4228
Rifleman's
Copse
STONE CL
BIGSTONE GR
THE MYRTLES
Tutshill
Park Grove
GRANVILLE TERR
SEDBURY LA
Meads
Farm
Tump
Farm
River Severn
TUTSHILL GDNS
CASTLE VIEW
SEVERN AVE
Wye Valley
Junction
SEDBURY LA
SEDBURY LA
Ladysmith
1
THE MARTINS
BEACHLEY RD
WYEBANK AVE
TUBULAR
COTTS
WYEBANK DR
EDMOND RD
Cumberland
Wood
94
54
55
56

61
74

73
147

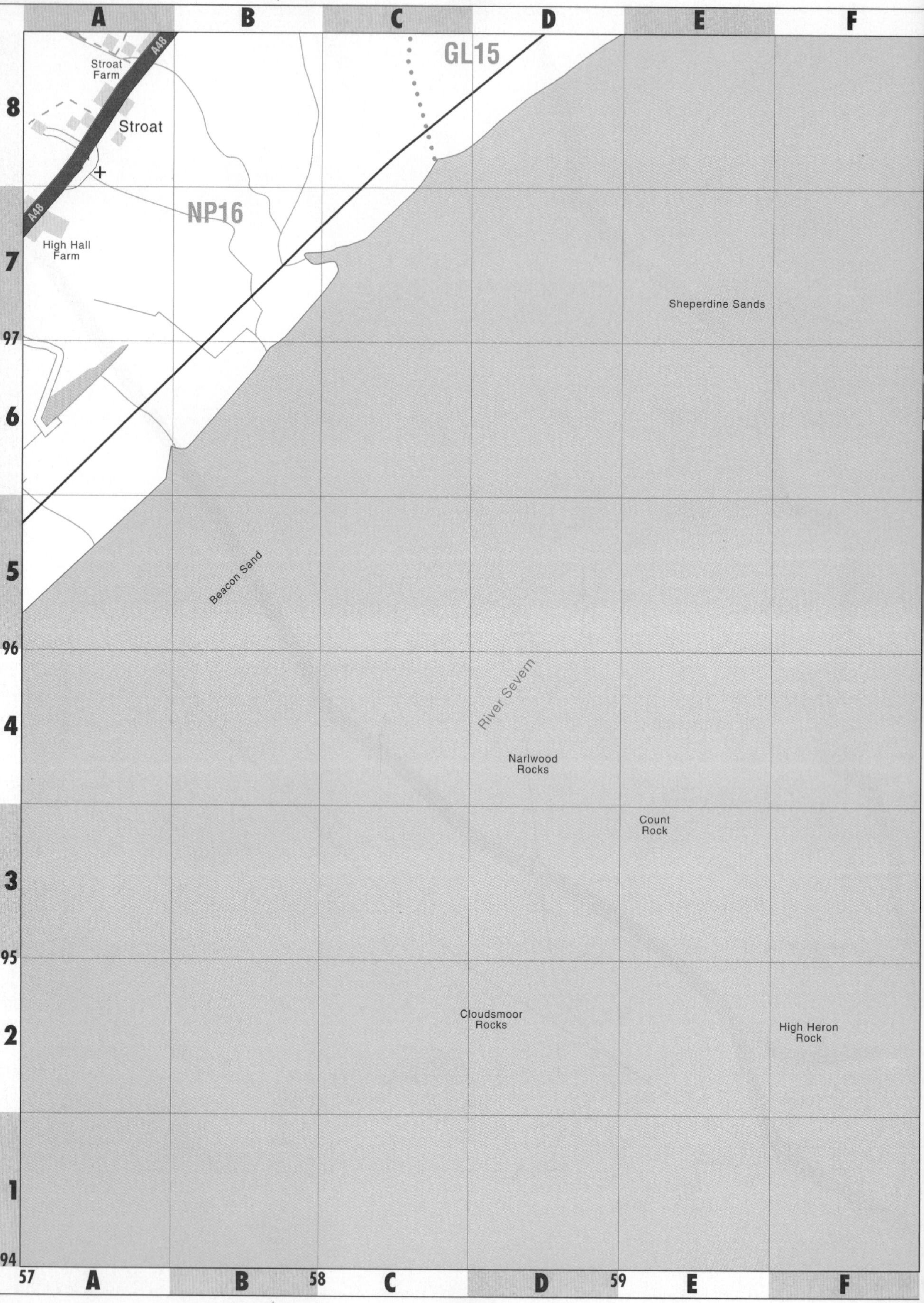

A B C D E F

GL15
Stroat Farm
Stroat
A48
NP16
High Hall Farm
Sheperdine Sands
Beacon Sand
River Severn
Narlwood Rocks
Count Rock
Cloudsmoor Rocks
High Heron Rock

8
7
97
6
5
96
4
3
95
2
1
94

57 A B 58 C D 59 E F

73
62

147
76

A
B
C
D
E
F
8
Hills Flats
7
97
GL13
6
River Severn
The Ledges
White House
Chapel House
Manor Farm
NUPDOWN RD
Severn Way
5
The Laurels
96
PH
Shepperdine Farm
North Ham Corner
4
Shepperdine Farm
Shepperdine
Brickhouse Farm
Shepperdine Withybed
3
BS35
95
Harecrest La
SHEPPERDINE RD
Jobscreen Farm
2
Lowgoods Farm
Power Station
Knight's Farm
Visitor Ctr
Mast
HILL LA
1
94
60
61
62

63
76

75
84

A B C D E F
8
7
97
6
5
96
4
3
95
2
1
94
63 64 65
River Severn
Severn Way
SEVERN LA
Willis Elm
WORLDSEND LA
Worldsend Farm
Blisbury Farm
BEVINGTON LA
Stample La
Pennyhay La
Bevington
Longpool La
Stuckmoor La
Dayhouse Farm
Brick House Farm
Manor Farm
Upper Hill
Cat Grove
Nupdown
Nupdown Farm
TRANTON LA
Upper Hill Farm
NUPDOWN RD
GL13
BS35
Yew Tree Farm
Hill Court
Scotlands Farm
Hill
Roundhouse Wood
HILL LA
Court Farm
Maniards Green
Church-hill Wood
WOODEND LA
Rockhampton Rhine
Beggarsbush La

75
64

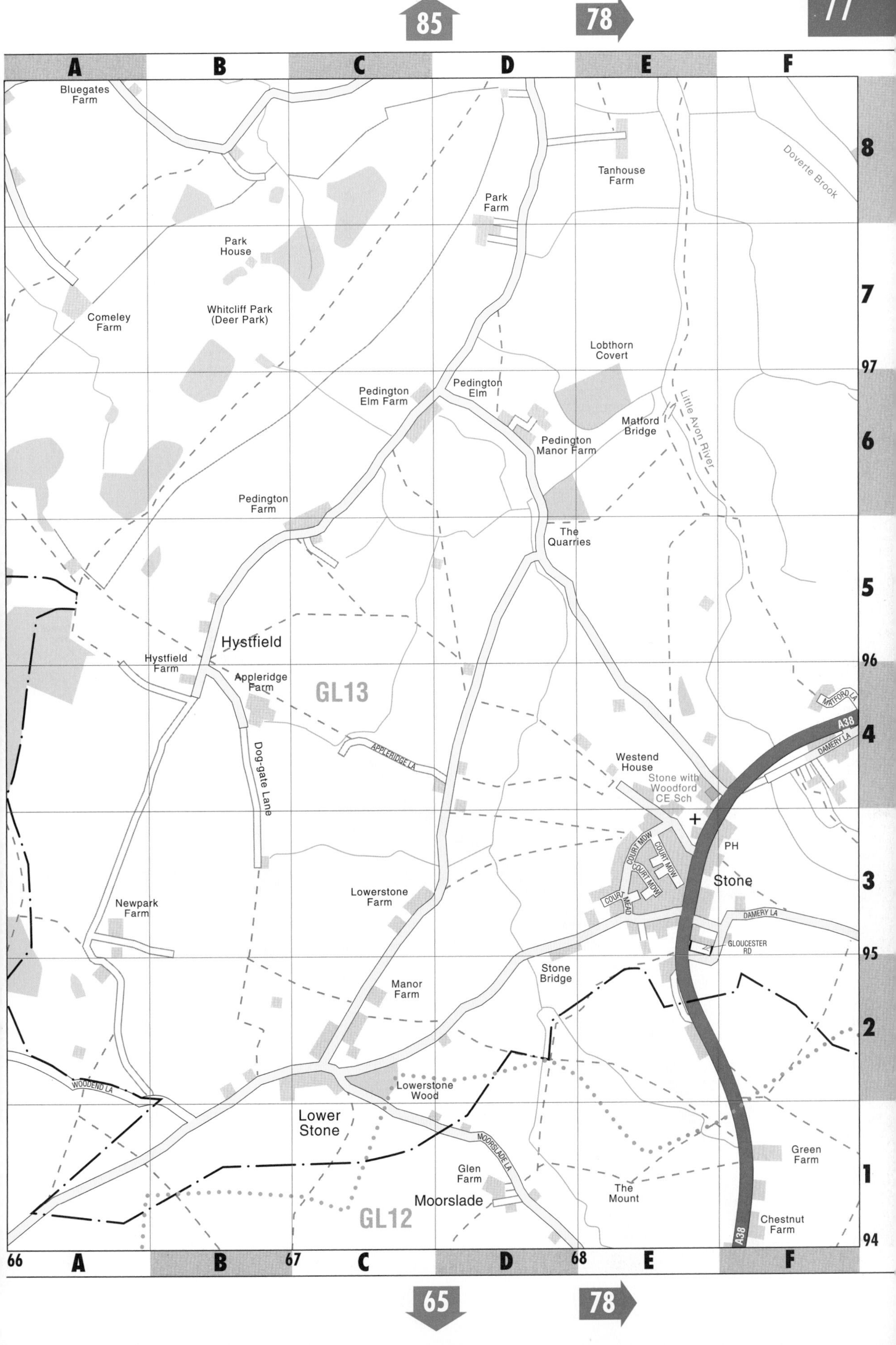
85
78
A
B
C
D
E
F
Bluegates Farm
Tanhouse Farm
Doverte Brook
Park Farm
Park House
Whitcliff Park (Deer Park)
Comeley Farm
Lobthorn Covert
Pedington Elm Farm
Pedington Elm
Little Avon River
Matford Bridge
Pedington Manor Farm
Pedington Farm
The Quarries
Hystfield
Hystfield Farm
Appleridge Farm
GL13
MATFORD LA
A38
DAMERY LA
APPLERIDGE LA
Dog-gate Lane
Westend House
Stone with Woodford CE Sch
PH
COURT MDW
COURT MEAD
Stone
Lowerstone Farm
Newpark Farm
DAMERY LA
GLOUCESTER RD
Stone Bridge
Manor Farm
Lowerstone Wood
WOODEND LA
Lower Stone
MOORSLADE LA
Green Farm
Glen Farm
The Mount
Moorslade
GL12
Chestnut Farm
8
7
97
6
5
96
4
3
95
2
1
94
66
67
68
65
78

77
86

A B C D E F

8
A38
CHURCH VIEW
CHURCH VIEW
Newport
Greenways
Goldwick Farm
Crossways
Hotel
Baynhamcourt Farm
7
CHAPEL HILL
Doverte Brook
Hogsdown Farm
Oakleaze Farm
97
M5
6
Lower Wick
HAYCROFT LA
GL13
GL11
Manor Farm
Swanley Farm
Lowerwick Farm
SWANLEY LA
Swanley
5
Middle Wick
Woodfordgreen Farm
Middlewick Farm
Whitehall Farm
96
PH
A38
Woodford
Wick Bridge
4
Michaelwood Farm
DAMERY LA
Harold's Brake
Woodford Farm
Michael Wood Service Area
MULE ST
3
Sweetbrier Brake
Middle Mill Farm
DAMERY LA
95
Furzeground Wood
2
Micheal Wood
Michaelwood Lodge Farm
DAMERY LA
Little Avon River
GL12
Crockley's Farm
Damery
1
Damery Bridge
Iron Mill Grove
M5
Daniel's Wood
94

69 A B 70 C D 71 E F

77
66

87
80

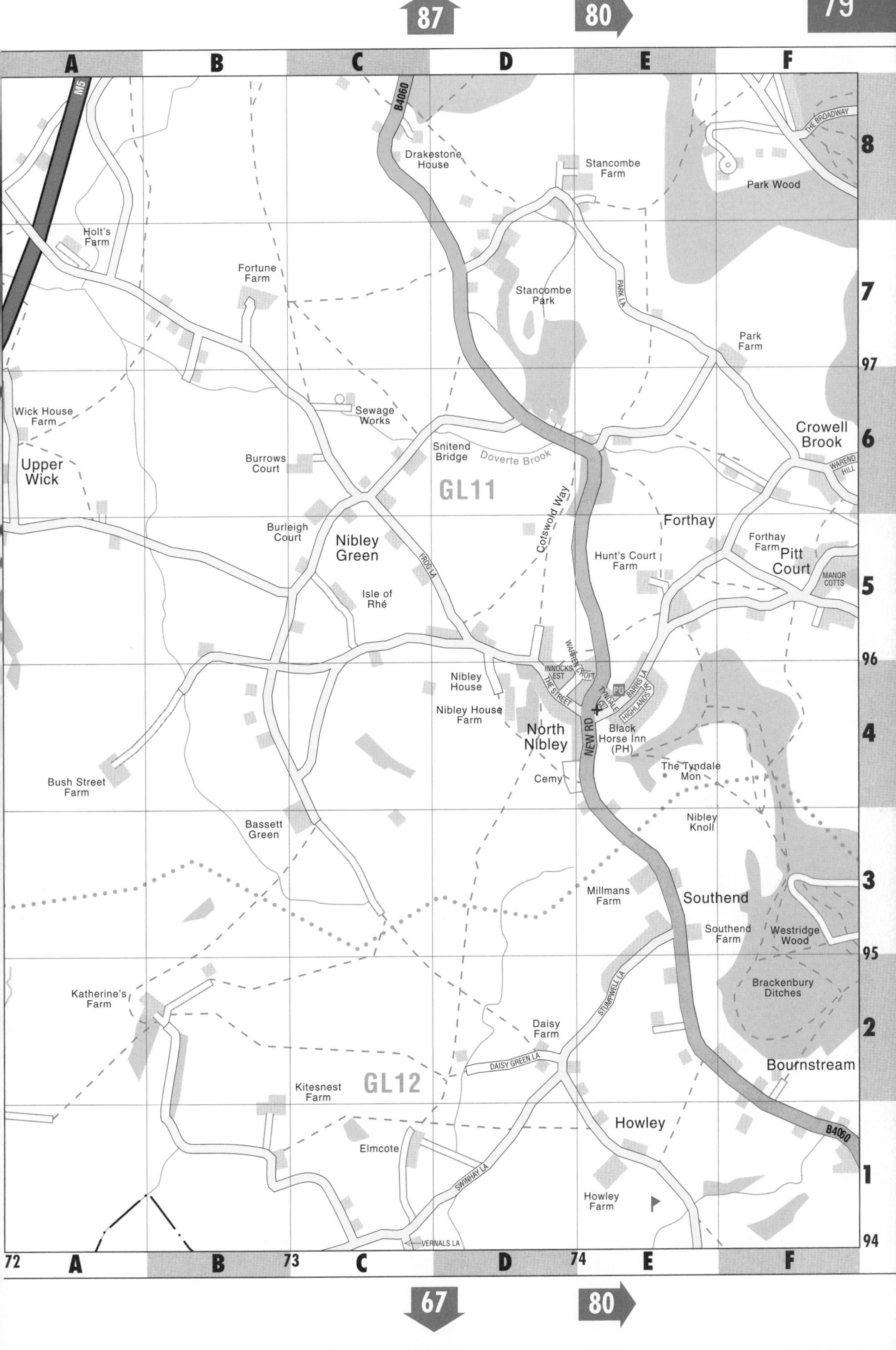
A B C D E F
8 7 97 6 5 96 4 3 95 2 1 94
72 73 74
M5
B4060
Drakestone House
Stancombe Farm
THE BROADWAY
Park Wood
Holt's Farm
Fortune Farm
Stancombe Park
PARK LA
Park Farm
Wick House Farm
Sewage Works
Crowell Brook
Upper Wick
Burrows Court
Snitend Bridge
Doverte Brook
GL11
WAREND HILL
Cotswold Way
Forthay
Burleigh Court
Nibley Green
FROG LA
Hunt's Court Farm
Forthay Farm
Pitt Court
MANOR COTTS
Isle of Rhé
WARREN CROFT
INNOCKS EST
THE STREET
TYNDALE CT
BARRS LA
HIGHLANDS
PO
Nibley House
Nibley House Farm
North Nibley
NEW RD
Black Horse Inn (PH)
Cemy
The Tyndale Mon
Bush Street Farm
Bassett Green
Nibley Knoll
Millmans Farm
Southend
Southend Farm
Westridge Wood
Brackenbury Ditches
STUMPWELL LA
Katherine's Farm
Daisy Farm
DAISY GREEN LA
Bournstream
Kitesnest Farm
GL12
Howley
Elmcote
SWINHAY LA
Howley Farm
VERNALS LA

79
88

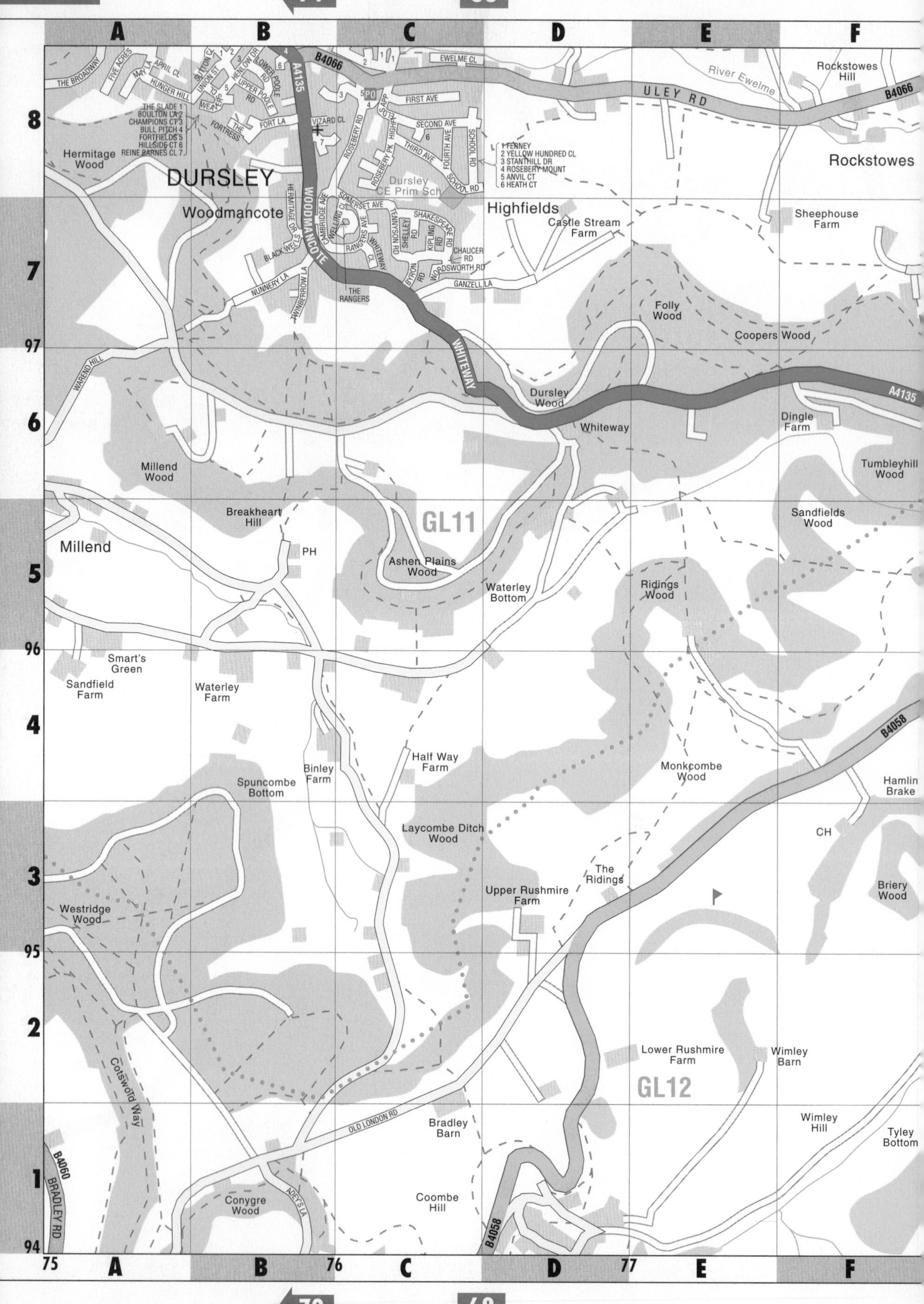
A
B
C
D
E
F
8
7
97
6
5
96
4
3
95
2
1
94
75
76
77
DURSLEY
Woodmancote
Hermitage Wood
Highfields
Castle Stream Farm
Rockstowes Hill
Rockstowes
Sheephouse Farm
River Ewelme
ULEY RD
B4066
A4135
WOODMANCOTE
WHITEWAY
Dursley CE Prim Sch
1 FERNEY
2 YELLOW HUNDRED CL
3 STANTHILL DR
4 ROSEBERY MOUNT
5 ANVIL CT
6 HEATH CT
THE SLADE 1
BOULTON LA 2
CHAMPIONS CT 3
BULL PITCH 4
FORTFIELDS 5
HILLSIDE CT 6
REINE BARNES CL 7
THE BROADWAY
FIVE ACRES
APRIL CL
HUNGER HILL
FORT LA
VIZARD CL
FIRST AVE
SECOND AVE
THIRD AVE
FOURTH AVE
SCHOOL RD
EWELME CL
ROSEBERY RD
SOMERSET AVE
SHAKESPEARE RD
TENNYSON RD
KIPLING RD
CHAUCER RD
WORDSWORTH RD
GANZELL LA
BYRON RD
NUNNERY LA
TWINBERROW LA
BLACK WELL
THE RANGERS
Folly Wood
Coopers Wood
Dursley Wood
Whiteway
Dingle Farm
Tumbleyhill Wood
Sandfields Wood
WAREND HILL
Millend Wood
Breakheart Hill
GL11
PH
Millend
Ashen Plains Wood
Waterley Bottom
Ridings Wood
Smart's Green
Sandfield Farm
Waterley Farm
Half Way Farm
Binley Farm
Spuncombe Bottom
Monkcombe Wood
B4058
Hamlin Brake
CH
Laycombe Ditch Wood
The Ridings
Upper Rushmire Farm
Briery Wood
Westridge Wood
Cotswold Way
Lower Rushmire Farm
Wimley Barn
GL12
OLD LONDON RD
Bradley Barn
Wimley Hill
Tyley Bottom
B4060
BRADLEY RD
Conygre Wood
ADEY'S LA
Coombe Hill

79
68

89
82

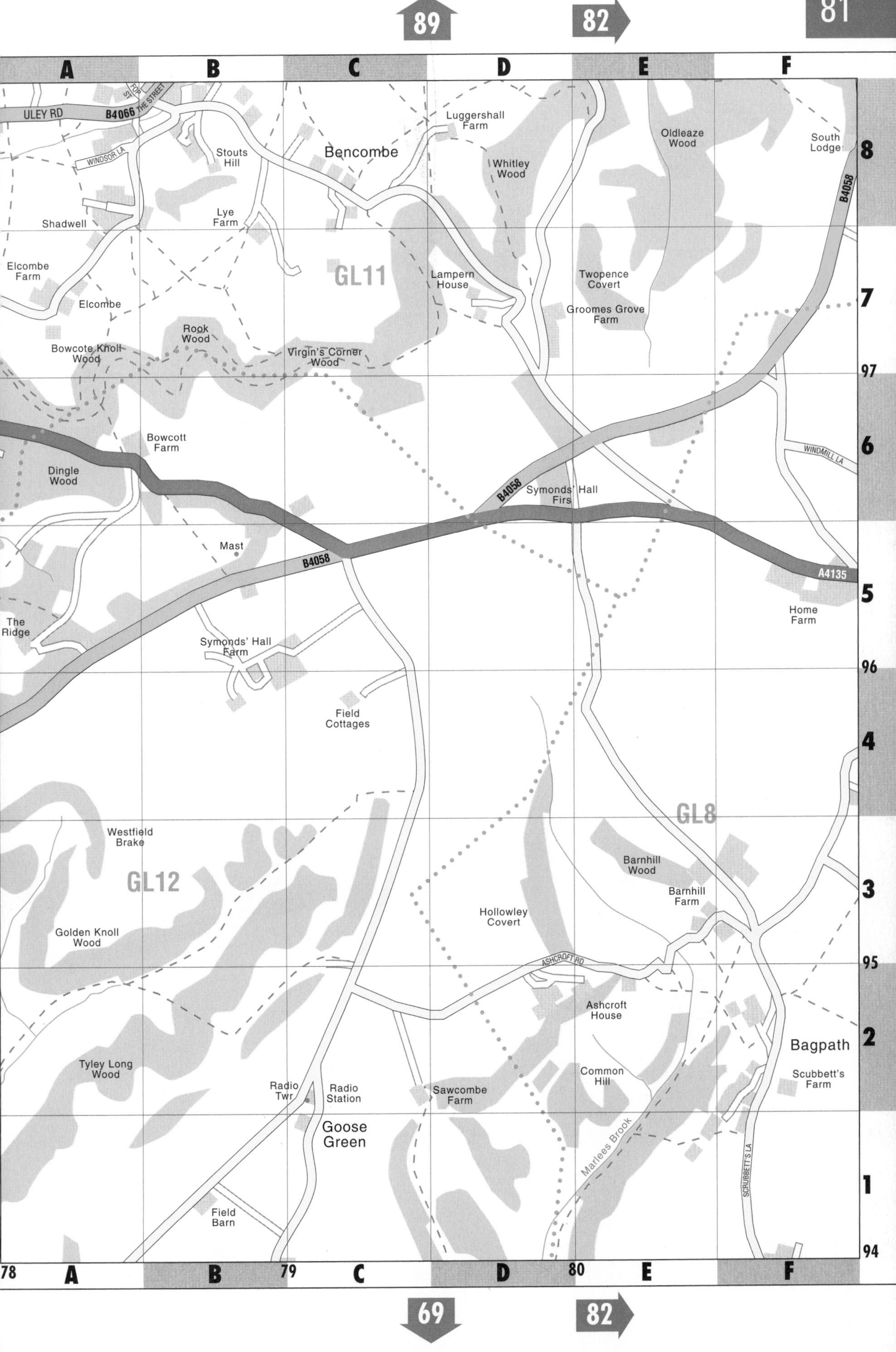
A
B
C
D
E
F
ULEY RD
B4066
THE STREET
WINDSOR LA
Stouts Hill
Bencombe
Luggershall Farm
Oldleaze Wood
South Lodge
Whitley Wood
B4058
Shadwell
Lye Farm
Elcombe Farm
GL11
Lampern House
Twopence Covert
Elcombe
Groomes Grove Farm
Rook Wood
Bowcote Knoll Wood
Virgin's Corner Wood
Bowcott Farm
WINDMILL LA
Dingle Wood
Symonds' Hall Firs
Mast
B4058
A4135
The Ridge
Symonds' Hall Farm
Home Farm
Field Cottages
GL8
Westfield Brake
Barnhill Wood
GL12
Barnhill Farm
Hollowley Covert
Golden Knoll Wood
ASHCROFT RD
Ashcroft House
Bagpath
Tyley Long Wood
Common Hill
Scubbett's Farm
Radio Twr
Radio Station
Sawcombe Farm
Goose Green
Marlees Brook
SCRUBBETT'S LA
Field Barn
8
7
97
6
5
96
4
3
95
2
1
94
78
79
80

69
82

81
90

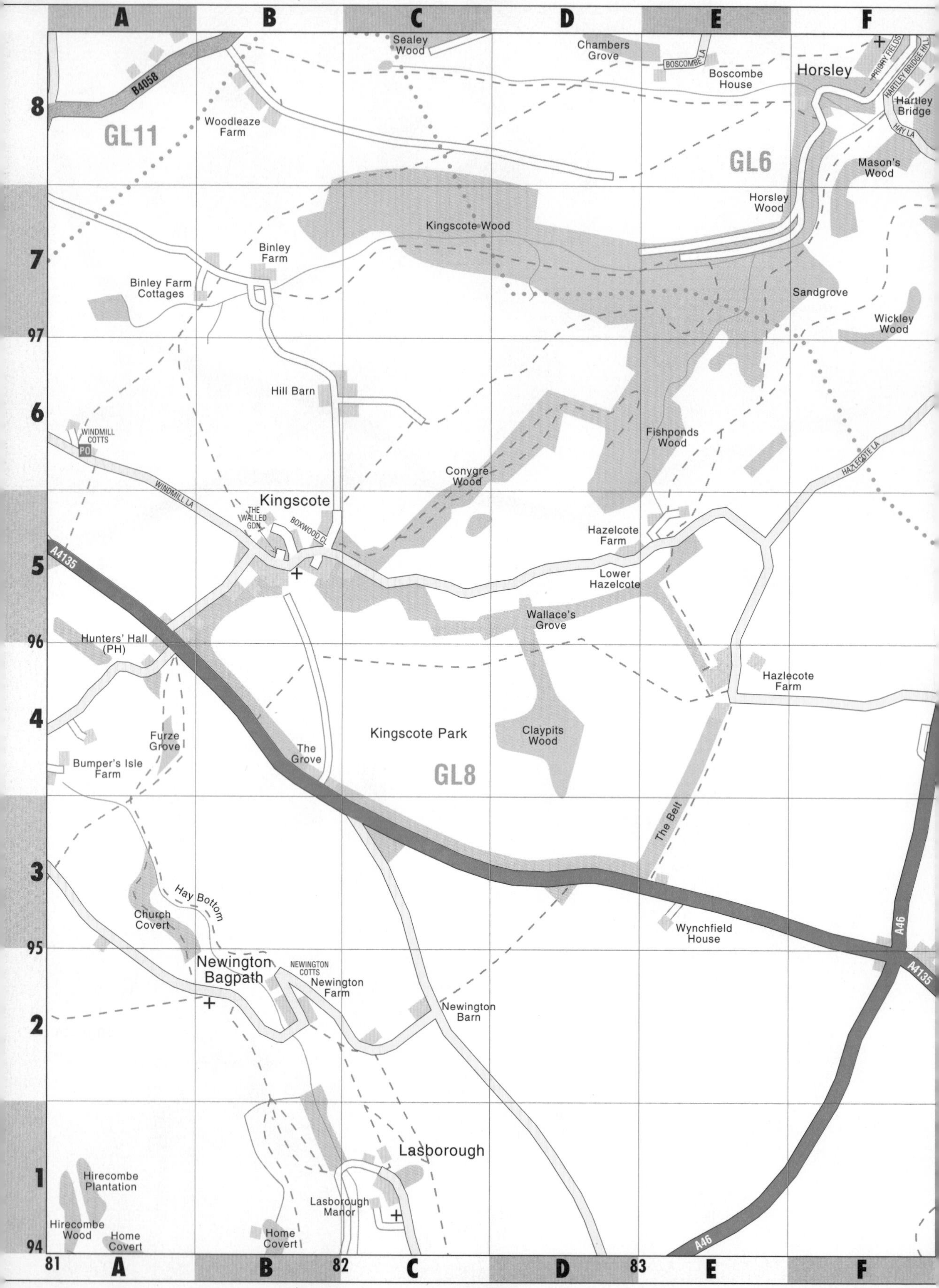

A B C D E F

8 7 97 6 5 96 4 3 95 2 1 94

Sealey Wood
Chambers Grove
BOSCOMBE LA
Boscombe House
Horsley
PRIORY FIELDS
HARTLEY BRIDGE HILL
Hartley Bridge
HAY LA
B4058
Woodleaze Farm
GL11
GL6
Mason's Wood
Horsley Wood
Kingscote Wood
Binley Farm
Binley Farm Cottages
Sandgrove
Wickley Wood
Hill Barn
WINDMILL COTTS
PO
Fishponds Wood
HAZLECOTE LA
Conygre Wood
WINDMILL LA
Kingscote
THE WALLED GDN
BOXWOOD CL
Hazelcote Farm
A4135
Lower Hazelcote
Wallace's Grove
Hunters' Hall (PH)
Hazlecote Farm
Furze Grove
Kingscote Park
Claypits Wood
Bumper's Isle Farm
The Grove
GL8
The Belt
Hay Bottom
Church Covert
Wynchfield House
A46
Newington Bagpath
NEWINGTON COTTS
Newington Farm
Newington Barn
Lasborough
Hirecombe Plantation
Lasborough Manor
Hirecombe Wood
Home Covert
Home Covert

81 A B 82 C D 83 E F

81
70

A
B
C
D
E
F
Park Wood
BARTONEND LA
A46
Barton End
Cold Harbour Barn
Westfield Barn
BATH RD
Upper Barton End
LONGLENGTH LA
HAY LA
Haylane Farm
Tiltups End
Tipputs Inn (PH)
GL6
Enoch's Barn
Pond Covert
HAZLECOTE LA
Ledgemoor Pond
Ledgemoor Wood
Knight's Bank
Ledgemoor Bottom
Orange Grove Covert
Carter's Bottom
Orange Grove Barn
Cranmore Covert
GL8
Longtree Bottom
Evan's Belt
Cranmore Dairy
Cranmore Cottages
Ledgemoor Road Cottages
Chavenage Green
Cranmore Farm
Union Gorse Covert
Calcot Farm
Calcot Manor Hotel
Broad Newell Covert
Macmillan Way
Babdown Farm
Beverston Old Brake
Chavenage La
Babdown Cottage
A4135
Beverston Castle Farm
8
7
97
6
5
96
4
3
95
2
1
94
84
85
86

147 92

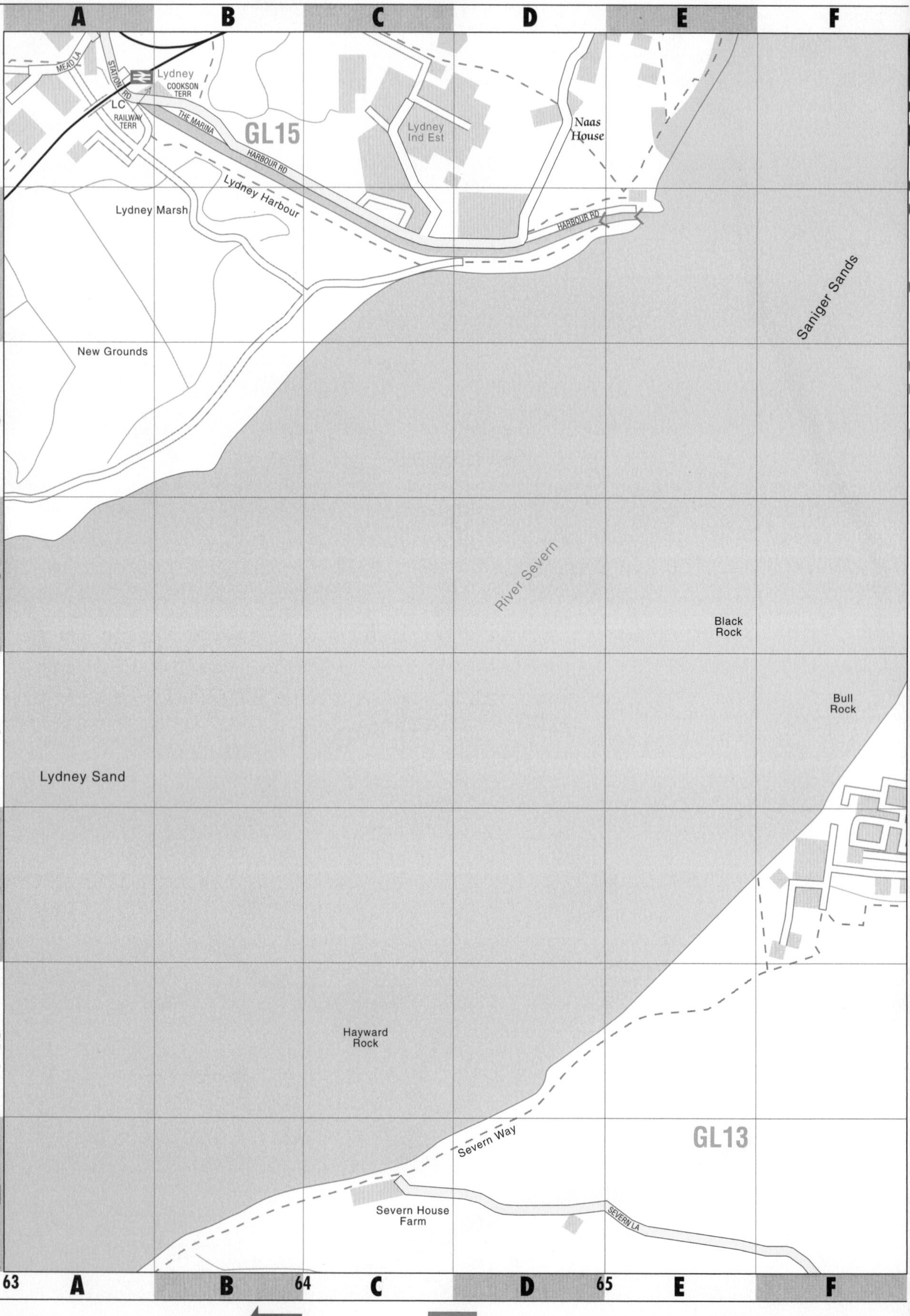

A B C D E F

8

7

01

6

5

00

4

3

99

2

1

98

Lydney
MEAD LA
STATION RD
COOKSON TERR
LC
RAILWAY TERR
THE MARINA
GL15
HARBOUR RD
Lydney Ind Est
Naas House
Lydney Marsh
Lydney Harbour
HARBOUR RD
New Grounds
Saniger Sands
River Severn
Black Rock
Bull Rock
Lydney Sand
Hayward Rock
Severn Way
GL13
Severn House Farm
SEVERN LA

63 A B 64 C D 65 E F

147 76

93
86
A
B
C
D
E
F
Newtown
Sharpness Prim Sch
Saniger Farm
Panthurst Farm
Severn Way
Oakhunger Farm
Westfield Brake
GL13
The Paddock
Rookery Farm
Wanswell
Berkeley Vale Com Sch
Hertsgrove Farm
Sugar-loaf Villa
Butler's Farm
Hainses
Pitbrook
Penny Grove
Abwell
Abwell Farm
Tintock Wood
Berkeley
The Fishers
Wickselm
Berkeley Power Station
Berkeley Pill
Hook Street
Lynch
Oakhunger
Cemy
Berkeley Prim Sch
Liby
TH
Jenner Mus
Long Bridge
Hamfield Farm
Berkeley Castle
Butterfly House
Floodgates Farm
Parham Brake
Kennels
Woodlands Farm
Ham
Salutation Inn (PH)
Fowler's Plantation
Brownsmill Farm
Bluegates Farm
Blackhall
Parham La
B4066
STAMBOURNE LA
VINECROFT
HALMORE LA
ROOKERY LA
SANIGER LA
STATION RD
OAKHUNGER LA
LYNCH RD
HAMFIELD LA
JUMPERS LA
HIGH ST
SALTER ST
MKT PL
CANONBURY ST
WOODLANDS LA
8
7
01
6
5
00
4
3
99
2
1
98
66
67
68
77
86

85
94

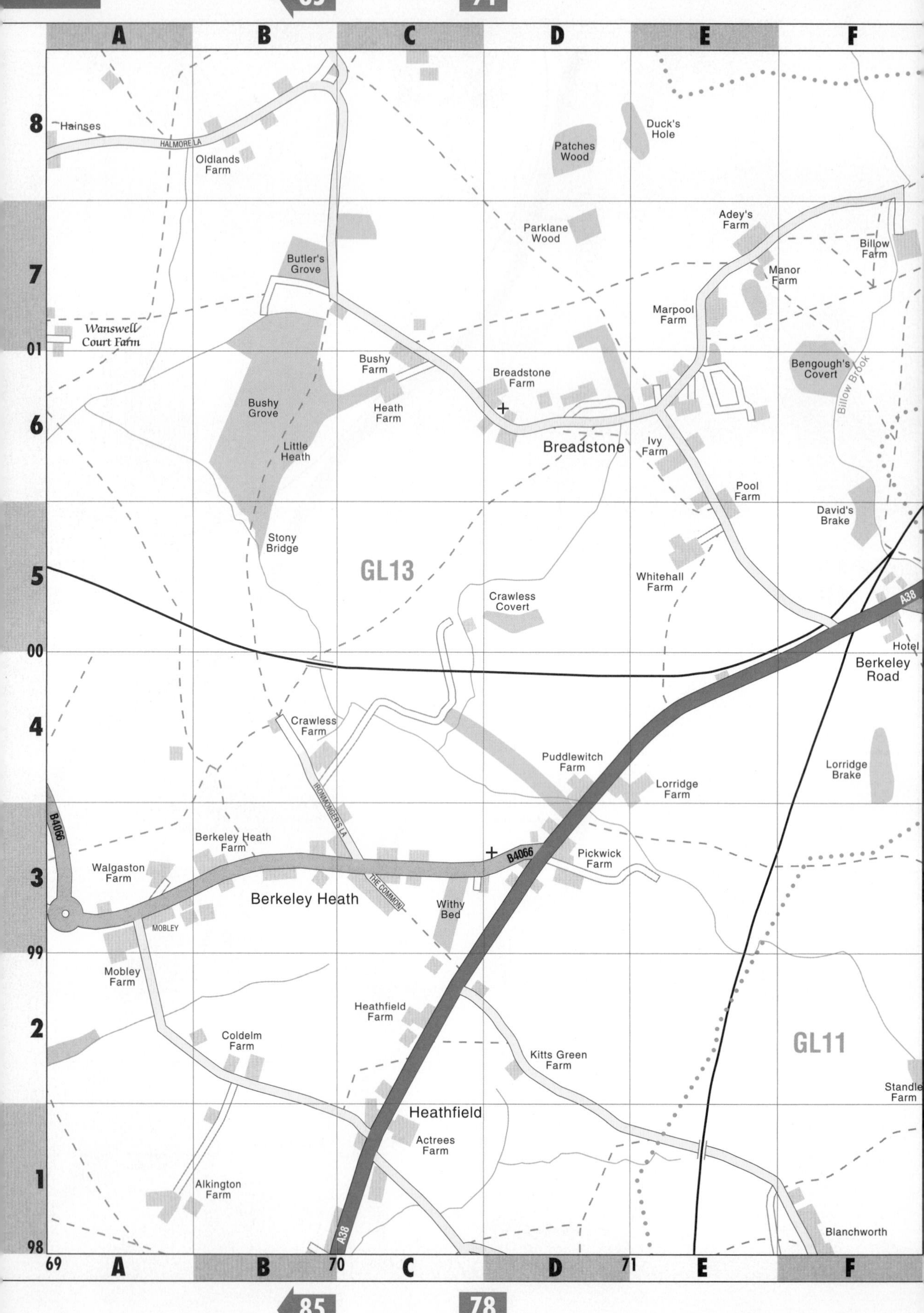
A
B
C
D
E
F
8
7
01
6
5
00
4
3
99
2
1
98
69
70
71
Hainses
HALMORE LA
Oldlands Farm
Duck's Hole
Patches Wood
Parklane Wood
Adey's Farm
Billow Farm
Butler's Grove
Manor Farm
Marpool Farm
Wanswell Court Farm
Bushy Farm
Breadstone Farm
Bengough's Covert
Billow Brook
Bushy Grove
Heath Farm
Breadstone
Ivy Farm
Little Heath
Pool Farm
David's Brake
Stony Bridge
GL13
Whitehall Farm
Crawless Covert
A38
Hotel
Berkeley Road
Crawless Farm
Puddlewitch Farm
Lorridge Brake
Lorridge Farm
IRONMONGER'S LA
B4066
Berkeley Heath Farm
Pickwick Farm
Walgaston Farm
Berkeley Heath
THE COMMON
Withy Bed
MOBLEY
Mobley Farm
Heathfield Farm
Coldelm Farm
Kitts Green Farm
GL11
Standle Farm
Heathfield
Actrees Farm
Alkington Farm
Blanchworth

85
78

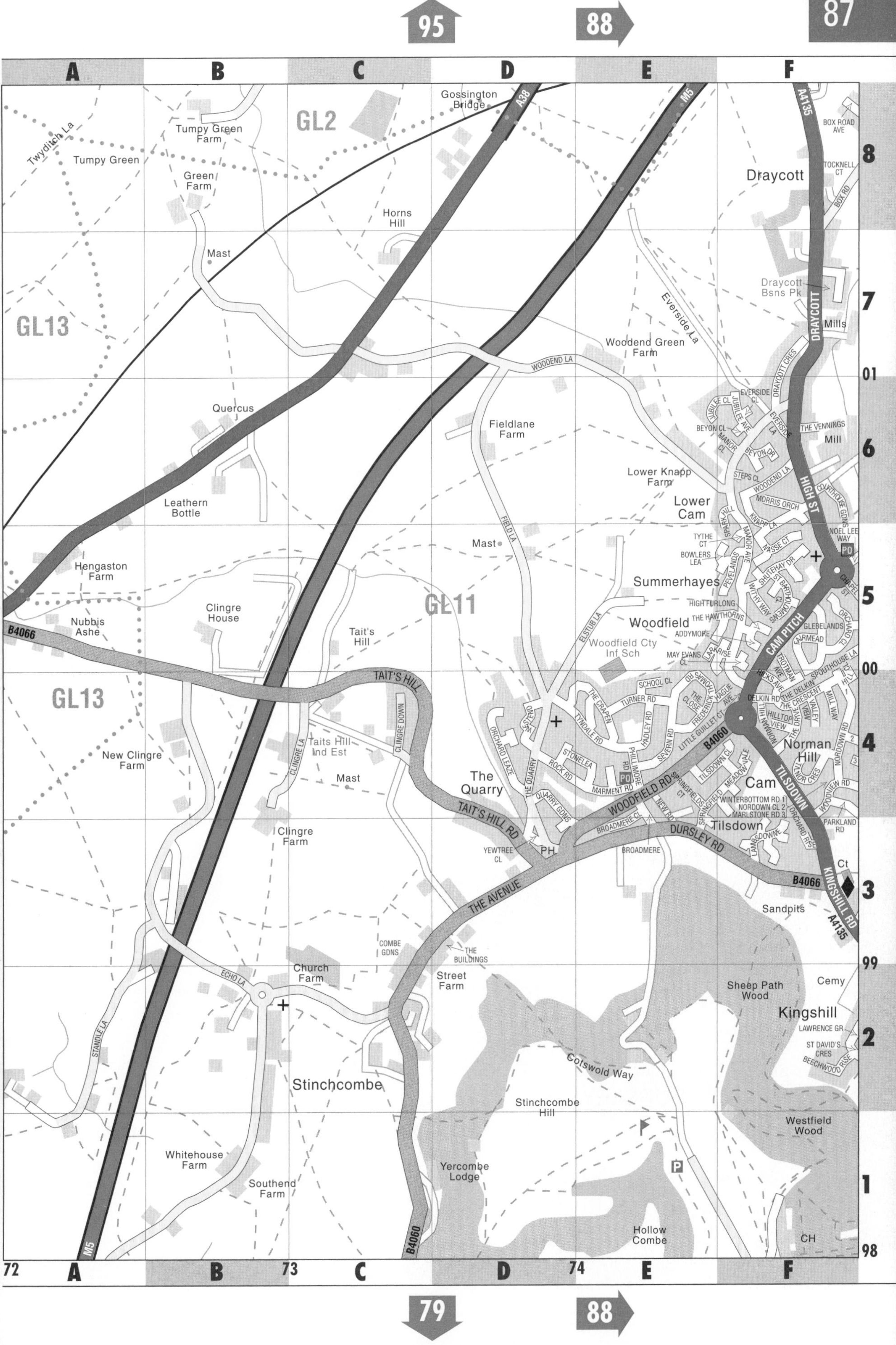
95
88
A
B
C
D
E
F
8
7
01
6
5
00
4
3
99
2
1
98
72
73
74
79
88
GL2
GL13
GL11
GL13
Twyditch La
Tumpy Green
Tumpy Green Farm
Green Farm
Gossington Bridge
A38
M5
A4135
Horns Hill
Mast
Draycott
Draycott Bsns Pk
DRAYCOTT
Mills
Everside La
Woodend Green Farm
WOODEND LA
Quercus
Fieldlane Farm
Leathern Bottle
Lower Knapp Farm
Lower Cam
HIGH ST
Mill
Hengaston Farm
Clingre House
Summerhayes
Woodfield
Woodfield Cty Inf Sch
Nubbis Ashe
B4066
Tait's Hill
TAIT'S HILL
CAM PITCH
New Clingre Farm
Taits Hill Ind Est
CLINGRE LA
CLINGRE DOWN
The Quarry
Norman Hill
Cam
Tilsdown
TILSDOWN
WOODFIELD RD
B4060
DURSLEY RD
TAIT'S HILL RD
Clingre Farm
PH
THE AVENUE
Sandpits
Ct
KINGSHILL RD
Church Farm
Street Farm
ECHO LA
STANDLE LA
Sheep Path Wood
Cemy
Kingshill
Cotswold Way
Stinchcombe
Stinchcombe Hill
Westfield Wood
Whitehouse Farm
Southend Farm
Yercombe Lodge
Hollow Combe
CH
B4060
M5
P
PO

87 96

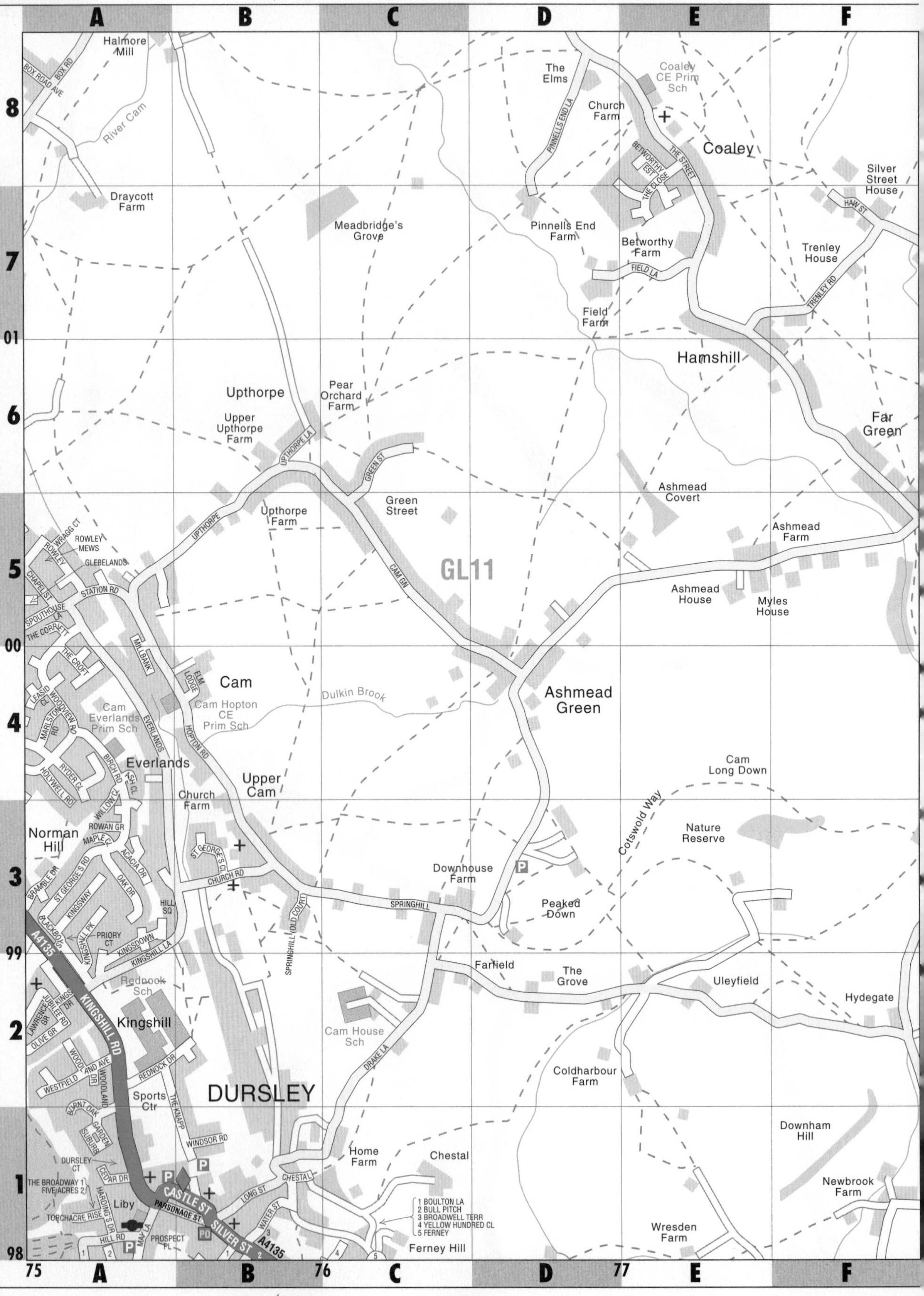

Halmore Mill
Draycott Farm
Meadbridge's Grove
The Elms
Church Farm
Coaley CE Prim Sch
Coaley
Silver Street House
Pinnells End Farm
Betworthy Farm
Trenley House
Field Farm
Hamshill
Upthorpe
Pear Orchard Farm
Upper Upthorpe Farm
Far Green
Green Street
Upthorpe Farm
Ashmead Covert
Ashmead Farm
GL11
Ashmead House
Myles House
Cam
Cam Hopton CE Prim Sch
Dulkin Brook
Ashmead Green
Cam Everlands Prim Sch
Everlands
Upper Cam
Church Farm
Cam Long Down
Norman Hill
Cotswold Way
Nature Reserve
Downhouse Farm
Peaked Down
Farfield
The Grove
Uleyfield
Rednock Sch
Hydegate
Kingshill
Cam House Sch
Coldharbour Farm
Sports Ctr
DURSLEY
Downham Hill
Home Farm
Chestal
Newbrook Farm
Liby
Wresden Farm
Ferney Hill
1 BOULTON LA
2 BULL PITCH
3 BROADWELL TERR
4 YELLOW HUNDRED CL
5 FERNEY
THE BROADWAY 1
FIVE ACRES 2
A4135

87 80

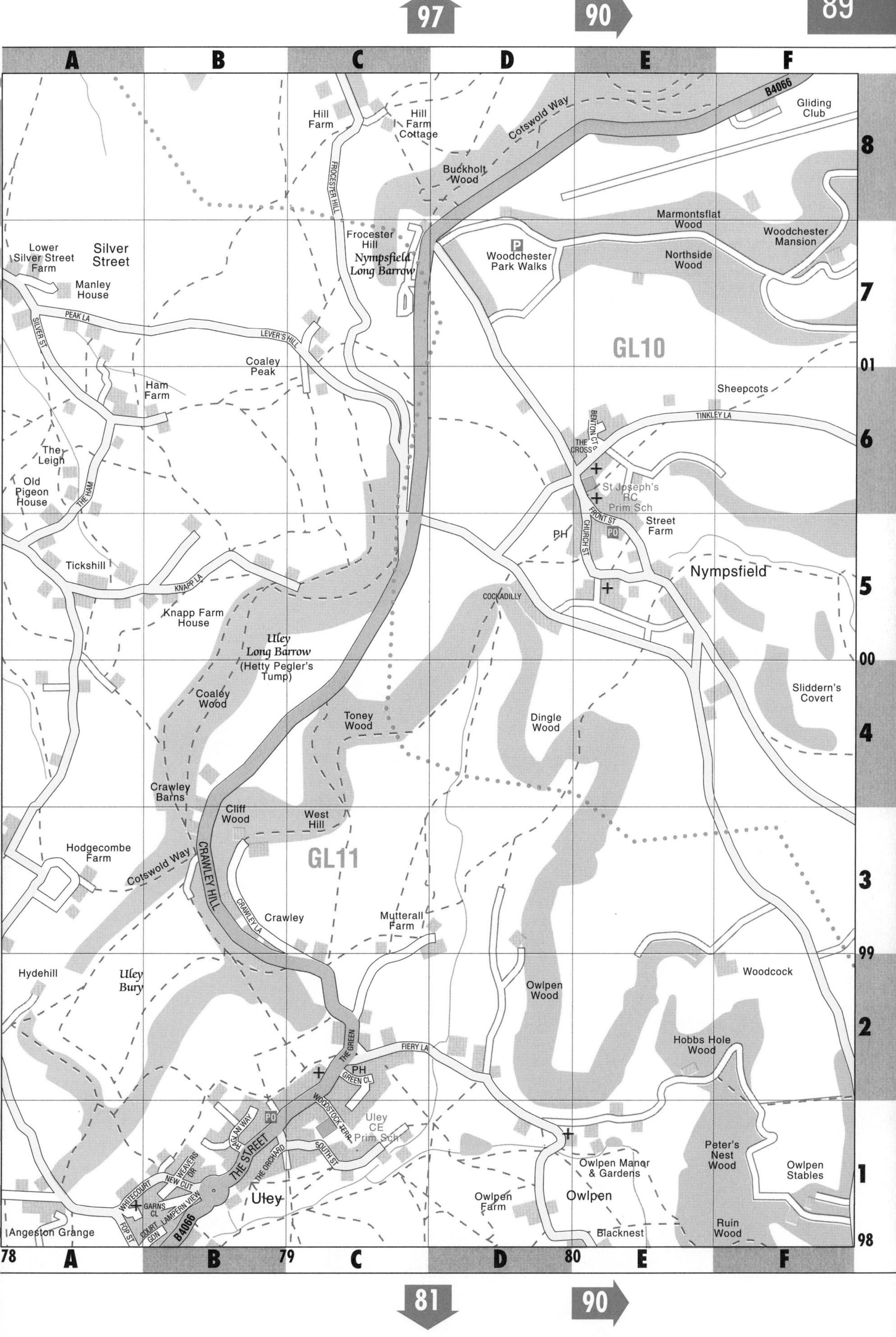
97
90
A
B
C
D
E
F
8
7
01
6
5
00
4
3
99
2
1
98
78
79
80
Hill
Farm
Hill
Farm
Cottage
Cotswold Way
B4066
Gliding
Club
Buckholt
Wood
FROCESTER HILL
Marmontsflat
Wood
Woodchester
Mansion
Frocester
Hill
Nympsfield
Long Barrow
Woodchester
Park Walks
Northside
Wood
Lower
Silver Street
Farm
Silver
Street
Manley
House
PEAK LA
SILVER ST
LEVER'S HILL
GL10
Coaley
Peak
Ham
Farm
Sheepcots
TINKLEY LA
BENTON CT
THE
CROSS
The
Leigh
Old
Pigeon
House
THE HAM
St Joseph's
RC
Prim Sch
FRONT ST
CHURCH ST
PH
PO
Street
Farm
Tickshill
KNAPP LA
Nympsfield
COCKADILLY
Knapp Farm
House
Uley
Long Barrow
(Hetty Pegler's
Tump)
Sliddern's
Covert
Coaley
Wood
Toney
Wood
Dingle
Wood
Crawley
Barns
Cliff
Wood
West
Hill
Hodgecombe
Farm
Cotswold Way
GL11
CRAWLEY HILL
CRAWLEY LA
Crawley
Mutterall
Farm
Hydehill
Uley
Bury
Woodcock
Owlpen
Wood
Hobbs Hole
Wood
THE GREEN
FIERY LA
PH
GREEN CL
WOODSTOCK TERR
PO
Uley
CE
Prim Sch
RAGLAN WAY
WEAVERS
DR
NEW CUT
THE STREET
THE ORCHARD
SOUTH ST
Peter's
Nest
Wood
Owlpen Manor
& Gardens
Owlpen
Stables
WHITECOURT
GARNS
CL
COURT
GDN
LAMPERN VIEW
FOP ST
B4066
Uley
Owlpen
Farm
Owlpen
Ruin
Wood
Angeston Grange
Blacknest
81
90

89
98

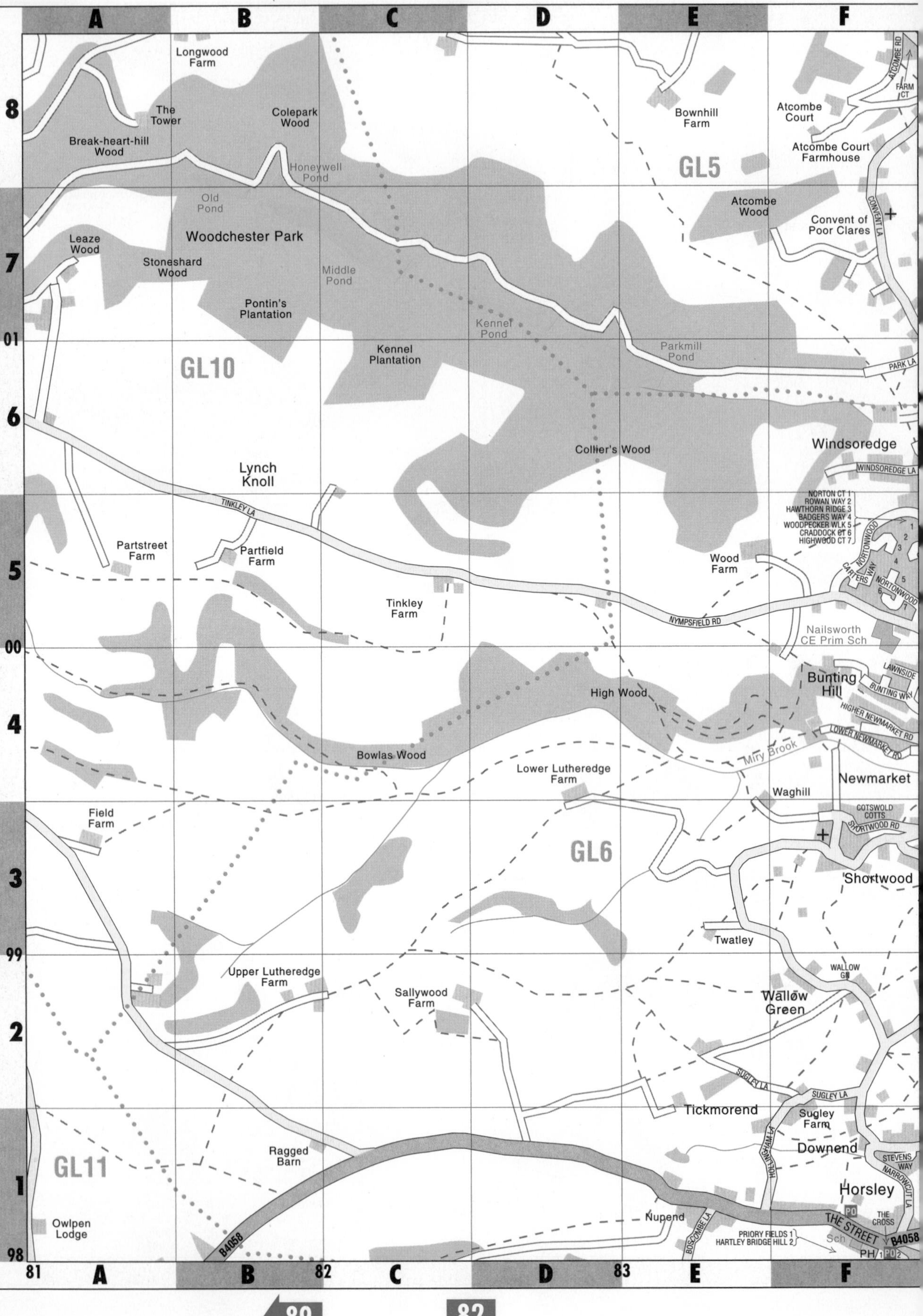

A B C D E F
8 7 01 6 5 00 4 3 99 2 1 98
Longwood Farm
The Tower
Colepark Wood
Break-heart-hill Wood
Honeywell Pond
Old Pond
Bownhill Farm
Atcombe Court
Atcombe Court Farmhouse
GL5
Atcombe Wood
Convent of Poor Clares
CONVENT LA
ATCOMBE RD
FARM CT
Leaze Wood
Woodchester Park
Stoneshard Wood
Middle Pond
Pontin's Plantation
Kennel Pond
Kennel Plantation
Parkmill Pond
PARK LA
GL10
Collier's Wood
Windsoredge
WINDSOREDGE LA
Lynch Knoll
TINKLEY LA
NORTON CT 1
ROWAN WAY 2
HAWTHORN RIDGE 3
BADGERS WAY 4
WOODPECKER WLK 5
CRADDOCK CT 6
HIGHWOOD CT 7
NORTONWOOD
CARTERS WAY
Partstreet Farm
Partfield Farm
Wood Farm
Tinkley Farm
NYMPSFIELD RD
Nailsworth CE Prim Sch
Bunting Hill
LAWNSIDE
BUNTING WAY
HIGHER NEWMARKET RD
LOWER NEWMARKET RD
High Wood
Bowlas Wood
Miry Brook
Lower Lutheredge Farm
Newmarket
Waghill
Field Farm
COTSWOLD COTTS
SHORTWOOD RD
GL6
Shortwood
Twatley
Upper Lutheredge Farm
Sallywood Farm
WALLOW GN
Wallow Green
SUGLEY LA
Tickmorend
Sugley Farm
HOLLINGHAM LA
Ragged Barn
Downend
STEVENS WAY
NARROWCUT LA
GL11
Horsley
PO
THE CROSS
Owlpen Lodge
Nupend
BOSCOMBE LA
THE STREET
B4058
PRIORY FIELDS 1
HARTLEY BRIDGE HILL 2
Sch
PH
81 82 83

89
82

99
148

A
B
C
D
E
F
8
7
01
6
5
00
4
3
99
2
1
98
84
85
86
St Chloe
Littleworth
Amberley
Amberley CE Sch
Minchinhampton Common
Whitfield's Tump
Long Barrow
Black Ditch
Jacob's Knowle
Beechknap
Claycombe
Burleigh
Hotel
Merrett's Mills
Inchbrook Trad Est
GL5
St Dominics RC Prim Sch
Theescombe
Inchbrook
Amberley Ct
Pinfarthings
Minchinhampton
Dunkirk Mills
Dunkirk Manor
Forest Green
Watledge
Cotswold Chine Home Specl Sch
Box
Forwood
Beaudesert Park Sch
Egypt
Box Farm
Box House
Worley
Nailsworth Mills Est
GL6
Spring Mill Ind Est
Ball's Green
Longfords Farm
Walkleywood
NAILSWORTH
Millbottom
Mast
Longford Mills
Hazel Wood
Fooks
Rockness
Midland Fishery
Harleywood
Windsorash
Whiteway
Rugger's Green Barn
GL8
Washpool
Brandhouse Farm
A46
STROUD RD
B4014
B4058
AVENING RD
BATH RD
HORSLEY RD
HORSLEY HILL
CIRENCESTER RD
WINDMILL RD
COMMON RD
SHIPTON'S GRAVE LA
TETBURY LA
OLD BRISTOL RD
1 BARN FIELD TERR
2 CHERRY TREE CL
1 BUTCHER HILL'S LA
2 CLISSOLD CT
3 PARK ROAD CRES
4 TANNER'S PL
5 UPPER PARK RD

83
148

Oldcroft
1 BRIERLEY WAY
2 CHURCH WLK
Shaphouse Farm
Needs Top
Hulks Farm
Soilwell Farm
Soilwell Manor
Little Purlieu
Purlieu End Farm
The Purlieu
Ten Acre Wood
Allaston Meend
Tingley Wood
Plummer's Brook
OLD DAM RD
A48
GROVE LA
ALLASTON RD
WINDSOR DR
Little Allaston
Billings Barn
Allaston
NEW MILLS
Driffield Farm
DRIFFIELD RD
Mast
Millrough Wood
Allaston Court
Primrose Hill CE Prim Sch
Nursehill Wood
Nursehill
Primrose Hill
HIGHFIELD LA
PH
PO
Cross Hands
GL15
Middle Forge
B4234
NEW RD
1 NODENS WAY
2 NERO CL
3 CAESARS CL
Rodley Manor
Highfield
Warren
Hurst Farm
Wellhouse Grove
THE SPRINGS
Newerne
Lydney
Lydney CE Prim Sch
FOREST RD
TUTHILL RISE 1
THE FOLDERS 2
HAWTHORN CT 3
Severnbanks Prim Sch
Warren Grove
Liby
LC
Lydney Town
HAMPTON MEWS
FAIRFIELD RD
Crump Farm
B4231
HIGH ST
Kears Wood
1 WYNTOUR'S PAR
2 DARTERS CL
3 HERBERT HOWELLS CL
4 STEEPLE VIEW
5 VICARAGE CL
Dean Forest Rly
Bathurst Park
Tutnalls
Whitecross Sch
CHURCH RD
NAAS LA
Plummer's Farm
Cliff Farm
CHURCH GDNS
St Mary's
CH
Iron Foundry
Naas Crossing (LC)
Naas Court
Naas
Lydney Junc
STATION RD
A
B
C
D
E
F
8
7
05
6
5
04
4
3
03
2
1
02
63
64
65

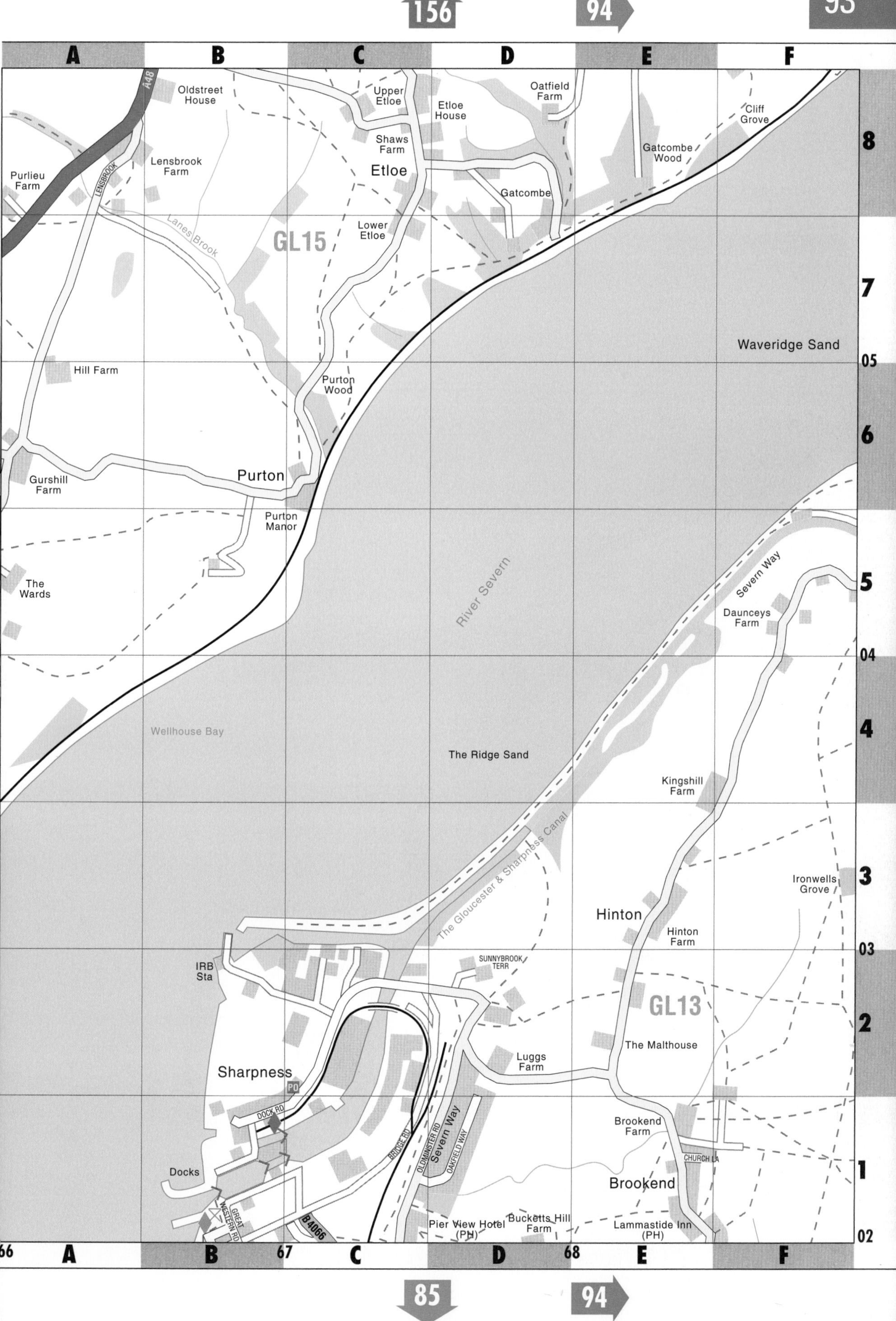
A
B
C
D
E
F
A48
Oldstreet House
Upper Etloe
Etloe House
Oatfield Farm
Cliff Grove
Shaws Farm
Gatcombe Wood
Purlieu Farm
Lensbrook Farm
Etloe
LENSBROOK
Gatcombe
Lanes Brook
GL15
Lower Etloe
Waveridge Sand
Hill Farm
Purton Wood
Gurshill Farm
Purton
Purton Manor
River Severn
Severn Way
The Wards
Dauncey Farm
Wellhouse Bay
The Ridge Sand
Kingshill Farm
The Gloucester & Sharpness Canal
Ironwells Grove
Hinton
Hinton Farm
IRB Sta
SUNNYBROOK TERR
GL13
The Malthouse
Luggs Farm
Sharpness
PO
DOCK RD
Brookend Farm
BRIDGE RD
OLDMINSTER RD
Severn Way
OAKFIELD WAY
CHURCH LA
Docks
Brookend
GREAT WESTERN RD
B4066
Pier View Hotel (PH)
Bucketts Hill Farm
Lammastide Inn (PH)
8
7
05
6
5
04
4
3
03
2
1
02
66
67
68

93
157

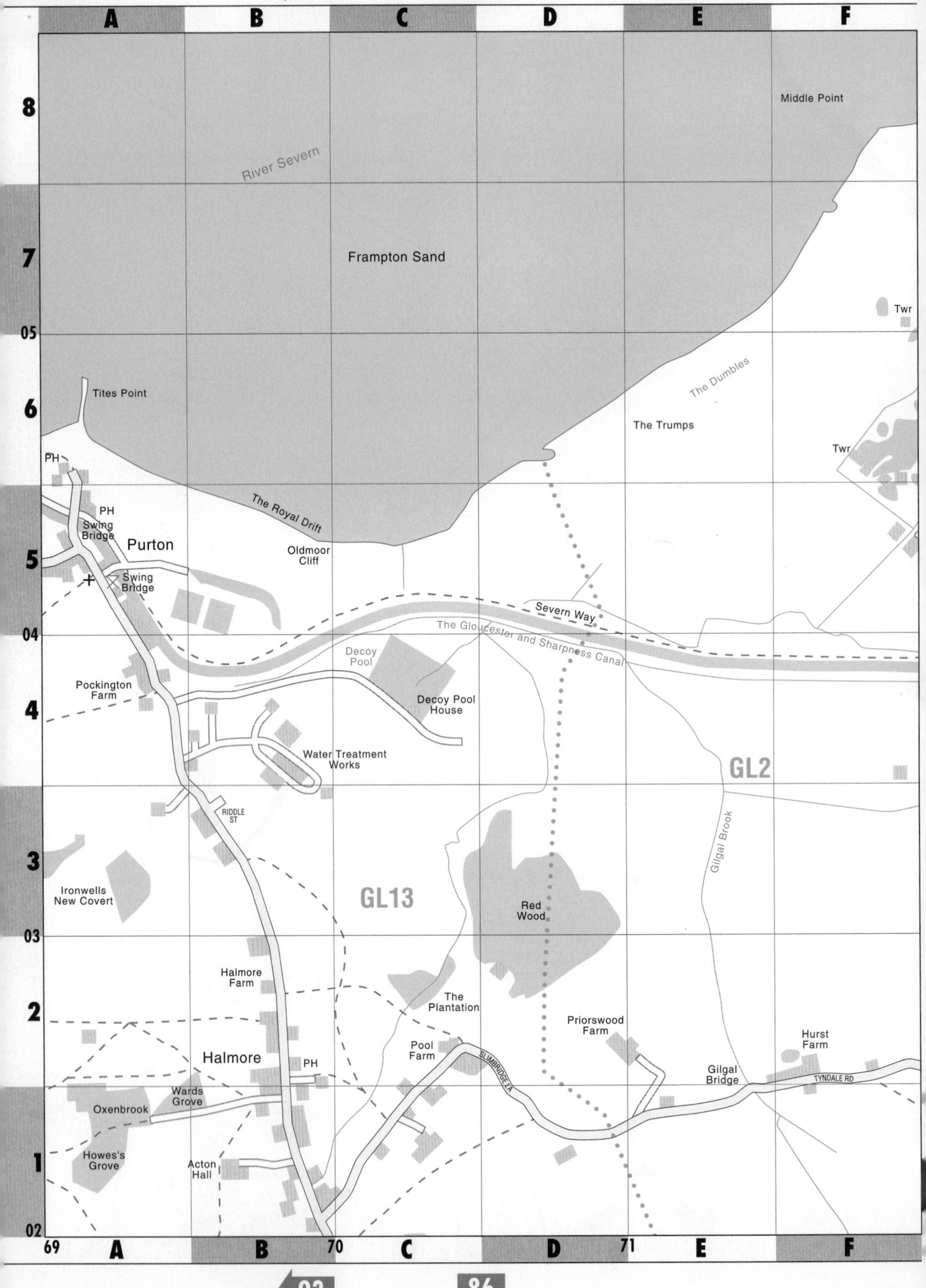

A B C D E F
8
7
05
6
5
04
4
3
03
2
1
02
Middle Point
River Severn
Frampton Sand
Twr
Tites Point
The Dumbles
The Trumps
Twr
PH
PH
Swing Bridge
Purton
The Royal Drift
Oldmoor Cliff
Swing Bridge
Severn Way
The Gloucester and Sharpness Canal
Decoy Pool
Pockington Farm
Decoy Pool House
Water Treatment Works
GL2
RIDDLE ST
Gilgal Brook
Ironwells New Covert
GL13
Red Wood
Halmore Farm
The Plantation
Priorswood Farm
Hurst Farm
Pool Farm
Halmore
PH
SLIMBRIDGE LA
Gilgal Bridge
TYNDALE RD
Wards Grove
Oxenbrook
Howes's Grove
Acton Hall
69 A B 70 C D 71 E F

93
86

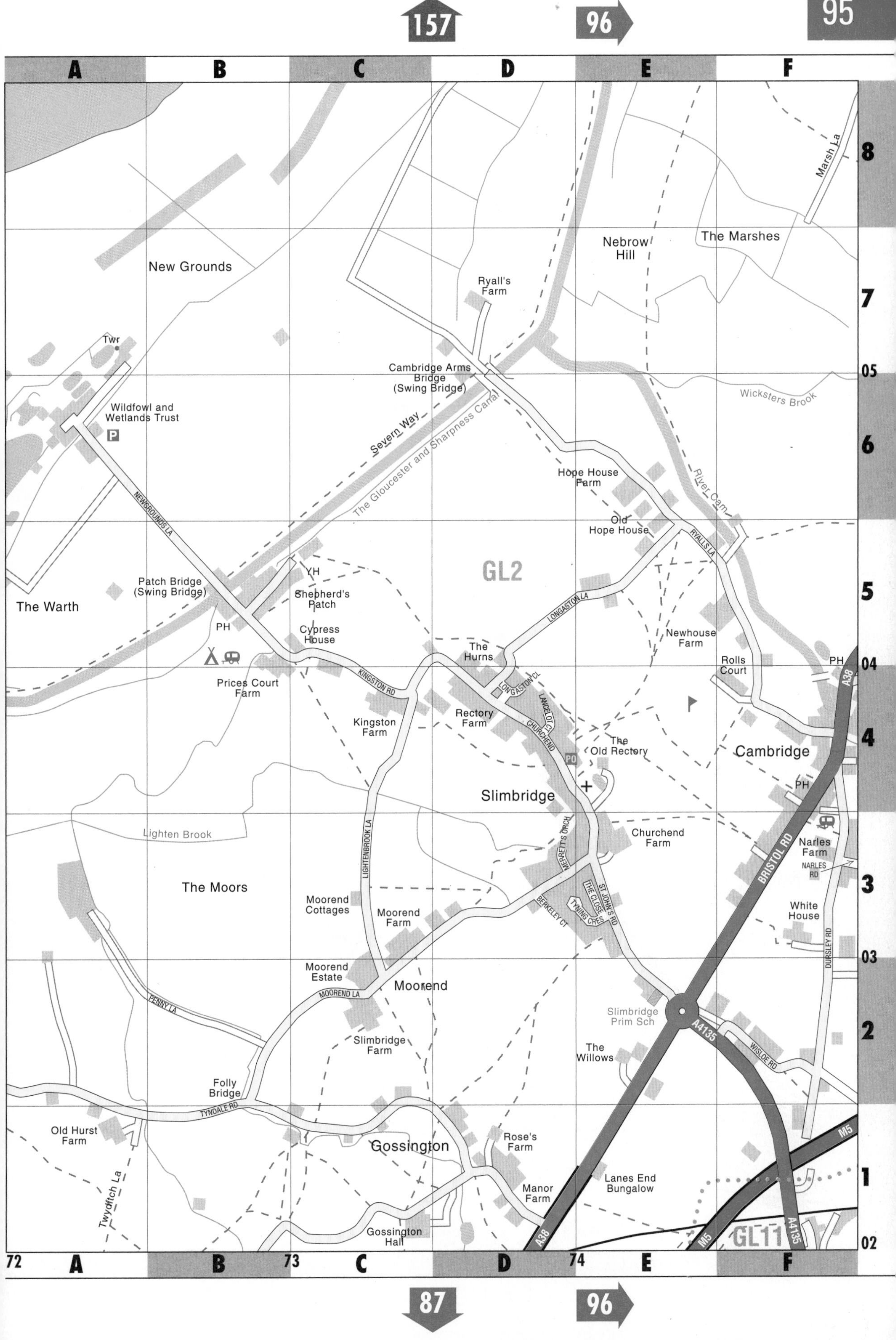
157
96
A B C D E F
8
7
05
6
5
04
4
3
03
2
1
02
72
73
74
New Grounds
Nebrow Hill
The Marshes
Marsh La
Ryall's Farm
Twr
Cambridge Arms Bridge (Swing Bridge)
Wicksters Brook
Wildfowl and Wetlands Trust
P
Severn Way
The Gloucester and Sharpness Canal
Hope House Farm
River Cam
Old Hope House
NEWGROUNDS LA
RYALLS LA
GL2
YH
Patch Bridge (Swing Bridge)
Shepherd's Patch
LONGASTON LA
The Warth
PH
Cypress House
Newhouse Farm
The Hurns
Rolls Court
PH
A38
Prices Court Farm
KINGSTON RD
LONGASTON CL
LANCELOT CT
CHURCHEND
Kingston Farm
Rectory Farm
The Old Rectory
Cambridge
PO
Slimbridge
PH
Lighten Brook
MERRETT'S ORCH
Churchend Farm
BRISTOL RD
Narles Farm
NARLES RD
The Moors
LIGHTENBROOK LA
Moorend Cottages
Moorend Farm
THE CLOSE
ST JOHN'S RD
TYNING CRES
BERKELEY CT
White House
DURSLEY RD
Moorend Estate
Moorend
MOOREND LA
PENNY LA
Slimbridge Prim Sch
A4135
WISLOE RD
Slimbridge Farm
The Willows
Folly Bridge
TYNDALE RD
Old Hurst Farm
Gossington
Rose's Farm
M5
Twyditch La
Lanes End Bungalow
Manor Farm
Gossington Hall
GL11
87
96

95
100

A
B
C
D
E
F
Old Withy Bed
Mincepie Covert
A38
Claypits
M5
Claypits Farm
Blackthorn Covert
8
Alkerton Court
Eastington
Puddleworth
BUDDON CL
BROADFIELD RD
BUSH CL
BUCKINGHAM CL
WENTSFIELD
COTSWOLD AVE
SPRING HILL
VICTORIA DR
Park's Farm
Green Farm
PO
ALKERTON TERR
ALKERTON RD
MIDDLECROFT
MILLEND LA
7
LEA CT
SWALLOW CROFT
Alkerton
Alkerton Farm
New House Farm
05
Bath Street
Wickster's Bridge
Wicksters Brook
BATH RD
6
Middle Street
Capehall Farm
New Covert
GL10
Hillhouse Farm
Elm Farm
GL2
5
Downton Farms
04
Cambridge House Farm
Beechmeadow Farm
4
Potgaston Farm
Woodman's Covert
Church Farm
PETER'S ST
Elmcote Farms
NARLES RD
3
River Cam
Long Covert
03
2
Waterend Farm
GL11
Westfield Farm
Coaley Mill
M5
Lapley Farm
1
Cam & Dursley
WEST END
BOX RD
Sewage Works
Farmcourt Covert
Corner Farm
02
75
76
77

95
88

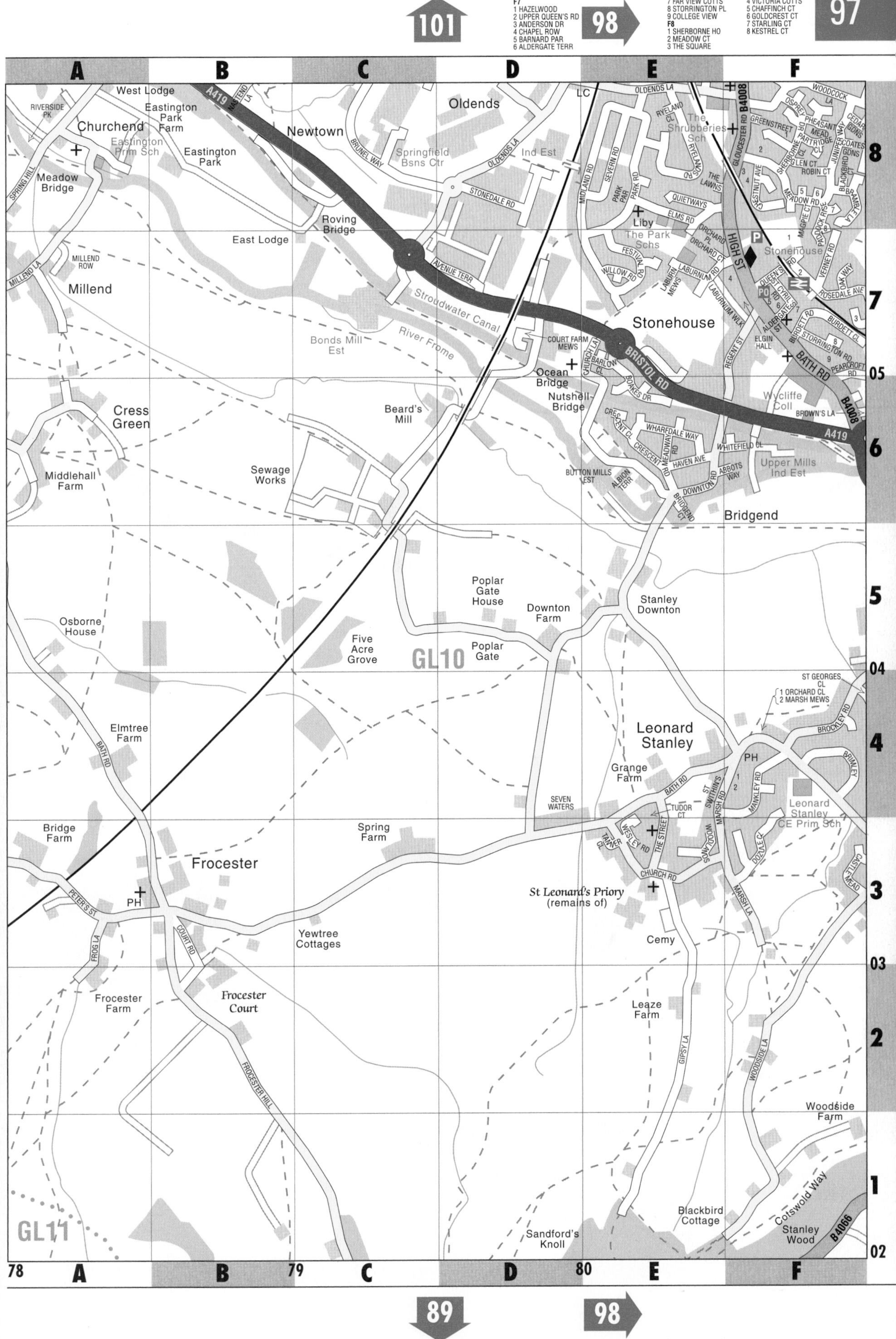
101
98
F7
1 HAZELWOOD
2 UPPER QUEEN'S RD
3 ANDERSON DR
4 CHAPEL ROW
5 BARNARD PAR
6 ALDERGATE TERR
7 FAR VIEW COTTS
8 STORRINGTON PL
9 COLLEGE VIEW
F8
1 SHERBORNE HO
2 MEADOW CT
3 THE SQUARE
4 VICTORIA COTTS
5 CHAFFINCH CT
6 GOLDCREST CT
7 STARLING CT
8 KESTREL CT
A
B
C
D
E
F
West Lodge
RIVERSIDE PK
Churchend
Eastington Park Farm
Eastington Prim Sch
Eastington Park
A419
NASTEND LA
Newtown
Oldends
Springfield Bsns Ctr
Ind Est
LC
OLDENDS LA
BRUNEL WAY
STONEDALE RD
SPRING HILL
Meadow Bridge
Roving Bridge
East Lodge
MILLEND ROW
MILLEND LA
Millend
AVENUE TERR
Stroudwater Canal
River Frome
Bonds Mill Est
COURT FARM MEWS
Ocean Bridge
Nutshell Bridge
Cress Green
Beard's Mill
Middlehall Farm
Sewage Works
BUTTON MILLS EST
ALBION TERR
RYELAND CL
RYELAND RD
The Shrubberies Sch
MIDLAND RD
SEVERN RD
PARK PAR
PARK RD
THE LAWNS
QUIETWAYS
ELMS RD
Liby
The Park Schs
FESTIVAL RD
WILLOW RD
ORCHARD PL
ORCHARD CT
LABURNUM MEWS
LABURNUM RD
LABURNUM WLK
Stonehouse
CHURCH LA
BARLOW CL
BOAKES DR
BRISTOL RD
CRESCENT CL
WHARFDALE WAY
MEADWAY
CRESCENT RD
HAVEN AVE
DOWNTON RD
ABBOTS WAY
WHITEFIELD CL
BRIDGEND CT
Bridgend
REGENT ST
HIGH ST
GLOUCESTER RD
B4008
WOODCOCK LA
OSPREY
GREENSTREET
PHEASANT MEAD
PARTRIDGE CL
SHERBORNE
GLEN CT
ROBIN CT
CHESTNUT AVE
JUNIPER WAY
CEDAR GDNS
COATES GDNS
BLACKBIRD CT
BRAMBLE LA
MEADOW RD
MAGPIE CT
PADDOCK RISE
VERNEY RD
OAK WAY
ROSEDALE AVE
QUEEN'S RD
ST CYRIL'S RD
ALDERGATE ST
ELGIN HALL
BURDETT RD
BURDETT CL
STORRINGTON RD
PEARCROFT RD
BATH RD
Wycliffe Coll
BROWN'S LA
Upper Mills Ind Est
Poplar Gate House
Downton Farm
Stanley Downton
Osborne House
Five Acre Grove
GL10
Poplar Gate
ST GEORGES CL
1 ORCHARD CL
2 MARSH MEWS
BROCKLEY RD
Elmtree Farm
Leonard Stanley
PH
BRIMLEY
Grange Farm
BATH RD
ST SWITHIN'S RD
MANKLEY RD
Leonard Stanley CE Prim Sch
SEVEN WATERS
TUDOR CT
Bridge Farm
Spring Farm
TANNER CL
WESLEY RD
THE STREET
WOODSTOCK
MARSH RD
DOZULE CL
CASTLE MEAD
Frocester
CHURCH RD
St Leonard's Priory (remains of)
MARSH LA
PETER'S ST
FROG LA
COURT RD
Yewtree Cottages
Cemy
Frocester Farm
Frocester Court
Leaze Farm
FROCESTER HILL
GIPSY LA
WOODSIDE LA
Woodside Farm
Cotswold Way
Blackbird Cottage
Stanley Wood
B4066
Sandford's Knoll
GL11
05
04
03
02
8
7
6
5
4
3
2
1
78
79
80
89
98

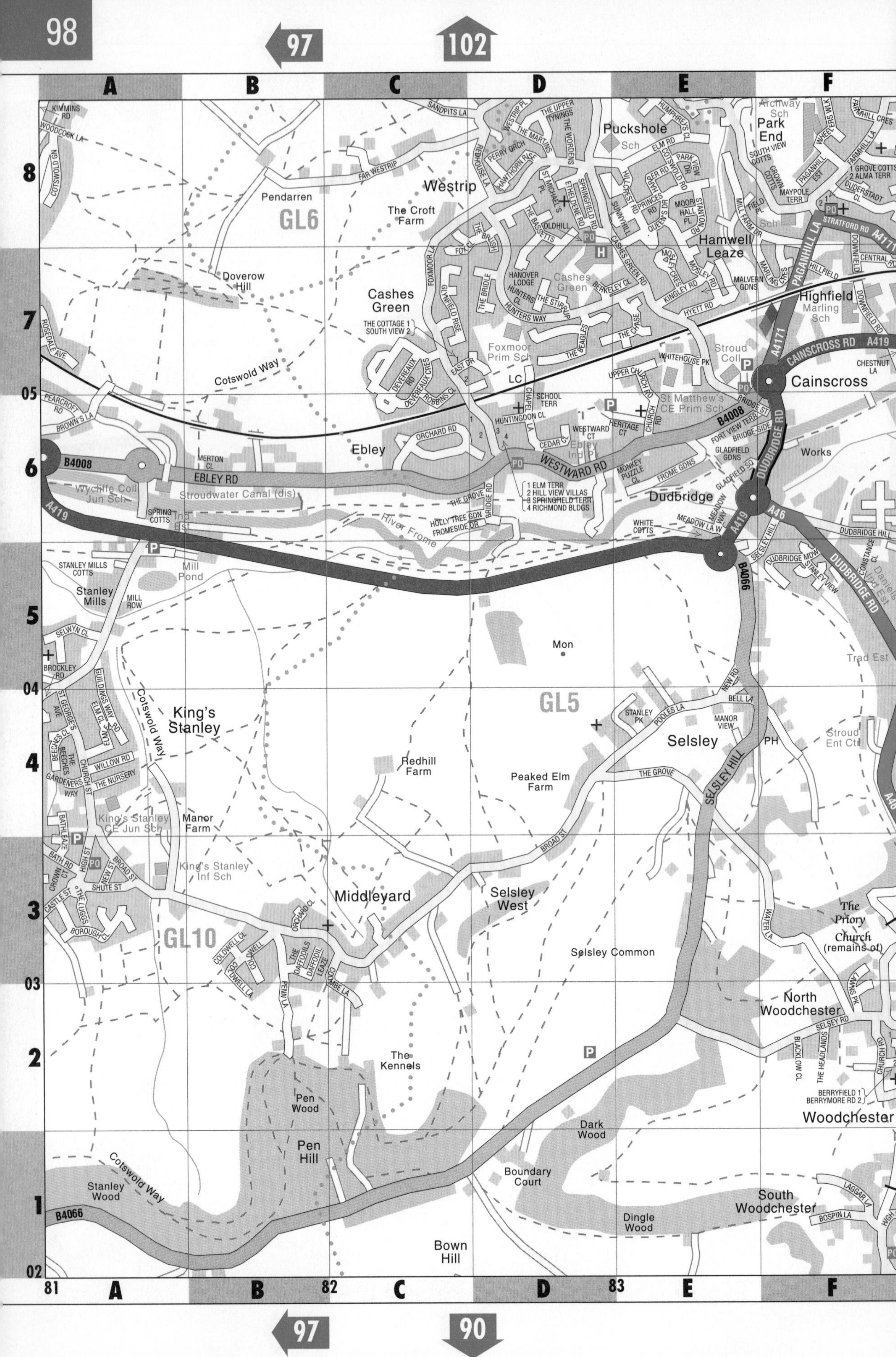
97
102
A
B
C
D
E
F
8
7
05
6
5
04
4
3
03
2
1
02
81
82
83
90
Puckshole
Westrip
Park End
Pendarren
GL6
The Croft Farm
Hamwell Leaze
Doverow Hill
Cashes Green
Highfield
Marling Sch
Foxmoor Prim Sch
Stroud Coll
Cotswold Way
Cainscross
St Matthew's CE Prim Sch
Ebley
EBLEY RD
WESTWARD RD
B4008
Works
Dudbridge
Wycliffe Coll Jun Sch
Stroudwater Canal (dis)
River Frome
A419
A46
A4171
CAINSCROSS RD
DUDBRIDGE RD
Stanley Mills
Mill Pond
Mon
GL5
Trad Est
King's Stanley
Selsley
Stroud Ent Ctr
Redhill Farm
Peaked Elm Farm
Manor Farm
King's Stanley CE Jun Sch
King's Stanley Inf Sch
Middleyard
Selsley West
GL10
The Priory Church (remains of)
Selsley Common
SELSLEY HILL
B4066
North Woodchester
The Kennels
Pen Wood
Woodchester
Dark Wood
Pen Hill
Boundary Court
Stanley Wood
South Woodchester
Dingle Wood
Bown Hill

C7
1 MERRYWALKS SH CTR
2 GLOUCESTER ST
3 LOCKING HILL
4 KING STREET PAR
5 GEORGE ST
6 CLARENDON CT
7 FAWKES PL
8 BEDFORD ST
9 KENDRICK ST
10 THREADNEEDLE ST
11 KINDRICK LA
12 THE SHAMBLES
13 SWAN LA
14 HIGH VEW LODGE
15 SPINNERS HO
16 WESLEY CT
17 WEAVERS HO
18 BLACKBOY
19 CASTLE VILLAS

103
148

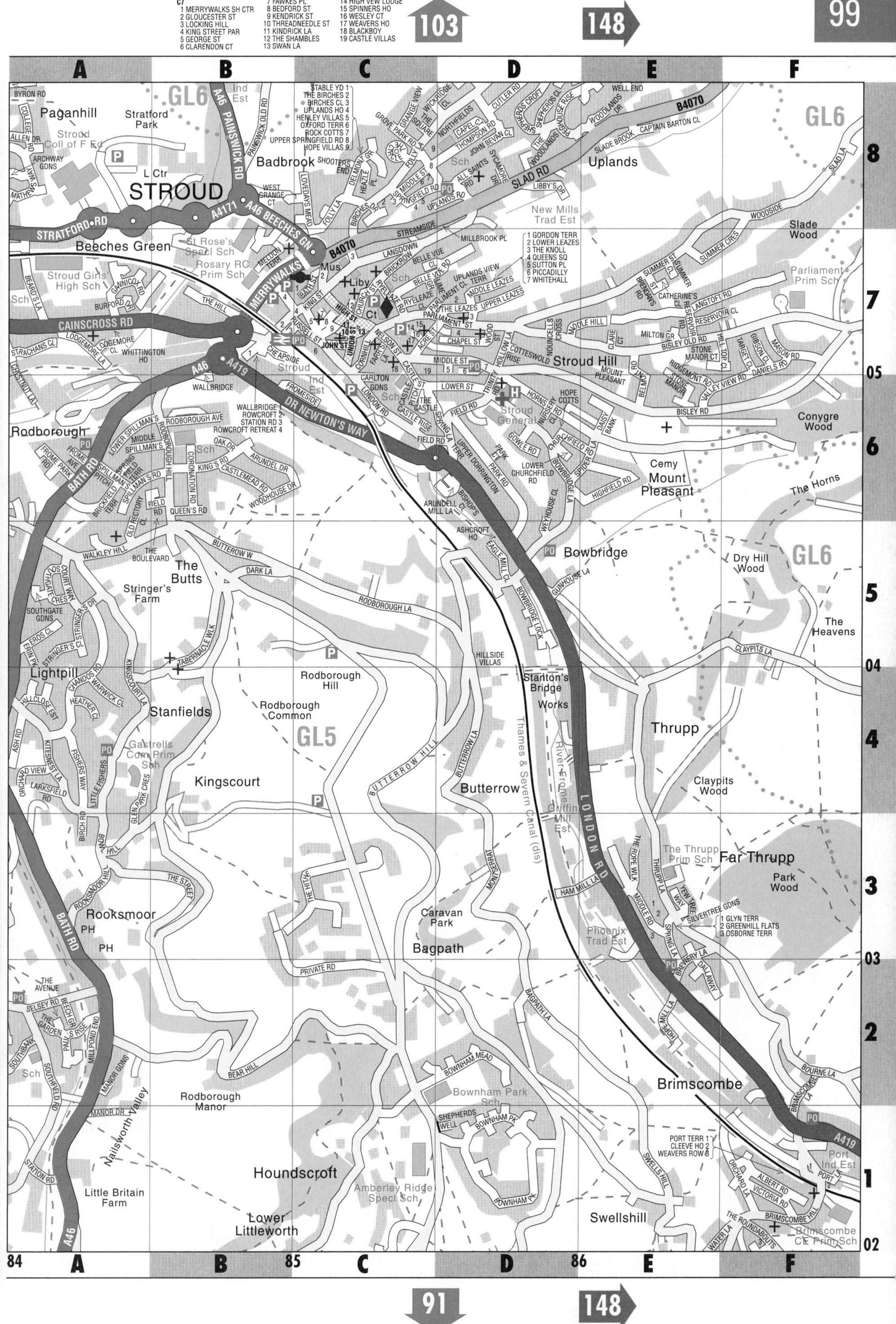

91
148

157
108

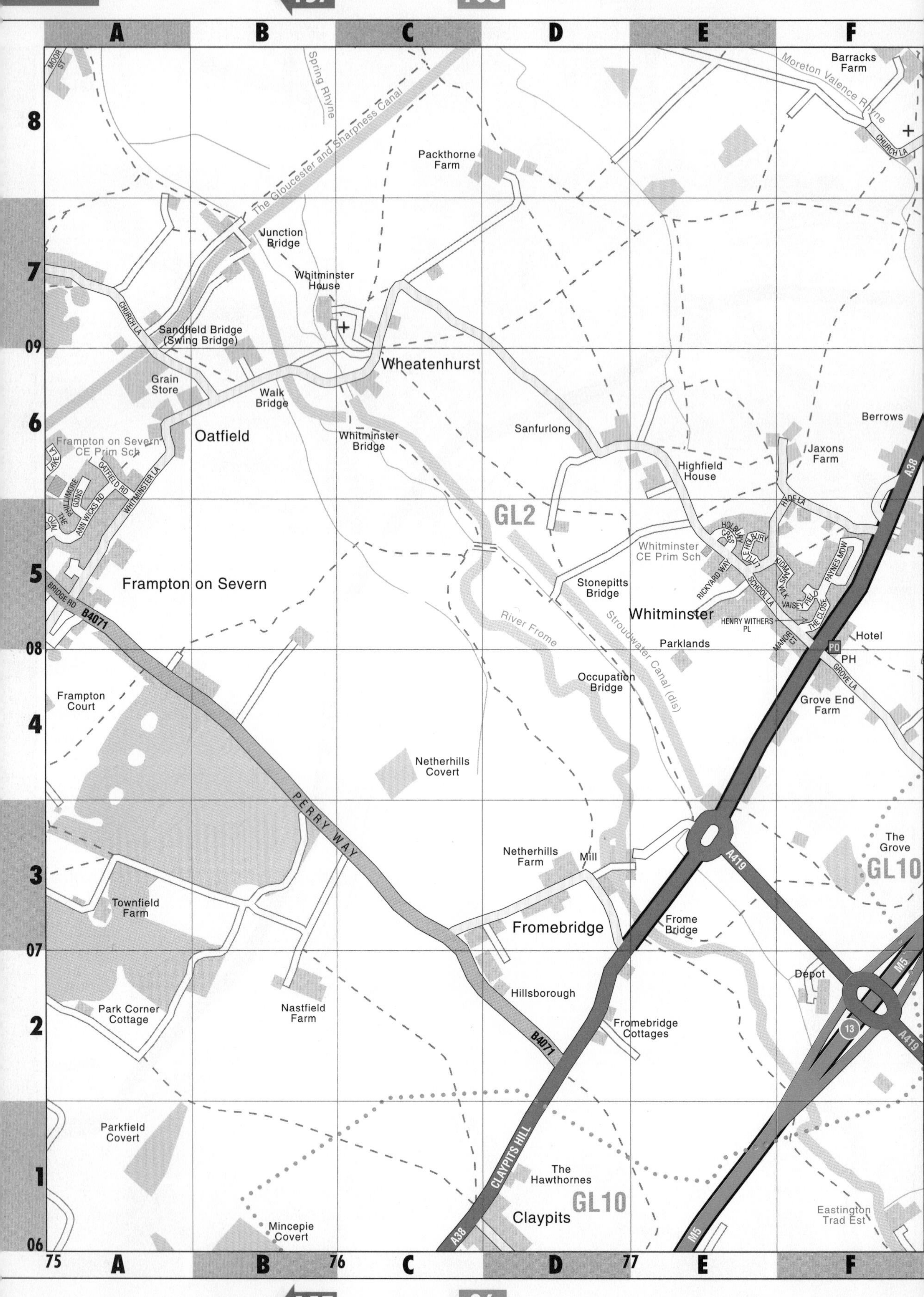

157
96

109
102

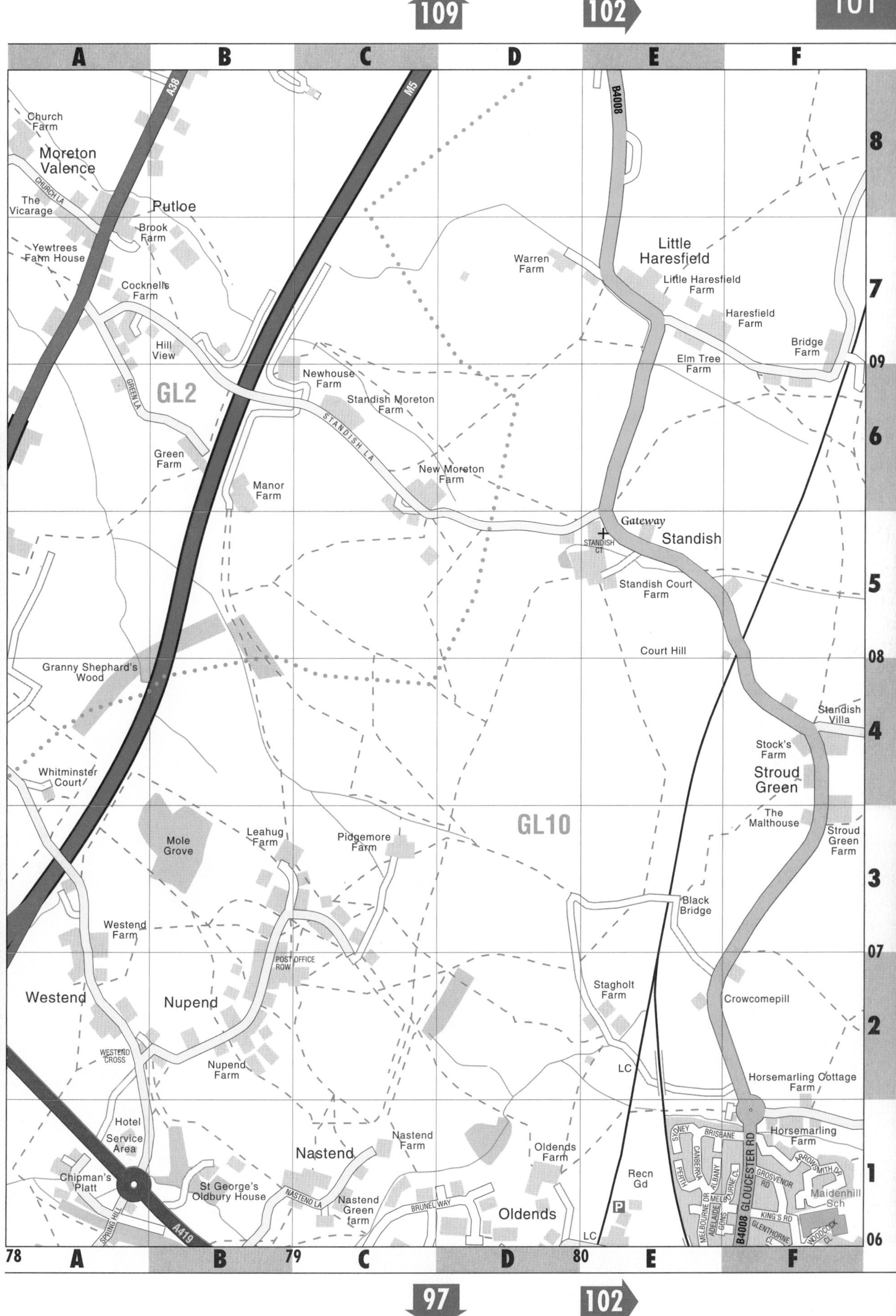

97
102

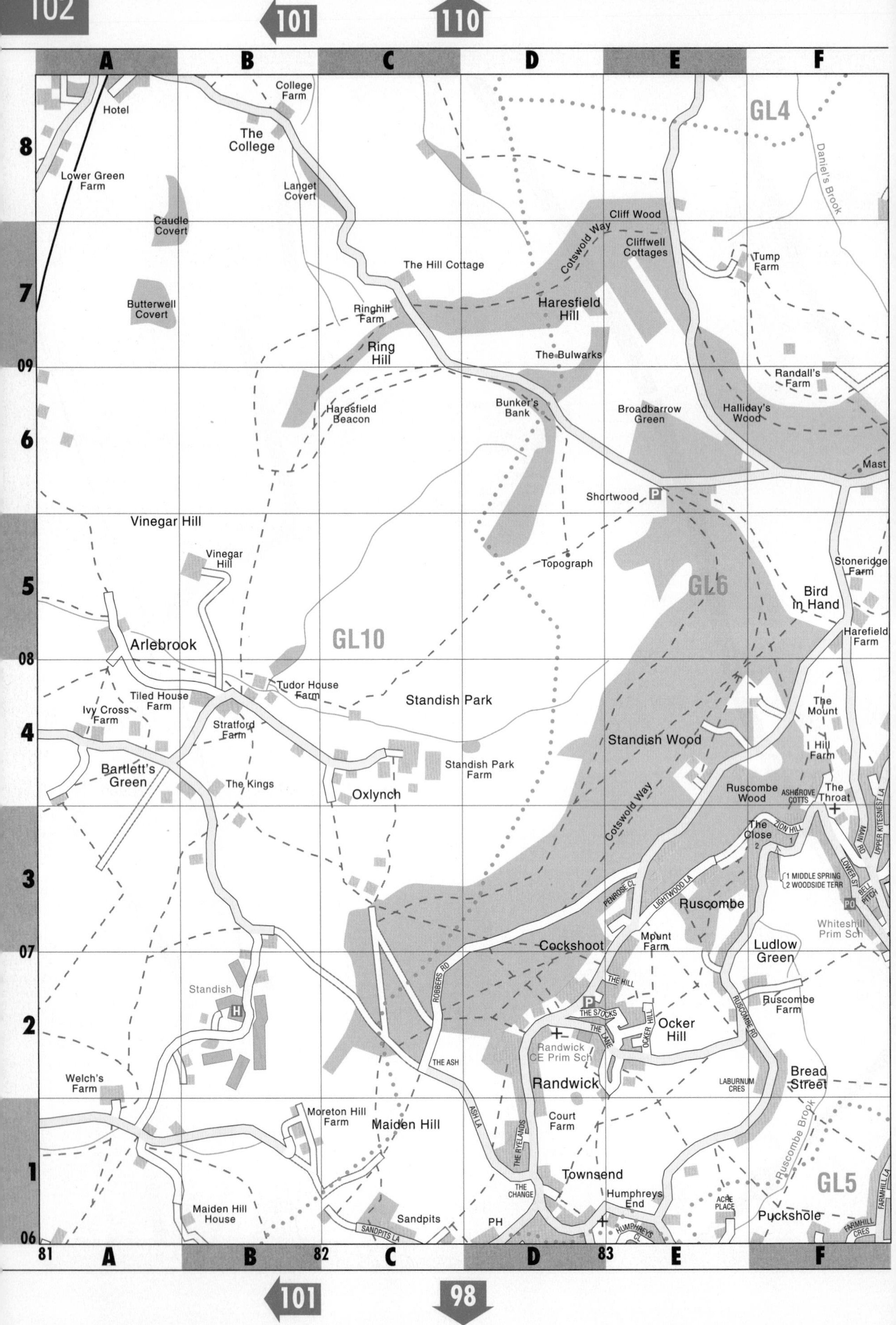
A
B
C
D
E
F
8
7
09
6
5
08
4
3
07
2
1
06
81
82
83
Hotel
College Farm
The College
Lower Green Farm
Langet Covert
Caudle Covert
Butterwell Covert
Cliff Wood
Cotswold Way
Cliffwell Cottages
Tump Farm
GL4
Daniel's Brook
The Hill Cottage
Ringhill Farm
Haresfield Hill
Ring Hill
The Bulwarks
Randall's Farm
Haresfield Beacon
Bunker's Bank
Broadbarrow Green
Halliday's Wood
Mast
Shortwood
P
Vinegar Hill
Vinegar Hill
Topograph
GL6
Stoneridge Farm
Bird in Hand
Arlebrook
GL10
Harefield Farm
Tudor House Farm
Tiled House Farm
Ivy Cross Farm
Standish Park
The Mount
Stratford Farm
Standish Wood
Hill Farm
Bartlett's Green
Standish Park Farm
The Kings
Oxlynch
Ruscombe Wood
ASHGROVE COTTS
The Throat
UPPER KITESNEST LA
The Close
ZION HILL
MAIN RD
LOWER ST
1 MIDDLE SPRING
2 WOODSIDE TERR
BELL PITCH
PO
PENROSE CL
LIGHTWOOD LA
Ruscombe
Whiteshill Prim Sch
Mount Farm
Cockshoot
Ludlow Green
ROBBERS RD
THE HILL
Standish
H
P
THE STOCKS
Ruscombe Farm
RUSCOMBE RD
OCKER HILL
Ocker Hill
THE LANE
Randwick CE Prim Sch
THE ASH
Welch's Farm
Randwick
LABURNUM CRES
Bread Street
Moreton Hill Farm
Maiden Hill
ASH LA
Court Farm
THE RYELANDS
Ruscombe Brook
GL5
Townsend
FARMHILL LA
THE CHANGE
Humphreys End
Maiden Hill House
ACRE PLACE
Puckshole
Sandpits
PH
SANDPITS LA
HUMPHREYS CL
FARMHILL CRES

111
104

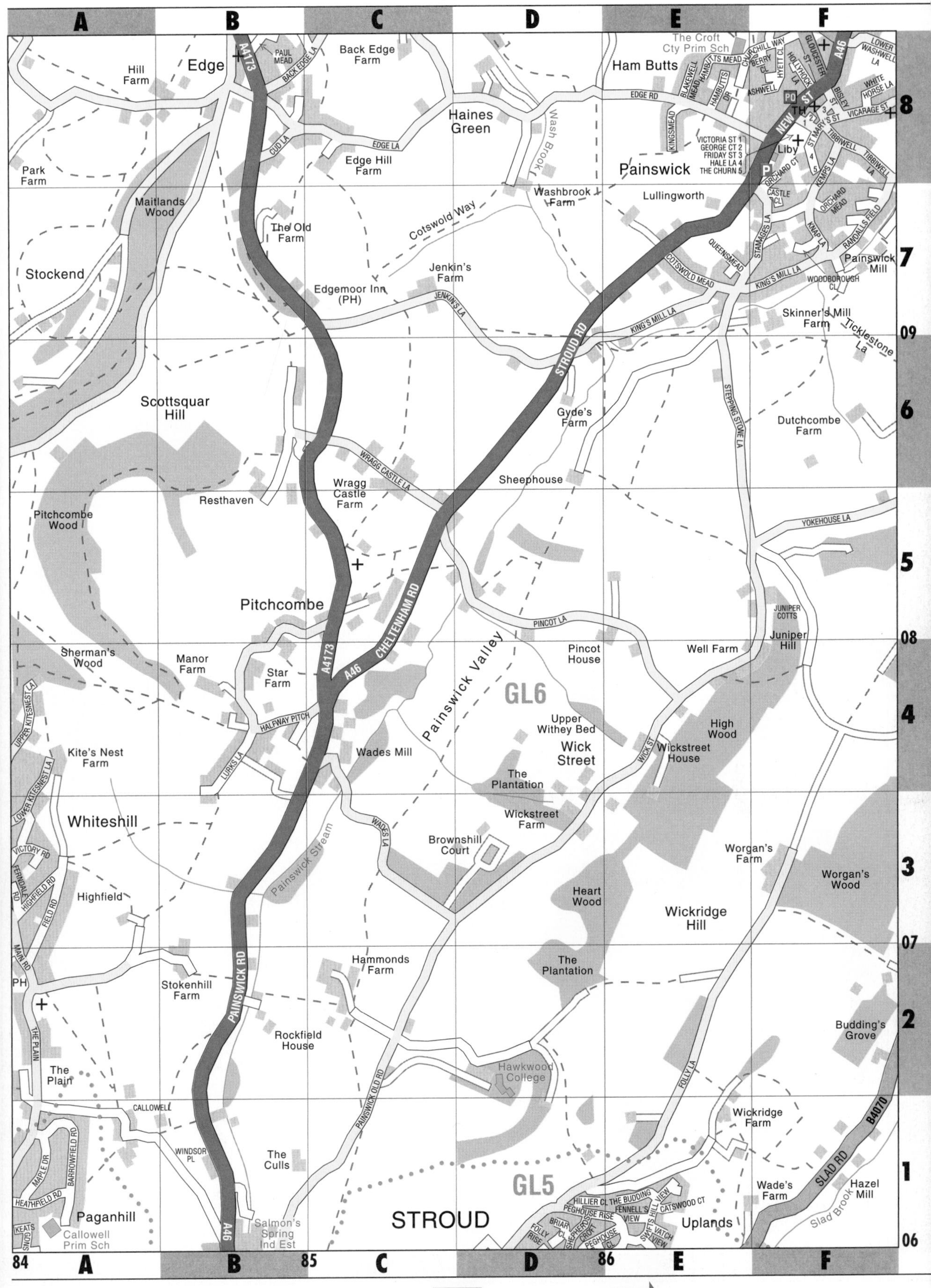

99
104

103
112

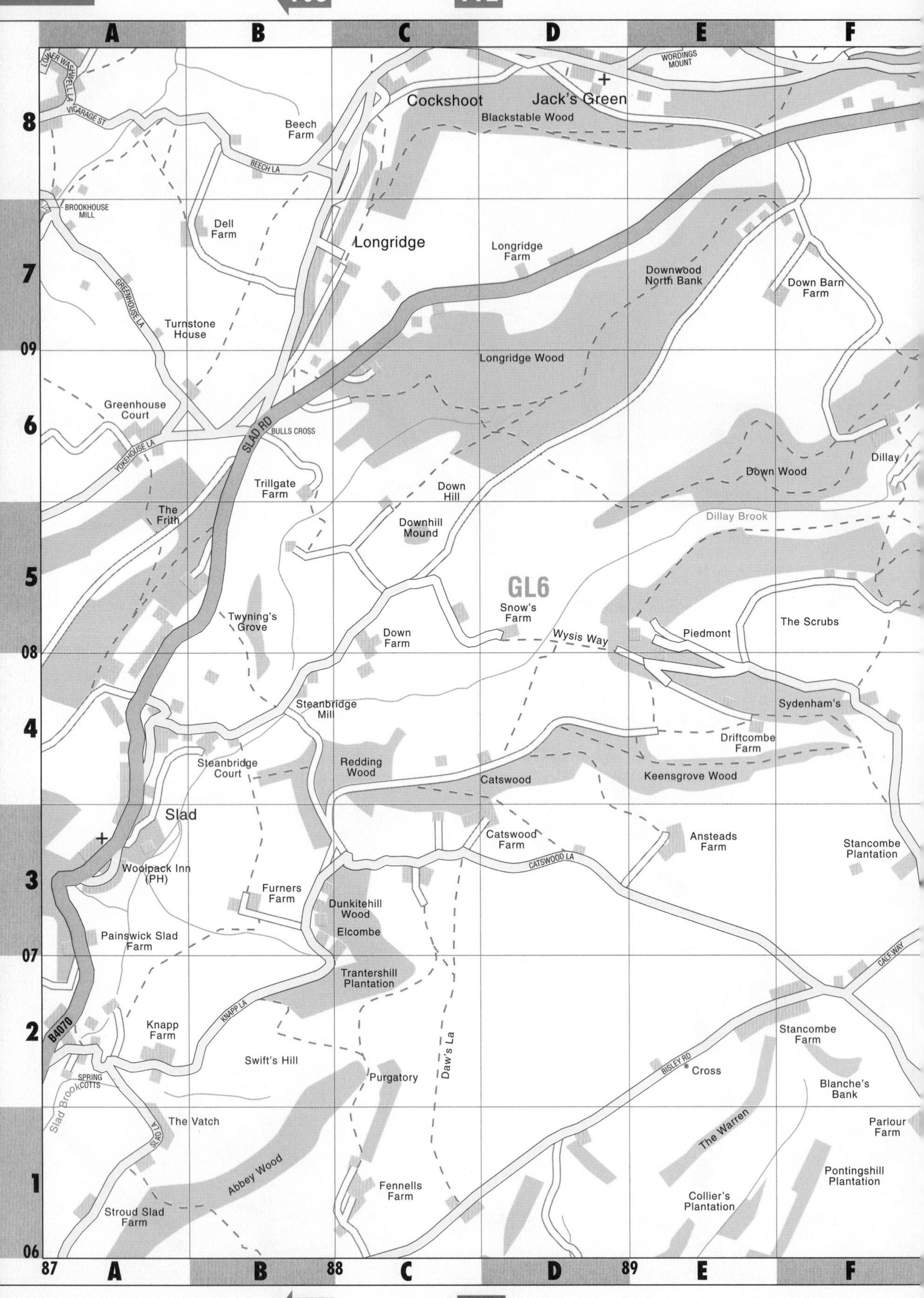

103
148

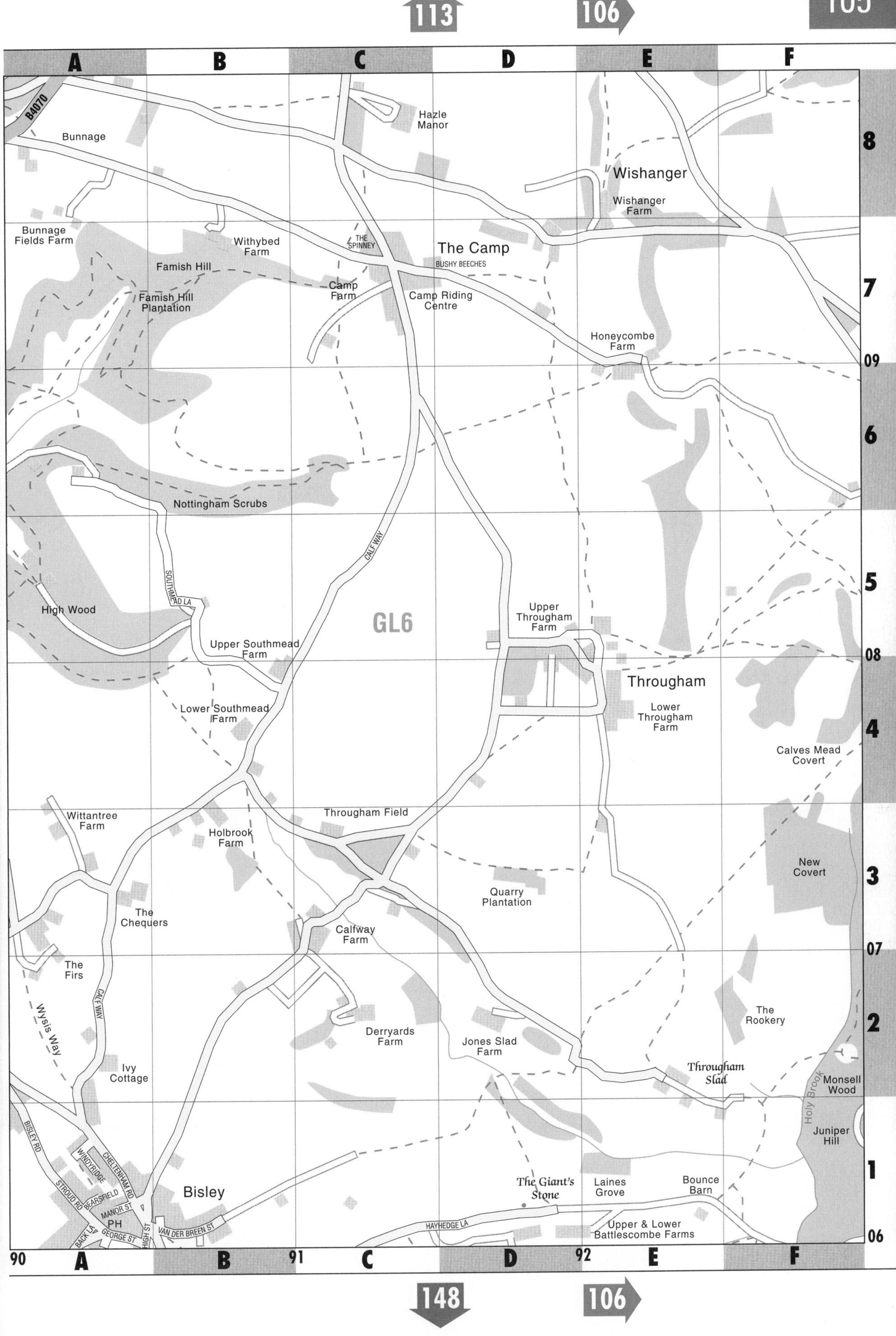
113
106
A
B
C
D
E
F
B4070
Bunnage
Hazle
Manor
Wishanger
Wishanger
Farm
Bunnage
Fields Farm
Withybed
Farm
THE
SPINNEY
The Camp
BUSHY BEECHES
Famish Hill
Camp
Farm
Camp Riding
Centre
Famish Hill
Plantation
Honeycombe
Farm
Nottingham Scrubs
CALF WAY
SOUTHMEAD LA
GL6
High Wood
Upper
Througham
Farm
Upper Southmead
Farm
Througham
Lower Southmead
Farm
Lower
Througham
Farm
Calves Mead
Covert
Wittantree
Farm
Througham Field
Holbrook
Farm
New
Covert
Quarry
Plantation
The
Chequers
Calfway
Farm
The
Firs
CALF WAY
Wysis Way
Derryards
Farm
Jones Slad
Farm
The
Rookery
Througham
Slad
Monsell
Wood
Ivy
Cottage
Holy Brook
Juniper
Hill
BISLEY RD
WINDYRIDGE
CHELTENHAM RD
STROUD RD
BEARSFIELD
MANOR ST
PH
BACK LA
GEORGE ST
HIGH ST
Bisley
VAN DER BREEN ST
The Giant's
Stone
HAYHEDGE LA
Laines
Grove
Bounce
Barn
Upper & Lower
Battlescombe Farms
8
7
09
6
5
08
4
3
07
2
1
06
90
91
92
148
106

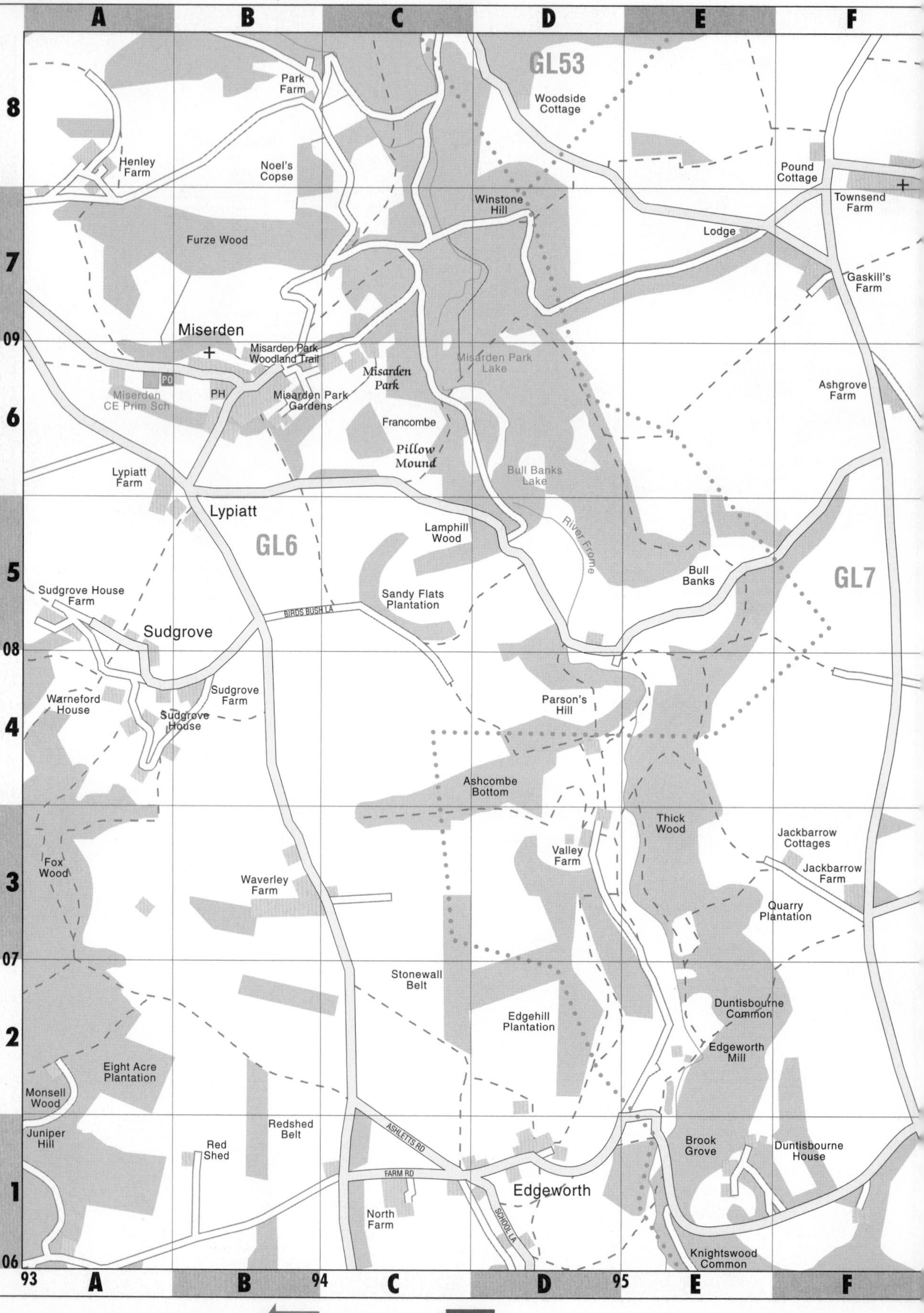

A B C D E F
8 7 09 6 5 08 4 3 07 2 1 06
93 94 95
GL53
Park Farm
Woodside Cottage
Henley Farm
Noel's Copse
Pound Cottage
Winstone Hill
Townsend Farm
Lodge
Furze Wood
Gaskill's Farm
Miserden
Misarden Park Woodland Trail
PO
Misarden Park Lake
Misarden Park
Ashgrove Farm
Miserden CE Prim Sch
PH
Misarden Park Gardens
Francombe
Pillow Mound
Lypiatt Farm
Bull Banks Lake
Lypiatt
GL6
Lamphill Wood
River Frome
Bull Banks
GL7
Sudgrove House Farm
Sandy Flats Plantation
BIRDS BUSH LA
Sudgrove
Warneford House
Sudgrove Farm
Parson's Hill
Sudgrove House
Ashcombe Bottom
Thick Wood
Jackbarrow Cottages
Valley Farm
Jackbarrow Farm
Fox Wood
Waverley Farm
Quarry Plantation
Stonewall Belt
Duntisbourne Common
Edgehill Plantation
Edgeworth Mill
Eight Acre Plantation
Monsell Wood
Redshed Belt
Juniper Hill
Red Shed
ASHLETTS RD
Brook Grove
Duntisbourne House
FARM RD
Edgeworth
North Farm
SCHOOL LA
Knightswood Common

115
158
A
B
C
D
E
F
Cot Abbey
Selscomb Wood
Cotswold Park
GL53
A417
PIKE RD
FOSS FIELD
Winstone
JACKBARROW RD
BACK LA
SCHOOL HILL
NOTCH RD
North Bank
Manor Farm
CROFT LA
South Bank
Cotswold Farm
PH
The Grove
Playing Field
Field's Copse
Rectory Farm
Field's Farm
EALY HILL
GL7
Long Furlong Barn
BURCOMBE LA
Yew Tree Farm
YH
Dix's Barn
Rendcombury
Abbots Farm
Duntisbourne Abbots
Sly's Wall Plantation
Ford's
Ford
Duntisbourne Leer
Nutbeam Farm
New Barn Farm
Beech Copse
CRABTREE LA
Manor Farm
WELSH WAY
Hoar Stone
Middle Duntisbourne
Longhill
LONGHILL RD
Rough Plantation
Macmillan Way
Duntisbourne Grove
Macmillan Way
Duntisbourne Rouse
8
7
09
6
5
08
4
3
07
2
1
06
96
97
98
149
158

157 116

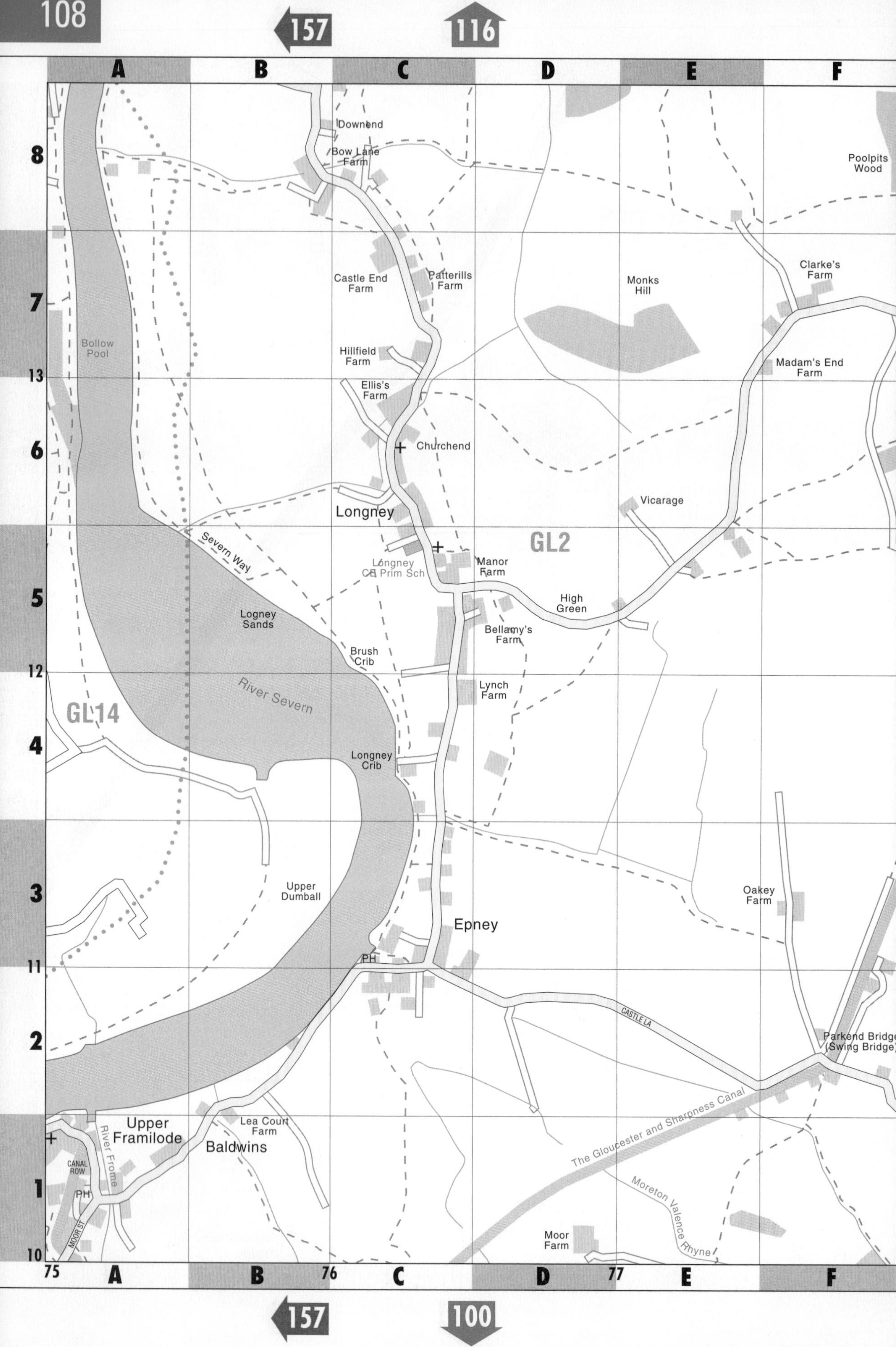

157 100

117
110

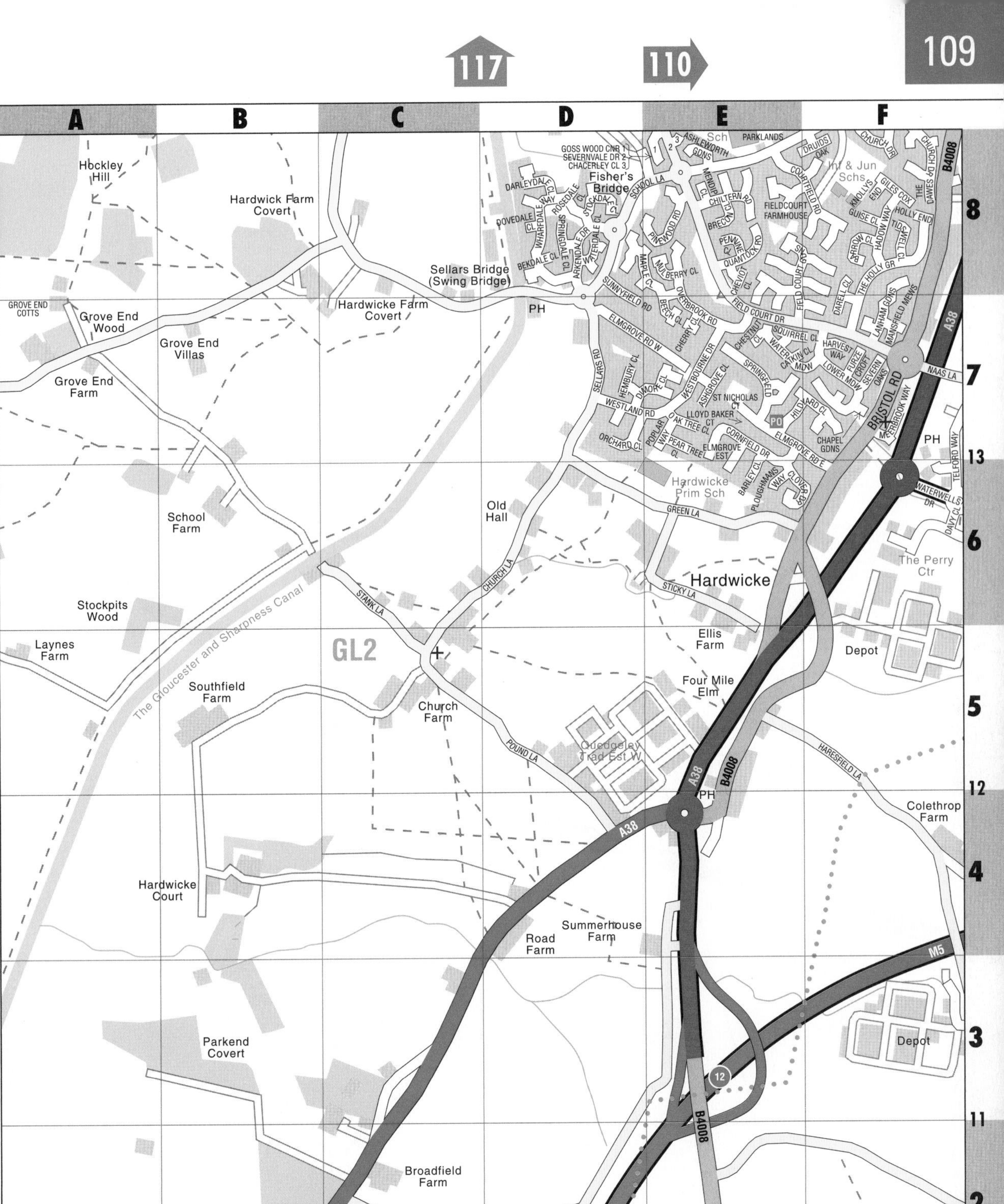

101
110

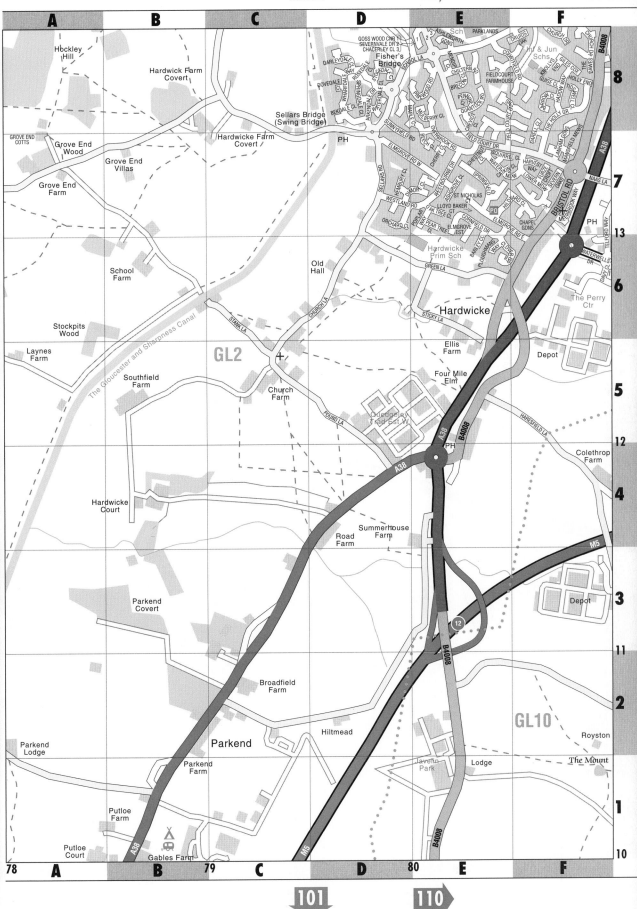

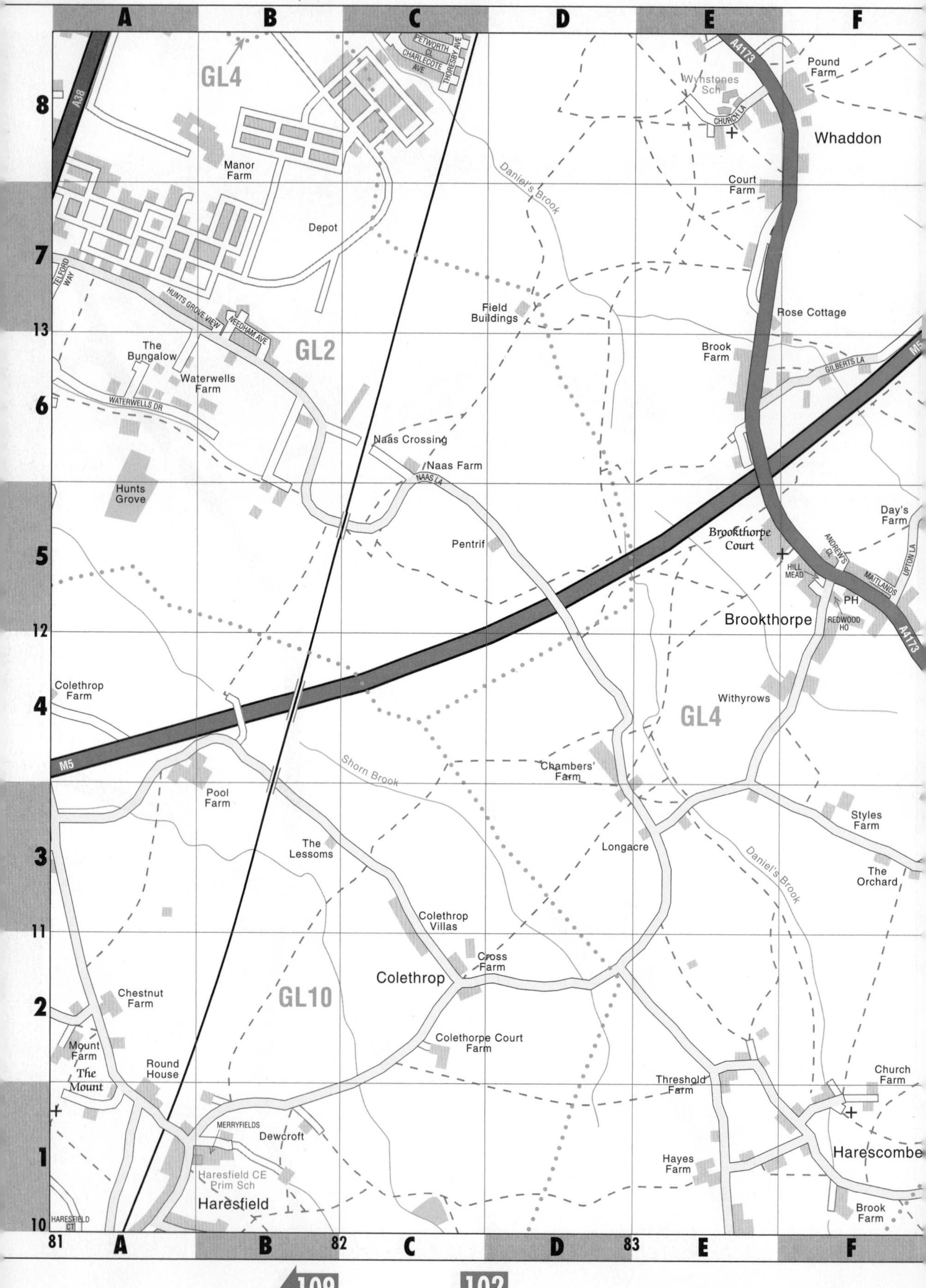

A B C D E F
8 7 13 6 5 12 4 3 11 2 1 10
GL4
A38
Manor Farm
Depot
PETWORTH CL
CHARLECOTE AVE
THORESBY AVE
Wynstones Sch
CHURCH LA
A4173
Pound Farm
Whaddon
Court Farm
Daniel's Brook
TELFORD WAY
HUNTS GROVE VIEW
NEEDHAM AVE
GL2
Field Buildings
Rose Cottage
Brook Farm
GILBERTS LA
M5
The Bungalow
Waterwells Farm
WATERWELLS DR
Naas Crossing
Naas Farm
NAAS LA
Hunts Grove
Pentrif
Brookthorpe Court
Day's Farm
ANDREW'S CL
UPTON LA
HILL MEAD
MAITLANDS
PH
Brookthorpe
REDWOOD HO
Colethrop Farm
Withyrows
GL4
M5
Shorn Brook
Chambers' Farm
Pool Farm
Styles Farm
The Lessoms
Longacre
Daniel's Brook
The Orchard
Colethrop Villas
Cross Farm
Colethrop
Chestnut Farm
GL10
Colethorpe Court Farm
Mount Farm
The Mount
Round House
Church Farm
Threshold Farm
MERRYFIELDS
Dewcroft
Hayes Farm
Harescombe
Haresfield CE Prim Sch
Haresfield
HARESFIELD CT
Brook Farm
81 A B 82 C D 83 E F

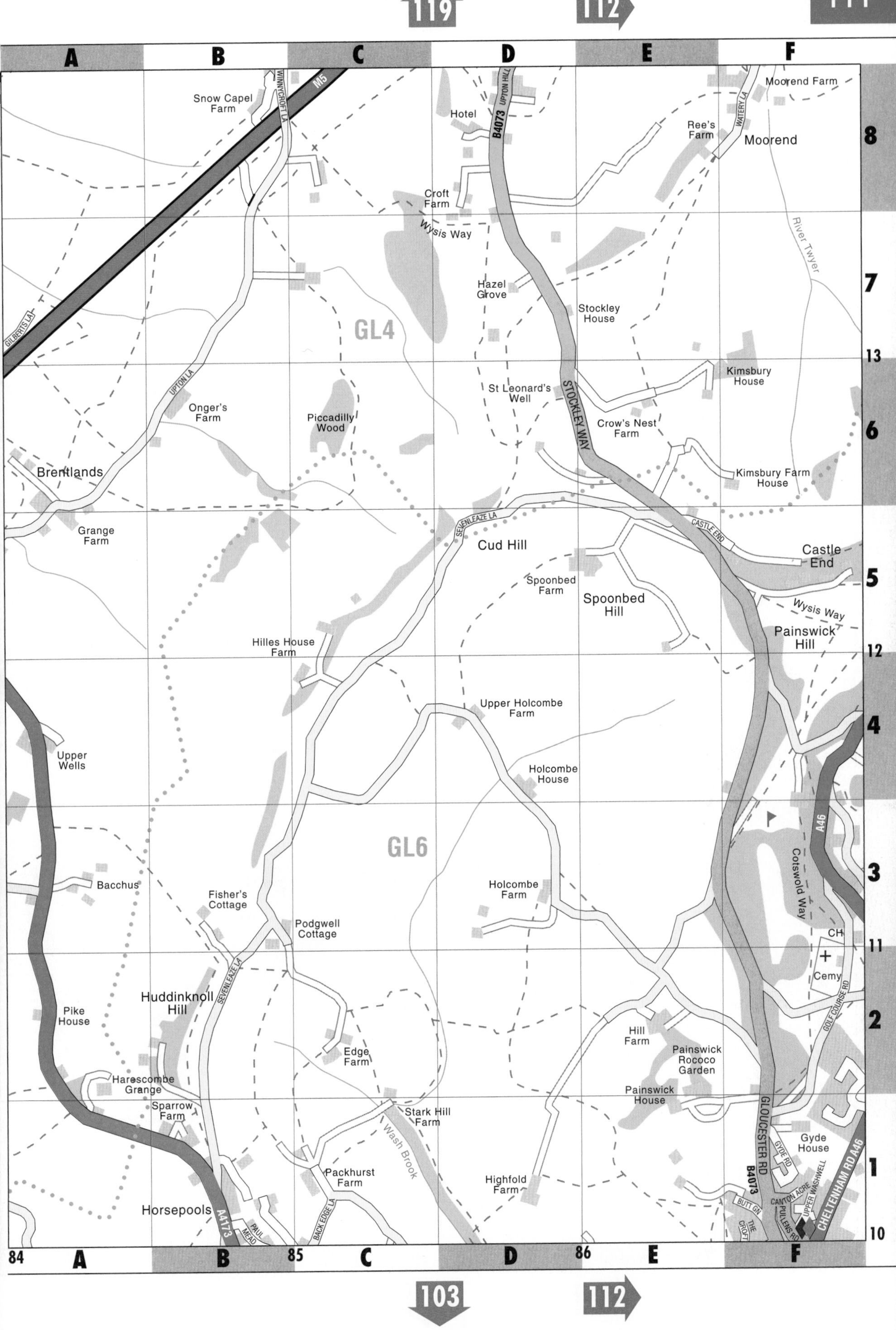
119
112
A
B
C
D
E
F
M5
WINNYCROFT LA
UPTON HILL
B4073
Snow Capel
Farm
Hotel
Moorend Farm
WATERY LA
Ree's
Farm
Moorend
8
Croft
Farm
Wysis Way
River Twyer
Hazel
Grove
Stockley
House
7
GILBERTS LA
GL4
13
UPTON LA
Onger's
Farm
Piccadilly
Wood
St Leonard's
Well
STOCKLEY WAY
Kimsbury
House
Crow's Nest
Farm
6
Brentlands
Kimsbury Farm
House
Grange
Farm
SEVENLEAZE LA
Cud Hill
CASTLE END
Castle
End
Spoonbed
Farm
Spoonbed
Hill
5
Wysis Way
Painswick
Hill
Hilles House
Farm
12
Upper Holcombe
Farm
4
Upper
Wells
Holcombe
House
A46
GL6
Cotswold Way
3
Bacchus
Holcombe
Farm
Fisher's
Cottage
Podgwell
Cottage
CH
11
Cemy
GOLF COURSE RD
Huddinknoll
Hill
SEVENLEAZE LA
Pike
House
Hill
Farm
Painswick
Rococo
Garden
2
Edge
Farm
Harescombe
Grange
Painswick
House
Sparrow
Farm
Stark Hill
Farm
GLOUCESTER RD
Wash Brook
Gyde
House
GYDE RD
1
Packhurst
Farm
Highfold
Farm
B4073
CANTON ACRE
UPPER WASHWELL
CHELTENHAM RD A46
BUTT GN
PULLENS RD
THE CROFT
Horsepools
A4173
PAUL MEAD
BACK EDGE LA
10
84
85
86
103
112

111
120

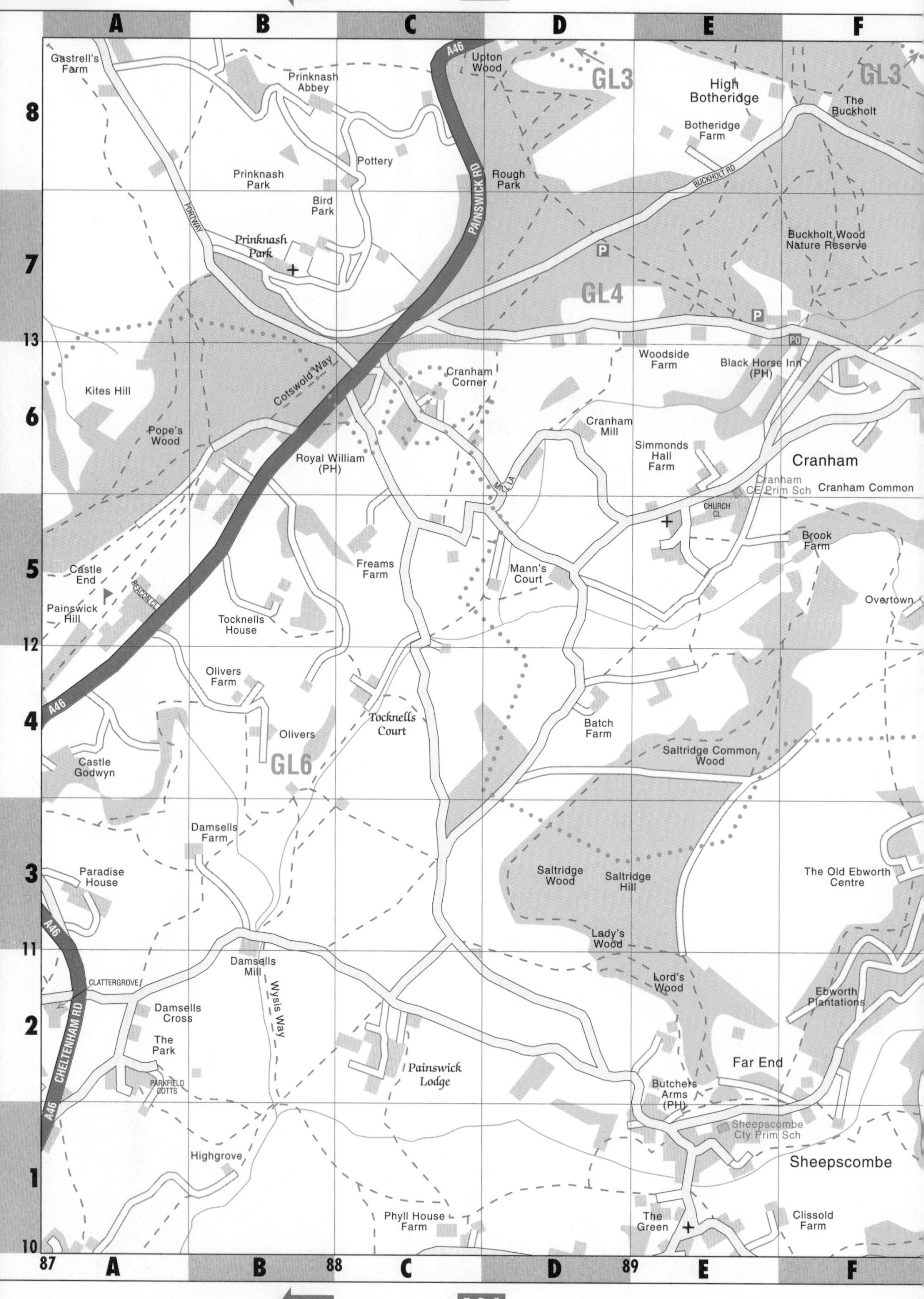

111
104

121
114

105
114

113
122

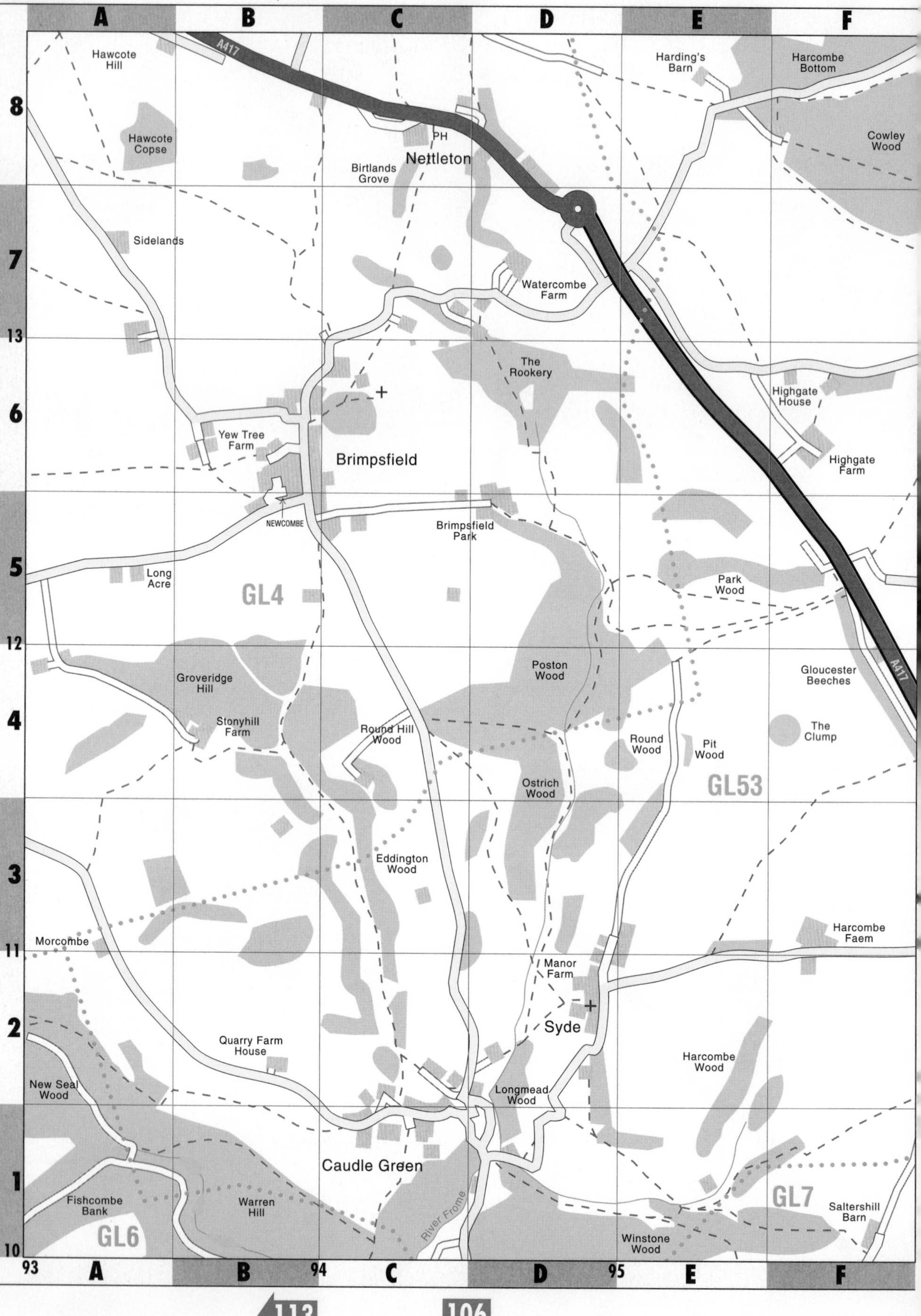

A B C D E F

8
7
13
6
5
12
4
3
11
2
1
10

Hawcote Hill
A417
Harding's Barn
Harcombe Bottom
Hawcote Copse
PH
Nettleton
Cowley Wood
Birtlands Grove
Sidelands
Watercombe Farm
The Rookery
Highgate House
Yew Tree Farm
Brimpsfield
Highgate Farm
NEWCOMBE
Brimpsfield Park
Long Acre
GL4
Park Wood
Groveridge Hill
Poston Wood
Gloucester Beeches
A417
Stonyhill Farm
Round Hill Wood
Round Wood
Pit Wood
The Clump
Ostrich Wood
GL53
Eddington Wood
Morcombe
Harcombe Faem
Manor Farm
Syde
Quarry Farm House
Harcombe Wood
New Seal Wood
Longmead Wood
Caudle Green
Fishcombe Bank
Warren Hill
River Frome
GL7
Saltershill Barn
GL6
Winstone Wood

93 A B 94 C D 95 E F

113
106

123
158
A
B
C
D
E
F
8
7
13
6
5
12
4
3
11
2
1
10
96
97
98
Lower Cockleford
A435
Cockleford Farm
Trout Farm
Churn Bank
River Churn
Butlers Hill Farm
Ward's Wood
Bubb's Hill Wood
Bubb's Hill
Butler's Farm
HIGH CROSS
High Cross
The Bungalow
Enfield Farm
HILL VIEW
Ward's Hey
Sparrowthorn
Slutswell
Ivy Cottage Farm
Elkstone
GL53
Manor Farm
Hillclose Grove
Paynters Cottage
Hall's Grove
Lion's Grove
Sadlers Farm
Hall's Grove
Combend Manor
Elkstone Farm
Hailer's Wood
Power's Wood
The Clumps
Westedge Wood
Ermin House Farm
Combend Farm
Pine Tree Cottage
Watercombe Farm
The Ash
Bromsley Wood
PH
Shewel Wood
Damson Grove
Adder Bank
Fosse Farm
Beechpike
PIKE RD
GL7
Winstone Radio Station
A417
GL7
107
158

165
124

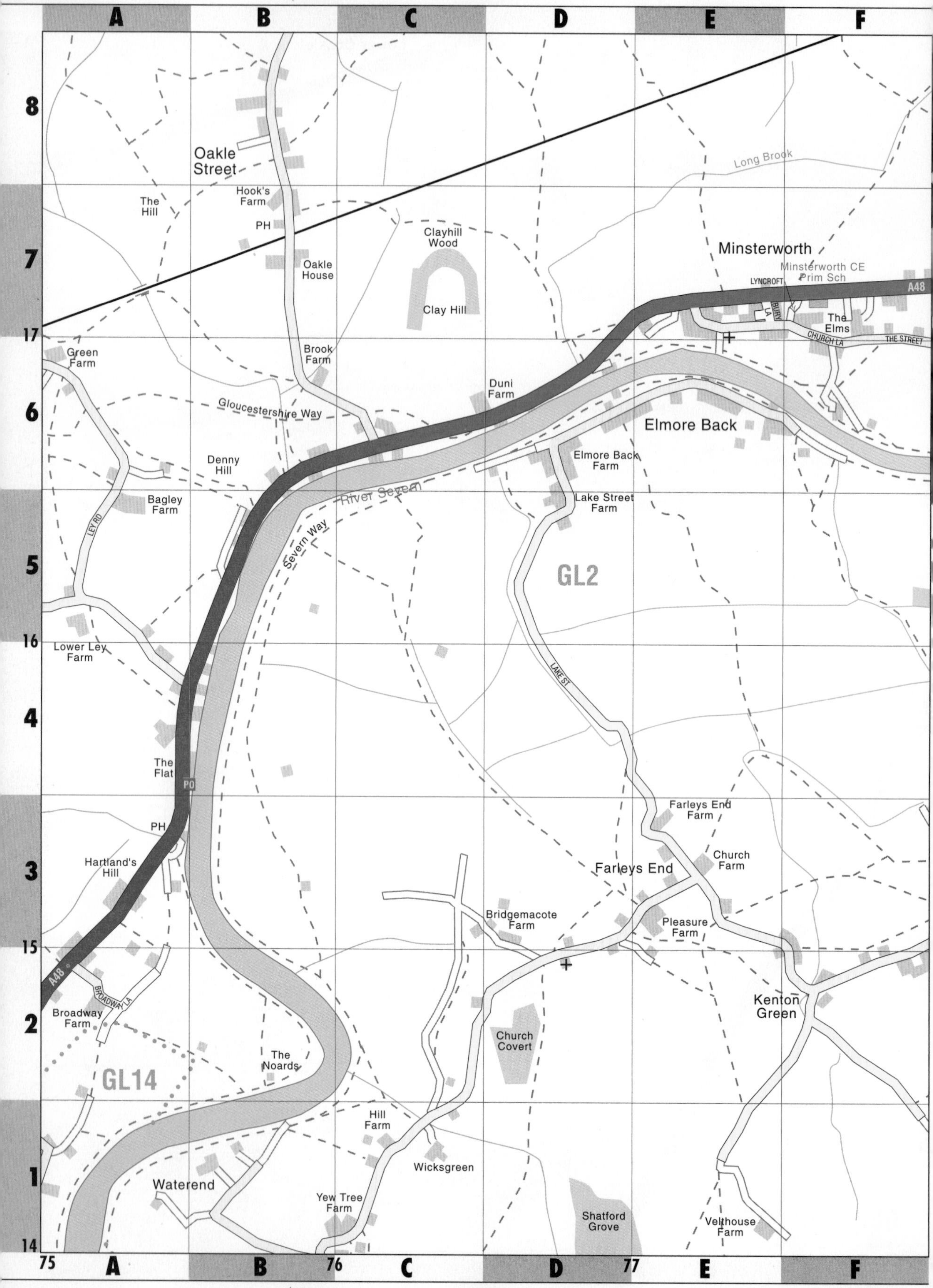

165
108

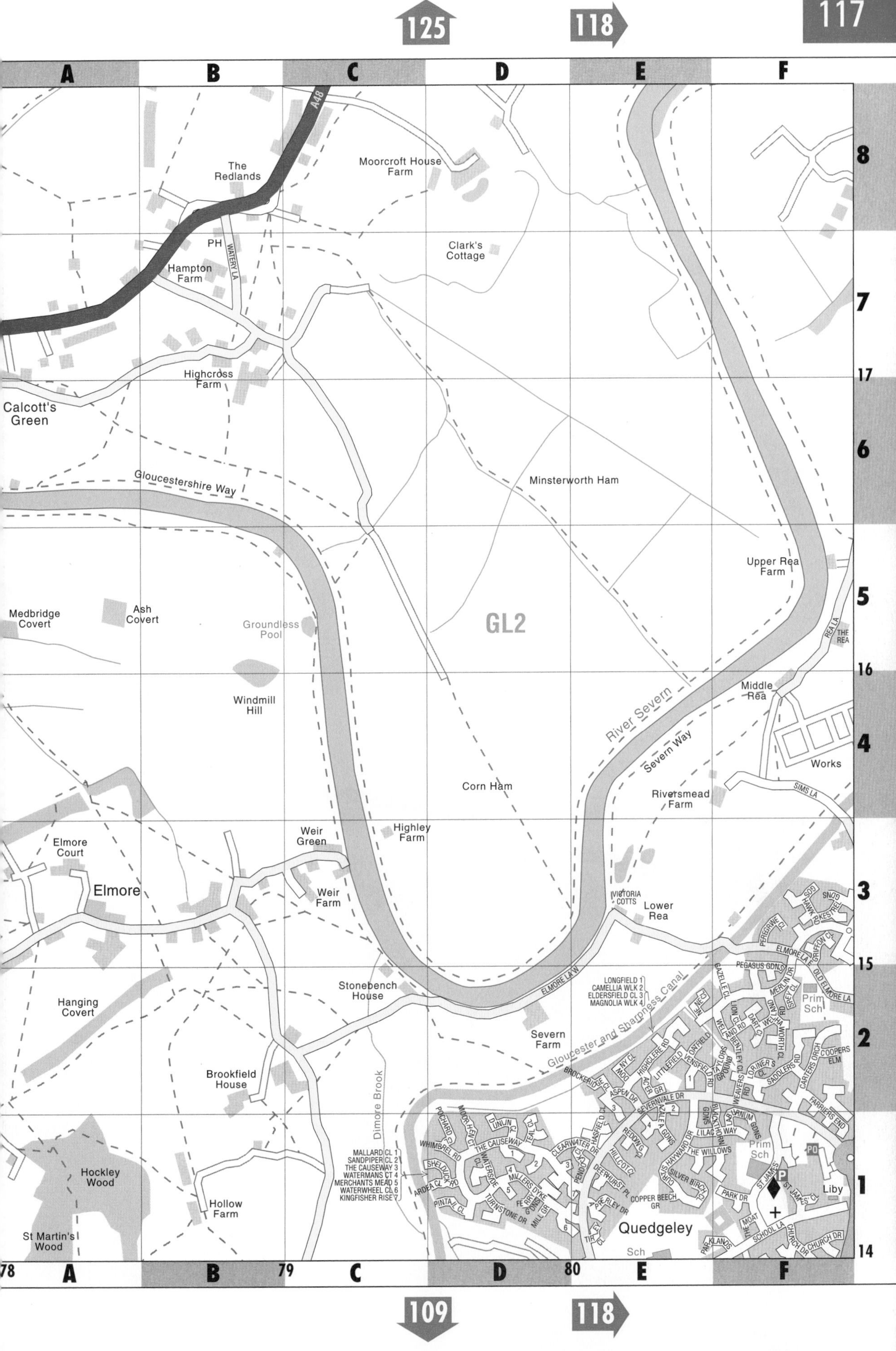
125
118
A
B
C
D
E
F
8
7
17
6
5
16
4
3
15
2
1
14
78
79
80
A48
The Redlands
Moorcroft House Farm
PH
WATERY LA
Hampton Farm
Clark's Cottage
Highcross Farm
Calcott's Green
Gloucestershire Way
Minsterworth Ham
Upper Rea Farm
Medbridge Covert
Ash Covert
Groundless Pool
GL2
REA LA
THE REA
Windmill Hill
Middle Rea
River Severn
Severn Way
Works
Corn Ham
SIMS LA
Riversmead Farm
Elmore Court
Weir Green
Highley Farm
Elmore
Weir Farm
VICTORIA COTTS
Lower Rea
Stonebench House
ELMORE LA W
LONGFIELD 1
CAMELLIA WLK 2
ELDERSFIELD CL 3
MAGNOLIA WLK 4
Gloucester and Sharpness Canal
Hanging Covert
Severn Farm
Brookfield House
Dimore Brook
Hockley Wood
MALLARD CL 1
SANDPIPER CL 2
THE CAUSEWAY 3
WATERMANS CT 4
MERCHANTS MEAD 5
WATERWHEEL CL 6
KINGFISHER RISE 7
Hollow Farm
St Martin's Wood
Quedgeley
Sch
Prim Sch
Liby
PO
ELMORE LA E
PEGASUS GDNS
OLD ELMORE LA
SEVERNVALE DR
THE WILLOWS
COPPER BEECH GR
PARK DR
SCHOOL LA
CHURCH DR
ST JAMES' CL
THE CAUSEWAY
TURNSTONE DR
MILL GR
BROCKERIDGE CL
CLEARWATER DR
DEERHURST PL
SILVER BIRCH CL
HAYWARD DR
LILAC WAY
WEAVERS RD
COOPERS ELM
SADDLERS RD
CARTERS ORCH
FARRIERS END
HIGHCLERE RD
LITTLEFIELD
ORTFIELD
PEREGRINE CL
GRIFFON CL
MERLIN DR
WHIMBREL RD
SHELDUCK RD
ARDEA CL
PINTAIL CL
POCHARD CL
MOORHEN CT
TEAL CL
DUNLIN CL
HILLCOT CL
ASPEN DR
A
B
C
D
E
F
109
118

For full street detail of the highlighted area see page 196.

F7
1 LLANDILO ST
2 CARMARTHEN ST
3 FARADAY CL
4 MASSEY PAR
5 DORA WLK
6 TARRINGTON RD

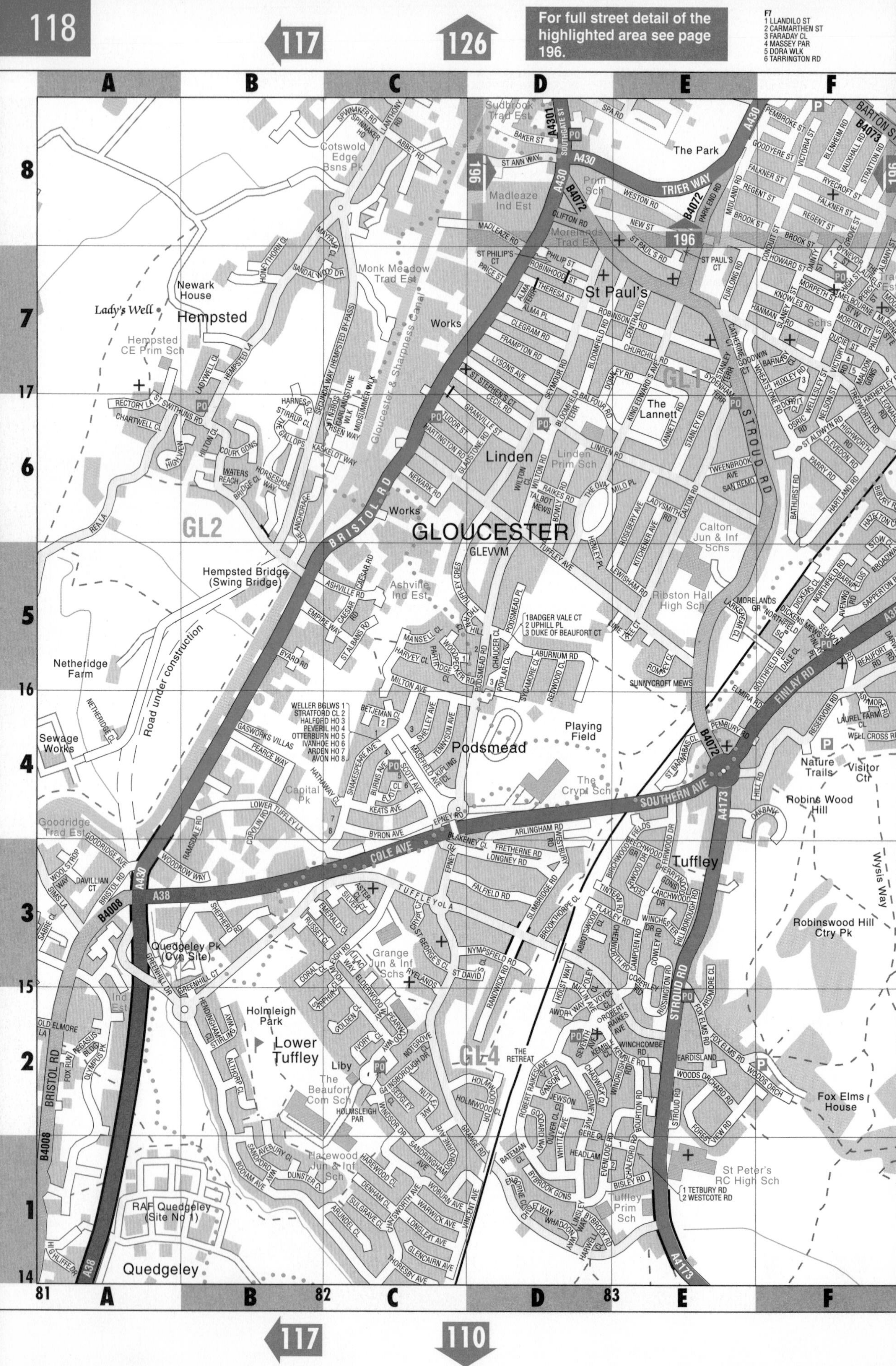

127
120

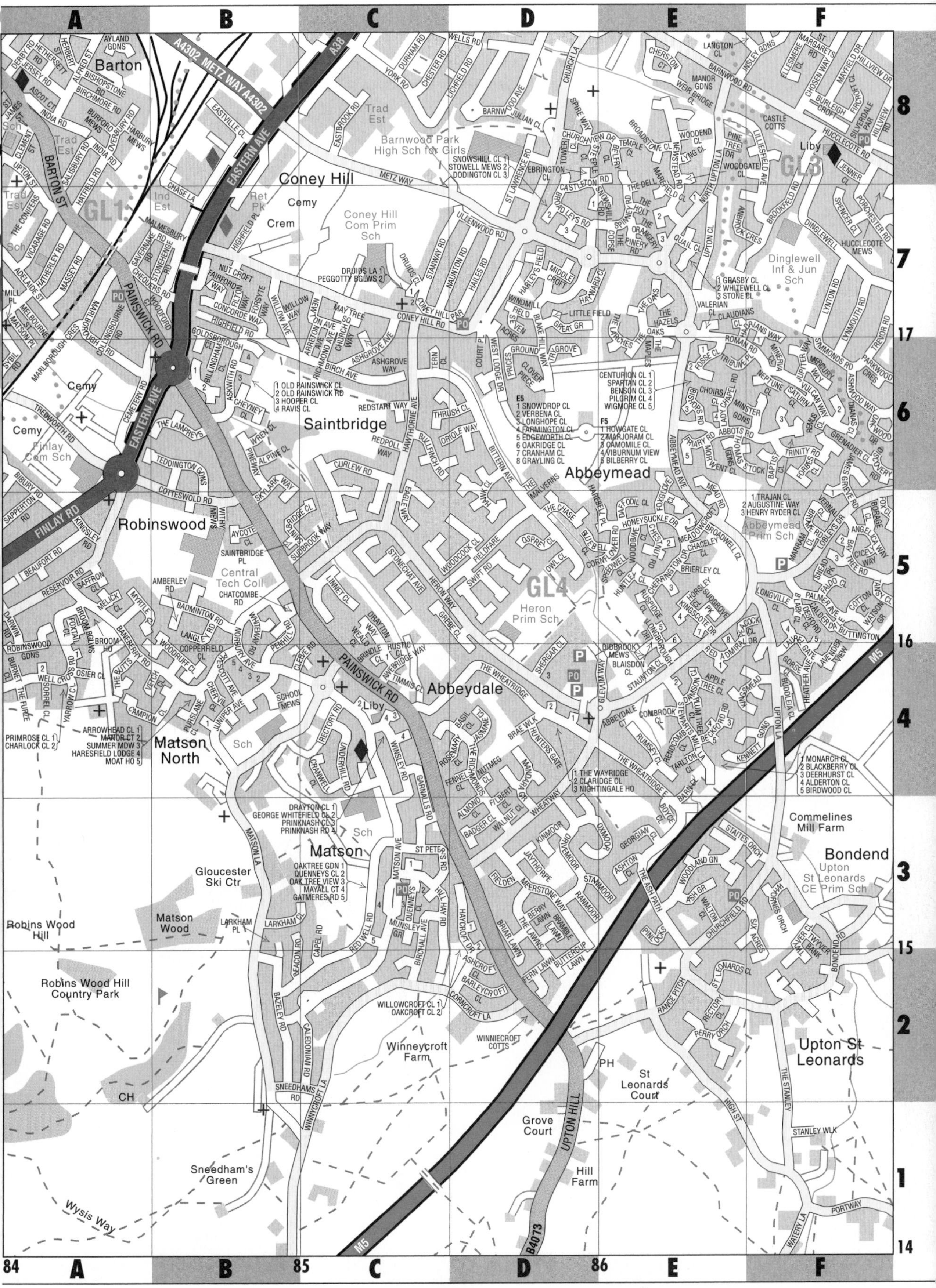

A B C D E F

Barton
Coney Hill
Saintbridge
Abbeymead
Robinswood
Abbeydale
Matson North
Matson
GL1
GL3
GL4
Dinglewell Inf & Jun Sch
Barnwood Park High Sch for Girls
Coney Hill Com Prim Sch
Finlay Com Sch
Central Tech Coll
Heron Prim Sch
Abbeymead Prim Sch
Gloucester Ski Ctr
Matson Wood
Robins Wood Hill
Robins Wood Hill Country Park
Commelines Mill Farm
Bondend
Upton St Leonards CE Prim Sch
Upton St Leonards
Winneycroft Farm
St Leonards Court
Grove Court
Hill Farm
Sneedham's Green
Wysis Way
A4302 METZ WAY A4302
EASTERN AVE
PAINSWICK RD
FINLAY RD
UPTON HILL
B4073
M5

1 SNOWSHILL CL
2 STOWELL MEWS
3 DODINGTON CL

1 DRUIDS LA
2 PEGGOTTY BGLWS

1 OLD PAINSWICK CL
2 OLD PAINSWICK RD
3 HOOPER CL
4 RAVIS CL

E5
1 SNOWDROP CL
2 VERBENA CL
3 LONGHOPE CL
4 FARMINGTON CL
5 EDGEWORTH CL
6 OAKRIDGE CL
7 CRANHAM CL
8 GRAYLING CL

F5
1 HOWGATE CL
2 MARJORAM CL
3 CAMOMILE CL
4 VIBURNUM VIEW
5 BILBERRY CL

1 CENTURION CL
2 SPARTAN CL
3 BENSON CL
4 PILGRIM CL
5 WIGMORE CL

1 GRASBY CL
2 WHITEWELL CL
3 STONE CL

1 TRAJAN CL
2 AUGUSTINE WAY
3 HENRY RYDER CL

1 ARROWHEAD CL
2 MANOR CT
3 SUMMER MDW
4 HARESFIELD LODGE
5 MOAT HO

1 PRIMROSE CL
2 CHARLOCK CL

1 THE WAYRIDGE
2 CLARIDGE CL
3 NIGHTINGALE HO

1 MONARCH CL
2 BLACKBERRY CL
3 DEERHURST CL
4 ALDERTON CL
5 BIRDWOOD CL

1 DRAYTON CL
2 GEORGE WHITEFIELD CL
3 PRINKNASH CL
4 PRINKNASH RD

1 OAKTREE GDN
2 QUENNEYS CL
3 OAK TREE VIEW
4 MAYALL CT
5 GATMERES RD

1 WILLOWCROFT CL
2 OAKCROFT CL

8 7 17 6 5 16 4 3 15 2 1 14

84 A B 85 C D 86 E F

111
120

A
B
C
D
E
F
The Noake
Noake Court Farm
Dean Farm
Hucclecote
GL51
Brockworth Court
Horsbere Brook
Playing Field
Brockworth
Brockworth Comp Sch
Liby
GLOUCESTER
Gloucester Bsns Pk
Airfield (dis)
Works
GL3
Watermead
Castle Hill
GL4
Droys Court
Abbotswood Farm
Green Street
Hotel
Nut Hill
Modewyke
Taena Pottery
Whitley Court
Cooper's Hill
Cooper's Hill Farm
Upton Wood
Brockworth Wood
Cooper's Hill Wood
Lakehouse Farm
Peaked Acres Cottage
Pincott Farm
Quarry (dis)
Great Witcombe Roman Villa
GL4
Cotswold Way
PAINSWICK RD
A46
A417
M5
1 HAMPTON CL
2 GREYSTONE LODGE
3 GRANSMOOR GRANGE
1 GLENVILLE PAR
2 MOGRIDGE CL
3 BLENHEIM HO
1 WHITWORTH MEWS
2 BERKELEY CL
WATERTON CL 1
GRIERSON CL 2
MONTGOMERY CL 3
GREENWOOD CL 4
THE PARADE 1
VICARAGE CT 2
POUND FARM CTYD 3
GLADIATOR CL 4
GANNET CL 5
BUCKHOLT WAY 6
HURRICANE RD
GOLF CLUB LA
VALIANT WAY
DELTA WAY
ERMIN ST
BROCKWORTH RD
BROCKWORTH COTTS
NUTHILL
PORTWAY
VALLEY LA
GREEN ST

129
122

113
122

121
130

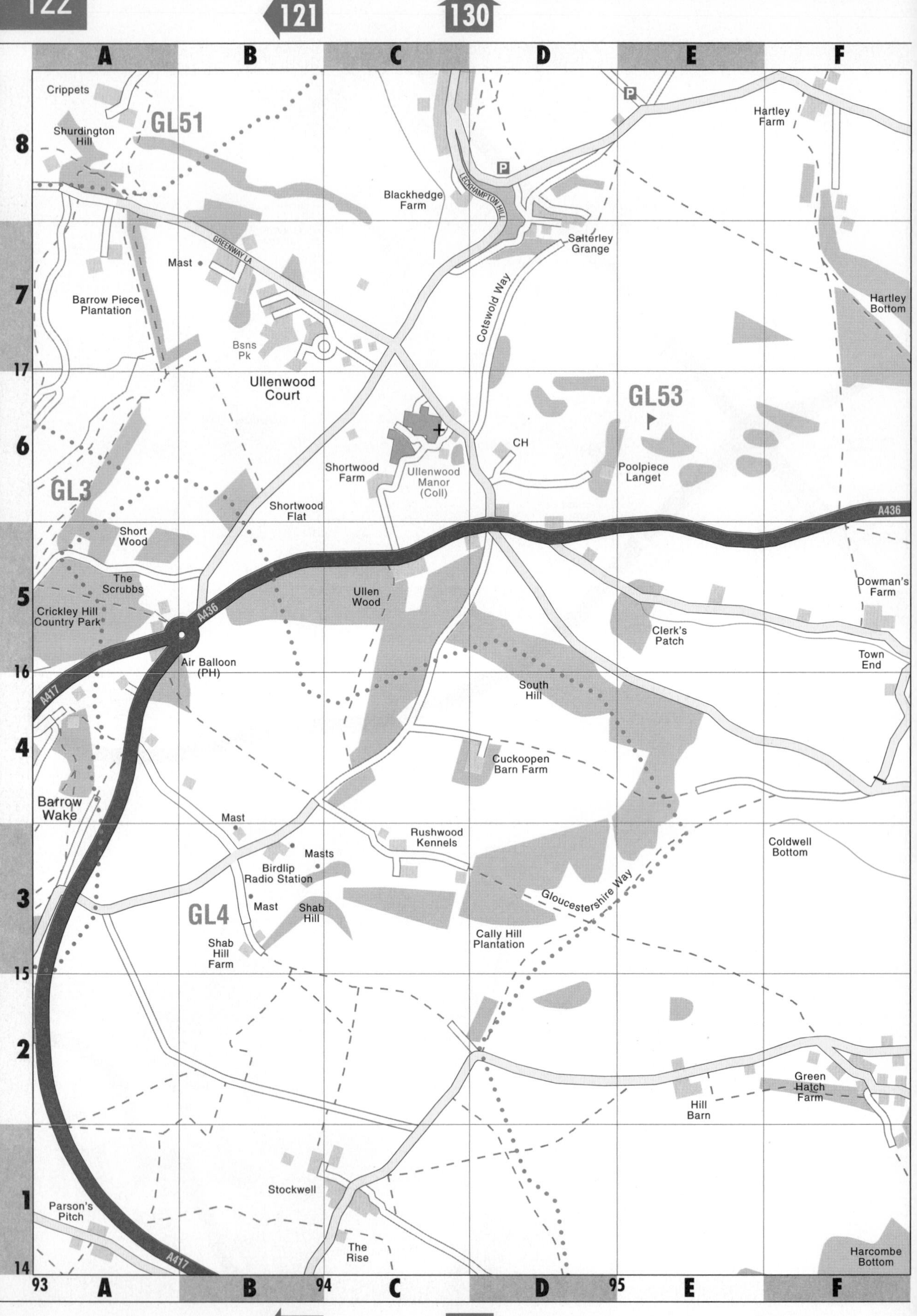

121
114

131
166

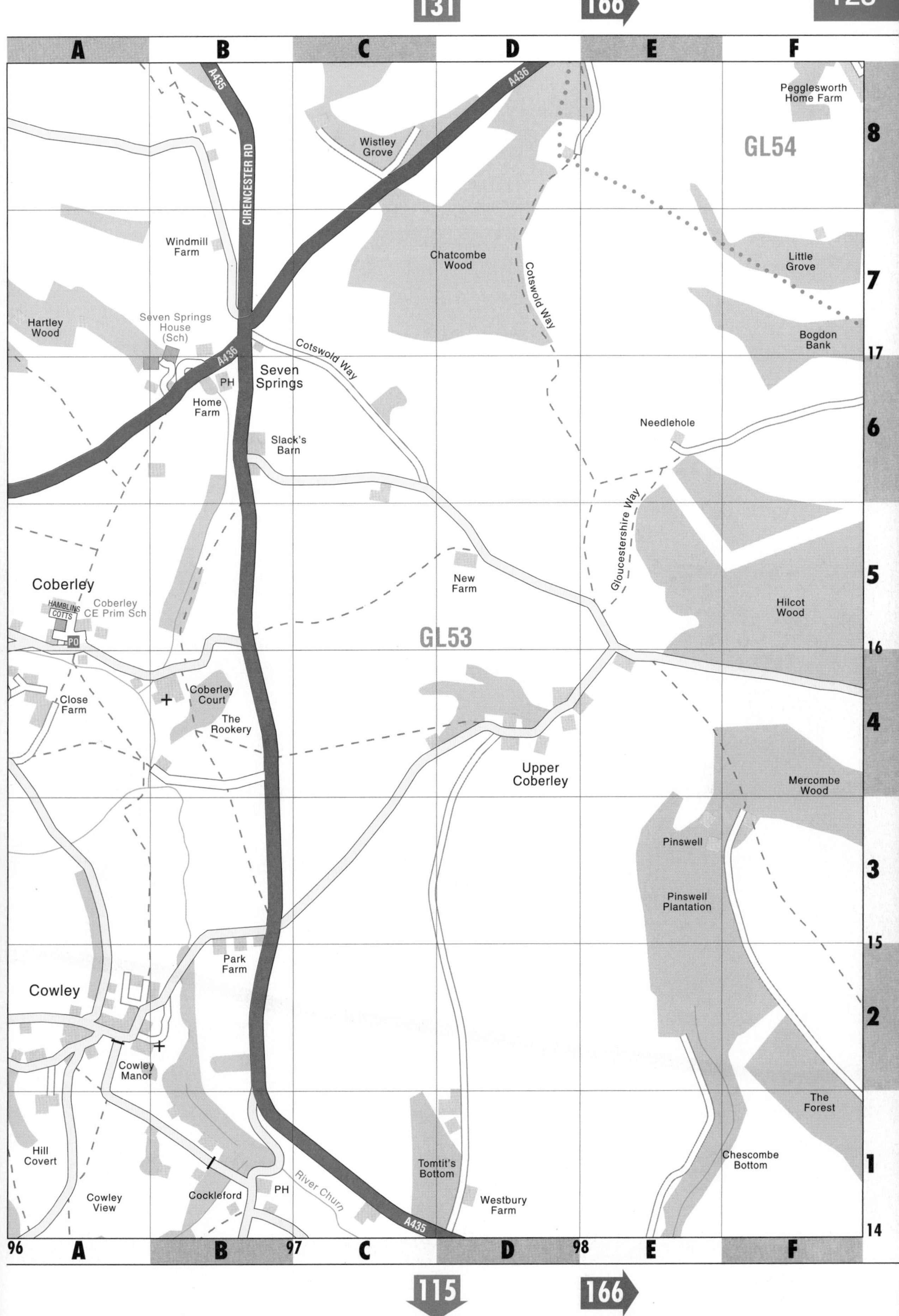
A
B
C
D
E
F
A435
A436
CIRENCESTER RD
Pegglesworth Home Farm
Wistley Grove
GL54
Windmill Farm
Chatcombe Wood
Cotswold Way
Little Grove
Hartley Wood
Seven Springs House (Sch)
Bogdon Bank
PH
Seven Springs
Home Farm
Needlehole
Slack's Barn
Gloucestershire Way
New Farm
Coberley
HAMBLINS COTTS
Coberley CE Prim Sch
Hilcot Wood
PO
GL53
Close Farm
Coberley Court
The Rookery
Upper Coberley
Mercombe Wood
Pinswell
Pinswell Plantation
Park Farm
Cowley
Cowley Manor
The Forest
Hill Covert
Tomtit's Bottom
Chescombe Bottom
Cowley View
Cockleford
PH
River Churn
Westbury Farm
8
7
17
6
5
16
4
3
15
2
1
14
96
97
98

115
166

165
171

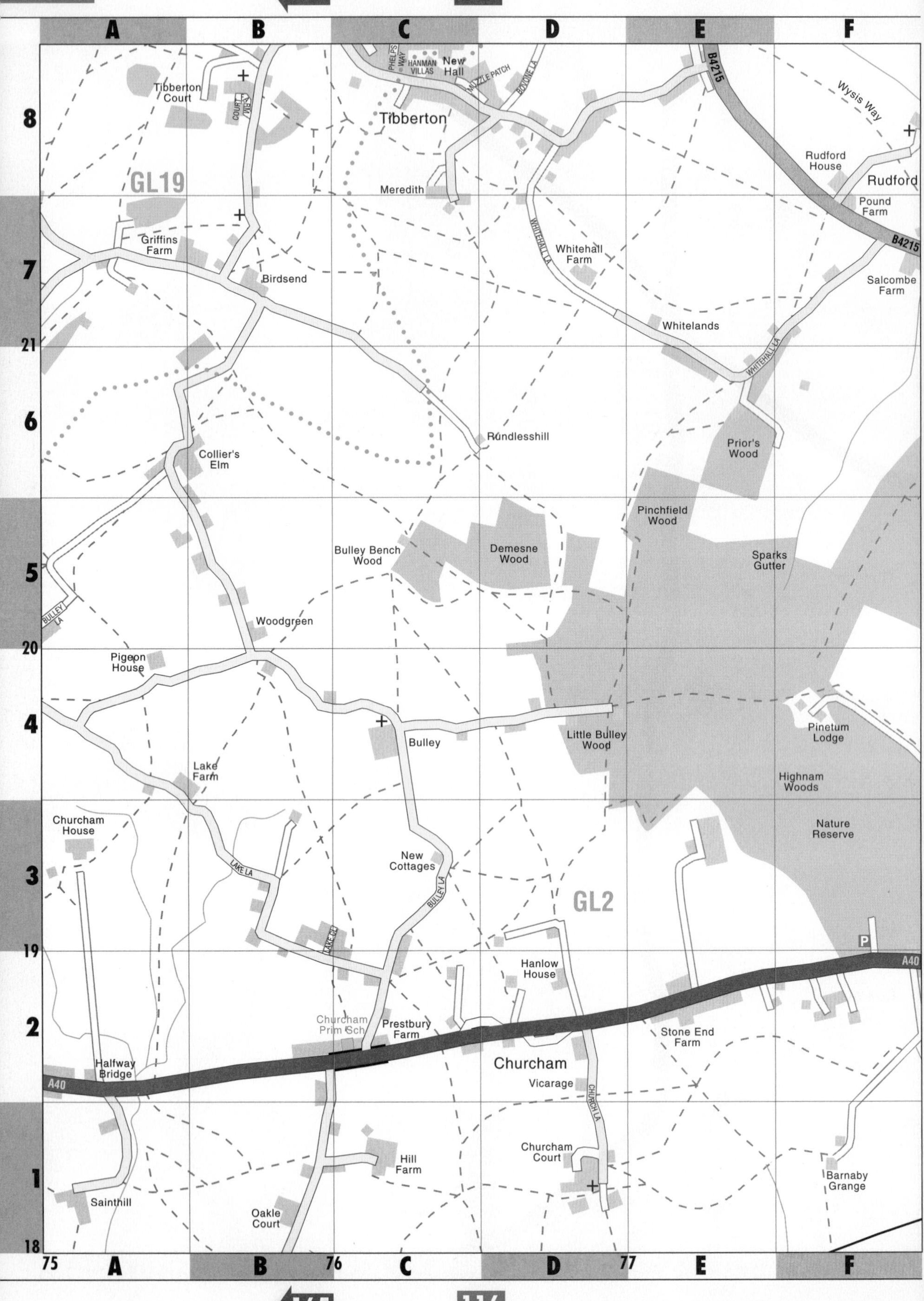

165
116

172
126

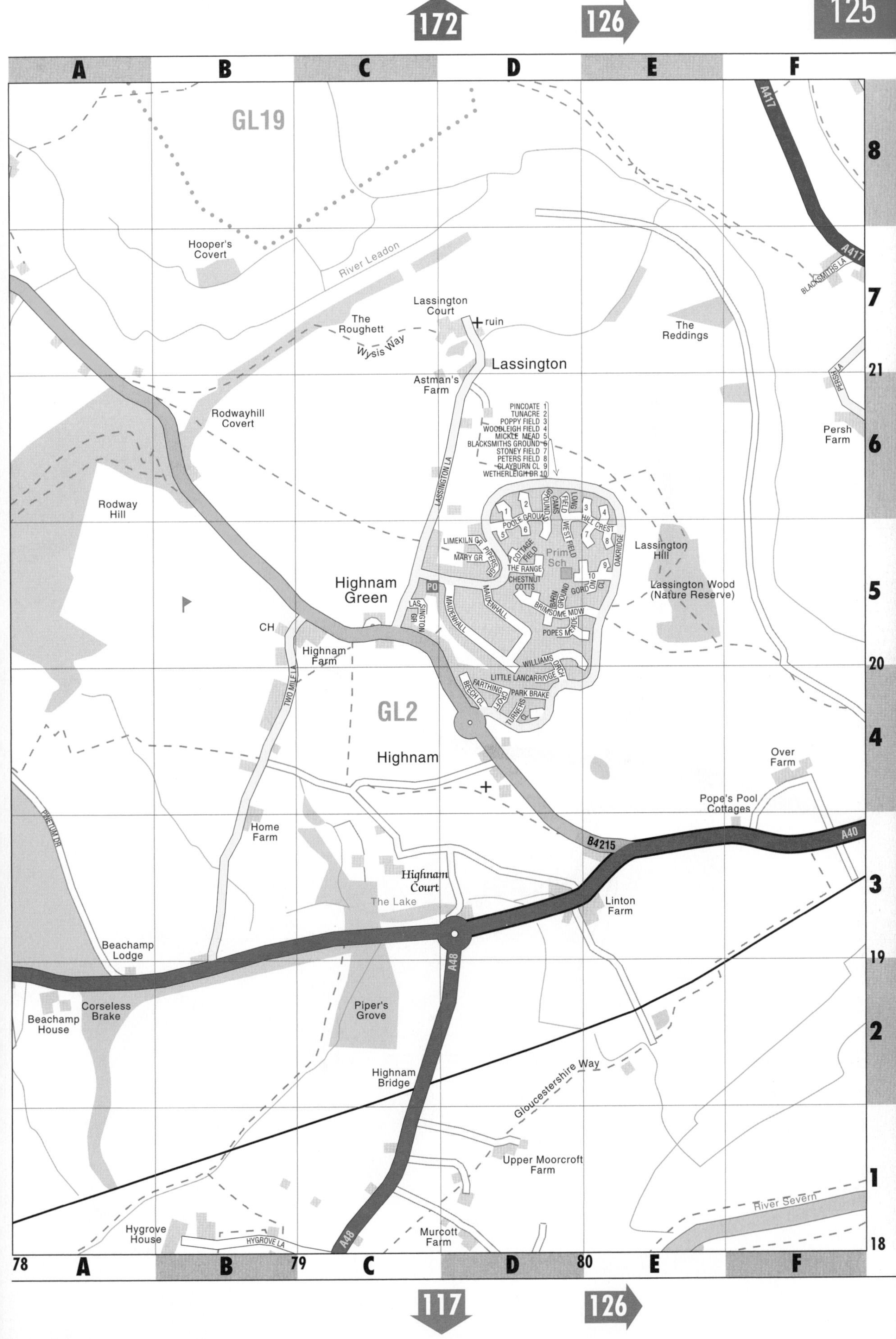

117
126

125
172

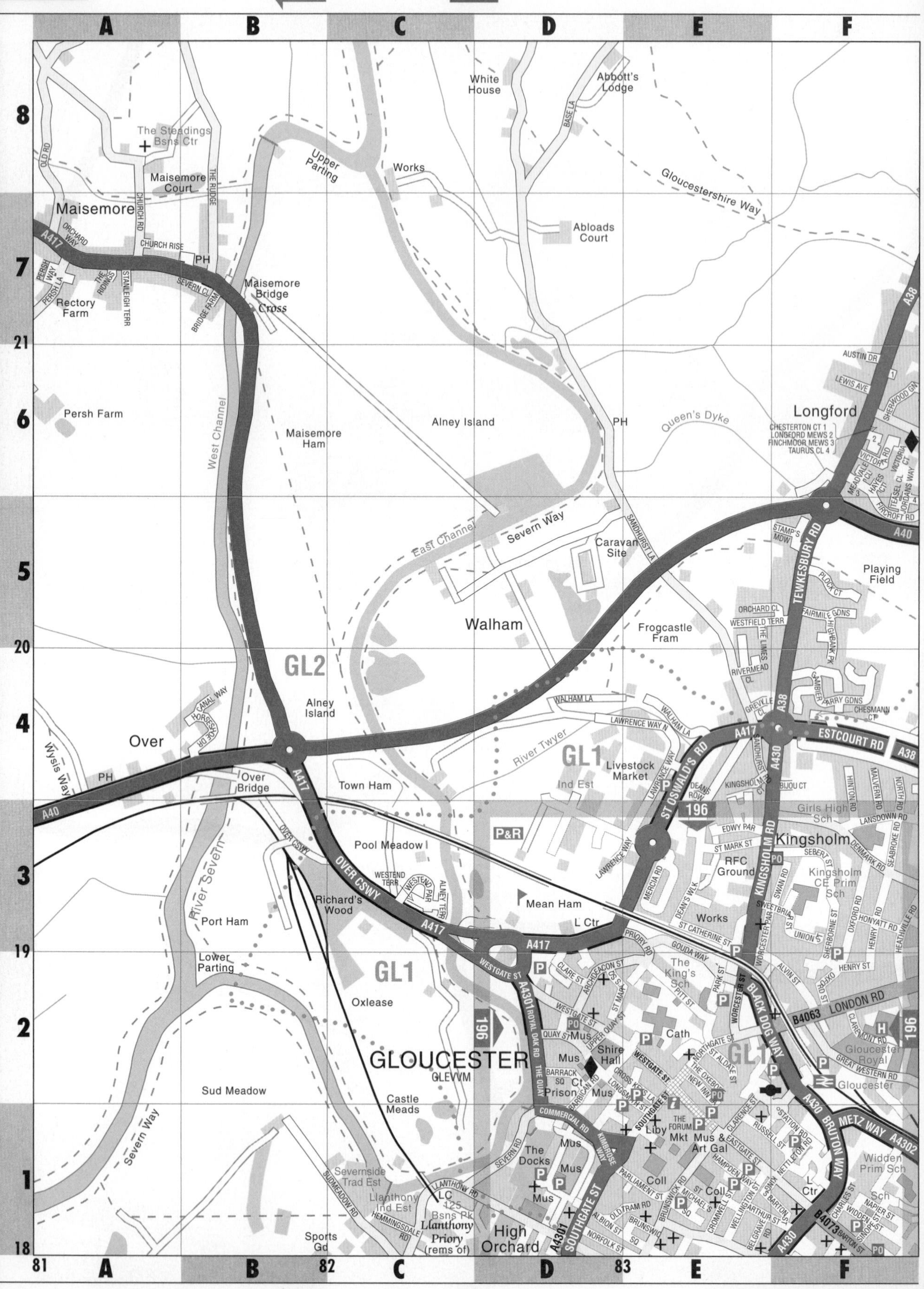

For full street detail of the highlighted area see page 196.

173 128

A B C D E F

Sewage Works

Gloucestershire Way

Hotel

TEWKESBURY RD

Broadboard Bridge

Drymeadow Farm

Drymeadow Lodge

Innsworth

Innsworth House Farm

GL3

Longford Bridge

Horsbere Brook

Sewage Works

Innsworth Tech Pk

Innsworth Jun Sch

1 CHAFFINCH CL
2 BULLFINCH WAY

GLENDOWER CL 1
FROBISHER MEWS 2

ARAGON WAY 1
PARR CL 2

Sports Gd

SHAMROCK CL 1
MISTLETOE MEWS 2
ELDERBERRY MEWS 3
BLAKELEY CT 4
HEATHDEAN RD 5
HAWTHORN DR 6

WENTWORTH CL 1
THE TULWORTHS 2
WOODCOTE 3
FOXCOTE 4
HORNBEAM MEWS 5

1 SHEEVAUN CL
2 LACCA CL

1 SAYLITTLE MEWS
2 MUTSILVER MEWS
3 PATSEAMUR MEWS

Larkfield Inf Sch

Paygrove Farm

CHELTENHAM RD E

B4063

A40

GL2

Schs

Playing Field

Oxstalls Com Sch

Allot Gdns

Longlevens

Liby

Longlevens Inf Sch

Longlevens Jun Sch

CHELTENHAM RD

ESTCOURT RD

Sir Thomas Rich's Sch

Elmbridge

Playing Fields

Wells' Bridge

LONDON RD

GL1

BARNWOOD RD

Elmbridge Inf & Jun Schs

Factory

GL4

St Peter's Inf & Jun Schs

Gloucestershire Royal

Wotton

Superstore

Barnwood

Hotel

GL3

EASTERN AVE

METZ WAY

A4302

A38

A417

84 85 86

A B C D E F

A1
1 MAGDALA RD
2 BECKSIDE CT
3 COUNTY CRES
4 MILLBROOK CL
5 ALINGTON CL

B2
1 ALDERNEY FLATS
2 KENCOURT CL
3 WESTMINSTER CT
4 WOTTON ELMS CT
5 BRADFORD RD

119 128

127
173

A
B
C
D
E
F
8
7
21
6
5
20
4
3
19
2
1
18
87
88
89
Bank View Farm
Bamfurlong
BAMFURLONG LA
M5
Jet Age Air Mus
GL2
Halfway Bridge
Blenheim House
Gloucestershire Airport
B4063
CH
FAIRWAYS DR
1 ST VINCENT WAY
2 VICTORY CL
A7
1 HANOVER WAY
2 BUCKINGHAM DR
3 MARLEYFIELD CL
4 APPLE TREE CL
5 JAPONICA CL
6 MIMOSA CT
7 BUDDLEIA CT
8 FORSYTHIA CL
9 KERRIS CT
10 CALENDULA CT
11 KILMINSTER CT
A40
11
CHELTENHAM RD E
INNSWORTH LA
WESTOVER CT
ORCHARD WAY
HOLTHAM AVE
Norman's Brook
Parton Farm
Parton Manor
Liby
Schs
CHADBOURNES
PARTON MEWS
BUTTERMILK LA
GARDINERS CL
ST JOHNS AVE
PARKLANDS
CRAVEN DR
GOODMOOR CRES
MARTINDALE RD
BERRYFIELD GLADE
GOLDEN VALE
QUINTON CL
PARTON RD
Home Farm
Gloucestershire Way
Churchdown
Parton Court
CHESFORD DR
Churchdown Sch
1 COCHRAN CL
2 SWORDFISH CL
3 SUNDERLAND CT
4 LYSANDER CT
5 EASTHOLM LAWNS
GL51
TALL ELMS CL 1
WATERMOOR CT 2
OAKHURST CL
Pirton Court
Pirton Brake
ST ANDREWS GN
MELVILLE RD
SUMMERLAND DR
STATION CL
BROOKFIELD LA
Chosen Hill Sch
STATION RD
PRIORY CT
CAVENDISH AVE
ALBEMARLE RD
THE AVENUE
BROOKFIELD RD
ANNE HATHAWAY DR
Teviotdale
JOHN DANIELS WAY
CHOSEN DR
CORDINGLEY CL
THE PIECE
THE MANOR
THE CHASE
BLACKSMITH LA
ORCHARD DR
OLDBURY ORCH
White House Farm
Witcombe Bridge
GL3
HOWCROFT
BARNHAY
CHURCH RD
DREWS CL 1
CHAPEL HAY CL 2
CHAPEL HAY LA
KINGSCOTE CL
CROFT CL
Chosen Hayes Farm
1 SWEETBRIAR HO
2 CHURCH VIEW
3 DUNSTAN GLEN
The Green
CRIFTYCRAFT LA
CRANHAM LA
BARROW HILL
Tinker's Hill
Woodfield Farm
Woodhouse Farm
Cemy
Zoons Court
Chosen Hill House
Mast
Churchdown Hill
HUCCLECOTE LA
BROCKWORTH RD
Woodlands Farm
A417
DEER PARK RD
COLWELL AVE
QUEENS CL
LARKHAY RD
Pressmead House

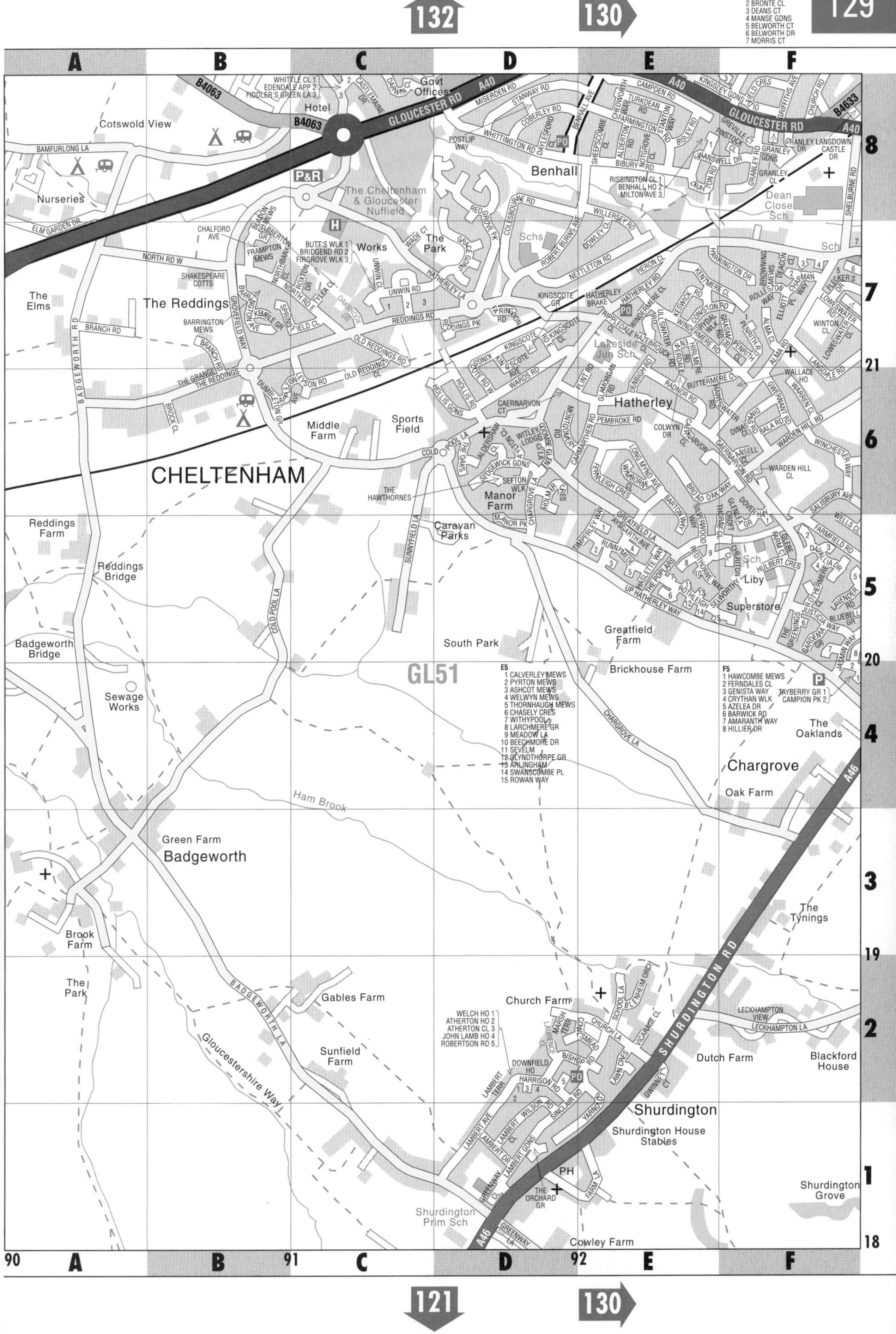
132
130
F7
1 DERWENT WLK
2 BRONTE CL
3 DEANS CT
4 MANSE GDNS
5 BELWORTH CT
6 BELWORTH DR
7 MORRIS CT
A
B
C
D
E
F
8
7
21
6
5
20
4
3
19
2
1
18
90
91
92
Cotswold View
Nurseries
Hotel
Govt Offices
GLOUCESTER RD
A40
B4063
B4633
BAMFURLONG LA
ELM GARDEN DR
The Cheltenham & Gloucester Nuffield
Benhall
Dean Close Sch
Works
The Park
Schs
The Elms
The Reddings
Lakeside Jun Sch
Hatherley
Middle Farm
Sports Field
CHELTENHAM
Manor Farm
Caravan Parks
Reddings Farm
Reddings Bridge
Badgeworth Bridge
Sewage Works
South Park
Greatfield Farm
Brickhouse Farm
GL51
E5
1 CALVERLEY MEWS
2 PYRTON MEWS
3 ASHCOT MEWS
4 WELWYN MEWS
5 THORNHAUGH MEWS
6 CHASELY CRES
7 WITHYPOOL
8 LARCHMERE GR
9 MEADOW LA
10 BEECHMORE DR
11 SEVELM
12 GLYNDTHORPE GR
13 ARLINGHAM
14 SWANSCOMBE PL
15 ROWAN WAY
F5
1 HAWCOMBE MEWS
2 FERNDALES CL
3 GENISTA WAY
4 CRYTHAN WLK
5 AZELEA DR
6 BARWICK RD
7 AMARANTH WAY
8 HILLIER DR
Liby
Superstore
The Oaklands
Chargrove
Oak Farm
Ham Brook
Green Farm
Badgeworth
Brook Farm
The Tynings
The Park
Gables Farm
Church Farm
Sunfield Farm
Gloucestershire Way
BADGEWORTH LA
SHURDINGTON RD
A46
Dutch Farm
Blackford House
Shurdington
Shurdington House Stables
Shurdington Prim Sch
Cowley Farm
Shurdington Grove
121
130

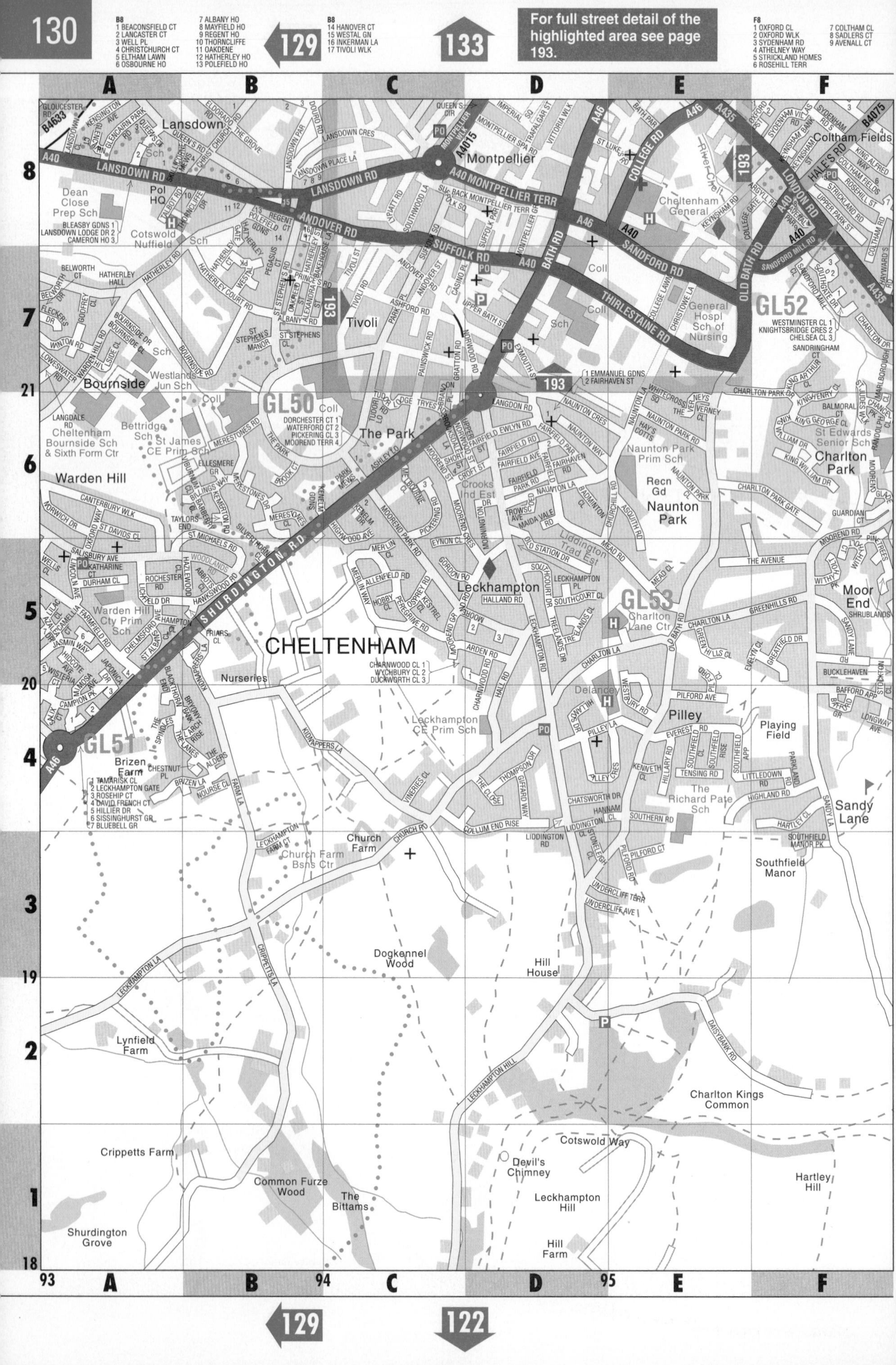

130
B8
1 BEACONSFIELD CT
2 LANCASTER CT
3 WELL PL
4 CHRISTCHURCH CT
5 ELTHAM LAWN
6 OSBOURNE HO
7 ALBANY HO
8 MAYFIELD HO
9 REGENT HO
10 THORNCLIFFE
11 OAKDENE
12 HATHERLEY HO
13 POLEFIELD HO
129
B8
14 HANOVER CT
15 WESTAL GN
16 INKERMAN LA
17 TIVOLI WLK
133
For full street detail of the highlighted area see page 193.
F8
1 OXFORD CL
2 OXFORD WLK
3 SYDENHAM RD
4 ATHELNEY WAY
5 STRICKLAND HOMES
6 ROSEHILL TERR
7 COLTHAM CL
8 SADLERS CT
9 AVENALL CT
A
B
C
D
E
F
8
7
21
6
5
20
4
3
19
2
1
18
93
94
95
Lansdown
Montpellier
Coltham Fields
Dean Close Prep Sch
Pol HQ
Cotswold Nuffield
Cheltenham General
Tivoli
GL52
GL50
GL51
GL53
Bournside
Westlands Jun Sch
Cheltenham Bournside Sch & Sixth Form Ctr
Bettridge Sch
St James CE Prim Sch
The Park
Warden Hill
Crooks Ind Est
Naunton Park Prim Sch
Recn Gd
Naunton Park
St Edwards Senior Sch
Charlton Park
Liddington Trad Est
Leckhampton
Moor End
Warden Hill Cty Prim Sch
CHELTENHAM
Charlton Lane Ctr
Nurseries
Delancey
Pilley
Playing Field
Leckhampton CE Prim Sch
Brizen Farm
The Richard Pate Sch
Sandy Lane
Church Farm
Church Farm Bsns Ctr
Southfield Manor
Dogkennel Wood
Hill House
Lynfield Farm
Charlton Kings Common
Cotswold Way
Crippetts Farm
Devil's Chimney
Common Furze Wood
The Bittams
Leckhampton Hill
Hartley Hill
Shurdington Grove
Hill Farm
LANSDOWN RD
ANDOVER RD
SUFFOLK RD
BATH RD
SANDFORD RD
THIRLESTAINE RD
LONDON RD
SHURDINGTON RD
LECKHAMPTON RD
LECKHAMPTON HILL
CRIPPETTS LA
LECKHAMPTON LA
DAISYBANK RD
129
122

B6
1 GROVELANDS CL
2 PORTURET WAY
3 SCHOOL ROAD FLATS
4 THE OLD SCHOOL MEWS
5 REABURN CL
6 COURTFIELD DR

134
166

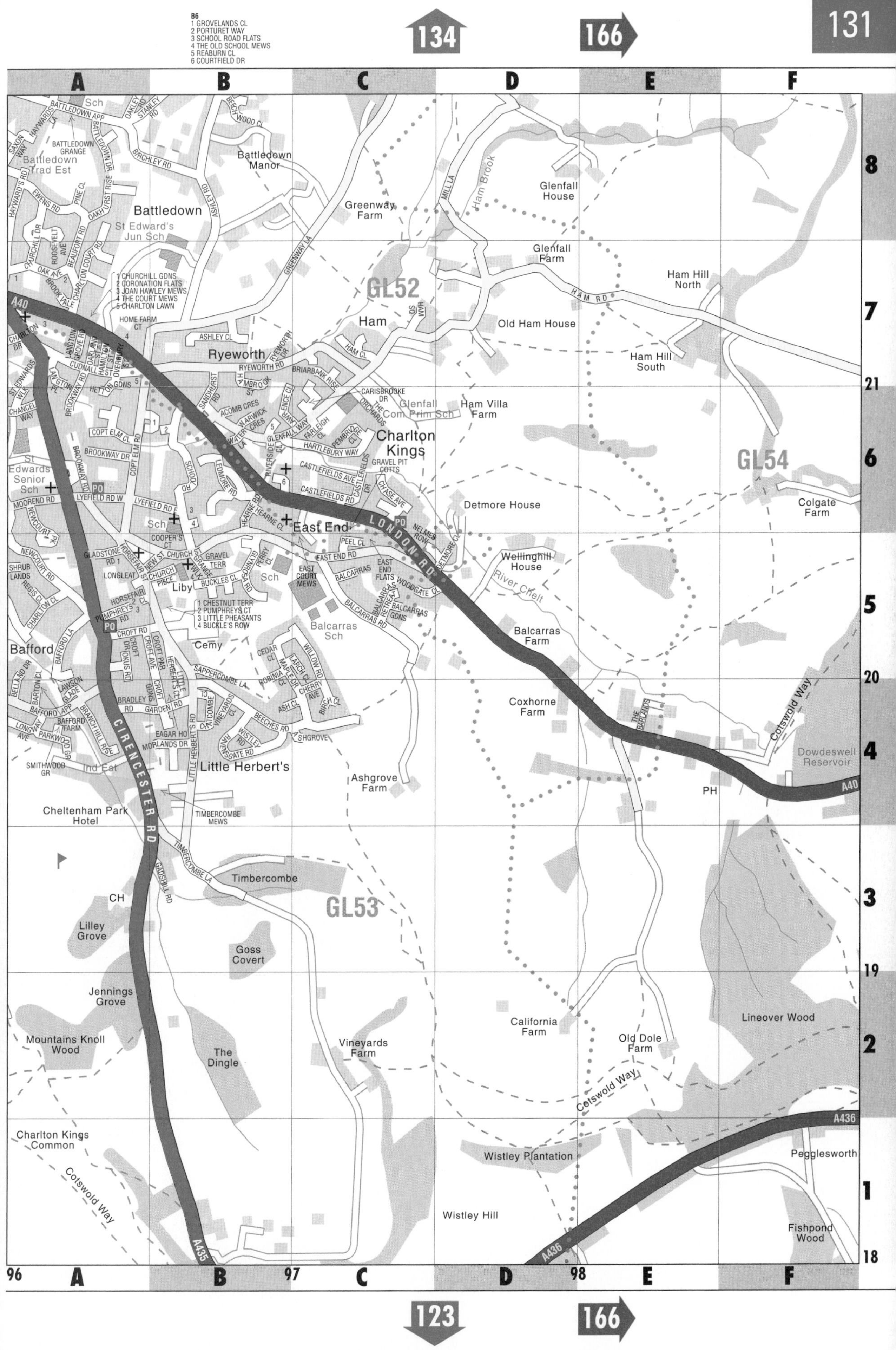

123
166

173
136

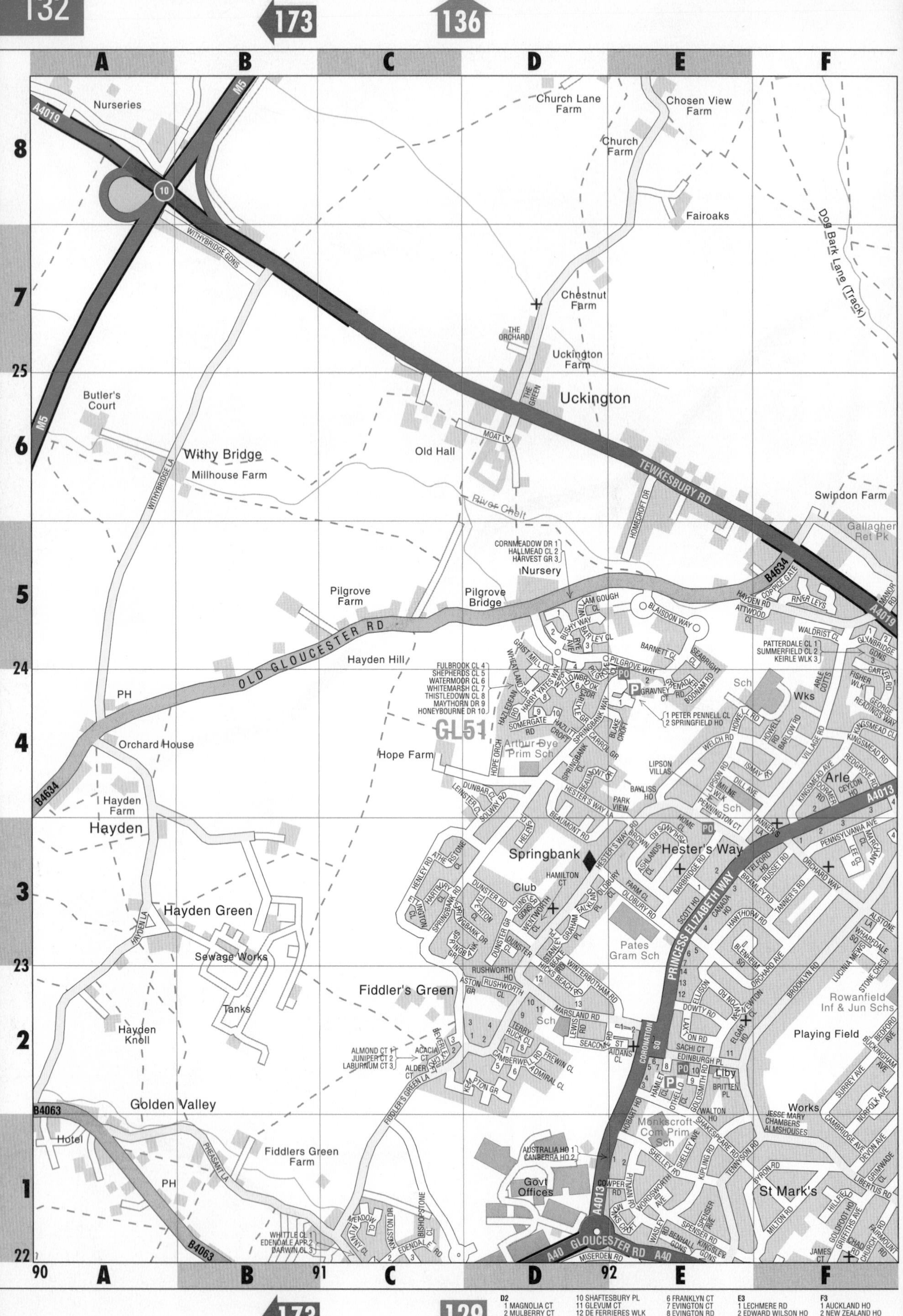

173
129

D2
1 MAGNOLIA CT
2 MULBERRY CT
3 SYCAMORE CT
4 REDWOOD CT
5 PEACOCK CL
6 SWALLOWTAIL CL
7 EMPEROR CL
8 HEAPEY CL
9 ROYAL CT
10 SHAFTESBURY PL
11 GLEVUM CT
12 DE FERRIERES WLK
13 DORINGTON WLK

E2
1 PAKISTAN HO
2 INDIA HO
3 TYLER CT
4 TASMANIA HO
5 GRESHAM CT
6 FRANKLYN CT
7 EVINGTON CT
8 EVINGTON RD
9 AMBERLEY RD
10 AMBERLEY CT
11 COATES HO
12 ARUNDEL HO
13 CHEPSTOW HO
14 EASTNOR HO

E3
1 LECHMERE RD
2 EDWARD WILSON HO
3 MONTREAL HO
4 QUEBEC HO
5 KENILWORTH HO
6 BERKELEY HO
7 SUDELEY HO

F3
1 AUCKLAND HO
2 NEW ZEALAND HO
3 LYGON WLK
4 BROOKLYN CL

F4
1 MARY GODWIN CT
2 RHODESIA HO
3 SOUTH AFRICA HO
4 GREVIL RD

For full street detail of the highlighted area see page 193.

137

134

Swindon
Home Farm
Swindon Village Prim Sch
Swindon Hall
Manor Farm
Hyde Brook
Sewage Works
Hyde Farm
Jardinerie
Kayte Farm
Gloucestershire Warwickshire Rly
Prestbury Park
Hall of Fame
Cheltenham Race Course
GL50
Hunting Butts
Wymans Brook
The Paddocks
Rosehill
Kingsditch
Kingsditch Ret Pk
Manor Park Bsns Ctr
Ashville Trad Est
Shaftesbury Ind Est
CHELTENHAM
Allot Gdns
Cleeve View Inf Sch
Marle Hill
Recn Ctr
Pittville Park
Pittville
Pittville Pump Room & Mus
Cleevemount
GL52
Tewkesbury Bridge
St Peter's
GL51
St Benedict's RC Sch & Sports Coll
Cheltenham Trade Pk
St Paul's
Rowanfield
Alstone
Alstone Lane Trad Est
Lansdown Ind Est
St George's Bsns Pk
The Catholic Sch of St Gregory the Great
Mus, Liby & Art Gal
Fairview
Overton Park
Bays Hill
Airthrie Sch
Cheltenham Spa
St John's CE Prim Sch

B1
1 SEDUM HO
2 HOMESPA HO
3 CHARLOTTE ROSE HO
4 RUTLAND CT
5 WINCHESTER HO
6 WESTERN CT
7 CHRIST CHURCH VILLAS
8 CHRIST CHURCH TERR

B2
1 ALSTONE CT
2 ST GEORGE'S CL
3 ST JOHN'S CT
4 OLD MILLBROOK TERR
5 GLOUCESTER COTTS

F2
1 CLAREMONT
2 TRESMORE
3 SELKIRK CT
4 TERHILL
5 HEATH LO
6 BERKELEY HO
7 ASKHAM CT
8 FAIRHAVENS CT
9 STAR CT
10 COTSWOLD LO
11 WESTBOURNE HO
12 ST ANNE'S
13 IRVING HO
14 GODWIN CL
15 THE GRYPHONS
16 BYRON CT
17 CADOGAN HO
18 ALL SAINT'S CT
19 LANDOR GDNS

130

134

133
138

A B C D E F

8
7
25
6
5
24
4
3
23
2
1
22

Southam
Thrift Wood
Cleve Cloud
Cleve Common
Nutterswood
Gloucestershire Warwickshire Rly
KAYTE LA
NEW RD
B4632
SOUTHAM LA
RATCLIFF LAWNS
THE CLOSE
SCHOOL LA
GRAVEL WLK
OLD RD
SUNSET LA
BENTLEY LA
Southam de la Bere (Hotel)
Hyde Brook
Cotswold Way
GL50
Queen's Wood
Southam Bridge
Cheltenham Race Course
White's Barn
SPRING LA
PARK LA
SHAW GREEN LA
Shaw Green
Knoll Holl House
QUEENWOOD GR
UPPER MILL LA
GRAVEL PIT LA
WATERSHOOT CL
APPLE ORCH
APPLE CL
ACACIA CL
LIME CL
BROADWAY
BRYMORE CL
LINDEN CL
LINDEN AVE
ELM CL
LAKE ST
BOWBRIDGE LA
Bow Bridge
GL52
THE HAYES
Prestbury
1 MORNINGSIDE CTYD
2 MORNINGSIDE CL
Lower Hill Farm
Whitehill
The Priory
THE BURGAGE
MILL ST
THE BANK
IDSALL DR
MILL LA
B4075
NEW BARN LA
CUMMING CT 1
BRYMORE AVE 2
NEW BARN AVE
NEW BARN CL
RUSHY HO
RUSHY MEWS
Liby
TATCHLEY LA
HIGH ST
THE STABLES
DEEP ST
ANN GOODRICH CL
BAY TREE CT
PRESTBURY GREEN DR
BLACKSMITHS LA
BEECH CL
LYNWORTH TERR
NOVERTON AVE
NOVERTON LA
LAUREL DR
GLEBE RD
FLORIDA DR
COURT RD
St Mary's CE Jun Sch
SOUTH VIEW WAY
FAWLEY DR
STUDLAND DR
PURBECK WAY
FINCHCROFT LA
FINCHCROFT CT
MUSCROFT RD
PICCADILLY WAY
Noverton
Noverton Farm
CLEEVEMOUNT RD
WELLAND LODGE RD
WELLAND CT
PRESTBURY RD
B4632
PRESCOTT WLK
CORONATION RD
KINDER HO
CHEVIOT RD
FIR TREE CL
YORK ROW
BOWEN CL
BETTRIDGE CT
CHILTERN RD
HONEYSUCKLE
IVY BANK
CORFE CL
GALLOPS LA
THREE SISTERS LA
ROBERTS RD
CLEEVE CLOUD LA
Lynworth
MENDIP RD
Sch
Sch
PENNINE RD
COTSWOLD RD
LYNWORTH PL
MENDIP CL
BUSH CT
BOUNCER'S LA
WHITEHORN DR
BRIAR
BRAMBLE RISE
HACKBERRY FIELD
WESTWOOD LA
BUTTERCROSS LA
CROMWELL RD
WILLOWHERB CL
CAM RD
CHELT RD
DART RD
PRIORS RD
Cemy
Crem
Piccadilly Farm
WYMAN'S RD
COLNE AVE
SEVERN RD
HAYES CT
THAMES RD
MEDWAY CT
Whaddon
TAMAR RD
PRIORS CT
BURMA AVE
SOMME RD
LADYSMITH RD
KIMBERLEY WLK
SALAMANCA RD
CHELTENHAM
ROBINS CL
WHADDON RD
EVENLODE AVE
CLYDE CRES
WINDRUSH RD
ISBOURNE RD
Sch
HAYES RD
HOMESPRING HO
CLEEVE VIEW RD
WHADDON AVE
CHURN AVE
AVON RD
MERSEY RD
HUMBER RD
IMJIN RD
ALEXANDRIA WLK
Oakley
Govt Offices
Cotswold Way
The Hewletts
Sch
LITTLEME RD
HEWLETT RD
JAMES DONOVAN CT
OAK CT
OAK MANOR DR
HILL VIEW RD
WESSEX DR
EXE
WESSEX
Oakley Farm
GL54
ELDON RD
ELDON AVE
HALES CL
HALE'S RD
BATTLEDOWN MEAD
Battledown Children's Ctr
GROVE DR
Lower Hewletts Farm
Hewletts Resr
AGGS HILL
HARP HILL
THE GROVE
OAKLEY RD
Battledown Hill
CAMP RD
GREENWAY LA
MILL LA
Northfield Farm
BATTLEDOWN PRIORS
BATTLEDOWN CL
Holy Apostles CE Prim Sch
STANLEY RD
ASHLEY RD
B4075

96 A B 97 C D 98 E F

A1
1 HOPWOOD GR
2 OAKDENE
3 OAK MANOR
4 RICHMOND DR
5 BARN FIELD

A3
1 CHELBURY MEWS
2 THE CONIFERS
3 FOSTER CT
4 NASEBY HO
5 LYNWORTH CT
6 GEORGE NAISEY HO
7 MENDIP HO
8 HANNAH BOOTE HO
9 LYNWORTH EXCHANGE

133
131

139
174

166
174

173
182

173
132

182
138

133
138

137
183

137
134

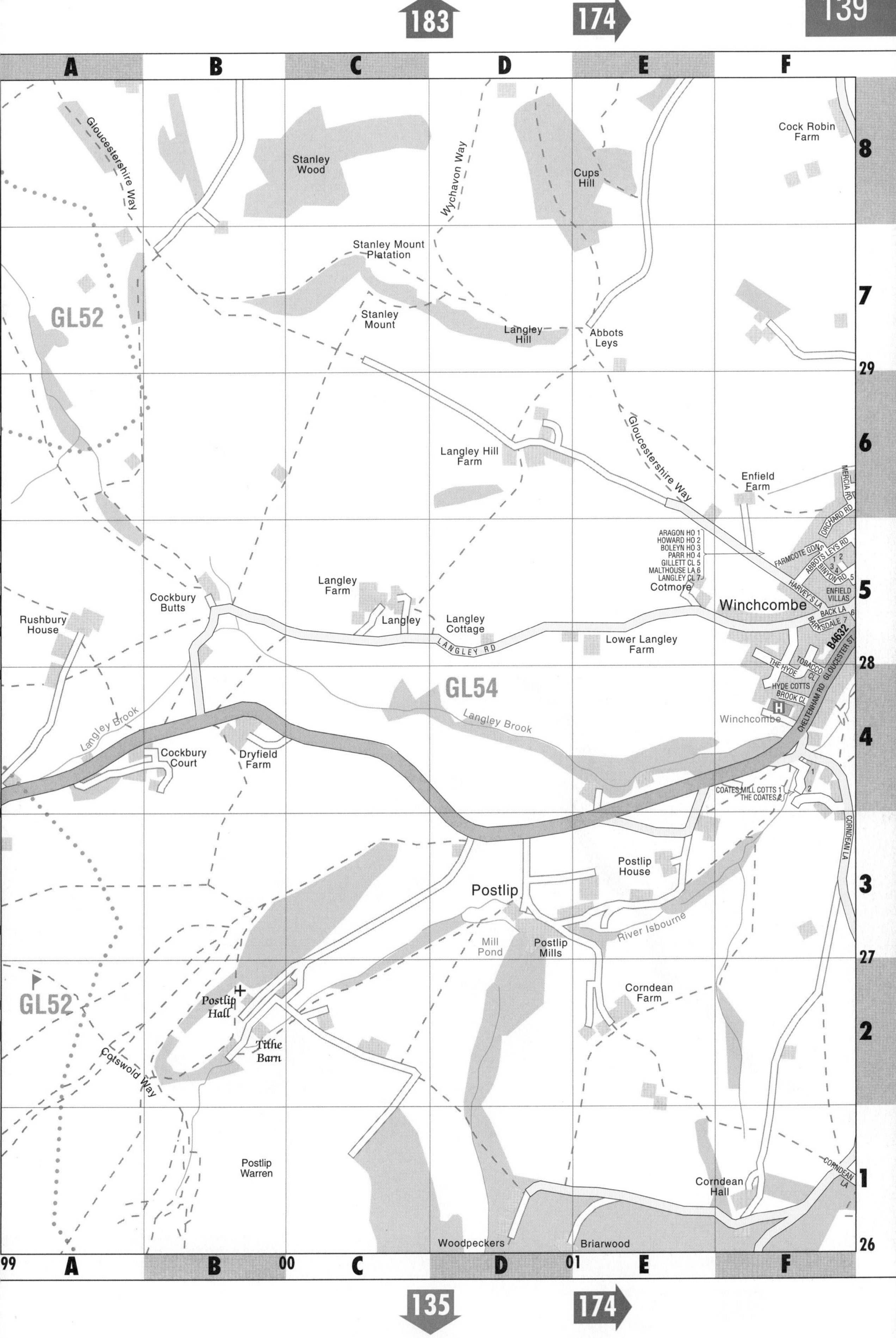

183
174
A
B
C
D
E
F
Gloucestershire Way
Stanley Wood
Wychavon Way
Cups Hill
Cock Robin Farm
8
Stanley Mount Platation
GL52
Stanley Mount
Langley Hill
Abbots Leys
7
29
Langley Hill Farm
Gloucestershire Way
Enfield Farm
6
ARAGON HO 1
HOWARD HO 2
BOLEYN HO 3
PARR HO 4
GILLETT CL 5
MALTHOUSE LA 6
LANGLEY CL 7
Cotmore
Winchcombe
Rushbury House
Cockbury Butts
Langley Farm
Langley
Langley Cottage
LANGLEY RD
Lower Langley Farm
5
B4632
28
GL54
Langley Brook
Langley Brook
Winchcombe
Cockbury Court
Dryfield Farm
4
COATES MILL COTTS 1
THE COATES 2
CORNDEAN LA
Postlip House
Postlip
3
Mill Pond
Postlip Mills
River Isbourne
27
GL52
Postlip Hall
Tithe Barn
Corndean Farm
Cotswold Way
2
Postlip Warren
Corndean Hall
CORNDEAN LA
1
Woodpeckers
Briarwood
26
99
00
01
135
174

83
148

C5
1 CHEVIOT CL
2 SUFFOLK CL
3 SHEPHERDS MEAD
4 JACOBS CL
5 COTSWOLD CL
6 TALBOY'S WLK
7 BERKELEY WAY

Scale: 1¾ inches to 1 mile
0 ¼ ½ mile
0 250m 500m 750m 1 km

A B C D E F

Avening
ORCHARD FIELD
HIGH ST
HAMPTON
FARM HILL
B4014
MAYS LA
Avening Court
GL7
Avening Park
WEST END
Mast
TETBURY HILL
STAR LA
1 NEW INN LA
2 POINT RD
3 POUND HILL
4 THE GROVE
5 MILL LA
ROUNDABOUT LA
Wickfield Wood
Macmilian Way
Longtree Barn
Star Farm
RIDGES LA
Grove Farm
Trull House
TRULL COTTS
A433
Troublehouse Covert
Holt Farm
Summerwell Farm
Warren Farm
OXLEAZE RD
CULKERTON
Colly Farm
PH
Purley Covert
Wr Twr
Tetbury Upton
Lowfield Farm
Lodge Farm
Upton Grove
UPTON GDNS 1
GROVE GDNS 2
CORONATION RD 3
HIGHFIELD RD 4
BLIND LA
Broadfield Farm
NEWNTON HILL
Highfield Farm
Hermit's Cave
LONGTREE CL
Sch
NORTHLANDS WAY
RYLAND CL
ILSOM COTTS
LONDON RD
WOODWARD CL
LOWFIELD RD
Ind Est
WEBB RD
CONYGAR RD
BRAYBROOKE CL
Great Larkhill Farm
ROMNEY
ST MARY'S RD
NORTHFIELD CL
HAMPTON ST
CIRENCESTER RD
Northfield
CHAVENAGE LA
MAGDALEN RD
A4135
NEWLEAZE GDNS
QUAIL MDWS
NORTHFIELD RD
NORTHLEAZE
SPRINGFIELDS
GL8
Addy's Firs
LINFOOT RD
SHERWOOD RD
Mus
COOMBE HO
LONDON RD
THE FERNS
HERD LA
Charlton House
LONG ST
CHIPPING ST
TETBURY
CHARLTON RD
NEW CHURCH ST
CHANTRY CT
Monarch's Way
Boldridge Farm
Tetbury
H
COTTON'S LA 1
BLACK HORSE HILL 2
THE BERRELLS 3
BERRELLS RD 4
SOUTHFIELD 5
CUTWELL
WEST ST
CHURCH ST
FOX HILL
The Folly Farm
Church Farm
HOOKSHOUSE LA
THE GREEN
Ind Est
NEWNTON RD
Ring & Bailey
CRUDWELL LA
GRANGE LA
Long Newnton
LONG FURLONG LA
Slads Farm
The Priory
PUMP LA
Newnton Farm
POWELLS WAY
Elmestree House
Close Farm
BATH RD
Oak Covert
Highgrove
Manor House
Thorn Covert
Doughton
Shipton Wood
Merchants Farm
BARBER LA
Estcourt House
Gilboa Farm
SN16
Manor Farm
Bell Farm
Tanner's
Eagle Lodge
WHITEHOUSE LA
B4014

8
97
7
96
6
95
5
94
4
93
3
92
2
91
1
90

87 88 89 90 91 92

Wiltshire STREET ATLAS

A B C D E F

71
59

B4
1 WISTARIA RD
2 WHEAT HILL
3 WINDSOR RD
4 OXLEASE CL
5 ELIZABETH GDNS
6 CHESTNUT CL
7 OXLEASE RD
8 FIVE TREES CL
9 MALTHOUSE WLK
10 ALEXANDER GDNS
11 COURT FIELD
12 HOLDER CL
13 CLOSE GDNS
14 WARNS CT
15 OLD BREWERY LA

C4
1 CLARRIE RD
2 COOKSPOOL
3 BARTLEY CROFT
4 THE RETREAT
5 BEECH TREE GDNS
6 CHERRY ORCHARD RD
7 PRIORY WAY
8 PARK CL
9 THE DAMSELLS
10 GUMSTOOL HILL
11 MARKET PL
12 SILVER ST

149
142

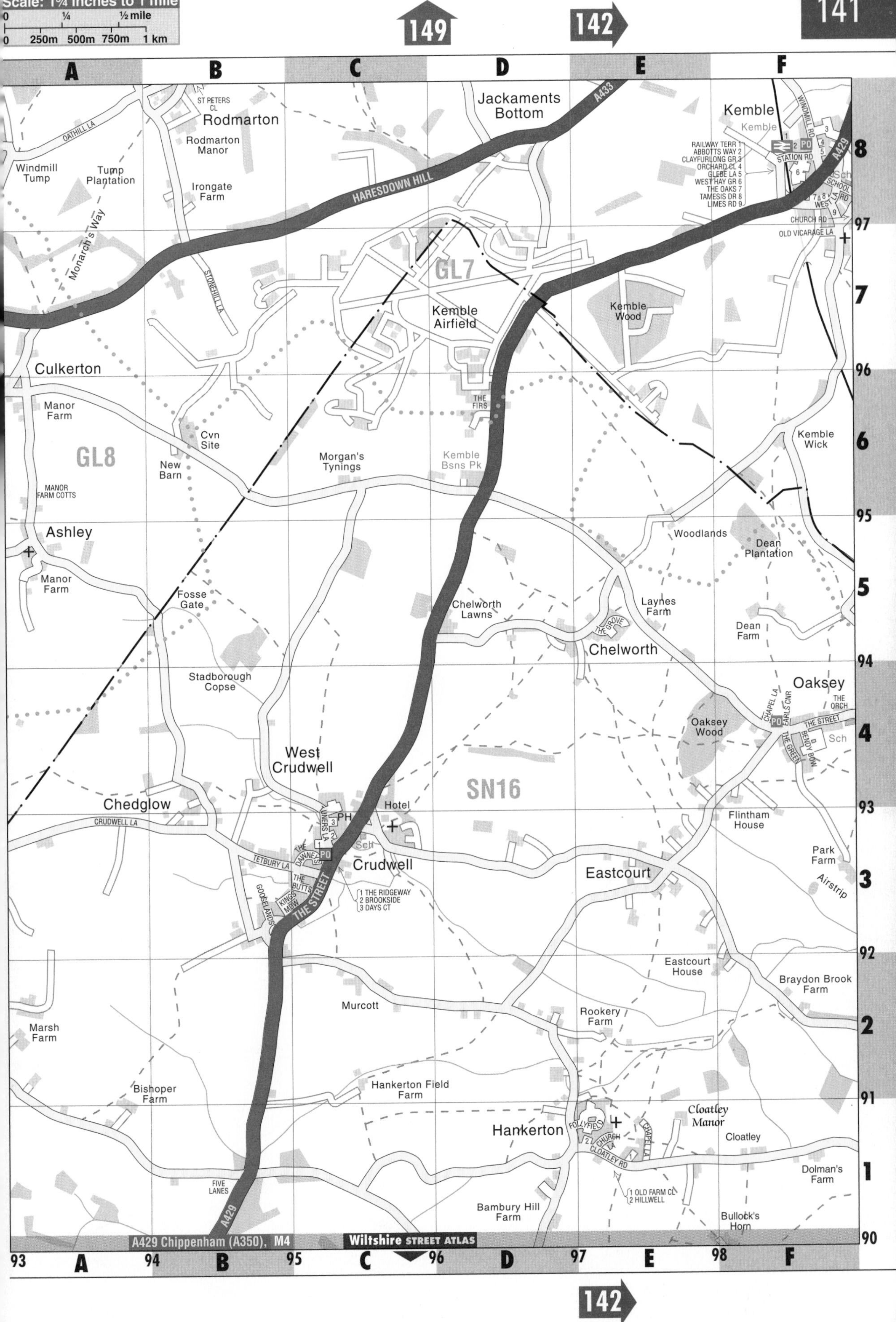
Scale: 1¾ inches to 1 mile
0 ¼ ½ mile
0 250m 500m 750m 1 km
A B C D E F
Jackaments Bottom
Kemble
Rodmarton
Rodmarton Manor
Irongate Farm
ST PETERS CL
OATHILL LA
Windmill Tump
Tump Plantation
Monarch's Way
HARESDOWN HILL
A433
A429
STONEHILL LA
GL7
Kemble Airfield
Kemble Wood
RAILWAY TERR 1
ABBOTTS WAY 2
CLAYFURLONG GR 3
ORCHARD CL 4
GLEBE LA 5
WEST HAY GR 6
THE OAKS 7
TAMESIS DR 8
LIMES RD 9
STATION RD
WINDMILL RD
SCHOOL RD
WEST LA
CHURCH RD
OLD VICARAGE LA
Culkerton
Manor Farm
GL8
Cvn Site
New Barn
THE FIRS
Morgan's Tynings
Kemble Bsns Pk
Kemble Wick
MANOR FARM COTTS
Ashley
Manor Farm
Woodlands
Dean Plantation
Fosse Gate
Chelworth Lawns
Laynes Farm
Dean Farm
THE GROVE
Chelworth
Stadborough Copse
Oaksey
Oaksey Wood
CHAPEL LA
EARLS CNR
THE STREET
THE ORCH
THE GREEN
BENDY BOW
Sch
West Crudwell
SN16
Chedglow
CRUDWELL LA
Hotel
PH
LUNERS LA
THE DANNEYS
TETBURY LA
Crudwell
Eastcourt
Flintham House
Park Farm
Airstrip
THE BUTTS
GOOSELANDS
KINGS MDW
THE STREET
1 THE RIDGEWAY
2 BROOKSIDE
3 DAYS CT
Eastcourt House
Braydon Brook Farm
Murcott
Rookery Farm
Marsh Farm
Bishoper Farm
Hankerton Field Farm
Cloatley Manor
Hankerton
FOLLYFIELD
CHURCH LA
CHAPEL LA
CLOATLEY RD
Cloatley
Dolman's Farm
FIVE LANES
1 OLD FARM CL
2 HILLWELL
Bambury Hill Farm
Bullock's Horn
A429 Chippenham (A350), M4
Wiltshire STREET ATLAS
93 94 95 96 97 98
90 91 92 93 94 95 96 97
1 2 3 4 5 6 7 8

142

141

150

Scale: 1¾ inches to 1 mile

0 ¼ ½ mile

0 250m 500m 750m 1 km

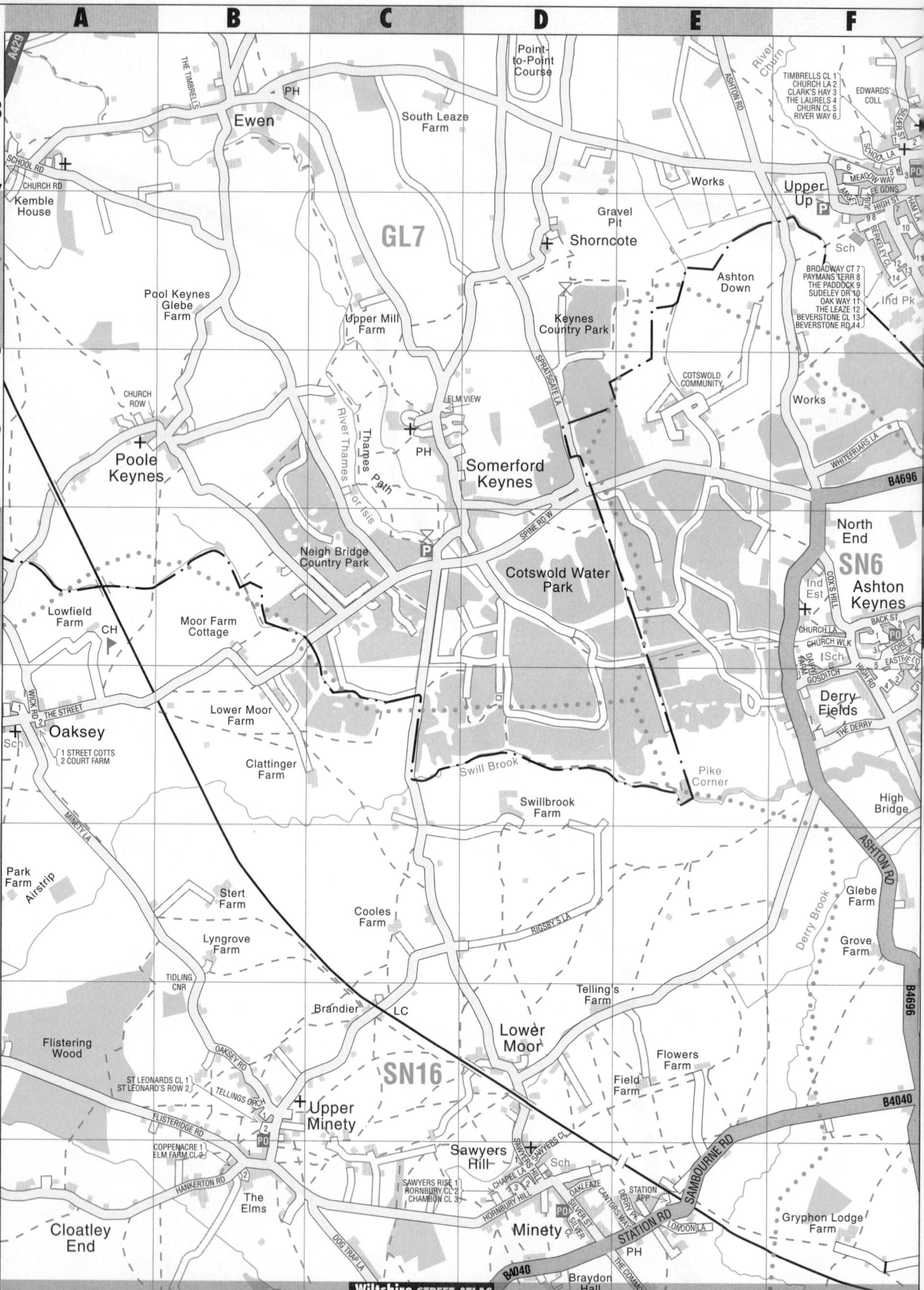

A B C D E F

A429

THE TIMBRELLS

PH

Ewen

Point-to-Point Course

South Leaze Farm

Ashton Rd

River Churn

TIMBRELLS CL 1
CHURCH LA 2
CLARK'S HAY 3
THE LAURELS 4
CHURN CL 5
RIVER WAY 6

EDWARDS' COLL

SILVER ST

SCHOOL LA

MEADOW WAY

HIGH ST

SCHOOL RD

CHURCH RD

Kemble House

Works

Upper Up

GL7

Gravel Pit

Shorncote

Sch

BERKELEY CL

BROADWAY CT 7
PAYMANS TERR 8
THE PADDOCK 9
SUDELEY DR 10
OAK WAY 11
THE LEAZE 12
BEVERSTONE CL 13
BEVERSTONE RD 14

Ind Pk

Ashton Down

Pool Keynes Glebe Farm

Upper Mill Farm

Keynes Country Park

SPRATSGATE LA

COTSWOLD COMMUNITY

CHURCH ROW

ELM VIEW

Works

River Thames

Thames Path

PH

Poole Keynes

Somerford Keynes

or Isis

WHITEFRIARS LA

B4696

SPINE RD W

Neigh Bridge Country Park

North End

SN6

Cotswold Water Park

Ind Est

COX'S HILL

Ashton Keynes

Lowfield Farm

CH

Moor Farm Cottage

CHURCH LA

CHURCH WLK

BACK ST

FORE ST

ISch

DAIRY FARM

GOSDITCH

HIGH RD

Derry Fields

THE DERRY

WICK RD

THE STREET

Oaksey

Sch

Lower Moor Farm

1 STREET COTTS
2 COURT FARM

Clattinger Farm

Swill Brook

Pike Corner

Swillbrook Farm

High Bridge

MINETY LA

Park Farm

Airstrip

Stert Farm

Cooles Farm

ASHTON RD

Glebe Farm

Derry Brook

Grove Farm

Lyngrove Farm

RIGSBY'S LA

TIDLING CNR

Telling's Farm

B4696

Brandier

LC

Flistering Wood

OAKSEY RD

Lower Moor

Flowers Farm

SN16

ST LEONARDS CL 1
ST LEONARD'S ROW 2

TELLINGS ORCH

Field Farm

Upper Minety

B4040

FLISTERIDGE RD

PO

COPPENACRE 1
ELM FARM CL 2

Sawyers Hill

SAWYERS HILL

SAWYERS CL

Sch

SAMBOURNE RD

HANKERTON RD

The Elms

SAWYERS RISE 1
HORNBURY CL 2
CHAMBON CL 3

CHAPEL LA

OAKLEAZE

STATION APP

HORNBURY HILL

SILVER ST

CANTORS WAY

DERRY PK

Gryphon Lodge Farm

Cloatley End

DOG TRAP LA

Minety

SILVER CL

STATION RD

LONDON LA

PH

THE COMMON

B4040

Braydon Hall

Wiltshire STREET ATLAS

99 A 00 B 01 C 02 D 03 E 04 F

141

F5
1 RICHMOND CT
2 THE LEAZE
3 COVE HOUSE GDNS
4 SADLERS FIELD
5 PARK PL
6 THE LOTTS

F4
1 PARK END
2 THAMES VIEW
3 THE MEAD
4 BIRCH GLADE

Scale: 1¾ inches to 1 mile
0 ¼ ½ mile
0 250m 500m 750m 1 km

151
144

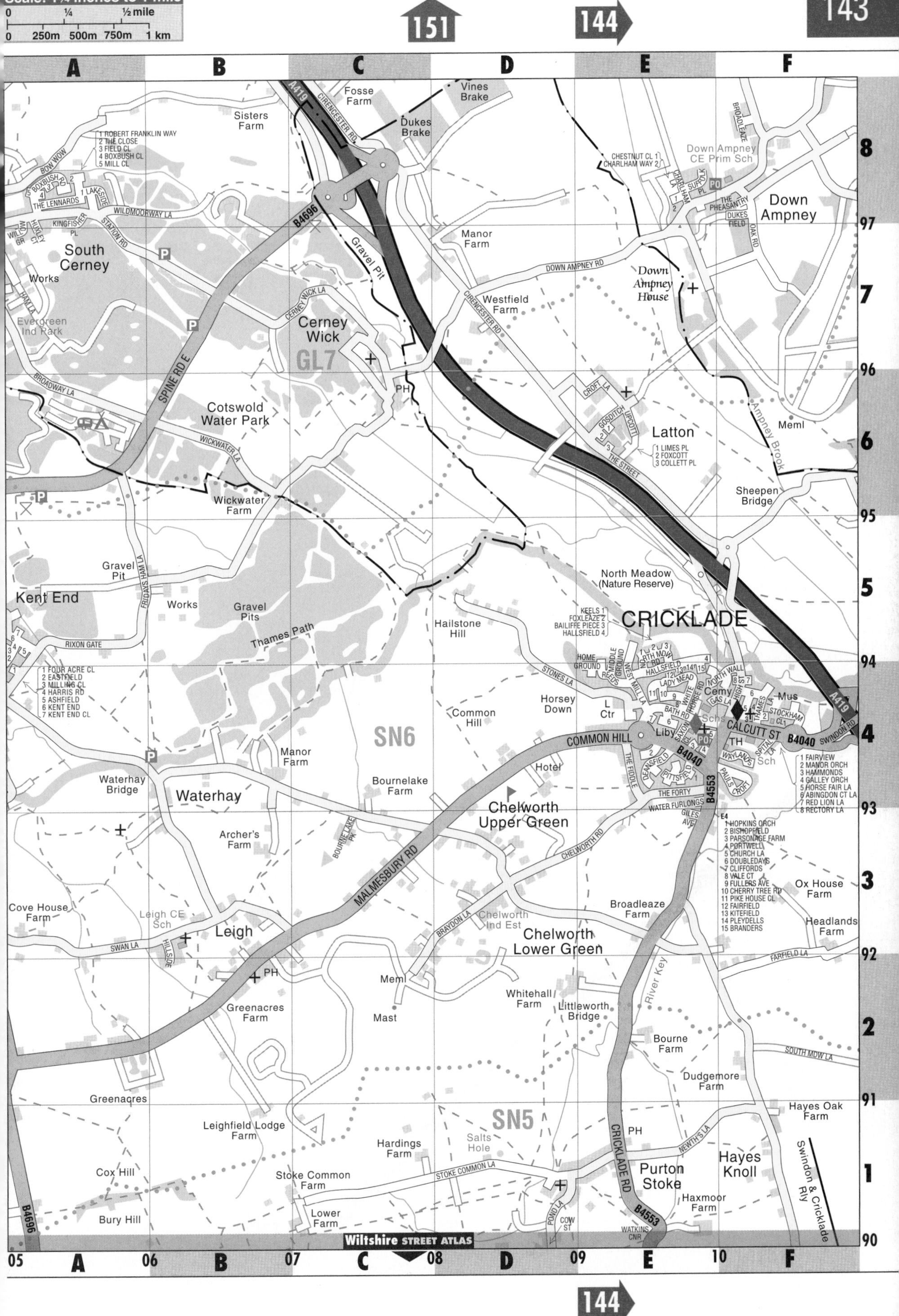

144

143
152

Scale: 1¾ inches to 1 mile
0 ¼ ½ mile
0 250m 500m 750m 1 km

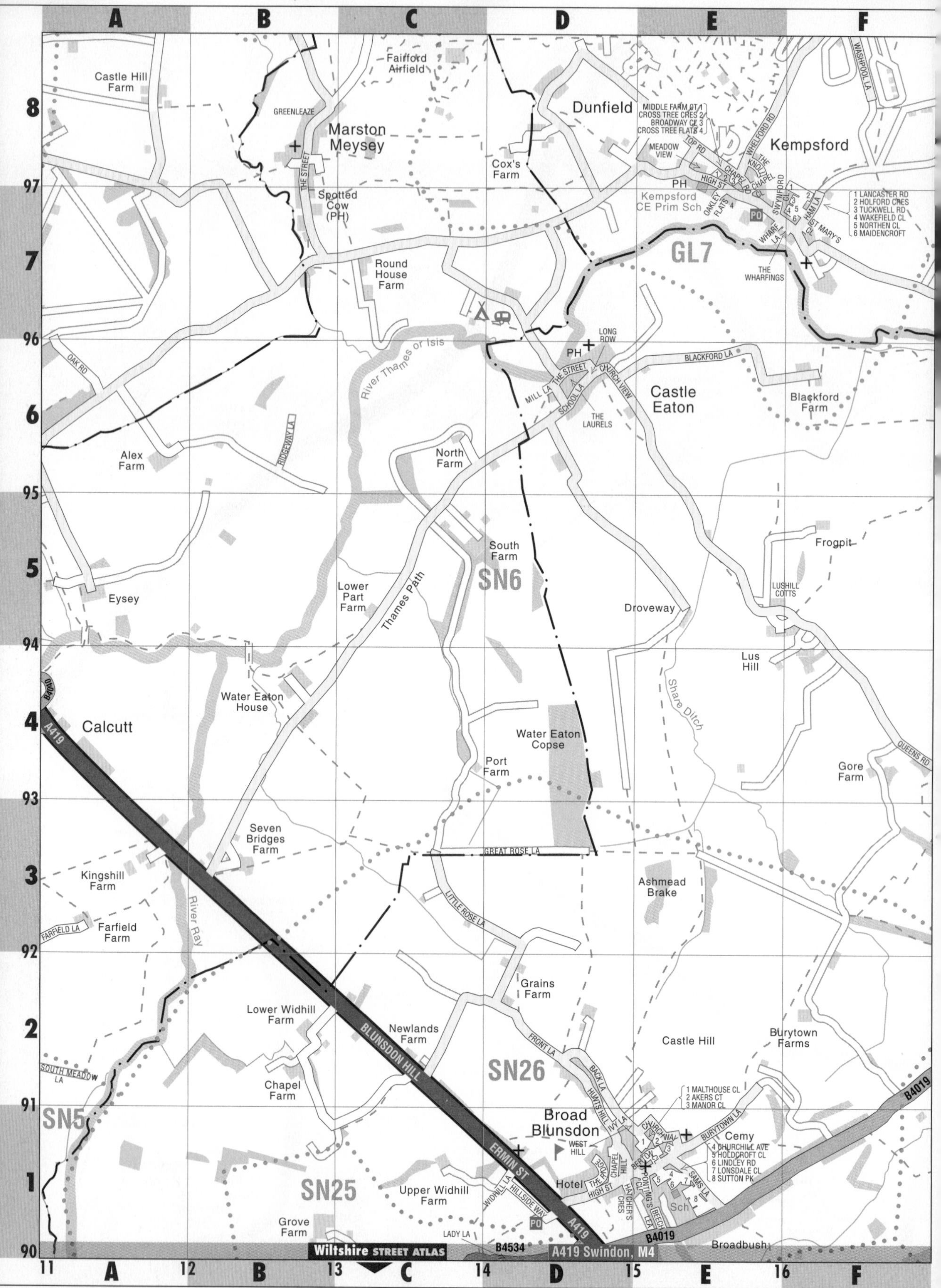

143

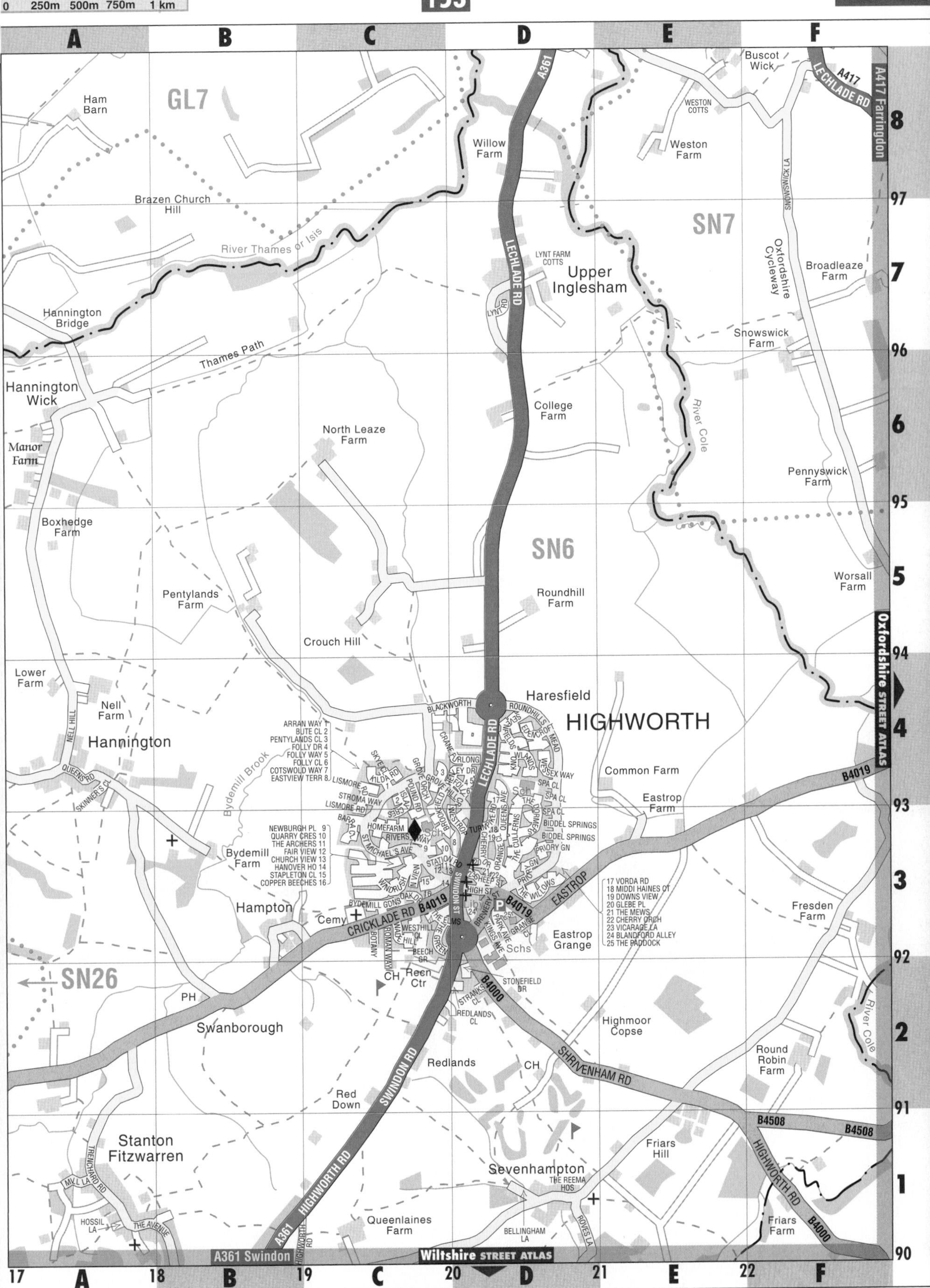
A
B
C
D
E
F
Ham Barn
GL7
Brazen Church Hill
River Thames or Isis
Hannington Bridge
Thames Path
Hannington Wick
Manor Farm
Boxhedge Farm
Pentylands Farm
Lower Farm
Nell Farm
NELL HILL
Hannington
QUEENS RD
SKINNER'S CL
Bydemill Brook
Bydemill Farm
Hampton
Cemy
PH
SN26
Swanborough
Stanton Fitzwarren
TRENCHARD RD
MILL LA
HOSSIL LA
THE AVENUE
A361 Swindon
North Leaze Farm
Crouch Hill
Willow Farm
A361
LECHLADE RD
LYNT FARM COTTS
LYNT RD
Upper Inglesham
College Farm
SN6
Roundhill Farm
Haresfield
HIGHWORTH
BLACKWORTH
ROUNDHILLS MEAD
CRANE FURLONG
ARRAN WAY 1
BUTE CL 2
PENTYLANDS CL 3
FOLLY DR 4
FOLLY WAY 5
FOLLY CL 6
COTSWOLD WAY 7
EASTVIEW TERR 8
LISMORE RD
STROMA WAY
SKYE CL
HILDA RD
POUND RD
GROVE ORCH
GROVE HILL
WESTROP
BARRA CL
HOMEFARM
RIVERSWAY
ST MICHAEL'S AVE
NEWBURGH PL 9
QUARRY CRES 10
THE ARCHERS 11
FAIR VIEW 12
CHURCH VIEW 13
HANOVER HO 14
STAPLETON CL 15
COPPER BEECHES 16
WINDRUSH
BYDEMILL GDNS
CRICKLADE RD
B4019
STATION RD
SWINDON ST
HIGH ST
SHEEP ST
BREWERY ST
PARK AVE
KINGS AVE
GRANGE CL
WESTHILL CL
BOTANY
ROMAN WAY
THE GREEN
THE ELMS
BEECH GR
CH
Recn Ctr
QUEENS AVE
THE CULLERNS
SPA CL
BIDDEL SPRINGS
PRIORY GN
THE WILLOWS
WESSEX WAY
EDENCROFT
KNOWLANDS
Sch
Schs
Lib
P
EASTROP
17 VORDA RD
18 MIDDI HAINES CT
19 DOWNS VIEW
20 GLEBE PL
21 THE MEWS
22 CHERRY ORCH
23 VICARAGE LA
24 BLANDFORD ALLEY
25 THE PADDOCK
Eastrop Grange
STONEFIELD DR
STRANKS CL
REDLANDS CL
B4000
Redlands
SWINDON RD
Red Down
HIGHWORTH RD
Queenlaines Farm
Sevenhampton
THE REEMA HOS
BELLINGHAM LA
ROVES LA
SHRIVENHAM RD
Highmoor Copse
Friars Hill
Common Farm
Eastrop Farm
B4019
Fresden Farm
Round Robin Farm
B4508
Friars Farm
River Cole
Buscot Wick
WESTON COTTS
Weston Farm
A417
LECHLADE RD
A417 Farringdon
SNOWSWICK LA
SN7
Oxfordshire Cycleway
Broadleaze Farm
Snowswick Farm
Pennyswick Farm
Worsall Farm
Oxfordshire STREET ATLAS
Wiltshire STREET ATLAS
8
97
7
96
6
95
5
94
4
93
3
92
2
91
1
90
17
18
19
20
21
22

154

Scale: 1¾ inches to 1 mile

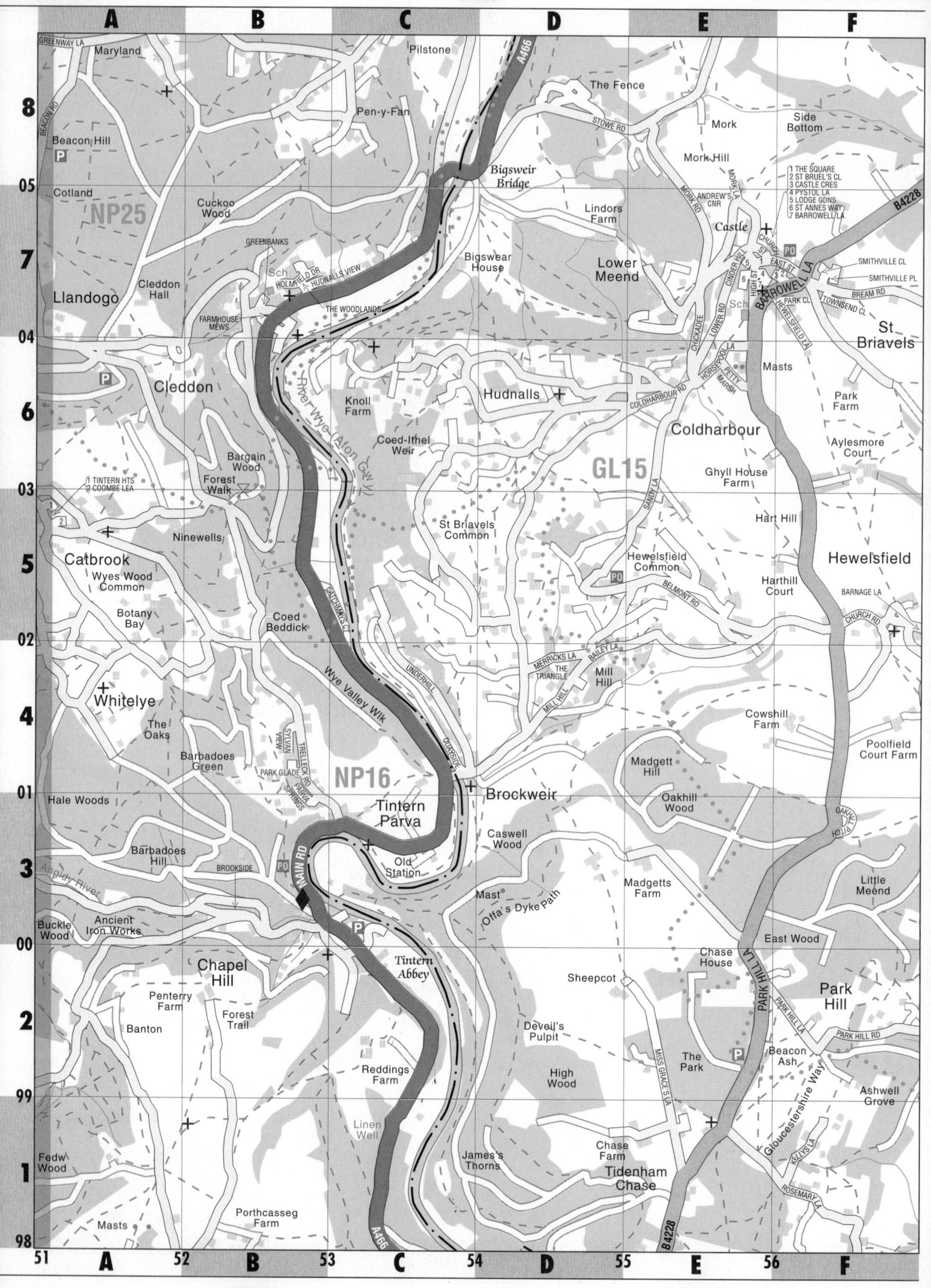

72

73

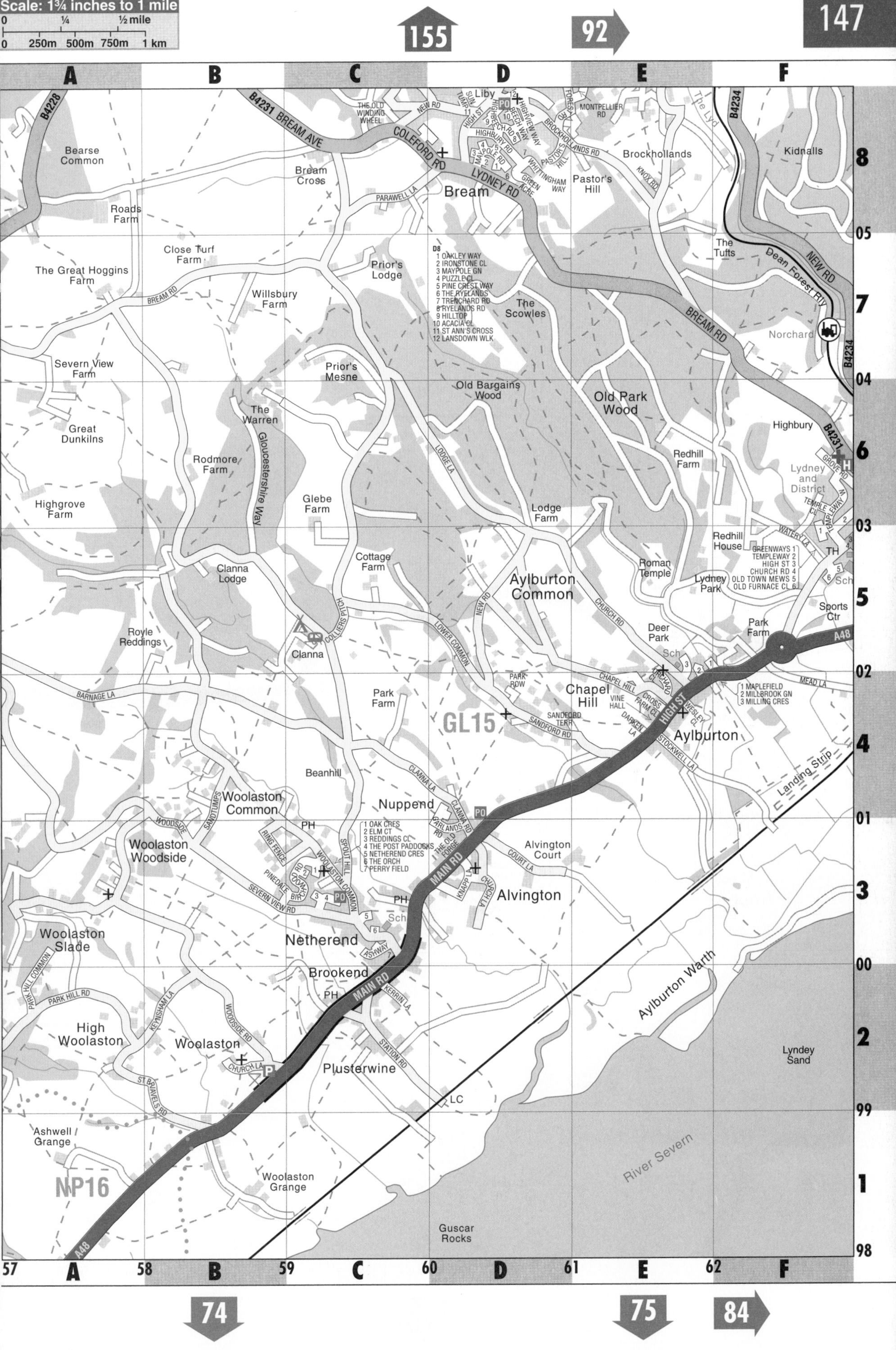
Scale: 1¾ inches to 1 mile
155
92
Bearse Common
Roads Farm
Close Turf Farm
The Great Hoggins Farm
Willsbury Farm
Bream Cross
Bream
Prior's Lodge
Liby
Brockhollands
Pastor's Hill
Kidnalls
The Tufts
Norchard
The Scowles
Severn View Farm
Prior's Mesne
Old Bargains Wood
Old Park Wood
Great Dunkilns
The Warren
Gloucestershire Way
Highbury
Rodmore Farm
Redhill Farm
Lydney and District
Highgrove Farm
Glebe Farm
Lodge Farm
Redhill House
Clanna Lodge
Cottage Farm
Roman Temple
Aylburton Common
Lydney Park
Sports Ctr
Royle Reddings
Clanna
Deer Park
Park Farm
Chapel Hill
GL15
Aylburton
Beanhill
Woolaston Common
Nuppend
Landing Strip
Woolaston Woodside
Alvington Court
Alvington
Woolaston Slade
Netherend
Brookend
Aylburton Warth
High Woolaston
Woolaston
Plusterwine
Lyndey Sand
Ashwell Grange
River Severn
NP16
Woolaston Grange
Guscar Rocks
D8
1 OAKLEY WAY
2 IRONSTONE CL
3 MAYPOLE GN
4 PUZZLE CL
5 PINE CREST WAY
6 THE RYELANDS
7 TRENCHARD RD
8 RYELANDS RD
9 HILLTOP
10 ACACIA CL
11 ST ANN'S CROSS
12 LANSDOWN WLK
GREENWAYS 1
TEMPLEWAY 2
HIGH ST 3
CHURCH RD 4
OLD TOWN MEWS 5
OLD FURNACE CL 6
1 MAPLEFIELD
2 MILLBROOK GN
3 MILLING CRES
1 OAK CRES
2 ELM CT
3 REDDINGS CL
4 THE POST PADDOCKS
5 NETHEREND CRES
6 THE ORCH
7 PERRY FIELD
B4231 BREAM AVE
COLEFORD RD
LYDNEY RD
BREAM RD
NEW RD
Dean Forest Rly
B4234
B4228
LODGE LA
CHURCH RD
BARNAGE LA
COLLIERS PITCH
LOWER COMMON
CLANNA LA
MAIN RD
HIGH ST
STOCKWELL LA
SANDFORD RD
COURT LA
CHURCH LA
STATION RD
WOODSIDE RD
ST BRIAVELS RD
PARK HILL RD
KENSHAM LA
SEVERN VIEW RD
SPOUT HILL
WOOLASTON COMMON
A48
57 58 59 60 61 62
05 04 03 02 01 00 99 98
8 7 6 5 4 3 2 1

99
104
105

B6
1 VELHURST DR
2 ASHLEY DR
3 CHASEWOOD CNR
4 BEECHWOOD DR
5 GREYS CL
6 DORINGTON CT
7 BURLEIGH VIEW
8 MUNDAY CL
9 FERRIS COURT VIEW

C6
1 SPARROW CL
2 ROBIN CL
3 PADIN CL
4 CUCKOO CL
5 HAWK CL
6 FOXES CL
7 ALDER WAY
8 STONECOTE RIDGE
9 FARRIERS CROFT

Scale: 1¾ inches to 1 mile
0 ¼ ½ mile
0 250m 500m 750m 1 km

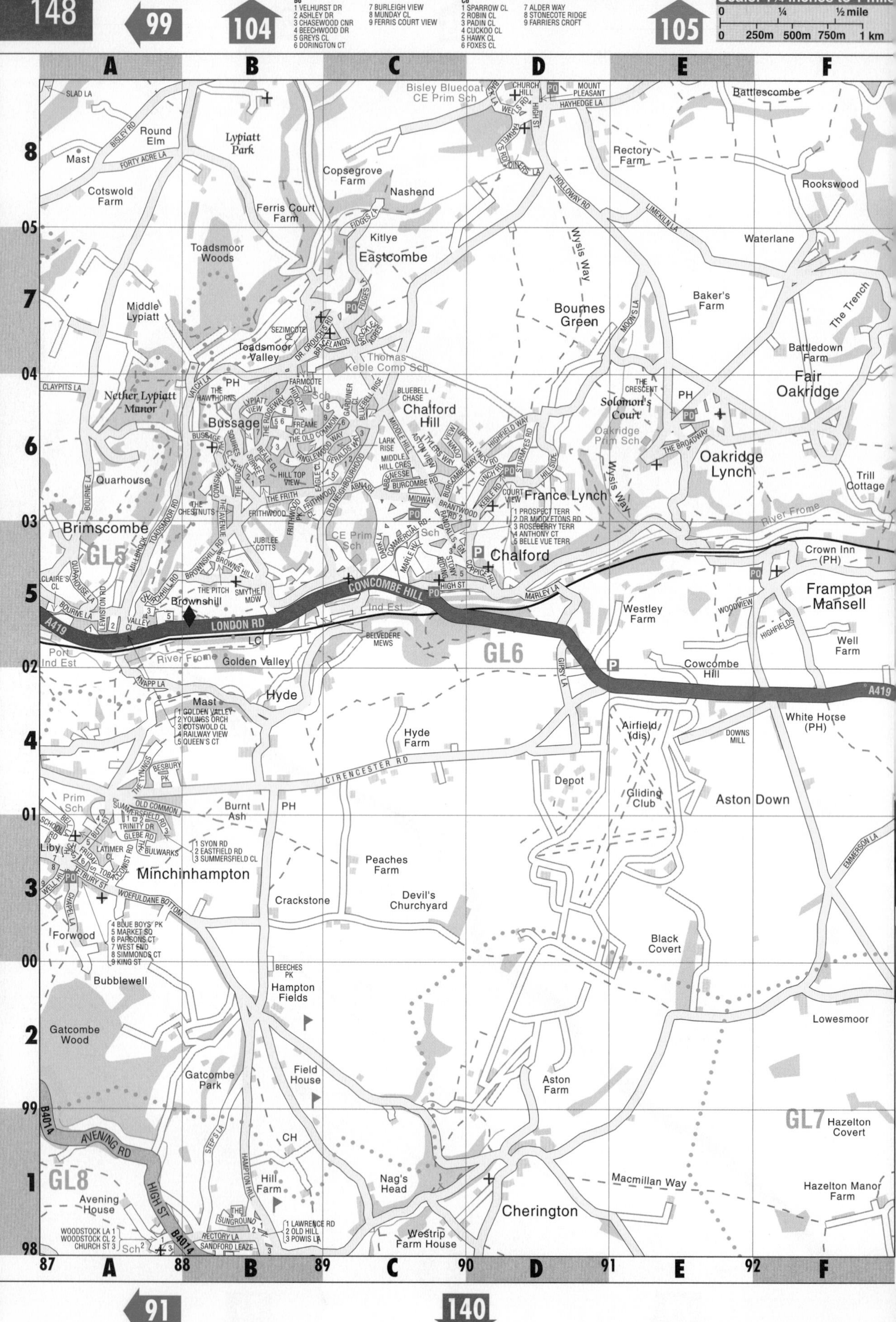

91
140

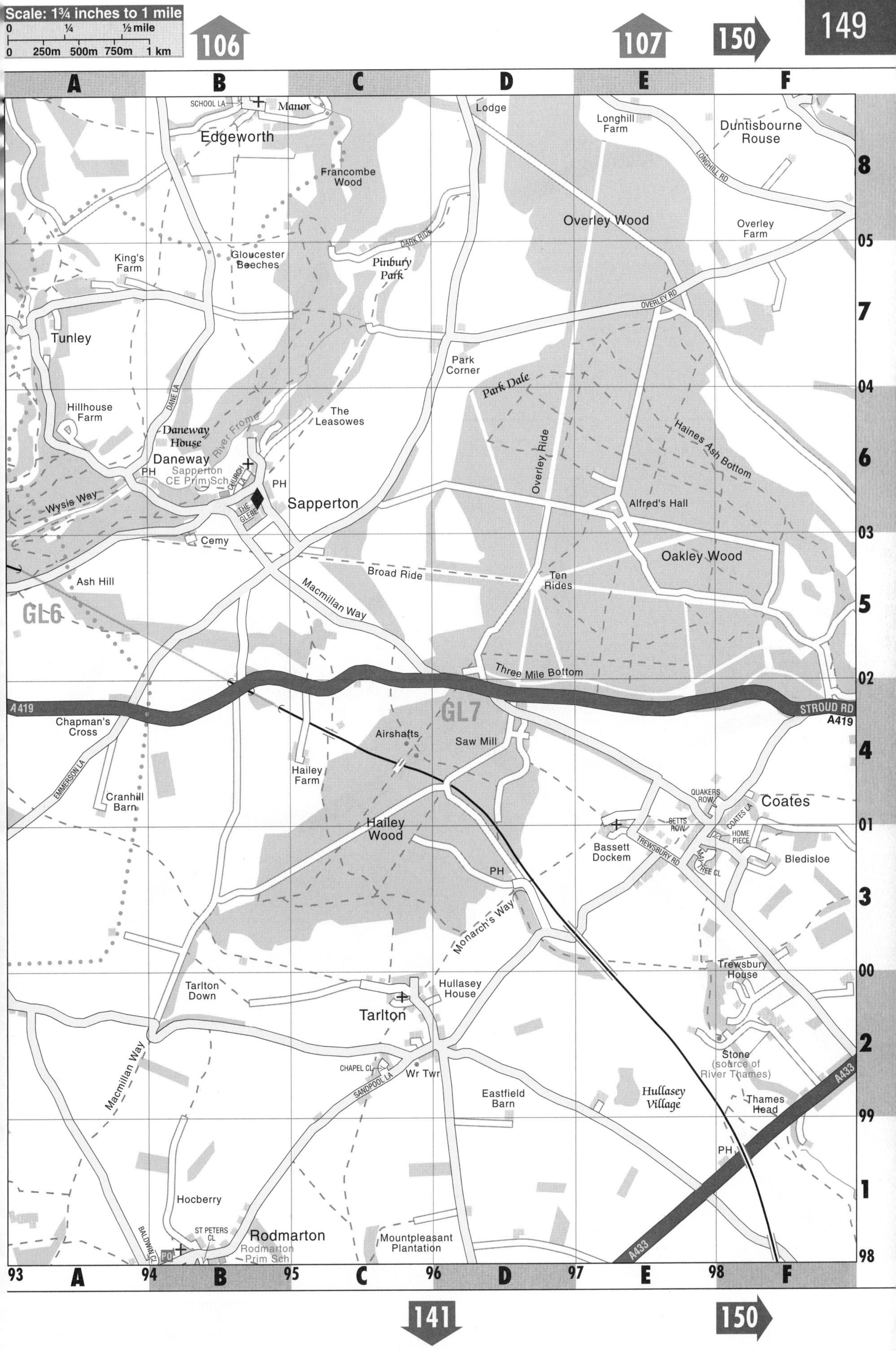
Scale: 1¾ inches to 1 mile
0 ¼ ½ mile
0 250m 500m 750m 1 km
106
107
150
A B C D E F
8
05
7
04
6
03
5
02
4
01
3
00
2
99
1
98
93 94 95 96 97 98
SCHOOL LA
Manor
Edgeworth
Lodge
Longhill Farm
Duntisbourne Rouse
LONGHILL RD
Francombe Wood
Overley Wood
Overley Farm
DARK RIDE
King's Farm
Gloucester Beeches
Pinbury Park
OVERLEY RD
Tunley
Park Corner
Park Dale
DANE LA
Hillhouse Farm
The Leasowes
Daneway House
River Frome
Haines Ash Bottom
Overley Ride
Daneway
PH
Sapperton CE Prim Sch
CHURCH LA
Wysis Way
THE GLEBE
Sapperton
Alfred's Hall
Cemy
Oakley Wood
Ash Hill
Broad Ride
Ten Rides
Macmillan Way
GL6
Three Mile Bottom
A419
GL7
STROUD RD
Chapman's Cross
Airshafts
Saw Mill
EMMERSON LA
Hailey Farm
Cranhill Barn
QUAKERS ROW
Coates
COATES LA
Hailey Wood
SETTS ROW
HOME PIECE
Bassett Dockem
TREWSBURY RD
TREE CL
Bledisloe
Monarch's Way
Trewsbury House
Tarlton Down
Hullasey House
Tarlton
Stone (source of River Thames)
CHAPEL CL
SANDPOOL LA
Wr Twr
A433
Eastfield Barn
Hullasey Village
Thames Head
Hocberry
BALDWIN CL
ST PETERS CL
Rodmarton
Rodmarton Prim Sch
PO
Mountpleasant Plantation

149
158

Scale: 1¾ inches to 1 mile
0 ¼ ½ mile
0 250m 500m 750m 1 km

A B C D E F

Grove Hill
Itlay
Mast
Peewits Hill
WARRENS GORSE COTTS
WELSH WAY
LYNCROFT FARM WKSHPS
CUTHAM LA
A435
Monarch's Way
The Sisters
WELSH WAY
A429
A417
DOWERS' LA
Daglingworth
Lower End
CH
Elden Wood
WHITE WAY
Wiggold
Raggedhedge Covert
DOWNS WAY
MILL VIEW
MEADOW VIEW
PRIORS CT
THE PADDOCKS
Baunton
Shooters Hill
STOW RD
Cemy
MANOR CL
BAUNTON LA
LINKS VIEW
STRATTON HTS
VAISEY RD
CHELTENHAM RD
Whiteway Farm
Stratton CE Prim Sch
GLOUCESTER RD
OVERHILL RD
Stratton
Yellow School Copse
THE WHITEWAY
PO
GLOUCESTER RD
BOWLING GREEN RD
Bowling Green
B4425
Ivy Lodge
Ewe Pens
ABBEY WAY
BURFORD RD
CHERRY TREE LA
Norcote
GROVE LA
A435
Pope's Seat
LONDON RD
A417
Cirencester Park
THOMAS ST
Liby
Mus
PO
UPPER CHURN SIDE
The Beeches
PHEASANT WAY
Kingshill Sch
GL7
CIRENCESTER
CORINIVM
CASTLE ST
DYER ST
LEWIS LA
Tech Coll
A419
TETBURY RD
SHEEP ST
QUERNS LA
VICTORIA RD
QUEEN ELIZABETH RD
New Mills
Mon
Deer Park Sch
Cirencester Coll
STROUD RD
Schs
NORTH HOME RD
A417
WITPIT LA
Royal Agricultural Coll
A419
A429
Cirencester Hosp
WATERMOOR RD
Jun & Inf Sch
PO
Prim Sch
Watermoor
A429
Kings Hill
KINGSHILL LA
BRISTOL RD
CHESTERTON LA
Cemy
Monarch's Way
APSLEY RD
A419 SWINDON RD
KINGSWAY
VILLAGE FARM
SPRINGFIELD RD
Prim Sch
SOMERFORD RD
PO
GRANHAMS LA
Chesterton
LOVE LA
Ind Est
Preston
Field Barn
A429 TETBURY RD
Chesterton Farm
SIDDINGTON RD
WILKINSON RD
Corinium Ctr
A433
A429
Siddington Sch
CIRENCESTER RD
A419
Siddington House
190
Upper Siddington
SPRATSGATE LA
POUND CL
JUBILEE FLATS
SOUTH CERNEY RD
PO
THE COMMON
Swallow Copse
Chesterton Plantation
PARK WAY
POST OFFICE SQ
THE TWENTIES
FRAZIER'S FOLLY
Twr
Siddington
Barracks
THOMPSON RD
HANNAH CRES
JACKSON RD
A433
ELIZABETH WAY
SIDDINGTON HALL
PH
BOWLY CRES
MOTTERSHEAD RD
NURSERY VIEW
CLARK'S LA
ASHTON RD
TRENCHARD GDNS
HAMBLEDON CL
Sewage Wks
Furzen Lease Farm
Point to Point Course
Dryleaze Farm
A429

8 05 7 04 6 03 5 02 4 01 3 00 2 99 1 98

99 A 00 B 01 C 02 D 03 E 04 F

190
190
190
190

For full street detail of the highlighted area see page 190.

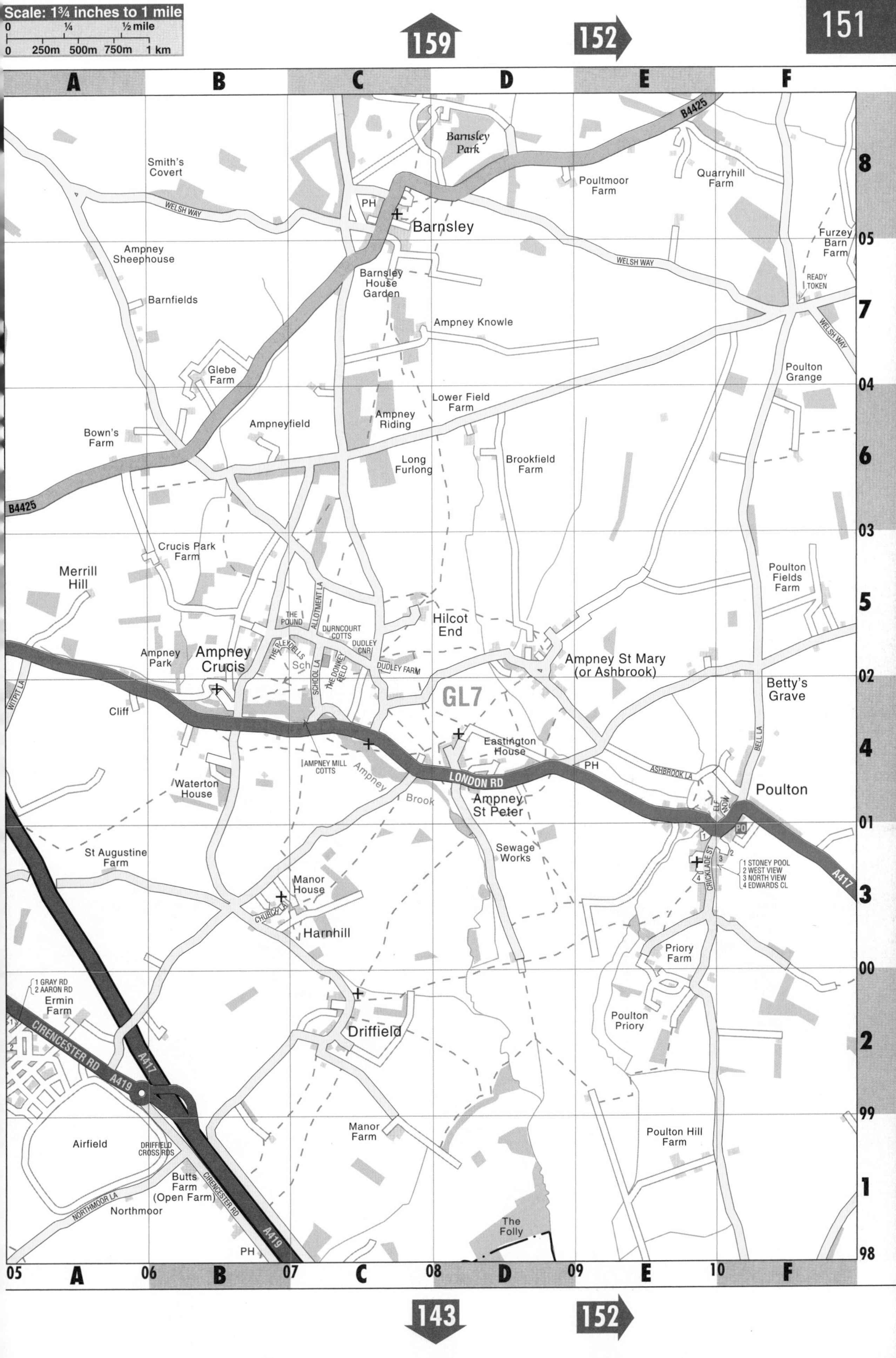

Scale: 1¾ inches to 1 mile
0 ¼ ½ mile
0 250m 500m 750m 1 km
159
152
A B C D E F
8 05 7 04 6 03 5 02 4 01 3 00 2 99 1 98
05 06 07 08 09 10
Barnsley Park
B4425
Smith's Covert
Poultmoor Farm
Quarryhill Farm
WELSH WAY
PH
Barnsley
Furzey Barn Farm
Ampney Sheephouse
Barnsley House Garden
WELSH WAY
READY TOKEN
Barnfields
Ampney Knowle
WELSH WAY
Glebe Farm
Poulton Grange
Lower Field Farm
Ampney Riding
Ampneyfield
Bown's Farm
Long Furlong
Brookfield Farm
B4425
Crucis Park Farm
Merrill Hill
Poulton Fields Farm
THE POUND
ALLOTMENT LA
DURNCOURT COTTS
Hilcot End
Ampney Park
Ampney Crucis
THE BEYDELLS
DUDLEY CNR
Sch
SCHOOL LA
THE DONKEY FIELD
DUDLEY FARM
Ampney St Mary (or Ashbrook)
WITPIT LA
Betty's Grave
GL7
Cliff
Eastington House
BELL LA
AMPNEY MILL COTTS
Ampney
PH
ASHBROOK LA
LONDON RD
Poulton
Waterton House
Brook
Ampney St Peter
ELF MDW
PO
Sewage Works
St Augustine Farm
CRICKLADE ST
1 STONEY POOL
2 WEST VIEW
3 NORTH VIEW
4 EDWARDS CL
A417
Manor House
CHURCH LA
Harnhill
Priory Farm
1 GRAY RD
2 AARON RD
Ermin Farm
Poulton Priory
Driffield
CIRENCESTER RD
A417
A419
Airfield
DRIFFIELD CROSS RDS
Manor Farm
Poulton Hill Farm
Butts Farm (Open Farm)
CIRENCESTER RD
NORTHMOOR LA
Northmoor
A419
The Folly
PH
143
152

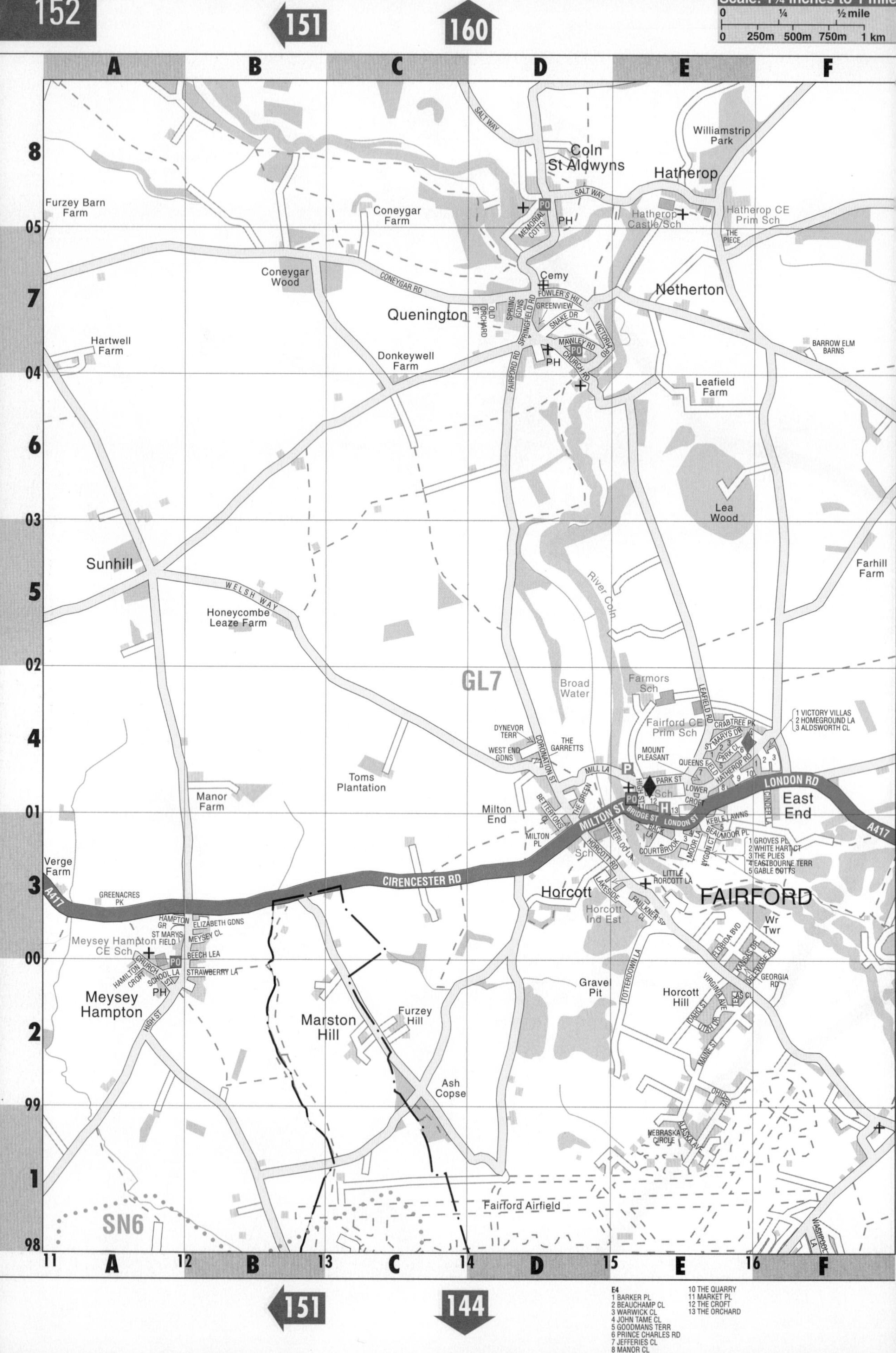
151
160
Scale: 1¾ inches to 1 mile
0 ¼ ½ mile
0 250m 500m 750m 1 km
A B C D E F
8
05
7
04
6
03
5
02
4
01
3
00
2
99
1
98
11 A 12 B 13 C 14 D 15 E 16 F
SALT WAY
Coln St Aldwyns
Hatherop
Williamstrip Park
Furzey Barn Farm
Coneygar Farm
PO
PH
MEMORIAL COTTS
Hatherop Castle Sch
Hatherop CE Prim Sch
THE PIECE
Coneygar Wood
CONEYGAR RD
Cemy
Netherton
FOWLER'S HILL
GREENVIEW
SNAKE DR
OLD ORCHARD CT
SPRING GDNS
SPRINGFIELD RD
Quenington
VICTORIA RD
MAWLEY RD
CHURCH RD
Hartwell Farm
Donkeywell Farm
FAIRFORD RD
BARROW ELM BARNS
Leafield Farm
Lea Wood
Sunhill
Farhill Farm
WELSH WAY
Honeycombe Leaze Farm
River Coln
GL7
Broad Water
Farmors Sch
LEAFIELD RD
Fairford CE Prim Sch
CRABTREE PK
1 VICTORY VILLAS
2 HOMEGROUND LA
3 ALDSWORTH CL
DYNEVOR TERR
CORONATION ST
THE GARRETTS
WEST END GDNS
MOUNT PLEASANT
ST MARYS DR
QUEENS FIELD
PARK CL
HATHEROP RD
MILL LA
P
PARK ST
Sch
Toms Plantation
Manor Farm
Milton End
BETTERTONS CL
THE GREEN
MILTON ST
HIGH ST
BRIDGE ST
LONDON ST
LOWER CROFT
H
CINDER LA
LONDON RD
East End
A417
KEBLE LAWNS
BEAUMOOR PL
MILTON PL
WATERLOO LA
BACK LA
COURTBROOK
MOOR LA
HORCOTT RD
AYGON CT
1 GROVES PL
2 WHITE HART CT
3 THE PLIES
4 EASTBOURNE TERR
5 GABLE COTTS
Verge Farm
CIRENCESTER RD
LITTLE HORCOTT LA
Horcott
LAKESIDE
FAULKNER ST
FAIRFORD
GREENACRES PK
Horcott Ind Est
Wr Twr
HAMPTON GR
ELIZABETH GDNS
ST MARYS FIELD
MEYSEY CL
Meysey Hampton CE Sch
BEECH LEA
STRAWBERRY LA
HAMILTON CROFT
CHURCH ST
SCHOOL LA
FLORIDA BVD
KANSAS DR
DELAWARE RD
GEORGIA RD
Meysey Hampton
HIGH ST
Gravel Pit
TOTTERDOWN LA
Horcott Hill
VIRGINIA AVE
TEXAS CL
IDAHO ST
UTAH DR
MAINE ST
Marston Hill
Furzey Hill
Ash Copse
OHIO AVE
NEBRASKA CIRCLE
ALASKA AVE
Fairford Airfield
SN6
WASHPOOL LA
151
144
E4
1 BARKER PL
2 BEAUCHAMP CL
3 WARWICK CL
4 JOHN TAME CL
5 GOODMANS TERR
6 PRINCE CHARLES RD
7 JEFFERIES CL
8 MANOR CL
9 CHURCHILL PL
10 THE QUARRY
11 MARKET PL
12 THE CROFT
13 THE ORCHARD

Scale: 1¾ inches to 1 mile

161

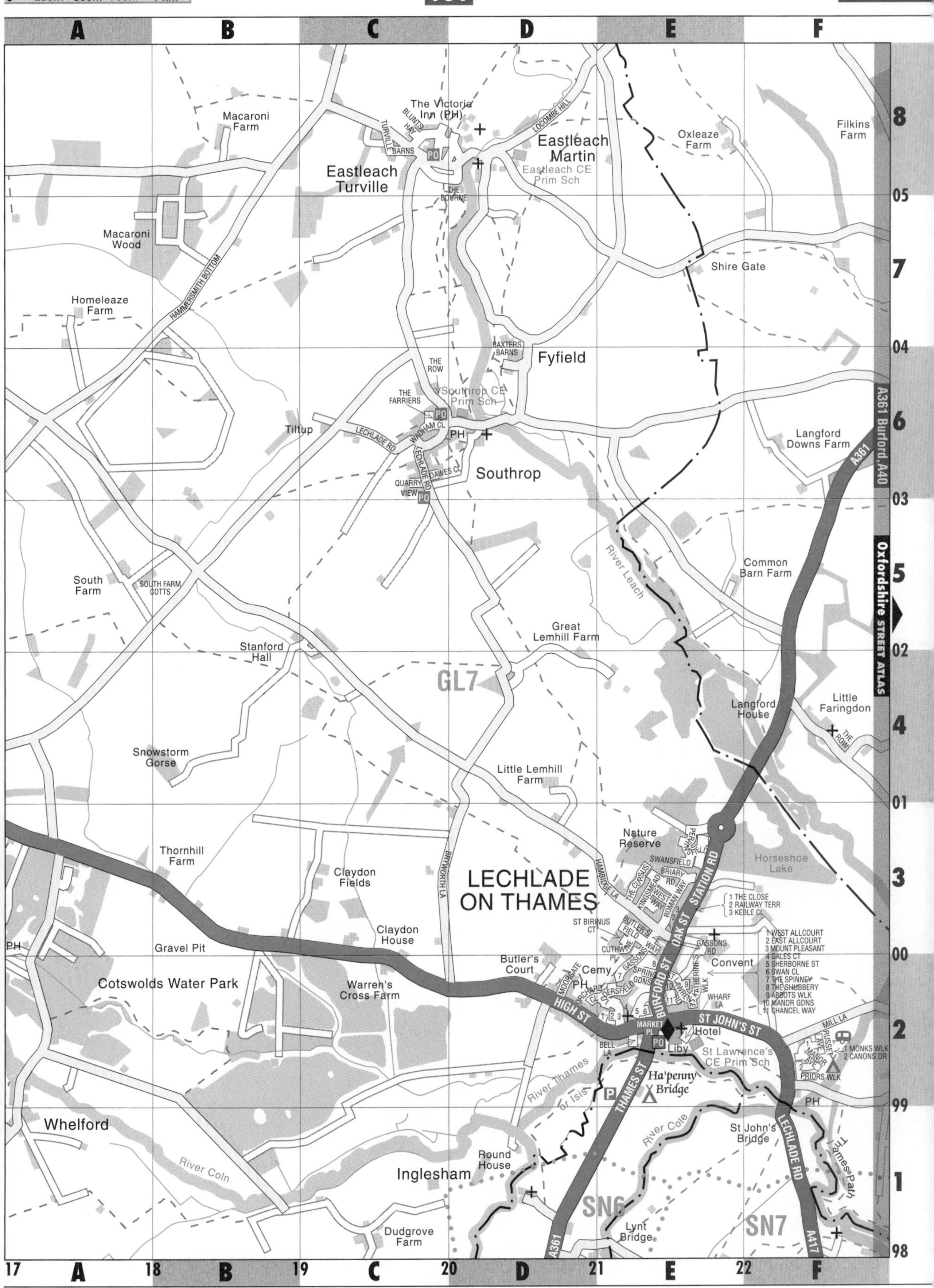

Macaroni Farm
The Victoria Inn (PH)
Eastleach Martin
Eastleach Turville
Eastleach CE Prim Sch
Oxleaze Farm
Filkins Farm
Macaroni Wood
Shire Gate
Homeleaze Farm
Fyfield
Southrop CE Prim Sch
Tiltup
Southrop
Langford Downs Farm
South Farm
SOUTH FARM COTTS
Common Barn Farm
River Leach
Great Lemhill Farm
Stanford Hall
GL7
Langford House
Little Faringdon
Snowstorm Gorse
Little Lemhill Farm
Nature Reserve
Thornhill Farm
Claydon Fields
LECHLADE ON THAMES
Horseshoe Lake
Claydon House
Gravel Pit
Butler's Court
Cemy
Convent
Cotswolds Water Park
Warren's Cross Farm
Hotel
Liby
St Lawrence's CE Prim Sch
Ha'penny Bridge
River Thames or Isis
Whelford
River Coln
Round House
Inglesham
River Cole
St John's Bridge
Thames Path
SN6
SN7
Lynt Bridge
Dudgrove Farm
A361 Burford, A40
Oxfordshire STREET ATLAS
1 THE CLOSE
2 RAILWAY TERR
3 KEBLE CL
1 WEST ALLCOURT
2 EAST ALLCOURT
3 MOUNT PLEASANT
4 GALES CT
5 SHERBORNE ST
6 SWAN CL
7 THE SPINNEY
8 THE SHRUBBERY
9 ABBOTS WLK
10 MANOR GDNS
11 CHANCEL WAY
1 MONKS WLK
2 CANONS DR
HIGH ST
ST JOHN'S ST
THAMES ST
BURFORD ST
OAK ST
STATION RD
LECHLADE RD
A361
A417

145

162

Scale: 1¾ inches to 1 mile

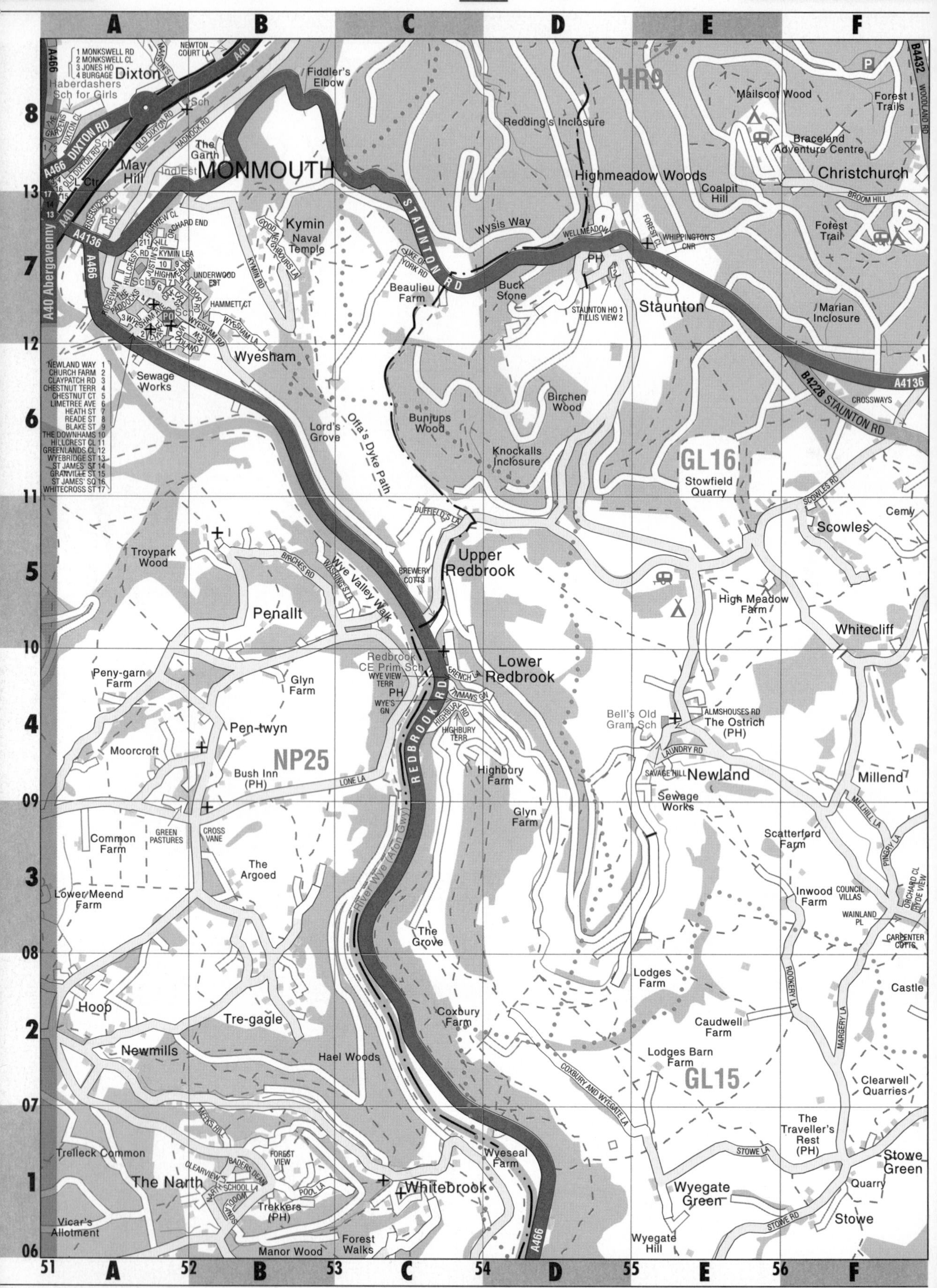

146

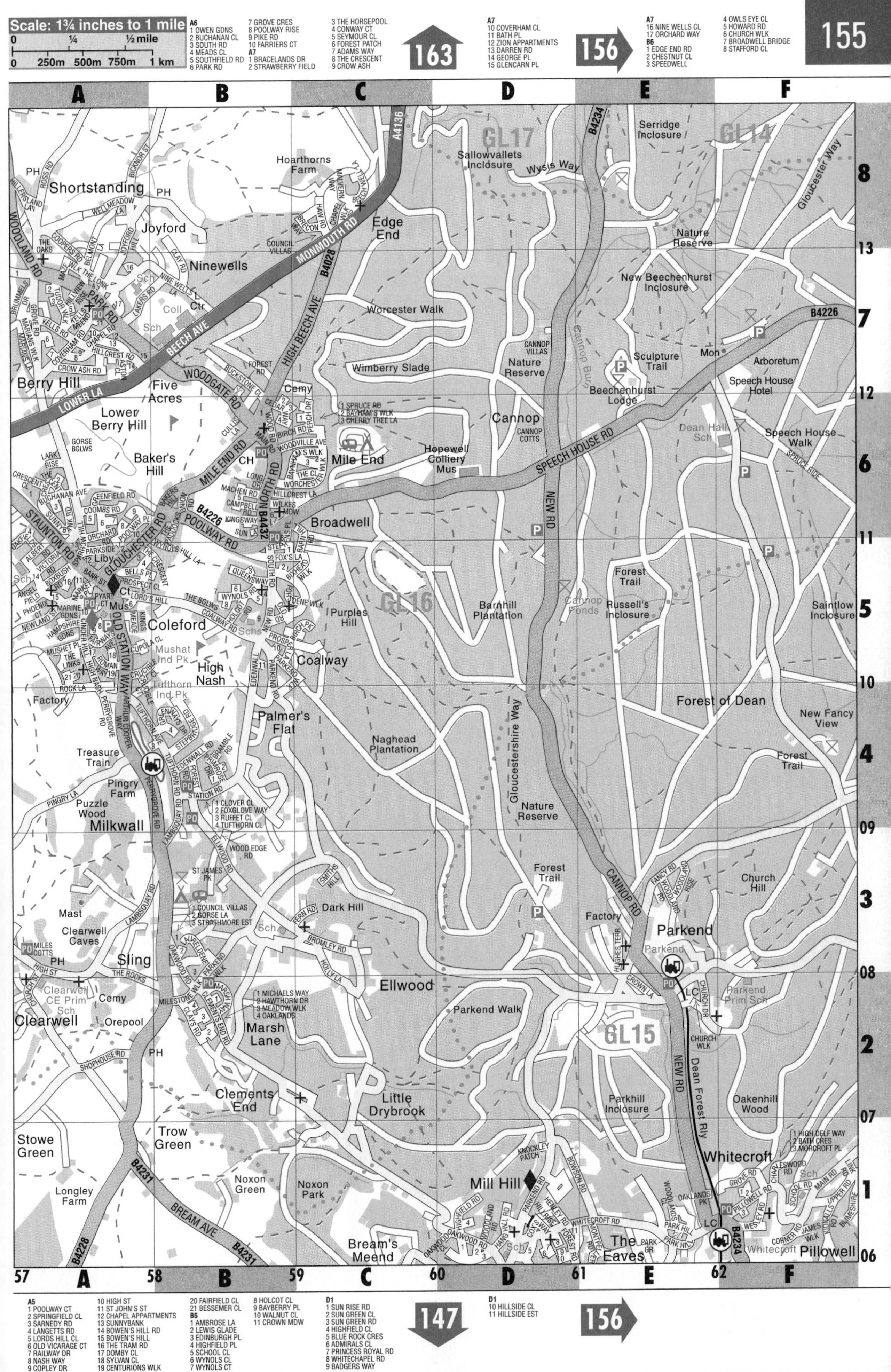

155
Scale: 1¾ inches to 1 mile
0 ¼ ½ mile
0 250m 500m 750m 1 km
A6
1 OWEN GDNS
2 BUCHANAN CL
3 SOUTH RD
4 MEADS CL
5 SOUTHFIELD RD
6 PARK RD
7 GROVE CRES
8 POOLWAY RISE
9 PIKE RD
10 FARRIERS CT
A7
1 BRACELANDS DR
2 STRAWBERRY FIELD
3 THE HORSEPOOL
4 CONWAY CT
5 SEYMOUR CL
6 FOREST PATCH
7 ADAMS WAY
8 THE CRESCENT
9 CROW ASH
163
A7
10 COVERHAM CL
11 BATH PL
12 ZION APPARTMENTS
13 DARREN RD
14 GEORGE PL
15 GLENCARN PL
156
A7
16 NINE WELLS CL
17 ORCHARD WAY
B6
1 EDGE END RD
2 CHESTNUT CL
3 SPEEDWELL
4 OWLS EYE CL
5 HOWARD RD
6 CHURCH WLK
7 BROADWELL BRIDGE
8 STAFFORD CL
Shortstanding
Joyford
Ninewells
Berry Hill
Five Acres
Lower Berry Hill
Baker's Hill
Coleford
Mushat Ind Pk
High Nash
Tufthorn Ind Pk
Coalway
Palmer's Flat
Broadwell
Mile End
Edge End
Hoarthorns Farm
Worcester Walk
Wimberry Slade
Purples Hill
Naghead Plantation
Treasure Train
Pingry Farm
Puzzle Wood
Milkwall
Mast
Clearwell Caves
Sling
Clearwell
Clearwell CE Prim Sch
Cemy
Orepool
Dark Hill
Ellwood
Marsh Lane
Clements End
Trow Green
Stowe Green
Longley Farm
Noxon Green
Noxon Park
Little Drybrook
Bream's Meend
Parkend Walk
Mill Hill
The Eaves
Whitecroft
Pillowell
Oakenhill Wood
Parkhill Inclosure
Parkend
Church Hill
Forest of Dean
New Fancy View
Forest Trail
Saintlow Inclosure
Russell's Inclosure
Cannop Ponds
Barnhill Plantation
Gloucestershire Way
Nature Reserve
Cannop
Hopewell Colliery Mus
Speech House Walk
Speech House Hotel
Arboretum
Sculpture Trail
Beechenhurst Lodge
New Beechenhurst Inclosure
Serridge Inclosure
Sallowvallets Inclosure
Wysis Way
Dean Forest Rly
GL14
GL15
GL16
GL17
B4226
B4228
B4231
B4234
B4028
B4432
A4136
MONMOUTH RD
BEECH AVE
LOWER LA
SPEECH HOUSE RD
NEW RD
CANNOP RD
BREAM AVE
57 58 59 60 61 62
06 07 08 09 10 11 12 13
A5
1 POOLWAY CT
2 SPRINGFIELD CL
3 SARNEDY RD
4 LANGETTS RD
5 LORDS HILL CL
6 OLD VICARAGE CT
7 RAILWAY DR
8 NASH WAY
9 COPLEY DR
10 HIGH ST
11 ST JOHN'S ST
12 CHAPEL APPARTMENTS
13 SUNNYBANK
14 BOWEN'S HILL RD
15 BOWEN'S HILL
16 THE TRAM RD
17 DOMBY CL
18 SYLVAN CL
19 CENTURIONS WLK
20 FAIRFIELD CL
21 BESSEMER CL
B5
1 AMBROSE LA
2 LEWIS GLADE
3 EDINBURGH PL
4 HIGHFIELD PL
5 SCHOOL CL
6 WYNOLS CL
7 WYNOLS CT
8 HOLCOT CL
9 BAYBERRY PL
10 WALNUT CL
11 CROWN MDW
D1
1 SUN RISE RD
2 SUN GREEN CL
3 SUN GREEN RD
4 HIGHFIELD CL
5 BLUE ROCK CRES
6 ADMIRALS CL
7 PRINCESS ROYAL RD
8 WHITECHAPEL RD
9 BADGERS WAY
D1
10 HILLSIDE CL
11 HILLSIDE EST
147
156

For full street detail of the highlighted area see page 191.

Scale: 1¾ inches to 1 mile
165
108
Newnham
Broadoak
Strand
Stantway
Gatwick
Stanley
Boxbush
Rodley
Framilode
Priding
Arlingham
Overton
Fretherne
Saul
Awre
Church End
River Severn
The Noose
Pimlico Sand
Arlingham Warth
Lower Dumball
Hock Cliff
Garden Cliff
Severn Way
GL14
GL2
The Gloucester and Sharpness Canal
94
95
100

115

166

Scale: 1¾ inches to 1 mile
0 ¼ ½ mile
0 250m 500m 750m 1 km

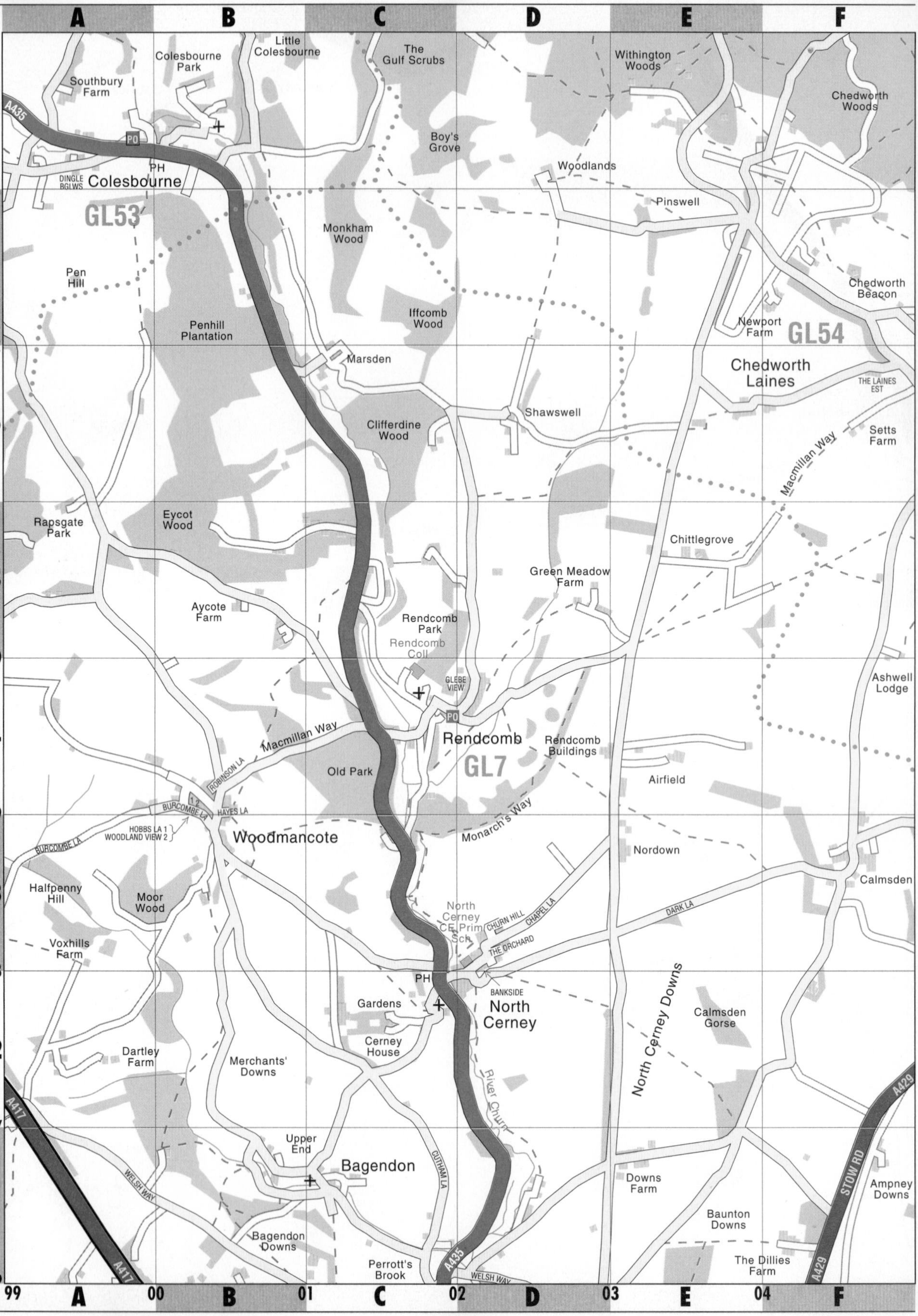

A B C D E F

8 13 7 12 6 11 5 10 4 09 3 08 2 07 1 06

99 A 00 B 01 C 02 D 03 E 04 F

107

150

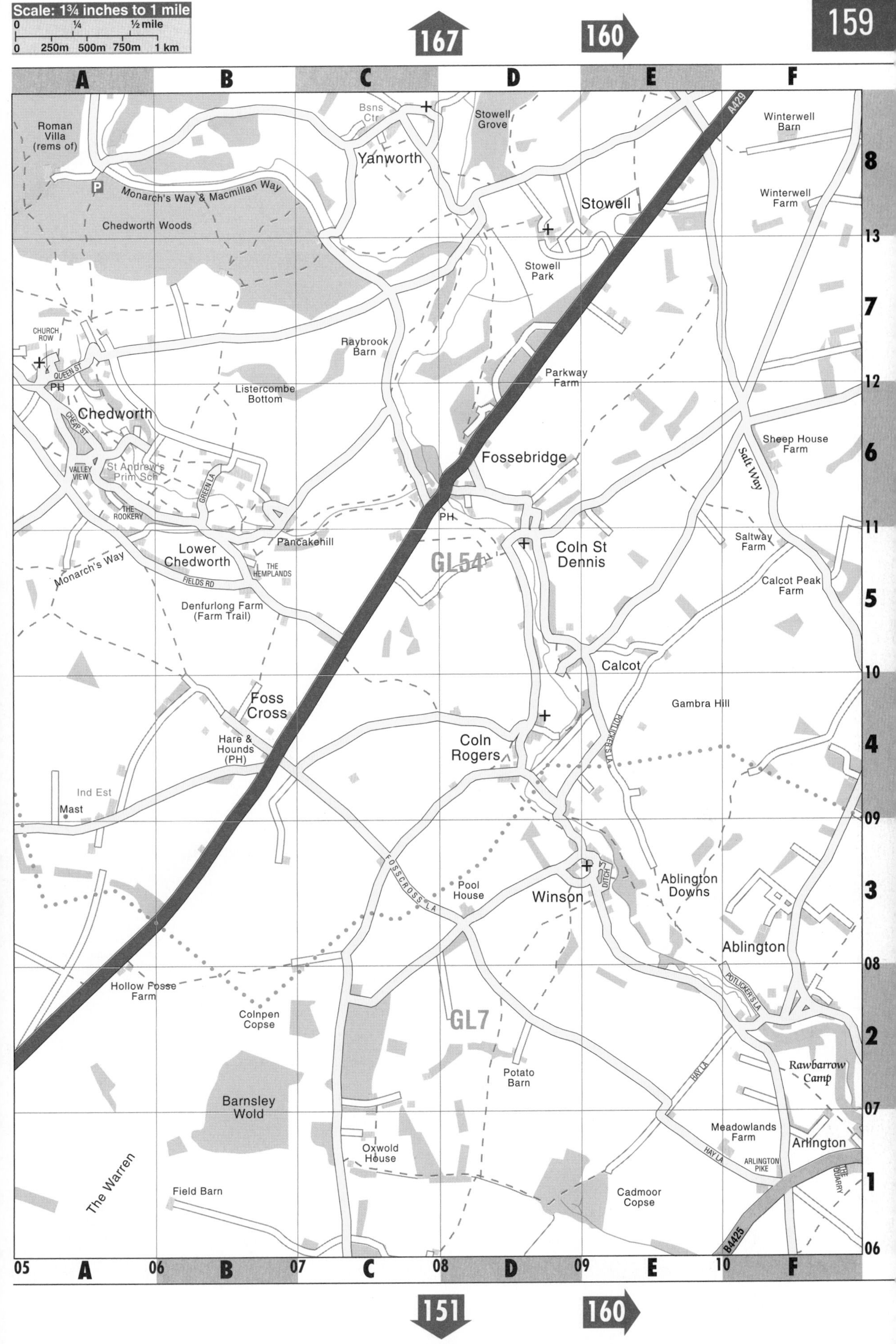

Scale: 1¾ inches to 1 mile
0 ¼ ½ mile
0 250m 500m 750m 1 km
167
160
A B C D E F
Roman Villa (rems of)
Bsns Ctr
Stowell Grove
Winterwell Barn
Yanworth
Monarch's Way & Macmillan Way
Chedworth Woods
Stowell
Winterwell Farm
Stowell Park
CHURCH ROW
QUEEN ST
Raybrook Barn
Parkway Farm
PH
Chedworth
CHEAP ST
Listercombe Bottom
VALLEY VIEW
St Andrew's Prim Sch
GREEN LA
THE ROOKERY
Fossebridge
Sheep House Farm
Salt Way
PH
Pancakehill
Lower Chedworth
Monarch's Way
FIELDS RD
THE HEMPLANDS
GL54
Coln St Dennis
Saltway Farm
Calcot Peak Farm
Denfurlong Farm (Farm Trail)
Calcot
Foss Cross
Gambra Hill
Hare & Hounds (PH)
Coln Rogers
POTLICKER'S LA
Ind Est
Mast
FOSSCROSS LA
Pool House
Winson
DITCH
Ablington Downs
Ablington
POTLICKER'S LA
Hollow Fosse Farm
Colnpen Copse
GL7
Potato Barn
HAY LA
Rawbarrow Camp
Barnsley Wold
Meadowlands Farm
Arlington
HAY LA
ARLINGTON PIKE
THE QUARRY
Oxwold House
The Warren
Field Barn
Cadmoor Copse
B4425
A429
8 13 7 12 6 11 5 10 4 09 3 08 2 07 1 06
05 A 06 B 07 C 08 D 09 E 10 F
151
160

159
168

Scale: 1¾ inches to 1 mile

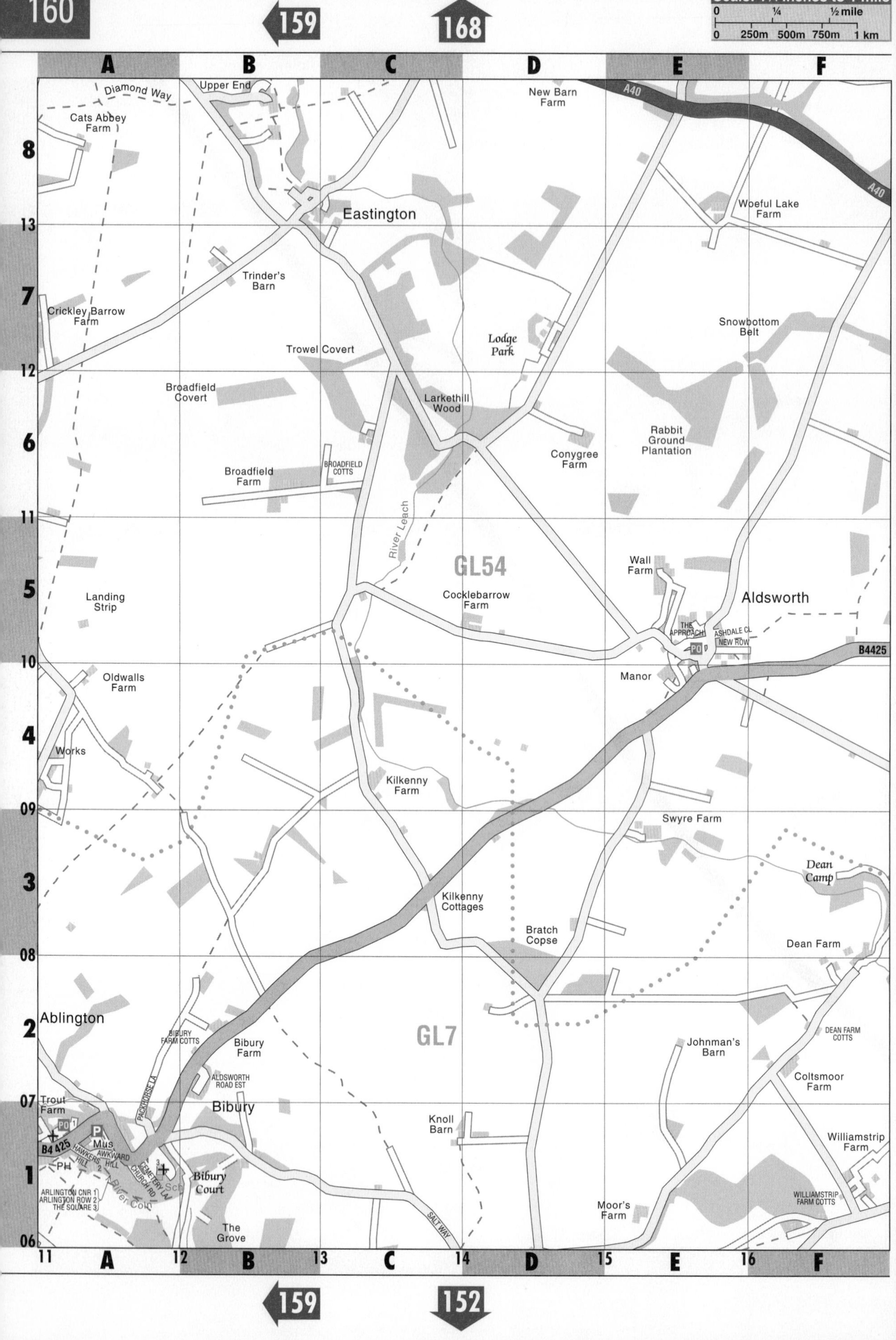

159
152

Scale: 1¾ inches to 1 mile
0 ¼ ½ mile
0 250m 500m 750m 1 km

169

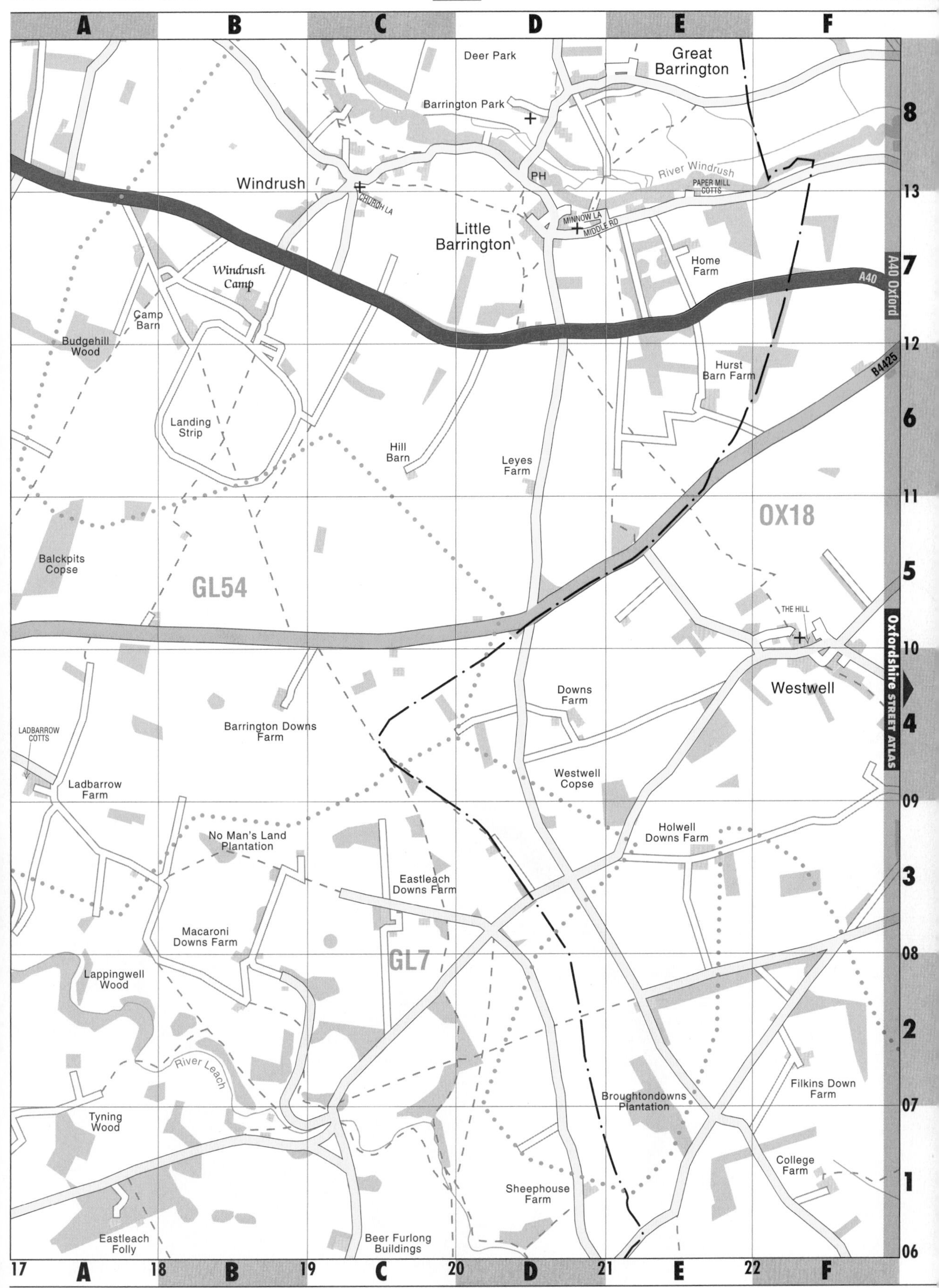
A B C D E F
Deer Park
Great Barrington
Barrington Park
PH
Windrush
CHURCH LA
River Windrush
PAPER MILL COTTS
MINNOW LA
MIDDLE RD
Little Barrington
Windrush Camp
Home Farm
A40
A40 Oxford
Camp Barn
Budgehill Wood
Hurst Barn Farm
B4425
Landing Strip
Hill Barn
Leyes Farm
OX18
Balckpits Copse
GL54
THE HILL
Westwell
Downs Farm
Oxfordshire STREET ATLAS
LADBARROW COTTS
Barrington Downs Farm
Ladbarrow Farm
Westwell Copse
No Man's Land Plantation
Holwell Downs Farm
Eastleach Downs Farm
Macaroni Downs Farm
GL7
Lappingwell Wood
River Leach
Filkins Down Farm
Broughtondowns Plantation
Tyning Wood
College Farm
Sheephouse Farm
Eastleach Folly
Beer Furlong Buildings
8 13 7 12 6 11 5 10 4 09 3 08 2 07 1 06
17 18 19 20 21 22

153

Scale: 1¾ inches to 1 mile
0 ¼ ½ mile
0 250m 500m 750m 1 km

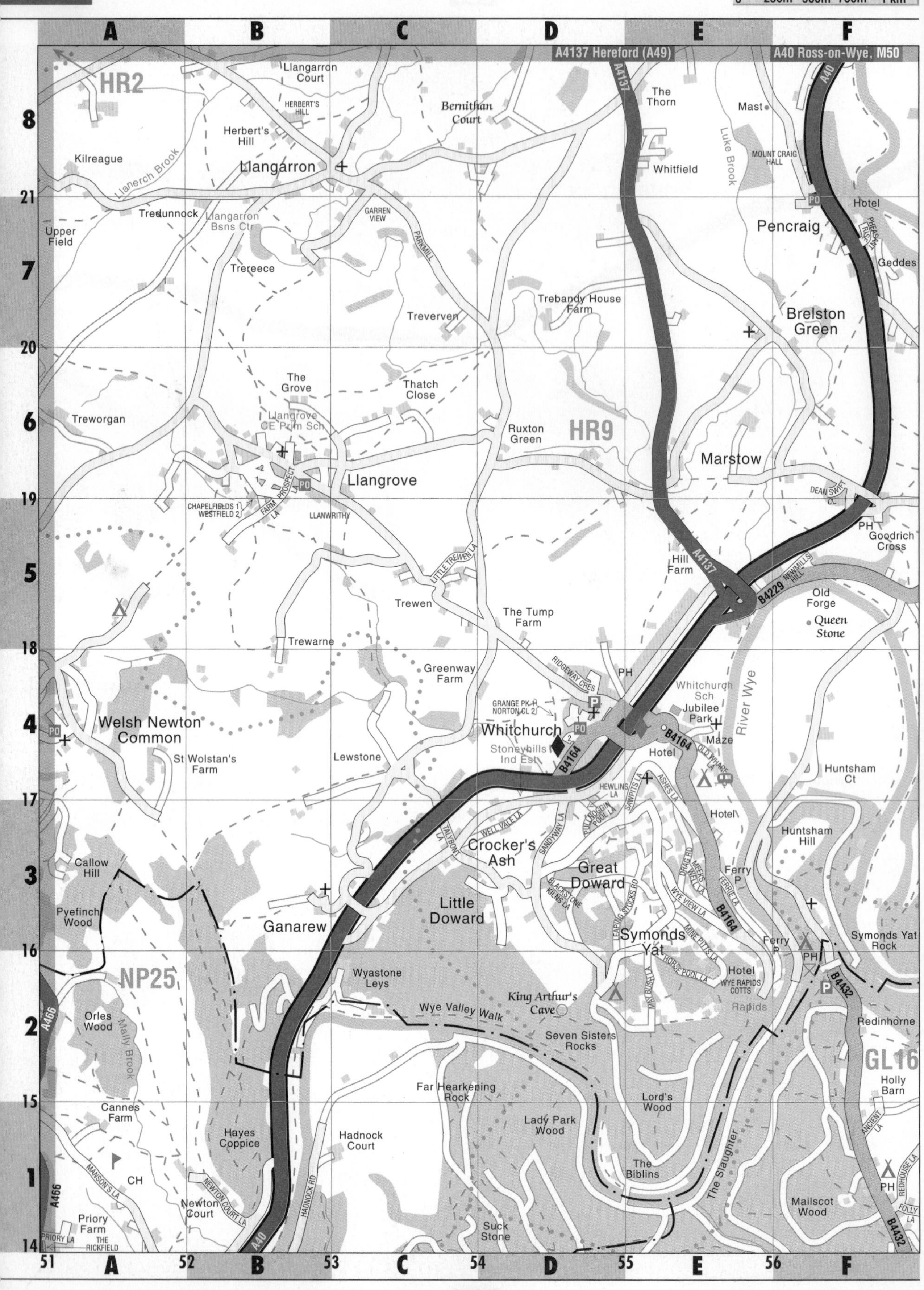

154

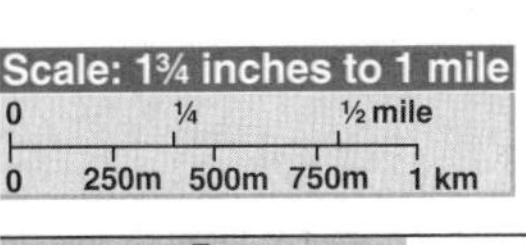

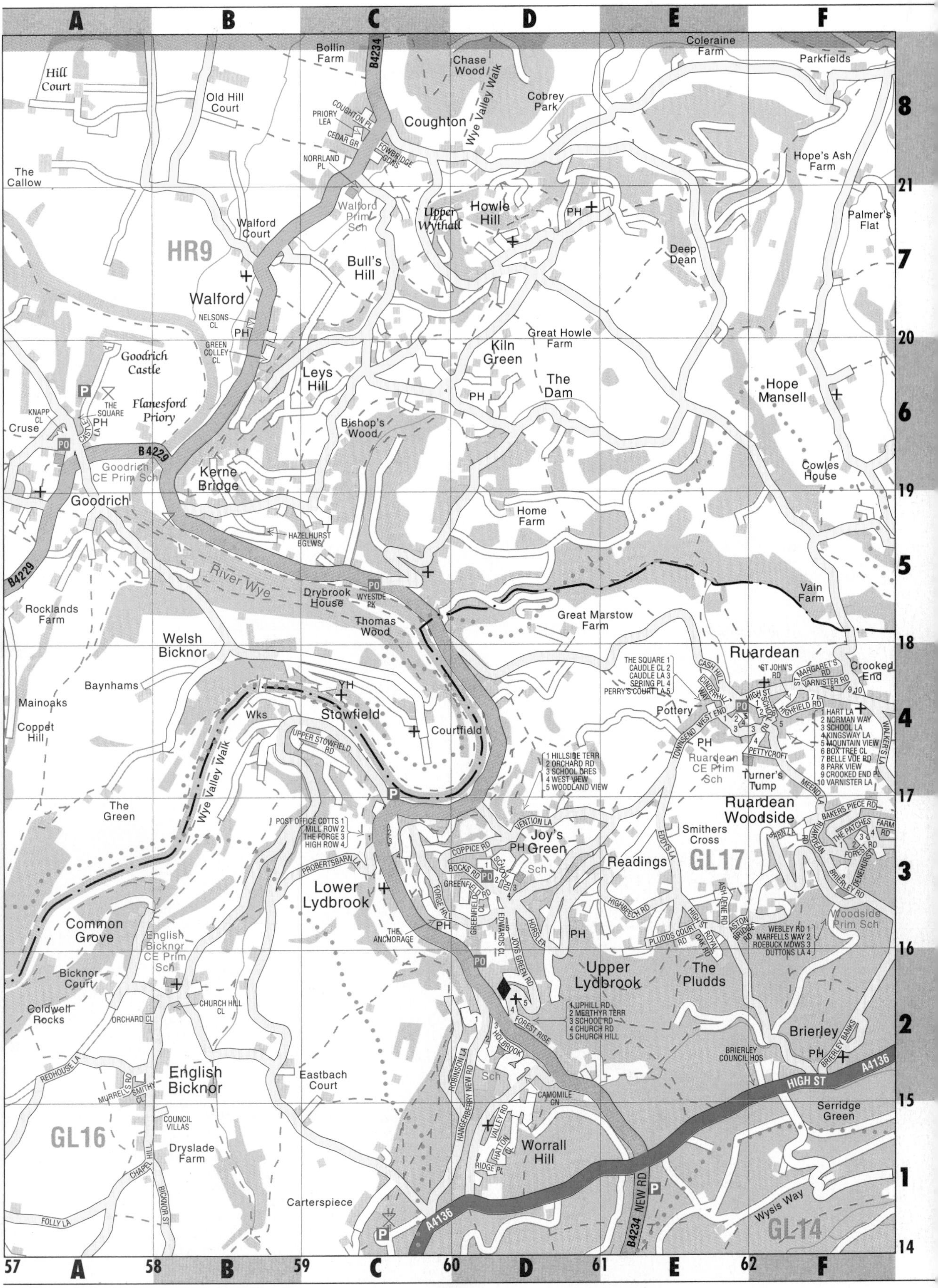

A B C D E F

Hill Court
Old Hill Court
Bollin Farm
B4234
Chase Wood
Wye Valley Walk
Coleraine Farm
Parkfields
Cobrey Park
Coughton
PRIORY LEA
COUGHTON PL
CEDAR GR
FOWBRIDGE GDNS
NORRLAND PL
8
Hope's Ash Farm
The Callow
21
Walford Prim Sch
Upper Wythall
Howle Hill
PH
Palmer's Flat
Walford Court
HR9
Bull's Hill
Deep Dean
7
Walford
NELSONS CL
PH
GREEN COLLEY CL
20
Great Howle Farm
Kiln Green
Goodrich Castle
Leys Hill
The Dam
Flanesford Priory
THE SQUARE
KNAPP CL
PH
CASTLE LA
PH
Hope Mansell
Cruse
PO
Bishop's Wood
6
B4229
Goodrich CE Prim Sch
Kerne Bridge
Cowles House
Goodrich
19
Home Farm
HAZELHURST BGLWS
B4229
River Wye
PO
WYESIDE PK
5
Drybrook House
Vain Farm
Rocklands Farm
Thomas Wood
Great Marstow Farm
Welsh Bicknor
18
THE SQUARE 1
CAUDLE CL 2
CAUDLE LA 3
SPRING PL 4
PERRY'S COURT LA 5
CASH HILL
Ruardean
ST JOHN'S RD
ST MARGARET'S RD
Crooked End
Baynhams
YH
CINDERHILL WAY
VARNISTER RD
Mainoaks
Stowfield
Pottery
PO
HIGH ST
SCHOOL RD
HIGHFIELD RD
Wks
1 HART LA
2 NORMAN WAY
3 SCHOOL LA
4 KINGSWAY LA
5 MOUNTAIN VIEW
6 BOX TREE CL
7 BELLE VUE RD
8 PARK VIEW
9 CROOKED END PL
10 VARNISTER LA
Coppet Hill
Courtfield
WEST END
4
UPPER STOWFIELD RD
TOWNSEND
PH
WALKER'S LA
1 HILLSIDE TERR
2 ORCHARD RD
3 SCHOOL CRES
4 WEST VIEW
5 WOODLAND VIEW
Ruardean CE Prim Sch
PETTYCROFT
Turner's Tump
MEEND LA
Wye Valley Walk
P
17
The Green
Ruardean Woodside
BAKERS PIECE RD
POST OFFICE COTTS 1
MILL ROW 2
THE FORGE 3
HIGH ROW 4
VENTION LA
Joy's Green
Smithers Cross
THE PATCHES
FARM
PH
EDDYS LA
GL17
COPPICE RD
FOREST RD
PROBERTSBARN LA
PO
SCHOOL RD
Sch
Readings
DENEHURST
3
Lower Lydbrook
ROCKS RD
GREENFIELD CL
BRIERLEY RD
FORGE HILL
HIGHBEECH RD
ASH DENE RD
Woodside Prim Sch
Common Grove
THE ANCHORAGE
PH
GREENFIELD RD
EDWARDS CL
HORSLEY
PH
PLUDDS COURT RD
OAK RD
ROYAL
ASTON BRIDGE RD
WEBLEY RD 1
MARFELLS WAY 2
ROEBUCK MDWS 3
DUTTONS LA 4
16
English Bicknor CE Prim Sch
JOYS GREEN RD
PO
Upper Lydbrook
The Pludds
Bicknor Court
Coldwell Rocks
CHURCH HILL CL
1 UPHILL RD
2 MERTHYR TERR
3 SCHOOL RD
4 CHURCH RD
5 CHURCH HILL
ORCHARD CL
FOREST RISE
2
Brierley
HOLBROOK
BRIERLEY BANKS
PH
BRIERLEY COUNCIL HOS
A4136
REDHOUSE LA
English Bicknor
Eastbach Court
ROBINSON LA
HANGERBERRY NEW RD
HIGH ST
MURRELL'S RD
SMITHY CL
Sch
CAMOMILE GN
15
Serridge Green
COUNCIL VILLAS
GL16
VALLEY RD
Dryslade Farm
Worrall Hill
HATTON CL
CHAPEL HILL
RIDGE PL
1
BICKNOR ST
NEW RD
P
Carterspiece
Wysis Way
FOLLY LA
A4136
P
B4234
GL14
14

57 A 58 B 59 C 60 D 61 E 62 F

155
164

163

170

Scale: 1¾ inches to 1 mile
0 ¼ ½ mile
0 250m 500m 750m 1 km

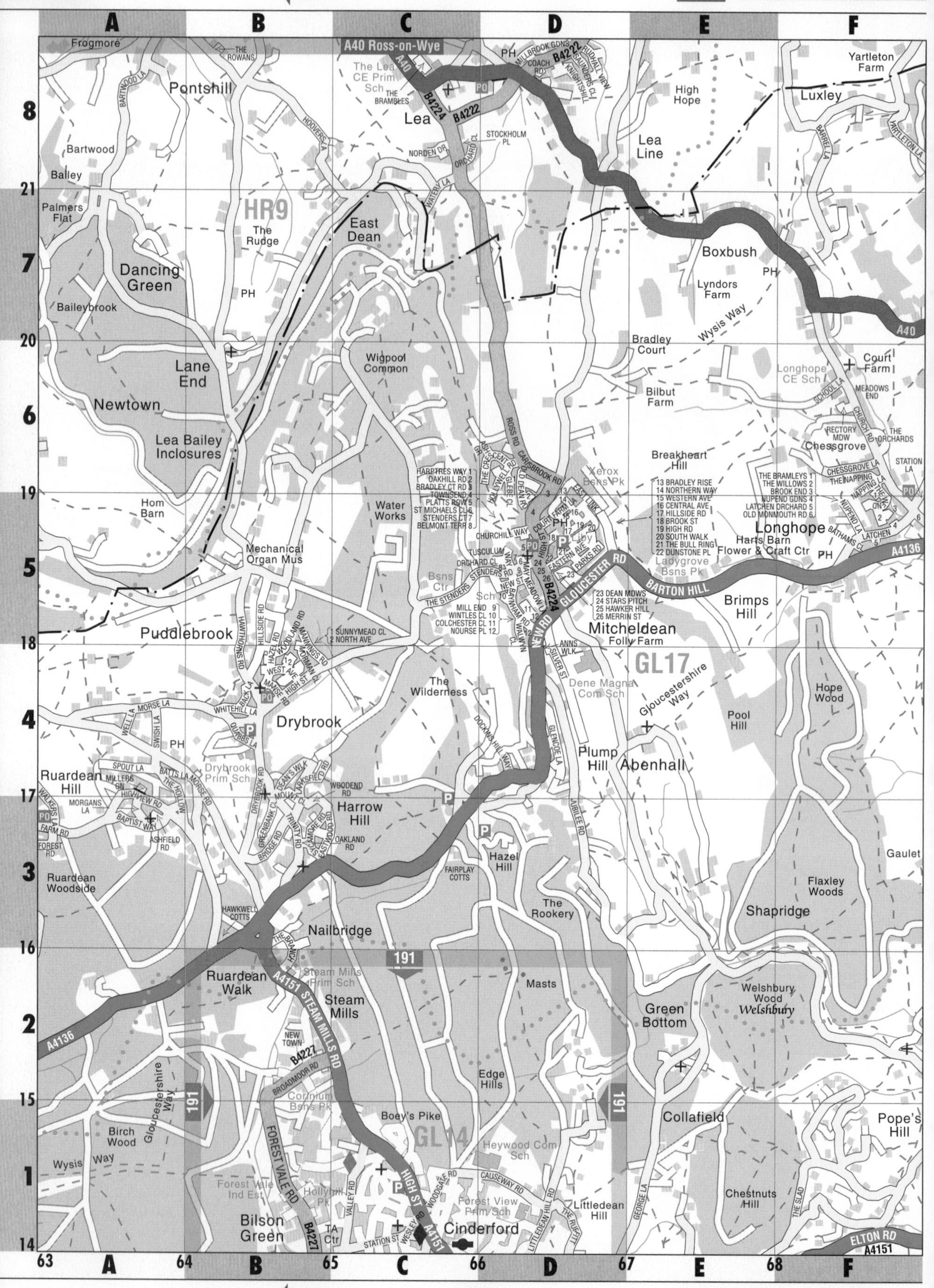

163

156

For full street detail of the highlighted area see page 191.

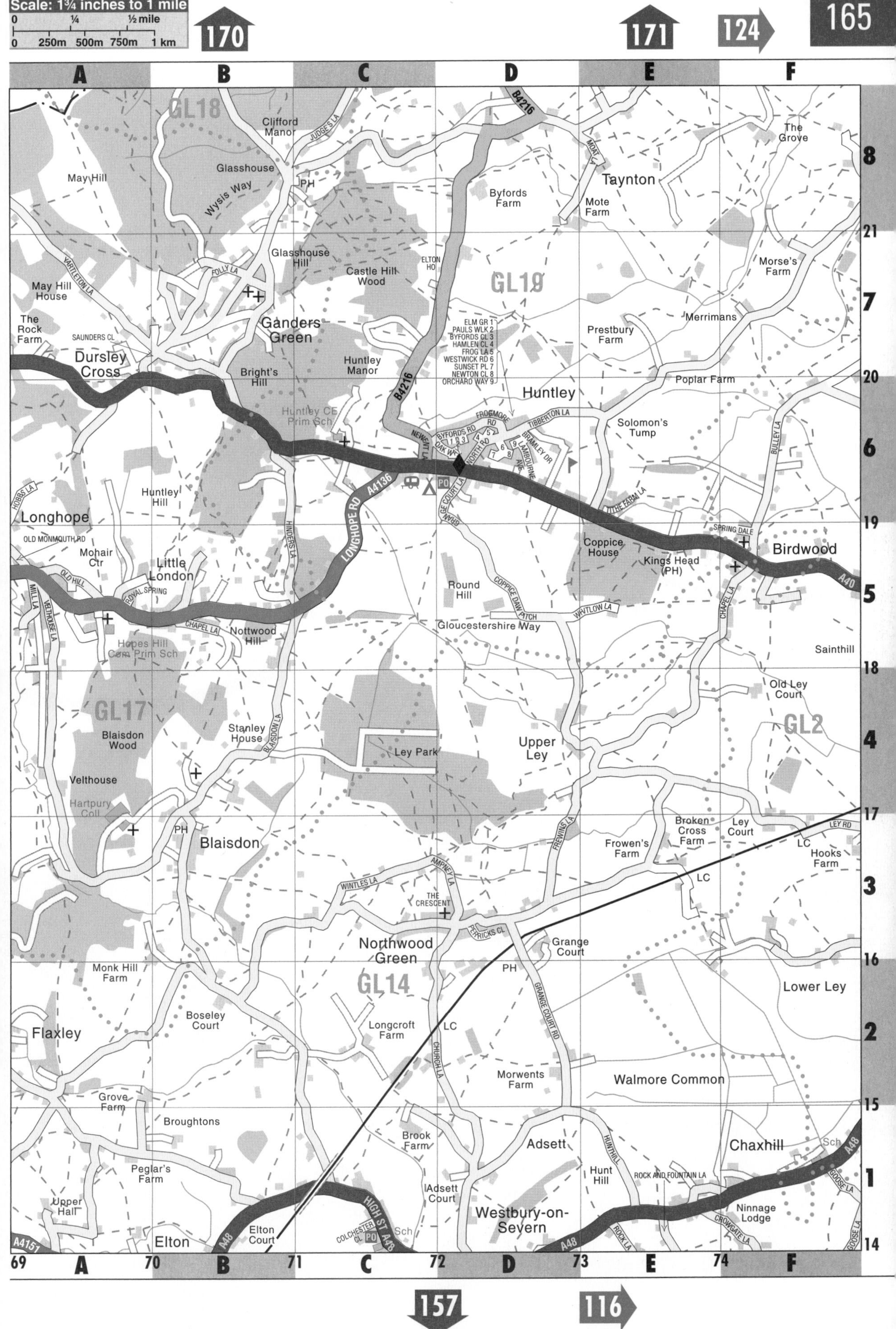

Scale: 1¾ inches to 1 mile
0
¼
½ mile
250m
500m
750m
1 km
170
171
124
165
A
B
C
D
E
F
GL18
Clifford Manor
JUDGE'S LA
The Grove
8
Glasshouse
Taynton
May Hill
Wysis Way
PH
Byfords Farm
Mote Farm
MOAT LA
21
Glasshouse Hill
Morse's Farm
FOLLY LA
ELTON HO
Castle Hill Wood
GL19
May Hill House
YARTLETON LA
7
The Rock Farm
Ganders Green
Merrimans
SAUNDERS CL
ELM GR 1
PAULS WLK 2
BYFORDS CL 3
HAMLEN CL 4
FROG LA 5
WESTWICK RD 6
SUNSET PL 7
NEWTON CL 8
ORCHARD WAY 9
Prestbury Farm
Dursley Cross
Huntley Manor
Bright's Hill
B4216
Poplar Farm
20
Huntley
Huntley CE Prim Sch
FROGMORE RD
TIBBERTON LA
Solomon's Tump
BYFORDS RD
OAK WY
NORTH RD
BRAMLEY DR
LAMBOURNE AVE
NEWENT LA
BULLEY LA
6
A4136
PO
GRANGE COURT LA
Huntley Hill
HOBBS LA
THE FARM LA
Longhope
LONGHOPE RD
19
OLD MONMOUTH RD
HINDERS LA
SPRING DALE
Coppice House
Birdwood
Mohair Ctr
Kings Head (PH)
Little London
OLD HILL
Round Hill
A40
ROYAL SPRING
COPPICE DAW PITCH
WHYTLOW LA
5
MILL LA
VELTHOUSE LA
CHAPEL LA
Nottwood Hill
Gloucestershire Way
Hopes Hill Com Prim Sch
Sainthill
18
Old Ley Court
GL17
GL2
Stanley House
BLAISDON LA
Blaisdon Wood
Upper Ley
4
Ley Park
Velthouse
Hartpury Coll
17
LEY RD
PH
Blaisdon
FREWINS LA
Broken Cross Farm
Ley Court
Frowen's Farm
LC
Hooks Farm
AMPNEY LA
WINTLES LA
LC
3
THE CRESCENT
PETRICKS CL
Grange Court
Northwood Green
16
Monk Hill Farm
PH
GL14
Lower Ley
GRANGE COURT RD
Boseley Court
Flaxley
Longcroft Farm
LC
2
CHURCH LA
Morwents Farm
Walmore Common
Grove Farm
15
Broughtons
Brook Farm
Adsett
Chaxhill
HUNTHILL
Sch
A48
Peglar's Farm
Hunt Hill
ROCK AND FOUNTAIN LA
1
GOOSE LA
Upper Hall
Adsett Court
Ninnage Lodge
HIGH ST A48
Westbury-on-Severn
CROWGATE LA
A4151
Elton
A48
Elton Court
COLCHESTER CL
PO
Sch
A48
ROCK LA
GOOSE LA
14
69
70
71
72
73
74
157
116

131
135
174

Scale: 1¾ inches to 1 mile

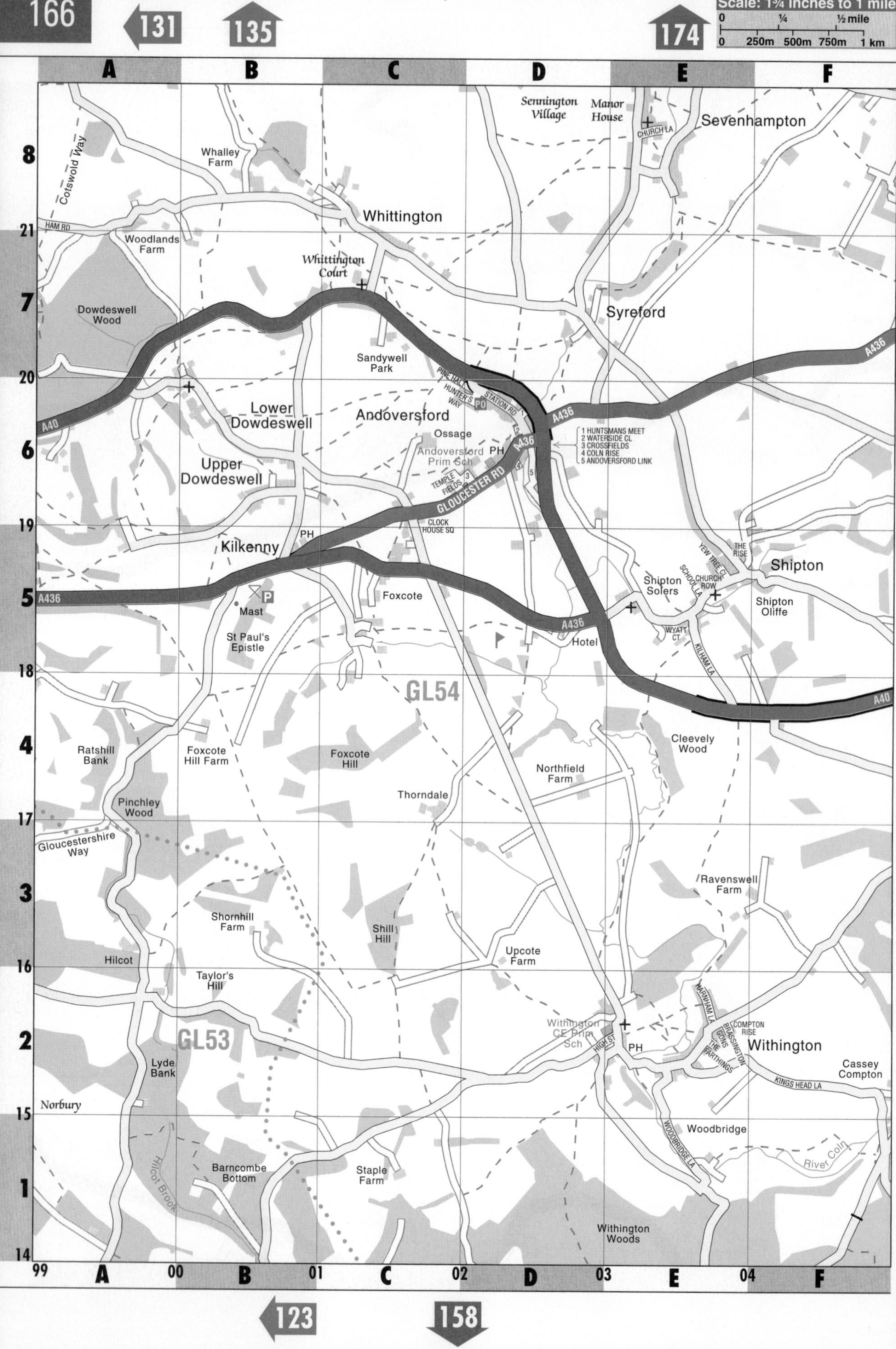

123
158

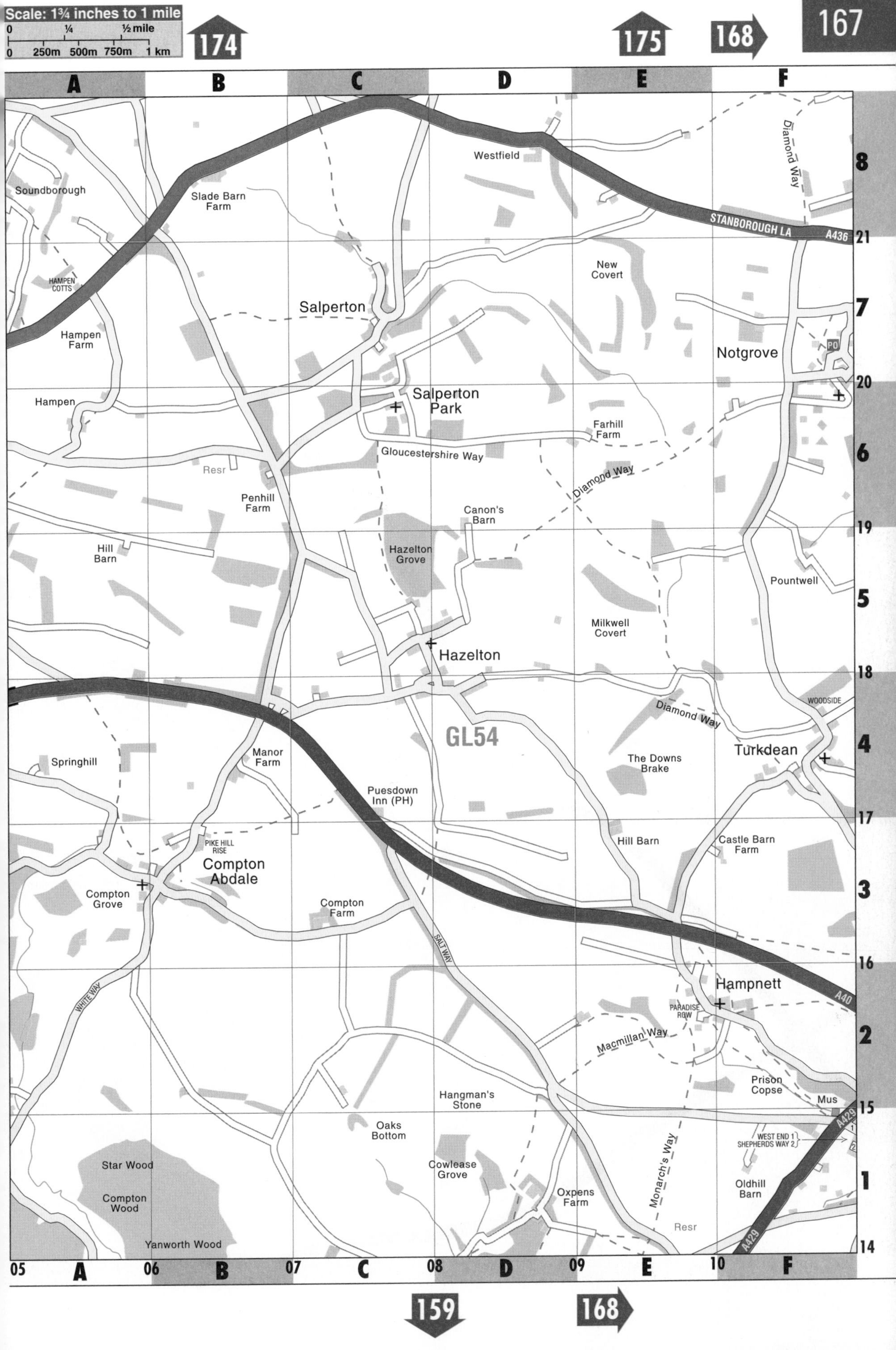

Scale: 1¾ inches to 1 mile
0
¼
½ mile
0
250m
500m
750m
1 km
174
175
168
A
B
C
D
E
F
8
21
7
20
6
19
5
18
4
17
3
16
2
15
1
14
05
06
07
08
09
10
Soundborough
Slade Barn Farm
Westfield
Diamond Way
STANBOROUGH LA
A436
HAMPEN COTTS
New Covert
Salperton
Hampen Farm
Notgrove
PO
Salperton Park
Hampen
Farhill Farm
Gloucestershire Way
Resr
Diamond Way
Penhill Farm
Canon's Barn
Hill Barn
Hazelton Grove
Pountwell
Milkwell Covert
Hazelton
WOODSIDE
Diamond Way
GL54
Turkdean
Manor Farm
Springhill
The Downs Brake
Puesdown Inn (PH)
PIKE HILL RISE
Compton Abdale
Hill Barn
Castle Barn Farm
Compton Grove
Compton Farm
SALT WAY
Hampnett
A40
WHITE WAY
PARADISE ROW
Macmillan Way
Prison Copse
Hangman's Stone
Mus
Oaks Bottom
A429
WEST END 1
SHEPHERDS WAY 2
Star Wood
Cowlease Grove
Monarch's Way
Oldhill Barn
Compton Wood
Oxpens Farm
Resr
Yanworth Wood
A429

168
167
175
F7
1 PERRYFIELD CT
2 THE NAIGHT
3 FOXES CL
4 SHERBORNE TERR
5 BOW LA
6 VICTORIA ST
7 CHADWAR GDNS
8 CLAPTON ROW
9 VICTORIA TERR
10 LETCH LA
11 BAINES CL
176
Scale: 1¾ inches to 1 mile
0 ¼ ½ mile
0 250m 500m 750m 1 km
A
B
C
D
E
F
8
21
7
20
6
19
5
18
4
17
3
16
2
15
1
14
Hill Farm
Upper Harford
Landing Strip
River Windrush
Aston Farm
Slaughter Farm
BEDDOME WAY 1
THE COURTYARD 2
STATION MDW 3
MARKET CL 4
THE AVENUE 5
PIECE HEDGE 6
LANSDOWN COTTS 7
A429
A436
Windrush Farm
Folly Farm
Camp Farm
A436 OLD GLOUCESTER RD
GREEN LANE CL
MOUSETRAP LA
SCHOOL HILL
HIGH ST
STATION RD
MOORE RD
Schs
Liby
Mus
POCKHILL LA
SHERBORNE ST
RISSINGTON RD
PO
Model Village
SPRINGFIELD
LETCH HILL DR
GASWORKS LA
BROADLANDS CT
Birdland
Gloucestershire Way
Macmillan Way
COUNCIL HOS
Cold Aston
BANGUP LA
CHAPEL LA
ASTON GR
Monarch's Way
Bangup Barn
Grove Farm
Tagmoor Farm
Marsh Farm
Fox Hill Farm
Shewhill Barn
Aston Grove
Bourton Hill Farm
Diamond Way
GL54
Macmillan Way
Sweetslade Farm
THE ORCHARD
Smith's Barn
Goms Hole
Clapton-on-the-Hill
Broadwater Bottom
Furzehill Wood
Leygore Manor
Starvall
The Fork
Upper Broadmoor
Monarch's Way
Farmington Grove
Northleach Downs
Haycroft Bottom
Sandy Hill Farm
Norbury
Camp Farm
A40
Hill House Farm
Haycroft House
Sherborne Brook
Farmington
HAYCROFT RD
FARMINGTON RD
NORTHLEACH
Empshill Farm
Folly Farm
The Oranges Farm
Sherborne Park
P
Mus
River Leach
Northleach CE Prim Sch
ALL ALONE
EAST END
NOSTLE RD
DUTTON LEYS
CRAIL VIEW
EASTINGTON RD
FALLOWS RD
BASSETT RD
HIGH ST
WEST END
MACARTHUR RD
TAYLER RD
WARD RD
FORTEY RD
GRAVENEY RD
A40
11
12
13
14
15
16
A1
1 GRACE DR
2 JESSOP DR
3 HAMMOND DR
4 MIDWINTER RD
5 BARNETT WAY
6 MAY'S CRES
7 GUGGLE LA
8 WALTON HOUSE BGLWS
9 WALTON HOUSE CT
10 BETTENSON RISE
11 ANTELOPE PADDOCK
12 THE ALLEN'S ALMHOUSES
13 FARMINGTON RISE
14 WALKERS GDN
15 BROOK CL
16 SHORT HEDGES CL
17 ASHWAY
167
160

Scale: 1¾ inches to 1 mile

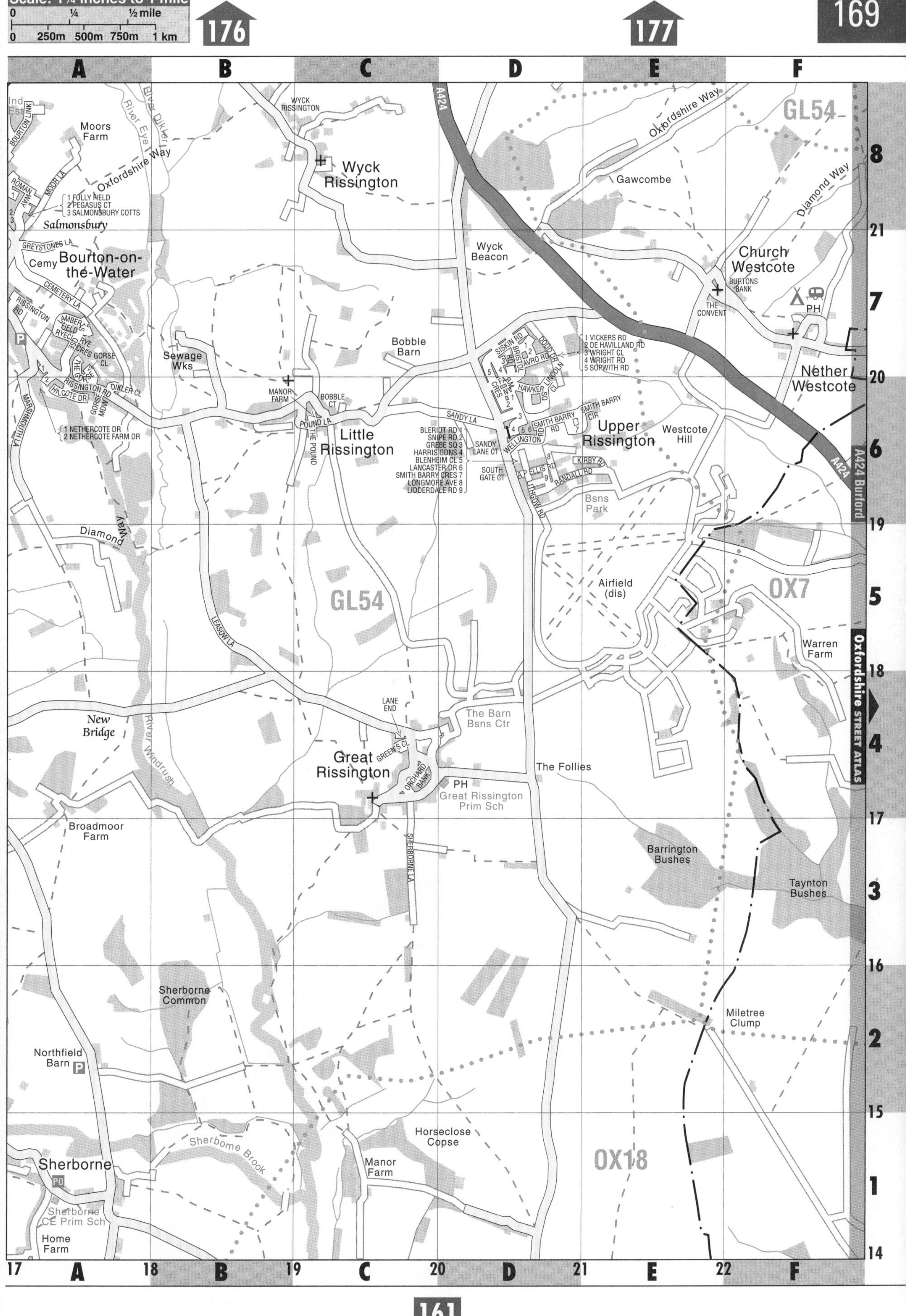

178

Scale: 1¾ inches to 1 mile

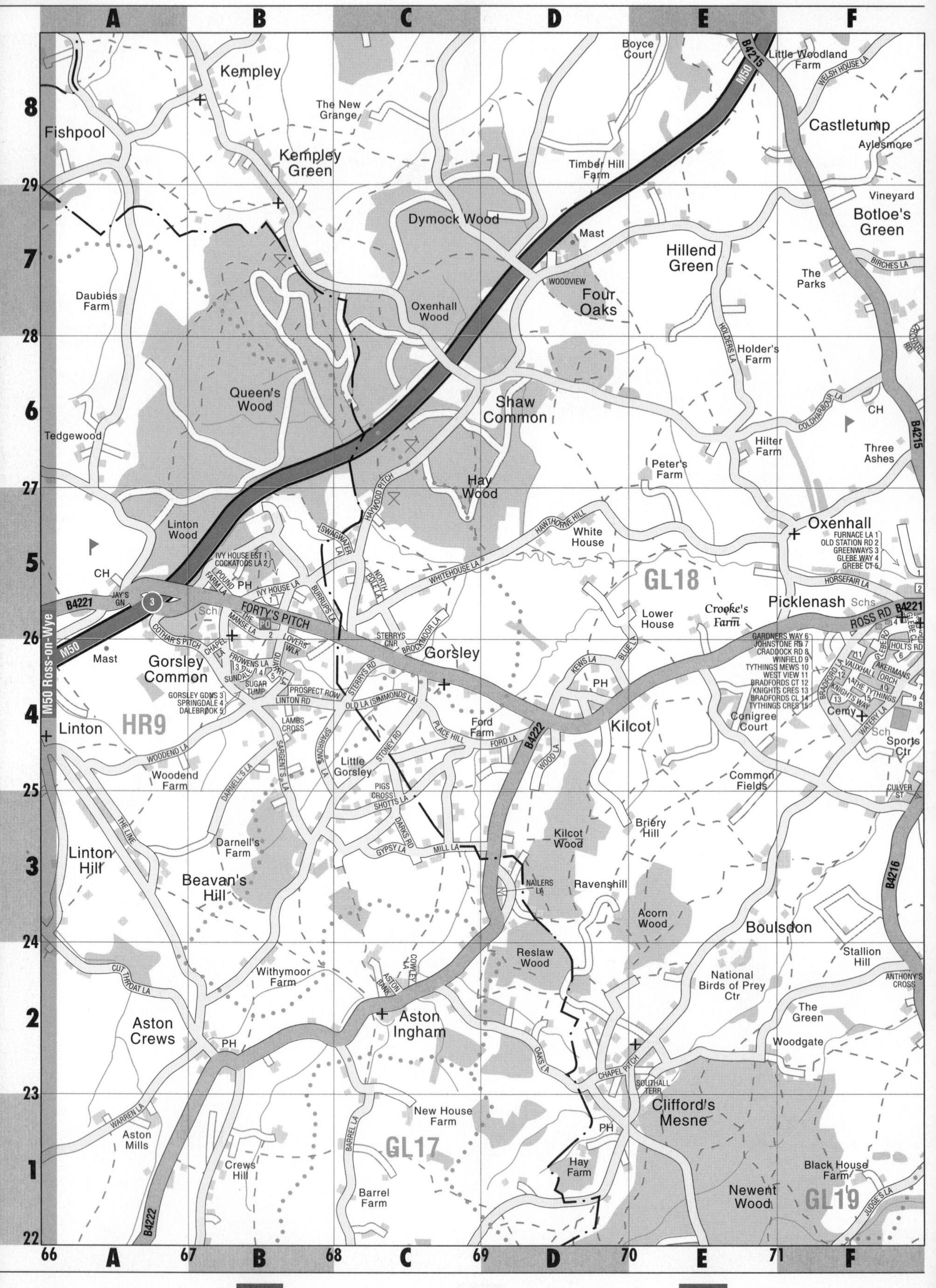

164

165

179
172

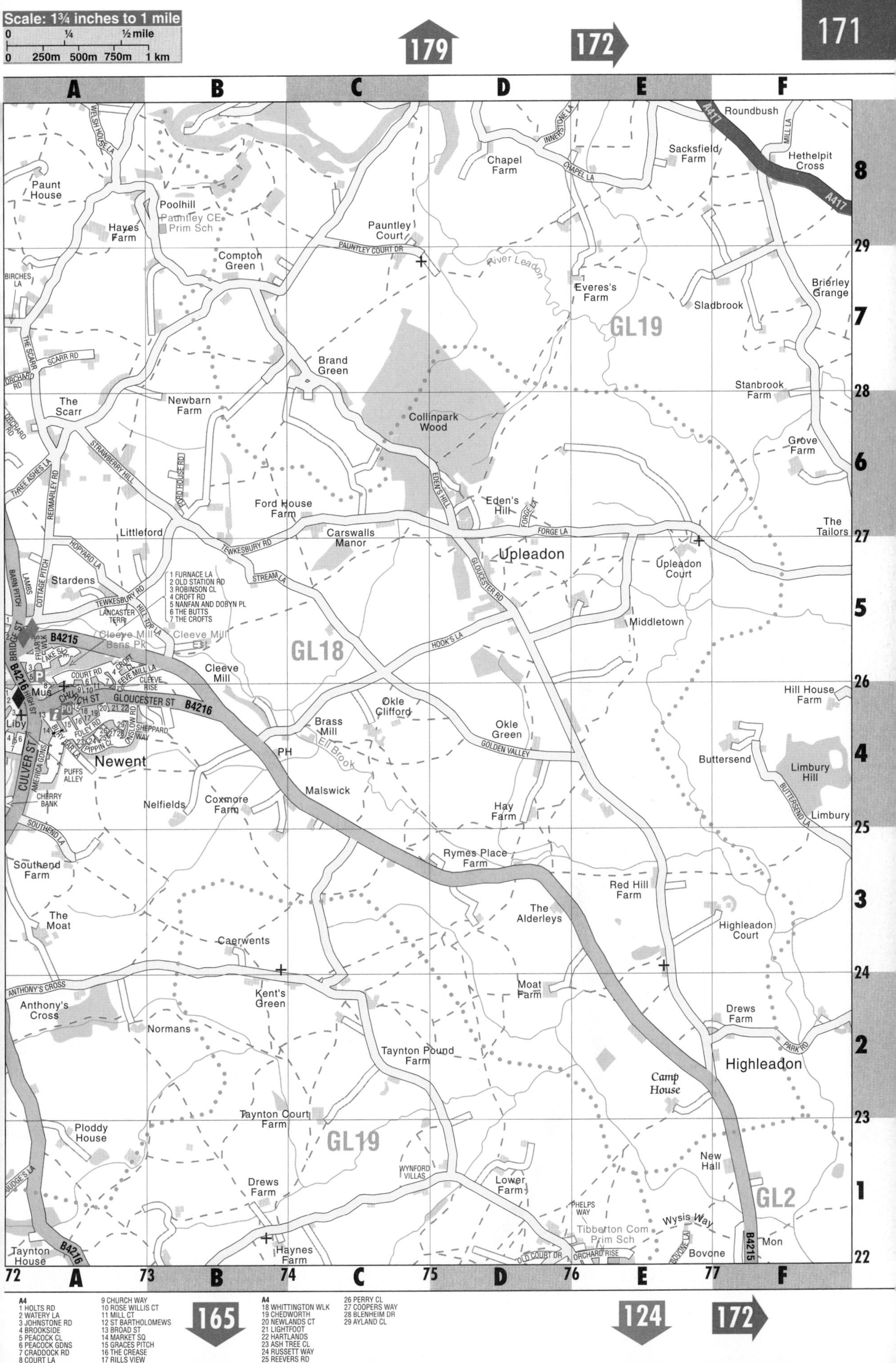

A4
1 HOLTS RD
2 WATERY LA
3 JOHNSTONE RD
4 BROOKSIDE
5 PEACOCK CL
6 PEACOCK GDNS
7 CRADDOCK RD
8 COURT LA
9 CHURCH WAY
10 ROSE WILLIS CT
11 MILL CT
12 ST BARTHOLOMEWS
13 BROAD ST
14 MARKET SQ
15 GRACES PITCH
16 THE CREASE
17 RILLS VIEW

A4
18 WHITTINGTON WLK
19 CHEDWORTH
20 NEWLANDS CT
21 LIGHTFOOT
22 HARTLANDS
23 ASH TREE CL
24 RUSSETT WAY
25 REEVERS RD
26 PERRY CL
27 COOPERS WAY
28 BLENHEIM DR
29 AYLAND CL

165
124
172

171
180

Scale: 1¾ inches to 1 mile
0 ¼ ½ mile
0 250m 500m 750m 1 km

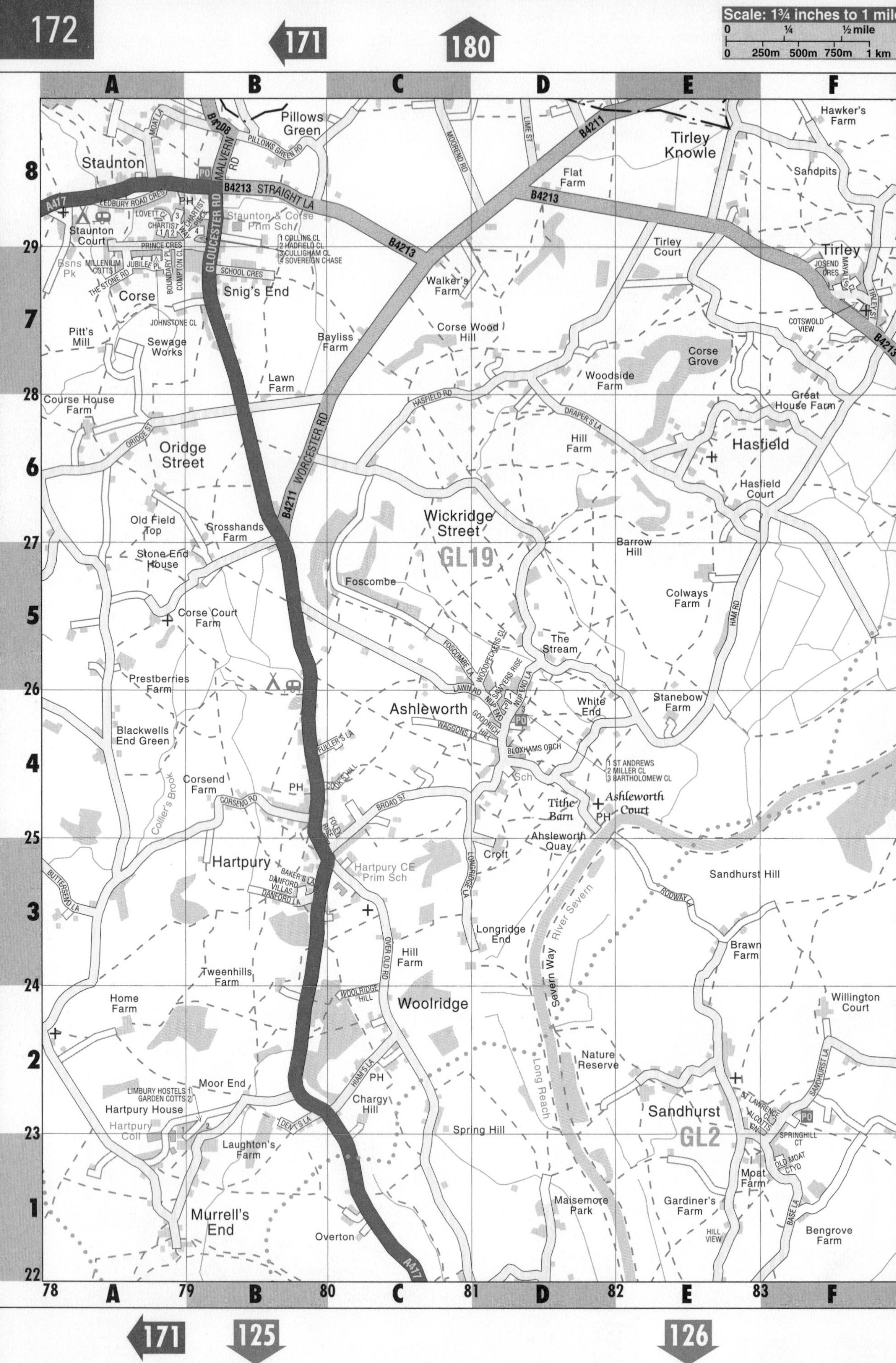

171
125
126

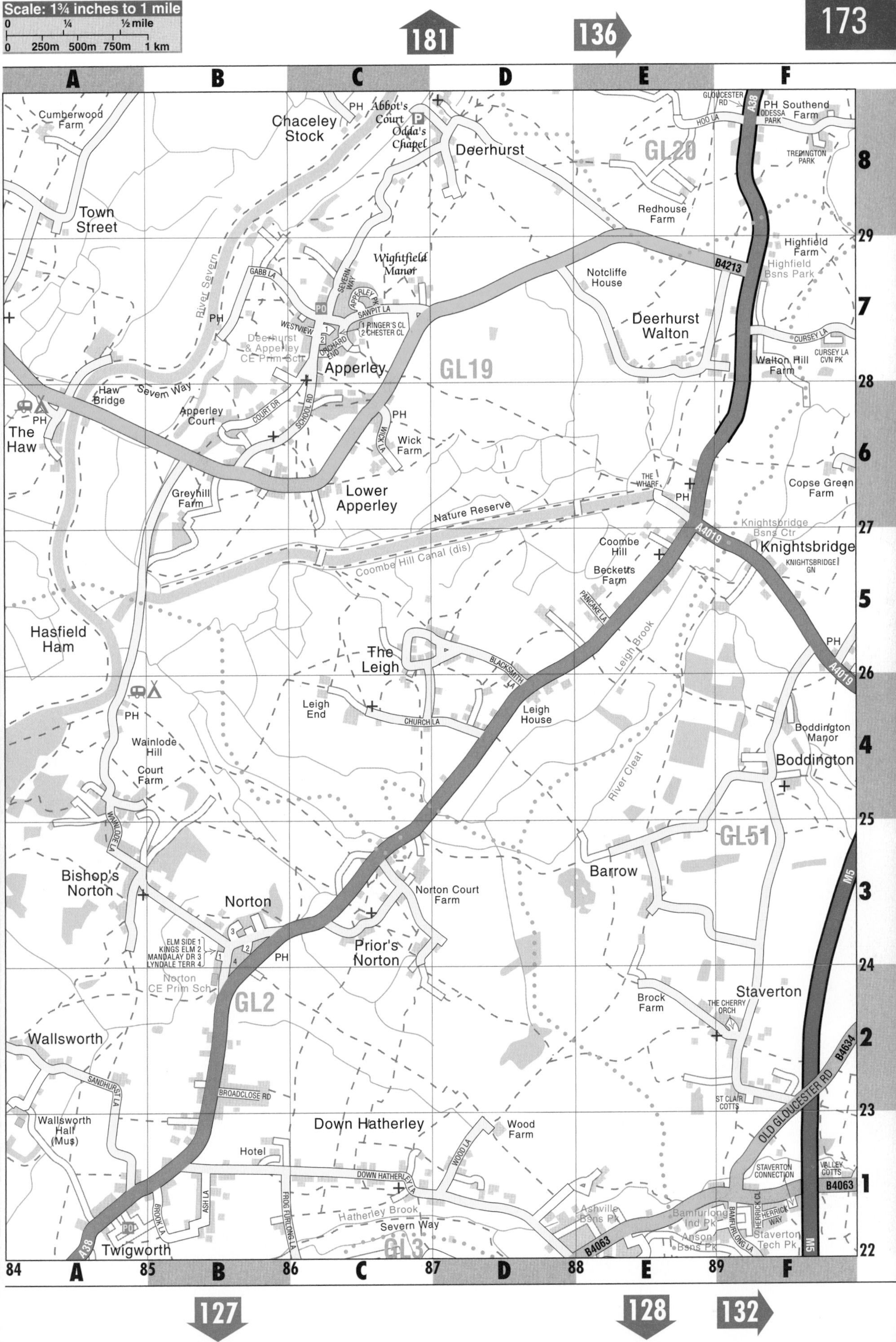
Scale: 1¾ inches to 1 mile
0 ¼ ½ mile
0 250m 500m 750m 1 km
181
136
A B C D E F
Cumberwood Farm
Chaceley Stock
Abbot's Court
Odda's Chapel
Deerhurst
Southend Farm
GL20
Tredington Park
Redhouse Farm
Town Street
Wightfield Manor
Highfield Farm
Highfield Bsns Park
Notcliffe House
B4213
Deerhurst Walton
River Severn
Gabb La
Severn Way
Apperley Pk
Sawpit La
Westview
Ringer's Cl
Chester Cl
Orchard End
Deerhurst & Apperley CE Prim Sch
Apperley
GL19
Cursey La
Cursey La Cvn Pk
Walton Hill Farm
Haw Bridge
Severn Way
Apperley Court
Court Dr
School Rd
The Haw
Wick La
Wick Farm
The Wharf
Copse Green Farm
Greyhill Farm
Lower Apperley
Nature Reserve
Knightsbridge Bsns Ctr
A4019
Knightsbridge
Knightsbridge Gn
Coombe Hill
Coombe Hill Canal (dis)
Becketts Farm
Pancake La
Hasfield Ham
Leigh Brook
The Leigh
Blacksmith La
Leigh End
Church La
Leigh House
Boddington Manor
Wainlode Hill
Boddington
Court Farm
River Cleat
Wainlode La
GL51
Bishop's Norton
Barrow
Norton Court Farm
M5
Norton
Elm Side
Kings Elm
Mandalay Dr
Lyndale Terr
Prior's Norton
Norton CE Prim Sch
GL2
Staverton
Brock Farm
The Cherry Orch
Wallsworth
Sandhurst La
B4634
Broadclose Rd
St Clair Cotts
Old Gloucester Rd
Wallsworth Hall (Mus)
Down Hatherley
Wood Farm
Hotel
Wood La
Down Hatherley La
Staverton Connection
Valley Cotts
B4063
Ash La
Brook La
Frog Furlong La
Hatherley Brook
Severn Way
Ashville Bsns Pk
Bamfurlong Ind Pk
Bamfurlong La
Herrick Cl
Herrick Way
Anson Bsns Pk
Staverton Tech Pk
A38
Twigworth
GL3
Gloucester Rd
Hoo La
Odessa Park
84 85 86 87 88 89
29 28 27 26 25 24 23 22
8 7 6 5 4 3 2 1
127
128
132

174
A7
1 CRISPIN CL
2 RATHMORE CL
3 BASSETT CL
4 CEDAR GR
5 SPITTLE LEYS
6 ORCHARD RD
7 MERCIA RD
8 BARNMEADOW RD
9 ABBOTS LEYS RD
10 SEYMOUR PL
11 BINYON RD
12 ST PETERS WAY
13 SUMMERS RD
139
A7
14 BLENHEIM CT
15 ABBEY VIEW
16 ENFIELD VILLAS
17 MALTHOUSE LA
18 ODDFELLOWS TERR
19 TYTHE TERR
184
A7
20 ABBEY CT
21 QUEENS SQ
22 CHANDOS ALMSHOUSES
23 ABBEY TERR
24 DENT'S TERR
25 STANCOMBE VIEW
26 CHANDOS ST
27 BULL LA
28 HAILES ST
29 KENULF RD
30 BICKS LA
31 SILK MILL CT
Scale: 1¾ inches to 1 mile
0 ¼ ½ mile
0 250m 500m 750m 1 km
A B C D E F
1 WHITMORE RD
2 CLARENDON RD
3 HUDDLESTON RD
4 ELDERSFIELD CL
5 GERVASE RD
EVESHAM RD
PH
B4078
B4632
Gloucestershire Warwickshire Rly
OTTERS FIELD
Winchcombe
Bsns Pk
Sch
ISBOURNE WAY
River Isbourne
NORTON CL
GRETTON RD
CRISPIN RD
GREET RD
BROADWAY RD
RIVERSIDE
PUCK PIT LA
Footbridge
Gloucestershire Way
STANCOMBE LA
Winchcombe
Liby
Sch
NORTH ST
HIGH ST
BACK LA
COWL LA
SILK MILL LA
CASTLE ST
GLOUCESTER ST
B4632
Mus
Mus
VINEYARD ST
RUSHLEY LA
Stancombe Wood
Sudeley Castle
St Kenelm's Well
HAILES GREEN BARNS
SALTER'S LA
Salter's Hill
Sudeley Hill
Round Hill
Hailes Wood
Beckbury
Farmcote
Little Farmcote
Slade Barn Farm
Pinnock Village
Pinnock Farm
B4077
Lynes Barn Farm
Cotswold Way
Sudeley Lodge
Beesmore Brook
Windrush Way
CORNDEAN LA
Parks Farm
Farmcote Wood Farm
Diamond Way
Guiting Wood
CAMPDEN LA
Deadmanbury Gate
Wadfield Farm
GL54
Waterhatch
Belas Knap Long Barrow
Humblebee
Cole's Hill
Spoonley Farm House
CRITCHFORD LA
Roel Hill Farm
Roel Farm
Goldwell Farm
Charlton Abbots
Holt Farm
ROEL GATE
Windrush Hill
Hawling
Whitehill Farm
Cotehay Farm
Brockhampton
Hawling Manor
Oxleaze
BROCKHAMPTON PK
PARK LA
PO
CHAPEL COTTS
NEW ROW
Southdown Farm
PO
B4068
8 29 7 28 6 27 5 26 4 25 3 24 2 23 1 22
02 03 04 05 06 07
135
166
167

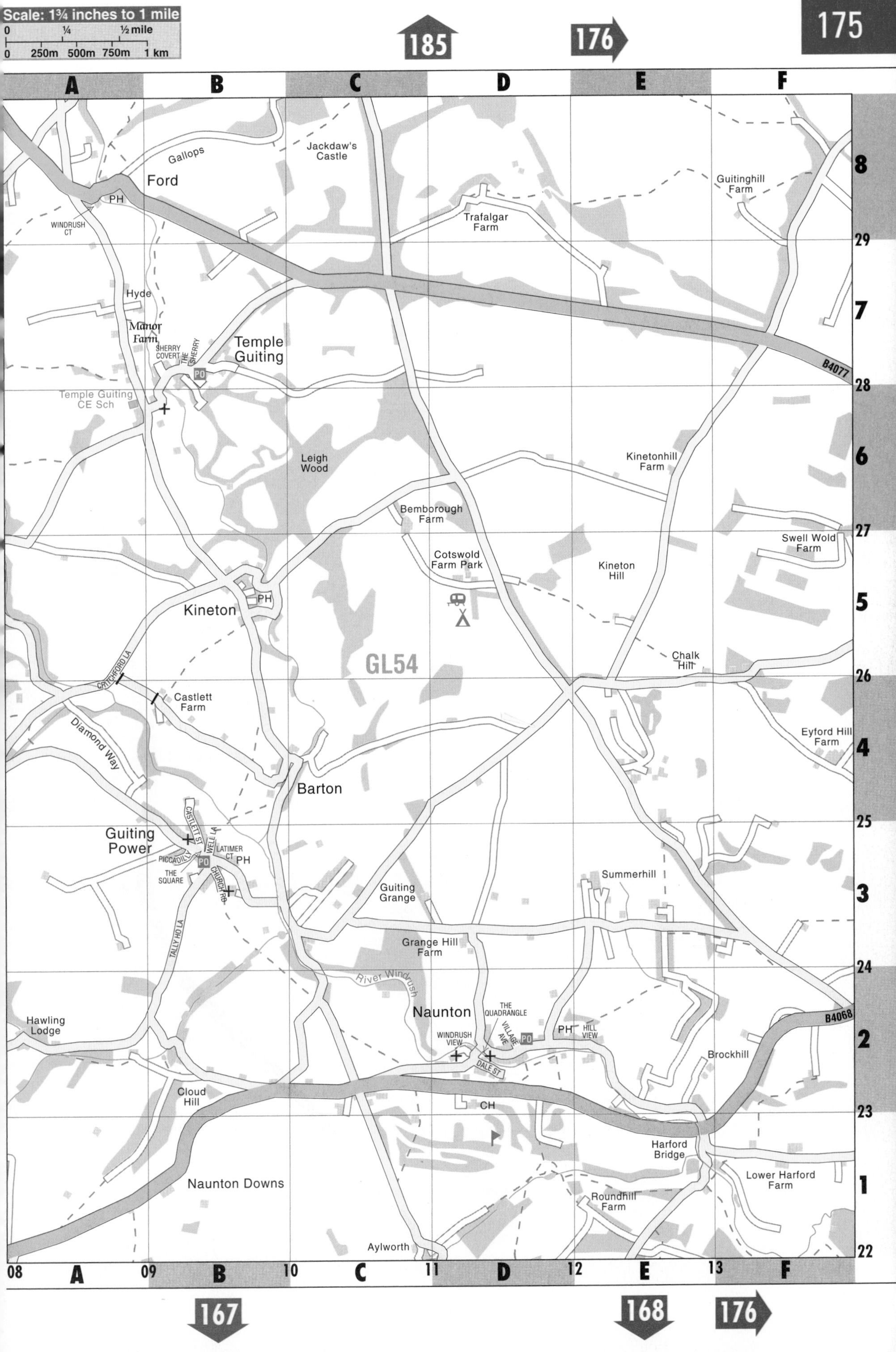
Scale: 1¾ inches to 1 mile
0 ¼ ½ mile
0 250m 500m 750m 1 km
185
176
A B C D E F
Jackdaw's Castle
Gallops
Ford
PH
WINDRUSH CT
Trafalgar Farm
Guitinghill Farm
Hyde
Manor Farm
SHERRY COVERT
THE SHERRY
Temple Guiting
PO
Temple Guiting CE Sch
B4077
Leigh Wood
Kinetonhill Farm
Bemborough Farm
Cotswold Farm Park
Swell Wold Farm
Kineton Hill
Kineton
PH
GL54
CRITCHFORD LA
Chalk Hill
Castlett Farm
Diamond Way
Eyford Hill Farm
Barton
Guiting Power
CASTLETT ST
WELL LA
LATIMER CT
PH
PICCADILLY
PO
THE SQUARE
CHURCH RD
Summerhill
Guiting Grange
TALLY HO LA
Grange Hill Farm
River Windrush
Naunton
THE QUADRANGLE
VILLAGE AVE
PO
PH
HILL VIEW
B4068
Hawling Lodge
WINDRUSH VIEW
DALE ST
Brockhill
Cloud Hill
CH
Harford Bridge
Naunton Downs
Lower Harford Farm
Roundhill Farm
Aylworth
8 29 7 28 6 27 5 26 4 25 3 24 2 23 1 22
08 09 10 11 12 13
167
168
176

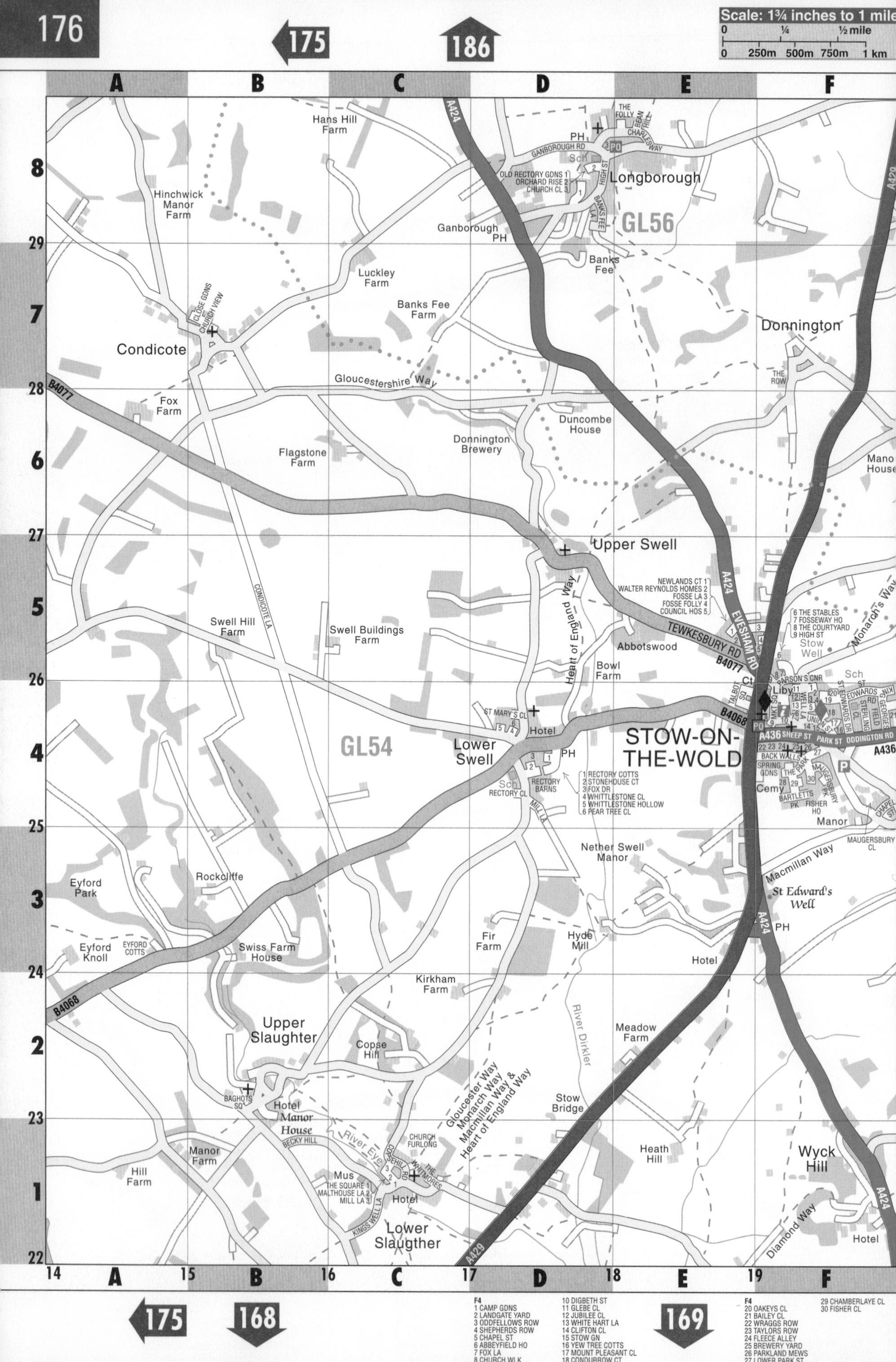

176
175
186
Scale: 1¾ inches to 1 mile
0 ¼ ½ mile
0 250m 500m 750m 1 km
A B C D E F
8 29 7 28 6 27 5 26 4 25 3 24 2 23 1 22
14 15 16 17 18 19
Hans Hill Farm
THE FOLLY
BEAN HILL
CHARLESWAY
GANBOROUGH RD
PH
Sch
PO
HIGH ST
OLD RECTORY GDNS 1
ORCHARD RISE 2
CHURCH CL 3
Longborough
BANKS FEE LA
GL56
Hinchwick Manor Farm
Ganborough PH
Banks Fee
Luckley Farm
Banks Fee Farm
CLOSE GDNS
CHURCH VIEW
Condicote
Donnington
THE ROW
Gloucestershire Way
B4077
Fox Farm
Duncombe House
Donnington Brewery
Flagstone Farm
Manor House
Upper Swell
A424
A429
NEWLANDS CT 1
WALTER REYNOLDS HOMES 2
FOSSE LA 3
FOSSE FOLLY 4
COUNCIL HOS 5
Heart of England Way
EVESHAM RD
TEWKESBURY RD
6 THE STABLES
7 FOSSEWAY HO
8 THE COURTYARD
9 HIGH ST
Monarch's Way
Stow Well
Swell Hill Farm
CONDICOTE LA
Swell Buildings Farm
Abbotswood
Bowl Farm
Sch
PARSON'S CNR
Ct
Liby
TALBOT SQ
ST EDWARDS DR
STERLING CL
FIELD RD
KING GEORGES
MKT SQ
WELL LA
UNION ST
ST MARY'S CL
B4068
Hotel
PO
A436
SHEEP ST
PARK ST
ODDINGTON RD
GL54
Lower Swell
STOW-ON-THE-WOLD
PH
BACK WALLS
SPRING GDNS
THE PARK
MAUGERSBURY PK
Cemy
BARTLETTS PK
FISHER HO
Manor
CHAPEL ST
MAUGERSBURY CL
Sch
RECTORY CL
RECTORY BARNS
MILL LA
1 RECTORY COTTS
2 STONEHOUSE CT
3 FOX DR
4 WHITTLESTONE CL
5 WHITTLESTONE HOLLOW
6 PEAR TREE CL
Nether Swell Manor
Macmillan Way
St Edward's Well
Eyford Park
Rockcliffe
Eyford Knoll
EYFORD COTTS
Swiss Farm House
Fir Farm
Hyde Mill
Hotel
Kirkham Farm
River Dikler
Meadow Farm
Upper Slaughter
Copse Hill
Gloucester Way
Monarch Way
Macmillan Way &
Heart of England Way
Stow Bridge
BAGHOTS SQ
Hotel
Manor House
BECKY HILL
River Eye
COPSEHILL RD
CHURCH FURLONG
THE WHITMORES
Manor Farm
Heath Hill
Wyck Hill
Hill Farm
Mus
THE SQUARE 1
MALTHOUSE LA 2
MILL LA 3
Hotel
KINGS WELL LA
Lower Slaughter
Diamond Way
Hotel
175
168
169
F4
1 CAMP GDNS
2 LANDGATE YARD
3 ODDFELLOWS ROW
4 SHEPHERDS ROW
5 CHAPEL ST
6 ABBEYFIELD HO
7 FOX LA
8 CHURCH WLK
9 CHURCH ST
10 DIGBETH ST
11 GLEBE CL
12 JUBILEE CL
13 WHITE HART LA
14 CLIFTON CL
15 STOW GN
16 YEW TREE COTTS
17 MOUNT PLEASANT CL
18 CONDURROW CT
19 SHEPHERDS WAY
F4
20 OAKEYS CL
21 BAILEY CL
22 WRAGGS ROW
23 TAYLORS ROW
24 FLEECE ALLEY
25 BREWERY YARD
26 PARKLAND MEWS
27 LOWER PARK ST
28 CHAMBERLAYNE HO
29 CHAMBERLAYE CL
30 FISHER CL

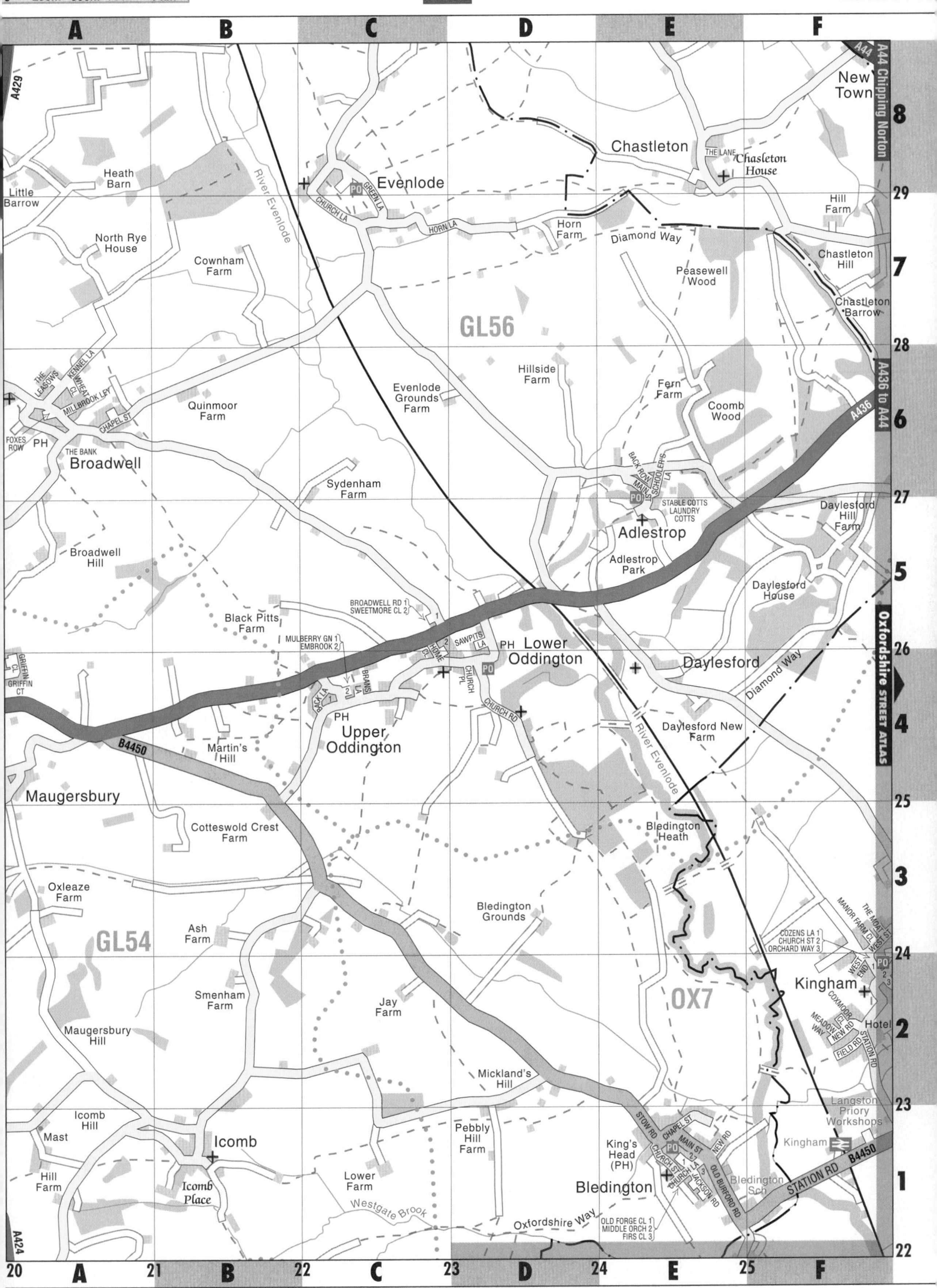
Chastleton
Chasleton House
Evenlode
Little Barrow
Heath Barn
North Rye House
Cownham Farm
Horn Farm
Diamond Way
Peasewell Wood
Hill Farm
Chastleton Hill
Chastleton Barrow
New Town
GL56
Hillside Farm
Fern Farm
Coomb Wood
Evenlode Grounds Farm
Quinmoor Farm
Broadwell
Sydenham Farm
Adlestrop
Adlestrop Park
Daylesford Hill Farm
Daylesford House
Broadwell Hill
Black Pitts Farm
Lower Oddington
Upper Oddington
Daylesford
Daylesford New Farm
River Evenlode
Martin's Hill
Maugersbury
Cotteswold Crest Farm
Bledington Heath
Oxleaze Farm
Bledington Grounds
Ash Farm
GL54
Smenham Farm
Jay Farm
OX7
Kingham
Hotel
Maugersbury Hill
Mickland's Hill
Langston Priory Workshops
Icomb Hill
Mast
Icomb
Icomb Place
Pebbly Hill Farm
King's Head (PH)
Lower Farm
Bledington
Hill Farm
Westgate Brook
Oxfordshire Way
Kingham
Bledington Sch
STATION RD
B4450
A44 Chipping Norton
A436 to A44
Oxfordshire STREET ATLAS
A429
A424
A436
A B C D E F
20 21 22 23 24 25
22 23 24 25 26 27 28 29

E8
1 NEW MILLS WAY
2 BRONTE DR
3 MARGARET RD
4 BARNETTS CL
5 LONG ACRES
6 LAWNSIDE RD
7 HODSES YD
8 MASEFIELD CL
9 WOODLEIGH CL
10 OATLEYS TERR
11 OATLEYS CRES
12 HARLING CT
13 FAIRFIELDS RD
14 ELMSDALE RD
15 CHESTNUT CL
16 ASTON CL
F8
1 BANK CRES
2 HOMEND CRES
3 ST MICHAELS
4 UPPERHALL CL
5 CHURCH ST
6 CHURCH RD
7 ST KATHERINE'S HOSPL THE ALMSHOUSES
8 UPPER CROSS
9 LEDBURY PK
10 BORN CT
11 SOUTH PAR
12 MABEL'S FURLONG
13 WARREN DR
14 LAMBOURNE CL
15 DUNNS COPSE
16 THE HOMEND
Scale: 1¾ inches to 1 mile
0 ¼ ½ mile
0 250m 500m 750m 1 km
A B C D E F
A4172 Leominster (A417)
Mast
A417 Hereford (A438)
A438 Hereford
A449 Great Malvern
LEDBURY
Aylton
COUNCIL HOS
Newbridge Park Farm
Flights Farm
Works
HALLWOOD DR
Coneygree Wood
Ledbury Heritage Ctr
Ledbury Park
LEADON WAY
Old Wharf
LEDDINGTON CT
Cemy
Lillands
Brook Farm
Old Lily Hall
Rowland's Green
Little Marcle
The Court
Hill House
Ind Est
E7
1 MILLER CRADDOCK WAY
2 RUSSET CL
3 FURLONG CT
4 BRAMLEY CL
5 KATHERINE'S WLK
6 WOODFIELD RD
7 FERNDOWN RD
8 SHEPHERD'S CL
Hazel Farm
F7
1 WINSTON CL
2 NEWTON CL
3 BLENHEIM DR
4 ORCHARD PL
5 TRAHERNE CL
6 SPRING GR
Dunbridge Farm
Robinscroft
HR8
Orlam Farm
Hall House Farm
Laddin Farm
Ludstock
Siddington Farm
PRESTON CROSS
White House
Argus Farm
Oldfields Cottage
Henberrow
Dinchall Farm
Preston Brook
VELDT HOUSE BARNS
Preston
Leddington
Mirabels Farm
Donnington
Noad Farm
PH
River Leadon
A449 Ross-on-Wye
Landing Strip
Tillputsend Cottage
Donnington Hall
Rosehill
Hellens
Hallwood Green
Greenway
The Vineyard
Much Marcle
Great Netherton
Tiller's Green
Broom's Green
Ockington Farm
B4024
Windcross Farm
Wilton Place
Bridges Farm
The Hill
Friar's Court
Stonehouse
CH
GL18
Shakesfield
Hill Ash
Knight's Green
CROWN CL 1
STONEBERROW PL 2
ST MARYS CL 3
THE WILLOWS
Kempley Brook
Allums
Dymock
The Pound
Ann Cam CE Prim Sch
WESTERN WAY
CROWFIELD LA
Kempley Court
Old Rock
Crowfield
Gamage Hall
Brookland
New Rock
Haind Park Wood
Normansland Farm
WELSH HOUSE LA
B4215
B4216
A4172
A449
A417
M50
66 67 68 69 70 71
30 31 32 33 34 35 36 37

Scale: 1¾ inches to 1 mile

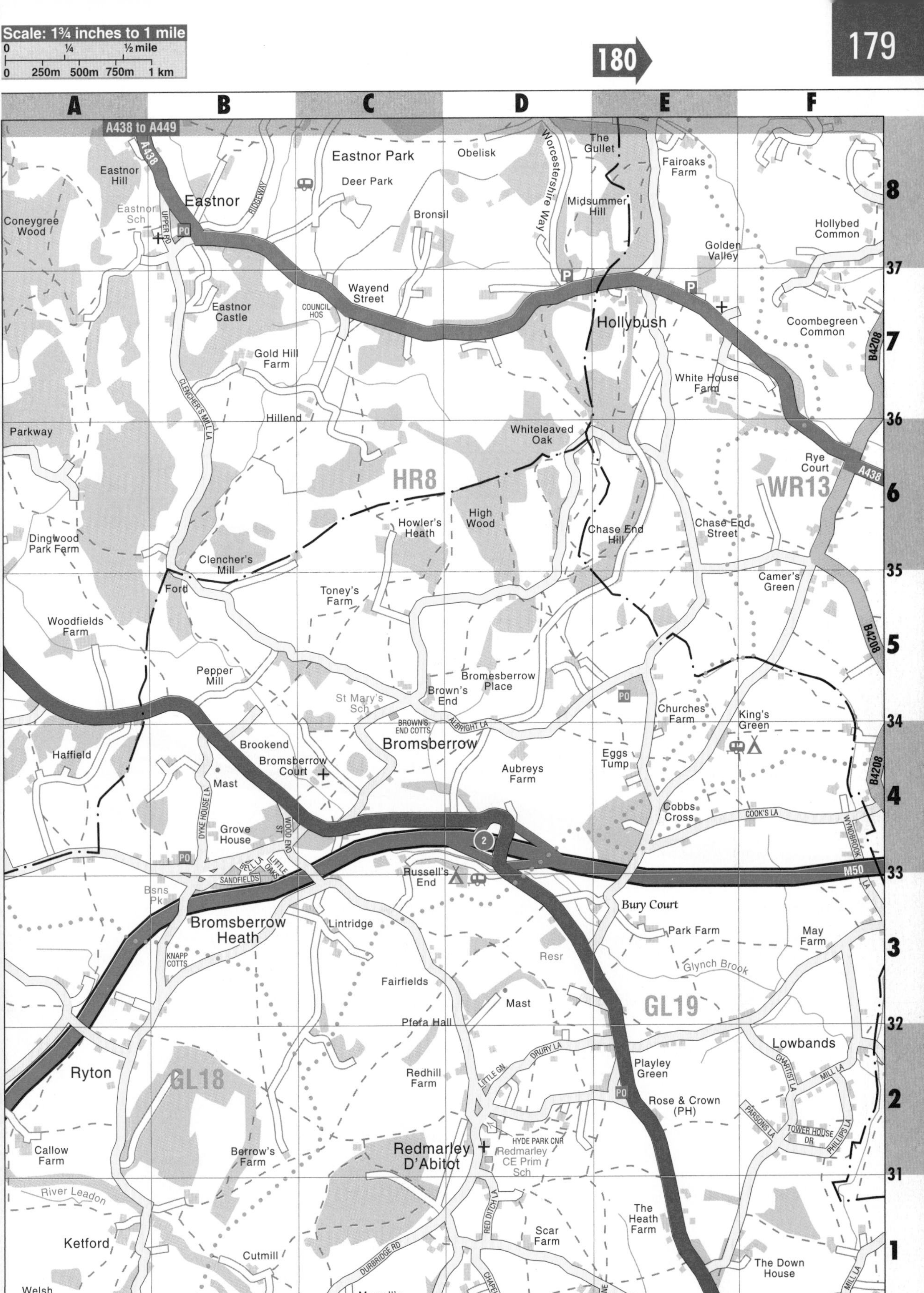

171
180

179

Scale: 1¾ inches to 1 mile
0 ¼ ½ mile
0 250m 500m 750m 1 km

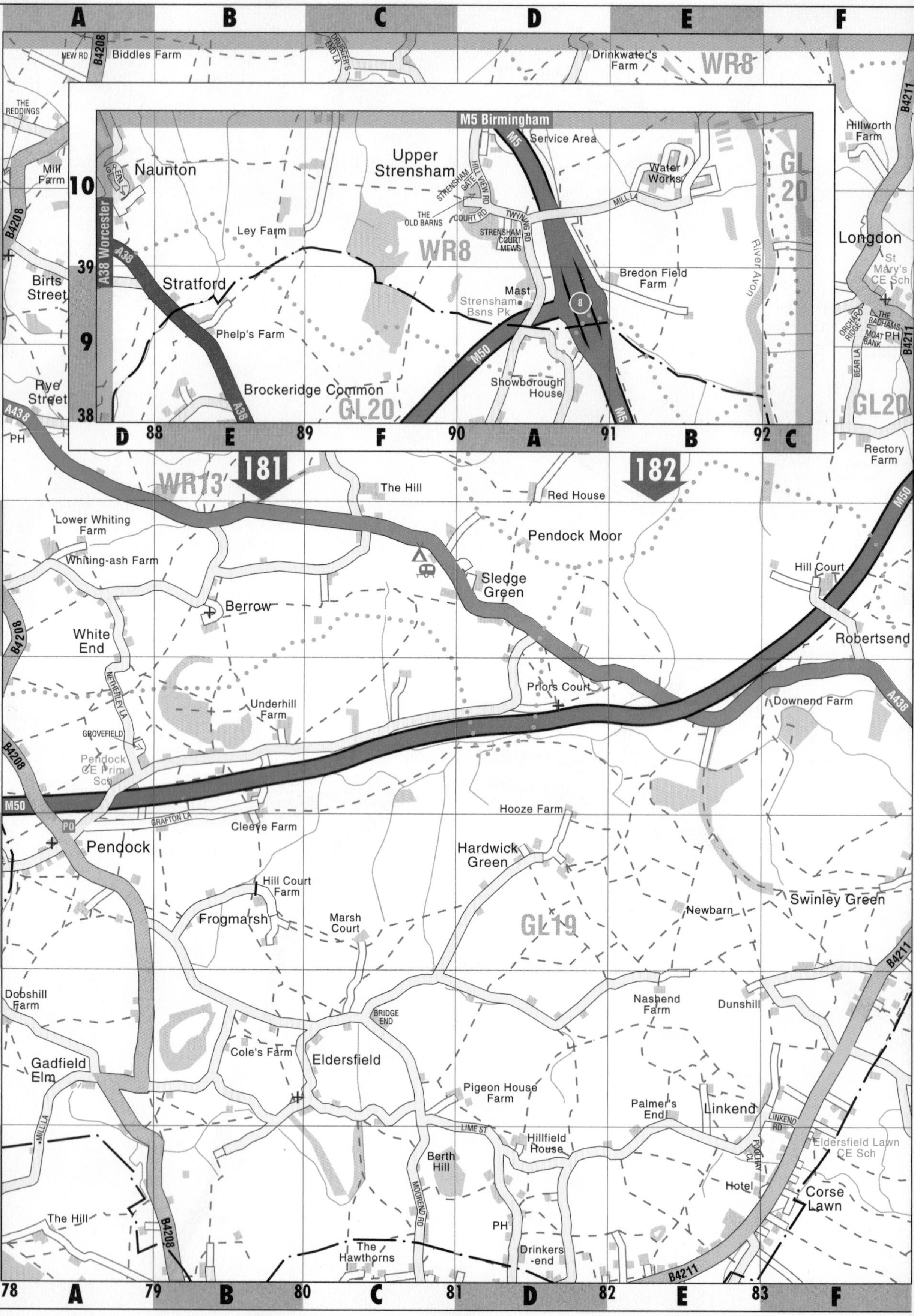

179

172

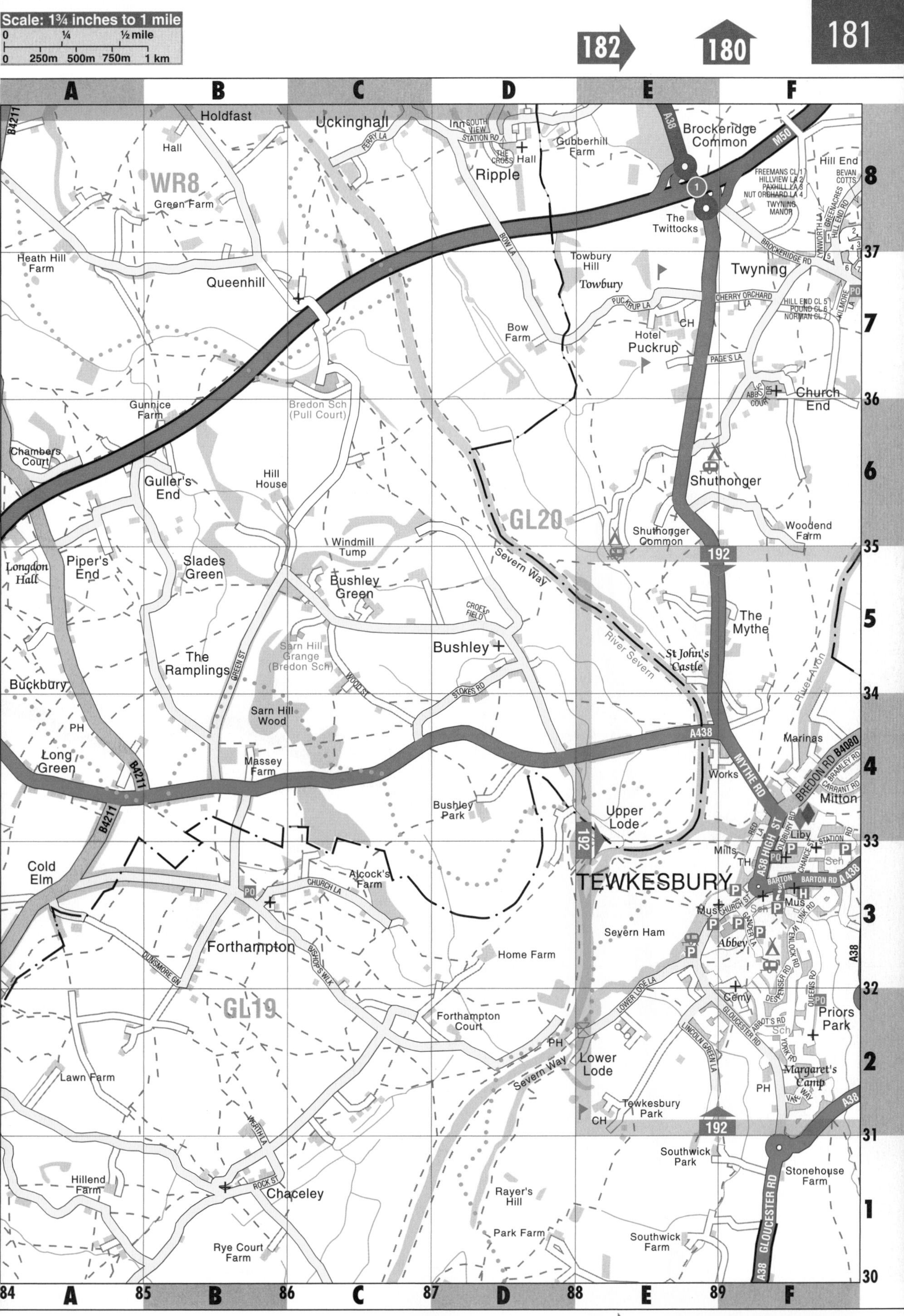

173

182

For full street detail of the highlighted area see page 192.

180
181

Scale: 1¾ inches to 1 mile
0 ¼ ½ mile
0 250m 500m 750m 1 km

A B C D E F

8 37 7 36 6 35 5 34 4 33 3 32 2 31 1 30

DINGLE LA
Hill End
HILL END RD
1 HILLVIEW LA
2 PAXHILL LA
3 THE MAYALLS
4 ORCHARD DR
5 HUDMAN'S CL
Downfield
DOWNFIELD LA
GOODIER'S LA
Twyning Green
FLEET LA
Twyning Sch
FLEET RD
PH
River Avon
M5
WR8
Manor House
Tythe Barn
Mill End
DOCK LA
Bredon
PERWELL CL
BACK LA
CHURCH ST
HIGH ST
PO
KEMERTON RD
B4080
MORETON LA
B4079
Westmancote
FARM LA
CHAPEL LA
HILL CL
Lower Westmancote
KEMERTON RD
PEPPERCORN ALLEY
BAYLISS RD
WING LA
JOB'S LA
Kemerton
Overbury Park
Overbury
Overbury Court
CHURCH ROW
GABLE ROW
Overbury CE Est Sch
SCHOOL LA
COLLEGE RD
ST GILES'S RD
CHERRY ORCH
VALLENDERS RD
FARM LA
OAK GDNS
BRASENOSE RD
JUBILEE DR
BLENHEIM DR
COTSWOLD CL
QUEENSWAY
1 WATERLOO CL
2 WELLINGTON LODGE CL
STATION COTTS 1
BREDON LODGE 2
STATION DR 3
GRAVEL PITS CL 4
BRICKNELL AVE 5
PLANTATION CRES 6
GLEBELAND DR 7
HOMESTEAD CL 8
THE CROFTLANDS 9
RUSSET CL 10
WATERLOO WAY 11
BROADACRE CL 12
ORCHARD CL 13
FLEET LA
CHELTENHAM RD
Gravel Pit
KINSHAM LA
CRASHMORE LA
Croft Farm Leisure and Water Park
TEWKESBURY RD
Bredon's Hardwick
PH
CHAPEL LA
Kinsham
Gravel Pit
Carrant Brook
192
Hardwick House
SALLIS CL 1
LAPWING CL 2
ROBIN CL 3
CURLEW CL 4
WAGTAIL DR 5
TAWNY CL 6
THE HOPYARD 7
PARK CL 8
WILLIS WLK 9
HARDWICK BANK RD
10 TUG WILSON CL
11 THISTLE DOWNS
12 THE PEAR ORCH
13 THE APPLE ORCH
14 CROMERS CL
15 WELL CL
16 SPRINGWATER CL
17 FARM CL
18 MONKEY MDW
19 WHEATSTONE CL
20 GEORGE DOWTY DR
21 SINDERBERRY DR
22 HUGHES CL
23 BOWLER RD
24 HAWTHORN WAY
25 BEVAN GDNS
Northway
GL20
Aston on Carrant
Mitton Lodge
KESTREL WAY
THE PARK
LONG EIGHTS
GRANGE RD
Sch
LC
26 REDWOOD CT
27 GRANGE CT
28 BRANNIGAN CT
Cowfield Farm
KENNET CL
NORTHWAY LA
B4080
BREDON RD
ARUNDEL RD
DERWENT DR
MANOR PK
BROOKSIDE
MITTON WAY
PO
Mitton
OAK DR
KINGSTON RD
WARREN RD
STEWARD RD
FAIRWAY
STANLEY RD
Ashchurch Ind Est
Ashchurch
Depot
1 ST GEORGES RD
2 ST ANDREWS CL
3 ST PATRICKS RD
Aston Cross
B4079
A46
PH
Mitton Manor Prim Sch
DELTA DR
BETA CL
GREEN LA
ALPHA CL
SHANNON WAY
GANNAWAY LA
Ind Est
Newtown
ALEXANDRA WAY
NORTH AVE
SOUTH AVE
ST DAVIDS RD
AUSTIN RD
Tirle Brook
ELLENDENE DR
A438
ASHCHURCH RD
9
A46
FITZHAMON PK
ST BARBARA'S
TIRLEBROOK GRANGE
Sch
Ashchurch
Pamington
A435
A438
A38
Schs
CHURCHILL RD
ROSEFIELD
1 ELMVIL RD
2 MILNE PASTURES
WESTFIELD AVE 29
SYCAMORE RD 30
CEDAR RD 31
VIRGINIA RD 32
ELM RD 33
VIRGINIA CL 34
CHERRY ORCH 35
HOWARD CL 36
HOWARD RD 37
LEE RD 38
LEE WLK 39
NORTHWAY TRAD EST 40
Natton
TEWKESBURY
Homedowns
LC
Walton Cardiff
SNOWDONIA RD
PALM RD
A38
MONTEREY CL
B4079
Tirle Brook
Claydon Farm
Gloucestershire Way
Oxenton
192
MONKS LA
LC
Fiddington
GL52
Crane Hill
Rudgeway Farm
CH
M5
LC
Bozard's Farm
WOOLSTONE LA
A435

90 91 92 93 94 95
A B C D E F

181
136
For full street detail of the highlighted area see page 192.
137

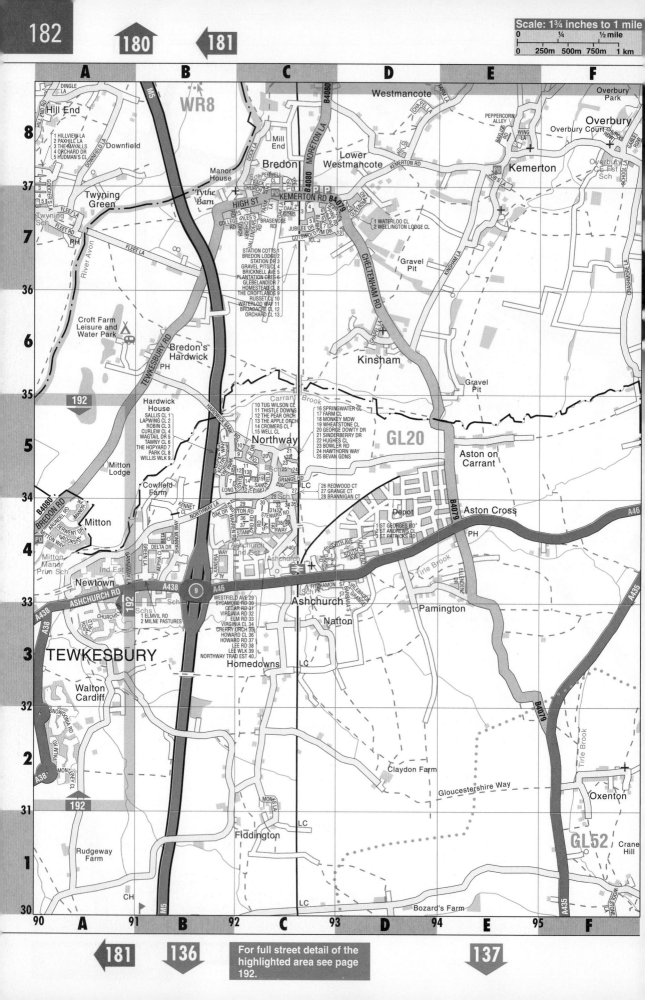

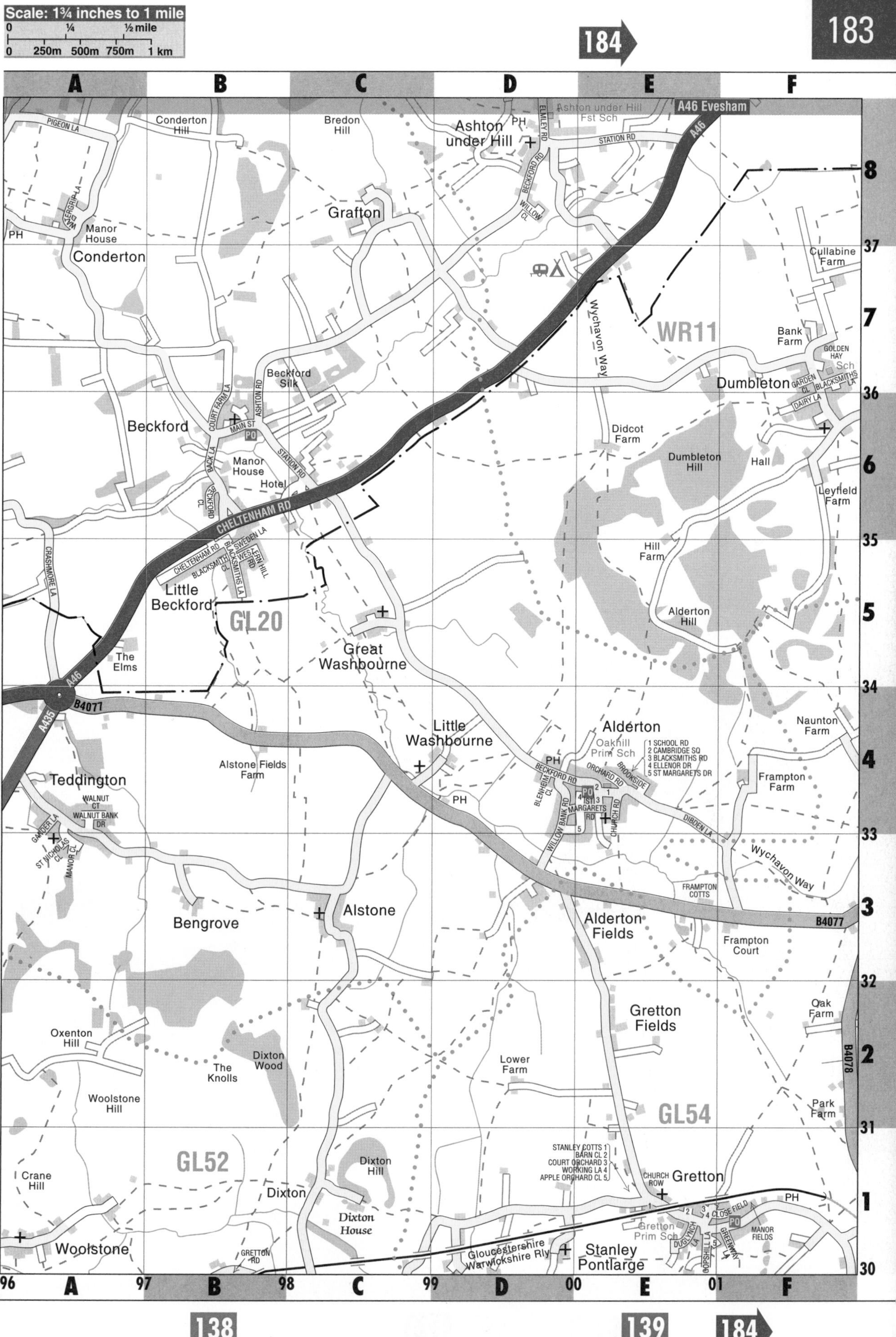
Scale: 1¾ inches to 1 mile
0 ¼ ½ mile
0 250m 500m 750m 1 km
184
A B C D E F
A46 Evesham
Conderton Hill
Bredon Hill
Ashton under Hill
Ashton under Hill Fst Sch
PH
PIGEON LA
ELMLEY RD
STATION RD
BECKFORD RD
WILLOW CL
Grafton
Manor House
PH
Conderton
8
37
Cullabine Farm
WR11
Wychavon Way
7
Bank Farm
GOLDEN HAY
Sch
Beckford Silk
Dumbleton
GARDEN CL
BLACKSMITHS LA
DAIRY LA
36
COURT FARM LA
ASHTON RD
MAIN ST
PO
Beckford
Didcot Farm
Manor House
Hotel
BACK LA
STATION RD
BECKFORD CL
Dumbleton Hill
Hall
6
Leyfield Farm
CHELTENHAM RD
CRASHMORE LA
CHELTENHAM RD
SWEDEN LA
BLACKSMITHS LA
WEST RD
FERN HILL
35
Hill Farm
Little Beckford
GL20
Alderton Hill
5
Great Washbourne
The Elms
A46
34
B4077
A435
Little Washbourne
Alderton
Oakhill Prim Sch
1 SCHOOL RD
2 CAMBRIDGE SQ
3 BLACKSMITHS RD
4 ELLENOR DR
5 ST MARGARETS DR
Naunton Farm
Alstone Fields Farm
Teddington
PH
BECKFORD RD
ORCHARD RD
BROOKSIDE
4
Frampton Farm
WALNUT CT
WALNUT BANK DR
GANDER LA
ST NICHOLAS CL
MANOR CL
BLENHEIM CL
WILLOW BANK RD
ST MARGARETS RD
CHURCH RD
DIBDEN LA
33
Wychavon Way
FRAMPTON COTTS
Bengrove
Alstone
Alderton Fields
B4077
3
Frampton Court
32
Oxenton Hill
Gretton Fields
Oak Farm
The Knolls
Dixton Wood
Lower Farm
B4078
2
Woolstone Hill
GL54
Park Farm
31
GL52
STANLEY COTTS 1
BARN CL 2
COURT ORCHARD 3
WORKING LA 4
APPLE ORCHARD CL 5
Crane Hill
Dixton Hill
CHURCH ROW
Gretton
Dixton
PH
1
Dixton House
Gretton Prim Sch
DUGLYNCH LA
GOPSHILL LA
CLOSE FIELD
GREENWAY LA
PO
MANOR FIELDS
Woolstone
GRETTON RD
Gloucestershire Warwickshire Rly
Stanley Pontlarge
30
96 A 97 B 98 C 99 D 00 E 01 F
138
139
184

183

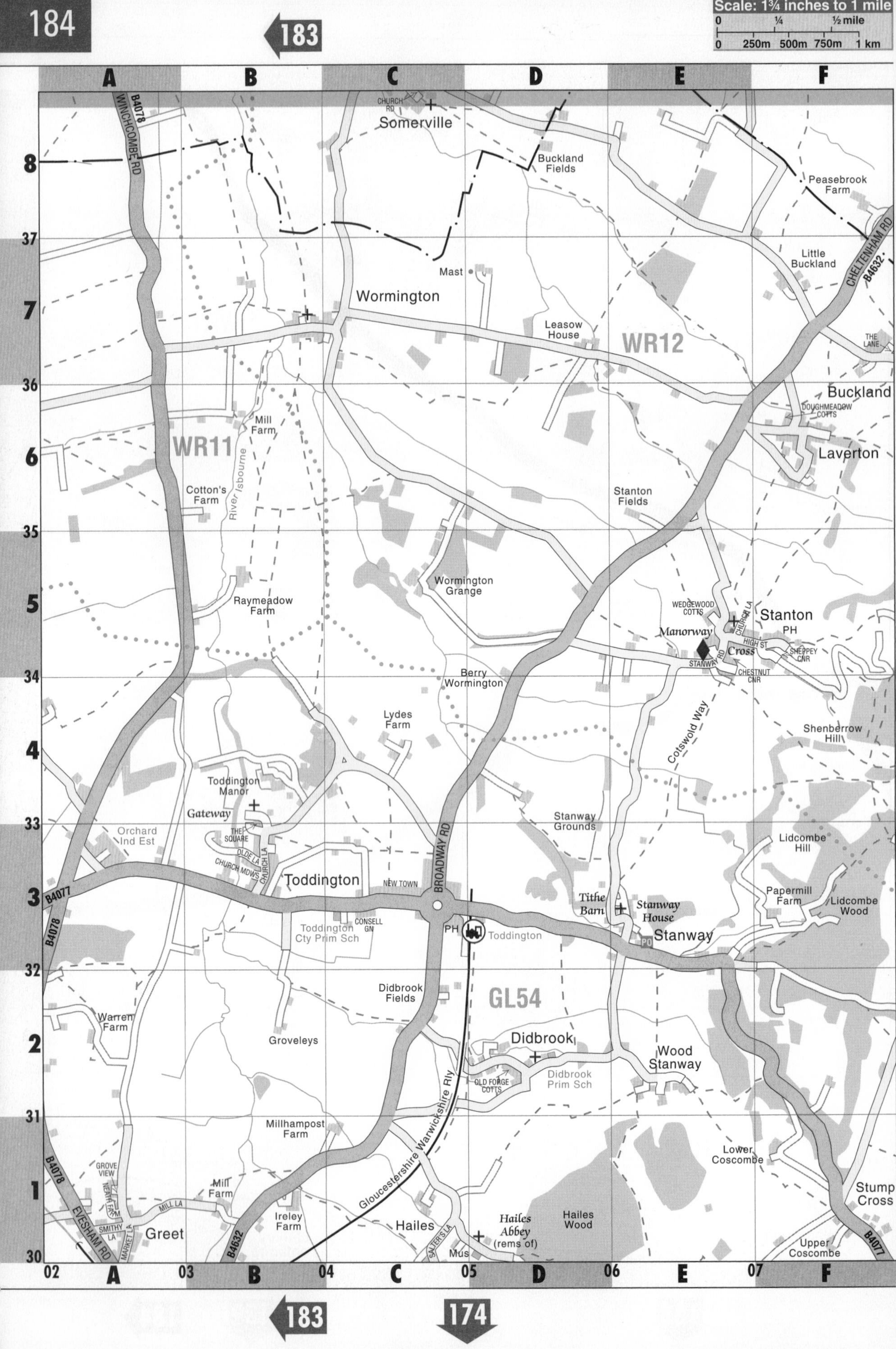

Scale: 1¾ inches to 1 mile
0 ¼ ½ mile
0 250m 500m 750m 1 km
A B C D E F
Somerville
Buckland Fields
Peasebrook Farm
Little Buckland
Mast
Wormington
Leasow House
WR12
Buckland
Laverton
WR11
Mill Farm
River Isbourne
Cotton's Farm
Stanton Fields
Wormington Grange
Raymeadow Farm
Stanton
PH
Manorway
Cross
Berry Wormington
Lydes Farm
Cotswold Way
Shenberrow Hill
Toddington Manor
Gateway
Orchard Ind Est
Stanway Grounds
Lidcombe Hill
Toddington
NEW TOWN
BROADWAY RD
Tithe Barn
Stanway House
Papermill Farm
Lidcombe Wood
Toddington Cty Prim Sch
PH
Toddington
Stanway
Didbrook Fields
GL54
Warren Farm
Groveleys
Didbrook
Wood Stanway
Didbrook Prim Sch
Millhampost Farm
Gloucestershire Warwickshire Rly
Lower Coscombe
Mill Farm
Stump Cross
Greet
Ireley Farm
Hailes
Hailes Abbey (rems of)
Hailes Wood
Mus
Upper Coscombe
EVESHAM RD
WINCHCOMBE RD
CHELTENHAM RD
02 03 04 05 06 07

183

174

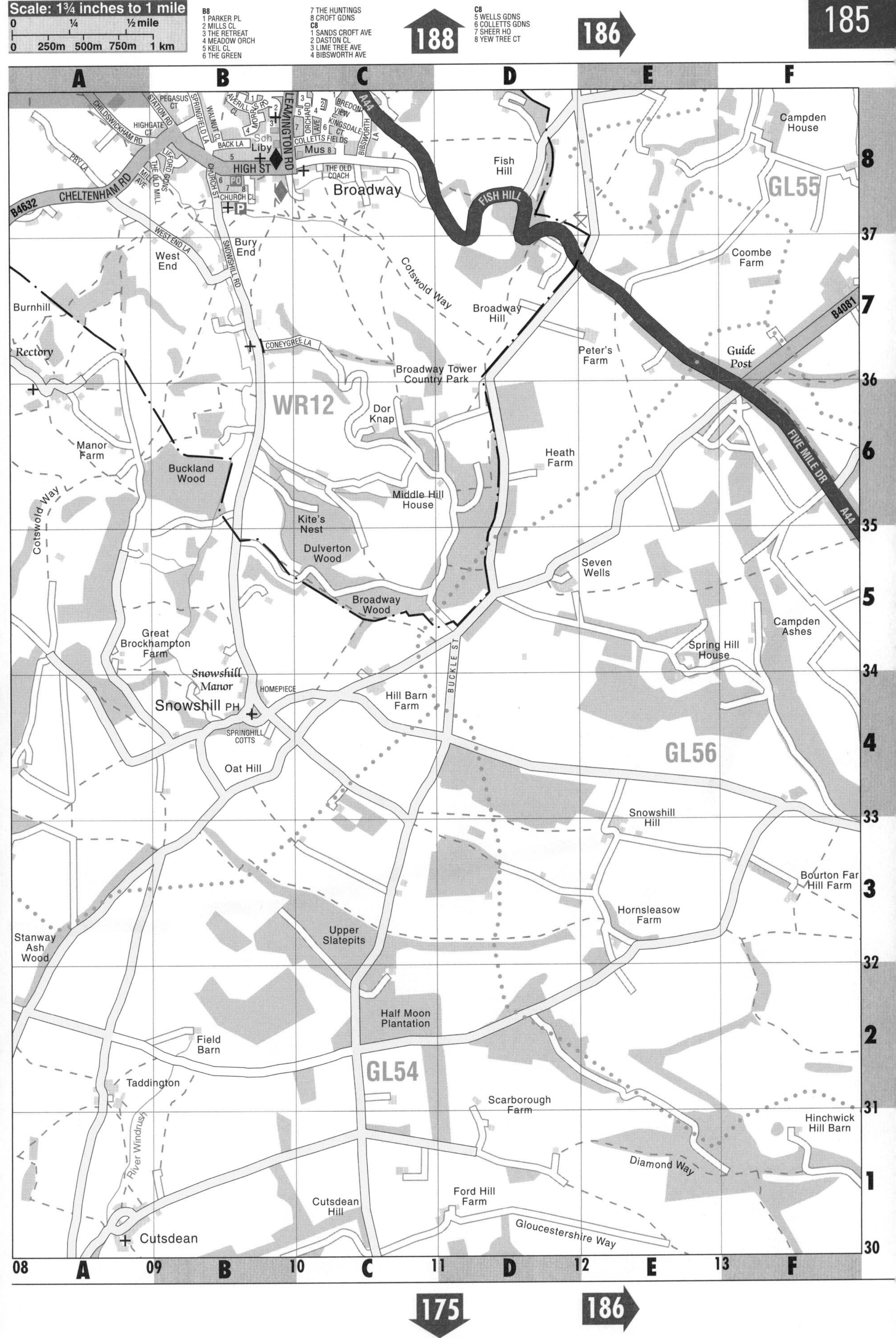
Scale: 1¾ inches to 1 mile
0 ¼ ½ mile
0 250m 500m 750m 1 km
B8
1 PARKER PL
2 MILLS CL
3 THE RETREAT
4 MEADOW ORCH
5 KEIL CL
6 THE GREEN
7 THE HUNTINGS
8 CROFT GDNS
C8
1 SANDS CROFT AVE
2 DASTON CL
3 LIME TREE AVE
4 BIBSWORTH AVE
C8
5 WELLS GDNS
6 COLLETTS GDNS
7 SHEER HO
8 YEW TREE CT
188
186
A
B
C
D
E
F
PEGASUS CT
STATION RD
CHILDSWICKHAM RD
HIGHGATE CT
SPRINGFIELD LA
WALNUT CL
AVERILL CL
MORRIS RD
LEAMINGTON RD
ORCHARD AVE
BREDON VIEW
KINGSDALE CT
COLLETTS FIELDS
BIBSWORTH LA
A44
BACK LA
Sch
Liby
Mus
HIGH ST
THE OLD COACH
PRY LA
LIFFORD GDNS
THE OLD MILL
MILL AVE
CHURCH ST
PO
CHURCH CL
Broadway
CHELTENHAM RD
B4632
Fish Hill
FISH HILL
Campden House
GL55
8
37
WEST END LA
West End
Bury End
SNOWSHILL RD
Cotswold Way
Broadway Hill
Coombe Farm
Burnhill
7
B4081
Rectory
CONEYGREE LA
Peter's Farm
Guide Post
Broadway Tower Country Park
36
WR12
Dor Knap
Manor Farm
Heath Farm
6
FIVE MILE DR
Buckland Wood
Middle Hill House
Cotswold Way
Kite's Nest
35
A44
Dulverton Wood
Seven Wells
5
Broadway Wood
Campden Ashes
Great Brockhampton Farm
Spring Hill House
BUCKLE ST
Snowshill Manor
34
HOMEPIECE
Hill Barn Farm
Snowshill PH
SPRINGHILL COTTS
4
Oat Hill
GL56
Snowshill Hill
33
Bourton Far Hill Farm
3
Hornsleasow Farm
Stanway Ash Wood
Upper Slatepits
32
Half Moon Plantation
Field Barn
2
GL54
Taddington
Scarborough Farm
31
Hinchwick Hill Barn
River Windrush
Diamond Way
1
Ford Hill Farm
Cutsdean Hill
Gloucestershire Way
Cutsdean
30
08
09
10
11
12
13
175
186

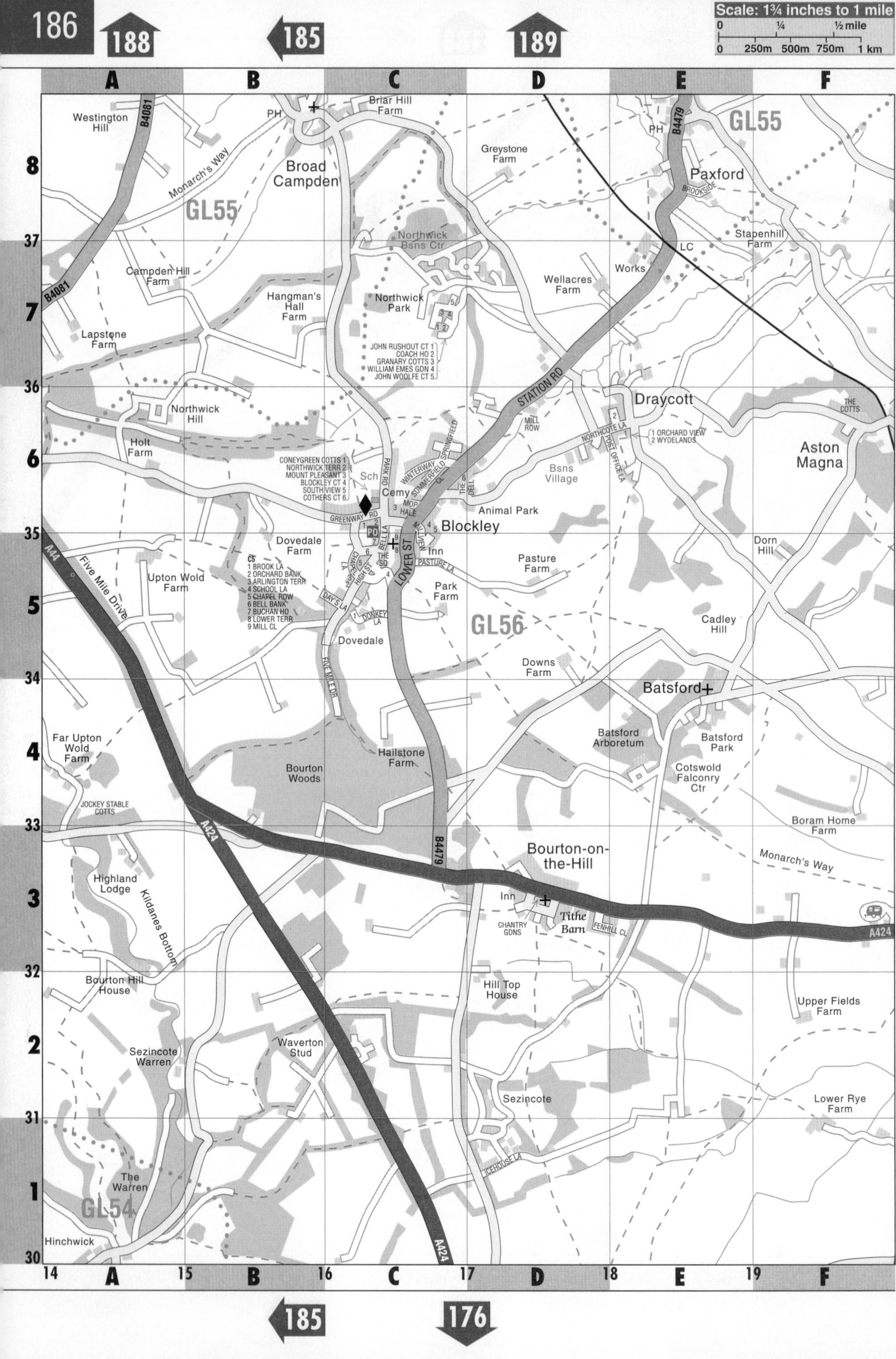
188
185
189
Scale: 1¾ inches to 1 mile
0 ¼ ½ mile
0 250m 500m 750m 1 km
A B C D E F
8
37
7
36
6
35
5
34
4
33
3
32
2
31
1
30
14 15 16 17 18 19
Westington Hill
B4081
PH
Briar Hill Farm
Greystone Farm
Broad Campden
Monarch's Way
GL55
B4479
Paxford
BROOKSIDE
Stapenhill Farm
LC
Works
Northwick Bsns Ctr
Campden Hill Farm
Hangman's Hall Farm
Northwick Park
Wellacres Farm
Lapstone Farm
JOHN RUSHOUT CT 1
COACH HO 2
GRANARY COTTS 3
WILLIAM EMES GDN 4
JOHN WOOLFE CT 5
STATION RD
Draycott
THE COTTS
Northwick Hill
MILL ROW
NORTHCOTE LA
1 ORCHARD VIEW
2 WYDELANDS
Holt Farm
CONEYGREEN COTTS 1
NORTHWICK TERR 2
MOUNT PLEASANT 3
BLOCKLEY CT 4
SOUTH VIEW 5
COTHERS CT 6
PARK RD
WINTERWAY
SUMMERFIELD CL
SPRINGFIELD
THE DELL
POST OFFICE LA
Bsns Village
Aston Magna
Sch
Cemy
MOP HALE
GREENWAY RD
Animal Park
PO
Blockley
MILL VIEW
LOWER ST
Inn
BELL LA
Dovedale Farm
C5
1 BROOK LA
2 ORCHARD BANK
3 ARLINGTON TERR
4 SCHOOL LA
5 CHAPEL ROW
6 BELL BANK
7 BUCHAN HO
8 LOWER TERR
9 MILL CL
CHAPEL LA
HIGH ST
THE SQ
PASTURE LA
Pasture Farm
Dorn Hill
A44
Five Mile Drive
Upton Wold Farm
DAY'S LA
DONKEY LA
Park Farm
GL56
Dovedale
FIVE MILE DR
Cadley Hill
Downs Farm
Batsford
Far Upton Wold Farm
Hailstone Farm
Batsford Arboretum
Batsford Park
Bourton Woods
Cotswold Falconry Ctr
JOCKEY STABLE COTTS
A424
Boram Home Farm
Bourton-on-the-Hill
Monarch's Way
Highland Lodge
Kildanes Bottom
Inn
Tithe Barn
CHANTRY GDNS
FENHILL CL
Bourton Hill House
Hill Top House
Upper Fields Farm
Sezincote Warren
Waverton Stud
Sezincote
Lower Rye Farm
ICEHOUSE LA
The Warren
GL54
Hinchwick
185
176

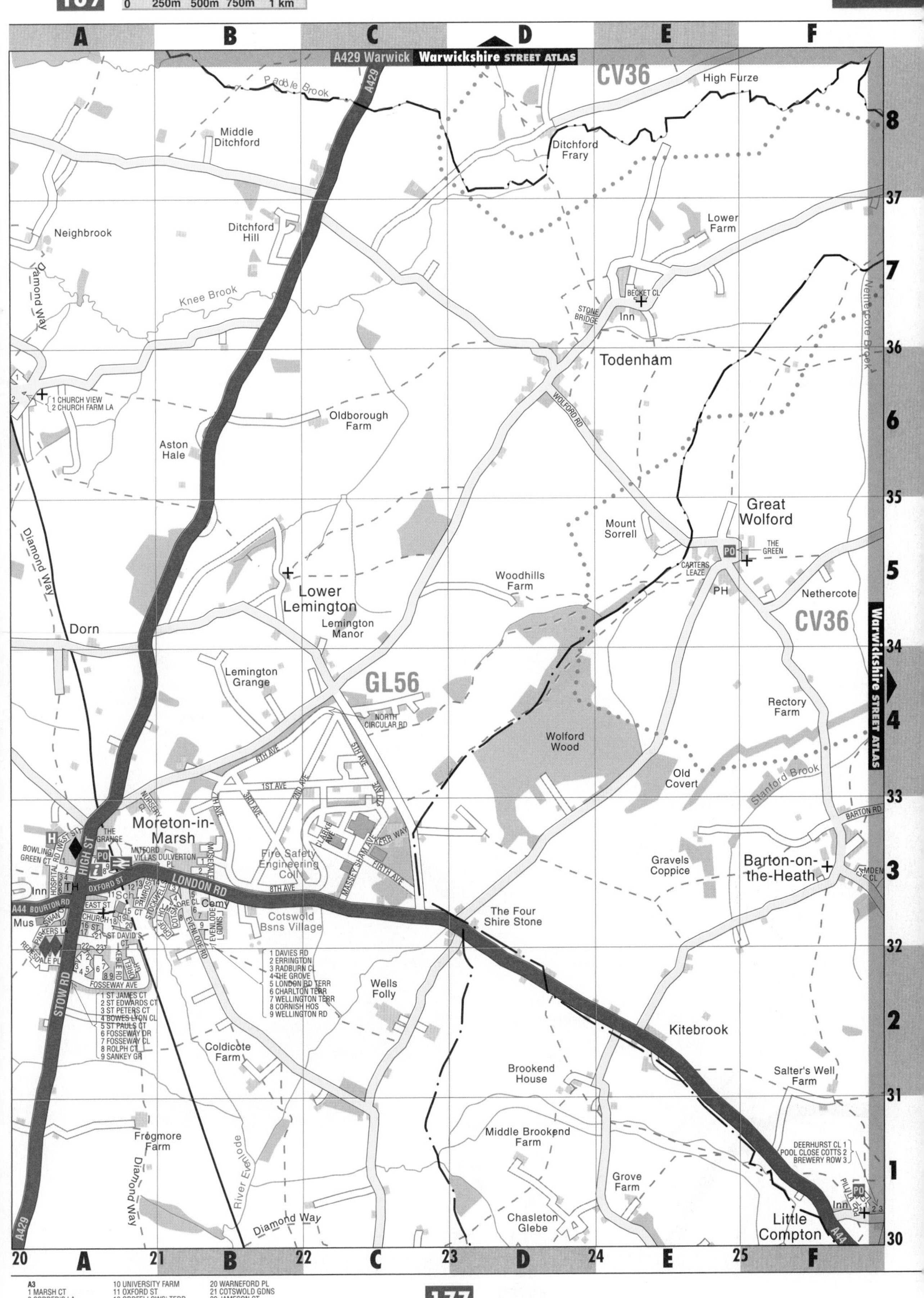

A3
1 MARSH CT
2 CORDER'S LA
3 DEVONSHIRE TERR
4 MANCHESTER CT
5 CORDER'S CL
6 REDESDALE MEWS
7 NEW RD
8 STATION RD
9 THE GREEN
10 UNIVERSITY FARM
11 OXFORD ST
12 ODDFELLOWS' TERR
13 TURNPIKE CL
14 CICESTER TERR
15 MEAD CL
16 STONEFARN CT
17 DUNSTALL HO
18 GRAY'S LA
19 ST GEORGE'S CL
20 WARNEFORD PL
21 COTSWOLD GDNS
22 JAMESON CT
23 TINKER'S CL

Scale: 1¾ inches to 1 mile

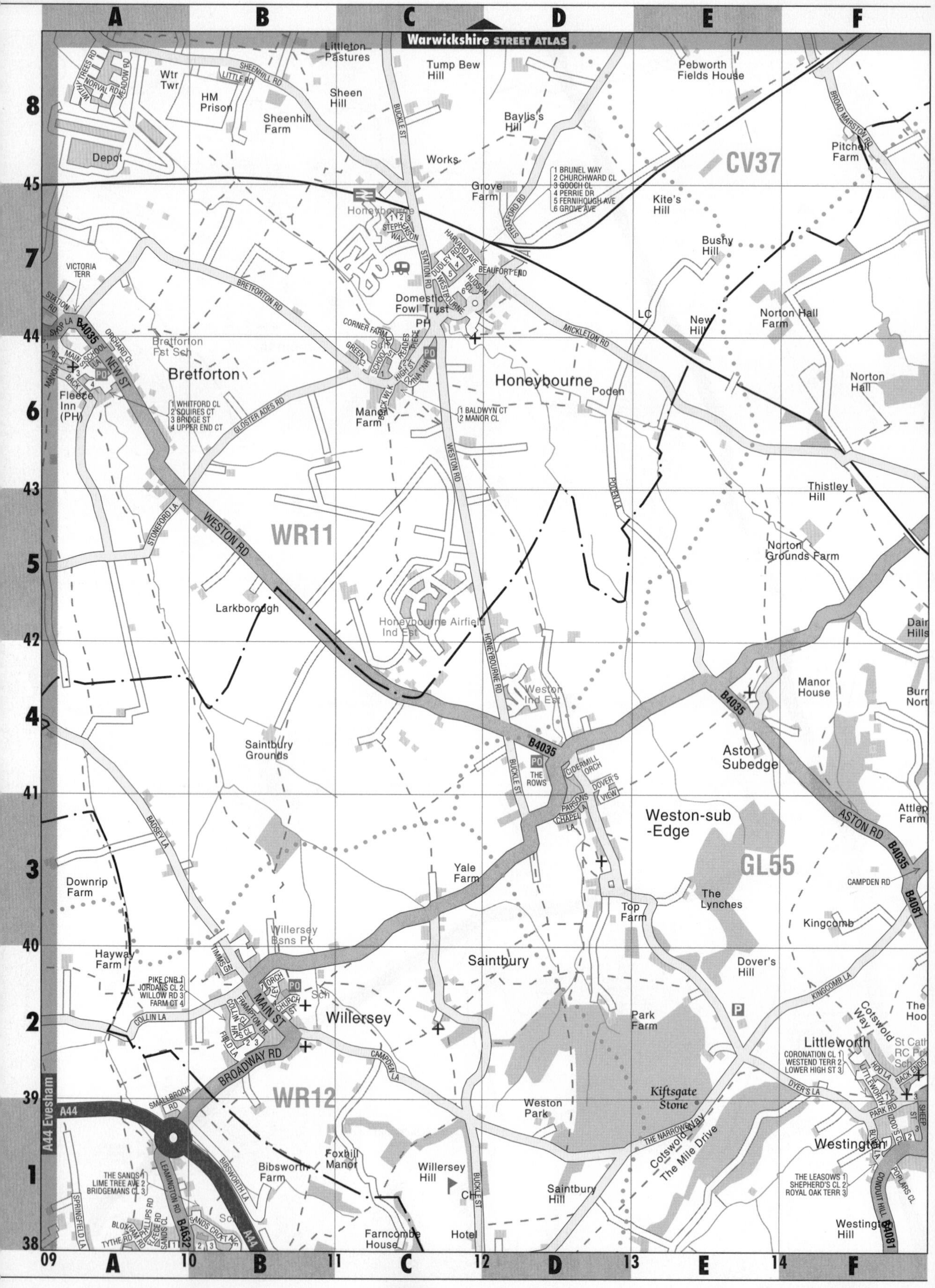

185
186

Scale: 1¾ inches to 1 mile
0 ¼ ½ mile
0 250m 500m 750m 1 km

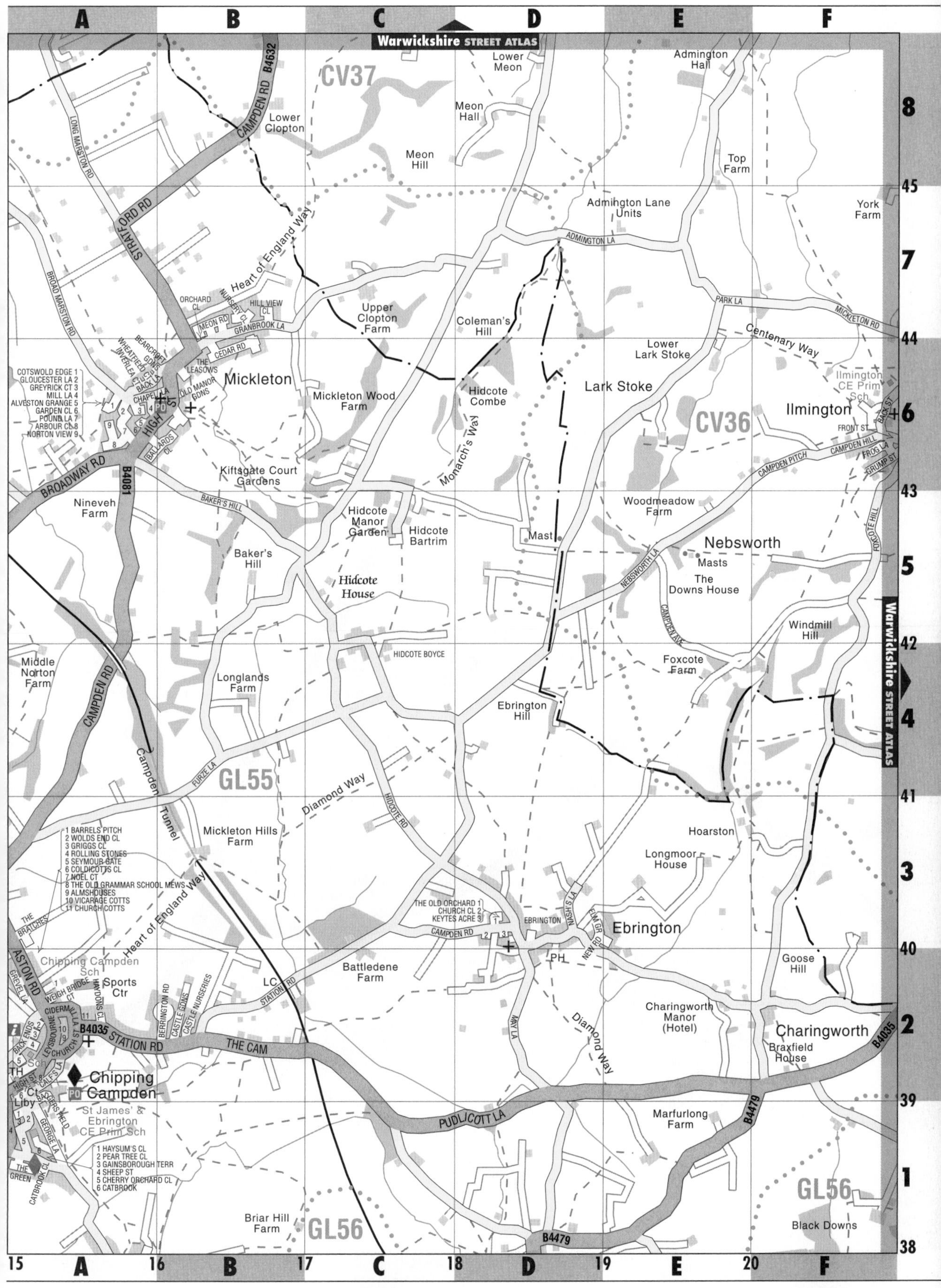

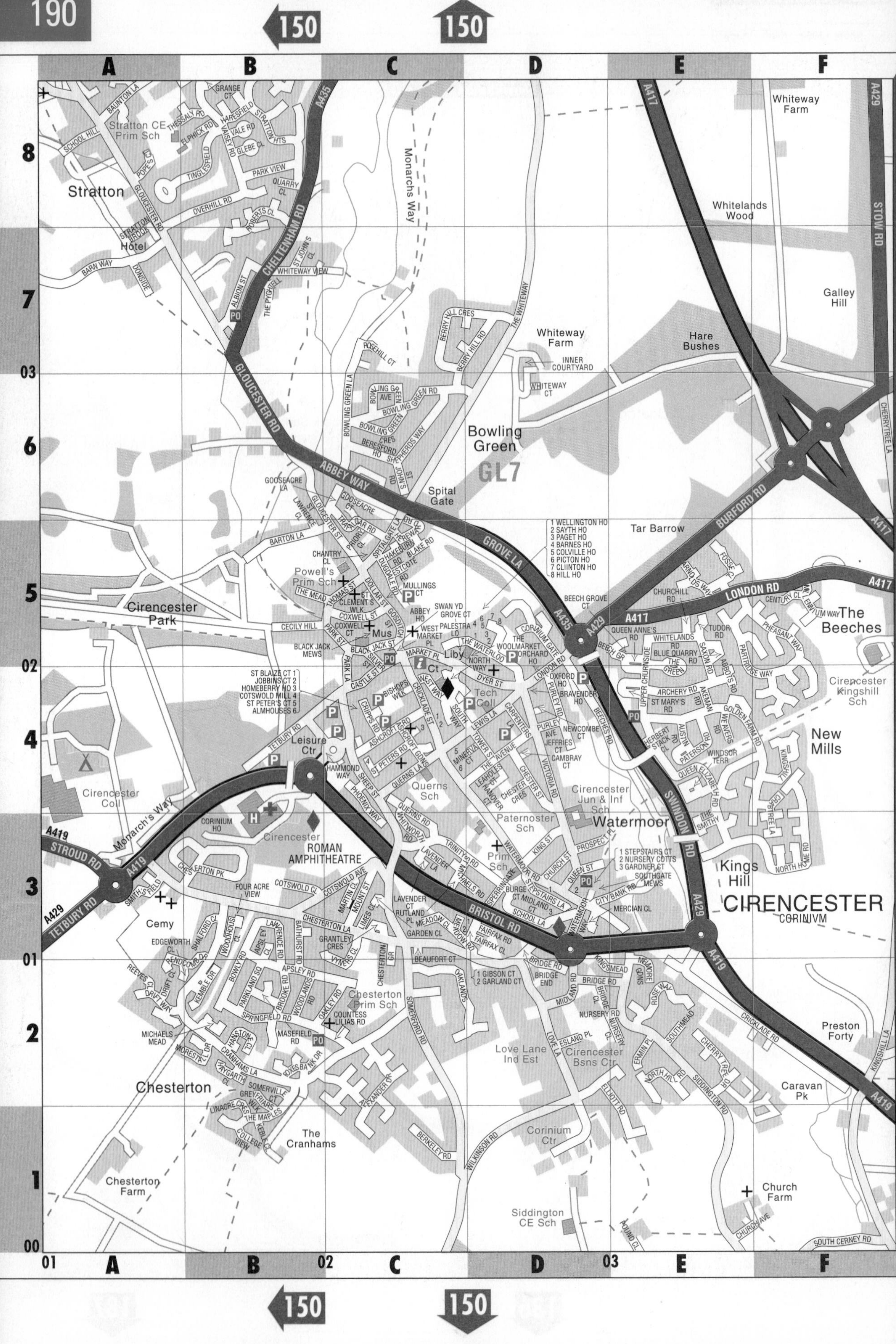
150
150
A
B
C
D
E
F
8
7
03
6
5
02
4
3
01
2
1
00
Stratton
Stratton CE Prim Sch
Hotel
Monarchs Way
Whiteway Farm
Whitelands Wood
STOW RD
Galley Hill
Hare Bushes
Whiteway Farm
INNER COURTYARD
WHITEWAY CT
Bowling Green
GL7
Spital Gate
CHELTENHAM RD
GLOUCESTER RD
ABBEY WAY
GROVE LA
BURFORD RD
LONDON RD
A417
A429
A435
A419
Tar Barrow
1 WELLINGTON HO
2 SAYTH HO
3 PAGET HO
4 BARNES HO
5 COLVILLE HO
6 PICTON HO
7 CLIINTON HO
8 HILL HO
Powell's Prim Sch
Cirencester Park
Mus
Liby
Ct
Tech Coll
The Beeches
Cirencester Kingshill Sch
New Mills
Leisure Ctr
Querns Sch
Cirencester Coll
Cirencester Jun & Inf Sch
Watermoor
Paternoster Sch
ROMAN AMPHITHEATRE
Cirencester
Prim Sch
1 STEPSTAIRS CT
2 NURSERY COTTS
3 GARDNER CT
SOUTHGATE MEWS
Kings Hill
CIRENCESTER
CORINIVM
STROUD RD
TETBURY RD
BRISTOL RD
SWINDON RD
Cemy
Chesterton Prim Sch
Love Lane Ind Est
Cirencester Bsns Ctr
Preston Forty
Caravan Pk
Chesterton
The Cranhams
Corinium Ctr
Chesterton Farm
Siddington CE Sch
Church Farm
SOUTH CERNEY RD
01
A
B
02
C
D
03
E
F
150
150

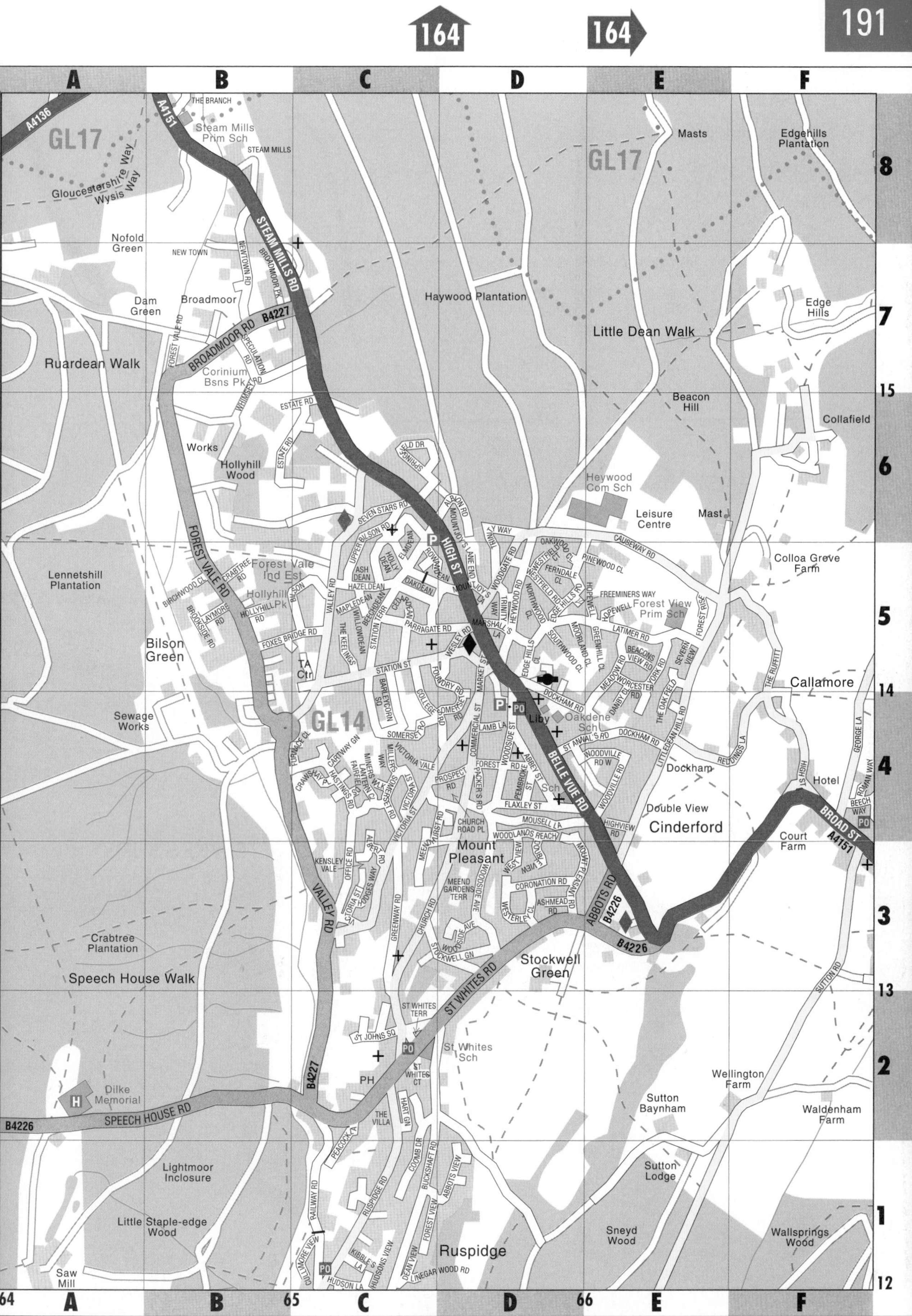
A
B
C
D
E
F
8
7
15
6
5
14
4
3
13
2
1
12
64
65
66
GL17
Gloucestershire Way
Wysis Way
THE BRANCH
Steam Mills Prim Sch
STEAM MILLS
STEAM MILLS RD
A4136
A4151
Masts
Edgehills Plantation
Nofold Green
NEW TOWN
Dam Green
Broadmoor
Haywood Plantation
Edge Hills
Little Dean Walk
Ruardean Walk
BROADMOOR RD
B4227
Corinium Bsns Pk
Beacon Hill
Collafield
Works
Hollyhill Wood
Heywood Com Sch
Leisure Centre
Mast
HIGH ST
Lennetshill Plantation
Forest Vale Ind Est
Hollyhill Pk
Colloa Grove Farm
Forest View Prim Sch
Bilson Green
TA Ctr
FOREST VALE RD
Sewage Works
GL14
Callamore
Liby
Oakdene Sch
Dockham
Hotel
BELLE VUE RD
Double View
Cinderford
Court Farm
BROAD ST
A4151
Mount Pleasant
VALLEY RD
Crabtree Plantation
Speech House Walk
Stockwell Green
ABBOTS RD
B4226
ST WHITES RD
St Whites Sch
Wellington Farm
Dilke Memorial
SPEECH HOUSE RD
B4226
B4227
PH
Sutton Baynham
Waldenham Farm
Lightmoor Inclosure
Sutton Lodge
Little Staple-edge Wood
Sneyd Wood
Wallsprings Wood
Ruspidge
Saw Mill

181 181 182

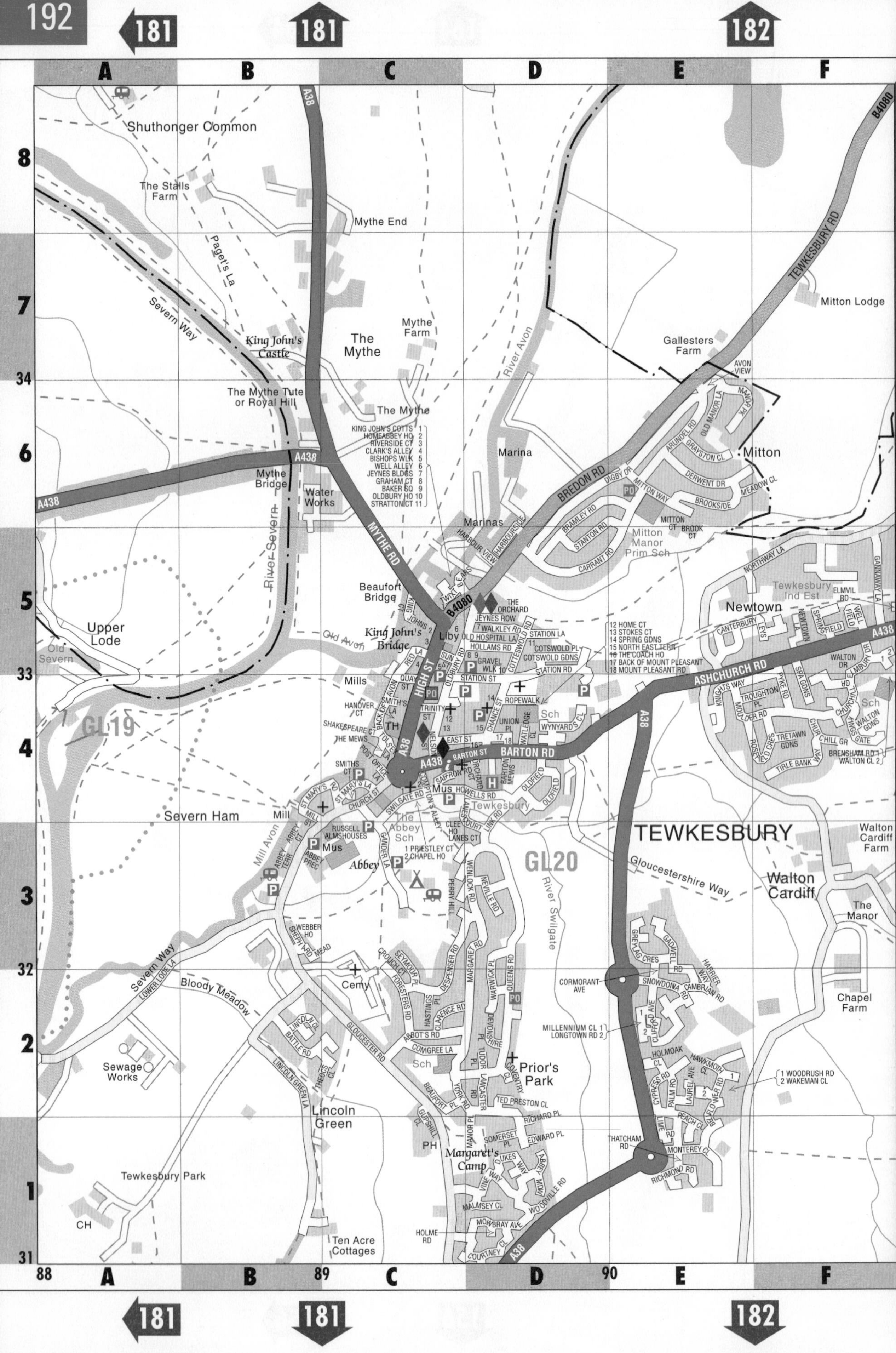

181 181 182

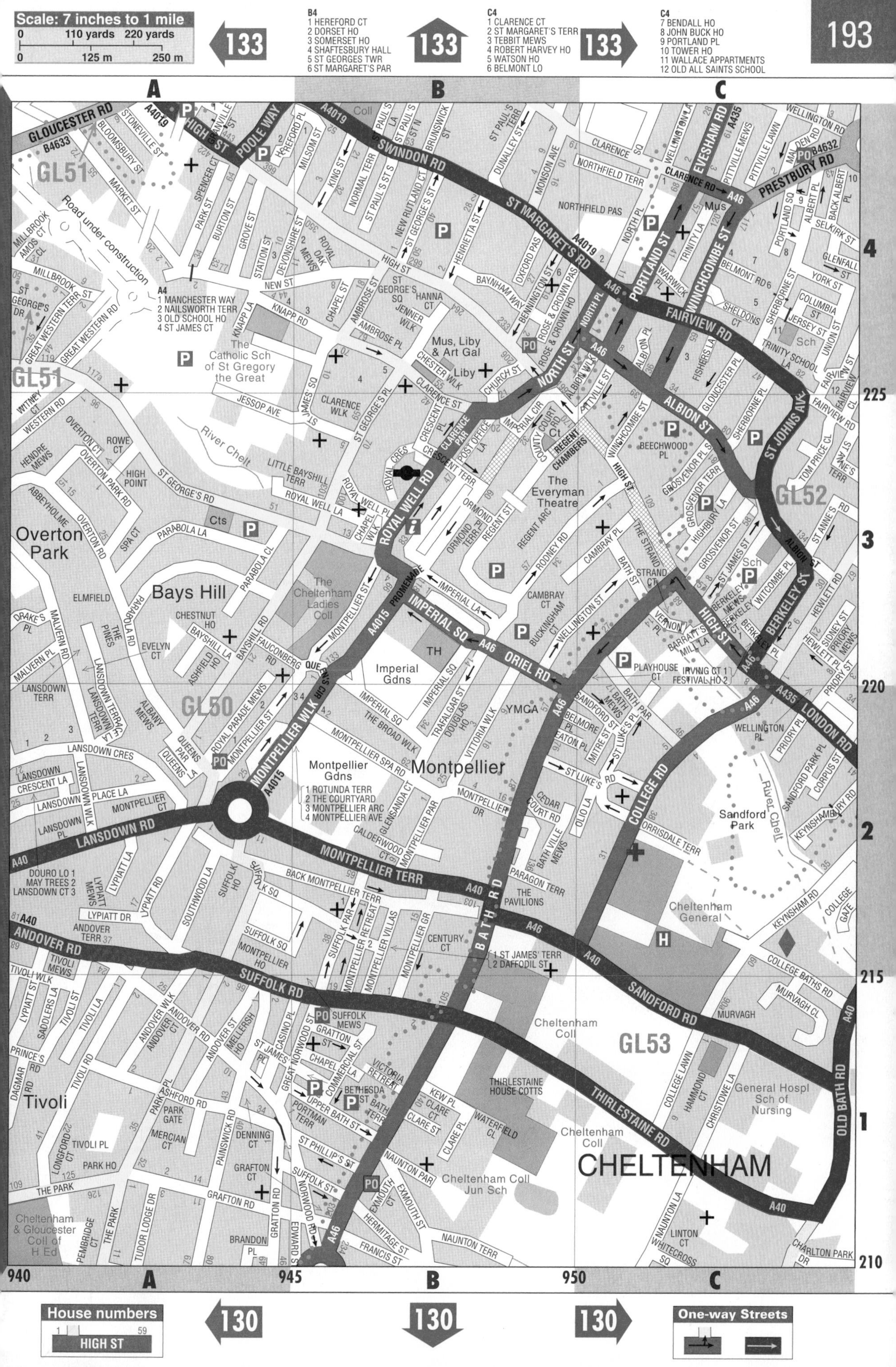

Scale: 7 inches to 1 mile
0 110 yards 220 yards
0 125 m 250 m
133
B4
1 HEREFORD CT
2 DORSET HO
3 SOMERSET HO
4 SHAFTESBURY HALL
5 ST GEORGES TWR
6 ST MARGARET'S PAR
133
C4
1 CLARENCE CT
2 ST MARGARET'S TERR
3 TEBBIT MEWS
4 ROBERT HARVEY HO
5 WATSON HO
6 BELMONT LO
133
C4
7 BENDALL HO
8 JOHN BUCK HO
9 PORTLAND PL
10 TOWER HO
11 WALLACE APPARTMENTS
12 OLD ALL SAINTS SCHOOL
193
A
B
C
GLOUCESTER RD
B4633
GL51
Road under construction
A4
1 MANCHESTER WAY
2 NAILSWORTH TERR
3 OLD SCHOOL HO
4 ST JAMES CT
The Catholic Sch of St Gregory the Great
River Chelt
Overton Park
Bays Hill
GL50
Lansdown Terr
LANSDOWN RD
A40
DOURO LO 1
MAY TREES 2
LANSDOWN CT 3
ANDOVER RD
SUFFOLK RD
Tivoli
Cheltenham & Gloucester Coll of H Ed
SWINDON RD
A4019
ST MARGARET'S RD
Mus, Liby & Art Gal
Liby
ROYAL WELL RD
The Cheltenham Ladies Coll
IMPERIAL SQ
TH
Imperial Gdns
Montpellier Gdns
1 ROTUNDA TERR
2 THE COURTYARD
3 MONTPELLIER ARC
4 MONTPELLIER AVE
Montpellier
MONTPELLIER WLK
A4015
MONTPELLIER TERR
BATH RD
1 ST JAMES' TERR
2 DAFFODIL ST
The Everyman Theatre
REGENT CHAMBERS
YMCA
ORIEL RD
A46
NORTH ST
PORTLAND ST
EVESHAM RD
A435
WINCHCOMBE ST
CLARENCE RD
PRESTBURY RD
B4632
FAIRVIEW RD
ALBION ST
ST JOHNS AVE
GL52
HIGH ST
BERKELEY ST
LONDON RD
PLAYHOUSE CT
IRVING CT 1
FESTIVAL HO 2
COLLEGE RD
Sandford Park
River Chelt
Cheltenham General
H
SANDFORD RD
GL53
Cheltenham Coll
THIRLESTAINE HOUSE COTTS
THIRLESTAINE RD
General Hospl Sch of Nursing
OLD BATH RD
Cheltenham Coll
CHELTENHAM
Cheltenham Coll Jun Sch
4
225
3
220
2
215
1
210
940
945
950
A
B
C
House numbers
1 59
HIGH ST
130
130
130
One-way Streets

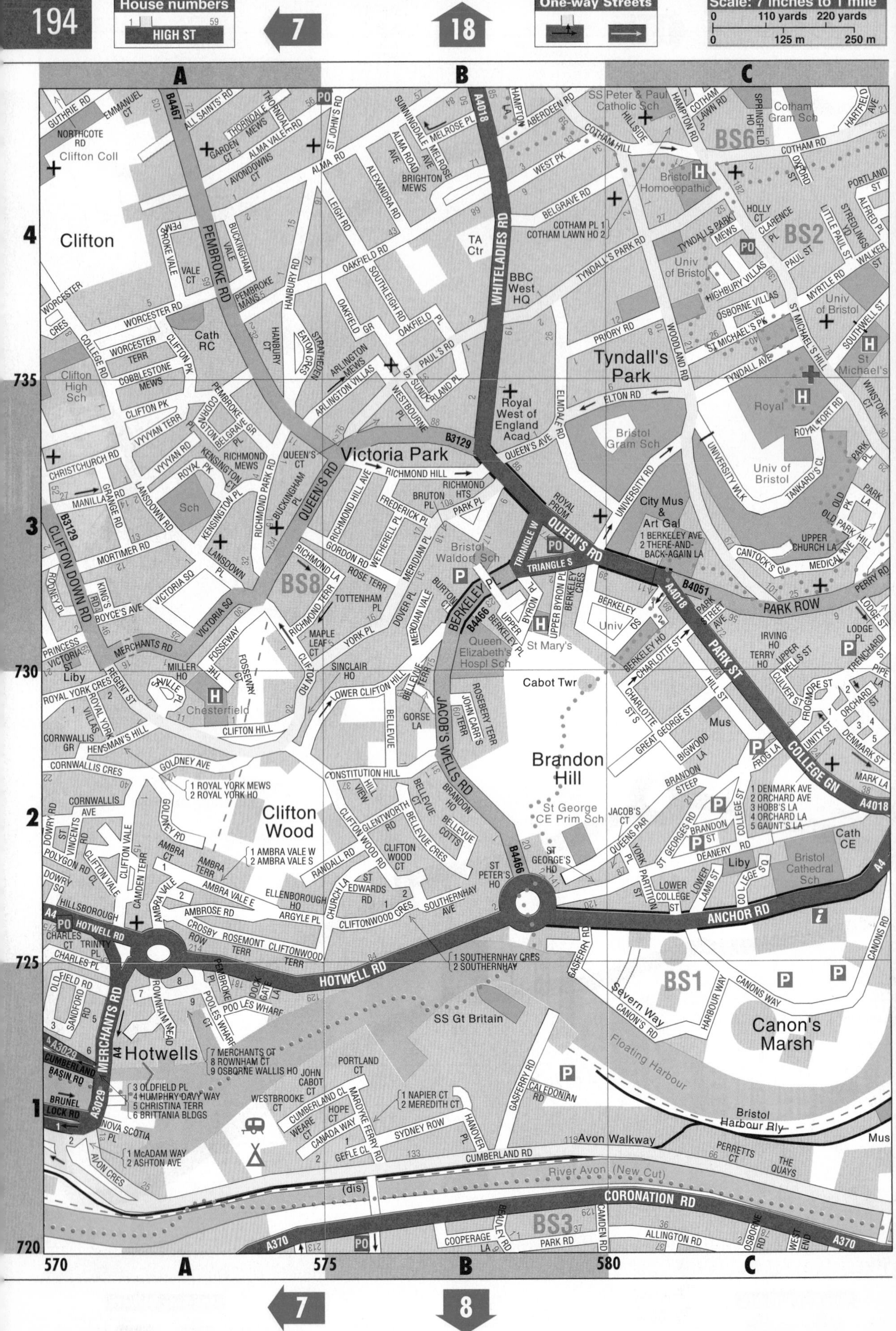
House numbers
HIGH ST
1
59
7
18
One-way Streets
Scale: 7 inches to 1 mile
0
110 yards
220 yards
125 m
250 m
A
B
C
4
3
2
1
735
730
725
720
570
575
580
Clifton
Clifton Coll
Clifton High Sch
Cath RC
Victoria Park
Tyndall's Park
Royal West of England Acad
Bristol Gram Sch
Univ of Bristol
Royal
St Michael's
Bristol Homoeopathic
Cotham Gram Sch
SS Peter & Paul Catholic Sch
TA Ctr
BBC West HQ
City Mus & Art Gal
1 BERKELEY AVE
2 THERE-AND-BACK-AGAIN LA
Bristol Waldorf Sch
Queen Elizabeth's Hospl Sch
St Mary's
Cabot Twr
Brandon Hill
St George CE Prim Sch
Clifton Wood
Chesterfield
Liby
Mus
Cath CE
Bristol Cathedral Sch
Hotwells
SS Gt Britain
Canon's Marsh
Floating Harbour
Bristol Harbour Rly
Avon Walkway
River Avon (New Cut)
BS1
BS2
BS3
BS6
BS8
PEMBROKE RD
WHITELADIES RD
QUEEN'S RD
PARK ROW
PARK ST
COLLEGE GN
ANCHOR RD
HOTWELL RD
MERCHANTS RD
CLIFTON DOWN RD
JACOB'S WELLS RD
CORONATION RD
CUMBERLAND RD
COTHAM HILL
TYNDALL'S PARK RD
ELTON RD
ALMA RD
WORCESTER RD
1 DENMARK AVE
2 ORCHARD AVE
3 HOBB'S LA
4 ORCHARD LA
5 GAUNT'S LA
1 ROYAL YORK MEWS
2 ROYAL YORK HO
1 AMBRA VALE W
2 AMBRA VALE S
1 SOUTHERNHAY CRES
2 SOUTHERNHAY
7 MERCHANTS CT
8 ROWNHAM CT
9 OSBORNE WALLIS HO
3 OLDFIELD PL
4 HUMPHRY DAVY WAY
5 CHRISTINA TERR
6 BRITTANIA BLDGS
1 NAPIER CT
2 MEREDITH CT
1 McADAM WAY
2 ASHTON AVE
A4018
B4467
B3129
B4466
B4051
A4
A3029
A370

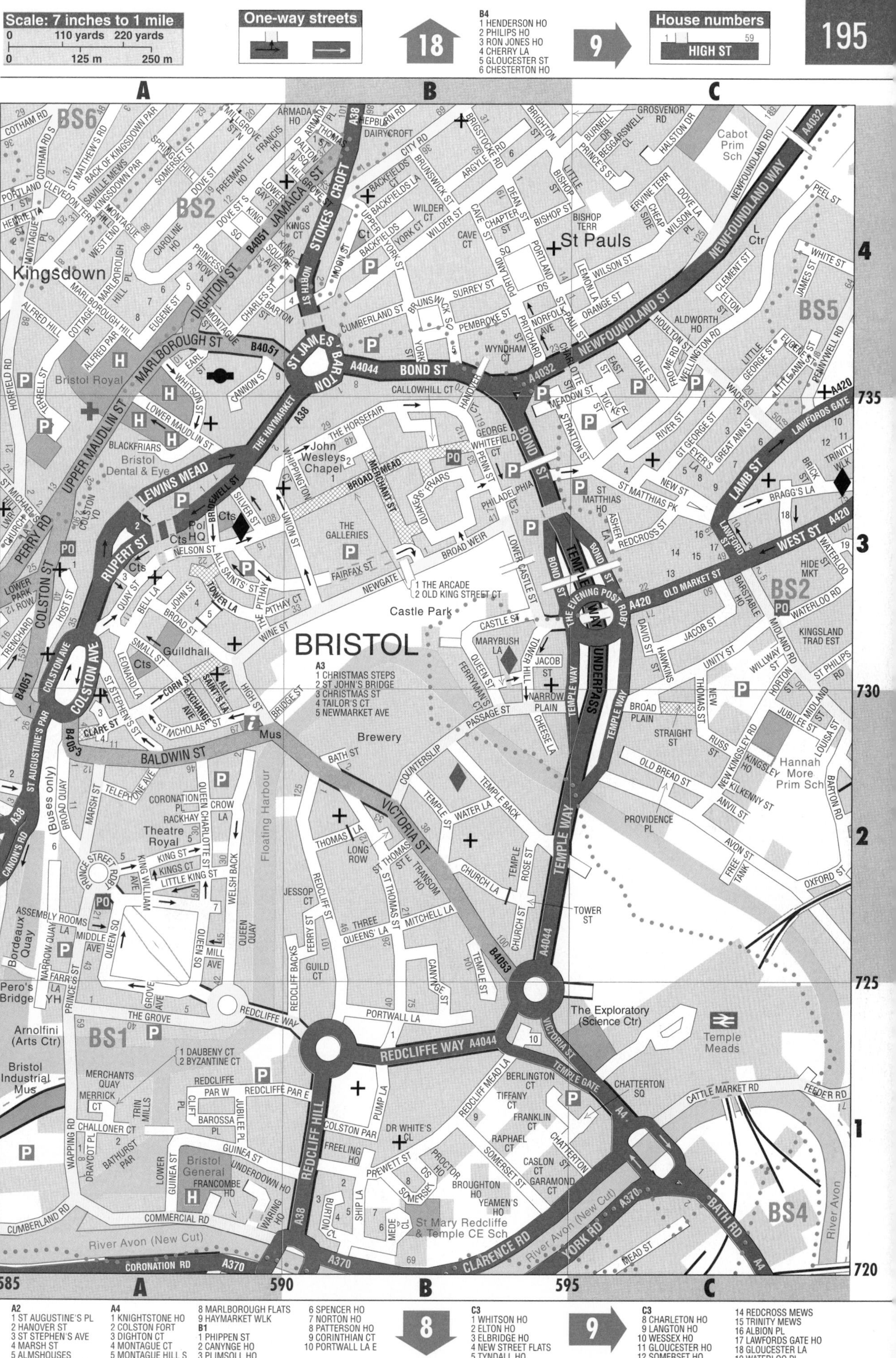
Scale: 7 inches to 1 mile
0 110 yards 220 yards
0 125 m 250 m
One-way streets
18
B4
1 HENDERSON HO
2 PHILIPS HO
3 RON JONES HO
4 CHERRY LA
5 GLOUCESTER ST
6 CHESTERTON HO
9
House numbers
1 59
HIGH ST
A
B
C
4
735
3
730
2
725
1
720
585
590
595
BS6
BS2
BS5
BS1
BS4
Kingsdown
St Pauls
Cabot Prim Sch
Bristol Royal
Bristol Dental & Eye
John Wesleys Chapel
THE GALLERIES
Castle Park
BRISTOL
Guildhall
Brewery
Floating Harbour
Theatre Royal
Hannah More Prim Sch
KINGSLAND TRAD EST
HIDE MKT
PROVIDENCE PL
The Exploratory (Science Ctr)
Temple Meads
Arnolfini (Arts Ctr)
Bristol Industrial Mus
Pero's Bridge
Bordeaux Quay
Bristol General
St Mary Redcliffe & Temple CE Sch
River Avon (New Cut)
River Avon
NEWFOUNDLAND WAY
NEWFOUNDLAND ST
BOND ST
ST JAMES' BARTON
THE HAYMARKET
LEWINS MEAD
RUPERT ST
COLSTON AVE
BALDWIN ST
VICTORIA ST
TEMPLE WAY
REDCLIFFE WAY
REDCLIFF HILL
CORONATION RD
CLARENCE RD
YORK RD
BATH RD
OLD MARKET ST
WEST ST
LAMB ST
STOKES CROFT
MARLBOROUGH ST
UPPER MAUDLIN ST
PERRY RD
A3
1 CHRISTMAS STEPS
2 ST JOHN'S BRIDGE
3 CHRISTMAS ST
4 TAILOR'S CT
5 NEWMARKET AVE
1 THE ARCADE
2 OLD KING STREET CT
1 DAUBENEY CT
2 BYZANTINE CT
A2
1 ST AUGUSTINE'S PL
2 HANOVER ST
3 ST STEPHEN'S AVE
4 MARSH ST
5 ALMSHOUSES
6 KING GEORGE V PL
7 QUEEN SQUARE AVE
A4
1 KNIGHTSTONE HO
2 COLSTON FORT
3 DIGHTON CT
4 MONTAGUE CT
5 MONTAGUE HILL S
6 MONTAGUE FLATS
7 EUGENE FLATS
8 MARLBOROUGH FLATS
9 HAYMARKET WLK
B1
1 PHIPPEN ST
2 CANYNGE HO
3 PLIMSOLL HO
4 ASTON HO
5 CHATTERTON HO
6 SPENCER HO
7 NORTON HO
8 PATTERSON HO
9 CORINTHIAN CT
10 PORTWALL LA E
8
C3
1 WHITSON HO
2 ELTON HO
3 ELBRIDGE HO
4 NEW STREET FLATS
5 TYNDALL HO
6 JOHN COZENS HO
7 HAVILAND HO
9
C3
8 CHARLETON HO
9 LANGTON HO
10 WESSEX HO
11 GLOUCESTER HO
12 SOMERSET HO
13 STEEVENS HO (ALMSHOUSES)
14 REDCROSS MEWS
15 TRINITY MEWS
16 ALBION PL
17 LAWFORDS GATE HO
18 GLOUCESTER LA
19 WATERLOO PL

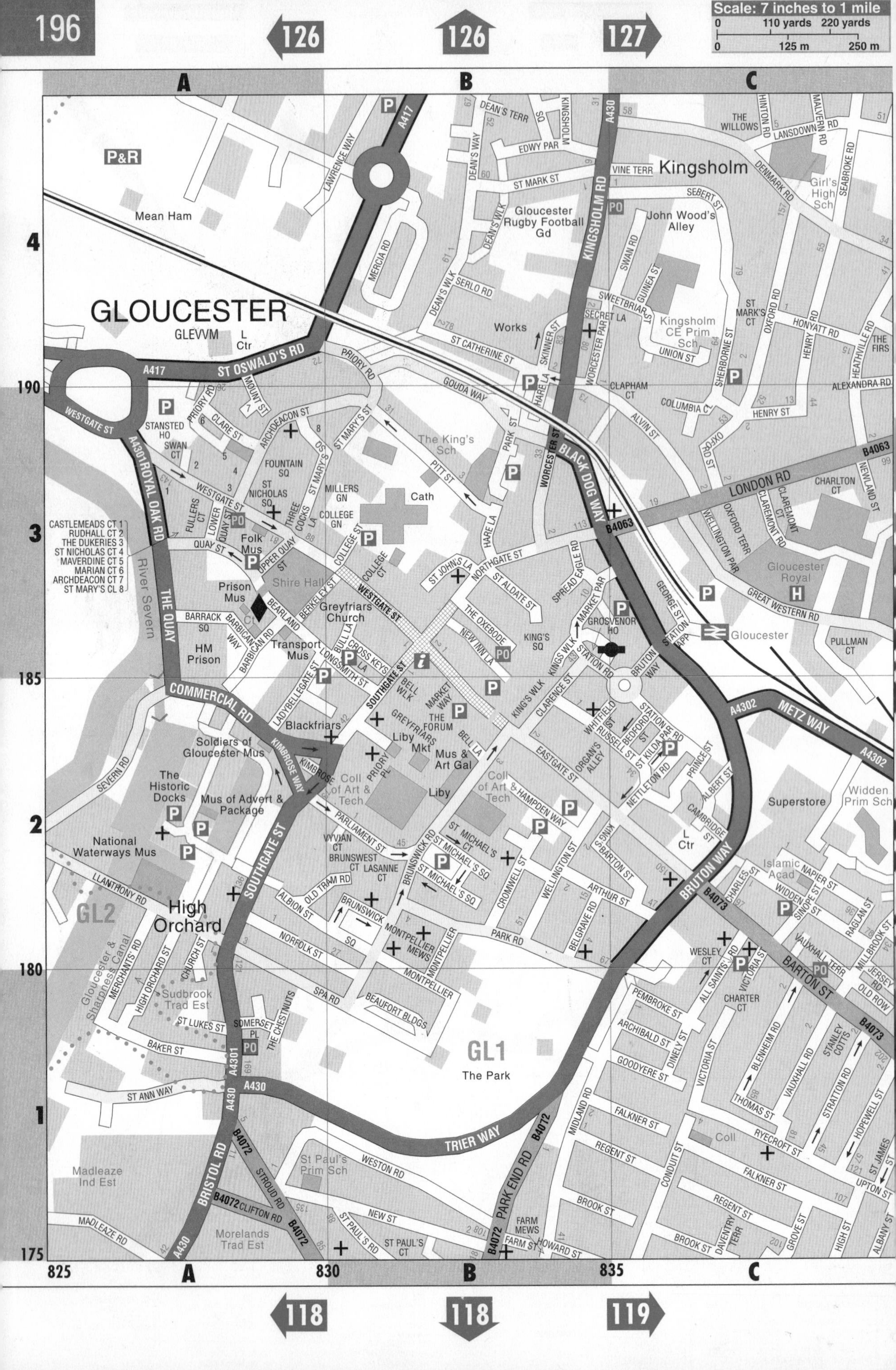

196
126
126
127
Scale: 7 inches to 1 mile
0
110 yards
220 yards
125 m
250 m
A
B
C
4
3
2
1
190
185
180
175
825
830
835
118
118
119
GLOUCESTER
GLEVVM
Kingsholm
Mean Ham
P&R
L Ctr
A417
ST OSWALD'S RD
WESTGATE ST
A430 ROYAL OAK RD
THE QUAY
River Severn
COMMERCIAL RD
KIMBROSE WAY
SOUTHGATE ST
BRISTOL RD
A430
A4301
B4072
STROUD RD
CLIFTON RD
TRIER WAY
PARK END RD
BRUTON WAY
BLACK DOG WAY
WORCESTER ST
KINGSHOLM RD
LONDON RD
B4063
METZ WAY
A4302
BARTON ST
B4073
LAWRENCE WAY
MERCIA RD
DEAN'S TERR
DEAN'S WAY
DEAN'S WLK
EDWY PAR
ST MARK ST
VINE TERR
Gloucester Rugby Football Gd
John Wood's Alley
SERLO RD
Works
ST CATHERINE ST
PRIORY RD
GOUDA WAY
SKINNER ST
HARE LA
SECRET LA
WORCESTER PAR
SWEETBRIAR ST
GUINEA ST
SWAN RD
SEBERT ST
Kingsholm CE Prim Sch
UNION ST
CLAPHAM CT
COLUMBIA CL
ALVIN ST
SHERBORNE ST
OXFORD RD
HENRY ST
HONYATT RD
ALEXANDRA RD
HEATHVILLE RD
THE FIRS
THE WILLOWS
HINTON RD
LANSDOWN RD
MALVERN RD
SEABROKE RD
DENMARK RD
Girl's High Sch
ST MARK'S CT
CHARLTON CT
NEWLAND ST
CLAREMONT RD
CLAREMONT CT
OXFORD TERR
WELLINGTON PAR
Gloucester Royal
GREAT WESTERN RD
Gloucester
PULLMAN CT
GEORGE ST
STATION APP
Superstore
Widden Prim Sch
Islamic Acad
NAPIER ST
WIDDEN ST
SINOPE ST
RAGLAN ST
VAUXHALL TERR
MILLBROOK ST
JERSEY RD
OLD ROW
ALBERT ST
CAMBRIDGE ST
PRINCE ST
STANSTED HO
SWAN CT
CLARE ST
ARCHDEACON ST
MOUNT ST
FOUNTAIN SQ
ST NICHOLAS SQ
THREE COCKS LA
ST MARY'S SQ
ST MARY'S ST
MILLERS GN
COLLEGE GN
The King's Sch
PITT ST
Cath
PARK ST
FULLERS CT
LOWER QUAY ST
QUAY ST
UPPER QUAY ST
Folk Mus
Shire Hall
Prison Mus
BARRACK SQ
BARBICAN WAY
BARBICAN RD
HM Prison
BEARLAND
BERKELEY ST
COLLEGE ST
COLLEGE CT
WESTGATE ST
Greyfriars Church
Transport Mus
LONGSMITH ST
LADYBELLEGATE ST
BULL LA
CROSS KEYS LA
SOUTHGATE ST
BELL WLK
MARKET WAY
THE FORUM
BELL LA
Blackfriars
GREYFRIARS
Liby
Mkt
Mus & Art Gal
PRIORY PL
Coll of Art & Tech
ST JOHN'S LA
NORTHGATE ST
ST ALDATE ST
THE OXEBODE
NEW INN LA
KING'S SQ
SPREAD EAGLE RD
MARKET PAR
GROSVENOR HO
KINGS WLK
KING'S WLK
STATION RD
BRUTON WAY
CLARENCE ST
WHITFIELD ST
BEDFORD ST
RUSSELL ST
ST KILDA PAR
NETTLETON RD
ORGAN'S ALLEY
EASTGATE ST
HAMPDEN WAY
CASTLEMEADS CT 1
RUDHALL CT 2
THE DUKERIES 3
ST NICHOLAS CT 4
MAVERDINE CT 5
MARIAN CT 6
ARCHDEACON CT 7
ST MARY'S CL 8
Soldiers of Gloucester Mus
The Historic Docks
Mus of Advert & Package
SEVERN RD
National Waterways Mus
LLANTHONY RD
GL2
High Orchard
PARLIAMENT ST
VYVIAN CT
BRUNSWEST CT
LASANNE CT
OLD TRAM RD
ALBION ST
BRUNSWICK RD
BRUNSWICK SQ
ST MICHAEL'S CT
ST MICHAEL'S SQ
CROMWELL ST
WELLINGTON ST
KINGS BARTON ST
ARTHUR ST
BELGRAVE RD
PARK RD
MONTPELLIER
MONTPELLIER MEWS
NORFOLK ST
SPA RD
BEAUFORT BLDGS
CHURCH ST
HIGH ORCHARD ST
MERCHANTS' RD
Gloucester & Sharpness Canal
Sudbrook Trad Est
ST LUKES ST
SOMERSET PL
THE CHESTNUTS
BAKER ST
ST ANN WAY
GL1
The Park
Madleaze Ind Est
MADLEAZE RD
Morelands Trad Est
St Paul's Prim Sch
WESTON RD
NEW ST
ST PAUL'S RD
ST PAUL'S CT
FARM MEWS
FARM ST
HOWARD ST
MIDLAND RD
FALKNER ST
REGENT ST
BROOK ST
CONDUIT ST
DAVENTRY TERR
PEMBROKE ST
ARCHIBALD ST
DINELY ST
GOODYERE ST
VICTORIA ST
ALL SAINTS RD
WESLEY CT
CHARLES ST
CHARTER CT
Coll
RYECROFT ST
BLENHEIM RD
VAUXHALL RD
THOMAS ST
STANLEY COTTS
STRATTON RD
HOPEWELL ST
ST JAMES
UPTON ST
GROVE ST
HIGH ST
ALBANY ST

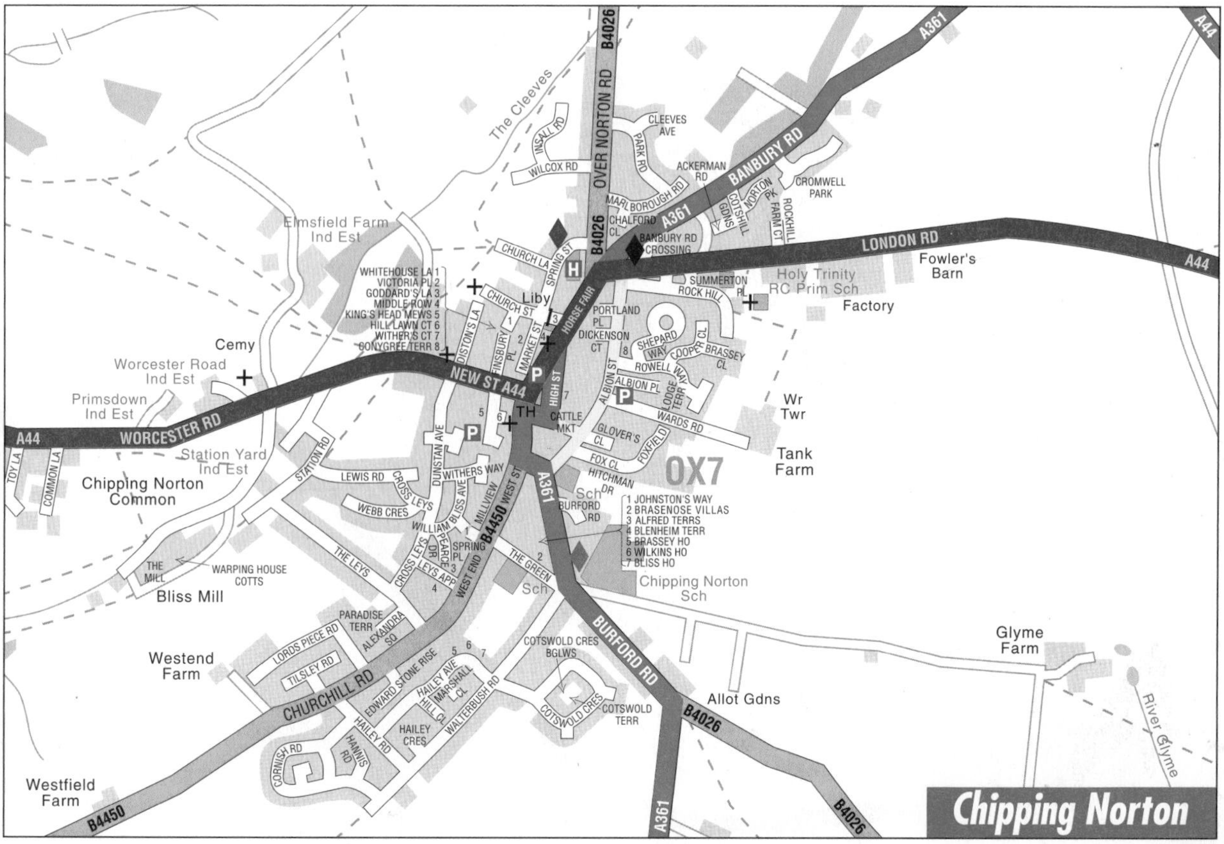
Chipping Norton
OX7
The Cleeves
INSALL RD
WILCOX RD
OVER NORTON RD
B4026
CLEEVES AVE
PARK RD
ACKERMAN RD
BANBURY RD
A361
CROMWELL PARK
MARLBOROUGH RD
CHALFORD CL
COTSHILL GDNS
NORTON PK
ROCKHILL FARM CT
BANBURY RD CROSSING
LONDON RD
A44
Fowler's Barn
Elmsfield Farm Ind Est
CHURCH LA
SPRING ST
HORSE FAIR
SUMMERTON PL
ROCK HILL
Holy Trinity RC Prim Sch
Factory
WHITEHOUSE LA 1
VICTORIA PL 2
GODDARD'S LA 3
MIDDLE ROW 4
KING'S HEAD MEWS 5
HILL LAWN CT 6
WITHER'S CT 7
CONYGREE TERR 8
CHURCH ST
Liby
PORTLAND PL
DICKENSON CT
SHEPARD WAY
COOPER CL
BRASSEY CL
Cemy
Worcester Road Ind Est
Primsdown Ind Est
DISTON'S LA
FINSBURY PL
MARKET ST
NEW ST A44
HIGH ST
ROWELL WAY
ALBION ST
ALBION PL
LODGE TERR
WARDS RD
Wr Twr
CATTLE MKT
TH
WORCESTER RD
GLOVER'S CL
FOXFIELD
FOX CL
Tank Farm
TOY LA
COMMON LA
Station Yard Ind Est
STATION RD
LEWIS RD
DUNSTAN AVE
WITHERS WAY
Chipping Norton Common
WEBB CRES
CROSS LEYS
BLISS AVE
MILLVIEW
WEST ST
B4450
HITCHMAN DR
Sch
BURFORD RD
1 JOHNSTON'S WAY
2 BRASENOSE VILLAS
3 ALFRED TERRS
4 BLENHEIM TERR
5 BRASSEY HO
6 WILKINS HO
7 BLISS HO
WILLIAM PEARCE DR
SPRING PL
LEYS APP
WEST END
THE GREEN
Chipping Norton Sch
THE MILL
WARPING HOUSE COTTS
THE LEYS
Bliss Mill
PARADISE TERR
ALEXANDRA SQ
LORDS PIECE RD
TILSLEY RD
Westend Farm
CHURCHILL RD
EDWARD STONE RISE
HAILEY AVE
MARSHALL CL
HILL CL
WATERBUSH RD
COTSWOLD CRES BGLWS
COTSWOLD CRES
COTSWOLD TERR
BURFORD RD
B4026
Allot Gdns
Glyme Farm
River Glyme
CORNISH RD
HAWKINS RD
HAILEY RD
HAILEY CRES
Westfield Farm
B4450
A361

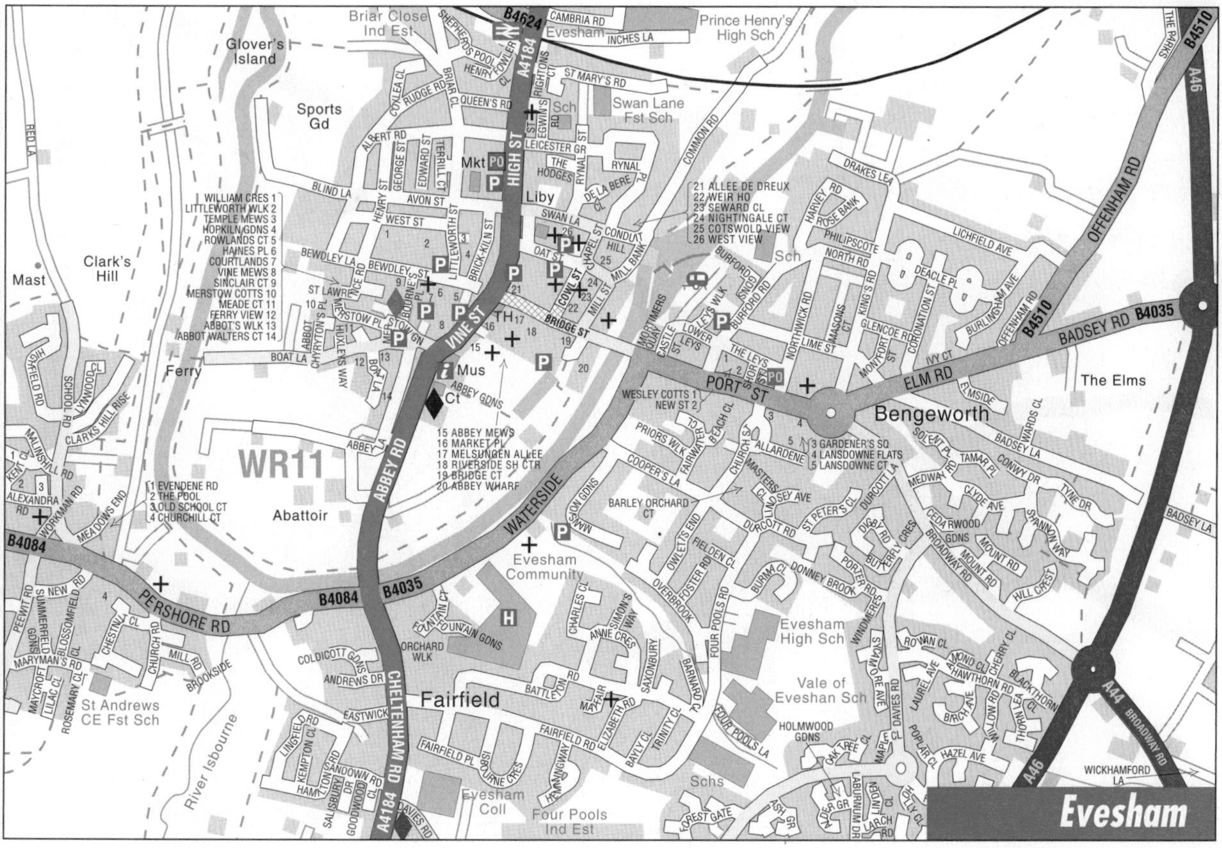
Evesham
WR11
Briar Close Ind Est
SHEPHERDS POOL
B4624
CAMBRIA RD
Evesham
INCHES LA
Prince Henry's High Sch
Glover's Island
HENRY CL
A4184
RIGHTONS
ST MARY'S RD
Sports Gd
CONLEA CL
RUDGE RD
BRIAR CL
QUEEN'S RD
Swan Lane Fst Sch
COMMON RD
RED LA
ALBERT RD
GEORGE ST
EDWARD ST
TERRILL CT
Mkt
PO
LEICESTER GR
THE HODGES
RYNAL ST
RYNAL PL
HIGH ST
DRAKES LEA
BLIND LA
AVON ST
Liby
DE LA BERE PL
21 ALLEE DE DREUX
22 WEIR HO
23 SEWARD CL
24 NIGHTINGALE CT
25 COTSWOLD VIEW
26 WEST VIEW
HARVEY RD
ROSE BANK
WILLIAM CRES 1
LITTLEWORTH WLK 2
TEMPLE MEWS 3
HOPKILN GDNS 4
ROWLANDS CT 5
HAINES PL 6
COURTLANDS 7
VINE MEWS 8
SINCLAIR CT 9
MERSTOW COTTS 10
MEADE CT 11
FERRY VIEW 12
ABBOT'S WLK 13
ABBOT WALTERS CT 14
HENRY ST
WEST ST
LITTLEWORTH ST
BRICK-KILN ST
SWAN LA
CONDUIT HILL
MILL BANK
PHILIPSCOTE
NORTH RD
LICHFIELD AVE
OFFENHAM RD
Clark's Hill
Mast
BEWDLEY LA
BEWDLEY ST
OAT ST
CHAPEL ST
BURFORD RD
Sch
DEACLE PL
ST LAWRENCE
VINE ST
COWL ST
MILL ST
MORTIMERS QUAY
CASTLE ST
LEYS WLK
LOWER LEYS
NORTHWICK RD
MASON'S CT
KING'S RD
CORONATION ST
BURLINGTON AVE
B4510
BADSEY RD
B4035
A46
MERSTOW PL
MERSTOW GN
BRIDGE ST
TH
GLENCOE RD
THE LEYS
SHORT ST
LIME ST
MONTFORT ST
IVY CT
ELM RD
ABBOT CHYRYTON'S PL
HUXLEY'S WAY
BOAT LA
BOAT LA
Mus
ABBEY GDNS
Ct
WESLEY COTTS 1
NEW ST 2
PORT ST
PO
Bengeworth
ELMSIDE
The Elms
WARDS CL
BADSEY LA
Ferry
HIGHFIELD RD
SCHOOL RD
KINWOOD CL
CLARKS HILL RISE
MALINSHILL RD
ABBEY LA
15 ABBEY MEWS
16 MARKET PL
17 MELSUNGEN ALLEE
18 RIVERSIDE SH CTR
19 BRIDGE CT
20 ABBEY WHARF
PRIORS WLK
FAIRWATER
BEACH CL
CHURCH ST
ALLARDENE
3 GARDENER'S SQ
4 LANSDOWNE FLATS
5 LANSDOWNE CT
SOLENT PL
TAMAR PL
CONWY DR
TYNE DR
KENT CL
ALEXANDRA RD
WORKMAN RD
1 EVENDENE RD
2 THE POOL
3 OLD SCHOOL CT
4 CHURCHILL CT
MEADOWS END
Abattoir
ABBEY RD
WATERSIDE
COOPER'S LA
MASTERS CL
LINDSEY AVE
ST PETER'S CL
DURCOTT LA
MEDWAY RD
CLYDE AVE
SHANNON WAY
BARLEY ORCHARD CT
MANSION GDNS
OWLET'S END
DURCOTT RD
DIGBY RD
BUTTERFLY CRES
CEDARWOOD GDNS
BROADWAY RD
MOUNT RD
BADSEY LA
B4084
Evesham Community
FIELDEN CL
FOSTER RD
DONNEY BROOK
PORTER RD
HILL CREST
PERSHORE RD
B4084
B4035
NEW RD
PEEWIT RD
SUMMERFIELD GDNS
BLOSSOMFIELD RD
CHESTNUT CL
CHURCH RD
MILL RD
BROOKSIDE
OVERBROOK
FOUR POOLS RD
FOUNTAIN CT
FOUNTAIN GDNS
ORCHARD WLK
CHARLES CL
ANNE CRES
ST SIMON'S WAY
SAXONBURY
Evesham High Sch
WINDMERE
SYCAMORE AVE
ROWAN CL
ALMOND CL
CHERRY CL
HAWTHORN RD
BLACKTHORN
COLDICOTT GDNS
ANDREWS DR
CHELTENHAM RD
BATTLETON RD
MAYFAIR
ELIZABETH RD
BARNARD CL
Vale of Evesham Sch
DAVIES RD
LAUREL AVE
BIRCH AVE
WILLOW RD
THORN LA
A44
MARYMAN'S RD
MAYCROFT
LILAC CL
ROSEMARY CL
St Andrews CE Fst Sch
River Isbourne
Fairfield
EASTWICK
FAIRFIELD RD
FAIRFIELD PL
BAYLY CL
TRINITY CL
FOUR POOLS LA
HOLMWOOD GDNS
OAK TREE CL
MAPLE CL
POPLAR CL
HAZEL AVE
WICKHAMFORD LA
A46
LINGFIELD RD
KEMPTON CL
HAM
ASCOT RD
SANDOWN RD
SALISBURY DR
GOODWOOD CL
A4184
DAVIES RD
HEMINGWAY
Evesham Coll
Four Pools Ind Est
Schs
FOREST GATE
ASH GR
ALDER GR
LABURNUM DR
LARCH RD

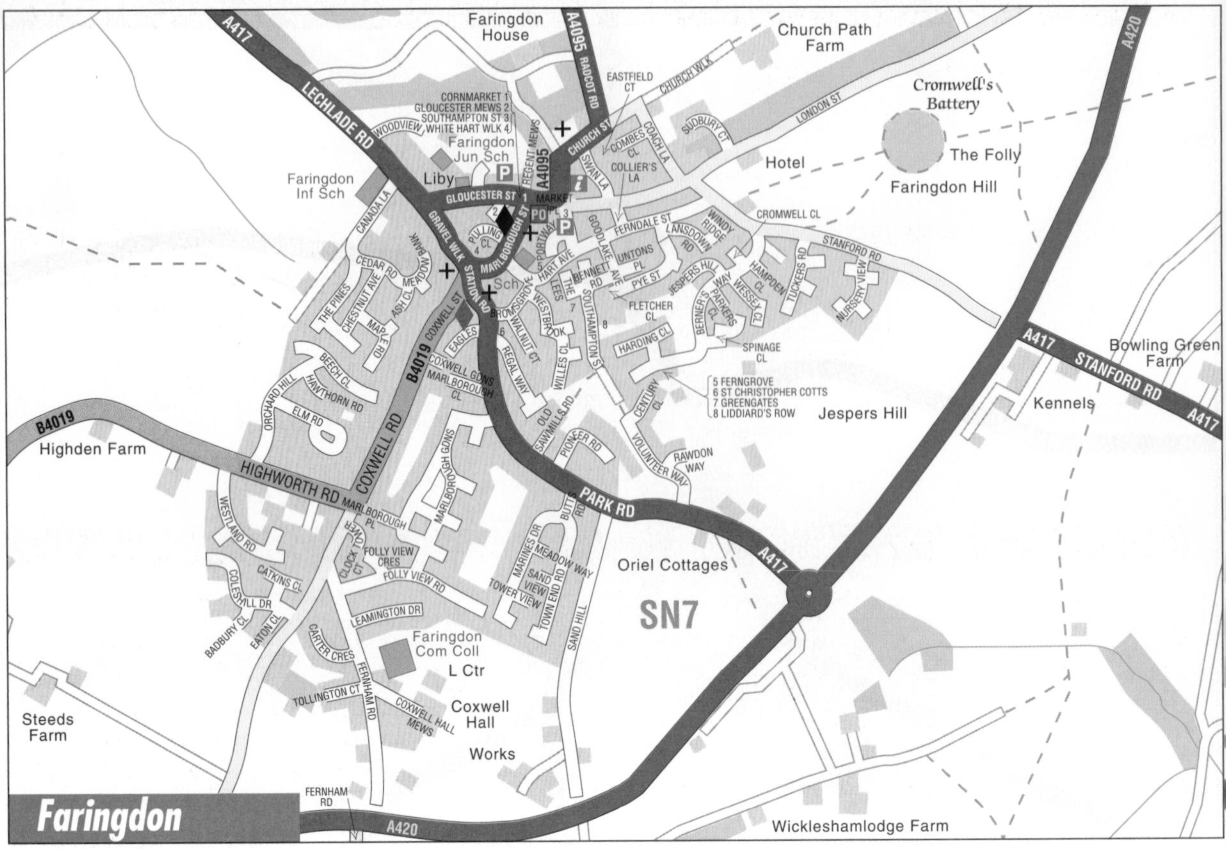

Faringdon

Faringdon House
Church Path Farm
A417
LECHLADE RD
A4095 RADCOT RD
EASTFIELD CT
CHURCH WLK
Cromwell's Battery
CORNMARKET 1
GLOUCESTER MEWS 2
SOUTHAMPTON ST 3
WHITE HART WLK 4
WOODVIEW
Faringdon Jun Sch
REGENT MEWS
CHURCH ST
COMBES CL
COACH LA
SUDBURY CT
LONDON ST
Hotel
The Folly
Faringdon Hill
Faringdon Inf Sch
Liby
SWAN LA
COLLIER'S LA
GLOUCESTER ST
MARKET PL
CANADA LA
GRAVEL WLK
PULLING CL
MARLBOROUGH ST
PORTWAY
FERNDALE ST
GOODLAKE AVE
LANSDOWN RD
WINDY RIDGE
CROMWELL CL
STANFORD RD
MEADOW BANK
CEDAR RD
STATION RD
HART AVE
UNTONS PL
BENNETT RD
PYE ST
JESPERS HILL
HAMPDEN CL
TUCKERS RD
NURSERY VIEW
THE PINES
CHESTNUT AVE
ASH CL
MAPLE RD
Sch
BROMSGROVE
WESTBROOK
LEES
THE
SOUTHAMPTON ST
FLETCHER CL
BERNERS WAY
PARKERS CL
WESSEX WAY
COXWELL ST
EAGLES
WALNUT CT
WILLES CL
HARDING CL
SPINAGE CL
A420
A417
STANFORD RD
Bowling Green Farm
Kennels
BEECH CL
HAWTHORN RD
B4019
COXWELL GDNS
MARLBOROUGH CL
REGAL WAY
OLD SAWMILLS RD
5 FERNGROVE
6 ST CHRISTOPHER COTTS
7 GREENGATES
8 LIDDIARD'S ROW
CENTURY CL
Jespers Hill
ORCHARD HILL
ELM RD
B4019
Highden Farm
HIGHWORTH RD
COXWELL RD
MARLBOROUGH GDNS
PIONEER RD
VOLUNTEER WAY
RAWDON WAY
PARK RD
WESTLAND RD
MARLBOROUGH PL
CLOCK TOWER CT
FOLLY VIEW CRES
FOLLY VIEW RD
MARINES DR
MEADOW WAY
SAND VIEW
TOWN END RD
TOWER VIEW
BUTTS RD
Oriel Cottages
A417
CATKINS CL
COLESHILL DR
BADBURY CL
EATON CL
LEAMINGTON DR
SN7
CARTER CRES
Faringdon Com Coll
L Ctr
SAND HILL
TOLLINGTON CT
FERNHAM RD
COXWELL HALL MEWS
Coxwell Hall
Works
Steeds Farm
FERNHAM RD
A420
Wickleshamlodge Farm

Faringdon

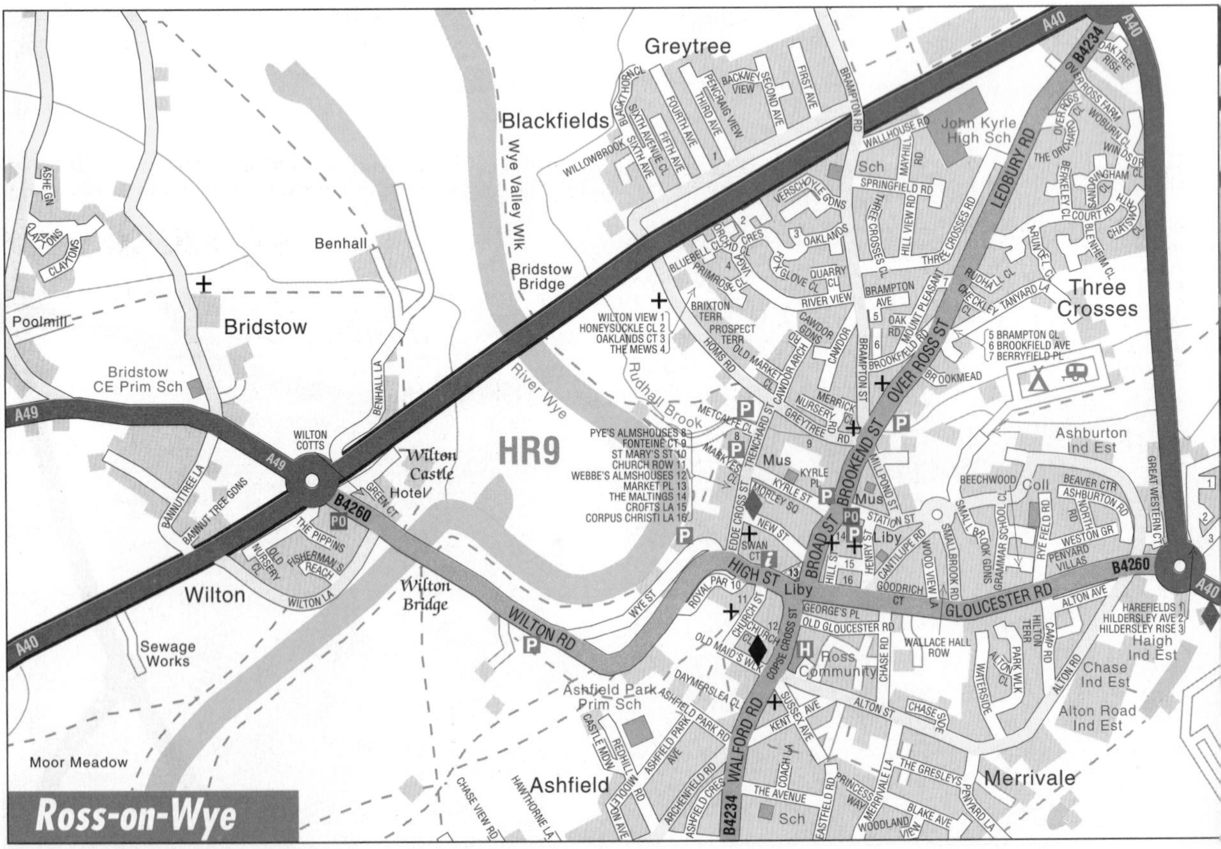

Ross-on-Wye

A40
B4234
OAK TREE RISE
Greytree
BACKNEY VIEW
SECOND AVE
FIRST AVE
BRAMPTON RD
PENCRAIG VIEW
THIRD AVE
FOURTH AVE
FIFTH AVE
SIXTH AVENUE CL
SIXTH AVE
BLACKTHORN CL
Blackfields
WILLOWBROOK
John Kyrle High Sch
WALLHOUSE RD
MAYHILL
Sch
LEDBURY RD
OVER ROSS FARM
WOBURN CL
THE ORCHARD
OVER ROSS
WINDSOR CL
SPRINGFIELD RD
BERKELEY CL
SANDRINGHAM CL
VERSCHOYLE GDNS
Wye Valley Wlk
OAKLANDS
HILL VIEW RD
THREE CROSSES RD
BERKELEY CL
COURT RD
BLENHEIM CL
CHATSWORTH CL
ASHE GN
CLAYTONS
Benhall
ORCHARD CL
QUARRY CL
FOXGLOVE CL
THREE CROSSES CL
MOUNT PLEASANT
RUDHALL CL
MUNTEL CL
Three Crosses
Bridstow Bridge
BLUEBELL CL
PRIMROSE CL
RIVER VIEW
BRAMPTON AVE
CHECKLEY
TANYARD LA
Poolmill
Bridstow
WILTON VIEW 1
HONEYSUCKLE CL 2
OAKLANDS CT 3
THE MEWS 4
BRIXTON TERR
PROSPECT TERR
OLD MARKET
CAWDOR GDNS
CAWDOR
OAK RD
BRAMPTON ST
BROOKFIELD RD
OVER ROSS ST
5 BRAMPTON CL
6 BROOKFIELD AVE
7 BERRYFIELD PL
Bridstow CE Prim Sch
River Wye
HOMS RD
CAWDOR ARCH
BROOKMEAD
BENHALL LA
A49
Rudhall Brook
NURSERY RD
MERRICK RD
METCALFE CL
GREYTREE RD
WILTON COTTS
HR9
PYE'S ALMSHOUSES 8
FONTEINE CT 9
ST MARY'S ST 10
CHURCH ROW 11
WEBBE'S ALMSHOUSES 12
MARKET PL 13
THE MALTINGS 14
CROFTS LA 15
CORPUS CHRISTI LA 16
TRENCHARD ST
Mus
KYRLE PL
BROOKEND ST
MILLPOND ST
Ashburton Ind Est
GREAT WESTERN CT
Wilton Castle
Hotel
GREEN CT
A49
B4260
BANNUTTREE LA
BANNUT TREE GDNS
THE PIPPINS
NURSERY CL
OLD MAYHILL
FISHERMAN'S REACH
MARKET
KYRLE ST
MORLEY SQ
EDDE CROSS ST
NEW ST
BROAD ST
STATION ST
Mus
Liby
BEECHWOOD
Coll
SMALLBROOK GDNS
SMALLBROOK RD
GRAMMAR SCH CL
RYE FIELD RD
BEAVER CTR
ASHBURTON RD
NORTH RD
WESTON GR
PENYARD VILLAS
CANTILUPE RD
WOOD VIEW LA
HENRY ST
HILL ST
SWAN CT
HIGH ST
Liby
GOODRICH CT
GLOUCESTER RD
B4260
A40
Wilton
WILTON LA
Wilton Bridge
WYE ST
ROYAL PAR
CHURCH ST
GEORGE'S PL
OLD GLOUCESTER RD
ALTON AVE
HAREFIELDS 1
HILDERSLEY AVE 2
HILDERSLEY RISE 3
Haigh Ind Est
HILTON TERR
CAMP RD
A40
Sewage Works
WILTON RD
OLD MAID'S WLK
CHURCH CL
COPSE CROSS ST
Ross Community
CHASE RD
WALLACE HALL ROW
WATERSIDE
ALTON CL
PARK WLK
ALTON RD
Chase Ind Est
Ashfield Park Prim Sch
DAYMERSLEA CL
ASHFIELD PARK RD
SUSSEX AVE
ALTON ST
CHASE SIDE
Alton Road Ind Est
KENT AVE
ASHFIELD PARK AVE
REDHILL RD
CASTLE MDW
WALFORD RD
COACH LA
THE GRESLEYS
Merrivale
Moor Meadow
CHASE VIEW RD
HAWTHORNE LA
Ashfield
MIDDLEFIELD
ARCHENFIELD RD
ASHFIELD CRES
THE AVENUE
EASTFIELD RD
PRINCESS WAY
MERRIVALE LA
BLAKE AVE
PENYARD LA
WOODLAND VIEW
B4234
Sch

Ross-on-Wye

Index

Church Rd **6** Beckenham BR2..........**53** C6

Place name
May be abbreviated on the map

Location number
Present when a number indicates the place's position in a crowded area of mapping

Locality, town or village
Shown when more than one place has the same name

Postcode district
District for the indexed place

Page and grid square
Page number and grid reference for the standard mapping

Public and commercial buildings are highlighted in magenta **Places of interest** are highlighted in blue with a star★

Abbreviations used in the index

Acad	**Academy**	Comm	**Common**	Gd	**Ground**	L	**Leisure**	Prom	**Prom**
App	**Approach**	Cott	**Cottage**	Gdn	**Garden**	La	**Lane**	Rd	**Road**
Arc	**Arcade**	Cres	**Crescent**	Gn	**Green**	Liby	**Library**	Recn	**Recreation**
Ave	**Avenue**	Cswy	**Causeway**	Gr	**Grove**	Mdw	**Meadow**	Ret	**Retail**
Bglw	**Bungalow**	Ct	**Court**	H	**Hall**	Meml	**Memorial**	Sh	**Shopping**
Bldg	**Building**	Ctr	**Centre**	Ho	**House**	Mkt	**Market**	Sq	**Square**
Bsns, Bus	**Business**	Ctry	**Country**	Hospl	**Hospital**	Mus	**Museum**	St	**Street**
Bvd	**Boulevard**	Cty	**County**	HQ	**Headquarters**	Orch	**Orchard**	Sta	**Station**
Cath	**Cathedral**	Dr	**Drive**	Hts	**Heights**	Pal	**Palace**	Terr	**Terrace**
Cir	**Circus**	Dro	**Drove**	Ind	**Industrial**	Par	**Parade**	TH	**Town Hall**
Cl	**Close**	Ed	**Education**	Inst	**Institute**	Pas	**Passage**	Univ	**University**
Cnr	**Corner**	Emb	**Embankment**	Int	**International**	Pk	**Park**	Wk, Wlk	**Walk**
Coll	**College**	Est	**Estate**	Intc	**Interchange**	Pl	**Place**	Wr	**Water**
Com	**Community**	Ex	**Exhibition**	Junc	**Junction**	Prec	**Precinct**	Yd	**Yard**

Index of localities, towns and villages

A

Abbots Leigh 7 A8
Ablington 159 F3
Acton Turville 35 F6
Adlestrop 177 E5
Alderton 183 E4
Aldsworth 160 E5
Almondsbury 40 B5
Alveston 51 B4
Amberley 91 C7
Ampney Crucis 151 B5
Andoversford 166 C6
Apperley 173 C7
Arlingham 157 B5
Ashchurch 182 C4
Ashleworth 172 C4
Ashton Keynes 142 F5
Ashton under Hill 183 D8
Aston Magna 186 F6
Aust 49 A6
Avening 140 A8
Avonmouth 26 D2
Awre 157 B3
Aylburton 147 E4

B

Badminton 46 F2
Bagendon 158 C1
Bamfurlong 128 F8
Barnsley 151 C8
Barton End 83 B8
Barton-on-the-Heath 187 F3
Bath 6 F1
Beachley 61 C3
Beckford 183 B6
Berkeley 85 F3
Berkeley Heath 86 B3
Berry Hill 155 A7
Bevington 76 F6
Bibury 160 B1
Birdwood 165 F5
Bishop's Cleeve 137 E3
Bisley 105 B1
Bitton 5 E8
Blakeney 156 E2
Bledington 177 E1
Blockley 186 C6
Boughspring 73 C7
Bourton-on-the-Hill 186 D3
Bourton-on-the-Water 169 A7
Bream 147 D8
Bredon 182 C8
Brentry 28 B2
Bretforton 188 A6
Brierley 163 F2
Brimpsfield 114 C6
Brimscombe 99 E2
Bristol 8 E7
Bristol 195 B3
Broad Blunsdon 144 D1
Broadway 185 C8
Broadwell 177 A6
Brockworth 120 F6
Bromberrow Heath 179 B3
Brookthorpe 110 F5
Burton 36 B3
Bushley 181 D5
Bussage 148 B6

C

Cam 87 F4
Cambridge 95 F4
Castle Eaton 144 E6
Chalford 148 D5
Charfield 67 B4
Charlton Abbots 174 A3
Charlton Kings 131 C6
Chastleton 177 E8
Chedworth 159 A6
Chedworth Laines 158 F6
Cheltenham 133 C4
Cheltenham 193 C1
Chelworth 141 E5
Chepstow 60 D6
Chipping Campden 189 A2
Chipping Sodbury 44 D1
Churcham 124 D2
Churchdown 128 D6
Cinderford 164 C1
Cinderford 191 E4
Cirencester 150 C4
Cirencester 190 F3
Clapton-on-the-Hill 168 F4
Clearwell 155 A2
Cleeve Hill 138 E2
Clifford's Mesne 170 E1
Coaley 88 E8
Coalpit Heath 31 D6
Coates 149 F4
Codrington 33 C2
Cold Ashton 13 F6
Cold Aston 168 B6
Coleford 155 B5
Colerne 15 F6
Colesbourne 158 A8
Coln Rogers 159 D4
Coln St Aldwyns 152 D8
Compton Abdale 167 B3
Condicote 176 A7
Cranham 112 F6
Cricklade 143 E5
Cromhall 66 A1
Crudwell 141 C3
Culkerton 141 A7

D

Daglingworth 150 A8
Didbrook 184 D2
Didmarton 57 C4
Doughton 140 A2
Down Ampney 143 F8
Down Hatherley 173 C1
Doynton 23 A1
Draycott (nr Dursley) 87 F8
Draycott (nr Moreton-in-Marsh) 186 E6
Drybrook 164 B4
Dumbleton 183 F7
Dundry 1 D2
Duntisbourne Abbots 107 C4
Dursley 88 B2
Dymock 178 D2
Dyrham 23 D4

E

Eastcombe 148 C7
Easter Compton 39 A2
Eastington 96 F8
Eastleach Turville 153 C8
Eastnor 179 B8
Easton-in-Gordano 16 A4
Ebrington 189 E3
Edge 103 B8
Edge End 155 C8
Edgeworth 106 D1
Elberton 50 A6
Elkstone 115 B5
Ellwood 155 C2
Elton 165 B1
Emersons Green 21 C6
English Bicknor 163 B2
Evenlode 177 C8
Ewen 142 B8

F

Fairford 152 E3
Falfield 65 E7
Forthampton 181 B3
Foss Cross 159 B4
Four Oaks 170 D7
Frampton Cotterell 31 B7
Frampton Mansell 148 F5
Frampton on Severn 100 A5
Fretherne 157 E4
Frocester 97 B3

G

Gloucester 126 D2
Gloucester 196 A4
Goodrich 163 A5
Gorsley 170 C4
Gotherington 138 B8
Great Rissington 169 C4
Great Wolford 187 F5
Greet 184 A1
Gretton 183 E1
Guiting Power 175 B3

H

Hallen 27 C5
Halmore 94 B2
Hambrook 30 C2
Hampnett 167 F2
Hankerton 141 D1
Hannington 145 A4
Hardwicke 109 E6
Haresfield 110 B1
Harnhill 151 C3
Harrow Hill 164 C3
Hartpury 172 B3
Hawkesbury Upton 56 A3
Hawling 174 E2
Henbury 27 E2
Henfield 31 D3
Hewelsfield 146 F5
Highleadon 171 F2
Highnam 125 C4
Highworth 145 D4
Hillesley 55 E8
Hinton 23 C6
Honeybourne 188 C6
Horsley 90 F1
Horton 45 B6
Hucclecote 120 B7
Huntley 165 D6

I

Ilmington 189 F6
Innsworth 127 D7
Iron Acton 42 D3

J

Joy's Green 163 D3

K

Kelston 6 C3
Kemble 141 F8
Kemerton 182 E8
Kempsford 144 F8
Keynsham 4 E3
Kilcot 170 D4
King's Stanley 98 A4
Kingham 177 F2
Kingscote 82 B5
Kingswood (nr Bristol) ..10 E8
Kingswood (nr Wooton-under-Edge) 67 E4
Kinsham 182 D6
Knightsbridge 173 F5

L

Latton 143 E6
Lea 164 C8
Lechlade on Thames ...153 D3
Ledbury 178 D8
Leigh 143 B3
Leigh Woods 7 D6
Leighterton 70 D3
Leonard Stanley 97 E4
Little Barrington 161 D7
Little Compton 187 F1
Little Rissington 169 C6
Little Witcombe 121 B4
Littledean 156 E8
Littleton-upon-Severn ..49 E8
Llandogo 146 A7
Llangarron 162 B8
Llangrove 162 C6
Logney 108 C6
Long Ashton 7 A1
Longborough 176 E8
Longdon 180 F7
Longford 126 F6
Longhope 164 F5
Longlevens 127 D4
Lowbands 179 F2
Lower Apperley 173 C6
Lower Hamswell 13 C3
Lower Lydbrook 163 C3
Lower Oddington 177 D4
Lower Redbrook 154 D4
Lower Slaughter 176 C1
Lower Swell 176 D4
Luckington 47 F4
Lydney 92 C3

M

Maiden Head 1 F1
Maisemore 126 A7
Marshfield 14 F8
Marston Meysey 144 C8
Meysey Hampton 152 A2
Mickleton 189 B6
Mile End 155 C6
Milkwall 155 A4
Minchinhampton 148 A3
Minety 142 D1
Minsterworth 116 F7
Miserden 106 B7
Mitcheldean 164 D5
Monmouth 154 B8
Moreton Valence 101 A8
Moreton-in-Marsh 187 A3
Much Marcle 178 A3

N

Nailsworth 91 C3
Naunton 175 D2
Netherend 147 C3
Newent 171 A4
Newland 154 E4
Newnham 157 A6
Newport 78 B8
North Cerney 158 D2
North Nibley 79 D4
Northleach 168 A1
Northway 182 C5
Northwood Green 165 C3
Norton 173 B3
Notgrove 167 F7
Nympsfield 89 F5

O

Oaksey 141 F4
Oldbury-on-Severn 63 C6
Oldcroft 156 B1
Olveston 50 B3
Overbury 182 F8

P

Painswick 103 E8
Parkend 155 E3
Paxford 186 E8
Penallt 154 B5
Pendock 180 A3
Pill 16 C4
Pillowell 155 F1
Pilning 38 D7
Pitchcombe 103 B5
Pitt Court 79 F5
Pontshill 164 B8
Poole Keynes 142 A6
Poolhill 171 B8
Popes Hill 164 F1
Poulton 151 F4
Prestbury 134 C5
Pucklechurch 22 B5

Q

Quedgeley 117 E1
Quenington 152 C7

R

Randwick 102 D2
Rangeworthy 52 F1
Redmarley D'Abitot 179 D2
Rendcomb 158 D4
Ripple 181 D8
Rockhampton 64 E7
Rodmarton 149 B1
Ruardean 163 F4
Ruardean Hill 164 A4
Ruardean Woodside ...163 F3
Rudford 124 F8
Ruspidge 156 C7
Ruspidge 191 D1

S

St Arvans 72 B6
St Briavels 146 F7
Saltford 5 D2
Sandhurst 172 E2
Sapperton 149 C6
Saul 157 F3
Sedbury 61 B8
Selsley 98 E4
Sevenhampton 166 E8
Severn Beach 38 B6
Sharpness 93 B2
Sheepscombe 112 F1
Sherborne 169 A1
Sherston 58 C1
Shipton 166 F5
Shipton Moyne 59 E8
Shirehampton 16 E7
Shurdington 129 E1
Siddington 150 E2
Slimbridge 95 D4
Sling 155 A3
Snowshill 185 B4
Somerford Keynes 142 D6
Sopworth 57 D1
South Cerney 143 A7
Southam 134 C8
Southrop 153 D6
Stanton 184 F5
Stanton Fitzwarren 145 A1
Staunton (nr Gloucester) 172 A8
Staunton (nr Monmouth) 154 E7
Staverton 173 F2
Stinchcombe 87 C2
Stoke Orchard 136 D5
Stone 77 E3
Stonehouse 97 E7
Stow-on-the-Wold 176 E4
Strand 157 C8
Stroat 74 A8
Stroud 99 B8
Sunhill 152 A5
Swindon 133 A7
Symonds Yat 162 E3

T

Tadwick 13 E1
Tarlton 149 C2
Taynton 165 E8
Teddington 183 A4
Temple Guiting 175 B7
Tetbury 140 C4
Tewkesbury 181 E3
Tewkesbury 192 E3
The Leigh 173 C5
The North 154 A1
Thornbury 64 D2
Thrupp 99 E4
Tibberton 124 C8
Tidenham 73 D4
Tidenham Chase 146 E1
Tintern Parva 146 C3
Tirley 172 F7
Tockington 50 C1
Toddington 184 B3
Todenham 187 E6
Tormarton 34 E2
Tortworth 66 C7
Tredington 136 A7
Turkdean 167 F4
Tutshill 73 A2
Twyning 181 F7
Tytherington 52 C5

U

Uckinghall 181 C8
Uckington 132 D6
Uley 89 B1
Upleadon 171 D5
Upper Framilode 108 A1
Upper Inglesham 145 D7
Upper Lydbrook 163 D2
Upper Minety 142 C2
Upper Oddington 177 C4
Upper Redbrook 154 C5
Upper Rissington 169 E6
Upper Soudley 156 D5
Upper Strensham 180 F10
Upton Cheyney 6 B8
Upton St Leonards 119 F2

V

Viney Hill 156 C1

W

Walford 163 B7
West Kington 25 F7
Westbury-on-Severn ..165 D1
Westerleigh 32 B4
Westmancote 182 D8
Weston-sub-Edge 188 D3
Westwell 161 F4
Whaddon 110 F8
Whitchurch (nr Monmouth) 162 D4
Whitchurch (nr Bristol) ..3 A4
Whitecroft 155 F1
Whiteshill 103 A3
Whitminster 100 E5
Wick 12 D6
Wickwar 54 B5
Willersey 188 B2
Winchcombe 174 B7
Windrush 161 B8
Winson 159 D3
Winstone 107 A8
Winterbourne 30 F6
Withington 166 F2
Woodchester 98 F2
Woodcroft 73 B4
Woodford 78 A4
Woodmancote (nr Cheltenham) 138 D4
Woodmancote (nr Cirencester) 158 B3
Woolaston 147 B2
Wooton-under-Edge 68 B6
Wyck Rissington 169 C8

Y

Yate 43 C1
Yorkley 156 A1

1

1st Ave GL56 .... 187 B4

2

2nd Ave GL56 .... 187 B4

3

3rd Ave GL56 .... 187 B3

5

5th Ave GL56 .... 187 C4

6

6th Ave GL56 .... 187 B4

7

7th Ave GL56 .... 187 B3

8

8th Ave GL56 .... 187 B3

1

125 Bsns Pk GL2 ...... 126 C1

A

A P Ellis Rd GL54 ...... 169 D6
Aaron Rd GL7 .... 150 F2
Abbenesse GL6 .... 148 C6
Abbey Cl BS31 .... 4 F6
Abbey Ct Bristol BS4 ...... 9 F5
Tewkesbury GL20 .... 192 B3
20 Winchcombe GL54 .... 174 A7
Abbey Ho
Cirencester GL7 .... 190 C5
5 Yate BS37 .... 32 D7
Abbey La BS35 .... 51 D6
Abbey Mdw GL20 ...... 192 D1
Abbey Mews GL12 .... 67 F4
Abbey Pk BS31 .... 4 F6
Abbey Prec GL20 ...... 192 B3
Abbey Rd Bristol BS9 ..... 17 F7
Gloucester GL2 .... 118 C8
Abbey Sch The GL20 ... 192 C4
Abbey St Cinderford GL14 191 D4
Kingswood GL12 .... 67 F5
Abbey Terr
Tewkesbury GL20 .... 192 B3
23 Winchcombe GL54 .... 174 A7
Abbey View 15 GL54 .... 174 A7
Abbey Way GL7 .... 190 C6
Abbeydale BS36 .... 30 E6
Abbeydale Ct GL4 ...... 119 E4
Abbeyfield Ho 6 GL54 .. 176 F4
Abbeyholme GL50 ..... 193 A3
Abbeymead Ave GL4 ... 119 E6
Abbeymead Cty Prim Sch
GL4 .... 119 F5
Abbeywood Dr BS9 ..... 17 C5
Abbeywood Pk BS34 .... 29 C2
Abbot's Rd GL20 .... 192 C2
Abbots Ave BS15 .... 10 C4
Abbots Cl Bristol BS14 ..... 3 A3
Cheltenham GL51 .... 130 B5
Abbots Court Dr GL20 .. 181 F7
Abbots Leigh Rd BS8 ..... 7 C7
Abbots Leys Rd GL54 ... 139 F5
Abbots Mews GL52 ..... 137 E2
Abbots Rd Bristol BS15 ... 10 C2
Cinderford GL14 .... 191 E3
Cirencester GL7 .... 190 E4
Gloucester GL4 .... 119 E6
Abbots View GL14 ..... 191 D1
Abbots Way Bristol BS9 ... 18 E6
Stonehouse GL10 .... 97 E6
Abbots Wlk GL7 .... 153 E2
Abbotsford Rd BS6 ...... 18 B1
Abbotswood Bristol BS15 . 10 D7
Yate BS37 .... 32 D7
Abbotswood Cl GL4 .... 118 D3
Abbotswood Inf Sch
BS37 .... 32 D6
Abbotswood Jun Sch
BS37 .... 32 D6
Abbotswood Rd GL3 ... 120 F4
Abbott Rd BS35 .... 38 A5
Abbotts Way GL7 ...... 141 F8
Aberdeen Rd BS6 ..... 194 B4
Abingdon Court La SN6 143 F4
Abingdon Rd BS16 ...... 20 A3
Ableton La BS35 .... 38 A5
Ableton Wlk BS9 .... 17 C5
Abnash GL6 .... 148 C6
Abon Ho BS9 .... 17 C4
Abraham Cl BS5 .... 9 B8
Abraham Fry Ho BS15 ... 10 E7
Abson Rd BS16 .... 22 D3
Acacia Ave BS16 .... 20 D4
Acacia Cl 10 Bream GL15 147 D8
Bristol BS16 .... 20 D3
Newnham GL14 .... 157 A7
Acacia Cl *continued*
Prestbury GL52 .... 134 A5
Acacia Ct
Cheltenham GL51 ...... 132 C2
Keynsham BS31 .... 4 C4
Acacia Dr GL11 .... 88 A3
Acacia Mews 4 BS16 ... 20 D4
Acacia Pk GL52 .... 137 D4
Acacia Rd BS16 .... 20 D4
Acer Gr GL2 .... 117 E2
Acid Rd BS11 .... 26 C4
Acomb Cres GL52 ...... 131 B6
Acorn Gr BS13 .... 1 E6
Acraman's Rd 7 BS3 ..... 8 C4
Acre Pl GL6 .... 102 E1
Acre St GL5 .... 99 C7
Acresbush Cl BS13 .... 2 A5
Acton Rd BS16 .... 20 A3
Adams Ct 5 BS8 .... 7 F6
Adams Hay 6 BS4 .... 9 D1
Adams Way 7 GL16 .... 155 A7
Adderly Gate BS16 ...... 21 B7
Addis Rd GL51 .... 133 B3
Addiscombe Rd BS14 ..... 3 B5
Addison Rd BS3 .... 8 E3
Addymore GL11 .... 87 F5
Adelaide Gdns GL10 ... 101 F1
Adelaide Pl
Bristol, Fishponds BS16 .... 19 F4
12 Bristol, Upper Easton BS5 9 B8
Adelaide St GL1 .... 119 A7
Adelaide Terr 1 BS16 ... 20 A4
Adey's La GL12 .... 68 B8
Admington La CV36 .... 189 D7
Admington Lane Units
CV36 .... 189 E7
Admiral Cl GL51 .... 132 D2
Admirals Cl 6 GL15 ... 155 D1
Adryen Ct 6 BS5 .... 9 C7
Aesops Orch GL52 ..... 138 C3
Agate St BS3 .... 8 B3
Aggs Hill GL54 .... 134 D1
Aggs La GL52 .... 138 A8
Aiken St BS5 .... 9 B6
Aintree Dr BS16 .... 30 F1
Air Balloon Ct 1 BS5 ... 10 A7
Air Balloon Hill Jun & Inf
Schs BS5 .... 10 A7
Air Balloon Rd BS5 ..... 10 A7
Airport Rd BS14 .... 3 A8
Airthrie Sch GL50 ...... 133 B1
Aisne Rd GL15 .... 156 B1
Akeman Rd GL7 .... 190 E4
Akeman Way BS11 ...... 16 C8
Akermans Orch GL18 ... 170 F4
Akers Ct SN26 .... 144 E1
Alanscourt BS30 .... 11 B5
Alard Rd BS4 .... 2 F7
Alaska Ave GL7 .... 152 E1
Albany GL10 .... 101 E1
Albany Gate BS34 ...... 29 E5
Albany Ho 7 GL50 ..... 130 B8
Albany Mews GL50 .... 193 A2
Albany Rd Bristol BS6 .... 18 F1
Cheltenham GL50 ...... 130 B7
Albany St Bristol BS15 ... 10 C8
Gloucester GL1 .... 118 F7
Albany Way BS30 .... 11 C5
Albemarle Gate GL50 .. 133 E4
Albemarle Rd GL3 ..... 128 D5
Albermarle Row 9 BS8 ... 7 F6
Albert Cres BS2 .... 9 B5
Albert Ct GL52 .... 133 F3
Albert Dr GL52 .... 133 F4
Albert Gr BS5 .... 9 F8
Albert Par BS5 .... 9 D8
Albert Park Pl BS6 ..... 18 F1
Albert Pk BS6 .... 18 F1
Albert Pl
1 Bristol, Bedminster BS3 .. 8 C3
Bristol, Eastfield BS9 ..... 18 A7
Cheltenham GL52 ...... 193 C4
Albert Rd Brimscombe GL5 99 F1
Bristol, Hanham BS15 .... 10 D5
Bristol, St Philip's Marsh
BS2 .... 9 A4
Bristol, Staple Hill BS16 ... 20 E4
Cheltenham GL52 ...... 133 F3
Cinderford GL14 .... 191 C3
Coleford GL16 .... 155 A5
Keynsham BS31 .... 4 E5
Ledbury HR8 .... 178 E8
Severn Beach BS35 ..... 38 A6
Albert St Bristol BS5 ...... 9 C8
Cheltenham GL50 ...... 133 D3
Gloucester GL1 .... 196 C2
Lydney GL15 .... 92 B3
Albert Terr BS16 .... 19 F4
Alberton Rd BS16 .... 19 F6
Albion Cl BS16 .... 20 F5
Albion Pl 16 Bristol BS2 . 195 C3
Cheltenham GL52 ...... 193 C4
Albion Rd Bristol BS5 .... 19 B1
Cinderford GL14 .... 191 D6
Albion St 6 Bristol BS5 ... 9 C8
Cheltenham GL52 ...... 193 C3
Cirencester GL7 .... 190 B7
Gloucester GL1 .... 196 A2
Albion Terr Bristol BS34 .. 40 B1
Stonehouse GL10 .... 97 E6
Albion Wlk GL50 ...... 193 C4
Albright La HR8 .... 179 D4
Alcotts Gn GL2 .... 172 F2
Alcove Rd BS16 .... 19 F3
Alder Cl GL2 .... 127 C4
Alder Ct GL51 .... 132 C2
Alder Dr BS5 .... 19 E1
Alder Way 7 GL6 ...... 148 C6
Aldercombe Rd BS9 ..... 17 C8
Alderdale GL15 .... 92 B4
Alderdown Cl BS11 ...... 17 A8
Aldergate St GL10 .... 97 F7
Aldergate Terr 6 GL10 ... 97 F7
Alderley Rd GL12 .... 68 D1
Alderman Knight Sch
GL20 .... 182 B4
Aldermoor Way BS30 .... 10 E4
Aldernay Ave BS4 .... 9 F4
Alderney Flats 1 GL2 .. 127 B2
Alders Gn GL2 .... 127 B5
Alders The Bristol BS16 ... 30 B1
Cheltenham GL53 ...... 130 B4
Aldershaw Cl GL51 .... 129 D6
Alderton Cl GL4 .... 119 E4
Alderton Rd Bristol BS7 ... 18 E8
Burton SN14 .... 36 D6
Cheltenham GL51 ...... 129 E8
Aldridge Cl GL50 ...... 133 C3
Aldsworth Cl GL7 ..... 152 F4
Aldsworth Road Est
GL7 .... 160 B2
Aldwick Ave BS13 .... 2 C3
Aldworth Ho BS2 ...... 195 C4
Alexander Dr GL7 ..... 190 C2
Alexander Gdns 10 GL8 . 140 B4
Alexander Hosea Prim Sch
The GL12 .... 54 B5
Alexandra Cl BS16 ...... 20 D4
Alexandra Gdns BS16 ... 20 D4
Alexandra Park Ctr BS16 . 19 F4
Alexandra Pk
Bristol, Cotham BS6 ...... 18 C2
Bristol, Ridgeway BS16 .... 19 F4
Alexandra Pl BS16 ...... 20 D4
Alexandra Rd Bristol BS8 194 B4
Bristol, Hanham BS15 .... 10 D5
Bristol, Highridge BS13 .... 1 F7
Bristol,Eastfield BS10 ..... 18 C8
Chepstow NP16 .... 60 F6
Coalpit Heath BS36 ...... 31 D7
Gloucester GL1 .... 127 A3
Alexandra St GL50 .... 130 B7
Alexandra Way
Northway GL20 .... 182 B4
Thornbury BS35 .... 64 B3
Alexandria Wlk GL52 .. 134 B2
Alford Rd BS4 .... 9 C2
Alfred Hill BS2 .... 195 A4
Alfred Lovell Gdns 7
BS30 .... 11 A4
Alfred Par BS2 .... 195 A4
Alfred Pl BS2 .... 194 C4
Alfred Rd
Bristol, Bedminster BS3 .... 8 D3
Bristol, Westbury Park BS6 . 18 A4
Alfred St
Bristol, Moorfields BS5 ..... 9 D8
Bristol, Newton BS2 .... 9 A6
Gloucester GL1 .... 119 A8
Algars Dr BS37 .... 42 E3
Algiers St BS3 .... 8 D3
Alice Cres NP16 .... 61 A4
Alington Ct 5 GL1 ..... 127 A1
Alkerton Rd GL10 .... 96 F7
Alkerton Terr GL10 ..... 96 F7
All Alone GL54 .... 168 A1
All Hallows Ct 11 BS5 .... 9 B8
All Hallows Rd BS5 .... 9 B8
All Saint's Ct 18 GL52 .. 133 F2
All Saints Rd
Blakeney GL15 .... 156 E2
Stroud GL5 .... 99 D8
All Saints' La BS1 ..... 195 A2
All Saints' Rd Bristol BS8 194 A4
Cheltenham GL52 ...... 133 F2
Gloucester GL1 .... 196 C1
All Saints' St BS1 ..... 195 A3
All Saints' Terr GL52 .. 133 F1
All Saints' Villas Rd
GL52 .... 133 F2
Allanmead Rd BS14 ...... 3 B8
Allaston Rd GL15 .... 92 B6
Allen Dr GL5 .... 99 A8
Allen's Almhouses The 12
GL54 .... 168 A1
Allendale Cl GL2 ...... 127 C4
Allenfield Rd GL53 .... 130 C5
Allengrove La SN14 ..... 47 C3
Allerton Cres BS14 ...... 3 B4
Allerton Gdns BS14 ...... 3 B5
Allerton Rd BS14 .... 3 B4
Allfoxton Rd BS7 .... 19 A3
Allington Dr BS30 ...... 10 F4
Allington Rd BS3 ...... 194 C1
Allison Ave BS4 .... 9 E4
Allison Rd BS4 .... 9 E3
Allotment La GL7 ..... 151 C5
Allsopp Cl GL14 ...... 156 F6
Alma Cl Bristol BS15 ..... 10 E8
Cheltenham GL51 ...... 129 F7
Alma Ct BS8 .... 18 B1
Alma Dr NP16 .... 61 A4
Alma Pl GL1 .... 118 D7
Alma Rd
Bristol, Clifton BS8 ..... 194 B4
Bristol, Kingswood BS15 ... 20 E1
Cheltenham GL51 ...... 129 F7
Alma Road Ave BS8 .... 194 B4
Alma St BS8 .... 18 B1
Alma Terr
Gloucester GL1 .... 118 D7
Stroud GL5 .... 98 F8
Alma Vale Rd BS8 ..... 194 A4
Almeda Rd BS5 .... 10 A6
Almhouses GL7 .... 190 C4
Almond Cl GL4 .... 119 D3
Almond Ct GL51 .... 132 C2
Almond Way BS16 .... 20 F5
Almond Wlk GL15 .... 92 B4
Almondsbury Bsns Ctr
BS32 .... 40 D3
Almondsbury CE Prim Sch
BS32 .... 40 A4
Almondsbury Intc BS32 .. 40 D4
Almondsbury Rdbt BS32 . 40 B3
Almorah Rd BS3 .... 8 E3
Almshouses
5 Bristol BS1 .... 195 A2
Chipping Campden GL55 .. 189 A2
Marshfield SN14 .... 14 E8
Wooton-u-E GL12 .... 68 B7
Almshouses Rd GL16 .. 154 E4
Alney Terr GL1 .... 126 C3
Alpha Cl GL20 .... 182 B4
Alpha Ctr The BS37 ..... 43 C3
Alpha Rd Bristol BS3 ..... 8 D4
Chepstow NP16 .... 60 F6
Alpine Cl GL4 .... 119 B6
Alpine Rd BS5 .... 19 C1
Alsop Rd 4 BS15 .... 20 D1
Alstone Ave GL51 ..... 133 B2
Alstone Croft GL51 .... 133 B2
Alstone Ct 1 GL51 .... 133 B2
Alstone La GL51 ...... 133 A2
Alstone Lane Trad Est
GL51 .... 133 A1
Althorp Cl GL4 .... 118 B2
Alton Rd BS7 .... 18 F5
Altringham Rd 8 BS5 .... 9 D8
Alverstoke BS14 .... 2 F7
Alverton Dr GL52 ..... 137 E2
Alveston Grange GL55 . 189 A6
Alveston Hill BS35 ...... 51 A6
Alveston Rd BS32 .... 50 D3
Alveston Wlk BS9 .... 17 B7
Alvin St GL1 .... 196 C3
Alwins Ct 2 BS30 .... 10 F4
Amaranth Way 7 GL51 . 129 F5
Amberley CE Sch GL5 ... 91 C7
Amberley Cl Bristol BS16 . 20 D7
Keynsham BS31 .... 4 E4
Amberley Ct 10 GL51 ... 132 E2
Amberley House Sch
BS8 .... 18 A1
Amberley Rd
Bristol, Kingswood BS16 ... 20 D7
Bristol, Patchway BS34 .... 29 B8
9 Cheltenham GL51 .... 132 E2
Gloucester GL4 .... 119 B5
Amberley Ridge Specl Sch
GL5 .... 99 C1
Amberley Way GL12 ..... 54 B4
Amble Cl BS15 .... 10 F7
Ambleside Ave BS10 ..... 28 B2
Ambra Ct BS8 .... 194 A2
Ambra Terr BS8 .... 194 A2
Ambra Vale BS8 ...... 194 A2
Ambra Vale E BS8 ..... 194 A2
Ambra Vale S BS8 ..... 194 A2
Ambra Vale W BS8 .... 194 A2
Ambrose La 1 GL16 ... 155 B5
Ambrose Pl GL50 ..... 193 B4
Ambrose Rd BS8 ...... 194 A2
Ambrose St GL50 ..... 193 B4
Amercombe Wlk BS14 .... 3 D7
America Gdns GL18 ... 171 A4
Amos Cl GL50 .... 193 A4
Ampney Crucis CE Prim Sch
GL7 .... 151 C5
Ampney La GL14 ...... 165 D3
Ampney Mill Cotts GL7 . 151 C4
Anbrook Cres GL4 ..... 119 E7
Anchor Cl BS5 .... 9 F6
Anchor Rd
Bristol, Canon's Marsh
BS1 .... 194 C2
Bristol, Kingswood BS15 ... 21 A2
Anchor Way BS20 .... 16 D4
Anchorage The
Gloucester GL2 .... 118 B6
Lower Lydbrook GL17 .... 163 C3
Ancient Rd GL16 ...... 162 F1
Andereach Cl BS14 ...... 3 B8
Anderson Cl GL52 .... 138 B3
Anderson Dr 3 GL10 .... 97 F7
Andorra Way GL3 ..... 128 B6
Andover Ct GL50 ..... 193 A1
Andover Rd Bristol BS4 ... 8 F2
Cheltenham GL50 ...... 193 A1
Andover St GL50 ..... 193 A1
Andover Terr GL50 .... 193 A2
Andover Wlk GL50 .... 193 A1
Andoversford Link
GL54 .... 166 D6
Andoversford Prim Sch
GL54 .... 166 D6
Andrew Millman Ct BS37 43 F1
Andrew's Cl GL4 ..... 110 F5
Andrew's Cnr GL15 .... 146 E7
Andruss Dr BS41 .... 1 D2
Angel Field GL16 ..... 155 A5
Angelica Way GL4 ..... 119 F5
Angels Gd BS4 .... 9 F6
Angers Rd BS4 .... 9 A3
Anglesea Pl 15 BS8 ..... 18 A2
Anlaby Ct GL52 .... 133 E3
Ann Cam CE Prim Sch
GL18 .... 178 D2
Ann Edwards Prim Sch
GL7 .... 142 F7
Ann Goodrich Cl GL52 . 134 C4
Ann Wicks Rd GL2 .... 100 A5
Anne Hathaway Dr GL3 . 128 E5
Anns Wlk GL17 .... 164 D4
Ansdell Dr GL3 .... 120 E6
Ansell Cl GL51 .... 129 F6
Anson Bsns Pk GL51 ... 173 E1
Anson Cl BS31 .... 5 D2
Anstey St BS5 .... 19 B1
Anstey's Rd BS15 .... 10 C5
Ansteys Cl BS15 .... 10 B5
Antelope Paddock 11
GL54 .... 168 A1
Anthea Rd BS5 .... 19 E2
Anthony Cl SN16 .... 58 C1
Anthony Ct GL6 .... 148 C5
Anthony's Cross GL18,
GL19 .... 171 A2
Antona Ct BS11 .... 16 D7
Antona Dr BS11 .... 16 D7
Antrim Rd BS9 .... 18 B6
Anvil St BS2 .... 195 C2
Apex Ct BS32 .... 40 D3
Apperley Cl BS37 .... 32 E8
Apperley Dr GL2 ...... 117 E1
Apperley Pk GL19 ..... 173 C7
Apple Cl GL52 .... 134 A5
Apple Orch GL52 ...... 134 A5
Apple Orch The GL20 .. 182 C5
Apple Orchard Cl GL54 . 183 E1
Apple Tree Cl
4 Churchdown GL3 .... 128 A7
Gloucester GL4 .... 119 E4
Woodmancote GL52 ..... 138 C2
Apple Yd The GL15 .... 156 A2
Appleby Wlk BS4 .... 2 D7
Appledore Cl BS14 .... 3 B8
Applegate BS10 .... 28 B3
Appleridge La GL13 ..... 77 C4
Appleton Ave GL51 .... 129 B6
Appleton Way GL3 .... 120 A6
Applin Gn BS16 .... 21 C6
Apprentice Cl NP16 ..... 61 B4
Approach The GL54 ... 160 E5
April Cl GL11 .... 80 A8
Apseleys Mead BS32 .... 40 C2
Apsley Cl GL7 .... 190 B3
Apsley Rd Bristol BS8 .... 18 A1
Cirencester GL7 .... 190 B2
Apsley St BS5 .... 19 C3
Aragon Ho GL54 ...... 139 F5
Aragon Way GL3 ...... 127 F7
Arbour Cl GL55 ...... 189 A6
Arbutus Dr BS9 .... 17 C8
Arcade The BS1 ...... 195 B3
Archdeacon Ct GL1 ... 196 A3
Archdeacon St GL1 ... 196 A3
Archer Ct BS30 .... 10 F3
Archer Wlk BS14 .... 3 E6
Archers La GL52 ...... 136 D5
Archers The SN6 ..... 145 C3
Archery Rd GL7 ...... 190 E4
Arches The 1 BS5 .... 9 B7
Archfield Ct BS6 .... 18 C1
Archfield Rd BS6 ...... 18 C1
Archibald St GL1 ..... 196 C1
Archway Cl GL14 ..... 156 C5
Archway Gdns GL5 ...... 99 A8
Archway Sch GL5 .... 98 F8
Ardea Cl GL2 .... 117 D1
Arden Cl BS32 .... 29 E6
Arden Ho GL2 .... 118 C4
Arden Rd GL53 .... 130 D5
Ardenton Wlk BS10 ..... 28 A3
Ardern Cl BS9 .... 17 B8
Ardmore BS8 .... 7 D7
Ardmore Cl GL4 ...... 118 E2
Argus Ct BS3 .... 8 C2
Argus Rd BS3 .... 8 C3
Argyle Ave BS5 .... 19 C2
Argyle Dr BS37 .... 43 E4
Argyle Pl BS8 .... 194 A2
Argyle Rd
Bristol, Chester Park BS16 . 20 B2
Bristol, St Pauls BS2 ..... 195 B4
Argyle St
5 Bristol, Eastville BS5 ... 19 C2
6 Bristol, Southville BS3 ... 8 C4
Argyll Pl GL2 .... 127 B2
Argyll Rd
Cheltenham GL53 ...... 130 F8
Gloucester GL2 .... 127 B2
Ariel Lodge Rd GL52 .. 133 F2
Arkells Ct GL12 .... 54 A6
Arkendale Dr GL2 ..... 109 D8
Arkle Cl GL50 .... 133 C5
Arle Ave GL51 .... 133 B2
Arle Cl GL51 .... 133 B2
Arle Cotts GL51 ...... 132 F4
Arle Dr GL51 .... 133 A3
Arle Gdns GL51 ...... 133 A3
Arle Rd GL51 .... 133 A3
Arley Cotts 4 BS6 ...... 18 D1
Arley Hill BS6 .... 18 D1
Arley Pk BS6 .... 18 D1
Arley Terr BS5 .... 19 E1
Arlingham 13 GL51 .... 129 E5
Arlingham Rd GL4 .... 118 D4
Arlingham Way BS34 .... 39 F1
Arlington Cnr GL7 .... 160 A1
Arlington Ct NP16 ...... 61 B8
Arlington Mans BS8 ... 194 B4
Arlington Mill Mus★ GL7 160 A1
Arlington Pike GL7 ... 159 F1
Arlington Rd BS4 .... 9 D5
Arlington Row★ GL7 ... 160 A1
Arlington Terr 3 GL56 . 186 C5
Arlington Villas BS8 .. 194 B3
Armada Cl GL3 .... 127 F7

Armada Ho BS2 195 B4
Armada Pl BS1 195 B4
Armada Rd BS14 3 A6
Armidale Ave 2 BS6 18 E1
Armidale Cotts 3 BS6 18 E1
Armoury Sq BS5 9 A8
Armscroft Cres GL2 127 B2
Armscroft Ct GL2 127 C1
Armscroft Gdns GL2 127 B1
Armscroft Pl GL2 127 B1
Armscroft Rd GL2 127 C1
Armscroft Way GL2 127 B1
Armstrong Cl BS35 51 D7
Armstrong Ct BS37 43 C3
Armstrong Dr BS30 11 B5
Armstrong Way BS37 43 B3
Arnall Dr BS10 27 F1
Arncliffe EPD BS10 18 C8
Arneside Rd BS10 28 C1
Arno's St BS4 9 A3
Arnold Ct BS37 44 B1
Arnold's La GL6 91 B3
Arnolds Field Trad Est GL12 54 A5
Arnolds Way GL7 190 E5
Arnolfini (Arts Ctr) BS1 195 A1
Arran Way SN6 145 C4
Arreton Ave GL4 119 C6
Arrowfield Cl BS14 3 A2
Arrowhead Cl GL4 119 B4
Arrowsmith Dr GL10 101 F1
Arthur Cooper Way GL16 155 A4
Arthur Dye Prim Sch GL51 132 D4
Arthur Skemp Cl BS5 9 B7
Arthur St
7 Bristol, Moorfields BS5 9 C8
Bristol, St Philip's Marsh BS2 9 A5
Gloucester GL1 196 B2
Arthurs Cl BS16 21 C6
Arthurswood Rd BS13 2 A4
Arundel Cl Bristol BS13 2 B5
Gloucester GL4 118 C1
Arundel Ct BS7 18 D3
Arundel Dr GL5 99 B6
Arundel Ho 12 GL51 132 E2
Arundel Rd Bristol BS7 18 D3
Tewkesbury GL20 192 E6
Arundel Wlk BS31 4 D5
Arundell Mill La GL5 99 D6
Ascot Cl BS16 30 F1
Ascot Ct GL1 119 A8
Ascot Rd BS10 28 E2
Ash Cl
Bristol, Hillfields BS16 20 C3
Bristol, Little Stoke BS34 29 D7
Charlton Kings GL53 131 C4
Chepstow NP16 60 E5
Dursley GL11 88 A4
Lydney GL15 92 B4
Yate BS37 43 D3
Ash Ct BS14 3 A6
Ash Dene Rd GL17 163 E3
Ash Gr Bristol BS16 20 D3
Mitcheldean GL17 164 D6
Upton St Leonards GL4 119 E3
Ash Grove Pl GL15 156 B1
Ash La Almondsbury BS32 39 D2
Down Hatherley GL2 173 B1
Randwick GL6 102 D1
Ash Path The GL4 119 E3
Ash Rd Bristol BS7 18 E5
Northway GL20 182 C4
Stroud GL5 99 A4
Ash Ridge Rd BS32 40 B3
Ash The GL6 102 C2
Ash Tree Cl 23 GL18 171 A4
Ash Wlk BS10 28 B3
Ashbourne Cl 2 BS30 11 C6
Ashbrook La GL7 151 F4
Ashburton Rd BS10 28 C1
Ashchurch Ind Est GL20 182 C4
Ashchurch Prim Sch GL20 182 C4
Ashchurch Rd GL20 182 B4
Ashchurch Sta GL20 182 C4
Ashcombe Cl 1 BS30 11 C6
Ashcombe Cres BS30 11 D6
Ashcot Mews 3 GL51 129 E5
Ashcott BS14 2 F7
Ashcroft Ave BS31 4 D5
Ashcroft Cl GL4 119 D2
Ashcroft Gdns GL7 190 C4
Ashcroft Ho GL5 99 D5
Ashcroft Rd Bristol BS9 17 C7
Cirencester GL7 190 C4
Wooton-u-E GL8,GL12 81 D3
Ashdale Cl GL54 160 E5
Ashdean GL14 191 C5
Ashdene Ave BS5 19 D3
Ashdown Ct BS9 17 F8
Asher La BS2 195 C3
Ashes La HR9 162 E4
Ashfield SN6 143 A5
Ashfield Cl GL52 138 A3
Ashfield Ho GL50 193 A3
Ashfield Pl BS6 18 F1
Ashfield Rd Bristol BS3 8 B3
Ruardean Hill GL17 164 A3
Ashfield Terr 8 BS3 8 B3
Ashford Rd Bristol BS34 29 A7
Cheltenham GL50 193 A1
Ashford Way BS15 11 A7
Ashgrove
Charlton Kings GL53 131 C4
Thornbury BS35 64 C1
Ashgrove Ave
Abbots Leigh BS8 7 B7
Bristol BS7 18 F4
Gloucester GL4 119 C6
Ashgrove Cl Bristol BS7 18 F4
Hardwicke GL2 109 E7
Ashgrove Cotts GL6 102 F4
Ashgrove Rd
Bristol, Ashley Down BS7 18 F4
Bristol, Bedminster BS3 8 B3
Ashgrove Way GL4 119 C6
Ashland Rd BS13 2 A4
Ashlands Cl GL51 132 E3
Ashlands Rd GL51 132 E3
Ashlea Mdws GL52 137 D4
Ashleigh La GL52 138 D1
Ashletts Rd GL6 106 C1
Ashleworth CE Prim Sch GL19 172 D4
Ashleworth Gdns GL2 109 E8
Ashley BS15 10 F8
Ashley Cl Bristol BS7 18 F4
Charlton Kings GL52 131 B7
Ashley Court Rd 2 BS7 18 F2
Ashley Down Jun & Inf Schs BS7 18 F5
Ashley Down Rd BS7 18 F4
Ashley Dr 2 GL6 148 B6
Ashley Grove Rd
7 Bristol BS2 18 F2
1 Bristol BS2 19 A1
Ashley Hill BS6,BS7 18 F2
Ashley Ho BS34 39 F1
Ashley Lo GL53 130 C6
Ashley Par BS2 18 F2
Ashley Pk BS6 18 F3
Ashley Rd Bristol BS6 18 E1
Cheltenham GL52 131 B8
Ashley St BS2 19 A1
Ashley Trad Est 6 BS2 18 F2
Ashman Cl 5 BS5 9 A8
Ashman Ct 1 BS16 19 E3
Ashmead GL2 127 B5
Ashmead Dr GL52 138 A8
Ashmead Ho 12 BS5 9 C7
Ashmead Rd
Cinderford GL14 191 D3
Keynsham BS31 5 B5
Ashmead Road Ind Est BS31 5 B5
Ashmead Way 8 BS1 7 F5
Ashmore Rd GL4 118 F4
Ashton BS16 30 C1
Ashton Ave BS1 194 A1
Ashton Cl GL4 119 E3
Ashton Court Est* BS41 7 C4
Ashton Dr BS3 7 F2
Ashton Gate Prim Sch BS3 8 A4
Ashton Gate Rd BS3 8 A4
Ashton Gate Terr 3 BS3 8 A4
Ashton Gate Trad Est BS3 7 E3
Ashton Gate Underpass BS3 7 F3
Ashton Keynes CE Prim Sch SN6 142 F5
Ashton Rd Beckford GL20 183 B6
Bristol, Ashton Gate BS3 7 F4
Bristol, Bower Ashton BS3 7 D3
Minety SN6 142 F3
Siddington GL7 150 E1
Ashton under Hill Fst Sch WR11 183 D8
Ashton Vale Prim Sch BS3 7 F2
Ashton Vale Rd BS3 7 E3
Ashton Vale Trad Est BS3 7 F1
Ashton Way BS31 4 E6
Ashville Bsns Pk GL2 173 E1
Ashville Ind Est GL2 118 C5
Ashville Rd Bristol BS3 8 A4
Gloucester GL2 118 C5
Ashville Trad Est GL51 133 B6
Ashway Netherend GL15 147 C3
17 Northleach GL54 168 A1
Ashwell GL6 103 F8
Ashwell Cl BS14 3 E6
Ashwicke BS14 3 A6
Ashwicke Rd SN14 15 B3
Ashwood Way GL3 119 F6
Askham Ct 7 GL52 133 F2
Askwith Rd GL4 119 B6
Aspen Cl SN14 15 F6
Aspen Dr GL2 117 E2
Asquith Rd GL53 130 E6
Assembly Rooms La BS1 195 A2
Aster Cl GL4 118 C3
Aston Bank HR9 170 C2
Aston Bridge Rd GL17 163 E3
Aston Cl Berry Hill GL16 155 A7
16 Ledbury HR8 178 E8
Aston Gr
Cheltenham GL51 132 D2
Cold Aston GL54 168 B6
Aston Ho 4 BS1 195 B1
Aston Rd GL55 188 F3
Aston View GL6 148 C6
Astor Cl GL3 120 D6
Astridge Rd GL3 121 A4
Astry Cl BS11 27 A1
Atchley St 17 BS5 9 B7
Atcombe Rd GL5 90 F8
Athelney Way 4 GL52 130 F8
Atherston BS30 11 D5
Atherstone Cl GL51 132 C3
Atherton Cl GL51 129 D2
Atherton Ho GL51 129 D2
Athlone Wlk BS4 8 E1
Atkins Cl BS14 3 E6
Atlantic Rd BS11 16 C8
Atlas Cl BS5 20 A2
Atlas Rd BS3 8 E3
Atlas St BS2 9 B5
Attwood Cl GL51 132 F5
Attwood Dr BS32 40 B1
Atwood Dr BS11 27 B2
Aubrey Ho 9 BS3 8 B3
Aubrey Meads BS30 5 E8
Aubrey Rd BS3 8 B3
Auburn Ave BS30 11 B3
Auburn Rd BS6 18 B1
Auckland Ho 1 GL51 132 F3
Audley Cl BS37 43 A8
Audrey Wlk BS9 18 D7
Augustine Way GL4 119 F6
Augustus Ho BS15 10 B6
Augustus Way GL15 92 B4
Aust Cres NP16 60 F5
Aust La BS9 18 A8
Aust Rd Olveston BS35 49 F5
Pilning BS35 48 D3
Austen Gr BS7 19 A8
Austen Ho BS7 19 A8
Austin Dr GL2 126 F6
Austin Rd
Ashchurch GL20 182 D4
Cirencester GL7 190 E4
Australia Ho GL51 132 E1
Avalon Rd BS5 10 B6
Avebury Cl GL4 118 B1
Avebury Rd BS3 7 F2
Avenall Ct 9 GL52 130 F8
Avenall Par GL53 130 F8
Avening Rd Bristol BS15 10 A8
Gloucester GL4 118 F5
Nailsworth GL6 91 E3
Avenue Ter GL10 97 D7
Avenue The
Bourton-on-t-W GL54 168 F8
Brimscombe GL6 148 B5
Bristol, Ashley Down BS7 18 E3
Bristol, Clifton BS8 18 A1
Bristol, Frenchay BS16 29 E1
Bristol, Little Stoke BS34 29 C6
Bristol, Patchway BS34 40 B2
Bristol, Sneyd Park BS9 17 E3
Bristol, St George BS5 9 F8
Cheltenham GL53 130 F5
Churchdown GL3 128 D5
Cirencester GL7 190 D4
Dursley GL11 87 D3
Gloucester GL2 127 C4
Keynsham BS31 4 E6
Stanton Fitzwarren SN6 145 A1
Woodchester GL5 99 A2
Yate BS37 43 D1
Averay Rd BS16 19 C4
Averill Cl WR12 185 B8
Avon Bsns Pk BS16 20 A3
Avon Cl Bristol BS5 9 F6
Keynsham BS31 4 F6
Avon Cres Bristol BS1 194 A1
Brockworth GL3 120 F5
Wickwar GL12 54 B6
Avon Ct BS16 20 B5
Avon Gorge Ind Est BS11 16 C7
Avon Gorge Nature Reserve* BS8 7 E7
Avon Gr BS9 17 D2
Avon Ho GL2 118 C4
Avon La BS31 5 F5
Avon Meads BS2 9 C5
Avon Mill La BS31 4 F6
Avon Pk BS5 9 D7
Avon Prim Sch BS11 16 D8
Avon Rd Bristol BS13 2 A6
Charfield GL12 67 A4
Cheltenham GL52 134 A2
Keynsham BS31 4 F5
Pill BS20 16 C5
Avon Rise SN14 47 E4
Avon Riverside Est BS11 16 C7
Avon St BS2 195 C2
Avon Trad Est BS2 9 A5
Avon Vale BS9 17 D4
Avon Valley Bsns Pk BS4 9 E6
Avon Valley Ctry Pk* BS31 5 D6
Avon Valley Rly* BS30 11 C3
Avon View Bristol BS15 10 B3
Tewkesbury GL20 192 E6
Avon Way
Bristol, Sneyd Park BS9 17 C4
Bristol, Southmead BS10 18 D7
Thornbury BS35 51 D7
Avonbank Ind Est BS11 16 B7
Avonbridge Trad Est BS11 16 C8
Avondale Bsns Ctr BS15 20 C2
Avondale Ct
Bristol, Oldland BS30 10 F3
Bristol, Sneyd Park BS9 17 D3
Avondown Cl BS10 28 D2
Avondown Ct BS3 8 C2
Avondowns Ct BS8 194 A4
Avonlea Bristol BS15 10 C5
Yate BS37 32 D8
Avonleaze BS9 17 B5
Avonleigh Ct 4 BS3 8 B2
Avonleigh Rd BS3 8 B2
Avonmouth CE Prim Sch BS11 16 C8
Avonmouth Rd
Avonmouth BS11 26 B1
Bristol BS11 16 C8
Avonmouth Sta BS11 26 B1
Avonmouth Way
Avonmouth BS11 26 D1
Bristol BS10 27 E3
Avonmouth Way W BS11 26 B1
Avonside Ind Est BS2 9 C6
Avonside Rd BS2 9 C6
Avonside Way BS4 9 F6
Avonsmere Residential Pk BS34 29 C3
Avonvale Rd BS5 9 C7
Avonwood Cl BS11 16 E6
Avro Rd GL54 169 D7
Awdelett Cl BS11 27 B1
Awdry Way GL4 118 D2
Awebridge Way GL4 119 C4
Awkward Hill GL7 160 A1
Awre Rd GL15 156 E1
Axbridge Rd BS4 8 F2
Axe Ct 4 BS35 51 C8
Axis BS14 2 D5
Aycote Cl GL4 119 B5
Ayford La SN14 14 F4
Ayland Cl 29 GL18 171 A4
Ayland Gdns GL1 119 A8
Aylburton CE Prim Sch GL15 147 E4
Aylesbury Cres BS3 8 B1
Aylesbury Rd BS3 8 B1
Aylmer Cres BS14 3 B6
Aylminton Wlk BS11 27 B2
Aylton Cl GL51 129 D6
Aysgarth Ave GL51 129 E5
Azalea Dr GL51 130 A5
Azalea Gdns GL2 117 E1
Aztec Ctr The BS32 40 A2
Aztec W BS32 40 A2

B

Back Albert Pl GL52 193 C4
Back Edge La GL6 103 B8
Back Ends GL55 189 A2
Back La Beckford GL20 183 B6
Bisley GL6 148 D8
Bredon GL20 182 C8
Bretforton WR11 188 A6
Broad Blunsdon SN26 144 D2
Broadway WR12 185 B8
Drybrook GL17 164 B4
Fairford GL7 152 E3
Keynsham BS31 4 E6
Leighterton GL8 70 C3
Lower Oddington GL56 177 C4
Marshfield SN14 14 F8
Mickleton GL55 189 A6
Pill BS20 16 C5
Pucklechurch BS16 22 C4
Wickwar GL12 54 A5
Winchcombe GL54 174 A7
Winstone GL7 107 A8
Back Montpellier Terr GL50 193 B2
Back Of Avon GL20 192 C4
Back Of Kingsdown Par BS6 195 A4
Back Of Mount Pleasant GL20 192 D4
Back Rd BS3 8 A4
Back Row GL56 177 E6
Back St
Ashton Keynes SN6 142 F5
Hawkesbury Upton GL9 56 A3
Ilmington CV36 189 F6
Newnham GL14 157 A6
Back Stoke La BS9 17 F6
Back The NP16 72 F1
Back Walls GL54 176 F4
Backfields BS2 195 B4
Backfields Ct BS2 195 B4
Backfields La BS2 195 B4
Backwell Wlk BS13 1 F8
Baden Hill Rd GL12 52 C6
Baden Rd
Bristol, Kingswood BS15 11 A7
Bristol, Redfield BS5 9 C7
Badenham Gr BS11 16 F8
Bader Ave GL3 128 C5
Bader Cl BS37 43 D3
Baders Dean NP25 154 B1
Badger Cl Bristol BS30 10 F3
Gloucester GL4 119 D3
Badger Vale Ct GL2 118 C5
Badger's La BS32 39 C3
Badgers Cl BS32 40 D3
Badgers Dene NP16 60 D8
Badgers Field GL55 189 A2
Badgers Mdw NP16 60 B6
Badgers Rise BS10 28 E4
Badgers Way
9 Bream GL15 155 D1
Nailsworth GL6 90 F5
Badgers Wlk BS4 9 D2
Badgeworth BS37 32 D6
Badgeworth La GL51 129 B2
Badgeworth Rd GL51 129 A7
Badhams The GL20 180 F7
Badminton BS16 30 C1
Badminton Cl GL53 130 D6
Badminton Ct BS37 43 C2
Badminton Ctr The BS37 43 C2
Badminton Rd
Bristol, Downend BS16 20 E7
Bristol, Montpelier BS2 18 F1
Badminton Rd *continued*
Chipping Sodbury BS37 34 B7
Frampton Cotterell BS36, BS37 31 C6
Gloucester GL4 119 B5
Badminton Road Trad Est BS37 43 B1
Badminton Sch BS9 18 A5
Badminton Wlk BS16 20 E7
Badock's Wood Prim Sch BS10 28 B1
Badsey La WR12 188 A3
Bafford App GL53 131 A4
Bafford Farm GL53 131 A4
Bafford Gr GL53 130 F4
Bafford La GL53 131 A5
Baglyn Ave BS15 20 F3
Bagnell Cl BS14 3 E5
Bagnell Rd BS14 3 E5
Bagpath La GL5 99 D2
Bagshots Sq GL54 176 B2
Bagstone Rd BS37,GL12 53 A2
Bagworth Dr BS30 10 F3
Bailey Cl 21 GL54 176 F4
Bailey Hill GL15 156 B1
Bailey La NP16,GL15 146 D4
Bailey's Court Prim Sch BS32 29 F6
Bailey's Hay NP16 60 B4
Baileys Court Rd BS32 29 F6
Baileys Ct BS32 29 F6
Baileys Mead Rd BS16 19 C5
Bailiffe Piece SN6 143 E5
Baines Cl 11 GL54 168 F7
Bakehouse La GL50 130 B7
Baker Sq GL20 192 D5
Baker St
Cheltenham GL51 133 C3
Gloucester GL2 196 A1
Baker's Hill GL55 189 B5
Baker's La GL19 172 B3
Bakers Ground BS34 30 A5
Bakers Hill GL16 155 B6
Bakers Piece Rd GL17 163 F3
Bakersfield BS30 11 B3
Bala Rd GL51 129 F6
Balaclava Rd BS16 19 F3
Balcarras GL53 131 C5
Balcarras Gdns GL53 131 C5
Balcarras Rd GL53 131 C5
Balcarras Retreat GL53 131 C5
Balcarras Sch GL53 131 C5
Baldwin Cl GL7 149 B1
Baldwin St BS1 195 A2
Baldwyn Ct WR11 188 C6
Balfour Rd Bristol BS3 8 B3
Gloucester GL1 118 D6
Ballards Cl GL55 189 A6
Ballast La BS11 26 E2
Ballinode Cl GL50 133 B5
Ballinska Mews GL2 127 D5
Balmain St BS4 9 A4
Balmoral Cl BS34 29 D4
Balmoral Ct Bristol BS16 21 A5
Cheltenham GL53 130 F6
Balmoral Mans 3 BS7 18 F2
Balmoral Rd
Bristol, Longwell Green BS30 10 F2
Bristol, Montpelier BS7 18 F2
Keynsham BS31 4 E4
Baltic Pl BS20 16 D4
Bamfield BS14 3 A6
Bamfurlong Ind Pk GL51 173 E1
Bamfurlong La
Bamfurlong GL51 129 A8
Cheltenham GL51 173 F1
Bampton Cl
Bristol, Emerson's Green BS16 21 C6
Bristol, Headley Park BS13 2 B7
Bampton Croft BS16 21 C6
Bampton Dr BS16 30 D1
Banady La GL52 136 E5
Baneberry Rd GL4 119 A4
Banfield Cl BS11 17 A8
Bangor Gr BS4 9 F5
Bangrove Wlk BS11 16 E8
Bangup La GL54 168 B6
Banister Gr BS4 2 D7
Bank Cres 1 HR8 178 F8
Bank Leaze Prim Sch BS11 27 B2
Bank Pl BS20 16 D4
Bank Rd Avonmouth BS11 26 D7
Bristol BS15 10 D8
Pilning BS35 38 E6
Bank Sq NP16 60 E8
Bank St Chepstow NP16 60 E8
Coleford GL16 155 A5
Bank The Broadwell GL56 177 A6
Prestbury GL52 134 C4
Banks Fee La GL56 176 D8
Bankside Bristol BS16 20 F4
North Cerney GL7 158 D3
Bankside Rd BS4 9 D3
Banner Rd BS6 18 E1
Bannerleigh La BS8 7 E6
Bannerleigh Rd BS8 7 E6
Bannerman Rd BS5 9 B8
Bannerman Road Prim Sch BS5 19 B1
Bannetts Tree Cres BS35 51 A5
Bantock Cl BS4 2 D6
Bantry Rd BS4 2 E8
Banwell Cl Bristol BS13 2 A8
Keynsham BS31 5 A2

Banwell Rd BS3 8 A3
Baptist Cl GL4 119 F6
Baptist St BS5 19 A1
Baptist Way GL17 164 A3
Barber La GL8 140 A2
Barberry Cl GL50 130 B6
Barbican Rd GL1 196 A3
Barbican Way GL1 196 A3
Barbour Gdns BS13 2 D3
Barbour Rd BS13 2 D3
Barbridge Rd GL51 132 E3
Barcroft Cl BS15 10 C8
Baregains La HR8 178 B8
Barker Ct 5 BS5 9 C7
Barker Pl 1 GL7 152 E4
Barker Wlk BS5 19 A1
Barker's Leys GL52 138 B4
Barkers Mead BS37 43 F4
Barkleys Hill BS16 19 C5
Barksdale GL54 139 F5
Barlands Ho BS10 27 F3
Barlands The GL52 131 E4
Barley Cl Bristol BS16 21 A6
Cheltenham GL51 132 D5
Frampton Cotterell BS36 31 C8
Hardwicke GL2 109 E6
Barley Close Prim Sch BS16 21 A6
Barley Croft BS9 17 F5
Barleycorn Sq GL14 191 C4
Barleycroft Cl GL4 119 D2
Barlow Cl GL10 97 E7
Barlow Rd GL51 132 F4
Barn Bsns Ctr The GL54 169 D4
Barn Cl Bristol BS16 21 B6
Gloucester GL4 119 E4
Gretton GL54 183 E1
Nailsworth GL6 91 B3
Barn End SN14 15 A8
Barn Field 5 GL52 134 A1
Barn Field Ave GL6 91 A4
Barn Field Rd GL6 91 A4
Barn Field Terr GL6 91 A4
Barn Ground GL2 125 D5
Barn Hill Rd GL16 155 C6
Barn La GL17 163 F3
Barn Owl Way BS34 29 F5
Barn Way GL7 190 A7
Barnabas St 12 BS2 18 E1
Barnaby Cl GL1 118 F7
Barnack Trad Est BS3 8 C1
Barnacre Dr GL3 127 F1
Barnage La GL15 147 A4
Barnard Par 5 GL10 97 F7
Barnard Wlk BS31 4 D4
Barnes Ho GL7 190 D5
Barnes St 2 BS5 9 D8
Barnes Wallis Way GL3 128 C5
Barnett Ave HR8 178 E8
Barnett Cl GL51 132 E5
Barnett Way
Gloucester GL4 127 D1
5 Northleach GL54 168 A1
Barnetts Cl 4 HR8 178 E8
Barnfields GL4 118 F5
Barnhay GL3 128 C4
Barnhill Cl BS37 44 A4
Barnhill Rd BS37 44 B1
Barnmeadow Rd 8 GL54 174 A7
Barnsley House Gdn★ GL7 151 C7
Barnstaple Ct BS4 2 E8
Barnstaple Rd BS4 2 E8
Barnstaple Wlk BS4 2 F8
Barnwood Ave GL4 119 D8
Barnwood CE Prim Sch GL4 127 D1
Barnwood Park Sch for Girls GL4 119 D8
Barnwood Rd
Gloucester GL2 127 C2
Yate BS37 32 C7
Barossa Pl BS1 195 A1
Barra Cl SN6 145 C3
Barrack Sq GL1 196 A3
Barrack's La BS11 16 D8
Barracks The GL15 156 A4
Barratt St BS5 19 C1
Barratt's Mill La GL53 193 C3
Barrel La GL17 164 F8
Barrels Pitch GL55 189 A2
Barrington Ave GL51 129 B7
Barrington Cl BS15 20 F2
Barrington Ct
11 Bristol, Knowle BS2 8 F4
Bristol, New Cheltenham BS15 20 E1
Barrington Dr GL3 119 F8
Barrington Mews GL51 129 B7
Barrow Cl GL2 109 F8
Barrow Elm Barns GL7 152 F7
Barrow Hill
Churchdown GL3 128 D3
Wick BS30 12 B5
Barrow Hill Cres BS11 16 C7
Barrow Hill Rd BS11 16 D6
Barrow Hospl BS48 1 A6
Barrow Rd BS2 9 A7
Barrowell La GL15 146 F7
Barrowfield Rd GL5 103 A1
Barrowmead Dr BS11 16 F7
Barrs Court Ave BS30 11 A5
Barrs Court Prim Sch BS30 10 F5
Barrs Court Rd BS30 11 A5
Barrs La GL11 79 E4
Barry Cl BS30 11 C1
Barry Rd BS30 11 C2
Barstable Ho BS2 195 C3
Bartholomew Cl GL19 172 D4
Bartlett's Rd BS3 8 C2
Bartletts Pk GL54 176 F4
Bartley Croft 3 GL8 140 C4
Bartley St BS3 8 D4
Barton Cl Alveston BS35 51 A5
1 Bristol BS4 9 F6
Charlton Kings GL53 131 A4
Winterbourne BS36 30 E5
Barton Ct BS5 9 C6
Barton Gn BS5 9 B7
Barton Hill GL17 164 E5
Barton Hill Inf Sch BS5 9 B6
Barton Hill Prim Sch BS5 9 B6
Barton Hill Rd BS5 9 B7
Barton Hill Trad Est 9 BS5 9 B6
Barton Ho BS5 9 C6
Barton La GL7 190 B5
Barton Manor BS2 9 A6
Barton Mews GL20 192 D4
Barton Rd
Barton-on-t-H GL56 187 F3
Bristol BS2 195 C2
Tewkesbury GL20 192 D4
Barton St Bristol BS1 195 A4
Gloucester GL1 119 A8
Tewkesbury GL20 192 C4
Barton The BS15 10 C4
Barton Vale 6 BS2 9 A6
Barton Way GL51 129 E6
Bartonend La GL6 91 A1
Bartonia Gr BS4 9 D1
Bartwood La HR9 164 A8
Barwick Ho BS11 16 E7
Barwick Rd 6 GL51 129 F5
Barwood Cl BS15 10 F8
Base La GL2 172 F1
Basil Cl GL4 119 D4
Bassett Cl 3 GL54 174 A7
Bassett Rd GL54 168 A1
Bassetts The GL5 98 D8
Batch The BS31 5 F3
Batchfield La BS16,BS37 22 D8
Bateman Cl GL4 118 D1
Bates Cl BS5 9 A8
Bath Bldgs BS6 18 E1
Bath Cres GL15 155 F1
Bath Hill BS31 4 F5
Bath Mews GL53 193 C2
Bath Par GL53 193 C2
Bath Pl
11 Berry Hill GL16 155 A7
Lydney GL15 92 B3
Bath Race Course★ BA1 6 F6
Bath Rd Bitton BA1,BA2,BS30 5 F7
Bristol, Brislington BS4 9 D2
Bristol, Brislington BS4,BS31 9 F1
Bristol,Longwell Green BS30 10 F3
Bristol,North Common BS30 11 D6
Bristol,Totterdown BS4,BS2 9 B4
Bristol,Willsbridge BS30 11 C1
Cheltenham GL50,GL53 193 B2
Chipping Sodbury BS37,GL9 34 C4
Colerne SN14 15 E2
Cricklade SN6 143 E4
Eastington GL10 96 F6
Leighterton GL8 70 B2
Leonard Stanley GL10 97 E4
Nailsworth GL6 91 B2
Saltford BS31 5 D3
Stonehouse GL10 97 F7
Tetbury GL8 140 B2
Thornbury BS35 51 B8
Wick BS30 12 E4
Woodchester GL5 99 A3
Bath St Bristol BS1 195 B2
Bristol, Ashton Gate BS3 8 A4
Bristol, Staple Hill BS16 20 E4
Cheltenham GL50 193 C3
Stroud GL5 99 C7
Bath Terr GL53 193 B1
Bath Ville Mews GL53 193 B2
Bathams Cl GL17 164 F5
Bathings The 1 BS35 51 C8
Bathleaze GL10 98 A3
Bathurst Par BS1 195 A1
Bathurst Park Rd GL15 92 A3
Bathurst Rd
Cirencester GL7 190 B3
Gloucester GL1 118 F6
Bathwell Rd BS4 9 A3
Batley Ct BS30 11 D4
Batsford Arboretum★ GL56 186 E4
Batten Ct BS37 44 C1
Batten's La BS5 10 A6
Battenburg Rd BS5 10 A8
Battens Rd BS5 10 B7
Battersby Way BS10 27 E2
Battersea Rd BS5 9 C8
Battle Rd GL20 192 B2
Battledown App GL52 131 A8
Battledown Cl GL52 134 A1
Battledown Dr GL52 131 A8
Battledown Grange GL52 131 A8
Battledown Mead GL52 134 A1
Battledown Priors GL52 134 A1
Battledown Trad Est GL52 131 A8
Batts La GL17 164 A4
Battson Rd BS14 3 E4
Baugh Gdns BS16 30 E1
Baugh Rd BS16 30 E1
Baunton La GL7 150 C7
Baxter Cl BS15 10 F8
Baxters Barns GL7 153 D6
Bay Gdns BS5 19 C2
Bay Tree Cl BS34 28 F7
Bay Tree Ct GL52 134 C4
Bay Tree Rd GL4 119 F5
Bayberry Pl 9 GL16 155 B5
Bayfield Gdns GL18 178 D2
Bayham Rd BS4 9 A3
Bayham's Wlk GL16 155 C6
Baylands GL13 85 D8
Bayleys Dr BS15 10 C6
Bayliss Ho GL51 132 E4
Bayliss Rd GL20 182 E8
Baynham Ct 3 BS15 10 B5
Baynham Rd GL17 164 D5
Baynham Way GL50 193 B4
Baynham's Wlk GL16 155 B6
Baynton Ho 2 BS5 9 B7
Baynton Mdw BS16 21 C6
Baynton Rd BS3 8 A4
Bays Hill GL13 85 D8
Bayshill La GL50 193 A3
Bayshill Rd GL50 193 A3
Bayswater Ave BS6 18 B3
Bayswater Rd BS7 18 F7
Bazeley Rd GL4 119 B2
Beach Ave BS35 38 A7
Beach Hill BS30 11 F3
Beach La BS30 12 C2
Beach Rd BS35 37 F7
Beachgrove Gdns BS16 20 C4
Beachgrove Rd BS16 20 B4
Beachley Rd
Beachley NP16 61 B4
Tutshill NP16 73 A1
Beachley Wlk BS11 16 D7
Beacon Cl GL6 112 A5
Beacon La BS16 30 C6
Beacon Rd
Gloucester GL4 119 B2
Llandogo NP25 146 A8
Beacon Rise Prim Sch BS15 10 D6
Beaconlea BS15 10 D6
Beacons View Rd GL14 191 E5
Beaconsfield Ct 1 GL50 130 B8
Beaconsfield Rd
Bristol, Clifton BS8 18 A1
Bristol, Knowle BS4 9 B3
Bristol, St George BS5 9 E7
Beaconsfield St 6 BS5 9 B6
Beagles The GL5 98 D7
Beale Cl Bristol BS14 3 E6
Bussage GL6 148 B6
Beale Rd GL51 132 D3
Beam St BS5 9 C7
Bean Acre The BS11 16 D8
Bean Hill GL56 176 E8
Bean St 11 BS5 19 A1
Beanhill Cres BS35 51 A5
Bear Hill GL5 99 B2
Bear La GL20 180 F6
Bear St GL12 68 B7
Bearbridge Rd BS13 1 F4
Bearcroft Gdn GL55 189 B6
Bearcroft Gdns GL55 189 B7
Beard's La GL5 99 A7
Bearland GL1 196 A3
Bearlands GL12 68 C6
Bearpacker Almshouses GL12 68 C8
Bearsfield GL6 105 A1
Beauchamp Cl 2 GL7 152 E4
Beauchamp Mdw GL15 92 C4
Beauchamp Rd BS7 18 D4
Beaudesert Park Sch GL6 91 C5
Beaufort Bristol BS16 30 C1
Chepstow NP16 60 E8
Beaufort Ave BS37 43 D2
Beaufort Bldgs
7 Bristol BS8 7 F7
Gloucester GL1 196 B1
Beaufort Cl BS5 9 D7
Beaufort Com Sch The GL4 118 B2
Beaufort Cres BS34 29 E4
Beaufort Ct Bristol BS16 21 A8
Cirencester GL7 190 C3
Beaufort Dr GL15 92 B2
Beaufort End WR11 188 C7
Beaufort Ho 11 BS5 9 B7
Beaufort Hts BS5 9 E7
Beaufort Mews BS37 44 B1
Beaufort Pl
Bristol, Frenchay BS16 30 B1
Bristol, Upper Easton BS5 9 A8
Chepstow NP16 60 E8
Tewkesbury GL20 192 C2
Beaufort Rd
Bristol, Clifton BS8 18 A1
Bristol, Horfield BS7 18 F6
Bristol, Kingswood BS15 20 C1
Bristol, St George BS5 9 F7
Bristol,Staple Hill BS16 20 E5
Bristol,Vinney Green BS16 21 A8
Charlton Kings GL52 131 A7
Frampton Cotterell BS36 31 A8
Gloucester GL4 119 A5
Yate BS37 43 D2
Beaufort St
Bristol, Bedminster BS3 8 C2
4 Bristol, Upper Easton BS5 9 A8
Beaufort Way BS10 18 D8
Beauley Rd BS3 8 B4
Beaumont Cl BS30 11 A3
Beaumont Dr GL51 132 D4
Beaumont Pl GL15 92 A2
Beaumont Rd
Cheltenham GL51 132 D3
Gloucester GL2 127 C5
Beaumont St BS5 9 A8
Beaumont Terr 6 BS5 9 A8
Beaumoor Pl GL7 152 E3
Beaver Cl BS36 30 F7
Beazer Cl 5 BS16 20 D3
Beck Cl BS16 21 C7
Beck Ho BS34 29 A8
Becket Cl GL56 187 E7
Becket Ct BS16 22 B5
Becketts La GL54 174 A8
Beckfield Farm BS37 42 F5
Beckford Cl GL20 183 B6
Beckford Gdns BS14 3 A3
Beckford Rd
Alderton GL20 183 D4
Ashton under Hill WR11 183 D8
Gloucester GL4 119 E4
Beckford Silk★ GL20 183 B6
Beckington Rd BS3 8 F2
Beckington Wlk BS3 8 F2
Beckside Ct 2 GL1 127 A1
Beckspool Rd BS16 30 C1
Becky Hill GL54 176 B1
Beddome Way GL54 168 F8
Bedford Ave GL51 133 A2
Bedford Cres BS7 18 F5
Bedford St
Gloucester GL1 196 C2
8 Stroud GL5 99 C7
Bedminster Down Rd BS3, BS13 8 B1
Bedminster Down Sch BS13 1 F7
Bedminster Par BS3 8 D4
Bedminster Pl 10 BS3 8 D4
Bedminster Rd BS3 8 C2
Bedminster Sta BS3 8 D3
Beech Ave GL16 155 B7
Beech Cl Alveston BS35 51 A5
Bristol BS30 11 A5
Hardwicke GL2 109 E7
Highnam GL2 125 D4
Prestbury GL52 134 C4
Beech Ct BS14 3 A5
Beech Gr Chepstow NP16 60 D7
Cirencester GL7 190 E5
Highworth SN6 145 C3
Woodchester GL5 99 A2
Beech Green Prim Sch GL2 117 F1
Beech Grove Ct GL7 190 E5
Beech Ho BS16 19 C5
Beech La GL6 104 B8
Beech Lea
Broad Blunsdon SN26 144 E1
Meysey Hampton GL7 152 B3
Beech Leaze BS35 51 A5
Beech Rd Bristol BS7 18 E5
Saltford BS31 5 E3
Yorkley GL15 156 A2
Beech Tree Gdns 5 GL8 140 C4
Beech Way Bream GL15 147 D8
Littledean GL14 156 E8
Beech Well La GL16 155 C8
Beechcroft BS41 1 D2
Beechcroft Rd GL2 127 B5
Beechcroft Wlk BS7 19 A8
Beechdean GL14 191 C5
Beechen Dr BS16 20 B3
Beechenhurst Lodge Visitor Ctr★ GL16 155 E7
Beeches Cl GL10 98 A4
Beeches Gn GL5 99 B8
Beeches Gr BS4 9 D2
Beeches Ind Est BS37 43 B2
Beeches Pk GL6 148 B2
Beeches Rd
Charlton Kings GL53 131 B4
Cirencester GL7 190 D4
Newnham GL14 157 A6
Beeches The
Bristol, Bradley Stoke BS32 29 D8
Bristol, Frenchay BS16 30 B1
Bristol, Oldland Common BS30 11 C2
Bristol, St Anne's Park BS4 9 E5
King's Stanley GL10 98 A4
Beechfield Cl BS41 7 C2
Beechfield Gr BS9 17 C8
Beechmore Dr 10 GL51 129 E5
Beechmount Ct BS14 3 B8
Beechmount Gr BS14 3 B8
Beechurst Ave GL52 133 F1
Beechurst Way GL52 137 D4
Beechwood Ave BS15 10 D5
Beechwood Cl Bristol BS14 3 C8
Cheltenham GL52 131 B8
Beechwood Dr 4 GL6 148 B6
Beechwood Gr
Gloucester GL4 118 E3
Wooton-u-E GL12 68 D8
Beechwood Pl GL50 193 C3
Beechwood Rd
Bristol BS16 20 B4
Easton-in-G BS20 16 A4
Beechwood Rise GL11 87 F2
Beehive Trad Est BS5 9 E7
Beek's La SN14,BA1 14 D5
Beesmoor Rd BS36 31 B6
Begbrook Dr BS16 19 F6
Begbrook La BS16 19 F6
Begbrook Pk BS16 20 A7
Begbrook Prim Sch BS16 19 F6
Beggar Bush La BS8 7 B6
Beggarswell Cl BS2 195 C4
Bekdale Cl GL2 109 D8
Belas Knap Long Barrow★ GL54 174 A4
Belfast Wlk BS4 2 E8
Belfrey The NP16 61 C7
Belfry BS30 11 B6
Belfry Ave BS5 10 A8
Belfry Cl GL4 119 E8
Belgrave Hill 5 BS8 18 A2
Belgrave Pl BS8 194 A3
Belgrave Rd Bristol BS8 194 B4
Gloucester GL1 196 B2
Bell Bank 6 GL56 186 C5
Bell Barn Rd BS9 17 D6
Bell Cl BS10 18 E7
Bell Hill BS16 19 C4
Bell Hill Rd BS5 9 F8
Bell La Blockley GL56 186 C5
Bristol BS1 195 A3
Bromberrow Heath GL18 179 B4
Gloucester GL1 196 B2
Lechlade on T GL7 153 E2
Minchinhampton GL6 148 A3
Poulton GL7 151 F4
Stroud GL5 98 E4
Bell Orch GL2 157 B6
Bell Pitch GL6 102 F3
Bell Rd BS36 31 C6
Bell Sq SN14 15 A8
Bell Wlk GL1 196 B2
Bell's Old Gram Sch GL16 154 E4
Bella Vista GL52 138 B3
Bellamy Ave BS13 2 C4
Bellamy Cl BS15 10 A5
Belland Dr Bristol BS14 2 F4
Charlton Kings GL53 131 A4
Belle Ct 7 BS2 8 F4
Belle Vue Cl GL5 99 C7
Belle Vue Cotts BS9 18 A7
Belle Vue Rd Bristol BS5 19 C1
Cinderford GL14 191 D4
Ruardean GL17 163 F4
Stroud GL5 99 C7
Belle Vue Terr GL6 148 C5
Bellevue BS8 194 B2
Bellevue Cl BS15 10 E7
Bellevue Cotts BS8 194 B2
Bellevue Cres BS8 194 B2
Bellevue Ct BS8 194 B2
Bellevue Pk BS4 9 D2
Bellevue Rd
Bristol, Kingswood BS15 10 F7
Bristol, St George BS5 10 A8
6 Bristol, Totterdown BS2 8 F4
Bellevue Terr
Bristol, Brislington BS4 9 D2
Bristol, Clifton Wood BS8 194 B2
Bristol, Totterdown BS2 8 F4
Bellfields La BS16 30 C1
Bellflower Rd GL20 192 E2
Bellhouse Wlk BS11 27 B1
Bellingham La SN6 145 D1
Bells Pl Cinderford GL14 156 C6
Coleford GL16 155 A5
Belluton Rd BS4 9 A3
Belmont Ave GL3 120 B7
Belmont Dr BS34 29 E5
Belmont La GL16 155 A8
Belmont Lo 6 GL52 193 C4
Belmont Pk BS7 28 F1
Belmont Rd
Bristol, Brislington BS4 9 C3
Bristol, Montpelier BS6 18 E2
Cheltenham GL52 193 C4
Hewelsfield GL15 146 E5
Stroud GL5 99 E6
Belmont St BS5 19 B1
Belmont Terr GL17 164 D5
Belmore Pl GL53 193 B2
Beloe Rd BS7 18 E5
Belroyal Ave BS4 9 F3
Belsher Dr BS15 11 A6
Belstone Wlk BS4 2 C8
Belton Rd BS5 9 B8
Belvedere Mews GL6 148 C5
Belvedere Rd BS6 18 B3
Belvoir Rd BS6 18 E2
Belworth Ct 5 GL51 129 F7
Belworth Dr GL51 130 A7
Bence Ct 2 BS15 10 B5
Bences Cl SN14 14 F8
Bendall Ho 7 GL52 193 C4
Bendy Bow SN16 141 F4
Benford Cl BS16 20 C6
Benhall Ave GL51 129 E8
Benhall Gdns GL51 132 E1
Benhall Ho GL51 129 F8
Benhall Inf Sch GL51 129 D7
Bennett Rd BS5 9 E7
Bennett Way BS1,BS8 7 F5
Bennett's Ct BS37 44 A1
Bennington St GL50 193 B4
Bensaunt Gr BS10 28 D4
Benson Cl GL4 119 E6
Bentley Cl Bristol BS14 2 F3
Quedgeley GL2 117 F2
Bentley La GL52 134 D7
Benton Ct GL10 89 E6
Benville Ave BS9 17 C8
Berchel Ho 4 BS3 8 D4

Berenda Dr BS30 ... 11 B3
Beresford Cl BS31 ... 5 E2
Beresford Ho GL7 ... 190 C6
Berkeley Ave Bristol BS8 194 C3
Bristol, Bishopston BS7 ... 18 D3
Berkeley Castle & Butterfly Ho★ GL13 ... 85 F2
Berkeley Cl Bristol BS16 ... 21 A8
Charfield GL12 ... 67 A5
Gloucester GL3 ... 120 C6
South Cerney GL7 ... 142 F7
Stroud GL5 ... 98 D7
Berkeley Cres
Bristol BS8 ... 194 B3
Lydney GL15 ... 92 B5
Berkeley Ct
Bristol, Bishopston BS7 ... 18 D3
Bristol, Upper Easton BS5 ... 9 B7
Cheltenham GL52 ... 193 C3
Slimbridge GL2 ... 95 D3
Berkeley Gdns BS31 ... 4 E4
Berkeley Gn
Bristol, Eastville BS5 ... 19 D2
Bristol, Frenchay BS16 ... 30 B1
Berkeley Gr BS5 ... 19 C2
Berkeley Ho Bristol BS1 ... 194 C3
7 Bristol, Staple Hill BS16 ... 20 D5
6 Cheltenham, Fairview GL52 ... 133 F2
6 Cheltenham, Hester's Way GL51 ... 132 E3
Berkeley Hospl GL13 ... 85 E3
Berkeley Mews GL52 ... 193 C3
Berkeley Pl Bristol BS8 ... 194 B3
Cheltenham GL52 ... 193 C3
Berkeley Prim Sch GL13 ... 85 E3
Berkeley Rd
Bristol, Bishopston BS7 ... 18 D3
Bristol, Kingswood BS15 ... 10 D7
Bristol, Mayfield Park BS16 ... 20 B2
Bristol, Staple Hill BS16 ... 20 D5
Bristol, Westbury Park BS6 ... 18 B4
Cirencester GL7 ... 190 C1
Berkeley Sq BS8 ... 194 B3
Berkeley St Bristol BS5 ... 19 C3
Cheltenham GL52 ... 193 C3
Gloucester GL1 ... 196 A3
Berkeley Sta GL13 ... 85 F5
Berkeley Vale Com Sch GL13 ... 85 E7
Berkeley Way Bristol BS16 21 B7
7 Tetbury GL8 ... 140 C5
Berkeleys Mead BS34 ... 30 A6
Berkhampstead Sch GL52 ... 134 A2
Berkley Ave BS8 ... 194 B3
Berkshire Rd BS7 ... 18 D3
Berlington Ct BS1 ... 195 B1
Berners Cl BS4 ... 2 D7
Berrells Rd GL8 ... 140 B3
Berrells The GL8 ... 140 B3
Berrington Rd GL55 ... 189 B2
Berrow Wlk BS3 ... 8 E2
Berrows Mead BS37 ... 43 A8
Berry Cl GL6 ... 103 F8
Berry Croft 5 BS3 ... 8 D4
Berry Hill Cres GL7 ... 190 C7
Berry Hill Prim Sch GL16 ... 155 A7
Berry Hill Rd GL7 ... 190 D7
Berry La BS7 ... 18 F6
Berry Lawn GL4 ... 119 D3
Berrycroft GL13 ... 85 E4
Berryfield GL5 ... 98 F2
Berryfield Glade GL3 ... 128 A6
Berrymore Rd GL5 ... 98 F2
Bertha's Field GL9 ... 57 B4
Berton Cl SN26 ... 144 E1
Berwick Cl BS10 ... 27 E8
Berwick Ct BS10 ... 27 B5
Berwick La BS10 ... 27 D7
Berwick Rd
Bishop's Cleeve GL52 ... 137 F5
Bristol BS5 ... 19 B2
Beryl Gr BS14 ... 3 C8
Beryl Rd BS3 ... 8 B3
Besbury Pk GL6 ... 148 A4
Besford Rd GL52 ... 138 E3
Besom La BS37 ... 32 D5
Bessemer Cl 21 GL16 ... 155 A5
Beta Cl GL20 ... 182 B4
Bethel Rd BS5 ... 9 F8
Bethesda St GL50 ... 193 B1
Betjeman Cl GL2 ... 118 C4
Betjeman Ct 2 BS30 ... 11 A5
Bettenson Rise 10 GL54 168 A1
Bettertons Cl GL7 ... 152 D3
Bettridge Ct GL52 ... 134 B3
Bettridge Sch GL51 ... 130 A6
Betts Gn BS16 ... 21 C7
Betworthy Est GL11 ... 88 E8
Beuchamp Mdw GL15 ... 92 C4
Bevan Cotts GL20 ... 181 F8
Bevan Ct BS34 ... 28 F2
Bevan Gdns GL20 ... 182 C5
Beverley Ave BS16 ... 30 F1
Beverley Cl BS5 ... 10 B6
Beverley Croft GL51 ... 132 C2
Beverley Gdns Bristol BS9 17 D7
Woodmancote GL52 ... 138 C3
Beverley Rd BS7 ... 18 F8
Beverly Ct 3 BS16 ... 20 D3
Beverston Gdns BS11 ... 27 B2
Beverstone BS15 ... 10 C8
Beverstone Cl GL7 ... 142 F7
Beverstone Rd GL7 ... 142 F7
Bevin Ct 5 BS2 ... 18 F1
Bevington Cl BS34 ... 39 E1
Bevington La GL13 ... 76 F7
Bevington Wlk BS34 ... 39 E1
Bewley Way GL3 ... 128 A6
Bexley Rd BS16 ... 20 B3
Beyon Cl GL11 ... 87 F6
Beyon Dr GL11 ... 87 F6
Bglws The GL16 ... 155 B5
Bhirraff Ct 14 BS6 ... 18 B1
Bibstone BS15 ... 11 A8
Bibsworth Ave 4 WR12 185 C8
Bibsworth La
Broadway WR12 ... 185 C8
Broadway WR12 ... 188 B1
Bibury Ave BS34 ... 29 B8
Bibury CE Prim Sch GL7 ... 160 A1
Bibury Cl BS9 ... 18 D7
Bibury Cres
Bristol, Hanham BS15 ... 10 C5
Bristol, Henleaze BS9 ... 18 D7
Bibury Farm Cotts GL7 ... 160 B2
Bibury Rd
Cheltenham GL51 ... 129 E8
Gloucester GL4 ... 119 A6
Bibury Trout Farm★ GL7 ... 160 A1
Bickerton Cl BS10 ... 27 F3
Bickford Cl BS30 ... 11 A6
Bickley Cl BS15 ... 10 C2
Bicknor St GL16 ... 155 A8
Bicks La 30 GL54 ... 174 A7
Biddel Springs SN6 ... 145 D3
Biddeston Rd BS7 ... 28 E1
Biddulph Way HR8 ... 178 E7
Bideford Cres BS4 ... 2 F8
Bidwell Cl BS10 ... 28 B3
Bifield Cl BS14 ... 3 F5
Bifield Gdns BS14 ... 3 E5
Bifield Rd BS14 ... 3 F5
Bigstone Cl NP16 ... 73 A2
Bigstone Gr NP16 ... 73 A2
Bigwood La BS1 ... 194 C2
Bijou Ct GL1 ... 126 F4
Bilberry Cl Bristol BS9 ... 17 C8
5 Gloucester GL4 ... 119 F5
Bilbie Cl BS10 ... 18 E7
Billand Cl BS13 ... 1 E3
Billbrook Rd GL3 ... 120 A7
Billingham Cl GL4 ... 119 B6
Billings Way GL50 ... 130 B6
Bilsham La BS35 ... 48 F2
Bilson GL14 ... 191 C5
Bindon Dr BS10 ... 28 D4
Binley Gr BS14 ... 3 D5
Binmead Gdns BS13 ... 2 B4
Binyon Rd GL54 ... 139 F5
Birbeck Rd BS9 ... 17 E5
Birch Ave GL4 ... 119 C6
Birch Cl Bristol BS34 ... 28 E7
Charlton Kings GL53 ... 131 C4
Ledbury HR8 ... 178 E8
Birch Croft BS14 ... 3 A3
Birch Ct BS31 ... 4 C4
Birch Dr Alveston BS35 ... 50 F4
Pucklechurch BS16 ... 22 B5
Birch Glade 4 SN6 ... 142 F4
Birch Ho BS16 ... 20 B5
Birch Pk GL16 ... 155 C5
Birch Rd
Bristol, Kingswood BS15 ... 20 E3
Bristol, Southville BS3 ... 8 B4
Dursley GL11 ... 88 A4
Mile End GL16 ... 155 C6
Woodchester GL5 ... 99 A3
Yate BS37 ... 43 D2
Birchall Ave GL4 ... 119 C3
Birchall Rd BS6 ... 18 C4
Birchdale Rd BS14 ... 3 A8
Birches Cl GL5 ... 99 C8
Birches Dr GL5 ... 99 C8
Birches La GL18 ... 170 F7
Birches Rd NP25 ... 154 B5
Birches The GL5 ... 99 C8
Birchfield Rd GL52 ... 138 A4
Birchills Trad Est BS4 ... 9 F1
Birchley Rd GL52 ... 131 B8
Birchmore Rd GL1 ... 119 A8
Birchwood Cl GL14 ... 191 B5
Birchwood Ct BS4 ... 9 F4
Birchwood Fields GL4 ... 118 E3
Birchwood Rd Bristol BS4 ... 9 F4
Netherend GL15 ... 147 C3
Bird Rd GL3 ... 120 B6
Birdale Cl BS10 ... 27 E3
Birdland★ GL54 ... 168 F7
Birdlip Fm GL4 ... 121 F1
Birdlip Ho GL1 ... 127 A2
Birdlip Prim Sch GL4 ... 121 F1
Birds Bush La GL6 ... 106 B5
Birdwell Prim Sch BS41 ... 1 A8
Birdwood BS15 ... 10 D6
Birdwood Cl GL4 ... 119 E4
Birdwood Gdns NP16 ... 60 C4
Birgage Rd GL9 ... 55 F2
Birkdale Bristol BS30 ... 11 B6
Yate BS37 ... 32 E8
Birkin St 5 BS2 ... 9 A6
Bishop Ct GL51 ... 133 A2
Bishop Manor Rd BS10 ... 18 D7
Bishop Rd
Bristol, Bishopston BS7 ... 18 D4
Bristol, Emerson's Green BS16 ... 21 C6
Shurdington GL51 ... 129 E2
Bishop Road Prim Sch BS7 ... 18 D4
Bishop St BS2 ... 195 B4
Bishop Terr BS2 ... 195 C4
Bishop's Cl GL5 ... 99 D6
Bishop's Cleeve Prim Sch GL52 ... 137 F3
Bishop's Wlk GL19 ... 181 C3
Bishop's Wood BS32 ... 40 C6
Bishops Cl
Bishop's Cleeve GL52 ... 138 A3
Bristol BS9 ... 17 E3
Chepstow NP16 ... 60 F4
Bishops Cove BS13 ... 1 F5
Bishops Dr GL52 ... 137 F3
Bishops Gate GL15 ... 92 A2
Bishops Knoll BS9 ... 17 C3
Bishops Mdw GL52 ... 137 E4
Bishops Mead NP16 ... 60 B4
Bishops Rd GL4 ... 119 E6
Bishops Wlk
Cirencester GL7 ... 190 C4
Tewkesbury GL20 ... 192 C5
Bishopsfield 2 SN6 ... 143 E4
Bishopstone Cl GL51 ... 132 C1
Bishopstone Rd GL1 ... 119 A8
Bishopsworth CE Jun Sch BS13 ... 1 F6
Bishopsworth Rd BS13 ... 2 A7
Bishopthorpe Rd BS10 ... 18 E7
Bishport Ave BS13 ... 2 C3
Bishport Cl BS13 ... 2 B4
Bishport Gn BS13 ... 2 C3
Bishton La NP16 ... 73 B3
Bisley BS37 ... 32 C7
Bisley Bluecoat CE Prim Sch GL6 ... 148 D8
Bisley Old Rd GL5 ... 99 E7
Bisley Rd Bisley GL6 ... 104 E2
Cheltenham GL51 ... 129 E8
Gloucester GL4 ... 118 E1
Bisley St GL6 ... 103 F8
Bissex Mead BS16 ... 21 B5
Bittern Ave GL4 ... 119 D6
Bitterwell Cl BS36 ... 31 D3
Bittlemead BS13 ... 2 F4
Bitton Sta BS30 ... 11 B1
Bixhead Wlk GL16 ... 155 C5
Blaby Cl GL4 ... 119 F5
Black Berry Field GL52 ... 134 C3
Black Dog Way GL1 ... 196 B3
Black Horse Hill GL8 ... 140 B3
Black Jack Mews GL7 ... 190 C5
Black Jack St GL7 ... 190 C5
Black Stone Kilns La HR9 ... 162 D3
Black Wells GL11 ... 80 B7
Blackacre BS14 ... 3 C4
Blackberry Ave 5 BS16 ... 19 E5
Blackberry Cl GL4 ... 119 E4
Blackberry Dr BS36 ... 31 C6
Blackberry Gr GL52 ... 137 E4
Blackberry Hill BS16 ... 19 E5
Blackberry Hill Hospl BS16 ... 19 F5
Blackbird Ave GL3 ... 127 D6
Blackbird Ct GL10 ... 97 F8
Blackboy 18 GL5 ... 99 C7
Blackboys GL11 ... 88 A3
Blackdown Ct BS14 ... 3 B5
Blackford La GL7 ... 144 E6
Blackfriars BS1 ... 195 A3
Blackfriars Church★ GL1 ... 196 A2
Blackhorse Cty Prim Sch BS16 ... 21 A8
Blackhorse Hill BS35, BS10 ... 28 B8
Blackhorse La BS16 ... 21 A8
Blackhorse Pl BS16 ... 21 A6
Blackhorse Rd
Bristol, Kingswood BS15 ... 10 D8
Bristol, Mangotsfield BS16 ... 21 A7
Blacklow Cl GL5 ... 98 F2
Blackmoor Rd BS8 ... 16 E2
Blackmoors La BS3 ... 7 E4
Blackquarries Hill GL12 ... 68 E7
Blackrock La BS14 ... 3 D1
Blacksmith Cl GL20 ... 183 B5
Blacksmith Hill GL12 ... 69 C7
Blacksmith La
Churchdown GL3 ... 128 D4
Leigh The GL19 ... 173 D5
Blacksmith's La BA1 ... 6 B3
Blacksmiths Ground GL2 ... 125 D5
Blacksmiths La
Beckford GL20 ... 183 B5
Dumbleton WR11 ... 183 F7
Highnam GL2 ... 125 F7
Prestbury GL52 ... 134 C4
Blacksmiths Rd GL20 ... 183 E4
Blackswarth Ho 6 BS5 ... 9 D7
Blackswarth Rd BS5 ... 9 D7
Blackthorn Cl BS13 ... 2 D5
Blackthorn Dr BS32 ... 29 D7
Blackthorn End GL53 ... 130 A4
Blackthorn Gdns GL2 ... 117 F1
Blackthorn Rd BS13 ... 2 D5
Blackthorn Wlk BS15 ... 20 E2
Blackwater Way GL2 ... 127 E5
Blackworth SN6 ... 145 D4
Bladon Mews GL51 ... 129 B7
Blagdon Cl BS3 ... 8 E2
Blagrove Cl BS13 ... 2 C3
Blagrove Cres BS13 ... 2 C3
Blaisdon BS37 ... 32 E7
Blaisdon Cl Bristol BS10 ... 28 A1
Blaisdon Cl *continued*
Gloucester GL4 ... 119 E4
Blaisdon La GL17 ... 165 B4
Blaisdon Way GL51 ... 132 E5
Blaise Castle Miniature Rly★ BS10 ... 27 E2
Blaise Castle Mus★ BS10 27 E2
Blaise Hamlet BS11 ... 27 D2
Blaise Prim Sch BS10 ... 27 F2
Blaise Wlk BS9 ... 17 C6
Blake Croft GL51 ... 132 E4
Blake Hill Way GL4 ... 119 D7
Blake Rd Bristol BS7 ... 19 B6
Cirencester GL7 ... 190 C5
Blake St NP25 ... 154 A7
Blakeley Ct GL3 ... 127 F6
Blakeney Cl GL4 ... 118 D3
Blakeney Hill Rd GL15 ... 156 D2
Blakeney Mills BS37 ... 43 E1
Blakeney Prim Sch GL15 ... 156 D1
Blakeney Rd
Bristol, Horfield BS7 ... 19 A7
Bristol, Patchway BS34 ... 39 E1
Blakes Rd BS35 ... 64 B1
Blakewell Mead GL6 ... 103 E8
Blanchards BS37 ... 33 D8
Blanchards Cotts BS37 ... 33 D8
Blandford Alley SN6 ... 145 D3
Blandford Cl 2 BS9 ... 18 B6
Blands Row BS35 ... 48 B1
Bleasby Gdns GL50 ... 130 A8
Bledington Sch OX7 ... 177 E1
Blenheim Cl
Alderton GL20 ... 183 D4
Upper Rissington GL54 ... 169 D6
Blenheim Ct Bristol BS32 ... 40 D3
14 Winchcombe GL54 ... 174 A7
Blenheim Dr
Bredon GL20 ... 182 C7
Bristol BS34 ... 29 B4
3 Ledbury HR8 ... 178 F7
28 Newent GL18 ... 171 A4
Yate BS37 ... 43 D3
Blenheim Ho GL3 ... 120 A7
Blenheim Orch GL51 ... 129 E2
Blenheim Rd Bristol BS6 ... 18 B3
Gloucester GL1 ... 196 C1
Blenheim Sq GL51 ... 132 E3
Blenheim St BS5 ... 19 A1
Blenman Cl BS16 ... 20 A7
Bleriot Rd GL54 ... 169 D6
Blethwin Cl BS10 ... 27 F1
Blimeshire GL15 ... 155 F1
Blind La
Chipping Campden GL55 ... 188 F1
Tetbury GL8 ... 140 C5
Blinkhorns Bridge La GL2 ... 127 B1
Blockley CE Sch GL56 ... 186 C6
Bloomfield Rd Bristol BS4 ... 9 D4
Gloucester GL1 ... 118 D7
Bloomfield Road Link BS4 9 C4
Bloomfield Terr GL1 ... 118 D6
Bloomsbury St GL51 ... 193 A4
Bloxham Rd WR12 ... 188 A1
Bloxhams Orch GL19 ... 172 D4
Bloy Sq BS5 ... 19 C1
Bloy St BS5 ... 19 C1
Blue Boys' Pk GL6 ... 148 A4
Blue Coat CE Prim Sch GL12 ... 68 B6
Blue La GL18 ... 170 D4
Blue Quarry Rd GL7 ... 190 E5
Blue Rock Cres 5 GL15 155 D1
Bluebell Chase GL6 ... 148 C6
Bluebell Cl Bristol BS9 ... 17 B6
Gloucester GL4 ... 119 D5
Thornbury BS35 ... 64 D2
Bluebell Dr NP16 ... 60 F5
Bluebell Gr GL51 ... 130 A5
Bluebell Rise GL6 ... 148 C6
Bluebells The BS32 ... 29 F7
Blundson Hill SN26 ... 144 C2
Blunts Hay GL7 ... 153 C8
Boakes Dr GL10 ... 97 E6
Bobble Ct GL54 ... 169 C6
Bockenem Cl BS35 ... 51 D7
Bodey Cl BS30 ... 11 A5
Bodiam Ave GL4 ... 118 B1
Bodmin Wlk BS4 ... 2 F8
Bodnam Rd GL51 ... 132 E4
Bodyce Rd 4 BS35 ... 51 A5
Boiling Wells La BS2 ... 19 A3
Boleyn Cl GL3 ... 127 F7
Boleyn Cotts GL51 ... 133 B7
Boleyn Ho GL54 ... 139 F5
Bolton Rd BS7 ... 18 E3
Bond St BS1 ... 195 B3
Bond's La SN14 ... 24 E1
Bondend Rd GL4 ... 119 F2
Bonds Mill Est GL10 ... 97 C7
Bonnington Wlk BS7 ... 19 B7
Bonville Bsns Ctr BS4 ... 9 F2
Bonville Rd BS4 ... 9 F2
Book End GL17 ... 164 F5
Boot La BS3 ... 8 D4
Bootenhay Rd GL52 ... 138 A4
Booth Rd BS3 ... 8 C4
Borage Cl GL4 ... 119 F5
Bordesley Rd BS14 ... 3 A3
Borleyton Wlk BS13 ... 1 F4
Born Ct 10 HR8 ... 178 F8
Borough Cl GL10 ... 98 A3
Borver Gr BS13 ... 2 B4
Boscombe Cres BS16 ... 20 F7
Boscombe La GL6 ... 90 E1
Bospin La GL5 ... 98 F1
Boston Rd BS7 ... 18 F8
Boswell St 4 BS5 ... 19 C2
Botany SN6 ... 145 C3
Botham Dr BS4 ... 9 E1
Boucher Pl 2 BS2 ... 19 A2
Boulters Rd BS13 ... 2 C4
Boulton La GL11 ... 88 B1
Boulton Rd GL50 ... 133 D5
Boulton's La 6 BS15 ... 10 D8
Boulton's Rd 5 BS15 ... 10 D8
Bouncer's La GL52 ... 134 B3
Boundary Cotts GL3 ... 121 A4
Boundary Pl GL19 ... 172 A7
Boundary Rd
Avonmouth BS11 ... 26 D3
Coalpit Heath BS36 ... 31 D7
Bourchier Gdns BS13 ... 2 B3
Bourne Cl Bristol BS15 ... 10 B8
Winterbourne BS36 ... 30 E7
Bourne La
Brimscombe GL5 ... 148 A5
Bristol BS5 ... 19 B2
Bourne Lake Pk SN6 ... 143 C3
Bourne Rd BS15 ... 10 B8
Bourne The GL7 ... 153 D8
Bourneville Rd BS5 ... 9 D8
Bournside Cl GL51 ... 130 A7
Bournside Dr GL51 ... 130 A7
Bournside Rd GL51 ... 130 B7
Boursland Cl BS32 ... 40 D2
Bourton Ave BS34 ... 29 C8
Bourton Cl BS34 ... 29 C8
Bourton Mead BS41 ... 7 A1
Bourton Rd
Gloucester GL4 ... 118 E2
Moreton-in-M GL56 ... 187 A3
Bourton Wlk BS13 ... 2 A8
Bourton-on-the-Water Prim Sch GL54 ... 168 F8
Bouverie St BS5 ... 9 B8
Boverton Ave GL3 ... 120 E6
Boverton Dr GL3 ... 120 D6
Boverton Rd BS34 ... 29 B4
Bovone La GL2 ... 124 D8
Bow La
5 Bourton-on-t-W GL54 ... 168 F7
Ripple GL20 ... 181 D8
Bow Wow GL7 ... 143 A8
Bowbridge La
Prestbury GL52 ... 134 B5
Stroud GL5 ... 99 D6
Bowbridge Lock GL5 ... 99 D5
Bowden Cl BS9 ... 17 C8
Bowden Pl BS16 ... 20 F7
Bowden Rd BS5 ... 19 E1
Bowen Cl GL52 ... 134 A3
Bowen's Hill 15 GL16 ... 155 A5
Bowen's Hill Rd 14 GL16 ... 155 A5
Bower Ashton Terr BS3 ... 7 F4
Bower Ct BS3 ... 8 A2
Bower Rd BS3 ... 8 A3
Bower Wlk BS3 ... 8 E3
Bowerleaze BS9 ... 17 C5
Bowes Lyon Cl GL56 ... 187 A2
Bowl Hill GL5 ... 99 A3
Bowldown Cotts GL8 ... 71 A5
Bowldown Rd GL8 ... 71 C3
Bowler Rd GL20 ... 182 C5
Bowlers Lea GL11 ... 87 F5
Bowling Green Ave GL7 190 C6
Bowling Green Cres GL7 ... 190 C6
Bowling Green Ct GL56 ... 187 A3
Bowling Green La GL7 ... 190 C6
Bowling Green Rd GL7 ... 190 C6
Bowling Hill BS37 ... 44 A1
Bowling Hill Bsns Pk BS37 ... 44 A1
Bowling Rd BS37 ... 33 B8
Bowly Cres GL7 ... 150 E2
Bowly Rd Cirencester GL7 190 B2
Gloucester GL1 ... 118 D6
Bowmead 7 BS4 ... 9 D1
Bownham Mead GL5 ... 99 D2
Bownham Park Sch GL5 ... 99 D2
Bownham Pk GL5 ... 99 D1
Bowood BS16 ... 30 C1
Bowring Cl BS13 ... 2 C3
Bowsland BS32 ... 40 E2
Bowsland Green Sch BS32 ... 40 E2
Bowsland Way BS32 ... 40 D2
Bowson Rd GL15 ... 155 D1
Bowstreet La BS35 ... 28 A8
Box Cres GL6 ... 91 F6
Box La GL6 ... 91 F5
Box Rd GL11 ... 88 A8
Box Road Ave GL11 ... 88 A8
Box Tree Cl GL17 ... 163 F4
Box Wlk BS31 ... 4 C4
Boxbush Cl GL7 ... 143 A8
Boxbush Rd
Coleford GL16 ... 155 A5
South Cerney GL7 ... 143 A8
Boxhedge Farm La BS36 ... 31 E3
Boxwell Rd GL8 ... 70 B4
Boxwood Cl GL8 ... 82 B5
Boyce Cl GL4 ... 119 E3
Boyce Dr BS2 ... 19 A2
Boyce's Ave BS8 ... 194 A3
Boyd Cl BS30 ... 12 B7
Boyd Rd BS31 ... 5 D3
Brabazon Rd BS34 ... 29 B2
Bracelands GL6 ... 148 C7
Bracelands Dr 1 GL16 ... 155 A7
Bracewell Gdns BS10 ... 28 C4
Bracey Dr BS16 ... 20 C6

Bracken Cl GL15 ....92 C3
Bracken Dr GL15 ....92 B3
Brackenbury Dr BS34 ....29 F5
Brackendene BS32 ....40 C1
Bracton Dr BS14 ....3 A5
Bradeston Gr BS16 ....20 A7
Bradford Rd 5 GL2 ....127 B2
Bradfords Cl GL18 ....170 F4
Bradfords Ct GL18 ....170 F4
Bradfords La GL18 ....170 F4
Bradhurst St 7 BS5 ....9 B6
Bradley Ave Bristol BS11 ..16 E6
Winterbourne BS36 ....30 E5
Bradley Cl GL2 ....127 C4
Bradley Court Rd GL17 .164 D6
Bradley Cres BS11 ....16 E6
Bradley Ct BS16 ....20 C5
Bradley Pavilions BS32 ..40 C2
Bradley Rd Bristol BS34 ..39 F1
Charlton Kings GL53 ....131 A4
Wooton-u-E GL12 ....68 A8
Bradley Rise GL17 ....164 D6
Bradley St GL12 ....68 A7
Bradley Stoke Way BS32 .29 E7
Bradshaw Cl GL2 ....127 E5
Bradstone Rd BS36 ....30 D5
Bradwell Gr BS10 ....18 C8
Brae Wlk GL4 ....119 D4
Braemar Ave BS7 ....28 F1
Braemar Cres BS7 ....28 F1
Braemor Ct BS9 ....18 A8
Bragg's La BS2 ....195 C3
Braikenridge Rd BS4 ....9 D4
Brainsfield BS9 ....17 F6
Brake Cl
Bristol, Bradley Stoke BS32 .29 E7
Bristol, Warmley Hill BS15 ..10 F7
Brake The
Coalpit Heath BS36 ....31 C5
Yate BS37 ....43 E5
Brakewell Gdns BS14 ....3 A4
Bramble Chase GL52 ..137 F4
Bramble Dr Bristol BS9 ..17 D3
Dursley GL11 ....88 A3
Bramble La Bristol BS9 ..17 C3
Stonehouse GL10 ....97 F8
Bramble Lawn GL4 ....119 D3
Bramble Rd GL16 ....155 B4
Bramble Rise GL52 ....134 C3
Brambles The
Berkeley GL13 ....85 E4
Keynsham BS31 ....4 D3
Lea HR9 ....164 C8
Brambling Wlk BS16 ....19 F6
Bramley Cl
Kingswood GL12 ....67 F4
4 Ledbury HR8 ....178 E7
Olveston BS35 ....50 A3
Pill BS20 ....16 C4
Bramley Ct 6 BS30 ....10 F4
Bramley Dr GL19 ....165 D6
Bramley Mews GL4 ....120 A6
Bramley Rd
Cheltenham GL51 ....132 F3
Tewkesbury GL20 ....192 D6
Bramleys The GL17 ....164 F5
Branch Hill Rise GL53 ..131 A4
Branch Rd
Bamfurlong GL51 ....129 A7
Cheltenham GL51 ....129 B7
Branch The GL17 ....164 B3
Branche Gr BS13 ....2 D3
Brandash Rd BS37 ....44 C1
Branders 15 SN6 ....143 E4
Brandon Cl GL3 ....128 A8
Brandon Ho BS8 ....194 B2
Brandon Pl GL50 ....193 A1
Brandon St BS1 ....194 C2
Brandon Steep BS1 ....194 C2
Brangwyn Gr BS7 ....19 B6
Branksome Cres BS34 ..29 B3
Branksome Dr
Bristol BS34 ....29 B3
Winterbourne BS36 ....30 E6
Branksome Rd BS6 ....18 B3
Brannigan Ct GL20 ....182 C5
Brans La GL56 ....177 C4
Branscombe Ct BS3 ....8 D2
Branscombe Rd BS9 ....17 C4
Bransdown Hill SN16 ....59 A3
Brantwood Rd GL6 ....148 C6
Branwhite Cl BS7 ....19 B7
Brasenose Rd GL20 ....182 C7
Brassington Gdns GL54 .166 E2
Bratches The GL55 ....189 A3
Bratton Rd BS4 ....2 D7
Braunton Rd BS3 ....8 C3
Bravender Ho GL7 ....190 D4
Bray Ave HR8 ....178 F8
Braybrooke Cl GL8 ....140 C4
Braydon Ave BS32 ....29 D7
Braydon La SN6 ....143 D3
Brayne Ct BS30 ....10 F3
Breach Rd BS3 ....8 A3
Breaches Gate BS32 ....29 F6
Breaches The BS20 ....16 B5
Bream Ave GL15 ....155 B1
Bream CE Prim Sch
GL15 ....155 D1
Bream Rd Bream GL15 ..147 E7
St Briavels GL15 ....147 B7
Brean Down Ave BS9 ..18 B5
Brecknock Rd BS4 ....9 A3
Brecon Cl Bristol BS9 ..18 B6
Quedgeley GL2 ....109 E8
Brecon Rd BS9 ....18 B6
Brecon Way GL16 ....155 C8
Bredon BS37 ....32 D7
Bredon Cl BS15 ....10 F7
Bredon Hancocks Endowed
Fst Sch GL20 ....182 C8
Bredon Lodge GL20 ....182 C7
Bredon Nook Rd BS10 ..18 C7
Bredon Rd GL20 ....192 D6
Bredon Sch (Pull Court)
GL20 ....181 C7
Bredon View WR12 ....185 C8
Bregawn Cl GL52 ....137 E2
Breinton Way GL2 ....127 D5
Brendon Cl BS30 ....11 C4
Brendon Rd BS3 ....8 D3
Brenner St BS5 ....19 B2
Brensham Ct GL3 ....120 A7
Brent Rd BS7 ....18 F5
Brentry Ave 5 BS5 ....9 B7
Brentry Hospl BS10 ....28 B2
Brentry La BS10 ....28 B3
Brentry Lo BS10 ....28 A3
Brentry Prim Sch BS10 ..28 B4
Brentry Rd BS16 ....19 F3
Brereton Way BS30 ....11 B4
Bretforton Fst Sch
WR11 ....188 A6
Bretforton Rd WR11 ....188 B7
Brewerton Cl BS10 ....28 C3
Brewery Cotts NP25 ....154 C5
Brewery Hill BS30 ....5 F7
Brewery La
Nailsworth GL6 ....91 B3
Thrupp GL5 ....99 E2
Brewery Row GL56 ....187 F1
Brewery St SN6 ....145 D3
Brewery Yd 25 GL54 ....176 F4
Briar Cl GL5 ....103 D1
Briar Ct BS20 ....16 C4
Briar Lawn GL4 ....119 D3
Briar Way BS16 ....20 C3
Briar Wlk Bristol BS16 ..20 C3
Prestbury GL52 ....134 C3
Briarbank Rise GL52 ....131 C7
Briarfield Ave BS15 ....10 C5
Briarleaze BS35 ....50 F2
Briars Cl GL3 ....128 A6
Briarside Ho BS10 ....28 D3
Briarside Rd BS10 ....28 D3
Briarwood BS9 ....17 F6
Briarwood Sch BS16 ....20 B3
Briary Rd GL7 ....153 E3
Briavels Gr BS6 ....18 F2
Brick Cotts BS35 ....62 E1
Brick St BS2 ....195 C3
Brick Wlk WR11 ....188 C6
Brickfield Terr GL5 ....99 A6
Brickfields GL12 ....68 B6
Bricknell Ave GL20 ....182 C7
Brickrow GL5 ....99 C7
Bridewell St BS1 ....195 A3
Bridge Cl
Cirencester GL7 ....190 D2
Gloucester GL2 ....118 B6
Whitchurch BS14 ....3 C4
Bridge End
Cirencester GL7 ....190 D3
Staunton GL19 ....180 C2
Bridge Farm GL2 ....126 B7
Bridge Farm Cl BS14 ....3 A3
Bridge Farm Inf Sch BS14 3 A4
Bridge Farm Jun Sch
BS14 ....3 A4
Bridge Rd
Bristol, Eastville BS5 ....19 B3
Bristol, Lower Soundwell
BS15 ....21 A3
Bristol, Shortwood BS16 ..21 C4
Cirencester GL7 ....190 D2
Frampton on Severn GL2 .157 F3
Harrow Hill GL17 ....164 B3
Leigh Woods BS8 ....7 E6
Sharpness GL13 ....93 C1
Stroud GL5 ....98 D6
Yate BS37 ....43 A2
Bridge St Blakeney GL15 .156 D1
Bretforton WR11 ....188 A6
Bristol BS1 ....195 A2
Bristol, Eastville BS5 ....19 D2
Cheltenham GL51 ....133 B4
Chepstow NP16 ....72 F1
Fairford GL7 ....152 E4
Ledbury HR8 ....178 E8
Nailsworth GL6 ....91 C4
Newent GL18 ....171 A5
Stroud GL5 ....98 E6
Bridge Valley Rd BS8 ....7 E8
Bridge Way BS36 ....31 B8
Bridge Wlk BS7 ....19 A8
Bridge-Side GL5 ....98 F6
Bridgeleap Rd BS16 ....20 F8
Bridgemans Cl WR12 ....188 B1
Bridgend Ct GL10 ....97 E6
Bridgend Rd GL51 ....129 C7
Bridges Ct 2 BS16 ....20 B4
Bridges Dr BS16 ....20 C6
Bridget Dr NP16 ....61 A7
Bridgman Gr BS34 ....29 B3
Bridgwater Rd BS41,BS13,
BS48 ....1 D6
Bridle The GL5 ....98 D7
Bridle Way BS35 ....50 F4
Briercliffe Rd BS9 ....17 D7
Brierley Banks GL17 ....163 F2
Brierley Cl GL4 ....119 E5
Brierley Council Hos
GL17 ....163 F2
Brierley Rd GL17 ....163 F3
Brierley Way GL15 ....156 B1
Brierly Furlong BS34 ....29 D3
Briery Leaze Rd BS14 ....3 A4
Bright St
Bristol, Barton Hill BS5 ....9 B7
Bristol, Kingswood BS15 ..10 D8
Brightlands GL14 ....157 A6
Brighton Cres BS3 ....8 B2
Brighton Mews BS8 ....194 B4
Brighton Pk 16 BS5 ....9 B8
Brighton Pl BS15 ....20 D1
Brighton Rd
Bristol, Patchway BS34 ....28 F8
Bristol, Redland BS6 ....18 C1
Cheltenham GL52 ....133 F1
Brighton St 13 BS2 ....18 E1
Brighton Terr 9 BS3 ....8 B2
Brigstocke Rd BS2 ....195 B4
Brimbles BS7 ....29 B2
Brimley GL10 ....97 F4
Brimscombe CE Prim Sch
GL5 ....99 F1
Brimscombe Hill GL5 ....91 E8
Brimscombe La GL5 ....99 F1
Brimsham Green Sec Sch
BS37 ....43 D4
Brimsome Mdw GL2 ..125 D5
Brindle Cl GL4 ....119 C4
Brinkmarsh La GL12 ....65 D2
Brinkworthy Rd BS16 ....19 E6
Brinmead Wlk BS13 ....1 F3
Brins Cl BS34 ....29 F4
Brinsham La BS37 ....44 A6
Brionne Way GL2 ....127 B5
Brisbane GL10 ....101 F1
Briscoes Ave BS13 ....2 D4
Brislington Hill BS4 ....9 E2
Brislington Ret Pk BS4 ....9 E1
Brislington Sch BS4 ....3 F8
Brislington Trad Est BS4 ..9 F2
Bristol & Anchor Ho 7
BS5 ....9 D8
Bristol Bsns Pk BS16 ....29 E1
Bristol Cathedral★ BS1 194 C2
Bristol Cathedral Sch
BS1 ....194 C2
Bristol City Coll Brunel Ctr
BS7 ....18 F4
Bristol City Fball Gd BS3 ..7 F3
Bristol City Mus & Art Gal★
BS8 ....194 C3
Bristol Dental Hospl
BS1 ....195 A3
Bristol Eye Hospl BS1 ..195 A3
Bristol Gate 1 BS8 ....7 F5
Bristol General Hospl
BS1 ....195 A1
Bristol Gram Sch BS8 ..194 C3
Bristol Harbour Rly★
BS1 ....194 C1
Bristol Hill BS4 ....9 D2
Bristol Homeopathic Hospl
BS8 ....194 C4
Bristol Ind Mus★ BS1 ..195 A1
Bristol Old Vic Theatre Sch
BS8 ....18 A1
Bristol Parkway N BS34 .30 A5
Bristol Parkway Sta BS34 29 E4
Bristol Rd Bristol BS16 ....30 C2
Cambridge GL2 ....95 F3
Cirencester GL7 ....190 D3
Cromhall GL12 ....53 B7
Frampton Cotterell BS36 ..42 B3
Gloucester GL1,GL2 ....118 C6
Keynsham BS31 ....4 E6
Luckington SN14 ....47 E3
Stonehouse GL10 ....97 E7
Thornbury BS35 ....51 B8
Upper Rissington GL54 ..169 D7
Whitchurch BS14 ....3 D3
Winterbourne BS16 ....30 D4
Bristol Royal Infmy BS2 195 A4
Bristol Vale Ctr For Ind
BS3 ....8 B1
Bristol Waldorf Sch
BS8 ....194 B3
Bristol Zoo Gdns★ BS8 ..17 F1
Bristow Broadway BS11 .26 C1
Bristowe Ho BS16 ....20 B5
Britannia Cres BS34 ....29 D5
Britannia Ct 1 BS16 ....20 D5
Britannia Rd
Bristol, Kingswood BS15 ..10 C8
Bristol, Lower Easton BS5 ..19 C1
Bristol, Patchway BS34 ....28 E7
Britannia Way GL52 ....138 B3
British Rd BS3 ....8 C3
British Sch The GL12 ....68 C6
Briton Cl NP16 ....61 A4
Brittania Bldgs BS8 ....194 A1
Britten Ct 10 BS30 ....10 F4
Britten Pl GL51 ....132 E2
Brittons Pass SN14 ....14 F8
Brixham Rd BS3 ....8 C1
Brixton Rd BS5 ....9 B8
Brixton Road Mews 22
BS5 ....9 B8
Brizen La GL53 ....130 B4
Broad Croft BS32 ....40 C2
Broad La
Coalpit Heath BS36 ....31 D5
Westerleigh BS37 ....32 A4
Yate BS37 ....43 C4
Broad Leys Rd GL4 ....119 D7
Broad Marston Rd GL55 189 A7
Broad Oak Rd BS13 ....1 F4
Broad Oak Way GL51 ..129 F6
Broad Oaks BS8 ....7 E6
Broad Plain BS2 ....195 C2
Broad Quay BS1 ....195 A2
Broad Rd BS15 ....20 C1
Broad St Bristol BS1 ....195 A3
Bristol, Staple Hill BS16 ..20 F4
Chipping Sodbury BS37 ....44 B1
Hartpury GL19 ....172 C4
King's Stanley GL10 ....98 A3
13 Newent GL18 ....171 A4
Stroud GL5 ....98 D3
Broad Weir BS1 ....195 B3
Broad Wlk BS4 ....9 A2
Broad Wlk The GL50 ....193 B2
Broadacre Cl GL20 ....182 C7
Broadbury Rd BS4 ....2 E8
Broadclose Rd GL2 ....173 B2
Broadfield Ave BS15 ....20 C1
Broadfield Cotts GL54 ..160 C6
Broadfield Rd Bristol BS4 ..9 A1
Eastington GL10 ....96 F8
Broadlands Ave BS31 ....4 D6
Broadlands Ct GL54 ....168 F7
Broadlands Dr BS11 ....27 A1
Broadlands Sch BS31 ....4 D6
Broadleas BS13 ....2 C7
Broadleaze Bristol BS11 ..16 E7
Down Ampney GL7 ....143 F8
Broadleys Ave BS9 ....18 C7
Broadmead BS1 ....195 B3
Broadmead La BS31 ....5 A6
Broadmere GL11 ....87 E4
Broadmere Cl GL11 ....87 E3
Broadmoor La BA1 ....6 F4
Broadmoor Pk GL14 ....191 B7
Broadmoor Rd GL14 ....191 B7
Broadoak Hill BS41 ....1 F2
Broadoak Wlk BS16 ....20 B4
Broadstone Cl GL4 ....119 E8
Broadstone Wlk BS13 ....2 D5
Broadwalk Sh Ctr BS4 ....9 B2
Broadway Gloucester GL4 118 F5
Saltford BS31 ....5 D3
Yate BS37 ....43 F2
Broadway Ave BS9 ....18 D6
Broadway Bears & Dolls
Mus★ WR12 ....185 C8
Broadway Cl
Kempsford GL7 ....144 E8
Prestbury GL52 ....134 A5
Broadway Fst Sch
WR12 ....188 B1
Broadway Inf Sch BS37 ..43 F2
Broadway La
Minsterworth GL2 ....116 A2
South Cerney GL7 ....143 A6
Broadway Rd
Bristol, Bishopston BS7 ..18 D3
Bristol, Bishopsworth BS13 ..1 F5
Mickleton GL55 ....189 A6
Toddington GL54 ....184 C3
Willersey WR12 ....188 B2
Winchcombe GL54 ....174 A7
Broadway The
Chalford GL6 ....148 E6
Dursley GL11 ....80 A8
North Nibley GL11 ....79 F8
Broadway Tower Ctry Pk★
WR12 ....185 D4
Broadways Dr BS16 ....19 F7
Broadwell Bridge 7
GL16 ....155 B6
Broadwell Cl GL4 ....119 E5
Broadwell Rd GL56 ....177 C5
Broadwell Terr GL11 ....88 B1
Brock Cl GL51 ....129 B6
Brockeridge Cl GL2 ....117 E2
Brockeridge Inf Sch
BS36 ....31 C7
Brockeridge Rd GL20 ..181 F7
Brockhampton Pk GL54 174 B1
Brockhollands Rd GL15 147 D8
Brockhurst Gdns BS15 ..10 A8
Brockhurst Rd BS15 ....10 A8
Brockley Acres GL6 ....148 C7
Brockley Cl BS34 ....29 C7
Brockley Ct GL56 ....186 C6
Brockley Rd
Leonard Stanley GL10 ....97 F4
Saltford BS31 ....5 D3
Brockley Wlk BS13 ....2 A8
Brockmoor La HR9 ....170 C4
Brockridge La BS36 ....31 C7
Brocks 4 BS4 ....9 D1
Brocks Rd BS13 ....2 C3
Brockworth BS37 ....32 C6
Brockworth Comp Sch
GL3 ....120 F6
Brockworth Cotts GL3 ..120 F4
Brockworth Cres BS16 ..19 F6
Brockworth Prim Sch
GL3 ....120 E5
Brockworth Rd GL3 ....128 E2
Brome Rd GL4 ....119 F5
Bromfield Wlk BS16 ....21 B7
Bromley Dr BS16 ....20 D8
Bromley Heath Ave BS16 20 D8
Bromley Heath Jun & Inf
Schs BS16 ....20 E8
Bromley Heath Rd BS16 .20 D8
Bromley Rd Bristol BS7 ..18 F5
Ellwood GL16 ....155 C3
Brompton Cl BS15 ....11 A8
Broncksea Rd BS7 ....28 F1
Bronte Cl 2 GL51 ....129 F7
Bronte Dr 2 HR8 ....178 E8
Brook Cl Long Ashton BS41 ..7 B1
15 Northleach GL54 ....168 A1
Winchcombe GL54 ....139 F4
Brook Ct
Cheltenham GL50 ....130 B6
Brook Ct *continued*
Tewkesbury GL20 ....192 E5
Brook Gate BS3 ....7 E1
Brook Hill BS6 ....18 F1
Brook Ho Bristol BS34 ....29 C8
3 Thornbury BS35 ....51 C8
Brook House (Dean Close
Sch) GL51 ....129 F7
Brook La
1 Blockley GL56 ....186 C5
Bristol, Montpelier BS6 ....18 F1
Bristol, Stapleton BS16 ....19 E6
Down Hatherley GL2 ....173 B1
Brook Lintons BS4 ....9 D3
Brook Rd
Bristol, Montpelier BS6 ....18 F1
Bristol, Southville BS3 ....8 D4
Bristol, Speedwell BS5 ....19 F1
Bristol, Warmley BS15 ....11 B8
Bristol,Hillfields BS16 ....20 B4
Bristol,Mangotsfield BS16 ..20 F6
Cheltenham GL51 ....133 A4
Brook St Bristol BS5 ....9 C7
Chipping Sodbury BS37 ....33 A8
Gloucester GL1 ....196 B1
Mitcheldean GL17 ....164 D5
Brook Vale GL52 ....131 A7
Brook Way BS32 ....29 D8
Brookcote Dr BS34 ....29 D6
Brookdale Rd BS13 ....2 B6
Brooke Rd GL7 ....190 B2
Brookfield SN6 ....145 C3
Brookfield Ave BS7 ....18 D3
Brookfield Cl BS37 ....44 C2
Brookfield La
2 Bristol BS6 ....18 D2
Churchdown GL3 ....128 E5
Brookfield Rd
3 Bristol, Montpelier BS6 .18 D2
Bristol, Patchway BS34 ....29 B8
Churchdown GL3 ....128 D5
Gloucester GL3 ....119 F7
Brookfield Senior Sch
GL51 ....130 A7
Brookfield Wlk BS30 ....11 C3
Brookhouse La SN14 ....24 D1
Brookhouse Mill GL6 ....104 A7
Brookland Rd BS6 ....18 D5
Brooklands Pk GL2 ....127 D5
Brooklea BS30 ....11 B3
Brookleaze BS9 ....17 C5
Brooklyn Cl 4 GL51 ....132 F3
Brooklyn Ct GL51 ....133 A4
Brooklyn Gdns GL51 ..133 A3
Brooklyn Rd Bristol BS13 ..2 B8
Cheltenham GL51 ....132 F2
Brookmead BS35 ....51 D7
Brookridge Ct 5 BS16 ..20 D4
Brookridge Ho BS10 ....27 F3
Brooksdale La GL53 ....130 C6
Brookside Alderton GL20 .183 E4
Crudwell SN16 ....141 C3
4 Newent GL18 ....171 A4
Paxford GL55 ....186 E8
Pill BS20 ....16 D3
Tewkesbury GL20 ....192 E6
Tintern Parva NP16 ....146 B3
Brookside Cotts GL5 ....91 B5
Brookside Dr BS36 ....31 B8
Brookside Rd Bristol BS4 ..9 E2
Cinderford GL14 ....191 B5
Brookside Villas GL2 ....127 B2
Brookthorpe BS37 ....32 D8
Brookthorpe Ave BS11 ..27 A1
Brookthorpe Cl GL4 ....118 D3
Brookview Wlk BS13 ....2 B7
Brookway Dr GL53 ....131 A6
Brookway Rd GL53 ....131 A6
Broom Bglws GL4 ....119 A5
Broom Hill Bristol BS16 ..19 E5
Coleford GL16 ....154 F7
Broom Ho GL4 ....119 A5
Broomhill Jun & Inf Schs
BS4 ....9 F3
Broomhill Rd BS4 ....10 A2
Brooms The BS16 ....31 A1
Brotherswood Ct BS32 ..40 D4
Broughton Ho BS1 ....195 B1
Brown Cl GL51 ....132 E3
Brown's End Cotts HR8 179 C5
Brown's La GL10 ....98 A6
Brown's Piece GL12 ....68 B7
Browne Ct 4 BS8 ....7 F6
Browning Ct BS7 ....19 B8
Browning Mews GL51 ..129 F7
Browns Hill GL6 ....148 B5
Brownshill Rd GL6 ....148 B5
Broxholme Wlk BS11 ....16 F8
Bruce Ave BS5 ....19 C1
Bruce Rd BS5 ....19 C1
Brummels Dr GL16 ....155 A7
Brunel Cl BS30 ....11 C7
Brunel Ct BS37 ....43 C2
Brunel Lock Rd BS1 ....7 F5
Brunel Rd Bristol BS13 ....2 A8
Chepstow NP16 ....60 E6
Brunel Way Bristol BS1,BS3 .7 F4
Honeybourne WR11 ....188 C7
Stonehouse GL10 ....101 C1
Thornbury BS35 ....51 B7
Brunswest Ct GL1 ....196 B2
Brunswick Pl 10 BS1 ....7 F5
Brunswick Rd GL1 ....196 B2
Brunswick Sq
Bristol BS2 ....195 B4

Brunswick Sq *continued*
Gloucester GL1 196 B2
Brunswick St Bristol BS2 195 B4
Bristol, Redfield BS5 9 C7
Cheltenham GL50 133 D3
Brush The GL5 98 D8
Bruton Cl BS5 9 F8
Bruton Pl BS8 194 B3
Bruton Way GL1 196 C2
Bryansons Cl BS16 19 D6
Bryant's Hill BS5 10 B6
Bryants Cl BS16 30 C1
Bryaston Cl GL51 133 A2
Bryerland Rd GL3 121 A4
Brymore Ave GL52 134 A5
Brymore Cl GL52 134 A5
Brynland Ave BS7 18 E4
Bryony Bank GL53 130 B4
Bryworth La GL7 153 C3
Buchan Ho 7 GL56 186 C5
Buchanan Ave GL16 155 A6
Buchanan Cl 2 GL16 155 A6
Buckholt Rd GL4 112 E8
Buckholt Way GL3 120 E5
Buckholt Wood Nature Reserve* GL4 112 F7
Buckingham Ave GL51 132 F2
Buckingham Cl GL10 96 E8
Buckingham Ct
Bristol BS32 40 D3
Cheltenham GL50 193 B3
Buckingham Dr
Bristol BS34 29 D5
2 Churchdown GL3 128 A7
Buckingham Gdns BS16 20 E6
Buckingham Ho BS34 28 F2
Buckingham Pl
Bristol BS8 194 A3
Bristol, Mangotsfield BS16 20 E6
Buckingham Rd BS4 9 D5
Buckingham St BS3 8 C2
Buckingham Vale BS8 194 A4
Buckland Cl GL52 137 F3
Buckle St
Broadway WR12,GL54, GL56 185 D5
Honeybourne WR11 188 C8
Weston-s-E GL55 188 D4
Buckle's Row GL53 131 B5
Bucklehaven GL53 130 F5
Buckles Cl GL53 131 B5
Buckshaft Rd GL14 191 C1
Buckstone Cl GL16 155 B7
Budd Ho 1 BS2 18 F1
Budding Rd GL10 96 E8
Budding The GL5 103 E1
Buddleia Cl GL4 119 F4
Buddleia Ct 7 GL3 128 A7
Bude Ave BS5 10 A8
Bude Rd BS34 29 B4
Buildings The GL11 87 D3
Bull La Bristol BS5 9 F6
Gloucester GL1 196 B3
Pill BS20 16 C4
27 Winchcombe GL54 174 A7
Bull Pitch GL11 88 B1
Bull Ring The GL17 164 D5
Bullens Cl BS32 40 D2
Buller Rd BS4 9 C2
Bulley La Birdwood GL2 165 F6
Churcham GL2 124 C3
Bullfinch Rd GL4 119 C6
Bullfinch Way GL3 127 D7
Bullingham Ct GL51 133 C3
Bulls Cross GL6 104 B6
Bully La BS37 53 D1
Bulwark Ave NP16 60 F5
Bulwark Rd NP16 60 E7
Bulwarks The GL6 148 A3
Bunting Hill GL6 91 A4
Bunting Way GL6 90 F4
Burbank Cl BS30 11 A3
Burchells Ave BS15 20 B1
Burchells Green Cl BS15 20 B1
Burchells Green Rd BS15 20 B1
Burcombe Cl BS36 31 D6
Burcombe La GL7 158 A3
Burcombe Rd GL6 148 C6
Burcombe Way GL6 148 C6
Burcott Rd BS11 26 D5
Burden Cl BS32 29 F6
Burdett Cl GL10 97 F7
Burdett Rd GL10 97 F7
Burfoot Rd BS14 3 E4
Burfoote Gdns BS14 3 E4
Burford Dr GL5 99 A7
Burford Gr BS11 16 F5
Burford Mews GL1 119 A8
Burford St GL7 153 E2
Burgage NP25 154 A8
Burgage Cl BS37 33 B8
Burgage The GL52 134 B5
Burge Ct GL7 190 D3
Burgess Green Cl BS4 9 E7
Burghill Rd BS10 28 A1
Burghley Ct BS36 30 E5
Burghley Rd BS6 18 E2
Burgis Rd BS14 3 D6
Burleigh Croft GL3 119 F8
Burleigh La GL5 91 F8
Burleigh Tor GL5 91 F7
Burleigh View 7 GL6 148 B6
Burleigh Way GL12 54 B5
Burley Ave BS16 20 F5
Burley Crest BS16 20 F5
Burley Gr BS16 20 F5
Burlington Ct 9 BS6 18 B2
Burlington Rd BS6 18 B2
Burltons The GL12 66 B2
Burma Ave GL52 134 B2
Burma Rd GL6 91 A4
Burnbush Cl BS14 3 E6
Burnbush Prim Sch BS14 3 D5
Burnell Dr BS2 195 C4
Burneside Cl BS10 28 C2
Burnet Cl GL4 119 A4
Burnett Bsns Pk BS31 5 B1
Burney Way BS30 11 A3
Burnham Cl BS15 20 F1
Burnham Dr BS15 20 F1
Burnham Rd BS11 16 D6
Burns Ave GL2 118 C4
Burnt Barn Rd NP16 60 F4
Burnt Oak GL11 88 A2
Burrington Wlk BS13 2 A8
Burrough Way BS36 30 E6
Burrups La HR9 170 B5
Burton Cl BS1 195 B1
Burton Ct Bristol BS8 194 B3
2 Bristol, Upper Eastville BS16 19 E3
Burton Rd GL9 35 F6
Burton St GL50 193 A4
Burtons Bank OX7 169 F7
Burwalls Rd BS8 7 E6
Bury Bar La GL18 171 A4
Bury Court Rd GL14 157 F6
Bury Hill BS36 30 F3
Bury Hill La BS37 44 A8
Bury Hill View BS16 30 E1
Bury La Doynton BS30 12 F7
Minsterworth GL2 116 E7
Burycourt Cl BS11 27 A1
Burytown La SN26 144 E1
Buscombe Gdns GL3 120 B7
Bush Ave BS34 29 D5
Bush Cl GL10 96 F8
Bush Ct Alveston BS32 50 F5
10 Bristol BS4 8 F4
Prestbury GL52 134 B3
Bush Hay GL3 128 B5
Bush Ind Est BS5 9 D8
Bushcombe Cl GL52 138 C3
Bushcombe La GL52 138 D4
Bushes La BS37 45 A6
Bushy Beeches GL6 105 D7
Bushy Ho BS2 8 F3
Bushy Pk BS4 8 F3
Bushy Way GL51 132 D5
Business Pk The BS13 2 E3
Bussage CE Prim Sch GL6 148 B6
Bussage Hill GL6 148 B6
Butcher Hill's La GL6 91 B3
Butcombe Wlk BS14 3 B5
Bute Cl SN6 145 C4
Butler Ho 5 BS5 9 F8
Butler's Field GL7 153 E3
Butlers Cl Bristol BS5 9 F7
Sherston SN16 58 C1
Butlers Mead GL15 156 E1
Butlers Wlk 3 BS5 9 F6
Butt Gn GL6 111 F1
Butt La BS35 64 C3
Butt St GL6 148 A3
Butt's La Dyrham SN14 24 B4
Woodmancote GL52 138 C4
Butt's Wlk GL51 129 C7
Buttercliffe Rise BS41 7 C3
Buttercross La GL52 134 D3
Buttercup Lawn GL4 119 D2
Butterfield Cl BS10 18 E7
Butterfield Rd BS10 18 E7
Butterfleld Cl BS36 31 B6
Buttermere Cl GL51 129 F6
Buttermilk La GL3 128 C6
Butterow W GL5 99 B5
Butterrow Hill GL5 99 C4
Butterrow La GL5 99 D4
Buttersend La GL19 171 F4
Butterworth Ct BS4 2 D7
Buttington GL4 119 F5
Buttington Hill NP16 61 B7
Buttington Rd NP16 61 A7
Buttington Terr NP16 61 B6
Button Cl BS14 3 A6
Button Mills Est GL10 97 E6
Butts Farm (Open Farm)* GL7 151 A1
Butts La GL15 156 E2
Butts The Crudwell SN16 141 C3
Gloucester GL4 119 A4
Newent GL18 171 A5
Buxton Wlk BS7 19 A8
Byard Rd GL2 118 B5
Bybrook Gdns GL4 118 D1
Bybrook Rd GL4 118 D1
Bydemill Gdns SN6 145 C3
Bye Mead BS16 21 B8
Bye St HR8 178 E8
Byfield Cl GL52 138 C2
Byfords Cl GL19 165 D6
Byfords Rd GL19 165 D6
Byron Ave GL2 118 C4
Byron Ct 16 GL52 133 F2
Byron Pl Bristol BS8 194 B3
Bristol, Staple Hill BS16 20 E4
Byron Rd
Cheltenham GL51 132 F1
Dursley GL11 80 C7
Byron St
Bristol, Redfield BS5 9 C7
5 Bristol, St Pauls BS2 19 A1
Byzantine Ct BS1 195 A1

C

Cabot Cl Bristol BS15 10 C7
Chipping Sodbury BS37 43 F1
Saltford BS31 5 D2
Cabot Ct BS7 28 F1
Cabot Gn BS5 9 B7
Cabot Ho 6 BS35 51 C8
Cabot Pk BS11 26 E5
Cabot Prim Sch BS2 195 C4
Cabot Twr* BS8 194 B2
Cabot Way Bristol BS8 7 F5
Pill BS20 16 D3
Cadbury Heath Cty Prim Sch BS30 11 B6
Cadbury Heath Rd BS30 11 B5
Cadbury Rd BS31 5 A2
Caddick Cl BS15 20 F2
Cade Cl
Bristol, Kingswood BS15 10 F6
Bristol, Stoke Gifford BS34 29 E5
Cadmium Rd BS11 26 C4
Cadogan Ho 17 GL52 133 F2
Cadogan Rd BS14 3 A8
Caen Rd BS3 8 E3
Caernarvon Cl GL51 129 E6
Caernarvon Ct GL51 129 D6
Caernarvon Rd
Cheltenham GL51 129 F6
Keynsham BS31 4 C4
Caerwent La NP16 60 F4
Caesar Rd GL2 118 C5
Caesars Cl GL15 92 C4
Caine Rd BS7 18 F7
Cains Cl BS15 10 E6
Cainscross Rd GL5 98 F7
Caird St NP16 60 E7
Cairn Gdns BS36 30 E4
Cairns Ct BS6 18 C4
Cairns Rd BS6 18 C4
Cairns' Cres 12 BS2 18 F1
Cakebridge Pl GL52 133 F3
Cakebridge Rd GL52 133 F4
Cala Trad Est BS3 7 F3
Calcott Rd BS4 9 A3
Calcutt St SN6 143 F4
Caldbeck Cl BS10 28 D2
Calder Cl BS31 5 A4
Calderdale GL4 119 F5
Calderwood Ct GL50 193 B2
Caldicot Cl
Bristol, Lawrence Weston BS11 27 C2
Bristol, Willsbridge BS30 11 B2
Caledonia Mews BS8 7 F6
Caledonia Pl BS8 7 F7
Caledonian Rd
Bristol BS1 194 B1
Gloucester GL4 119 C2
Calendula Ct 10 GL3 128 A7
Calf Way GL6 105 C5
Calf's La GL55 189 A2
California Rd BS30 11 B3
Callicroft Inf Sch BS34 28 F8
Callicroft Jun Sch BS34 28 F8
Callicroft Rd BS34 29 A7
Callington Rd BS4 9 D1
Callowell GL6 103 A1
Callowell Prim Sch GL5 103 A1
Callowhill Ct BS1 195 B3
Calspick Way GL2 127 D5
Calton Jun & Inf Schs GL1 118 E5
Calton Rd GL1 118 E6
Calverley Mews 1 GL51 129 E5
Cam & Dursley Sta GL10 96 A1
Cam Everlands Prim Sch GL11 88 A4
Cam Gn GL11 88 C5
Cam Hopton CE Prim Sch GL11 88 B4
Cam House Sch GL11 88 C2
Cam Pitch GL11 87 F5
Cam Rd GL52 134 B3
Cam The GL55 189 B2
Camberley Cl GL3 120 A8
Camberley Dr BS36 30 F8
Camberley Rd BS4 2 D8
Camberwell Rd GL51 132 D2
Camborne Rd BS7 19 A7
Cambourne Pl GL15 92 B2
Cambray Ct
Cheltenham GL50 193 B3
Cirencester GL7 190 D4
Cambray Pl GL50 193 C3
Cambrian Dr BS37 43 E3
Cambrian Rd GL20 192 E2
Cambridge Ave
Cheltenham GL51 132 F1
Dursley GL11 80 B7
Cambridge Cres BS9 18 A7
Cambridge Pk BS6 18 B3
Cambridge Rd BS7 18 E4
Cambridge Sq GL20 183 E4
Cambridge St
8 Bristol, Redfield BS5 9 C7
Bristol, Totterdown BS3 8 F4
Gloucester GL1 196 C2
Cambridge Way GL6 91 F6
Camden Cl GL56 187 F3
Camden Rd BS3 194 B1
Camden Terr BS8 194 A2
Camelford Rd BS5 19 D1
Camellia Ct GL51 130 A5
Camellia Wlk GL2 117 E2
Cameron Ho GL50 130 A8
Cameron Wlk BS7 19 C6
Cameroons Cl BS31 4 E4
Camerton Cl BS31 5 E3
Camerton Rd BS5 19 D1
Camomile Cl 3 GL4 119 F5
Camomile Gn GL17 163 D2
Camp Gdns 1 GL54 176 F4
Camp La SN14 24 C4
Camp Rd Bristol BS8 7 F7
Charlton Kings GL52 134 C1
Chepstow NP16 60 F6
Thornbury BS35 63 B6
Camp View BS36 30 E4
Campbell Cl GL3 127 E7
Campbell Ct BS11 26 F1
Campbell Farm BS11 26 F1
Campbell Farm Dr BS11 26 F1
Campbell Rd GL16 155 B6
Campbell St BS2 18 E1
Campden Ave CV36 189 E5
Campden Hill CV36 189 F6
Campden La
Hawling GL54 174 D5
Willersey WR12 188 C2
Campden Pitch CV36 189 F6
Campden Rd
Cheltenham GL51 129 E8
Chipping Campden GL55 189 A4
Ebrington GL55 189 C3
Gloucester GL4 118 E3
Mickleton GL55 189 B8
Campion Cl
Gloucester GL4 119 B4
Thornbury BS35 64 D2
Campion Dr BS32 40 D2
Campion Pk GL51 130 A4
Campion Wlk BS4 2 D6
Cams Ground GL2 125 D6
Camwal Ind Est BS2 9 A5
Camwal Rd BS2 9 A5
Canada Ho GL51 132 E3
Canada Way BS1 194 B1
Canal Row GL2 108 A1
Canal Way GL2 126 B4
Canberra GL10 101 E1
Canberra Gr BS34 29 B4
Canberra Ho GL51 132 E1
Candy Ct BS4 9 D5
Canford La BS9 17 E8
Canford Rd BS9 17 F8
Cann La BS30 11 E6
Cannans Cl BS36 30 E7
Canning Rd GL2 127 E5
Cannon St Bristol BS1 195 A4
Bristol, Bedminster BS3 8 C4
Cannop Cotts GL16 155 D6
Cannop Rd GL15 155 E3
Cannop Villas GL16 155 D7
Canon Pk GL13 85 F4
Canon St BS5 9 C8
Canon's Rd BS1 194 C1
Canon's Wlk BS15 20 F2
Canonbury St GL13 85 F3
Canons Dr GL7 153 F2
Canons Rd BS1 194 C2
Canons Way BS1 194 C1
Canowie Rd BS6 18 B3
Cantell Gr BS14 3 F5
Canterbury Cl BS37 43 E3
Canterbury Ct BS16 19 E6
Canterbury Leys GL20 192 E5
Canterbury St 5 BS5 9 B6
Canterbury Wlk GL51 130 A6
Canters Leaze GL12 54 B4
Cantock's Cl BS8 194 C3
Canton Acre GL6 111 F1
Cantors Ct GL52 137 F2
Cantors Dr GL52 137 E2
Cantors Way SN16 142 E1
Canvey Cl BS10 18 E7
Canynge Ho 2 BS1 195 B1
Canynge Rd BS8 7 F8
Canynge Sq BS8 7 F8
Canynge St BS1 195 B2
Capel Cl BS15 11 B8
Capel Ct GL5 99 D8
Capel Rd Bristol BS11 27 B1
Gloucester GL4 119 C2
Capgrave Cl BS4 10 A3
Capgrave Cres BS4 10 A3
Capital Pk GL2 118 B4
Captain Barton Cl GL5 99 E8
Captains Green Rd GL15 156 A2
Caraway Gdns BS5 19 C2
Cardigan Rd BS9 18 B6
Cardill Cl BS13 2 A8
Cares Cl GL52 138 A4
Carfax Ct BS6 18 A3
Carisbrook Rd GL17 164 D6
Carisbrooke Dr GL52 131 C6
Carisbrooke Rd Bristol BS4 2 D7
Gloucester GL3 120 A7
Carlow Rd BS4 2 E8
Carlton Ct 3 BS9 18 A7
Carlton Gdns GL5 99 C6
Carlton Ho 2 BS9 18 A7
Carlton Pk BS5 9 C8
Carlton Pl GL50,GL51 133 C3
Carlton St GL52 133 F1
Carlyle Gr GL51 132 D4
Carlyle Rd BS5 19 C1
Carmarthen Cl BS37 43 F4
Carmarthen Gr BS30 11 B1
Carmarthen Rd
Bristol BS9 18 A5
Carmarthen Rd *continued*
Cheltenham GL51 129 E6
Carmarthen St 2 GL1 118 F7
Carnarvon Rd BS6 18 D2
Carne Pl GL4 127 C1
Caroline Cl
Chipping Sodbury BS37 44 B2
Keynsham BS31 4 C4
Caroline Ho BS2 195 A4
Carpenter Cotts GL16 154 F3
Carpenters Cl SN16 58 D1
Carpenters La
Cirencester GL7 190 D4
Keynsham BS31 4 E5
Carr Ho 3 BS2 18 F1
Carrant Brook Jun Sch GL20 182 C5
Carrant Rd GL20 192 D5
Carrick Ho 7 BS8 7 F6
Carrington Rd BS3 8 A3
Carrol Gr GL51 132 D4
Carroll Ct BS16 29 E1
Carsons Rd BS16 21 B2
Carter Rd GL51 132 F4
Carter Wlk BS32 29 D8
Carters Leaze CV36 187 E5
Carters Orch GL2 117 F2
Carters Way GL6 90 F5
Cartledge Rd 6 BS5 19 C1
Cartway Gn GL14 191 C4
Cary Ct 2 BS2 18 F1
Casey Cl GL1 127 B1
Cash Hill GL17 163 E4
Cashes Green Hospl GL5 98 D7
Cashes Green Prim Sch GL5 98 D8
Cashes Green Rd GL5 98 E7
Cashmore Ho 8 BS5 9 B7
Casino Pl GL50 193 A1
Casion Ct BS1 195 B1
Cassell Rd BS16 20 C5
Cassey Bottom La BS5 10 A7
Casson Dr BS16 19 E8
Castle Cl Bristol BS10 27 E2
Painswick GL6 103 F7
Castle Coombe BS35 64 C1
Castle Cotts GL3 119 F8
Castle Cres GL15 146 F7
Castle Ct Bristol BS4 9 C4
Thornbury BS35 64 B1
Castle End GL6 111 E5
Castle Farm Cl GL8 70 C3
Castle Farm La BS41 1 B2
Castle Farm Rd BS15 10 C2
Castle Gdns
Chepstow NP16 72 D1
Chipping Campden GL55 189 B2
Castle Hill Dr GL3 120 F4
Castle Hill Prim Sch GL3 120 E4
Castle La Goodrich HR9 163 A6
Marshfield SN14 24 E2
Moreton Valence GL2 108 E2
Castle Mead GL10 97 F3
Castle Nurseries GL55 189 B2
Castle Pitch GL5 99 C6
Castle Prim Sch BS31 4 D4
Castle Rd
Bristol, Kingswood BS15 20 D2
Bristol, Oldland Common BS30 11 D3
Pucklechurch BS16 22 C6
Castle Rise GL5 99 C6
Castle Sch The BS35 64 B2
Castle Sixth Form Ctr BS35 64 B1
Castle St Bristol BS1 195 B3
Cirencester GL7 190 C4
Dursley GL11 88 B1
King's Stanley GL10 98 A3
Stroud GL5 99 C6
Thornbury BS35 64 B1
Winchcombe GL54 174 A7
Castle The GL5 99 C6
Castle View NP16 73 A1
Castle Villas 19 GL5 99 C7
Castlefields Ave GL52 131 C6
Castlefields Dr GL52 131 C6
Castlefields Rd GL52 131 C6
Castleford Gdns NP16 72 F2
Castleford Hill NP16 72 E2
Castlegate Ho BS4 9 E3
Castlemaine Dr GL51 129 C8
Castlemead Rd GL5 99 B6
Castlemeads Ct GL1 196 A3
Castleton Rd GL4 119 D8
Castlett St GL54 175 B3
Catbrain Hill BS10 28 B6
Catbrain La BS10 28 B6
Catbrook GL55 189 A1
Catbrook Cl GL55 189 A1
Catchmays Ct NP16, NP25 146 C5
Catchpot La BS37 34 A6
Cater Rd BS13 2 B6
Cathedral Church of St Peter & the Holy Family* GL1 196 B3
Cathedral Church of The Holy & Undivided Trinity BS1 194 C2
Cathedral Gram Sch BS1 194 C2
Catherine Ct GL1 118 E7
Catherine Hill BS35 49 F2
Catherine Mead St BS3 8 D4
Catherine St BS11 16 C8
Catherine's Cl GL5 99 E7

Catholic Sch of St Gregory the Great The GL50 ... 193 A4
Catkin Cl GL2 ... 109 E7
Catley Gr BS41 ... 7 B2
Cato St BS5 ... 19 B2
Catswood Ct GL5 ... 103 E1
Catswood La GL6 ... 104 D3
Cattistock Dr BS5 ... 10 A6
Cattle Market Rd BS1 ... 195 C1
Cattybrook Rd BS16 ... 21 D5
Cattybrook St
6 Bristol BS5 ... 9 B7
23 Bristol BS5 ... 9 B8
Caudle Cl GL17 ... 163 E4
Caudle La GL17 ... 163 E4
Causeway Rd GL14 ... 191 E5
Causeway The
Coalpit Heath BS36 ... 31 D7
Quedgeley GL2 ... 117 D1
Causley Dr BS30 ... 11 A5
Cavan Wlk BS4 ... 8 D1
Cave Ct BS2 ... 195 B4
Cave Dr BS16 ... 20 D6
Cave Gr BS16 ... 21 B7
Cave St BS2 ... 195 B4
Cavendish Ave GL3 ... 128 D5
Cavendish Cl BS31 ... 5 D2
Cavendish Gdns BS9 ... 17 C4
Cavendish Rd
Bristol, Henleaze BS9 ... 18 A5
Bristol, Patchway BS34 ... 28 F8
Caves Cotts BS16 ... 20 E7
Cecil Ave BS5 ... 19 F1
Cecil Rd Bristol, Clifton BS8 ... 7 F8
Bristol, Kingswood BS15 ... 10 D8
Gloucester GL1 ... 118 D6
Cecily Hill GL7 ... 190 B5
Cedar Cl
Bristol, Oldland BS30 ... 11 B4
Bristol, Patchway BS34 ... 28 F7
Charlton Kings GL53 ... 131 B5
Chepstow NP16 ... 60 E5
Stroud GL5 ... 98 D6
Cedar Court Rd GL53 ... 193 B2
Cedar Ct
Bristol, Mangotsfield BS16 ... 20 E6
Bristol, Westbury on Trym BS9 ... 17 F8
Bristol,Combe Dingle BS9 ... 17 D7
Bristol,Sneyd Park BS9 ... 17 C4
Ledbury HR8 ... 178 F8
Cedar Dr Dursley GL11 ... 88 A1
Keynsham BS31 ... 4 D4
Cedar Gdns GL10 ... 97 F8
Cedar Gr Bristol BS9 ... 17 D5
Walford HR9 ... 163 C8
4 Winchcombe GL54 ... 174 A7
Cedar Hall BS16 ... 20 C8
Cedar Pk BS9 ... 17 D5
Cedar Rd
Brockworth GL3 ... 120 D7
Mickleton GL55 ... 189 B6
Northway GL20 ... 182 C4
Cedar Row BS11 ... 16 F6
Cedar Way Mile End GL16 ... 155 B6
Pucklechurch BS16 ... 22 C5
Winterbourne BS36 ... 30 D5
Cedardean GL14 ... 191 C5
Cedars The
Gloucester GL3 ... 120 A8
Wooton-u-E GL12 ... 68 C8
Cedarwood Dr GL4 ... 118 E3
Celandine Bank GL52 ... 138 B4
Celandine Cl BS35 ... 64 D2
Celandine Ct NP16 ... 60 F5
Celestine Rd BS37 ... 43 C3
Celia Terr BS4 ... 9 F6
Cemetery La Bibury GL7 ... 160 A1
Bourton-on-t-W GL54 ... 169 A7
Cemetery Rd Bristol BS4 ... 9 A3
Gloucester GL4 ... 119 A6
Cennick Ave BS15 ... 20 E1
Centaurus Rd BS34 ... 28 D7
Central Ave Bristol BS15 ... 10 C5
Mitcheldean GL17 ... 164 D5
Severn Beach BS10 ... 38 A3
Central Cross Dr GL50, GL52 ... 133 E3
Central Pk BS14 ... 3 B7
Central Rd
Gloucester GL1 ... 118 E7
Stroud GL5 ... 98 F7
Central Tech Coll GL4 ... 119 B5
Central Trad Est BS4 ... 9 B4
Central Way Bristol BS10 ... 18 E8
Cheltenham GL51 ... 133 B3
Centre The BS31 ... 4 F5
Centurion Cl GL4 ... 119 E6
Centurion Rd GL15 ... 92 B4
Centurions Wlk 19 GL16 ... 155 A5
Century Cl GL7 ... 190 F5
Century Ct GL50 ... 193 B2
Ceres Cl BS30 ... 10 F2
Cerimon Gate BS34 ... 29 E5
Cerney House Gdns* GL7 ... 158 C2
Cerney La BS11 ... 16 E5
Cerney Wick La GL7 ... 143 C7
Cesson Cl BS37 ... 33 C8
Ceylon Ho GL51 ... 132 F4
Chaceley Cl
Gloucester GL4 ... 119 E5
Quedgeley GL2 ... 109 E8
Chad Rd GL51 ... 132 F1
Chadbournes GL3 ... 128 B6
Chadleigh Gr BS4 ... 2 D7
Chadwick Cl GL4 ... 118 D2
Chaffinch Cl GL3 ... 127 D7
Chaffinch Ct 5 GL10 ... 97 F8
Chaingate La BS37 ... 43 A6
Chakeshill Cl BS10 ... 28 C3
Chakeshill Dr BS10 ... 28 C4
Chalcombe Cl BS34 ... 29 C8
Chalcroft Ho 1 BS3 ... 8 A4
Chalcroft Wlk BS13 ... 1 E4
Chalet The BS10 ... 27 F3
Chalfield Cl BS31 ... 5 A2
Chalford Ave GL51 ... 129 B7
Chalford Cl BS37 ... 32 D8
Chalford Hill Prim Sch GL6 ... 148 C5
Chalford Rd GL4 ... 118 E1
Chalks Rd BS5 ... 9 D8
Challender Ave BS10 ... 27 F2
Challoner Ct BS1 ... 195 A1
Chamberlayne Cl 29 GL54 ... 176 F4
Chamberlayne Ho 28 GL54 ... 176 F4
Chambon Cl SN16 ... 142 D1
Champion Rd BS15 ... 21 A2
Champions Ct GL11 ... 80 B8
Champneys Ave BS10 ... 27 F3
Chamwell Sch GL2 ... 127 B5
Chamwells Ave GL2 ... 127 B4
Chamwells Wlk GL2 ... 127 B4
Chance St GL20 ... 192 D4
Chancel Cl Bristol BS9 ... 17 D3
Gloucester GL4 ... 127 C1
Chancel Pk GL53 ... 130 F6
Chancel Way
Charlton Kings GL53 ... 131 A6
Lechlade on T GL7 ... 153 E2
Chancery St BS5 ... 9 B7
Chandag Inf Sch BS31 ... 5 A4
Chandag Jun Sch BS31 ... 5 A4
Chandag Rd BS31 ... 5 A4
Chandler Rd GL52 ... 137 F2
Chandos Almshouses 22 GL54 ... 174 A7
Chandos Dr GL3 ... 120 E5
Chandos Rd Bristol BS6 ... 18 C1
Keynsham BS31 ... 4 E7
Stroud GL5 ... 99 A4
Chandos St 26 GL54 ... 174 A7
Chandos Trad Est BS2 ... 9 A5
Change The GL6 ... 102 D1
Channel View NP16 ... 60 E5
Channell's Hill BS9 ... 18 A8
Channon's Hill BS16 ... 19 F4
Chantry Cl
Cirencester GL7 ... 190 C5
Lydney GL15 ... 92 A1
Chantry Ct GL8 ... 140 C4
Chantry Gate GL52 ... 137 E2
Chantry Gdns GL56 ... 186 D3
Chantry Gr BS11 ... 27 C2
Chantry La BS16 ... 30 F1
Chantry Rd Bristol BS8 ... 18 B1
Thornbury BS35 ... 64 B2
Chapel Appartments 12 GL16 ... 155 A5
Chapel Barton 7 BS3 ... 8 B2
Chapel Cl Bristol BS15 ... 11 B8
Chepstow NP16 ... 60 B5
Kempsford GL7 ... 144 E8
Monmouth NP25 ... 154 A7
Tarlton GL7 ... 149 C2
Chapel Cotts GL54 ... 174 B1
Chapel Ct
Bristol, Brentry BS10 ... 28 D3
Bristol, St Philip's Marsh BS2 ... 9 A5
Chapel Gdns Bristol BS10 ... 28 A1
Quedgeley GL2 ... 109 F7
Chapel Green La BS6 ... 18 B2
Chapel Hay Cl GL3 ... 128 C4
Chapel Hay La GL3 ... 128 D4
Chapel Hill
Aylburton GL15 ... 147 E4
Broad Blunsdon SN26 ... 144 D1
English Bicknor GL16 ... 163 A1
Newport GL13 ... 78 B7
Chapel Ho GL20 ... 192 C4
Chapel La
Acton Turville GL9 ... 36 A6
Blockley GL56 ... 186 C5
Bristol, Clay Hill BS5 ... 19 E2
Bristol, Frenchay BS16 ... 20 C7
Bristol, Lawrence Weston BS11 ... 27 C2
Bristol, Warmley BS15 ... 11 B8
Bristol,Fishponds BS16 ... 20 A4
Cheltenham GL50 ... 193 B1
Chepstow NP16 ... 60 B5
Chipping Sodbury BS37 ... 34 A7
Churcham GL2 ... 165 F5
Cold Aston GL54 ... 168 B6
Gorsley HR9 ... 170 B4
Hankerton SN16 ... 141 E1
Hillesley GL12 ... 55 E8
Hinton SN14 ... 23 C5
Kinsham GL20 ... 182 D6
Longhope GL17 ... 165 B5
Mickleton GL55 ... 189 A6
Minchinhampton GL6 ... 148 A3
Minety SN16 ... 142 D1
North Cerney GL7 ... 158 D3
Oaksey SN16 ... 141 F4
Staunton GL19 ... 171 E8
Stroud GL5 ... 98 D6
Thornbury BS35 ... 65 A1
Westmancote GL20 ... 182 D8
Weston-s-E GL55 ... 188 D3
Woodmancote GL52 ... 138 C3
Chapel Pitch GL18 ... 170 D2
Chapel Rd
Berry Hill GL16 ... 155 A7
Bristol, Bishopsworth BS13 ... 2 A6
Bristol, Hanham BS15 ... 10 C5
2 Bristol, Lower Easton BS5 ... 19 B1
Kempsford GL7 ... 144 E8
Thornbury BS35 ... 63 C5
Viney Hill GL15 ... 156 C1
Chapel Row
5 Blockley GL56 ... 186 C5
Luckington SN14 ... 47 E4
Pill BS20 ... 16 C4
4 Stonehouse GL10 ... 97 F7
Chapel St
Bledington OX7 ... 177 E1
Bristol BS2 ... 9 A5
Broadwell GL56 ... 177 A6
Cheltenham GL50 ... 193 B4
Dursley GL11 ... 88 A5
5 Stow-on-t-W GL54 ... 176 F4
Stroud GL5 ... 99 D7
Thornbury BS35 ... 51 B8
Chapel Way BS4 ... 9 E6
Chapel Wlk
Cheltenham GL50 ... 193 B3
Didmarton GL9 ... 57 B3
Edge End GL16 ... 155 C8
Chapelfields HR9 ... 162 B6
Chaplin Rd BS5 ... 19 B1
Chapman Way GL51 ... 129 F7
Chapter St BS2 ... 195 B4
Charbon Gate BS34 ... 29 F5
Charborough Ct BS34 ... 29 A2
Charborough Rd BS34 ... 28 F2
Charborough Road Prim Sch BS34 ... 28 F2
Charbury Wlk BS11 ... 16 E5
Chard Ct BS14 ... 3 B6
Chardstock Ave BS9 ... 17 D8
Chardwar Gdns 7 GL54 ... 168 F7
Charfield 4 BS15 ... 11 A8
Charfield Prim Sch GL12 ... 66 F5
Charfield Rd Bristol BS10 ... 28 D1
Kingswood GL12 ... 67 E5
Chargrove 3 Bristol BS30 ... 11 C6
Yate BS37 ... 32 D7
Chargrove La GL51 ... 129 E4
Charis Ave BS10 ... 18 C7
Charlecombe Ct BS9 ... 17 F6
Charlecombe Rd BS9 ... 17 F6
Charlecote Ave GL4 ... 110 C8
Charlecote Cnr GL52 ... 137 E3
Charles Ave BS34 ... 29 E4
Charles Cl BS35 ... 64 C3
Charles Ct BS8 ... 194 A2
Charles England Ho BS34 ... 28 F7
Charles Pl BS8 ... 194 A2
Charles Rd BS34 ... 29 B3
Charles St Bristol BS1 ... 195 A4
Cheltenham GL51 ... 133 C3
Gloucester GL1 ... 196 C2
Charlesway GL56 ... 176 E8
Charleswood Rd GL15 ... 155 F1
Charleton Ho 8 BS2 ... 195 C3
Charlham La GL7 ... 143 E8
Charlham Way GL7 ... 143 E8
Charlock Cl GL4 ... 119 A4
Charlotte Rose Ho 3 GL50 ... 133 B1
Charlotte St
Bristol, Brandon Hill BS1 ... 194 C3
Bristol, St Pauls BS2 ... 195 C4
Charlotte St S BS1 ... 194 C2
Charlton Ave BS34 ... 28 F2
Charlton Cl GL53 ... 131 A5
Charlton Court Rd GL52 ... 131 A7
Charlton Ct Bristol BS34 ... 39 F1
Gloucester GL1 ... 196 C3
Charlton Down Cotts GL8 ... 71 E4
Charlton Dr GL53 ... 130 F7
Charlton Gdns BS10 ... 28 D4
Charlton Kings Cty Jun Sch GL53 ... 131 B5
Charlton Kings Inf Sch GL52 ... 131 B6
Charlton La Bristol BS10 ... 28 A3
Cheltenham, Leckhampton GL53 ... 130 D5
Charlton Lane Ctr GL53 ... 130 E5
Charlton Lawn GL53 ... 131 A7
Charlton Mead Ct BS10 ... 28 D4
Charlton Mead Dr BS10 ... 28 D3
Charlton Park Dr GL53 ... 130 F7
Charlton Park Gate GL53 ... 130 F6
Charlton Pk BS31 ... 4 D5
Charlton Pl BS10 ... 28 D4
Charlton Rd
Bristol, Brentry BS10 ... 28 C3
Bristol, Kingswood BS15 ... 20 B1
Keynsham BS31,BS14 ... 4 C3
Tetbury GL8 ... 140 B4
Charlton St 16 BS5 ... 9 B7
Charlton Terr GL56 ... 187 B3
Charlton Way GL2 ... 127 C5
Charminster Rd BS16 ... 20 B3
Charmouth Ct BS3 ... 8 D1
Charnell Rd BS16 ... 20 E4
Charnhill Brow BS16 ... 21 A4
Charnhill Cres BS16 ... 20 F4
Charnhill Dr BS16 ... 20 F4
Charnhill Ridge BS16 ... 21 A4
Charnhill Vale BS16 ... 20 F4
Charnwood BS16 ... 21 A4
Charnwood Cl GL53 ... 130 D5
Charnwood Ct GL15 ... 92 B5
Charnwood Rd Bristol BS14 ... 3 B4
Cheltenham GL53 ... 130 D5
Charter Ct GL1 ... 196 C1
Charter Wlk BS14 ... 3 A6
Charterhouse Rd 5 BS5 ... 9 D8
Chartist La GL19 ... 179 F2
Chartist Piece GL19 ... 172 B8
Chartist Way GL19 ... 172 A8
Chartists Way NP16 ... 60 E5
Chartley BS9 ... 17 D2
Chartwell Cl GL2 ... 118 A6
Chase Ave GL52 ... 131 C6
Chase La Gloucester GL4 ... 119 B7
Wickwar GL12 ... 54 C6
Chase Rd BS15 ... 20 D2
Chase The Bristol BS16 ... 20 C3
Churchdown GL3 ... 128 D4
Gloucester GL4 ... 119 D5
Stroud GL5 ... 98 E7
Chasefield La 1 BS16 ... 20 B4
Chasely Cres 6 GL51 ... 129 E5
Chasewood Cnr 3 GL6 ... 148 B6
Chatcombe BS37 ... 32 E7
Chatcombe Cl GL53 ... 131 B4
Chatcombe Rd GL4 ... 119 B5
Chatsworth Ave GL4 ... 118 C1
Chatsworth Dr GL53 ... 130 D4
Chatsworth Pk BS35 ... 64 C3
Chatsworth Rd
Bristol, Arno's Vale BS4 ... 9 C4
Bristol, Hillfields BS16 ... 20 B3
Chatterton Gn BS14 ... 2 F3
Chatterton Ho 5 BS1 ... 195 B1
Chatterton Rd BS37 ... 43 D1
Chatterton Sq BS1 ... 195 C1
Chatterton St BS1 ... 195 C1
Chaucer Cl GL1 ... 118 D5
Chaucer Rd GL11 ... 80 C7
Chaundey Gr BS13 ... 2 B5
Chavenage BS15 ... 21 A1
Chavenage La GL8 ... 140 B4
Cheap St GL54 ... 159 A6
Cheapside Bristol BS2 ... 195 C4
Stroud GL5 ... 99 B7
Cheapside St 8 BS3 ... 8 F4
Cheddar Gr BS13 ... 2 A8
Cheddar Grove Sch BS13 ... 2 A8
Chedworth Bristol BS15 ... 20 F3
19 Newent GL18 ... 171 A4
Yate BS37 ... 32 B7
Chedworth Rd Bristol BS7 ... 19 A6
Gloucester GL4 ... 118 E3
Chedworth Way GL51 ... 129 E8
Cheese La BS2 ... 195 B2
Chelbury Mews 1 GL52 ... 134 A3
Chelford Gr BS34 ... 29 B8
Chelmer Gr BS31 ... 4 F4
Chelmsford Ave GL51 ... 130 A5
Chelmsford Wlk BS4 ... 9 F5
Chelsea Cl
Cheltenham GL53 ... 130 F7
Keynsham BS31 ... 5 A5
Chelsea Pk BS5 ... 9 C8
Chelsea Rd BS5 ... 19 B1
Chelston Rd BS4 ... 2 D7
Chelt Rd GL52 ... 134 B3
Cheltenham & Gloucester Coll of H Ed
Cheltenham, Cleevemount GL52 ... 133 F4
Cheltenham, The Park GL53 ... 130 C6
Cheltenham & Gloucester Coll of H Ed (Francis Close Hall) GL50 ... 133 D3
Cheltenham & Gloucester Nuffield Hospl The GL51 ... 129 C7
Cheltenham Bournside Sch & Sixth Form Ctr GL51 ... 130 A6
Cheltenham Coll GL53 ... 193 B1
Cheltenham Coll Jun Sch GL53 ... 193 B1
Cheltenham Cres 2 BS6 ... 18 D1
Cheltenham General Hospl GL53 ... 193 C2
Cheltenham Kingsmead Sch GL51 ... 132 F4
Cheltenham La BS6 ... 18 D2
Cheltenham Ladies Coll The GL50 ... 193 B3
Cheltenham Mus & Art Gal* GL50 ... 193 B4
Cheltenham Race Course GL50,GL52 ... 134 A6
Cheltenham Racecourse Hall of Fame* GL50 ... 133 F6
Cheltenham Rd
Bagendon GL7 ... 150 D7
Beckford GL20 ... 183 B6
Bishop's Cleeve GL52 ... 137 F3
Bisley GL6 ... 105 A1
Bredon GL20 ... 182 D7
Bristol BS6 ... 18 E1
Broadway WR12 ... 185 A8
Gloucester GL2 ... 127 D3
Painswick GL6 ... 112 A2
Pitchcombe GL6 ... 103 C4
Winchcombe GL54 ... 139 F4
Cheltenham Rd E GL3 ... 128 A7
Cheltenham Spa Sta GL51 ... 133 A1
Cheltenham Trade Pk GL51 ... 133 B3
Chelvy Cl BS13 ... 2 D3
Chelwood Rd Bristol BS11 ... 16 D7
Saltford BS31 ... 5 E4
Chelworth Ind Est SN6 ... 143 D3
Chelworth Rd SN6 ... 143 E3
Chepstow Bulwark* NP16 ... 60 F6
Chepstow Castle* NP16 ... 72 E1
Chepstow Com Hospl NP16 ... 60 D8
Chepstow Comp Sch NP16 ... 72 D2
Chepstow Ho 13 GL51 ... 132 E2
Chepstow Mus* NP16 ... 72 F1
Chepstow Pk BS16 ... 30 F1
Chepstow Race Course* NP16 ... 72 C3
Chepstow Rd BS4 ... 2 D8
Chepstow Sta NP16 ... 60 F8
Chepstow Wlk BS31 ... 4 D5
Chequers Cl BS30 ... 11 C3
Chequers Ct BS34 ... 30 A6
Chequers Rd GL4 ... 119 B7
Cherington Bristol BS15 ... 10 B5
Yate BS37 ... 32 D6
Cherington Rd BS10 ... 18 D7
Cheriton Cl GL51 ... 129 F5
Cheriton Pl
Bristol, Eastfield BS9 ... 18 B7
Bristol, Warmley BS30 ... 11 C6
Cherrington Dr GL4 ... 119 E5
Cherry Ave GL53 ... 131 C4
Cherry Bank GL18 ... 171 A4
Cherry Blossom Cl GL52 ... 137 F5
Cherry Cl GL2 ... 109 E7
Cherry Garden La BS30 ... 11 B2
Cherry Garden Prim Sch BS30 ... 11 C2
Cherry Garden Rd BS30 ... 11 C1
Cherry Gdns Bristol BS30 ... 11 C1
Gloucester GL3 ... 120 A8
Cherry Gr BS16 ... 21 A6
Cherry La 4 BS1 ... 195 B4
Cherry Orch
Bredon GL20 ... 182 C7
Highworth SN6 ... 145 D3
Wooton-u-E GL12 ... 68 C7
Cherry Orch The GL51 ... 173 F2
Cherry Orchard Cl GL55 ... 189 A1
Cherry Orchard La
3 Bristol BS5 ... 9 F8
Luckington SN14 ... 47 C5
Twyning GL20 ... 181 F7
Cherry Orchard Rd 6 GL8 ... 140 C4
Cherry Rd BS37 ... 44 A1
Cherry Tree Cl
Bristol BS16 ... 20 C2
Keynsham BS31 ... 4 C4
Nailsworth GL6 ... 91 A4
Cherry Tree La GL16 ... 155 C6
Cherry Tree Rd 10 SN6 ... 143 E4
Cherry Wlk GL15 ... 92 A4
Cherry Wood BS30 ... 11 B2
Cherrytree Cres BS16 ... 20 C2
Cherrytree Ct BS16 ... 22 C5
Cherrytree La GL7 ... 150 F5
Cherrytree Rd BS16 ... 20 C2
Cherrywood Gdns GL4 ... 118 E3
Cherston Ct GL4 ... 119 E8
Chertsey Rd BS6 ... 18 B1
Chervil Cl GL4 ... 119 B4
Cherwell Cl BS35 ... 51 C7
Cherwell Rd BS31 ... 5 A4
Chesford Dr GL3 ... 128 C6
Chesham Way BS15 ... 20 D1
Cheshire Cl BS37 ... 43 E3
Cheshire Rd GL3 ... 127 E6
Chesils The GL54 ... 174 A8
Chesley Hill BS30 ... 11 F7
Chesmann Ct GL1 ... 126 F4
Chessel Cl BS32 ... 40 C2
Chessel Ct 6 BS3 ... 8 B2
Chessel St BS3 ... 8 B3
Chessell Ave BS35 ... 38 C7
Chessgrove La GL17 ... 164 F6
Chessington Ave BS14 ... 3 B5
Chestal GL11 ... 88 B1
Chester Cl GL19 ... 173 C7
Chester Cres GL7 ... 190 D4
Chester Ct 4 BS5 ... 9 C7
Chester Park Jun & Inf Schs BS16 ... 20 A3
Chester Park Rd BS16 ... 20 B2
Chester Pk BS5 ... 19 E1
Chester Rd Bristol BS5 ... 19 E1
Gloucester GL4 ... 119 C8
Chester St Bristol BS5 ... 19 B2
Cirencester GL7 ... 190 D4
Chester Wlk GL50 ... 193 B4
Chesterfield Ave BS6 ... 18 E2
Chesterfield Hospl BS8 ... 194 A2
Chesterfield Rd
Bristol, Mangotsfield BS16 ... 20 E5
Bristol, Montpelier BS6 ... 18 E2
Chestermaster Cl BS32 ... 40 A5
Chesters BS30 ... 11 A4
Chesterton Ct GL2 ... 126 F6
Chesterton Gr GL7 ... 190 C3
Chesterton Ho 6 BS2 ... 195 B4
Chesterton La GL7 ... 190 C3
Chesterton Pk GL7 ... 190 B4
Chesterton Prim Sch GL7 ... 190 C2
Chestnut Ave GL10 ... 97 F8
Chestnut Cl Bristol BS14 ... 3 F5
Down Ampney GL7 ... 143 E8
15 Ledbury HR8 ... 178 E8

Chestnut Cl *continued*
2 Mile End GL16 .155 B6
Nailsworth GL6 .91 B4
Quedgeley GL2 .109 E7
6 Tetbury GL8 .140 B4
Chestnut Cnr WR12 .184 E5
Chestnut Cotts GL2 .125 D5
Chestnut Ct Bristol BS16 .21 A5
Monmouth NP25 .154 A7
Chestnut Dr
Chipping Sodbury BS37 .44 A1
Thornbury BS35 .64 C1
Chestnut Hill GL6 .91 B4
Chestnut Ho Bristol BS13 .2 D3
Cheltenham GL50 .193 A3
Chestnut La GL5 .98 F7
Chestnut Park Est GL12 .67 F4
Chestnut Pl GL53 .130 B4
Chestnut Rd
Bristol, Lower Soundwell BS15 .20 F3
Bristol, Mangotsfield BS16 .20 D6
Gloucester GL4 .119 E5
Long Ashton BS41 .7 B2
Chestnut Terr
Charlton Kings GL53 .131 A5
Monmouth NP25 .154 A7
Chestnut Way BS15 .20 F3
Chestnut Wlk Bristol BS13 .2 A6
Saltford BS31 .5 E3
Chestnuts The
Bussage GL6 .148 B6
Gloucester GL1 .196 A1
Chetwode Cl BS10 .28 D3
Chetwood Ho BS5 .9 C6
Chevening Cl BS34 .29 D4
Cheviot Cl Quedgeley GL2 109 E8
1 Tetbury GL8 .140 C5
Cheviot Dr BS35 .51 E8
Cheviot Rd GL52 .134 B4
Cheviot Way BS30 .11 C5
Chew Cotts BS31 .4 F5
Chewton Cl BS16 .20 B3
Chewton Rd BS31 .4 F2
Cheyne Rd BS9 .17 D6
Cheyney Cl GL4 .119 B6
Chichester Ho BS4 .9 F6
Chichester Way BS37 .43 D3
Chickadee GL15 .146 E7
Chicknalls La GL15 .156 F3
Childer Rd HR8 .178 D8
Childswickham Rd WR12 .185 A8
Chillington Ct BS34 .39 E1
Chillwood Cl BS37 .42 E3
Chiltern Ave GL52 .137 E4
Chiltern Cl
Bristol, Warmley BS30 .11 C5
Bristol, Whitchurch BS14 .3 B4
Chiltern Pk BS35 .51 E8
Chiltern Rd
Prestbury GL52 .134 B3
Quedgeley GL2 .109 E8
Chilton Rd BS4 .3 A8
Chilwood Cl BS37 .42 E3
China Cnr WR11 .188 C6
Chine The BS16 .19 D5
Chine View BS16 .20 F8
Chiphouse Rd BS15 .20 F3
Chippenham Rd SN14 .15 A8
Chipperfield Dr BS15 .20 F1
Chipping Campden Sch GL55 .189 A2
Chipping Cl GL12 .68 B7
Chipping Edge Est BS37 .44 C1
Chipping Gdns GL12 .68 B7
Chipping Sodbury Sch BS37 .33 B8
Chipping St GL8 .140 C4
Chipping The GL12 .67 F4
Chippings The BS16 .19 D5
Chisbury St BS5 .19 C3
Chislet Way GL4 .118 D1
Chittening Rd BS11 .26 E7
Chock La BS9 .18 A7
Choirs Cl GL4 .119 E6
Chosen Dr GL3 .128 B5
Chosen Hill Sch GL3 .128 E5
Chosen View Rd GL51 .133 B5
Chosen Way GL3 .119 F8
Christ CE Prim Sch GL50 .133 B1
Christ Church CE Inf Sch BS16 .20 D5
Christ Church CE Prim Sch
Bristol BS8 .194 B3
Chalford GL6 .148 C5
Christ Church Rd GL50 .130 B8
Christ Church Terr 8 GL50 .133 B1
Christ Church Villas 7 GL50 .133 B1
Christ the King Prim Sch BS35 .64 D1
Christchurch Ave BS16 .20 D5
Christchurch CE Prim Sch BS15 .10 B4
Christchurch Ct 4 GL50 .130 B8
Christchurch Jun Sch BS16 .20 D5
Christchurch La BS16 .20 D5
Christchurch Rd BS8 .194 A3
Christina Terr BS8 .194 A1
Christmas St 3 BS1 .195 A3
Christmas Stps 1 BS1 .195 A3
Christmas Tree BS34 .28 D6
Christowe La GL53 .193 C1
Chubb Cl BS30 .10 F5
Chuch Wlk GL12 .68 C7
Church Ave
Bristol, Sneyd Park BS9 .17 E4
3 Bristol, Upper Easton BS5 .19 B1
Bristol, Warmley BS30 .11 D7
Cirencester GL7 .190 E1
Falfield GL12 .65 E7
Church Cl Bristol BS10 .27 E2
Broadway WR12 .185 B8
Cranham GL4 .112 E5
Ebrington GL55 .189 D3
Frampton Cotterell BS36 .31 B8
Longborough GL56 .176 D8
Church Cotts GL55 .189 A2
Church Dr Bristol BS5 .9 E8
Parkend GL15 .155 E2
Quedgeley GL2 .117 F1
Church Farm NP25 .154 A7
Church Farm Bsns Ctr GL53 .130 C3
Church Farm La GL56 .187 A6
Church Farm Paddock BS30 .5 E7
Church Farm Rd BS16 .21 C6
Church Furlong GL54 .176 C1
Church Gdns GL15 .92 A2
Church Hill Bisley GL6 .148 D8
Bristol BS4 .9 E2
Burton SN14 .36 B3
Olveston BS35 .49 F3
Upper Lydbrook GL17 .163 D2
Church Hill Cl GL16 .163 B2
Church La
Ashton Keynes SN6 .142 F5
Badminton GL9 .46 E5
Berkeley GL13 .85 E3
Bitton BS30 .5 E7
Bledington OX7 .177 E1
Bristol BS1 .195 B2
Bristol, Bedminster BS3 .8 D3
Bristol, Bromley Heath BS16 30 F1
Bristol, Clifton Wood BS8 .194 B2
Bristol, Henbury BS10 .27 E2
Chipping Sodbury BS37 .34 B8
Churcham GL2 .124 D1
Coalpit Heath BS36 .31 C6
5 Cricklade SN6 .143 E4
Cromhall GL12 .66 A1
Evenlode GL56 .177 C7
Forthampton GL19 .181 C3
Gloucester GL4 .119 D8
Hambrook BS16 .30 E2
Hankerton SN16 .141 E1
Hardwicke GL2 .109 D6
Harnhill GL7 .151 B3
Leigh The GL19 .173 C4
Long Ashton BS41 .7 C2
Marshfield SN14 .15 A8
Minsterworth GL2 .116 F7
Moreton Valence GL2 .101 A8
Netherend GL15 .147 D3
Northwood Green GL14 .165 C2
Rangeworthy BS37 .52 F1
Sapperton GL7 .149 B6
Saul GL2 .100 A7
Sevenhampton GL54 .166 E8
Sharpness GL13 .93 E1
Shurdington GL51 .129 E2
Sopworth SN14 .57 D1
South Cerney GL7 .142 F8
St Arvans NP16 .72 B6
Stanton WR12 .184 E5
Stonehouse GL10 .97 E7
Toddington GL54 .184 B3
Whaddon GL4 .110 E8
Wickwar GL12 .54 A6
Windrush OX18 .161 C7
Winterbourne BS16 .30 C6
Woolaston GL15 .147 B2
Church Leaze BS11 .16 D6
Church Mdws
Toddington GL54 .184 B3
Whitchurch BS14 .3 C4
Church Par BS4 .9 E2
Church Piece GL53 .131 B5
Church Pl Pill BS20 .16 C4
Upper Oddington GL56 .177 D4
Church Rd Abbots Leigh BS8 7 A8
Alderton GL20 .183 E4
Almondsbury BS32 .40 A5
Alveston BS35 .51 A1
Arlingham GL2 .157 B5
Aylburton GL15 .147 E5
Bibury GL7 .160 A1
Bishop's Cleeve GL52 .137 F4
Bitton BS30 .5 E7
Bristol, Bedminster BS3 .8 C3
Bristol, Bishopsworth BS13 .2 A6
Bristol, Filton BS34 .29 A3
Bristol, Frenchay BS16 .20 C7
Bristol, Hanham BS15 .10 B5
Bristol, Horfield BS7 .18 E5
Bristol, Kingswood BS15 .10 E8
Bristol, Moorfields BS5 .9 D8
Bristol, Sneyd Park BS9 .17 D3
Bristol, Stoke Gifford BS34 .29 E4
Bristol, Upper Soundwell BS16 .20 E3
Bristol, Westbury-on-T BS9 .18 A7
Cheltenham, Leckhampton GL53 .130 C3
Cheltenham, St Mark's GL51 .129 F8
Church Rd *continued*
Chepstow NP16 .72 F1
Churchdown GL3 .128 C4
Cinderford GL14 .191 C3
Doynton BS30 .23 A1
Dundry BS41 .1 D2
Dursley GL11 .88 B3
Easter Compton BS35 .39 A1
Easton-in-G BS20 .16 A4
Frampton Cotterell BS36 .31 C8
Gloucester GL2 .127 C4
Guiting Power GL54 .175 B3
Hewelsfield GL15 .146 F5
Kemble GL7 .141 F8
6 Ledbury HR8 .178 F8
Leigh Woods BS8 .7 D6
Leonard Stanley GL10 .97 E3
Longhope GL17 .164 F6
Luckington SN14 .47 F4
Lydney GL15 .92 A2
Maisemore GL2 .126 A7
Nailsworth GL6 .91 A6
Newnham GL14 .157 A6
Oldbury-on-S BS35 .63 B5
Pilning BS35 .38 B7
Quenington GL7 .152 D7
Severn Beach BS35 .38 A6
Stanton WR12 .184 C8
Stroud GL5 .98 E6
Swindon GL51 .133 B6
Thornbury BS35 .64 B2
Upper Lydbrook GL17 .163 D2
Upper Oddington GL56 .177 D4
Upper Soudley GL14 .156 C5
Whitchurch BS14 .3 B4
Wick BS30 .12 B6
Winterbourne BS36 .30 E4
Woodchester GL5 .98 F2
Yate BS37 .43 F2
Yate, Goose Green BS37 .43 E3
Church Rise GL2 .126 A7
Church Road Pl GL14 .191 D4
Church Row
Chedworth GL54 .159 A7
Gretton GL54 .183 E1
Nailsworth GL6 .91 A6
Overbury GL20 .182 F8
Poole Keynes GL7 .142 A6
Shipton GL54 .166 E5
Church Sq GL15 .156 E2
Church St Avening GL8 .148 A1
Bledington OX7 .177 E1
Bredon GL20 .182 C7
Bristol BS1 .195 B2
Bristol, Lower Easton BS5 .19 B1
Bristol, Redfield BS5 .9 B6
Broadway WR12 .185 B8
Charlton Kings GL53 .131 B5
Cheltenham GL50 .193 B4
Chipping Campden GL55 .189 A2
Cirencester GL7 .190 D3
Clearwell GL16 .155 A2
Gloucester GL2 .196 A2
King's Stanley GL10 .98 A4
Kingham OX7 .177 F2
5 Ledbury HR8 .178 F8
Littledean GL14 .156 E8
Meysey Hampton GL7 .152 A2
Moreton-in-M GL56 .187 A3
Nailsworth GL6 .91 C4
Newent GL18 .171 A4
Nympsfield GL10 .89 E5
Sherston SN16 .58 C1
St Briavels GL15 .146 E7
9 Stow-on-t-W GL54 .176 F4
Stroud GL5 .99 C7
Tetbury GL8 .140 B3
Tewkesbury GL20 .192 C4
Willersey WR12 .188 B2
Wooton-u-E GL12 .68 B7
Church View
Almondsbury BS32 .39 F4
Aston Magna GL56 .187 A6
Bristol, Filton BS34 .29 A3
Bristol, Staple Hill BS16 .20 D5
Castle Eaton SN6 .144 D6
Churchdown GL3 .128 D4
Condicote GL54 .176 B7
Highworth SN6 .145 C3
Hillesley GL12 .55 D8
Newport GL13 .78 C8
Thornbury GL13 .64 E7
Church Way
Blakeney GL15 .156 E2
Gloucester GL4 .119 C7
9 Newent GL18 .171 A4
Church Wlk
Ashton Keynes SN6 .142 F5
6 Coleford GL16 .155 B6
Littledean GL14 .156 E8
Parkend GL15 .155 E2
Pill BS20 .16 C4
8 Stow-on-t-W GL54 .176 F4
Viney Hill GL15 .156 C1
Churcham Prim Sch GL2 .124 C2
Churchdown La GL3 .120 C8
Churchdown Sch GL3 .128 B5
Churchdown Village Inf Sch GL3 .128 C5
Churchdown Village Jun Sch GL3 .128 C4
Churchdown Wlk BS11 .16 E5
Churchend GL2 .95 D4
Churchend La GL12 .66 F3
Churchfarm Cl BS37 .43 F3
Churchfield Rd
Stroud GL5 .99 D6
Churchfield Rd *continued*
Upton St Leonards GL4 .119 E3
Churchfields GL52 .138 A4
Churchhill Rd GL5 .148 A5
Churchill Ave SN26 .144 E1
Churchill Cl Bristol BS30 .11 A5
Nailsworth GL6 .91 B4
Churchill Dr Bristol BS9 .17 D7
Cheltenham GL52 .131 A7
Churchill Gdns GL52 .131 A7
Churchill Gr GL20 .192 F4
Churchill Mdw HR8 .178 E8
Churchill Pl 9 GL7 .152 E4
Churchill Rd Bristol BS4 .9 C4
Cheltenham GL53 .130 E6
Cirencester GL7 .190 E5
Gloucester GL1 .118 E7
Nailsworth GL6 .91 B4
Churchill Way
Mitcheldean GL17 .164 D5
Painswick GL6 .103 F8
Churchpath Rd BS20 .16 C4
Churchside BS16 .20 B7
Churchview Dr GL4 .119 D8
Churchward Cl
9 Bristol BS15 .10 B5
Honeybourne WR11 .188 C7
Churchward Rd BS37 .43 B3
Churchway SN26 .144 E1
Churchways BS14 .3 C4
Churchways Ave BS7 .18 E6
Churchways Cres BS7 .18 E6
Churclands 8 BS3 .8 B2
Churn Ave GL52 .134 A2
Churn Cl GL7 .142 F8
Churn Hill GL7 .158 D3
Churn The GL6 .103 F8
Churston Cl BS14 .3 A3
Cicely Way GL4 .119 F5
Cicester Terr 14 GL56 .187 A3
Cidermill Cl NP16 .60 F4
Cidermill La GL55 .189 A2
Cidermill Orch GL55 .188 D4
Cinder Hill Coleford GL16 155 A5
St Briavels GL15 .146 E7
Cinder La GL7 .152 F4
Cinderford Rd GL15 .156 D2
Cinderhill Way GL17 .163 E4
Circle The GL5 .99 C8
Circuit 32 BS5 .9 B8
Circular Rd BS9 .17 E2
Cirencester Bsns Ctr GL7 .190 D2
Cirencester Coll GL7 .190 A4
Cirencester Hosp GL7 .190 B4
Cirencester Jun & Inf Sch GL7 .190 D3
Cirencester Kingshill Sch GL7 .190 F5
Cirencester Rd
Charlton Kings GL53 .131 A4
Fairford GL7 .152 C3
Latton SN6 .143 D7
Little Witcombe GL3 .121 A4
Minchinhampton GL6 .148 C4
South Cerney GL7 .151 A2
Tetbury GL8 .140 C4
City Bank Rd GL7 .190 D3
City Bsns Pk BS5 .9 A8
City of Bristol Coll South Bristol Ctr at Bedminster BS3 .8 E2
City Rd BS2 .195 B4
Claire's Cl GL5 .148 A5
Clamp The BS30 .11 C3
Clanage Rd BS3 .7 E4
Clanna La GL15 .147 C4
Clanna Rd GL15 .147 D4
Clapham Ct GL1 .196 C3
Clapton Row 8 GL54 .168 F7
Clapton Wlk BS9 .17 C5
Clare Ave BS7 .18 C3
Clare Ct Cheltenham GL53 193 B1
Stroud GL5 .99 E7
Clare Pl GL53 .193 B1
Clare Rd
Bristol, Cotham BS6 .18 D1
Bristol, Kingswood BS15 .20 C2
Bristol, Lower Easton BS5 .19 B2
Clare St Bristol BS1 .195 A2
Bristol, Moorfields BS5 .9 C8
Cheltenham GL53 .193 B1
Gloucester GL1 .196 A3
Clare Wlk BS35 .64 B2
Claremont 1 GL52 .133 F2
Claremont Ave BS7 .18 D3
Claremont Ct Bristol BS9 .18 C5
Gloucester GL1 .196 C3
Claremont Rd Bristol BS7 .18 D3
Gloucester GL1 .196 C3
Claremont Specl Sch BS9 .18 C5
Claremont St BS5 .19 A1
Claremont Terr 10 BS5 .9 D7
Clarence Ave BS16 .20 E5
Clarence Ct
1 Cheltenham GL52 .193 C4
Wooton-u-E GL12 .68 B7
Clarence Gdns BS16 .20 E5
Clarence Par GL50 .193 B3
Clarence Pl BS2 .194 C4
Clarence Rd Bristol BS1 .195 B1
Bristol, Kingswood BS15 .20 B1
Bristol, Staple Hill BS16 .20 E5
Bristol, Upper Easton BS2 .9 A7
Cheltenham GL52 .193 C4
Tewkesbury GL20 .192 C2
Wooton-u-E GL12 .68 B7
Clarence Sq GL50 .193 C4
Clarence St
Cheltenham GL50 .193 B4
Gloucester GL1 .196 B2
Clarence Wlk GL50 .193 B3
Clarendon Cl NP16 .61 A4
Clarendon Ct 6 GL5 .99 C7
Clarendon Rd Bristol BS6 .18 C2
Winchcombe GL54 .174 A8
Claridge Cl GL4 .119 D4
Clarington Mews GL50 .133 E3
Clark Dr BS16 .19 F7
Clark St BS5 .9 A8
Clark's Alley GL20 .192 C5
Clark's Hay GL7 .142 F8
Clark's La Blakeney GL15 156 D1
Siddington GL7 .150 D2
Clarke Ave GL56 .187 C3
Clarke St BS3 .8 D4
Clarke Way GL50 .133 D3
Clarken Coombe BS41 .7 B3
Clarkia Cl GL3 .127 F7
Clarrie Rd 1 GL8 .140 C4
Clattergrove GL6 .112 A2
Clatworthy Dr BS14 .3 A7
Claudians Cl GL4 .119 E7
Claudius Way GL15 .92 B4
Clavell Rd BS10 .27 F2
Claverham Rd BS16 .20 A5
Claverton Rd BS31 .5 E2
Claverton Rd W BS31 .5 D3
Clay Bottom BS5 .19 E2
Clay Hill BS5 .19 E2
Clay La Bitton BS30 .5 D8
Bristol, Little Stoke BS34 .29 C7
Bristol, Willsbridge BS30 .11 D1
Thornbury BS35 .64 E1
Clay Pit Rd BS6 .18 A3
Clay Rd GL16 .155 B7
Clayburn Cl GL2 .125 E5
Claydon Gn BS14 .2 F3
Clayfield BS37 .43 E5
Clayfield Rd BS4 .9 E3
Clayfurlong Gr GL7 .141 F8
Claymore Cres BS15 .20 B1
Claypatch Rd NP25 .154 A7
Claypiece Rd BS13 .2 A4
Claypit Hill BS37 .33 B7
Claypits Hill GL2,GL10 .100 D1
Claypits La GL6 .99 F5
Claypool Rd BS15 .10 E7
Clays Rd GL16 .155 B2
Clayton St
Avonmouth BS11 .26 A1
21 Bristol BS5 .9 B8
Clearview NP25 .154 B1
Clearwater Dr GL2 .117 E1
Clearwell Caves* GL16 155 A3
Clearwell CE Prim Sch GL16 .155 A2
Cleave St BS2 .19 A2
Clee Ho GL20 .192 C3
Cleeve Ave BS16 .20 E7
Cleeve Cloud La GL52 .134 D3
Cleeve Ct GL52 .137 F3
Cleeve Gdns BS16 .20 D7
Cleeve Gr BS31 .4 D5
Cleeve Hill BS16 .20 D7
Cleeve Hill Extension BS16 .20 E6
Cleeve Ho GL5 .99 F1
Cleeve La BS30 .22 D1
Cleeve Lake Ct GL52 .137 E4
Cleeve Lawns BS16 .20 D7
Cleeve Lodge Cl BS16 .20 E6
Cleeve Lodge Rd BS16 .20 E6
Cleeve Mill Bsns Pk GL18 .171 A5
Cleeve Mill Est GL18 .171 B5
Cleeve Mill La GL18 .171 B5
Cleeve Park Rd BS16 .20 E7
Cleeve Rd Bristol BS4 .9 B3
Bristol, Frenchay BS16 .20 C8
Bristol, Mangotsfield BS16 .20 E6
Gloucester GL4 .119 B4
Gotherington GL52 .138 A7
Yate BS37 .43 E1
Cleeve Rise GL18 .171 A4
Cleeve Sch GL52 .138 A2
Cleeve View GL52 .136 E5
Cleeve View Inf Sch GL51 .133 C4
Cleeve View Rd GL52 .134 A2
Cleeve Wood Rd BS16 .20 D7
Cleevecroft Ave GL52 .138 A3
Cleeveland St GL51 .133 C3
Cleevelands Ave GL50 .133 E4
Cleevelands Cl GL50 .133 E5
Cleevelands Dr GL50 .133 E5
Cleevemont GL52 .133 E5
Cleevemont Cl GL52 .133 F3
Cleevemount Rd GL52 .133 F4
Clegram Rd GL1 .118 D7
Clematis Ct GL52 .137 E3
Clement St Bristol BS2 .195 C4
Gloucester GL1 .119 A8
Clements End Rd GL16 .155 B2
Clencher's Mill La HR8 .179 B7
Clent Ct GL52 .133 F1
Cleve Ct
3 Bristol, Clifton Wood BS8 .7 F6
Bristol, Filton BS34 .29 B4
Cleve House Sch BS4 .9 B3
Cleve Rd BS34 .29 A4
Clevedale BS16 .20 D7
Clevedale Ct BS16 .20 D7
Clevedon Rd Bristol BS7 .18 D4
Gloucester GL1 .118 F6

Clevedon Sq GL51 ... 133 A2
Clevedon Terr BS6 ... 195 A4
Cleveland Cl BS35 ... 51 E8
Clewson Rise BS14 ... 2 F3
Cliff Court Dr BS16 ... 20 B7
Cliff View NP16 ... 61 B7
Clifford Ave GL20 ... 192 E2
Clifford Gdns BS11 ... 16 E6
Clifford Rd BS16 ... 20 C4
Cliffords 7 SN6 ... 143 E4
Clift House Rd BS3 ... 8 A4
Clift House Spur BS3 ... 7 F4
Clift Pl BS1 ... 195 A1
Clift Rd BS3 ... 8 A4
Clifton Cl 1 Bristol BS8 ... 7 F7
14 Stow-on-t-W GL54 ... 176 F4
Clifton Coll BS8 ... 194 A4
Clifton College Prep Sch BS8 ... 17 F1
Clifton Down BS8 ... 7 F7
Clifton Down Rd BS8 ... 194 A3
Clifton Down Sh Ctr 11 BS8 ... 18 B1
Clifton Down Sta BS8 ... 18 B1
Clifton High Gr BS9 ... 17 E5
Clifton High Sch BS8 ... 194 A4
Clifton Hill BS8 ... 194 A2
Clifton Metro 10 BS8 ... 18 B1
Clifton Park Rd BS8 ... 7 F8
Clifton Pk BS8 ... 194 A3
Clifton Pl BS5 ... 9 A8
Clifton Rd Bristol BS8 ... 194 A2
Gloucester GL1 ... 196 A1
Clifton St
Bristol, Bedminster BS3 ... 8 C3
Bristol, Upper Easton BS5 ... 9 A8
Clifton Suspension Bridge★ BS8 ... 7 E7
Clifton Vale BS8 ... 194 A2
Clifton Vale Cl BS8 ... 194 A2
Clifton View 1 BS3 ... 8 F4
Clifton Wood Ct BS8 ... 194 B2
Clifton Wood Rd BS8 ... 194 B2
Cliftonwood Cres BS8 ... 194 B2
Cliftonwood Terr BS8 ... 194 A2
Cliinton Ho GL7 ... 190 D5
Clingre Down GL11 ... 87 C4
Clingre La GL11 ... 87 C4
Clinton Rd BS3 ... 8 C2
Clissold Ct GL6 ... 91 B3
Clive Rd BS14 ... 3 C8
Cloatley Rd SN16 ... 141 E1
Clock House Sq GL54 ... 166 C6
Cloisters Rd BS36 ... 30 F6
Cloisters The GL52 ... 137 E4
Clomoney Way GL2 ... 127 D5
Clonmel Rd BS4 ... 8 D1
Close Gdns
Condicote GL54 ... 176 B7
13 Tetbury GL8 ... 140 B4
Close The
Bristol, Henbury BS10 ... 28 A5
Bristol, Little Stoke BS34 ... 29 C6
Bristol, Patchway BS32 ... 40 C1
Bristol, Upper Soundwell BS16 ... 20 D3
Cheltenham GL53 ... 130 D4
Coaley GL11 ... 88 E7
Coalpit Heath BS36 ... 31 C6
Coleford GL16 ... 155 C6
Dursley GL11 ... 87 E4
Lechlade on T GL7 ... 153 E3
Slimbridge GL2 ... 95 E3
South Cerney GL7 ... 143 A8
Southam GL52 ... 134 C8
Whitminster GL2 ... 100 F5
Clothier Rd BS4 ... 9 F2
Cloud The GL12 ... 68 B7
Clouds Hill Ave BS5 ... 9 E8
Clouds Hill Rd BS5 ... 9 F8
Clovelly Cl BS5 ... 9 F8
Clovelly Rd BS5 ... 9 F8
Clover Cl
Cinderford GL14 ... 156 C6
Milkwall GL16 ... 155 B4
Clover Dr GL2 ... 109 E6
Clover Ground BS9 ... 18 B7
Clover Leaze BS32 ... 29 D6
Clover Piece GL4 ... 119 D6
Cloverdale Dr BS30 ... 11 A3
Cloverlea Bsns Ctr BS36 ... 31 C3
Cloverlea Rd BS30 ... 11 C5
Clyde Ave BS31 ... 4 F4
Clyde Cres GL52 ... 134 A2
Clyde Ct 2 BS3 ... 8 C3
Clyde Gdns BS5 ... 10 B6
Clyde Gr BS34 ... 28 F2
Clyde Ho 7 BS35 ... 51 C8
Clyde La BS6 ... 18 C2
Clyde Mews 3 BS6 ... 18 C2
Clyde Rd
Bristol, Knowle BS4 ... 9 A3
Bristol, Redland BS6 ... 18 B2
Brockworth GL3 ... 120 F5
Frampton Cotterell BS36 ... 31 B8
Clyde Terr
3 Bristol, Bedminster BS3 ... 8 C3
Bristol, Knowle BS4 ... 9 A3
Clydesdale Cl BS14 ... 3 A6
Co-operation Rd BS5 ... 19 C1
Coach Cl GL13 ... 85 E3
Coach Ho GL56 ... 186 C7
Coach Ho The GL20 ... 192 D4
Coach Rd HR9 ... 164 D8
Coaley CE Prim Sch GL11 ... 88 E8
Coaley Rd BS11 ... 16 D5
Coalsack La BS36 ... 31 B3
Coalville Rd BS36 ... 31 D7
Coalway Inf Sch GL16 ... 155 B5
Coalway Prim Sch GL16 ... 155 B5
Coalway Rd GL16 ... 155 B5
Coape Rd BS14 ... 3 F5
Coates Gdns GL10 ... 97 F8
Coates Ho 11 GL51 ... 132 E2
Coates La GL7 ... 149 F4
Coates Mill Cotts GL54 ... 139 F4
Coates The GL54 ... 139 F4
Coates Wlk BS4 ... 2 D6
Cobbler's Cl The GL52 ... 138 A7
Cobblestone Mews BS8 ... 194 A4
Cobden St BS5 ... 9 C7
Coberley BS15 ... 10 C6
Coberley CE Prim Sch GL53 ... 123 A5
Coberley Rd
Cheltenham GL51 ... 129 D8
Gloucester GL4 ... 118 E3
Cobham Ct GL51 ... 133 B3
Cobham Rd GL51 ... 133 B3
Cobhorn Dr BS13 ... 1 F4
Cobourg Rd BS6 ... 18 F2
Cochran Cl GL3 ... 128 C5
Cock La SN14 ... 23 D5
Cock Rd BS15 ... 10 F6
Cockadilly GL10 ... 89 D5
Cockatoos La HR9 ... 170 B5
Codrington Pl BS8 ... 194 A3
Codrington Rd BS7 ... 18 D3
Cody Ct 1 BS15 ... 10 B5
Cogan Rd BS16 ... 20 E3
Cogsall Rd BS14 ... 3 F6
Colchester Cl
Mitcheldean GL17 ... 164 D5
Northwood Green GL14 ... 165 C1
Colchester Cres BS4 ... 2 D7
Cold Pool La
Bamfurlong GL51 ... 129 B5
Cheltenham GL51 ... 129 D6
Coldharbour La
Bristol BS16 ... 19 E8
Newent GL18 ... 170 F6
Coldharbour Rd
Bristol BS6 ... 18 B4
St Briavels GL15 ... 146 E6
Coldicotts Cl GL55 ... 189 A2
Coldpark Gdns BS13 ... 1 E5
Coldpark Rd BS13 ... 1 E5
Coldray Cl GL1 ... 127 B1
Coldrick Cl BS14 ... 2 F3
Coldwell GL10 ... 98 B3
Coldwell Cl GL10 ... 98 B3
Coldwell La GL10 ... 98 B3
Cole Ave GL2 ... 118 C3
Cole Rd BS2 ... 9 B6
Colebridge Ave GL2 ... 127 C3
Colebrook Rd BS15 ... 10 C8
Coleford Rd Bream GL15 ... 147 C8
Bristol BS10 ... 28 D1
Tutshill NP16 ... 72 F2
Colemead BS13 ... 2 B5
Coleridge Ho BS34 ... 40 A1
Coleridge Rd BS5 ... 19 C3
Colerne Dr GL3 ... 120 B7
Colesborne Cl BS37 ... 32 E8
Colesbourne Rd GL51 ... 129 D8
Coleshill Dr BS13 ... 2 B5
Colin Cl BS35 ... 64 C1
Colin Rd GL4 ... 127 D1
Coll of St Matthias Inf Sch BS16 ... 20 A5
Collard Ho 2 BS16 ... 19 F4
College Ave BS16 ... 20 A5
College Baths Rd GL53 ... 193 C2
College Ct Bristol BS16 ... 20 A5
Gloucester GL1 ... 196 B3
College Fields Bristol BS8 ... 7 F8
Gloucester GL2 ... 127 D4
College Gate GL53 ... 193 C2
College Gn Bristol BS1 ... 194 C2
Gloucester GL1 ... 196 B3
College Lawn GL53 ... 193 C1
College Park Dr BS10 ... 27 F1
College Rd Bredon GL20 ... 182 B7
Bristol, Clifton BS8 ... 7 F8
Bristol, Fishponds BS16 ... 20 A5
Bristol, Westbury on Trym BS9 ... 18 A7
Cheltenham GL53 ... 193 C2
Cinderford GL14 ... 191 C4
Stroud GL5 ... 99 A8
College Sq BS1 ... 194 C2
College St Bristol BS1 ... 194 C2
Gloucester GL1 ... 196 B3
College View
Cirencester GL7 ... 190 B1
9 Stonehouse GL10 ... 97 F7
Collett Cl BS15 ... 10 B5
Collett Pl SN6 ... 143 E6
Collett Way BS37 ... 43 C3
Colletts Dr GL51 ... 133 B3
Colletts Fields WR12 ... 185 C8
Colletts Gdns 6 WR12 ... 185 C8
Colliers Break BS16 ... 21 B5
Colliers Pitch GL15 ... 147 C5
Colliers Wood GL6 ... 91 A5
Collin Cl WR12 ... 188 B2
Collin La WR12 ... 188 A2
Collin Rd BS4 ... 9 D4
Collingbourne Rd GL4 ... 119 A7
Collingwood Ave BS15 ... 20 E1
Collingwood Cl
Chepstow NP16 ... 61 A5
Saltford BS31 ... 5 E2
Collingwood Rd 4 BS6 ... 18 B1
Collins Ave BS34 ... 29 C6
Collins Cl GL19 ... 172 A8
Collins St BS11 ... 16 B8
Collinson Rd BS13 ... 2 B5
Colliter Cres BS3 ... 8 B2
Collum End Rise GL53 ... 130 D4
Coln House Specl Sch GL7 ... 152 D3
Coln Rise GL54 ... 166 D6
Coln Sq BS35 ... 51 C8
Colne Ave GL52 ... 134 A3
Colne Gn BS31 ... 5 A4
Colston Ave BS1 ... 195 A2
Colston Cl Bristol BS16 ... 20 D3
Winterbourne BS36 ... 30 E4
Colston Ct BS7 ... 18 D3
Colston Dale BS16 ... 19 E4
Colston Fort 2 BS2 ... 195 A4
Colston Hill BS16 ... 19 D4
Colston Mews BS6 ... 18 E1
Colston Par BS1 ... 195 B1
Colston Rd BS5 ... 19 C1
Colston St Bristol BS1 ... 195 A3
Bristol, Upper Soundwell BS16 ... 20 D3
Colston Yd BS1 ... 195 A3
Colston's Girls Sch BS6 ... 18 E1
Colston's Prep Sch BS16 ... 19 D5
Colston's Prim Sch BS6 ... 18 D1
Colston's Sch BS16 ... 19 C4
Colstone Ct 3 BS16 ... 19 E3
Colsty Mdw GL15 ... 156 D1
Coltham Cl 7 GL52 ... 130 F8
Coltham Fields GL52 ... 130 F8
Coltham Rd GL52 ... 130 F8
Colthurst Dr BS15 ... 10 E5
Coltman Cl GL1 ... 127 B1
Colts Gn BS37 ... 33 E8
Columbia Cl GL1 ... 196 C3
Columbia St GL52 ... 193 C4
Colville Ho GL7 ... 190 D5
Colwell Ave GL3 ... 128 A1
Colwyn Dr GL51 ... 129 E6
Colwyn Rd 2 BS5 ... 19 C1
Colyton Ct BS3 ... 8 D1
Comb Paddock BS9 ... 18 B7
Combe Cross Wlk BS13 ... 2 B3
Combe Gdns GL11 ... 87 C3
Combermere BS35 ... 51 D8
Combfactory La 13 BS5 ... 9 B8
Combrook Cl GL4 ... 119 E4
Commercial Rd
Bristol BS1 ... 195 A1
Chalford GL6 ... 148 C5
Gloucester GL1 ... 196 A2
Commercial St
Cheltenham GL50 ... 193 B1
Cinderford GL14 ... 191 D4
Common (East) The BS32 ... 40 C1
Common Hill SN6 ... 143 E4
Common La BS20 ... 16 B2
Common Mead La BS16 ... 30 A1
Common Rd Bristol BS15 ... 10 B3
Minchinhampton GL6 ... 91 E6
Winterbourne BS36 ... 30 F7
Common The
Berkeley Heath GL13 ... 86 C3
Bristol, Frenchay BS16 ... 20 B7
Bristol, Patchway BS32 ... 40 C1
Minety SN16 ... 142 E1
Siddington GL7 ... 150 E2
Commonfield Rd BS11 ... 27 B1
Commonmead La BS37 ... 33 F8
Compton Cl
Churchdown GL3 ... 128 A8
Staunton GL19 ... 172 A7
Compton Dr BS9 ... 17 C7
Compton Gn BS31 ... 4 E4
Compton Lodge 3 BS6 ... 18 B1
Compton Rd GL51 ... 133 B4
Compton Rise GL54 ... 166 E2
Compton St BS5 ... 9 C7
Compton's Alley GL20 ... 192 C4
Comyn Wlk BS16 ... 20 A5
Concord GL6 ... 91 A3
Concorde Dr BS10 ... 28 B1
Concorde Rd BS34 ... 28 E7
Concorde Way GL4 ... 119 B7
Condicote La GL54 ... 176 B5
Condor Ho BS7 ... 19 C7
Condover Rd BS4 ... 10 A3
Conduit Hill GL55 ... 188 F1
Conduit Pl 2 BS2 ... 19 A1
Conduit Rd BS2 ... 19 A1
Conduit St GL1 ... 196 C1
Condurrow Ct 18 GL54 ... 176 F4
Cone The BS10,BS34 ... 28 C6
Coney Hill Com Prim Sch GL4 ... 119 C7
Coney Hill Par GL4 ... 119 C7
Coney Hill Rd GL4 ... 119 C7
Coneygar Rd GL7 ... 152 C7
Coneygree BS13 ... 1 F6
Coneygree La WR12 ... 185 B7
Coneygreen Cotts GL56 ... 186 C6
Congleton Rd BS5 ... 9 D8
Conham Hill BS15 ... 10 A5
Conham Rd BS4,BS5,BS15 ... 9 F5
Conham Vale BS15 ... 10 A5
Conifer Cl Bristol BS16 ... 20 D6
Frampton Cotterell BS36 ... 42 A1
Conifers The
2 Cheltenham GL52 ... 134 A3
Gloucester GL1 ... 119 A7
Conigree La GL20 ... 192 C2
Coniston Ave BS9 ... 17 E6
Coniston Cl BS30 ... 11 D6
Coniston Prim Sch BS34 ... 39 F1
Coniston Rd Bristol BS34 ... 39 F1
Cheltenham GL51 ... 129 E7
Gloucester GL2 ... 127 C4
Connaught Rd BS4 ... 2 E8
Consell Gn GL54 ... 184 C3
Constable Cl BS31 ... 4 F6
Constable Rd BS7 ... 19 B6
Constance Cl GL5 ... 98 F5
Constantine Ave BS34 ... 29 E5
Constitution Hill BS8 ... 194 B2
Convent Cl BS10 ... 27 D3
Convent La GL5 ... 90 F7
Convent The OX7 ... 169 E7
Conway Ct 4 GL16 ... 155 A7
Conway Gn BS31 ... 5 A3
Conway Rd Bristol BS4 ... 9 C4
Gloucester GL3 ... 120 A8
Conygar Rd GL8 ... 140 C4
Conygre Gr BS34 ... 29 C3
Conygre Rd BS34 ... 29 B3
Cook Cl BS30 ... 11 C4
Cook St BS11 ... 16 C8
Cook's Folly Rd BS9 ... 17 D3
Cook's Hill GL19 ... 172 C4
Cook's La GL19 ... 179 F4
Cooke's Dr BS35 ... 39 A1
Cooks Cl BS32 ... 40 D3
Cooks La BS36 ... 31 D3
Cooks Orch GL1 ... 127 A3
Cooksley Rd BS5 ... 9 C8
Cookson Terr GL15 ... 84 B8
Cookspool 2 GL8 ... 140 C4
Cookworthy Cl 2 BS5 ... 9 B6
Coomb Dr GL14 ... 191 C1
Coomb Rocke BS9 ... 17 D6
Coombe Ave BS35 ... 64 B2
Coombe Bridge Ave BS9 ... 17 D6
Coombe Cl BS10 ... 27 D3
Coombe Dale BS9 ... 17 C6
Coombe Gdns BS9 ... 17 E6
Coombe Glen La GL51 ... 129 D6
Coombe Ho GL8 ... 140 B4
Coombe La Bristol BS9 ... 17 E6
Easton-in-G BS8 ... 16 A1
King's Stanley GL10 ... 98 C2
Wooton-u-E GL12 ... 68 D8
Coombe Lea NP16 ... 146 A5
Coombe Meade GL52 ... 138 B3
Coombe Rd Bristol BS5 ... 19 C2
Wooton-u-E GL12 ... 68 C8
Coombe Terr GL12 ... 68 C8
Coombe Way BS10 ... 27 F1
Coombes Way BS30 ... 11 D4
Coombs Rd GL16 ... 155 A6
Cooper Rd Bristol BS9 ... 17 F7
Thornbury BS35 ... 51 B7
Cooper's Ct
Brockworth GL3 ... 120 E5
Charlton Kings GL53 ... 131 B5
Cooper's Hill★ GL3 ... 120 E2
Cooper's View GL3 ... 120 E5
Cooperage La BS3 ... 194 B1
Cooperage Rd BS5 ... 9 D7
Coopers Dr BS37 ... 43 F5
Coopers Elm GL2 ... 117 F2
Coopers Mill GL5 ... 91 A6
Coopers Rd GL16 ... 155 A8
Coopers Way 27 GL18 ... 171 A4
Coots The BS14 ... 3 E6
Cope Pk BS32 ... 40 C5
Copeland Dr BS14 ... 3 B5
Copford La BS41 ... 7 B1
Copley Ct BS15 ... 10 E5
Copley Dr 9 GL16 ... 155 A5
Copley Gdns BS7 ... 19 B6
Coppenacre SN16 ... 142 B1
Copper Beech Gr GL2 ... 117 E1
Copper Beeches SN6 ... 145 C3
Copperfield Cl GL4 ... 119 B4
Coppice Daw Pitch GL19 ... 165 D5
Coppice Gate GL51 ... 132 F5
Coppice Hill GL6 ... 148 D5
Coppice Rd GL17 ... 163 D3
Coppice The
Bristol, Bradley Stoke BS32 ... 29 E7
Bristol, Highridge BS13 ... 1 E4
Copse Rd Bristol BS4 ... 9 B3
Keynsham BS31 ... 5 C4
Copse The GL4 ... 119 E7
Copsehill Rd GL54 ... 176 C1
Copt Elm Cl GL53 ... 131 A6
Copt Elm Rd GL53 ... 131 A6
Copthorne Cl BS14 ... 3 B5
Coral Cl GL4 ... 118 B3
Corbet Cl BS11 ... 27 C2
Corbett Ho 11 BS5 ... 9 C7
Corder's La 2 GL56 ... 187 A3
Corders Cl 5 GL56 ... 187 A3
Cordingley Cl GL3 ... 128 C5
Cordwell Wlk BS10 ... 18 D7
Corey Cl 6 BS2 ... 18 F1
Corfe Cl GL52 ... 134 C4
Corfe Cres BS31 ... 4 E4
Corfe Pl BS30 ... 11 B1
Corfe Rd BS4 ... 2 D7
Coriander Dr Bristol BS34 ... 30 A7
Innsworth GL3 ... 127 F7
Coriander Wlk BS5 ... 19 C2
Corinium Bsns Pk GL14 ... 191 B7
Corinium Cntr GL7 ... 190 D1
Corinium Gate GL7 ... 190 D5
Corinium Ho GL7 ... 190 B3
Corinium Mus★ GL7 ... 190 C5
Corinthian Ct 9 BS1 ... 195 B1
Corker's Hill 9 BS5 ... 9 F6
Cormorant Ave GL20 ... 192 E2
Corn St BS1 ... 195 A3
Corncroft La GL4 ... 119 D2
Corndean La GL54 ... 174 A5
Corner Farm Dr WR11 ... 188 C6
Corner Rd GL15 ... 155 F1
Cornfield Cl BS32 ... 40 C1
Cornfield Dr
Bishop's Cleeve GL52 ... 137 E4
Hardwicke GL2 ... 109 E7
Cornfields The GL52 ... 137 E4
Cornflower Rd GL4 ... 119 E5
Cornhill GL5 ... 99 C7
Cornhill Dr BS14 ... 3 A7
Cornish Gr BS14 ... 3 E6
Cornish Hos
Cinderford GL14 ... 156 C6
Moreton-in-M GL56 ... 187 B3
Cornish Rd BS14 ... 3 E6
Cornish Wlk BS14 ... 3 E6
Cornleaze BS13 ... 2 A5
Cornmeadow Dr GL51 ... 132 D5
Cornwall Ave GL51 ... 133 A2
Cornwall Cres BS37 ... 43 F3
Cornwall Rd BS7 ... 18 D4
Cornwallis Ave BS8 ... 194 A2
Cornwallis Cres BS8 ... 7 F6
Cornwallis Gr BS8 ... 194 A2
Corolin Rd GL2 ... 118 B4
Coronation Ave
Bristol BS16 ... 20 A4
Keynsham BS31 ... 4 D4
Coronation Cl
Bristol BS30 ... 11 A5
Chipping Campden GL55 ... 188 F2
Coronation Flats GL52 ... 131 A7
Coronation Gr GL2 ... 127 B2
Coronation Pl BS1 ... 195 A2
Coronation Rd
Bristol BS3 ... 194 B1
Bristol, Cadbury Heath BS30 ... 11 B5
Bristol, Mangotsfield BS16 ... 20 E5
Bristol, Warmley BS15 ... 11 A7
Cinderford GL14 ... 191 D3
Prestbury GL52 ... 134 B4
Stroud GL5 ... 99 B6
Tetbury GL8 ... 140 B5
Coronation Sq GL51 ... 132 E2
Coronation St GL7 ... 152 D4
Corpus St GL52 ... 193 C2
Corriett The GL11 ... 88 A5
Corsend Rd GL19 ... 172 B4
Corsley Wlk BS4 ... 2 F8
Corston Wlk BS11 ... 16 D7
Cossham Cl BS35 ... 64 C2
Cossham Meml Hospl BS16 ... 20 C2
Cossham Rd Bristol BS5 ... 9 D7
Pucklechurch BS16 ... 22 C4
Cossham St BS16 ... 21 B5
Cossham Wlk BS5 ... 20 A1
Cossington Rd BS4 ... 2 F8
Cossins Rd BS6 ... 18 B3
Costers Cl BS35 ... 51 A5
Costiland Dr BS13 ... 1 F6
Cote Dr BS9 ... 18 A4
Cote House La BS9 ... 18 A5
Cote La BS9 ... 18 A5
Cote Lea Pk BS9 ... 18 B7
Cote Paddock BS9 ... 17 F4
Cote Pk BS9 ... 17 E6
Cote Rd BS9 ... 18 A4
Cotham Brow BS6 ... 18 D1
Cotham Gdns 15 BS6 ... 18 B1
Cotham Gr BS6 ... 18 D1
Cotham Gram Sch BS6 ... 194 C4
Cotham Gram Sch Charnwood Annexe BS6 ... 18 C1
Cotham Hill BS6 ... 194 C4
Cotham Lawn Ho BS6 ... 194 C4
Cotham Lawn Rd BS6 ... 18 C1
Cotham Pk BS6 ... 18 C1
Cotham Pk N BS6 ... 18 C1
Cotham Pl BS6 ... 194 C4
Cotham Rd BS6 ... 194 C4
Cotham Rd S BS6 ... 195 A4
Cotham Side BS6 ... 18 D1
Cotham Vale BS6 ... 18 C1
Cothar's Pitch HR9 ... 170 A5
Cothers Ct GL56 ... 186 C6
Cotman Wlk BS7 ... 19 B6
Cotrith Gr BS10 ... 27 E3
Cotsmore Cl GL56 ... 187 B3
Cotswold Ave
Cirencester GL7 ... 190 C3
Eastington GL10 ... 96 F7
Cotswold Bsns Village GL56 ... 187 B3
Cotswold Chine Home Specl Sch GL6 ... 91 D5
Cotswold Cl
Bredon GL20 ... 182 C7
Brimscombe GL5 ... 148 A5
Cirencester GL7 ... 190 B3
5 Tetbury GL8 ... 140 C5
Cotswold Com GL7 ... 142 E6
Cotswold Cotts GL6 ... 90 F3
Cotswold Ct BS37 ... 44 B1
Cotswold Edge GL55 ... 189 A6
Cotswold Edge Bsns Pk GL2 ... 118 C8
Cotswold Falconry Ctr★ GL56 ... 186 E4
Cotswold Farm Pk★ GL54 ... 175 D5

Cotswold Gdns
Gloucester GL2 .... 127 D5
21 Moreton-in-M GL56 .. 187 A3
Tewkesbury GL20 .... 192 D5
Wooton-u-E GL12 .... 68 C7
Cotswold Gn GL10 ...... 98 A8
Cotswold La BS37 .... 34 A8
Cotswold Lo 10 GL52 .... 133 F2
Cotswold Mead GL6 .... 103 E7
Cotswold Mill GL7 ..... 190 C4
Cotswold Nuffield Hospl
GL51 .... 130 A8
Cotswold Pl GL20 ...... 192 D5
Cotswold Rd Bristol BS3 ... 8 D3
Cheltenham GL52 .... 134 B3
Chipping Sodbury BS37 ..... 33 B8
Stroud GL5 .... 98 E8
Cotswold Sch The GL54 . 168 F8
Cotswold View
Bristol, Filton BS34 .... 29 A3
Bristol, Kingswood BS15 ... 20 D2
Charfield GL12 .... 67 B5
Tirley GL19 .... 172 F7
Wickwar GL12 .... 54 B6
Woodmancote GL52 ..... 138 B3
Cotswold Water Pk★
GL7 .... 142 D5
Cotswold Way SN6 ..... 145 C3
Cotswolds Countryside Mus★
GL54 .... 167 F2
Cotswolds Motoring Mus
The★ GL54 .... 168 F7
Cotswolds Water Pk★
GL7 .... 153 A2
Cottage Field GL2 ..... 125 D5
Cottage Pitch GL18 .... 171 A5
Cottage Pl BS2 .... 195 A4
Cottage Rake Ave GL50 . 133 C5
Cottage The GL5 .... 98 C7
Cotteswold Rd
Gloucester GL4 .... 119 B5
Tewkesbury GL20 .... 192 D5
Cotteswold Rise GL5 .... 99 D7
Cottington Ct BS15 ...... 10 E5
Cottisford Rd BS5 .... 19 B4
Cottle Gdns BS14 .... 3 F6
Cottle Rd BS14 .... 3 F6
Cotton Cl GL4 .... 119 F5
Cotton's La GL8 .... 140 B3
Cottonwood Dr BS30 .... 11 A3
Cottrell Ave BS15 .... 20 C2
Cottrell Rd BS5 .... 19 C3
Cotts The GL56 .... 186 F6
Coughton Pl HR9 ...... 163 C8
Coulson Wlk BS15 ...... 20 C2
Coulson's Cl BS14 .... 3 A3
Coulson's Rd BS14 .... 3 A3
Council Hos
Cold Aston GL54 .... 168 B6
Eastnor HR8 .... 179 C7
Ledbury HR8 .... 178 A8
Stow-on-t-W GL54 ...... 176 F5
Council Villas
Clearwell GL16 .... 154 F3
Edge End GL16 .... 155 C8
English Bicknor GL16 .... 163 B1
Sling GL16 .... 155 B3
Counterpool Rd BS15 .... 10 C7
Counterslip BS1 .... 195 B2
Counterslip Gdns BS14 ... 3 C6
Countess Lilias Rd GL7 . 190 C2
Countess Wlk BS16 ...... 19 D6
County Court Rd GL50 .. 193 B3
County Cres 3 GL1 ..... 127 A1
County St BS4 .... 9 A4
Court Ave BS34 .... 29 F5
Court Cl BS7 .... 18 E7
Court Dr GL19 .... 173 B6
Court Farm Oaksey SN16 142 A4
Tibberton GL19 .... 124 B8
Court Farm La
Beckford GL20 .... 183 B6
Mitcheldean GL17 ...... 164 D5
Court Farm Mews GL10 . 97 D7
Court Farm Rd
Bristol, Longwell Green
BS30 .... 10 E2
Bristol, Whitchurch BS14 .... 2 F3
Court Field 11 GL8 ..... 140 B4
Court Gdn GL11 .... 89 B1
Court Gdns
Gloucester GL2 .... 118 B6
St Arvans NP16 .... 72 B6
Strand GL14 .... 157 C8
Court Gdns The GL2 .... 157 B5
Court La Netherend GL15 147 D3
8 Newent GL18 .... 171 A4
Wick BS30 .... 12 B6
Court Mdw Stone GL13 ... 77 F3
Wooton-u-E GL12 .... 68 C7
Court Mead GL13 .... 77 E3
Court Mews The GL52 .. 131 A7
Court Orch Gretton GL54 183 E1
Wooton-u-E GL12 .... 68 C7
Court Pl GL4 .... 119 D7
Court Rd
Bristol, Horfield BS7 ...... 18 F6
Bristol, Kingswood BS15 ... 10 D7
Bristol, Oldland Common
BS30 .... 11 C3
Brockworth GL3 .... 120 E6
Frampton Cotterell BS36 ... 30 F8
Frocester GL10 .... 97 B3
Lydney GL15 .... 92 B5
Newent GL18 .... 171 A5
Court Rd *continued*
Prestbury GL52 .... 134 C4
Upper Strensham WR8 ... 180 D7
Court St SN16 .... 58 C1
Court View GL6 .... 148 D6
Court View Cl BS32 ...... 40 A5
Court Way GL5 .... 99 A5
Courtbrook GL7 .... 152 E3
Courtenay Rd BS31 .... 5 B2
Courtenay St GL50 ..... 133 D3
Courteney Cres BS4 .... 2 D7
Courtfield Dr 6 GL52 .. 131 B6
Courtfield Gr BS16 ...... 20 A4
Courtfield Rd GL2 ...... 109 F8
Courthouse Gdns GL11 .. 87 F6
Courtiers Dr GL52 ..... 138 A3
Courtlands Bristol BS32 .. 40 C1
Keynsham BS31 .... 4 E5
Courtlands La BS3 .... 7 E4
Courtlands Unit BS4 ...... 2 D8
Courtney Cl GL20 ...... 192 D1
Courtney Prim Sch BS15 . 10 F7
Courtney Rd BS15 .... 10 E7
Courtney Way BS15 ..... 11 A7
Courtside Mews BS6 ..... 18 C1
Courtyard The
Bourton-on-t-W GL54 .... 168 F8
Cheltenham GL50 .... 193 A2
Stow-on-t-W GL54 ...... 176 F5
Courville Cl BS35 .... 51 A4
Cousins Cl BS10 .... 27 D3
Cousins La BS5 .... 9 F8
Cousins Mews BS4 .... 9 F6
Cousins Way BS16 .... 21 B8
Cousley Cl GL3 .... 120 A7
Couzens Cl BS37 .... 44 B2
Couzens Pl BS34 .... 29 F5
Cove House Gdns 3
SN6 .... 142 F5
Coventry Cl GL20 ...... 192 D2
Coventry Wlk BS4 .... 9 F6
Coverham Cl 10 GL16 ... 155 A7
Coverham Rd GL16 ..... 155 A7
Cow La GL5 .... 91 A6
Cowcombe Hill GL6 .... 148 C5
Cowdray Rd BS4 .... 2 D7
Cowhorn Hill BS30 ...... 11 C4
Cowl La GL54 .... 174 A7
Cowler Wlk BS13 .... 1 F4
Cowley Cl GL51 .... 129 E7
Cowley La HR9 .... 170 C2
Cowley Rd GL4 .... 118 E3
Cowling Dr BS14 .... 3 C5
Cowling Rd BS14 .... 3 D5
Cowlsmead GL51 .... 129 E2
Cowper Rd Bristol BS6 ... 18 C1
Cheltenham GL51 .... 132 E1
Cowper St BS5 .... 9 C7
Cowship La GL12 .... 53 D6
Cowslip Mdw GL52 ..... 138 B3
Cowswell La GL6 .... 148 B6
Cox Ct BS30 .... 10 F4
Cox's Hill SN6 .... 142 F5
Cox's Way Bream GL15 .. 155 D1
Gloucester GL4 .... 120 A6
Coxbury & Wyegate La
GL15 .... 154 D2
Coxgrove Hill BS16 ...... 21 F7
Coxmoor Cl OX7 .... 177 F2
Coxwell Ct GL7 .... 190 C5
Coxwell St GL7 .... 190 C5
Cozens La OX7 .... 177 F2
Crab Tree Pl GL50 ..... 133 C3
Crabtree Cl BS41 .... 1 D1
Crabtree La
Cirencester GL7 .... 190 F3
Dundry BS41 .... 1 D2
Duntisbourne Abbots GL7 . 107 B3
Crabtree Pk GL7 .... 152 E4
Crabtree Rd GL14 ...... 191 B5
Crabtree Wlk BS5 .... 19 D2
Craddock Ct GL6 .... 90 F5
Craddock Rd 7 GL18 ... 171 A4
Cradock Cl BS30 .... 11 B4
Craftes Ct BS5 .... 19 E1
Craig Yr Afon NP16 ...... 60 E7
Crail View GL54 .... 168 A1
Cranberry Wlk BS9 ...... 17 C8
Cranbourne Rd BS34 .... 28 F7
Cranbrook Rd BS6 .... 18 C3
Crandell Cl BS10 .... 27 F4
Crane Cl BS15 .... 11 B8
Crane Furlong SN6 ..... 145 D4
Cranford Cl GL52 ...... 138 C3
Cranford Ct 1 BS9 ...... 18 B6
Cranham BS37 .... 32 C7
Cranham CE Prim Sch
GL4 .... 112 E6
Cranham Cl Bristol BS15 .. 20 F2
7 Gloucester GL4 .... 119 E5
Cranham Dr BS34 .... 40 C1
Cranham La GL3 .... 128 D3
Cranham Rd Bristol BS10 . 18 C8
Cheltenham GL52 .... 133 F1
Cranhams La GL7 ...... 190 B2
Cranleigh Court Inf Sch
BS37 .... 43 D3
Cranleigh Court Rd BS37 43 D2
Cranleigh Gdns BS9 ..... 17 E4
Cranleigh Rd BS14 .... 3 B5
Cranley GL50 .... 133 E3
Cranmoor Gn BS35 ...... 38 D7
Cranmore Ave BS31 .... 4 E6
Cranmore Cres BS10 ..... 28 D1
Cranside Ave BS6 .... 18 C4
Cransley Cres BS9 ...... 18 C7
Crantock Ave BS13 .... 2 B8
Crantock Dr BS32 .... 40 B5
Crantock Rd BS37 .... 43 D1
Cranwell Cl GL4 .... 119 C4
Cranwell Gr BS14 .... 3 A5
Crapen The GL11 .... 87 E4
Crashmore La GL20 ..... 182 F7
Crates Cl BS15 .... 10 E8
Craven Cl BS30 .... 10 F5
Craven Dr GL3 .... 128 B6
Craven Way BS30 .... 10 F5
Crawley Hill GL11 .... 89 B3
Crawley La GL11 .... 89 B3
Crawshay Pl GL14 ...... 191 C4
Craydon Gr BS14 .... 3 D4
Craydon Rd BS14 .... 3 D5
Craydon Wlk BS14 .... 3 D5
Crease The 16 GL18 .... 171 A4
Crediton Cres BS4 .... 8 F1
Credon Rd GL3 .... 127 E1
Crescent Cl
Coleford GL16 .... 155 A6
Stonehouse GL10 .... 97 E6
Crescent Pl GL50 .... 193 B3
Crescent Rd Bristol BS16 . 20 C6
Stonehouse GL10 .... 97 E6
Crescent Terr GL50 ..... 193 B3
Crescent The
8 Berry Hill GL16 ...... 155 A7
Bristol, Frenchay BS16 .... 29 F1
Bristol, Henleaze BS9 ..... 18 C6
Bristol, Sea Mills BS9 ..... 17 C6
Bristol, Upper Soundwell
BS16 .... 20 D3
Brockworth GL3 .... 120 D6
Chalford GL6 .... 148 E6
Coleford GL16 .... 155 A5
Coleford GL16 .... 155 A6
Dursley GL11 .... 87 F4
Mitcheldean GL17 ...... 164 D6
Northwood Green GL14 .. 165 D3
Olveston BS35 .... 50 D4
Sharpness GL13 .... 85 D8
Wick BS30 .... 12 C7
Crescentdale GL2 ...... 127 A5
Crest The Bristol BS4 ..... 9 C2
West Kington SN14 ...... 25 F3
Crest Way GL4 .... 127 F1
Creswicke Ave BS15 ..... 10 C5
Creswicke Rd BS4 .... 2 E7
Crew's Hole Rd BS5 ...... 9 E7
Cribbs Causeway Ctr
BS34 .... 28 A6
Cribbs Cswy BS10 .... 28 A6
Cricklade Rd Bristol BS7 . 18 E4
Cirencester GL7 .... 190 E2
Cricklade SN5 .... 143 E1
Highworth SN6 .... 145 C3
Cricklade St
Cirencester GL7 .... 190 C4
Poulton GL7 .... 151 E3
Crickley Hill Ctry Pk★
GL3 .... 122 A5
Criftycraft La GL3 ...... 128 C3
Crippetts La GL51 ...... 130 B3
Cripps Rd Bristol BS3 ..... 8 C3
Cirencester GL7 .... 190 C4
Crispin Cl Gloucester GL2 127 C5
1 Winchcombe GL54 .... 174 A7
Crispin La BS35 .... 64 B1
Crispin Rd GL54 .... 174 A7
Crispin Way BS15 .... 20 F2
Critchford La GL54 .... 175 A5
Crockerne CE Prim Sch
BS20 .... 16 C4
Crockerne Dr BS20 ...... 16 C3
Crockerne Ho BS20 ...... 16 D4
Croft Ave Bristol BS16 ... 19 C4
Charlton Kings GL53 .... 131 B5
Croft Cl Bitton BS30 ...... 5 D8
Churchdown GL3 .... 128 D4
Newent GL18 .... 171 A5
Croft Cty Prim Sch The
GL6 .... 103 E8
Croft Dr GL53 .... 131 A5
Croft Farm Leisure & Water
Pk★ GL20 .... 182 A6
Croft Gdns
8 Broadway WR12 ..... 185 B8
Charlton Kings GL53 .... 131 B4
Croft Hall Sch GL7 ..... 152 E4
Croft Holm GL56 .... 187 B3
Croft La Latton SN6 .... 143 E6
Winstone GL7 .... 107 A7
Croft Par GL53 .... 131 B5
Croft Rd
Charlton Kings GL53 .... 131 A5
Newent GL18 .... 171 A5
Croft St GL53 .... 130 D6
Croft The
Bristol, Mangotsfield BS16 . 20 F5
Bristol, Oldland Common
BS30 .... 11 C3
Dursley GL11 .... 88 A4
12 Fairford GL7 .... 152 E4
Painswick GL6 .... 111 F1
Croft Thorne Cl GL51 .. 129 F5
Croft View BS9 .... 18 C6
Crofters Wlk BS32 ...... 29 D8
Croftlands The GL20 ... 182 C7
Crofton Ave BS7 .... 18 F6
Crofton Fields BS36 ..... 30 E6
Crofts End Ind Est BS5 .. 19 E1
Crofts End Rd BS5 ...... 19 E1
Crofts Field GL20 ...... 181 D5
Crofts The GL18 .... 171 A5
Crokeswood Wlk BS11 ... 27 A1
Crome Rd BS7 .... 19 B7
Cromer Rd BS5 .... 19 C2
Cromers Cl GL20 ...... 182 C5
Cromhall La GL12 .... 65 D1
Cromwell Ct BS15 .... 10 E5
Cromwell Rd
Bristol, Montpelier BS6 .... 18 E2
Bristol, St George BS5 .... 10 A8
Cheltenham GL52 .... 134 A3
Chepstow NP16 .... 60 E5
Cromwell St Bristol BS3 ... 8 C3
Gloucester GL1 .... 196 B2
Cromwell View BS6 ...... 18 E2
Cromwells Hide BS16 .... 19 E5
Crooked End Pl GL17 ... 163 F4
Crooks Ind Est GL53 ... 130 D6
Croomes Hill BS16 ...... 20 D6
Cropthorne Rd BS7 ...... 29 A1
Cropthorne Rd S BS7 .... 19 A8
Crosby Row BS8 .... 194 A2
Cross Elms La BS9 ...... 17 E5
Cross Farm Cl GL15 .... 147 E4
Cross Hands Rd BS35 ... 38 D7
Cross Keys La GL1 ..... 196 B3
Cross Lanes BS20 .... 16 C4
Cross St Bristol BS15 .... 20 D1
Keynsham BS31 .... 4 F7
Cross The Horsley GL6 .... 90 F1
Nympsfield GL10 .... 89 E6
Ripple GL20 .... 181 D8
Cross Tree Cres GL7 ... 144 E8
Cross Tree Flats GL7 ... 144 E7
Cross Tree Gr BS32 ..... 29 D8
Cross Vane NP25 .... 154 B3
Cross Wlk BS14 .... 3 A6
Crosscombe Dr BS13 ...... 2 C3
Crossfield Rd BS16 ...... 20 E3
Crossfields GL54 .... 166 D6
Crossleaze Rd BS15 ..... 10 C3
Crossley Cl BS36 .... 30 F7
Crossman Ave BS36 ...... 30 E5
Crossways GL16 .... 154 F6
Crossways Jun & Inf Sch
BS35 .... 64 D1
Crossways Rd Bristol BS4 . 9 A1
Thornbury BS35 .... 64 D1
Crouch Ct GL20 .... 192 C3
Crow Ash 9 GL16 ...... 155 A7
Crow Ash Rd GL16 ..... 155 A7
Crow La Bristol BS1 .... 195 A2
Henbury BS10 .... 27 F2
Crow Mdw GL12 .... 67 F4
Crowfield GL52 .... 138 B4
Crowfield La GL18 ..... 178 E2
Crowgate La GL14 ...... 157 F8
Crowley Way BS11 .... 26 B1
Crown Cl
Bishop's Cleeve GL52 .... 137 F3
Dymock GL18 .... 178 D2
Crown Cotts GL5 .... 98 F8
Crown Ct GL10 .... 98 A3
Crown Dr GL52 .... 137 F2
Crown Gdns BS30 .... 11 B7
Crown Hill BS5 .... 9 F8
Crown Hill Wlk BS5 ..... 19 F1
Crown Ind Est BS30 ...... 11 C7
Crown La Bristol BS16 ... 20 D4
Parkend GL15 .... 155 E2
Yorkley GL15 .... 156 A1
Crown Mdw 11 GL16 ... 155 B5
Crown Rd
Bristol, Upper Soundwell
BS15 .... 20 D2
Bristol, Warmley BS30 .... 11 C6
Crowndale Rd BS4 .... 9 A3
Crownleaze BS16 .... 20 D3
Crows Gr BS32 .... 40 D3
Crowther Pk BS7 .... 19 A4
Crowther Rd BS7 .... 19 A4
Crowther St 4 BS3 ...... 8 B3
Crowthers Ave BS37 ..... 43 E3
Croydon Ho 1 BS5 .... 9 B8
Croydon St BS5 .... 9 B8
Crucible Cl GL16 ...... 155 A5
Crucible Ct GL16 ...... 155 A5
Crudwell CE Prim Sch
SN16 .... 141 C3
Crudwell La GL8 .... 140 F3
Crump Pl GL15 .... 92 C2
Crunnis The BS32 .... 29 E6
Crusty La BS20 .... 16 C5
Crypt Ct GL4 .... 118 C3
Crypt Sch The GL2 ..... 118 D4
Crypt The GL18 .... 178 D2
Crythan Wlk 4 GL51 ... 129 F5
Cuckoo Cl 4 GL6 ...... 148 C6
Cuckoo La BS36 .... 30 F3
Cuckoo Row GL6 .... 91 F6
Cud La GL6 .... 103 B8
Cudnall St GL53 .... 131 A7
Cuffington Ave BS4 .... 9 D4
Culkerton GL8 .... 140 F6
Cullerns The SN6 ...... 145 D3
Culleysgate La BS30 ..... 12 F6
Cullimore View GL14 ... 191 C1
Cullingham Cl GL19 .... 172 A8
Cullis La GL16 .... 155 B6
Culross Cl GL50 .... 133 E4
Culver Hill GL5 .... 91 A8
Culver St Bristol BS1 ... 194 C2
Newent GL18 .... 171 A4
Culverhay GL12 .... 68 B7
Culverhill Rd BS37 ...... 44 A1
Culverhill Sch BS37 ..... 32 D7
Culvers Rd BS31 .... 4 E6
Culvert The BS32 .... 29 D8
Culverwell Rd BS13 ...... 2 A4
Cumberland Basin Rd BS8 7 F5
Cumberland Cl BS1 .... 194 A1
Cumberland Cres GL51 . 133 A2
Cumberland Gr 5 BS6 .. 18 F2
Cumberland Pl 6 BS8 .... 7 F6
Cumberland Rd BS1 .... 194 B1
Cumberland St BS2 .... 195 B4
Cumbria Cl BS35 .... 64 E1
Cumming Ct GL52 ...... 134 A4
Cunningham Gdns BS16 . 20 B5
Cupola Cl GL16 .... 155 A5
Curland Gr BS14 .... 3 B5
Curlew Cl Bristol BS16 ... 19 F6
Northway GL20 .... 182 B5
Curlew Rd GL4 .... 119 C6
Cursey La GL51 .... 136 B5
Cursey Lane Cvn Pk
GL51 .... 173 F7
Cursus The GL7 .... 153 E3
Curtis Hayward Dr GL2 . 117 E1
Curtis La BS34 .... 30 A4
Custom Cl BS14 .... 3 A7
Cut & Fry Rd GL15 ..... 156 B1
Cut Throat La HR9 ..... 170 A2
Cutham La GL7 .... 158 C1
Cuthwine Pl GL7 .... 153 E3
Cutler Rd Bristol BS13 ..... 1 F6
Stroud GL5 .... 99 D8
Cutlers Brook Jun Sch
BS2 .... 19 A2
Cutsdean Cl GL52 ...... 137 D4
Cutsheath Rd GL12 ...... 52 C8
Cutters Row BS3 .... 8 E4
Cutwell GL8 .... 140 B3
Cylde Pk BS6 .... 18 B2
Cynder Way BS16 .... 31 A1
Cypress Ct BS9 .... 17 D3
Cypress Gdns BS8 .... 7 E6
Cypress Gr BS9 .... 18 C6
Cypress Rd GL20 ...... 192 E2
Cypress Wlk SN14 .... 15 F6
Cyrus Ct BS16 .... 21 B7

D

Daffodil Cl GL4 .... 119 E5
Daffodil Leaze GL10 ..... 98 B3
Daffodil St GL50 ...... 193 B2
Daffodils The GL10 ...... 98 B3
Dagmar Rd GL50 .... 193 A1
Daines Ct 4 BS16 ...... 19 E3
Dainty St GL1 .... 118 F7
Dairy Farm SN6 .... 142 F4
Dairy La WR11 .... 183 F6
Dairycroft BS2 .... 195 B4
Daisy Bank GL5 .... 99 E6
Daisy Green La GL12 .... 79 D2
Daisy Rd BS5 .... 19 C2
Daisybank Rd GL53 ..... 130 E2
Dakin Cl BS4 .... 8 E1
Dakota Dr BS14 .... 3 A4
Dalby Ave BS3 .... 8 D4
Daldry Gdns BS35 .... 50 A3
Dale Cl GL4 .... 118 F5
Dale St Bristol BS2 .... 195 C4
Bristol, St George BS5 ...... 9 F8
Temple Guiting GL54 .... 175 D2
Dale Wlk GL52 .... 138 A3
Dalebrook HR9 .... 170 B4
Dalkeith Ave BS15 ...... 20 C1
Dallaway GL5 .... 99 E2
Dalrymple Rd 11 BS2 .... 18 E1
Dalston Rd BS3 .... 8 B4
Dalton Sq BS2 .... 195 B4
Damery La Stone GL13 ... 77 F3
Woodford GL13 .... 78 A4
Dampier Rd BS3 .... 8 A3
Damsells The 9 GL8 ... 140 C4
Damson Cl GL4 .... 119 E4
Danbury Cres BS10 ...... 28 C1
Danbury Wlk BS10 ...... 28 C1
Danby Cl Cinderford GL14 191 E4
Yorkley GL15 .... 156 B2
Danby Ho BS7 .... 19 A5
Danby Rd GL15 .... 156 B2
Dancey Mead BS13 .... 1 F6
Dancey Rd GL3 .... 127 F6
Dane Cl GL2 .... 127 C5
Dane La GL7 .... 149 B6
Danes Cl NP16 .... 60 D8
Danes Hill NP16 .... 61 B7
Danford La GL19 .... 172 B3
Danford Villas GL19 .... 172 B3
Dangerfield Ave BS13 ..... 1 F6
Daniels Ind Est GL5 ...... 98 F5
Daniels Rd GL5 .... 99 F7
Dapps Hill BS31 .... 4 F5
Dapwell La BS14,BS31 ..... 4 A1
Darell Cl GL2 .... 109 F7
Darell Gdns GL2 .... 157 F3
Dark La Chalford GL6 ... 148 C5
Nailsworth GL6 .... 91 A4
North Cerney GL7 ...... 158 E3
Stroud GL5 .... 99 B5
Swindon GL51 .... 133 A7
Dark Ride GL7 .... 149 C8
Darken La GL15 .... 147 E4
Darks Rd GL18 .... 170 C3
Darley Cl BS10 .... 27 D3
Darleydale Cl GL2 ..... 109 D8
Darnell's La HR9 ...... 170 B4
Darnley Ave BS7 .... 18 F6
Darren Rd 13 GL16 ..... 155 A7
Dart Cl Quedgeley GL2 .. 117 F2
Thornbury BS35 .... 51 B8
Dart Rd GL52 .... 134 B3
Darters Cl GL15 .... 92 A2
Dartmoor St BS3 .... 8 B3
Dartmouth Wlk BS31 ...... 4 D4
Darwin Cl GL51 .... 129 C8
Darwin Rd GL4 .... 119 A5

Daston Cl 2 WR12 .....185 C8
Daubeny Cl BS16 ....20 B5
Daubeny Ct BS1 ....195 A1
Davallia Dr GL51 ....129 F5
Daventry Rd BS4 ....8 F1
Daventry Terr GL1 .....196 C1
Davey St BS2 ....18 F1
Davey Terr 8 BS2 ....18 F1
David French Ct GL51 ..130 A5
David St BS2 ....195 C3
David's La BS35 ....51 A4
David's Rd BS14 ....3 C6
Davids Cl BS35 ....51 A4
Davies Dr BS4 ....9 F5
Davies Rd GL56 ....187 B3
Davillian Ct GL2 ....118 A3
Davin Cres BS20 ....16 C3
Davis Cl BS30 ....10 F5
Davis Ct BS35 ....64 C2
Davis St BS11 ....16 B8
Davron Ct BS3 ....8 E4
Davy Cl GL2 ....109 F6
Dawes Cl GL7 ....153 C6
Dawes Ct 2 BS8 ....7 F6
Dawes The GL2 ....109 F8
Dawley Cl BS36 ....30 E7
Dawlish Rd BS3 ....8 D2
Dawn Rise BS15 ....21 A1
Dawneys The SN16 .....141 C3
Daws Ct BS16 ....20 B4
Day House La GL12 .....55 C8
Day's La GL56 ....186 C5
Day's Rd BS2 ....9 A6
Daylesford Cl GL51 ....129 D8
Days Ct SN16 ....141 C3
Days Road Commercial Ctr BS2 ....9 A7
De Clifford Rd BS11 .....27 C2
De Ferrieres Wlk 12 GL51 ....132 D2
De Havilland Rd GL54 ..169 D7
De La Warre Ct 11 BS4 ....9 F6
De Verose Ct BS15 ......10 E4
Deacon Cl
Cheltenham GL51 ....129 F7
Winterbourne BS36 ....30 E5
Deacons Pl GL52 ....137 E2
Deakin Cl GL51 ....133 B7
Dean Ave BS35 ....64 C2
Dean Cl BS15 ....10 B4
Dean Close Prep Sch GL51 ....130 A8
Dean Close Sch
Cheltenham GL51 ....129 F8
Cheltenham GL51 ....130 A8
Dean Cres 8 Bristol BS3 ...8 C4
1 Bristol BS3 ....8 D4
Littledean GL14 ....156 E8
Dean Ct Lydney GL15 .....92 B5
Yate BS37 ....43 C3
Dean Farm Cotts GL7 ..160 F2
Dean Forest Rly★ GL15 ..92 A2
Dean Hall Sch GL16 ....155 F6
Dean Heritage Mus★ GL14 ....156 D5
Dean La Bristol BS3 ....8 C4
Stoke Orchard GL52 .....136 E5
Dean Mdws GL17 ....164 D5
Dean Rd Avonmouth BS11 .26 C5
Newnham GL14 ....156 F6
Yate BS37 ....43 C3
Dean St
Bristol, Bedminster BS3 ....8 C4
Bristol, St Pauls BS2 .....195 B4
Dean Swift Cl HR9 .....162 F6
Dean View GL14 ....191 C1
Dean's Dr BS5 ....20 A2
Dean's Quarry GL5 ......91 F7
Dean's Terr GL1 ....196 B4
Dean's Way GL1 ....196 B4
Dean's Wlk GL1 ....196 B4
Dean's Wlk GL17 ......164 B4
Deanery Cl BS15 ....11 B8
Deanery Rd Bristol BS1 .194 C2
Bristol, Warmley BS15 .....11 B8
Deanhill La BA1 ....6 F2
Deanna Ct BS16 ....20 E6
Deans Ct 3 GL51 ......129 F7
Deans Gdns NP16 ....72 D1
Deans Hill NP16 ....60 D8
Deans Mead BS11 ....17 A8
Deans Row GL1 ....126 E4
Deans Way GL52 ....137 F3
Deansfield SN6 ....143 E4
Debecca's La BS20 ......16 B4
Deep Coombe Rd BS3 ....8 A2
Deep Pit Rd BS5 ....19 F2
Deep St GL52 ....134 B4
Deer Park Rd GL3 .....128 A1
Deer Park Sch GL7 .....150 B4
Deer Pk GL15 ....156 A2
Deerhurst Bristol BS15 ...20 E3
Yate BS37 ....32 C8
Deerhurst & Apperley CE Prim Sch GL19 ......173 C7
Deerhurst Cl
Gloucester GL4 ....119 E4
Little Compton GL56 .....187 F1
Deerhurst Pl GL2 ......117 E1
Deering Cl BS11 ....27 B1
Deers Wood Cty Prim Sch BS15 ....21 A2
Deerswood BS15 ....21 A2
Delabere Ave BS16 ......20 B5
Delabere Rd GL52 .....138 A2
Delancey Hospl GL53 ..130 D4
Delavale Rd GL54 .....174 A7
Deleware Rd GL7 ......152 E2
Delius Gr BS4 ....2 D7
Delkin Rd GL11 ....87 F4
Delkin The GL11 ....87 F4
Dell Prim Sch The NP16 .72 E1
Dell The Blockley GL56 ...186 C6
Bredon GL20 ....182 C8
Bristol, Bradley Stoke BS32 .29 E7
Bristol, Oldland Common BS30 ....11 C5
Bristol, Westbury on Trym BS9 ....17 F5
Gloucester GL4 ....119 E7
Dell View NP16 ....60 E8
Delmont Gr GL5 ....99 C8
Delphinium Dr GL52 ...137 E3
Delta Dr GL20 ....182 B4
Delta Way GL3 ....120 C6
Delvin Rd BS10 ....18 C8
Denbigh Dr NP16 ....61 A5
Denbigh Rd GL51 ......129 E6
Denbigh St BS2 ....18 F1
Dene Cl BS31 ....4 F3
Dene Magna Com Sch GL17 ....164 D4
Dene Rd BS14 ....3 C4
Denehurst GL17 ....163 F3
Denfurlong Farm (Farm Trail)★ GL54 ......159 B5
Denham Cl
Gloucester GL4 ....118 C1
Woodmancote GL52 .....138 C3
Denleigh Cl BS14 ....3 A4
Denley Cl GL52 ....137 F2
Denmark Ave BS1 .....194 C2
Denmark Ct GL1 ....127 A3
Denmark Dr NP16 ....61 B7
Denmark Pl BS7 ....18 E3
Denmark Rd GL1 ......196 C4
Denmark St BS1 ....194 C2
Denning Ct GL50 ......193 A1
Dennisworth BS16 ......22 B5
Dennor Pk BS14 ....3 B7
Denny Isle Dr BS35 .....38 A6
Denston Wlk BS13 ....2 A7
Dent's La GL19 ....172 B2
Dent's Terr 24 GL54 ....174 A7
Denton Patch BS16 .....21 B7
Dentwood Gr BS9 ....17 B8
Denvale Trad Pk BS4 .....2 E7
Denys Ct BS35 ....50 A3
Derby Ct GL1 ....127 A1
Derby Rd Bristol BS7 .....18 E3
Gloucester GL1 ....127 A1
Derby St BS5 ....9 D7
Derham Rd BS13 ....2 A5
Dermot St 11 BS2 ....18 F1
Derrick Rd BS15 ....10 D8
Derricke Rd BS14 ....3 F6
Derry Pk SN16 ....142 E1
Derry Rd BS3 ....8 B2
Derry The SN6 ....142 F4
Derwent Cl Bristol BS34 ..29 A8
Brockworth GL3 ....120 E5
Derwent Ct BS35 ....51 D8
Derwent Dr GL20 ......192 E6
Derwent Gr BS31 ....5 A5
Derwent Rd BS5 ....19 F1
Derwent Wlk 1 GL51 ...129 F7
Desford Cl GL4 ....119 F5
Despenser Rd GL20 ....192 C2
Detmore Cl GL53 ....131 D5
Devaney Cl BS4 ....9 F5
Devauden Rd NP16 ......72 B7
Devereaux Cres GL5 .....98 C7
Devereaux Rd GL5 ......98 C7
Deveron Gr BS31 ....5 A4
Devil's Chy★ GL53 .....130 D1
Devil's Elbow The GL6 ...91 E4
Devil's La GL12 ....67 A2
Devon Ave GL51 ....133 A2
Devon Gr BS5 ....9 C8
Devon Rd BS5 ....19 C1
Devon Road Trad Est 1 BS5 ....19 C1
Devonshire Bldgs BS3 ....8 E4
Devonshire Pl GL20 ....192 D2
Devonshire Rd BS6 .....18 B4
Devonshire St GL50 ....193 A4
Devonshire Terr 3 GL56 ....187 A3
Dewey Cl GL52 ....138 B3
Dewfalls Dr BS32 ....40 D1
Dial La BS16 ....20 D6
Diamond Rd BS5 ....9 F7
Diamond St BS3 ....8 C3
Diamonite Ind Pk BS16 ..20 A3
Diana Gdns BS32 ....29 E8
Dianas Cl GL4 ....119 F6
Dibden Cl BS16 ....21 A8
Dibden La
Alderton GL20,GL54 .....183 E4
Bristol BS16 ....21 B7
Dibden Rd BS16 ....21 A7
Dickens Cl Bristol BS7 ....19 A8
Gloucester GL4 ....118 F5
Dickens Mews GL4 .....118 F5
Didbrook Mews GL4 ...119 E4
Didbrook Prim Sch GL54 ....184 D2
Didsbury Cl BS10 ....27 F1
Digbeth St 10 GL54 ....176 F4
Digby Dr GL20 ....192 E6
Dighton Ct 3 BS2 ......195 A4
Dighton Gate BS34 ......29 E5
Dighton St BS2 ....195 A4
Dikler Cl GL54 ....169 A6
Dilke Meml Hospl
Cinderford GL14 ....191 A2
Dilke Meml Hospl *continued*
Ruspidge GL14 ....156 B7
Dill Ave GL51 ....132 E4
Dillon Ct 17 BS5 ....9 D7
Dimore Cl GL2 ....109 E7
Dinas Cl GL51 ....129 F6
Dinas Rd GL51 ....129 F6
Dinely St GL1 ....196 C1
Dingle Bglws GL53 ....158 A8
Dingle Cl BS9 ....17 C6
Dingle Ct BS13 ....1 F7
Dingle La GL20 ....182 A8
Dingle Rd BS9 ....17 D7
Dingle The Bristol BS9 ...17 D7
Winterbourne BS36 ....30 F3
Yate BS37 ....43 F4
Dingle View BS9 ....17 C7
Dinglewell GL3 ....119 F7
Dinglewell Inf & Jun Sch GL3 ....119 F7
Dinglewood Cl BS9 .....17 D7
Dings Wlk 4 BS2 ....9 A6
Discovery Rd GL4 ......119 F6
Distel Cl GL50 ....133 C5
District Ctr BS32 ....29 E8
Ditch La GL7 ....159 E3
Dixon Rd BS4 ....9 F2
Dixton Cl NP25 ....154 A8
Dixton Rd NP25 ....154 A8
Dock Gate La BS8 .....194 A1
Dock La GL20 ....182 C8
Dock Rd GL13 ....93 B1
Dockham Rd GL14 .....191 D4
Dockins Hill Way GL17 .164 D4
Docks Ind Est BS11 .....26 E7
Dodd Dr GL54 ....169 D7
Dodington Cl GL4 .....119 D7
Dodington La BS37 .....33 D5
Dodington Rd BS37 .....33 B7
Dodisham Wlk BS16 .....20 B6
Dog La GL3 ....121 D5
Dog Trap La SN16 .....142 C1
Dollar St GL7 ....190 C5
Dolman Cl BS10 ....27 F3
Domby Cl 17 GL16 ....155 A5
Domestic Fowl Trust★ WR11 ....188 C7
Dominion Rd BS16 ......19 F3
Donald Rd BS13 ....1 F7
Doncaster Rd BS10 .....18 C8
Doncombe Hill SN14 ....15 F7
Doncombe La SN14 .....15 F7
Donegal Rd BS4 ....8 D1
Dongola Ave BS7 ....18 E4
Dongola Rd BS7 ....18 E4
Donkey Field The GL7 ..151 C5
Donkey La GL56 ....186 C5
Donnington Wlk BS31 ....4 D4
Donside GL7 ....190 A7
Doone Rd BS7 ....18 F8
Dora Wlk 5 GL1 ....118 F7
Dorcas Ave BS34 ....29 F5
Dorchester Ct GL50 ....130 C6
Dorchester Rd BS7 .....19 A7
Dorester Cl BS10 ....28 C4
Dorian Cl BS7 ....18 E7
Dorian Rd BS7 ....18 E7
Dorian Way BS7 ....18 E8
Dorington Ct 6 GL6 ....148 B6
Dorington Wlk 13 GL51 .132 D2
Dormer Cl BS36 ....31 D6
Dormer Rd Bristol BS5 ...19 B3
Cheltenham GL51 ....132 F4
Dormers The SN6 ......145 D3
Dorney Rd GL1 ....118 E7
Dorrit Cl GL1 ....118 F6
Dorset Ave GL51 ......133 A2
Dorset Gr 9 BS2 ....19 A2
Dorset Ho 2 GL50 .....193 B4
Dorset Rd
Bristol, Kingswood BS15 ...20 D1
Bristol, Westbury on Trym BS9 ....18 B6
Dorset St 6 BS3 ....8 B3
Dorset Way BS37 ....44 A3
Double View GL14 .....191 D3
Doubledays 6 SN6 .....143 E4
Doughmeadow Cotts WR12 ....184 F6
Douglas Ho GL50 ......193 B2
Douglas Rd
Bristol, Horfield BS7 ......18 F7
Bristol, Kingswood BS15 ...10 D7
Doulton Way BS14 ....3 B5
Douro Lo GL50 ....193 A2
Douro Rd GL50 ....133 B1
Dove La Bristol, Redfield BS5 9 C7
Bristol, St Pauls BS2 .....195 C4
Dove St BS2 ....195 A4
Dove St S BS2 ....195 A4
Dovecote BS37 ....32 F7
Dovedale BS35 ....51 D8
Dovedale Cl GL2 ......109 D8
Dover Hay GL51 ......129 F5
Dover Pl BS8 ....194 B3
Dover's View GL55 ....188 D4
Dovercourt Rd BS7 .....19 A6
Doverdale Dr GL2 .....127 D4
Doveswell Gr BS13 ....2 A4
Doveton St 9 BS3 ....8 D4
Dovey Ct BS30 ....11 C5
Dowdeswell Cl BS10 ....27 F3
Dowding Cl BS37 ....44 C2
Dowding Way GL3 .....128 C5
Dowers' La GL7 ....150 A8
Dowling Rd BS13 ....2 D3
Down Ampney CE Prim Sch GL7 ....143 F8
Down Ampney Rd GL7 .143 D7
Down Farm Ho BS36 ....30 D6
Down Hatherley La GL2 173 C1
Down Leaze 2 BS35 ....51 A5
Down Rd Alveston BS35 ...51 A5
Marshfield SN14 ....25 C2
Winterbourne BS36 ....30 F4
Down The Alveston BS35 ..50 F5
Tockington BS32 ....50 D3
Down View Bristol BS7 ....18 F3
Chalford GL6 ....148 C6
Downend Lower Sec Sch BS16 ....20 F5
Downend Park Rd BS16 .20 D5
Downend Pk BS7 ....18 F5
Downend Rd
Bristol, Fishponds BS16 ...20 C5
Bristol, Horfield BS7 ......18 F5
Bristol, Kingswood BS15 ...20 D1
Downend Upper Sec Sch BS16 ....20 F7
Downfield Bristol BS9 ....17 C7
Keynsham BS31 ....4 D5
Stroud GL5 ....98 F7
Downfield Cl 1 BS35 ....51 A5
Downfield Dr BS36 ......31 B8
Downfield Ho GL51 ....129 D2
Downfield La GL20 .....182 A8
Downfield Lodge BS8 ...18 A1
Downfield Rd Bristol BS8 .18 A1
Stroud GL5 ....98 F7
Downhams The NP25 ...154 A7
Downland Cl BS4 ....2 D6
Downleaze
Bristol, Downend BS16 ....20 D8
Bristol, Stoke Bishop BS9 ..17 F3
Downleaze Dr BS37 .....33 B8
Downleaze Rd BS9 ......17 F3
Downman Rd BS7 ....19 A5
Downs Cl 3 BS35 ....51 A5
Downs Cote Ave BS9 ....17 F6
Downs Cote Dr BS9 .....17 F6
Downs Cote Gdns BS9 ...18 A6
Downs Cote Pk BS9 .....18 A6
Downs Cote View BS9 ...18 A6
Downs Ct BS9 ....18 B6
Downs Mill GL6 ....148 E4
Downs Pk E BS6 ....18 A4
Downs Pk W BS6 ....18 A4
Downs Rd Bristol BS9 ....18 A6
Dundry BS41 ....1 D2
Downs The GL12 ....53 F7
Downs View SN6 ......145 D3
Downs Way GL7 ....150 D7
Downside Cl BS30 ......10 F5
Downside Rd BS8 ....18 A1
Downsview Ct BS8 ......18 A1
Downton Rd Bristol BS4 ...8 D1
Stonehouse GL10 ....97 E6
Downy Cl GL2 ....117 E2
Dowry Pl 3 BS8 ....7 F5
Dowry Rd BS8 ....194 A2
Dowry Sq BS8 ....194 A2
Dowty Rd GL51 ....132 E2
Doynton La SN14 ....23 B3
Dozule Cl GL10 ....97 F3
Dr Brown's Cl GL6 ......91 F6
Dr Brown's Rd GL6 .....91 F7
Dr Crawfords Way GL6 ..91 F6
Dr Crouch's Rd GL6 ...148 B7
Dr Middletons Rd GL6 .148 C5
Dr Newton's Way GL5 ...99 C6
Dr White's Cl BS1 .....195 B1
Drag Rd HR9 ....162 E3
Dragon Ct BS5 ....19 E1
Dragon Rd BS36 ....30 D5
Dragon Wlk BS5 ....19 F1
Dragons Hill Cl BS31 .....4 F5
Dragons Hill Ct BS31 .....4 F5
Dragons Hill Gdns BS31 ..4 F5
Dragonswell Rd BS10 ...28 A2
Drake Cl Innsworth GL3 ..127 F7
Saltford BS31 ....5 D2
Drake La GL11 ....88 C2
Drake Rd BS3 ....8 A3
Drakes Pl GL50 ....193 A3
Draper Ct 3 BS5 ....9 C7
Draper's La GL19 ......172 D6
Drapers Ct GL52 ....138 B3
Draycot Pl BS1 ....195 A1
Draycott GL11 ....87 F7
Draycott Bsns Pk GL11 ..87 F7
Draycott Cres GL11 .....87 F7
Draycott Rd BS7 ....18 F5
Draydon Rd BS4 ....2 D8
Drayton Cl Bristol BS14 ...3 B8
Cheltenham GL51 ....133 B6
Gloucester GL4 ....119 C4
Drayton Rd Bristol BS9 ...17 C8
Cheltenham GL51 ....129 E8
Drayton Way GL4 ......119 C5
Drews Cl GL3 ....128 C4
Drews Ct GL3 ....128 C4
Driffield Cross Rds GL7 151 B1
Driffield Rd GL15 ....92 C5
Drift Cl GL7 ....190 A2
Drift Way GL7 ....190 A2
Drifton Hill SN14 ....25 F7
Drive The
Bristol, Hengrove BS14 .....3 C6
Bristol, Henleaze BS9 .....18 B5
Dursley GL11 ....87 F4
Drivemoor GL4 ....119 D3
Druetts Cl BS10 ....18 E6
Drugger's End La WR13 180 C8
Druid Cl BS9 ....17 E5
Druid Hill BS9 ....17 E5
Druid Rd BS9 ....17 D4
Druid Stoke Ave BS9 ....17 D5
Druid Woods BS9 ....17 C5
Druids Cl GL4 ....119 C7
Druids La GL4 ....119 C7
Druids Oak GL2 ....109 F8
Drummond Ct BS30 .....10 F4
Drummond Rd
Bristol, Fishponds BS16 ....19 F3
Bristol, St Pauls BS2 ......18 E1
Drury La GL19 ....179 D2
Dry Meadow La GL3 ...127 C7
Drybrook Rd GL17 .....164 B4
Drybrook Sch GL17 ....164 B4
Dryland Mews GL3 .....120 B6
Dryleaze Keynsham BS31 ...4 E7
Wooton-u-E GL12 ....68 A7
Yate BS37 ....43 E5
Dryleaze Ct GL12 ....68 A7
Dryleaze Gdns GL12 ....68 A7
Dryleaze Ho GL12 ......68 A7
Dryleaze Rd BS16 ......19 F6
Dubbers La BS5 ....19 E2
Dublin Cres BS9 ....18 B6
Duchess Rd BS8 ....18 A1
Duchess Way BS16 ......19 D6
Ducie Rd
Bristol, Redfield BS5 ....9 B7
Bristol, Staple Hill BS16 ...20 E5
Ducie St GL1 ....118 F7
Duck St GL12 ....52 C5
Duckmoor Rd BS3 ....8 A3
Duckworth Cl GL53 ....130 D5
Dudbridge Hill GL5 .....98 F6
Dudbridge Mdw GL5 ....98 F5
Dudbridge Rd GL5 ......98 F5
Duderstadt Cl GL5 ......98 F8
Dudley Cl BS31 ....4 E4
Dudley Cnr GL7 ....151 C5
Dudley Ct 3 BS30 ....10 F4
Dudley Farm GL7 ......151 C5
Dudley Gr BS7 ....19 A8
Dudley Rd WR11 ....188 C7
Duffield's La NP25 .....154 C5
Dugar Wlk BS6 ....18 C3
Dugdale Rd GL7 ....190 C5
Duglynch La GL54 .....183 E1
Duke of Beaufort Ct GL1 ....118 D5
Duke Of York Rd GL16 ..154 C7
Duke St GL52 ....133 F1
Dukeries The GL1 .....196 A3
Dukes Field GL7 ....143 F8
Dukes Way GL20 ....192 D1
Dulverton Pl GL56 .....187 B3
Dulverton Rd BS7 ....18 D4
Dumaine Ave BS34 ......29 E5
Dumbleton Gr GL51 ....129 B6
Dunalley Par GL50 .....133 D3
Dunalley Prim Sch GL50 ....133 E3
Dunalley St GL50 ......193 B4
Dunbar Cl GL51 ....132 D4
Duncombe La BS15 .....20 B2
Duncombe Rd BS15 .....20 B1
Duncroft Rd GL3 ......127 F1
Dundas Cl BS10 ....27 E2
Dundonald Rd BS6 ......18 B3
Dundridge Gdns BS5 ....10 A6
Dundridge La BS5 ......10 A6
Dundry CE Prim Sch BS41 1 D2
Dundry Cl BS15 ....10 D6
Dundry La BS41 ....1 C3
Dundry View BS4 ....9 A1
Dunford Rd BS3 ....8 D3
Dunkeld Ave BS34 ....28 F2
Dunkerry Rd BS3 ....8 D3
Dunkirk Rd BS16 ....19 F3
Dunlin Cl GL2 ....117 D1
Dunmail Prim Sch BS10 .28 C2
Dunmail Rd BS10 ....28 C2
Dunmore St 3 BS2 ....8 F4
Dunns Copse 15 HR8 ...178 F8
Dunsdown La SN14 ......24 B5
Dunsmore Gn GL19 ....181 B3
Dunstall Ho 17 GL56 ...187 A3
Dunstan Glen GL3 .....128 D4
Dunster Cl
Cheltenham GL51 ....132 D3
Gloucester GL4 ....118 B1
Dunster Gdns Bristol BS30 11 B2
Cheltenham GL51 ....132 D3
Dunster Gr GL51 ......132 D3
Dunster Rd Bristol BS4 ....2 F8
Cheltenham GL51 ....132 D3
Keynsham BS31 ....4 E4
Dunstone Pl GL17 .....164 D5
Durand Cl GL2 ....127 C6
Durand Ct GL12 ....68 A7
Durban Rd BS34 ....28 F8
Durbin Wlk BS5 ....9 A8
Durbridge Rd GL19 ....179 C1
Durdham Ho BS6 ....18 A3
Durdham Pk BS6 ....18 A3
Durham Cl GL51 ......130 A5
Durham Gr BS31 ....4 D4
Durham Rd 10 Bristol BS2 19 A2
Charfield GL12 ....67 A5
Gloucester GL4 ....119 C8
Durleigh Cl BS13 ....2 A7
Durley Hill BS31 ....4 C7
Durley La BS31 ....4 D7
Durn's Rd GL12 ....68 C7
Durncourt Cotts GL7 ...151 C5
Durnford Ave BS3 ....8 A4
Durnford St BS3 ....8 A4

Dursley CE Prim Sch
GL11 80 C8
Dursley Cl BS37 43 E1
Dursley Ct GL11 88 A1
Dursley Rd Bristol BS11 16 E5
Dursley GL11 87 E3
Slimbridge GL2 95 F3
Durville Rd BS13 2 B6
Durweston Wlk BS14 3 C8
Dutton Cl BS14 3 D6
Dutton Leys GL54 168 A1
Dutton Rd BS14 3 D6
Dutton Wlk BS14 3 D6
Duttons La GL17 163 F3
Dye House Rd GL12 67 F5
Dyer St GL7 190 D4
Dyer's La
Chipping Campden GL55 188 F2
Yate BS37 43 A4
Dyers Cl BS13 2 D4
Dyersbrook GL12 68 B7
Dyke House La GL18 179 B4
Dylan Thomas Ct 4
BS30 11 A5
Dynevor St GL1 118 F7
Dynevor Terr GL7 152 D4
Dyrham BS16 30 C1
Dyrham Cl
Bristol, Henleaze BS9 18 D6
Bristol, Kingswood BS15 10 F8
Thornbury BS35 64 C3
Dyrham Par BS34 29 C8
Dyrham Park* SN14 23 F5
Dyrham Rd BS15 10 F8

E

Eagar Ho GL53 131 B4
Eagle Cl GL6 148 B6
Eagle Cres BS16 22 C5
Eagle Dr BS34 28 E8
Eagle Mill Cl GL5 99 D5
Eagle Rd BS4 9 D2
Eagle Way GL4 119 C5
Eagles Wood Bsns Pk
BS32 40 C3
Ealy Hill GL7 107 C5
Eardisland Rd GL4 118 E2
Earl Russell Way BS5 9 B7
Earl St BS1 195 A4
Earls Cnr SN16 141 F4
Earlsmead BS16 19 E4
Earlstone Cl BS30 11 A4
Earlstone Cres BS30 11 A4
Early Way BS7 18 E8
Earthcott Rd BS35 51 F1
Easedale Cl BS10 28 D2
East Allcourt GL7 153 E2
East Approach Dr GL52 133 F4
East Court Mews GL52 131 C5
East Croft BS9 18 C7
East Ct BS3 7 F3
East Dr GL5 98 C7
East Dundry La BS41 2 A1
East Dundry Rd BS13,BS14 2 F2
East End GL54 168 A1
East End Flats GL53 131 C5
East End Rd GL52,GL53 131 C5
East Gable GL52 138 B3
East Gr BS6 18 F1
East Hill BS9 18 B7
East Link GL17 164 D5
East Par BS9 17 C6
East Park Dr BS5 19 C2
East Pk
Bristol, Lower Easton BS5 19 C2
Bristol, Rose Green BS5 19 D1
East Priory Cl BS9 18 A7
East Ridge Dr BS13 1 F5
East Shrubbery 3 BS6 18 B2
East St Avonmouth BS11 26 A1
Bristol, Bedminster BS3 8 D4
Bristol, St Pauls BS2 195 C4
Moreton-in-M GL56 187 A3
St Briavels GL15 146 F7
Tewkesbury GL20 192 C4
East View Bristol BS16 20 F6
Newnham GL14 156 F7
East Wlk BS37 43 E1
Eastbourne Rd 9 BS5 9 B8
Eastbourne Terr GL7 152 E3
Eastbrook Rd GL4 119 C8
Eastbury Cl BS35 64 C1
Eastbury Rd Bristol BS16 20 A4
Thornbury BS35 64 C1
Eastcote Pk BS14 3 B5
Eastcott Way GL3 128 A6
Eastern Ave
Gloucester GL4 119 B8
Mitcheldean GL17 164 D5
Eastern Way GL14 156 C6
Eastfield
Ashton Keynes SN6 142 F5
Bristol BS9 18 B7
Eastfield Dr BS37 43 E4
Eastfield Rd
Bristol, Eastfield BS9 18 B7
Bristol, Montpelier BS6 18 D2
Bristol, Westbury on Trym
BS9 18 A7
Minchinhampton GL6 148 A3
Eastfield Terr BS9 18 B6
Eastgate Ctr BS5 19 B3
Eastgate Office Ctr BS5 19 B3
Eastgate St GL1 196 B2
Eastholm Lawns GL3 128 C5
Eastington Prim Sch
GL10 97 A8
Eastington Rd GL54 168 A1
Eastington Trad Est
GL10 100 F1
Eastlake Cl BS7 19 B7
Eastland Ave BS35 64 C2
Eastland Rd BS35 64 C2
Eastleach CE Prim Sch
GL7 153 D8
Eastleigh Cl BS16 20 E4
Eastleigh Rd
Bristol, Brentry BS10 28 D1
Bristol, Staple Hill BS16 20 E3
Eastley Cl GL12 65 E7
Eastlyn Rd BS13 2 B8
Eastmead Ct BS9 17 E4
Eastmead La BS9 17 E4
Eastnor Castle* HR8 179 B7
Eastnor CE Prim Sch
HR8 179 B8
Eastnor Ho 14 GL51 132 E2
Eastnor Rd BS14 3 A3
Easton Bsns Ctr BS5 9 B8
Easton CE Prim Sch BS5 9 A8
Easton Hill Rd BS35 64 D1
Easton Rd Bristol BS5 9 B8
Pill BS20 16 C4
Easton Sq SN16 58 D1
Easton Town SN16 58 D1
Easton Way BS5 9 A8
Eastover Cl BS9 18 A8
Eastrop SN6 145 D3
Eastrop Cty Inf Sch
SN6 145 D3
Eastview Terr SN6 145 D3
Eastville Cl GL4 119 B8
Eastwood Cres BS4 9 F3
Eastwood Rd Bristol BS4 9 F4
Harrow Hill GL17 164 B3
Eaton Cl
Bristol, Fishponds BS16 20 B4
Bristol, Stockwood BS14 3 E5
Eaton Cres BS8 194 A4
Eaton Pl GL53 193 B2
Eaton St 10 BS3 8 C3
Ebenezer La BS9 17 E5
Ebenezer St BS5 9 D7
Ebley Ind Pk GL5 98 D6
Ebley Rd GL10 98 B6
Ebor Rd GL2 127 C1
Ebrington GL55 189 D3
Ebrington Cl GL4 119 D8
Eccleston Ho 1 BS5 9 B6
Echo La GL11 87 B2
Eclipse Ct BS16 20 C4
Eclipse Office Pk BS16 20 C4
Eddys La GL17 163 E3
Eden Gr BS7 29 A1
Eden's Hill GL18 171 D6
Edencroft SN6 145 D4
Edendale App GL51 129 C8
Edendale Rd GL51 132 C1
Edenwall GL16 155 B5
Edenwall Rd GL16 155 B4
Edge End Rd 1 GL16 155 B6
Edge Hills Cl GL14 191 D5
Edge Hills Rd GL14 191 D5
Edge La GL6 103 C8
Edge Rd GL6 103 E8
Edgecombe Cl BS15 20 F1
Edgecorner La SN14 36 A3
Edgecumbe Rd BS6 18 D2
Edgefield Cl BS14 2 F3
Edgefield Rd BS14 2 F3
Edgeware Rd
Bristol, Southville BS3 8 C4
Bristol, Staple Hill BS16 20 D4
Edgewood Cl
Bristol, Hengrove BS14 3 B8
Bristol, Longwell Green
BS30 11 A3
Edgeworth BS37 32 C6
Edgeworth Cl
Cirencester GL7 190 B2
5 Gloucester GL4 119 E5
Edinburgh Pl
Cheltenham GL51 132 E2
3 Coleford GL16 155 B5
Edinburgh Rd BS31 4 E4
Edington Gr BS10 28 A2
Edmond Rd NP16 61 B8
Edmund Cl BS16 20 D6
Edmund Ct BS16 22 B6
Edna Ave BS4 9 E3
Edward Bird Ho BS7 19 B6
Edward Ct BS31 4 F4
Edward Pl GL20 192 D1
Edward Rd
Bristol, Arno's Vale BS4 9 B4
Bristol, Kingswood BS15 10 E8
Edward St
Bristol, Eastville BS5 19 D2
Bristol, Redfield BS5 9 C7
Cheltenham GL50 193 B1
Edward Wilson Ho 2
GL51 132 E3
Edwards Cl
Joy's Green GL17 163 D3
Poulton GL7 151 E3
Edwards Ct 16 BS5 9 D7
Edwards' Coll GL7 142 F8
Edwin Short Cl BS30 5 E8
Edwy Par GL1 196 B4
Effingham Rd BS6 18 E2
Egerton Brow BS7 18 D4
Egerton Rd BS7 18 D4
Eggshill La BS37 43 D1
Eglin Croft BS13 2 B4
Egypt Ho GL6 91 B4
Eighth Ave
Bristol, Filton BS7 29 B1
Bristol, Hengrove BS14 3 A7
Eirene Terr BS20 16 D4
Elberton BS15 11 A8
Elberton Rd Bristol BS9 17 B7
Elberton BS35 49 F5
Elbridge Ho 3 BS2 195 C3
Elbury Ave BS15 20 C2
Elderberry Mews GL3 127 F6
Elderberry Wlk BS10 28 C3
Eldersfield Cl
Quedgeley GL2 117 E2
Winchcombe GL54 174 A8
Eldersfield Lawn CE Sch
GL19 180 F1
Elderwood Dr BS30 11 A3
Elderwood Rd BS14 3 B7
Elderwood Way GL4 118 C2
Eldon Ave GL52 134 A1
Eldon Rd GL52 133 F1
Eldon Terr BS3 8 D3
Eldon Way BS4 9 C5
Eldonwall Trad Est BS4 9 C5
Eldorado Cres GL50 133 B1
Eldorado Rd GL50 133 B1
Eldred Cl BS9 17 D5
Eleventh Ave BS7 29 B1
Elf Mdw GL7 151 F4
Elfin Rd BS16 20 A5
Elgar Cl Bristol BS4 2 D6
Ledbury HR8 178 E8
Elgar Ho GL51 132 E2
Elgin Ave BS7 28 F1
Elgin Hall GL10 97 F7
Elgin Pk BS6 18 B2
Elgin Rd BS16 20 B2
Eliot Cl Bristol BS7 29 A1
Gloucester GL2 118 C4
Elizabeth Cl BS35 51 D8
Elizabeth Cres BS34 29 E4
Elizabeth Gdns
Meysey Hampton GL7 152 B3
5 Tetbury GL8 140 B4
Elizabeth Ho BS20 16 D4
Elizabeth Way
Bristol BS16 21 B3
Siddington GL7 150 E2
Elizabeths Mews 12 BS4 9 F6
Elkstone Wlk BS30 11 C2
Ellacombe Rd BS30 10 F2
Ellan Hay Rd BS34 30 A6
Ellbridge Cl BS9 17 D5
Ellenborough Ho BS8 194 A2
Ellenborough Rd GL52 138 A2
Ellendene Dr GL20 182 E4
Ellenor Dr GL20 183 E4
Ellerncroft Rd
Kingswood GL12 67 F8
Wooton-u-E GL12 68 A8
Ellesmere BS35 51 C8
Ellesmere Cl GL3 119 F8
Ellesmere Gr GL50 130 B6
Ellesmere Rd
1 Bristol, Hengrove BS4 9 D1
1 Bristol, Kingswood BS15 10 D8
Ellfield Cl BS13 1 F6
Ellicks Cl BS32 40 E2
Ellicott Rd BS7 18 F5
Ellingham Ct GL52 133 E3
Ellinghurst Cl BS10 28 A2
Elliott Ave BS16 30 C1
Elliott Pl GL51 129 F7
Elliott Rd GL7 190 E1
Ellis Ave BS13 2 A8
Ellison Cl GL4 120 A6
Ellison Rd GL51 132 E2
Elliston La BS6 18 C2
Elliston Rd BS6 18 C2
Ellsbridge Cl BS31 5 B5
Ellsbridge Ho Norton
Radstock Coll BS31 5 B5
Ellsworth Rd BS10 27 F2
Ellwood Prim Sch
Ellwood GL16 155 B3
Sling GL16 155 B3
Ellwood Rd GL16 155 B3
Ellyott Ct 5 BS16 19 E3
Elm Cl Bristol BS34 29 D7
Cheltenham GL51 133 B3
Chipping Sodbury BS37 44 A1
King's Stanley GL10 98 A4
Prestbury GL52 134 A5
Tutshill NP16 73 A2
Elm Ct
Bristol, Hengrove BS14 3 A6
Bristol, Redland BS6 18 B2
Cheltenham GL52 133 F4
Keynsham BS31 4 C4
Netherend GL15 147 C3
Elm Dr GL3 120 D7
Elm Farm Cl SN16 142 B1
Elm Garden Dr GL51 129 A7
Elm Gr Ebrington GL55 189 D3
Huntley GL19 165 D6
Elm Hayes BS13 1 F6
Elm La BS6 18 B2
Elm Lodge GL11 88 B4
Elm Park Prim Sch BS36 30 E6
Elm Pk BS34 29 A2
Elm Rd
Bristol, Horfield BS7 18 E5
Bristol, Kingswood BS15 10 E6
Northway GL20 182 C4
Elm Rd *continued*
Stroud GL5 98 E8
Tutshill NP16 73 A2
Elm Side GL2 173 B3
Elm St GL51 133 B4
Elm Terr GL5 98 D6
Elm Tree Ave BS16 21 A7
Elm View GL7 142 C6
Elm Wood BS37 32 E8
Elmbridge Inf Sch GL2 127 C2
Elmbridge Jun Sch GL2 127 C2
Elmbridge Rd GL2 127 C3
Elmbury Dr GL20 192 F5
ElMCroft Cres BS7 19 A4
Elmdale NP16 72 E1
Elmdale Cres BS35 64 C1
Elmdale Gdns 2 BS16 20 A4
Elmdale Rd Bristol BS8 194 B3
Bristol, Bedminster BS3 8 B2
Elmdean GL14 191 C5
Elmfield Bristol BS15 10 E6
Cheltenham GL50 193 A3
Elmfield Ave GL51 133 C4
Elmfield Cl BS15 10 E6
Elmfield Jun Sch GL51 133 C4
Elmfield Rd Bristol BS9 18 A8
Cheltenham GL51 133 C4
Elmfield Sch for Deaf
Children BS10 18 B8
Elmgrove Ave 10 BS5 9 B8
Elmgrove Dr BS37 43 F2
Elmgrove Est GL2 109 E7
Elmgrove Pk 1 BS6 18 D1
Elmgrove Rd
Bristol, Fishponds BS16 19 E3
Bristol, Redland BS6 18 D1
Gloucester GL3 120 A6
Elmgrove Rd E GL2 109 E7
Elmgrove Rd W GL2 109 D7
Elmhirst Gdns BS37 44 A2
Elmhurst Ave BS5 19 D3
Elming Down Cl BS32 29 D6
Elmira Rd GL4 118 F4
Elmlea Ave BS9 17 F5
Elmlea Jun & Inf Schs
BS9 17 F5
Elmlea Rd GL10 98 A4
Elmleaze GL2 127 D3
Elmleigh Ave BS16 21 B5
Elmleigh Cl BS16 21 B5
Elmleigh Rd BS16 21 B5
Elmley Rd WR11 183 D8
Elmore Bristol BS15 20 F2
Yate BS37 32 D8
Elmore La E GL2 117 F3
Elmore La W GL2 117 D2
Elmore Rd
Bristol, Horfield BS7 19 A6
Bristol, Patchway BS34 39 F1
Elms Gr BS34 40 B1
Elms Rd GL10 97 E8
Elms The
Bristol, Frenchay BS16 30 C1
Bristol, Henbury BS10 27 F2
Highworth SN6 145 C3
Elmsdale Rd 14 HR8 178 E8
Elmtree Cl BS15 20 D1
Elmtree Cotts GL12 68 D3
Elmtree Dr BS13 1 F5
Elmtree Way BS15 20 D1
Elmvil Rd GL20 182 B4
Elphick Rd GL7 190 B8
Elsbert Dr BS13 1 E6
Elstree Rd BS5 19 E1
Elstub La GL11 87 E5
Eltham Lawn 5 GL50 130 B8
Elton Ho 2 Bristol BS2 195 C3
Huntley GL19 165 D7
Elton La BS7 18 D2
Elton Rd Bristol BS8 194 C3
Bristol, Bishopston BS7 18 D2
Bristol, Kingswood BS15 20 C1
Elton GL14 157 A8
Littledean GL14 156 E8
Elton St BS2 195 C4
Elvard Cl BS13 2 A4
Elvard Rd BS13 2 A4
Elvaston Rd BS3 8 E3
Elwell La BS40,BS41 1 A1
Ely Gr BS9 17 B7
Embassy Rd BS5 19 E1
Embassy Wlk BS5 19 E1
Embleton Prim Sch BS10 28 C2
Embleton Rd BS10 28 C2
Embrook GL56 177 C4
Emerald Cl GL4 118 C3
Emerson Green Prim Sch
BS16 21 B7
Emerson Sq BS7 19 A8
Emersons Green La BS16 21 B6
Emersons Way BS16 21 C7
Emery Rd BS4 9 F1
Emet Gr BS16 21 B6
Emet La BS16 21 B6
Emlyn Rd BS5 19 C2
Emma-Chris Way BS34 29 C2
Emmanuel Ct BS8 194 A4
Emmanuel Gdns GL53 130 D6
Emmerson La GL6 149 A4
Emmett Wood BS14 3 B3
Emperor Cl 7 GL51 132 D2
Empire Cres BS15 10 E4
Empire Way GL2 118 C5
Emra Cl BS5 19 F1
Enborne Cl GL4 118 D1
Enfield Rd BS16 20 A3
Enfield Villas GL54 139 F5
Engine Common La BS37 43 C5
England's Cres BS36 30 E7
English Bicknor CE Prim Sch
GL16 163 B2
Englishcombe Rd BS13 2 C3
Ennerdale Ave GL2 127 D5
Ennerdale Rd Bristol BS10 28 D2
Cheltenham GL51 129 E7
Enterprise Way GL51 133 B3
Epney Cl BS34 39 F1
Epney Rd GL4 118 C3
Epsom Cl BS16 30 F1
Epworth Rd BS10 28 A3
Equinox BS32 40 C3
Erin Pk GL5 99 A5
Erin Wlk BS4 2 D8
Ermin Pk GL3 120 D6
Ermin Pl GL7 190 E2
Ermin St
Broad Blunsdon SN26 144 D1
Brockworth GL3 120 E5
Ermin Way GL3 121 B4
Ermine Par GL3 120 D6
Ermine Way BS11 16 C7
Erminster Dr GL3 120 A7
Ermleet Rd 1 BS6 18 C2
Ernest Barker Cl 14 BS5 9 B7
Ernestville Rd BS16 19 F3
Eros Cl GL5 99 A5
Errington GL56 187 B3
Ervine Terr BS2 195 C4
Eskdale BS35 51 D7
Esland Pl GL7 190 D2
Essery Rd BS5 19 C2
Essex Ave GL51 133 A2
Essex Cl GL3 128 A8
Essex Pl GL54 168 F8
Esson Rd BS15 20 B1
Estate Rd GL14 191 B6
Estcote Rd GL7 190 C5
Estcourt Cl GL1 127 A4
Estcourt Gdns BS16 19 D5
Estcourt Rd GL1 127 A3
Estoril BS37 43 F1
Estune Wlk BS41 7 A2
Etheldene Rd GL5 98 D8
Etheridge Pl GL1 127 B1
Etloe Rd BS6 18 A4
Eton Rd BS4 9 D3
Ettington Cl GL51 132 C3
Ettricke Dr BS16 20 B5
Eugene Flats 7 BS2 195 A4
Eugene St
Bristol, Kingsdown BS2 195 A4
Bristol, St Pauls BS2,BS5 195 C4
Evans Cl BS4 9 F5
Evans Rd BS6 18 B2
Eve Rd BS5 19 B1
Evelyn Cl GL53 130 F5
Evelyn Ct GL50 193 A3
Evelyn Rd BS10 18 C7
Evening Post Rdbt The
BS2 195 C3
Evenlode Ave GL52 134 A2
Evenlode Gdns
Bristol BS11 16 F5
Moreton-in-M GL56 187 B3
Evenlode Rd
Gloucester GL4 118 D1
Moreton-in-M GL56 187 B3
Evenlode Way BS31 5 A3
Evercreech Rd BS14 3 B4
Everest Ave BS16 19 E4
Everest Cl GL6 91 E6
Everest Rd Bristol BS16 19 E4
Cheltenham GL53 130 E4
Evergreen Ind Pk GL7 143 A7
Everlands GL11 88 A4
Everside Cl GL11 87 F6
Everside La GL11 87 F6
Everyman Theatre The
GL50 193 B3
Evesham Rd
Bishop's Cleeve GL52 137 F5
Cheltenham GL50,GL52 133 E5
Greet GL54 184 A1
Stow-on-t-W GL54 176 E5
Evington Ct 7 GL51 132 E2
Evington Rd 8 GL51 132 E2
Ewens Rd GL52 131 A8
Ewlyn Rd GL53 130 D6
Exchange Ave BS1 195 A2
Exeter Bldgs BS6 18 B2
Exeter Rd BS3 8 B4
Exley Cl BS30 11 D5
Exmoor St BS3 8 B3
Exmouth Ct GL53 193 B1
Exmouth Rd BS4 8 F1
Exmouth St GL53 193 B1
Exploratory (Science Ctr)
The* BS1 195 C1
Exton Cl BS14 3 B5
Eyer's La BS2 195 C3
Eyford Cotts GL54 176 A3
Eynon Cl GL53 130 C5

F

Faber Gr BS13 2 C4
Fabian Dr BS34 29 E5
Factory Rd BS36 30 F7
Failand Cres BS9 17 C5
Failand La BS20 16 A1
Failand Wlk BS9 17 C6
Fair Furlong BS13 2 A4
Fair Furlong Prim Sch
BS13 2 B4
Fair Lawn BS30 11 B4

Fair View Chepstow NP16 60 D6
Highworth SN6 145 C3
Fair View Cl GL6 91 B5
Fair View Dr BS6 18 C2
Fairacre Cl BS7 19 B5
Fairacres Cl BS31 4 F5
Fairfax Cl GL7 190 D3
Fairfax Rd GL7 190 D3
Fairfax St BS1 195 B3
Fairfield 12 SN6 143 E4
Fairfield Ave GL53 130 D6
Fairfield Cl
20 Coleford GL16 155 A5
Marshfield SN14 15 A8
Fairfield High Sch BS6 18 F2
Fairfield Par GL53 130 D6
Fairfield Park Rd GL53 130 D6
Fairfield Pl BS3 8 B4
Fairfield Rd
Bristol, Montpelier BS6 18 F2
Bristol, Southville BS3 8 C4
Cheltenham GL53 130 D6
Chepstow NP16 60 E6
Lydney GL15 92 A3
Fairfield St GL53 130 D6
Fairfield Wlk GL53 130 D6
Fairfields GL14 191 C4
Fairfields Rd 13 HR8 178 E8
Fairfoot Rd BS4 9 A3
Fairford CE Prim Sch GL7 152 E4
Fairford Cl BS15 20 F2
Fairford Cres BS34 29 C8
Fairford Hospl GL7 152 E4
Fairford Rd Bristol BS11 16 D7
Quenington GL7 152 D7
Fairford Way GL4 119 B7
Fairhaven BS37 43 F1
Fairhaven Ave GL3 120 E6
Fairhaven Rd Bristol BS6 18 C4
Cheltenham GL53 130 D6
Fairhaven St GL53 130 D6
Fairhavens Ct 8 GL52 133 F2
Fairlawn Ave BS34 29 A3
Fairlawn Rd BS6 18 F2
Fairlyn Dr BS15 20 F3
Fairmead GL11 87 F5
Fairmile Gdns GL2 126 F5
Fairmount Rd GL51 132 F1
Fairoaks BS30 11 A3
Fairplay Cotts GL17 164 C3
Fairview SN6 143 F4
Fairview Cl
Cheltenham GL52 193 C3
Monmouth NP25 154 A7
Fairview Ho BS9 17 F8
Fairview Rd Bristol BS15 10 F8
Cheltenham GL52 193 C4
Fairview St GL52 193 C4
Fairwater Pk GL4 127 D1
Fairway Bristol BS4 9 D1
Northway GL20 182 C4
Fairway Cl BS30 11 B4
Fairway Ind Ctr BS34 28 F3
Fairways BS31 5 E2
Fairways Ave GL16 155 A5
Falcon Cl
Bristol, Patchway BS34 28 E8
Bristol, Westbury on Trym BS9 17 F8
Innsworth GL3 127 C6
Falcon Ct BS9 18 A7
Falcon Dr BS34 28 E8
Falcon La HR8 178 C8
Falcon Way BS35 64 D2
Falcon Wlk BS34 39 E1
Falcondale Rd BS9 17 F7
Falcondale Wlk BS9 18 A8
Falconride Prim Sch BS15 20 F1
Faldo Cl GL4 119 F5
Falfield Rd Bristol BS4 9 C3
Gloucester GL4 118 D3
Falfield Wlk BS10 18 C8
Falkland Pl GL51 132 D3
Falkland Rd 4 BS6 18 F2
Falkner St GL1 196 C1
Fallodon Ct BS9 18 B5
Fallodon Way BS9 18 B5
Fallowfield BS30 11 D5
Fallows Rd GL54 168 A1
Falmouth Rd BS7 18 E4
Fancy Rd GL15 155 E3
Fane Cl BS10 28 A3
Fanshawe Rd BS14 3 A7
Far Handstones BS30 11 A4
Far Sandfield GL3 128 C5
Far View Cotts 7 GL10 97 F7
Far Wells Rd GL6 148 D8
Far Westrip GL6 98 C8
Faraday Cl 3 GL1 118 F7
Faraday Rd 2 BS8 7 F5
Farendell Rd BS16 31 B1
Farfield La SN6 143 F2
Faringdon Rd GL51 129 D7
Farington Rd BS10 18 D7
Farleigh Cl GL52 131 C6
Farleigh La GL12 66 C2
Farleigh Rd BS31 4 D4
Farleigh Wlk BS13 2 A8
Farley Cl BS34 29 C7
Farm Cl Bristol BS16 21 B6
Cheltenham GL51 132 E3
Northway GL20 182 C5
Farm Ct Bristol BS16 20 E7
Willersey WR12 188 B2
Woodchester GL5 90 F8
Farm Hill GL8 140 A8
Farm La Bredon GL20 182 C7
Cheltenham GL51,GL53 130 B4
Easter Compton BS35 38 E2
Kemerton GL20 182 E8
Leighterton GL8 70 C3
Llangrove HR9 162 B5
Shurdington GL51 129 E1
Farm Lees GL12 67 A6
Farm Mews GL1 196 B1
Farm Rd Bristol BS16 20 E7
Edgeworth GL6 106 C1
Ruardean Woodside GL17 163 F3
Farm St GL1 196 B1
Farman Cres GL54 169 D6
Farmcote GL12 55 D8
Farmcote Cl GL6 148 B6
FarMCote Gdns GL54 139 F5
Farmer Rd BS13 1 E4
Farmfield Rd GL51 130 A5
Farmhill Cres GL5 98 F8
Farmhill La GL5 102 F1
Farmhouse Mews NP25 146 B7
Farmington Cl 4 GL4 119 E5
Farmington Rd
Cheltenham GL51 129 E8
Northleach GL54 168 A1
Farmington Rise 13 GL54 168 A1
Farmors Sch GL7 152 E4
Farmwell Cl BS13 2 B5
Farnaby Cl BS4 2 C7
Farndale BS5 10 A6
Farne Cl BS9 18 B5
Farr St BS11 16 B8
Farr's La Bristol BS1 195 A2
Stroud GL5 99 C7
Farrant Ave GL3 128 A6
Farrant Cl BS4 2 D6
Farriers Croft 9 GL6 148 C6
Farriers Ct 10 GL16 155 A6
Farriers End GL2 117 F1
Farriers Reach GL52 137 D4
Farriers The GL7 153 C6
Farthing Croft GL2 125 D4
Farthings The GL54 166 E2
Fauconberg Rd GL50 193 A3
Faulkner's Cl GL7 152 E3
Fawkes Cl BS15 11 B8
Fawkes Pl 7 GL5 99 C7
Fawley Dr GL52 134 C4
Featherbed La BS35 63 B6
Featherstone Rd 4 BS16 19 F4
Feeder Rd BS2 9 A5
Felix Rd BS5 9 B8
Felstead Rd BS10 28 E1
Feltham Rd BS16 22 C6
Felton Gr BS13 2 A8
Fenbrook Cl BS16 30 B1
Fenhill Cl GL56 186 D3
Fennel Cl GL4 119 D4
Fennel Dr BS34 30 A7
Fennell Gr BS10 28 A2
Fennell's View GL5 103 E1
Fenshurst Gdns BS41 1 A8
Fenton Cl BS31 5 D3
Fenton Rd BS7 18 D4
Fermaine Ave BS4 9 F3
Fern Cl BS10 28 B3
Fern Ct NP16 60 F5
Fern Gr BS32 29 D8
Fern Lawn GL4 119 D2
Fern Rd Bristol BS16 20 D5
Ellwood GL16 155 C3
Fern St BS2 18 F1
Fernbank Ct 2 BS6 18 C2
Fernbank Rd BS6 18 C2
Fernbrook Cl BS16 30 B1
Ferndale Ave BS30 11 A3
Ferndale Cl
Almondsbury BS32 40 D7
Cinderford GL14 191 D5
Gloucester GL2 127 B5
Ferndale Rd Bristol BS34 29 A2
Whiteshill GL6 103 A3
Ferndales Cl 2 GL51 129 F5
Ferndene BS32 40 C2
Ferndown BS37 43 E1
Ferndown Cl BS11 17 A7
Ferndown Rd 7 HR8 178 E7
Ferney GL11 80 C8
Fernhill BS32 40 C7
Fernhill Ct
Almondsbury BS32 40 C7
Bristol BS11 27 B1
Fernhill La BS11 27 B1
Fernhurst Rd BS5 19 F1
Fernihough Ave WR11 188 C7
Fernlea Gdns BS20 16 B4
Fernleaze BS36 31 C6
Fernleigh Cres GL51 129 E6
Fernleigh Ct 1 BS6 18 B2
Ferns The GL8 140 B4
Fernsteed Rd BS13 1 F6
Ferrie La HR9 162 E3
Ferris Court View 9 GL6 148 B6
Ferry Gdns GL2 117 D1
Ferry La GL20 181 C8
Ferry Rd BS15 10 D1
Ferry St BS1 195 B2
Ferry Steps Ind Est BS2 9 A4
Ferry Way NP16 61 B4
Ferryman's Ct BS2 195 B2
Festival Ho GL52 193 C3
Festival Rd GL10 97 E7
Fewster Rd GL6 91 B4
Fewster Sq GL6 91 B4
Fiddes Rd BS6 18 C4
Fiddle The SN6 143 E4
Fiddler's Green La GL51 132 C1
Fidges La GL6 148 C7
Field Cl Gretton GL54 183 E1
South Cerney GL7 143 A8
Field Court CE Inf Sch GL2 109 F8
Field Court Dr GL2 109 E7
Field Court Gdns GL2 109 E8
Field Court Jun Sch GL2 109 F8
Field End GL3 128 A7
Field Farm Cl BS34 29 F4
Field La Bristol BS30 10 F3
Coaley GL11 88 E7
Dursley GL11 87 D5
Dyrham SN14 23 F6
Littleton-u-S BS35 50 A8
Tytherington BS35 51 E3
Field Pl GL5 98 F8
Field Rd Bristol BS15 20 C1
Kingham OX7 177 F2
Stroud, Bowbridge GL5 99 D6
Stroud, Rodborough GL5 99 B6
Whiteshill GL6 103 A3
Field View BS5 9 A8
Field View Dr BS16 20 C6
Fieldcote Dr GL3 120 A7
Fieldcourt Farmhouse GL2 109 E8
Fielden GL4 119 D3
Fieldfare GL4 119 D5
Fieldgate Rd GL52 138 A4
Fields La WR12 188 B2
Fields Rd GL54 159 B5
Fieldways GL6 91 A4
Fiennes Cl BS16 20 E4
Fiery La GL11 89 C2
Fifth Ave Bristol, Filton BS7 29 A1
Bristol, Hengrove BS14 3 B7
Fifth Way BS11 26 E2
Filbert Cl GL4 119 D3
Filby Dr BS34 29 C8
Filton Abbey Wood Sta BS7 29 B1
Filton Ave BS7,BS34 19 A7
Filton Avenue Jun & Inf Schs BS7 19 A7
Filton Coll N BS34 29 A4
Filton Coll S BS34 29 A4
Filton Gr BS7 18 F6
Filton High Sch BS34 29 D3
Filton Hill Prim Sch BS34 29 B4
Filton La BS34 29 D2
Filton Park Sch BS34 28 F2
Filton Rd
Bristol, Frenchay BS16 29 F2
Bristol, Harry Stoke BS34 29 D2
Bristol, Horfield BS7 18 F8
Filton Way GL4 119 B7
Filwood Broadway BS4 2 E8
Filwood Ct BS16 20 B3
Filwood Dr BS15 10 F8
Filwood Rd BS16 20 A3
Finch Cl BS35 64 C2
Finch Rd
Chipping Sodbury BS37 33 A8
Innsworth GL3 127 D7
Finchcroft Ct GL52 134 D4
Finchcroft La GL52 134 C4
Finchmoor Mews GL2 126 F6
Finlay Com Sch GL4 119 A6
Finlay Pl GL4 118 F5
Finlay Rd GL4 118 F5
Finstock Cl GL51 129 F8
Fir Rd SN14 15 F6
Fir Tree Cl Bristol BS34 28 F7
Cheltenham GL52 134 A4
Fir Tree La BS5 10 A7
Fir View Rd GL14 156 C6
Fircroft Cl GL3 119 F8
Fircroft Rd GL2 126 F5
Fire Engine La BS36 31 D7
Fire Safety Engineering Coll GL56 187 C3
Fire Station La BS11 26 B2
Firethorne Cl GL2 127 B5
Firework Cl BS15 11 B8
Firfield St BS4 9 A4
Firgrove Cres BS37 44 A2
Firgrove Wlk GL51 129 C7
Firs Cl OX7 177 E1
Firs Ct BS31 4 C4
Firs Rd GL5 91 C5
Firs The Bristol BS16 20 E6
Gloucester GL1 196 C4
Kemble GL7 141 D6
Swindon GL51 133 B7
First Ave
Bristol, Hengrove BS14 3 A7
Bristol, St Anne's BS4 9 E5
Dursley GL11 80 C8
First Way BS11 26 C1
Firth Ave GL56 187 C3
Firwood Dr GL4 118 E3
Fish Hill WR12 185 D8
Fisher Ave BS15 21 A1
Fisher Cl 30 GL54 176 F4
Fisher Rd BS15 21 A1
Fisher Wlk GL51 132 F4
Fisherman's Wlk NP16 60 F5
Fishers La GL52 193 C4
Fishers Rd GL13 85 E4
Fishers Way GL5 99 A4
Fishponds Rd BS5 19 D3
Fishponds Trad Est BS5 19 E2
Fishpool Hill BS10 28 B4
Fitchett Wlk BS10 27 F3
Fitzgerald Rd BS3 8 F3
Fitzhamon Pk GL20 182 C4
Fitzharding Rd BS20 16 E3
Fitzhardinge Way GL13 85 E4
Fitzosborn Cl NP16 60 D7
Fitzroy Rd BS16 20 B2
Fitzroy St BS4 9 A4
Fitzroy Terr 7 BS6 18 B2
Five Acre Dr BS16 20 A7
Five Acres GL11 80 A8
Five Lanes SN16 141 B1
Five Mile Dr GL56 186 C5
Five Trees Cl 8 GL8 140 B4
Flaxley Rd GL4 118 E3
Flaxley St GL14 191 D4
Flaxman Cl BS7 19 B6
Flaxpits La BS36 30 E5
Flecker's Dr GL51 129 F7
Fleece Alley 24 GL54 176 F4
Fleece Inn* WR11 188 A6
Fleece Rd WR12 188 A1
Fleet La GL20 182 A7
Fleet Rd GL20 182 A7
Fleming Cl GL2 127 C6
Flint Rd GL51 129 E6
Flisteridge Rd SN16 142 B2
Florence Brown Specl Sch BS4 2 D8
Florence Pk
Almondsbury BS32 40 C5
Bristol BS6 18 B4
Florence Rd BS16 20 E3
Florida Bvd GL7 152 E3
Florida Dr GL52 134 C4
Flower Way GL2 127 B4
Flowers Hill BS4 9 E1
Flowers Hill Cl BS4 9 E1
Flowers Hill Trad Est BS4 9 E1
Flowerwell Rd BS13 2 B5
Folders The GL15 92 B3
Foley Cl GL4 118 D3
Foley Rd GL18 171 A4
Foley Rise GL19 172 C4
Folk Mus* GL1 196 A3
Folland Ave GL3 120 B6
Folleigh Cl BS41 7 B2
Folleigh Dr BS41 7 B2
Folleigh La BS41 7 B2
Folliot Cl BS16 20 A7
Folly Bridge Cl BS37 43 D2
Folly Brook Rd BS16 31 B1
Folly Cl SN6 145 D4
Folly Cres SN6 145 D4
Folly Dr SN6 145 D4
Folly Farm Waterfowl* GL54 168 B7
Folly Field GL54 169 A8
Folly La Bristol BS2 9 A6
Cheltenham GL50 133 D3
English Bicknor GL16 163 A1
Huntley GL17 165 B7
Stroud GL5,GL6 103 E2
Folly Rd BS37 42 A5
Folly Rise GL5 103 D1
Folly The Bristol BS16 20 F7
Cold Ashton SN14 13 F6
Longborough GL56 176 E8
Saltford BS31 5 F2
Folly Way SN6 145 D4
Follyfield SN16 141 E1
Fontana Cl BS30 11 B3
Fonthill Prim Sch BS10 28 E2
Fonthill Rd BS10 28 D2
Fontmell Ct BS14 3 D7
Fontwell Dr BS16 30 F1
Footes La BS36 31 B7
Footshill Cl BS15 10 C6
Footshill Dr BS15 10 C7
Footshill Rd BS15 10 C6
Fop St GL11 89 A1
Forbes Cl GL4 119 F6
Ford House Rd GL18 171 B6
Ford La Bristol BS16 21 B6
Gorsley GL18 170 D4
Ford St BS5 9 C6
Forde Cl BS30 10 F5
Fordell Pl BS4 9 A3
Fordwich Cl NP16 72 B5
Fore St SN6 142 F5
Forest Ave BS16 20 B3
Forest Cl GL16 154 E7
Forest Dr BS10 28 C3
Forest Edge BS15 10 C4
Forest Hills BS32 40 B5
Forest Patch 6 GL16 155 A7
Forest Rd Bream GL15 147 D8
Bristol, Fishponds BS16 20 B4
Bristol, Kingswood BS15 10 D7
Cinderford GL14 191 D4
Lydney GL15 92 A3
Mile End GL16 155 B7
Milkwall GL16 155 B4
Ruardean Woodside GL17 163 F3
Forest Rise
Cinderford GL14 191 E5
Upper Lydbrook GL17 163 D2
Forest Vale Ind Est GL14 191 B5
Forest Vale Rd GL14 191 B5
Forest View
Cinderford GL14 191 C1
Narth The NP25 154 B1
Forest View Prim Sch GL14 191 E5
Forest View Rd
Berkeley GL13 85 E4
Gloucester GL4 118 E1
Forest Wlk
Bristol, Fishponds BS16 20 B2
Bristol, Kingswood BS15 10 C7
Foresters Rd GL20 192 C2
Forge Gdns NP16 72 B6
Forge Hill GL17 163 C3
Forge La GL18 171 D6
Forge The GL17 163 C3
Forsdene Wlk GL16 155 B5
Forsyte Way GL4 119 B7
Forsythia Cl 8 GL3 128 A7
Fort La GL11 80 B8
Fort View Terr GL5 98 E6
Fortey Rd GL54 168 A1
Fortfield Rd BS14 3 B5
Fortfields GL11 80 B8
Forthill Way BS30 11 C2
Fortina Cl GL50 133 C5
Fortress The GL11 80 B8
Forty Acre La
Alveston BS35 51 B3
Stroud GL6 148 A8
Forty The SN6 143 E4
Forty's Pitch HR9 170 B5
Forum The GL1 196 B2
Foscombe La GL19 172 C5
Foss Ct 7 BS5 9 F8
Foss Field GL7 107 A8
Foss La BS35 63 E6
Fosscross La GL54,GL7 159 C3
Fosse Cl Cirencester GL7 190 E5
Gloucester GL4 119 E6
Fosse Folly GL54 176 F5
Fosse La GL54 176 F5
Fossedale Ave BS14 3 C6
Fosseway Ave GL56 187 A2
Fosseway Cl GL56 187 A2
Fosseway Ct BS8 194 A2
Fosseway Dr GL56 187 A2
Fosseway Ho GL54 176 F5
Fosseway The BS8 194 A3
Foster Cl GL52 138 A5
Foster Ct 3 GL52 134 A3
Foster St BS5 19 B2
Foundry La BS5 19 F2
Foundry Rd GL14 191 D5
Fountain Cres GL12 68 C6
Fountain Ct Bristol BS32 40 C3
2 Yate BS37 32 D7
Fountain Sq GL1 196 A3
Fountain St GL6 91 C4
Fountain Way NP16 60 F4
Fountaine Ct 3 BS5 19 C2
Fountains Dr BS30 10 F6
Four Acre Ave BS16 20 E8
Four Acre Cl SN6 143 A4
Four Acre Cres BS16 30 E1
Four Acre Rd BS16 20 E8
Four Acre View GL7 190 B3
Four Acres BS13 1 E4
Four Acres Cl BS13 1 F4
Four Acres Prim Sch BS13 1 E4
Four Seasons Sq BS37 43 E1
Fourth Ave
Bristol, Filton BS7 29 A1
Bristol, Hengrove BS14 3 B7
Dursley GL11 80 C8
Fourth Way BS11 26 E1
Fowbridge Gdns HR9 163 C8
Fowler's Hill GL7 152 D7
Fox & Hounds La BS31 4 F5
Fox Ave BS37 43 D2
Fox Cl Bristol BS4 9 F5
Gloucester GL4 119 F5
Stroud GL5 98 C7
Fox Ct BS30 10 F3
Fox Den Rd BS34 29 D3
Fox Dr GL54 176 D4
Fox Elms Rd GL4 118 E2
Fox Hill GL8 140 C3
Fox Ho BS4 9 E3
Fox La 7 GL54 176 F4
Fox Rd BS5 19 B1
Fox Run GL2 118 A2
Fox's La GL16 155 B5
Foxborough Gdns BS32 40 D2
Foxcombe Rd BS14 3 B4
Foxcote Bristol BS15 10 F7
Gloucester GL2 127 B5
Foxcote Hill CV36 189 F5
Foxcote Rd BS3 8 A3
Foxcott SN6 143 E6
Foxcroft Cl BS32 29 F6
Foxcroft Rd BS5 9 D8
Foxe Rd BS36 31 B8
Foxes Bank Dr GL7 190 B2
Foxes Bridge Rd GL14 191 B5
Foxes Cl
3 Bourton-on-t-W GL54 168 F7
6 Chalford GL6 148 C6
Foxes Dell GL6 91 A5
Foxes Row GL56 177 A6
Foxfield Ave BS32 40 D3
Foxglove Cl Bristol BS16 19 E5
Gloucester GL4 119 E5
Thornbury BS35 64 D2
Foxglove Way GL16 155 B4
Foxgrove Dr GL52 134 A1
Foxholes La BS32 50 C4
Foxleaze SN6 143 E5
Foxleigh Cres GL2 127 E5
Foxmoor GL52 137 E4
Foxmoor La GL5 98 C7
Foxmoor Prim Sch GL5 98 D7
Foxtail Cl GL4 119 A5

Foxwell Dr GL3 120 A8
Foye Ho BS8 7 E6
Fraley Rd BS9 18 A7
Frampton Cotterell CE Sch BS36 31 A8
Frampton Cotts GL20 183 E3
Frampton Cres BS16 20 C4
Frampton Ct
[8] Bristol, Longwell Green BS30 10 F4
[15] Bristol, Redfield BS5 9 D7
Frampton Dr WR12 188 B2
Frampton End Rd BS37 42 D2
Frampton Mews GL51 129 B7
Frampton on Severn CE Prim Sch GL2 100 A6
Frampton Rd GL1 118 D7
France La GL9 56 B2
Frances Ct GL52 133 F1
Frances Greeves Ct BS10 27 F1
Francis Ct BS5 9 F7
Francis Ho BS2 195 A4
Francis Pl BS30 10 F4
Francis Rd
Bristol, Bedminster BS3 8 C2
Bristol, Westbury on Trym BS10 18 C8
Francis St GL53 193 B1
Francis Way BS30 11 D6
Francombe Gr BS10 18 E6
Francombe Ho BS1 195 A1
Frank Brookes Rd GL51 133 A4
Franklin Ct BS1 195 B1
Franklyn Ct
[6] Bristol BS16 19 E3
[6] Cheltenham GL51 132 E2
Franklyn La [10] BS2 18 F1
Franklyn St BS2 18 F1
Fraser St BS3 8 D3
Frayne Rd BS3 8 A4
Frazier's Folly GL7 150 E2
Freame Cl GL6 148 B6
Frederick Pl BS8 194 B3
Frederick Thomas Rd GL11 87 E4
Fredrick St BS4 9 A4
Free Tank BS2 195 C2
Freeland Bldgs [1] BS5 19 C2
Freeland Pl BS8 7 F6
Freeling Ho BS1 195 B1
Freemans Cl GL20 181 F8
Freemantle Gdns BS5 19 C3
Freemantle Ho BS2 195 A4
Freemantle Rd BS5 19 C3
Freeminers Way GL14 191 D5
Freestone Rd BS2 9 A6
Freezinghill La BS30 13 B4
Fremantle La [8] BS6 18 D1
Fremantle Rd BS6 18 D1
Fremantle Sq BS6 18 D1
French La NP25 154 C4
Frenchay CE Prim Sch BS16 20 B7
Frenchay Cl BS16 20 B7
Frenchay Hill BS16 20 C7
Frenchay Hospl BS16 20 B8
Frenchay Park Rd BS16 19 F6
Frenchay Rd BS16 20 C6
Freshland Way BS15 10 B8
Fretherne Rd GL4 118 D3
Frewin Cl GL51 132 D2
Frewins La GL14 165 D3
Friar's Wlk GL18 171 A5
Friars Cl GL51 130 B5
Friars Ho [4] BS37 32 D7
Friary Grange Pk BS36 30 E6
Friary Rd Bristol BS7 18 D4
Gloucester GL4 119 E6
Friday St Arlingham GL2 157 C6
Minchinhampton GL6 148 A3
Painswick GL6 103 F8
Fridays Ham La SN6 143 A5
Friendly Row BS20 16 C5
Friendship Rd BS4 9 A2
Friezewood Rd BS3 8 A4
Fripp Cl BS5 9 B6
Frith La GL12 53 F3
Frith The GL6 148 B6
Frithwood GL6 148 B6
Frithwood Cl GL6 148 B6
Frithwood Pk GL6 148 B6
Frobisher Mews GL3 127 F8
Frobisher Rd BS3 8 A3
Frocester Hill GL10 89 C8
Frog Furlong La GL2, GL3 127 E8
Frog La Bristol BS1 194 C2
Coalpit Heath BS36 31 E7
Frocester GL10 97 A3
Huntley GL19 165 D6
Ilmington CV36 189 F6
North Nibley GL11 79 C5
Frogmarsh La GL5 91 A8
Frogmore Rd GL19 165 D6
Frogmore St BS1 194 C2
Frome Ave GL5 99 A6
Frome Ct BS35 51 C8
Frome Gdns GL5 98 E6
Frome Glen BS36 30 E4
Frome Park Rd GL5 99 A6
Frome Pl [1] BS16 19 E5
Frome Rd BS37 44 C1
Frome St BS2 195 C4
Frome Valley Rd BS16 19 F6
Frome View BS36 31 B7
Frome Villas BS16 20 C7
Frome Way BS36 30 E5
Fromebank Jun Sch BS37 43 D3
Fromeside GL5 99 C6
Fromeside Dr GL5 98 D6
Fromeside Pk BS16 20 B7
Front La SN26 144 D2
Front St Ilmington CV36 189 F6
Nympsfield GL10 89 E5
Froomshaw Rd BS16 20 A7
Frowens La HR9 170 B4
Fry Ct [2] BS3 8 C4
Fry's Cl BS16 19 D4
Fry's Hill BS4 9 D2
Frys Hill BS15 20 E2
Fulbrook Cl GL51 132 D5
Fulford Rd BS13 2 C5
Fulford Specl Sch BS13 2 C4
Fulford Wlk BS13 2 B5
Fuller's La GL19 172 B4
Fullers Ave [9] SN6 143 E4
Fullers Ct GL1 196 A3
Fulmar Cl BS35 64 D2
Furber Ct BS5 10 B6
Furber Rd BS5 10 B6
Furber Ridge BS5 10 B6
Furber Vale BS5 10 B6
Furlong Ct [3] HR8 178 E7
Furlong La GL52 137 F3
Furlong Rd GL1 118 E7
Furlong The BS6 18 D6
Furlongs The GL12 69 C3
Furnace Cl GL14 191 C4
Furnace La GL18 171 A5
Furnace Valley GL15 156 D1
Furnwood BS5 10 A6
Furze Croft GL2 109 F7
Furze La GL55 189 B4
Furze Rd BS16 20 C3
Furze The GL4 119 A4
Furzewood Rd BS15 10 F8
Fussell Ct BS15 10 F8
Fylton Croft BS14 3 B3

G

Gabb La GL19 173 B7
Gable Cl BS35 39 A2
Gable Cotts GL7 152 E3
Gable Point GL52 138 B3
Gable Rd [7] BS5 19 A1
Gable Row GL20 182 F8
Gadshill Dr BS34 29 E5
Gadshill Rd Bristol BS5 19 C2
Charlton Kings GL53 131 B3
Gadwell Rd GL20 192 E3
Gages Cl BS15 10 F7
Gages Rd BS15 10 F7
Gainsborough Dr GL4 118 C2
Gainsborough Rd BS31 4 F5
Gainsborough Sq BS7 19 B7
Gainsborough Terr GL55 189 A1
Gales Ct GL7 153 E2
Gallagher Ret Pk GL51 132 F5
Galleries The BS1 195 B3
Galley Orch SN6 143 F4
Gallivan Cl BS34 29 B8
Gallops La GL52 134 D4
Gallops The GL2 118 B6
Galway Rd BS4 8 E1
Gambier Parry Gdns GL2 126 F4
Gambles La GL52 138 D2
Gambril La GL12 65 F5
Ganborough Rd GL56 176 D8
Gander Cl BS13 2 B5
Gander La
Teddington GL20 183 A4
Tewkesbury GL20 192 C3
Gannaway La GL20 192 F5
Gannet Cl GL3 120 E5
Gannicox Rd GL5 99 A7
Ganzell La GL11 80 C7
Garamond Ct BS1 195 B1
Garden City Way NP16 60 E8
Garden Cl Bristol BS9 17 C5
Cirencester GL7 190 C3
Dumbleton WR11 183 F7
Mickleton GL55 189 A6
Garden Cotts GL19 172 A2
Garden Ct BS8 194 A4
Garden Rd GL53 131 B4
Garden Suburb GL11 88 A1
Garden The GL5 99 A2
Garden Way GL2 127 B4
Gardeners Way
King's Stanley GL10 98 A4
Newent GL18 170 F4
Gardeners Wlk BS41 7 B1
Gardenia Gr GL51 129 F5
Gardens The
Bristol, Frenchay BS16 29 F1
[4] Bristol, Upper Sounwell BS16 20 D3
Cheltenham GL50 133 E4
Monmouth NP25 154 A8
Gardiner Cl GL6 148 C6
Gardiners Cl GL3 128 A6
Gardner Ave BS13 1 F7
Gardner Ct GL7 190 D3
Gardner's La GL51 133 C4
Garfield Rd BS5 10 A8
Garland Ct GL7 190 C3
Garlands Rd GL15 147 D3
Garlandstone Wlk GL1 118 C6
Garnalls Rd GL4 119 C4
Garnet St BS3 8 B3
Garnett Pl BS16 20 F7
Garns Cl GL11 89 B1
Garren View HR9 162 C7
Garrett Dr BS32 29 D7
Garretts The GL7 152 D4
Garth Rd BS13 2 A8
Garton Ho [3] BS16 20 D5
Garvey Cl NP16 60 F4
Garvey Ho [14] BS5 9 C7
Gas La Bristol BS2 9 A6
Cricklade SN6 143 F4
Gasferry Rd BS1 194 B1
Gaskins The BS7 19 A5
Gassons Rd GL7 153 E3
Gassons Way GL7 153 E2
Gaston Ave BS31 4 F6
Gaston La SN16 58 D1
Gastons The BS11 17 A8
Gastrells Com Prim Sch GL5 99 A4
Gasworks La GL54 168 F7
Gasworks Villas GL2 118 B4
Gatcombe Cl GL52 137 E3
Gatcombe Dr BS34 29 E4
Gatcombe Rd BS13 2 B5
Gatehouse Ave BS13 2 A5
Gatehouse Cl BS13 2 A5
Gatehouse Ct BS13 2 B5
Gatehouse Sh Ctr BS13 2 B5
Gatehouse Way BS13 2 A5
Gatesby Mead BS34 29 E5
Gathorne Rd BS3 8 B4
Gatmeres Rd GL4 119 C3
Gatton Rd BS2 19 A1
Gatton Way GL3 127 F1
Gatwick Cl GL14 157 E8
Gaunt's La BS1 194 C2
Gaunts Earthcott La BS32 41 B5
Gaunts Rd BS37 33 B8
Gay Elms Prim Sch BS13 2 A4
Gay Elms Rd BS13 2 A4
Gayner Rd BS7 29 A1
Gays Rd BS15 10 B4
Gaythorne Cres BS37 43 D2
Gaywood Ho [7] BS3 8 B3
Gazelle Cl GL2 117 F2
Gazzard Cl BS36 30 E7
Gazzard Rd BS36 30 E7
Gee Moors BS15 10 F7
Gefle Cl BS1 194 B1
General Hospl Sch of Nursing GL53 193 C1
Genista Way [3] GL51 129 F5
Geoffrey Cl BS13 1 E6
George & Dragon La [11] BS5 9 D7
George Ct [12] Bristol BS6 18 B1
Painswick GL6 103 F8
George Dowty Dr GL20 182 C5
George La
Chipping Campden GL55 189 A1
Cinderford GL14 164 E1
Marshfield SN14 24 E1
George Naisey Ho [6] GL52 134 A3
George Pl [14] GL16 155 A7
George Rd GL15 156 A2
George Readings Way GL51 133 A4
George St Bisley GL6 105 A1
Bristol BS5 9 C8
Gloucester GL1 196 C3
Nailsworth GL6 91 C4
[5] Stroud GL5 99 C7
George Whitefield Cl GL4 119 C4
George Whitefield Ct BS1 195 B3
Georgia Rd GL7 152 E2
Georgian Cl GL4 119 E3
Georgian House (Mus)★ BS1 194 C2
Gerald Rd BS3 8 A3
Geralds Way GL6 148 C6
Gere Cl GL4 118 D2
Gerrard Cl BS4 2 D7
Gerrish Ave
Bristol, Redfield BS5 9 C8
Bristol, Staple Hill BS16 20 F5
Gervase Rd GL54 174 A8
Gibbet La BS14 3 D1
Gibbs Ct [14] BS5 9 D7
Gibbsfold Rd BS13 2 C4
Gibraltar Way NP16 61 B4
Gibson Cl GL5 99 F7
Gibson Ct GL7 190 D3
Gibson Rd Bristol BS6 18 D1
Innsworth GL3 127 E7
Giddynap La GL5 91 A7
Giffard Ho BS34 29 D6
Giffard Way GL53 130 D4
Gifford Cl Gloucester GL2 127 C5
Rangeworthy BS37 43 A8
Gifford Ct BS34 29 D2
Gifford Rd BS10 27 F4
Giffords Pl BS13 2 A7
Gilbert Hill GL13 85 E4
Gilbert Rd
Bristol, Kingswood BS15 20 D1
Bristol, Redfield BS5 9 C8
Gloucester GL2 127 C5
Gilberts La GL4 110 F6
Gilda Cl BS14 3 C5
Gilda Cres BS14 3 B6
Gilda Par BS14 3 C5
Gilda Sq W BS14 3 B5
Gilder Rd GL52 138 A2
Gilders Paddock GL52 137 F4
Giles Ave SN6 143 E3
Giles Cox GL2 109 F8
Gill Ave BS16 20 B6
Gillard Cl BS15 10 B8
Gillard Rd BS15 10 B8
Gillebank Cl BS14 3 D5
Gillett Cl GL54 139 F5
Gillingham Hill [6] BS15 10 B5
Gillingstool BS35 51 C8
Gillingstool Prim Sch BS35 51 B8
Gillray Cl BS7 19 B6
Gilpin Ave GL3 127 F1
Gilpin Cl BS15 20 F1
Gilroy Cl BS30 11 B3
Gilslake Ave BS10 28 B3
Gilton Ho BS4 9 E2
Gimson Cl GL4 118 D2
Gingell's Gn [4] BS5 10 A8
Gipsy La Chalford GL6 148 D4
Leonard Stanley GL10 97 E2
Gipsy Patch La BS34 29 C6
Glades The BS5 19 E2
Gladfield Gdns GL5 98 E6
Gladfield Sq GL5 98 E6
Gladiator Cl GL3 120 E5
Gladstone Dr BS16 20 E3
Gladstone La BS36 31 C7
Gladstone Rd
Bristol, Hengrove BS14 3 B6
[2] Bristol, Kingswood BS15 20 D1
Charlton Kings GL53 131 A5
Gloucester GL1 118 D6
Gladstone St
Bristol, Bedminster BS3 8 B3
Bristol, Kingswood BS16 20 D3
[12] Bristol, Redfield BS5 9 D7
Glaisdale Rd BS16 20 A5
Glamorgan Rd GL51 129 E6
Glanville Gdns BS15 10 E7
Glass House La BS2 9 B5
Glastonbury Cl BS30 10 F5
Glavum Works Trad Est GL1 118 F7
Glebe Cl Cirencester GL7 190 B8
Frampton on Severn GL2 157 F1
Long Ashton BS41 7 C2
Mitcheldean GL17 164 D6
Newent GL18 170 F5
[11] Stow-on-t-W GL54 176 F4
Glebe Farm Ct GL51 129 F5
Glebe Field BS32 40 A5
Glebe Inf Sch GL18 170 F5
Glebe La GL7 141 F8
Glebe Orch HR8 178 A3
Glebe Pl SN6 145 D3
Glebe Rd Bristol BS5 9 E8
Long Ashton BS41 7 C2
Minchinhampton GL6 148 A3
Newent GL18 170 F4
Prestbury GL52 134 B4
Glebe The Pilning BS35 38 C7
Sapperton GL7 149 B6
Glebe View GL7 158 C4
Glebe Way GL18 170 F5
Glebe Wlk BS31 4 C4
Glebeland Dr GL20 182 C7
Glebelands GL11 87 F5
Glebelands Rd BS34 29 A3
Gledemoor Dr BS36 31 D7
Glen Brook BS9 17 D4
Glen Ct GL10 97 F8
Glen Dr BS9 17 D5
Glen Hospl The BS6 18 A2
Glen La BS4 9 D2
Glen Park Cres GL5 99 A4
Glen Park Gdns BS5 10 A8
Glen Pk
Bristol, Eastville BS5 19 C2
Bristol, St George BS5 10 A8
Glen The
Bristol, Hanham BS15 10 B4
Bristol, Redland BS6 18 B3
Saltford BS31 5 F1
Yate BS37 43 E2
Glena Ave BS4 9 B2
Glenarm Rd BS4 9 E2
Glenarm Wlk BS4 9 E2
Glenavon Pk BS9 17 C4
Glenburn Rd BS15 20 B1
Glencairn Ave GL4 118 C1
Glencairn Ct GL50 130 A8
Glencairn Park Rd GL50 130 A8
Glencarn Pl [15] GL16 155 A7
Glencoe La GL17 164 D4
Glencoyne Sq BS10 28 C2
Glendale [16] Bristol BS8 7 F6
Bristol, Downend BS16 20 E8
Bristol, Hillfields BS16 20 C3
Glendare St BS5 9 C6
Glendevon Rd BS14 3 A3
Glendower Cl GL3 127 F8
Gleneagles BS37 43 E1
Gleneagles Dr BS10 27 D3
Gleneagles Rd BS30 11 B6
Glenfall BS37 32 D7
Glenfall Com Prim Sch GL52 131 C6
Glenfall St GL52 133 F2
Glenfall Way GL52 131 B6
Glenfrome Prim Sch BS5 19 B4
Glenfrome Rd BS2 19 B3
Glenlea Gr GL51 129 F5
Glenroy Ave BS15 20 B1
Glensanda Ct GL50 193 B2
Glenside Cl BS16 20 C7
Glenside Pk [3] BS16 19 E5
Glentworth Rd
Bristol BS8 194 B2
Bristol, Redland BS6 18 C2
Glenview Rd BS4 9 D2
Glenville Par GL3 120 A7
Glenwood BS16 20 C3
Glenwood Dr BS30 11 B4
Glenwood Rd BS10 18 C7
Glevum Cl GL2 127 B4
Glevum Ct [11] GL51 132 D2
Glevum Way GL4 119 E4
Glevum Works (Trad Est) GL1 119 A7
Gloster Ades Rd WR11 188 B6
Gloster Ave BS5 19 D3
Gloucester Bsns Pk GL3 120 B6
Gloucester Cl BS34 29 D5
Gloucester Coll of Arts & Tech
Cheltenham GL50 130 B6
Gloucester GL1 196 B2
Gloucester Cotts [5] GL50 133 B2
Gloucester Docks The★ GL1 196 A2
Gloucester Ho [11] BS2 195 C3
Gloucester House Mews GL12 68 A8
Gloucester La
[18] Bristol BS2 195 C3
Mickleton GL55 189 A6
Gloucester Mus & Art Gal★ GL1 196 B2
Gloucester Pl GL52 193 C4
Gloucester Prison Mus★ GL1 196 A3
Gloucester Rd
Almondsbury BS32,BS35 40 C6
Andoversford GL54 166 D6
Avonmouth BS11 26 A1
Bristol, Bishopston BS7 18 E4
Bristol, Patchway BS34 29 B7
Bristol, Staple Hill BS16 20 E3
Cheltenham GL51 132 D1
Coleford GL16 155 A5
Mitcheldean GL17 164 D5
Painswick GL6 111 F1
Sharpness GL13 85 C8
Staunton GL19 172 B8
Stone GL13 77 F3
Tadwick BA1 13 F2
Tewkesbury GL20 181 F1
Tutshill NP16 73 A2
Upleadon GL18 171 D5
Gloucester Rd N BS7, BS34 29 A4
Gloucester Road Prim Sch GL51 133 B2
Gloucester Row
[6] Bristol BS8 7 F7
Kingswood GL12 67 F8
Gloucester Royal Hospl GL1 196 C3
Gloucester Rugby Football Gd GL1 196 B4
Gloucester Ski Ctr★ GL4 119 B3
Gloucester St
[8] Bristol, Clifton BS8 7 F7
Bristol, Eastville BS5 19 D3
[5] Bristol, St Pauls BS2 195 B4
Cirencester GL7 190 B6
Newent GL18 171 A4
Painswick GL6 103 F8
[2] Stroud GL5 99 C7
Winchcombe GL54 174 A7
Wooton-u-E GL12 68 A7
Gloucester Sta GL1 196 C3
Gloucestershire & Warwickshire Rly★ GL54 184 C1
Gloucestershire Airport GL51 128 D8
Gloucestershire Coll of Arts & Tech GL51 133 B2
Gloucestershire Constabulary HQ GL51 130 A8
Gloucestershire Royal Hospl GL1 127 A2
Glyn Terr GL5 99 E3
Glyn Vale BS3 8 E1
Glynbridge Gdns GL51 132 F5
Glyndthorpe Gr [12] GL51 129 E5
Glynfield Rise GL5 98 C7
Glynrosa Rd GL53 131 B5
Goddard Way GL4 118 D2
Godfrey Cl GL51 130 A7
Godfrey Ct [7] BS30 10 F4
Godwin Cl [14] GL52 133 F2
Godwin Rd GL54 174 A8
Goffenton Dr BS16 20 B6
Goldcrest Ct [6] GL10 97 F8
Goldcrest Rd BS37 32 F7
Golden Cl GL4 118 C2
Golden Farm Rd GL7 190 E4
Golden Hay WR11 183 F7
Golden Hill BS6 18 C5
Golden La GL12 67 F4
Golden Miller Rd GL50 133 C5
Golden Vale GL3 128 B6
Golden Valley
Brimscombe GL5 148 A5
Newent GL18 171 D4
Golden Valley La BS30 11 F2
Goldfinch Way BS16 22 C4
Goldfoot Ho GL51 132 F1

Goldney Ave
Bristol, Clifton BS8 ... 194 A2
Bristol, Warmley BS30 ... 11 C7
Goldney Ct 7 BS16 ... 19 E3
Goldney Rd BS8 ... 194 A2
Goldsborough Cl GL4 ... 119 B6
Goldsbury Wlk BS11 ... 27 A1
Goldsmith Rd GL51 ... 132 E2
Golf Club La
Brockworth GL3 ... 120 C5
Saltford BS31 ... 5 E2
Golf Course La BS34 ... 28 F3
Golf Course Rd GL6 ... 111 F2
Gooch Cl WR11 ... 188 C7
Gooch Ct BS30 ... 11 C3
Good Neighbours La NP25 ... 154 B7
Good Shepherd Cl BS7 ... 18 C4
Goodeve Pk BS9 ... 17 D3
Goodeve Rd BS9 ... 17 D3
Goodhind St BS5 ... 9 A8
Goodier's La GL20 ... 182 A7
Goodmans Terr 5 GL7 ... 152 E4
Goodmoor Cres GL3 ... 128 A6
Goodneston Rd BS16 ... 20 A3
Goodrich Castle* HR9 ... 163 A6
Goodrich CE Prim Sch HR9 ... 163 A6
Goodrich Cl BS37 ... 43 B1
Goodrich Hill GL19 ... 172 D4
Goodridge Ave GL2 ... 118 A3
Goodridge Trad Est GL2 ... 118 A4
Goodring Hill BS11 ... 27 A1
Goodwin Ct GL1 ... 118 E7
Goodwin Dr BS14 ... 2 F4
Goodwood Gdns BS16 ... 30 F1
Goodyere St GL1 ... 196 C1
Goolden St BS4 ... 9 A3
Goose Acre BS32 ... 29 F6
Goose Gn Bristol BS30 ... 21 C1
Yate BS37 ... 43 E3
Goose Green Way BS37 ... 43 E4
Goose La GL14 ... 157 F8
Gooseacre Ct GL7 ... 190 C6
Gooseacre La GL7 ... 190 C6
Goosegreen BS36 ... 31 C8
Gooseland Cl BS14 ... 2 F3
Gooselands SN16 ... 141 B3
Gopshill La GL54 ... 183 E1
Gordano Gdns BS20 ... 16 B4
Gordon Ave BS5 ... 19 E1
Gordon Cl Bristol BS5 ... 19 E1
Highnam GL2 ... 125 E5
Gordon Rd Bristol BS8 ... 194 B3
14 Bristol, St Pauls BS2 ... 18 F1
Bristol, Whitehall BS5 ... 19 D1
Cheltenham GL53 ... 130 C5
Gordon Terr GL5 ... 99 D7
Gore Rd BS3 ... 8 A3
Gore's Marsh Rd BS3 ... 8 A2
Gorham Cl BS11 ... 27 C2
Gorlands Rd BS37 ... 44 C1
Gorlangton Cl BS14 ... 3 A7
Gorse Bglws GL16 ... 155 A6
Gorse Cl
Bourton-on-t-W GL54 ... 169 A7
Gloucester GL4 ... 119 F4
Gorse Cover Rd BS35 ... 38 A7
Gorse Hill BS16 ... 20 C3
Gorse La Bristol BS8 ... 194 B2
Cold Ashton BS30,SN14 ... 13 D7
Sling GL16 ... 155 B3
Gorse Mdw GL54 ... 169 A6
Gorse The GL54 ... 169 A7
Gorsley Gdns HR9 ... 170 B4
Gorsley Goff's Prim Sch HR9 ... 170 B5
Gosditch
Ashton Keynes SN6 ... 142 F4
Latton SN6 ... 143 E6
Gosditch St GL7 ... 190 C5
Gosforth Cl BS10 ... 28 B1
Gosforth Rd BS10 ... 28 B1
Goshawk Rd GL2 ... 117 F3
Goslet Rd BS14 ... 3 E5
Goss Wood Cnr GL2 ... 109 E8
Gotherington Fields GL52 ... 137 E8
Gotherington La GL52 ... 138 A5
Gotherington Prim Sch GL52 ... 138 B7
Gotley Rd BS4 ... 9 D2
Gott Dr BS4 ... 9 D5
Gouda Way GL1 ... 196 B4
Gould Dr GL20 ... 182 C5
Goulston Rd BS13 ... 2 A5
Goulston Wlk BS13 ... 2 A5
Goulter St BS5 ... 9 B6
Gourney Cl BS11 ... 27 B2
Gover Rd BS15 ... 10 C3
Govier Way BS35 ... 38 C4
Gower Cotts NP16 ... 72 F2
Gowle Rd GL5 ... 99 D6
Grace Cl BS37 ... 44 C1
Grace Ct BS16 ... 20 D6
Grace Dr Bristol BS15 ... 11 A8
1 Northleach GL54 ... 168 A1
Grace Gdns GL51 ... 129 D7
Grace Park Rd BS4 ... 9 D1
Grace Rd BS16 ... 20 C5
Graces Pitch 15 GL18 ... 171 A4
Graeme Cl BS16 ... 20 A4
Grafton Ct GL50 ... 193 B1
Grafton La GL19 ... 180 B3
Grafton Rd
Cheltenham GL50 ... 193 A1
Gloucester GL2 ... 127 B3
Graham Ct GL20 ... 192 D5
Graham Gdns GL2 ... 127 B3
Graham Pl GL51 ... 132 D3
Graham Rd
4 Bristol, Bedminster BS3 ... 8 C3
21 Bristol, Upper Easton BS5 ... 19 B1
Grahamstown Gr NP16 ... 61 B8
Grahamstown Rd NP16 ... 61 B8
Grainger Ct BS11 ... 16 E7
Grampian Cl BS30 ... 11 C4
Granary Cotts GL56 ... 186 C7
Granbrook La GL55 ... 189 B7
Granby Hill BS8 ... 7 F6
Grandmother's Rock La BS30 ... 12 D2
Grange Ave
Bristol, Hanham BS15 ... 10 D5
Bristol, Little Stoke BS34 ... 29 C6
Grange Cl Bristol BS32 ... 40 C2
Highworth SN6 ... 145 D3
Minchinhampton GL6 ... 91 F6
Grange Cl N BS9 ... 18 B6
Grange Com Sch BS30 ... 11 B7
Grange Court La GL19 ... 165 D6
Grange Court Rd
Bristol BS9 ... 18 A6
Westbury-on-S GL14 ... 165 D2
Grange Ct Bristol BS15 ... 10 D5
Bristol, Henleaze BS9 ... 18 B6
Bristol, Westbury-on-T BS9 ... 18 A8
Northway GL20 ... 182 C5
Grange Dr
Bishop's Cleeve GL52 ... 137 F3
Bristol BS16 ... 20 C6
Grange Inf Sch GL4 ... 118 C2
Grange Jun Sch GL4 ... 118 C3
Grange La GL8 ... 140 B3
Grange Pk
Bristol, Frenchay BS16 ... 20 C8
Bristol, Westbury on Trym BS9 ... 18 B6
St Arvans NP16 ... 72 A6
Whitchurch HR9 ... 162 D4
Grange Rd
Bristol, Bishopsworth BS13 ... 2 A5
Bristol, Clifton BS8 ... 194 A3
Gloucester GL4 ... 118 D1
Northway GL20 ... 182 C5
Saltford BS31 ... 5 C3
St Arvans NP16 ... 72 A6
Grange The Bristol BS9 ... 17 D7
Cheltenham GL51 ... 129 B6
Gloucester GL2 ... 127 B2
Moreton-in-M GL56 ... 187 A3
Grange View GL5 ... 99 C8
Grange Wlk GL53 ... 131 B5
Grangefield Sch GL52 ... 137 E3
Grangeville Cl BS30 ... 11 B3
Grangewood Cl BS16 ... 20 C6
Granley Cl GL51 ... 129 F8
Granley Dr GL51 ... 129 F8
Granley Gdns GL51 ... 129 F8
Granley Rd GL51 ... 129 F8
Granna La GL52 ... 138 D8
Granny's La BS15 ... 10 E6
Gransmoor Grange GL3 ... 120 B7
Grantham Ho BS15 ... 20 C1
Grantham La BS15 ... 10 C8
Grantham Rd BS15 ... 20 C1
Grantley Cres GL7 ... 190 C3
Grantson Cl BS4 ... 9 E2
Granville Chapel 5 BS8 ... 7 F5
Granville Cl BS15 ... 10 B3
Granville St Bristol BS5 ... 9 C6
Cheltenham GL50 ... 133 C3
Gloucester GL1 ... 118 D6
Monmouth NP25 ... 154 A7
Granville Terr NP16 ... 73 A1
Grasby Cl GL4 ... 119 E7
Grasmere Cl BS10 ... 18 A8
Grasmere Rd
Cheltenham GL51 ... 129 F7
Gloucester GL2 ... 127 C4
Grasmere Way NP16 ... 61 A4
Grass Meers Dr BS14 ... 3 A4
Grassington Dr BS37 ... 33 A8
Grassmere Gdns BS30 ... 11 D6
Gratitude Rd BS5 ... 19 C1
Gratton Rd GL50 ... 193 A1
Gratton St GL50 ... 193 B1
Gravel Hill Rd BS37 ... 44 A5
Gravel Pit Cotts GL52 ... 131 C6
Gravel Pit La GL52 ... 134 C5
Gravel Pits Cl GL20 ... 182 C7
Gravel Terr GL53 ... 131 B5
Gravel Wlk
Southam GL52 ... 134 C8
Tewkesbury GL20 ... 192 D5
Graveney Cl BS4 ... 9 D1
Graveney Rd GL54 ... 168 A1
Gravney Ct GL51 ... 132 E4
Gray Cl Bristol BS10 ... 27 E2
Innsworth GL3 ... 127 E7
Gray Rd GL7 ... 151 A2
Gray's La 18 GL56 ... 187 A3
Grayle Rd BS10 ... 28 A2
Grayling Cl 8 GL4 ... 119 E5
Grayling Ho BS9 ... 17 F7
Grayston Cl GL20 ... 192 E6
Great Ann St BS2 ... 195 C3
Great Brockeridge BS9 ... 17 F6
Great Dowles BS30 ... 11 A4
Great George St
Bristol, Brandon Hill BS1 ... 194 C2
Bristol, St Pauls BS2 ... 195 C3
Great Gr GL4 ... 119 D7
Great Hayles Rd BS14 ... 3 A6
Great Leaze BS30 ... 11 A4
Great Mdw BS34 ... 30 A6
Great Meadow Rd BS32 ... 29 F6
Great Norwood St GL50 ... 193 B1
Great Park Rd BS32 ... 40 C3
Great Rissington Prim Sch GL54 ... 169 D4
Great Rose La SN26 ... 144 D3
Great Stoke BS34 ... 30 A5
Great Stoke Way
Bristol, Great Stoke BS34 ... 30 A5
Bristol, Harry Stoke BS34 ... 29 D3
Great Western Ct BS34 ... 29 F4
Great Western La BS5 ... 9 C6
Great Western Railway Mus* GL16 ... 155 A5
Great Western Rd
Cheltenham GL50 ... 193 A4
Gloucester GL1 ... 196 C3
Sharpness GL13 ... 93 B1
Great Western Terr GL50 ... 193 A4
Great Weston Bsns Pk BS37 ... 43 B3
Great Witcombe Roman Villa* GL3 ... 120 F1
Greatfield Dr GL53 ... 130 F5
Greatfield La GL51 ... 129 E5
Greatfield Park Prim Sch GL51 ... 129 F5
Grebe Cl GL4 ... 119 D5
Grebe Sq GL54 ... 169 D6
Green Acre Bream GL15 ... 147 D8
Brockworth GL3 ... 120 E5
Green Bank GL3 ... 120 E4
Green Cl Bristol BS7 ... 19 A8
Brockworth GL3 ... 120 E4
Honeybourne WR11 ... 188 C6
Uley GL11 ... 89 C2
Green Colley Cl HR9 ... 163 B6
Green Croft BS5 ... 20 A1
Green Dell Cl BS10 ... 27 D3
Green Dragon Rd BS36 ... 30 D5
Green Gdns GL3 ... 120 E4
Green Hayes BS37 ... 33 C8
Green Hill BS35 ... 51 A4
Green La Avonmouth BS11 ... 26 B1
Chedworth GL54 ... 159 B6
Churchdown GL3 ... 128 C4
Easter Compton BS35 ... 38 C1
Evenlode GL56 ... 177 C7
Gloucester GL3 ... 120 A6
Hardwicke GL2 ... 109 E6
Little Witcombe GL3 ... 121 C3
Marshfield SN14 ... 14 E8
Moreton Valence GL2 ... 101 A6
Naunton WR8 ... 180 A7
Rangeworthy BS37,GL12 ... 53 B2
Severn Beach BS35 ... 38 B8
Sherston SN16 ... 58 C1
Tewkesbury GL20 ... 182 B4
Tytherington GL12 ... 52 B8
Winterbourne BS16 ... 30 C7
Green Lane Cl GL54 ... 168 F8
Green Meadow Bank GL52 ... 137 E3
Green Pastures NP25 ... 154 A3
Green Pippin Cl GL2 ... 127 C2
Green Side BS16 ... 21 A6
Green St Bristol BS3 ... 8 F4
Brockworth GL3 ... 120 E3
Bushley GL19,GL20 ... 181 B5
Chepstow NP16 ... 60 E8
Dursley GL11 ... 88 C6
Green The
Bishop's Cleeve GL52 ... 137 F3
Bristol, New Cheltenham BS15 ... 20 E2
Bristol, Stoke Gifford BS34 ... 29 E4
6 Broadway WR12 ... 185 B8
Chepstow NP16 ... 60 B5
Chipping Campden GL55 ... 189 A1
Cirencester GL7 ... 190 E5
Cromhall GL12 ... 53 B8
Fairford GL7 ... 152 D4
Frampton on Severn GL2 ... 157 F2
Great Wolford CV36 ... 187 E5
Highworth SN6 ... 145 C3
9 Moreton-in-M GL56 ... 187 A3
Newnham GL14 ... 156 F6
Oaksey SN16 ... 141 F4
Olveston BS35 ... 50 A2
Pill BS20 ... 16 D4
Tetbury GL8 ... 140 C4
Uckington GL51 ... 132 D6
Uley GL11 ... 89 C2
Green Way GL3 ... 120 E5
Green Wlk BS4 ... 9 A1
Green's Cl GL54 ... 169 C4
Greenacre Rd BS14 ... 3 A3
Greenacres Bristol BS9 ... 17 E7
Twyning GL20 ... 181 F8
Greenacres Park Homes BS36 ... 31 E5
Greenacres Pk GL7 ... 152 A3
Greenaways GL18 ... 170 F5
Greenbank Ave BS5 ... 19 C1
Greenbank Ave W BS5 ... 19 C1
Greenbank Cl GL17 ... 164 B3
Greenbank Rd
Bristol, Hanham BS15 ... 10 D5
Bristol, Lower Easton BS5 ... 19 D2
Bristol, Southville BS3 ... 8 A4
Greenbank View BS5 ... 19 D2
Greenbanks NP25 ... 146 B7
Greendale Rd
Bristol, Bedminster BS3 ... 8 E2
Greendale Rd *continued*
Bristol, Redland BS6 ... 18 B3
Greenditch Ave BS13 ... 2 C5
Greenditch St BS35 ... 49 D1
Greendown BS5 ... 10 A7
Greenfield Ave BS10 ... 18 D8
Greenfield Cl GL17 ... 163 D3
Greenfield Rd
Bristol BS10 ... 28 D1
Coleford GL16 ... 155 A6
Joy's Green GL17 ... 163 D3
Greenhaven 5 BS5 ... 19 C1
Greenhill BS35 ... 51 A4
Greenhill Cl GL14 ... 191 E5
Greenhill Ct GL4 ... 118 B2
Greenhill Down BS35 ... 51 A5
Greenhill Dr GL2 ... 118 A3
Greenhill Flats GL5 ... 99 E3
Greenhill Gdns BS35 ... 51 A4
Greenhill Gr BS3 ... 8 A2
Greenhill Ho GL52 ... 137 F3
Greenhill La
Alveston BS35 ... 50 F4
Bristol BS11 ... 27 C1
Greenhill Par 5 BS35 ... 51 A5
Greenhill Rd BS35 ... 51 A5
Greenhills Cl GL53 ... 130 E5
Greenhills Rd GL53 ... 130 F5
Greenhouse La GL6 ... 104 A7
Greenings The GL51 ... 129 F5
Greenlands Cl NP25 ... 154 A7
Greenlands Way BS10 ... 27 F4
Greenleaze Bristol BS4 ... 9 B1
Marston Meysey SN6 ... 144 B8
Greenleaze Ave BS16 ... 30 D1
Greenleaze Cl BS16 ... 30 D1
Greenmore Rd BS4 ... 9 B2
Greenore BS15 ... 10 C7
Greenpark Rd BS10 ... 28 E1
Greenridge Cl BS13 ... 1 E4
Greenside Cl BS10 ... 27 D3
Greensplott Rd BS11 ... 26 E7
Greenstreet GL10 ... 97 F8
Greenview Bristol BS30 ... 11 A2
Quenington GL7 ... 152 D7
Greenway GL52 ... 138 B3
Greenway Bush La BS3 ... 8 B4
Greenway Cl GL51 ... 129 D1
Greenway Dr BS10 ... 18 D8
Greenway Ho 10 BS6 ... 18 B2
Greenway La
Charlton Kings GL52 ... 131 C7
Cheltenham GL53 ... 122 B7
Cold Ashton SN14 ... 13 D5
Gretton GL54 ... 183 F1
Llandogo NP25 ... 146 A8
Shurdington GL51 ... 129 D1
Greenway Pk BS10 ... 18 D8
Greenway Rd
Blockley GL56 ... 186 C6
Bristol BS6 ... 18 B2
Cinderford GL14 ... 191 C3
Greenway The BS16 ... 20 C3
Greenways
Aylburton GL15 ... 147 F5
Bristol BS15 ... 21 A1
Winchcombe GL54 ... 174 A8
Greenways Dr GL16 ... 155 B4
Greenways Rd BS37 ... 43 E3
Greenwood Cl Bristol BS7 ... 18 E7
Gloucester GL3 ... 120 B6
Greenwood Dr BS35 ... 50 F4
Greenwood Rd BS4 ... 9 A1
Greet Rd GL54 ... 174 A8
Gregory Ct BS30 ... 11 A6
Grenadier Cl GL4 ... 119 F6
Grenadier Rd GL51 ... 132 E4
Grenville Cl Bristol BS5 ... 9 F8
Innsworth GL3 ... 127 F8
Grenville Pl 7 BS1 ... 7 F5
Grenville Rd BS6 ... 18 E3
Gresham Ct 5 GL51 ... 132 E2
Gretton Prim Sch GL54 ... 183 E1
Gretton Rd
Gotherington GL52 ... 138 C8
Winchcombe GL54 ... 174 A8
Greve Ct 5 BS30 ... 10 F4
Grevel La GL55 ... 189 A2
Grevil Rd 4 GL51 ... 132 F4
Greville Cl GL2 ... 126 E4
Greville Ct GL51 ... 129 F8
Greville Rd BS3 ... 8 B4
Greville St BS3 ... 8 C4
Greyfriars GL1 ... 196 B2
Greyfriars Church* GL1 ... 196 B3
Greyfriars Wlk GL7 ... 190 B2
Greyhound Gdns GL2 ... 127 D5
Greylag Cres GL20 ... 192 E3
Greylands Rd BS13 ... 1 F7
Greyrick Ct GL55 ... 189 A6
Greys Cl 5 GL6 ... 148 B6
Greystoke Ave BS10 ... 28 C1
Greystoke Gdns BS10 ... 18 A8
Greystone Lodge GL3 ... 120 B7
Greystones BS16 ... 30 E1
Greystones La GL54 ... 169 A7
Grierson Cl GL3 ... 120 B6
Griffin Cl GL54 ... 177 A4
Griffin Ct GL54 ... 177 A4
Griffin Mill Est GL5 ... 99 D4
Griffiths Ave GL51 ... 132 F1
Griffon Cl GL2 ... 117 F3
Griggfield Wlk BS14 ... 3 A7
Griggs Cl GL55 ... 189 A2
Grimsbury Park Specl Sch BS30 ... 11 B7
Grimsbury Rd BS15 ... 11 A7
Grimwade Cl GL51 ... 132 F1
Grindell Rd BS5 ... 9 D7
Grinfield Ave BS13 ... 2 C4
Grinfield Cl BS13 ... 2 C4
Grinfield Ct BS13 ... 2 C4
Grisedale Cl GL2 ... 127 D5
Grist Mill Cl GL51 ... 132 D5
Grittleton Rd BS7 ... 18 E8
Grosvenor Ct 2 BS6 ... 18 B1
Grosvenor Ho GL1 ... 196 B3
Grosvenor Pl S GL52 ... 193 C3
Grosvenor Rd Bristol BS2 ... 18 F1
Gloucester GL2 ... 127 B2
Stonehouse GL10 ... 101 F1
Grosvenor St GL52 ... 193 C3
Grosvenor Terr GL52 ... 193 C3
Grove Ave Bristol BS1 ... 195 A1
Bristol, Coombe Dingle BS9 ... 17 C7
3 Bristol, Fishponds BS16 ... 19 F4
Honeybourne WR11 ... 188 C7
Grove Bank BS16 ... 30 C1
Grove Cotts GL5 ... 98 F8
Grove Cres
7 Coleford GL16 ... 155 A6
Gloucester GL4 ... 127 D1
Grove Ct BS9 ... 17 E5
Grove End Cotts GL2 ... 109 A7
Grove Gdns GL8 ... 140 B5
Grove Hill SN6 ... 145 C4
Grove Ind Est The BS34 ... 29 B8
Grove La Cirencester GL7 ... 190 D5
Hinton SN14 ... 23 C6
Lydney GL15 ... 92 B6
Whitminster GL2 ... 100 F4
Grove Leaze BS11 ... 16 D6
Grove Orch SN6 ... 145 C4
Grove Park Ave BS4 ... 9 D2
Grove Park Rd Bristol BS4 ... 9 D2
Stroud GL5 ... 99 C8
Grove Park Terr BS16 ... 19 F4
Grove Pk
Bristol, Brislington BS4 ... 9 D2
Bristol, Redland BS6 ... 18 C2
Grove Rd Aylburton GL15 ... 147 F6
Berry Hill GL16 ... 155 A7
Bristol, Coombe Dingle BS9 ... 17 D8
Bristol, Fishponds BS16 ... 19 F4
Bristol, Redland BS6 ... 18 A2
Innsworth GL3 ... 127 F6
Whitecroft GL15 ... 155 F1
Grove St
Cheltenham GL50 ... 193 A4
Gloucester GL1 ... 196 C1
Grove The Avening GL8 ... 140 B8
Bristol BS1 ... 195 A1
Bristol, Oldland BS30 ... 11 A4
Bristol, Patchway BS34 ... 29 B7
Cheltenham, Battledown GL52 ... 134 A1
Cheltenham, Lansdown GL50 ... 130 B8
Chelworth SN16 ... 141 E5
Moreton-in-M GL56 ... 187 B3
Rangeworthy BS37 ... 43 A8
Selsley GL5 ... 98 E4
Stroud GL5 ... 98 D6
Grove View Bristol BS16 ... 19 E6
Greet GL54 ... 184 A1
Grovefield GL19 ... 180 A4
Grovefield Way GL51 ... 129 B7
Grovelands GL4 ... 127 E1
Grovelands Cl 1 GL53 ... 131 B6
Groves Pl GL7 ... 152 E3
Groves The BS13 ... 2 D4
Grovesend Rd BS35 ... 51 D8
Grump St CV36 ... 189 F6
Gryphons The 15 GL52 ... 133 F2
Guardian Ct GL53 ... 130 F6
Guernsey Ave BS4 ... 9 F4
Guest Ave BS16 ... 21 B7
Guestriss Cotts GL50 ... 133 C5
Guggle La 7 GL54 ... 168 A1
Guild Ct BS1 ... 195 B2
Guildford Rd BS4 ... 9 E6
Guildings Way GL10 ... 98 A4
Guinea La Bristol BS16 ... 20 A4
Bristol BS16 ... 20 A5
Guinea St Bristol BS1 ... 195 A1
Gloucester GL1 ... 196 C4
Guise Ave GL3 ... 120 F4
Guise Cl GL2 ... 109 F8
Gullimores Gdns BS13 ... 2 B4
Gullivers Pl BS37 ... 33 A8
Gullon Wlk BS13 ... 1 F5
Gullons Cl BS13 ... 2 A6
Gully La BS35 ... 64 E7
Gully The BS36 ... 30 F7
Gullybrook La 3 BS5 ... 9 B6
Gumstool Hill 10 GL8 ... 140 C4
Gunhouse La GL5 ... 99 D5
Gunning Cl BS15 ... 10 D6
Gunter's Hill BS5 ... 10 A6
Gupshill Cl GL20 ... 192 C2
Gurney Ave GL4 ... 118 D2
Gustav Holst Birthplace Mus* GL52 ... 193 C4
Guthrie Rd BS8 ... 194 A4
Gwentlands Cl NP16 ... 60 E7
Gwernant Rd GL51 ... 129 F6
Gwilliam St BS3 ... 8 D3
Gwinnett Ct GL51 ... 129 E2
Gwy Ct NP16 ... 72 F1
Gwyn St BS2 ... 18 E1
Gyde Rd GL6 ... 111 F1
Gypsy La Gorsley GL18 ... 170 C3

Gypsy La *continued*
Marshfield SN14 14 F7

H

Haberdashers Sch for Girls NP25 154 A8
Haberdashers' Agincourt Sch NP25 154 A8
Haberfield Hill BS8 16 E2
Haberfield Ho 1 BS8 7 F6
Hacket Hill BS35 51 F8
Hacket La BS35 51 F8
Hadfield Cl GL19 172 A8
Hadley Ct BS30 11 B6
Hadley Rd GL11 87 E4
Hadnock Rd NP25 154 A8
Hadnock Road Ind Est NP25 154 A8
Hadow Way GL2 109 F8
Hadrian Cl Bristol BS9 17 C4
Lydney GL15 92 B4
Hadrians Way GL4 119 F7
Hague Ave GL11 87 F4
Haig Cl BS9 17 B7
Hailes Abbey & Mus* GL54 184 D1
Hailes Green Barns GL54 174 C8
Hailes Rd GL4 119 D7
Hailes St 28 GL54 174 A7
Hakeburn Rd GL7 190 C5
Halbrow Cres BS16 20 C5
Haldon Cl BS3 8 D1
Hale Cl BS15 10 D4
Hale La GL6 103 F8
Hale's Rd GL52 134 A1
Hales Cl GL52 134 A1
Hales Horn Cl BS32 29 D6
Halfacre Cl BS14 3 A3
Halfacre La BS14 3 B4
Halford Ho GL2 118 C4
Halfway Pitch GL6 103 B4
Halifax Rd BS37 43 D4
Hall End La BS37 53 D2
Hall La
Cold Ashton BA1,SN14 13 E2
Horton BS37 45 E5
Lower Hamswell BA1 13 B3
Hall Rd GL53 130 D4
Hall St BS3 8 C2
Halland Rd GL53 130 D5
Hallards Cl BS11 16 F8
Hallen Cl BS10 27 D3
Hallen Dr BS9 17 C7
Hallen Ind Est BS10 27 A7
Hallen Rd BS10 27 D4
Hallmead Cl GL51 132 D5
Halls Rd BS15 10 D8
Hallsfield SN6 143 E4
Hallwood Dr HR8 178 D8
Halmore La GL13 86 A8
Halsbury Rd BS6 18 B4
Halstock Ave BS16 19 F3
Halston Dr BS2 195 C4
Halswell Gdns BS13 2 B4
Halt End BS14 3 C3
Halwyn Cl BS9 17 D5
Ham Cl GL52 131 C7
Ham Farm La BS16 21 B6
Ham Gn BS20 16 D3
Ham La Bristol BS16 19 E6
Doynton BS30 22 E1
Dundry BS41 1 D3
Kempsford GL7 144 F7
South Cerney GL7 142 F7
Thornbury BS35 63 C7
Ham Mill La GL5 99 E3
Ham Rd Ashleworth GL19 172 E5
Charlton Kings GL52,GL54 131 E7
Ham Sq GL52 131 C7
Ham The GL11 89 A6
Hambidge La GL7 153 E3
Hamble Cl BS35 51 C8
Hambledon Cl GL7 150 F2
Hamblins Cotts GL53 123 A5
Hambrook La BS34 30 A3
Hambrook Prim Sch BS16 30 D3
Hambrook St GL52 131 B7
Hambutts Dr GL6 103 E8
Hambutts Mead GL6 103 E8
Hamer St GL1 127 B1
Hamfallow Ct GL13 85 D8
Hamfield La GL13 85 D3
Hamilton Croft GL7 152 A2
Hamilton Ct GL51 132 D3
Hamilton Rd
Bristol, Southville BS3 8 B4
Bristol, Upper Easton BS5 9 B8
Hamilton St GL53 131 A7
Hamlen Cl GL19 165 D6
Hamlet Cl GL51 132 E2
Hammersmith Bottom GL7 153 B7
Hammersmith Rd BS5 9 D8
Hammett Ct NP25 154 B7
Hammond Cl BS4 9 E1
Hammond Ct GL53 193 C1
Hammond Dr 3 GL54 168 A1
Hammond Gdns BS9 17 E7
Hammond Way
Cirencester GL7 190 C4
Gloucester GL4 127 D1
Hammonds SN6 143 F4
Hampden Cl BS37 43 D4
Hampden Rd BS4 9 B3
Hampden Way GL1 196 B2
Hampen Cotts GL54 167 A7
Hampshire Gdns GL16 155 A5
Hampshire Way BS37 43 F4
Hampstead Rd BS4 9 C3
Hampton Cl Bristol BS30 11 A5
Cheltenham GL51 130 A5
Gloucester GL3 120 B7
Hampton Cnr BS11 16 E6
Hampton Ct BS6 18 B1
Hampton Gr GL7 152 A3
Hampton Hill GL8 148 B1
Hampton La 17 BS6 18 B1
Hampton Mews GL15 92 B3
Hampton Pk BS6 18 B1
Hampton Pl GL3 128 A8
Hampton Rd BS6 18 B1
Hampton St Bristol BS15 20 D1
Tetbury GL8 140 B4
Hams Rd Keynsham BS31 4 F7
Lydney GL15 92 B3
Hanbury Cl BS15 10 D5
Hanbury Ct BS8 194 A4
Hanbury Ho NP16 60 E8
Hanbury Rd BS8 194 A4
Handel Ave 2 BS5 9 D7
Handel Rd BS31 4 E5
Handford Way BS30 11 B3
Hanford Ct BS14 3 D7
Hang Hill Rd GL15 155 D1
Hangerberry New Rd GL17 163 D1
Hanham Abbots Jun Sch BS15 10 C4
Hanham Bsns Pk BS15 10 B5
Hanham Hall Hospl BS15 10 D4
Hanham High Sch BS15 10 C4
Hanham Rd BS15 10 D7
Hankerton Rd SN16 142 B1
Hanley La NP16 73 E6
Hanman Rd GL1 118 F7
Hanman Villas GL2 124 C8
Hanna Ct GL50 193 B4
Hannah Boote Ho 8 GL52 134 A3
Hannah Cres GL7 150 F2
Hannah More Prim Sch BS1 195 B2
Hannah Pl GL3 127 E7
Hannam Cl GL53 130 E4
Hanover Cl NP16 72 D1
Hanover Ct Bristol BS1 195 B3
Bristol, Filton BS34 29 A3
14 Cheltenham GL51 130 B8
Cirencester GL7 190 D4
Tewkesbury GL20 192 C4
Tutshill NP16 61 A8
Hanover Gdns GL6 91 B4
Hanover Ho Bristol BS2 9 A7
Highworth SN6 145 C3
Hanover Lodge GL5 98 D7
Hanover Pl BS1 194 B1
Hanover St
2 Bristol BS1 195 A2
Bristol, Barton Hill BS5 9 C7
Cheltenham GL50 133 D3
Hanover Way 1 GL3 128 A7
Hanstone Cl GL7 190 B2
Happerton La BS20 16 D2
Harbour Rd GL15 84 B8
Harbour View GL20 192 D5
Harbour Wall BS9 17 B4
Harbour Way BS1 194 C1
Harbourside GL20 192 E5
Harbury Mews GL1 119 A8
Harbury Rd BS9 18 C7
Harcombe Hill BS36 30 E4
Harcombe Rd BS36 30 D5
Harcourt Ave BS5 10 A6
Harcourt Cl BS31 5 E2
Harcourt Hill BS6 18 C3
Harcourt Rd BS6 18 B3
Harden Rd BS14 3 E5
Hardenhuish Rd BS4 9 D5
Harding Pl BS31 5 B5
Harding's Dr GL11 88 A1
Hardington Dr BS31 5 A2
Hardwick Ave NP16 60 E7
Hardwick Bank Rd GL20 182 B5
Hardwick Bldg (Cheltenham & Gloucester Coll of H Ed) GL50,GL51 133 C3
Hardwick Cl
Bristol, Brislington BS4 9 E3
Bristol, North Common BS30 11 D5
Hardwick Hill NP16 60 E7
Hardwick Hill La NP16 60 E8
Hardwick Rd BS20 16 C5
Hardwicke BS37 32 C7
Hardwicke Prim Sch GL2 109 E6
Hardy Ave BS3 8 A4
Hardy Ct BS30 10 F5
Hardy La BS32 50 A1
Hardy Rd
Bishop's Cleeve GL52 138 A4
Bristol BS3 8 B2
Hare La GL1 196 B3
Harebell Pl GL4 119 E5
Hareclive Prim Sch BS13 2 C4
Hareclive Rd BS13 2 C4
Harefield Cl BS15 10 C2
Harescombe BS37 32 E7
Haresdown Hill GL7 141 C8
Haresfield GL7 190 B8
Haresfield CE Prim Sch GL10 110 B1
Haresfield Ct GL10 110 A1
Haresfield La GL2,GL10 109 F5
Haresfield Lodge GL4 119 B4
Harewood Cl GL4 118 C1
Harewood Ho BS6 18 A3
Harewood Jun & Inf Sch GL4 118 C1
Harewood Rd BS5 20 A1
Harford Cl BS9 17 C7
Harford Dr BS16 30 C1
Harlech Way BS30 11 B2
Harleston St 1 BS5 9 A8
Harley Ct 3 BS8 7 F7
Harley Mews 2 BS8 7 F7
Harley Pl 4 BS8 7 F7
Harleys Field GL4 119 D7
Harling Ct 12 HR8 178 E8
Harmer Cl BS10 27 F3
Harness Cl GL2 118 B6
Harnham La GL54 166 E2
Harnhill Cl BS13 2 B4
Harold Rd GL15 156 B2
Harolds Way BS15 10 C6
Harp Hill GL52 134 B1
Harper Rd GL5 98 E8
Harpfield Cl GL52 137 F3
Harpfield Rd GL52 137 F2
Harptree Ct 5 BS30 11 A4
Harptree Gr BS3 8 B2
Harptres Way GL17 164 D6
Harrier Way GL20 192 E2
Harrington Ave BS14 3 E6
Harrington Cl BS30 5 E8
Harrington Dr GL51 129 F7
Harrington Gr BS14 3 E6
Harrington Rd BS14 3 E6
Harrington Wlk BS14 3 E6
Harris Barton BS36 31 B7
Harris Cl GL3 128 C5
Harris Ct BS30 10 F4
Harris Gdns GL54 169 D6
Harris Rd SN6 143 A5
Harrison Cl Bristol BS16 21 B6
Newnham GL14 156 F6
Harrison Rd GL51 129 D2
Harrison Way GL15 92 C2
Harrow Rd BS4 9 D3
Harrowdene Rd BS4 9 B3
Harry Stoke Rd BS34 29 E2
Harry Yates Way GL51 132 D4
Hart Gn GL14 191 C2
Hart La GL17 163 F4
Hartbury Cl GL51 132 C3
Hartcliffe Rd BS4 2 E8
Hartcliffe Sch BS13 2 E4
Hartcliffe Way BS3,BS4, BS13 2 C7
Hartcliffe Wlk BS4 2 F8
Hartfield Ave BS6 194 C4
Hartgill Cl BS13 2 B3
Hartington Pk BS6 18 C2
Hartington Rd GL1 118 C6
Hartland Ho BS5 9 C6
Hartland Rd GL1 118 F6
Hartlands 22 GL18 171 A4
Hartlebury Way GL52 131 C6
Hartley Bridge Hill GL6 82 F8
Hartley Cl
Cheltenham GL53 130 F4
Chipping Sodbury BS37 44 C1
Hartpury CE Prim Sch GL19 172 C3
Hartpury Coll
Hartpury GL19 172 A1
Longhope GL17 165 A4
Harts Barn Flower & Craft Ctr* GL17 164 E5
Harts Croft BS37 43 F4
Harvard Ave WR11 188 C7
Harvest Cl BS32 40 D1
Harvest Gr GL51 132 D5
Harvest Way GL2 109 F7
Harvesters View GL52 137 D4
Harvey Cl GL2 118 C5
Harvey's La GL54 139 F5
Harwell Cl GL4 118 D1
Harwood Ho 13 BS5 9 B7
Haselbury Gr BS31 5 E2
Hasfield Cl GL2 117 E1
Hasfield Rd GL19 172 C6
Haskins Ct 4 BS30 11 A4
Haslemere Ind Est BS11 26 C2
Haslette Way GL51 129 E5
Hasnett Rd HR8 178 E8
Hassell Dr BS2 9 A7
Hastings Cl BS3 8 C1
Hastings Pl GL20 192 C2
Hastings Rd Bristol BS3 8 C1
Cinderford GL14 191 C4
Hatcher's Cres SN26 144 D1
Hatchet La BS34 29 E4
Hatchet Rd BS34 29 E5
Hatchmere BS35 51 D8
Hatfield Rd GL1 119 A7
Hathaway Cl GL2 118 C4
Hatherley BS37 32 E7
Hatherley Brake GL51 129 E7
Hatherley Court Rd GL51 130 B7
Hatherley Ct GL51 130 B7
Hatherley Gate GL51 130 B8
Hatherley Hall GL51 130 A7
Hatherley Ho 2 GL51 130 B8
Hatherley Inf Sch GL1 119 A7
Hatherley La GL51 129 D7
Hatherley Rd Bristol BS7 18 E4
Cheltenham GL51 129 F7
Gloucester GL1 119 A7
Hatherley St GL50 130 B7
Hatherop GL7 152 E8
Hatherop Castle Sch GL7 152 E8
Hatherop CE Prim Sch GL7 152 E8
Hatherop Rd GL7 152 E4
Hathorn Rd GL3 120 B6
Hathway Wlk BS5 9 A8
Hatters' La BS37 44 C1
Hatton Cl GL17 163 D1
Havelock Rd GL3 120 A8
Haven Ave GL10 97 E6
Haven Ct GL2 127 C3
Haven The BS15 20 E1
Haverstock Rd BS4 9 A3
Haviland Ho 7 BS2 195 C3
Haw La BS35 50 B3
Haw Rd GL16 155 C8
Haw St Coaley GL11 88 F7
Wooton-u-E GL12 68 A7
Hawburn Cl BS4 9 D2
Hawcombe Mews 1 GL51 129 F5
Haweswater Cl BS30 11 D6
Haweswater Rd GL51 129 F6
Hawk Cl 5 Chalford GL6 148 C6
Gloucester GL4 119 D5
Hawker Hill GL17 164 D5
Hawker Sq GL54 169 D6
Hawkers Hill GL7 160 A1
Hawkesbury Grange GL9 56 A2
Hawkesbury Prim Sch GL9 55 F3
Hawkesbury Rd
Bristol BS16 19 E3
Hillesley GL12 55 D6
Hawkesley Dr BS34 29 D6
Hawkfield Bsns Pk BS14 2 D5
Hawkfield Cl BS14 2 D5
Hawkfield Rd BS13 2 D5
Hawkfield Way BS14 2 D5
Hawkins Cl BS30 11 C5
Hawkins Cres BS32 29 E8
Hawkins La GL14 157 A7
Hawkins St BS2 195 C3
Hawkley Dr BS32 40 D3
Hawkmoor La BS16 19 E8
Hawkmoth Cl GL20 192 E2
Hawkridge Dr BS16 22 C5
Hawksmoor Cl BS14 3 A6
Hawkswood Rd GL51 130 B5
Hawksworth Dr BS15 10 B5
Hawkwell Cotts GL17 164 B3
Hawkwood Coll GL6 103 D2
Haworth Cl GL2 117 F2
Hawthorn Ave BS15 10 B5
Hawthorn Cl Bristol BS34 28 E7
Charfield GL12 67 A4
Chepstow NP16 60 E4
Hawthorn Cres BS35 64 C2
Hawthorn Ct GL15 92 B3
Hawthorn Dr
Innsworth GL3 127 F6
Sling GL16 155 B2
Woodmancote GL52 138 B3
Hawthorn Rd GL51 132 E3
Hawthorn Ridge GL6 90 F5
Hawthorn Rise GL5 98 D8
Hawthorn Way
Bristol BS34 29 E5
Northway GL20 182 C5
Hawthorne Ave GL4 119 C6
Hawthorne Cl BS16 22 C5
Hawthorne Gdns BS16 20 F4
Hawthorne Hill GL18 170 D5
Hawthorne St BS4 9 A3
Hawthornes The
Bristol BS16 20 F4
Cheltenham GL51 129 D6
Hawthorns La BS31 4 E5
Hawthorns Rd GL17 164 B5
Hawthorns The
Bishop's Cleeve GL52 137 E4
Bussage GL6 148 B6
Dursley GL11 87 F5
Lydney GL15 92 B3
Hay Ct BS20 16 A4
Hay La Ablington GL7 159 E1
Horsley GL6 83 A7
Hay Leaze BS37 43 D4
Hay St SN14 15 A8
Hay's Cotts GL53 130 E6
Haycombe BS14 2 F6
Haycroft Cl GL52 137 E4
Haycroft Dr GL4 119 D3
Haycroft La GL13 78 C6
Haycroft Rd Bristol BS34 29 A3
Northleach GL54 168 F2
Haydale Gdns GL2 127 C5
Hayden La GL51 132 A3
Hayden Rd GL51 132 F5
Haydock Cl BS16 30 F1
Haydon Ct 12 BS8 18 A2
Haydon Gdns BS7 19 B5
Haydons Cl GL55 189 A2
Haye's La GL9 46 F2
Hayeley Dr BS32 29 E6
Hayes Cl BS2 9 A7
Hayes Ct Bristol BS34 29 A7
Cheltenham GL52 134 A2
Gloucester GL2 126 F6
Hayes La GL7 158 B4
Hayes Rd
Cheltenham GL52 134 A2
Hayes Rd *continued*
Nailsworth GL6 91 A5
Hayes The
Prestbury GL52 134 C5
Sedbury NP16 61 B8
Hayfield SN14 15 A8
Hayfield Way GL52 137 E5
Haygarth Cl GL7 190 B2
Hayhedge La GL6 148 D8
Haylea Rd GL52 137 D4
Hayleigh Ho BS13 2 C4
Haymarket The BS1 195 A3
Haymarket Wlk 9 BS1 195 A4
Haymead La GL8 70 D5
Haymes Dr GL52 138 C1
Haymes Rd GL52 138 C1
Haynes Ho 2 BS16 20 D4
Haynes La BS16 20 D5
Hays Cl WR12 188 B2
Haysum's Cl GL55 189 A1
Hayter Ct BS10 28 D3
Haythorn Ct BS16 20 F5
Haythorne Ct 8 BS16 19 E3
Haytor Pk BS9 17 D6
Hayward Cl GL4 119 D7
Hayward Ind Est 1 BS16 20 D3
Hayward Rd
Bristol, Barton Hill BS5 9 C7
Bristol, Staple Hill BS16 20 D3
Hayward's Rd GL52 131 A8
Haywards La GL52 131 A8
Haywood Pitch HR9 170 C5
Hazebrouck Cl GL51 129 E7
Hazel Ave BS6 18 B2
Hazel Cl GL2 127 B5
Hazel Cote Rd BS14 3 B4
Hazel Cres BS35 64 D1
Hazel Ct GL4 127 D1
Hazel Gdns BS35 51 A4
Hazel Gr BS7 19 A8
Hazel La Alveston BS35 50 F2
Tockington BS32 50 E3
Hazel Rd GL17 164 B4
Hazelbury Dr BS30 11 C6
Hazelbury Rd BS14 3 C7
Hazelcroft GL3 128 B6
Hazeldean GL14 191 C5
Hazeldene Rd BS34 29 A7
Hazelgrove BS36 30 E5
Hazelhurst Bglws HR9 163 B5
Hazels The GL4 119 E7
Hazelton Cl GL4 118 F6
Hazelton Rd BS7 18 D3
Hazelwood 1 GL10 97 F7
Hazelwood Ct BS9 17 D3
Hazelwood Rd BS9 17 D3
Hazle Cl HR8 178 E7
Hazlecote La GL6,GL8 82 F6
Hazledean Rd GL51 132 D4
Hazlewood Cl GL51 130 B5
Hazlitt Croft GL51 132 D4
Headford Ave BS5 10 B7
Headford Rd BS4 8 D1
Headington Cl BS15 10 D4
Headlam Cl GL4 118 D1
Headland The NP16 61 A4
Headlands The GL5 98 F2
Headley Ct BS13 2 B6
Headley La BS13 2 B7
Headley Park Ave BS13 2 B7
Headley Park Prim Sch BS13 2 B6
Headley Park Rd BS13 2 A7
Headley Rd BS13 2 A6
Headley Wlk BS13 2 B7
Healey Dr SN14 23 C6
Heapey Cl 8 GL51 132 D2
Hearne Cl GL53 131 B6
Hearne Rd GL53 131 B6
Heart Meers BS14 3 B5
Heath Cl BS36 30 E6
Heath Ct BS16 20 D7
Heath Gdns Bristol BS16 20 D8
Coalpit Heath BS36 31 C5
Heath House La BS7,BS16 19 C5
Heath House Priory Hospl BS16 19 B4
Heath Lo 5 GL52 133 F2
Heath Rd
Bristol, Downend BS16 20 D8
Bristol, Eastville BS5 19 B3
Bristol, Hanham BS15 10 B4
Heath Ridge BS41 7 A2
Heath Rise BS30 11 B5
Heath St Bristol BS5 19 C3
Monmouth NP25 154 A7
Heath Wlk BS16 20 D7
Heathcote Dr BS36 31 D7
Heathcote La BS36 31 D7
Heathcote Rd
Bristol, Chester Park BS16 20 B2
Bristol, Staple Hill BS16 20 E5
Heathcote Wlk BS16 20 C2
Heathdean Rd GL3 127 F6
Heather Ave
Frampton Cotterell BS36 31 B6
Gloucester GL4 119 F4
Heather Cl Bristol BS15 10 B8
Chepstow NP16 60 F5
Stroud GL5 99 A4
Heatherdene BS14 2 F7
Heathfield Cl BS31 4 C5
Heathfield Cres BS14 3 B4
Heathfield Rd GL5 103 A1
Heathfields BS16 20 D8
Heathville Rd GL1 127 A3
Heazle Pl GL5 99 C8
Hebden Cl GL3 120 F5

Heber St BS5 9 C7
Hebron Rd 9 BS3 8 C3
Hedgeditch La GL8 59 D7
Hedgemead Cl BS16 19 D5
Hedgemead View BS16 19 E5
Hedgerow The GL2 127 B4
Hedwick Ave BS5 9 E7
Hedwick St BS5 9 E7
Heggard Cl BS13 2 A5
Helens Cl GL51 132 D3
Hellens* HR8 178 A4
Hellier Wlk BS13 2 C3
Hembury Cl GL2 109 D7
Hemming Way GL52 137 F3
Hemmings Par 4 BS5 9 B7
Hemmingsdale Rd GL2 126 C1
Hemplands The GL54 159 B5
Hemplow Cl BS14 3 D7
Hempstead CE Prim Sch GL2 118 A7
Hempsted La GL2 118 B7
Hempton La BS32 40 B2
Henacre Rd BS11 16 F8
Henbury Ct BS10 27 E3
Henbury Gdns BS10 27 E2
Henbury Hill BS9 27 F1
Henbury Manor Sch BS10 27 E2
Henbury Rd
Bristol, Hanham BS15 10 B5
Bristol, Henbury BS10 27 F2
Bristol, Westbury on Trym BS9 18 A8
Henbury Road Henbury Hill BS9 17 F8
Henbury Sch BS10 27 E3
Hencliffe Rd BS14 3 D7
Hencliffe Way BS15 10 B3
Henderson Ho 1 BS2 195 B4
Henderson Rd BS15 10 B5
Hendingham Cl GL4 118 B2
Hendre Mews GL50 193 A3
Hendre Rd BS3 8 A2
Hendrick Dr NP16 61 A8
Heneage La GL12 65 F8
Henfield Cres BS30 11 B3
Henfield Rd BS36 31 C4
Hengaston St BS3 8 B2
Hengrove Ave BS14 3 B8
Hengrove La BS14 3 B8
Hengrove Rd BS4 9 A2
Hengrove Sch BS14 3 B7
Hengrove Way BS14 2 E6
Henleaze Ave BS9 18 A5
Henleaze Gdns BS9 18 A5
Henleaze Jun & Inf Schs BS9 18 C5
Henleaze Park Dr BS9 18 C6
Henleaze Pk BS9 18 C5
Henleaze Rd BS9 18 B6
Henleaze Terr BS9 18 B7
Henley Dr SN6 145 D4
Henley Gr BS9 18 B5
Henley Pl GL1 118 D5
Henley Rd Bream GL15 155 D1
Cheltenham GL51 132 C3
Henley Villas GL5 99 C8
Henlow Dr GL11 80 B8
Hennessy Cl BS14 2 F3
Henrietta St
Bristol, Kingsdown BS2 195 A4
5 Bristol, Lower Easton BS5 19 B1
Cheltenham GL50 193 B4
Henry Rd GL1 196 C4
Henry Ryder Cl GL4 119 F6
Henry St Bristol BS3 8 F4
Gloucester GL1 196 C3
Henry Williamson Ct 1 BS30 11 A5
Henry Withers Pl GL2 100 F5
Henshaw Cl BS15 20 C2
Henshaw Rd BS15 20 C2
Henshaw Wlk BS15 20 C2
Hensman's Hill BS8 194 A2
Hentley Tor GL12 68 C6
Hepburn Rd BS2 195 B4
Herald Cl BS9 17 D5
Herapath St BS5 9 C6
Herbert Cres BS5 19 D3
Herbert Howells Cl GL15 92 A2
Herbert St
Bristol, Southville BS3 8 D4
Bristol, Whitehall BS5 9 C8
Gloucester GL1 119 A8
Herbert's Hill HR9 162 B8
Herberts Way GL15 156 B1
Hercules Cl BS34 29 D6
Herd La GL8 140 C4
Hereford Ct 1 GL50 193 B4
Hereford Pl GL50 193 A4
Hereford Rd BS2 19 A2
Hereford St BS3 8 D3
Hereward Rd GL7 190 C5
Heritage Ct GL5 98 E6
Herkomer Cl BS7 19 B7
Hermes Cl BS31 5 D2
Hermitage Cl BS11 16 E7
Hermitage Dr GL11 80 B7
Hermitage Rd BS16 20 E5
Hermitage St GL53 193 B1
Heron Cl GL51 129 E7
Heron Prim Sch GL4 119 D5
Heron Rd BS5 19 B1
Heron Way
Chipping Sodbury BS37 33 A8
Gloucester GL4 119 C5
Herrick Cl GL51 173 F1
Herrick Way GL51 173 F1
Herridge Cl BS13 2 B4
Herridge Rd BS13 2 B4
Hersey Gdns BS13 1 E3
Hersta Cl GL7 190 E4
Hertford Rd GL52 138 A4
Hesding Cl BS15 10 C3
Hester's Way La GL51 132 D4
Hester's Way Prim Sch GL51 132 E4
Hester's Way Rd GL51 132 E3
Hestercombe Rd BS13 2 B6
Hethersett Rd GL1 119 A8
Hetton Gdns GL53 131 A7
Hewelsfield La GL15 146 F7
Hewland Ct BS11 27 C2
Hewlett Pl GL52 193 C3
Hewlett Rd GL52 133 F1
Hewlett Way GL14 156 C6
Hewling La HR9 162 D3
Heyford Ave BS5 19 B4
Heyron Wlk BS13 2 B4
Heywood Com Sch GL14 191 E6
Heywood Rd
Cinderford GL14 191 D5
Pill BS20 16 C4
Heywood Terr BS20 16 C4
Hiam's La GL19 172 C2
Hiatt Rd GL6 91 F7
Hibbs Cl SN14 14 F8
Hickley Gdns GL3 120 E6
Hickling Ct 8 BS15 20 D1
Hicks Ave Bristol BS16 21 B8
Dursley GL11 87 F4
Hicks Beach Rd GL51 132 D2
Hicks Common Rd BS36 30 E5
Hicks Ct BS30 10 F4
Hidcote Ave GL51 130 A5
Hidcote Boyce GL55 189 C4
Hidcote Cl GL6 148 B6
Hidcote Manor Gdns* GL55 189 C5
Hidcote Rd GL55 189 C3
Hide Mkt BS2 195 C3
High Beech Ave
Edge End GL16 155 C8
Mile End GL16 155 C7
High Beech La NP16 60 D6
High Cross GL53 115 B7
High Delf Way GL15 155 F1
High Elm BS15 10 E6
High Furlong GL11 87 F5
High Gr BS9 17 B7
High Nash GL16 155 A5
High Orchard St GL2 196 A1
High Pk BS14 9 B1
High Point GL50 193 A3
High Rd
Ashton Keynes SN6 142 F4
Mitcheldean GL17 164 D5
High Row GL17 163 C3
High Sch for Girls GL1 196 C4
High St Arlingham GL2 157 B6
Avening GL8 148 A1
Aylburton GL15 147 E4
Badminton GL9 46 E2
Berkeley GL13 85 E3
Bisley GL6 148 D8
Bitton BS30 5 E8
Blakeney GL15 156 E1
Blockley GL56 186 C5
Bourton-on-t-W GL54 168 F7
Bream GL15 147 D8
Bredon GL20 182 C7
Brierley GL17 163 F2
Bristol BS1 195 A2
Bristol, Clifton BS8 18 A2
Bristol, Jefferies Hill BS15 10 C5
Bristol, Kingswood BS15 10 E8
Bristol, Lower Easton BS5 19 B1
Bristol, Oldland Common BS30 11 D4
Bristol, Shirehampton BS11 16 E6
Bristol, Staple Hill BS16 20 D4
Bristol, Warmley BS15 11 B8
Bristol, Westbury on Trym BS9 18 A7
Broad Blunsdon SN26 144 D1
Broadway WR12 185 B8
Chalford GL6 148 C5
Cheltenham GL50,GL52 193 B4
Chepstow NP16 60 E8
Chipping Campden GL55 189 A2
Chipping Sodbury BS37 44 B1
Cinderford GL14 191 D5
Clearwell GL16 155 A3
10 Coleford GL16 155 A5
Cricklade SN6 143 F4
Doynton BS30 22 F1
Drybrook GL17 164 B4
Dursley GL11 87 F6
Dyrham SN14 23 D4
Fairford GL7 152 E4
Gloucester GL1 118 F7
Hawkesbury Upton GL9 55 F3
Highworth SN6 145 D3
Hillesley GL12 55 D8
Honeybourne WR11 188 C6
Iron Acton BS37 42 D4
Kempsford GL7 144 E7
Keynsham BS31 4 E6
King's Stanley GL10 98 A3
Kingswood GL12 67 F4
Lechlade on T GL7 153 E2
Ledbury HR8 178 F8
Littledean GL14 191 F4
Longborough GL56 176 D8
High St *continued*
Lydney GL15 92 A3
Marshfield SN14 14 F8
Meysey Hampton GL7 152 A2
Mickleton GL55 189 B6
Minchinhampton GL6 148 A3
Mitcheldean GL17 164 D5
Moreton-in-M GL56 187 A3
Newent GL18 171 A4
Newnham GL14 157 A7
Northleach GL54 168 A1
Northwood Green GL14 165 C1
Prestbury GL52 134 C4
Ruardean GL17 163 F4
Saltford BS31 5 F3
Saul GL2 157 F4
South Cerney GL7 142 F7
St Briavels GL15 146 E7
Stanton WR12 184 F5
Stonehouse GL10 97 F7
Stow-on-t-W GL54 176 F5
Stroud GL5 99 C7
Tewkesbury GL20 192 C4
Thornbury BS35 51 B8
Upper Lydbrook GL17 163 E3
Upton St Leonards GL4 119 E1
Wick BS30 12 D6
Wickwar GL12 54 A5
Winchcombe GL54 174 A7
Winterbourne BS36 30 D6
Withington GL54 166 D2
Woodchester GL5 98 F1
Wooton-u-E GL12 68 B7
High Vew Lodge 14 GL5 99 C7
High View Chepstow NP16 60 E8
Gloucester GL2 118 A6
Higham St 4 BS2 8 F4
Highbank Pk GL2 126 F5
Highbeech Rd
Bream GL15 147 D8
Upper Lydbrook GL17 163 E3
Highbury La GL52 193 C3
Highbury Rd
Bream GL15 147 D8
Bristol, Bedminster BS3 8 C2
Bristol, Horfield BS7 18 F7
Lower Redbrook NP25 154 C4
Highbury Terr NP25 154 C4
Highbury Villas BS2 194 C4
Highclere Rd GL2 117 E2
Highcroft 4 Bristol BS30 11 C6
Minchinhampton GL6 91 F7
Highcroft Jun Sch BS36 31 C8
Highdale Cl BS14 3 B4
Higher Newmarket Rd GL6 90 F4
Highett Dr BS5 19 A1
Highfield GL15 156 D1
Highfield Ave BS15 10 D5
Highfield Bsns Pk GL19 173 F7
Highfield Cl 4 GL15 155 D1
Highfield Gdns BS30 11 C2
Highfield Gr BS7 18 D5
Highfield La Horton BS37 45 E7
Lydney GL15 92 C5
Highfield Pl
4 Coleford GL16 155 B5
Gloucester GL4 119 B7
Highfield Rd
Bream GL15 155 D1
Chipping Sodbury BS37 44 A1
Gloucester GL4 119 B7
Keynsham BS31 4 F2
Lydney GL15 92 C4
Ruardean GL17 163 F4
Stroud GL5 99 E6
Tetbury GL8 140 B5
Whiteshill GL6 103 A3
Highfield Villas GL14 156 F6
Highfield Way GL6 148 D6
Highfields
Frampton Mansell GL6 148 F5
Hawkesbury Upton GL9 55 F2
Highfields App GL11 80 C8
Highfields Cl BS34 29 F3
Highgate Ct WR12 185 B8
Highgrove St BS4 9 A4
Highgrove The GL52 137 E3
Highgrove Way GL3 127 F8
Highland Cres 3 BS8 18 A2
Highland Pl 13 BS8 18 A2
Highland Rd GL53 130 F4
Highland Sq 4 BS8 18 A2
Highlands Dr GL11 79 E4
Highlands Rd BS41 7 A2
Highleaze Rd BS30 11 C4
Highliffe Dr GL2 118 A1
Highmead Gdns BS13 1 E4
Highmeadow NP25 154 A7
Highmore Ct BS7 19 B7
Highmore Gdns BS7 19 C7
Highnam CE Prim Sch GL2 125 D5
Highnam Cl BS34 40 B1
Highnam Woods (Nature Reserve)* GL2 124 F4
Highridge Cres BS13 1 F5
Highridge Gn BS13 1 E6
Highridge Inf Sch BS13 1 F6
Highridge Pk BS13 1 F6
Highridge Rd
Bristol, Bedminster BS3 8 B2
Bristol, Withywood BS13, BS41 1 E4
Highridge Wlk BS13 1 E7
Highview Rd Bristol BS15 20 F2
Cinderford GL14 191 E4
Ruardean Hill GL17 164 A3
Highview Rd *continued*
Yorkley GL15 156 A2
Highview Way GL15 147 D8
Highwall La BS14,BS31 3 F1
Highway BS37 43 F2
Highwood Ave GL53 130 C5
Highwood Ct GL6 90 F5
Highwood La BS10,BS34 28 D7
Highwood Rd BS34 28 F7
Highworth Cres BS37 32 D8
Highworth Rd Bristol BS4 9 D6
Gloucester GL1 118 F6
Highworth SN6 145 F1
Stanton Fitzwarren SN6 145 B1
Highworth Warneford Comp Sch SN6 145 D3
Hilcote Dr GL54 169 A6
Hildyard Cl GL2 109 E7
Hilhouse BS9 17 C6
Hill Ave BS3 8 E3
Hill Burn BS9 18 C6
Hill Cl Dursley GL11 87 F4
Westmancote GL20 182 D8
Hill Court Rd GL52 133 E4
Hill Crest Bristol BS4 9 B1
Highnam GL2 125 E5
Hill Ct GL52 133 E4
Hill End Cl GL20 181 F7
Hill End Dr BS10 27 D3
Hill End Rd GL20 181 F8
Hill Gr BS9 18 C6
Hill Hay Rd GL4 119 C3
Hill Ho GL7 190 D5
Hill House Rd BS16 20 F5
Hill La
Chipping Sodbury BS37 34 B7
Thornbury BS35 76 A2
Hill Lawn BS4 9 D3
Hill Mead GL4 110 F5
Hill Pk GL15 156 A2
Hill Rd Dundry BS41 1 D2
Dursley GL11 88 A1
Gloucester GL4 118 F4
Wooton-u-E GL12 68 C6
Hill Sq GL11 88 A3
Hill St Bristol BS1 194 C2
Bristol, Kingswood BS15 10 F8
Bristol, St George BS5 9 F8
Bristol, Totterdown BS3 8 F4
Lydney GL15 92 A3
Hill The Almondsbury BS32 40 B4
Randwick GL6 102 E2
Stroud GL5 99 B7
Westwell OX18 161 F5
Hill Top NP16 60 D7
Hill Top Cl GL5 99 F7
Hill Top La GL18 171 B5
Hill Top Rd GL50 133 D5
Hill Top View GL6 148 B6
Hill View Bristol BS8 194 B2
Bristol, Filton BS34 29 A3
Bristol, Henleaze BS9 18 C6
Bristol, Upper Soundwell BS16 20 D2
Elkstone GL53 115 B6
Lydney GL15 92 A3
Naunton GL54 175 E2
Sandhurst GL2 172 E1
Hill View Cl BS30 11 C4
Hill View Rd Bristol BS13 2 A8
Cheltenham GL52 134 B2
Pucklechurch BS16 22 C5
Upper Strensham WR8 180 D7
Hill View Villas GL5 98 D6
Hill's Barton BS13 8 A1
Hillands Dr GL53 130 D4
Hillary Rd GL53 130 E4
Hillborough Rd GL4 118 E3
Hillbrook Rd 5 BS35 51 D8
Hillburn Rd BS5 10 A8
Hillclose Est GL5 99 A4
Hillcot Cl GL2 117 E1
Hillcrest Berkeley GL13 85 F4
Thornbury BS35 64 B1
Hillcrest Cl NP25 154 A7
Hillcrest La GL16 155 B6
Hillcrest Rd
Berry Hill GL16 155 A7
Monmouth NP25 154 A7
Stroud GL5 98 E8
Hillcroft Cl BS15 10 E4
Hillersland La GL16 155 A8
Hillesley Prim Sch GL12 55 E8
Hillesley Rd GL12 67 F4
Hillfield Cheltenham GL51 132 F1
Stroud GL5 98 F7
Hillfield Court Rd GL1 127 A3
Hillfield Ct GL1 127 A3
Hillfields Ave BS16 20 C3
Hillfields Prim Sch BS16 20 C2
Hillgrove St BS2 195 B4
Hillgrove St N BS2 195 A4
Hillier Cl GL5 103 D1
Hillier Dr 8 GL51 129 F5
Hillmill La GL12 69 B4
Hillrise GL15 155 D1
Hills Cl BS31 5 A5
Hillsborough BS8 194 A2
Hillsborough Rd BS4 9 C4
Hillsdon Rd BS9 17 F8
Hillside Bristol BS6 194 C4
Bristol, Mangotsfield BS16 21 A5
Burton SN14 36 A4
Chalford GL6 148 D6
Leigh SN6 143 B3
Hillside Ave BS15 10 C8
Hillside Cl
10 Bream GL15 155 D1
Hillside Cl *continued*
Cheltenham GL51 130 A7
Frampton Cotterell BS36 31 C7
Woodmancote GL52 138 C3
Hillside Ct GL11 80 B8
Hillside Est 11 GL15 155 D1
Hillside Gdns GL52 138 C3
Hillside Ho 5 BS6 18 D1
Hillside La BS36 31 C7
Hillside Rd Bristol BS5 10 A7
Drybrook GL17 164 B5
Long Ashton BS41 7 B2
Mitcheldean GL17 164 D5
Hillside St BS4 9 A4
Hillside Terr GL17 163 D3
Hillside Villas GL5 99 D5
Hillside Way SN26 144 D1
Hilltop 9 GL15 147 D8
Hilltop Gdns
Bristol, St George BS5 10 A7
Bristol, Upper Soundwell BS16 20 D2
Hilltop Rd BS16 20 D2
Hilltop View Bristol BS5 10 A7
Dursley GL11 87 F4
Hillview Ave GL3 120 D6
Hillview Cty Prim Sch GL3 120 A8
Hillview Dr GL3 120 A8
Hillview La GL20 181 F8
Hillview Rd GL3 120 A8
Hillview Rise GL16 155 A7
Hillwell SN16 141 E1
Hillyfield Rd BS13 2 A6
Hilton Cl GL2 118 B6
Hilton Ct 5 BS5 9 B8
Hinders La GL17,GL19 165 B5
Hine Gdns GL52 133 F3
Hinton Cl BS31 5 E3
Hinton Ct GL13 85 C8
Hinton Dr BS30 11 C6
Hinton La 12 BS8 7 F6
Hinton Rd
Bristol, Fishponds BS16 20 A4
Bristol, Lower Easton BS5 19 C1
Gloucester GL1 126 F4
Hisnams Field GL52 137 F3
Hitchen Cl SN14 14 F8
Hitchen Hollow NP16 61 B4
Hitchings GL15 156 D2
Hithe The GL5 99 C3
Hither Mead BS36 31 B6
Hobart Ho GL51 132 E2
Hobb's La BS1 194 C2
Hobbs La Bristol BS30 21 B1
Longhope GL17 165 A6
Woodmancote GL7 158 B4
Hobby Cl GL53 130 C5
Hobhouse Cl BS9 18 C7
Hobwell La BS41 7 C2
Hocker Hill St NP16 60 E8
Hockeys La BS16 20 A4
Hoddon La BS16 22 D5
Hodges Way GL14 191 C3
Hodses Yd 7 HR8 178 E8
Hogarth Wlk BS7 19 C7
Hogues Wlk BS13 2 B4
Holbeach Way BS14 3 A2
Holbrook GL17 163 D2
Holbrook Cres BS13 2 D4
Holbrook La BS30 12 B7
Holbury Cres GL2 100 E5
Holcombe BS14 3 A5
Holcombe Gr BS31 4 D5
Holcot Cl 8 GL16 155 B5
Holcot Rd GL16 155 B5
Holdcroft Cl SN26 144 E1
Holdenhurst Rd BS15 20 C1
Holder Cl 12 GL8 140 B4
Holder Rd GL52 137 F2
Holders La GL18 170 E6
Holford Cres GL7 144 F7
Holford Ct BS14 3 B5
Hollams Rd GL20 192 D5
Holland Ct GL1 127 A3
Hollidge Gdns 3 BS3 8 D4
Hollies Hill GL6 91 C4
Hollies The BS15 10 E6
Hollingham La GL6 90 E1
Hollins Cl NP16 72 F1
Hollis Cl BS41 1 A8
Hollis Gdns
Cheltenham GL51 129 D6
Luckington SN14 47 E4
Hollis Rd GL51 129 D6
Hollister's Dr BS13 2 D4
Hollow La GL5 99 D7
Hollow Rd
Almondsbury BS32 40 A4
Bristol BS15 10 E8
Hollow The GL17 164 A4
Holloway Hill SN14 25 F7
Holloway Rd Bisley GL6 148 D8
Severn Beach BS35 38 C4
Hollows The BS36 31 D2
Hollway Cl BS14 3 E5
Hollway Rd BS14 3 E5
Holly Cl Alveston BS35 50 F4
Bristol BS5 20 A2
Chepstow NP16 60 E5
Pucklechurch BS16 22 C5
Holly Cres BS15 20 E1
Holly Ct BS2 194 C4
Holly Dr SN14 15 F6
Holly End GL2 109 F8

Holly Gn BS15 ....21 A1
Holly Gr BS16 ....20 C3
Holly Gr The GL2 ....109 F8
Holly Hill BS37 ....42 E3
Holly Hill Rd BS15 ....20 F1
Holly Ho BS11 ....27 C2
Holly La GL16 ....155 C3
Holly Lodge Cl BS5 .....20 A2
Holly Lodge Rd BS5 .....19 F2
Holly Tree Gdn GL5 .....98 D6
Holly Tree Pl GL15 .....156 B1
Holly Wlk BS31 ....4 D4
Hollybush Cl GL9 ....36 A6
Hollybush La Bristol BS9 ..17 E5
Bristol BS9 ....17 F4
Hollydean GL14 ....191 C5
Hollyguest Rd BS15 .....10 E6
Hollyhill Pk GL14 ......191 B5
Hollyhill Rd GL14 ......191 B5
Hollyhock La GL6 ......103 F8
Hollyleigh Ave BS34 .....28 F2
Hollymead La BS9 ......17 E4
Hollyridge BS14 ....3 C6
Hollywell Rd GL17 .....164 D6
Hollywood La BS10,BS35 .28 A7
Hollywood Rd BS4 ....9 D2
Holm La BS35 ....49 B2
Holmdale Rd BS34 ....29 C3
Holme Rd GL20 ....192 D1
Holmer Cres GL51 .....129 D6
Holmes Ct BS9 ....18 B5
Holmes Gr BS9 ....18 B5
Holmes Hill Rd BS5 ......9 F8
Holmes St BS5 ....9 B6
Holmesdale Rd BS3 ......8 E3
Holmfield Dr NP25 .....146 B7
Holmleigh Rd GL4 .....118 C3
Holmoak Cl GL20 ......192 E2
Holmoak Rd BS31 ....4 C4
Holmsleigh Par GL4 ...118 C2
Holmwood BS15 ....10 C5
Holmwood Cl
Gloucester GL4 ....118 D2
Winterbourne BS36 ......30 D6
Holmwood Dr GL4 .....118 D2
Holmwood Gdns BS9 ....18 B8
Holroyd Ho BS3 ....8 D3
Holsom Cl BS14 ....3 F6
Holsom Rd BS14 ....3 F6
Holst Gdns BS4 ....2 D7
Holst Way GL4 ....118 D3
Holt The
Bishop's Cleeve GL52 ....137 E2
Gloucester GL4 ....119 E7
Holtham Ave GL3 ......128 B7
Holton Rd BS7 ....19 A6
Holts Rd GL18 ....170 F4
Holy Apostles CE Prim Sch
GL52 ....131 A8
Holy Cross Catholic Prim Sch
BS3 ....8 C4
Holy Family Prim Sch
BS34 ....29 B8
Holy Trinity Prim Sch
Bristol BS32 ....40 C2
Cheltenham GL52 ....193 C4
Holy Well Cl BS4 ....9 E6
Holymead Inf Sch BS4 ....9 D2
Holymead Jun Sch BS4 ...9 D3
Holyrood Cl BS34 ....29 D4
Holywell Rd Dursley GL11 .88 A4
Wooton-u-E GL12 ....68 C8
Home Cl Bristol BS10 .....28 E2
Cheltenham GL51 ....132 E3
Upper Oddington GL56 ...177 C5
Home Ct GL20 ....192 C4
Home Farm Ct GL52 .....131 A7
Home Farm Rd BS8 ......7 B8
Home Farm Way BS35 ...39 A1
Home Field Cl BS16 .....21 B6
Home Ground
Bristol, Eastfield BS9 ......18 B7
Bristol, Shirehampton BS11 16 D7
Cricklade SN6 ....143 E4
Home Mead
Bristol, Cadbury Heath
BS30 ....11 A4
Bristol, Filwood Park BS4 ...2 E7
Home Orch BS37 ....43 D2
Home Piece GL7 ....149 E3
Homeabbey Ho GL20 ...192 C5
Homeapple Hill BS30 .....11 F6
Homeavon Ho BS31 ......4 F5
Homeberry Ho GL7 .....190 C4
Homecroft Dr GL51 .....132 E6
Homefarm SN6 ....145 C3
Homefield Nailsworth GL6 .91 A3
Thornbury BS35 ....51 D8
Yate BS37 ....43 E3
Homefield Cl BS31 ....5 E3
Homefield Dr BS16 ......20 A5
Homefield Rd
Pucklechurch BS16 ....22 B5
Saltford BS31 ....5 F3
Homeground BS16 ....21 B6
Homeground La GL7 ....152 F4
Homeleaze Rd BS10 .....28 D3
Homemead Dr BS4 ....9 D1
Homend Cres 2 HR8 ....178 F8
Homend The 16 HR8 ....178 F8
Homepiece WR12 ....185 B4
Homespa Ho 2 GL50 ....133 B1
Homespring Ho GL52 ...134 A2
Homestead Cl GL20 .....182 C7
Homestead Gdns BS16 ...20 B8
Homestead Rd BS34 .....29 A3
Homestead The BS31 .....4 F2
Honey Garston Cl BS13 ..2 B4
Honey Garston Rd BS13 ..2 B4
Honey Hill Rd BS15 .....10 F8
Honey Suckle La BS16 ...19 E5
Honeyborne Way GL12 ..54 B5
Honeybourne Airfield Ind Est
WR11 ....188 C5
Honeybourne Dr GL51 ..132 D4
Honeybourne Fst Sch
WR11 ....188 C6
Honeybourne Rd WR11 .188 D4
Honeybourne Sta WR11 188 C7
Honeymead BS14 ....3 C6
Honeysuckle Cl
Bristol BS32 ....40 E2
Prestbury GL52 ....134 C3
Honeysuckle Dr GL4 ...119 E5
Honeysuckle Way GL52 .137 F5
Honeythorn Cl GL2 .....118 B7
Honister Ho BS34 ....29 A8
Honiton Rd BS16 ....20 A3
Honyatt Rd GL1 ....196 C4
Hoo La
Chipping Campden GL55 ..188 F2
Tewkesbury GL20 ....173 E8
Hook's La GL18 ....171 D5
Hookshouse La
Doughton GL8 ....71 E4
Tetbury GL8 ....140 A3
Hooper Cl GL4 ....119 B6
Hooper Rd BS14 ....3 D5
Hoovers La HR9 ....164 B8
Hop Gdn The NP16 ......60 F4
Hope Cotts GL5 ....99 D6
Hope Ct BS1 ....194 B1
Hope Mill La GL5 ....99 E2
Hope Orch GL51 ....132 D4
Hope Rd Bristol BS3 ......8 C2
Yate BS37 ....43 A2
Hope Sq BS8 ....7 F6
Hope St GL51 ....133 B3
Hope Villas GL5 ....99 C8
Hopechapel Hill 10 BS8 ...7 F6
Hopes Cl GL15 ....92 C2
Hopes Hill Com Prim Sch
GL17 ....165 A5
Hopetoun Rd BS2 ....18 F3
Hopewell GL14 ....191 E5
Hopewell Cl NP16 ....61 A4
Hopewell Colliery Mus★
GL16 ....155 D6
Hopewell Gdns BS11 ....16 F7
Hopewell St GL1 ....196 C1
Hopkin Cl BS35 ....51 D7
Hopkins Ct 13 BS6 ....18 B1
Hopkins Orch 1 SN6 ....143 E4
Hopland Cl BS30 ....11 B3
Hopp's Rd BS15 ....10 D7
Hopton Rd GL11 ....88 B4
Hopwood Gr 1 GL52 ....134 A1
Hopyard La GL18 ......171 A5
Hopyard The GL20 .....182 B5
Horcott Ind Est GL7 ....152 D3
Horcott Rd GL7 ....152 D3
Horesham Gr BS13 ....2 C5
Horfield CE Prim Sch
BS10 ....18 D7
Horfield Ct BS7 ....18 E4
Horfield Rd BS2 ....195 A4
Horley Rd BS2 ....19 A2
Horn La GL56 ....177 C7
Hornbeam Mews GL2 ...127 B5
Hornbeam Wlk BS31 ......4 C3
Hornbeams The BS16 ....30 B1
Hornbury Cl SN16 ......142 D1
Hornbury Hill SN16 ....142 D1
Horns Rd GL5 ....99 D6
Horsbere Rd GL3 ......120 B8
Horse Fair La SN6 ......143 F4
Horse La BS35 ....64 D5
Horse Lane Orch HR8 ...178 F8
Horse Pool La HR9 .....162 E2
Horse St BS37 ....44 C1
Horsecroft Gdns BS30 ...11 A6
Horsefair Cl GL53 ......131 A5
Horsefair La GL18 ......170 F5
Horsefair St GL53 ......131 A5
Horsefair The BS1 ......195 B3
Horsepool La
Doynton BS30 ....12 F8
St Briavels GL15 ....146 E6
Horsepool Rd BS13 ....1 E3
Horsepool The 3 GL16 .155 A7
Horseshoe Dr Bristol BS9 17 C4
Gloucester GL2 ....126 B4
Horseshoe La BS37 ......44 B1
Horseshoe Way GL2 ....118 B6
Horsford Rd GL12 ....67 B5
Horslea GL17 ....163 D3
Horsley CE Prim Sch GL6 90 F1
Horsley Cl GL4 ....119 E5
Horsley Hill GL6 ....91 A1
Horsley Rd GL6 ....91 A2
Hortham La BS32 ....40 E5
Horton Ct★ BS37 ....45 D7
Horton Hill BS37 ....45 C5
Horton Prim Sch BS37 ..45 C5
Horton Rd
Chipping Sodbury BS37 ...44 C2
Chipping Sodbury, Little
Sodbury End BS37 ......44 D4
Gloucester GL1 ....127 A2
Horton St BS2 ....195 C3
Horwood Ct 3 BS30 .....11 A4
Horwood La GL12 ....54 B4
Hosey Wlk BS13 ....2 A5
Hospital Rd GL56 ......187 A3
Host St BS1 ....195 A3
Hot Water La BS15 ......21 A3
Hottom Gdns BS7 ....19 A7
Hotwell Rd BS8 ....194 B1
Hotwells Prim Sch BS8 ...7 F6
Houlton St BS2 ....195 C4
Hounds Cl BS37 ....44 B1
Hounds Rd BS37 ....44 B1
Howard Ave BS5 ....9 E8
Howard Cl
Northway GL20 ....182 C4
Saltford BS31 ....5 D3
Howard Ho GL54 ....139 F5
Howard Pl GL3 ....120 A7
Howard Rd
Bristol, Southville BS3 ......8 C4
Bristol, Staple Hill BS16 ...20 D4
Bristol, Westbury Park BS6 .18 B4
5 Coleford GL16 ....155 B6
Northway GL20 ....182 C4
Thornbury BS35 ....64 C2
Howard St Bristol BS5 ....19 E1
Gloucester GL1 ....118 F7
Howcroft GL3 ....128 C4
Howecroft Ct BS9 ....17 E4
Howecroft Gdns BS9 ....17 E4
Howell Rd
Cheltenham GL51 ....132 E4
Cheltenham GL51 ....132 F4
Howell's La GL15 ....156 E3
Howells Mead BS16 .....21 B7
Howells Rd GL20 ....192 D4
Howes Cl BS30 ....11 A6
Howett Rd 16 BS5 ....9 C7
Howgate Cl 1 GL4 .....119 F5
Howmead GL13 ....85 E4
Howsmoor La Bristol BS16 21 B8
Bristol BS16 ....21 C8
Hoylake BS37 ....32 E8
Hoylake Dr BS30 ....11 B6
Hucclecote La GL3 .....128 D2
Hucclecote Mews GL3 ..119 F7
Hucclecote Rd GL3 .....120 B7
Huckford La BS36 ....31 A4
Huckford Rd BS36 ....30 E5
Huckley Way BS32 ....29 F6
Hudd's Hill Gdns 2 BS5 ..9 F8
Hudd's Hill Rd BS5 ....9 F8
Hudd's Vale Rd BS5 ......9 E8
Huddleston Rd GL54 ...174 A8
Hudman's Cl GL20 ......182 A7
Hudnalls View NP25 ....146 B7
Hudson Cl
Chipping Sodbury BS37 ...32 F8
Honeybourne WR11 .....188 C7
Hudson La GL14 ....191 C1
Hudson St GL50 ....133 D3
Hudsons View GL14 .....191 C1
Hughenden Rd
Bristol, Clifton BS8 ....18 A2
Bristol, Horfield BS7 .....18 E5
Hughes Cl GL20 ....182 C5
Hughes Cres NP16 ....60 E7
Hughes Terr GL15 ......155 E3
Hulbert Cl Bristol BS4 ....10 A2
Swindon GL51 ....133 A7
Hulbert Cres GL51 .....129 F5
Hulse Rd BS4 ....9 D1
Humber Pl GL3 ....120 F5
Humber Rd GL52 ....134 A2
Humber Way BS11 ......26 D5
Humberstan Wlk BS11 ...16 E8
Humphreys Cl GL5 ......98 E8
Humphry Davy Way 6
BS8 ....7 F5
Humphrys Barton BS4 ....9 F5
Hung Rd BS11 ....16 E5
Hunger Hill GL11 ....80 A8
Hungerford Cl BS4 ....3 E8
Hungerford Cres BS4 .....9 E1
Hungerford Gdns BS4 ....3 E8
Hungerford Rd BS4 ......3 E8
Hungerford St GL50 ....133 D3
Hungerford Wlk BS4 .....9 E1
Hunter's Way
Andoversford GL54 ......166 C6
Bristol BS34 ....29 B3
Hunters Cl Bristol BS15 ...10 C5
Stroud GL5 ....98 D7
Hunters Dr BS15 ....20 F1
Hunters Gate GL4 ......119 D4
Hunters Mead GL9 ....56 A2
Hunters Rd
Bishop's Cleeve GL52 ....137 E4
Bristol BS15 ....10 C5
Hunters Rd E BS15 ......10 C4
Hunters Way GL5 ....98 D7
Huntfield Rd NP16 ....60 D8
Hunthill GL14 ....165 E1
Huntingdon Cl GL5 ......98 D6
Huntingham Rd BS13 .....1 F4
Huntings The 7 WR12 ..185 B8
Huntley CE Prim Sch
GL19 ....165 C6
Huntley Cl GL4 ....119 E5
Hunts Ground Rd BS34 ..29 F4
Hunts Grove View GL2 ..110 B7
Hunts Hill SN26 ....144 D1
Hunts La BS7 ....18 E6
Huntscote Rd GL51 .....133 A5
Huntsfield Cl GL50 .....133 E4
Huntsmans Cl GL52 .....138 A4
Huntsmans Meet GL54 ..166 D6
Hurcombe Way GL3 ....120 E6
Hurle Cres BS8 ....18 B1
Hurle Rd BS8 ....18 B1
Hurlingham Rd BS7 ......18 F2
Hurn La BS31 ....5 A3
Hurricane Rd GL3 ......120 C5
Hursley Hill BS14 ....3 D1
Hursley La BS14 ....3 E1
Hurst Cl GL2 ....127 D5
Hurst Rd BS4 ....2 F8
Hurst Wlk BS4 ....2 F8
Hurston Rd BS4 ....2 D7
Hurstwood Rd BS16 .....20 D5
Hutton Cl Bristol BS9 .....17 E7
Keynsham BS31 ....5 A2
Huxley Ct GL7 ....143 A8
Huxley Rd GL1 ....118 F7
Huxley Way GL52 ....137 D4
Huyton Rd BS5 ....19 E3
Hyatts Way GL52 ....138 A3
Hyde Ave BS35 ....64 B3
Hyde Cl GL1 ....127 A2
Hyde Cotts GL54 ....139 F4
Hyde La Gloucester GL1 ..127 A2
Newnham GL14 ....156 F7
Swindon GL50,GL51 .....133 D7
Whitminster GL2 ....100 F6
Hyde Park Cnr GL19 ...179 D2
Hyde The GL54 ....139 F5
Hyde View GL16 ....154 F3
Hyde's La SN14 ....14 A6
Hyett Cl GL6 ....103 F8
Hyett Rd GL5 ....98 E7
Hygrove La GL2 ....125 B1
Hyland Gr BS9 ....17 F8

I

Icehouse La GL56 ......186 D1
Icombe Cl GL52 ....137 F3
Ida Rd 2 BS5 ....9 C8
Idaho St GL7 ....152 E2
Iddesleigh Rd BS6 ......18 B3
Idsall Dr GL52 ....134 C4
Idstone Rd BS16 ....20 B4
Iford Cl BS31 ....5 E3
Ilchester Cres BS13 ......8 B1
Ilchester Rd BS13 ....2 B8
Iles Cl BS15 ....10 D4
Ilex Cl BS13 ....1 F6
Ilmington CE Prim Sch
CV36 ....189 F6
Ilminster Ave BS4 ....2 F8
Ilminster Avenue Prim Sch
BS4 ....3 A8
Ilsom Cotts GL8 ....140 D5
Ilsyn Gr BS14 ....3 D7
Imber Court Cl BS14 .....3 B8
Imjin Rd GL52 ....134 B2
Imperial Arc BS3 ....8 D4
Imperial Cir GL50 ......193 B3
Imperial La GL50 ......193 B3
Imperial Rd
8 Bristol, Clifton BS6 .....18 B1
Bristol, Knowle BS14 ......3 C8
Imperial Sq GL50 ....193 B2
Imperial Wlk BS14 ....9 B1
Inchbrook Hill GL5,GL6 ..91 A6
Inchbrook Trad Est GL5 ..91 A7
India Ho 2 GL51 ....132 E2
India Rd GL1 ....119 A8
Ingleside Rd BS15 ....20 C1
Inglestone Rd GL12 ......54 B5
Ingmire Rd BS5 ....19 B3
Ingst Hill BS35 ....49 B3
Ingst Rd BS35 ....49 D4
Inkerman Cl BS7 ....18 E7
Inkerman La 16 GL50 ...130 B8
Inn Cotts BS11 ....17 A7
Inner Ctyd GL7 ....190 D7
Inner Down The BS12 ...50 D3
Inner Loop Rd NP16 .....61 B6
Innerstone La GL19 .....171 D8
Innocks Est GL11 ....79 D4
Innox Gdns BS13 ....2 A5
Inns Court Ave BS4 ......2 D7
Inns Court Dr BS4 ....2 D6
Innsworth Jun Sch GL3 127 D6
Innsworth La GL3 ......127 D7
Innsworth Tech Pk GL3 .127 C6
Insley Gdns GL3 ....119 F8
Instow Rd BS4 ....2 E8
Instow Wlk BS4 ....2 E8
International Sch of
Choueifat SN14 ....15 C4
International Trad Est
BS11 ....26 B2
Interplex 16 BS32 ....40 C3
Inverlea Ct GL55 ....189 A6
Ipswich Dr BS4 ....9 E6
Irby Rd BS3 ....8 A3
Irena Rd BS16 ....19 F3
Ireton Rd BS3 ....8 B3
Iron Acton CE Prim Sch
BS37 ....42 E4
Iron Acton Way BS37 .....43 B3
Iron Hogg La GL12 ......65 C3
Iron Mills GL6 ....91 E3
Ironchurch Rd BS11 .....26 C5
Ironmonger's La GL13 ...86 B4
Ironmould La BS4 ....10 A1
Ironstone Cl 2 GL15 ....147 D8
Irving Cl BS16 ....20 E4
Irving Ct GL52 ....193 C3
Irving Ho Bristol BS1 ....194 C3
13 Cheltenham GL52 .....133 F2
Isbourne Rd GL52 ....134 B2
Isbourne Way GL54 .....174 B8
ISF Rd BS11 ....26 C3
Islamic Acad GL1 ....196 C2
Island Gdns BS16 ....19 C4
Islay Cres SN6 ....145 C4
Isleys Ct BS30 ....10 F3
Islington Rd BS3 ....8 C4
Ismay Rd GL51 ....132 F4
Ison Hill Rd BS10 ....27 D3
Itchington Rd
Alveston BS35 ....51 F4
Tytherington GL12 ....52 B4
Itton Rd NP16 ....72 B2
Ivanhoe Ho GL2 ....118 C4
Ivor Rd BS5 ....9 C8
Ivory Cl GL4 ....118 C2
Ivy Bank GL52 ....134 C3
Ivy House Est HR9 .....170 B5
Ivy House La HR9 ......170 B5
Ivy La Bristol BS16 ....20 A3
Broad Blunsdon SN26 ...144 D1
Ivy Lodge Barns GL4 ...121 F1
Ivy Terr BS37 ....32 B4
Ivywell Rd BS9 ....17 E3
Izod's Cl GL55 ....188 F1

J

Jack Knight Ho BS7 .....18 F5
Jackbarrow Rd GL7 ....107 A8
Jackson Cl BS35 ....38 D7
Jackson Cres GL3 ......127 E6
Jackson Rd
Bledington OX7 ....177 E1
South Cerney GL7 ....150 F2
Jacob St Bristol BS2 ....195 B3
Bristol BS2 ....195 C3
Jacob's Ct BS1 ....194 C2
Jacob's Wells Rd BS8 ..194 B2
Jacobs Cl 4 GL8 ....140 C5
Jamaica St BS2 ....195 B4
James Cl BS16 ....20 E4
James Ct
Cheltenham GL51 ....132 F1
Yorkley GL15 ....156 B1
James Donovan Ct
GL52 ....134 A2
James Grieve Rd GL4 ...119 F6
James Orch GL13 ....85 E3
James Rd BS16 ....20 E3
James St
Bristol, Baptist Mills BS2 ..19 A2
Bristol, St Pauls BS5 .....195 C4
James Way GL3 ....120 C6
James Wlk GL15 ....155 F1
Jameson Ct 22 GL56 ....187 A3
Jane St BS5 ....9 B7
Japonica Cl 5 GL3 .....128 A7
Japonica Dr GL51 ......130 A5
Jardine Dr GL52 ....137 E4
Jarvis St BS5 ....9 B6
Jasmin Way GL51 ....130 A5
Jasmine Cl GL4 ....119 D4
Jasmine Gr BS11 ....27 C2
Jasper St BS3 ....8 B3
Javelin Pk GL2 ....109 E1
Javelin Way GL3 ....120 F5
Jay's Gn HR9 ....170 A5
Jay's Mead GL12 ....68 C7
Jays The GL12 ....52 B6
Jaythorpe GL4 ....119 D3
Jean Rd BS4 ....9 E2
Jefferies Cl 7 GL7 .....152 E4
Jefferies Hill Bottom
BS15 ....10 B5
Jeffery Ct BS30 ....11 B6
Jeffreys Ct 9 BS16 ......19 E3
Jeffries Ct GL7 ....190 D4
Jellicoe Ave BS16 ....19 E8
Jena Ct BS31 ....5 D3
Jenkin's La GL6 ....103 C7
Jenner Cl
Chipping Sodbury BS37 ...33 D8
Gloucester GL3 ....119 F8
Jenner Ct GL13 ....85 E3
Jenner Mus★ GL13 ......85 E3
Jenner Wlk GL50 ....193 B4
Jersey Ave Bristol BS4 .....9 F4
Cheltenham GL52 ....133 F2
Jersey Rd GL1 ....119 A8
Jersey St GL52 ....193 C4
Jesse Mary Chambers
Almshouses GL51 ....132 F1
Jesson Rd GL52 ....138 A3
Jessop Ave GL50 ....193 A3
Jessop Ct BS1 ....195 B2
Jessop Dr 2 GL54 ......168 A1
Jessop Underpass BS3 ...7 F4
Jet Age Air Mus★ GL2 .128 C8
Jewson Cl GL4 ....118 D2
Jeynes Bldgs GL20 .....192 D5
Jeynes Row GL20 ......192 D5
Jim O'Neil Ho BS11 .....16 D7
Joan Hawley Mews
GL52 ....131 A7
Job's La GL20 ....182 E8
Jobbins Ct GL7 ....190 C4
Jocelyn Rd BS7 ....18 F7
Jockey La BS5 ....10 A7
Jockey Stable Cotts
GL56 ....186 A4
John Bevan Cl GL5 ......99 D8
John Buck Ho 8 GL52 ..193 C4
John Cabot Ct BS1 .....194 A1
John Cabot Cty Tech Coll
BS15 ....10 C7
John Carr's Terr BS8 ...194 B2
John Cozens Ho 6 BS2 195 C3
John Daniels Way GL3 .128 B4
John James Ct BS7 ......19 B7
John Lamb Ho GL51 ...129 D2

John Masefield High Sch HR8 178 F8
John Moore Countryside Mus* GL20 192 C4
John Rushout Ct GL56 186 C7
John St Bristol BS1 195 A3
Bristol, Baptist Mills BS2 19 A2
Bristol, Two Mile Hill BS15 10 C8
Stroud GL5 99 C7
John Tame Cl 4 GL7 152 E4
John Wesley Rd BS5 10 B6
John Wesleys Chapel BS1 195 B3
John Woolfe Ct GL56 186 C7
Johnson Dr BS30 10 F5
Johnson Rd BS16 21 C6
Johnsons La BS5 19 D1
Johnsons Rd BS5 19 C1
Johnsons Way GL15 156 B2
Johnstone Cl GL19 172 A7
Johnstone Rd 3 GL18 171 A4
Joiners La GL6 148 D8
Jones Ho NP25 154 A8
Jordan Wlk BS32 29 D8
Jordans Cl WR12 188 B2
Jordans Way GL2 126 F5
Jorrocks Ind Est BS37 32 C4
Josend Cres GL19 172 F7
Joy Hill BS8 7 F6
Joy's Green Prim Sch GL17 163 D3
Joyford Hill GL16 155 A8
Joyner Rd GL51 133 A4
Joys Green Rd GL17 163 D2
Jubilee Ave GL11 87 F6
Jubilee Cl Dursley GL11 87 F6
Ledbury HR8 178 F7
12 Stow-on-t-W GL54 176 F4
Jubilee Cotts GL6 148 B5
Jubilee Cres BS16 21 A6
Jubilee Dr Bredon GL20 182 C7
Thornbury BS35 64 D1
Jubilee Flats GL7 150 E2
Jubilee Gdns
South Cerney GL7 142 F7
Yate BS37 44 A2
Jubilee Ho BS34 29 C8
Jubilee La GL12 53 B7
Jubilee Maze* HR9 162 E4
Jubilee Pk* HR9 162 E4
Jubilee Pl Bristol BS1 195 A1
Staunton GL19 172 A7
Jubilee Rd
Bristol, Baptist Mills BS2 19 A1
Bristol, Knowle BS4 9 C2
Bristol, St George BS5 9 F7
Bristol, Staple Hill BS15 20 E3
Dursley GL11 88 A2
Lydney GL15 92 C3
Mitcheldean GL17 164 D3
Nailsworth GL6 91 A5
Jubilee St BS2 195 C2
Jubilee Way
Avonmouth BS11 26 B2
Sharpness GL13 85 D8
Judge's La
Longhope GL18 170 F1
Taynton GL18 171 A1
Julian Cl Bristol BS9 17 E3
Gloucester GL4 119 D8
Julian Ct BS9 17 E3
Julian Rd BS9 17 E3
Julius Rd BS7 18 D3
Julius Way GL15 92 B4
Jumpers La GL13 85 E3
Junction Rd BS4 9 C4
Juniper Ave GL4 119 B4
Juniper Cotts GL6 103 F5
Juniper Ct 2 Bristol BS5 19 C2
Cheltenham GL51 132 C2
Juniper Way Bristol BS34 30 A7
Stonehouse GL10 97 F8
Juno Dr GL15 92 B5
Jupiter Rd BS34 28 E7
Jupiter Way GL4 119 F6
Justice Ave BS31 5 E3
Justice Rd BS16 20 A3
Justicia Way GL51 129 F5
Justin's Hill NP25 154 A7
Jutland Rd BS11 26 B1

K

Kansas Dr GL7 152 E2
Karelean Ct BS10 28 D3
Kaskelot Way GL1 118 C6
Katharine Ct GL51 130 A5
Kathdene Gdns BS7 18 F3
Katherine Cl GL3 127 F8
Katherine Dr GL12 67 A5
Katherine Lady Berkeley's Sch GL12 67 F6
Katherine"s Wlk 5 HR8 178 E7
Katherine's Wlk GL7 153 E2
Kaybourne Cres GL3 128 D5
Kayte Cl GL52 137 F2
Kayte La GL52 138 A2
Keats Ave GL2 118 C4
Keats Gdns GL5 103 A1
Keble Ave BS13 1 F5
Keble Cl Cirencester GL7 190 B1
Lechlade on T GL7 153 E3
Keble Lawns GL7 152 E3
Keble Rd Chalford GL6 148 D6
Moreton-in-M GL56 187 A2
Keel Cl BS5 9 F6
Keelings The GL14 191 C5
Keels SN6 143 E5
Keen's Gr BS35 38 C7
Keep The BS30 11 D5
Keepers Mill GL52 138 B3
Keil Cl 5 WR12 185 B8
Keinton Wlk BS10 28 A2
Keirle Wlk GL51 132 F5
Kelbra Cres BS36 31 B6
Kellaway Ave BS7 18 D5
Kellaway Cres BS9 18 D6
Kellaway Ct BS6 18 D5
Kells Meend GL16 155 A7
Kells Rd GL16 155 A7
Kellys La NP16 146 F1
Kelston Cl Saltford BS31 5 D4
Yate BS37 32 D7
Kelston Gdns BS10 18 D8
Kelston Gr BS15 10 E6
Kelston Rd Bath BA1 6 E1
Bristol BS10 18 D8
Keynsham BS31 4 D5
Kelston Wlk BS16 20 C4
Kemble Bsns Pk SN16 141 D6
Kemble Cl Bristol BS15 10 E6
Gloucester GL4 118 D2
Kemble Dr GL7 190 B2
Kemble Gdns BS11 16 F5
Kemble Gr GL51 129 B7
Kemble Ho BS34 39 F1
Kemble Prim Sch GL7 141 F8
Kemble Rd GL4 118 E2
Kemble Sta GL7 141 F8
Kemerton Rd
Bredon GL20 182 C7
Cheltenham GL50 130 B6
Westmancote GL20 182 D8
Kempe's Cl BS41 7 A2
Kemperleye Way BS32 29 D7
Kemps La GL6 103 F8
Kempsford Acre GL52 138 B3
Kempsford CE Prim Sch GL7 144 E8
Kempton Cl Bristol BS16 30 F1
Thornbury BS35 64 B3
Kempton Gr GL51 132 D2
Kencot Wlk BS13 2 B3
Kencourt Cl 2 GL2 127 B2
Kendal Rd Bristol BS7 19 A7
Gloucester GL2 127 C4
Kendall Gdns BS16 20 D4
Kendall Rd BS16 20 D4
Kendon Dr BS10 18 D7
Kendon Way BS10 18 D8
Kendrick St 9 GL5 99 C7
Kenelm Dr GL53 130 C6
Kenelm Gdns GL53 130 B6
Kenelm Rise GL54 174 A8
Kenilworth BS37 32 F8
Kenilworth Ave GL2 127 B3
Kenilworth Cl BS31 4 D4
Kenilworth Dr BS30 11 B2
Kenilworth Ho 5 GL51 132 E3
Kenilworth Rd BS6 18 C1
Kenmare Rd BS4 8 E1
Kenmore Cres BS7 28 E1
Kenmore Dr BS7 28 E1
Kenmore Gr BS7 28 E1
Kenn Court Bsns Pk BS4 2 E7
Kenn Rd BS5 10 A7
Kennard Cl BS15 10 C7
Kennard Rd BS15 10 C8
Kennard Rise BS15 10 C8
Kennedy Cl GL3 127 F1
Kennedy Ho BS37 43 F1
Kennedy Way BS37 43 F1
Kennel Dr GL9 46 E2
Kennel La
Broadwell GL56 177 A6
Brockworth GL3 120 E4
Kennel Lodge Rd BS3 7 E4
Kennerwell La GL12 68 E3
Kennet Cl GL20 182 B4
Kennet Rd BS31 5 A4
Kennet Way 4 BS35 51 D8
Kenneth Cl GL53 130 E4
Kenneth Rd BS4 9 D2
Kennett Gdns GL4 119 F4
Kennington Ave
Bristol, Bishopston BS7 18 F4
3 Bristol, Two Mile Hill BS15 20 D1
Kennion Rd BS5 10 A7
Kennmoor Cl BS30 11 A6
Kensal Ave BS3 8 E3
Kensal Rd BS3 8 E3
Kensington Ave GL50 130 A8
Kensington Cl BS35 64 B2
Kensington Ct BS8 194 A3
Kensington Park Rd BS4 9 C2
Kensington Pk 12 BS5 19 A1
Kensington Pl BS8 194 A3
Kensington Rd
Bristol, Redland BS6 18 C1
3 Bristol, St George BS5 10 A8
6 Bristol, Staple Hill BS16 20 D4
Kensley Vale GL14 191 C3
Kent Ave BS37 43 F3
Kent Cl Bristol BS34 29 D4
Churchdown GL3 128 D5
Kent End SN6 143 A5
Kent End Cl SN6 143 A5
Kent Rd BS7 18 E4
Kent St BS3 8 C3
Kentmere Cl GL51 129 E7
Kenton Dr GL2 127 C5
Kenton Ho BS34 39 F1
Kenton Mews BS9 18 C5
Kents Gn BS15 20 E2
Kenulf Rd 29 GL54 174 A7
Keppel Cl BS31 5 D2
Keriston Ave GL3 128 A6
Kerr Way GL56 187 C3
Kerrin La GL15 147 C2
Kerris Ct 9 GL3 128 A7
Kerry Rd BS4 8 E1
Kersteman Rd BS6 18 C3
Kerstin Cl GL50 133 C5
Kestrel Cl Bristol BS34 28 E8
Cheltenham GL53 130 C5
Chipping Sodbury BS37 32 F8
Thornbury BS35 64 D2
Kestrel Ct 8 GL10 97 F8
Kestrel Dr BS16 22 C4
Kestrel Gdns GL2 117 F3
Kestrel Par GL3 127 D6
Kestrel Way GL20 182 B5
Keswick Cl GL2 127 B3
Keswick Rd GL51 129 E7
Keswick Wlk BS10 28 C2
Ketch Rd BS3 8 F3
Kevin Cl GL4 127 D1
Kew Pl GL53 193 B1
Kew Wlk BS4 3 C8
Kews La GL18 170 D4
Kewstoke Rd BS9 17 E4
Keynes Ctry Pk* GL7 142 D7
Keynsham Bank GL52 130 F8
Keynsham By-Pass BS31 4 E7
Keynsham Hospl BS31 4 F4
Keynsham La GL15 147 B2
Keynsham Prim Sch BS31 4 D5
Keynsham Rd
Bristol BS30,BS31 5 A8
Cheltenham GL53 193 C2
Keynsham St GL52 130 F8
Keynsham Sta BS31 4 F6
Keynshambury Rd GL52 193 C2
Keys Ave BS7 18 F7
Keytes Acre GL55 189 D3
Kibble's La GL14 191 C1
Kidnalls Rd GL15 155 F1
Kidnams Wlk GL2 100 F5
Kidnappers La GL53 130 B4
Kidney Hill BS37 32 A3
Kiftsgate Court Gdns* GL55 189 C6
Kilbirnie Rd BS14 3 A3
Kilburn Ct 17 BS5 9 B8
Kilburn St 19 BS5 9 B8
Kilda Rd SN6 145 C4
Kildare Rd BS4 8 D1
Kilham La GL54 166 E5
Kilkenny St BS2 195 C2
Killcott Rd GL12 55 E8
Kilmersdon Rd BS13 2 B4
Kilminster Ct 11 GL3 128 A7
Kilminster Rd
Bristol BS11 16 D7
Stroud GL5 99 F7
Kilmore La GL20 181 F7
Kiln Cl BS15 20 B2
Kiln Ct BS5 9 B8
Kilnhurst Cl BS30 10 F2
Kilvert Cl BS4 9 D5
Kimberley Ave BS16 20 C5
Kimberley Cl Bristol BS16 20 F7
Gloucester GL2 127 D4
Lydney GL15 92 B3
Kimberley Cres BS16 20 C5
Kimberley Dr GL15 92 B3
Kimberley Rd
Bristol, Fishponds BS16 20 C5
Bristol, Kingswood BS15 20 D1
Kimberley Wlk GL52 134 C2
Kimbrose GL1 196 A2
Kimbrose Way GL1 196 A2
Kimmins Rd GL10 98 A8
Kinder Ho GL52 134 B4
Kindrick La 11 GL5 99 C7
King Alfred Way GL52 130 F8
King Alfreds Rd NP16 61 A8
King Arthur Cl GL53 130 F7
King Dick's La 6 BS5 9 F8
King Edmund Com Sch BS37 43 E1
King Edward Cl BS14 3 A6
King Edward's Ave GL1 118 E7
King George Cl GL53 130 F6
King George V Pl 6 BS1 195 A2
King George's Rd BS13 1 F5
King Georges Field GL54 176 F4
King Henry Cl GL53 130 F6
King John's Cotts GL20 192 C5
King John's Rd BS15 20 B2
King Johns Ct GL20 192 C5
King La BS37 45 A7
King Rd BS4 9 C1
King Road Ave BS11 26 B2
King Sq BS2 195 A4
King Square Ave BS2 195 A4
King St Avonmouth BS11 26 A1
Bristol BS1 195 A2
Bristol, Lower Easton BS5 19 C1
Bristol, St George BS15 10 B8
Cheltenham GL50 193 B4
Cirencester GL7 190 D3
Minchinhampton GL6 148 A3
Stroud GL5 99 C7
King Street Par 4 GL5 99 C7
King William Ave BS1 195 A2
King William Dr GL53 130 F6
King William St BS3 8 B4
King's Ave BS6,BS7 18 C4
King's Barton St GL1 196 C2
King's Dr BS7 18 C4
King's Head La BS13 1 F7
King's Mill La GL6 103 E7
King's Parade Ave 1 BS8 18 B1
King's Parade Mews BS8 18 A1
King's Rd
Bristol, Clifton BS8 194 A3
Bristol, Kensington Park BS4 9 C3
Cheltenham GL52 133 F1
Stonehouse GL10 101 F1
Stroud GL5 99 B6
King's Sch The GL1 196 B3
King's Sq GL1 196 B3
King's Stanley CE Jun Sch GL10 98 A4
King's Stanley Inf Sch GL10 98 A3
Kingcomb La GL55 188 F2
Kingfisher Cl Bristol BS32 40 E2
Thornbury BS35 64 D2
Kingfisher Dr BS16 19 E6
Kingfisher Pl GL7 143 A8
Kingfisher Rd BS37 33 A8
Kingfisher Rise GL2 117 E1
Kingham Sta OX7 177 F1
Kingley Rd GL5 98 E7
Kingrove Cres BS37 33 C8
Kingrove La BS37 33 C7
Kings Ave Bristol BS15 10 B4
Highworth SN6 145 D3
Kings Chase BS15 10 D8
Kings Court Prim Sch BS37 32 E8
Kings Ct Bristol BS1 195 A2
Bristol, Little Stoke BS34 29 C6
Bristol, St Pauls BS1 195 B4
Kings Dr Bristol BS15 10 B4
Dursley GL11 88 A2
Kings Elm GL2 173 B3
Kings Gate GL20 192 F4
Kings Head La GL54 166 F2
Kings Mdw
Bourton-on-t-W GL54 168 F8
Crudwell SN16 141 B3
Kings Mead GL14 156 F6
Kings Meade GL16 155 A5
Kings Park Ave BS2 9 C6
Kings Sq BS30 5 D8
Kings Well La GL54 176 C1
Kings Weston Ave BS11 16 E8
Kings Weston La
Avonmouth BS11 26 E3
Bristol BS11 17 A8
Kings Weston Rd BS11, BS10 27 C1
Kings Wlk Bristol BS13 1 E7
Gloucester GL1 196 B3
Kingsclere Dr GL52 137 E3
Kingscote BS37 32 D6
Kingscote Ave GL51 129 D7
Kingscote Cl
Cheltenham GL51 129 D7
Churchdown GL3 128 D4
Kingscote Dr GL4 119 E5
Kingscote Gr GL51 129 D7
Kingscote Pk BS5 10 B6
Kingscote Rd E GL51 129 D7
Kingscote Rd W GL51 129 D6
Kingscourt Cl BS14 3 A4
Kingscourt La GL5 99 A4
Kingscroft Rd GL3 120 A7
Kingsdale Ct WR12 185 C8
Kingsditch La GL51 133 A5
Kingsditch Ret Pk GL51 133 A5
Kingsdown GL11 88 A3
Kingsdown Par BS6 195 A4
Kingsfield La
Bristol, Longwell Green BS15 10 E5
Bristol, Mount Hill BS30 10 E4
Kingsfield Sch BS15 11 A8
Kingshill GL7 190 F4
Kingshill Ho BS4 9 B1
Kingshill La
Cirencester GL7 150 F4
Dursley GL11 88 A2
Kingshill Pk GL11 88 A3
Kingshill Rd Bristol BS4 9 B1
Dursley GL11 88 A2
Kingsholm CE Prim Sch GL1 196 C4
Kingsholm Ct GL1 126 E4
Kingsholm Rd
Bristol BS10 18 D8
Gloucester GL1 196 B4
Kingsholm Sq GL1 196 B4
Kingsholme Rd BS15 20 D1
Kingsland Cl 1 BS2 9 A6
Kingsland Rd BS2 9 A6
Kingsland Road Bridge 3 BS2 9 A6
Kingsland Trad Est BS2 195 C3
Kingsleigh Ct BS15 10 F7
Kingsleigh Gdns BS15 10 F7
Kingsleigh Pk BS15 10 F7
Kingsley Gdns GL51 129 E8
Kingsley Ho Bristol BS2 195 C2
Bristol, Westbury on Trym BS9 18 A8
Kingsley Pl 1 BS3 8 C4
Kingsley Rd
Bristol, Lower Easton BS5 19 C1
Bristol, Montpelier BS6 18 D2
Gloucester GL4 119 A5
Kingsmark La NP16 72 D1
Kingsmarsh Ho 3 BS5 9 B7
Kingsmead
Cirencester GL7 190 E2
Gloucester GL4 119 F4
Lechlade on T GL7 153 E3
Painswick GL6 103 E8
Kingsmead Ave GL51 132 F4
Kingsmead Cl GL51 132 F4
Kingsmead Ind Est GL51 133 A4
Kingsmead Rd Bristol BS5 20 A1
Cheltenham GL51 132 F4
Kingsmead Wlk BS5 20 A1
Kingsmill BS9 17 D5
Kingston Ave BS31 5 C3
Kingston Cl BS16 21 A7
Kingston Dr Bristol BS16 21 A7
Cheltenham GL51 132 C1
Kingston Rd Bristol BS3 8 C4
Northway GL20 182 C4
Slimbridge GL2 95 C4
Kingstone Ave GL3 127 F1
Kingstree St BS4 9 A4
Kingsville Rd GL51 133 A5
Kingsway
Bristol, Little Stoke BS34 29 C6
Bristol, St George BS5 10 B7
Cirencester GL7 150 F3
Coleford GL16 155 B6
Dursley GL11 88 A3
Kingsway Ave BS15 10 B8
Kingsway Cres BS15 10 C8
Kingsway La GL17 163 F4
Kingsway Sh Prec BS5 10 B7
Kingswear Rd BS3 8 D2
Kingsweston Down Nature Res* BS9,BS11 27 C1
Kingsweston Specl Sch BS11 17 A8
Kingswood Abbey Gatehouse* GL12 67 F5
Kingswood Cl GL52 137 F3
Kingswood Cty Prim sch GL12 67 F5
Kingswood Rd GL12 55 D8
Kingswood Trad Est 6 BS15 20 D1
Kington La BS35 63 E1
Kington Rd BS35 63 E3
Kinmoor GL4 119 D3
Kinsale Rd BS14 3 C7
Kinsale Wlk BS4 8 E1
Kinsham La GL20 182 E7
Kinvara Rd BS4 2 E8
Kipling Cl GL2 118 C4
Kipling Rd Bristol BS7 29 B1
Cheltenham GL51 132 E1
Dursley GL11 80 C7
Kirby Rd GL54 169 E6
Kirkby Rd BS11 27 A1
Kirkstone Gdns BS10 28 C2
Kirkstone Ho BS34 29 A8
Kirtlington Rd BS5 19 B3
Kitchener Ave GL1 118 E5
Kite Hay Cl BS16 19 E5
Kitefield 13 SN6 143 E4
Kites Cl BS32 40 C2
Kitesnest La GL5 99 A4
Klondyke Ave GL15 92 B3
Knap La Cromhall GL12 66 B3
Painswick GL6 103 F7
Knapp Cl HR9 163 A6
Knapp Cotts GL18 179 B3
Knapp La
Brimscombe GL5 148 A4
Cheltenham GL50 193 A4
Coaley GL11 89 B5
Dursley GL11 87 F6
Netherend GL15 147 D3
Stroud GL6 104 B2
Knapp Rd
Cheltenham GL50 193 A4
Thornbury BS35 64 D1
Thornbury,Crossways BS35 64 E2
Wooton-u-E GL12 68 C7
Knapp The Dursley GL11 88 B1
Yate BS37 43 F5
Knapps La BS5 19 E2
Knighton Rd BS10 28 E1
Knights Cl BS9 18 B6
Knights Cres GL18 170 F4
Knights Way
Newent GL18 170 F4
Tewkesbury GL20 192 E4
Knightsbridge Bsns Ctr GL51 173 F5
Knightsbridge Cres GL53 130 F7
Knightsbridge Gn GL51 173 F5
Knightsbridge Pk BS13 2 E4
Knightshill HR9 164 D8
Knightstone Ct BS5 19 D2
Knightstone Gdns BS4 9 B2
Knightstone Ho 1 BS2 195 A4
Knightstone Mount BS5 10 A6
Knightstone Rise 4 BS5 9 F8
Knightstone Sq BS14 3 C5
Knightwood Rd BS34 29 F5
Knockdown Rd SN16 58 C1
Knockley Patch GL15 155 D1
Knole Cl BS32 39 F4
Knole La BS10 28 B3
Knole Pk BS32 39 F3
Knoll Ct BS9 17 D3
Knoll Hill BS9 17 D3
Knoll The Kempsford GL7 144 E8

Knoll The *continued*
Stroud GL5 99 D7
Knollys End GL2 109 F8
Knovill Cl BS11 27 B2
Knowlands SN6 145 D4
Knowle Jun Sch BS4 9 A3
Knowle Park Jun & Inf Schs BS4 9 A1
Knowle Rd BS4 8 F3
Knowles Rd GL1 118 F7
Knowsley Rd BS16 19 E3
Knox Rd GL15 147 E8
Kyderminster Rd GL54 174 A8
Kyght Cl BS15 11 A8
Kylross Ave BS14 3 B5
Kymin Lea NP25 154 A7
Kymin Rd NP25 154 B7
Kynges Mill Cl BS16 20 A7
Kyngstone Ct 10 BS16 19 E3

L

La Maison BS5 20 A2
Labbott The BS31 4 E5
Laburnum Cres GL6 102 F2
Laburnum Ct GL51 132 C2
Laburnum Gdns GL2 117 F2
Laburnum Gr BS16 20 B4
Laburnum Mews GL10 97 E7
Laburnum Rd Bristol BS15 10 C5
Gloucester GL1 118 D5
Stonehouse GL10 97 E7
Laburnum Way NP16 60 E5
Laburnum Wlk
Keynsham BS31 4 C3
Stonehouse GL10 97 E7
Lacca Cl GL2 127 D5
Lacey Rd BS14 3 F6
Lacock Dr BS30 10 F5
Lacy Cl GL2 127 C6
Ladbarrow Cotts GL54 161 A4
Ladd Cl BS15 10 F7
Ladden Ct BS35 51 C8
Ladder The GL6 91 C4
Ladies Mile BS8 17 F1
Ladman Gr BS14 3 E6
Ladman Rd BS14 3 E5
Lady Chapel Rd GL4 119 E6
Lady La SN26 144 D1
Lady Margaret Ct NP16 60 F4
Lady Mead SN6 143 E4
Ladybellegate St GL1 196 A2
Ladygrove Bsns Pk GL17 164 E5
Ladysmith Rd Bristol BS6 18 B4
Cheltenham GL52 134 B2
Gloucester GL1 118 E6
Ladywell Cl GL2 118 B7
Laggar La GL5 98 F1
Laines Est The GL54 158 F6
Lake Cl GL2 124 B3
Lake La Churcham GL2 124 B3
Frampton on Severn GL2 157 F3
Lake Rd BS10 18 C8
Lake Side GL18 171 A5
Lake St Prestbury GL52 134 B5
Quedgeley GL2 116 D4
Lake Terr GL2 157 F3
Lake View Rd BS5 9 D8
Lakemead Gdns BS13 1 F4
Lakemead Gr BS13 1 F6
Lakers Rd GL16 155 A7
Lakers Sch GL16 155 B7
Lakeside Bristol BS16 19 E3
Fairford GL7 152 D3
South Cerney GL7 143 A8
Lakeside Ave GL15 92 C2
Lakeside Ct GL52 133 F4
Lakeside Dr GL15 92 C2
Lakeside Jun Sch GL51 129 E7
Lakewood Cres BS10 18 B8
Lakewood Rd BS10 18 B8
Lamb Hill BS5 9 F7
Lamb La GL14 191 D4
Lamb St BS2 195 C3
Lambert Ave GL51 129 D1
Lambert Cl GL51 129 D1
Lambert Dr GL51 129 D1
Lambert Gdns GL51 129 D1
Lambert Pl BS4 2 D6
Lambert Terr GL51 129 D2
Lamberts Field GL54 169 A7
Lambley Rd BS5 9 E8
Lambourn Cl Bristol BS3 8 D3
Gloucester GL2 127 E3
Lambourn Rd BS31 5 A4
Lambourne Ave GL19 165 D6
Lambourne Cl 14 HR8 178 F8
Lambrook Rd BS16 20 A4
Lambs Barn Pitch GL18 171 A5
Lambs Cross HR9 170 B4
Lambsdowne GL11 87 F3
Lambsquay Rd GL16 155 A3
Lamord Gate BS34 29 E5
Lampern View GL11 89 B1
Lampeter Rd BS9 18 A7
Lampreys The GL4 119 B6
Lampton Ave BS13 2 E3
Lampton Gr BS13 2 E3
Lampton Rd BS41 7 A1
Lanaway Rd BS16 20 B6
Lancashire Rd BS7 18 E3
Lancaster Cl BS34 29 D4
Lancaster Ct
2 Cheltenham GL50 130 B8
Lydney GL15 92 B5
Lancaster Dr Lydney GL15 92 B5
Upper Rissington GL54 169 D6
Lancaster Rd Bristol BS2 19 A2
Kempsford GL7 144 F7
Tewkesbury GL20 192 D2
Yate BS37 43 E3
Lancaster St 10 BS5 9 C7
Lancaster Terr GL18 171 A5
Lancaster Way NP16 60 D8
Lancaut La NP16 72 F6
Lancelot Ct GL2 95 D4
Lancelot Rd BS16 19 E8
Land The BS36 31 C7
Landgate Yd 2 GL54 176 F4
Landor Gdns 19 GL52 133 F2
Landseer Ave BS7 19 B7
Lane End GL54 169 C4
Lane The
Broadway WR12 184 F7
Chastleton GL56 177 E8
Easter Compton BS35 38 F2
Randwick GL6 102 D2
Lanercost Rd BS10 28 C2
Lanes Ct GL20 192 C3
Lanes The GL53 130 B4
Lanesborough Rise BS14 3 D7
Lanescourt GL20 192 D3
Langdale Ct BS34 29 A8
Langdale Gdns GL2 127 C5
Langdale Rd Bristol BS16 19 F4
Cheltenham GL51 129 F6
Langdon Rd GL53 130 D6
Langdown Ct BS14 3 E5
Langet GL7 142 F7
Langetts Rd 4 GL16 155 A5
Langfield Cl BS10 27 E3
Langford Rd BS13 1 F8
Langford Way BS15 10 E7
Langham Ho NP16 60 F5
Langham Rd BS4 9 B2
Langhill Ave BS4 2 D7
Langley Cl GL54 139 F5
Langley Cres BS3 7 E1
Langley Mow BS16 21 B7
Langley Rd
Gloucester GL4 119 B5
Winchcombe GL54 139 D5
Langsdown Ho 7 BS2 18 F1
Langston Priory Workshops OX7 177 F1
Langthorn Cl BS36 31 C7
Langtoft Rd GL5 99 E7
Langton Cl GL4 119 E8
Langton Court Rd BS4 9 D5
Langton Ct 11 BS16 19 E3
Langton Grove Rd GL52 131 A7
Langton Ho 9 BS2 195 C3
Langton Pk BS3 8 C4
Langton Pl GL53 131 A7
Langton Rd BS4 9 D5
Langton Way BS4 9 F6
Lanham Gdns GL2 109 F7
Lannett Rd GL1 118 E6
Lansdown Stroud GL5 99 C7
Yate BS37 32 E8
Lansdown Castle Dr GL51 129 F8
Lansdown Cl Bristol BS15 20 D2
Cheltenham GL51 130 A8
Lansdown Cotts GL54 168 F8
Lansdown Cres GL50 193 A2
Lansdown Crescent La GL50 193 A2
Lansdown Ct GL50 193 A2
Lansdown Ho BS15 20 D2
Lansdown Ind Est GL51 133 A1
Lansdown La BS30 12 C1
Lansdown Lodge Dr GL51 130 A8
Lansdown Par GL50 130 B8
Lansdown Pl Bristol BS8 194 A3
Cheltenham GL50 193 A2
Lansdown Place La GL50 193 A2
Lansdown Rd
Bristol, Clifton BS8 194 A3
Bristol, Kingswood BS15 20 D2
Bristol, Redland BS6 18 C1
6 Bristol, Upper Easton BS5 9 B8
Cheltenham GL51 130 A8
Gloucester GL1 127 A3
Pucklechurch BS16 22 C6
Saltford BS31 5 E3
Lansdown Terr
Bristol BS6 18 D5
Cheltenham GL50 193 A2
Cheltenham GL50 193 A3
Lansdown Terrace La GL50 193 A2
Lansdown View BS15 10 F8
Lansdown Wlk
12 Bream GL15 147 D8
Cheltenham GL50 193 A2
Lansdowne BS16 30 C1
Lansdowne Ct 2 BS5 9 B8
Lantern Cl Berkeley GL13 85 E3
Cinderford GL14 191 C4
Lapdown La GL9 34 D1
Laphams Ct 11 BS30 10 F4
Lapwing Cl Bristol BS32 40 D2
Northway GL20 182 B5
Lapwing Gdns BS16 19 F6
Larch Cl GL53 131 C5
Larch Rd Bristol BS15 20 E3
Colerne SN14 15 F6
Larch Rise GL53 130 B4
Larch Way BS34 28 E7
Larches The GL4 119 E6
Larchmere Gr 8 GL51 129 E5
Larchwood Dr GL4 118 E3
Lark Rise Chalford GL6 148 C6
Coleford GL16 155 A6
Yate BS37 43 F4
Lark's Field BS16 19 E5
Lark's La BS37 42 B7
Larkfield BS36 31 D7
Larkfield Ave NP16 60 E7
Larkfield Cty Inf Sch GL3 127 E6
Larkfield Ho NP16 60 D7
Larkfield Pk NP16 60 D7
Larkham Cl GL4 119 B3
Larkham Pl GL4 119 B3
Larkhay Rd GL3 120 A8
Larkhill Cl NP16 60 E7
Larkrise GL11 87 F5
Larksfield Rd
Harrow Hill GL17 164 B4
Stroud GL5 99 A4
Larksleaze Rd BS30 10 F2
Larkspear Cl GL1 118 E5
Larkspur Cl BS35 64 D1
Larput Pl GL50 133 D3
Lasanne Ct GL1 196 B2
Lasbury Gr BS13 2 C5
Lasne Cres GL3 120 F4
Lassington Gr GL2 125 C5
Lassington La GL2 125 D6
Lassington Wood (Nature Reserve)* GL2 125 E5
Latchen GL17 164 F5
Latchen Orch GL17 164 F5
Latchmoor Ho BS13 2 A8
Latimer Cl Bristol BS4 9 E4
Minchinhampton GL6 148 A3
Latimer Ct GL54 175 B3
Latimer Rd GL14 191 E5
Latteridge La
Iron Acton BS37 42 A7
Tytherington BS35 51 F1
Latteridge Rd BS37 42 D4
Latton Rd BS7 18 F8
Latymer Croft GL3 128 B5
Launceston Ave BS15 10 B5
Launceston Rd BS15 20 B1
Laundry Cotts GL56 177 E5
Laundry Rd GL16 154 E4
Laura Cl GL2 127 B4
Laurel Ave GL20 192 E2
Laurel Dr Colerne SN14 15 F6
Prestbury GL52 134 B4
Laurel Farm Cl GL4 118 F4
Laurel Gate GL4 119 F5
Laurel Pk NP16 72 B6
Laurel St BS15 10 D8
Laureldene GL16 155 B3
Laurels The
Bristol, Catbrain BS10 28 A6
Bristol, Mangotsfield BS16 21 A6
Castle Eaton SN6 144 D6
Gloucester GL1 118 F7
South Cerney GL7 142 F8
Laurence Cl GL51 129 D2
Laurie Cres BS9 18 D6
Laurie Lee Ct 3 BS30 11 A5
Lavender Cl BS35 64 D1
Lavender Ct Bristol BS5 19 F1
Cirencester GL7 190 C3
Lavender La GL7 190 C3
Lavender Mews GL52 137 E3
Lavender Rd GL51 129 F5
Lavender View GL4 119 F4
Lavender Way BS32 29 F7
Lavenham Rd BS37 43 B2
Lavers Cl BS15 10 E6
Lavington Dr GL2 127 E4
Lavington Rd BS5 10 B6
Lawford Ave BS34 29 C6
Lawford St BS2 195 C3
Lawfords Gate BS2 195 C3
Lawfords Gate Ho 17 BS2 195 C3
Lawn Ave BS16 20 B5
Lawn Cres GL51 129 E2
Lawn Rd
Ashleworth GL19 172 D4
Bristol BS16 20 B5
Lawns Pk GL5 98 F2
Lawns Rd BS37 43 F2
Lawns The Bristol BS11 16 E7
Gloucester GL4 119 D3
Gotherington GL52 138 B7
Stonehouse GL10 97 E8
Lawnside GL6 91 A4
Lawnside Rd 6 HR8 178 E8
Lawnwood Ind Units 14 BS5 9 B8
Lawnwood Rd 15 BS5 9 B8
Lawrence Ave BS5 19 B1
Lawrence Cl Bristol BS15 21 A2
Charlton Kings GL52 131 B6
Lawrence Dr BS37 43 B2
Lawrence Gr Bristol BS9 18 B5
Dursley GL11 88 A2
Lawrence Hill BS5 9 B7
Lawrence Hill Ind Pk BS5 9 B8
Lawrence Hill Rdbt BS5 9 A7
Lawrence Hill Sta BS5 9 B7
Lawrence Rd
Avening GL8 148 B1
Cirencester GL7 190 B3
Lawrence Way GL1 126 E4
Lawrence Way N GL1 126 E4
Lawrence Weston Rd
Avonmouth BS11 26 E5
Bristol BS11 27 A3
Bristol BS11 27 C1
Lawrence Weston Sch BS11 27 B1
Lawrence's Mdw GL52 138 A8
Lawson Cl BS31 5 C2
Lawson Glade GL53 131 A4
Laxey Rd BS7 18 F7
Laxton Cl BS35 50 A3
Laxton Dr GL12 67 F4
Laxton Rd
Cheltenham GL51 132 E2
Gloucester GL4 120 A6
Laymore Rd GL14 191 B5
Laynes Rd GL3 120 A7
Lays Bsns Ctr BS31 4 C4
Lays Dr BS31 4 C5
Lea CE Prim Sch The HR9 164 C8
Lea Cres GL2 127 C5
Lea Croft BS13 2 A4
Lea Ct GL10 96 E7
Lea Rd GL3 120 F5
Leacey Ct GL3 128 A7
Leacy Mews GL3 128 A7
Leadon Cl GL3 120 F5
Leadon Way HR8 178 E7
Leafield Rd GL7 152 E4
Leaholes Ct GL7 190 D4
Leaholme Gdns BS14 3 A3
Leaman Cl BS37 44 B1
Leamington Rd WR12 188 A1
Leap Vale BS16 21 A8
Leap Valley Cres BS16 21 A8
Leaping Stocks Rd HR9 162 D3
Lear Cl BS30 11 B5
Lears Dr GL52 138 A3
Leaside Cl GL11 88 A4
Leasow La GL54 169 B5
Leasows The
Broadwell GL56 177 A6
Chipping Campden GL55 188 F1
Mickleton GL55 189 B6
Leaze Cl GL13 85 E3
Leaze Ct GL15 92 C2
Leaze The
2 Ashton Keynes SN6 142 F5
South Cerney GL7 142 F7
Yate BS37 43 D2
Leazes The GL5 99 D7
Lechlade Rd
Highworth SN6 145 D4
Lechlade on T GL7 153 F1
Southrop GL7 153 C6
Upper Inglesham SN6 145 D7
Lechmere Rd 1 GL51 132 E3
Leckhampton CE Prim Sch GL53 130 D4
Leckhampton Farm Ct GL51 130 B3
Leckhampton Gate GL51 130 A4
Leckhampton Hill GL53 130 D2
Leckhampton La GL51 130 A2
Leckhampton Pl GL53 130 D5
Leckhampton Rd GL53 130 D5
Leckhampton View GL51 129 F2
Leda Ave BS14 3 A7
Ledbury Heritage Ctr* HR8 178 F8
Ledbury Pk 9 HR8 178 F8
Ledbury Prim Sch HR8 178 E8
Ledbury Rd BS16 20 C4
Ledbury Road Cres GL19 172 A8
Leddington Ct HR8 178 D7
Ledmore Rd GL53 131 B6
Lee Cl Bristol BS34 28 F8
Cheltenham GL51 132 F3
Lee Rd GL20 182 C4
Leechpool Way BS37 43 E5
Leeming Way BS11 16 C8
Lees Ct BS15 20 E1
Lees Hill BS15 20 E2
Lees La BS30 11 D5
Leicester Sq BS16 20 D3
Leicester St 6 BS3 8 D4
Leicester Wlk BS4 9 F5
Leigh CE Sch SN6 143 B3
Leigh Court Bsns Ctr BS8 17 A2
Leigh La Cold Ashton BA1 14 B3
Westerleigh BS37 32 B1
Leigh Rd BS8 194 B4
Leigh St BS3 8 A4
Leigh Woods Forest Walks* BS8 17 C1
Leighterton Prim Sch GL8 70 C3
Leighton Rd
Bristol, Knowle BS4 9 B2
Bristol, Southville BS3 8 B4
Cheltenham GL52 133 F1
Leinster Ave BS4 2 D8
Leinster Cl GL51 132 D4
Leisure Cntr* GL7 190 B4
Leisure Rd BS5 10 E5
Lemon La BS2 195 C4
Lena Ave 3 BS5 19 C1
Lena St BS5 19 C1
Lennards The GL7 143 A8
Lennox Way BS11 26 B1
Lenover Gdns BS13 2 B4
Lensbrook GL15 93 A8
Leonard La BS1 195 A3
Leonard Rd Bristol BS5 9 D7
Gloucester GL1 118 F6
Leonard Stanley CE Prim Sch GL10 97 F4
Leonards Ave BS5 19 C1
Leopold Rd BS6 18 E2
Lescren Way BS11 26 D1
Letch Hill Dr GL54 168 F7
Letch La 10 GL54 168 F7
Leven Cl GL2 127 D4
Lever's Hill GL11 89 B7
Lewin St 9 BS5 9 D7
Lewington Rd BS16 20 C4
Lewins Mead BS1 195 A3
Lewis Ave GL2 126 F6
Lewis Cl BS30 11 D5
Lewis Glade 2 GL16 155 B5
Lewis La GL7 190 D4
Lewis Rd Bristol BS13 2 A8
Cheltenham GL51 132 D2
Lewis St BS2 9 B5
Lewis Way NP16 60 F4
Lewisham Rd GL1 118 E5
Lewisham Terr GL13 85 C8
Lewiston Rd GL5 148 A5
Lewton La BS36 30 E7
Ley La BS35 49 F3
Ley Orch WR12 188 B2
Ley Rd GL2 116 A5
Leyland Wlk BS13 1 F4
Leys The GL13 85 E4
Leysbourne GL55 189 A2
Leyson Rd GL51 129 C6
Leyton Villas BS6 18 B2
Libby's Dr GL5 99 D8
Libertus Ct GL51 133 A1
Libertus Rd GL51 133 A1
Liberty Ind Pk BS3 8 A1
Lichfield Dr GL51 130 A5
Lichfield Rd Bristol BS4 9 E6
Gloucester GL4 119 D8
Lidderdale Rd GL54 169 D6
Liddington Cl GL53 130 D4
Liddington Rd
Cheltenham GL53 130 D4
Gloucester GL2 127 E3
Liddington Trad Est GL53 130 D5
Lifford Gdns WR12 185 B8
Lightenbrook La GL2 95 C3
Lightfoot 21 GL18 171 A4
Lightwood La GL6 102 E3
Lilac Cl Bristol BS10 28 C1
Cheltenham GL51 130 A5
Lilac Ct BS31 4 C4
Lilac Way Gloucester GL4 118 C3
Quedgeley GL2 117 F1
Lillian St 5 BS5 9 C8
Lilliesfield Ave GL3 119 F8
Lilliput Ave BS37 33 A8
Lilliput Ct BS37 33 B8
Lilly Hall La HR8 178 C7
Lilstock Ave BS7 18 F4
Lilton Wlk BS13 8 A1
Lilymead Ave BS4 9 A3
Limber Hill GL50 133 C5
Limbury Hostels GL19 172 A2
Lime Ave GL9 35 B8
Lime Cl Brentry BS10 28 B3
Prestbury GL52 134 A5
Lime Croft BS37 43 F4
Lime Ct BS31 4 C4
Lime Gr Alveston BS35 50 F4
Stroud GL5 99 C7
Lime Kiln Cl BS34 29 D3
Lime Kiln Gdns BS32 40 D2
Lime Rd
Bristol, Hanham BS15 10 A5
Bristol, Southville BS3 8 B4
Tewkesbury GL20 192 E1
Lime St GL19 180 D1
Lime Tree Ave 3 WR12 185 C8
Lime Tree Ct GL1 118 E5
Lime Tree Gr BS20 16 D3
Lime Trees Rd BS9 18 D6
Lime Way GL15 92 B4
Limekiln Gr GL2 125 D5
Limekiln La GL6 148 E8
Limekiln Rd BS37,GL12 53 C2
Limerick Rd BS6 18 C2
Limes Cl GL7 190 C3
Limes Pl SN6 143 E6
Limes Rd GL7 141 F8
Limes The Badminton GL9 46 E2
Bristol BS16 30 B1
Gloucester, Barnwood GL4 127 C1
Gloucester, Kingsholm GL2 126 E5
Limetree Ave NP25 154 A7
Linacre Cres GL7 190 B2
Lincoln Ave GL51 130 A5
Lincoln Cl Keynsham BS31 4 C4
Tewkesbury GL20 192 B2
Upper Rissington GL54 169 D6
Lincoln Ct BS16 19 D6
Lincoln Green La GL20 192 B2
Lincoln St BS5 9 B7
Lincombe Ave BS16 20 D6
Lincombe Rd BS16 20 C6
Linden Ave GL52 134 A5
Linden Cl
Bristol, Mayfield Park BS16 20 A2
Bristol, Stockwood BS14 3 E6
Chepstow NP16 60 E5
Colerne SN14 15 F6
Prestbury GL52 134 B5
Winterbourne BS36 30 E6
Linden Dr BS32 29 E8

Linden Ho BS16 19 C5
Linden Prim Sch GL1 118 D6
Linden Rd Bristol BS6 18 B4
Gloucester GL1 118 D6
Lindon Ho BS4 9 E3
Lindrea St 3 BS3 8 B3
Lindsay Rd BS7 19 A4
Line The HR9 170 A3
Linegar Wood Rd GL14 191 C1
Lines Way BS14 3 C3
Linfoot Rd GL8 140 B4
Lingfield Pk BS16 30 F2
Link Rd Bristol BS34 28 F3
Pillowell GL15 155 F1
Tewkesbury GL20 192 D4
Yate BS37 43 F1
Linkend Rd GL19 180 F2
Links The GL16 155 A5
Links View GL7 150 C7
Linley Rd SN26 144 E1
Linnell Cl BS7 19 B6
Linnet Cl Bristol BS34 28 E8
Gloucester GL4 119 C5
Linsley Way GL4 118 D1
Lintern Cres BS30 11 B6
Lintham Dr BS15 10 F6
Linton Ct GL53 193 C1
Linton Rd HR9 170 B4
Linwell Cl GL50 133 B5
Linworth Rd GL52 138 A3
Lion Cl GL2 117 F2
Lipson Rd GL51 132 E4
Lipson Villas GL51 132 E4
Lisburn Rd BS4 8 E1
Lisle Pl GL12 68 A7
Lismore Rd SN6 145 C4
Litfield Pl BS8 7 F7
Litfield Rd BS8 7 F8
Lithgow Rd GL54 169 D6
Little Acorns GL52 137 E5
Little Acre GL12 68 A8
Little Ann St BS2,BS5 195 C4
Little Bayshill Terr GL50 193 B3
Little Birch Croft BS14 3 A5
Little Bishop St BS2 195 B4
Little Bristol Cl GL12 67 B4
Little Bristol La GL12 67 B4
Little Caroline Pl 4 BS8 7 F5
Little Cleevemount GL52 133 F3
Little Dowles BS30 11 A4
Little Elmbridge GL2 127 E3
Little Field GL4 119 D7
Little Fishers GL5 99 A4
Little George St BS2 195 C4
Little Gn GL19 179 D2
Little Green La BS35 38 A7
Little Guillet Ct GL11 87 F4
Little Hayes BS16 20 B6
Little Headley Cl BS13 2 B7
Little Herbert's Cl GL53 131 B5
Little Herbert's Rd GL53 131 B4
Little Holbury GL2 100 E5
Little Horcott La GL7 152 E3
Little King St BS1 195 A2
Little Lancarridge GL2 125 D4
Little Marcle Rd HR8 178 E8
Little Mdw BS34 30 A6
Little Mead BS11 27 B1
Little Mus★ GL20 192 C4
Little Normans GL2 127 C5
Little Oaks GL18 179 B4
Little Orch GL52 137 E4
Little Paradise BS3 8 D3
Little Parr Cl BS16 19 C5
Little Paul St BS2 194 C4
Little Pheasants GL53 131 A5
Little Rd WR11 188 B8
Little Rose La SN26 144 C3
Little Stoke La BS34 29 D6
Little Stoke Prim Sch BS34 29 D6
Little Stoke Rd BS9 17 E4
Little Trewen La HR9 162 C5
Little Withey Mead BS9 17 F5
Little Wlk GL2 127 C5
Littlecote Cl GL52 137 E3
Littlecross Ho BS3 8 B4
Littledean BS37 32 E7
Littledean CE Prim Sch GL14 156 E8
Littledean Hall★ GL14 156 E7
Littledean Hill Rd GL14 191 E4
Littledown Rd GL53 130 F4
Littlefield GL2 117 E2
Littleton Ct BS34 39 F1
Littleton La BS41 1 C1
Littleton Rd BS3 8 D2
Littleton St 4 BS5 19 C1
Littlewood Cl BS14 3 B3
Littleworth GL55 188 F2
Livia Way GL15 92 B4
Llanarth Villas 3 BS6 18 D1
Llandilo St 1 GL1 118 F7
Llandogo Jun & Inf Sch NP25 146 B7
Llangarron Bsns Ctr HR9 162 B7
Llangrove CE Prim Sch HR9 162 B6
Llanthony Cotts GL20 136 B7
Llanthony Ind Est GL2 126 C1
Llanthony Priory★ GL2 126 C1
Llanthony Rd GL2 126 C1
Llanwrithy HR9 162 C5
Llewellyn Ct BS9 18 A8
Lloyd Baker Ct GL2 109 E7
Lobb Ct GL1 127 A1
Lobleys Dr GL4 120 A5
Lock Gdns BS13 1 E7
Lock's La BS37 41 E4
Lockemor Rd BS13 2 F4
Locking Hill 3 GL5 99 C7
Lockingwell Rd BS31 4 D5
Lockleaze Rd BS7 19 A6
Lockleaze Sch BS7 19 C7
Locombe Hill GL7 153 D8
Locombe Pl GL12 68 C6
Lodersfield GL7 153 E2
Lodge Causeway Trad Ctr BS16 19 F3
Lodge Cswy BS16 20 A3
Lodge Ct BS9 17 E4
Lodge Dr Bristol BS30 11 C2
Long Ashton BS41 7 B2
Lodge Gdns GL15 146 E7
Lodge Hill BS15 20 C2
Lodge La GL15 147 D6
Lodge Pl BS1 194 C3
Lodge Rd Bristol BS15 20 C1
Wick BS30 22 B1
Yate BS37 43 A3
Lodge St BS1 194 C3
Lodge Wlk BS16 20 D6
Lodgemore Cl GL5 99 A7
Lodgemore La GL5 99 A7
Lodgeside Ave BS15 20 C1
Lodgeside Gdns BS15 20 C1
Lodore Rd BS16 19 F3
Lodway BS20 16 C4
Lodway Cl BS20 16 C5
Lodway Gdns BS20 16 C4
Lodway Rd BS4 9 C2
Logan Rd BS7 18 D3
Logus Ct 14 BS30 10 F4
Loiterpin GL15 156 D2
Lombard St BS3 8 D4
Lomond Rd BS7 28 F1
London La SN16 142 E1
London Rd
Bristol, St Pauls BS2 18 F1
Bristol, Warmley BS30 11 D7
Charlton Kings GL52,GL53 131 C5
Cheltenham GL52 130 F8
Fairford GL7 152 F4
Gloucester GL1,GL2 127 A2
Moreton-in-M GL56 187 B3
Stroud GL5 99 C6
Tetbury GL8 140 C5
Thrupp GL5 99 E3
Wick BS30 12 E6
London Road Terr GL56 187 B3
London St Bristol BS15 10 D8
Fairford GL7 152 E3
Lone La NP25 154 C4
Long Acres 5 HR8 178 E8
Long Acres Cl BS9 17 D7
Long Ashton Rd BS41 7 B2
Long Beach Rd BS30 11 B3
Long Cl
Bristol, Fishponds BS16 20 C6
Bristol, Little Stoke BS32 29 E6
Long Croft BS37 43 D4
Long Cross BS11 27 B2
Long Dr GL16 155 B6
Long Eaton Dr BS14 3 B7
Long Eights GL20 182 C5
Long Field GL2 125 D6
Long Furlong GL52 137 F7
Long Furlong La GL8 140 B3
Long Handstones BS30 11 A4
Long Marston Rd CV37, GL55 189 A8
Long Mdw BS16 19 D6
Long Mead BS37 43 E5
Long Mynd Ave GL51 129 E6
Long Rd BS16 21 A5
Long Row Bristol BS1 195 B2
Castle Eaton SN6 144 D6
Long St Dursley GL11 88 B1
Tetbury GL8 140 B4
Wooton-u-E GL12 68 B7
Longacre Rd BS14 3 A3
Longaston Cl GL2 95 D4
Longaston La GL2 95 E5
Longborough CE Prim Sch GL56 176 D8
Longborough Dr GL4 119 E4
Longcross GL12 66 B1
Longden Rd BS16 20 F6
Longfield GL2 117 E2
Longfield Rd BS7 18 E3
Longford BS37 32 C8
Longford Ave BS10 18 D8
Longford Ct GL50 193 A1
Longford La GL2 127 A5
Longford Mews GL2 126 F6
Longhill Rd GL7 149 E8
Longhope CE Prim Sch GL17 164 F6
Longhope Cl 3 GL4 119 E5
Longhope Rd GL19 165 C6
Longland Ct GL2 127 B4
Longland Gdns GL2 127 B4
Longlands Cl GL52 138 B4
Longlands Ho 13 BS5 9 C7
Longlands Rd GL52 138 B4
Longleat GL53 131 A5
Longleat Ave GL4 118 C1
Longleat Cl BS9 18 C5
Longlength La GL6 83 C8
Longlevens Inf Sch GL2 127 D4
Longlevens Jun Sch GL2 127 C4
Longmead Ave BS7 18 D5
Longmead Croft BS13 1 F4
Longmead Rd BS16 31 B1
Longmeadow Rd BS31 4 C4
Longmoor Ct BS3 8 A2
Longmoor Rd BS3 8 A2
Longmore Ave GL54 169 D6
Longney CE Prim Sch GL2 108 C5
Longney Pl BS34 39 F1
Longney Rd GL4 118 D3
Longreach Gr BS14 3 D6
Longridge La GL19 172 C3
Longs Dr BS37 43 C2
Longs View GL12 67 A5
Longsmith St GL1 196 B3
Longtown Rd GL20 192 E2
Longtree Cl GL8 140 B5
Longville Cl GL4 119 F5
Longway Ave
Bristol BS13,BS14 2 F4
Charlton Kings GL53 131 A4
Longwell Green Prim Sch BS30 10 F3
Longwell Ho BS30 10 F3
Longwood BS4 10 A2
Lonk The GL16 155 A7
Lons The BS30 11 C1
Lonsdale Bsns Ctr BS15 20 C2
Lonsdale Cl SN26 144 E1
Lonsdale Rd GL2 127 C2
Loop Rd NP16 61 B5
Lorain Wlk BS10 27 F2
Lord Eldon Dr NP16 60 F4
Lord's Hill GL16 155 A5
Lord's Hill Cl 5 GL16 155 A5
Lords Gn GL52 138 C3
Loriners Cl GL2 117 F2
Lorton Cl BS10 28 B1
Lorton Rd BS10 28 B1
Lotts The 7 SN6 142 F5
Loughman Cl BS15 10 E8
Louisa St BS2 195 C2
Louise Ave BS16 21 A5
Love La
Chipping Sodbury BS37 33 A8
Cirencester GL7 190 D2
Yate BS37 44 A4
Love Lane Ind Est GL7 190 D2
Lovedays Mead GL5 99 C8
Lovell Ave BS30 11 D4
Lovell's Hill BS15 10 B5
Loveringe Cl BS10 27 F4
Lovers Wlk HR9 170 B4
Lovett Cl GL19 172 A8
Lowbourne BS14 2 F6
Lowdilow La GL51 136 E1
Lower Ashley Rd
Bristol, Baptist Mills BS2, BS5 19 A1
18 Bristol, St Pauls BS2 18 F1
Lower Berrycroft GL13 85 E3
Lower Castle St BS1 195 B3
Lower Chapel La BS36 31 C7
Lower Chapel Rd BS15 10 C5
Lower Cheltenham Pl BS6 18 F1
Lower Church La BS2 195 A3
Lower Church St NP16 72 F1
Lower Churchfield Rd GL5 99 D6
Lower Clifton Hill BS8 194 B2
Lower Cock Rd BS15 10 F7
Lower College St BS1 194 C2
Lower Comm GL15 147 D5
Lower Court Rd BS32 40 A5
Lower Croft GL7 152 E4
Lower Fallow Cl BS14 2 F3
Lower Gay St BS2 195 A4
Lower Grove Rd BS16 19 F4
Lower Guinea St BS1 195 A1
Lower Hanham Rd BS15 10 C6
Lower High St
Bristol BS11 16 D7
Chipping Campden GL55 189 A2
Lower House Cres BS34 29 B4
Lower Kitesnest La GL6 103 A3
Lower Knole La BS10 28 A3
Lower Lamb St BS1 194 C2
Lower Leazes GL5 99 D7
Lower Lode La GL20 192 A2
Lower Maudlin St BS1 195 A3
Lower Mdw GL2 109 F7
Lower Mill St GL51 133 B3
Lower Moor Rd BS37 43 E4
Lower Newmarket Rd GL6 90 F4
Lower Park Row BS1 195 A3
Lower Park St 27 GL54 176 F4
Lower Poole Rd GL11 80 B8
Lower Quay St GL1 196 A3
Lower Rd Berry Hill GL16 155 A7
Ledbury HR8 178 E8
St Briavels GL15 146 E7
Upper Soudley GL14 156 C5
Yorkley GL15 156 A2
Lower Redland Mews 2 BS6 18 B2
Lower Redland Rd BS6 18 B2
Lower Sidney St BS3 8 A4
Lower Spillman's GL5 99 A6
Lower St Blockley GL56 186 C5
Stroud GL5 99 D6
Whiteshill GL6 102 F3
Lower Station Rd
4 Bristol, Ridgeway BS16 20 A4
Bristol, Staplehill BS16 20 C4
Lower Stone Cl BS36 31 C7
Lower Terr 8 GL56 186 C5
Lower Thirlmere Rd BS34 29 A8
Lower Tockington Rd BS32 50 B1
Lower Tuffley La GL2 118 B4
Lower Washwell La GL6 104 A8
Loweswater Cl GL51 129 F7
Loweswater Rd GL51 129 F7
Lowfield Rd GL8 140 B5
Lowlis Cl BS10 27 F3
Lowther Rd BS10 28 C2
Loxton Sq BS14 3 A6
Lucas Cl BS4 9 D1
Luccombe Hill BS6 18 B2
Lucinia Mews GL51 132 F3
Luckington Court Gdns★ SN14 47 F5
Luckington Cty Prim Sch SN14 47 E5
Luckington Rd BS7 18 E8
Luckley Ave BS13 2 C5
Luckwell Prim Sch BS3 8 A3
Luckwell Rd BS3 8 B3
Lucky La BS3 8 D4
Ludgate Hill GL12 68 B7
Ludlow Cl
Bristol, St Pauls BS2 18 F1
Bristol, Willsbridge BS30 11 B2
Keynsham BS31 4 D5
Ludlow Ct BS30 11 B1
Ludlow Rd BS7 19 A7
Ludwell Cl BS36 30 D5
Luggs The GL10 98 A3
Luke La GL3 127 E6
Lullington Rd BS4 9 B2
Lulsgate Rd BS13 2 A8
Lulworth Cres BS16 20 F8
Lulworth Rd BS31 4 E4
Lurgan Wlk BS4 8 D1
Lurks La GL6 103 B4
Lushill Cotts SN6 144 E5
Lux Furlong BS9 17 B7
Luxton St BS5 9 B8
Lych Gate Mews GL15 92 A2
Lydbrook Cl BS37 32 D8
Lydbrook Prim Sch GL17 163 D2
Lyddington Rd BS7 18 F8
Lyde Green Rdbt BS16 21 B8
Lydfield Rd GL15 92 B3
Lydford Wlk BS3 8 C2
Lydiard Croft BS15 10 C4
Lydney & District Hospl GL15 147 F6
Lydney CE Com Prim Sch GL15 92 A3
Lydney Ind Est GL15 84 C8
Lydney Junc Sta★ GL15 92 A1
Lydney Rd Bream GL15 147 D8
Bristol, Southmead BS10 28 D1
Bristol, Staple Hill BS16 20 E4
Lydney Sta GL15 84 A8
Lydney Town Sta★ GL15 92 A3
Lydstep Terr BS3 8 C4
Lye La GL52 138 D1
Lyefield Rd E GL53 131 B6
Lyefield Rd W GL53 131 A6
Lygon Ct GL7 152 E3
Lygon Wlk 3 GL51 132 F3
Lyley Ho GL12 68 A7
Lynch Ct BS30 10 F4
Lynch Rd Berkeley GL13 85 D3
Chalford GL6 148 D6
Lyncombe Wlk BS16 20 B2
Lyncroft GL2 116 F7
Lyncroft Farm Wkshps GL7 150 C8
Lyndale Ave BS9 17 D5
Lyndale Rd Bristol BS5 9 D8
Yate BS37 43 D1
Lyndale Terr
Cheltenham GL51 133 A2
Norton GL2 173 B3
Lynde Cl BS13 2 B4
Lyndhurst Cl GL52 138 B3
Lyndhurst Rd Bristol BS9 17 F7
Keynsham BS31 4 F3
Lyndley Chase GL52 137 D4
Lyng Cl GL4 119 E8
Lynmouth Rd
3 Bristol BS2 19 A2
Gloucester GL3 119 F7
Lynn Rd BS16 19 D5
Lynt Farm Cotts SN6 145 D7
Lynt Rd SN6 145 D7
Lynton 3 BS15 11 A8
Lynton Pl 9 BS5 9 C8
Lynton Rd Bristol BS3 8 D2
Gloucester GL3 119 F7
Lynton Way BS16 30 B1
Lynwood Rd Bristol BS3 8 B2
Lydney GL15 92 A5
Lynworth Ct 5 GL52 134 A3
Lynworth Exchange 9 GL52 134 A3
Lynworth La GL20 181 F8
Lynworth Pl GL52 134 A3
Lynworth Prim Sch GL52 134 B3
Lynworth Terr GL52 134 B4
Lyons Court Rd BS14 3 D7
Lypiatt Dr GL50 193 A2
Lypiatt La GL50 193 A2
Lypiatt Mews GL50 193 A2
Lypiatt Rd GL50 193 A2
Lypiatt St GL50 193 A1
Lypiatt View GL6 148 B6
Lyppiatt Rd BS5 9 D8
Lyppincourt Rd BS10 28 A3
Lysander Ct GL3 128 C5
Lysander Rd BS10,BS34 28 C6
Lysander Wlk BS34 29 E5
Lysons Ave GL1 118 D7
Lytchet Dr BS16 20 F8
Lytes Cary Rd BS31 5 A3
Lytton Gr Bristol BS7 19 A8
Keynsham BS31 5 A5
Lyveden Gdns BS13 2 B5
Lyvedon Way BS41 7 B1

M

Mabel's Furlong 12 HR8 178 F8
Macarthur Rd GL54 168 A1
Macauley Rd BS7 19 A8
Macdonald Wlk 3 BS15 10 D8
Macey's Rd BS13 2 D3
Machen Rd GL16 155 B6
Machin Cl BS10 27 F3
Machin Gdns BS10 28 A3
Machin Rd BS10 28 A3
Mackenzie Way GL51 133 A5
Mackie Ave BS34 29 B2
Mackie Gr BS34 29 B2
Mackie Rd BS34 29 B2
Macrae Ct BS15 10 E8
Macrae Rd BS20 16 E4
Madeline Rd BS16 19 F2
Madison Cl BS37 43 D2
Madleaze Ind Est GL1 196 A1
Madleaze Rd GL1 196 A1
Madocke Rd NP16 61 A7
Maesbury BS15 10 E6
Maesbury Rd BS31 5 A2
Maesknoll La BS14 3 B1
Maesknoll Rd BS4 9 A2
Magdala Rd 1 GL1 127 A1
Magdalen Rd GL8 140 B4
Magdalene Pl BS2 18 F1
Maggs Cl BS10 28 C3
Maggs La Bristol BS5 19 E2
Whitchurch BS14 3 C4
Magnolia Cl NP16 60 F5
Magnolia Ct 1 GL51 132 D2
Magnolia Wlk GL2 117 E1
Magpie Bottom La
Bristol BS15 10 C6
Bristol BS5 10 B6
Magpie Ct GL10 97 F8
Maida Vale Rd GL53 130 D6
Maiden Way BS11 16 C8
Maidencroft GL7 144 F7
Maidenhall GL2 125 D5
Maidenhead Rd BS13 2 D3
Maidenhill Sch GL10 101 F1
Maidstone St BS3 8 F3
Main Rd Bristol BS16 21 D5
Mile End GL16 155 B6
Netherend GL15 147 D3
Pillowell GL15 155 F1
Tintern Parva NP16 146 B3
Whiteshill GL6 102 F3
Woolaston GL15 147 C2
Main St Adlestrop GL56 177 E6
Beckford GL20 183 B6
Bledington OX7 177 E1
Bretforton WR11 188 A6
Willersey WR12 188 B2
Main View BS36 31 D7
Mainard Sq GL2 127 C5
Maine St GL7 152 E2
Maisemore BS37 32 E6
Maisemore Ave BS34 40 B1
Maitlands GL4 110 F5
Makin Cl BS30 11 C5
Malago Rd BS3 8 D3
Malago Vale Est BS3 8 D3
Malago Wlk BS13 1 E4
Malden Rd GL52 133 E3
Maldon Gdns GL1 118 F7
Maldowers La 2 BS5 10 A8
Malet Cl GL2 127 C5
Mall The Bristol, Clifton BS8 7 F7
Bristol, Cribbs Causeway BS34 28 D6
Mallard Cl
Bristol, Crofts End BS5 19 F1
Bristol, Patchway BS32 40 D2
Chipping Sodbury BS37 33 A8
Quedgeley GL2 117 D1
Malleson Rd GL52 137 F8
Mallow Cl BS35 64 D2
Malmains Dr BS16 30 B1
Malmesbury Cl
Bristol, Bishopston BS6 18 C4
Bristol, Longwell Green BS30 10 F5
Malmesbury Rd
Cheltenham GL51 133 A5
Gloucester GL4 119 B7
Leigh SN6 143 C3
Malmsey Cl GL20 192 D1
Malthouse Cl SN26 144 E1
Malthouse La
Cheltenham GL50 133 D3
Lower Slaughter GL54 176 C1
17 Winchcombe GL54 174 A7
Malthouse Wlk 9 GL8 140 B4
Malvern Ct BS5 9 F7
Malvern Dr Bristol BS30 11 C5
Thornbury BS35 51 D8

Malvern Gdns GL5 98 E7
Malvern Pl GL50 193 A3
Malvern Rd
Bristol, Brislington BS4 9 D3
Bristol, St George BS5 9 F7
Cheltenham GL50 133 B1
Gloucester GL1 126 F4
Staunton GL19 172 B8
Malvern St GL51 133 B4
Malvern View Bsns Pk GL52 137 C4
Malvern Way GL16 155 C8
Malverns The GL4 119 D6
Manchester Ct 4 GL56 187 A3
Manchester Pk GL51 133 B4
Manchester Way 1 GL50 193 A4
Mancroft Ave BS11 16 F7
Mandalay Dr GL2 173 B3
Mandara Gr GL4 119 D4
Mandarin Way GL50 133 C5
Mandeville Cl GL2 127 C6
Mangotsfield CE Sch BS16 21 B6
Mangotsfield Rd BS16 21 A5
Mangotsfield Sch BS16 21 B4
Manilla Rd BS8 194 A3
Mankley Rd GL10 97 F4
Manley Gdns GL2 127 C5
Mannings Rd GL17 164 B4
Manor Ave Dursley GL11 87 F5
Lechlade on T GL7 153 F2
Manor Cl
Broad Blunsdon SN26 144 E1
Cirencester GL7 150 C7
Coalpit Heath BS36 31 C6
Dursley GL11 87 F6
Easton-in-G BS20 16 A4
8 Fairford GL7 152 E4
Honeybourne WR11 188 C6
Sherston SN16 58 C1
Teddington GL20 183 A3
Tockington BS32 50 C1
Manor Cl The BS8 7 A8
Manor Cotts Pitt Ct GL11 79 F5
Sopworth SN14 57 D1
Manor Court Dr BS7 18 E7
Manor Ct
Bristol, Fishponds BS16 19 E4
9 Bristol, Upper Easton BS5 19 B1
Gloucester GL4 119 B4
Swindon GL51 133 A6
Whitminster GL2 100 F5
Manor Dr GL5 99 A1
Manor Farm Bristol BS32 29 D8
Little Rissington GL54 169 C6
Manor Farm Cl OX7 177 F3
Manor Farm Cotts GL8 141 A6
Manor Farm Cres BS32 40 D1
Manor Field GL54 183 F1
Manor Gardens Ho BS16 20 A5
Manor Gdns
Gloucester GL4 119 E8
Lechlade on T GL7 153 E2
Newnham GL14 156 F6
Woodchester GL5 99 A2
Manor Gr
Bristol, Mangotsfield BS16 21 A4
Bristol, Patchway BS34 40 B2
Manor Ho 6 BS5 19 B1
Manor La
Bretforton WR11 188 A6
Charfield GL12 67 A4
Gotherington GL52 138 B7
Winterbourne BS36 30 F7
Wooton-u-E GL12 68 C7
Manor Orch SN6 143 F4
Manor Park Bsns Ctr GL51 133 A5
Manor Pk Bristol BS6 18 B3
Cheltenham GL51 129 D5
Gloucester GL2 127 E4
Tewkesbury GL20 192 E6
Tockington BS32 50 C1
Manor Pl Bristol BS16 30 C1
Tewkesbury GL20 192 D1
Manor Prim Sch The BS36 31 D6
Manor Rd Abbots Leigh BS8 7 A8
Bristol, Bishopston BS7 18 E4
Bristol, Bishopsworth BS13 2 A6
Bristol, Fishponds BS16 20 A5
Bristol, Mangotsfield BS16 21 A4
Cheltenham GL51 133 A6
Lydney GL15 92 C3
Rangeworthy BS37 43 A7
Saltford BS31 5 C2
Wick BS30 12 C5
Manor St GL6 105 A1
Manor The GL3 128 C4
Manor View
St Arvans NP16 72 B5
Stroud GL5 98 E4
Manor Way BS37 44 C2
Manor Wlk BS35 64 B3
Manse Gdns 4 GL51 129 F7
Manse La The HR9 170 B5
Manse Rd GL17 164 B4
Mansel Cl BS31 5 C3
Mansell Cl GL2 118 C5
Manser St GL50 133 D3
Mansfield Mews GL2 109 F7
Mansfield St BS3 8 C2
Manson's La NP25 162 A1
Manston Cl BS14 3 C7
Manworthy Rd BS4 9 D3
Manx Rd BS7 18 F8
Maple Ave Bristol BS16 20 C3
Chepstow NP16 60 E5
Thornbury BS35 64 C1
Maple Cl
Bristol, Little Stoke BS34 29 C7
Bristol, Oldland BS30 11 B4
Bristol, Stockwood BS14 3 D5
Dursley GL11 88 A3
Hardwicke GL2 109 E8
Maple Ct Bristol BS9 17 F8
Gloucester GL2 127 E4
5 Bristol BS15 20 D1
Maple Dr
Brockworth GL3 120 D7
Charlton Kings GL53 131 B5
Stroud GL5 103 A1
Maple Leaf Ct BS8 194 A3
Maple Rd
Bristol, Horfield BS7 18 E5
Bristol, St Anne's BS4 9 D5
Maple Wlk Keynsham BS31 4 D4
Pucklechurch BS16 22 C5
Mapledean GL14 191 C5
Maplefield GL15 147 E5
Mapleleaze BS4 9 D3
Maplemeade BS7 18 C4
Mapleridge La BS37 44 D7
Maples The
Cirencester GL7 190 B1
Gloucester GL4 119 E6
Maplestone Rd BS14 3 A3
Mapstone Cl BS16 30 B3
Marbeck Rd BS10 28 B1
Marchant Cl GL51 132 F3
Mardale Cl BS10 28 C2
Marden Rd BS31 5 A4
Mardon Rd BS4 9 D6
Mardyke Ferry Rd BS1 194 B1
Marefield Cl GL4 119 E7
Marfells Way GL17 163 F3
Margaret Rd Bristol BS13 1 F4
3 Ledbury HR8 178 E8
Tewkesbury GL20 192 D3
Margate St BS3 8 F3
Margery La GL15 154 F2
Margrett Rd GL50 133 D3
Marguerite Rd BS13 1 F7
Marian Ct GL1 196 A3
Marian La GL16 155 A7
Marians Wlk GL16 155 A7
Marigold Wlk BS3 8 A2
Marina Gdns BS16 19 E3
Marina The GL15 84 B8
Marine Gdns GL16 155 A5
Marine Par BS20 16 C5
Mariner's Way BS20 16 C5
Mariners Dr BS9 17 D4
Mariners Way NP16 61 A4
Mariners' Path BS9 17 E3
Marion Rd BS15 10 B3
Marion Wlk BS5 10 A7
Marissal Cl BS10 27 E3
Marissal Rd BS10 27 E3
Mariston Way BS30 11 C6
Marjoram Cl 2 GL4 119 F5
Marjoram Pl BS32 29 F7
Mark La BS1 194 C2
Market Cl GL54 168 F8
Market La GL54 184 A1
Market Par GL1 196 B3
Market Pl Berkeley GL13 85 E3
Cirencester GL7 190 C5
Coleford GL16 155 A5
11 Fairford GL7 152 E4
Lechlade on T GL7 153 E2
Marshfield SN14 15 A8
11 Tetbury GL8 140 C4
Market Sq Bristol BS16 20 C3
Minchinhampton GL6 148 A3
14 Newent GL18 171 A4
Stow-on-t-W GL54 176 F4
Market St
Cheltenham GL50 193 A4
Cinderford GL14 191 D5
Ledbury HR8 178 E8
Nailsworth GL6 91 B3
Wooton-u-E GL12 68 B7
Market Way GL1 196 B2
Marketside BS2 9 B4
Markham Cl BS11 16 C7
Marklands BS9 17 E3
Marksbury Rd BS3 8 D2
Marlborough Ave 13 BS16 19 E3
Marlborough Cl
Bishop's Cleeve GL52 137 E3
Charlton Kings GL53 130 F6
Marlborough Cres GL4 119 A7
Marlborough Dr BS16 30 B1
Marlborough Flats 8 BS2 195 A4
Marlborough Hill BS2 195 A4
Marlborough Hill Pl BS2 195 A4
Marlborough Pl GL52 133 F1
Marlborough Rd GL4 119 A7
Marlborough St
Bristol, Eastville BS5 19 E3
Bristol, Kingsdown BS2 195 A4
Marlbrook Prim Sch BS35 64 C2
Marle Hill GL6 148 C5
Marle Hill Par GL50 133 D3
Marle Hill Rd GL50 133 D3
Marlepit Gr BS13 1 F6
Marley La GL6 148 D5
Marleyfield Cl 3 GL3 128 A7
Marleyfield Way GL3 128 A7
Marlfield Wlk BS13 1 E7
Marling Cl GL5 91 C8
Marling Cres GL5 98 F7
Marling Rd BS5 9 F8
Marling Sch GL5 98 F7
Marlstone Rd GL11 88 A4
Marlwood Dr BS10 28 A3
Marlwood Sch BS32 50 F5
Marmaduke St BS3 8 F3
Marment Rd GL11 87 E4
Marmion Cres BS10 27 F3
Marne Cl BS14 3 D5
Marram Cl GL4 119 F5
Marsh Cl
Cheltenham GL51 133 C3
Winterbourne BS36 30 E5
Marsh Comm BS35 38 D6
Marsh Ct 1 GL56 187 A3
Marsh Dr GL51 133 C4
Marsh Gdns GL51 133 C3
Marsh La
Bristol, Ashton Vale BS3 8 B2
Bristol, Redfield BS5 9 C6
Burton SN14,GL9 36 C4
Cheltenham GL51 133 C3
Easton-in-G BS20 16 A4
Frampton on Severn GL2 157 F1
Leonard Stanley GL10 97 F3
Marsh Mews GL10 97 F4
Marsh Rd Bristol BS3 7 F3
Chepstow NP16 60 F5
Leonard Stanley GL10 97 E4
Marsh St Avonmouth BS11 16 C8
4 Bristol BS1 195 A2
Marsh Terr GL51 129 D2
Marsh Way GL16 155 B2
Marshacre La BS35 49 F6
Marshall Ho 1 BS16 19 F4
Marshall Wlk BS4 2 D7
Marshall's La GL14 191 D5
Marsham Way BS30 10 F4
Marshfield CE Prim Sch SN14 15 A8
Marshfield La BS30 12 D1
Marshfield Rd
Bristol, Frenchay BS16 20 C8
Bristol, Hillfields BS16 20 C4
Tormarton GL9 34 E1
Marshmouth La GL54 169 A6
Marshwall La BS32 39 E6
Marsland Rd GL51 132 D2
Marston Rd Bristol BS4 9 B3
Cheltenham GL52 133 F4
Martcombe Rd BS20 16 C2
Marten Cl GL4 120 A5
Marten Rd NP16 60 E6
Martin Cl Bristol BS34 28 E8
Cirencester GL7 190 C3
Martin Ct 12 BS16 19 E3
Martin St 2 BS3 8 B3
Martin's Rd BS15 10 C5
Martindale Rd GL3 128 B6
Martingale Rd BS4 9 D4
Martins Cl BS15 10 C5
Martins The Stroud GL5 98 D8
Tutshill NP16 73 A1
Martins Way HR8 178 E7
Martlock Cres BS3 8 C1
Martock Rd Bristol BS3 8 C2
Keynsham BS31 5 A3
Martor Ind Est SN14 25 A2
Marwood Rd BS4 2 E8
Mary Carpenter Pl 15 BS2 18 F1
Mary Ct 1 BS5 9 D8
Mary Godwin Ct 1 GL51 132 F4
Mary Gr GL2 125 D5
Mary Rose Ave GL3 127 F7
Mary St BS5 9 D8
Marybrook St GL13 85 E3
Marybush La BS2 195 B3
Marygold Leaze BS30 11 A4
Mascot Rd BS3 8 D3
Masefield Ave GL2 118 C4
Masefield Cl 8 HR8 178 E8
Masefield Rd GL7 190 B2
Masefield Way BS7 19 A6
Maskelyne Ave BS10 18 D7
Mason Ct GL13 85 E3
Mason Rd GL5 99 F7
Masons View BS36 30 F7
Massey Par 4 GL1 118 F7
Massey Rd GL1 119 A7
Massey Sham Ave GL56 187 C3
Matchells Cl BS4 9 E6
Materman Rd BS14 3 E5
Matford Cl Bristol BS10 28 D4
Winterbourne BS36 30 E5
Matford La GL13 77 F4
Mathern Cres NP16 60 B4
Mathern Rd NP16 60 D5
Mathern Way NP16 60 E5
Mathews Way GL5 99 A8
Matson Ave GL4 119 C3
Matson La GL4 119 B3
Matson Pl GL1 119 A7
Matthew's Rd 17 BS5 9 C7
Matthews Cl BS14 3 F6
Maud's Elm Ho GL51 133 B4
Maugersbury Cl GL54 176 F4
Maugersbury Pk GL54 176 F4
Maules La BS16 29 F2
Maunsell Rd BS11 27 B2
Maurice Rd BS6 18 E2
Mautravers Cl BS32 29 D7
Maverdine Ct GL1 196 A3
Mawdeley Ho 11 BS3 8 C4
Mawley Rd GL7 152 D7
Maxse Rd BS4 9 B2
May Bush La HR9 162 E2
May Evans Cl GL11 87 F5
May Gr GL12 67 B5
May La Dursley GL11 88 A1
Ebrington GL55 189 D2
May Meadow La GL17 164 D5
May Park Prim Sch BS5 19 C2
May St BS15 20 C1
May Tree Cl GL7 149 E3
May Tree Sq GL4 119 C7
May Tree Wlk BS31 4 C3
May Trees GL50 193 A2
May's Cres 6 GL54 168 A1
Mayall Ct GL4 119 C3
Mayalls Cl GL19 172 F7
Mayalls The GL20 182 A7
Maybank Rd BS37 43 D1
Maybec Gdns BS5 10 A6
Maybourne BS4 10 A2
Maycliffe Pk BS6 18 F2
Mayfair Cl GL2 118 C8
Mayfield Ave BS16 20 A2
Mayfield Cl GL52 137 F2
Mayfield Ct BS16 20 A3
Mayfield Dr GL3 119 F8
Mayfield Ho 8 GL50 130 B8
Mayfield Pk BS16 20 A2
Mayfield Pk N BS16 20 A2
Mayfield Pk S BS16 20 A2
Mayfields BS31 4 E5
Mayhill Ind Est NP25 154 A7
Maynard Cl BS13 2 C5
Maynard Rd BS13 2 C5
Mayors Bldgs BS16 20 B5
Maypole Gn 3 GL15 147 D8
Maypole Rd GL15 147 D8
Maypole Terr GL5 98 F8
Mays La GL8 140 B8
Maythorn Dr GL51 132 D4
Maytree Ave BS13 2 B7
Maytree Cl BS13 2 B7
Mayville Ave BS34 29 A3
Maywood Ave 3 BS16 20 B4
Maywood Cres BS16 20 B4
Maywood Rd BS16 20 C4
Maze St BS5 9 B6
Maze Wlk GL16 155 A7
McAdam Way BS1 7 F5
Mead Cl Bristol BS11 16 E6
Cheltenham GL53 130 E5
15 Moreton-in-M GL56 187 A3
Mead Ct Bsns Pk BS35 51 B8
Mead La Aylburton GL15 147 F4
Lydney GL15 84 A8
Saltford BS31 5 F4
Tockington BS35 49 D2
Mead Rd Bristol BS34 29 F5
Cheltenham GL53 130 E5
Chipping Sodbury BS37 44 C1
Gloucester GL4 119 E5
Mead Rise BS3 8 F4
Mead St BS3 195 C1
Mead The Alveston BS35 51 A5
3 Ashton Keynes SN6 142 F4
Bristol BS34 29 B4
Cirencester GL7 190 B5
Dundry BS41 1 D2
Mead Way BS35 51 B7
Meade-King Gr GL52 138 B3
Meadgate BS16 21 B7
Meadow Cl Bristol BS16 20 F7
Cheltenham GL51 132 C1
Cirencester GL7 190 C3
Tewkesbury GL20 192 E6
Viney Hill GL15 156 C1
Meadow Court Dr BS30 11 C3
Meadow Ct 2 GL10 97 F8
Meadow Gr BS11 16 D7
Meadow La 9 GL51 129 E5
Meadow La W GL5 98 E6
Meadow Mead
Frampton Cotterell BS36 31 B8
Yate BS37 43 E5
Meadow Orch 4 WR12 185 B8
Meadow Rd
Chipping Sodbury BS37 44 A1
Cinderford GL14 191 E5
Cirencester GL7 190 C3
Cromhall GL12 66 B4
Honeybourne WR11 188 A8
Stonehouse GL10 97 F8
Meadow St
Avonmouth BS11 26 A1
Bristol BS2 195 C4
Meadow Vale Bristol BS5 20 A1
Dursley GL11 87 F4
Meadow View
Cirencester GL7 150 D7
Frampton Cotterell BS36 31 D7
Kempsford GL7 144 E8
Meadow Way Bristol BS32 29 E7
Churchdown GL3 128 B7
Kingham OX7 177 F2
South Cerney GL7 142 F8
Stroud GL5 98 E6
Meadow Wlk
Chepstow NP16 60 D8
Sling GL16 155 B2
Meadoway GL52 137 E2
Meadowbank GL15 92 C3
Meadowcroft Bristol BS16 21 A8
Gloucester GL4 119 E5
Meadowland Rd BS10 27 E4
Meadowleaze GL2 127 D3
Meadows End GL17 164 F6
Meadows Prim Sch The BS30 5 D8
Meadows The BS15 10 D4
Meadowside 2 BS35 51 D8
Meadowside Dr BS14 3 A3
Meadowside Prim Sch GL2 117 F2
Meadowsweet Ave BS34 29 B3
Meads Cl
Bishop's Cleeve GL52 138 A3
4 Coleford GL16 155 A6
Meads Ct NP16 60 E6
Meads The Bristol BS16 20 F7
Burton SN14 36 B3
Leighterton GL8 70 C3
Meadvale Cl GL2 126 F6
Meadway BS9 17 C6
Meadway Rd GL10 97 E6
Meardon Rd BS14 3 E6
Mechanical Organ Mus* GL17 164 B5
Mede Cl BS1 195 B1
Medical Ave BS2,BS8 194 C3
Medina Cl BS35 51 C7
Medoc Cl GL50 133 C5
Medway Cl BS31 5 A3
Medway Cres GL3 120 F5
Medway Ct
Cheltenham GL52 134 A2
Thornbury BS35 51 D8
Medway Dr
Frampton Cotterell BS36 31 B7
Keynsham BS31 5 A3
Meeks Hill NP25 154 B1
Meeks Well La HR9 162 E3
Meend Gardens Terr GL14 191 D3
Meend La GL17 163 F4
Meendhurst Rd GL14 191 C4
Meerbrook Way GL2 109 F7
Meere Bank BS11 27 B1
Meerstone Way GL4 119 D3
Meg Thatcher's Gdns BS5 10 B7
Meg Thatchers Cl BS5 10 B7
Melbourne Cl
Cheltenham GL53 130 C6
Stonehouse GL10 101 F1
Melbourne Dr
Chipping Sodbury BS37 44 C1
Stonehouse GL10 101 E1
Melbourne Rd BS7 18 D4
Melbourne St GL1 119 A7
Melbourne St E GL1 118 F7
Melbourne St W GL1 118 F7
Melbury Rd BS4 9 A2
Meldon Terr GL5 99 B7
Melick Cl GL4 119 A5
Melita Rd BS6 18 E3
Mellent Ave BS13 2 C3
Mellersh Ho GL50 193 A1
Mells Cl BS31 5 A2
Melmore Gdns GL7 190 E2
Melody Way GL2 127 E5
Melrose Ave Bristol BS8 194 B4
Yate BS37 44 A2
Melrose Cl BS37 44 A2
Melrose Pl BS8 194 B4
Melton Cres BS7 19 A7
Melville GL54 168 F8
Melville Rd Bristol BS6 18 B1
Churchdown GL3 128 B5
Melville Terr BS3 8 C3
Melvin Sq BS4 8 E1
Memorial Cl BS15 10 B4
Memorial Cotts GL7 152 D8
Memorial Rd BS15 10 B4
Mendip Cl
Cheltenham GL52 134 A3
Keynsham BS31 4 D5
Quedgeley GL2 109 E8
Mendip Cres BS16 21 A8
Mendip Ho 7 GL52 134 A3
Mendip Rd Bristol BS3 8 D3
Cheltenham GL52 134 A3
Mendip View BS30 12 C7
Mendip View Ave BS16 20 A3
Meon Rd GL55 189 B7
Mercer Ct BS14 3 B8
Merchant St BS1 195 B3
Merchants Ct BS8 194 A1
Merchants Mead GL2 117 D1
Merchants Quay BS1 195 A1
Merchants Rd
Bristol, Clifton BS8 194 A3
Bristol, Hotwells BS8 194 A1
Merchants The SN14 47 E4
Merchants Trad Pk BS2 9 C6
Merchants' Rd GL2 196 A2
Mercia Dr BS2 19 A2
Mercia Rd
Gloucester GL1 196 B4
Winchcombe GL54 139 F6
Mercian Cl GL7 190 D3
Mercian Ct GL50 193 A1
Mercian Way NP16 61 A7
Mercier Cl BS37 43 F2
Mercury Way GL4 119 F6
Meredith Ct BS1 194 A1
Merestones Cl GL50 130 B6
Merestones Dr GL50 130 B6
Merestones Rd GL50 130 B6
Merevale Rd GL2 127 C3
Merfield Rd BS4 9 B2
Meridian Pl BS8 194 B3
Meridian Rd BS6 18 C1

Meridian Vale BS8 .....194 B3
Meriet Ave BS13 ....2 B4
Merioneth St BS3 ....8 F3
Meriton St BS2 ....9 B5
Merlin Cl Bristol BS9 .....17 F8
Cheltenham GL53 ....130 C5
Merlin Ct BS10 ....18 B7
Merlin Dr GL2 ....117 F2
Merlin Haven GL12 ....68 A7
Merlin Rd BS10,BS34 .....28 C6
Merlin Ridge BS16 ......22 C4
Merlin Way
Cheltenham GL53 ....130 C5
Chipping Sodbury BS37 ....32 F8
Merrett Ct BS7 ....19 B6
Merrett's Orch GL2 .....95 D3
Merrick Ct BS1 ....195 A1
Merricks La NP16 ......146 D4
Merrimans Rd BS11 .....16 D8
Merrin St GL17 ....164 D5
Merriville Gdns GL51 ...133 A3
Merriville Rd GL51 .....133 A3
Merryfields GL10 ......110 B1
Merrywalks GL5 ....99 B7
Merrywalks Sh Ctr 1
GL5 ....99 C7
Merryweather Cl BS32 ...29 D8
Merryweathers BS4 ......9 E2
Merrywood Cl 5 BS3 .....8 C4
Merrywood Rd BS3 ....8 C4
Merrywood Sch BS4 ......8 F1
Mersey Rd GL52 ....134 A2
Merstham Rd 12 BS2 ....19 A2
Merthyr Terr GL17 .....163 D2
Merton Cl GL10 ....98 B6
Merton Rd BS7 ....18 E5
Mertons The GL14 .....156 F6
Mervyn Rd BS7 ....18 E4
Meryl Ct BS6 ....18 B1
Meteor Way GL3 ....120 E5
Metford Gr BS6 ....18 B3
Metford Pl BS6 ....18 C3
Metford Rd BS6 ....18 C3
Metz Way GL1,GL4 ......119 B8
Mews The
Highworth SN6 ....145 D3
Tewkesbury GL20 ....192 C4
Meysey Cl GL7 ....152 B3
Meysey Hampton CE Sch
GL7 ....152 A3
Michaelmas Ct GL1 ....127 A3
Michaels Mead GL7 ....190 B2
Michaels Way GL16 ....155 B2
Mickle Mead GL2 ......125 D5
Mickleton Rd
Honeybourne WR11 .....188 D7
Ilmington CV36 ....189 F7
Mid Gloucester Tech Coll
GL7 ....190 D4
Middi Haines Ct SN6 ...145 D3
Middle Ave BS1 ....195 A2
Middle Croft GL4 ......119 D7
Middle Farm Ct GL7 ...144 E8
Middle Ground SN6 ....143 E4
Middle Hill Chalford GL6 .148 C6
Stroud GL5 ....99 E7
Middle Hill Cres GL6 ...148 C6
Middle Leazes GL5 .....99 D7
Middle Orch OX7 ......177 E1
Middle Rd Bristol BS15 ...20 F3
Little Barrington OX18 ....161 D7
Thrupp GL5 ....99 E3
Middle Spillman's GL5 ..99 A6
Middle Spring GL6 .....102 F3
Middle St Chepstow NP16 .60 E8
Stroud, Bowbridge GL5 ....99 D7
Stroud, Uplands GL5 ......99 C8
Middle Tynings GL6 .....91 A4
Middle Way NP16 ....60 F5
Middlecroft GL10 ....96 F7
Middledown Rd SN14 ...24 C1
Middleford Ho BS13 ......2 C4
Middlehay Ct GL52 .....137 E3
Middlemoor Mill GL5 ....91 A6
Middleton Lawn GL3 ...127 E6
Middleton Rd BS11 ......16 F8
Midland Ct GL7 ....190 D3
Midland Rd Bristol BS2 ..195 C3
Bristol, Staple Hill BS16 ...20 D4
Cirencester GL7 ....190 D2
Gloucester GL1 ....196 B1
Stonehouse GL10 ....97 E8
Midland St BS2 ....195 C2
Midland Terr BS16 .....19 F3
Midland Way BS35 ......51 C7
Midsummer Wlk GL1 ...118 C6
Midway GL6 ....148 C6
Midwinter Ave GL51 ...133 C3
Midwinter Gdns GL50 ..133 C5
Midwinter Rd 4 GL54 ..168 A1
Mildred St BS5 ....9 C7
Mile End Rd GL16 ......155 B6
Mile Wlk BS14 ....3 A6
Miles Cotts GL16 ......155 A3
Miles Ct BS30 ....10 F4
Miles Rd BS8 ....18 A1
Milestone Sch The GL2 .127 B5
Milestone Wlk GL16 ....155 B2
Milford Ave BS30 ....12 B7
Milford Cl GL2 ....127 B5
Milford St BS3 ....8 C4
Mill Ave Bristol BS1 .....195 A2
Broadway WR12 ....185 A8
Mill Cl 9 Blockley GL56 ..186 C5
Frampton Cotterell BS36 ...31 C7
South Cerney GL7 ....143 A8
Wooton-u-E GL12 ....68 C6
Mill Cres BS37 ....32 B4
Mill Ct 11 GL18 ....171 A4
Mill End GL17 ....164 D5
Mill Farm Dr GL5 ....98 E8
Mill Gr GL2 ....117 D1
Mill Hill NP16 ....146 D4
Mill Ho 10 BS5 ....19 A1
Mill La Avening GL8 .....140 B8
Bitton BS30 ....5 E8
Bristol, Bedminster BS3 ....8 D4
Bristol, Warmley BS30 ....11 C5
Brockworth GL3 ....120 F6
Castle Eaton SN26 ......144 D6
Charlton Kings GL54 .....131 D8
Chipping Sodbury BS37 ....33 E6
Cranham GL4 ....112 D6
Doynton BS30 ....22 F1
Fairford GL7 ....152 D4
Falfield GL12 ....65 F7
Frampton Cotterell BS36 ...42 B1
Gorsley GL18 ....170 C3
Greet GL54 ....184 A1
Lechlade on T GL7 ....153 F2
Longhope GL17 ....165 A5
Lowbands GL19 ....179 F2
Lower Slaughter GL54 ...176 C1
Lower Swell GL54 ....176 D4
Mickleton GL55 ....189 A6
Prestbury GL52 ....134 D4
Stanton Fitzwarren SN6 ..145 A1
Staunton GL19 ....179 F1
Stoke Orchard GL51,GL52 .136 D5
Tockington BS32 ....50 B1
Upper Strensham WR8 ...180 E7
Upton Cheyney BS30 ......11 F1
Winchcombe GL54 ....174 A7
Mill Pitt Gdns GL3 .....120 A8
Mill Pl GL1 ....119 A7
Mill Rd BS36 ....30 D4
Mill Row Blockley GL56 ..186 D6
King's Stanley GL10 ....98 A5
Lower Lydbrook GL17 ....163 C3
Mill St Gloucester GL1 ...127 A1
Prestbury GL52 ....134 C5
Tewkesbury GL20 ....192 B4
Mill Stps BS36 ....30 E4
Mill View
Cirencester GL7 ....150 D7
Northleach GL54 ....168 A1
Mill Way GL11 ....87 F4
Millard Cl BS10 ....28 D2
Millbank GL11 ....88 A4
Millbank Cl BS4 ....9 E3
Millbook Ct 1 BS6 ......18 E1
Millbridge Rd GL3 .....120 A7
Millbrook GL5 ....148 A5
Millbrook Ave BS4 ....9 F3
Millbrook Cl Bristol BS30 .11 C6
4 Gloucester GL1 ......127 A1
Millbrook Ct GL50 .....193 A4
Millbrook Gdns
Cheltenham GL50 ....133 B2
Lea HR9 ....164 D8
Millbrook Gn GL15 .....147 E5
Millbrook Ley GL56 .....177 A6
Millbrook Pl GL5 ....99 D7
Millbrook Rd BS37 ......43 B2
Millbrook St
Cheltenham GL50 ....193 A4
Gloucester GL1 ....127 A1
Millend GL15 ....156 E1
Millend La GL10 ....97 A7
Millend Row GL10 ......97 A7
Millenium Cotts GL19 ..172 A7
Millennium Cl GL20 ...192 E2
Millennium Way GL7 ...190 F5
Miller Cl
Ashleworth GL19 ....172 D4
Gloucester GL2 ....127 D5
Miller Craddock Way 1
HR8 ....178 E7
Miller Ho BS8 ....194 A2
Millers Cl BS20 ....16 C4
Millers Dr BS30 ....11 D5
Millers Dyke GL2 ......117 D1
Millers Gn
Drybrook GL17 ....164 A4
Gloucester GL1 ....196 B3
Millers Way GL14 ......191 C4
Millfield BS35 ....64 C2
Millfield Dr BS30 ....11 C6
Millfields GL3 ....120 A8
Millground Rd BS13 ......1 F5
Millham Rd GL52 ......138 A4
Millhill La GL16 ....154 F3
Millhouse Dr GL50 .....133 C5
Milliman Cl BS13 ....2 C5
Millin Ave GL4 ....118 D2
Milling Cl SN6 ....143 A5
Milling Cres GL15 .....147 E5
Millmead Ho BS13 ....2 C4
Millpond End GL5 ....99 A2
Millpond Prim Sch BS5 ..19 A1
Millpond St 9 BS5 ....19 A1
Millpool Ct BS10 ....28 B1
Millpool Ct EPD BS9 ....18 B8
Mills Cl 2 WR12 ....185 B8
Millview GL56 ....186 C6
Millward Gr BS16 ....20 C4
Milne Pastures GL20 ...182 B4
Milne Wlk GL51 ....132 E4
Milner Gn BS30 ....11 A5
Milner Rd BS7 ....18 F5
Milo Pl GL1 ....118 E6
Milsom St Bristol BS5 .....9 A8
Cheltenham GL50 ....193 B4
Milton Ave
Cheltenham GL51 ....129 F8
Gloucester GL2 ....118 C5
Milton Cl BS37 ....43 D2
Milton Gr GL5 ....99 E7
Milton Pk 1 BS5 ....9 C7
Milton Pl GL7 ....152 D3
Milton Rd Bristol BS7 ....18 E6
Cheltenham GL51 ....132 F1
Yate BS37 ....43 D2
Milton St GL7 ....152 D3
Miltons Cl BS13 ....2 D4
Milverton Gdns BS6 .....18 F2
Milward Rd BS31 ....4 E6
Mimosa Ave GL51 ......130 A4
Mimosa Ct 6 GL3 ......128 A7
Mina Rd BS2 ....19 A2
Minchinhampton Prim Sch
GL6 ....148 A3
Mine Pitts La HR9 .....162 E3
Minehead Rd BS4 ....8 F1
Miners Wlk GL14 ......191 C4
Minerva Cl GL4 ....119 F6
Minerva Ct GL7 ....190 D4
Minerva Wlk GL15 ......92 B5
Minetts Ave GL52 .....138 A3
Minety CE Prim Sch
SN16 ....142 D1
Minety La SN16 ....142 A3
Miniature World Model
Village★ GL54 ....168 F7
Minnow La OX18 ......161 D7
Minor's La BS10 ....27 A8
Minsmere Rd BS31 ....5 A4
Minster Cl GL52 ....137 E4
Minster Ct 1 BS37 ......32 D7
Minster Gdns GL4 .....119 F6
Minsterworth CE Prim Sch
GL2 ....116 F7
Minstrel Way GL3 .....127 F8
Minto Rd BS2 ....19 A2
Minto Road Ind Ctr 8
BS2 ....19 A2
Minton Cl BS14 ....3 B5
Misarden Park Gdns★
GL6 ....106 B6
Misarden Park Woodland
Trail★ GL6 ....106 B6
Miserden CEPrim Sch
GL6 ....106 A6
Miserden Rd GL51 .....132 D1
Miss Grace's La NP16 ..146 E2
Mission Rd BS37 ....43 B4
Mistletoe Mews GL3 ...127 F6
Mitcheldean Endowed Prim
Sch GL17 ....164 D5
Mitchell La BS1 ....195 B2
Mitchell Wlk BS30 ....11 D7
Mitford Villas GL56 ....187 A3
Mitre Pitch GL12 ....68 C7
Mitre St GL53 ....193 C2
Mitton Ct GL20 ....192 E6
Mitton Manor Prim Sch
GL20 ....192 E6
Mitton Way GL20 ......192 E6
Mivart St BS5 ....19 B2
Moat Bank GL20 ....180 F7
Moat Ho GL4 ....119 B4
Moat La Huntley GL19 ...165 E8
Staunton GL19 ....172 A8
Uckington GL51 ....132 D6
Moat Prim Sch The GL4 119 B4
Moat The Kingham OX7 ...177 F3
Quedgeley GL2 ....117 F1
Mobley GL13 ....86 A3
Modecombe Gr BS10 ....27 F3
Moffat Rd GL6 ....91 A4
Mogg St BS2 ....19 A2
Mogridge Cl GL3 ......120 A7
Molesworth Cl BS13 .....2 A4
Molesworth Dr BS13 .....2 A4
Monarch Cl GL4 ....119 E4
Monica Dr GL50 ....133 E4
Monk Meadow Trad Est
GL2 ....118 C7
Monk Rd BS7 ....18 D4
Monk's Park Ave BS7 ....18 E8
Monkey Mdw GL20 .....182 C5
Monkey Puzzle Cl GL5 ...98 E6
Monks Ave BS15 ....10 B8
Monks Croft GL51 ......132 E1
Monks Ho 3 BS37 ....32 D7
Monks La GL20 ....182 C2
Monks Park Sch BS7 ....18 F8
Monks Park Way BS7 ....18 E8
Monks Wlk GL7 ....153 F2
Monkscroft Com Prim Sch
GL51 ....132 E1
Monkswell Cl NP25 .....154 A8
Monkswell Rd NP25 ....154 A8
Monkton Rd BS15 ....10 B5
Monmouth Com Sch
NP25 ....154 A8
Monmouth Hill BS32 ....39 E4
Monmouth Rd Bristol BS7 18 D4
Edge End GL16 ....155 C8
Keynsham BS31 ....4 D5
Pill BS20 ....16 C5
Monmouth St BS3 ....8 F3
Monsdale Cl BS10 ....28 A3
Monsdale Dr BS10 ......28 A2
Monson Ave GL50 .....193 B4
Montague Cl BS34 ......29 E5
Montague Ct 4 BS2 ....195 A4
Montague Flats 6 BS2 .195 A4
Montague Hill BS2 .....195 A4
Montague Hill S 5 BS2 195 A4
Montague Pl BS6 ......195 A4
Montague Rd BS31 ....5 D2
Montague St BS1 ......195 A4
Monterey Cl GL20 ......192 E1
Montfort Rd GL2 ....127 B5
Montgomery Cl GL3 ....120 B6
Montgomery Rd GL51 ..129 D6
Montgomery St BS3 ......8 F3
Montpelier Sta BS6 .....18 E2
Montpellier GL1 ....196 B1
Montpellier Arc GL50 ..193 B2
Montpellier Ave GL50 ..193 B2
Montpellier Ct GL50 ...193 A2
Montpellier Dr GL50 ...193 B2
Montpellier Gr GL50 ...193 B2
Montpellier Ho GL50 ...193 A2
Montpellier Mews GL1 .196 B2
Montpellier Par GL50 ..193 B2
Montpellier Rd GL15 ...155 E1
Montpellier Retreat
GL50 ....193 B2
Montpellier Spa Rd
GL50 ....193 B2
Montpellier St GL50 ...193 B3
Montpellier Terr GL50 ..193 B2
Montpellier Villas GL50 .193 B2
Montpellier Wlk GL50 ..193 A2
Montreal Ave BS7 ....19 A8
Montreal Ho 3 GL51 ...132 E3
Montreaux Ho 2 BS5 ...10 A7
Montrose Ave BS6 ....18 C1
Montrose Dr BS30 ....11 B6
Montrose Pk BS4 ....9 D2
Montroy Cl BS9 ....18 C6
Montserrat GL5 ....99 D3
Moon St BS2 ....195 B4
Moon's La GL6 ....148 E7
Moor Court Dr GL52 ...133 F2
Moor Croft Dr BS30 .....10 F3
Moor Gr BS11 ....17 A8
Moor Hall Pl GL5 ....98 E8
Moor La
Bourton-on-t-W GL54 ....169 A8
Fairford GL7 ....152 E3
Tockington BS32 ....40 A8
Moor St Chepstow NP16 ..60 E8
Gloucester GL1 ....118 F7
Saul GL2 ....157 F4
Moordell Cl BS37 ....43 D1
Moore Cottage Hospl
GL54 ....168 F8
Moore Rd GL54 ....168 F7
Moorend Cres GL53 ....130 C6
Moorend Gdns BS11 .....16 F7
Moorend Glade GL53 ...130 F6
Moorend Gr GL53 ......130 C5
Moorend La GL2 ....95 C2
Moorend Park Rd GL53 .130 C6
Moorend Rd
Charlton Kings GL53 .....130 F6
Cheltenham GL53 ....130 C5
Hambrook BS16 ....30 D3
Staunton GL19 ....180 C1
Moorend St GL53 ......130 C6
Moorend Terr GL53 ....130 C6
Moorfield Ave GL15 ...156 D1
Moorfield Rd GL3 .....120 F5
Moorfields Ho BS5 ....9 C7
Moorgate GL7 ....153 D2
Moorgrove Ho BS9 ......17 C7
Moorhen Ct GL2 ....117 D1
Moorhill St 17 BS5 ......19 B1
Moorhouse La BS10 .....27 B4
Moorings The BS20 .....16 C4
Moorland Cl GL14 .....191 D5
Moorland Rd BS37 ......43 D1
Moorlands Rd
Bristol, Mayfield Park BS16 .20 A2
Bristol, Ridgeway BS16 ....19 F3
Moorpark Ave BS37 .....43 D1
Moors Ave GL51 ....133 A4
Moorslade La GL12 .....77 D1
Mop Hale GL56 ....186 C6
Mopla Rd NP16 ....72 F2
Moravian Ct 4 BS15 ....10 D8
Moravian Rd BS15 ......10 D8
Morcroft Pl GL15 ......155 F1
Morden Wlk BS14 ....3 D7
Morelands Gr GL1 .....118 E5
Morelands Trad Est
GL1 ....196 A1
Morestall Dr GL7 ......190 B2
Moreton Cl
Bishop's Cleeve GL52 ....138 A2
Bristol BS14 ....3 A4
Moreton La GL20 ......182 C8
Moreton-in-Marsh District
Hospl GL56 ....187 A3
Moreton-in-Marsh Sta
GL56 ....187 A3
Morgan Cl BS31 ....5 D2
Morgan St BS2 ....18 F1
Morgan's Way GL14 ....156 C6
Morgans La GL17 ......164 A3
Mork La GL15 ....146 E7
Mork Rd GL15 ....146 E7
Morlands Dr GL53 .....131 B4
Morley Ave Bristol BS16 ..21 A4
Churchdown GL3 ....128 A6
Morley Cl
Bristol, Little Stoke BS34 ..29 C7
Bristol, Staple Hill BS16 ...20 D4
Morley Rd
Bristol, Southville BS3 ......8 C4
Bristol, Staple Hill BS16 ...20 D3
Morley Sq BS7 ....18 E4
Morley St
Bristol, Baptist Mills BS2 ..18 F1
Bristol, Barton Hill BS5 .....9 B7
Morley Terr 1 BS15 .....20 D1
Morman Cl GL17 ....164 B4
Morningside Cl GL52 ...134 C4
Morningside Ctyd GL52 134 C4
Mornington Dr GL53 ...130 D6
Mornington Rd 14 BS8 ..18 A2
Mornington Terr GL14 ..157 A6
Morpeth Rd BS4 ....2 D8
Morpeth St GL1 ....118 F7
Morris Cl GL15 ....156 B2
Morris Ct 7 GL51 ......129 F7
Morris Hill Cl GL51 ....133 B6
Morris Orch GL11 ....87 F6
Morris Rd Bristol BS7 ....19 A5
Broadway WR12 ....185 B8
Morse La GL17 ....164 A4
Morse Rd Bristol BS5 .....9 C7
Drybrook GL17 ....164 B4
Mortimer Rd
Bristol, Clifton BS8 ......194 A3
Bristol, Filton BS34 ....29 B2
Gloucester GL2 ....127 C5
Morton Mill BS35 ....64 C3
Morton St Bristol BS5 .....9 B7
Gloucester GL1 ....118 F7
Thornbury BS35 ....64 C4
Morton Way BS35 ......64 D1
Morwent Cl GL4 ....119 E6
Mosedale GL56 ....187 B3
Moselle Dr GL3 ....128 A6
Mosley Cres GL5 ....98 E7
Mosley Rd GL5 ....98 E7
Motor Mus (The Bugatti
Trust)★ GL52 ....138 E8
Motorway Distribution Ctr
BS11 ....26 C2
Mottershead Dr GL3 ...127 E6
Mottershead Rd GL7 ...150 F2
Moulder Rd GL20 ......192 E4
Mount Cl
Frampton Cotterell BS36 ...30 F8
Harrow Hill GL17 ....164 B4
Mount Craig Hall HR9 ..162 F8
Mount Cres BS36 ....30 E5
Mount Gdns BS15 ....10 D6
Mount Hill Rd BS15 .....10 D6
Mount Pleasant
Bisley GL6 ....148 D8
Blockley GL56 ....186 C6
Chepstow NP16 ....60 E8
Fairford GL7 ....152 E4
Hallen BS10 ....27 C4
Lechlade on T GL7 ....153 E2
Lydney GL15 ....92 C2
Pill BS20 ....16 D4
Stroud GL5 ....99 E7
Wooton-u-E GL12 ....68 C7
Mount Pleasant Cl
Lydney GL15 ....92 C2
17 Stow-on-t-W GL54 ....176 F4
Mount Pleasant Rd
Cinderford GL14 ....191 D3
Tewkesbury GL20 ....192 D4
Mount Pleasant Terr BS3 .8 C4
Mount St Cirencester GL7 190 C3
Gloucester GL1 ....196 A3
Mount Way
Chepstow NP16 ....60 D8
Chepstow NP16 ....72 D1
Mountain View GL17 ...163 F4
Mountbatten Cl BS37 ...43 D3
Mounteney's La GL12 ...54 D7
Mountjoy's La GL14 ....191 D5
Mountjoy's Lane End
GL14 ....191 D5
Mounton Cl NP16 ....60 D7
Mounton Dr NP16 ....60 D7
Mounton House Sch
NP16 ....60 B7
Mounton Hts NP16 ......60 D8
Mounton Rd NP16 ....60 D8
Mousell La GL14 ......191 D4
Mousetrap La GL54 ....168 F8
Mow Barton Bristol BS13 ..1 F6
Yate BS37 ....43 D2
Mowberry Cl GL2 ......127 C5
Mowbray Ave GL20 ....192 D1
Mowbray Rd BS14 ....3 C7
Mowcroft Rd BS13 ....2 D4
Moxham Dr BS13 ....2 C4
Moyle Old School La
NP16 ....73 A4
Muirfield Bristol BS30 ....11 A6
Yate BS37 ....32 E8
Mulberry Cl Bristol BS15 ..10 E8
Hardwicke GL2 ....109 E8
Mulberry Ct 2 GL51 ...132 D2
Mulberry Dr BS15 ......20 F1
Mulberry Gn GL56 .....177 C4
Mulberry Wlk BS9 ......17 C8
Mule St GL13 ....78 B3
Muller Ave BS7 ....18 F4
Muller Rd BS5,BS7 ......19 B3
Mullings Ct GL7 ....190 C5
Mulready Cl BS7 ....19 C6
Mumbleys Hill BS35 ....50 E7
Mumbleys La
Thornbury, Alveston Down
BS35 ....50 E6
Thornbury,Kington BS35 ...50 E8
Munday Cl 8 GL6 ......148 B6
Munsley Gr GL4 ....119 C3
Murford Ave BS13 ....2 B4
Murford Wlk BS13 ....2 B4
Murray Cl GL52 ....137 F5
Murray St 9 BS3 ....8 C4
Murrells Rd GL16 ......163 A2
Murvagh GL53 ....193 C1

Murvagh Cl GL53 ......193 C1
Mus of Advert & Package★ GL1 ......196 A2
Muscroft Rd GL52 ......134 D4
Musgrove Cl BS11 ......27 C2
Mushat Ind Pk GL16 ......155 B5
Mushet Pl GL16 ......155 A5
Mutsilver Mews GL2 ......127 E5
Muzzle Patch GL2 ......124 C8
Myers Rd GL1 ......127 A1
Myrtle Cl GL4 ......119 A5
Myrtle Dr BS11 ......16 E5
Myrtle Hill BS20 ......16 C5
Myrtle Pl NP16 ......72 F1
Myrtle Rd BS2 ......194 C4
Myrtle St BS3 ......8 B3
Myrtles The NP16 ......73 A2
Mythe Rd GL20 ......192 C5
Mythe Terr GL14 ......157 A6

N

Naas La Lydney GL15 ......92 D2
Quedgeley GL2,GL4 ......110 C6
Nags Head Hill BS5 ......10 A7
Nailers La GL18 ......170 D3
Nailsea Cl BS13 ......2 A7
Nailsworth Ave BS37 ......43 E1
Nailsworth CE Prim Sch GL6 ......90 F5
Nailsworth Mills Est GL6 91 C4
Nailsworth Terr 2 GL50 ......193 A4
Naishcombe Hill BS30 ......12 C7
Naite The BS35 ......63 D6
Nanfan & Dobyn Pl GL18 ......171 A5
Napier Ct BS1 ......194 B1
Napier Miles Rd BS11 ......17 A8
Napier Rd
Avonmouth BS11 ......26 B1
Bristol, Baptist Mills BS5 ......19 B2
Bristol, Redland BS6 ......18 B2
Napier Sq BS11 ......26 A1
Napier St Bristol BS5 ......9 B6
Gloucester GL1 ......196 C2
Napping La GL17 ......164 F6
Napping The GL17 ......164 F6
Narles Rd GL2 ......96 A3
Narrow La BS16 ......20 E4
Narrow Plain BS2 ......195 B2
Narrow Quay BS1 ......195 A2
Narroways Rd BS2 ......19 A3
Narrowcut La GL6 ......90 F1
Narrows The GL55 ......188 E1
Narth La NP25 ......154 B1
Naseby Ho 4 GL52 ......134 A3
Naseby Wlk BS5 ......19 F1
Nash Cl BS31 ......5 A5
Nash Dr BS7 ......19 C7
Nash Way 8 GL16 ......155 A5
Nash's La GL55 ......189 D3
Nasse Ct GL11 ......87 F5
Nastend La GL10 ......101 C1
National Birds of Prey Ctr★ GL18 ......170 E2
National Waterways Mus★ GL1 ......196 A2
Nature Cl GL3 ......120 E5
Naught The 2 GL54 ......168 F7
Naunton Cres GL53 ......130 D6
Naunton La GL53 ......130 D6
Naunton Par GL53 ......193 B1
Naunton Park Cl GL53 ......130 E6
Naunton Park Prim Sch GL53 ......130 E6
Naunton Park Rd GL53 ......130 E6
Naunton Rd GL4 ......119 D7
Naunton Terr GL53 ......193 B1
Naunton Way GL53 ......130 D6
Naval Temple★ NP25 ......154 B7
Neads Dr BS30 ......11 C5
Neale Way BS11 ......26 C1
Neate Ct BS34 ......29 C8
Neath Farm GL54 ......184 A1
Neath Rd BS5 ......9 D8
Nebraska Circ GL7 ......152 E1
Nebsworth La CV36 ......189 E5
Needham Ave GL2 ......110 B6
Neigh Bridge Ctry Pk★ GL7 ......142 C5
Nell Hill SN6 ......145 A4
Nelmes Row GL53 ......131 C5
Nelson Ho 8 BS16 ......20 D5
Nelson Par 11 BS3 ......8 D4
Nelson Rd 3 Bristol BS16 20 D4
Bristol BS16 ......20 D5
Nelson St Bristol BS1 ......195 A3
Bristol, Ashton Vale BS3 ......8 A2
Chepstow NP16 ......60 F8
Gloucester GL1 ......118 F6
Stroud GL5 ......99 C7
Tewkesbury GL20 ......192 C4
Nelsons Cl HR9 ......163 B7
Nene Cl GL2 ......117 E2
Neptune Cl GL4 ......119 F6
Nero Cl GL15 ......92 C4
Neston Wlk BS4 ......2 F8
Netham Park Ind Est BS5 ......9 D6
Netham Rd BS5 ......9 D6
Netham View Ind Pk BS5 ......9 D7
Nethercote Dr GL54 ......169 A7
Nethercote Farm Dr GL54 ......169 A6
Netherend Cres GL15 ......147 C3
Netherhope La NP16 ......73 B5
Netheridge Cl GL2 ......118 A4
Netherley La GL19 ......180 A4
Netherwood Cl GL51 ......133 A3
Netherwood Gdns GL51 133 A3
Netting La GL2 ......157 B6
Nettlestone Cl BS10 ......27 E4
Nettleton & Burton CE Prim Sch SN14 ......36 B2
Nettleton Rd Burton SN14 ......36 B2
Cheltenham GL51 ......129 E7
Gloucester GL1 ......196 C2
Nevalan Dr BS5 ......10 A6
Nevil Rd BS7 ......18 E4
Neville Rd Bristol BS15 ......20 E2
Tewkesbury GL20 ......192 D3
New Barn Ave GL52 ......134 A4
New Barn Cl GL52 ......134 A4
New Barn La GL52 ......134 A4
New Bldgs BS16 ......19 F4
New Brunswick Ave BS5 ......10 B7
New Charlotte St BS3 ......8 D4
New Cheltenham Rd BS15 ......20 E1
New Church St GL8 ......140 B4
New Cut GL11 ......89 B1
New Fosseway Rd BS14 ......3 B6
New Fosseway Sch BS14 ......3 B6
New Inn La Avening GL8 ......140 B8
Gloucester GL1 ......196 B3
New John St 15 BS3 ......8 C3
New Kingsley Rd BS2 ......195 C2
New La BS35 ......51 C5
New Leaze BS32 ......40 C3
New Mills GL15 ......92 A6
New Mills La GL12 ......55 E8
New Mills Trad Est GL5 ......99 D8
New Mills Way 1 HR8 ......178 E8
New Queen St
Bristol, Bedminster BS3 ......8 E4
Bristol, St George BS15 ......10 B8
New Rd Aylburton GL15 ......147 D5
Blakeney GL15 ......156 D1
Bledington OX7 ......177 E1
Bream GL15 ......147 D8
Bristol, Filton BS34 ......28 F3
Bristol, Harry Stoke BS34 ......29 D3
Coleford GL16 ......155 B5
Coleford, Cannop GL15, GL16 ......155 D6
Dursley GL11 ......87 E4
Ebrington GL55 ......189 D3
Kingham OX7 ......177 F2
Kingswood GL12 ......67 F6
Minchinhampton GL6 ......91 F5
7 Moreton-in-M GL56 ......187 A3
North Nibley GL11 ......79 E4
Olveston BS35 ......50 A2
Parkend GL15 ......155 E2
Pendock WR13 ......180 A8
Pill BS20 ......16 C4
Popes Hill GL17 ......164 D5
Rangeworthy BS37 ......43 A8
Rangeworthy BS37 ......53 C1
Stroud GL5 ......98 E5
Tytherington GL12 ......52 C6
Whitecroft GL15 ......147 F7
Woodmancote GL52 ......138 C2
Yorkley GL15 ......156 A1
New Row Aldsworth GL54 160 E5
Brockhampton GL54 ......174 B1
New Rutland Ct GL50 ......193 B4
New Siblands Sch BS35 ......64 D1
New St Bretforton WR11 ......188 A6
Bristol BS2 ......195 C3
Charfield GL12 ......67 A6
Charlton Kings GL53 ......131 B5
Cheltenham GL50 ......193 A4
Gloucester GL1 ......196 B1
King's Stanley GL10 ......98 A3
Ledbury HR8 ......178 E8
Mitcheldean GL17 ......164 D5
Painswick GL6 ......103 F8
Sharpness GL13 ......85 C8
New Stadium Rd BS5 ......19 B2
New Station Rd BS16 ......20 A4
New Station Way BS16 ......20 A4
New Street Flats 4 BS2 ......195 C3
New Thomas St BS2 ......195 C2
New Town
Cinderford GL14 ......191 B7
Toddington GL54 ......184 C3
New Tyning La BS37 ......45 C4
New Walls BS4 ......8 F4
New Wlk BS15 ......10 B5
New Zealand Ho 2 GL51 ......132 F3
Newark Pk★ GL12 ......69 A7
Newark Rd GL1 ......118 C6
Newbrick Rd BS34 ......30 A5
Newbridge Cl BS4 ......9 D5
Newbridge Ho BS9 ......17 C4
Newbridge Park Farm★ HR8 ......178 A8
Newbridge Rd BS4 ......9 E6
Newbridge Trad Est BS4 ......9 D5
Newburgh Pl SN6 ......145 C3
Newbury Rd BS7 ......19 A7
Newcombe GL4 ......114 B5
Newcombe Ct GL7 ......190 D4
Newcombe Dr BS9 ......17 C4
Newcombe Rd BS9 ......17 F7
Newcourt Pk GL53 ......131 A6
Newcourt Rd GL53 ......131 A5
Newent Ave BS15 ......10 C7
Newent Comm Sch GL18 ......170 F4
Newent La GL19 ......165 C6
Newerne St GL15 ......92 B3
Newfoundland Rd
6 Bristol BS2 ......19 A1
Bristol BS2 ......195 C4
Newfoundland St BS2 ......195 C4
Newfoundland Way BS2 ......195 C4
Newgate BS1 ......195 B3
Newgrounds La GL2 ......95 B6
Newhouse Farm Ind Est NP16 ......60 F3
Newington Cotts GL8 ......82 B2
Newland Dr BS13 ......2 A4
Newland Rd BS13 ......2 A3
Newland St
Coleford GL16 ......155 A5
Gloucester GL1 ......196 C3
Newland Way NP25 ......154 A7
Newland Wlk BS13 ......2 A3
Newlands Ave BS36 ......31 C7
Newlands Ct
20 Newent GL18 ......171 A4
Stow-on-t-W GL54 ......176 E5
Newlands Rd BS31 ......4 D4
Newlands The BS16 ......20 B7
Newleaze BS34 ......29 A2
Newleaze Gdns GL8 ......140 B4
Newlyn Ave BS9 ......17 D5
Newlyn Way BS37 ......43 F2
Newlyn Wlk BS4 ......9 B1
Newman Cl BS37 ......32 B4
Newmarket Ave 5 BS1 ......195 A3
Newmarket Rd GL6 ......91 A4
Newmills Hill HR9 ......162 F5
Newnham Cl BS14 ......3 D7
Newnham Pl BS34 ......39 F1
Newnton Hill GL8 ......140 D5
Newnton Rd GL8 ......140 C3
Newpit La BS30 ......11 F2
Newport Rd
Chepstow NP16 ......60 D7
Pill BS20 ......16 C5
Newport St BS3 ......8 E3
Newquay Rd BS4 ......8 F1
Newry Wlk BS4 ......8 E1
Newsome Ave BS20 ......16 C4
Newstead Rd GL4 ......119 E8
Newth's La SN5 ......143 E1
Newton Ave GL4 ......119 C7
Newton Cl Bristol BS15 ......21 A1
Cheltenham GL51 ......132 E2
Huntley GL19 ......165 D6
2 Ledbury HR8 ......178 F7
Newton Court La NP25 ......162 B1
Newton Dr BS30 ......11 A5
Newton Rd Bristol BS30 ......11 A5
Cheltenham GL51 ......132 E2
Newton St BS5 ......9 A8
Newtown GL12 ......67 A5
Newtown La GL20 ......192 F5
Newtown Rd GL14 ......191 B7
Niblett Cl BS15 ......10 F6
Niblett's Hill BS5 ......10 A6
Nibley La BS37 ......42 F3
Nibley Rd BS11 ......16 E5
Nicholas La BS5 ......10 A6
Nicholas Rd BS5 ......19 B1
Nicholas St BS3 ......8 E4
Nicholettes BS30 ......11 D5
Nicholls Ct BS36 ......30 E7
Nicholls La BS36 ......30 E6
Nicolson Cl GL3 ......127 E6
Nigel Pk BS11 ......16 E7
Nightingale Cl Bristol BS4 ......9 E6
Frampton Cotterell BS36 ......31 A6
Thornbury BS35 ......64 D2
Nightingale Croft GL3 ......127 D6
Nightingale Ct BS4 ......9 D3
Nightingale Ho GL4 ......119 D4
Nightingale La BS36 ......31 A8
Nind La GL12 ......68 B4
Nine Elms Rd GL2 ......127 E4
Nine Tree Hill 6 BS1 ......18 E1
Nine Wells Cl 16 GL16 ......155 A7
Nine Wells Rd GL16 ......155 B7
Ninth Ave BS7 ......29 B1
Noake Rd GL3 ......120 A8
Noble Ave BS30 ......11 C4
Nodens Way GL15 ......92 C4
Noel Ct GL55 ......189 A2
Noel Lee Way GL11 ......87 F5
Norbury Ave GL4 ......119 B4
Norchard Sta GL15 ......147 F7
Norden Dr HR9 ......164 C8
Nordown Cl GL11 ......87 F4
Nordown Rd GL11 ......87 F4
Norfolk Ave
Bristol, Montpelier BS6 ......18 E2
Bristol, St Pauls BS2 ......195 B4
Cheltenham GL51 ......132 F2
Norfolk Gr BS31 ......4 C4
Norfolk Pl BS3 ......8 C3
Norfolk St GL1 ......196 A2
Norland Rd BS8 ......7 F8
Norley Rd BS7 ......18 F7
Normal Terr GL50 ......193 B4
Norman Ball Way GL1 ......127 B1
Norman Cl GL20 ......181 F7
Norman Gr BS15 ......20 D2
Norman Hill GL11 ......87 F4
Norman Rd
Bristol, Baptist Mills BS2 ......19 A2
Bristol, Warmley BS30 ......11 B8
Saltford BS31 ......5 E3
Norman Way GL17 ......163 F4
Normanby Rd 20 BS5 ......19 B1
Normandy Way NP16 ......72 D1
Normanton Rd 16 BS8 ......18 A2
Norrisville Rd 5 BS6 ......18 E1
Norrland Pl HR9 ......163 C8
Norse Way NP16 ......61 B7
Nortenham Cl GL52 ......137 D4
North Ave
Ashchurch GL20 ......182 D4
Drybrook GL17 ......164 B4
North Cerney Prim Sch GL7 ......158 D3
North Circular Rd GL56 187 C4
North Croft BS30 ......11 D4
North Ct BS32 ......40 D3
North Devon Rd BS16 ......20 A5
North East Rd BS35 ......64 C2
North East Terr GL20 ......192 D4
North End Gdns SN16 ......58 C1
North Gr BS20 ......16 C4
North Green St 11 BS8 ......7 F6
North Hall Mews GL52 ......133 F2
North Hill Rd GL7 ......190 E2
North Home Rd GL7 ......190 F3
North Leaze BS41 ......7 B2
North Meadow Rd SN6 ......143 E5
North Par BS37 ......43 E2
North Pk BS15 ......20 E1
North Pl GL50 ......193 C4
North Pole La HR9 ......170 C5
North Rd
6 Bristol, Ashton Gate BS3 ......8 A4
Bristol, Montpelier BS6 ......18 E2
Bristol, Stoke Gifford BS34 ......29 F4
Coleford GL16 ......155 B6
Gloucester GL1 ......126 F4
Huntley GL19 ......165 D6
Leigh Woods BS8 ......7 D7
Thornbury BS35 ......64 C2
Winterbourne BS36 ......30 F7
Yate BS37 ......43 B3
Yate, Engine Common BS37 ......43 B5
North Rd E GL51 ......129 C7
North Rd W GL51 ......129 B7
North St Bristol BS1 ......195 B4
Bristol, Bedminster BS3 ......8 B3
Bristol, Downend BS16 ......20 E5
Bristol, Oldland Common BS30 ......11 C4
Cheltenham GL50 ......193 B4
Wickwar GL12 ......54 A6
Winchcombe GL54 ......174 A7
North Stoke La BS30 ......6 B8
North Upton La GL4 ......119 E8
North View Bristol BS6 ......18 A4
Bristol, Mangotsfield BS16 ......20 E5
Bristol, Upper Soundwell BS16 ......20 D4
Highworth SN6 ......145 C3
Poulton GL7 ......151 F3
North Wall SN6 ......143 F4
North Way Bristol BS34 ......29 B4
Cirencester GL7 ......190 C4
North Wlk BS37 ......43 E1
Northavon Bsns Ctr BS37 43 C3
Northbank Cl GL51 ......129 B7
Northbridge Bsns Ctr BS37 ......43 C2
Northbrook Rd GL4 ......127 C1
Northcot La GL56 ......186 D6
Northcote Rd
Bristol, Clifton BS8 ......17 F1
Bristol, Mangotsfield BS16 ......20 F6
Bristol, St George BS5 ......9 E7
Northcote St 18 BS5 ......19 B1
Northen Cl GL7 ......144 F7
Northend Ave BS15 ......20 D2
Northend Gdns BS15 ......20 D2
Northend Rd BS15 ......20 E1
Northern Way GL17 ......164 D5
Northfield BS37 ......32 D8
Northfield Ave BS15 ......10 D5
Northfield Cl GL8 ......140 C4
Northfield Ho 10 BS3 ......8 C4
Northfield La SN14 ......24 F1
Northfield Pas GL50 ......193 C4
Northfield Rd Bristol BS5 ......10 B7
Gloucester GL4 ......118 F5
Tetbury GL8 ......140 C4
Northfield Sq GL4 ......118 F5
Northfield Terr GL50 ......193 C4
Northfields GL5 ......99 D8
Northfields Rd GL6 ......91 A5
Northgate St GL1 ......196 B3
Northington La GL14 ......157 B3
Northlands Way GL8 ......140 C5
Northleach CE Prim Sch GL54 ......168 A1
Northleach Wlk BS11 ......16 F5
Northleaze GL8 ......140 C4
Northleaze Prim Sch BS41 7 B2
Northmead La BS37 ......42 D6
Northmoor La GL7 ......151 A1
Northover Ct BS35 ......38 E6
Northover Rd BS9 ......28 A1
Northumberland Rd BS6 18 D2
Northumbria Dr BS9 ......18 B4
Northview Cty Prim Sch SN6 ......145 D4
Northville Rd BS7 ......29 A1
Northway Inf Sch GL20 ......182 C4
Northway La GL20 ......182 B4
Northwick Bsns Ctr GL56 ......186 C8
Northwick Rd Bristol BS7 ......18 F8
Pilning BS35 ......48 E1
Northwick Terr GL56 ......186 C6
Northwood Cl GL14 ......191 D5
Northwoods Wlk BS10 ......28 D3
Norton CE Prim Sch GL2 ......173 B2
Norton Cl Bristol BS15 ......10 F7
Whitchurch HR9 ......162 D4
Winchcombe GL54 ......174 A8
Norton Ct GL6 ......90 F5
Norton Ho 7 Bristol BS1 195 B1
Bristol, Patchway BS34 ......39 F1
Cheltenham GL51 ......133 A2
Norton La BS14 ......3 C2
Norton Rd BS4 ......9 A3
Norton Ridge GL6 ......91 A5
Norton View GL55 ......189 A6
Nortonwood GL6 ......90 F5
Norval Rd WR11 ......188 A8
Norwich Dr Bristol BS4 ......9 E6
Cheltenham GL51 ......130 A6
Norwood Rd GL50 ......193 B1
Nostle Rd GL54 ......168 A1
Notch Rd GL7,GL53 ......107 C8
Notgrove Cl
Cheltenham GL51 ......129 E8
Gloucester GL4 ......118 C2
Notley Pl GL3 ......120 A7
Nottingham Rd
Bishop's Cleeve GL52 ......137 F5
Bristol BS7 ......18 E3
Nottingham St BS3 ......8 F3
Nouncells Cross GL5 ......99 D7
Nourse Cl GL53 ......130 B4
Nourse Pl GL17 ......164 D5
Nova Scotia Pl BS1 ......194 A1
Nova Way BS11 ......26 B1
Nover's Lane Inf Sch BS4 ......2 C7
Nover's Lane Jun Sch BS4 ......2 C7
Novers Cres BS4 ......2 C8
Novers Hill BS4 ......2 C8
Novers Hill Trad Est BS3 ......8 C1
Novers La BS4 ......2 D7
Novers Park Dr BS4 ......2 C8
Novers Park Rd BS4 ......2 D8
Novers Rd BS4 ......2 C8
Noverton Ave GL52 ......134 D4
Noverton La GL52 ......134 D4
Nugent Hill BS6 ......18 D1
Nunnery La GL11 ......80 B7
Nunney Cl BS31 ......5 A2
Nunny Cl GL51 ......132 C1
Nup End GL19 ......172 D4
Nup End La GL19 ......172 D4
Nupdown Rd BS35 ......75 E5
Nupend Gdns GL17 ......164 F5
Nupend La GL17 ......164 F5
Nurseries The
Bishop's Cleeve GL52 ......137 E2
Tytherington GL12 ......52 B5
Nursery Cl
Cirencester GL7 ......190 E2
Mickleton GL55 ......189 B7
Moreton-in-M GL56 ......187 A4
Stroud GL5 ......99 D6
Nursery Cott GL7 ......190 D3
Nursery Gdns BS10 ......28 A3
Nursery Rd GL7 ......190 E2
Nursery The Bristol BS3 ......8 B3
King's Stanley GL10 ......98 A4
Nursery View GL7 ......150 E2
Nut Croft GL4 ......119 B7
Nut Orchard La GL20 ......181 F8
Nutfield Gr BS34 ......29 B2
Nutgrove Ave BS3 ......8 E3
Nuthatch Dr BS16 ......19 F6
Nuthatch Gdns BS16 ......20 A6
Nuthill GL4 ......120 B2
Nutley Ave GL4 ......118 C2
Nutmeg Cl GL4 ......119 D4
Nympsfield BS15 ......20 E2
Nympsfield Long Barrow★ GL11 ......89 C7
Nympsfield Rd
Gloucester GL4 ......118 D3
Nailsworth GL6 ......90 E5

O

O'brien Rd GL51 ......133 A4
Oak Ave GL52 ......131 A7
Oak Cl Bristol BS34 ......29 D7
Chepstow NP16 ......60 E5
Yate BS37 ......43 D3
Oak Cres
Monmouth NP25 ......154 A7
Netherend GL15 ......147 C3
Oak Ct Bristol BS14 ......3 A5
Cheltenham GL52 ......134 A1
Oak Dr Brockworth GL3 ......120 D6
Dursley GL11 ......88 A3
Highworth SN6 ......145 C3
Stroud GL5 ......99 B6
Tewkesbury GL20 ......182 B4
Oak Field The GL14 ......191 E5
Oak Gdns GL20 ......182 C7
Oak Gr BS20 ......16 C5
Oak Ho Bristol BS13 ......2 D4
Brockworth GL3 ......120 D6
Oak La Bredon GL20 ......182 C7
Bristol BS5 ......19 F2
Oak Lodge BS37 ......32 D8
Oak Manor 3 GL52 ......134 A1
Oak Manor Dr GL52 ......134 A1
Oak Mdw GL15 ......92 B6
Oak Rd Bristol BS7 ......18 E5
Colerne SN14 ......15 F5
Down Ampney GL7 ......143 F7
Marston Meysey SN6 ......144 A6

Oak St GL7 .....153 E2
Oak Tree Ave BS16 .....22 B4
Oak Tree Cl Bristol BS15 ..10 C3
Hardwicke GL2 .....109 E7
Oak Tree View GL4 .....119 C3
Oak Tree Wlk BS31 .....4 D3
Oak Way Huntley GL19 ..165 D6
Littledean GL14 .....156 E8
South Cerney GL7 .....142 F7
Stonehouse GL10 .....97 F7
Oakbank GL4 .....118 F4
Oakbrook Dr GL51 .....129 C7
Oakcroft Cl GL4 .....119 D3
Oakdale Ave BS16 .....20 D8
Oakdale Cl BS16 .....20 E8
Oakdale Ct BS16 .....20 D7
Oakdale Rd
Bristol, Downend BS16 .....20 E8
Bristol, Hengrove BS14 .....3 A8
Oakdean GL14 .....191 C5
Oakdene
2 Cheltenham, Fairview GL52 .....134 A1
11 Cheltenham, Lansdown GL51 .....130 B8
Oakdene Ave BS5 .....19 D3
Oakdene Sch GL14 .....191 D4
Oakenhill Rd BS4 .....9 E2
Oakenhill Wlk BS4 .....9 E2
Oakes La GL9 .....35 B5
Oakfield Ave NP16 .....72 D1
Oakfield Bsns Pk BS15 ..10 D7
Oakfield Gr BS8 .....194 B4
Oakfield Pl BS8 .....194 B4
Oakfield Rd
Bishop's Cleeve GL52 .....138 A4
Bristol, Clifton BS8 .....194 B4
Bristol, Kingswood BS15 ...10 D7
Keynsham BS31 .....4 F2
Oakfield St GL50 .....130 B7
Oakfield Way GL13 .....93 D1
Oakfields GL16 .....155 A6
Oakford La SN14 .....15 B2
Oakhanger Dr BS11 .....27 B1
Oakhill Ave BS30 .....11 C2
Oakhill Inf Sch WR11 ...183 F7
Oakhill La BS10 .....27 C4
Oakhill Pitch GL15 .....146 F3
Oakhill Prim Sch GL20 .183 E4
Oakhill Rd GL17 .....164 D5
Oakhunger La GL13 .....85 C4
Oakhurst Cl GL3 .....128 A5
Oakhurst Rd BS9 .....17 F5
Oakhurst Rise GL52 .....131 A8
Oakland Ave GL52 .....133 F3
Oakland Bsn Pk BS37 ...43 B3
Oakland Dr HR8 .....178 E8
Oakland Rd
6 Bristol, Redland BS6 ...18 B1
Bristol, St George BS5 .....9 E8
Harrow Hill GL17 .....164 B3
Oakland St GL53 .....131 A7
Oaklands Cirencester GL7 190 C2
Sling GL16 .....155 B2
Oaklands Cl BS16 .....21 B5
Oaklands Dr
Almondsbury BS32 .....40 A4
Bristol, Frenchay BS16 .....20 A7
Bristol, Oldland Common BS30 .....11 C2
Oaklands Pk GL15 .....155 E1
Oaklands Rd BS16 .....21 A5
Oaklea Rd GL15 .....156 B2
Oakleaze
Coalpit Heath BS36 .....31 D7
Minety SN16 .....142 D1
Oakleaze Rd BS35 .....64 C1
Oakleigh Ave BS5 .....19 D1
Oakleigh Gdns BS30 .....11 C2
Oakley Cl 20 GL54 .....176 F4
Oakley Flats GL7 .....144 E7
Oakley Rd Bristol BS7 .....18 F7
Cheltenham GL52 .....134 B1
Cirencester GL7 .....190 C2
Oakley Way 1 GL15 .....147 D8
Oakmeade Pk BS4 .....9 B2
Oakridge GL2 .....125 E5
Oakridge Cl Bristol BS15 .11 A7
6 Gloucester GL4 .....119 E5
Oakridge Prim Sch GL6 148 E6
Oaks La GL18 .....170 D2
Oaks The Berry Hill GL16 .155 A8
Cheltenham GL51 .....129 D6
Gloucester GL4 .....119 E7
Kemble GL7 .....141 F8
Oaksey CE Prim Sch SN16 .....141 F4
Oaksey Rd SN16 .....142 B2
Oaktree Cres BS32 .....40 C2
Oaktree Ct BS11 .....16 E7
Oaktree Gdn GL4 .....119 C3
Oaktree Gdns BS13 .....1 E5
Oakwood Ave BS9 .....18 C6
Oakwood Cl Bream GL15 155 D1
Cinderford GL14 .....191 D5
Oakwood Dr GL3 .....119 F6
Oakwood Gdns BS36 .....31 E7
Oakwood Pk BS16 .....20 A3
Oakwood Rd
Bream GL15 .....155 D1
Bristol BS9 .....18 B6
Sling GL16 .....155 B3
Oatfield GL2 .....117 E2
Oatfield Rd GL2 .....100 A6
Oatground GL12 .....68 C7
Oathill La GL7 .....141 A8
Oatlands Ave BS14 .....3 A6
Oatleys Cres 11 HR8 .....178 E8
Oatleys Rd HR8 .....178 E8
Oatleys Terr 10 HR8 .....178 E8
Oberon Ave BS5 .....19 E2
Ocker Hill GL6 .....102 E2
Octagon The NP16 .....60 F5
Octavia Pl GL15 .....92 B4
Oddfellows Row 3 GL54 .....176 F4
Oddfellows Terr 18 GL54 .....174 A7
Oddfellows' Terr 12 GL56 .....187 A3
Oddington Rd GL54 .....176 F4
Odessa Pk GL20 .....173 F8
Offa's Mead Prim Sch NP16 .....61 A8
Offas Cl NP16 .....61 A7
Office Rd GL14 .....191 C3
Ogbourne Cl GL2 .....127 E3
Ohio Ave GL7 .....152 E2
Okebourne Cl BS10 .....28 B4
Okebourne Rd BS10 .....28 B4
Okus Rd GL53 .....131 A5
Old All Saints Sch 12 GL52 .....193 C4
Old Ashley Hill BS6 .....18 F2
Old Aust Rd BS32 .....40 C6
Old Barns The WR8 .....180 D7
Old Barrow Hill BS11 .....16 D7
Old Bath Rd GL53 .....130 E5
Old Bell Chambers NP16 .60 E8
Old Bread St BS2 .....195 C2
Old Brewery La 15 GL8 .140 B4
Old Bristol Rd GL6 .....91 B3
Old Bulwark Rd NP16 .....60 E7
Old Burford Rd OX7 .....177 E1
Old Cheltenham Rd GL2 .....127 D4
Old Coach Cl NP16 .....61 C2
Old Coach Rd NP16 .....61 C3
Old Coach The WR12 ...185 C8
Old Comm GL6 .....148 C4
Old Comm The GL6 .....148 C6
Old Common The GL6 .....148 B6
Old Court Dr GL19 .....171 D1
Old Dam Rd GL15 .....92 D7
Old Dean Rd GL17 .....164 D6
Old Dixton Rd NP25 .....154 A8
Old Down Hill BS32 .....50 B2
Old Down Rd GL9 .....35 C8
Old Elmore La GL2 .....117 F2
Old Farm Cl SN16 .....141 E1
Old Farm La BS5 .....10 B6
Old Forge Cl OX7 .....177 E1
Old Forge Cotts
Didbrook GL54 .....184 D2
Stoke Orchard GL52 .....136 E5
Old Forge The GL15 .....147 D3
Old Furnace Cl GL15 .....147 F5
Old Gloucester Rd
Alveston BS35 .....51 B5
Bourton-on-t-W GL54 .....168 E7
Bristol BS16 .....30 B2
Bristol BS16 .....30 B4
Frampton Cotterell BS36 ...41 D3
Staverton GL51 .....173 F1
Thornbury BS35 .....65 B2
Uckington GL51 .....132 B5
Old Gram School Mews The
The GL55 .....189 A2
Old Hill Avening GL8 .....148 B1
Longhope GL17 .....165 A5
Old Horsley Rd GL6 .....91 B3
Old Hospital La GL20 ...192 D5
Old Inchbrook Sch GL6 ..91 A5
Old King Street Ct BS1 .195 B3
Old La BS16 .....21 C6
Old La (Simmonds La) HR9,GL18 .....170 C4
Old Lodge Ct GL50 .....133 E3
Old London Rd GL12 .....80 C1
Old Manor Cl GL12 .....67 A5
Old Manor Gdns GL55 ..189 B6
Old Manor La GL20 .....192 E6
Old Market GL6 .....91 B4
Old Market St BS2 .....195 C3
Old Mill Cl BS37 .....32 B4
Old Mill Mus The★ GL54 .....176 C1
Old Mill The WR12 .....185 B8
Old Millbrook Terr 4 GL50 .....133 B2
Old Moat Ctyd GL2 .....172 F1
Old Monmouth Rd GL17 165 A5
Old Neighbourhood GL6 .....148 C6
Old Oak Cl NP16 .....60 F5
Old Orchard Ct GL7 .....152 D7
Old Orchard The GL55 ..189 D3
Old Painswick Cl GL4 ..119 B6
Old Painswick Rd GL4 ..119 B6
Old Park Hill BS2 .....194 C3
Old Park Rd BS11 .....16 D7
Old Pk BS2 .....194 C3
Old Police Sta The BS4 .....9 A3
Old Priory Rd BS20 .....16 B4
Old Quarry Ind Units The GL8 .....140 C3
Old Quarry Rd BS11 .....16 E7
Old Quarry Rise BS11 ...16 E7
Old Rd Coleford GL16 .....155 B5
Maisemore GL2 .....126 A8
Southam GL52 .....134 C8
Old Rectory Cl GL5 .....99 A5
Old Rectory Gdns GL56 .176 D8
Old Rectory Rd GL12 .....67 F4
Old Reddings Cl GL51 ..129 C7
Old Reddings Rd GL51 .129 C7
Old Row GL1 .....196 C1
Old School Cl GL6 .....91 B4
Old School Ho 3 GL50 .193 A4
Old School Mews The 4 GL53 .....131 B6
Old Sneed Ave BS9 .....17 D4
Old Sneed Cotts BS9 .....17 E4
Old Sneed Pk BS9 .....17 D4
Old Sneed Rd BS9 .....17 D4
Old Sodbury CE Prim Sch BS37 .....34 B8
Old Station Dr GL53 ...130 D5
Old Station Rd GL18 .....171 A5
Old Station Way GL16 ..155 A5
Old Town GL12 .....68 B7
Old Town Mews GL15 ...147 F5
Old Tram Rd GL1 .....196 A2
Old Vicarage Ct
6 Coleford GL16 .....155 A5
Whitchurch BS14 .....3 C4
Old Vicarage Gn BS31 .....4 E6
Old Vicarage La GL7 .....141 F7
Old Vicarage Pl BS8 .....18 A1
Old Vicarage The
Bristol BS6 .....18 E1
Olveston BS35 .....50 A3
Old Winding Wheel The GL15 .....147 C8
Oldacre Dr GL52 .....138 A4
Oldacre Rd BS14 .....3 A3
Oldbridge Rd BS14 .....3 C3
Oldbury Chase BS30 .....11 A2
Oldbury Cl GL51 .....132 D3
Oldbury Court Dr BS16 ..20 B6
Oldbury Court Prim Sch BS16 .....20 C7
Oldbury Court Rd BS16 ..20 A5
Oldbury Ho GL20 .....192 D5
Oldbury La
Thornbury BS35 .....64 B4
Wick BS30 .....12 D5
Oldbury Orch GL3 .....128 D4
Oldbury Power Station Visitor Ctr★ BS35 .....75 B1
Oldbury Prim Sch BS35 ..63 B5
Oldbury Rd
Cheltenham GL51 .....132 E3
Tewkesbury GL20 .....192 C5
Oldbury-on-Severn Prim Sch BS35 .....63 B4
Oldcroft Rd GL15 .....156 B1
Olde La GL54 .....184 B3
Oldends La GL10 .....97 D8
Oldfield GL20 .....192 D4
Oldfield Cres GL51 .....129 F8
Oldfield Girls Sch BA1 .....6 F1
Oldfield Pl BS8 .....7 F5
Oldfield Rd BS8 .....194 A1
Oldfields La BS35 .....41 D7
Oldhill GL5 .....98 D8
Oldlands Ave BS36 .....31 C6
Oldmead Wlk BS13 .....1 E7
Oldminster Rd GL13 .....93 D1
Oldown Cty Pk★ BS32 ...50 C4
Oldwood La BS37 .....43 B8
Olio La GL53 .....193 C2
Olive Gdns BS35 .....50 F4
Olive Gr GL11 .....88 A2
Oliver Cl GL4 .....118 D2
Ollney Rd GL6 .....91 F6
Olveston Prim Sch BS35 .50 A3
Olveston Rd BS7 .....18 E5
Olympus Cl BS34 .....29 D6
Olympus Pk GL2 .....118 A2
Olympus Rd BS34 .....28 D7
Onslow Rd GL18 .....171 A4
Oram Ct BS30 .....10 F4
Orange Cl SN6 .....145 D3
Orange St BS2 .....195 C4
Orangery The GL4 .....119 E7
Orch The
Netherend GL15 .....147 C3
Oaksey SN16 .....141 F4
Orchard Ave Bristol BS1 .194 C2
Broadway WR12 .....185 C8
Cheltenham GL51 .....132 F2
Chepstow NP16 .....60 E5
Thornbury BS35 .....64 D1
Orchard Bank
2 Blockley GL56 .....186 C5
Great Rissington GL54 ...169 C4
Orchard Bvd BS30 .....11 B4
Orchard Cl
Aylburton GL15 .....147 E4
Bredon GL20 .....182 D7
Bretforton WR11 .....188 A6
Bristol, Kingswood BS15 ...10 E8
Bristol, Westbury on Trym BS9 .....17 F5
Charfield GL12 .....67 A5
Clearwell GL16 .....154 F3
Dursley GL11 .....87 F5
English Bicknor GL16 .....163 A2
Gloucester GL2 .....126 F5
Hardwicke GL2 .....109 D7
Kemble GL7 .....141 F8
Keynsham BS31 .....4 D6
King's Stanley GL10 .....98 B3
Lea HR9 .....164 C8
Lechlade on T GL7 .....153 D2
Leonard Stanley GL10 .....97 F4
Mickleton GL55 .....189 B7
Mitcheldean GL17 .....164 D5
Winterbourne BS36 .....30 E5
Woodcroft NP16 .....73 A4
Yate BS37 .....43 F2
Orchard Cres BS11 .....16 D7
Orchard Ct
Bristol, Filton BS34 .....29 A2
18 Bristol, Redfield BS5 .....9 D7
Painswick GL6 .....103 F8
Stonehouse GL10 .....97 E7
Tewkesbury GL20 .....192 D4
Yate BS37 .....43 B3
Orchard Dr Aust BS35 .....49 A7
Churchdown GL3 .....128 D4
Twyning GL20 .....182 A7
Orchard End
Apperley GL19 .....173 C7
Monmouth NP25 .....154 A7
Orchard Farm Cl NP16 ...61 B7
Orchard Field GL8 .....140 B8
Orchard Gate GL15 .....156 D2
Orchard Gdns BS15 .....10 F8
Orchard Gr The GL51 ...129 D1
Orchard Grange BS35 .....64 B2
Orchard Ho GL7 .....190 D5
Orchard Ind Est GL54 ..184 A3
Orchard La Bristol BS1 ..194 C2
Ledbury HR8 .....178 E8
Orchard Lea
6 Alveston BS35 .....51 A5
Pill BS20 .....16 D4
Orchard Leaze GL11 .....87 D4
Orchard Mead
Nailsworth GL6 .....91 B4
Painswick GL6 .....103 F7
Orchard Pl
4 Ledbury HR8 .....178 F7
Stonehouse GL10 .....97 E7
Orchard Rd
Alderton GL20 .....183 E4
Bishop's Cleeve GL52 .....137 F3
Bristol, Ashley Down BS7 ..18 E4
Bristol, Kingswood BS15 ...10 E8
Bristol, St George BS5 .....9 F8
Coalpit Heath BS36 .....31 D7
Coleford GL16 .....155 A6
Gloucester GL2 .....127 E4
Joy's Green GL17 .....163 D3
Lydney GL15 .....92 B2
Newent GL18 .....171 A7
Pucklechurch BS16 .....22 B5
Stroud GL5 .....98 C6
Winchcombe GL54 .....139 F6
Orchard Ridge GL20 .....180 F7
Orchard Rise
Chepstow NP16 .....60 B5
Dursley GL11 .....87 F3
Longborough GL56 .....176 D8
Newnham GL14 .....156 F6
Olveston BS35 .....50 A3
Tibberton GL19 .....171 E1
Orchard Springs GL6 .....91 A4
Orchard Sq BS5 .....9 D7
Orchard St Bristol BS1 ..194 C2
Wooton-u-E GL12 .....68 B7
Orchard The Bristol BS34 .29 F5
Clapton-on-t-H GL54 .....168 F4
13 Fairford GL7 .....152 E4
Frampton Cotterell BS36 ...31 C8
North Cerney GL7 .....158 D3
Pill BS20 .....16 C4
Tewkesbury GL20 .....192 D5
Tytherington GL12 .....52 B5
Uckington GL51 .....132 D7
Uley GL11 .....89 B1
Orchard Vale BS15 .....10 F7
Orchard View
Draycott GL56 .....186 E6
Stroud GL5 .....99 A4
Orchard View Ham Green Hospl BS20 .....16 E4
Orchard Way
17 Berry Hill GL16 .....155 A7
Cheltenham GL51 .....132 F3
Churchdown GL3 .....128 B7
Huntley GL19 .....165 D6
Kingham OX7 .....177 F2
Maisemore GL2 .....126 A7
Orchard Wlk GL12 .....67 F4
Orchards The
Bristol, Kingswood BS15 ...10 F7
Bristol, Shirehampton BS11 .16 E6
Charlton Kings GL52 .....131 C6
Longhope GL17 .....164 F6
Lydney GL15 .....92 A3
Orchid Mdw NP16 .....60 B5
Organ's Alley GL1 .....196 B2
Oridge St GL19 .....172 A6
Oriel Gr GL56 .....187 A2
Oriel Rd GL50 .....193 B3
Oriole Way GL4 .....119 D6
Orion Dr BS34 .....29 D6
Orland Way BS30 .....11 A3
Orlebar Gdns BS11 .....27 B2
Orlham La HR8 .....178 D6
Ormerod Rd Bristol BS9 ..17 E5
Sedbury NP16 .....61 B7
Ormond Pl GL50 .....193 B3
Ormond Terr GL50 .....193 B3
Ormonds Cl BS32 .....40 E1
Ormsley Cl BS34 .....29 C8
Orpen Gdns BS7 .....19 B5
Orpen Pk BS32 .....40 B3
Orpheus Ave BS34 .....29 D6
Orrisdale Terr GL53 .....193 C2
Orwell Dr BS31 .....5 A4
Orwell St BS3 .....8 E3
Osborne Ave BS7 .....18 F3
Osborne Cl BS34 .....29 D4
Osborne Rd
Bristol, Clifton BS8 .....18 A1
Bristol, Southville BS3 .....8 C4
Severn Beach BS35 .....38 A7
Osborne Terr
10 Bristol BS3 .....8 B2
Thrupp GL5 .....99 E3
Osborne Villas BS2 .....194 C4
Osborne Wallis Ho BS8 .194 A1
Osbourne Ave GL4 .....118 C1
Osbourne Ho 6 GL50 ..130 B8
Osier Cl GL4 .....119 A4
Osprey Cl GL4 .....119 D5
Osprey Ct BS14 .....2 D5
Osprey Dr GL10 .....97 F8
Osprey Pk BS35 .....64 D3
Osprey Rd 15 Bristol BS5 .....9 C7
Cheltenham GL53 .....130 C5
Osric Rd GL1 .....118 F6
Othello Cl GL51 .....132 E2
Otter Rd GL4 .....120 A5
Otterburn Ho GL2 .....118 C4
Otterford Cl BS14 .....3 B5
Otters Field GL54 .....174 A8
Ottery Cl BS11 .....27 A1
Ottrells Mead BS32 .....40 C3
Our Lady of Lourdes Prim RC Sch BS15 .....10 E7
Our Lady of the Rosary Cath Prim Sch BS11 .....17 A8
Our Lady of the Rosary Prim Sch BS11 .....27 A1
Oval App GL2 .....157 F3
Oval The
Frampton on Severn GL2 .100 A5
Gloucester GL1 .....118 D6
Over Bridge★ GL2 .....126 B4
Over Cswy GL1 .....126 C3
Over La BS35 .....39 D2
Over Old Rd GL19,GL2 ..172 C3
Overbrook Cl GL4 .....127 C1
Overbrook Dr GL52 .....133 F3
Overbrook Rd GL2 .....109 E7
Overbury CE Fst Sch GL20 .....182 F8
Overbury Rd GL1 .....119 A8
Overbury St GL53 .....131 A7
Overhill BS20 .....16 D4
Overhill Rd GL7 .....190 B8
Overley Rd GL7 .....149 E7
Overndale Rd BS16 .....20 C6
Overndale Sch BS37 .....34 A7
Overnhill Ct BS16 .....20 D5
Overnhill Rd BS16 .....20 D5
Overnhurst Ct 2 BS16 ..20 D5
Overton 5 BS4 .....9 D1
Overton Ct GL50 .....193 A3
Overton La GL2 .....157 E5
Overton Park Rd GL50 ..193 A3
Overton Rd Bristol BS6 ...18 E2
Cheltenham GL50 .....193 A3
Owen Gdns 1 GL16 .....155 A6
Owen Gr BS9 .....18 B5
Owen St 18 BS5 .....9 B8
Owl Cl GL4 .....119 D5
Owlpen Manor & Gdns★ GL11 .....89 E1
Owls End Rd GL52 .....138 A4
Owls Eye Cl 4 GL16 .....155 B6
Owls Head Rd BS15 .....10 E6
Oxbarton BS34 .....29 F5
Oxbutts Ind Est GL52 ...138 B4
Oxebode The GL1 .....196 B3
Oxen Leaze BS32 .....40 E2
Oxford Cl 1 GL52 .....130 F8
Oxford Ho GL7 .....190 D4
Oxford Pas GL50 .....193 B4
Oxford Pl
19 Bristol, Clifton BS8 .....7 F6
14 Bristol, Upper Easton BS5 .....19 B1
Oxford Rd GL1 .....196 C4
Oxford St Bristol BS2 ...194 C4
7 Bristol, Barton Hill BS5 ...9 C7
Bristol, Knowle BS3 .....8 F4
Bristol, Newton BS2 .....9 A6
Cheltenham GL52 .....130 F8
Chepstow NP16 .....60 E8
Gloucester GL1 .....196 C3
Lydney GL15 .....92 A2
Moreton-in-M GL56 .....187 A3
Oxford Terr
Gloucester GL1 .....196 C3
Stroud GL5 .....99 C8
Oxford Way GL51 .....130 A6
Oxford Wlk 2 GL52 .....130 F8
Oxleaze BS13 .....2 D4
Oxleaze Cl 4 GL8 .....140 B4
Oxleaze La BS41 .....1 E3
Oxleaze Rd Culkerton GL8 140 F6
7 Tetbury GL8 .....140 B4
Oxmead Cl GL52 .....138 B4
Oxmoor GL4 .....119 E3
Oxstalls Com Sch GL1 ..127 A4
Oxstalls Dr GL2 .....127 A5
Oxstalls La GL2 .....127 B4
Oxstalls Way GL2 .....127 B4
Ozleworth BS15 .....11 A8

P

Packer's Rd GL14 .....191 D4
Packhorse La GL7 .....160 A1
Paddock Cl
Bristol, Emerson's Green BS16 .....21 C6
Bristol, Patchway BS32 .....40 E2
Paddock Gdn BS14 .....2 F4

Paddock Gdns
Alveston BS35 51 A5
Gloucester GL2 127 D5
Paddock Rise GL10 97 F8
Paddock The
Chepstow NP16 60 D6
Coleford GL16 155 B6
Highworth SN6 145 D3
South Cerney GL7 142 F7
Paddocks La GL50 133 D5
Paddocks The
Cirencester GL7 150 D7
Monmouth NP25 154 A7
Thornbury BS35 64 D1
Padin Cl 3 GL6 148 C6
Padmore Ct 7 BS5 9 D7
Padstow Rd BS4 2 F8
Paganhill Est GL5 98 F8
Paganhill La GL5 98 F7
Page Ct BS16 20 F4
Page Rd BS16 20 D4
Page's La GL20 181 F7
Pages Mead BS11 16 C8
Paget Ho GL7 190 D5
Pagets Rd GL52 138 A2
Painswick Ave BS34 29 B8
Painswick Dr BS37 43 E1
Painswick Old Rd GL6 103 C1
Painswick Rd
Brockworth GL3 120 D3
Cheltenham GL50 193 A1
Gloucester GL4 119 C4
Stroud GL6 103 B2
Painswick Rococo Gdn★ GL6 111 E2
Pakistan Ho 1 GL51 132 E2
Palestra Lo GL7 190 C5
Palm Rd GL20 192 E2
Palmdale Cl BS30 11 A3
Palmer Ave GL4 119 F5
Palmers Cl BS30 11 A6
Palmers Leaze BS34 30 A6
Palmerston Rd BS6 18 C4
Palmerston St 6 BS3 8 C3
Palmyra Rd BS3 8 B2
Pancake La GL19 173 E5
Paper Mill Cotts OX18 161 E7
Paquet Ho BS20 16 D5
Parabola Cl GL50 193 A3
Parabola La GL50 193 A3
Parabola Rd GL50 193 A3
Parade The
Bristol, Bishopsworth BS13 2 A6
Bristol, Patchway BS34 39 F1
Bristol, Shirehampton BS11 16 E6
Brockworth GL3 120 E5
Chipping Sodbury BS37 44 A1
Gloucester GL2 127 E4
Paradise Row GL54 167 E2
Paragon Terr GL53 193 B2
Paragon The BS8 7 F6
Parawell La GL15 147 C8
Parbrook Ct BS14 3 B5
Parfitt's Hill 8 BS5 9 F6
Park Ave
Bristol, Eastville BS5 19 D3
Bristol, Knowle BS3 8 E3
Bristol, Patchway BS32 40 A2
Bristol, St George BS5 9 E8
Frampton Cotterell BS36 31 B6
Gloucester GL2 127 C5
Highworth SN6 145 D3
Winterbourne BS36 30 E7
Park Brake GL2 125 D4
Park Cl
Bristol, Cadbury Heath BS30 11 B5
Bristol, Kingswood BS15 10 E7
Fairford GL7 152 E4
Keynsham BS31 4 D5
Northway GL20 182 B5
St Briavels GL15 146 F7
8 Tetbury GL8 140 C4
Park Cres
Bristol, Cadbury Heath BS30 11 B5
Bristol, Frenchay BS16 30 C1
Bristol, St George BS5 9 E8
Park Ct Lydney GL15 92 A3
Stroud GL5 99 D6
Park Dr GL2 117 F1
Park End 1 SN6 142 F4
Park End Rd GL1 196 B1
Park Farm GL54 168 F8
Park Farm Ct 13 BS30 10 F4
Park Farm Village Gn BS36 31 B6
Park Gate GL50 193 A1
Park Glade NP16 146 B4
Park Gr Bristol BS9 18 C5
Whitecroft GL15 155 E1
Park Hill Bristol BS11 16 F6
Whitecroft GL15 155 E1
Park Hill Comm GL15 147 A2
Park Hill La NP16,GL15 146 E2
Park Hill Rd
Tidenham Chase GL15 146 F2
Woolaston GL15 147 A2
Park Ho GL50 193 A1
Park Inf Sch The GL10 97 E7
Park Jun Sch GL10 97 E7
Park La Bristol BS2 194 C3
Brockhampton GL54 174 A1
Cirencester GL7 190 C4
Ilmington CV36 189 E7
Park La *continued*
North Nibley GL11 79 E7
Prestbury GL52 134 B6
Winterbourne BS36 31 B6
Woodchester GL5 90 F6
Wooton-u-E GL12 69 A8
Park Mews GL50 130 C6
Park Par GL10 97 E8
Park Pl
5 Ashton Keynes SN6 142 F5
Bristol, Kingsdown BS8 194 B3
Bristol, Upper Eastville BS5 19 E3
Bristol, Victoria Park BS2 194 C3
Cheltenham GL50 193 A1
Park Prim Sch The BS15 10 E8
Park Rd Berry Hill GL16 155 A7
Blockley GL56 186 C6
Bristol BS3 194 B1
Bristol, Cadbury Heath BS30 11 B5
Bristol, Kingswood BS15 10 D8
Bristol, Northville BS7 29 A1
Bristol, Shirehampton BS11 16 F6
Bristol, Staple Hill BS16 20 E5
Bristol, Stapleton BS16 19 D5
Chipping Campden GL55 188 F1
6 Coleford GL16 155 A6
Cromhall GL12 66 B4
Gloucester GL1 196 B2
Highleadon GL19 171 F2
Keynsham BS31 4 E4
Nailsworth GL6 91 C3
Stonehouse GL10 97 E8
Stroud GL5 99 D6
Thornbury BS35 64 B2
Park Road Cres GL6 91 C3
Park Row Aylburton GL15 147 D4
Bristol BS1 194 C3
Frampton Cotterell BS36 31 A8
Park St Bristol BS1 194 C3
Bristol, St George BS5 9 F8
Bristol, Totterdown BS4 9 A3
Cheltenham GL50 193 A4
Cirencester GL7 190 C5
Fairford GL7 152 E4
Gloucester GL1 196 B3
Hawkesbury Upton GL9 56 A2
Iron Acton BS37 42 D4
Stow-on-t-W GL54 176 F4
Park Street Ave BS1 194 C3
Park Terr GL6 91 F6
Park The
Bristol, Frenchay BS16 30 B1
Bristol, Kingswood BS15 10 E8
Bristol, Patchway BS32 40 C3
Bristol, Willsbridge BS30 11 B1
Cheltenham GL50 130 B6
Keynsham BS31 4 E6
Northway GL20 182 B5
Stow-on-t-W GL54 176 F4
Park View Bristol BS15 10 E7
Cheltenham GL51 132 E4
Chepstow NP16 72 C1
Cirencester GL7 190 B8
Ruardean GL17 163 F4
Saul GL2 157 F4
Sedbury NP16 61 B8
Yate BS37 32 E8
Park View Ave BS35 64 C2
Park View Dr GL5 98 E8
Park View Rd GL13 85 D3
Park View Terr BS5 9 E8
Park Way Bristol BS30 11 B5
Siddington GL7 150 D2
Park Wood Cl BS14 2 F4
Parkbury Cl GL51 133 A2
Parkend Prim Sch GL15 155 F2
Parkend Rd Bream GL15 155 D1
Coleford GL16 155 B5
Yorkley GL15 156 A2
Parkend Sta GL15 155 E3
Parkend Wlk
Coleford GL16 155 B5
Sling GL16 155 B3
Parker Pl 1 WR12 185 B8
Parker St 5 BS3 8 B3
Parkers Ave BS30 12 C7
Parkers Barton BS5 9 B6
Parkers Cl BS10 28 E4
Parkers La GL56 187 A3
Parkfield Ave 3 BS5 9 D7
Parkfield Cotts GL6 112 A2
Parkfield Rd BS16 22 A6
Parkhouse La BS31 4 C2
Parkhurst Ave 4 BS16 20 B4
Parkland Mews 26 GL54 176 F4
Parkland Rd
Cheltenham GL53 130 F4
Dursley GL11 87 F4
Parkland Sq GL7 190 B2
Parkland Way BS35 64 C3
Parklands Bristol BS15 10 E8
Churchdown GL3 128 A6
Quedgeley GL2 117 F1
Wooton-u-E GL12 68 B8
Quedgeley GL2 109 E8
Parklands Cl NP16 60 B4
Parklands Rd BS3 7 E4
Parkmill HR9 162 C7
Parks Rd GL17 164 D5
Parkside GL16 155 A5
Parkside Ave BS36 30 E6
Parkside Cl GL3 127 F6
Parkside Dr GL3 127 F6
Parkside Gdns BS5 19 B4
Parkstone Ave BS7 18 F6
Parkwall Cres BS30 10 F4
Parkwall Rd BS30 11 A4
Parkway BS34 30 A4
Parkway N BS34 30 A4
Parkway Trad Est 10 BS2 18 F2
Parkwell Cty Prim Sch BS30 11 A4
Parkwood Cres GL3 119 F6
Parkwood Gr GL53 131 A4
Parliament Prim Sch GL5 99 F7
Parliament St Bristol BS4 9 A4
Gloucester GL1 196 B2
Stroud GL5 99 D7
Parliment Cl GL5 99 C7
Parnall Cres BS37 43 C2
Parnall Rd BS16 20 A3
Parnall Road Ind Est BS16 20 A3
Parnell Rd BS16 19 E7
Parr Cl GL3 127 F7
Parr Ho GL54 139 E5
Parragate Rd GL14 191 C5
Parry Rd GL1 118 F6
Parry's Cl BS9 17 E5
Parry's La BS9 17 F5
Parrys Gr BS9 17 E5
Parslow Barton 4 BS5 10 A7
Parson St BS3 8 B2
Parson Street Prim Sch BS3 8 C2
Parson Street Sta BS3 8 B2
Parson's Cnr GL54 176 F5
Parsonage Farm 3 SN6 143 E4
Parsonage Rd BS41 7 C2
Parsonage St GL11 88 A1
Parsons Ave BS34 29 F5
Parsons Ct GL6 148 A3
Parsons La
Redmarley D'Abitot GL19 179 F2
Weston-s-E GL55 188 D3
Parsons Paddock BS14 3 A7
Parsons Wlk BS30 11 D7
Partition St BS1 194 C2
Parton Dr GL3 128 C5
Parton Manor Inf Sch GL3 128 B6
Parton Manor Jun Sch GL3 128 B6
Parton Mews GL3 128 B6
Parton Rd GL3 128 C6
Partridge Cl
Gloucester GL2 118 C5
Stonehouse GL10 97 F8
Partridge Rd BS16 22 C4
Partridge Way GL7 190 E4
Parva Springs NP16 146 B4
Passage Leaze BS11 16 D6
Passage Rd
Arlingham GL2 157 B6
Bristol, Brentry BS10 27 F3
Bristol, Westbury on Trym BS9 18 A8
Saul GL2 157 F4
Passage Road Brentry Hill BS9,BS10 28 A2
Passage St BS2 195 B2
Pastor's Hill GL15 147 D8
Pasture La GL56 186 C5
Patch Ct BS16 21 A8
Patch Elm La BS37 42 F7
Patch La BS37 43 A8
Patcham High Sch BS32 40 B1
Patches The GL17 163 F3
Patchway BS34 29 B8
Patchway Brook BS32 40 C2
Patchway CE Prim Sch BS34 40 C1
Patchway Sta BS34 29 C6
Patchway Trad Est BS34 28 E7
Paternoster Sch GL7 190 D3
Paterson Rd GL7 190 E4
Pates Ave GL51 133 B2
Pates Gram Sch GL51 132 E3
Patseamur Mews GL2 127 E5
Patterdale Cl GL51 132 F5
Patterson Ho 8 BS1 195 B1
Paul Mead GL6 111 B1
Paul St Bristol BS2 194 C4
Gloucester GL1 118 F7
Paul's Rise GL5 99 A2
Pauls Croft SN6 143 F4
Pauls Wlk GL19 165 D6
Paulton Dr BS7 18 C4
Paultow Ave BS3 8 E3
Paultow Rd BS3 8 E3
Pauntley CE Prim Sch GL18 171 B8
Pauntley Court Dr GL19 171 C7
Pavey Cl BS13 2 C4
Pavey Rd BS13 2 C4
Pavilion Rd NP16 61 C2
Pavilions The GL53 193 B2
Pawlett Rd BS13 2 C3
Pawlett Wlk BS13 2 C3
Paxhill La GL20 182 A8
Paxton BS16 19 E8
Paybridge Rd BS13 1 F4
Paygrove La GL2 127 D5
Paymans Terr GL7 142 F7
Payne Dr BS5 9 B7
Paynes Mdw GL2 100 F5
Paynes Pitch GL3 128 D4
Peach Cl GL20 192 E1
Peache Ct BS16 20 E6
Peache Rd BS16 20 F6
Peacock Cl
5 Cheltenham GL51 132 D2
Gloucester GL4 119 E5
5 Newent GL18 171 A4
Peacock Gdns 6 GL18 171 A4
Peacock La GL14 191 C1
Peacocks La BS15 10 C7
Peak La GL11 89 A7
Peakstile Piece GL52 138 B3
Pear Orch The GL20 182 C5
Pear Tree Cl
Chipping Campden GL55 189 A1
Hardwicke GL2 109 E7
Lower Swell GL54 176 D4
Woodmancote GL52 138 C3
Pear Tree Hey BS37 43 E5
Pear Tree Rd BS32 40 C2
Pearce Way GL2 118 B4
Pearces Hill BS16 20 B7
Pearcroft Rd GL10 98 A6
Pearl St BS3 8 B3
Pearsall Rd BS30 10 E2
Peart Cl Bristol BS13 1 E5
Gloucester GL1 127 B1
Peart Dr BS13 1 E4
Peartree La
Bristol, Lower Soundwell BS15 20 F2
Bristol, St George BS5 10 B6
Pearwood Way GL4 118 C2
Pecked La GL52 138 A3
Peel Cl GL53 131 C5
Peel St BS5 195 C4
Peg Hill BS37 43 F4
Pegasus Bldg GL2 118 A2
Pegasus Ct
Bourton-on-t-W GL54 169 A8
Broadway WR12 185 B8
Cheltenham GL51 130 B7
Gloucester GL4 127 E1
Pegasus Gdns GL2 117 F2
Pegasus Rd BS34 28 D7
Peggotty Bglws GL4 119 C7
Peghouse Cl GL5 103 D1
Peghouse Rise GL5 103 D1
Pelham Cres GL3 128 A6
Pemberton Ct BS16 20 C5
Pembery Rd BS3 8 B3
Pembridge Cl GL52 131 C6
Pembridge Ct GL50 193 A1
Pembroke Ave BS11 16 E6
Pembroke Gate BS8 18 A1
Pembroke Gr BS8 194 A3
Pembroke Jun & Inf Sch NP16 60 E6
Pembroke Mans BS8 194 A4
Pembroke Pl BS8 194 A1
Pembroke Rd
Bristol, Clifton BS8 194 A4
Bristol, Kingswood BS15 20 E2
Bristol, Shirehampton BS11 16 E6
Bristol, Southville BS3 8 C4
Cheltenham GL51 129 E6
Chepstow NP16 60 E6
Pembroke St Bristol BS2 195 B4
Cinderford GL14 191 D4
Gloucester GL1 196 C1
Pembroke Vale BS8 194 A4
Pembury Rd GL4 118 E4
Pen Park Rd BS10 28 D2
Pen Park Sch BS10 28 D2
Penard Way BS15 10 F7
Penby Lawn GL14 156 F6
Penda Pl NP16 61 A8
Pendennis Ave BS16 20 D4
Pendennis Ho 5 BS16 20 D5
Pendennis Pk BS4 9 D2
Pendennis Rd BS16 20 D5
Pendil Cl GL50 133 B6
Pendock CE Prim Sch GL19 180 A4
Pendock Cl Bristol BS30 11 C1
Quedgeley GL2 117 E1
Pendock Ct BS16 21 B7
Pendock Rd Bristol BS16 20 C6
Winterbourne BS36 30 E5
Penfield Rd BS2 19 A2
Penharva Cl GL51 133 A3
Penhill Rd GL4 119 B5
Penlea Ct BS11 16 D7
Penmoel La NP16 73 A3
Penmoyle Gdns NP16 73 A4
Penn Dr BS16 30 C1
Penn La GL10 98 B2
Penn St BS1 195 B3
Pennard Ct BS14 3 B5
Penngrove BS30 11 A3
Pennine Cl GL2 109 E8
Pennine Rd Bristol BS30 11 C4
Cheltenham GL52 134 B3
Pennington Ct GL51 132 E4
Pennlea BS13 2 C7
Pennsylvania Ave GL51 132 F3
Penny Cl GL2 127 D4
Penny La GL2 95 B2
Pennyroyal Gr BS16 19 E4
Pennywell Ct 3 BS5 9 A8
Pennywell Rd BS5 9 A8
Penpole Ave BS11 16 E6
Penpole Cl BS11 16 D7
Penpole La BS11 16 E7
Penpole Pk BS11 16 E7
Penpole Pl BS11 16 E6
Penrith Cl GL51 129 F7
Penrith Gdns BS10 18 D8
Penrith Rd GL51 129 F7
Penrose BS14 2 F7
Penrose Cl GL6 102 E3
Penrose Dr BS32 29 D7
Penrose Rd GL3 127 D6
Pensfield Pk BS10 28 D4
Pensford Ct BS14 3 D5
Pensile Rd GL6 91 D4
Pentagon The BS9 17 B5
Pentathlon Way GL50 133 D5
Penterry La NP16 72 B7
Penterry Pk NP16 60 D8
Pentire Ave BS13 2 A6
Pentland Ave BS35 51 E8
Pentwyn Cl NP16 60 B6
Pentylands Cl SN6 145 C4
Peppercorn Alley GL20 182 E8
Pepys Cl BS31 5 D2
Perch Dr GL16 155 C6
Percival Rd BS8 7 F8
Percy St 8 Bristol BS3 8 D4
Gloucester GL1 118 F7
Percy Walker Ct BS16 20 C6
Peregrine Cl GL2 117 F3
Peregrine Rd GL53 130 C5
Perretts Ct BS1 194 C1
Perricks Cl GL14 165 D3
Perrie Dr WR11 188 C7
Perrinpit Rd BS36 41 E2
Perrinsfield GL7 153 E3
Perrott Rd BS15 21 A1
Perry Cl
Charlton Kings GL53 131 B5
26 Newent GL18 171 A4
Winterbourne BS36 30 D4
Perry Court Inf Sch BS14 3 A6
Perry Court Jun Sch BS14 3 A6
Perry Ctr The GL2 109 F6
Perry Field GL15 147 C3
Perry Hill GL20 192 C3
Perry Orch Stroud GL5 98 D8
Upton St Leonards GL4 119 E2
Perry Rd BS1 195 A3
Perry St BS5 9 A8
Perry Way GL2 100 B3
Perry's Court La GL17 163 E4
Perrycroft Ave BS13 2 A6
Perrycroft Rd BS13 2 A6
Perryfield Ct 1 GL54 168 F7
Perrygrove Rd GL16 155 A4
Perrymans Cl BS16 20 A6
Perrys Lea BS32 40 D2
Persh La GL2 125 F6
Persh Way GL2 126 A7
Perth GL10 101 E1
Perwell Cl GL20 182 C8
Pesley Cl BS13 2 A4
Peter Pennell Cl GL51 132 E4
Peter's St GL10 96 E3
Peter's Terr BS5 9 B7
Petercole Dr BS13 2 A6
Peters Field GL2 125 E5
Peterson Sq BS13 2 C3
Petersway Gdns BS5 10 A6
Petherton Cl BS15 10 E7
Petherton Gdns BS14 3 B7
Petherton Rd BS14 3 B7
Petherton Road Inf Sch BS14 3 B7
Pethick Ho BS4 2 F8
Pettigrove Gdns BS15 10 E7
Pettigrove Rd BS15 10 E6
Petty La GL52 138 F3
Petty Marsh GL15 146 E6
Pettycroft GL17 163 F4
Petworth Cl GL4 110 C8
Pevelands GL11 87 F5
Pevensey Wlk BS4 2 D7
Peverell Cl BS10 27 F3
Peverell Dr BS10 27 F3
Peveril Ho GL2 118 C4
Pheasant La GL51 132 B1
Pheasant Mead GL10 97 F8
Pheasant Rise HR9 162 F7
Pheasant Way GL7 190 F5
Pheasantry The GL7 143 F8
Phelps Way GL19 171 E1
Philadelphia Ct BS1 195 B3
Philip St
Bristol, Bedminster BS3 8 D4
Bristol, St Philip's Marsh BS2 9 B5
Gloucester GL1 118 D7
Philip's Cl GL15 156 B1
Philippa Cl BS14 3 A7
Philips Ho 2 BS2 195 B4
Phillimore Gdns GL2 100 A5
Phillimore Rd GL11 87 E4
Phillips La GL19 179 F2
Phillips Rd WR12 188 A1
Phippen St 1 BS1 195 B1
Phipps St BS3 8 B4
Phoenix Ct GL16 155 A5
Phoenix Dr NP16 61 A4
Phoenix Gr BS6 18 C5
Phoenix Ho BS5 9 B6
Phoenix Trad Est GL5 99 E3
Phoenix Way GL7 190 C4
Piccadilly
Guiting Power GL54 175 B3
Stroud GL5 99 D7
Piccadilly Way GL52 134 D4
Pickedmoor La BS35 63 E5
Pickering Cl GL53 130 C6
Pickering Rd GL53 130 C6
Picklenash Jun Sch GL18 170 F5
Picton Ho GL7 190 D5
Picton La BS6 18 E1
Picton St BS6 18 E1
Piece Hedge GL54 168 F8
Piece The
Churchdown GL3 128 D4
Coln St Aldwyns GL7 152 E7
Piercefield Ave NP16 72 C1
Piercefield Terr NP16 72 B5

Pigeon House Dr BS13 ...2 D4
Pigeon La GL20 ...183 A8
Pigott Ave BS13 ...2 A4
Pigs Cross GL18 ...170 C3
Pike Cnr WR12 ...188 B2
Pike Hill Rise GL54 ...167 B3
Pike House Cl 11 SN6 ...143 E4
Pike La GL6 ...91 B3
Pike Rd 9 Coleford GL16 155 A6
Winstone GL7,GL53 ...115 A1
Pile Marsh BS5 ...9 D7
Pilford Ave GL53 ...130 E4
Pilford Cl GL53 ...130 E5
Pilford Ct GL53 ...130 E3
Pilford Rd GL53 ...130 E3
Pilgrim Cl GL4 ...119 E6
Pilgrims Way Bristol BS16 20 D8
Shirehampton BS11 ...16 C7
Pilgrims Wharf BS4 ...9 E7
Pilgrove Cl GL51 ...132 D4
Pilgrove Way GL51 ...132 E5
Pilkington Cl BS34 ...29 C2
Pill La GL56 ...187 F1
Pill Rd Abbots Leigh BS8 ...16 F1
Pill BS20 ...16 E2
Pill St BS20 ...16 D4
Pillcroft Cl GL3 ...121 A4
Pillcroft Rd GL3 ...121 A4
Pilley Cres GL53 ...130 D4
Pilley La GL53 ...130 D4
Pillingers Rd BS15 ...10 C7
Pillowell Prim Sch GL15 155 F1
Pillowell Rd GL15 ...155 F1
Pillows Green Rd GL19 .172 B8
Pilning St BS35 ...39 C8
Pilning Sta BS35 ...38 F5
Pimpernel Mead BS32 ...29 E7
Pincoate GL2 ...125 D6
Pincot La GL6 ...103 D5
Pincots La GL12 ...54 B3
Pine Bank GL52 ...138 B4
Pine Cl Cheltenham GL52 .131 A8
Thornbury BS35 ...64 C1
Pine Crest Way 5 GL15 147 D8
Pine Ct BS31 ...4 C4
Pine Gr BS7 ...29 A1
Pine Grove Pl BS7 ...18 D3
Pine Halt GL54 ...166 C6
Pine Rd BS10 ...28 B3
Pine Ridge Cl BS9 ...17 C4
Pine Tree Dr GL4 ...119 E8
Pine Tree Way GL15 ...156 C1
Pinecroft BS14 ...2 F7
Pinedale GL15 ...147 B3
Pineholt Gate GL3 ...120 B7
Pinemount Rd GL3 ...120 A7
Pinery Rd GL4 ...119 E7
Pines La BS35 ...50 D3
Pines Rd BS30 ...11 C1
Pines The
Cheltenham GL50 ...193 A3
Greet GL54 ...174 A8
Pinetrees GL53 ...130 F5
Pinetum Dr GL2 ...125 A3
Pineway GL4 ...119 B6
Pinewood BS15 ...20 F1
Pinewood Cl Bristol BS9 ..18 B7
Cinderford GL14 ...191 E5
Pinewood Rd GL2 ...109 E8
Pinewood Way SN14 ...15 F7
Pingry La GL16 ...155 A4
Pinhay Rd BS13 ...2 B6
Pinkers Mead BS16 ...21 C6
Pinkhams Twist BS14 ...3 A5
Pinlocks GL4 ...119 E3
Pinnell Gr BS16 ...21 C7
Pinnells End La GL11 ...88 D8
Pintail Cl GL2 ...117 D1
Pioneer Pk BS4 ...9 C5
Pipe La BS1 ...194 C2
Piper Rd BS37 ...43 E3
Pipers Gr GL2 ...125 D5
Pippin Cl Gloucester GL4 .120 A6
Newent GL18 ...171 A4
Pippin Ct 4 BS30 ...10 F4
Pippins Rd GL20 ...182 C7
Pirton Cres GL3 ...128 B5
Pirton La GL3 ...128 B5
Pitch & Pay La BS9 ...17 E3
Pitch & Pay Pk BS9 ...17 E3
Pitch La BS6 ...18 D1
Pitch The GL6 ...148 B5
Pitchcombe BS37 ...32 C7
Pitchcombe Gdns BS9 ..17 D7
Pithay Ct BS1 ...195 A3
Pithay The BS1 ...195 A3
Pitlochry Cl BS7 ...28 F1
Pitman Pl GL12 ...68 C6
Pitman Rd GL51 ...132 E1
Pitt Ho GL52 ...133 F1
Pitt Rd BS7 ...18 E5
Pitt St GL1 ...196 B3
Pittsfield SN6 ...143 E4
Pittville Cir GL52 ...133 F2
Pittville Circus Rd GL52 133 F2
Pittville Cl BS35 ...64 C3
Pittville Cres GL52 ...133 F3
Pittville Crescent La
GL52 ...133 F3
Pittville Ct GL52 ...133 F4
Pittville Lawn GL52 ...133 E3
Pittville Mews GL52 ...193 C4
Pittville Pump Room & Mus*
GL52 ...133 E4
Pittville Sch GL52 ...133 F4
Pittville St GL52 ...193 C4
Pitville Pl 16 BS6 ...18 B1
Pixash Bsns Ctr BS31 ...5 B5
Pixash La BS31 ...5 C5
Place Hill GL18 ...170 C4
Plain The Stroud GL6 ...103 A2
Thornbury BS35 ...64 B1
Plantation Cres GL20 ...182 C7
Platts Row GL17 ...164 D5
Players Cl BS16 ...30 B3
Playford Gdns BS11 ...16 E8
Playhouse Ct GL53 ...193 C3
Pleasant Ho 4 BS16 ...20 D5
Pleasant Rd BS16 ...20 D5
Pleasant Stile GL14 ...156 E7
Pleydells 14 SN6 ...143 E4
Pleydells The GL7 ...151 B5
Plies The GL7 ...152 E3
Plimsoll Ho
3 Bristol BS1 ...195 B1
5 Bristol, Woolcott Park
BS6 ...18 B1
Plock Ct GL2 ...126 F5
Ploughmans Way GL2 ..109 E6
Plover Cl BS37 ...43 C2
Plowright Ho 7 BS15 ...10 B5
Pludds Court Rd GL17 ..163 E3
Plum Tree Cl GL4 ...119 E4
Plummer's Hill BS5 ...9 E8
Plumpton Ct BS16 ...30 F1
Pochard Cl GL2 ...117 D1
Pockhill La GL54 ...168 F7
Poden La WR11 ...188 D6
Podsmead Pl GL1 ...118 D5
Podsmead Rd GL1 ...118 D5
Poets' Cl BS5 ...9 D8
Point Rd GL8 ...140 B8
Polar Gdns SN14 ...47 E4
Polden Ho BS3 ...8 D3
Polefield Gdns GL51 ...130 B8
Polefield Ho 13 GL51 ...130 B8
Pollards La GL15 ...156 D1
Polly Barnes Cl 4 BS15 .10 B5
Polly Barnes Hill BS15 ...10 B5
Polygon Rd BS8 ...194 A2
Polygon The
Avonmouth BS11 ...26 D1
15 Bristol BS8 ...7 F6
Pomfrett Gdns BS14 ...3 E5
Pomphrey Hill BS16 ...21 C4
Pond La SN5 ...143 D1
Ponsford Rd BS4 ...9 B1
Ponting Cl BS5 ...20 A1
Ponting's Cl SN26 ...144 E1
Pool Cl GL56 ...187 F1
Pool Close Cotts GL56 ..187 F1
Pool Cnr BS32 ...50 B2
Pool Ho BS34 ...29 A8
Pool La NP25 ...154 B1
Pool Rd BS15 ...20 E3
Poole Court Dr BS37 ...43 E2
Poole Ground GL2 ...125 D6
Poole St BS11 ...16 B8
Poole Way GL50 ...193 A4
Pooles La GL5 ...98 E4
Pooles Wharf BS8 ...194 A1
Pooles Wharf Ct BS8 ...194 A1
Poolhay Cl GL19 ...180 E1
Poolway Ct 1 GL16 ...155 A5
Poolway Pl GL16 ...155 A6
Poolway Rd GL16 ...155 B6
Poolway Rise 8 GL16 ..155 A6
Pope's Ct GL7 ...190 A8
Popes Cl GL50 ...133 D3
Popes Meade GL2 ...125 D5
Poplar Ave BS9 ...17 D6
Poplar Cl Bristol BS30 ...11 C6
Gloucester GL1 ...118 D5
Poplar Dr
Pucklechurch BS16 ...22 B5
Woodmancote GL52 ...138 C3
Poplar La GL12 ...54 B4
Poplar Pl BS16 ...20 A3
Poplar Rd
Bristol, Hanham BS15 ...10 A5
Bristol, Highridge BS13 ...1 F7
Bristol, North Common
BS30 ...11 D6
Bristol, Speedwell BS5 ...19 F1
Poplar Terr BS15 ...10 F8
Poplar Way Colerne SN14 .15 F5
Hardwicke GL2 ...109 E7
Poplars Cl GL55 ...188 F1
Poplars The
Cheltenham GL51 ...129 E5
Easton-in-G BS20 ...16 B4
Poppy Field GL2 ...125 E6
Poppy Mead BS32 ...29 E7
Porchester Rd GL3 ...119 F7
Porlock Rd BS3 ...8 D3
Port Elizabeth Ho BS10 ..28 B1
Port Ind Est GL5 ...99 F1
Port La GL5 ...99 F1
Port Side Cl 5 BS5 ...9 F6
Port Terr GL5 ...99 F1
Port View BS20 ...16 C5
Port Wall* NP16 ...60 F8
Portbury Gr BS11 ...16 D6
Portbury Wlk BS11 ...16 D6
Portishead Way BS3 ...7 E3
Portland Ct BS1 ...194 B1
Portland Pl Bristol BS16 ..20 D3
9 Cheltenham GL52 ...193 C4
Portland Sq Bristol BS2 .195 B4
Cheltenham GL52 ...193 C4
Portland St
Bristol, Clifton BS8 ...7 F7
Bristol, Staple Hill BS16 ..20 D3
Cheltenham GL52 ...193 C4
Portman Terr GL50 ...193 B1
Portmeirion Cl BS14 ...3 B5
Porturet Way 2 GL53 ..131 B6
Portview Rd BS11 ...16 B8
Portwall La BS1 ...195 B1
Portwall La E 10 BS1 ...195 B1
Portwall Rd NP16 ...60 E8
Portway
Bristol, Shirehampton BS11 16 C6
Bristol, Sneyd Park BS8 ...17 C3
Upton St Leonards GL4 ...112 B7
Portway Com Sch BS11 ..16 E7
Portway La BS37 ...44 E2
Portway Rdbt BS11 ...16 C8
Portwell 4 SN6 ...143 E4
Post Office Cotts GL17 .163 C3
Post Office La
Cheltenham GL50 ...193 B3
Cleeve Hill GL52 ...138 E3
Draycott GL56 ...186 D6
Tewkesbury GL20 ...192 C4
Post Office Row GL2 ...101 B2
Post Office Sq GL7 ...150 E2
Post Paddocks The
GL15 ...147 C3
Postlip Way GL51 ...129 D8
Potlicker's La
Ablington GL7 ...159 F2
Coln Rogers GL54,GL7 ...159 E4
Potters Croft NP16 ...61 B4
Potters Field Rd GL52 ..138 C3
Potters Pond GL12 ...68 C7
Pound Cl Brockworth GL3 120 E4
Ledbury HR8 ...178 E8
Siddington GL7 ...150 E2
Twyning GL20 ...181 F7
Pound Dr BS16 ...19 F5
Pound Farm Ctyd GL3 ..120 E5
Pound Farm La HR9 ...170 B5
Pound Hill GL8 ...140 B8
Pound La Arlingham GL2 .157 B5
Bristol BS16 ...19 F4
Hardwicke GL2 ...109 D5
Little Rissington GL54 ...169 C6
Mickleton GL55 ...189 A6
Pound Mdw HR8 ...178 E8
Pound Rd Bristol BS15 ...20 F2
Highworth SN6 ...145 C4
Pound The
Almondsbury BS32 ...40 A5
Ampney Crucis GL7 ...151 B5
Little Rissington GL54 ...169 C6
Thornbury BS35 ...63 B6
Pountney Dr BS5 ...9 B8
Pow's Rd BS15 ...10 D7
Powell's Prim Sch GL7 .190 C5
Powells Way GL8 ...140 D3
Powis La GL8 ...148 B1
Poyntz Ct BS30 ...10 F3
Poyntz Rd BS4 ...2 F8
Pratten's La 1 BS16 ...20 D4
Preacher Cl BS5 ...10 B6
Preddy's La BS5 ...10 A6
Prescott BS37 ...32 D8
Prescott Ave GL4 ...119 B4
Prescott Wlk GL52 ...134 B4
Press Moor Dr BS30 ...10 F4
Prestbury BS37 ...32 D8
Prestbury Green Dr
GL52 ...134 C4
Prestbury Rd GL52 ...134 A4
Preston Cl NP16 ...60 F4
Preston Cross HR8 ...178 B6
Preston Wlk BS4 ...9 A1
Prestwick Cl BS4 ...9 D1
Pretoria Rd BS34 ...28 F8
Prewett St BS1 ...195 B1
Price St GL1 ...118 D7
Prices Ground GL4 ...119 D6
Priddy Ct BS14 ...3 B5
Priddy Dr BS14 ...3 B5
Priestley Ct GL20 ...192 C4
Priestwood Cl BS10 ...28 A3
Primrose Cl
Bristol, Patchway BS32 ...40 D2
Bristol, St George BS15 ...10 C8
Gloucester GL4 ...119 A4
Primrose Ct GL56 ...187 A3
Primrose Dr
Milkwall GL16 ...155 B4
Thornbury BS35 ...64 D2
Primrose Hill CE Prim Sch
GL15 ...92 B5
Primrose Hill Rd GL15 ...92 A5
Primrose La BS15 ...20 C1
Primrose Terr BS15 ...20 C1
Primrose Way GL15 ...92 B5
Prince Albert Ct GL3 ..120 C6
Prince Charles Rd 6
GL7 ...152 E4
Prince Cres GL19 ...172 A8
Prince St Bristol BS1 ...195 A1
Gloucester GL1 ...196 C2
Prince Street Rdbt BS1 195 A2
Prince's Bldgs 17 BS8 ...7 F6
Prince's Rd GL50 ...130 B7
Prince's St Bristol BS2 ..195 C4
Cheltenham GL52 ...133 F1
Princes Ct BS30 ...10 F4
Princes Rd GL5 ...98 E8
Princes' La BS8 ...7 F6
Princes' Pl BS7 ...18 E3
Princess Cl BS31 ...4 E4
Princess Elizabeth Way
GL51 ...132 E3
Princess Gdns BS16 ...19 D6
Princess Row BS2 ...195 A4
Princess Royal Rd 7
GL15 ...155 D1
Princess St
Bristol, Bedminster BS3 ...8 E4
Bristol, Newton BS2 ...9 A7
Princess Victoria St BS8 ..7 F6
Prinknash Abbey* GL4 .112 B8
Prinknash Cl GL4 ...119 C4
Prinknash Ct 6 BS37 ...32 D7
Prinknash Rd GL4 ...119 C4
Prior Park Prep Sch
SN6 ...143 F4
Prior's Hill 11 BS6 ...18 D1
Priors Ct Cirencester GL7 150 D7
Prestbury GL52 ...134 B3
Priors Lea BS37 ...43 E1
Priors Rd GL52 ...134 B3
Priors Wlk GL7 ...153 F2
Priory Ave BS9 ...18 A7
Priory Cl Chepstow NP16 ..72 D1
Cirencester GL7 ...190 C5
Priory Court Rd BS9 ...18 A7
Priory Ct
Bristol, Hanham BS15 ...10 C3
Bristol, Knowle BS4 ...9 B2
Churchdown GL3 ...128 D5
Dursley GL11 ...88 A3
Priory Dene BS9 ...18 A7
Priory Fields GL6 ...82 F8
Priory Gdns
Bristol, Horfield BS7 ...18 F8
Bristol, Shirehampton BS11 16 D7
Easton-in-G BS20 ...16 B4
Priory Gn SN6 ...145 D3
Priory Ind Est GL8 ...140 C4
Priory La
Bishop's Cleeve GL52 ...138 A4
Monmouth NP25 ...162 A1
Priory Lea HR9 ...163 C8
Priory Mews GL52 ...193 C3
Priory Pl
Cheltenham GL52 ...193 C2
Gloucester GL1 ...196 B2
Priory Rd
Bristol, Knowle BS4 ...9 B2
Bristol, Shirehampton BS8 .16 D6
Bristol, Tyndall's Park
BS8 ...194 C4
Easton-in-G BS20 ...16 B4
Gloucester GL1 ...196 A3
Gloucester GL1 ...196 B4
Keynsham BS31 ...4 E7
Priory St GL52 ...193 C3
Priory Terr GL52 ...133 F1
Priory Way 7 GL8 ...140 C4
Priory Wlk GL52 ...133 F1
Pritchard St BS2 ...195 B4
Private Rd GL5 ...99 C2
Probertsbarn La GL17 ..163 C3
Probyn Cl BS16 ...20 A7
Proctor Cl BS4 ...9 D1
Proctor Ho BS1 ...195 B1
Promenade GL50 ...193 B3
Promenade The BS7 ...18 D2
Prospect Ave BS15 ...20 B1
Prospect Cl
Coleford GL16 ...155 A5
Easter Compton BS35 ...39 A2
Frampton Cotterell BS36 ...30 F8
Winterbourne BS36 ...30 E4
Prospect Cres BS15 ...20 F2
Prospect La
Frampton Cotterell BS36 ..30 F8
Llangrove HR9 ...162 B6
Prospect Pl
7 Bristol, Bedminster BS3 ..8 C3
1 Bristol, Montpelier BS6 .18 D2
Bristol, Whitehall BS5 ...9 C8
Cirencester GL7 ...190 D3
Dursley GL11 ...88 A1
Prospect Rd
Cinderford GL14 ...191 D4
Severn Beach BS35 ...38 A5
Prospect Row HR9 ...170 B4
Prospect Terr GL6 ...148 C5
Prosper La GL16 ...155 B5
Providence La BS41 ...7 A1
Providence Pl BS2 ...195 C2
Providence View BS41 ...7 A1
Prudham St 7 BS5 ...19 C1
Pry La WR12 ...185 A8
Puck Pit La GL54 ...174 A7
Pucklechurch CE Prim Sch
BS16 ...22 C6
Pucklechurch Trad Est
BS16 ...22 B4
Puckrup La GL20 ...181 E7
Pudlicott La GL55 ...189 D1
Puffs Alley GL18 ...171 A4
Pullar Cl GL52 ...137 F4
Pullar Ct GL52 ...137 F4
Pullen Ct GL52 ...138 A7
Pullens Rd GL6 ...111 F1
Pullin Ct BS30 ...11 D4
Pullins Gn BS35 ...64 B1
Pullman Ct GL1 ...196 C3
Pullnoggin Pool La
HR9 ...162 D3
Pump La Bristol BS1 ...195 B1
Tetbury GL8 ...140 E3
Tockington BS32 ...50 D4
Pump Sq BS20 ...16 D5
Pumphreys Ct GL53 ...131 A5
Pumphreys Rd GL53 ...131 A5
Purbeck Way GL52 ...134 C4
Purcell Rd GL3 ...128 A8
Purcell Wlk BS4 ...2 D7
Purdown Rd BS7 ...18 F5
Purley Ave GL7 ...190 D4
Purley Rd GL7 ...190 D4
Pursey Dr BS32 ...29 F6
Purslane Cl GL4 ...119 B4
Purton Cl BS15 ...10 E6
Purton Pl GL15 ...92 C2
Purton Rd BS7 ...18 D2
Puxley Cl BS14 ...3 E6
Puzzle Cl 4 GL15 ...147 D8
Puzzle Wood* GL16 ...155 A4
Pwllmeyric Cl NP16 ...60 B5
Pyart Ct GL16 ...155 A5
Pye Croft BS32 ...40 E3
Pyecroft Ave BS9 ...18 C7
Pyghtell The GL7 ...190 B7
Pyke Rd GL20 ...192 F4
Pylers Way GL15 ...92 B2
Pylle Hill Cres BS3 ...8 F4
Pynne Cl BS14 ...3 F5
Pynne Rd BS14 ...3 F5
Pyracantha Wlk BS14 ...3 A6
Pyrton Mews 2 GL51 ..129 E5
Pystol La GL15 ...146 E7

Q

Quabbs La GL17 ...164 B4
Quadrangle The
Naunton GL54 ...175 D2
Westerleigh BS37 ...32 C4
Quadrant BS32 ...40 B3
Quadrant E BS16 ...20 C3
Quadrant The
Bristol, Patchway BS32 ...40 A3
Bristol, Westbury Park BS6 .18 B3
Quadrant W BS16 ...20 C3
Quail Cl GL4 ...119 E7
Quail Mdws GL8 ...140 B4
Quaker La BS35 ...64 B1
Quaker's Cl BS16 ...20 D8
Quaker's Rd BS16 ...20 E8
Quakers Row GL7 ...149 E4
Quakers' Friars BS1 ...195 B3
Quantock Cl BS30 ...11 C5
Quantock Rd Bristol BS3 ..8 D3
Quedgeley GL2 ...109 E8
Quarhouse La GL5 ...148 A5
Quarries The BS32 ...40 C6
Quarrington Rd BS7 ...18 E5
Quarry Barton BS16 ...30 C4
Quarry Cl GL7 ...190 B8
Quarry Cres SN6 ...145 C3
Quarry Gdns GL11 ...87 D4
Quarry La Bristol BS11 ..27 C1
Gorsley HR9 ...170 B4
Winterbourne BS36 ...30 E4
Quarry Mead BS35 ...50 F5
Quarry Rd Alveston BS35 .50 F5
Bristol, Frenchay BS16 ...20 C7
Bristol, Kingswood BS15 ..10 D6
Chipping Sodbury BS37 ...44 A1
Quarry Stps 8 BS8 ...18 A2
Quarry The Ablington GL7 159 F1
Bristol BS11 ...27 C1
Dursley GL11 ...87 D4
10 Fairford GL7 ...152 E4
Quarry View GL7 ...153 C6
Quarry Way
Bristol, Emerson's Green
BS16 ...31 A1
Bristol, Fishponds BS16 ...19 E5
Quat Goose La GL51 ...133 B7
Quay St Bristol BS1 ...195 A3
Gloucester GL1 ...196 A3
Tewkesbury GL20 ...192 C4
Quay The GL1 ...196 A3
Quays The BS1 ...194 C1
Quayside NP16 ...146 C4
Quayside La 4 BS5 ...9 F6
Quebec Ho 4 GL51 ...132 E3
Quedgeley BS37 ...32 C8
Quedgeley Trad Est W
GL2 ...109 D5
Queen Ann Rd BS5 ...9 B6
Queen Anne's Rd GL7 ..190 E5
Queen Charlotte St BS1 195 A2
Queen Charlton La BS14 ..3 E2
Queen Elizabeth Rd
GL7 ...190 E4
Queen Elizabeth's Hospital
Sch BS8 ...194 B3
Queen Margaret Prim Sch
GL20 ...192 C2
Queen Quay BS1 ...195 A2
Queen Sq Bristol BS1 ...195 A2
Saltford BS31 ...5 F3
Queen Square Ave 7
BS1 ...195 A2
Queen St Avonmouth BS11 .26 A1
Bristol BS2 ...195 B3
Bristol, Eastville BS5 ...19 D3
Bristol, St George BS15 ...10 B8
Chedworth GL54 ...159 A7
Cheltenham GL51 ...133 C3
Cirencester GL7 ...190 D3
Lydney GL15 ...92 B4
Queen Victoria Rd BS6 ..18 A4
Queen Victoria St BS2 ...9 A6
Queen's Ave BS8 ...194 B3
Queen's Cir GL50 ...193 B2
Queen's Ct
Brimscombe GL5 ...148 A5
Bristol BS8 ...194 B3
Ledbury HR8 ...178 E8
Queen's Dr Bristol BS7 ..18 C5
Stroud GL5 ...98 E8

Queen's Rd Bristol BS8 . . 194 B3
Bristol, Ashley Down BS7 . . 18 F5
Bristol, Bishopsworth BS13, BS41 . . . . 1 F4
Bristol, Cadbury Heath BS30 . . . . 11 B4
Bristol, St George BS5 . . . . . . 9 F7
Cheltenham GL50 . . . . 130 B8
Chepstow NP16 . . . . 60 E6
Pucklechurch BS16 . . . . 22 B5
Stonehouse GL10 . . . . 97 F7
Stroud GL5 . . . . 99 B6
Queen's Retreat GL51 . . 133 B2
Queen's Way HR8 . . . . . 178 E8
Queens Acre GL14 . . . . . 156 F6
Queens Ave SN6 . . . . 145 D3
Queens Cl GL3 . . . . 128 A1
Queens Ct GL50 . . . . 130 A8
Queens Down Ct BS4 . . . . . 9 C3
Queens Down Gdns BS4 . . 9 C3
Queens Dr BS15 . . . . 10 B4
Queens Field GL7 . . . . . . 152 E4
Queens Gate BS9 . . . . 17 D5
Queens La GL50 . . . . 193 A2
Queens Par Bristol BS1 . 194 C2
Cheltenham GL50 . . . . 193 A2
Queens Rd Bristol BS4 . . . . 9 C2
Broad Blunsdon SN6 . . . . . 144 F4
Hannington SN6 . . . . 145 A4
Keynsham BS31 . . . . 4 D4
Tewkesbury GL20 . . . . 192 D2
Queens Sq Stroud GL5 . . . 99 D7
21 Winchcombe GL54 . . . . 174 A7
Queens Way GL12 . . . . 68 B7
Queens Wlk BS35 . . . . 64 B3
Queensdale Cres BS4 . . . . 9 A1
Queensdown Gdns BS4 . . . 9 C2
Queenshill Rd BS4 . . . . 9 A1
Queensholm Ave BS16 . . . 30 E1
Queensholm Cl BS16 . . . . 30 E1
Queensholm Cres BS16 . . 30 E1
Queensholm Dr BS16 . . . . 30 E1
Queensmead
Bredon GL20 . . . . 182 D7
Painswick GL6 . . . . 103 E7
Queensway Bristol BS34 . . 29 D6
Coleford GL16 . . . . 155 B5
Queenwood Gr GL52 . . . 134 D5
Quenneys Cl GL4 . . . . . . 119 C3
Querns La GL7 . . . . 190 C4
Querns Rd GL7 . . . . 190 C3
Querns Sch GL7 . . . . 190 C4
Quickthorn Cl BS14 . . . . . . 3 A6
Quietways GL10 . . . . 97 E8
Quilter Gr BS4 . . . . 2 D7
Quinton Cl GL3 . . . . 128 B6

R

Rackham Cl BS7 . . . . 19 B6
Rackhay BS1 . . . . 195 A2
Radburn Cl GL56 . . . . . . 187 B3
Radley Rd BS16 . . . . 20 B4
Radnor Bsns Ctr BS7 . . . . 18 E5
Radnor Rd
Bristol, Horfield BS7 . . . . . . 18 E5
Bristol, Westbury on Trym BS9 . . . . 18 B5
Cheltenham GL51 . . . . 129 E6
Raeburn Rd BS5 . . . . 10 B6
Rag La GL12 . . . . 53 D5
Raglan La BS5 . . . . 10 A7
Raglan Pl Bristol BS7 . . . 18 D3
Thornbury BS35 . . . . 51 B8
Raglan Rd BS7 . . . . 18 D3
Raglan St GL1 . . . . 196 C2
Raglan Way
Chepstow NP16 . . . . 60 F5
Uley GL11 . . . . 89 B1
Raglan Wlk BS31 . . . . 4 D4
Ragnal La GL6 . . . . 91 A3
Raikes Rd GL1 . . . . 118 D6
Railton Jones Cl BS34 . . . 29 E3
Railway Cotts BS37 . . . . . 33 E8
Railway Dr 7 GL16 . . . . 155 A5
Railway Rd GL14 . . . . . . 191 C1
Railway Terr Bristol BS16 . 20 C4
Kemble GL7 . . . . 141 F8
Lechlade on T GL7 . . . . . . 153 E3
Lydney GL15 . . . . 84 A8
Railway View GL5 . . . . . . 148 A5
Rainbow Ct BS37 . . . . 43 B3
Raleigh Cl Innsworth GL3 127 F8
Saltford BS31 . . . . 5 D2
Raleigh Rd BS3 . . . . 8 B4
Ralph Rd BS7 . . . . 18 F4
Ram Hill BS36 . . . . 31 D4
Ram Hill Bsns Pk BS36 . . 31 D5
Ramsdale Rd GL2 . . . . . . 118 B4
Ramsey Rd BS7 . . . . 18 F7
Rance Pitch GL4 . . . . 119 E2
Randall Cl BS15 . . . . 20 F2
Randall Rd Bristol BS8 . . 194 B2
Upper Rissington GL54 . . . 169 D6
Randalls Field GL6 . . . . . 103 F7
Randalls Gn GL6 . . . . . . 148 C5
Randolph Ave Bristol BS13 . 2 B5
Yate BS37 . . . . 43 D4
Randolph Cl Bristol BS13 . . 2 B5
Charlton Kings GL53 . . . . . 130 F6
Randwick CE Prim Sch GL6 . . . . 102 D2
Randwick Rd GL4 . . . . . . 118 D3
Range The GL2 . . . . 125 D5
Rangers Ave GL11 . . . . 80 C7
Rangers The GL11 . . . . 80 C7
Rangers Wlk BS15 . . . . . . 10 C4
Rangeworthy CE Prim Sch BS37 . . . . 52 F1
Ranmoor GL4 . . . . 119 D3
Rannoch Rd BS7 . . . . 28 F1
Raphael Ct BS1 . . . . 195 B1
Ratcliff Lawns GL52 . . . . 134 B8
Ratcliffe Dr BS34 . . . . 29 E5
Rathbone Cl BS36 . . . . 31 C5
Rathmore Cl 2 GL54 . . . 174 A7
Raven Ct BS9 . . . . 17 F8
Ravendale Dr BS30 . . . . . . 11 B2
Ravenglass Cres BS10 . . . 28 D2
Ravenhead Dr BS14 . . . . . . 3 B8
Ravenhill Ave BS3 . . . . 8 F2
Ravenhill Rd BS3 . . . . 8 F3
Ravenscourt Rd BS34 . . . 29 B7
Ravensgate Rd GL53 . . . 131 B4
Ravenswood BS30 . . . . . . 11 B3
Ravenswood Rd BS6 . . . . 18 C1
Ravis Cl GL4 . . . . 119 B6
Rawnsley Ho 13 BS5 . . . . 19 A1
Rayleigh Rd BS9 . . . . 17 E7
Raymend Rd BS3 . . . . 8 E3
Raymend Wlk BS3 . . . . 8 E2
Raymill BS4 . . . . 10 A2
Raymond Ho BS16 . . . . 20 F4
Raynes Rd BS3 . . . . 8 A3
Raysfield Inf Sch BS37 . . . 32 F8
Raysfield Jun Sch BS37 . . 32 F8
Rea La GL2 . . . . 118 A6
Rea The GL2 . . . . 117 F5
Reaburn Cl 5 GL52 . . . . 131 B6
Read Way GL52 . . . . 137 F2
Read's Row GL12 . . . . 55 D7
Reade St NP25 . . . . 154 A7
Reades Piece WR11 . . . . 188 C6
Ready Token GL7 . . . . 151 F7
Rectory Barns GL54 . . . . 176 D4
Rectory Cl
Lower Swell GL54 . . . . 176 D4
Upton St Leonards GL4 . . . 119 E2
Yate BS37 . . . . 43 F3
Rectory Cotts GL54 . . . . 176 D4
Rectory Ct GL52 . . . . 138 A4
Rectory La Avening GL8 . . 148 B1
Bristol BS34 . . . . 29 A3
Cricklade SN6 . . . . 143 F4
Cromhall GL12 . . . . 53 A8
Gloucester GL2 . . . . 118 A6
Rectory Mdw GL17 . . . . . 164 F6
Rectory Rd
Easton-in-G BS20 . . . . 16 B3
Frampton Cotterell BS36 . . . 31 A8
Gloucester GL4 . . . . 119 C4
Red Admiral Dr GL4 . . . . 119 E4
Red Ditch La GL19 . . . . . 179 D1
Red House La
Almondsbury BS32 . . . . 40 B4
Bristol BS9 . . . . 17 E6
Red La GL20 . . . . 192 C5
Red Lion La SN6 . . . . 143 F4
Red Maids Jun Sch BS9 . . 18 A6
Red Maids Sch BS9 . . . . . 18 A6
Red Rover Cl GL50 . . . . . 133 C5
Red Well Rd GL4 . . . . 119 C3
Redbrook CE Prim Sch NP25 . . . . 154 C4
Redcar Ct BS16 . . . . 30 F1
Redcatch Rd BS4 . . . . 8 F2
Redcliff Backs BS1 . . . . . 195 B2
Redcliff Cres BS3 . . . . 8 E4
Redcliff Hill BS1 . . . . 195 B1
Redcliff Mead La BS1 . . 195 B1
Redcliff St BS1 . . . . 195 B2
Redcliffe Par E BS1 . . . . 195 A1
Redcliffe Par W BS1 . . . . 195 A1
Redcliffe Way BS1 . . . . . 195 B1
Redcross Mews 14 BS2 . 195 C3
Redcross St BS2 . . . . 195 C3
Redding Cl GL2 . . . . 117 E1
Reddings Cl GL15 . . . . . . 147 C3
Reddings La GL14 . . . . . . 191 F4
Reddings Pk GL51 . . . . . . 129 D7
Reddings Rd GL51 . . . . . . 129 C7
Reddings The Bristol BS15 20 F8
Cheltenham GL51 . . . . 129 B6
Chepstow NP16 . . . . 60 F5
Pendock WR13 . . . . 180 A8
Redesdale Mews 6 GL56 . . . . 187 A3
Redesdale Pl GL56 . . . . . 187 A2
Redfield Edge Prim Sch BS30 . . . . 11 D4
Redfield Hill BS30 . . . . . . 11 E3
Redfield Rd BS34 . . . . 29 B7
Redford Cres BS13 . . . . 1 F3
Redford La BS16 . . . . 22 D4
Redford Wlk BS13 . . . . 1 F3
Redgrove Pk GL51 . . . . . 129 D8
Redgrove Rd GL51 . . . . . 132 F4
Redham La BS35 . . . . 38 F8
Redhill Cl BS16 . . . . 19 E3
Redhill Dr BS16 . . . . 19 E3
Redhill La BS35 . . . . 49 E6
Redhouse La
English Bicknor GL16 . . . . 163 A2
Stroud GL5 . . . . 98 D8
Redland Cl GL2 . . . . 127 B4
Redland Court (Girls High Sch) BS6 . . . . 18 C2
Redland Court Rd BS6 . . . 18 C2
Redland Gr BS6 . . . . 18 C2
Redland Green Rd BS6 . . . 18 B3
Redland High Jun Sch BS6 . . . . 18 C2
Redland High Sch BS6 . . 18 C2
Redland Hill BS6 . . . . 18 B2
Redland Pk BS6 . . . . 18 B2
Redland Rd BS6 . . . . 18 C2
Redland Sta BS6 . . . . 18 C2
Redland Terr 8 BS6 . . . . . 18 B2
Redlands Cl SN6 . . . . 145 D2
Redlynch La BS31 . . . . 4 D2
Redmarley CE Prim Sch GL19 . . . . 179 D2
Redmarley Rd GL18 . . . . 171 A6
Rednock Dr GL11 . . . . 88 A2
Rednock Sch GL11 . . . . . . 88 A2
Redpoll Way GL4 . . . . . . 119 C6
Redshelf Wlk BS10 . . . . . . 28 C3
Redstart Way GL4 . . . . . 119 C6
Redthorne Way GL51 . . . 129 E5
Redwick & Northwick CE Sch BS35 . . . . 48 D2
Redwick Cl BS11 . . . . 27 C2
Redwick Gdns BS35 . . . . . 38 C7
Redwick Rd BS35 . . . . 38 C8
Redwind Way GL2 . . . . . . 127 D5
Redwing Gdns BS16 . . . . . 19 E6
Redwood Cl Bristol BS30 . 11 A3
Chepstow NP16 . . . . 60 E5
Gloucester GL1 . . . . 118 D5
Redwood Ct
4 Cheltenham GL51 . . . . 132 D2
Northway GL20 . . . . 182 C5
Redwood Ho Bristol BS13 . . 2 D3
Brookthorpe GL4 . . . . 110 F5
Reed Cl BS10 . . . . 18 D6
Reed Ct BS30 . . . . 10 F3
Reed's Row GL12 . . . . 55 D7
Reedley Rd BS9 . . . . 17 F5
Reedling Cl BS16 . . . . 19 E6
Reeds SN6 . . . . 143 E4
Reema Hos The SN6 . . . 145 D1
Reevers Rd 25 GL18 . . . 171 A4
Reeves Cl GL7 . . . . 190 A2
Regency Dr BS4 . . . . 10 A2
Regent Arc GL50 . . . . 193 B3
Regent Chambers GL50 193 B3
Regent Ct GL51 . . . . 130 B8
Regent Ho 9 GL50 . . . . . 130 B8
Regent Rd BS3 . . . . 8 D4
Regent St
Bristol, Clifton BS8 . . . . . . 194 A2
Bristol, Kingswood BS15 . . . 10 D8
Cheltenham GL50 . . . . 193 B3
Gloucester GL1 . . . . 196 C1
Lydney GL15 . . . . 92 B3
Stonehouse GL10 . . . . 97 F7
Regent Way NP16 . . . . 60 E8
Regents BS31 . . . . 4 F6
Regents Cl BS35 . . . . 64 B2
Regis Cl GL53 . . . . 131 A5
Reine Barnes Cl GL11 . . . 80 B8
Remenham Dr BS9 . . . . . . 18 B5
Remenham Pk BS9 . . . . . . 18 B5
Remus Cl GL4 . . . . 119 F6
Rendcomb Cl GL4 . . . . . . 119 E4
Rendcomb Coll GL7 . . . . 158 C4
Rendcomb Dr GL7 . . . . . 190 B2
Rendle Ho BS16 . . . . 20 F4
Rene Rd 12 BS5 . . . . 19 B1
Repton Rd BS4 . . . . 9 D3
Reservoir Cl GL5 . . . . 99 E7
Reservoir Rd
Gloucester GL4 . . . . 118 F4
Stroud GL5 . . . . 99 E7
Restway Wall NP16 . . . . . . 60 E8
Retort Rd BS11 . . . . 26 C3
Retreat The
3 Broadway WR12 . . . . . 185 B8
Gloucester GL4 . . . . 118 D2
4 Tetbury GL8 . . . . 140 C4
Reynold's Wlk BS7 . . . . . . 19 A7
Reynolds Cl BS31 . . . . 5 A5
Rhode Cl BS31 . . . . 5 A3
Rhodesia Ho 2 GL51 . . . 132 F4
Ribble Cl GL3 . . . . 120 F5
Ribblesdale BS35 . . . . 51 D8
Ribston Hall High Sch GL1 . . . . 118 E5
Ricardo Rd GL6 . . . . 91 F7
Richard Pate Sch The GL53 . . . . 130 E4
Richard Pl GL20 . . . . 192 D1
Richards Rd GL51 . . . . . . 133 B4
Richeson Cl BS10 . . . . 27 F2
Richeson Wlk BS10 . . . . . . 27 F2
Richmond Ave
Bristol, Montpelier BS6 . . . . 18 F2
Bristol, Stoke Gifford BS34 . 29 E5
Gloucester GL4 . . . . 119 C6
Richmond Bldgs GL5 . . . . 98 D6
Richmond Cl BS31 . . . . 4 D4
Richmond Ct
1 Ashton Keynes SN6 . . . 142 F5
7 Bristol, Clifton BS8 . . . . 18 A2
2 Bristol, Knowle BS3 . . . . . 8 F4
Richmond Dale 6 BS8 . . . 18 A2
Richmond Dr 4 GL52 . . . 134 A1
Richmond Gdns GL2 . . . 127 D5
Richmond Hill BS8 . . . . . 194 B3
Richmond Hill Ave BS8 . 194 B3
Richmond Hts BS8 . . . . . 194 B3
Richmond La BS8 . . . . . . 194 B3
Richmond Mews BS8 . . . 194 A3
Richmond Park Rd BS8 194 A3
Richmond Rd
Bristol, Mangotsfield BS16 . 21 A5
Bristol, Montpelier BS6 . . . 18 E1
Bristol, St George BS5 . . . . . 9 E7
Tewkesbury GL20 . . . . 192 E1
Richmond St BS3 . . . . 8 F4
Richmond Terr
Avonmouth BS11 . . . . 26 B1
Bristol BS8 . . . . 194 A3
Richmonds The GL4 . . . . 119 D4
Rickfield The NP25 . . . . 162 A1
Rickyard Way GL2 . . . . . 100 E5
Riddle St GL13 . . . . 94 B3
Ride The BS15 . . . . 21 A2
Ridge Jun Sch The BS37 . 43 F2
Ridge Pl GL17 . . . . 163 D1
Ridge The Bristol BS11 . . . 16 E7
Broad Blunsdon SN26 . . . . 144 D1
Bussage GL6 . . . . 148 B6
Coalpit Heath BS36 . . . . 31 C7
Ridge's La GL8 . . . . 140 C7
Ridgehill BS9 . . . . 18 C6
Ridgemeade BS14 . . . . 3 B4
Ridgemont Rd GL5 . . . . . . 99 E6
Ridgemount Cl GL3 . . . . 120 E5
Ridgeview BS41 . . . . 7 B2
Ridgeway
Coalpit Heath BS36 . . . . 31 D7
Eastnor HR8 . . . . 179 B8
Monmouth NP25 . . . . 154 A7
Yate BS37 . . . . 44 A2
Yorkley GL15 . . . . 156 B2
Ridgeway Cres HR9 . . . . 162 D4
Ridgeway Ct BS10 . . . . . . 28 A1
Ridgeway Gdns BS14 . . . . . 3 C5
Ridgeway Ind Ctr BS5 . . . 19 E2
Ridgeway La Bristol BS14 . . 3 B5
Marston Meysey SN6 . . . . 144 B6
Ridgeway Par BS5 . . . . . . 19 E3
Ridgeway Rd Bristol BS16 . 19 F3
Long Ashton BS41 . . . . 7 A2
Ridgeway The
Bristol BS10 . . . . 28 A1
Bussage GL6 . . . . 148 B6
Crudwell SN16 . . . . 141 C3
Eastcombe GL6 . . . . 148 B7
Ridgewood BS9 . . . . 17 D3
Riding Barn Hill BS30 . . . 12 A6
Ridingleaze BS11 . . . . 27 A1
Ridings Cl BS37 . . . . 44 D1
Ridings High Sch The BS36 . . . . 30 D6
Ridings Rd BS36 . . . . 31 C6
Ridings The Bristol BS13 . . . 1 E4
Coalpit Heath BS36 . . . . 31 C6
Maisemore GL2 . . . . 126 A7
Nailsworth GL6 . . . . 91 C3
Ridler Rd GL15 . . . . 92 C2
Rigsby's La SN16 . . . . . . 142 C3
Rills View 17 GL18 . . . . . 171 A4
Ring Fence GL15 . . . . 147 B3
Ringer's Cl GL19 . . . . 173 C7
Ringfield Cl GL6 . . . . 91 C3
Ringspit La BS14 . . . . 3 E1
Ringwood Cres BS10 . . . . 28 D1
Ripley Rd BS5 . . . . 20 A1
Ripon Ct BS16 . . . . 30 F2
Ripon Rd BS4 . . . . 9 E6
Rippledale Cl GL51 . . . . . 129 E7
Risdale Rd BS3 . . . . 7 F1
Rise The GL54 . . . . 166 E5
Risedale BS15 . . . . 10 D5
Rising Sun La GL52 . . . . 138 E2
Rissington Cl GL51 . . . . . 129 E8
Rissington Rd
Bourton-on-t-W GL54 . . . . 169 A6
Gloucester GL4 . . . . 118 E3
Rivelands Rd GL51 . . . . . 133 B7
River Leys GL51 . . . . 132 F5
River Rd BS37 . . . . 44 A1
River St BS2 . . . . 195 C3
River Terr BS31 . . . . 4 F5
River View Bristol BS16 . . 19 E5
Chepstow NP16 . . . . 60 E8
River Way GL7 . . . . 142 F8
Riverdale GL14 . . . . 157 A6
Riverland Dr BS13 . . . . 1 F5
Riverleaze BS9 . . . . 17 C5
Rivermead Cl GL2 . . . . . . 126 E4
Rivers Way SN6 . . . . 145 C3
Riverside GL54 . . . . 174 A7
Riverside Bsns Pk BS4 . . . 9 D6
Riverside Cl Bristol BS11 . . 16 F5
Charlton Kings GL52 . . . . . 131 B6
Riverside Cotts BS15 . . . . 10 B1
Riverside Ct 2 Bristol BS4 . 9 F6
Tewkesbury GL20 . . . . 192 C5
Riverside Mews BS4 . . . . . 9 F6
Riverside Pk
Eastington GL10 . . . . 97 A8
Monmouth NP25 . . . . 154 A7
Severn Beach BS35 . . . . . . 37 F6
Riverside Stps BS4 . . . . . . 9 E7
Riverside Way BS15 . . . . . 10 C3
Riverside Wlk 6 BS5 . . . . . 9 F6
Riversley Rd GL2 . . . . . . 127 C2
Riversmeet GL3 . . . . 120 F5
Riverview Way GL51 . . . 133 A4
Riverwood Rd BS16 . . . . . 30 C1
Riviera Cres BS16 . . . . 20 E4
Rixon Gate SN6 . . . . 143 A5
Roach's La GL9 . . . . 46 D2
Road Hill SN14 . . . . 15 D1
Road Two BS10 . . . . 38 A3
Robbers Rd GL6 . . . . 102 C2
Robbins Cl Bristol BS32 . . 29 F6
Marshfield SN14 . . . . 14 F8
Stroud GL5 . . . . 98 C6
Robbins Ct BS16 . . . . 21 B6
Robel Ave BS36 . . . . 31 A8
Robert Burns Ave GL51 . 129 D7
Robert Ct Bristol BS16 . . . 21 B7
Leigh Woods BS8 . . . . 7 D7
Robert Franklin Way GL7 . . . . 143 A8
Robert Harvey Ho 4 GL52 . . . . 193 C4
Robert Raikes Ave
Gloucester GL4 . . . . 118 D2
Gloucester GL4 . . . . 118 E2
Robert St
Bristol, Baptist Mills BS5 . . . 19 B2
15 Bristol, Russell Town BS5 . 9 B7
Roberts Cl
Bishop's Cleeve GL52 . . . . 137 F4
Cirencester GL7 . . . . 190 B8
Roberts Rd
Innsworth GL3 . . . . 127 E7
Prestbury GL52 . . . . 134 D3
Robertson Dr BS4 . . . . 9 F6
Robertson Rd Bristol BS5 . 19 C2
Shurdington GL51 . . . . 129 D2
Robin Cl
Bristol, Brentry BS10 . . . . . 28 B2
Bristol, Stockwood BS14 . . . . 3 D6
2 Chalford GL6 . . . . 148 C6
Northway GL20 . . . . 182 B5
Robin Ct GL10 . . . . 97 F8
Robin Way BS37 . . . . 33 A7
Robinhood St GL1 . . . . . 118 D7
Robinia Cl GL53 . . . . 131 B5
Robinia Wlk BS14 . . . . 3 A7
Robins Cl GL52 . . . . 134 A2
Robins End GL3 . . . . 127 D7
Robins Wood Hill Ctry Pk* GL4 . . . . 119 A2
Robinson Cl GL18 . . . . . . 171 A5
Robinson Dr BS5 . . . . 9 A8
Robinson La
Upper Lydbrook GL17 . . . . 163 D2
Woodmancote GL7 . . . . . . 158 B4
Robinson Rd GL1 . . . . . . 118 E7
Robinswood Gdns GL4 . 119 A4
Robinswood Hill Ctry Pk* GL4 . . . . 118 F3
Robinswood Prim Sch GL4 . . . . 119 C3
Rochester Rd Bristol BS4 . . 9 F5
Cheltenham GL51 . . . . 130 A5
Rock & Fountain La GL14 . . . . 157 E8
Rock Cl BS4 . . . . 9 E2
Rock Cotts Pill BS20 . . . . . 16 E4
Stroud GL5 . . . . 99 C8
Rock Ho BS10 . . . . 28 C3
Rock La Bristol BS34 . . . . 29 F4
Coleford GL16 . . . . 155 A5
Elton GL14 . . . . 157 E8
Northwood Green GL14 . . . 165 E1
Rock Rd Dursley GL11 . . . . 87 D4
Keynsham BS31 . . . . 4 E5
Wick BS30 . . . . 12 D8
Rock St
Forthampton GL19 . . . . . . 181 B1
Thornbury BS35 . . . . 51 B8
Rock The BS4 . . . . 9 E3
Rock Villa La NP16 . . . . . . 72 F1
Rockhill Est BS31 . . . . 4 F4
Rockingham Gdns BS11 . . 17 A8
Rockland Gr BS16 . . . . 19 D5
Rockland Rd BS16 . . . . 20 D7
Rocklease BS35 . . . . 64 B1
Rockleaze BS9 . . . . 17 E2
Rockleaze Ave BS9 . . . . . . 17 E3
Rockleaze Ct BS9 . . . . 17 E3
Rockleaze Rd BS9 . . . . 17 E3
Rockness Hill GL6 . . . . 91 A2
Rocks Rd GL17 . . . . 163 D3
Rocks The GL16 . . . . 155 A3
Rockside Ave BS16 . . . . . . 20 F8
Rockside Dr BS9 . . . . 18 C6
Rockside Gdns
Bristol BS16 . . . . 20 F8
Frampton Cotterell BS36 . . . 31 C8
Rockstowes Way BS10 . . . 28 D3
Rockwell Ave BS11 . . . . . . 27 B1
Rockwood Ho BS37 . . . . . . 44 A4
Rockwood Rd NP16 . . . . . 60 E7
Rodborough BS37 . . . . 32 C7
Rodborough Ave GL5 . . . . 99 B6
Rodborough Com Prim Sch GL5 . . . . 99 B6
Rodborough Hill GL5 . . . . 99 B6
Rodborough La GL5 . . . . . 99 C5
Rodborough Way BS15 . . . 11 A7
Rodbourne Rd BS10 . . . . . 18 E6
Rodford Prim Sch BS37 . . 32 D7
Rodford Way BS37 . . . . . . 32 D7
Rodfords Mead BS14 . . . . . 3 A7
Rodley Rd GL15 . . . . 92 C3
Rodley Sq GL15 . . . . 92 C3
Rodmarton Prim Sch GL7 . . . . 149 B1
Rodmead Wlk BS13 . . . . . . 2 A4
Rodney Ave BS15 . . . . 10 A8
Rodney Cl GL2 . . . . 127 B4
Rodney Cres BS34 . . . . . . 29 A4
Rodney Pl BS8 . . . . 194 A3
Rodney Rd Bristol BS15 . . . 10 A8
Cheltenham GL50 . . . . 193 B3
Saltford BS31 . . . . 5 E2
Rodney Wlk BS15 . . . . 20 A1
Rodway Hill BS16 . . . . 21 B3
Rodway Hill Rd BS16 . . . . 21 A4
Rodway La GL19,GL2 . . . . 172 E3
Rodway Rd
Bristol, Mangotsfield BS16 . 21 A5
Bristol, Patchway BS34 . . . . 28 F7
Rodway View BS15 . . . . . . 20 F3
Roebuck Mdws GL17 . . . 163 F3
Roegate Dr BS4 . . . . 9 E6

Roegate Ho BS5 ....20 A1
Roel Gate GL54 ....174 D3
Rogers Cl BS30 ....11 B5
Rokeby Ave BS6 ....18 C1
Rollers The GL6 ....91 B4
Rolleston Way GL51 ....129 F7
Rolling Stones GL55 ....189 A2
Rolph Ct GL56 ....187 A2
Roman Amphitheatre★ GL7 ....190 B4
Roman Farm Ct BS11 ....27 C2
Roman Farm Rd BS4 ....2 E7
Roman Hackle Ave GL50 ....133 C5
Roman Rd Bristol BS5 ....19 B1
Cheltenham GL51 ....133 A1
Gloucester GL4 ....119 E6
Roman Way
Bourton-on-t-W GL54 ....169 A8
Bristol BS9 ....17 C4
Coleford GL16 ....155 A5
Highworth SN6 ....145 C3
Lechlade on T GL7 ....153 E3
Littledean GL14 ....191 F4
Roman Wlk
Bristol, Brislington BS4 ....9 C3
Bristol, Stoke Gifford BS34 .29 E5
Romney Ave BS7 ....19 B6
Romney Avenue Inf Sch BS7 ....19 B6
Romney Avenue Jun Sch BS7 ....19 B6
Romney Cl GL1 ....118 E5
Romney Rd GL8 ....140 B4
Ron Jones Ho 3 BS1 ....195 B4
Ronald Rd BS16 ....19 F6
Ronayne Wlk BS16 ....20 C6
Rookery La Pilning BS35 ....39 A6
Pucklechurch BS30,SN14 ....22 F4
Sharpness GL13 ....85 E7
St Briavels GL15 ....154 F2
Rookery Rd Bristol BS4 ....9 A3
Innsworth GL3 ....127 D6
Rookery The GL54 ....159 A6
Rookery Way BS14 ....2 F4
Rooksmoor Hill GL5 ....99 A3
Roosevelt Ave GL52 ....131 A8
Rope Wlk The GL5 ....99 E3
Ropewalk GL20 ....192 D4
Rosary RC Prim Sch GL5 99 B7
Rosary The BS16 ....21 D7
Rose & Crown Ho GL50 .193 B4
Rose & Crown Pas GL50 193 B4
Rose Acre BS10 ....28 A3
Rose Cl BS36 ....30 E4
Rose Green Cl BS5 ....19 E2
Rose Green Rd BS5 ....19 D2
Rose Hill Sch GL12 ....68 D2
Rose La BS36 ....31 D6
Rose Mead BS7 ....19 A7
Rose Meare Gdns BS13 ....1 E7
Rose Oak Dr BS36 ....31 D7
Rose Oak Gdns BS36 ....31 D7
Rose Oak La BS36 ....31 D7
Rose Rd BS5 ....9 E7
Rose Terr BS8 ....194 B3
Rose Tree Ho BS16 ....20 F4
Rose Way GL7 ....190 E2
Rose Willis Ct 10 GL18 .171 A4
Rose Wlk BS16 ....20 C3
Rosebay Mead BS16 ....19 E5
Roseberry Pk BS5 ....9 D8
Roseberry Rd BS5 ....9 C7
Roseberry Terr GL6 ....148 C5
Rosebery Ave Bristol BS2 .19 A1
Gloucester GL1 ....118 E6
Rosebery Mount GL11 ....80 C8
Rosebery Pk GL11 ....80 C8
Rosebery Rd GL11 ....80 C8
Rosebery Terr BS8 ....194 B2
Rosedale Ave GL10 ....98 A7
Rosedale Cl GL2 ....109 D8
Rosedale Rd BS16 ....20 C3
Rosefield Cres GL20 ....192 F4
Rosehill Ct GL7 ....190 C7
Rosehill St GL52 ....130 F8
Rosehill Terr 6 GL52 ....130 F8
Rosehip Ct GL51 ....130 A4
Rosehip Way GL52 ....137 E4
Roselarge Gdns BS10 ....28 A2
Rosemary Cl Bristol BS32 .29 F7
Gloucester GL4 ....119 D4
Rosemary La Bristol BS5 .19 C2
Stroat NP16 ....146 F1
Rosemary Terr GL12 ....68 B7
Rosemont Terr BS8 ....194 A2
Rosemount Ct BS15 ....10 B8
Rosery Cl BS9 ....18 A8
Rosery The BS16 ....20 C3
Rosevear BS2 ....9 A7
Roseville Ave BS30 ....11 A2
Rosewood Ave BS35 ....50 F5
Roshni Gar E 16 BS5 ....19 B1
Roshni Gar W 15 BS5 ....19 B1
Rosling Rd BS7 ....18 E6
Roslyn Rd BS6 ....18 C1
Ross Cl BS37 ....44 B1
Ross Rd Berry Hill GL16 ..155 A8
Mitcheldean GL17 ....164 D6
Newent GL18 ....170 F5
Rossall Ave BS34 ....29 C6
Rossall Rd BS4 ....9 D3
Rossiter Wood Ct BS11 ..27 B2
Rossiter's La BS5 ....10 A6
Rosslyn Way BS35 ....64 C3
Rothermere Cl GL51 ....129 F5
Rothleigh GL51 ....129 E5
Rotunda Terr GL50 ....193 A2
Rougemont Gr NP16 ....60 F4
Rounceval St BS37 ....44 A1
Roundabout La GL8 ....140 C8
Roundabouts The GL5 ....99 F1
Roundhills Mead SN6 ..145 D4
Roundmoor Cl BS31 ....5 D3
Roundmoor Gdns BS14 ....3 D7
Roundways BS36 ....31 D6
Rousham Rd BS5 ....19 A3
Roves La SN6 ....145 D1
Row The Aust BS35 ....49 A7
Lechlade on T GL7 ....153 F4
Longborough GL56 ....176 F7
Southrop GL7 ....153 C6
St Arvans NP16 ....72 B6
Rowacres BS14 ....2 F6
Rowan Cl BS16 ....20 A2
Rowan Ct 9 Bristol BS5 ....9 B7
Yate BS37 ....43 C3
Rowan Dr NP16 ....60 E5
Rowan Gdns GL3 ....120 E6
Rowan Gr GL11 ....88 A3
Rowan Ho BS13 ....2 D4
Rowan Tree Ho BS16 ....20 F4
Rowan Way Bristol BS15 ..10 B3
15 Cheltenham GL51 ....129 E5
Nailsworth GL6 ....90 F5
Rowan Wlk BS31 ....4 C4
Rowandean GL14 ....191 C5
Rowanfield Exchange GL51 ....133 A2
Rowanfield Inf & Jun Schs GL51 ....133 A2
Rowanfield Rd GL51 ....133 A1
Rowans The Bristol BS16 ..30 B1
Pontshill HR9 ....164 B8
Woodmancote GL52 ....138 B3
Rowberrow BS14 ....2 F7
Rowcroft GL5 ....99 B7
Rowcroft Retreat GL5 ....99 B7
Rowe Ct GL50 ....193 A3
Rowland Ave BS16 ....19 D4
Rowlandson Gdns BS7 ..19 B6
Rowley GL11 ....88 A5
Rowley Mews GL11 ....88 A5
Rowley St BS3 ....8 C3
Rownham Cl BS3 ....7 E4
Rownham Ct BS8 ....194 A1
Rownham Hill BS8 ....7 E6
Rownham Mead BS8 ....194 A1
Rows The GL55 ....188 D4
Roxton Dr GL51 ....129 C7
Roy King Gdns BS30 ....11 C6
Royal Agricultural Coll GL7 ....150 B4
Royal Albert Rd BS6 ....18 A4
Royal Cl BS10 ....27 D3
Royal Cres GL50 ....193 B3
Royal Ct 9 GL51 ....132 D2
Royal Forest of Dean Coll GL16 ....155 B7
Royal Fort Rd BS2,BS8 ..194 C3
Royal Hospl for Sick Children BS2 ....194 C3
Royal La GL1 ....127 A2
Royal Oak Mews GL50 ..193 B4
Royal Oak Rd
Gloucester GL1 ....196 A3
Upper Lydbrook GL17 ....163 E3
Royal Oak Terr GL55 ....188 F1
Royal Parade Mews GL50 ....193 A2
Royal Pk BS8 ....194 A3
Royal Prom BS8 ....194 B3
Royal Rd BS16 ....21 A6
Royal Spring GL17 ....165 A5
Royal Well La GL50 ....193 B3
Royal Well Pl GL50 ....193 B3
Royal Well Rd GL50 ....193 B3
Royal West of England Acad BS8 ....194 B3
Royal York Cres BS8 ....7 F6
Royal York Ho BS8 ....194 A2
Royal York Mews BS8 ..194 A2
Royal York Villas BS8 ..194 A2
Royate Hill BS5 ....19 D2
Roycroft Rd BS34 ....29 B2
Royston Wlk BS10 ....28 D2
Rozel Rd BS7 ....18 E5
Ruardean CE Prim Sch GL17 ....163 E4
Ruardean Rd GL17 ....163 F3
Rubens Cl BS31 ....5 A5
Ruby St BS3 ....8 B3
Rudford Cl BS34 ....40 B1
Rudge Cl BS15 ....20 F2
Rudge The GL2 ....126 B8
Rudgeway Pk BS35 ....50 F1
Rudgewood Cl BS13 ....2 D4
Rudgleigh Ave BS20 ....16 C4
Rudgleigh Rd BS20 ....16 C4
Rudhall Ct GL1 ....196 A3
Rudhall Gr BS10 ....18 E7
Rudhall View HR9 ....164 D8
Rudthorpe Rd BS7 ....18 E5
Ruffet Cl GL16 ....155 B4
Ruffet Rd BS36 ....31 B4
Ruffet's Cl NP16 ....60 D8
Ruffitt The GL14 ....191 F5
Rugby Rd BS4 ....9 D3
Rumsey Cl GL4 ....119 E4
Runnings Rd GL51 ....133 A5
Runnings The GL51 ....133 A6
Runnymead Ave BS4 ....9 D2
Runnymede Bristol BS15 ..20 E1
Cheltenham GL51 ....129 E5
Runswick Rd BS4 ....9 C3
Rupert St Bristol BS1 ....195 A3
Rupert St *continued*
Bristol, Redfield BS5 ....9 C7
Ruscombe Rd GL6 ....102 E2
Rush Cl BS32 ....40 D2
Rusham BS13 ....1 F4
Rushley La GL54 ....174 A7
Rushmead La SN14 ....24 F2
Rushton Dr BS36 ....31 D7
Rushworth Cl GL51 ....132 D2
Rushworth Ho GL51 ....132 D2
Rushy BS30 ....11 A4
Rushy Ho GL52 ....134 A4
Rushy Mews GL52 ....134 A4
Rushy Way BS16 ....31 A1
Rushyleaze GL15 ....92 B2
Ruskin Gr BS7 ....19 A8
Ruskin Ho BS34 ....29 A8
Ruspidge Cl GL4 ....119 E5
Ruspidge Rd GL14 ....156 C6
Russ St BS2 ....195 C2
Russell Almshouses GL20 ....192 C3
Russell Ave BS15 ....10 E7
Russell Cl GL9 ....57 B3
Russell Gr BS6 ....18 C5
Russell Pl GL51 ....133 C3
Russell Rd
Bristol, Chester Park BS16 .20 B2
Bristol, Westbury Park BS6 .18 B4
Russell St
Cheltenham GL51 ....133 C3
Gloucester GL1 ....196 B2
Stroud GL5 ....99 C7
Russell Town Ave BS5 ....9 B8
Russell Town Ind Pk 18 BS5 ....9 C7
Russet Ave GL7 ....153 F2
Russet Cl Bredon GL20 ..182 C7
Gloucester GL4 ....118 B3
2 Ledbury HR8 ....178 E7
Olveston BS35 ....50 A3
Russet Ct GL12 ....67 F4
Russet Rd GL51 ....132 F3
Russett Way 24 GL18 ....171 A4
Rustic Cl GL4 ....119 C4
Rutherford Cl BS30 ....11 A3
Rutherford Way GL51 ..133 A5
Ruthven Rd BS4 ....2 E8
Rutland Ave BS30 ....11 A2
Rutland Ct 4 GL50 ....133 B1
Rutland Pl GL7 ....190 C3
Rutland Rd BS7 ....18 E3
Ryalls La GL2 ....95 E5
Rydal Ho BS34 ....29 A8
Rydal Rd GL2 ....127 B4
Rydal Wlk GL51 ....129 E7
Ryde Rd BS4 ....9 B2
Ryder Cl GL11 ....88 A4
Ryder Row GL3 ....127 E6
Rye Ave GL51 ....132 D5
Rye Cl BS13 ....1 E6
Rye Cres GL54 ....169 A7
Ryeclose GL54 ....169 A7
Ryecroft Ct BS36 ....31 C7
Ryecroft Rd BS36 ....31 C8
Ryecroft Rise BS41 ....7 B1
Ryecroft St GL1 ....196 C1
Ryedown La BS30 ....11 D2
Ryelands GL4 ....118 C3
Ryelands Cl GL10 ....97 E8
Ryelands Rd
8 Bream GL15 ....147 D8
Stonehouse GL10 ....97 E8
Ryelands The
6 Bream GL15 ....147 D8
Randwick GL6 ....102 D1
Ryeleaze Cl GL5 ....99 C7
Ryeleaze Rd GL5 ....99 C7
Ryeworth Dr GL52 ....131 B7
Ryeworth Rd GL52 ....131 B7
Ryland Cl GL8 ....140 C5
Ryland Pl 1 BS2 ....19 A2
Rylestone Cl BS36 ....30 F8
Rylestone Gr BS9 ....17 F5
Rysdale Rd BS9 ....17 F6

S

Sabre Cl GL2 ....118 A3
Sabrina Way Bristol BS9 ..17 C4
Lydney GL15 ....92 B4
Sachi Ct GL51 ....132 E2
Sackville App GL50 ....133 D4
Saddlers La GL50 ....193 A1
Saddlers Rd GL2 ....117 F2
Sadlers Ct 8 GL52 ....130 F8
Sadlers Field 4 SN6 ....142 F5
Sadlier Cl BS11 ....17 A8
Saffron Cl GL4 ....119 A5
Saffron Rd GL20 ....192 C4
Sages Mead BS32 ....29 E8
Saintbridge Cl GL4 ....119 B5
Saintbridge Pl GL4 ....119 B5
SS Gt Britain★ BS1 ....194 B1
SS Peter & Paul Catholic Sch BS8 ....194 C4
SS Peter & Paul RC Cath★ BS8 ....194 A4
St Agnes Ave BS4 ....8 F2
St Agnes Cl BS4 ....8 F2
St Agnes Wlk BS4 ....8 F2
St Aidan's Cl BS5 ....10 B6
St Aidan's Rd BS5 ....10 B6
St Aidans Cl GL51 ....132 E2
St Alban's Rd BS6 ....18 B4
St Albans Cl GL51 ....130 A5
St Albans Rd GL2 ....118 C5
St Aldams Dr BS16 ....22 B5
St Aldate St GL1 ....196 B3
St Aldwyn Rd GL1 ....118 F6
St Aldwyn's Cl BS7 ....18 F8
St Andrew CE Jun Sch SN26 ....144 E1
St Andrew's Ave NP16 ....60 E7
St Andrew's CE Prim Sch GL12 ....66 A1
St Andrew's Prim Sch GL54 ....159 A6
St Andrew's Rd
Avonmouth BS11 ....26 B1
Avonmouth BS11 ....26 B4
Bristol BS6 ....18 E2
St Andrews
Ashleworth GL19 ....172 D4
Bristol BS30 ....11 B6
Yate BS37 ....43 F1
St Andrews Cl GL20 ....182 C4
St Andrews Gate Rdbt BS11 ....26 C2
St Andrews Gn GL3 ....128 B5
St Andrews Road Sta BS11 ....26 B4
St Andrews Trad Est BS11 ....26 C2
St Ann St NP16 ....72 F1
St Ann Way GL1 ....196 A1
St Ann's Cross 11 GL15 .147 D8
St Annal's Rd GL14 ....191 E4
St Anne's 12 GL52 ....133 F2
St Anne's Ave BS31 ....4 D6
St Anne's CE Prim Sch BS30 ....11 C3
St Anne's Cl Bristol BS30 .11 B4
Cheltenham GL52 ....133 F2
St Anne's Ct BS31 ....4 D6
St Anne's Dr
Coalpit Heath BS36 ....31 C5
Wick BS30 ....12 B7
St Anne's Inf Sch BS4 ....9 D5
St Anne's Park Prim Sch BS4 ....9 E5
St Anne's Park Rd BS4 ....9 E5
St Anne's Rd
Bristol, St Anne's Park BS4 ..9 D6
Bristol, St George BS5 ....10 B6
Cheltenham GL52 ....193 C3
St Anne's Terr Bristol BS4 ..9 E5
Cheltenham GL52 ....193 C3
St Annes Cl 7 Bristol BS5 .9 F6
Brockworth GL3 ....120 E6
St Annes Ct BS4 ....9 D5
St Annes Dr BS30 ....11 C2
St Annes Way GL15 ....146 E7
St Anthony's Dr BS30 ....12 B7
St Anthony's Sch GL14 .191 D4
St Arild's Rd GL9 ....57 B4
St Aubin's Ave BS4 ....9 F3
St Augustine of Canterbury RC Sch BS16 ....20 F7
St Augustine's Par BS1 .195 A2
St Augustine's Pl 1 BS1 ....195 A2
St Barbara's Cl GL20 ....182 D4
St Barnabas CE Prim Sch BS6 ....18 F1
St Barnabas Cl
Bristol, Knowle BS4 ....8 F1
Bristol, Warmley BS30 ....11 C7
Gloucester GL1 ....118 E4
St Bartholomew's Rd BS7 ....18 F3
St Bartholomews 12 GL18 ....171 A4
St Bartholomews Cl GL11 87 F5
St Bede's RC Sch BS11 ..27 B2
St Bede's Rd BS15 ....20 D2
St Benedict's Catholic Sch & Sports Coll GL51 ....133 A3
St Bernadette RC Prim Sch BS14 ....3 B6
St Bernadette RC Sch BS14 ....3 B6
St Bernard's RC Sch BS11 ....16 E6
St Bernard's Rd BS11 ....16 E6
St Birinus Ct GL7 ....153 E3
St Blaize Ct GL7 ....190 C4
St Bonaventure's RC Prim Sch BS7 ....18 D4
St Brelades Gr BS4 ....9 F5
St Brendan's Rd GL5 ....99 E7
St Brendan's Sixth Form Coll BS4 ....10 A1
St Brendan's Way BS11 ..26 B1
St Brendans Rdbt BS11 ..26 C1
St Briavels Dr BS37 ....32 D8
St Briavels Parochial CE Prim Sch GL15 ....146 E7
St Briavels Rd GL15 ....147 B2
St Bruel's Cl GL15 ....146 F7
St Cadoc Ho BS31 ....4 F5
St Catharine's RC Prim Sch GL55 ....188 F2
St Catherine St GL1 ....196 B4
St Catherine's Ind Est BS3 8 D3
St Catherine's Mead BS20 ....16 D3
St Catherine's Terr BS3 ..8 D3
St Catherines Pl 7 BS3 ..8 D4
St Christopher's Specl Sch BS6 ....18 B4
St Clair Cotts GL51 ....173 F2
St Clement's Wlk GL7 ..190 C5
St Clements Ct
6 Bristol BS16 ....20 D3
St Clements Ct *continued*
Keynsham BS31 ....4 E4
St Clements Rd BS31 ....4 F4
St Cloe Mead GL5 ....91 B8
St Cloes Pitch GL5 ....91 A8
St Cyril's Rd GL10 ....97 F7
St David's Ave BS30 ....11 B5
St David's Cl
Chepstow NP16 ....60 E7
Gloucester GL4 ....118 D3
St David's Cres BS4 ....9 F6
St David's Ct GL56 ....187 A3
St David's Prim Sch GL56 ....187 A3
St David's Rd BS35 ....64 C1
St Davids Cl GL51 ....130 A6
St Davids Rd GL20 ....182 C4
St Dominics RC Prim Sch GL5 ....91 A7
St Dunstan's Rd BS3 ....8 C2
St Edward's Rd BS8 ....194 B2
St Edward's Sch GL52 ..131 A7
St Edwards Ct GL56 ....187 A2
St Edwards Dr GL54 ....176 F4
St Edwards Jun Sch GL52 ....131 B7
St Edwards Rd GL54 ....176 F4
St Edwards Senior Sch GL53 ....130 F6
St Edwards Wlk GL53 ....131 A6
St Edyth's Rd BS9 ....17 C6
St Ewens Rd NP16 ....60 E6
St Fagans Ct BS30 ....11 B2
St Francis Dr Wick BS30 ..12 B7
Winterbourne BS36 ....30 F6
St Francis Rd
5 Bristol BS3 ....8 A4
Keynsham BS31 ....4 D6
St Gabriel's Rd BS5 ....9 B8
St George CE Prim Sch BS1 ....194 B2
St George Com Sch BS5 ..9 C8
St George Rd NP16 ....60 E7
St George's Ave GL10 ....98 A4
St George's Bsns Pk GL51 ....133 A2
St George's Cl
2 Cheltenham GL51 ....133 B2
Dursley GL11 ....88 B3
Gloucester GL4 ....118 C3
19 Moreton-in-M GL56 ..187 A3
St George's Dr GL51 ....133 B2
St George's Hill BS20 ....16 A3
St George's Ho BS8 ....194 B2
St George's Pl GL50 ....193 B3
St George's Rd
Cheltenham GL50 ....193 A3
Dursley GL11 ....88 A3
Keynsham BS31 ....4 D6
St George's Sq GL50 ....193 B4
St George's St GL50 ....193 B4
St Georges Ave 10 BS5 ....9 F6
St Georges Ho BS5 ....9 E8
St Georges Ind Est BS11 .26 B3
St Georges Rd
Ashchurch GL20 ....182 C4
Bristol BS1 ....194 C2
Brockworth GL3 ....120 E5
St Georges Twr 5 GL50 .193 B4
St Georges Way NP16 ....61 B4
St Giles Barton GL12 ....55 D8
St Giles's Rd GL20 ....182 C7
St Gregory's Rd BS7 ....18 F8
St Gregory's Wlk BS7 ....18 F8
St Helen's Wlk BS5 ....20 A1
St Helena Rd BS6 ....18 B4
St Helens CE Prim Sch BS35 ....51 A4
St Helens Dr Bristol BS30 .11 C2
Wick BS30 ....12 C7
St Helier Ave BS4 ....9 F3
St Hilary Cl BS9 ....17 D5
St Ivel Way BS30 ....11 C6
St James CE Prim Sch
Cheltenham GL50 ....130 B6
Chipping Campden GL55 ..189 A2
St James Cl BS35 ....64 C3
St James Ct Bristol BS32 .40 C3
4 Cheltenham GL50 ....193 A4
Moreton-in-M GL56 ....187 A2
St James Pk GL16 ....155 B3
St James St
Cheltenham GL52 ....193 C3
Gloucester GL1 ....119 A8
St James' GL2 ....117 F1
St James' & Ebrington CE Prim Sch GL55 ....189 A1
St James' Barton BS1 ..195 B4
St James' CE Jun Sch GL1 ....119 A8
St James' Cl GL2 ....117 F1
St James' Pl GL50 ....193 A1
St James' Sq
Cheltenham GL50 ....193 B3
Monmouth NP25 ....154 A7
St James' St NP25 ....154 A7
St James' Terr GL50 ....193 B2
St James's Pl BS16 ....21 A5
St James's St BS16 ....21 A5
St John St
Hawkesbury Upton GL9 ....56 A3
Thornbury BS35 ....64 B1
St John's Bridge 2 BS1 195 A3
St John's CE Prim Sch
Bristol BS8 ....18 A2

St John's CE Prim Sch *continued*
Cheltenham GL52 ... 193 C3
St John's Cl
Bishop's Cleeve GL52 ... 137 F4
Cirencester GL7 ... 190 B7
St John's Cres BS3 ... 8 E2
St John's Ct 3 GL50 ... 133 B2
St John's Gdns NP16 ... 72 D1
St John's Ho 6 BS5 ... 9 D8
St John's La Bristol BS3 ... 8 E2
Gloucester GL1 ... 196 B3
St John's Mead CE Prim Sch BS37 ... 44 B1
St John's Prim Sch BS31 ... 4 E5
St John's Rd Bristol BS8 ... 18 A1
Bristol, Bedminster BS3 ... 8 C3
Bristol, Southville BS3 ... 8 D4
Cirencester GL7 ... 190 C6
Ruardean GL17 ... 163 F4
Slimbridge GL2 ... 95 E3
St John's St Bristol BS3 ... 8 C3
11 Coleford GL16 ... 155 A5
Lechlade on T GL7 ... 153 E2
St John's-on-the-hill Sch NP16 ... 72 F2
St Johns Ave
Cheltenham GL52 ... 193 C3
Churchdown GL3 ... 128 A6
St Johns CE Prim Sch GL16 ... 155 A5
St Johns Ct Bristol BS16 ... 20 A3
Keynsham BS31 ... 4 E6
St Johns Sq GL14 ... 191 C2
St Johns Way BS37 ... 44 C2
St Joseph's RC Prim Sch BS16 ... 20 B3
St Joseph's RC Prim Sch GL10 ... 89 E6
St Joseph's Rd BS10 ... 28 B3
St Judes Wlk GL53 ... 130 F6
St Katherine's Hospl The Alms Houses 7 HR8 ... 178 F8
St Katherine's Sch BS20 ... 16 E3
St Kenya Ct BS31 ... 4 F5
St Keyna Rd BS31 ... 4 E5
St Kilda Par GL1 ... 196 C2
St Kingsmark Ave NP16 ... 72 D1
St Ladoc Rd BS31 ... 4 D6
St Laud Cl BS9 ... 17 D5
St Lawrence Cl
Cirencester GL7 ... 190 B5
Sandhurst GL2 ... 172 F2
St Lawrence La NP16 ... 60 C7
St Lawrence Pk NP16 ... 60 C8
St Lawrence Rd
Chepstow NP16 ... 60 C8
Gloucester GL4 ... 119 D8
Lechlade on T GL7 ... 153 E2
St Lawrence's CE Prim Sch GL7 ... 153 E2
St Leonard's Rd
Bristol, Horfield BS7 ... 18 E5
Bristol, Lower Easton BS5 ... 19 C2
St Leonard's Row SN16 ... 142 B2
St Leonards Cl
Upper Minety SN16 ... 142 B2
Upton St Leonards GL4 ... 119 E2
St Lucia Cl BS7 ... 18 E7
St Lucia Cres BS7 ... 18 E7
St Luke St 12 BS5 ... 9 B7
St Luke's Cres BS3 ... 8 F4
St Luke's Ct BS3 ... 8 E4
St Luke's Gdns BS4 ... 9 E2
St Luke's Pl GL53 ... 193 C2
St Luke's Rd Bristol BS3 ... 8 E4
Cheltenham GL53 ... 193 C2
St Lukes St GL1 ... 196 A1
St Margaret's Cl BS31 ... 4 D6
St Margaret's Dr BS9 ... 18 C5
St Margaret's Par 6 GL50 ... 193 B4
St Margaret's Rd
Cheltenham GL50 ... 193 B4
Ruardean GL17 ... 163 F4
St Margaret's Terr 2 GL52 ... 193 C4
St Margarets Dr GL20 ... 183 E4
St Margarets Rd
Alderton GL20 ... 183 E4
Gloucester GL3 ... 119 F8
St Mark St GL1 ... 196 B4
St Mark's Ave 1 BS5 ... 19 B1
St Mark's CE Jun Sch GL51 ... 129 D7
St Mark's Ct GL1 ... 196 C4
St Mark's Gr 8 BS5 ... 19 B1
St Mark's Rd BS5 ... 19 B1
St Mark's Terr 11 BS5 ... 19 B1
St Marks Church Ho 4 BS5 ... 19 B1
St Marks Cl BS31 ... 4 E6
St Marks Ho 13 BS5 ... 19 B1
St Martin's Gdns BS4 ... 9 B1
St Martin's La SN14 ... 14 F8
St Martin's Pk SN14 ... 14 F8
St Martin's Rd BS4 ... 9 B2
St Martin's Wlk BS4 ... 9 B1
St Martins Cl BS4 ... 9 B1
St Martins Terr GL50 ... 133 E3
St Mary Redcliffe & Temple CE Sch BS1 ... 195 B1
St Mary Redcliffe Prim Sch BS3 ... 8 E4
St Mary St Chepstow NP16 ... 60 E8
St Mary St *continued*
Thornbury BS35 ... 51 B8
St Mary Street Arc NP16 ... 60 E8
St Mary's Abbey Church★ GL20 ... 192 C3
St Mary's CE Inf Sch GL52 ... 134 B3
St Mary's CE Jun Sch GL52 ... 134 B4
St Mary's CE Prim Sch
Bromberrow Heath HR8 ... 179 C5
Tetbury GL8 ... 140 B4
St Mary's CE Prim Sch BS37 ... 43 E2
St Mary's CE Sch GL20 ... 180 F7
St Mary's Cl GL1 ... 196 A3
St Mary's Cl
Kempsford GL7 ... 144 F7
Lower Swell GL54 ... 176 D4
St Mary's Halt★ GL15 ... 92 A2
St Mary's Hill GL5 ... 91 A7
St Mary's Hospl BS8 ... 194 B3
St Mary's La GL20 ... 192 C4
St Mary's RC Jun & Inf Sch NP16 ... 60 E7
St Mary's RC Prim Sch WR12 ... 185 B8
St Mary's Rd Bristol BS11 ... 16 D7
Cirencester GL7 ... 190 E4
Leigh Woods BS8 ... 7 D6
Tetbury GL8 ... 140 B4
Tewkesbury GL20 ... 192 B4
St Mary's Sch BS35 ... 64 A2
St Mary's Sq
Gloucester GL1 ... 196 A3
Lydney GL15 ... 92 C3
St Mary's St
Gloucester GL1 ... 196 B3
Painswick GL6 ... 103 F8
St Mary's Way BS37 ... 43 F2
St Mary's Wlk BS11 ... 16 D6
St Marys Cl GL18 ... 178 D2
St Marys Dr GL7 ... 152 E4
St Marys Field GL7 ... 152 A3
St Marys RC Prim Sch
Bristol BS34 ... 30 A7
Innsworth GL3 ... 127 F6
St Marys Way BS35 ... 64 B1
St Mathias Ho BS2 ... 195 C3
St Matthew's Ave 10 BS6 ... 18 D1
St Matthew's CE Prim Sch GL5 ... 98 E7
St Matthew's Rd BS6 ... 195 A4
St Matthias & Dr Bell's CE Prim Sch BS16 ... 20 A4
St Matthias Pk BS2 ... 195 C3
St Maur Gdns NP16 ... 72 D1
St Michael's Ave SN6 ... 145 C3
St Michael's CE Prim Sch BS34 ... 29 E5
St Michael's Cl
Mitcheldean GL17 ... 164 D5
Winterbourne BS36 ... 30 E7
St Michael's Ct GL1 ... 196 B2
St Michael's Hill BS2 ... 194 C4
St Michael's Hospl BS2 ... 194 C4
St Michael's Pk BS2 ... 194 C4
St Michael's Pl GL5 ... 98 D8
St Michael's Sq GL1 ... 196 B2
St Michaels 3 HR8 ... 178 F8
St Michaels Ave GL52 ... 138 A3
St Michaels CE Prim Sch BS36 ... 30 E6
St Michaels Cl BS7 ... 18 E4
St Michaels Ct BS15 ... 10 B8
St Michaels Rd
Cheltenham GL51 ... 130 B5
Cirencester GL7 ... 190 C3
St Nicholas Cl GL20 ... 183 A3
St Nicholas Ct
Gloucester GL1 ... 196 A3
Hardwicke GL2 ... 109 E7
St Nicholas Dr GL50 ... 133 D5
St Nicholas of Tolentine RC Prim Sch BS5 ... 9 A8
St Nicholas Pk 10 BS5 ... 19 B1
St Nicholas Rd BS14 ... 3 C4
St Nicholas Sq GL1 ... 196 A3
St Nicholas St BS1 ... 195 A2
St Nicholas' Rd BS2 ... 18 F1
St Nicholas's Church Mus BS1 ... 195 A2
St Oswald's Ct BS13 ... 2 A8
St Oswald's Ct BS6 ... 18 B3
St Oswald's Rd Bristol BS6 ... 18 B3
Gloucester GL1 ... 196 A4
St Patrick's RC Prim Sch BS5 ... 9 D7
St Patricks Ct BS31 ... 4 E5
St Patricks Rd GL20 ... 182 C4
St Paul St BS2 ... 195 B4
St Paul's Ct GL1 ... 118 E7
St Paul's La GL50 ... 133 D3
St Paul's Par GL50 ... 133 D3
St Paul's Prim Sch GL1 ... 196 A1
St Paul's RC Prim Sch BS37 ... 32 E8
St Paul's Rd Bristol BS8 ... 194 B4
2 Bristol, Southville BS3 ... 8 D4
Cheltenham GL50 ... 133 D3
Gloucester GL1 ... 118 E7
St Paul's St N GL50 ... 133 D3
St Paul's St S GL50 ... 193 B4
St Paul's Terr GL50 ... 193 B4
St Pauls Ct GL56 ... 187 A2
St Peter's CE Sch GL14 ... 157 A7
St Peter's Cl GL14 ... 157 A6
St Peter's Cres BS36 ... 31 B8
St Peter's Ct GL7 ... 190 C4
St Peter's Ho BS8 ... 194 B2
St Peter's Inf & Jun Schs GL1 ... 127 B2
St Peter's RC High Sch GL4 ... 118 E1
St Peter's Rd GL4 ... 119 C3
St Peter's Rise BS13 ... 2 B7
St Peter's Sq GL51 ... 133 A4
St Peter's Wlk 3 BS9 ... 18 B6
St Peters Cl
Cheltenham GL51 ... 133 B4
Rodmarton GL7 ... 149 B1
St Peters Ct GL56 ... 187 A2
St Peters Rd GL7 ... 190 C4
St Peters Way 12 GL54 ... 174 A7
St Philip's Cl GL3 ... 120 A8
St Philip's Ct GL1 ... 118 D7
St Philips Central BS2 ... 9 A5
St Philips Cswy BS2 ... 9 B5
St Phillip's St GL50 ... 193 B1
St Phillips Rd BS2 ... 9 A7
St Pias X RC Prim Sch BS13 ... 2 A5
St Pierre Dr BS30 ... 11 B6
St Ronan's Ave BS6 ... 18 C1
St Rose's Specl Sch GL5 ... 99 B7
St Sampson's Jun & Inf Schs SN6 ... 143 E4
St Saviour's Rise BS36 ... 31 B6
St Silas St BS2 ... 9 A5
St Stephen's Ave 3 BS1 ... 195 A2
St Stephen's CE Jun Sch BS15 ... 20 D2
St Stephen's Ct GL1 ... 118 D7
St Stephen's Manor GL51 ... 130 B7
St Stephen's Rd
Bristol BS16 ... 20 D2
Cheltenham GL51 ... 130 B7
St Stephen's St BS1 ... 195 A2
St Stephens Bsns Ctr BS30 ... 11 C5
St Stephens Cl
Bristol BS16 ... 20 E3
Cheltenham GL50 ... 130 B7
St Swithin's GL10 ... 97 E4
St Swithins Rd GL15 ... 156 B1
St Swithuns Rd GL2 ... 118 A6
St Tecla Rd NP16 ... 60 E6
St Teresa's RC Prim Sch BS7 ... 28 E1
St Tewdric Rd NP16 ... 60 E7
St Tewdrics Pl NP16 ... 60 B4
St Thomas More Catholic Prim Sch GL51 ... 132 D2
St Thomas More RC Sch BS7 ... 19 A3
St Thomas St BS1 ... 195 B2
St Thomas St E BS1 ... 195 B2
St Ursula's High Sch BS9 ... 18 A6
St Vincent Way GL3 ... 128 A8
St Vincent's Hill 1 BS6 ... 18 A2
St Vincent's Rd BS8 ... 194 A2
St Vincents Trad Est BS2 ... 9 D6
St Werburgh's Pk BS2 ... 19 A2
St Werburgh's Rd BS2 ... 18 F2
St Werburgh's Sch BS5 ... 19 A2
St Whites Ct GL14 ... 191 C2
St Whites Rd GL14 ... 191 D3
St Whites Sch GL14 ... 191 C2
St Whites Terr GL14 ... 191 C2
St Whytes Rd BS4 ... 2 D8
Salamanca Rd GL52 ... 134 B2
Salcombe Rd BS4 ... 9 A1
Salem Rd BS36 ... 30 F7
Salisbury Ave Bristol BS15 ... 10 B8
Cheltenham GL51 ... 130 A5
Salisbury Gdns BS16 ... 20 E5
Salisbury Pk BS16 ... 20 E6
Salisbury Rd
Bristol, Mangotsfield BS16 ... 20 E6
Bristol, Redland BS6 ... 18 D2
Bristol, St Anne's BS4 ... 9 D5
Gloucester GL1 ... 119 A8
Salisbury St
Bristol, Pile Marsh BS5 ... 9 E7
Bristol, Russell Town BS5 ... 9 B6
Salix Ct GL51 ... 130 A4
Sallis Cl GL20 ... 182 B5
Sallybarn Cl BS30 ... 10 E2
Sallys Way BS36 ... 30 F7
Sallysmead Cl BS13 ... 2 B4
Salmon's Spring Ind Est GL6 ... 103 B1
Salmons Way BS16 ... 21 B8
Salmonsbury Cotts GL54 ... 169 A8
Salt Way
Coln St Aldwyns GL7 ... 152 D8
Compton Abdale GL54 ... 167 D3
Salter St GL13 ... 85 E3
Salter's La GL54 ... 174 C8
Salterley Grange GL53 ... 122 D7
Saltford CE Prim Sch BS31 ... 5 E2
Saltford Ct BS31 ... 5 E3
Salthrop Rd BS7 ... 18 E4
Saltmarsh Dr BS11 ... 27 A1
Saltwell Ave BS14 ... 3 C5
Salvia Cl GL3 ... 127 F6
Sambourne La BS20 ... 16 C4
Sambourne Rd SN16 ... 142 E1
Samian Way BS34 ... 29 E5
Sampson House Bsns Pk BS10 ... 27 D7
Sampsons Rd BS13 ... 2 D4
Sams La SN26 ... 144 E1
Samuel St 3 BS5 ... 9 C8
Samuel White Rd BS15 ... 10 C4
Samuel Whites Inf Sch BS15 ... 10 C4
Samuel Wright Cl BS30 ... 11 D5
San Andreas BS34 ... 28 E6
San Remo GL1 ... 118 E6
Sanctuary Gdns BS9 ... 17 D3
Sand Hill BS4 ... 9 C4
Sandalwood Dr GL2 ... 118 B7
Sandbach Rd BS4 ... 9 D4
Sandbed Rd BS2 ... 19 A2
Sandburrows Rd BS13 ... 1 F6
Sandburrows Wlk BS13 ... 1 F6
Sandcroft BS14 ... 2 F6
Sandfield Rd GL3 ... 128 D5
Sandfield The GL20 ... 182 C5
Sandfields GL18 ... 179 B3
Sandford Leaze GL8 ... 148 B1
Sandford Mill Cl GL53 ... 130 F7
Sandford Mill Rd GL53 ... 130 F7
Sandford Park Pl GL52 ... 193 C2
Sandford Rd
Aylburton GL15 ... 147 D4
Bristol BS8 ... 194 A1
Cheltenham GL53 ... 193 C1
Sandford St GL53 ... 193 C2
Sandford Terr GL15 ... 147 D4
Sandford Way GL4 ... 118 B1
Sandgate Rd BS4 ... 9 D3
Sandholme Cl BS16 ... 20 E8
Sandholme Rd BS4 ... 9 D4
Sandhurst BS37 ... 32 D8
Sandhurst Cl BS34 ... 40 B1
Sandhurst La
Down Hatherley GL2 ... 173 A2
Gloucester GL2 ... 126 F5
Sandhurst Rd Bristol BS4 ... 9 D4
Charlton Kings GL52 ... 131 B6
Gloucester GL1 ... 126 E4
Sandling Ave BS7 ... 19 A7
Sandown Cl BS16 ... 30 F1
Sandown Rd
Bishop's Cleeve GL52 ... 137 F4
Bristol, Brislington BS4 ... 9 D4
Bristol, Filton BS34 ... 29 C3
Sandpiper Cl GL2 ... 117 D1
Sandpits La
Hawkesbury Upton GL9 ... 56 A2
Randwick GL6 ... 102 C1
Sherston SN16 ... 58 C1
Stroud GL6 ... 98 C8
Sandpool La GL7 ... 149 C2
Sandringham Ave
Bristol BS16 ... 20 E8
Gloucester GL4 ... 118 C1
Sandringham Ct GL53 ... 130 F7
Sandringham Pk BS16 ... 20 E8
Sandringham Rd
Bristol, Brislington BS4 ... 9 D4
Bristol, Longwell Green BS30 ... 10 F2
Bristol, Stoke Gifford BS34 ... 29 D4
Sands Cl WR12 ... 188 A1
Sands Croft Ave WR12 ... 188 B1
Sands Hill SN14 ... 23 E3
Sands La BS36 ... 41 F1
Sands The WR12 ... 188 A1
Sandstar Cl GL2 ... 127 D5
Sandstone Rise BS36 ... 30 E4
Sandtumps GL15 ... 147 B4
Sandwich Rd BS4 ... 9 D4
Sandy Cl BS32 ... 29 E6
Sandy La Aust BS35 ... 49 A7
Aust BS35 ... 49 A8
Bristol BS5 ... 19 C3
Cheltenham GL53 ... 130 F4
Easton-in-G BS20 ... 16 A1
Hewelsfield GL15 ... 146 E5
Upper Rissington GL54 ... 169 D6
Sandy La Ct GL54 ... 169 D6
Sandy Lane Rd GL53 ... 130 F5
Sandy Lodge BS37 ... 32 E8
Sandy Park Rd BS4 ... 9 C3
Sandy Pluck La GL51 ... 121 B8
Sandycroft Rd GL3 ... 128 A7
Sandyleaze Bristol BS9 ... 17 E7
Gloucester GL2 ... 127 D3
Sandyway La HR9 ... 162 D3
Saniger La Berkeley GL13 ... 85 D6
Sharpness GL13 ... 85 C7
Sankey Gr GL56 ... 187 A2
Sappercombe La GL53 ... 131 B5
Sapperton CE Prim Sch GL7 ... 149 B6
Sapperton Rd GL4 ... 118 F5
Sapphire Cl GL4 ... 118 C2
Sarah St BS5 ... 9 B7
Sargent St BS3 ... 8 E4
Sargent's La HR9,GL18 ... 170 B4
Sarn Hill Grange (Bredon Sch) GL20 ... 181 C5
Sarnedy Rd 3 GL16 ... 155 A5
Sarum Cres BS10 ... 28 C1
Sassoon Ct BS30 ... 10 F5
Satchfield Cl BS10 ... 27 F2
Satchfield Cres BS10 ... 27 F2
Satellite Bsns Pk BS5 ... 9 D6
Sates Way BS9 ... 18 C6
Saturn Cl GL4 ... 119 F6
Saul Prim Sch GL2 ... 157 F4
Saunders Cl
Huntley GL17 ... 165 A7
Lea HR9 ... 164 D8
Saunders Rd BS16 ... 20 E4
Saunton Wlk BS4 ... 2 E8
Savage Hill GL16 ... 154 E4
Savages Wood BS32 ... 29 E8
Savages Wood Rd BS32 ... 29 D8
Savernake Rd GL4 ... 119 A7
Saville Cl GL50 ... 133 E4
Saville Gate Cl BS9 ... 17 F4
Saville Mews BS6 ... 195 A4
Saville Pl BS8 ... 194 A2
Saville Rd BS9 ... 17 F3
Savoy Rd BS4 ... 9 D4
Saw Mill La BS35 ... 64 B1
Sawpit La GL19 ... 173 C7
Sawpits La GL56 ... 177 D5
Sawpitts La HR9 ... 162 E4
Sawyers Cl SN16 ... 142 D1
Sawyers Hill SN16 ... 142 D1
Sawyers Rise
Ashleworth GL19 ... 172 D4
Minety SN16 ... 142 D1
Saxon Cl Cricklade SN6 ... 143 E4
Gloucester GL2 ... 127 C5
Saxon Pl NP16 ... 61 A7
Saxon Rd Bristol BS2 ... 19 A2
Cirencester GL7 ... 190 E5
Saxon Way Bristol BS32 ... 40 C1
Cheltenham GL52 ... 131 A8
Say Wlk BS30 ... 11 D7
Sayers Cres GL3 ... 120 E5
Saylittle Mews GL2 ... 127 E5
Sayth Ho GL7 ... 190 D5
SBI Ctr BS15 ... 10 B5
Scandrett Cl BS10 ... 27 E2
Scantleberry Cl BS16 ... 20 D8
Scar Hill GL6 ... 91 D4
Scarr Rd GL18 ... 171 A7
Scarr The GL18 ... 171 A7
School Cl
Bristol, Eastville BS5 ... 19 D2
Bristol, Patchway BS34 ... 29 C8
Bristol, Whitchurch BS14 ... 2 F4
5 Coleford GL16 ... 155 B5
Dursley GL11 ... 87 E4
School Cres
Joy's Green GL17 ... 163 D3
Lydney GL15 ... 92 B5
Staunton GL19 ... 172 B7
School Hill
Bourton-on-t-W GL54 ... 168 F7
Chepstow NP16 ... 60 E8
Cirencester GL7 ... 190 A8
Winstone GL7 ... 107 A8
School Hill Ind Est NP16 ... 60 E8
School La
Ampney Crucis GL7 ... 151 C5
Badminton GL9 ... 46 E2
4 Blockley GL56 ... 186 C5
Bretforton WR11 ... 188 A6
2 Bristol BS16 ... 19 E5
Castle Eaton SN6 ... 144 D6
Cirencester GL7 ... 190 D3
Edgeworth GL6 ... 106 D1
Hardwicke GL2 ... 109 E8
Longhope GL17 ... 164 F6
Meysey Hampton GL7 ... 152 A2
Narth The NP25 ... 154 B1
Overbury GL20 ... 182 F8
Ruardean GL17 ... 163 F4
Shipton GL54 ... 166 E5
Shurdington GL51 ... 129 E2
South Cerney GL7 ... 142 F8
Southam GL52 ... 134 C8
Whitminster GL2 ... 100 E5
School Mead GL51 ... 133 A2
School Mews GL4 ... 119 B4
School of Christ the King RC Prim Sch BS4 ... 2 E8
School Rd Alderton GL20 ... 183 E4
Apperley GL19 ... 173 C6
Bishop's Cleeve GL52 ... 138 A4
Bristol BS15 ... 10 C8
Bristol, Broom Hill BS4 ... 9 E3
Bristol, Cadbury Heath BS30 ... 11 A4
Bristol, Oldland Common BS30 ... 11 C3
Bristol, Totterdown BS4 ... 9 A3
Charlton Kings GL53 ... 131 B6
Dursley GL11 ... 80 C8
Frampton Cotterell BS36 ... 31 A8
Joy's Green GL17 ... 163 D3
Kemble GL7 ... 141 F8
Minchinhampton GL6 ... 148 A3
Ruardean GL17 ... 163 F4
Upper Lydbrook GL17 ... 163 D2
Whitecroft GL15 ... 155 F1
Wooton-u-E GL12 ... 68 B7
School Road Flats 3 GL53 ... 131 B6
School St WR11 ... 188 C6
School Terr GL5 ... 98 D6
School Way BS35 ... 38 A6
School Wlk Bristol BS5 ... 19 D1
Yate BS37 ... 43 E2
Schooler's La GL56 ... 177 E6
Scop The BS32 ... 40 B5
Scott Ave GL2 ... 118 C4
Scott Ct BS30 ... 10 F5
Scott Ho GL51 ... 132 E3
Scott Lawrence Cl BS16 ... 20 A7
Scott Way BS37 ... 32 F8
Scott Wlk BS30 ... 11 D7
Scowles Rd GL16 ... 154 F6
Scrubbett's La GL8 ... 69 F8
Sea Mills Inf Sch BS9 ... 17 C7
Sea Mills Jun Sch BS9 ... 17 C5
Sea Mills La BS9 ... 17 C5
Sea Mills Sta BS9 ... 17 B4
Seabright Cl GL51 ... 132 E5

Seabroke Rd GL1 ... 196 C4
Seabrook Rd GL3 ... 120 E5
Seacome Rd GL51 ... 132 D2
Seagry Cl BS10 ... 28 E1
Searle Court Ave BS4 ... 9 E4
Seaton Ct BS3 ... 8 D1
Seaton Rd BS5 ... 19 C1
Seawalls BS9 ... 17 D2
Seawalls Rd BS9 ... 17 D2
Sebert St GL1 ... 196 C4
Second Ave Bristol BS14 ... 3 B7
Dursley GL11 ... 80 C8
Second Way BS11 ... 26 D1
Secret La GL1 ... 196 B4
Secunda Way (Hempsted By-Pass) GL2 ... 118 C7
Sedbury Bsns Pk NP16 ... 61 B8
Sedbury La NP16 ... 73 A1
Seddon Rd 4 BS2 ... 19 A2
Sedgefield Gdns BS16 ... 30 F1
Sedgewick Gdns GL51 ... 129 D6
Sedgley Cl GL4 ... 118 C2
Sedgley Rd GL52 ... 137 F4
Sedgwick Ho BS11 ... 16 E7
Sedum Ho 1 GL50 ... 133 B1
Sefton Park Jun & Inf Schs BS7 ... 18 F3
Sefton Park Rd BS7 ... 18 F3
Sefton Wlk GL51 ... 129 D6
Selborne Rd
Bishop's Cleeve GL52 ... 137 F4
Bristol BS7 ... 18 F5
Selbrooke Cres BS16 ... 20 C6
Selby Rd BS5 ... 19 F1
Selden Rd BS14 ... 3 E5
Selkirk Cl GL52 ... 133 F2
Selkirk Ct 3 GL52 ... 133 F2
Selkirk Gdns GL52 ... 133 F2
Selkirk Rd BS15 ... 20 C1
Selkirk St GL52 ... 133 F2
Sellars Rd GL2 ... 109 D7
Selley Wlk BS13 ... 2 A5
Selsey Rd GL5 ... 98 F2
Selsley Hill GL5 ... 98 E4
Selworthy Bristol BS15 ... 10 E7
Cheltenham GL51 ... 129 E5
Selworthy Cl BS31 ... 4 D5
Selworthy Rd BS4 ... 9 B2
Selwyn Cl GL10 ... 98 A5
Selwyn Rd GL4 ... 118 F5
Seneca Pl 1 BS5 ... 9 D7
Seneca St BS5 ... 9 D7
Seneca Way GL50 ... 133 B5
Septimus Bldgs BS14 ... 2 D5
Serlo Rd GL1 ... 196 B4
Serridge La BS36 ... 31 D4
Setts Row GL7 ... 149 E3
Sevelm 11 GL51 ... 129 E5
Seven Acres GL4 ... 119 D7
Seven Springs House (Sch) GL53 ... 123 B7
Seven Stars Rd GL14 ... 191 C6
Seven Waters GL10 ... 97 D4
Sevenacres Rd GL6 ... 91 A4
Sevenfields SN6 ... 145 D4
Sevenleaze La Edge GL6 111 B2
Gloucester GL4,GL6 ... 111 D5
Seventh Ave
Bristol, Filton BS7 ... 29 B1
Bristol, Hengrove BS14 ... 3 A7
Gloucester GL4 ... 118 D2
Severn Ave NP16 ... 73 A1
Severn Beach Prim Sch BS35 ... 38 A6
Severn Beach Sta BS35 ... 38 A6
Severn Cl Charfield GL12 ... 67 A4
Maisemore GL2 ... 126 B7
Severn Cres NP16 ... 60 F7
Severn Dr Berkeley GL13 ... 85 E4
Thornbury BS35 ... 64 B2
Severn Grange BS10 ... 27 D3
Severn La Berkeley GL13 ... 84 E1
Bevington GL13 ... 76 F8
Severn Oaks GL2 ... 109 F7
Severn Rd
Avonmouth BS11 ... 26 C4
Bristol BS11 ... 16 D6
Cheltenham GL52 ... 134 A3
Dursley GL11 ... 87 E4
Gloucester GL1 ... 196 A2
Hallen BS10 ... 27 A7
Lydney GL15 ... 92 B2
Pill BS20 ... 16 C5
Severn Beach BS35 ... 37 F3
Sharpness GL13 ... 85 B8
Stonehouse GL10 ... 97 E8
Severn St GL14 ... 157 A6
Severn Terr GL14 ... 157 A6
Severn Vale Sch GL2 ... 109 E8
Severn View GL14 ... 191 E5
Severn View Rd
Thornbury BS35 ... 64 C2
Woolaston GL15 ... 147 B3
Yorkley GL15 ... 156 B2
Severn Way
Apperley GL19 ... 173 C7
Bristol BS34 ... 39 F1
Keynsham BS31 ... 5 A5
Severnbank Ave GL15 ... 92 C3
Severnbanks Prim Sch GL15 ... 92 C3
Severnleigh Gdns BS9 ... 17 F3
Severnside Trad Est
Avonmouth BS11 ... 26 C5
Gloucester GL2 ... 126 C1
Severnvale Dr GL2 ... 117 E2
Severnwood Gdns BS35 ... 38 A5
Sevier St BS2 ... 18 F2
Seymour Ave BS7 ... 18 E4
Seymour Cl 5 GL16 ... 155 A7
Seymour Gate GL55 ... 189 A2
Seymour Pl
Tewkesbury GL20 ... 192 C3
10 Winchcombe GL54 ... 174 A7
Seymour Rd
Bristol, Ashley Down BS7 ... 18 E4
Bristol, Kingswood BS15 ... 20 C1
Bristol, Staple Hill BS16 ... 20 E4
Bristol, Upper Easton BS5 ... 19 A1
Gloucester GL1 ... 118 D7
Seyton Wlk BS34 ... 29 E5
Sezincote* GL56 ... 186 D2
Sezincote Cl GL6 ... 148 B6
Shackel Hendy Mews BS16 ... 21 B5
Shackleton Ave BS37 ... 32 F8
Shackleton Cl GL3 ... 128 C5
Shadwell Rd BS7 ... 18 D3
Shaft Rd BS35 ... 38 A8
Shaftesbury Ave BS6 ... 18 E1
Shaftesbury Hall 4 GL50 ... 193 B4
Shaftesbury Ind Est GL51 ... 133 B6
Shaftesbury Pl 10 GL51 ... 132 D2
Shaftesbury Terr 8 BS5 ... 9 D7
Shakespeare Ave
Bristol BS7 ... 19 A8
Gloucester GL2 ... 118 C4
Shakespeare Cotts GL51 ... 129 B7
Shakespeare Ct GL20 ... 192 C4
Shakespeare Rd
Cheltenham GL51 ... 132 E1
Dursley GL11 ... 80 C7
Shaldon Rd BS7 ... 19 A4
Shalford Cl GL7 ... 190 B3
Shallowbrooks La SN14 ... 47 F8
Shallows The BS31 ... 5 F3
Shambles Mus The* GL18 ... 171 A4
Shambles The 12 GL5 ... 99 C7
Shamrock Cl GL3 ... 127 F6
Shamrock Rd BS5 ... 19 D3
Shanklin Dr BS34 ... 29 B3
Shannon Ct BS35 ... 51 D8
Shannon Way GL20 ... 182 B4
Shapcott Cl BS4 ... 9 B1
Shaplands BS9 ... 17 F4
Sharland Cl BS9 ... 17 E3
Sharland Gr BS13 ... 2 C4
Sharpness Prim Sch GL13 ... 85 D8
Sharps Way NP16 ... 60 F5
Shaw Cl 3 BS5 ... 9 B8
Shaw Green La GL52 ... 134 C5
Shaymoor La BS35 ... 39 A4
Shearmore Cl BS7 ... 19 A7
Shearwater Gr GL3 ... 127 E6
Sheene Ct 18 BS3 ... 8 C3
Sheene La BS3 ... 8 C3
Sheene Way BS3 ... 8 C3
Sheenhill Rd WR11 ... 188 B8
Sheens Mdw GL14 ... 156 F7
Sheep Fair La SN14 ... 14 F8
Sheep St Cirencester GL7 190 C4
Highworth SN6 ... 145 D3
Stow-on-t-W GL54 ... 176 F4
Sheeps Croft BS13 ... 2 A5
Sheepscombe Cl GL51 ... 129 E8
Sheepscombe Cty Prim Sch GL6 ... 112 E1
Sheepwood Cl BS10 ... 28 A2
Sheepwood Rd BS10 ... 28 A2
Sheer Ho 7 WR12 ... 185 C8
Sheevaun Cl GL2 ... 127 D5
Sheiling Sch The BS35 ... 64 B2
Shelburne Rd GL51 ... 129 F8
Sheldare Barton BS5 ... 10 B7
Sheldons Ct GL52 ... 193 C4
Sheldrake Dr BS16 ... 19 E6
Shelduck Rd GL2 ... 117 D1
Shellard Rd BS34 ... 29 A2
Shellards La BS35 ... 51 E2
Shellards Rd BS30 ... 10 F3
Shelley Ave
Cheltenham GL51 ... 132 E1
Gloucester GL2 ... 118 C4
Shelley Cl BS5 ... 9 F8
Shelley Ho BS34 ... 40 A1
Shelley Rd
Cheltenham GL51 ... 132 E1
Dursley GL11 ... 80 C7
Shelley Way BS7 ... 19 A8
Shellmor Ave BS34 ... 40 B1
Shellmor Cl BS32 ... 40 D1
Shephard Mead GL20 ... 192 B3
Shepherd Rd GL2 ... 118 B3
Shepherd's Cl GL55 ... 188 F1
Shepherd's Leaze GL12 ... 68 C6
Shepherdine Cl GL15 ... 92 C3
Shepherds Cl Bristol BS16 20 E5
Cheltenham GL51 ... 132 D4
8 Ledbury HR8 ... 178 E7
Stroud GL5 ... 99 D8
Shepherds Croft GL5 ... 99 D8
Shepherds Mead 3 GL8 ... 140 C5
Shepherds Row 4 GL54 176 F4
Shepherds Way
Cirencester GL7 ... 190 C6
Innsworth GL3 ... 127 F7
Northleach GL54 ... 167 F1
19 Stow-on-t-W GL54 ... 176 F4
Shepherds Well GL5 ... 99 D1
Shepherds Wlk GL12 ... 68 C6
Sheppard Rd BS16 ... 20 C6
Sheppard Way
Minchinhampton GL6 ... 91 F7
Newent GL18 ... 171 A4
Shepperdine Rd BS35 ... 75 D2
Sheppey Cnr WR12 ... 184 F5
Shepton Wlk BS3 ... 8 C2
Sherborne CE Prim Sch GL54 ... 169 A1
Sherborne Cl GL10 ... 97 F8
Sherborne Ho 1 GL10 ... 97 F8
Sherborne La GL54 ... 169 C3
Sherborne Pl GL52 ... 193 C3
Sherborne St
Bourton-on-t-W GL54 ... 168 F7
Cheltenham GL52 ... 193 C4
Gloucester GL1 ... 196 C4
Lechlade on T GL7 ... 153 E2
Sherborne Terr 4 GL54 ... 168 F7
Sherbourne Ave BS32 ... 29 E7
Sherbourne Cl BS15 ... 20 F2
Sherbourne St BS5 ... 9 E7
Sherbourne's Brake BS32 ... 29 E6
Shergar Cl GL4 ... 119 D4
Sheridan Rd BS7 ... 19 A8
Sheridan Way BS30 ... 11 A2
Sherrin Way BS13 ... 1 E3
Sherrings The BS34 ... 29 B8
Sherry Covert GL54 ... 175 B7
Sherry The GL54 ... 175 B7
Sherston Cl BS16 ... 20 B5
Sherston Rd Bristol BS7 ... 18 E8
Luckington SN14 ... 47 F5
Sherwell Rd BS4 ... 9 E3
Sherwood Cl BS31 ... 4 E5
Sherwood Gn GL2 ... 126 F6
Sherwood Rd Bristol BS15 20 B1
Keynsham BS31 ... 4 E5
Tetbury GL8 ... 140 B4
Shetland Rd BS10 ... 28 D1
Shield Ret Ctr BS34 ... 29 A3
Shield Road Prim Sch BS7 ... 29 A1
Shields Ave BS7 ... 29 A1
Shiels Dr BS32 ... 29 D7
Shilton Cl BS15 ... 10 F7
Shimsey Cl BS16 ... 20 C6
Ship La BS1 ... 195 B1
Shipham Cl BS14 ... 3 B5
Shipley Mow BS16 ... 21 B6
Shipley Rd BS9 ... 18 A8
Shipman Ct BS16 ... 20 E4
Shipton's Grave La GL6 ... 91 C1
Shipway Ct GL52 ... 137 F4
Shire Gdns BS11 ... 16 D8
Shire Hill SN14 ... 25 A7
Shire Way BS37 ... 32 D6
Shirehampton Inf Sch BS11 ... 16 D6
Shirehampton Rd BS9 ... 17 C6
Shirehampton Sta BS11 ... 16 D5
Shooters End GL5 ... 99 C8
Shop La Badminton GL9 ... 46 E2
Bretforton WR11 ... 188 A7
Shophouse Rd GL15, GL16 ... 155 A2
Shorland Ho BS8 ... 18 A1
Short Hedges Cl 16 GL54 ... 168 A1
Short La BS41 ... 7 A2
Short St Bristol BS2 ... 9 A5
Cheltenham GL53 ... 130 C6
Short Way BS35 ... 51 B7
Shorthill Rd BS37 ... 32 C4
Shortlands Rd BS11 ... 27 A1
Shortwood Hill BS16 ... 21 E4
Shortwood Rd Bristol BS13 ... 2 E3
Nailsworth GL6 ... 91 A3
Pucklechurch BS16 ... 22 A4
Shortwood View BS15 ... 10 F8
Shortwood Wlk BS13 ... 2 E3
Shotts La GL18 ... 170 C3
Showering Cl BS14 ... 3 D5
Showering Rd BS14 ... 3 D5
Shrivenham Rd SN6 ... 145 D2
Shrubberies Sch The GL10 ... 97 E8
Shrubbery Cotts 4 BS6 ... 18 B2
Shrubbery Ct 6 BS16 ... 20 D5
Shrubbery Rd BS16 ... 20 D5
Shrublands GL53 ... 130 F5
Shubbery The GL7 ... 153 E2
Shurdington Prim Sch GL51 ... 129 D1
Shurdington Rd
Brockworth GL3 ... 121 A5
Cheltenham GL51 ... 130 B5
Shurdington GL51 ... 129 E2
Shute St GL10 ... 98 A3
Shutehay Dr GL11 ... 87 F5
Shuter Rd BS13 ... 1 E5
Shutter La GL52 ... 137 F8
Sibland BS35 ... 51 D8
Sibland Cl 3 BS35 ... 51 D8
Sibland Rd BS35 ... 51 D8
Sibland Way BS35 ... 51 D8
Sibree Cl GL6 ... 148 B6
Sidcot BS4 ... 10 A2
Siddington CE Sch GL7 190 D1
Siddington Hall GL7 ... 150 E2
Sideland Cl BS14 ... 3 E6
Sidelands Rd BS16 ... 20 C6
Sidings The GL12 ... 67 B5
Sidmouth Ct BS3 ... 8 D1
Sidmouth Gdns BS3 ... 8 D2
Sidmouth Rd BS3 ... 8 E2
Sidney St
Cheltenham GL52 ... 193 C3
Gloucester GL1 ... 127 A1
Signal Rd BS16 ... 20 F4
Silbury Rd BS3 ... 7 E2
Silbury Rise BS31 ... 5 A2
Silcock Cl GL3 ... 127 F7
Silcox Rd BS13 ... 2 C4
Silk Mill Ct 31 GL54 ... 174 A7
Silk Mill La GL54 ... 174 A7
Silklands Gr BS9 ... 17 C6
Silley's Cl NP16 ... 72 F2
Silver Birch Cl GL2 ... 117 E1
Silver Cl Gloucester GL4 ... 118 C3
Minety SN16 ... 142 D1
Silver St Arlingham GL2 ... 157 C6
Bristol BS1 ... 195 A3
Cirencester GL7 ... 190 C5
Coaley GL11 ... 89 A7
Dursley GL11 ... 88 B1
Littledean GL14 ... 156 E8
Minety SN16 ... 142 D1
Mitcheldean GL17 ... 164 D5
South Cerney GL7 ... 142 F8
12 Tetbury GL8 ... 140 C4
Thornbury BS35 ... 64 B1
Silverbirch Cl BS34 ... 29 D7
Silverdale Par GL3 ... 119 F8
Silverhill Brake BS35 ... 50 E1
Silverhill Rd BS10 ... 27 E4
Silverhill Sch BS37 ... 50 E1
Silverhill Sch (Jun) BS36 30 E7
Silverthorn Cl GL53 ... 130 B5
Silverthorne La BS2 ... 9 A6
Silverthorne Wharf BS2 ... 9 B6
Silverton Ct BS4 ... 8 F1
Silvertree Gdns GL5 ... 99 E3
Silverwood Way GL51 ... 129 E5
Simmonds Ct GL6 ... 148 A3
Simmonds Rd GL3 ... 119 F6
Simmonds View BS34 ... 29 F5
Simon Rd GL2 ... 127 C5
Simplex Ind Est The BS30 ... 11 D4
Sims La GL2 ... 117 F4
Sinclair Ho
Bristol, Clifton Wood BS8 ... 194 A2
Bristol, Filton BS34 ... 29 A2
Sinclair Rd GL51 ... 129 D1
Sinderberry Dr GL20 ... 182 C5
Sinope St GL1 ... 196 C2
Sion Hill BS8 ... 7 F7
Sion La BS8 ... 7 F7
Sion Pl BS8 ... 7 F7
Sion Rd 10 BS3 ... 8 C3
Sir Bernard Lovell Sch BS30 ... 11 C4
Sir Bernard Lovell Sch (annexe) BS30 ... 11 D5
Sir Bevil Grenville's Mon* BA1 ... 13 A1
Sir John's La Bristol BS5 ... 19 B4
Bristol BS7 ... 19 B5
Sir Thomas Rich's Sch GL2 ... 127 D3
Sir William Romney's Sch GL8 ... 140 C5
Siskin Rd GL54 ... 169 D7
Sissinghurst Gr GL51 ... 130 A5
Sisson End GL2 ... 127 D2
Sisson Rd GL2 ... 127 C2
Siston Cl BS15 ... 21 A2
Siston Comm Bristol BS15 21 A2
Bristol BS30 ... 21 B1
Siston Ctr The BS15 ... 21 A2
Siston La BS30 ... 21 F2
Siston Pk BS15 ... 21 A2
Sivell Cl GL2 ... 127 A6
Six Acres GL4 ... 119 F3
Sixth Ave
Bristol, Filton BS7 ... 29 B1
Bristol, Hengrove BS14 ... 3 A7
Skillicorne Mews GL50 ... 130 B8
Skinner St GL1 ... 196 B4
Skinner's Cl SN6 ... 145 A4
Skippon Ct BS15 ... 10 E5
Skye Cl SN6 ... 145 C4
Skylark Way GL4 ... 119 B6
Slad La GL5,GL6 ... 99 F8
Slad Rd GL5 ... 99 D8
Slad The GL14 ... 156 E8
Slade Brook GL5 ... 99 E8
Slade Rd GL15 ... 156 B2
Slade The GL11 ... 80 B8
Slaney St GL1 ... 118 F7
Sleep La BS14 ... 3 D3
Slimbridge Cl BS37 ... 32 F7
Slimbridge La GL13 ... 94 D2
Slimbridge Prim Sch GL2 ... 95 E2
Slimbridge Rd GL4 ... 118 D3
Sloan St BS5 ... 9 D8
Slough La SN14 ... 13 F5
Slymbridge Ave BS10 ... 28 A3
Small La BS16 ... 19 E5
Small St Bristol BS1 ... 195 A3
Bristol, St Philip's Marsh BS2 ... 9 A5
Smallbrook Rd WR12 ... 188 A1
Smarts Gn BS37 ... 33 C8
Smeaton Rd BS1 ... 7 F5
Smith Barry Cir GL54 ... 169 E6
Smith Barry Cres GL54 ... 169 D6
Smith Barry Rd GL54 ... 169 D6
Smith's Field GL7 ... 190 A3
Smith's La GL20 ... 192 C4
Smithcourt Dr BS34 ... 29 D6
Smithmead BS13 ... 2 B5
Smiths Ct GL20 ... 192 C4
Smiths Hill GL16 ... 155 C3
Smithville Cl GL15 ... 146 F7
Smithville Pl GL15 ... 146 F7
Smithwood Gr GL53 ... 131 A4
Smithy Cl GL16 ... 163 A2
Smithy La GL54 ... 184 A1
Smithy The
Blakeney GL15 ... 156 E2
Cirencester GL7 ... 190 E3
Smithyman Ct GL14 ... 157 A6
Smoke La BS11 ... 26 D6
Smooth Stones NP16 ... 60 A7
Smyth Rd BS3 ... 8 A3
Smyth Terr 3 BS3 ... 8 C4
Smythe Croft BS14 ... 3 A3
Smythe Mdw GL6 ... 148 B5
Smythe Rd GL51 ... 133 B6
Smyths Cl BS11 ... 26 B1
Snake Dr GL7 ... 152 D7
Snead Pk GL4 ... 119 F5
Sneedhams Rd GL4 ... 119 B2
Snipe Rd GL54 ... 169 D6
Snowberry Wlk BS5 ... 19 E1
Snowdon Cl BS16 ... 19 F4
Snowdon Gdns GL3 ... 128 A7
Snowdon Rd BS16 ... 19 F4
Snowdonia Rd GL20 ... 192 E2
Snowdrop Cl 1 GL4 ... 119 E5
Snowshill Cl GL4 ... 119 D7
Snowshill Dr GL52 ... 137 F3
Snowshill Manor* WR12 ... 185 B4
Snowshill Rd
Broadway WR12 ... 185 B7
Gloucester GL4 ... 119 E7
Snowswick La SN6 ... 145 F8
Soapers La BS35 ... 51 B8
Soaphouse Ind Est BS5 ... 9 E8
Sodbury Rd GL12 ... 54 A4
Soldiers of Gloucester Mus* GL1 ... 196 A2
Solent Way BS35 ... 51 D7
Solon Ct BS13 ... 1 F5
Solway Rd GL51 ... 132 D4
Somerby Cl BS32 ... 29 D7
Somerdale Ave BS4 ... 9 A1
Somerdale Rd BS31 ... 4 F7
Somerdale Rd N BS30,BS31 4 F8
Somerford Ct BS10 ... 27 F1
Somerford Rd GL7 ... 190 C2
Somergate Rd GL51 ... 132 D4
Somermead BS3 ... 8 C1
Somerset Ave
Cheltenham GL51 ... 133 A2
Dursley GL11 ... 80 C7
Yate BS37 ... 43 F3
Somerset Cl GL12 ... 67 F4
Somerset Cres BS34 ... 29 F5
Somerset Ho
12 Bristol BS2 ... 195 C3
3 Cheltenham GL50 ... 193 B4
Somerset Pl
Gloucester GL1 ... 196 A1
Tewkesbury GL20 ... 192 D1
Somerset Rd Bristol BS4 ... 9 B3
Cinderford GL14 ... 191 C4
Somerset Sq BS1 ... 195 B1
Somerset St Bristol BS1 ... 195 B1
Bristol, Kingsdown BS2 ... 195 A4
Somerset Terr BS3 ... 8 D3
Somerset Way NP16 ... 60 F4
Somerton Cl BS15 ... 10 E7
Somerton Rd BS7 ... 18 E6
Somerville Cl BS31 ... 5 E2
Somerville Ct GL7 ... 190 B2
Somme Rd GL52 ... 134 B2
Sommerville Rd BS7 ... 18 E3
Sommerville Rd S 1 BS6 18 F2
Sopwith Rd GL54 ... 169 D7
Sopworth Rd SN14 ... 47 E5
Soren Larsen Way GL1 ... 118 C6
Sorrel Cl Gloucester GL4 ... 119 A4
Thornbury BS35 ... 64 D2
Soudley Prim Sch GL14 156 D5
Soundwell Coll
Bristol, Filton BS34 ... 29 D3
Bristol, Upper Soundwell BS16 ... 20 E2
Soundwell Rd BS15,BS16 ... 20 D2
Soundwell Tech Coll (Downend division) BS16 ... 21 A8
Soundwell Tech Coll (Kingswood annexe) BS15 ... 10 E8
South Africa Ho 3 GL51 ... 132 F4
South Ave
Ashchurch GL20 ... 182 D4
Yate BS37 ... 43 B1
South Bristol Trad Pk BS3 ... 7 F3
South Cl GL2 ... 127 B4
South Croft BS9 ... 18 C7
South Ct BS32 ... 40 D3
South Dene BS9 ... 17 E6
South Farm Cotts GL7 ... 153 B5
South Gate Ct GL54 ... 169 D6
South Gloucestershire Central Teaching Unit BS16 ... 21 A5
South Gr Bristol BS6 ... 18 C5
Pill BS20 ... 16 C4
South Green St 8 BS8 ... 7 F6
South Hayes BS5 ... 19 B4

South Liberty La BS3 .....8 A1
South Mdw La SN5 .....143 F2
South Meadow La SN5 .144 A2
South Par
11 Ledbury HR8 ....178 F8
Yate BS37 ....43 E1
South Rd
Almondsbury BS32 ......40 E6
11 Bristol, Bedminster BS3 ..8 C3
Bristol, Kingswood BS15 ...10 D8
Bristol, Redland BS6 ......18 C2
3 Coleford GL16 ....155 A6
Coleford, Broadwell GL16 .155 B5
Lydney GL15 ....92 A4
South St Bristol BS3 ....8 B3
Uley GL11 ....89 C1
South Street Prim Sch
BS3 ....8 B3
South Terr 6 BS6 ....18 B2
South View
Blockley GL56 ....186 C6
Bristol BS16 ....20 E5
Frampton Cotterell BS36 ...31 B7
Ripple GL20 ....181 D8
Stroud GL5 ....98 C7
South View Bsns Pk
BS16 ....20 F5
South View Cotts GL5 ...98 E8
South View Cres BS36 ...31 D6
South View Rise BS36 ...31 D6
South View Way GL52 ..134 C4
South Way GL7 ....190 C4
South Wlk
Mitcheldean GL17 ....164 D5
Yate BS37 ....43 E1
Southall Terr GL18 .....170 E2
Southam La GL52 ....134 B8
Southbank GL5 ....99 A2
Southbow Ho 2 BS3 .....8 A3
Southbrook Rd GL4 .....127 C1
Southcourt Cl GL53 ....130 D5
Southcourt Dr GL53 ....130 D5
Southdown Rd BS9 ......17 F8
Southend Ho GL12 ......54 A5
Southend La GL18 ......171 A4
Southend The HR8 .....178 F8
Southern Ave GL4 ......118 E4
Southern Rd GL53 .....130 E4
Southernhay
Bristol, Clifton Wood BS8 .194 B2
Bristol, Staple Hill BS16 ..20 D4
Southernhay Ave BS8 ..194 B2
Southernhay Cres BS8 .194 B2
Southey Ave BS15 ....20 E1
Southey Ct BS15 ....20 D1
Southey St BS2 ....18 F2
Southfield
Minchinhampton GL6 ......91 F6
Tetbury GL8 ....140 B3
Southfield App GL53 ...130 E4
Southfield Ave BS15 ....20 E2
Southfield Cl GL53 ....130 E4
Southfield Ct BS9 ......18 A7
Southfield Manor Pk
GL53 ....130 F3
Southfield Prim Sch
SN6 ....145 D3
Southfield Rd
Bristol, Cotham BS6 ......18 D1
Bristol, Westbury on Trym
BS9 ....18 A7
5 Coleford GL16 ....155 A6
Gloucester GL4 ....118 F5
Woodchester GL5 ....99 A2
Southfield Rise GL53 ...130 E4
Southgate Cres GL5 .....99 A5
Southgate Dr GL53 ....130 F7
Southgate Gdns GL5 ....99 A5
Southgate Mews GL7 ..190 D3
Southgate St GL1 .....196 A2
Southlands BS4 ....9 B1
Southleigh Rd BS8 .....194 B4
Southmead GL7 ....190 E2
Southmead Hospl BS10 ..18 E8
Southmead La GL6 .....105 B5
Southmead Rd BS10,BS34 28 E1
Southmead Way BS10 ...18 D8
Southover Cl BS9 ....18 A8
Southrop CE Prim Sch
GL7 ....153 D6
Southsea Rd BS34 ......29 A8
Southside GL8 ....59 E7
Southside Cl BS9 ....17 B8
Southville Pl BS3 ....8 D4
Southville Prim Sch BS3 ..8 C4
Southville Rd BS3 ....8 C4
Southway Dr BS15 ......11 D5
Southwell St BS2 ......194 C4
Southwood Ave BS9 .....17 C8
Southwood Cl GL14 ....191 D5
Southwood Dr BS9 .....17 B8
Southwood Dr E BS9 ....17 C8
Southwood La GL50 ....193 A2
Sovereign Chase GL19 .172 B8
Spa Cl SN6 ....145 D4
Spa Ct GL50 ....193 A3
Spa Gdns GL20 ....192 F4
Spa Rd GL1 ....196 B1
Spalding Cl BS7 ....19 A3
Spaniorum View BS35 ...38 F2
Spar Rd Avonmouth BS11 ..26 D4
Yate BS37 ....43 D2
Spark Hill GL11 ....87 F6
Sparrow Cl 1 GL6 ......148 C6
Sparrow Hill GL16 .....155 A5
Sparrows La HR9,GL18 ..170 B4
Spartan Cl GL4 ....119 E6
Spartley Dr BS13 ....1 F6
Spartley Wlk BS13 ....1 F6
Speculation Rd GL14 ..191 B7
Speech House Rd
Coleford GL16 ....155 D6
Ruspidge GL14,GL16 .....156 A7
Speedwell 3 GL16 .....155 B6
Speedwell Ave 5 BS5 ....9 D7
Speedwell Cl
Gloucester GL4 ....119 E5
Thornbury BS35 ....64 D2
Speedwell Rd BS5,BS15 ..20 A1
Speedwell Sch BS15 ....20 A1
Spencer Cl GL3 ....119 F7
Spencer Ct GL50 ....193 A4
Spencer Ho 6 BS1 .....195 B1
Spencer's Ct BS35 ......51 B5
Spenser Ave GL51 .....132 E1
Spenser Rd GL51 ......132 E1
Sperringate GL7 ......190 D3
Spey Cl Quedgeley GL2 ...117 F2
Thornbury BS35 ....51 C8
Spider La GL5 ....99 E6
Spillman's Pitch GL5 ....99 A6
Spillman's Rd GL5 ......99 A6
Spindles The GL53 ....130 A4
Spine Rd W GL7 ....142 D5
Spine Road E GL7 .....143 B7
Spinnaker Ho GL2 .....118 C8
Spinnaker Rd GL2 .....118 C8
Spinners Ho 15 GL5 .....99 C7
Spinney Croft BS13 ....1 F5
Spinney Ct GL5 ....99 F1
Spinney Rd GL4 ....119 E7
Spinney The Bristol BS32 .29 E7
Cheltenham GL52 ......133 E4
Frampton Cotterell BS36 ...31 B7
Lechlade on T GL7 ......153 E2
Stroud GL6 ....105 C7
Spire Way GL4 ....119 D8
Spires View 4 BS16 .....19 E5
Spital La SN6 ....143 F4
Spitalgate La GL7 .....190 C5
Spittle Leys 5 GL54 ...174 A7
Spout Hill GL15 ....147 C3
Spout La GL17 ....164 A4
Spouthouse La GL11 ....88 A5
Spratsgate La
Siddington GL7 ....150 D2
Somerford Keynes GL7 ..142 D6
Spread Eagle Rd GL1 ..196 B3
Spring Cotts
Stonehouse GL10 ....98 A6
Stroud GL6 ....104 A2
Spring Dale GL2 ......165 F5
Spring Field Terr GL5 ...99 A6
Spring Gdns Bristol BS4 ..9 A1
Lechlade on T GL7 .....153 E2
Quenington GL7 ....152 D7
Tewkesbury GL20 ......192 D4
Spring Gr 6 HR8 ......178 F7
Spring Hill
Bristol, Kingsdown BS2 ..195 A4
Bristol, Upper Soundwell
BS15 ....20 E2
Eastington GL10 ....97 A8
Nailsworth GL6 ....91 B4
Spring Ho 2 BS35 ......51 C8
Spring La
Cleeve Hill GL52 ....138 E2
Dundry BS41 ....2 A1
Prestbury GL52 ....134 B6
Stroud GL5 ....99 D6
Thrupp GL5 ....99 E3
Spring Meadow Rd GL15 92 A4
Spring Mill Ind Est GL6 ..91 D3
Spring Pl GL17 ....163 E4
Spring St BS3 ....8 E4
Spring Street Pl BS3 .....8 E4
Springbank Cl GL51 ...132 D4
Springbank Dr GL51 ...132 C3
Springbank Gr GL51 ...132 C3
Springbank Rd GL51 ...132 C3
Springbank Way GL51 ..132 D4
Springdale HR9 ....170 B4
Springdale Cl GL2 .....109 D8
Springfield
Blockley GL56 ....186 C6
Bourton-on-t-W GL54 ...168 F7
Dursley GL11 ....87 E4
Hardwicke GL2 ....109 E7
Tewkesbury GL20 ......192 F5
1 Thornbury BS35 ....51 D8
Springfield Ave
Bristol, Horfield BS7 ......18 F5
Bristol, Mangotsfield BS16 .21 A7
Bristol, Shirehampton BS11 16 D6
Springfield Bsns Ctr
GL10 ....97 C8
Springfield Cl
Bristol BS16 ....21 A7
Cheltenham GL51 ......129 C7
2 Coleford GL16 ....155 A5
Springfield Cotts BS30 ...6 A8
Springfield Dr GL14 ...191 C6
Springfield Gr BS6 ......18 C5
Springfield Ho
Bristol BS6 ....194 C4
Cheltenham GL51 ......132 E4
Springfield La WR12 ...185 B8
Springfield Lawn BS11 ..16 D6
Springfield Pl GL4 .....121 F1
Springfield Rd
Bristol, Cotham BS6 ......18 D1
Bristol, Mangotsfield BS16 .21 A7
Cirencester GL7 ....190 B2
Springfield Rd *continued*
Lydney GL15 ....92 A4
Pill BS20 ....16 C4
Quenington GL7 ....152 D7
Stroud GL5 ....99 C8
Stroud, Westrip GL5 .....98 D8
Springfield Terr GL5 ....98 D6
Springfields Bristol BS34 .29 A2
Tetbury GL8 ....140 C4
Springfields Ct GL11 ....87 E4
Springhill GL11 ....88 C3
Springhill (Old Court)
GL11 ....88 B3
Springhill Cl GL6 ....91 B4
Springhill Cotts WR12 ..185 B4
Springhill Cres GL6 .....91 B4
Springhill Ct GL2 ......172 F1
Springleaze
Bristol, Knowle BS4 ....9 A1
Bristol, Mangotsfield BS16 .21 A7
Springs The GL15 ....92 A4
Springvale GL54 ....168 F8
Springville Cl BS30 ......11 A3
Springwater Cl GL20 ...182 C5
Springwater Park Trad Est
BS5 ....9 E7
Springwell Gdns GL3 ...128 B6
Springwood Dr BS10 ....27 D3
Spruce Rd GL16 ....155 C6
Spruce Ride
Coleford GL16 ....155 F6
Ruspidge GL14,GL16 .....156 A5
Spruce Way BS34 ....28 F7
Sq The GL56 ....186 C5
Square The Bibury GL7 ..160 A1
Bristol BS4 ....9 A1
Goodrich HR9 ....163 A6
Guiting Power GL54 .....175 B3
Ruardean GL17 ....163 E4
St Briavels GL15 ....146 E7
3 Stonehouse GL10 ......97 F8
Stroud GL5 ....99 C8
Toddington GL54 ......184 B3
Squires Cl GL6 ....148 B6
Squires Ct
Bretforton WR11 ....188 A6
Bristol BS30 ....10 F4
Squires Leaze BS35 .....64 D2
Squirrel Cl GL2 ....109 E7
Stable Cotts GL56 .....177 E5
Stable Yd GL5 ....99 C8
Stables The
Prestbury GL52 ....134 C4
Stow-on-t-W GL54 ......176 F5
Stackpool Rd BS3 ....8 C4
Stadium Rd BS6 ....18 C5
Stafford Cl 8 GL16 ....155 B6
Stafford Cres BS35 .....64 B1
Stafford Rd BS2 ....19 A2
Stafford St BS3 ....8 D4
Staffords Ct BS30 ......11 A6
Stag Hill GL15 ....156 A2
Stainer Cl BS4 ....2 D7
Staites Orch GL4 ......119 E3
Stamage's La GL6 .....103 F7
Stambourne La GL13 ....85 E8
Stamp's Mdw GL2 .....126 F5
Stanborough La GL54 ..167 F8
Stanbridge Cl BS16 .....20 F6
Stanbridge Cty Prim Sch
BS16 ....20 F6
Stanbridge Rd BS16 .....20 F6
Stanbury Ave BS16 ......20 C5
Stanbury Mews GL3 ....120 B6
Stanbury Rd BS3 ....8 E3
Stancombe La GL54 ....174 B7
Stancombe View 25
GL54 ....174 A7
Standfast Rd BS10 ......27 F3
Standish Ave BS34 ......40 C1
Standish Cl BS10 ....27 F1
Standish Ct GL10 ......101 E5
Standish Hospl GL10 ...102 B2
Standish La GL2,GL10 ..101 C6
Standle La GL11 ....87 A2
Standon Way BS10 ......28 C2
Stane Way BS11 ....16 C7
Stanfield Cl BS7 ....19 C6
Stanford Cl BS36 ....30 F8
Stanford Pl BS4 ....2 D7
Stanford Rd Lydney GL15 .92 A3
Northway GL20 ....182 C4
Stanhope Rd BS30 ......10 F2
Stanhope St BS2 ....9 A5
Stank La GL2 ....109 C6
Stanleigh Terr GL2 ....126 A7
Stanley Ave
Bristol, Bishopston BS7 ....18 E3
Bristol, Filton BS34 ....29 B2
Stanley Chase BS5 ......19 E2
Stanley Cotts
Gloucester GL1 ....196 C1
Gretton GL54 ....183 E1
Stanley Cres BS34 ......29 B2
Stanley Gdns BS30 .....11 B4
Stanley Hill BS4 ....9 A4
Stanley Mead BS32 .....40 E2
Stanley Mills Cotts GL10 .98 A5
Stanley Park Rd BS16 ...20 E3
Stanley Pk Bristol BS5 ...19 C1
Stroud GL5 ....98 E4
Stanley Pl GL51 ....132 D3
Stanley Rd
Bristol, Cotham BS6 ......18 C1
Bristol, Warmley BS15 ....11 B8
Cheltenham GL52 ......134 B1
Gloucester GL1 ....118 E6
Stanley St 5 BS3 ....8 C3
Stanley St N 12 BS3 ......8 C3
Stanley St S BS3 ....8 C2
Stanley Terr Bristol BS3 ...8 C2
Gloucester GL1 ....118 E7
Stanley The GL4 ....119 F2
Stanley View GL5 ....98 F5
Stanley Wlk GL4 ......119 F1
Stanmoor GL4 ....119 E3
Stansby Cres GL3 .....128 A6
Stanshaw Cl BS16 ....20 A7
Stanshaw Rd BS16 ......20 A7
Stanshawe Cres BS37 ...43 E1
Stanshawes Court Dr
BS37 ....32 E8
Stanshawes Dr BS37 ....43 D1
Stanshaws Cl BS32 ......40 C2
Stansted Ho GL1 ....196 A3
Stanthill Dr GL11 ....80 C8
Stanton Cl BS15 ....20 F1
Stanton Dr GL51 ......133 A7
Stanton Rd Bristol BS10 ..28 E2
Stroud GL5 ....98 E8
Tewkesbury GL20 ......192 D5
Stanton Way GL51 .....129 E8
Stantway La GL14 .....157 E8
Stanway BS30 ....11 C1
Stanway Rd
Cheltenham GL51 ......129 D8
Gloucester GL4 ....119 C7
Stanton WR12 ....184 E5
Stanway Wood Dr GL52 137 E3
Stanwick Cres GL51 ....133 B5
Stanwick Dr GL51 .....133 B5
Stanwick Gdns GL51 ...133 B4
Staple Gr BS31 ....4 D5
Staple Grove Cres BS5 ..10 B7
Staple Hill Cty Prim Sch
BS16 ....20 D4
Staplehill Rd BS16 ......20 B4
Staples Rd BS37 ....43 D2
Stapleton Cl Bristol BS16 .19 D5
Highworth SN6 ....145 C3
Stapleton Rd
Bristol, Baptist Mills BS5 ...19 B1
Bristol, Eastville BS5 ......19 C3
Stapleton Road Junc
BS5 ....19 B1
Star Barn Rd BS36 ......30 E7
Star Ct 9 GL52 ....133 F2
Star Hill GL6 ....91 A5
Star La Avening GL8 ....140 B8
Bristol BS16 ....19 F3
Pill BS20 ....16 D4
Starling Ct 7 GL10 .....97 F8
Stars Pitch GL17 ......164 D5
Station App
Gloucester GL1 ....196 C3
Minety SN16 ....142 E1
Station Avenue S 3
BS16 ....20 A4
Station Cl Bristol BS15 ...11 C8
Chipping Sodbury BS37 ...33 D8
Churchdown GL3 ....128 D5
Station Cotts GL20 ....182 C7
Station Ct BS5 ....9 E8
Station Dr GL20 ....182 C7
Station La Bristol BS7 ...19 A4
Longhope GL17 ....164 F5
Tewkesbury GL20 ......192 D5
Station Mdw GL54 .....168 F8
Station Rd
Acton Turville GL9 ......35 F8
Andoversford GL54 .....166 D6
Ashton under Hill WR11 ..183 E8
Beckford GL20 ....183 B6
Berkeley GL13 ....85 E5
Bishop's Cleeve GL52 ...138 B4
Blockley GL56 ....186 D6
Bourton-on-t-W GL54 ...168 F8
Bretforton WR11 ....188 A7
Bristol, Ashley Down BS7 ..18 F4
Bristol, Brislington BS4 .....9 D2
Bristol, Filton BS34 ....29 A3
Bristol, Fishponds BS16 ...20 A4
Bristol, Henbury BS10 .....27 F4
Bristol, Montpelier BS6 ....18 E2
Bristol, Newleaze BS34 ....29 B2
Bristol, Patchway BS34 ....29 C7
Bristol, Shirehampton BS11 16 D5
Bristol, Shirehampton BS11 .16 E6
Bristol, Staple Hill BS15 ...20 F3
Bristol, Warmley BS30 .....11 C7
Broadway WR12 ....185 B8
Charfield GL12 ....67 B5
Chepstow NP16 ....60 F8
Chipping Campden GL55 .189 A2
Churchdown GL3 ....128 C5
Coalpit Heath BS36 ......31 C5
Dursley GL11 ....88 A5
Gloucester GL1 ....196 C2
Highworth SN6 ....145 C3
Honeybourne WR11 ....188 C7
Iron Acton BS37 ....42 D3
Kemble GL7 ....141 F8
Keynsham BS31 ....4 E6
Kingham OX7 ....177 F1
Kingham OX7 ....177 F2
Lechlade on T GL7 .....153 E3
Lydney GL15 ....84 A8
Milkwall GL16 ....155 B4
Minety SN16 ....142 E1
8 Moreton-in-M GL56 ...187 A3
Nailsworth GL6 ....91 C4
Newnham GL14 ....156 F7
Pill BS20 ....16 C4
Pilning BS35 ....38 F4
Ripple GL20 ....181 D8
Severn Beach BS35 ......38 A6
Station Rd *continued*
South Cerney GL7 ......143 A7
Stroud GL5 ....99 B7
Tewkesbury GL20 ......192 D5
Wickwar GL12 ....54 B7
Winterbourne BS36 ......30 E4
Woodchester GL5 ....99 A1
Woolaston GL15 ....147 C2
Yate BS37 ....43 C2
Station Road Bsns Ctr
BS15 ....21 A3
Station Road Workshops
BS15 ....21 A3
Station St
Cheltenham GL50 ......193 A4
Cinderford GL14 ....191 C5
Tewkesbury GL20 ......192 D4
Station Terr
Cinderford GL14 ....191 C5
Dymock GL18 ....178 D2
Station Yard Ind Est
NP16 ....60 F8
Staunton & Corse CE Prim
Sch GL19 ....172 B8
Staunton Cl GL4 ......119 E4
Staunton Fields BS14 .....3 C4
Staunton Ho GL16 .....154 D7
Staunton La BS14 ....3 D3
Staunton Rd
Coleford GL16 ....154 F6
Monmouth GL16,NP25 ...154 C7
Staunton Way BS14 ......3 D4
Staveley Cres BS10 .....28 C2
Staverton Cl BS32 ....40 C1
Staverton Connection
GL51 ....173 F1
Staverton Tech Pk GL51 173 F1
Staverton Way BS15 .....11 A7
Stavordale Gr BS14 ......3 B6
Staynes Cres BS15 ......10 E8
Steadings Bsns Ctr The
GL2 ....126 A8
Steam Mills GL14 .....191 B8
Steam Mills Prim Sch
GL14 ....191 B8
Steam Mills Rd GL14 ..191 B7
Stean Bridge Rd BS32 ...29 E6
Steanbridge BS32 ....29 D6
Steel Ave GL15 ....92 B3
Steel Ct BS30 ....10 F3
Steel Mills BS31 ....4 F4
Steep St NP16 ....60 E8
Steeple Cl GL4 ....119 D8
Steeple View GL15 ......92 A2
Steevens Ho (almshouses) 13
BS2 ....195 C3
Stella Gr BS3 ....8 A2
Stella Way GL52 ....137 D4
Stenders Cl GL17 ......164 D5
Stenders Rd GL17 .....164 D5
Stenders The GL17 ....164 C5
Step's La GL8 ....148 B1
Stepaside NP16 ....60 C3
Stepbridge Rd GL16 ...155 B4
Stephen St BS5 ....9 C8
Stephens Dr BS30 ....10 F5
Stephens Pl GL16 .....155 B5
Stephenson Way WR11 .188 C7
Stepney Rd BS5 ....19 C1
Stepney Wlk BS5 ....19 C1
Stepping Stone La GL6 .103 E6
Stepping Stones The BS4 .9 E6
Steps Cl GL11 ....87 F6
Stepstairs Ct GL7 .....190 D3
Stepstairs La GL7 .....190 D3
Sterling Cl GL54 ......176 F4
Sterling Ct GL51 ......133 B2
Sterncourt Rd BS16 .....20 A7
Sterrys Cnr HR9 ....170 C4
Sterrys Rd HR9 ....170 C4
Stevans Cl GL2 ....127 A5
Stevens Cres BS3 ....8 F4
Stevens Way GL6 ....90 F1
Stevens Wlk BS32 ......29 D8
Steward Rd GL20 ......182 C4
Stewarts Mill La GL4 ..119 E4
Stibbs Ct BS30 ....10 F4
Stibbs Hill BS5 ....10 A7
Sticky La GL2 ....109 E6
Stidcot La GL12 ....52 D5
Stidcote La GL12 ....52 E5
Stile Acres BS11 ....27 A1
Stillhouse La BS3 ....8 D4
Stillingfleet Rd BS13 .....2 C5
Stillman Cl BS13 ....1 E4
Stinchcombe BS37 ......43 E1
Stirling Cl BS37 ....43 D4
Stirling Rd BS4 ....9 C3
Stirling Way
Gloucester GL4 ....118 B2
Keynsham BS31 ....4 E4
Stirrup Cl GL2 ....118 B6
Stirrup The GL5 ....98 D7
Stock Hill BS35 ....63 C1
Stock La GL13 ....85 E3
Stockdale Cl GL2 .....109 D8
Stocken Cl GL3 ....120 B6
Stockham Cl SN6 ......143 F4
Stockholm Pl HR9 .....164 C8
Stockley Way GL4,GL6 .111 D6
Stocks The GL6 ....102 D2
Stockton Cl
Bristol, Oldland BS30 .....11 B3
Bristol, Whitchurch BS14 ...2 F4
Charlton Kings GL53 ....130 F4
Stockwell Ave BS16 .....21 A6
Stockwell Cl BS16 ....20 F7
Stockwell Dr BS16 ......21 A6

Stockwell Gn GL14 .....191 D3
Stockwell La
Aylburton GL15 ....147 E4
Woodmancote GL52 .....138 D3
Stockwells GL56 ....187 A3
Stockwood Cres BS4 .....8 F2
Stockwood Green Prim Sch BS14 ...3 E4
Stockwood Hill BS31 ....4 C7
Stockwood La BS14 ......3 E5
Stockwood Mews BS4 ....9 F5
Stockwood Rd BS4,BS14 ..4 A7
Stoke Bishop CE Prim Sch BS9 ...17 D5
Stoke Bridge Ave BS34 ..29 D6
Stoke Common La SN5 .143 D1
Stoke Cotts BS9 ......17 E4
Stoke Gr BS9 ....17 E6
Stoke Hamlet BS9 ......17 F6
Stoke Hill BS9 ......17 E3
Stoke La
Bristol, Broomhill BS16 ....19 E7
Bristol, Patchway BS34 ....29 C8
Bristol, Westbury on Trym BS9 ....17 F6
Stoke Lodge Jun & Inf Sch BS34 ....29 C8
Stoke Mdws BS32 .....40 D1
Stoke Paddock Rd BS9 ..17 D6
Stoke Park Cl GL52 ....137 F4
Stoke Park Ct GL52 ....137 F4
Stoke Park Rd BS9 .....17 F4
Stoke Park Rd S BS9 ....17 E3
Stoke Rd
Bishop's Cleeve GL52 ....137 C4
Bishop's Cleeve GL52 ....137 E4
Bristol BS8,BS9 ......18 A2
Stoke View BS34 ......29 A3
Stoke View Pk 5 BS16 ....19 F4
Stoke View Rd BS16 ....19 F3
Stokefield Cl BS35 .....64 B1
Stokeleigh Wlk BS9 .....17 C5
Stokemead BS34 ......29 C8
Stokes Croft BS1 .....195 B4
Stokes Ct 1 Bristol BS30 .11 A4
Tewkesbury GL20 ......192 C4
Stokes Rd GL20 ....181 D5
Stone Bridge GL56 ....187 D7
Stone Cl GL4 ....119 E7
Stone Cres GL51 ......132 F2
Stone House Mews BS37 44 B1
Stone La BS36 ....30 F3
Stone Manor GL5 ......99 E6
Stone Manor Ct GL5 ....99 E7
Stone Monolith BS34 ....28 E6
Stone Rd The GL19 .....172 A7
Stone with Woodford CE Sch GL13 ....77 E4
Stone's Cotts BS10 .....27 C4
Stoneberrow Pl GL18 ..178 D2
Stoneberry Rd BS14 .....3 B3
Stonebridge Pk BS5 ....19 E2
Stonechat Ave GL4 .....119 C5
Stonechat Gdns BS16 ...19 E6
Stonecote Ridge 8 GL6 .....148 C6
Stonecroft Cl GL52 .....137 E4
Stonedale Rd GL10 .....97 D8
Stonefarn Ct 16 GL56 ...187 A3
Stonefield Dr SN6 ......145 D2
Stoneford La WR11 .....188 A5
Stonehenge Rd GL4 ....119 B7
Stonehill BS15 ....10 E4
Stonehill Ctr BS30 ......10 E4
Stonehill La GL7 ....141 B7
Stonehouse Ct GL54 ...176 D4
Stonehouse Sta GL10 ....97 F7
Stonelea GL11 ....87 E4
Stoneleigh Cl GL53 ....130 D3
Stoneleigh Cres BS4 .....9 A2
Stoneleigh Dr BS30 .....10 F5
Stoneleigh Rd BS4 ......9 A2
Stoneleigh Wlk BS4 .....9 A2
Stones La SN6 ....143 D4
Stoneville St GL51 .....193 A4
Stoney Field GL2 ......125 E5
Stoney Pool GL7 ......151 E3
Stoney Rd GL18 ....170 C4
Stoney Stile Rd BS35 ....51 A5
Stoneyfield Cl BS20 .....16 B5
Stoneyfields BS20 ......16 B4
Stoneyhills Ind Est HR9 162 D4
Stony Riding GL6 ......148 C5
Stores Rd BS11 ....26 C4
Storrington Pl 8 GL10 ...97 F7
Storrington Rd GL10 .....97 F7
Stothard Rd BS7 ....19 B7
Stottbury Rd BS7 ......19 A3
Stoulgrove La NP16 .....73 A4
Stoulton Gr BS10 ....28 A3
Stourden Cl BS16 ....20 A7
Stourton Dr BS30 ....10 F4
Stover Rd BS37 ....43 B2
Stover Trad Est BS37 ....43 B2
Stow Cl GL4 ....118 F6
Stow Ct GL51 ....133 A1
Stow Gn 15 GL54 ......176 F4
Stow Hill Rd GL12 ......52 B6
Stow Rd Bledington OX7 .177 E1
Cirencester GL7 ....150 E7
Moreton-in-M GL56 .....187 A2
Stow-on-the-Wold Prim Sch GL54 ....176 F4
Stowe La GL15 ....154 E1
Stowe Rd GL15 ....146 D8
Stowell Hill Rd GL12 ....52 B6
Stowell Mews GL4 .....119 D7
Stowick Cres BS11 .....27 C1
Strachans Cl GL5 ....99 A7
Stradbrook Ave BS5 .....10 B7
Stradling Rd BS11 ......27 C2
Straight La GL19 ......172 B8
Straight St BS2 ....195 C2
Straits Par BS16 ....20 B5
Strand Ct GL53 ....193 C3
Strand La GL14 ....157 C8
Strand The GL50 ......193 C3
Stranks Cl SN6 ....145 D2
Stratford Cl Bristol BS14 ..2 F3
Gloucester GL2 ....118 C4
Stratford Ct BS9 ....17 F8
Stratford Rd
Honeybourne WR11 .....188 D7
Mickleton GL55 ....189 A7
Stroud GL5 ....99 A8
Stratheden BS8 ....194 A4
Strathmore Rd BS7 .....18 F5
Stratmore Est GL16 ....155 B3
Stratton Brook GL7 ....190 A7
Stratton CE Prim Sch GL7 ....190 A8
Stratton Cl BS34 ....29 C7
Stratton Ct GL20 ......192 D5
Stratton Rd
Gloucester GL1 ....196 C1
Saltford BS31 ....5 E3
Stratton St BS2 ....195 B3
Strawberry Field 2 GL16 ....155 A7
Strawberry Hill GL18 ...171 A6
Strawberry La
Dundry BS13,BS41 ....1 E3
Meysey Hampton GL7 ....152 B2
Strawbridge Rd 10 BS5 ....9 B7
Stream Cl BS10 ....28 D3
Stream La GL18 ....171 B5
Stream Side BS16 ....20 F6
Stream The BS16 ....30 B2
Streamfield GL12 ....68 B8
Streamleaze Ct BS35 ....51 B8
Streamleaze BS35 ....51 C8
Streamside
Bishop's Cleeve GL52 ....137 F4
Stroud GL5 ....99 C7
Streamside Rd BS37 ....44 A1
Streamside Wlk BS4 .....9 E3
Stredlings Yd BS2 .....194 C4
Street Cotts SN16 .....142 A4
Street The Alveston BS35 ..51 B5
Burton SN14 ....36 B4
Castle Eaton SN6 ......144 D6
Coaley GL11 ....88 E8
Crudwell SN16 ....141 C3
Didmarton GL9 ....57 C3
Frampton on Severn GL2 ..157 F2
Horsley GL6 ....90 F1
Latton SN6 ....143 E6
Leighterton GL8 ....70 C3
Leonard Stanley GL10 ....97 E3
Luckington SN14 ....47 E4
Marston Meysey SN6 ....144 B8
Minsterworth GL2 ......116 F7
North Nibley GL11 ......79 D4
Oaksey SN16 ....142 A4
Olveston BS35 ....50 A3
Shipton Moyne GL8 .....59 D8
Uley GL11 ....89 B1
Woodchester GL5 ....99 B3
Strensham Bsns Pk WR8 ....180 D7
Strensham Court Mews WR8 ....180 D7
Strensham Gate WR8 ..180 D7
Stretford Ave BS5 ....9 D8
Stretford Rd BS5 ....9 D8
Strickland Homes 5 GL52 ....130 F8
Strickland Rd GL52 ....130 F8
Stride Cl BS35 ....38 A6
Striguil Rd NP16 ....60 E6
Stringer's Cl GL5 ....99 A5
Stringer's Dr GL5 ....99 A5
Strode Comm BS35 .....50 F5
Strode Gdns BS35 ......50 F5
Stroma Way SN6 ......145 C4
Strongbow Rd NP16 .....60 E6
Stroud Coll GL5 ....99 A7
Stroud Coll of F Ed GL5 .99 A8
Stroud Ent Ctr GL5 ......98 F4
Stroud General Hospl GL5 ....99 D6
Stroud Girls' High Sch GL5 ....99 A7
Stroud Rd Bisley GL6 ...105 A1
Bristol, Patchway BS34 ....28 F8
Bristol, Shirehampton BS11 .16 E5
Cirencester GL7 ......150 B4
Gloucester GL1,GL4 ....118 E6
Nailsworth GL6 ....91 B5
Painswick GL6 ....103 D6
Stroud Sta GL5 ....99 B7
Stroud Valley Prim Sch
Stroud GL5 ....99 C6
Stroud GL5 ....99 C7
Stuart Cl NP16 ....72 D1
Stuart St BS5 ....9 C7
Studland Ct BS9 ....18 B6
Studland Dr GL52 .....134 C4
Stump La GL3 ....120 B8
Stumpwell La GL12 .....79 E2
Sturden La BS16 ....30 C3
Sturdon Rd BS3 ....8 A3
Sturmer Cl BS37 ....43 E4
Sturmey Way BS20 .....16 E3
Sturminster Cl BS14 ......3 D6
Sturminster Rd BS14 .....3 D7
Sturmyes Rd GL6 ......148 D6
Sudbrook Trad Est GL2 .196 A1
Sudbrook Way GL4 ....119 C5
Sudeley Castle* GL54 ..174 B6
Sudeley Dr GL7 ....142 F7
Sudeley Ho 7 GL51 ....132 E3
Sudgrove Pk GL4 ......119 E5
Sudmeadow Rd GL2 ...126 C1
Suffolk Cl 2 GL8 .....140 C5
Suffolk Ho GL50 ......193 A2
Suffolk Mews GL50 ....193 B1
Suffolk Par GL50 ......193 B2
Suffolk Pl GL7 ....143 E8
Suffolk Rd GL50 ....193 A1
Suffolk Sq GL50 ....193 A2
Suffolk St GL50 ....193 B1
Sugar Tump HR9 ......170 B4
Sugley La GL6 ....90 F2
Sulgrave Cl GL4 ......118 C1
Sullivan Cl BS4 ....2 D8
Summer Cl GL5 ....99 E7
Summer Cres GL5 ......99 E7
Summer Hill BS4 ....9 A4
Summer La SN14 ....36 F3
Summer Mdw GL4 .....119 B4
Summer St 4 Bristol BS3 ..8 C4
Stroud GL5 ....99 E7
Summerfield Cl
Blockley GL56 ....186 C6
Cheltenham GL51 ......132 F5
Summerhayes BS30 .....11 D5
Summerhill Jun & Inf Schs BS5 .....9 E8
Summerhill Rd BS5 ......9 F8
Summerhill Terr BS5 .....9 F7
Summerhouse La NP16 ...60 F4
Summerland Dr GL3 ...128 C5
Summerleaze
Bristol BS16 ....20 C3
Keynsham BS31 ....4 E7
Lydney GL15 ....92 B2
Summerleaze Rd GL15 ..92 B2
Summers Dr BS30 ......23 A1
Summers Mead BS37 ....43 E4
Summers Rd
4 Bristol BS2 ....19 A1
13 Winchcombe GL54 ....174 A7
Summers Terr 3 BS2 ...19 A1
Summersfield Cl GL6 ..148 A3
Summersfield Rd GL6 ..148 A4
Sun Green Cl 2 GL15 ..155 D1
Sun Green Rd 3 GL15 ..155 D1
Sun La GL16 ....155 B6
Sun Rise Rd 1 GL15 ...155 D1
Sun St Cheltenham GL51 .133 C3
Tewkesbury GL20 ......192 C5
Sun Tump GL15 ....147 D8
Sundale HR9 ....170 B4
Sundays Hill BS32 .....40 A4
Sundayshill La GL12 ....65 D7
Sunderland Ct GL3 ....128 C5
Sunderland Pl BS8 ....194 B3
Sundridge Pk BS37 .....32 E8
Sunground The GL8 ....148 B1
Sunningdale Bristol BS8 .194 B4
Yate BS37 ....32 E8
Sunningdale Dr BS30 ....11 B6
Sunny Bank Bristol BS15 ..20 B1
Wick BS30 ....12 B7
Sunny Hill BS9 ....17 C7
Sunny Wlk BS15 ....20 B1
Sunnybank Bristol BS16 ..20 E6
18 Coleford GL16 ......155 A5
Westerleigh BS37 ......32 A3
Sunnybank Rd GL16 ...155 A6
Sunnybrook Terr GL13 ...93 D2
Sunnycroft Cl GL52 ....138 A2
Sunnycroft Mews GL1 ..118 E5
Sunnydene BS4 ....9 D4
Sunnyfield La GL51 ....129 C5
Sunnyfield Rd GL2 .....109 D8
Sunnyhill GL5 ....98 E8
Sunnyhill Dr BS11 ......16 E6
Sunnyhill Ho E BS11 ....16 E6
Sunnyhill Ho W BS11 ....16 E6
Sunnymead Bristol BS30 ..11 D6
Keynsham BS31 ....4 F3
Sunnymead Cl GL17 ....164 B4
Sunnyside Bristol BS9 ....17 E5
Frampton Cotterell BS36 ..31 B8
Sunnyside La Bristol BS16 30 C2
Yate BS37 ....43 C1
Sunnyvale Dr BS30 .....11 B3
Sunridge BS16 ....20 D6
Sunrise Gr BS4 ....9 D4
Sunset La GL52 ....134 C8
Sunset Pl GL19 ....165 D6
Surrey Ave GL51 ......132 F2
Surrey Rd BS7 ....18 E3
Surrey St BS2 ....195 B4
Sussex Ave GL51 ......133 A2
Sussex Gdns GL3 .....120 B7
Sussex Pl BS2 ....18 F1
Sussex St BS2 ....9 A6
Sutherland Ave
Bristol BS16 ....20 E7
Yate BS37 ....43 D4
Sutherland Pl 9 BS8 ...18 A2
Sutton Ave BS4 ....9 D4
Sutton Cl GL11 ....80 B8
Sutton Pk SN26 ....144 E1
Sutton Pl GL5 ....99 D7
Sutton Rd
Littledean GL14 ....191 F3
Upper Soudley GL14 ....156 C5
Swagwater La HR9 ....170 C5
Swainswick BS14 ....2 F6
Swaish Dr 2 BS30 ......11 A4
Swallow Cres GL3 .....127 D6
Swallow Croft GL10 .....96 F7
Swallow Ct BS14 ....3 F6
Swallow Dr BS34 ....28 E8
Swallow Pk BS35 ....64 D3
Swallows Ct BS34 ....29 E4
Swallowtail Cl 6 GL51 .132 D2
Swan Cl
Lechlade on T GL7 .....153 E2
Moreton-in-M GL56 ....187 A3
Swan Ct GL1 ....196 A3
Swan Field BS37 ....43 F2
Swan La Blakeney GL15 ..156 E2
Leigh SN6 ....143 A3
Stoke Orchard GL52 ....136 D5
13 Stroud GL5 ....99 C7
Winterbourne BS36 .....30 C8
Swan Rd Gloucester GL1 .196 C4
Lydney GL15 ....92 A3
Swan Yd GL7 ....190 C5
Swane Rd BS14 ....3 F6
Swanley La GL13 ....78 B5
Swanmoor Cres BS10 ...28 A4
Swanscombe Pl 14 GL51 ....129 E5
Swansfield GL7 ....153 E3
Swanswell Dr GL51 ....129 E8
Sweden La GL20 ......183 B5
Sweetbriar Cl GL52 ....137 E4
Sweetbriar Ho GL3 ....128 D4
Sweetbriar St GL1 .....196 C4
Sweetmore Cl GL56 ....177 C5
Sweets Cl BS15 ....20 E2
Sweets Rd BS15 ....20 E2
Swell CE Prim Sch GL54 ....176 D4
Swells Hill GL5 ....99 E1
Swift Rd GL4 ....119 D5
Swifts Hill View GL5 ...103 E1
Swilgate Rd GL20 .....192 C4
Swindon Cl GL51 ......133 C3
Swindon La GL50 ......133 D5
Swindon Manor GL51 ..133 A6
Swindon Rd
Cheltenham GL51 ......133 B4
Cirencester GL7 ....190 E3
Cricklade SN6 ....143 F4
Highworth SN6 ....145 C2
Swindon St
Cheltenham GL51 ......133 C3
Highworth SN6 ....145 D3
Swindon Village Prim Sch GL51 ....133 B7
Swinhay La GL12 ....67 B8
Swish La GL17 ....164 A4
Swiss Dr BS3 ....7 F2
Swiss Rd BS3 ....7 F1
Swordfish Cl GL3 .....128 C5
Swynford Cl GL7 ......144 E7
Sybil Rd GL1 ....119 A6
Sycamore Ave NP16 ....60 E5
Sycamore Cl
Bristol, Hanham BS15 ....10 B3
Bristol, Whitehall BS5 ....19 E1
Gloucester GL1 ....118 D5
Sycamore Ct Bristol BS7 ..18 E3
3 Cheltenham GL51 ....132 D2
St Arvans NP16 ....72 B5
Sycamore Dr Bristol BS34 .28 F7
Stroud GL5 ....99 D8
Thornbury BS35 ....64 C1
Sycamore Rd
Harrow Hill GL17 ......164 B3
Northway GL20 ....182 C4
Sydenham Hill BS6 .....18 D1
Sydenham La BS6 ......18 E1
Sydenham Rd
Bristol, Cotham BS6 .....18 E1
Bristol, Knowle BS4 ......9 A3
3 Cheltenham GL52 ....130 F8
Sydenham Rd S GL52 ...130 F8
Sydenham Terr GL1 ....118 E7
Sydenham Villas Rd GL52 ....130 F8
Sydenham Way BS15 ....10 C3
Sydney GL10 ....101 E1
Sydney Ho BS20 ....16 D4
Sydney Row BS1 ......194 B1
Sylvan Cl 18 GL16 .....155 A5
Sylvan View NP16 .....146 B4
Sylvan Way BS9 ....17 B7
Sylvia Ave BS3 ....8 F3
Symes Ave BS13 ....2 C4
Symington Rd BS16 .....20 B5
Symn La GL12 ....68 B7
Synwell La GL12 ....68 C7
Syon Rd GL6 ....148 A3
Syston Way BS15 ......20 D1

T

Tabernacle Pitch GL12 ...68 B7
Tabernacle Rd
Bristol BS15 ....10 C6
Wooton-u-E GL12 ....68 B8
Tabernacle Wlk GL5 ....99 B5
Tabrams Pitch GL6 .....91 C4
Tackley Rd BS5 ....19 B3
Tadwick La BA1 ....13 E1
Taena Pottery* GL4 ....120 B2
Tailor's Ct 4 BS1 .....195 A3
Tainmor Cl GL2 ....127 E5
Tait's Hill GL11 ....87 C4
Tait's Hill Rd GL11 .....87 D4
Taits Hill Ind Est GL11 ..87 C4
Talbot Ave BS15 ....20 C1
Talbot Mews GL1 .....118 D6
Talbot Rd Bristol BS4 .....9 C2
Cheltenham GL51 ......130 A8
Talbot Sq GL54 ....176 E4
Talboy's Wlk 6 GL8 ....140 C5
Talgarth Rd BS7 ....18 F4
Tall Elms Cl GL3 ......128 B5
Tallard's Pl NP16 ....61 A8
Tallis Gr BS4 ....2 D6
Tallis Rd GL3 ....127 F8
Tally Ho La GL54 .....175 B3
Talybont La HR9 ......162 C3
Tamar Cl BS35 ....51 D7
Tamar Dr BS31 ....5 A4
Tamar Rd Bristol BS2 .....9 C6
Brockworth GL3 ....120 F5
Cheltenham GL52 ......134 A2
Tamarisk Cl GL51 .....130 A4
Tamesis Dr GL7 ....141 F8
Tamsin Ct BS31 ....4 F5
Tamworth Rd BS31 ......4 E4
Tandey Wlk GL3 ......127 E6
Tanglewood Way GL6 ..148 B6
Tanhouse La BS37 ......43 D7
Tankard's Cl BS8 .....194 C3
Tanner Cl BS30 ....10 F5
Tanner's La GL51 .....132 F3
Tanner's Pl GL6 ....91 C3
Tanner's Rd GL51 .....132 F3
Tanners Cl GL3 ....120 E6
Tanners Ct Bristol BS16 ..30 B1
Thornbury BS35 ....51 B8
Tanners La SN14 ....14 F8
Tanners Wlk SN14 ......14 F8
Tannery Cl GL10 ....97 E3
Tanorth Cl BS14 ....3 A3
Tanorth Rd BS14 ....2 F3
Tansy Cl GL4 ....119 F5
Tanyard The BS30 ......11 B2
Tapscott Ct GL12 ....68 A7
Tapsters BS30 ....11 A4
Tara Cl BS36 ....41 F1
Target Cl GL5 ....99 F7
Tarlton Cl GL4 ....119 E4
Tarn Ho BS34 ....29 A8
Tarnock Ave BS14 ....3 A7
Tarragon Pl BS32 ......29 F7
Tarrington Rd 6 GL1 ..118 F7
Tasmania Ho 4 GL51 ..132 E2
Tatchley La GL52 .....134 B4
Taunton Wlk BS7 ......19 A7
Taurus Cl GL2 ....126 F5
Taverner Cl BS4 ....2 D7
Tavistock Rd BS4 ....8 F1
Tavistock Wlk BS4 ......8 F1
Tawny Cl GL20 ....182 B5
Tayberry Gr GL51 .....129 F4
Tayler Rd GL54 ....168 A1
Taylor Cl BS15 ....10 F8
Taylor Gdns BS13 ....1 F4
Taylors End GL50 .....130 B6
Taylors Ground GL2 ...117 F2
Taylors Row 23 GL54 ...176 F4
Tayman Cl BS10 ....18 E6
Tayman Ridge BS30 ......5 D8
Taynton Cl BS30 ....11 C2
Teal Cl Bristol BS32 .....40 D2
Quedgeley GL2 ....117 D1
Teasel Cl GL2 ....126 F5
Teasel Mead BS32 ......29 E7
Tebbit Mews 2 GL52 ...193 C4
Ted Preston Cl GL20 ...192 D2
Teddington Gdns GL4 ..119 B6
Teewell Ave BS16 ....20 E4
Teewell Cl BS16 ....20 E4
Teewell Ct BS16 ....20 E4
Teewell Hill BS16 ....20 E4
Teignmouth Rd BS4 .....8 F1
Telephone Ave BS1 ....195 A2
Telford Ho GL51 ....132 F3
Telford Way GL2 ......109 F7
Telford Wlk BS5 ....20 A1
Tellings Orch SN16 ....142 B2
Teme Rd GL52 ....134 A2
Tempest Dr NP16 ......60 D8
Templar Rd BS37 ....43 E3
Temple Back BS1 .....195 B2
Temple Cl
Aylburton GL15 ....147 F6
Gloucester GL4 ....119 E8
Temple Ct BS31 ....4 E5
Temple Gate BS1 .....195 B1
Temple Guiting CE Prim Sch GL54 ....175 A6
Temple Hill Inf Sch BS31 ..4 F5
Temple Jun Sch BS31 ....4 F6
Temple Meads Sta BS1 .195 C1
Temple Rose St BS1 ...195 B2
Temple St Bristol BS1 ...195 B2
Bristol, Bedminster BS3 ....8 B2
Keynsham BS31 ....4 F5
Temple Way BS2 ......195 B2
Temple Way Underpass BS2 ....195 C3
Templefields GL54 ....166 C6
Templeland Rd BS13 ......1 F5
Templeway GL15 ......147 F6
Templeway W GL15 ....147 F6
Tenby Rd BS31 ....4 D4
Tenby St BS5 ....9 B7
Tennessee Gr BS6 ......18 C5
Tennis Rd BS4 ....9 A2
Tenniscourt Rd BS15 ....21 A1
Tennyson Ave GL2 .....118 C4
Tennyson Cl BS31 ......4 F6
Tennyson Rd Bristol BS7 ..18 E5

Tennyson Rd *continued*
Cheltenham GL51 132 E1
Dursley GL11 80 C7
Tensing Rd GL53 130 E4
Tenth Ave BS7 29 B1
Tereslake Gn BS10 28 D4
Terhill 4 GL52 133 F2
Tern Cl GL4 119 C6
Terrace The
Nailsworth GL6 91 A2
Wooton-u-E GL12 68 D8
Terrell Gdns 13 BS5 9 D7
Terrell St BS2 195 A4
Terris Ct BS34 29 E4
Terry Ho BS1 194 C3
Terry Ruck Cl GL51 132 D2
Tetbury Cl BS34 29 C7
Tetbury Hill GL8 140 B8
Tetbury Hospl GL8 140 C3
Tetbury La
Crudwell SN16 141 B3
Leighterton GL8 70 C3
Nailsworth GL6 91 C2
Tetbury Police Mus★
GL8 140 B4
Tetbury Rd Bristol BS15 10 B8
Cirencester GL7 150 B3
Cirencester GL7 190 B4
Gloucester GL4 118 E1
Sherston SN16 58 D1
Tetbury St GL6 148 A3
Teviot Rd BS31 5 A4
Tewkesbury CE Prim Sch
GL20 192 D4
Tewkesbury Hospl
GL20 192 D4
Tewkesbury Ind Est
GL20 192 F5
Tewkesbury Mus★
GL20 192 C4
Tewkesbury Rd
11 Bristol BS2 19 A2
Cheltenham GL51 133 A4
Gloucester GL2 126 F5
Newent GL18 171 B5
Northway GL20 182 B6
Stow-on-t-W GL54 176 E5
Uckington GL51 132 E6
Tewkesbury Sch GL20 182 B4
Tewther Rd BS13 2 D3
Texas Cl GL7 152 E2
Teyfant Com Sch BS13 2 E4
Teyfant Rd BS13 2 E4
Teyfant Wlk BS13 2 E4
Thackeray Wlk BS7 19 A8
Thames Cl GL12 67 A4
Thames Ho 9 BS35 51 C8
Thames La SN6 143 F4
Thames Rd GL52 134 A2
Thames St GL7 153 E2
Thames View 2 SN6 142 F4
Thanet Rd BS3 8 B2
Thatcham Rd GL20 192 E1
Thatchers Cl BS5 10 B7
Thatchers End GL52 138 B3
Theatre Royal BS1 195 A2
Theescombe Hill GL5 91 B6
Theocs Cl GL20 192 C2
There-and-Back-Again La
BS1 194 C3
Theresa Ave BS7 18 E4
Theresa St GL1 118 D7
Thessaly Rd GL7 190 B8
Theyer Cl GL3 120 E5
Theynes Croft BS41 7 B1
Thicket Ave BS16 20 C3
Thicket Rd BS16 20 C4
Thicket Wlk BS35 64 C1
Thiery Rd BS4 9 C2
Thingwall Pk BS16 19 E3
Third Ave
Bristol, Filton BS7 29 A1
Bristol, Hengrove BS14 3 B7
Dursley GL11 80 C8
Third Way BS11 26 C2
Thirlestaine House Cotts
GL53 193 B1
Thirlestaine Rd GL53 193 C1
Thirlmere Ct BS30 11 D6
Thirlmere Rd Bristol BS34 29 A8
Cheltenham GL51 129 E7
Thistle Downs GL20 182 C5
Thistle St 1 BS3 8 B3
Thistledown Cl GL51 132 D4
Thomas Ave BS16 21 B8
Thomas Keble Comp Sch
GL6 148 C7
Thomas La BS1 195 B2
Thomas Moore Cl GL3 128 A8
Thomas Pring Wlk 1
BS5 20 A1
Thomas St
Bristol, Kingsdown BS2 195 B4
7 Bristol, Russell Town BS5 9 B7
Bristol, St Pauls BS2 18 F1
Chepstow NP16 60 E8
Cirencester GL7 190 C5
Gloucester GL1 196 C1
Thomas St N 12 BS2 18 D1
Thomas Stock Gdns
GL4 119 E6
Thomond Cl GL51 133 C4
Thompson Dr GL53 130 D4
Thompson Rd Bristol BS14 3 E6
South Cerney GL7 150 F2
Thompson Rd *continued*
Stroud GL5 99 D8
Thompson Way GL3 127 E6
Thomson Rd 7 BS5 9 B8
Thoresby GL52 133 E5
Thoresby Ave GL4 110 C8
Thorn Cl BS37 43 D1
Thorn Tree Dr NP16 60 F4
Thornbury Cl GL51 133 B2
Thornbury Hospl BS35 64 C1
Thornbury Ind Pk BS35 51 B7
Thornbury Mus★ BS35 51 B8
Thornbury Rd BS35 51 A5
Thorncliffe 10 GL51 130 B8
Thorncliffe Dr GL51 130 B8
Thorndale BS8 194 A4
Thorndale Mews BS8 194 A4
Thornhaugh Mews 5
GL51 129 E5
Thornhayes Cl BS36 31 A8
Thornhill Cl GL1 118 D5
Thornhills The BS16 20 B6
Thornleigh Rd BS7 18 E5
Thornmead Gr BS10 28 A2
Thorns Farm BS37 43 E1
Thornwell Jun Sch NP16 60 F5
Thornwell Rd NP16 60 F5
Thornycroft Cl BS7 19 B7
Thorpe Lodge 9 BS6 18 D1
Threadneedle St 10 GL5 99 C7
Three Ashes La GL18 171 A6
Three Cocks La GL1 196 A3
Three Queens' La BS1 195 B2
Three Sisters La GL52 134 D3
Three Wells Rd BS13 1 F4
Thrissell St BS5 9 A8
Throgmorton Rd BS4 2 F8
Thrupp La GL5 99 E3
Thrupp Prim Sch The
GL5 99 E3
Thrush Cl GL4 119 D6
Thurlestone BS14 3 A6
Thurlow Rd BS5 19 C2
Thurston's Barton BS5 19 E1
Tibberton BS15 11 A8
Tibberton Com Prim Sch
GL19 171 E1
Tibberton Gr GL51 129 B7
Tibberton La GL19 165 D6
Tibbiwell La GL6 103 F8
Tibbott Rd BS14 3 D5
Tibbott Wlk BS14 3 D5
Tiberius Ave GL15 92 B4
Tichborne Rd BS5 9 C7
Tide Gr BS11 17 A8
Tidenham Way BS34 39 F1
Tidling Cnr SN16 142 B3
Tidswell Cl GL2 109 F8
Tiffany Ct BS1 195 B1
Tilley Cl BS31 5 A2
Tilling Rd BS10 18 E7
Tilling Wlk BS10 18 E7
Tillis View GL16 154 D7
Tilney Rd GL50 133 D4
Tilnor Cres GL11 87 F4
Tilsdown GL11 87 F4
Tilsdown Cl GL11 87 F4
Tilting Rd BS35 64 B2
Timber Dene BS16 19 D4
Timbercombe La GL53 131 B3
Timbercombe Mews
GL53 131 B4
Timberscombe Wlk BS14 3 C5
Timbrells Cl GL7 142 F8
Timbrells The GL7 142 B8
Timmis Cl GL4 119 C4
Timms Gn WR12 188 B2
Timperley Way GL51 129 E5
Timsbury Rd BS3 8 E2
Tindell Ct 12 BS30 10 F4
Tinglesfield GL7 190 B8
Tinker's Cl 23 GL56 187 A3
Tinkley La GL10 90 B5
Tinmans Gn NP25 154 C4
Tintagel Cl BS31 4 D4
Tintern Abbey★ NP16 146 C2
Tintern Ave 4 BS5 9 D8
Tintern Cl BS30 10 F6
Tintern Hts NP16 146 A5
Tintern Old Sta★ NP16 146 C3
Tintern Rd GL4 118 E3
Tippetts Rd BS15 10 D6
Tirle Bank Way GL20 192 F4
Tirlebrook Grange
GL20 182 D4
Tirlebrook Prim Sch
GL20 192 F4
Tirley Cl GL2 117 E1
Tirley Ho BS34 39 F1
Tirley St GL19 172 F7
Tithe Farm La GL19 165 E6
Tiverton Cl GL51 132 D3
Tiverton Wlk BS16 20 A2
Tivoli La GL50 193 A1
Tivoli Mews GL50 193 A2
Tivoli Pl GL50 193 A1
Tivoli Rd GL50 193 A1
Tivoli St GL50 193 A1
Tivoli Wlk 17 GL50 130 B8
Toadsmoor Rd GL5 148 A5
Tobacco Cl GL54 139 F4
Tobacconist Rd GL6 148 A3
Tobyfield Cl GL52 138 A3
Tobyfield La GL52 138 A3
Tobyfield Rd GL52 138 A3
Tockington La BS32 40 A7
Tockington Manor Sch
BS32 50 C2
Tockington Park La BS32 40 E8
Tocknell Ct GL11 87 F8
Toddington Cl BS37 32 D8
Toddington Cty Prim Sch
GL54 184 C3
Toddington Sta★ GL54 184 D3
Toghill La BS30 13 A8
Toll Down Way SN14 36 A3
Toll House Ct 4 BS3 8 A4
Tolsey La GL20 192 C4
Tom Price Cl GL52 193 C3
Tomlin Pl GL15 156 B1
Tommy Taylor's La
GL50 133 D4
Tone Dr GL3 120 F5
Tooke Rd GL6 91 E7
Top Rd Kempsford GL7 144 E8
Upper Soudley GL14 156 C5
Torchacre Rise GL11 88 A1
Tormarton Cres BS10 27 F4
Tormarton Intc GL9 34 B1
Tormarton Rd GL9 35 E6
Toronto Rd BS7 19 A8
Torpoint Rd BS3 8 D2
Torrance Cl BS30 11 D6
Torridge Rd BS31 5 A4
Torrington Ave BS4 2 F8
Tortworth Farming Mus★
GL12 66 B6
Tortworth Prim Sch
GL12 66 C7
Tortworth Rd BS7 18 E5
Torwood House Sch BS6 18 A3
Totshill Dr BS13 2 E4
Totshill Gr BS13 2 E4
Tottenham Pl BS8 194 B3
Totterdown Bridge Ind Est
BS2 9 A4
Totterdown La GL7 152 E2
Touching End La SN14 14 F8
Touchstone Ave BS34 29 F5
Tower Cl GL4 119 D8
Tower Hill BS2 195 B3
Tower Ho 10 GL52 193 C4
Tower House Dr GL19 179 F2
Tower La Bristol BS1 195 A3
Bristol, Cadbury Heath
BS30 11 B6
Tower Rd Bristol BS15 20 C1
Yorkley GL15 156 A2
Tower Rd N BS30 11 B7
Tower Rd S BS30 11 B5
Tower St Bristol BS1 195 B2
Cirencester GL7 190 D4
Towerleaze BS9 17 D3
Townsend
Almondsbury BS32 39 F4
Mitcheldean GL17 164 D5
Ruardean GL17 163 E4
Townsend Cl Bristol BS14 3 F5
St Briavels GL15 146 F7
Townsend La BS32 40 A5
Townsend Rd BS14 3 F5
Townsend St GL51 133 C3
Townwell GL12 66 B2
Tozers Hill BS4 9 C2
Tracy Cl BS14 2 F7
Trafalgar Dr GL3 127 F8
Trafalgar Rd GL7 190 C5
Trafalgar St GL50 193 B2
Trafalgar Terr 3 BS3 8 B2
Traherne Cl 5 HR8 178 F7
Trajan Cl GL4 119 F6
Tralee Wlk BS4 8 D1
Tram Rd The 16 GL16 155 A5
Tramway Rd Bristol BS4 9 C3
Cinderford GL14 156 C6
Upper Soudley GL14 156 C5
Tranmere Ave BS10 28 A4
Tranmere Gr BS10 28 A3
Transom Ho BS1 195 B2
Transport Mus★ GL1 196 A3
Tranton La GL13 76 C4
Tratman Wlk BS10 27 F3
Travers Cl BS4 2 D6
Travers Wlk BS34 29 F5
Treasure Train★ GL16 155 A4
Tredegar Rd BS16 20 B3
Tredington Pk GL20 173 F8
Tredington Prim Sch
GL20 136 B6
Tredworth Jun & Inf Schs
GL1 118 F7
Tredworth Rd GL1 118 F6
Tree Leaze BS37 43 F2
Treefield Pl 5 BS2 19 A2
Treelands Cl GL53 130 D5
Treelands Dr GL53 130 D5
Tregarth Rd BS3 7 F1
Trelawney Ave 3 BS5 9 D8
Trelawney Pk BS4 9 D3
Trelawney Rd BS6 18 C1
Trelleck Rd NP16 146 B4
Trellick Wlk BS16 19 E8
Tremes Cl SN14 14 F8
Trench La BS32 40 E2
Trenchard Gdns GL7 150 F2
Trenchard Rd
7 Bream GL15 147 D8
Saltford BS31 5 D3
Stanton Fitzwarren SN6 145 A1
Trenchard St BS1 194 C3
Trendlewood Pk BS16 19 E5
Trenley Rd GL11 88 F7
Trent Dr BS35 51 D7
Trent Gr BS31 5 A4
Trent Rd GL3 120 F5
Trentham Cl 7 BS2 19 A2
Tresham Cl BS32 40 D2
Tresmore 2 GL52 133 F2
Tretawn Gdns GL20 192 F4
Trevanna Rd BS3 7 F1
Trevelyan Wlk
Bristol, Henbury BS10 27 F3
Bristol, Stoke Gifford BS34 30 A5
Treverdowe Wlk BS10 27 D3
Trevethin Cl BS15 10 D7
Trevisa Cres GL13 85 E3
Trevisa Gr BS10 28 C4
Trevor Rd GL3 119 F7
Trewint Gdns BS4 2 F8
Trewsbury Rd GL7 149 E3
Triangle S BS8 194 B3
Triangle The
Hewelsfield GL15 146 D4
Longlevens GL2 127 C3
Triangle W BS8 194 B3
Tribune Pl GL4 119 E6
Trident Cl BS16 31 A1
Trier Way GL1 196 B1
Trin Mills BS1 195 A1
Trinder Rd BS20 16 B4
Trinity CE Prim Sch GL9 36 A6
Trinity Coll BS9 17 E4
Trinity Dr GL6 148 A3
Trinity La GL52 193 C4
Trinity Mews 15 BS2 195 C3
Trinity Pl BS8 194 A2
Trinity Rd Bristol BS2 9 A7
Cirencester GL7 190 C3
Gloucester GL4 119 F6
Harrow Hill GL17 164 B3
Stroud GL5 99 D6
Trinity School La GL52 193 C4
Trinity St Bristol BS2 9 A7
Tewkesbury GL20 192 C4
Trinity Way GL14 191 D5
Trinity Wlk BS2 195 C3
Troon BS37 32 E8
Troon Dr BS30 11 B6
Troopers' Hill Rd BS5 10 A7
Trotman Ave GL11 87 F5
Troughton Pl GL20 192 E4
Trowbridge Rd BS10 28 C1
Trowbridge Wlk BS10 28 C1
Trowscoed Ave GL53 130 D6
Trubshaw Ct GL3 128 C5
Trull Cotts GL8 140 F7
Truro Rd BS3 8 B3
Tryes Rd GL50 130 C6
Trygrove GL4 119 D6
Trym Bank BS9 17 D7
Trym Cross Rd BS9 17 C5
Trym Rd BS9 18 A7
Trym Side BS9 17 C5
Trymleaze BS9 17 C5
Trymwood Cl BS10 27 F2
Trymwood Par BS9 17 D6
Tubular Cotts NP16 73 A1
Tucker St BS2 195 C3
Tuckett La BS16 20 C7
Tuckwell Rd GL7 144 F7
Tudor Cl BS30 11 C3
Tudor Ct GL10 97 E4
Tudor Dr NP16 72 C1
Tudor Lo GL50 130 C6
Tudor Lodge Dr GL50 193 A1
Tudor Lodge Rd GL50 130 C6
Tudor Pl GL20 192 D2
Tudor Rd
Bristol, Hanham BS15 10 C5
Bristol, Lower Easton BS5 19 C1
Bristol, St Pauls BS2 18 F1
Cirencester GL7 190 E5
Monmouth NP25 154 B7
Tudor St GL1 118 C6
Tudor Wlk GL16 155 A7
Tuffley Ave GL1 118 D5
Tuffley Cres GL1 118 C5
Tuffley La GL4 118 C3
Tuffley Prim Sch GL4 118 D1
Tuffley Rd BS10 18 C8
Tufthorn Ave GL16 155 A4
Tufthorn Cl GL16 155 B4
Tufthorn Ind Pk GL16 155 B4
Tufthorn Rd GL16 155 B4
Tufton Ave BS11 17 A8
Tug Wilson Cl GL20 182 C5
Tugela Rd BS13 1 F7
Tulworths The GL2 127 B5
Tunacre GL2 125 D6
Tunbridge Way BS16 21 A8
Tuners La SN16 141 C3
Tunstall Cl BS9 17 E4
Turkdean Rd GL51 129 E8
Turley Rd BS5 19 D1
Turnberry BS30 11 B6
Turnberry Wlk 3 BS4 9 D1
Turnbridge Cl BS10 28 D4
Turnbridge Rd BS10 28 C3
Turnbury BS37 32 E8
Turner Cl BS31 5 A5
Turner Dr BS37 43 B1
Turner Gdns BS7 19 B6
Turner Rd GL11 87 E4
Turners Cl GL2 125 D4
Turners Ct 9 BS30 10 F4
Turnpike Ave GL12 68 C6
Turnpike Cl
Chepstow NP16 72 C1
13 Moreton-in-M GL56 187 A3
Yate BS37 43 E2
Turnpike End NP16 61 B4
Turnpike Gate GL12 54 B6
Turnpike Rd SN6 145 D3
Turnstone Dr GL2 117 D1
Turtlegate Ave BS13 1 E4
Turtlegate Wlk BS13 1 E4
Turville Barns GL7 153 C8
Turville Dr BS7 19 A6
Tuscany Ho BS6 18 A3
Tusculum Way GL17 164 D5
Tuthill Rise GL15 92 B3
Tutnalls St GL15 92 B3
Tutshill Gdns NP16 73 A1
Tweed Cl BS35 51 C8
Tweenbrook Ave GL1 118 E6
Tweeny La BS30 11 D6
Twenties The GL7 150 E2
Twenty Acres Rd BS10 28 B2
Twickenham Rd BS6 18 C5
Twigworth CE Prim Sch
GL2 127 A8
Twinberrow La GL11 80 B7
Twixtbears GL20 192 C5
Two Acres Rd BS14 3 A7
Two Hedges Rd GL52 138 A3
Two Mile Ct BS15 10 C8
Two Mile Hill Jun & Inf Schs
BS15 10 C8
Two Mile La GL2 125 B4
Twomile Hill Rd BS15 10 B8
Twyning Manor GL20 181 F8
Twyning Rd WR8 180 D7
Twyning Sch GL20 182 A7
Twynings The BS15 20 E2
Twyver Bank GL4 119 F3
Twyver Cl GL4 119 F3
Tybalt Way BS34 29 E5
Tylea Cl GL51 129 C7
Tyler Cl BS15 10 E5
Tyler Ct 3 GL51 132 E2
Tyler St BS2 9 A6
Tyler's La BS16 20 D5
Tylers Way Chalford GL6 148 C6
Sedbury NP16 61 B8
Yate BS37 43 F5
Yorkley GL15 156 B2
Tyndale Ave Bristol BS16 20 A4
Yate BS37 43 D3
Tyndale Cl GL11 79 E4
Tyndale Ct 7 BS6 18 B1
Tyndale Mon The★ GL11 79 E4
Tyndale Rd Bristol BS15 20 E2
Dursley GL11 87 E4
Gloucester GL3 120 A8
Slimbridge GL2 95 B1
Tyndale View BS35 51 B8
Tyndall Ave BS8 194 C4
Tyndall Ho 5 BS2 195 C3
Tyndall Rd BS5 9 B8
Tyndall's Park Rd BS8 194 C4
Tyndalls Park Mews
BS2 194 C4
Tyndalls Way BS10 18 E8
Tyne Ho 8 BS35 51 C8
Tyne Rd BS7 18 D3
Tyne St BS2 19 A2
Tyning Cl Bristol BS14 3 A7
Yate BS37 43 E2
Tyning Cres GL2 95 E3
Tyning Hengrove Jun Sch
BS14 3 A7
Tyning Rd Bristol BS3 8 F3
Saltford BS31 5 E2
Tynings Ct GL3 128 D5
Tynings Cty Prim Sch
BS16 20 E4
Tynings Rd GL6 91 A4
Tynings The GL6 148 A4
Tynte Ave BS13 2 E3
Tyntesfield Rd BS13 2 A8
Tyrone Wlk BS4 2 E8
Tyrrel Way BS34 29 E5
Tythe Ct Dursley GL11 87 F5
Marshfield SN14 15 A8
Tythe Rd WR12 188 A1
Tythe Terr 19 GL54 174 A7
Tytherington Rd BS35 52 A6
Tythings Cres GL18 170 F4
Tythings Mews GL18 170 F4
Tythings The GL18 170 F4

U

Uley CE Prim Sch GL11 89 C1
Uley Long Barrow (Hetty Pegler's Tump)★ GL11 89 B5
Uley Rd GL11 80 E8
Ullenwood Court Bsns Pk
GL53 122 B7
Ullenwood Manor (Coll)
GL53 122 C6
Ullenwood Rd GL4 119 D7
Ullswater Cl Bristol BS30 11 D6
Yate BS37 43 E3
Ullswater Rd Bristol BS10 28 C1
Cheltenham GL51 129 E7
Underbanks BS20 16 D4
Undercliff Ave GL53 130 D3
Undercliff Terr GL53 130 D3
Underdown Ho BS1 195 A1
Underhill NP16 146 C4
Underhill Rd
Charfield GL12 67 A5
Gloucester GL4 119 C4
Underwood Cl BS35 51 A4
Underwood Est NP25 154 B7
Unicorn Bsns Pk BS4 9 D5
Union Pl GL20 192 D4
Union Rd 2 Bristol BS2 9 A6
Coleford GL16 155 B6
Union St Bristol BS1 195 B3

Union St *continued*
Cheltenham GL52 .... 193 C4
Dursley GL11 .... 80 B8
Gloucester GL1 .... 196 C4
Stow-on-t-W GL54 .... 176 F4
Stroud GL5 .... 99 C7
Unity Ct BS31 .... 5 A5
Unity Rd BS31 .... 5 A6
Unity St
Bristol, Canon's Marsh BS1 .... 194 C2
Bristol, Kingswood BS15 ... 10 C8
Bristol, Newton BS2 ..... 195 C3
Univ of Bristol BS8 .... 194 C3
Univ of Bristol Dept of Economics BS8 .... 194 C3
Univ of Bristol Dept of Ed BS8 .... 194 C3
Univ of Bristol Sch of Vetinary Science BS2 . 194 C4
Univ of the West of England
Bristol, Bower Ashton BS3 ... 7 E4
Bristol, Redland BS6 ...... 18 B2
Univ of the West of England Faculty of Health & Social Care BS16 .... 19 E5
Univ of the West of England Frenchay Campus BS16 . 29 E1
Univ of the West of England, St Matthias BS16 ...... 20 A5
University Cl BS9 .... 17 F4
University Farm 10 GL56 .... 187 A3
University Rd BS8 ..... 194 C3
University Wlk BS8 .... 194 C3
Unlawater La GL14 ..... 157 A7
Unwin Cl GL51 .... 129 C7
Unwin Rd GL51 .... 129 C7
Up Hatherley Way GL51 129 E5
Upcott SN6 .... 143 E6
Upfield Prep Sch GL5 ... 98 F8
Uphill Pl GL1 .... 118 D5
Uphill Rd Bristol BS7 ..... 18 F5
Upper Lydbrook GL17 .... 163 D2
Upjohn Cres BS13 .... 2 D3
Uplands Com Prim Sch GL5 .... 99 D8
Uplands Dr BS31 .... 5 F2
Uplands Ho GL5 .... 99 C8
Uplands Rd Bristol BS16 .. 20 D3
Saltford BS31 .... 5 F2
Stroud GL5 .... 99 D8
Uplands View Terr GL5 .. 99 D7
Upper Bath Rd BS35 .... 51 B8
Upper Bath St GL50 .... 193 B1
Upper Belgrave Rd BS8 . 18 A2
Upper Belmont Rd BS7 .. 18 E3
Upper Berkeley Pl BS8 . 194 B3
Upper Bilson Rd GL14 . 191 C6
Upper Byron Pl BS8 .... 194 B3
Upper Chapel La BS36 ... 31 C7
Upper Cheltenham Pl BS6 .... 18 E1
Upper Church La BS2 . 194 C3
Upper Church Rd GL5 ... 98 E7
Upper Church St NP16 ... 60 F8
Upper Cranbrook Rd BS6 18 B4
Upper Cross 8 HR8 .... 178 F8
Upper Dorrington Terr GL5 .... 99 D6
Upper End Ct WR11 .... 188 A6
Upper Hayes Rd GL6 .... 91 A4
Upper Horfield Prim Sch BS7 .... 19 A8
Upper Kitesnest La GL6 102 F4
Upper Leazes GL5 ...... 99 D7
Upper Lynch Rd GL6 .. 148 D6
Upper Maudlin St BS2 . 195 A3
Upper Mill La GL52 .... 134 E5
Upper Mills Ind Est GL10 97 F6
Upper Myrtle Hill BS20 .. 16 C4
Upper Nelson St NP16 ... 60 E8
Upper Norwood St GL53 .... 130 C6
Upper Park Rd GL6 ..... 91 C3
Upper Park St GL52 .... 130 F8
Upper Perry Hill BS3 ..... 8 C4
Upper Poole Rd GL11 .... 80 B8
Upper Quay St GL1 .... 196 A3
Upper Queen's Rd 2 GL10 .... 97 F7
Upper Rd Eastnor HR8 .. 179 B8
Pillowell GL15 .... 155 F1
Upper Rodley Rd GL14 . 157 F8
Upper Sandhurst Rd BS4 . 9 D4
Upper Springfield Rd GL5 .... 99 C8
Upper St Bristol BS4 ...... 9 A4
Dyrham SN14 .... 23 D4
Upper Station Rd BS16 . 20 D4
Upper Stone Cl BS36 .... 31 C7
Upper Stowfield Rd GL17 .... 163 C4
Upper Sydney St BS3 ..... 8 B3
Upper Terr BS11 .... 27 B1
Upper Tockington Rd BS32 .... 50 A2
Upper Tynings GL6 ...... 91 A4
Upper Tynings The GL5 . 98 D8
Upper Washwell GL6 .. 111 F1
Upper Wells St BS1 .... 194 C2
Upper York St BS2 ..... 195 B4
Upperfield Rd GL51 .... 133 A5
Upperhall Cl 4 HR8 .... 178 F8
Upthorpe GL11 .... 88 B5
Upthorpe La GL11 .... 88 B6
Upton Cl GL4 .... 119 E7
Upton Gdns GL8 .... 140 B5
Upton Hill GL4 .... 119 D1
Upton La
Brookthorpe GL4 .... 111 B6
Gloucester GL4 .... 119 F4
Maiden Head BS41 .... 1 F1
Upton Rd BS3 .... 8 B4
Upton St GL1 .... 119 A8
Upton St Leonards CE Prim Sch GL4 .... 119 F3
Urfords Dr BS16 .... 20 C6
Usk Ct 5 BS35 .... 51 C8
Usk Way GL3 .... 120 F5
Utah Dr GL7 .... 152 E2

V

Vaisey Field GL2 .... 100 F5
Vale Bank GL2 .... 157 B6
Vale Ct Bristol BS8 ...... 194 A4
8 Cricklade SN6 .... 143 E4
Vale La BS3 .... 2 C8
Vale Rd GL7 .... 190 B8
Vale St BS4 .... 9 A4
Vale The BS16 .... 21 F6
Valentine Cl Bristol BS14 ... 3 B5
Chepstow NP16 .... 61 A4
Valerian Cl Bristol BS11 ... 16 F6
Gloucester GL4 .... 119 E7
Valiant Way GL3 .... 120 C7
Vallenders Rd GL20 .... 182 C7
Valley Cl GL5 .... 148 A5
Valley Cotts GL51 ...... 173 F1
Valley Ent Pk NP25 ..... 154 A8
Valley Gdns BS16 .... 20 F8
Valley La GL4 .... 120 A1
Valley Rd
Bristol, Bedminster Down BS13 .... 2 A8
Bristol, Mangotsfield BS16 . 21 A5
Bristol, Warmley BS30 .... 11 D6
Cinderford GL14 .... 191 C3
Leigh Woods BS8 .... 7 C7
Lydney GL15 .... 92 C2
Upper Lydbrook GL17 .... 163 D1
Wooton-u-E GL12 .... 68 C8
Valley View
Chedworth GL54 .... 159 A6
Dursley GL11 .... 87 F4
Valley View Rd GL5 ...... 99 F6
Valls The BS32 .... 29 F6
Valma Rocks BS5 .... 10 A6
Van Der Breen St GL6 .. 105 B1
Vandyck Ave BS31 .... 4 F6
Varley Ave GL3 .... 120 B6
Varnister La GL17 ...... 163 F4
Varnister Rd GL17 ...... 163 F4
Vassall Ct BS16 .... 20 B5
Vassall Rd BS16 .... 20 B5
Vatch La GL5 .... 148 B7
Vatch View GL5 .... 103 E1
Vattingstone La BS35 .... 50 F5
Vaughan Cl BS10 .... 27 F3
Vauxhall GL18 .... 170 F4
Vauxhall La NP16 .... 60 D8
Vauxhall Rd
Chepstow NP16 .... 60 D8
Gloucester GL1 .... 196 C1
Vauxhall Terr
2 Bristol BS3 .... 8 A4
Gloucester GL1 .... 196 C1
Vayre Cl BS37 .... 44 C1
Veldt House Barns HR8 . 178 B5
Velhurst Dr 1 GL6 ..... 148 B6
Velthouse La GL17 ..... 165 A5
Vennings The GL11 ...... 87 F6
Venns Acre GL12 .... 68 B6
Vensfield Rd GL2 ...... 117 E2
Vention La GL17 .... 163 D3
Ventnor Ave 1 BS5 .... 9 F8
Ventnor Rd
Bristol, Filton BS34 .... 29 B3
Bristol, St George BS5 .... 19 F1
Venton Ct 5 BS15 .... 10 B5
Vera Rd BS16 .... 19 F2
Verbena Cl 2 GL4 ...... 119 E5
Vernal Cl GL4 .... 119 F5
Vernals La GL12 .... 67 C8
Verney Cl GL53 .... 130 E6
Verney Rd GL10 .... 97 F7
Verneys The GL53 ...... 130 E6
Vernon Cl BS31 .... 5 D3
Vernon Pl GL53 .... 193 C3
Vernon St 5 BS2 .... 8 F4
Verrier Rd BS5 .... 9 C7
Vertican Rd GL3 .... 127 D6
Vervain Cl GL3 .... 128 A7
Verwood Dr BS30 .... 11 C2
Vetch Cl GL4 .... 119 A4
Viburnum Cl GL50 ..... 130 B6
Viburnum View 4 GL4 .. 119 F5
Vicarage Cl
Churchdown GL3 .... 128 C4
Lydney GL15 .... 92 A2
Shurdington GL51 .... 129 E2
Vicarage Cotts
Bristol BS16 .... 20 D5
Chipping Campden GL55 . 189 A2
Vicarage Ct
8 Bristol BS15 .... 10 B5
Brockworth GL3 .... 120 E5
Vicarage La
Arlingham GL2 .... 157 B5
Brockworth GL3 .... 120 E6
Frampton on Severn GL2 . 157 F1
Highworth SN6 .... 145 D3
Hillesley GL12 .... 55 D8
Olveston BS35 .... 50 B3
Vicarage Rd
Bristol, Bishopsworth BS13 .. 2 A6
Bristol, Hanham BS15 ..... 10 B5
Bristol, Southville BS3 ...... 8 B4
Bristol, Whitehall BS5 ...... 9 C8
Coalpit Heath BS36 .... 31 C6
Gloucester GL1 .... 119 A7
Leigh Woods BS8 .... 7 D6
Pilning BS35 .... 38 C7
Vicarage St GL6 .... 104 A8
Vicars Cl BS16 .... 20 B4
Vickers Rd GL54 .... 169 D7
Victor Ho BS34 .... 29 C7
Victor Rd BS3 .... 8 C3
Victor St
8 Bristol, Barton Hill BS5 ... 9 B6
Bristol, St Philip's Marsh BS2 .... 9 A4
Victoria Ave BS5 .... 9 C7
Victoria Cl BS35 .... 64 B3
Victoria Cotts
Quedgeley GL2 .... 117 E3
4 Stonehouse GL10 .... 97 F8
Victoria Cres BS35 ...... 38 A6
Victoria Ct
6 Bristol, Cotham BS6 .... 18 D1
Bristol, Redland BS6 ...... 18 A3
Gloucester GL2 .... 126 F6
Victoria Dr GL10 .... 96 F7
Victoria Gdns 7 BS6 .... 18 D1
Victoria Gr BS3 .... 8 E4
Victoria Ho BS31 .... 4 F4
Victoria Par BS5 .... 9 C8
Victoria Park Com Jun & Inf Schs BS3 .... 8 E3
Victoria Pk
Bristol, Fishponds BS16 ... 20 A5
Bristol, Kingswood BS15 ... 20 D1
Victoria Pl Bristol BS3 .... 8 C3
Cheltenham GL52 .... 133 F1
Victoria Rd
Avonmouth BS11 .... 16 B7
Brimscombe GL5 .... 99 F1
Bristol, Hanham BS15 ..... 10 C5
Bristol, St Philip's Marsh BS2 .... 9 A5
Bristol, Warmley BS30 .... 11 D5
Chepstow NP16 .... 60 F5
Cirencester GL7 .... 190 D4
Coleford GL16 .... 155 A5
Gloucester GL2 .... 126 F6
Ledbury HR8 .... 178 E8
Lydney GL15 .... 92 A3
Quenington GL7 .... 152 D7
Saltford BS31 .... 5 D3
Victoria Retreat GL50 .. 193 B1
Victoria Sq BS8 .... 194 A3
Victoria St
6 Bourton-on-t-W GL54 .. 168 F7
Bristol BS1 .... 195 B2
Bristol, Staple Hill BS16 ... 20 D5
Cheltenham GL50 .... 133 D3
Cinderford GL14 .... 191 C3
Cinderford GL14 .... 191 C4
Gloucester GL1 .... 196 C1
Painswick GL6 .... 103 F8
Victoria Terr
9 Bourton-on-t-W GL54 .. 168 F7
Bretforton WR11 .... 188 A7
14 Bristol, Clifton BS8 ...... 7 F6
Bristol, St Philip's Marsh BS2 .... 9 B5
Cheltenham GL52 .... 133 F1
Victoria Vale GL14 ..... 191 C4
Victoria Wlk BS6 .... 18 D1
Victory Cl GL3 .... 128 A8
Victory Rd
Gloucester GL1 .... 118 F7
Whiteshill GL6 .... 103 A3
Victory Villas GL7 ..... 152 F4
View Ct BS30 .... 12 C6
Vigor Rd BS13 .... 2 B5
Villa The GL14 .... 191 C2
Villa Way HR8 .... 178 E7
Village Ave GL54 ...... 175 D2
Village Cl BS37 .... 43 D1
Village Farm GL7 ...... 150 F3
Village Rd GL51 .... 132 F4
Villiers Rd BS5 .... 19 B1
Vilner La BS35 .... 51 B7
Vilverie Mead GL52 .... 137 D4
Vimpany Cl BS10 .... 27 F3
Vimpennys La BS35 ..... 38 E1
Vincent Ave GL4 .... 118 D1
Vincent Cl BS11 .... 27 C2
Vincent Ct 2 BS16 ...... 20 D3
Vine Cotts NP16 .... 60 E8
Vine Ct GL50 .... 133 C3
Vine Hall GL15 .... 147 E4
Vine Terr GL1 .... 196 C4
Vine Way GL20 .... 192 D1
Vinecroft GL13 .... 85 E8
Viner's La GL9 .... 36 B5
Vineries Cl GL53 ...... 130 C4
Vines The GL3 .... 120 B7
Vineyard La GL12 .... 67 F5
Vineyard St GL54 ...... 174 A7
Vineyards Cl GL53 ..... 131 B4
Vining Wlk 4 BS5 .... 9 B8
Vinney La BS37 .... 44 F8
Vinny Ave BS16 .... 21 A7
Vintery Leys BS9 .... 18 B7
Virginia Ave GL7 ...... 152 E2
Virginia Cl BS37 .... 44 A1
Virginia Rd GL20 ...... 182 C4
Vittoria Wlk GL50 ..... 193 B2
Vivian St BS3 .... 8 D3
Vizard Cl GL11 .... 80 B8
Vorda Rd SN6 .... 145 D4
Vowell Cl BS13 .... 2 B4
Voxwell La GL52 ...... 137 E3
Voyce Cl GL4 .... 118 D2
Vulcan Way GL4 .... 119 F6
Vyners Cl GL7 .... 190 C2
Vyvian Ct GL1 .... 196 B2
Vyvyan Rd BS8 .... 194 A3
Vyvyan Terr BS8 .... 194 A3

W

Wade Ct GL51 .... 129 C7
Wade Hill SN6 .... 145 C3
Wade Rd BS37 .... 43 A3
Wade St BS2 .... 195 C3
Wadehurst Ind Pk BS2 .... 9 A7
Wades La GL6 .... 103 C3
Wades Rd BS34 .... 29 B3
Wadham Cl GL7 .... 153 C6
Wadham Dr BS16 .... 30 B1
Wadham Gr BS16 .... 21 B5
Waggons La GL19 ...... 172 C4
Wagtail Dr GL20 .... 182 B5
Wainbridge Cres BS35 .. 38 D7
Wainbrook Dr BS5 ...... 19 D2
Wainland Pl GL16 ...... 154 F3
Wainlode La GL2 ...... 173 A3
Wakefield Cl GL7 ...... 144 F7
Wakeford Rd 1 BS16 .... 21 A7
Wakeman Cl GL20 ..... 192 E2
Walden Rd BS31 .... 5 A4
Waldrist Cl GL51 ...... 132 F5
Walford Prim Sch HR9 . 163 C7
Walham La GL1 .... 126 E4
Walk Mill La GL12 ...... 67 F4
Walk The GL12 .... 67 F5
Walker Cl
Bristol, Downend BS16 .... 21 A7
Bristol, Upper Easton BS5 .. 9 B8
Walker Ct BS16 .... 20 F5
Walker St BS2 .... 194 C4
Walker Way BS35 .... 51 B7
Walker's La GL17 ...... 163 F4
Walkers Gdn 14 GL54 ... 168 A1
Walkley Hill GL5 .... 99 A5
Walkley Rd GL20 ...... 192 D5
Wallace Appartments 11 GL52 .... 193 C4
Wallace Ho GL51 ...... 129 F6
Wallbank Ho GL1 ...... 127 A3
Wallbridge Stroud GL5 ... 99 B6
Stroud GL5 .... 99 B7
Wallcroft Ho BS6 .... 18 A3
Walled Gdn The GL8 ..... 82 B5
Wallingford Rd BS4 .... 2 D7
Walliscote Ave BS9 ...... 18 C6
Walliscote Rd BS9 .... 18 C6
Wallow Gn Horsley GL6 ... 90 F2
Nailsworth GL6 .... 90 F2
Wallscourt Rd BS34 ..... 29 B2
Wallscourt Rd S BS34 ... 29 B1
Wallsend La SN14 .... 24 C5
Wallsworth Hall Nature in Art Mus★ GL2 .... 173 A1
Walmore Hill Prim Sch GL2 .... 165 F1
Walnut Ave BS37 .... 44 A2
Walnut Bank Dr GL20 .. 183 A4
Walnut Cl Bristol BS15 .... 20 F1
Broadway WR12 .... 185 B8
Cheltenham GL52 .... 133 E4
10 Coleford GL16 .... 155 B5
Easton-in-G BS20 .... 16 A3
Frampton Cotterell BS36 ... 31 C6
Gloucester GL4 .... 119 D3
Keynsham BS31 .... 4 C4
Thornbury BS35 .... 64 D1
Walnut Cres BS15 .... 10 F8
Walnut Ct GL20 .... 183 A4
Walnut Dr SN14 .... 15 F6
Walnut La BS15 .... 11 A8
Walnut Tree Cl BS32 ..... 40 A5
Walnut Wlk Bristol BS13 ... 2 A6
Keynsham BS31 .... 4 C4
Walsh Ave BS14 .... 3 A7
Walshe Ave BS37 .... 44 C1
Walsingham Rd BS6 ..... 18 E2
Walter Reynold Homes GL54 .... 176 E5
Walter St BS3 .... 8 A4
Walton Ave BS4 .... 9 D5
Walton Cl Bristol BS30 ... 11 C1
Keynsham BS31 .... 4 D4
Upton St Leonards GL4 ... 119 E3
Walton Dr GL20 .... 192 F5
Walton Gdns GL20 ...... 192 F4
Walton Heath BS37 ...... 43 F1
Walton Ho GL51 .... 132 E2
Walton House Bglws 8 GL54 .... 168 A1
Walton House Ct 9 GL54 .... 168 A1
Walton Rd BS11 .... 16 D6
Walton Rise BS9 .... 18 A7
Walton St BS5 .... 19 B1
Walwyn Cl GL17 .... 164 D5
Wandsdyke Prim Sch BS14 .... 2 F4
Wansbeck Rd BS31 .... 5 A4
Wanscow Wlk BS9 ...... 18 B6
Wansdyke Ct BS14 .... 3 B5
Wansdyke Workshops BS31 .... 5 A6
Wapley Hill BS37 .... 32 E4
Wapley Rd BS37 .... 33 B3
Wapping Rd BS1 .... 195 A1
Ward Ave GL3 .... 127 E6
Ward Cl GL52 .... 138 A4
Ward Rd GL54 .... 168 A1
Warden Hill Cl GL51 ... 129 F6
Warden Hill Cty Prim Sch GL51 .... 130 A5
Warden Hill Rd GL51 .. 130 A6
Warden Rd BS3 .... 8 C4
Wardour Rd BS4 .... 2 D8
Wards Rd GL51 .... 129 D6
Ware Ct BS36 .... 30 D5
Warend Hill Dursley GL11 . 80 A6
North Nibley GL11 .... 79 F6
Waring Ho BS1 .... 195 A1
Warman Cl BS14 .... 3 F6
Warman Rd BS14 .... 3 F6
Warmington Rd BS14 ...... 3 C8
Warminster Rd BS2 ..... 19 A2
Warmley CE Prim Sch BS30 .... 11 C6
Warmley Tower Specl Sch BS30 .... 11 B7
Warneford Pl 20 GL56 .. 187 A3
Warner Cl BS15 .... 10 F6
Warns Ct 14 GL8 .... 140 B4
Warns The BS30 .... 11 A4
Warren Cl Bristol BS32 ... 40 D3
Cheltenham GL51 .... 129 F6
Innsworth GL3 .... 128 A7
Warren Croft GL11 ...... 79 E4
Warren Dr 13 HR8 ..... 178 F8
Warren Gdns BS14 .... 3 F5
Warren La HR9 .... 170 A1
Warren Rd Bristol BS34 ... 29 B3
Northway GL20 .... 182 B4
Warren Slade NP16 ...... 60 F5
Warren Way BS37 .... 43 E3
Warrens Gorse Cotts GL7 .... 150 B8
Warrington Rd BS4 .... 9 D2
Warth La Arlingham GL2 . 157 C6
Pilning BS35 .... 48 D3
Warwick Ave
7 Bristol BS5 .... 19 B1
Gloucester GL4 .... 118 C1
Warwick Cl Bristol BS30 ... 11 B2
Chepstow NP16 .... 60 D6
3 Fairford GL7 .... 152 E4
Stroud GL5 .... 99 A4
Thornbury BS35 .... 64 A1
Warwick Cres GL52 .... 131 B6
Warwick Pl
Cheltenham GL52 .... 193 C4
Tewkesbury GL20 .... 192 D3
Warwick Rd
Bristol, Baptist Mills BS5 ... 19 B1
Bristol, Redland BS6 ...... 18 B1
Keynsham BS31 .... 4 D4
Washing Pound La BS14 .. 3 B4
Washing's La NP25 ..... 154 C5
Washingpool Hill BS35 .. 50 E1
Washingpool Hill Rd BS32 .... 50 D2
Washingpool La BS11 ... 26 F7
Washington Ave BS5 .... 19 C1
Washpool La
Fairford GL7 .... 152 F1
Kempsford GL7 .... 144 F8
Wasley Rd GL51 .... 132 E1
Watch Elm Cl BS32 ...... 29 E6
Watchhouse Rd BS20 .... 16 D4
Watchill Ave BS13 .... 1 F6
Watchill Cl BS13 .... 1 F6
Water Furlongs SN6 ... 143 E4
Water La Brimscombe GL5 . 99 E1
Bristol BS1 .... 195 B2
Bristol, Brislington BS4 ..... 9 D2
Bristol, Hanham Green BS15 .... 10 B2
Bristol, Knowle BS3 .... 8 F3
Charlton Kings GL52 ..... 131 B6
Pill BS20 .... 16 C4
Woodchester GL5 .... 98 F3
Wooton-u-E GL12 .... 68 B6
Water Mdw GL2 .... 109 E7
Water St GL11 .... 88 B1
Water's La BS9 .... 18 A7
Waterbridge Rd BS13 ..... 1 F4
Watercress Rd BS2 ...... 18 F3
Waterdale Cl Bristol BS9 . 18 C7
Hardwicke GL2 .... 109 D8
Waterdale Gdns BS9 .... 18 C7
Waterfield Cl GL53 ..... 193 B1
Waterford Cl BS35 .... 51 D8
Waterford Ct GL53 ..... 130 C6
Waterford Rd BS9 .... 18 B6
Watergrip La GL20 ..... 183 A8
Waterloo Cl GL20 ...... 182 D7
Waterloo Ho BS20 .... 16 D5
Waterloo La GL7 .... 152 E3
Waterloo Pl 19 BS2 .... 195 C3
Waterloo Rd BS2 ...... 195 C3
Waterloo St Bristol BS2 . 195 C3
9 Bristol, Clifton BS8 ...... 7 F7
Cheltenham GL51 .... 133 B3
Waterloo The GL7 ..... 190 D5
Waterloo Way GL20 .... 182 D7
Watermans Ct GL2 ..... 117 D1
Watermead GL15 .... 92 A3
Watermill Cl GL12 .... 65 E7
Watermoor Cl GL51 .... 132 D4
Watermoor Ct GL3 ..... 128 B5
Watermoor Prim Sch GL7 .... 190 D3
Watermoor Rd GL7 .... 190 D3

Watermoor Way GL7 190 D3
Watermore Cl BS36 31 C7
Waters Rd BS15 10 C8
Waters Reach GL2 118 B6
Waters Way NP16 60 E7
Watershoot Cl GL52 134 A5
Waterside Cl
Andoversford GL54 166 D6
Quedgeley GL2 117 D1
Waterside Dr BS32 40 A1
Waterton Cl GL3 120 B6
Waterwells Dr GL2 110 A6
Waterwheel Cl GL2 117 D1
Watery La Aylburton GL15 147 F5
Doynton BS30 13 A8
Frampton on Severn GL2 157 F2
Gloucester GL4 111 F8
Lea HR9 164 C8
Minsterworth GL2 117 B7
Newent GL18 170 F4
Wathen Rd BS6 18 F3
Watkins Cnr SN5 143 E1
Watkins Yd BS9 18 A8
Watledge Bank GL6 91 B5
Watledge Cl GL20 192 D4
Watledge Rd GL6 91 B5
Watley's End Rd BS36 30 F7
Watling Way BS11 16 D7
Watson Ave BS4 9 D4
Watson Gr GL4 119 F5
Watson Ho 5 GL52 193 C4
Watson's Rd BS30 10 F3
Watters Cl BS36 31 D6
Watts Cl GL3 120 B7
Wavell Cl BS37 43 D3
Waveney Rd BS31 5 A3
Waverley Rd
Bristol, Cotham BS6 18 C1
Bristol, Shirehampton BS11 16 E6
Gloucester GL2 127 C2
Yate BS37 43 B2
Waverley St 8 BS5 19 A1
Waycroft Prim Sch BS14 3 E5
Wayford Cl BS31 5 A3
Waylands SN6 143 F4
Wayleaze
Coalpit Heath BS36 31 D7
Westerleigh BS37 32 F3
Wayridge The GL4 119 D4
Wayside Cl BS36 31 B7
Weald Cl GL4 119 C5
Weare Ct BS1 194 A1
Weathers The BS35 63 D5
Weavers Cl Dursley GL11 80 B8
Kingswood GL12 67 F4
Weavers Dr GL11 89 B1
Weavers Ho 17 GL5 99 C7
Weavers Rd
Cirencester GL7 190 E4
Quedgeley GL2 117 F2
Weavers Row GL5 99 F4
Weavings La GL14 156 C6
Webb Rd GL8 140 B5
Webb St BS5 9 A8
Webber Ho GL20 192 B3
Webbs Heath BS30 11 E8
Webbs Wood BS32 29 F7
Webbs Wood Rd BS32 29 F7
Webley Rd GL17 163 F3
Wedgewood Cotts
WR12 184 E5
Wedgewood Rd BS16 30 D1
Wedgwood Cl BS14 3 B5
Wedgwood Dr GL2 127 C4
Wedmore Cl BS15 10 F7
Wedmore Rd BS31 5 D4
Wedmore Vale BS3 8 E2
Weedon Cl 6 BS2 19 A2
Weigh Bridge Ct GL55 189 A2
Weight Rd 2 BS5 9 C7
Weir Bridge Cl GL4 119 E8
Weir La SN14 14 F8
Welch Ho GL51 129 D2
Welch Rd GL51 132 E4
Well Alley GL20 192 C5
Well Cl Chepstow NP16 60 F4
Long Ashton BS41 7 B1
Northway GL20 182 C5
Well Cross Rd GL4 119 A4
Well Hill GL6 148 A3
Well House Cl BS9 17 E3
Well La Badminton GL9 46 E5
Drybrook GL17 164 A4
Guiting Power GL54 175 B3
Stow-on-t-W GL54 176 F4
Well Pl GL50 133 B1
Well Vale La HR9 162 D3
Welland Ct GL52 134 A4
Welland Dr GL52 134 A4
Welland Lodge Rd GL52 134 A4
Welland Rd Keynsham BS31 4 F4
Quedgeley GL2 117 F2
Wellbrook Rd GL52 137 F5
Weller Bglws GL2 118 C4
Wellesley Prim Sch BS37 32 D6
Wellesley Rd GL50 133 E3
Wellesley St GL1 118 F6
Wellfield GL20 192 F5
Wellgarth Rd BS4 9 A2
Wellgarth Wlk BS4 9 A2
Welling Cl GL11 80 C7
Wellington Ave BS6 18 E1
Wellington Cres BS7 18 E6
Wellington Dr Bristol BS9 18 D6
Yate BS37 43 B2
Wellington Hill BS7 18 E6
Wellington Hill W BS9 18 D7
Wellington Ho GL7 190 D5
Wellington La Bristol BS6 18 E1
Cheltenham GL52 133 E3
Wellington Lodge Cl
GL20 182 D7
Wellington Mews BS11 16 D5
Wellington Par GL1 196 C3
Wellington Pk BS8 18 A2
Wellington Pl Bristol BS16 30 B1
Cheltenham GL52 193 C2
Wellington Rd
Bristol, Kingswood BS15 20 D2
Bristol, St Pauls BS2 195 C4
Cheltenham GL52 133 E3
Moreton-in-M GL56 187 B3
Upper Rissington GL54 169 D6
Yate BS37 43 E3
Wellington Sq GL50 133 E3
Wellington St
Cheltenham GL50 193 C3
Gloucester GL1 196 B2
Wellington Terr
18 Bristol BS8 7 F6
Moreton-in-M GL56 187 B3
Newnham GL14 156 F6
Wellington Wlk BS10 18 C7
Wellmeadow GL16 154 D7
Wellmeadow La GL16 155 A8
Wells Cl Bristol BS14 3 C5
Cheltenham GL51 129 F5
Wells Gdns 5 WR12 185 C8
Wells Rd Bisley GL6 148 D8
Bristol BS4 9 B2
Gloucester GL4 119 C8
Maiden Head BS41 1 E1
Wells St BS3 8 A4
Wellsprings Ho GL2 127 C3
Wellsprings Rd GL2 127 C3
Wellstead Ave BS37 43 D1
Wellsway BS31 4 F3
Wellsway Sec Sch BS31 5 A5
Welsford Ave BS16 19 D4
Welsford Rd BS16 19 C4
Welsh Back BS1 195 A2
Welsh House La GL18 170 F8
Welsh St NP16 72 D1
Welsh Way
Bagendon GL7 158 D1
Fairford GL7 152 B5
Sunhill GL7 151 F7
Welton Wlk BS15 20 C2
Welveland La GL4 127 E1
Welwyn Gdns BS13 2 C3
Welwyn Mews 4 GL51 129 E5
Wench Ford Forest Trail*
GL15 156 C2
Wend The GL17 164 F5
Wendover Gdns GL50 133 B1
Wenlock Rd GL20 192 D3
Wenmore Cl BS16 30 D1
Wentforth Dr 2 BS15 20 C2
Wentsfield GL10 96 F7
Wentworth Bristol BS30 11 A6
Yate BS37 43 E1
Wentworth Cl
Cheltenham GL51 132 D3
Gloucester GL2 127 B5
Wentworth Rd BS7 18 D3
Werth La GL19 181 B1
Wescott Gr BS11 27 C2
Wesley Ave BS15 10 D5
Wesley Cl Aylburton GL15 147 E4
7 Bristol, Upper Soundwell
BS16 20 D3
Bristol, Whitehall BS5 19 D1
Wesley Ct
Gloucester GL1 196 C2
16 Stroud GL5 99 C7
Wesley Hill BS15 20 D1
Wesley La BS30 11 B5
Wesley Pl BS8 18 A2
Wesley Rd Bristol BS7 18 E4
Cinderford GL14 191 D5
Leonard Stanley GL10 97 E3
Whitecroft GL15 155 F1
Wesley St BS3 8 C3
Wesley Theological Coll
BS10 27 F1
Wessex Ave BS7 18 F7
Wessex Dr GL52 134 B2
Wessex Ho 10 BS2 195 C3
Wessex Way SN6 145 D4
West Allcourt GL7 153 E2
West Approach Dr GL52 133 E4
West Ave GL17 164 B4
West Broadway BS9 18 D6
West Coombe BS9 17 D6
West Country Water Pk*
BS36 40 F2
West Croft BS9 18 C7
West Dene BS9 17 E6
West Dr GL50 133 E3
West Dundry La BS41 1 E2
West End Avening GL8 140 A8
Bristol, Kingsdown BS2 195 A4
Bristol, Southville BS3 194 C1
Coaley GL11 96 D1
Kingham OX7 177 F2
Minchinhampton GL6 148 A3
Northleach GL54 168 A1
Ruardean GL17 163 E4
Thornbury BS35 63 C6
West End Gdns GL7 152 D4
West End La
Broadway WR12 185 B7
Gloucester GL3 120 B6
West Field GL2 125 D5
West Gr BS6 18 F1
West Grange Ct GL5 99 B8
West Hay Gr GL7 141 F8
West Hill SN26 144 D2
West La GL7 141 F8
West Leaze Pl BS32 29 E6
West Littleton Rd SN14 24 E2
West Lodge Dr GL4 119 D6
West Mall BS8 7 F7
West Market Pl GL7 190 C5
West Mill La SN6 143 E4
West Par BS9 17 C7
West Park Rd BS16 20 E5
West Pk BS8 194 B4
West Point Row BS32 40 C3
West Priory Cl BS9 18 A7
West Ridge BS36 31 C7
West Rocke Ave BS9 17 D6
West Shrubbery 5 BS6 18 B2
West St Bristol BS2 195 C3
Bristol, Bedminster BS3 8 C3
2 Bristol, Kingswood BS15 10 D8
Bristol, Oldland Common
BS30 11 C4
Kingham OX7 177 F3
Tetbury GL8 140 B4
Tytherington GL12 52 B5
West Town Ave BS4 9 D1
West Town Dr 2 BS4 9 D1
West Town Gr BS4 3 D8
West Town La BS4 9 D1
West Town Lane Jun & Inf
Schs BS4 9 C1
West Town Pk BS4 9 D1
West Town Rd BS11 16 C7
West Tynings GL6 91 A4
West View Alveston BS35 50 F4
Cinderford GL14 191 D3
Joy's Green GL17 163 D3
Newent GL18 170 F4
Newnham GL14 156 F7
Poulton GL7 151 F3
Wooton-u-E GL12 68 C7
West View Rd Bristol BS3 8 B3
Keynsham BS31 4 E5
West Way
Bristol BS10,BS34 28 E4
Cirencester GL7 190 C4
Lechlade on T GL7 153 E3
West Wlk BS37 43 E1
Westacre Cl BS10 28 A2
Westal Gn 15 GL50 130 B8
Westal Pk GL51 130 B7
Westbourne WR11 188 C7
Westbourne Ave BS31 4 E5
Westbourne Cl 2 BS16 21 A7
Westbourne Dr
Cheltenham GL52 133 F2
Hardwicke GL2 109 E7
Westbourne Gr 8 BS3 8 C3
Westbourne Ho 11 GL52 133 F2
Westbourne Pl BS8 194 B3
Westbourne Rd
Bristol, Downend BS16 20 F8
8 Bristol, Upper Easton BS5 9 B8
Westbourne Terr BS16 20 B7
Westbrook Rd BS4 3 D8
Westbrooke Ct BS1 194 A1
Westbury Court Rd BS9 18 A7
Westbury Ct BS9 18 A7
Westbury Hill BS9 18 A7
Westbury La BS9 17 C7
Westbury Park Prim Sch
BS6 18 B3
Westbury Pk BS6 18 A4
Westbury Rd Bristol BS6 18 A4
Cheltenham GL53 130 E4
Gloucester GL4 118 D3
Westbury-on-Severn CE
Prim Sch GL14 165 C1
Westbury-on-Trym CE Prim
Sch BS9 18 A8
Westcote Rd GL4 118 E1
Westcourt Dr BS30 11 B4
Westdown Gdns GL52 133 F1
Westend GL11 87 D4
Westend Cross GL10 101 A2
Westend La BS35 63 B6
Westend Par GL1 126 C3
Westend Rd GL12 53 E5
Westend Terr
Chipping Campden GL55 188 F2
Gloucester GL1 126 C3
Westering Cl BS16 21 A5
Westerleigh Cl BS16 20 F7
Westerleigh Rd
Bristol BS16 20 F6
Henfield BS36 31 D2
Pucklechurch BS16 22 C7
Westerleigh BS36,BS37 32 B5
Yate BS37 32 C8
Westerley Cl GL14 191 D3
Western Approach
Distribution Pk BS35 38 C4
Western Ave
Chepstow NP16 60 F5
Frampton Cotterell BS36 42 A1
Mitcheldean GL17 164 D5
Western Ct 6 GL50 133 B1
Western Dr BS14 2 E6
Western Grange BS34 29 A3
Western Hill Rd GL20 183 B5
Western Rd Bristol BS7 18 E6
Cheltenham GL50 193 A3
Western Way GL18 178 D2
Westfield Dursley GL11 88 A2
Llangrove HR9 162 B6
Westfield Ave
Brockworth GL3 120 D6
Northway GL20 182 C4
Westfield Cl Bristol BS15 10 D5
Keynsham BS31 4 C5
Westfield Cotts GL51 136 B3
Westfield Ct GL14 191 D5
Westfield La BS34 29 E3
Westfield Pk BS6 18 B1
Westfield Pl BS8 7 F7
Westfield Rd Bristol BS9 18 A8
Brockworth GL3 120 D6
Cinderford GL14 191 D5
Westfield Terr GL2 126 E5
Westfield Way BS32 40 D2
Westfields GL12 68 A7
Westgate St GL1 196 A3
Westhill Cl SN6 145 C3
Westland Ave BS30 11 C4
Westland Rd GL2 109 D7
Westlands Jun Sch
GL51 130 A7
Westleigh Cl Bristol BS10 28 D1
Yate BS37 43 C1
Westleigh Ct BS37 43 C1
Westleigh Pk BS14 3 B8
Westleigh Rd BS10 28 D1
Westmarsh BS35 63 B5
Westmarsh La BS35 63 B5
Westmead Rd Bristol BS5 10 B7
Gloucester GL2 127 D5
Westminster Cl
1 Bristol BS9 18 A7
Cheltenham GL53 130 F7
Westminster Ct 3 GL2 127 B2
Westminster Rd BS5 9 D8
Westmoreland Rd BS6 18 B3
Westmorland Ho BS6 18 A3
Westmorland Terr BS37 34 D7
Weston Ave 4 BS5 9 D7
Weston Cl BS9 17 C7
Weston Cotts SN7 145 E8
Weston Cres BS7 18 E6
Weston Ind Est WR11 188 D4
Weston Park Prim Sch
BS11 16 F8
Weston Rd
Bretforton WR11 188 B5
Gloucester GL1 196 B1
Honeybourne WR11 188 C6
Long Ashton BS41 7 A1
Westonbirt GL8 58 D8
Westonbirt Arboretum*
GL8 58 B8
Westonbirt Sch GL8 58 E8
Westonian Ct BS9 17 C4
Westons Brake BS16 31 A1
Westons Hill Dr BS16 31 A1
Westons Way BS15 10 F7
Westover Cl BS9 27 F1
Westover Ct GL3 128 B7
Westover Dr BS9 28 A1
Westover Gdns BS9 17 F8
Westover Rd BS9 28 A1
Westover Rise BS9 28 A1
Westpoint Trad Est BS15 10 D7
Westridge Rd GL12 68 A8
Westrip Pl GL5 98 D8
Westrop SN6 145 D3
Westrop Cty Prim Sch
SN6 145 C3
Westview GL19 173 C7
Westward BS41 7 B2
Westward Ct GL5 98 D6
Westward Dr BS20 16 C4
Westward Gdns BS41 7 B2
Westward Rd Bristol BS13 1 F7
Stroud GL5 98 D6
Westwick Rd GL19 165 D6
Westwing Sch BS32 50 E8
Westwood Cres BS4 9 D5
Westwood La GL52 134 D3
Westwood Rd BS4 3 D8
Wetherby Ct BS16 30 F1
Wetherell Pl BS8 194 B3
Wetherleigh Dr GL2 125 E5
Wexford Rd BS4 2 D8
Weyhouse Cl GL5 99 D5
Weymouth Rd BS3 8 D2
Whaddon Ave GL52 134 A2
Whaddon Dr GL52 133 F2
Whaddon Prim Sch
GL52 134 B2
Whaddon Rd GL52 134 A2
Whaddon Road Ground
(Cheltenham Town FC)
GL52 133 F3
Whaddon Way GL4 118 D1
Wharf La Kempsford GL7 144 E7
Lechlade on T GL7 153 E2
Wharf Rd 6 BS16 19 F4
Wharf The GL19 173 E6
Wharfdale Sq GL51 132 F3
Wharfdale Way
Hardwicke GL2 109 D8
Stonehouse GL10 97 E6
Wharfedale BS35 51 D8
Wharfings The GL7 144 E7
Wharnecliffe Cl BS14 3 B5
Wharnecliffe Gdns BS14 3 B5
Whartons 8 BS4 9 D1
Whatley Ct 9 BS8 18 B1
Whatley Rd BS8 18 B1
Wheat Cl GL56 177 A6
Wheat Hill 2 GL8 140 B4
Wheatfield Ct GL55 189 A6
Wheatfield Dr BS32 40 D1
Wheatfield Prim Sch
BS32 40 D1
Wheathill Cl BS31 4 D5
Wheatland Dr GL51 132 D4
Wheatridge E The GL4 119 E4
Wheatridge The GL4 119 D4
Wheatsheaf Dr GL52 137 D4
Wheatstone Cl GL20 182 C5
Wheatstone Rd GL1 118 F7
Wheatway GL4 119 D3
Wheelers Wlk GL5 98 F8
Whelford Rd GL7 144 E8
Whimbrel Rd GL2 117 D1
Whimsey Rd GL14 191 B6
Whinchat Gdns BS16 19 F6
Whip La GL6 91 B5
Whippington Ct BS1 195 B3
Whippington's Cnr
GL16 154 E7
Whitby Rd BS4 9 C5
Whitchurch District Ctr
BS14 3 A5
Whitchurch La
Bristol, Bishopsworth BS13 2 B5
Bristol, Hartcliffe BS13 2 C5
Bristol, Whitchurch BS14 2 E5
Dundry BS41 2 C1
Whitchurch Prim Sch
BS14 3 C4
Whitchurch Rd BS13 2 A6
Whitchurch Sch HR9 162 E4
White Cotts GL5 98 E6
White Cross Rd GL15 92 A2
White Hart Ct GL7 152 E3
White Hart Ho GL51 133 C3
White Hart La 13 GL54 176 F4
White Hart St GL51 133 C3
White Horse La GL6 103 F8
White Horse Rd SN6 143 E4
White Lodge Rd BS16 20 F4
White St BS5 195 C4
White Tree Rd BS9 18 B4
Whitebeam Cl GL2 127 B5
Whitebeam Ct BS5 9 E8
Whitechapel Rd 8
GL15 155 D1
Whitecourt GL11 89 A1
Whitecroft GL6 91 B4
Whitecroft Rd GL15 155 E1
Whitecroft Sta GL15 155 F1
Whitecroft Way BS15 11 A7
Whitecross Ave BS14 3 C6
Whitecross Sch GL15 92 A2
Whitecross Sq GL53 193 C1
Whitecross St NP25 154 A7
Whitefield Ave
Bristol, Hanham BS15 10 D5
Bristol, Speedwell BS5 20 A1
Whitefield Cl GL10 97 F6
Whitefield Rd BS5 20 A2
Whitefields
Bishop's Cleeve GL52 137 D4
Chipping Sodbury BS37 44 C1
Whitefriars La SN6 142 F6
Whitegates BS36 30 D6
Whitehall GL5 99 D7
Whitehall Ave BS5 19 E1
Whitehall Gdns BS5 19 D1
Whitehall La GL2 124 E6
Whitehall Prim Sch BS5 19 D1
Whitehall Rd BS5 9 C8
Whitehall Trad Est 4 BS5 9 C8
Whitehill La GL17 164 B4
Whitehouse La Bristol BS3 8 D4
Gorsley HR9,GL18 170 C5
Tetbury GL8 140 C1
Whitehouse Pk GL5 98 E7
Whitehouse Pl BS3 8 E4
Whitehouse Prim Sch
BS13 2 C5
Whitehouse Rd BS35 38 C7
Whitehouse St BS3 8 E4
Whitehouse Way GL52 138 B3
Whiteladies Rd BS8 194 B4
Whitelands La GL51 121 D7
Whitelands Rd GL7 190 E5
Whiteleaze BS10 18 C8
Whitemarsh Cl GL51 132 D4
Whitemead Ho 3 BS3 8 A3
Whites Hill BS5 10 A6
Whiteshill BS16 30 D3
Whiteshill Prim Sch
GL6 102 F3
Whitethorn Cott GL51 133 A7
Whitethorn Dr GL52 134 C3
Whitewall La BS35 64 F1
Whitewater Rd GL8 70 C4
Whiteway GL11 80 C6
Whiteway Cl
Bristol, St Anne's Park BS4 9 E6
Bristol, St George BS5 10 A8
Dursley GL11 80 C7
Whiteway Ct
1 Bristol BS5 10 A8
Cirencester GL7 190 D6
Whiteway Mews BS5 10 A8
Whiteway Rd
Bristol BS5,BS15 20 A1
Gloucester GL4 119 B5
Whiteway View GL7 190 B7
Whitewell Cl GL4 119 E7
Whitewood Rd BS5 19 F1
Whitfield Cl 8 BS16 20 D3
Whitfield Fishponds Com Sch
BS16 19 F4
Whitfield Rd BS35 64 C2
Whitfield St GL1 196 B2
Whitford Cl WR11 188 A6

Whiting Rd BS13 2 A4
Whitland Ave BS13 2 B5
Whitland Rd BS13 2 B5
Whitley Cl BS37 43 C3
Whitley Mead BS34 29 E3
Whitlow La GL19 165 E5
Whitmead Gdns BS13 2 C4
Whitminster CE Prim Sch GL2 100 E5
Whitminster La GL2 100 A6
Whitmore Ave BS4 10 A3
Whitmore Rd GL54 174 A8
Whitmores The GL54 176 C1
Whitson Ho 1 BS2 195 C3
Whitson St BS1 195 A4
Whittingham Hall GL14 156 E5
Whittington Ho GL5 99 A7
Whittington Rd
Bristol BS16 20 C6
Cheltenham GL51 129 D8
Whittington Way GL15 147 D8
Whittington Wlk 18 GL18 171 A4
Whittle Ave GL4 118 D2
Whittle Cl GL51 129 C8
Whittles La GL2 157 F2
Whittlestone Cl GL54 176 D4
Whittlestone Hollow GL54 176 D4
Whittock Rd BS14 3 D6
Whittock Sq BS14 3 D7
Whittucks Cl BS15 10 D4
Whittucks Rd BS15 10 C4
Whitwell Rd BS14 3 B8
Whitworth Mews GL3 120 C6
Whitworth Rd GL7 190 C3
Whornes Orch GL4 119 F3
Whytes Cl BS9 18 A8
Wick CE Prim Sch BS30 12 B6
Wick Cres BS4 9 F3
Wick House Cl BS31 5 D3
Wick La
Lower Apperley GL19 173 C6
Upton Cheyney BS30 12 A2
Wick Rd Bristol BS4 9 D4
Oaksey SN16 142 A4
Pilning BS35 38 C7
Wick St GL6 103 E4
Wickets The
Bristol, Filton BS7 28 F1
Bristol, Upper Soundwell BS15 20 D2
Wicketts The BS7 28 F2
Wickfield La GL52 138 F4
Wickham Cl BS37 33 D8
Wickham Ct BS16 19 D5
Wickham Glen BS16 19 D5
Wickham Hill BS16 19 D5
Wickham View BS16 19 D4
Wicklow Rd BS4 2 E8
Wickridge Cl GL5 99 C8
Wickwar Rd
Kingswood GL12 67 E4
Rangeworthy BS37 53 B1
Yate BS37 44 B5
Wickwater La GL7 143 B6
Widcombe BS14 3 A6
Widcombe Cl 3 BS5 10 A7
Widden Prim Sch GL1 196 C2
Widden St GL1 196 C2
Widhill La SN26 144 D1
Widmore Rd BS13 2 B5
Wigmore Cl GL4 119 E6
Wigton Cres BS10 28 C2
Wilbye Gr BS4 2 D7
Wilcox Cl BS15 10 C6
Wildcroft Ho BS9 18 B4
Wildcroft Rd BS9 18 B4
Wilder Ct BS2 195 B4
Wilder St BS2 195 B4
Wildfowl & Wetlands Trust★ GL2 95 A6
Wildlife Wlk GL3 120 E4
Wildmoorway La GL7 143 A8
Wilkes Ave GL3 120 A8
Wilkes Mdw GL16 155 B6
Wilkinson Rd GL7 190 D1
Willada Cl BS3 8 B2
Willcox Dr GL52 138 B3
Willersey Bsns Pk WR12 188 B3
Willersey CE Prim Sch WR12 188 B2
Willersey Rd GL51 129 E8
William Emes Gdn GL56 186 C7
William Gough Cl GL51 132 D5
William Mason Cl 18 BS5 9 B7
William St
Bristol, Bedminster BS3 8 E4
Bristol, Fishponds BS16 20 B3
Bristol, Newton BS2 9 A6
8 Bristol, Redfield BS5 9 C8
Bristol, St Pauls BS2 18 F1
Bristol, Totterdown BS3 8 F4
Williams Cl BS30 10 F3
Williams Orch GL2 125 D5
Williamson Rd BS7 18 F3
Williamstrip Farm Cotts GL7 160 F1
Willinton Rd BS4 2 F8
Willis Est BS2 18 F3
Willis Rd BS15 20 F2
Willis Wlk GL20 182 C5
Willment Way BS11 26 D1
Willmott Cl BS14 2 F3
Willoughby Cl
Alveston BS35 51 A4
Bristol BS13 2 B7
Willoughby Rd BS7 18 E5
Willow Ave GL4 119 B7
Willow Bank BS10 18 C7
Willow Bank Rd GL20 183 D4
Willow Bed Cl BS16 20 B6
Willow Cl
Ashton under Hill WR11 183 D8
Bristol, Patchway BS34 28 E7
Bristol, Warmley BS30 11 D6
Charfield GL12 67 A4
Chepstow NP16 60 D6
Dursley GL11 88 A3
Wick BS30 12 B6
Woodmancote GL52 138 B3
Willow Ct BS7 19 A7
Willow Gr 1 Bristol BS16 20 C2
South Cerney GL7 143 A8
Willow Ho BS13 2 D4
Willow Hts GL15 92 B5
Willow Park Dr GL52 137 F4
Willow Rd Bristol BS15 10 C3
Charlton Kings GL53 131 C5
King's Stanley GL10 98 A4
Stonehouse GL10 97 E7
Willersey WR12 188 B2
Willow Sh Ctr The BS16 20 E6
Willow Way
Coalpit Heath BS36 31 C6
Gloucester GL4 119 B7
Willow Wlk Bristol BS10 28 B3
Keynsham BS31 4 D4
Willowbrook Dr GL51 132 D4
Willowcroft Cl GL4 119 D3
Willowdean GL14 191 C5
Willowherb Cl GL52 134 C3
Willowleaze GL2 127 D3
Willows The
Bristol, Bradley Stoke BS32 29 D8
Bristol, Frenchay BS16 30 B1
Dymock GL18 178 D2
Gloucester GL1 196 C4
Highworth SN6 145 D3
Longhope GL17 164 F5
Quedgeley GL2 117 E1
Yate BS37 43 D2
Wills Dr BS5 9 A8
Willsbridge Hill BS30 11 A2
Willsbridge Mill★ BS30 11 A2
Willway St Bristol BS2 195 C3
Bristol, Bedminster BS3 8 D4
Wilmot Ct BS30 11 A6
Wilmots Way BS20 16 D4
Wilmott Ho BS20 16 D4
Wilshire Ave BS15 10 D5
Wilson Pl BS2 195 C4
Wilson Rd GL51 129 D1
Wilson St BS2 195 C4
Wilton Cl Bristol BS10 28 C1
Gloucester GL1 118 D6
Wilton Rd GL1 118 D6
Wiltshire Ave BS37 44 A3
Wiltshire Pl BS15 20 E3
Wilverley Ind Est BS4 9 E1
Wimbledon Rd BS6 18 C5
Wimborne Cl GL51 129 E6
Wimborne Rd BS3 8 C1
Winash Cl BS14 3 D7
Wincanton Cl BS16 30 F1
Wincel Rd GL54 174 A7
Winchcombe Abbey CE Prim Sch GL54 174 A7
Winchcombe Folk & Police Mus★ GL54 174 A7
Winchcombe Hospl GL54 139 F4
Winchcombe Railway Mus★ GL54 174 A7
Winchcombe Rd
Dumbleton WR11 184 A8
Frampton Cotterell BS36 31 B8
Gloucester GL4 118 E2
Winchcombe Sch GL54 174 A8
Winchcombe St GL52 193 C4
Winchcombe Sta GL54 174 A8
Winchester Ave BS4 9 D3
Winchester Ct BS16 19 E6
Winchester Dr GL4 118 E3
Winchester Ho 5 GL50 133 B1
Winchester Rd BS4 9 D3
Winchester Way GL51 129 F6
Wincombe Trad Est BS2 9 A4
Wincroft BS30 11 C4
Windcliff Cres BS11 16 E7
Windermere Cl GL51 129 E7
Windermere Rd
Bristol BS34 29 A8
Cheltenham GL51 129 E7
Gloucester GL2 127 C4
Windermere Way BS30 11 D6
Windfall Way GL2 127 C2
Windmill Cl BS3 8 E4
Windmill Cotts GL8 82 A6
Windmill Farm Bsns Ctr BS3 8 D4
Windmill Field GL4 119 D7
Windmill Hill BS3 8 D3
Windmill La Bristol BS10 27 D3
Kingscote GL8 82 A6
Windmill Rd Kemble GL7 141 F8
Minchinhampton GL6 91 E6
Windrush SN6 145 C3
Windrush Ct
Temple Guiting GL54 175 A8
Thornbury BS35 51 C8
Windrush Gn BS31 5 A4
Windrush Rd
Cheltenham GL52 134 A2
Gloucester GL4 118 E2
Windrush Rd continued
Keynsham BS31 5 A4
Windrush View GL54 175 D2
Windsor Ave Bristol BS5 10 B6
Keynsham BS31 4 E4
Windsor Cl BS34 29 E4
Windsor Cres BS10 27 C4
Windsor Ct
18 Bristol, Clifton BS8 7 F6
Bristol, Downend BS16 20 E7
Wick BS30 12 C7
Windsor Dr Lydney GL15 92 B6
Yate BS37 43 D2
Windsor Gr 20 BS5 9 B8
Windsor La GL11 81 A8
Windsor Pl
Bristol, Clifton BS8 7 F6
Bristol, Mangotsfield BS16 21 A5
Stroud GL6 103 B1
Windsor Rd
Bristol, Longwell Green BS30 10 F2
Bristol, Montpelier BS6 18 E2
Dursley GL11 88 B1
3 Tetbury GL8 140 B4
Windsor St GL52 133 F3
Windsor Terr
Bristol, Clifton BS8 7 F6
Bristol, Totterdown BS3 8 F4
Cirencester GL7 190 E4
Windsoredge La GL6 91 A6
Windyridge GL6 105 A1
Windyridge Gdns GL50 133 C5
Windyridge Rd GL50 133 C5
Wine St BS1 195 A3
Wineberry Cl BS5 19 D1
Winfield GL18 170 F4
Winfield Rd BS30 11 C7
Winford Gr BS13 2 A8
Winford La BS41 1 C1
Winford Terr BS41 1 C5
Wing La GL20 182 E8
Wingfield Rd BS3 8 E2
Winkworth Pl 4 BS2 18 F1
Winniecroft Cotts GL4 119 D2
Winnycroft La GL4 119 C1
Winsbury Way BS32 40 D1
Winscombe Cl BS31 4 D6
Winsdor Dr GL4 118 C2
Winsford St 2 BS5 9 A8
Winsham Cl BS14 3 B5
Winsley Rd Bristol BS6 18 D1
Gloucester GL4 119 C4
Winstanley Ho 4 BS5 9 B6
Winston Cl 1 HR8 178 F7
Winston Rd GL3 128 B5
Winstone Ct BS2 194 C3
Winstonian Rd GL52 133 F2
Winterbotham Rd
Cheltenham GL51 132 D2
Dursley GL11 87 F4
Winterbourne Hill BS36 30 D5
Winterbourne Rd BS34 29 E6
Winterspring La GL12 68 F3
Winterstoke Cl 5 BS3 8 B2
Winterstoke Ctr 1 BS3 8 B2
Winterstoke Ho 1 BS3 8 A3
Winterstoke Rd BS3 8 A2
Winterstoke Underpass BS3 7 F4
Winterway GL56 186 C6
Wintle's Hill GL14 157 D8
Wintles Cl GL17 164 D5
Wintles La GL14 165 C3
Winton Cl GL51 130 A7
Winton Rd GL51 130 A7
Winton St BS4 8 F4
Wintour Cl NP16 72 D1
Wirewood Cl NP16 73 A2
Wirewood Cres NP16 73 A2
Wishford Cl GL2 127 E4
Wisloe Rd GL2 95 F2
Wistaria Ave BS37 44 A1
Wistaria Rd 1 GL8 140 B4
Wisteria Ct GL51 130 A4
Wisteria Way GL3 128 A7
Wistley Rd GL53 131 B4
Witch Hazel Rd BS13 2 E3
Witchell Rd BS5 9 C7
Witcombe BS37 32 C7
Witcombe Cl BS15 20 F1
Witcombe Pl GL52 193 C3
Witham Rd BS31 5 A3
Witherlies Rd BS16 19 F6
Withers The GL52 137 F4
Withey Cl W BS9 17 F5
Witheys The BS14 3 C4
Withington CE Prim Sch GL54 166 E2
Withington Cl BS30 11 C2
Withleigh Rd BS4 9 B2
Withy Cl E BS9 17 F6
Withy Mews GL4 119 B5
Withy Trees Rd WR11 188 A8
Withy Way GL11 87 F5
Withybridge Gdns GL51 132 B7
Withybridge La GL51 132 A6
Withyfield Rd GL52 138 A4
Withyholt Ct GL53 130 F5
Withyholt Pk GL53 130 F5
Withymead Rd SN14 15 A8
Withypool 7 GL51 129 E5
Withypool Gdns BS14 3 B5
Withys The BS20 16 D4
Withywood Com Sch BS13 2 A5
Withywood Gdns BS13 1 F4
Withywood Rd BS13 1 F4
Witley Lodge Cl GL51 129 D6
Witney Cl BS31 5 D3
Witney Ct GL50 193 A3
Witpit La GL7 150 F4
Woburn Ave GL4 118 C1
Woburn Cl BS30 10 F5
Woburn Rd BS5 19 B3
Woefuldane Bottom GL6 148 A3
Wolds End Cl GL55 189 A2
Wolferton Rd BS7 18 F2
Wolford Rd GL56 187 D6
Wolfridge Gdns BS10 28 A4
Wolfridge La BS35 50 F4
Wolfridge Ride BS35 50 F4
Wolseley Lodge GL2 127 B2
Wolseley Rd Bristol BS7 18 D3
Gloucester GL2 127 C2
Wood Edge Rd GL16 155 B3
Wood End St GL18 179 B4
Wood End Wlk BS9 17 C6
Wood La
Down Hatherley GL2 173 D1
Gorsley GL18 170 D4
Horton BS37 55 A1
Nailsworth GL6 91 C3
Wood Rd Bristol BS15 10 D8
Mile End GL16 155 B6
Wood St Bristol BS5 19 B2
Bushley GL20 181 C5
Stroud GL5 99 D7
Woodbine Cl GL4 119 E5
Woodbine Rd BS5 9 D8
Woodborough Cl GL6 103 F7
Woodborough St BS5 19 B1
Woodbridge La GL54 166 E1
Woodbridge Rd BS4 9 A2
Woodbury La BS8 18 A2
Woodchester Bristol BS15 20 E3
Yate BS37 32 E7
Woodchester CE Prim Sch GL5 99 A2
Woodchester Mansion★ GL10 89 F7
Woodchester Park Walks★ GL10 89 D7
Woodchester Pk★ GL10 90 B7
Woodchester Rd BS10 18 C7
Woodcock Cl
Gloucester GL4 119 D5
Stonehouse GL10 101 F1
Woodcock La GL10 97 F8
Woodcote Bristol BS15 10 D6
Gloucester GL2 127 B5
Woodcote Rd BS16 20 B3
Woodcote Wlk BS16 20 B2
Woodcroft Ave BS5 19 D1
Woodcroft Cl Bristol BS4 9 E4
Woodcroft NP16 73 A4
Woodcroft La NP16 73 A4
Woodcroft Rd BS4 9 E4
Woodcroft Terr NP16 73 B4
Woodend BS15 10 D6
Woodend Cl GL4 119 E8
Woodend La Awre GL14 157 B2
Dursley GL11 87 D7
Dursley GL11 87 F6
Gorsley HR9 170 A4
Rockhampton BS35 76 E1
Woodend Rd
Frampton Cotterell BS36 31 C7
Harrow Hill GL17 164 B3
Woodfield Cty Inf Sch GL11 87 E5
Woodfield Rd Bristol BS6 18 B2
Dursley GL11 87 E4
6 Ledbury HR8 178 E7
Woodford Ct GL4 119 B7
Woodgate Cl
Charlton Kings GL52 131 C5
Gloucester GL4 119 E8
Woodgate Rd
Cinderford GL14 191 D5
Mile End GL16 155 B7
Woodgrove Rd BS10 27 D2
Woodhall Cl BS16 20 F6
Woodhouse Ave BS32 40 D7
Woodhouse Cl
Almondsbury BS32 40 D6
Cirencester GL7 190 B3
Woodhouse Dr GL5 99 B6
Woodhouse Gr BS7 18 E6
Woodington Ct 1 BS30 10 F4
Woodland Ave
Bristol BS15 20 D2
Dursley GL11 88 A2
Woodland Cl BS15 20 C2
Woodland Ct BS9 17 C3
Woodland Dr GL11 88 A2
Woodland Gn GL4 119 E3
Woodland Gr BS9 17 D6
Woodland Pl GL15 156 B2
Woodland Rd
Berry Hill GL16 155 A7
Bream GL15 155 D1
Bristol BS8 194 C4
Coleford GL16 154 F8
Cromhall GL12 66 B4
Drybrook GL17 164 B4
Parkend GL15 155 E3
Woodland Rise
Lydney GL15 92 B4
Parkend GL15 155 E3
Woodland Terr
Bristol, Kingswood BS15 10 E7
Bristol, Redland BS6 18 B2
Woodland View
Joy's Green GL17 163 D3
Monmouth NP25 154 A7
Woodland View continued
Woodmancote GL7 158 B4
Woodland Way BS15 20 C2
Woodlands
Bristol, Downend BS16 20 E6
Bristol, Patchway BS32 40 D3
Leonard Stanley GL10 97 E3
Narth The NP25 154 B1
Tytherington GL12 52 B6
Woodlands Cl
St Arvans NP16 72 B6
Whitecroft GL15 155 E1
Woodlands Ct BS32 40 B3
Woodlands Dr GL5 99 E8
Woodlands La
Almondsbury BS32 40 E5
Berkeley GL13 85 A1
Bristol BS32 40 C3
Woodlands Pk BS32 40 C3
Woodlands Rd
Charfield GL12 67 A4
Cheltenham GL51 130 B5
Cirencester GL7 190 B2
Tytherington GL12 52 B6
Woodlands Reach GL14 191 D4
Woodlands Rise BS16 20 D6
Woodlands The
Llandogo NP25 146 B7
Stroud GL5 99 D8
Woodleaze BS9 17 B6
Woodleigh BS35 64 C1
Woodleigh Cl 9 HR8 178 E8
Woodleigh Field GL2 125 E6
Woodleigh Gdns BS14 3 C6
Woodleigh Rd HR8 178 E8
Woodmancote
Dursley GL11 80 B7
Yate BS37 32 D8
Woodmancote Rd 4 BS6 18 E1
Woodmancote Sch GL52 138 B4
Woodmancote Vale GL52 138 B3
Woodmans Cl BS37 33 B8
Woodmans Rd BS37 33 C8
Woodmans Vale BS37 33 C8
Woodmans Way GL52 137 F3
Woodmarsh Cl BS14 3 A4
Woodmead Gdns BS13 2 C4
Woodmead La BS30 23 A1
Woodpecker Cres BS16 22 C4
Woodpecker Rd GL2 118 C5
Woodpecker Wlk GL6 90 F5
Woodpeckers Cl GL19 172 D5
Woodrow Way GL2 118 A3
Woodruff Cl GL4 119 B4
Woodrush Rd GL20 192 E2
Woods Cl SN16 58 C1
Woods Orch GL4 118 F2
Woods Orchard Rd GL4 118 E2
Woodside Bristol BS9 17 D3
Stroud GL5 99 F8
Turkdean GL54 167 F4
Woolaston GL15 147 B3
Woodside Ave GL14 191 D3
Woodside Gr BS10 27 D3
Woodside La GL10 97 F2
Woodside Prim Sch GL17 163 F3
Woodside Rd
Bristol, Downend BS16 20 C7
Bristol, Kingswood BS15 10 C7
Bristol, St Anne's Park BS4 9 E6
Coalpit Heath BS36 31 E6
Woolaston GL15 147 B2
Woodside St GL14 191 D4
Woodside Terr GL6 102 F3
Woodstock Ave BS6 18 C1
Woodstock Cl
Avening GL8 148 A1
Bristol BS15 10 F8
Woodstock La GL8 148 A1
Woodstock Rd
Bristol, Kingswood BS15 10 F7
Bristol, Redland BS6 18 C2
Woodstock Sch BS15 10 E7
Woodstock Terr GL11 89 C1
Woodview
Four Oaks GL18 170 D7
Frampton Mansell GL6 148 F5
Woodview Cl BS11 16 E7
Woodview Rd GL11 88 A4
Woodville Ave GL16 155 C6
Woodville Rd
Cinderford GL14 191 E4
Tewkesbury GL20 192 D1
Woodville Rd W GL14 191 E4
Woodward Ave BS37 43 B1
Woodward Cl GL8 140 B5
Woodward Dr BS30 10 F4
Woodwell Rd BS11 16 E5
Woodyleaze Dr BS15 10 D6
Woolaston Comm GL15 147 C3
Woolaston Prim Sch GL15 147 C3
Woolcot St BS6 18 B2
Woollard La BS14 3 E1
Woolley Rd BS14 3 E5
Woolmarket The GL7 190 D5
Woolridge Hill GL19 172 C2
Woolstone La GL52 137 F8
Woolstrop Way GL2 118 A3
Woolthorpe La GL2 157 C6
Wootton Cres BS4 9 E6
Wootton Pk BS14 9 B1

Wootton Rd BS4 ....9 F6
Worcester Cl BS16 ......20 B2
Worcester Cres BS8 ....194 A4
Worcester Par GL1 .....196 B4
Worcester Rd
Bristol, Clifton BS8 ......194 A4
Bristol, Kingswood BS15 ...20 D1
Cinderford GL14 ....191 E5
Hartpury GL19 ....172 B6
Ledbury HR8 ....178 F8
Worcester St GL1 ......196 B3
Worcester Terr BS8 ....194 A4
Worcester Wlk GL16 ...155 C6
Wordens The GL5 ....98 D8
Wordings Mount GL6 ...104 E8
Wordsworth Ave GL51 ..132 E1
Wordsworth Ho BS34 ....29 A8
Wordsworth Rd
Bristol BS7 ....19 B7
Dursley GL11 ....80 C7
Working La GL54 ....183 E1
Workshop Rd BS11 ......26 C4
World of Mechanical Music Mus★ GL54 ....168 A1
World's End La BS31 .....5 C5
Worldsend La GL13 .....76 E7
Worley Ridge GL6 ....91 A4
Wormwood Hill GL6 .....91 A1
Worrall Mews 10 BS8 ....18 A2
Worrall Pl 11 BS8 ....18 A2
Worrall Rd BS8 ....18 A2
Worrel's La BS16 ....30 D3
Worsley St BS5 ....9 D7
Worthing Rd BS34 ....28 F8
Worthy Cl BS15 ....10 F6
Worthy Rd BS11 ....26 D7
Worthys The BS34 ....30 A6
Wortley Rd GL12 ....68 C6
Wortley Terr GL12 ....68 C6
Wotton Cres GL12 ....68 C6
Wotton Ct GL4 ....127 D1
Wotton Elms Ct 4 GL2 .127 B2
Wotton Heritage Ctr★ GL12 ....68 B7
Wotton Rd Charfield GL12 .67 B5
Iron Acton BS37 ....42 F5
Kingswood GL12 ....67 F5
Wragg Castle La GL6 ...103 C6
Wragg Ct GL11 ....88 A5
Wraggs Row 22 GL54 ...176 F4
Wraxall Gr BS13 ....2 A8
Wraxall Rd BS30 ....11 A6
Wren Cl Bristol BS16 .....19 E7
Gloucester GL4 ....119 B6
Wren Dr BS16 ....20 A6
Wren Terr GL3 ....127 D6
Wrenbert Rd BS16 ......20 D5
Wright Cl GL54 ....169 D7
Wright Rd GL54 ....169 D7
Wright Way BS16 ....19 E8
Wrington Cl BS34 ....29 C7
Wrington Cres BS13 ......2 A7
Wroughton Dr BS13 ......2 D4
Wroughton Gdns BS13 ...2 D4
Wroxham Dr BS34 ......29 C8
Wyatt Ave BS13 ....1 F5
Wyatt Cl BS13 ....1 F5
Wyatt Ct GL54 ....166 E5
Wyatts View BS4 ....9 E6
Wychbury Cl GL53 .....130 D5
Wychwood BS15 ....10 E6
Wyck Beck Rd BS10 .....28 A3
Wyck Rissington GL54 ..169 C6
Wycliffe Coll GL10 ......97 F6
Wycliffe Coll Jun Sch GL10 ....98 A6
Wycliffe Rd BS9 ....18 B7
Wycliffe Row 9 BS3 ......8 F4
Wycombe Gr BS4 ....9 D2
Wydelands GL56 ....186 E6
Wye Cres NP16 ....60 E7
Wye Croft Cl BS10 ......28 D3
Wye Ct BS35 ....51 C8
Wye Rapids Cotts HR9 .162 E2
Wye Rd GL3 ....120 F5
Wye Valley Link Rd NP16 .60 E5
Wye View Ho NP16 ......61 A7
Wye View La HR9 ......162 E3
Wye View Terr NP25 ....154 C4
Wye's Gn NP25 ....154 C4
Wyebank Ave NP16 ......73 A1
Wyebank Cl NP16 ....61 A8
Wyebank Cres NP16 .....61 A8
Wyebank Dr NP16 ....73 A1
Wyebank Pl NP16 ....61 A8
Wyebank Rd NP16 ....61 A8
Wyebank Rise NP16 .....61 A8
Wyebank View NP16 .....61 A8
Wyebank Way NP16 .....61 A7
Wyebridge St NP25 ....154 A7
Wyedale Ave BS9 ....17 C7
Wyedean Cl GL15 ....92 C2
Wyedean Sch NP16 ....61 A8
Wyelands View NP16 ....60 B4
Wyesham Ave NP25 ....154 A7
Wyesham Inf Sch NP25 .154 A7
Wyesham Jun Sch NP25 ....154 A7
Wyesham La NP25 .....154 B7
Wyesham Rd NP25 .....154 B7
Wyeside Commercial Ctr NP25 ....154 A7
Wyeside Pk HR9 ....163 C5
Wykis Ct BS15 ....10 E5
Wyman's La GL51 ......133 B6
Wyman's Rd GL52 ......134 A3
Wymans Ct GL50 ....133 C5
Wymbush Cres BS13 .....2 C5
Wymbush Gdns BS13 .....2 C5
Wyndam Ct BS2 ....195 B4
Wyndbrook La GL19 ....179 F4
Wyndcliffe View NP16 ...72 B5
Wyndecliffe Ho NP16 ....61 A7
Wyndham Cres
Bristol BS4 ....10 A3
Easton-in-G BS20 ....16 B4
Wynford Villas GL19 ....171 C1
Wynols Cl 6 GL16 .....155 B5
Wynols Ct 7 GL16 .....155 B5
Wynols Hill La GL16 ...155 B5
Wynols Rd GL16 ....155 B5
Wynstones Sch GL4 ....110 E8
Wynstones The BS15 ....10 C7
Wyntour Ho NP16 ....61 A8
Wyntour's Par GL15 .....92 A2
Wynyards Cl GL20 .....192 D4
Wyvern Rd NP16 ....61 B1
Wyvern Villas BS9 ....18 A8

X

Xerox Bsns Pk GL17 ....164 D5

Y

Yanleigh Cl BS13 ....1 D6
Yanley La BS41,BS13 ......1 C7
Yarlington Cl GL52 .....137 E4
Yarnold Terr GL51 ......133 A4
Yarnolds GL51 ....129 E1
Yarrow Cl GL4 ....119 A4
Yartleton La GL17 ......165 A7
Yate Rd BS37 ....42 F3
Yate Rocks BS37 ....43 F7
Yate Sta BS37 ....43 C2
Yeamen's Ho BS1 ......195 B1
Yellow Hundred Cl GL11 .80 C8
Yelverton Rd BS4 ....9 E1
Yeomans Cl BS9 ....17 D5
Yeomanside Cl BS14 .....3 C5
Yeomeads BS41 ....7 A1
Yetts The NP16 ....61 B8
Yew Tree Cl
Cheltenham GL50 ....133 C5
Shipton GL54 ....166 E5
Yew Tree Cotts 16 GL54 .176 F4
Yew Tree Ct Bristol BS14 ...3 B5
8 Broadway WR12 .....185 C8
Gotherington GL52 ......138 A8
Yew Tree Dr Bristol BS15 ..20 F3
Yew Tree Gdns BS20 .....16 C4
Yew Tree Way
Churchdown GL3 ....128 A5
Thrupp GL5 ....99 E3
Yewcroft Cl BS14 ....3 A4
Yewtree Cl GL11 ....87 D3
Yokehouse La GL6 .....104 A6
York Ave BS7 ....18 F4
York Bldgs BS3 ....8 E4
York Cl
Bristol, Bromley Heath BS16 30 F1
Bristol, Stoke Gifford BS34 .29 D4
Yate BS37 ....43 E4
York Ct BS2 ....195 B4
York Gdns Bristol BS8 .....7 F6
Winterbourne BS36 ....30 F8
York Pl
Bristol, Brandon Hill BS1 .194 C2
Bristol, Clifton BS8 ......194 B3
York Rd
Bristol, Bedminster BS3 .....8 E4
Bristol, Lower Easton BS5 ..19 C1
Bristol, Montpelier BS6 ....18 E1
Bristol, Staple Hill BS16 ...20 E4
Cinderford GL14 ....191 E5
Gloucester GL4 ....119 C8
Tewkesbury GL20 ....192 C2
York Row GL52 ....134 A4
York St
Bristol, Baptist Mills BS2 ..19 A2
9 Bristol, Barton Hill BS5 ...9 C7
2 Bristol, Clifton BS8 .....18 A2
Bristol, St Pauls BS2 .....195 B4
Cheltenham GL52 ....193 C4
Yorkley La GL15 ....156 A1
Yorkley Prim Sch GL15 .156 A1
Yorkley Wood Rd GL15 .156 A1
Youngs Ct BS16 ....21 B8
Youngs Orch GL5 ......148 A5

Z

Zetland Rd BS6 ....18 D2
Zinc Rd BS11 ....26 C3
Zinnia Cl GL3 ....127 F7
Zion Appartments 12 GL16 ....155 A7
Zion Hill GL6 ....102 F3
Zoons Rd GL3 ....120 A8

NG NH NJ NK
NM NN NO NP
NR NS NT NU
NX NY NZ
SC SD SE TA
SH SJ SK TF TG
SM SN SO SP TL TM
SR SS ST SU TQ TR
SW SX SY SZ TV

Using the Ordnance Survey National Grid

Any feature in this atlas can be given a unique reference to help you find the same feature on other Ordnance Survey maps of the area, or to help someone else locate you if they do not have a Street Atlas.

The grid squares in this atlas match the Ordnance Survey National Grid and are at 500 metre intervals. The small figures at the bottom and sides of every other grid line are the National Grid kilometre values (**00** to **99** km) and are repeated across the country every 100 km (see left).

To give a unique National Grid reference you need to locate where in the country you are. The country is divided into 100 km squares with each square given a unique two-letter reference. Use the administrative map to determine in which 100 km square a particular page of this atlas falls.

The bold letters and numbers between each grid line (**A** to **F**, **1** to **8**) are for use within a specific Street Atlas only, and when used with the page number, are a convenient way of referencing these grid squares.

Example The railway bridge over DARLEY GREEN RD in grid square B1

Step 1: Identify the two-letter reference, in this example the page is in **SP**

Step 2: Identify the 1 km square in which the railway bridge falls. Use the figures in the southwest corner of this square: Eastings **17**, Northings **74**. This gives a unique reference: **SP 17 74**, accurate to 1 km.

Step 3: To give a more precise reference accurate to 100 m you need to estimate how many tenths along and how many tenths up this 1 km square the feature is (to help with this the 1 km square is divided into four 500 m squares). This makes the bridge about **8** tenths along and about **1** tenth up from the southwest corner.

This gives a unique reference: **SP 178 741**, accurate to 100 m.

Eastings (read from left to right along the bottom) come before Northings (read from bottom to top). If you have trouble remembering say to yourself "Along the hall, THEN up the stairs"!

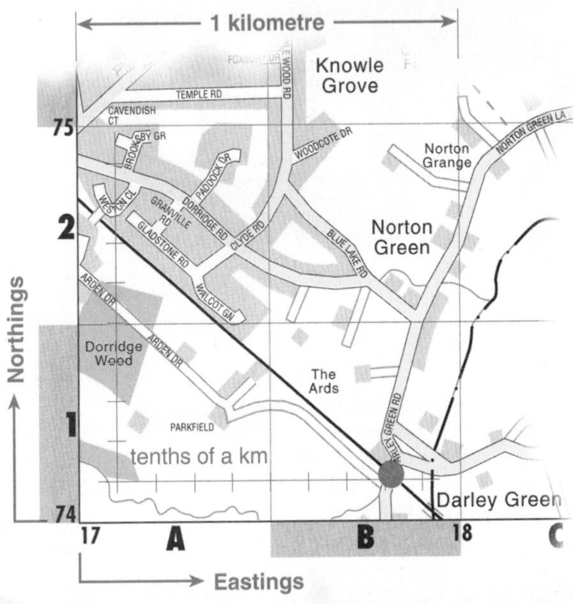

Street Atlases from Philip's

Philip's publish an extensive range of regional and local street atlases which are ideal for motoring, business and leisure use. They are widely used by the emergency services and local authorities throughout Britain.

Key features include:

- **Superb county-wide mapping at an extra-large scale of 3½ inches to 1 mile, or 2½ inches to 1 mile in pocket editions**
- **Complete urban and rural coverage, detailing every named street in town and country**
- **Each atlas available in two handy sizes – standard spiral and pocket paperback**

'The mapping is very clear... great in scope and value'

★★★★ **BEST BUY** **AUTO EXPRESS**

1 Bedfordshire
2 Berkshire
3 Birmingham and West Midlands
4 Bristol and Bath
5 Buckinghamshire
6 Cambridgeshire
7 Cardiff, Swansea and The Valleys
8 Cheshire
9 Cornwall
10 Derbyshire
11 Devon
12 Dorset
13 County Durham and Teesside
14 Edinburgh and East Central Scotland
15 North Essex
16 South Essex
17 Glasgow and West Central Scotland
18 Gloucestershire
19 North Hampshire
20 South Hampshire
21 Hertfordshire
22 East Kent
23 West Kent
24 Lancashire
25 Leicestershire and Rutland
26 London
27 Greater Manchester
28 Merseyside
29 Norfolk
30 Northamptonshire
31 Nottinghamshire
32 Oxfordshire
33 Somerset
34 Staffordshire
35 Suffolk
36 Surrey
37 East Sussex
38 West Sussex
39 Tyne and Wear and Northumberland
40 Warwickshire
41 Worcestershire
42 Wiltshire and Swindon
43 East Yorkshire and Northern Lincolnshire
44 North Yorkshire
45 South Yorkshire
46 West Yorkshire

How to order

The Philip's range of street atlases is available from good retailers or directly from the publisher by phoning 01903 828503